REEDS

Practical Boat O

SMALL ALMANAC

C000001017

2022

EDITORS

Perrin Towler & Mark Fishwick

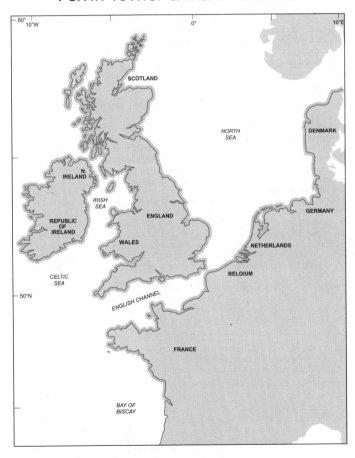

THE UNITED KINGDOM AND IRELAND
PLUS DENMARK TO THE GIRONDE

PLEASE SEE IMPORTANT SAFETY NOTE ON PAGE 2

REEDS
Practical BoatOwner
SMALL CRAFT ALMANAC
2022

Editors: Perrin Towler & Mark Fishwick

The Editors would like to thank the many official bodies who have kindly provided essential information in the preparation of this Almanac. They include the UK Hydrographic Office, Trinity House, Northern Lighthouse Board, Irish Lights, HM Nautical Almanac Office, HM Stationery Office, HM Customs, Meteorological Office and the Maritime and Coastguard Agency.

Information from the Admiralty List of Lights, Admiralty Tide Tables and the Admiralty List of Radio Signals is reproduced with the permission of the UK Hydrographic Office and the Controller of HMSO. Extracts from the following are published by permission of the Controller of HM Stationery Office: International Code of Signals, 1969; Meteorological Office Weather Services for Shipping. Phases of the Moon and Sun/Moon rising and setting times are included by permission of HM Nautical Almanac Office. UK and Foreign tidal predictions are supplied by the UK Hydrographic Office, Taunton TA1 2DN. Acknowledgment is also made to the following authorities for permission to use tidal predictions stated: Danmarks Meteorologiske Institut, Denmark: Esbjerg. SHOM, France: Dunkerque, Dieppe, Le Havre, Cherbourg, St Malo, Brest, Pointe de Grave, Authorisation (2021-158). Rijkswaterstaat, The Netherlands: Vlissingen, and Hoek van Holland. BSH, Hamburg and Rostock: Helgoland, Wilhelmshaven and Cuxhaven (BSH, Federal Maritime and Hydrographic Agency of Germany) [Licence number 11123/2012-10]. Vlaamse Hydrografie, Belgium: Zeebrugge. **Warning**: The UK Hydrographic Office has not verified the reproduced data and does not accept any liability for the accuracy of reproduction or any modifications made thereafter.

Corrections Any necessary corrections will be published on the website www.reedsalmanacs.co.uk. Data in this almanac is corrected up to Edition 25/2021 of the *Admiralty Notices to Mariners.*

IMPORTANT SAFETY NOTE AND LEGAL DISCLAIMER

This Almanac provides basic navigational data for planning and executing passages. The tidal prediction data has been reproduced by permission of national hydrographic offices. Chartlets illustrate items in the text, orientate the user and highlight key features; they should not be relied on for navigational purposes and must always be used in conjunction with a current, corrected navigational chart. Any waypoint or position listed in this Almanac must first be plotted on the appropriate chart to assess its accuracy, safety in the prevailing circumstances and relevance to the Skipper's intentions.

Navigational guidance or suggestions are based on the accumulated experience of editors, agents, harbour masters and users. They are generic and in compiling a passage plan or pilotage notebook all other available publications and information should be consulted. They take no account of the characteristics of individual vessels nor the actual or forecast meteorological conditions, sea or tidal state. These need to be checked with appropriate local authorities for the intended area of operation prior to departure.

While every care has been taken in compiling the Almanac, it is a human endeavour with many contributors. Despite rigorous checking there may be inadvertent errors or inaccuracies, and omissions resulting from the time of notification in relation to the publication date. To the extent that the editors or publisher become aware of these, corrections will be published on the website www.reedsalmanacs.co.uk (requires registration). Readers should therefore regularly check the website between January and June for any such corrections. Data in this Almanac is corrected up to Weekly Edition 25/2021 of Admiralty Notices to Mariners.

The publisher, editors and their agents accept no responsibility for any errors or omissions, or for any accident, loss or damage (including without limitation any indirect, consequential, special or exemplary damages) arising from the use or misuse of, or reliance upon, the information contained in this Almanac.

The use of any data in this Almanac is entirely at the discretion of the Skipper or other individual with responsibility for the command, conduct or navigation of the vessel in which it is relied upon.

Correspondence Letters on general matters should be addressed to info@reedsalmanacs.co.uk, or on nautical issues to editor.britishisles@reedsalmanacs.co.uk (British Isles excluding Channel Islands) or editor.continental@ reedsalmanacs.co.uk (Denmark to Gironde, including Channel Islands).

Practical Boat Owner is published every four weeks by Future PLC, 161 Marsh Wall, London E14 9AP. For subscription enquiries call +44 (0)330 333 1113 quoting code BL32.

MIXTE
Issu de sources responsables
FSC® C051148
www.fsc.org

ISBN 978 1 4729 9060 0 A CIP catalogue record for this book is available from the British Library.

Reeds and Adlard Coles are registered trade marks of Bloomsbury Publishing Plc.

Managing editor: Chris Stevens
Cartography & production: Chris Stevens

Adlard Coles
50 Bedford Square, London, WC1B 3DP
29 Earlsfort Terrace, Dublin 2, Ireland
Tel: +44 (0)1865 411010 www.reedsalmanacs.co.uk

Foreword

Welcome to the *Reeds PBO Small Craft Almanac 2022* – the ideal compact almanac for your bookshelf covering UK waters, Ireland and the European coast from Denmark to France.

Compiled using the same trusted data as published in the full-size *Reeds Almanac*, you'll find all the tide times you need, complete with tidal curves, pilotage and waypoints for major hazards and port entrances, plus detailed tidal atlases and tips on how to negotiate tricky headlands.

There are also contact details for harbour authorities and marinas, information on how to obtain and interpret weather forecasts, and at-a-glance checklists for safety procedures and first aid. With all this and more in one compact source, updated monthly via our website www.pbo.co.uk, this is a book no cruiser can afford to be without.

Together with the editors at Reeds, all of us at *Practical Boat Owner* wish you fair winds and sunny skies for the 2022 season.

Rob Melotti
Editor
Practical Boat Owner
Britain's biggest-selling boating magazine

Contents

ABBREVIATIONS

AC, ACA	Admiralty chart, chart agent
AC	Shore power (electrical)
ACN	Adlard Coles Nautical
Al	Alternating lt
ALL	Admiralty list of lights
ALRS	Admiralty list of radio signals
ASD	Admiralty sailing directions (Pilot)
ATT	Admiralty tide tables
ATT	Atterisage (landfall/SWM) buoy
Bcn, Bn	Beacon
Bkwtr	Breakwater
BST	British summer time (DST)
CD	Chart datum
Cf	Compare, cross-refer to
CG	Coastguard
Ch	Channel (VHF)
chan.	Channel (navigational)
COG	Course over the ground
CROSS	Centre régional opérationnel de surveillance et sauvetage (MRCC)
CRS	Coast radio station(s)
DF	Direction finding
Dia	Diaphone (fog signal)
Dir Lt	Directional light
DSC	Digital selective calling
DST	Daylight saving time
DZ	Danger zone (buoy)
E	East
ECM	East cardinal mark (buoy/beacon)
ED	Existence doubtful, European datum
EPIRB	Emergency pos'n indicating radio bn
F	Fixed light. Beaufort wind force
FFL	Fixed and flashing lt
Fl	Flashing light
FM	Frequency modulation
FV	Fishing vessel
G	Green. Gravel
GMDSS	Global maritime distress & safety system
H, Hrs, h	Hour(s)
H24	Continuous
HAT	Highest astronomical tide
Hbr	Harbour
Hd	Head, headland
HF	High frequency
HJ	Day service, sunrise to sunset
HO	Office hours, Hydrographic office
ht	Height
HW	High water
HX	No fixed hours
Hz	Hertz
IALA	Int'l association of lt ho authorities
IDM	Isolated danger mark (buoy/bcn)
IMO	Int'l maritime organisation
Inmarsat	Int'l maritime satellite system
IPTS	Int'l port traffic signals
Is, I	Island, Islet
Iso	Isophase light
ITZ	Inshore traffic zone
Kn	Knot(s)
Lanby	Large automatic navigational buoy
Lat	Latitude
LB	Lifeboat
Ldg	Leading (lt)
LF	Low frequency
Long	Longitude
LT	Local time
Lt(s)	Light(s)
Lt F	Light float
Lt Ho	Lighthouse
Lt V	Light vessel
LW	Low water
M	Sea mile(s)
m	Metre(s)
MCA	Maritime & Coastguard Agency
Météo	Météorologie/weather
MF	Medium frequency
MHWN	Mean HW neaps
MHWS	Mean HW springs
MHz	Megahertz
MLWN	Mean LW neaps
MLWS	Mean LW springs
MMSI	Maritime mobile service identity
Mo	Morse
MRCC	Maritime rescue co-ordination centre
MRSC	Maritime rescue sub-centre (not in UK)
MSI	Maritime safety information
N	North
NCM	North cardinal mark (buoy/bcn)
Oc	Occulting light
PHM	Port-hand mark (buoy/bcn)
Pt(e), (a)	Point(e), Punta
Q	Quick flashing
R	Red. River
Ra	Coast radar station
Racon	Radar transponder beacon
RG	Emergency RDF station
R/T	Radiotelephony
S	South
s	second(s) of time
SAR	Search and rescue
SCM	South cardinal mark (buoy/bcn)
SHM	Starboard-hand mark (buoy/bcn)
Sig Stn	Signal station
SMS	Short message service (texting)
SNSM	Société nationale de sauvetage enmer (French LB service)
SOG	Speed over the ground
SOLAS	Safety of life at sea (Convention)
SPM	Special mark (buoy/bcn)
SRR	SAR Region
SSB	Single sideband (radio)
Stn	Station
SWM	Safe water mark, landfall buoy
Tfc	Traffic
TSS	Traffic separation scheme
UQ	Ultra quick flashing lt
UT	Universal time
VHF	Very high frequency
VNF	Voie navigable de France (canals)
VQ	Very quick flashing lt
VTS	Vessel traffic service
W	West, White
WCM	West cardinal mark (buoy/bcn)
WGS	World geodetic system (datum)
WIP	Work in progress
WPT	Waypoint
Y	Yellow, orange, amber

5

GENERAL VOCABULARY. See also weather vocabulary on page 106

ENGLISH	GERMAN	FRENCH	DUTCH
ASHORE			
Ashore	An Land	A terre	Aan land
Airport	Flughafen	Aéroport	Vliegveld
Bank	Bank	Banque	Bank
Boathoist	Bootskran	Travelift	Botenlift
Boatyard	Bootswerft	Chantier naval	Jachtwerf
Bureau de change	Wechselstelle	Bureau de change	Geldwisselkantoor
Bus	Bus	Autobus	Bus
Chandlery	Yachtausrüster	Shipchandler	Scheepswinkel
Chemist	Apotheke	Pharmacie	Apotheek
Dentist	Zahnarzt	Dentiste	Tandarts
Doctor	Arzt	Médecin	Dokter
Engineer	Motorenservice	Ingénieur/mécanique	Ingenieur
Ferry	Fähre	Ferry/transbordeur	Veer/Pont
Garage	Autowerkstatt	Station service	Garage
Harbour	Hafen	Port	Haven
Hospital	Krankenhaus	Hôpital	Ziekenhuis
Mast crane	Mastenkran	Grue	Masten kraan
Post office	Postamt	Bureau de poste/PTT	Postkantoor
Railway station	Bahnhof	Gare de chemin de fer	Station
Sailmaker	Segelmacher	Voilier	Zeilmaker
Shops	Geschäfte	Boutiques	Winkels
Slip	Slip	Cale	Helling
Supermarket	Supermarkt	Supermarché	Supermarkt
Taxi	Taxi	Taxi	Taxi
Village	Ort	Village	Dorp
Yacht club	Yachtclub	Club nautique	Jacht club
NAVIGATION			
Abeam	Querab	A côté	Naast
Ahead	Voraus	Avant	Voor
Astern	Achteraus	Arrière	Achter
Bearing	Peilung	Cap	Peiling
Buoy	Tonne	Bouée	Boei
Binoculars	Fernglas	Jumelles	Verrekijker
Channel	Kanal	Chenal	Kanaal
Chart	Seekarte	Carte	Zeekaart
Compass	Kompass	Compas	Kompas
Compass course	Kompass Kurs	Cap du compas	Kompas koers
Current	Strömung	Courant	Stroom
Dead reckoning	Koppelnavigation	Estime	Gegist bestek
Degree	Grad	Degré	Graden
Deviation	Deviation	Déviation	Deviatie
Distance	Entfernung	Distance	Afstand
Downstream	Flußabwärts	En aval	Stroom afwaards
East	Ost	Est	Oost
Ebb	Ebbe	Jusant	Eb
Echosounder	Echolot	Sondeur	Dieptemeter
Estimated position	Gegißte Position	Point estimé	Gegiste positie
Fathom	Faden	Une brasse	Vadem
Feet	Fuß	Pieds	Voet
Flood	Flut	Flot	Vloed
Handbearing compass	Handpeilkompass	Compas de relèvement	Handpeil kompas

ENGLISH	GERMAN	FRENCH	DUTCH
Harbour guide	Hafenhandbuch	Guide du port	Havengids
High water	Hochwasser	Pleine mer	Hoog water
Latitude	Geographische Breite	Latitude	Breedte
Leading lights	Feuer in Linie	Alignement	Geleide lichten
Leeway	Abdrift	Dérive	Drift
Lighthouse	Leuchtturm	Phare	Vuurtoren
List of lights	Leuchtfeuer Verzeichnis	Liste des feux	Lichtenlijst
Log	Logge	Loch	Log
Longitude	Geographische Länge	Longitude	Lengte
Low water	Niedrigwasser	Basse mer	Laag water
Metre	Meter	Mètre	Meter
Minute	Minute	Minute	Minuut
Nautical almanac	Nautischer Almanach	Almanach nautique	Almanak
Nautical mile	Seemeile	Mille nautique	Zeemijl
Neap tide	Nipptide	Marée de morte-eau	Dood tij
North	Nord	Nord	Noord
Pilot	Lotse	Pilote	Loods/Gids
Pilotage book	Handbuch	Instructions nautiques	Vaarwijzer
RDF	Funkpeiler	Radio gonio	Radio richtingzoeker
Radar	Radar	Radar	Radar
Radio receiver	Radio, Empfänger	Récepteur radio	Radio ontvanger
Radio transmitter	Sender	Emetteur radio	Radio zender
River outlet	Flußmündung	Embouchure	Riviermond
South	Süd	Sud	Zuid
Spring tide	Springtide	Marée de vive-eau	Springtij/ springvloed
Tide	Tide, Gezeit	Marée	Getijde
Tide tables	Tidenkalender	Annuaire des marées	Getijdetafel
True course	Wahrer Kurs	Vrai cap	Ware Koers
Upstream	Flußaufwärts	En amont	Stroom opwaards
VHF	UKW	VHF	Marifoon
Variation	Mißweisung	Variation	Variatie
Waypoint	Wegpunkt	Point de rapport	Waypoint/Route punt
West	West	Ouest	West

OFFICIALDOM

Certificate of registry	Schiffszertifikat	Acte de franchisation	Zeebrief
Check in	Einklarieren	Enregistrement	Check-in
Customs	Zoll	Douanes	Douane
Declare	Verzollen	Déclarer	Aangeven
Harbour master	Hafenmeister	Capitaine du port	Havenmeester
Insurance	Versicherung	Assurance	Verzekering
Insurance certificate	Versicherungspolice	Certificat d'assurance	Verzekeringsbewijs
Passport	Paß	Passeport	Paspoort
Police	Polizei	Police	Politie
Pratique	Verkehrserlaubnis	Pratique	Verlof tot ontscheping
Prohibited area	Sperrgebiet	Zone interdite	Verboden gebied
Register	Register	Liste de passagers	Register
Ship's log	Logbuch	Livre de bord	Logboek
Ship's papers	Schiffspapiere	Papiers de bateau	Scheepspapieren
Surveyor	Gutachter	Expert maritime	Opzichter

Chapter 1 – Navigation

PASSAGE PLANNING AND SOLAS V

All passages by any vessel that goes to sea *must* be planned. 'Going to sea' is defined as proceeding beyond sheltered waters. Even in very familiar waters every passage, however short, should be properly planned. Before you set sail you need to determine where you are going, how to get there and what factors may influence the plan.

Full passage planning requirements may be found in Chapter V of the International Convention for Safety of Life at Sea (SOLAS), but more digestible guidance for small craft is in the MCA's Pleasure Craft Information Pack at: **www.dft.gov.uk/mca/pleasure_craft_information_packdec07-2.pdf.**

Although the passage plan does not have to be recorded on paper, in the event of legal action a written plan is clear proof that the required planning has been completed; it can also be referred to during the passage. A suggested passage planning form is overleaf. When completed this would constitute, with due consideration of the points below, a reasonable passage plan. The blank form may be photocopied and modified to suit individual needs.

Although spot checks on small craft are unlikely, the MCA could, following an accident or incident, take action under the Merchant Shipping Act if it could be proved that the skipper did not have a reasonable passage plan.

Passage planning considerations

All passage plans should at least consider the following:

• **Weather.** Before setting out check the weather forecast and know how to get regular updates during the passage.

• **Tides.** Check tidal predictions and determine if there are any limiting depths at your port of departure, during the passage and at the port of arrival (and at alternative ports, if applicable). Tidal streams will almost certainly affect the plan.

• **Vessel.** Confirm she is suitable for the intended trip, is properly equipped, and has sufficient fuel, water and food on board.

• **Crew.** Take into account your crew's experience, expertise and stamina. Cold,

tiredness and seasickness can be debilitating – and skippers are not immune.

• **Navigation.** Make sure you are aware of all navigational dangers by consulting up to date charts, pilot books and this Almanac. Never *rely* on GPS for fixing your position.

• **Contingency plan.** Consider bolt holes which can be entered *safely* in an emergency, if the weather deteriorates or mutiny threatens.

• **Information ashore.** Make sure someone ashore knows your plans, when they should become concerned and what action to take if necessary. Be sure to join the Coastguard Voluntary Identification Scheme (Form CG66).

"The winds and waves are always on the side of the ablest navigators." (Edward Gibbon)

Passage planning form

The following notes amplify some of the items on the form:

• The height of tide affects the depth, and tidal streams may hinder sensible progress – off headlands or in narrow passages, for example. On longer passages, which cross main tidal streams, determine the net effect of the streams and calculate a course to steer – more efficient than trying to maintain a track.

• Note which harbours and marinas have restricted times of access due to bars, sills or locks. These may affect your ETA and, probably, your ETD.

• Prepare a detailed pilotage plan for entry/exit of any unfamiliar harbour; a sketch is invaluable.

• Squinting into the setting sun can make pilotage very difficult. At night, light from a full moon can help enormously.

• Know when you expect to see lights at night – a good check on progress. See table of dipping/rising lights.

• Look up and note relevant VHF channels and/or phone numbers for ports of departure and arrival.

PASSAGE PLANNING FORM

DATE:............................ FROM: .... TO: .... DIST: ....M

ALTERNATIVE DESTINATION(S): ....

WEATHER FORECAST: ....

....

FORECASTS AVAILABLE DURING PASSAGE: ....

....

TIDES

DATE:............................	DATE:............................	DATE: ....
PLACE:...........................	PLACE:	PLACE: ....
HW	HW	HW ....
LW	LW	LW ....
HW	HW	HW ....
LW	LW	LW ....
COEFFICIENT:		
HEIGHT OF TIDE AT:		
.... hrs .... m	.... hrs .... m	.... hrs .... m

DEPTH CONSTRAINTS: ....

TIDAL STREAMS AT: ....

TURNS .... AT .... TOTAL SET (FM .... TO ....): ....° .... M

TURNS .... AT .... TOTAL SET (FM .... TO ....): ....° .... M

NET TIDAL STREAM FOR PASSAGE: ....° .... M

ESTIMATED TIME: ....hrs ETD: .... ETA: ....

SUN/MOON

SUNRISE: .... SUNSET: ....

MOONRISE: .... MOONSET: .... PHASE: ....

WAYPOINTS	NO	NAME	TRACK/DISTANCE (TO NEXT WAYPOINT)
	....	....	.... / ....
	....	....	.... / ....
	....	....	.... / ....
	....	....	.... / ....
	....	....	.... / ....

DANGERS   CLEARING BEARINGS/RANGES/DEPTHS

....

....

LIGHTS/MARKS EXPECTED ....

....

....

COMMUNICATIONS   PORT/MARINA .... VHF .... ☎ ....

PORT/MARINA .... VHF .... ☎ ....

NOTES (CHARTS PREPARED & PAGE NUMBERS OF RELEVANT PILOTS/ALMANACS/ETC): ....

....

....

DISTANCES (M) ACROSS THE ENGLISH CHANNEL

ENGLAND FRANCE/CI	Longships	Falmouth	Fowey	Plymouth bkwtr	Salcombe	Dartmouth	Torbay	Weymouth	Poole Hbr Ent	Needles Lt Ho	Nab Tower	Littlehampton	Shoreham	Brighton	Newhaven	Eastbourne	Folkestone	Dover
Le Conquet	114	118	134	142	139	152	158	181	199	203	236	256	260	264	269	281	313	318
L'Aberwrac'h	101	103	114	120	122	133	142	171	191	197	197	236	246	247	248	258	297	301
Roscoff	110	97	101	97	91	100	107	130	144	149	165	184	193	197	200	211	246	252
Trébeurden	118	105	107	100	95	103	110	128	148	148	168	186	197	201	206	218	257	262
Tréguier	131	114	112	102	93	99	104	116	132	136	153	170	182	187	192	211	252	253
Lézardrieux	139	124	119	107	97	102	105	117	129	133	150	167	179	184	189	208	249	250
St Q.-Portrieux	151	134	128	120	109	114	115	128	133	136	151	174	180	185	188	200	238	242
St Malo	172	152	145	132	118	121	124	125	130	133	148	170	176	182	185	195	235	240
St Helier	156	133	124	110	95	97	100	103	108	110	125	145	155	160	163	175	211	218
St Peter Port	140	113	105	89	75	71	73	81	87	90	105	126	135	139	142	155	190	196
Braye (Alderney)	149	129	107	90	74	72	71	63	68	71	86	108	115	120	123	135	173	178
Cherbourg	173	144	130	111	98	94	93	67	64	63	72	89	99	102	107	120	153	158
St Vaast	194	165	151	134	119	117	119	86	78	72	69	84	91	94	97	104	140	147
Ouistreham	231	203	190	173	158	155	159	121	111	100	88	93	94	94	93	96	132	133
Deauville	238	210	198	181	164	163	160	127	114	103	89	90	89	87	87	89	124	126
Le Havre	239	210	197	180	164	162	165	125	112	98	84	84	83	82	82	83	119	120
Fécamp	246	218	206	188	173	169	165	127	111	98	81	72	69	66	63	63	98	98
Dieppe	273	243	231	214	200	194	191	151	133	121	97	86	76	72	67	62	78	80
Boulogne	294	264	247	231	216	204	202	161	143	132	101	86	77	73	65	54	28	28
Calais	307	276	261	244	229	218	214	174	155	143	114	99	91	86	78	64	29	24

NOTES

1. This Table applies to Areas 1–3, and 14–16, each of which also contains its own internal Distance Table. Approximate distances in nautical miles are by the most direct route, while avoiding dangers and allowing for Traffic Separation Schemes.

2. For ports within the Solent, add the appropriate distances given in Area 2 to those shown above under either Needles Lighthouse or Nab Tower.

AREA 1 *South West England - Isles of Scilly to Anvil Point*

SELECTED LIGHTS, BUOYS & WAYPOINTS

ISLES OF SCILLY TO LAND'S END

Bishop Rock ☆ Fl (2) 15s 44m **20M**; part obsc 204°-211°, obsc 211°-233° and 236°-259°; Gy ○ twr with helo platform; *Racon T, 18M, 254°-215°*; 49°52'·37N 06°26'·74W; 992351137.
Round Rk ⚓ 49°53'·10N 06°25'·19W.
Old Wreck ⚓ VQ; 49°54'·26N 06°22'·81W.

ST AGNES and ST MARY'S

Peninnis Hd ⚓ Fl 20s 36m 9M; 231°-117° but part obsc 048°-083° within 5M; W ○ twr on B frame, B cupola; 49°54'·28N 06°18'·21W.
Gugh ⚓ Fl (5) Y 20s; 49°53'·52N 06°18'·73W.
Spanish Ledge ⚓ Q (3) 10s; *Bell;* 49°53'·94N 06°18'·86W.
Woolpack ⚓ Fl G 5s; 49°54'·40N 06°19'·37W.
Bartholomew Ledges ⚓ QR 12m; 49°54'·37N 06°19'·89W.
N Bartholomew ⚓ Fl R 5s; 49°54'·49N 06°19'·99W.
Bacon Ledge ⚓ Fl (4) R 5s; 49°55'·22N 06°19'·26W.
Ldg lts 097·3°: Front, Iso RW (vert) 2s; W △, 49°55'·12N 06°18'·50W. Rear, Oc WR (vert) 10s; Or X on W bcn.
Crow Rock ⚓ Fl (2) 10s; 49°56'·26N 06°18'·49W.
Hats ⚓ VQ (6) + L Fl 10s; 49°56'·21N 06°17'·14W.

AROUND TRESCO, BRYHER and ST MARTIN'S

Tresco Flats, Hulman ⚓ Fl G 4s, 49°56'·29N 06°20'·30W.
Little Rag Ledge ⚓ Fl (2) R 5s, 49°56'·44N 06°20'·43W.
Bryher, Bar ⚓ Q (3) 10s, 49°57'·37N 06°20'·84W.
Bryher, Church Quay ⚓ Q (3) 10s; 49°57'·18N 06°20'·97W.
Spencers Ledge ⚓ Q (6) + L Fl 15s; 49°54'·78N 06°22'·06W.
Steeple Rock ⚓ Q (9) 15s; 49°55'·46N 06°24'·24W.
Round Island ☆ Fl 10s 55m **18M**, also shown in reduced vis; 021°-288°; W ○ twr; *Horn (4) 60s*; 49°58'·74N 06°19'·39W.
St Martin's, Higher Town quay ⚓ Fl R 5s, 49°57'·45N 06°16'·84W.

SCILLY to LAND'S END

Seven Stones Lt V ⚓ Fl (3) 30s 12m **15M**; R hull; *Horn (3) 60s*; *Racon O, 15M;* 50°03'·63N 06°04'·32W; 992351023.
Wolf Rock ☆ Fl 15s 34m **16M**; H24; *Horn 30s*; *Racon T, 10M;* 49°56'·72N 05°48'·55W; 992351128.
Longships ☆ Fl (2) WR 10s 35m **W15M**, R11M; 189°-R-327°-W- 189°; also shown in reduced vis; Gy ○ twr with helicopter platform; *Horn 10s*; 50°04'·01N 05°44'·81W.
Carn Base ⚓ Q (9) 15s; 50°01'·48N 05°46'·18W.
Runnel Stone ⚓ Q (6) + L Fl 15s; *Whis;* 50°01'·18N 05°40'·36W.

LAND'S END TO PLYMOUTH

Tater-du ☆ Fl (3) 15s 34m **20M**; 241°-072°; W ○ twr. FR 31m 9M, 060°-072° over Runnel Stone; 50°03'·14N 05°34'·67W.

NEWLYN

Low Lee ⚓ Q (3) 10s; 50°05'·56N 05°31'·38W.
S Pier ⚓ Fl 5s 10m 9M; W ○ twr; 253°-336°; 50°06'·18N 05°32'·57W.
N Pier ⚓ F WG 4m 2M; 238°-G-248°, 50°06'·18N 05°32'·62W.

PENZANCE

S Pier ☆ Fl WR 5s 11m **W17M**, R12M; 159°-R (unintens)-224°-R-268°-W-344·5°-R-shore; 50°07'·06N 05°31'·68W.
Mountamopus ⚓ Q (6) + L Fl 15s; 50°04'·62N 05°26'·25W.
Lizard ☆ Fl 3s 70m **26M**; 250°-120°, partly visible 235°-250°; W 8-sided twr; *Horn 30s;* 49°57'·61N 05°12'·13W.
Manacle ⚓ Q (3) 10s; *Bell;* 50°02'·81N 05°01'·91W.

FALMOUTH

St Anthony Head ☆ Iso WR 15s 22m, **W16M**, R14M, H24; 295°-W-004°-R (over Manacles)-022°-W-172°; W 8-sided twr; *Horn 30s;* 50°08'·46N 05°00'·96W.
Black Rock ⚓ Fl(2) 10s 3M; IDM B bn; 50°08'·72N 05°02'·00W.
Black Rock ⚓ Fl R 2·5s; 50°08'·68N 05°01'·74W.
Castle ⚓ Fl G 2·5s; 50°08'·99N 05°01'·62W.
St Mawes ⚓ Q (6) + L Fl 15s; 50°09'·10N 05°01'·42W.
The Governor ⚓ VQ (3) 5s; 50°09'·15N 05°02'·40W.
West Narrows ⚓ Fl (2) R 10s; 50°09'·39N 05°02'·07W.
East Narrows ⚓ Fl (2) G 10s; 50°09'·43N 05°01'·90W.
The Vilt ⚓ Fl (4) G 15s; 50°09'·99N 05°02'·28W.
Northbank ⚓ Fl R 4s; 50°10'·34N 05°02'·26W.
St Just ⚓ QR; 50°10'·44N 05°01'·72W.
Mylor appr chan ⚓ Fl G 6s; 50°10'·79N 05°02'·70W. ⚓ Fl R 5s.
Messack ⚓ Fl G 15s; 50°11'·31N 05°02'·22W.
Carrick ⚓ Fl (2) G 10s; 50°11'·59N 05°02'·74W.
Pill ⚓ Fl (3) G 15s; 50°12'·05N 05°02'·40W.
Turnaware Bar ⚓ Fl G 5s; 50°12'·40N 05°02'·15W.
Dock Basin Dir ⚓ 266°: WRG 2s 15m, 10M; 258°-Iso G-226°-Al WG-264°-Iso W-268°-Al WR-270°-Iso R-274°; 50°09'·38N 05°03'·29W.
N Arm ⚓ QR 5m 3M; 50°09'·42N 05°03'·20W.
Inner Hbr Dir ⚓ 233°: WRG 3s 5m, 9M; 226°-Iso G-231°-Iso W-236°-Iso R-241°; 50°09'·20N 05°03'·94W.
Falmouth Haven Marina ⚓ 2 FR (vert); 50°09'·27N 05°03'·91W.
Falmouth Marina ⚓ VQ (3) 5s; 50°09'·91N 05°04'·99W.

DODMAN POINT and MEVAGISSEY

Naval gunnery targets SSE of Dodman Point:
'A' ⚓ Fl Y 10s; 50°08'·53N 04°46'·37W.
'B' ⚓ Fl Y 5s; 50°10'·30N 04°45'·00W.
'C' ⚓ Fl Y 2s; 50°10'·40N 04°47'·51W.
Gwineas ⚓ Q (3) 10s; *Bell;* 50°14'·48N 04°45'·40W.
Mevagissey, Victoria Pier ⚓ Fl (2) 10s 9m 12M; *Dia 30s;* 50°16'·15N 04°46'·92W.

FOWEY

Cannis Rk ⚓ Q (6) + L Fl 15s; *Bell;* 50°18'·45N 04°39'·88W.
Fowey ⚓ L Fl WR 5s 28m W11M, R9M; 284°-R-295°-W-028°-R-054°; W 8-sided twr, R lantern; 50°19'·63N 04°38'·83W.
St Catherine's Pt ⚓ Fl R 2·5s 15m 2M; vis 150°-295°; 50°19'·69N 04°38'·66W.
Lamp Rock ⚓ Fl G 5s 3m 2M; vis 357°-214°; 50°19'·70N 04°38'·41W. Whitehouse Pt ⚓ Iso WRG 3s 11m W11M, R/G8M; 017°-G-022°- W-032°-R-037°; R col; 50°19'·98N 04°38'·28W.

POLPERRO, LOOE, EDDYSTONE and WHITSAND BAY

Udder Rock ⚓ VQ (6) + L Fl 10s; *Bell;* 50°18'·93N 04°33'·85W.

POLPERRO, W pier ⚡ FW 4m 4M; FR when hbr closed in bad weather; 50°19'·86N 04°30'·96W.

Spy House Pt ⚡ Iso WR 6s 30m 7M; W288°-060°, R060°-288°; 50°19'·81N 04°30'·69W.

LOOE, Ranneys ⚓ Q (6) + L Fl 15s; 50°19'·85N 04°26'·37W.

Mid Main ⚓ Q (3) 10s 2M; 50°20'·56N 04°26'·94W.

Banjo Pier ☆ Oc WR 3s 8m **W15M**, R12M; 207°-R267°-W-313°-R-332°; 50°21'·06N 04°27'·06W.

White Rock ⚡ Fl R 3s 5m 2M; 50°21'·03N 04°27'·09W.

Eddystone ☆ Fl (2) 10s 41m **17M**. Same twr, Iso R 10s 28m 8M; vis 110°-133° over Hand Deeps; Gy twr, helicopter platform; *Horn 30s; Racon T, 10M;* 50°10'·84N 04°15'·94W; 992351125.

Hand Deeps ⚓ Q (9) 15s; 50°12'·68N 04°21'·10W.

PLYMOUTH

PLYMOUTH SOUND, WESTERN CHANNEL

Draystone ⚲ Fl (2) R 5s; 50°18'·85N 04°11'·07W.

Knap ▲ Fl G 5s; 50°19'·56N 04°10'·02W.

Plymouth bkwtr W head, ⚡ Fl WR 10s 19m W12M, R9M; 262°-W-208°-R-262°; W ◯ twr. Same twr, Iso 4s 12m 10M; vis 033°-037°; *Horn 15s;* 50°20'·07N 04°09'·52W.

Maker ⚡ Fl (2) WRG 15s 29m, W11M, R/G6M; 270°-G330°-W-004°-R-050°; W twr, R stripe; 50°20'·51N 04°10'·87W.

Queens Ground ⚲ Fl (2) R 10s; 50°20'·29N 04°10'·08W.

New Ground ⚲ Fl R 2s; 50°20'·47N 04°09'·43W.

Melampus ⚲ Fl R 4s; 50°21'·15N 04°08'·72W.

PLYMOUTH SOUND, EASTERN CHANNEL

Wembury Pt ⚡ Oc Y 10s 45m; occas; 50°19'·01N 04°06'·63W.

West Tinker ⚓ VQ (9) 10s; 50°19'·25N 04°08'·64W.

East Tinker ⚓ Q (3) 10s; 50°19'·20N 04°08'·30W.

Whidbey ⚓ Oc (2) WRG 10s 29m, W8M, R/G6M; H24; 000°-G-137·5°-W-139·5°-R-159°; Or and W col; 50°19'·53N 04°07'·27W.

The Breakwater, E head ⚓ L Fl WR 10s 9m W8M, R6M; 190°-R-353°-W-001°-R-018°-W-190°; 50°20'·01N 04°08'·24W.

Staddon Pt ⚓ Oc WRG 10s 15m W8M, R/G5M; H24. 348°-G-038°-W-050°-R-090°; W structure, R bands; 50°20'·17N 04°07'·54W.

Withyhedge Dir ⚡ 070° (for W Chan): WRG 13m W13M, R/G5M; H24; 060°-FG-065°-Al WG (W phase increasing with brg) -069°-FW-071°-Al WR (R phase increasing with brg)-075°-F R 080°; W ▽, orange stripe on col. Same col, Fl (2) Bu 5s; vis 120°-160°; 50°20'·75N 04°07'·44W.

SMEATON PASS (W of Mount Batten and S of The Hoe)

Ldg lts 349°. Front, Mallard Shoal ⚓ Q WRG 5m W10M, R/G3M; W △, Or bands; 233°-G-043°- R-067°- G-087°-W-099°-R-108° (ldg sector); 50°21'·60N 04°08'·33W. Rear, 396m from front, Hoe ⚓ Oc G 1·3s 11m 3M, 310°-040°; W ▽, Or bands; 50°21'·81N 04°08'·39W.

S Mallard ⚓ VQ (6) + L Fl 10s; 50°21'·51N 04°08'·30W.

W Mallard ▲ QG; 50°21'·57N 04°08'·36W.

S Winter ⚓ Q (6) + L Fl 15s; 50°21'·40N 04°08'·55W.

NE Winter ⚲ QR; 50°21'·54N 04°08'·50W.

NW Winter ⚓ VQ (9) 10s; 50°21'·55N 04°08'·70W.

ENTRANCE TO THE CATTEWATER

QAB (Queen Anne's Battery) ldg lts ⚡ 048·5°. Front, FR; Or/W bcn; 50°21'·84N 04°07'·84W. Rear, Oc R 8s 14m 3M; 139m NE.

Fishers Nose ⚡ Fl (3) R 10s 6m 4M; 50°21'·80N 04°08'·01W. Also F Bu ≠ 026·5° with F Bu 50°22'·00N 04°07'·86W, for Cobbler Chan.

DRAKE CHANNEL, THE BRIDGE and THE NARROWS

Ravenness Dir ⚡ 225°: WRG 11m, W13M, R/G5M; vis 217°-FG-221°-Al WG-224° (W phase inc with brg)-FW-226°-Al WR-229° (R phase inc with bearing)-FR-237°; H24; W ▽, O stripe col. In fog, 160°-FW-305°; power failure QY; 50°21'·14N 04°10'·07W.

Asia ⚲ Fl (2) R 5s; 50°21'·47N 04°08'·85W.

St Nicholas ⚲ QR; 50°21'·55N 04°09'·20W.

N Drakes Is ⚲ Fl R 4s; 50°21'·52N 04°09'·38W.

E Vanguard ▲ QG; 50°21'·47N 04°09'·70W.

W Vanguard ▲ Fl G 3s; 50°21'·49N 04°09'·98W.

Devils Point ⚓ QG 5m 3M; Fl 5s in fog; 50°21'·59N 04°10'·04W. Battery ⚲ Fl R 2s; 50°21'·52N 04°10'·21W.

The Bridge Channel

No 1, ⚓ QG 4m; 50°21'·03N 04°09'·53W. No 2, ⚓ QR 4m. No 3, ⚓ Fl (3) G 10s 4m. No 4, ⚓ Fl (4) R 10s 4m; 50°21'·09N 04°09'·63W.

Mount Wise, Dir ⚡ 343°: WRG 7m, W13M, R/G5M; H24. 331°-FG-338°-Al WG-342° (W phase increasing with brg)-FW-344°-Al WR-348° (R phase increasing with bearing)-FR-351°. In fog, 341·5°-FW-344·5°; 50°21'·96N 04°10'·33W.

Ocean Court Dir Q WRG 15m, W11M, R/G3M; 010°-G-080°-W-090°-R-100°; 50°21'·85N 04°10'·11W.

PLYMOUTH TO START POINT

RIVER YEALM

Sand bar ⚲ Fl R 5s; 50°18'·59N 04°04'·12W.

SALCOMBE

Sandhill Pt Dir ⚡ 000°: Fl WRG 2s 27m W/R/G 8M; 337·5°-G-357·5°-W-002·5°-R-012·5°; R/W ◇ on W mast, rear daymark; 50°13'·77N 03°46'·67W. Front daymark, Pound Stone R/W ⚓.

Bass Rk ⚲ Fl R 5s; 50°13'·47N 03°46'·71W.

Wolf Rk ▲ Fl G 5s; 50°13'·53N 03°46'·58W.

Blackstone Rk ⚓; 50°13'·61N 03°46'·51W.

Ldg lts 042·5°, front Fl 2s 5m 8M, 50°14'·53N 03°45'·31W; rear Fl 5s 45m 8M.

Start Pt ☆ Fl (3) 10s 62m **18M**; 184°-068°. Same twr: FR 55m 9M; 210°-255° over Skerries Bank; *Horn 30s;* 50°13'·34N 03°38'·54W.

START POINT TO PORTLAND BILL

DARTMOUTH

Kingswear Dir ⚡ 328°: Iso WRG 3s 9m 8M; 318°-G-325°-W-331°-R-340°; W ◯ twr; 50°20'·81N 03°34'·09W.

Mewstone ⚓ VQ (6) + L Fl 10s; 50°19'·92N 03°31'·89W.

West Rock ⚓ Q (6) + L Fl 15s; 50°19'·86N 03°32'·47W.

Homestone ⚲ QR; 50°19'·61N 03°33'·55W.

Castle Ledge ▲ Fl G 5s; 50°19'·99N 03°33'·11W.

Checkstone ⚲ Fl (2) R 5s; 50°20'·45N 03°33'·81W.

Dir ⚡ 104·5°: FW 5m 9M; vis 102°-107°; 50°20'·65N 03°33'·80W.

BRIXHAM

Berry Head ☆ Fl (2) 15s 58m **18M**; vis 100°-023°; W twr; 50°23'·98N 03°29'·01W. R lts on radio mast 5·7M NW, inland of Paignton.

Victoria bkwtr ⚓ Oc R 15s 9m 6M; W twr; 50°24'·33N 03°30'·78W.

No 1 ▲ Fl G; 50°24'·30N 03°30'·89W.

No 2 ⬡ Fl R; 50°24'·32N 03°30'·83W.

PAIGNTON and TORQUAY

▲ QG (May-Sep); 50°27'·42N 03°31'·80W, 85m off Haldon Pier.

Haldon Pier (E) ⚓ QG 9m 6M; 50°27'·43N 03°31'·73W.

Princess Pier (W) ⚓ QR 9m 6M; 50°27'·46N 03°31'·73W.

TEIGNMOUTH

Outfall ⚓ Fl Y 5s; 50°31'·97N 03°27'·77W, 288°/1·3M to hbr ent.

Bar ▲ Fl G 2s; 50°32'·44N 03°29'·25W.

Trng wall, middle ⚓ Oc R 6s 4m 3M; 50°32'·33N 03°29'·93W.

The Point ⚓ Oc G 6s 3M & FG (vert); 50°32'·42N 03°30'·05W.

RIVER EXE to SIDMOUTH and AXMOUTH

Exe ⬡ Mo(A) 10s; 50°35'·86N 03°23'·79W.

No 1 ▲ 50°36'·03N 03°23'·77W.

No 2 ⬡ 50°36'·01N 03°23'·87W.

Exmouth Dir ⚓ 305°: WRG 6m, 6M; 299°-Iso G-304°-Iso W-306°-Iso R-311°; W col, 50°36'·99N 03°25'·34W.

No 10 ⬡ Fl R 3s; 50°36'·73N 03°24'·77W.

No 12 Warren Pt ⬡ 50°36'·91N 03°25'·41W.

Sidmouth ⚓ Fl R 5s 5m 2M; 50°40'·48'N 03°14'·43W.

Axmouth jetty ⚓ Fl G 4s 7m 2M; 50°42'·12N 03°03'·29W.

LYME REGIS

Outfall ⚓ Q (6) + L Fl 15s; 50°43'·17N 02°55'·66W.

Ldg lts 284°: Front, Victoria Pier ⚓ Oc WR 8s 6m, W9M, R7M; 284°-R-104°-W-284°; Bu col; 50°43'·19N 02°56'·17W. Rear, FG 8m 9M.

WEST BAY (BRIDPORT)

W pier root, Dir ⚓ 336°: F WRG 5m 4M; 165°-G-331°-W-341°-R-165°; 50°42'·62N 02°45'·89W.

W pier outer limit ⚓ Iso R 2s 5m 4M; 50°42'·51N 02°45'·83W.

E pier outer limit ⚓ Iso G 2s 5m 4M; 50°42'·53N 02°45'·80W.

PORTLAND BILL TO ANVIL POINT

Portland Bill lt ho ☆ Fl (4) 20s 43m **18M**. vis 221°-141°. W ○ twr; *Dia 30s*; 50°30'·85N 02°27'·38W. Same twr, FR 19m 13M; 265°-291° over Shambles.

W Shambles ⚓ Q (9) 15s; *Bell*; 50°29'·78N 02°24'·41W.

E Shambles ⚓ Q (3) 10s; *Bell*; 50°31'·26N 02°20'·08W.

PORTLAND HARBOUR

Outer Bkwtr Fort Head (N end) ⚓ QR 14m 5M; 013°-268°; 50°35'·11N 02°24'·87W.

NE Bkwtr (A Hd) ⚓ Fl 2·5s 22m 10M; 50°35'·16N 02°25'·07W.

NE Bkwtr (B Hd) ⚓ Oc R 15s 11m 5M; 50°35'·65N 02°25'·88W.

N Arm (C Hd) ⚓ Oc G 10s 11m 5M; 50°35'·78N 02°25'·95W.

WEYMOUTH

Ldg lts 239·6°: both FR 5/7m 7M; Front 50°36'·46N 02°26'·87W, S Pier hd ⚓ Q 10m 9M; 50°36'·58N 02°26'·49W. IPTS 190m SW.

LULWORTH RANGE TO ANVIL POINT

Targets: DZ 'A' ⬡, Fl Y 2s, 50°33'·34N 02°06'·52W.
off DZ 'B' ⬡, Fl Y 10s, 50°32'·11N 02°05'·92W.
St Alban's Hd DZ 'C' ⬡, Fl Y 5s, 50°32'·76N 02°04'·56W.

Anvil Pt ⚓ Fl 10s 45m 9M; vis 237°-076° (H24); W ○ twr and dwelling; 50°35'·51N 01°57'·60W. Measured mile close west.

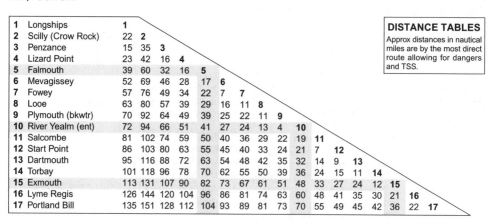

		1	2	3	4	5	6	7	8	9	10	11	12	13	14	15	16	17
1	Longships	1																
2	Scilly (Crow Rock)	22	2															
3	Penzance	15	35	3														
4	Lizard Point	23	42	16	4													
5	Falmouth	39	60	32	16	5												
6	Mevagissey	52	69	46	28	17	6											
7	Fowey	57	76	49	34	22	7	7										
8	Looe	63	80	57	39	29	16	11	8									
9	Plymouth (bkwtr)	70	92	64	49	39	25	22	11	9								
10	River Yealm (ent)	72	94	66	51	41	27	24	13	4	10							
11	Salcombe	81	102	74	59	50	40	36	29	22	19	11						
12	Start Point	86	103	80	63	55	45	40	33	24	21	7	12					
13	Dartmouth	95	116	88	72	63	54	48	42	35	32	14	9	13				
14	Torbay	101	118	96	78	70	62	55	50	39	36	24	15	11	14			
15	Exmouth	113	131	107	90	82	73	67	61	51	48	33	27	24	12	15		
16	Lyme Regis	126	144	120	104	96	86	81	74	63	60	48	41	35	30	21	16	
17	Portland Bill	135	151	128	112	104	93	89	81	73	70	55	49	45	42	36	22	17

DISTANCE TABLES

Approx distances in nautical miles are by the most direct route allowing for dangers and TSS.

SELECTED LIGHTS, BUOYS & WAYPOINTS

SWANAGE TO ISLE OF WIGHT

SWANAGE

Pier Hd ⚡ 2 FR (vert) 6m 3M; 50°36'·56N 01°56'·95W.
Peveril Ledge ⚓ QR; 50°36'·41N 01°56'·10W.

POOLE BAR and SWASH CHANNEL

Poole Bar (No 1) ⬣ QG; 50°39·29N 01°55'·14W.
(Historic wreck) ⚓ Fl Y 5s; 50°39'·70N 01°54'·86W.
No 2 ⬢ Fl R 2s; 50°39'·23N 01°55'·24W.
No 3 ⬣ Fl G 3s; 50°39'·76N 01°55'·49W.
No 4 ⬢ Fl R 2s; 50°39'·72N 01°55'·60W.
Training Bank ⚓ 2 FR (vert); 50°39'·82N 01°55'·86W.
No 5 ⬣Fl G 5s; 50°40'·19N 01°55'·81W.
No 6 ⬢ Fl R 4s; 50°40'·14N 01°55'·91W.
Hook Sands (No 7) ⬣ Fl G 3s; 50°40'·50N 01°56'·16W.
Channel (No 8) ⬢ Fl R 2s; 50°40'·45N 01°56'·27W.
Swash (No 9) ⚓ Q (9) 15s; 50°40'·88N 01°56'·70W.
No 10 ⬢ Fl R 4s; 50°40'·84N 01°56'·86W.

EAST LOOE CHANNEL

East Hook ⬢ 50°40'·58W 01°55'·23W.
East Looe 1 ⬣ Fl G 5s; 50°41'·09N 01°55'·82W.
East Looe 2 ⬢ Fl R 4s; 50°41'·07N 01°55'·83W.
East Looe 3 (Limit 10kn) ⬣ Fl G 3s; 50°41'·07N 01°56'·17W.
East Looe 4 (Limit 10kn) ⬢ Fl R 2s; 50°41'·05N 01°56'·17W.
North Hook ⬢ Fl (2) R 5s; 50°40'·97N 01°56'·51W.

BROWNSEA ROADS

No 12 ⬢ Q R; 50°40'·94N 01°57'·17W.
No14 ⬢ Fl R 2s; 50°41'·03N 01°57'·32W.
N Haven ⚓ Q (9) 15s 5m; 50°41'·15N 01°57'·39W.
Brownsea ⚓ Q (3) 10s; 50°41'·14N 01°57'·39W.
Brownsea Island Dir lt 299°F WRG; 296·5°-G-297·8°-AltWG-298·8°-W-299·2°-AltWR-300·2°-R-301·5°; 50°41'·16N 01°57'·67W (only shown for commercial vessels); 2FR(vert); 301·5°-296·5° (H24).

MIDDLE SHIP CHANNEL

Bell (No 15) ⚓ Q (6) + L Fl 15s; 50°41'·36N 01°57'·12W.
No 16 ⬢ VQ R; 50°41'·43N 01°57'·25W.
No 17 ⬣ Fl G 3s; 50°41'·68N 01°57'·02W.
Aunt Betty (No 22) ⚓ Q (3)10s; 50°41'·96N 01°57'·39W.
Diver (No 25) ⚓ Q (9) 15s; 50°42'·29N 01°58'·32W.

NORTH CHANNEL

Salterns Marina Outer Bkwtr Hd ⚡ 2 FR (vert) 2M; Tfc sigs; 50°42'·23N 01°57'·10W.
Parkstone YC platform ⚡ Q 8m 1M; 50°42'·37N 01°58'·08W.
Stakes (No 29) ⚓ Q (6) + L Fl 15s; 50°42'·43N 01°59'·00W.

POOLE BAY

Flag Hd Chine ⚓ Fl (2); 50°41'·79N 01°55'·10W.
Bournemouth Rocks ⬢ 50°42'·32N 01°53'·40W.
Christchurch Ledge ⚓ 50°41'·57N 01°41'·55W (Apr-Oct).
⚓(x2) Fl(5) Y 20s; 50°37'·98N 01°43'·02W; (265°Needles F'wy).

WESTERN APPROACHES TO THE SOLENT

NEEDLES CHANNEL

Needles Fairway ⚓ L Fl 10s; *Bell*; 50°38'·24N 01°38'·98W.

SW Shingles ⚓ Fl R 2·5s; 50°39'·29N 01°37'·52W.
Bridge ⚓ VQ (9) 10s; *Racon (T) 10M*; 50°39'·63N 01°36'·88W.

NEEDLES ☆ 50°39'·73N 01°35'·50W; Oc (2) WRG 20s 24m
W17M, R14M, R13M G14M; ○ Twr, R band and lantern; vis: shore-R-300°-W-083°-R (unintens)-212°-W-217°-G-224° (H24). Horn (2) 30s.
Shingles Elbow ⬢ Fl (2) R 5s; 50°40'·37N 01°36'·05W.
Mid Shingles ⬢ Fl (3) R 10s; 50°41'·21N 01°34'·66W.
Warden ⬣ Fl G 2·5s; *Bell*; 50°41'·48N 01°33'·55W.
NE Shingles ⚓ Q (3) 10s; 50°41'·96N 01°33'·41W.

Hurst Point ☆ 50°42'·48N 01°33'·03W; FL (4) WR 15s 23m
W13M, R11M; W ○ Twr; vis:080°-W(unintens)-104°, 234°-W-244°-R-250°- W-053°. Same structure, Iso WRG 4s 19m
W21M, R18M, G17M; vis: 038·8°-G-040·8°-W-041·8°-R-043·8°; By day W7M, R5M, G5M.

NORTH CHANNEL

North Head ⬣ Fl (3) G 10s; 50°42'·69N 01°35'·52W.

THE WESTERN SOLENT

Note: Numerous yellow yacht racing buoys are laid throughout the Solent (seasonal, Mar-Dec). Most, but not all, are lit Fl Y 4s.

SOLENT MARKS

Sconce ⚓ Q; *Bell*; 50°42'·53N 01°31'·43W.
Black Rock ⬣ Fl G 5s; 50°42'·57N 01°30'·59W.
Lymington Bank ⬢ Fl (2) R 5s; *Bell*; 50°43'·10N 01°30'·85W.
Solent Bank ⬢ Fl (3) R 10s; 50°44'·23N 01°27'·37W.
Hamstead Ledge ⬣ Fl (2) G 5s; 50°43'·87N 01°26'18W.
Newtown River ⚓ Q (9) 15s; 50°43'·75N 01°24'·96W.
W Lepe ⬢ Fl R 5s; 50°45'·24N 01°24'·09W.
Salt Mead ⬣ Fl (3) G 10s; 50°44'·51N 01°23'·04W.
Gurnard Ledge ⬣ Fl (4) G 15s; 50°45'·51N 01°20'·59W.
E Lepe ⬢ Fl (2) R 5s; *Bell*; 50°45'·93N 01°21'·07W.
Lepe Spit ⚓ Q (6) + L Fl 15s; 50°46'·78N 01°20'·64W.
Gurnard ⚓ Q; 50°46'·22N 01°18'·84W.

YARMOUTH

East Fairway ⬢ Fl R 2s; 50°42'·62N 01°29'·95W.
Poole Belle ⬢ Fl Y 5s; 50°42'·54N 01°30'·17W.
Pier Head, centre, ⚡ 2 FR (vert) 2M; G col. High intensity FW (occas); 50°42'·51N 01°29'·97W.
Ldg Lts 187·6° Front FG 5m 2M; 50°42'·36N 01°30'·06 W. Rear, 63m from front, FG 9m 2M; both W ◇.

LYMINGTON

Ldg Lts 319·5°, Or posts. Front, FR 12m 8M; 50°45'·19N 01°31'·65W. vis: 309·5°-329·5°. Rear, FR 17m 8M.
Jack in the Basket ⚓ Fl R 2s 9m; 50°44'·27N 01°30'·57W.
No 1 ⚓ Fl G 2s 2m 3M; G △ on pile; 50°44'·41N 01°30'·48W.
No 2 (Cross Boom) ⚓ Fl R 2s 4m 3M; 50°44'·36N 01°30'·58W.
Yacht Haven ldg lts 244°. Front FY 4m; R △; 50°45'·09N 01°31'·53W. Rear, 22m from front, FY 6m; R ▽.

BEAULIEU RIVER

Millennium Dir lt 334°. ⚡ OcWRG 4s 13m W4M, R3M, G3M; vis: 318°-G-330°-W-337°-R-348°; 50°47'·12N 01°21'·90W.
Beaulieu Spit E ⚓ Fl R 5s 3M; R dolphin; 50°46'·85N 01°21'·76W.

No 1 ⚓ 50°46'·91N 01°21'·70W.
No 2 ⚓ 50°46'·92N 01°21'·78W.

COWES

Prince Consort ⚓ VQ; 50°46'·41N 01°17'·56W.
Trinity House ⚓ Fl Y 5s; 50°46'·31N 01°17'·75W.
No 1 ⚓ Q G; 50°46'·07N 01°18'·03W.
No 2 ⚓ Q R; 50°46'·07N 01°17'·87W.
No 2A ⚓ LFl R 10s; 50°45'·92N 01°17'·70W.
No 4A Tide gauge ⚓ L Fl R 5s; 50°45'·76N 01°17'·63W.
EC 11 ⚓ Q (6) + L Fl 15s; 50°45'·80N 01°17'·67W.
E Cowes Bkwtr Hd ⚓ 2F R; 50°45'·88N 01°17'·52W.
EC 8 ⚓ Fl R 4s; 50°45'·87N 01°17'·58W.
EC 7 ⚓ Fl G 4s; 50°45'·90N 01°17'·60W.
EC 3 ⚓ Q (3) 10s; 50°45'·99N 01°17'·51W.
EC 2 ⚓ Fl R 3s; 50°46'·06N 01°17'·04W.
EC 1 ⚓ Fl G 3s; 50°46'·08N 01°17'·05W.
Shrape Bn ⚓ LFl R 10S 3m 3M; 50°46'·09N 01°16'·90W.

CENTRAL SOLENT AND SOUTHAMPTON WATER

Note: Numerous yellow yacht racing buoys are laid throughout the Solent (seasonal, Mar-Dec). Most, but not all, are lit Fl Y 4s.

SOLENT MARKS

Lepe Spit ⚓ Q(6) + L Fl 15s; 50°46'·78N 01°20'·64W.
NE Gurnard ⚓ Fl(3) R 10s; 50°47'·06N 01°19'·42W.
South Bramble ⚓ Fl G 2·5s; 50°46'·98N 01°17'·72W.
W Bramble ⚓ VQ(9) 10s; *Racon (T) 3M*; 50°47'·20N 01°18'·65W; AIS.
Thorn Knoll ⚓ Fl G 5s; 50°47'·50N 01°18'·44W.
Bourne Gap ⚓ Fl R 3s; 50°47'·83N 01°18'·34W.
West Knoll ⚓ Fl Y 2·5s; 50°47'·43N 01°17'·84W.
North Thorn ⚓ QG; 50°47'·92N 01°17'·84W.
East Knoll ⚓ Fl(2) G 10s; 50°47'·96N 01°16'·86W.
Stanswood Outfall ⚓ Iso R 10s 6m 5M; 4 FR Lts; 50°48'·26N 01°18'·82W.

CALSHOT REACH

East Knoll ⚓ 50°47'·96N 01°16'·83W.
CALSHOT SPIT ⚓ Fl 5s 5m 10M; R hull, Lt Twr amidships; *Horn (2) 60s*; 50°48'·35N 01°17'·64W.
Calshot ⚓ VQ; 50°48'·44N 01°17'·03W.
Castle Point ⚓ IQ R 10s; 50°48'·71N 01°17'·67W.
Reach ⚓ Fl (3) G 10s; 50°49'·05N 01°17'·65W.
Black Jack ⚓ Fl (2) R 4s; 50°49'·13N 01°18'·09W.
Hook ⚓ QG; *Horn (1) 15s*; 50°49'·52N 01°18'·30W.
Coronation ⚓ Fl Y 5s; 50°49'·55N 01°17'·62W.
Bald Head ⚓ Fl G 2·5s; 50°49'·80N 01°18'·06W.

RIVER HAMBLE

Hamble Pt ⚓ Q (6) + L Fl 15s; 50°50'·15N 01°18'·66W.
Hamble Common ⚓ Dir 351·7°, Oc (2) WRG 12s 5m W4M; R4M; G4M; vis: 348·7°-G-350·7°-W-352·7°-R-354·7°; 50°51'·00N 01°18'·84W.
Sailing Club Dir lt 028·9° ⚓ Iso WRG 6s 5m W4M, R4M, G4M: vis: 025·9°-G-027·9°-W-029·9°-R-031·9°; 50°51'·10N 01°18'·34W.

SOUTHAMPTON WATER

Fawley Terminal SE ⚓ 2 FR(vert) 9m 10M; 50°50'·06N 01°19'·42W.
Fawley Deep ⚓ Fl (2) G 4s; 50°50'·42N 01°19'·19W.
Greenland ⚓ Iso G 2s; 50°51'·11N 01°20'·38W.
Cadland ⚓ Fl R 3s; 50°51'·02N 01°20'·54W.
After Barn ⚓ Fl (2) G 4s; 50°51'·53N 01°20'·81W.

Lains Lake ⚓ Fl (2) R 4s; 50°51'·59N 01°21'·65W.
Hound ⚓ Fl (3) G 10s; 50°51'·68N 01°21'·52W.
Netley ⚓ Fl G 3s; 50°52'·03N 01°21'·81W.
Deans Elbow ⚓ Oc R 4s; 50°52'·20N 01°22'·85W.
NW Netley ⚓ Q G; 50°52'·31N 01°22'·73W.
Moorhead ⚓ Q G; 50°52'·55N 01°22'·90W.
Test ⚓ Fl (2) R 4s; 50°52'·59N 01°23'·45W.
Weston Shelf ⚓ Fl (2) G 4s; 50°52'·71N 01°23'·26W.

HYTHE

Hythe Pier Hd ⚓ 2 FR (vert) 12m 5M; 50°52'·49N 01°23'·61W.
Hythe Marina Ent ⚓ Q (3) 10s; 50°52'·63N 01°23'·88W.
Hythe Knock ⚓ Fl R 3s; 50°52'·83N 01°23'·81W.

SOUTHAMPTON and RIVER ITCHEN

Swinging Ground No 1 ⚓ Oc G 4s; 50°53'·00N 01°23'·44W.
E side. No 1 ⚓ QG; 50°53'·15N 01°23'·40W.
No 2 ⚓ Fl G 5s 2M; 50°53'·29N 01°23'·38W.
No 3 ⚓ Fl G 7s; 50°53'·48N 01°23'·28W.
No 4 ⚓ QG 4m 2M; 50°53'·62N 01°23'·16W.

SOUTHAMPTON and RIVER TEST

QE II Terminal, S end 4 FG (vert) 16m 3M; 50°53'·00N 01°23'·71W.
Gymp ⚓ QR; 50°53'·07N 01°24'·16W.
Town Quay Ldg Lts 329°, both F 12/22m 3/2M.
Gymp Elbow ⚓ Oc R 4s; 50°53'·43N 01°24'·61W.
Dibden Bay ⚓ Q; 50°53'·70N 01°24'·92W.

THE EASTERN SOLENT

Note: Numerous yellow yacht racing buoys are laid throughout the Solent (seasonal, Mar-Dec). Most, but not all, are lit Fl Y 4s.

SOLENT MARKS

West Ryde Middle ⚓ Q (9) 15s; 50°46'·48N 01°15'·79W.
Norris ⚓ Fl (3) R 10s; 50°45'·97N 01°15'·51W.
N Ryde Middle ⚓ Fl (4) R 20s; 50°46'·61N 01°14'·31W.
South Ryde Middle ⚓ Fl G 5s; 50°46'·13N 01°14'·16W.
Peel Bank ⚓ Fl (2) R 5s; 50°45'·49N 01°13'·35W.
SE Ryde Middle ⚓ VQ (6)+L Fl 10s; 50°45'·93N 01°12'·10W.
NE Ryde Middle ⚓ Fl (2) R 10s; 50°46'·21N 01°11'·88W.
Mother Bank ⚓ Fl R 3s; 50°45'·49N 01°11'·21W.
Browndown ⚓ Fl G 15s; 50°46'·57N 01°10'·95W.
Fort Gilkicker ⚓ Oc G 10s 7M; 50°46'·43N 01°08'·47W.
N Sturbridge ⚓ VQ; 50°45'·33N 01°08'·23W.
Ryde Sands ⚓ Fl R 10s; 50°44'·56N 01°07'·26W.
Ryde Sands ⚓ L Fl R 12s; 50°44'·16N 01°05'·99W.
No Man's Land Fort ⚓ Iso R 2s 21m 8M; 50°44'·40N 01°05'·70W.
Horse Sand Fort ⚓ Iso G 2s 21m 8M; 50°45'·01N 01°04'·34W.
Saddle ⚓ VQ (3) G 10s; 50°45'·05N 01°04'·94W.

NORTH CHANNEL and HILLHEAD

Calshot ⚓ VQ; *Bell (1) 30s*; 50°48'·44N 01°17'·03W.
Hillhead ⚓ Fl R 2·5s; 50°48'·07N 01°16'·00W.
E Bramble ⚓ VQ (3) 5s; 50°47'·23N 01°13'·64W.

WOOTTON CREEK

Wootton Beacon ⚓ Q 1M; (NB); 50°44'·53N 01°12'·16W.
Dir lt Oc WRG 10s vis: 220·8°-G-224·3°-W-225·8°-R-230·8°; 50°44'·03N 01°12'·86W.

RYDE

Ryde Pier 2 FR (vert) mark corners. In fog FY from N corner, vis: 045°-165°, 200°-320°; 50°44'·34N 01°09'·72W.

Leisure Hbr E side ⚓ 2 FR (vert) 7m 1M. FY 6m shown when depth of water in Hbr greater than 1m; 2 FY 6m when depth exceeds 1·5m; 50°43'·99N 01°09'·29W.

PORTSMOUTH APPROACHES

Horse Sand ▲ Fl G 2·5s; 50°45'·62N 01°05'·12W.
Outer Spit (OSB) ⚲ Q (6) + L Fl 15s; 50°45'·44N 01°05'·46W.
Mary Rose ⚲ Fl Y 5s; 50°45'·80N 01°06'·22W.
Boyne ▲ Fl G 5s; 50°46'·04N 01°05'·26W.
Spit Refuge ⚲ Fl R 5s; 50°46'·21N 01°05'·68W.
Spit Sand Fort ⚓ Fl R 5s; 18m 7M. 50°46'·24N 01°05'·94W.
Castle ▲ Fl (2) G 6s; 50°46'·50N 01°05'·40W.
Southsea S Castle Pile ⚓ Dir 348° WRG 17m 11M day 6M, pile vis: 340°-FG-343°-Al WG (W phase inc with brg)-347°-FW-349°-AlWR(R phase incr with brg)-354°-FR-356°; H24; same structure Fl G 5s; 50°46'·66N 01°05'·65W.
No 1 Bar (NB) ▲ Fl (3) G 10s; 50°46'·77N 01°05'·81W.
No 2 ⚲ Fl (3) R 10s; 50°46'·66N 01°06'·15W.
No 3 ▲ QG; 50°47'·08N 01°06'·23W.
No 4 ⚲ QR; 50°46'·98N 01°06'·48W.
BC Outer ⚲ Oc R 15s; 50°47'·32N 01°06'·68W.

PORTSMOUTH HARBOUR

Fort Blockhouse ⚓ Dir 323° WRG 4s 6m WRG 12M; vis: 313°- Oc G-317°-Fl G (phase dec with brg)-321°- Oc W-325°-Fl R (phase inc with brg)-329°-Oc R-333°; 50°47'·37N 01°06'·74W.
Ballast ⚲ Fl R 2·5s; 50°47'·62N 01°06'·83W.
Hbr Ent ⚓ Dir 333·75° WRG 2s 2m 12M; vis: 323·75°-Iso G-329·75°-Fl G (phase dec with brg)-332·75°-Iso (main chan)-334·75°-Fl R (phase inc with brg)-337·75°-Iso R-343·75°; H24; same structure Fuel Jetty ⚓ 2F R (vert) 8m 4M; 50°47'·85N 01°06'·98W.

EASTERN APPROACHES to THE SOLENT

Outer Nab 1 ⚲ VQ (9) 10s; 50°38'·18N 00°56'·88W.
Outer Nab 2 ⚲ VQ (3) 5s; 50°38'·43N 00°57'·70W.
Nab Tower ⚓ Fl 10s 17m 12M; *Horn (2) 30s; RACON T*; 50°40'·08N 00°57'·15W; 992351136.
N 2 ⚲ Fl Y 2·5s. 6M; 50°41'·03N 00°56'·74W.
N 1 ⚲ Fl Y (4)10s; 50°41'·26N 00°56'·52W.
N 4 ⚲ Fl Y 7·5s; 50°41'·86N 00°57'·24W.

N 3 ⚲ Fl (3) Y 15s; 50°41'·63N 00°56'·74W.
N 5 ⚲ Fl Y 5s; 50°41'·99N 00°56'·97W.
N 7 ⚲ Fl Y 2·5s; 50°42'·35N 00°57'·20W.
New Grounds ⚲ VQ (3) 5s; 50°41'·84N 00°58'·49W.
Nab End ⚲ Fl R 5s; *Whis*; 50°42'·63N 00°59'·49W.
Dean Tail ▲ Fl G 5s; 50°42'·99N 00°59'·17W.
Dean Tail S ⚲ VQ (6) + L Fl 10s; 50°43'·04N 00°59'·58W.
Dean Tail N ⚲ Q; 50°43'·13N 00°59'·57W.
Horse Tail ▲ Fl (2) G 10s; 50°43'·23N 01°00'·23W.
Nab East ⚲ Fl (2) R 10s; 50°42'·86N 01°00'·80W.
Dean Elbow ▲ Fl (3) G 15s; 50°43'·69N 01°01'·88W.
St Helens ⚲ Fl (3) R 15s; 50°43'·36N 01°02'·41W.
Horse Elbow ▲ QG; 50°44'·26N 01°03'·88W.
Cambrian Wreck ⚲ 50°44'·43N 01°03'·43W.
Warner ⚲ QR; *Whis*; 50°43'·87N 01°03'·99W.

BEMBRIDGE

St Helen's Fort ☆ (IOW) Fl (3) 10s 16m 8M; large ○ stone structure; 50°42'·30N 01°05'·05W.

SOUTH EAST COAST of the ISLE OF WIGHT

St Catherine's Point ☆ 50°34'·54N 01°17'·87W; Fl 5s 41m **25M**; vis: 257°-117°; FR 35m 13M (same Twr) vis: 099°-116°.
Ventnor Haven W Bwtr ⚓ 2 FR (vert) 3M; 50°35'·50N 01°12'·30W.
Sandown Pier Hd ⚓ 2 FR (vert) 7m 2M; 50°39'·05N 01°09'·18W.
W Princessa ⚲ Q (9) 15s; 50°40'·16N 01°03'·65W.
Bembridge Ledge ⚲ Q (3) 10s; 50°41'·15N 01°02'·81W

LANGSTONE and APPROACHES

Eastney Pt Fraser Trials Range ⚓ FR, Oc (2) Y 10s, and FY Lts (occas) when firing taking place; 50°47'·19N 01°02'·22W.
Winner ⚲; 50°45'·10N 01°00'·10W.
Roway Wk ⚲ Fl (2) 5s; 50°46'·11N 01°02'·28W.
Langstone Fairway ⚲ L Fl 10s; 50°46'·32N 01°01'·36W.
Eastney Pt Outfall ⚓ QR 2m 2M; 50°47'·23N 01°01'·68W.
East Milton ⚲ Fl (4) R 10s; 50°48'·16N 01°01'·76W.
NW Sinah ▲ Fl G 5s; 50°48'·14N 01°01'·58W.

DISTANCE TABLES
Approx distances in nautical miles are by the most direct route allowing for dangers and TSS.

		1	2	3	4	5	6	7	8	9	10	11	12	13	14	15	16	17	18
1	Portland Bill	1																	
2	Weymouth	8	2																
3	Swanage	23	22	3															
4	Poole Hbr ent	28	26	6	4														
5	Needles Lt Ho	35	34	14	14	5													
6	Lymington	42	40	21	21	7	6												
7	Yarmouth (IOW)	40	39	19	19	6	2	7											
8	Beaulieu River ent	46	45	25	25	12	7	7	8										
9	Cowes	49	46	28	28	15	9	9	3	9									
10	Southampton	55	54	34	34	21	15	15	9	9	10								
11	R. Hamble (ent)	53	51	32	32	19	12	12	6	6	4	11							
12	Portsmouth	58	57	37	37	24	18	18	11	9	18	15	12						
13	Langstone Hbr	61	59	40	40	27	22	22	15	12	16	13	5	13					
14	Chichester Bar	63	62	42	42	29	24	24	17	15	20	17	8	5	14				
15	Bembridge	59	58	38	38	25	19	19	12	10	19	15	6	6	8	15			
16	Nab Tower	60	63	39	39	30	25	25	18	16	21	18	10	7	6	6	16		
17	St Catherine's Pt	45	44	25	25	14	18	18	27	25	30	27	19	20	19	17	15	17	
18	Littlehampton	79	79	60	61	46	44	45	38	36	41	38	31	27	24	28	22	35	18

CHICHESTER ENTRANCE
West Pole (tripod) ⚓ Fl R 5s 14m 7M; 50°45'·45N 00°56'·59W.
Bar ⚓ Fl(2) R 10s 10m 4M; 50°46'·02N 00°56'·38W.
Eastoke ⚓ QR; 50°46'·68N 00°56'·11W.
West Winner ⚓ QG; Tide gauge. 50°46'·88N 00°55'·98W.

EMSWORTH CHANNEL
Fishery ⚓ Q (6) + L Fl 15s; 50°47'·38N 00°56'·07W.
NW Pilsey ⚓ Fl G 5s; 50°47'·50N 00°56'·20W.
Verner ⚓ Fl R 10s; 50°48'·20N 00°56'·63W.
Marker Pt ⚓ Fl (2) G 10s 8m; 50°48'·91N 00°56'·72W.
Emsworth ⚓ Q (6) + L Fl 15s; tide gauge; 50°49'·66N 00°56'·76W.

THORNEY CHANNEL
Camber ⚓ Q (6) + L Fl 15s; 50°47'·87N 00°54'·06W.
Pilsey ⚓ Fl (2) R 10s ; 50°47'·98N 00°54'·24W.
Thorney ⚓ Fl G 5s; 50°48'·20N 00°54'·28W.

CHICHESTER CHANNEL
NW Winner ⚓ Fl G 10s; 50°47'·19N 00°55'·92W.
N Winner ⚓ Fl (2) G 10s; 50°47'·31N 00°55'·83W.
Mid Winner ⚓ Fl (3) G 10s; 50°47'·40N 00°55'·72W.
Stocker ⚓ Fl (3) R 10s; 50°47'·45N 00°55'·52W.
Copyhold ⚓ Fl (4) R 10s; 50°47'·50N 00°54'·93W.
East Head Spit ⚓ Fl (4) G 10s; 50°47'·45N 00°54'·82W.
Snowhill ⚓ Fl G 5s; 50°47'·52N 00°54'·34W.
Sandhead ⚓ Fl R 10s; 50°47'·67N 00°54'·25W.
Chalkdock ⚓ Fl (2) G 10s; 50°48'·49N 00°53'·30W.

AREA 3 *South East England – Selsey Bill to North Foreland*

SELECTED LIGHTS, BUOYS & WAYPOINTS

OWERS TO BEACHY HEAD
SELSEY BILL and THE OWERS
S Pullar ⚓ VQ (6) + L Fl 10s; 50°38'·84N 00°49'·29W.
Pullar ⚓ Q (9) 15s; 50°40'·47N 00°50'·09W.
Boulder ⚓ Fl G 2·5s; 50°41'·56N 00°49'·09W.
Street ⚓ QR; 50°41'·69N 00°48'·89W.
Mixon Bn ⚓ Q(6) + L Fl 15s; 50°42'·37N 00°46'·32E.
Owers ⚓ Q (6) + L Fl 15s; *Bell*; *Racon (O) 10M*; 50°38'·59N 00°41'·09W.
E Borough Hd ⚓ Q (3) 10s *Bell*; 50°41'·54N 00°39'·09W.

LITTLEHAMPTON
West Pier Hd ⚓ QR 7m 6M; 50°47'·88N 00°32'·46W.
Training Wall Hd ⚓ QG 10m 2M; 50°47'·87N 00°32'·38W.
Ldg lts 346°. Front, E Pier Hd ☆ FG 6m 7M; B col. Rear, 64m from front, Oc W 7·5s 9m10M; W twr; vis: 290°-W-042°; 50°48'·09N 00°32'·51W.
Outfall ⚓ Fl Y 5s; 50°46'·27N 00°30'·53W.
Littlehampton ☆ Fl (5) Y 20s 9m 5M; 50°46'·19N 00°29'·54W.

WORTHING and SHOREHAM
Met Mast ☆ Fl Y 5s 12m 2M; 50°41'·29N 00°20'·59W.
Outfall ⚓ Fl R 2·5s 3m; 50°48'·38N 00°20'·34W.
Express ⚓ Fl Y 5s; (Apr-Oct); 50°47'·28N 00°17'·09W.
W Bkwtr Head ☆ Fl R 5s 7m 7M; 50°49'·49N 00°14'·89W.
Ldg Lts 355°. Middle Pier Front, Oc 5s 8m 10M; W watch-house, R base; tidal Lts, tfc sigs; *Horn 20s*. Rear, 192m from front, Fl 10s 12m 10M; Gy twr vis: 283°-103°; 50°49'·85N 00°14'·89W.
Outfall ⚓ 50°49'·47N 00°14'·39W.
Shoreham Outfall ⚓ Q (6) + L Fl 15s; 50°47'·88N 00°13'·72W.

BRIGHTON and BRIGHTON MARINA
Black Rk Ledge ⚓ Fl Y 4s; 50°48'·07N 00°06'·46W.
W Bkwtr Hd ☆ QR 10m 7M; W ◯ structure, R bands; *Horn (2) 30s*; 50°48'·50N 00°06'·38W.
E Bkwtr Hd ☆ QG 8m 7M.
Saltdean Outfall ⚓ Fl Y 5s; 50°46'·72N 00°02'·13W.

NEWHAVEN
Bkwtr Head ☆ Oc (2) 10s 17m 12M; 50°46'·56N 00°03'·50E.
E Pier Hd ☆ Iso G 10s 12m 6M; W twr; 50°46'·81N 00°03'·59E.

OFFSHORE MARKS
CS 1 ⚓ Fl Y 2·5s; *Whis*; 50°33'·69N 00°03'·92W.
GREENWICH ⚓ 50°24'·54N 00°00'·10E; Fl 5s 12m **15M**; Riding light FW; R hull; *Racon (M) 10M*; *Horn 30s*; 992351032.
CS 2 ⚓ Fl Y 5s; 50°39'·14N 00°32'·60E.
CS 3 ⚓ Fl Y 10s; 50°52'·04N 01°02'·18E.

BEACHY HEAD TO DUNGENESS
Beachy Head ☆ 50°44'·03N 00°14'·49E; Fl (2) 20s 31m **16M**; W round twr, R band and lantern; vis: 248°-101°; (H24).
Royal Sovereign ☆ Fl 20s 28m 12M; W ◯ twr, R band on W cabin on col; *Horn (2) 30s*; 50°43'·45N 00°26'·09E.
Royal Sovereign ⚓ QR; 50°44'·23N 00°25'·84E.

EASTBOURNE and SOVEREIGN HARBOUR
SH ⚓ L Fl 10s; 50°47'·40N 00°20'·71E.
Martello Tower ☆ Fl (3) 15s 12m 7M; 50°47'·24N 00°19'·83E.
Dir lt 260·5° Fl WRG 5s 4m 1M; vis: 255°-G-259°-W-262°-R-265°; 50°47'·28N 00°19'·71E.
S Bkwtr Hd ☆ Fl (4) R 12s 3m 6M; 50°47'·30N 00°20'·03E.
St Leonard's Outfall ⚓ Fl Y 5s; 50°49'·31N 00°31'·95E.

HASTINGS
Ldg Lts 356·3°. Front, FR 14m 4M; 50°51'·29N 00°35'·38E.
Rear, West Hill, 357m from front, FR 55m 4M; W twr.

RYE
Rye Fairway, L Fl 10s; 50°54'·04N 00°48'·04E.
W Groyne Hd No 2 ☆ LFl R 7s 7m 6M; 50°55'·58N 00°46'·55E; 992351156.
E Arm Hd No 1 ⚓ Q (9) 15s 7m 5M; G △; *Horn 7s*; 50°55'·73N 00°46'·46E.
Dungeness Outfall ⚓ Q (6) + L Fl 15s; 50°54'·45N 00°58'·21E.
Dungeness ☆ 50°54'·81N 00°58'·56E; Fl 10s 40m **21M**; B ◯ twr, W bands and lantern, floodlit; Part obsc 078°-shore; (H24). F RG 37m 10M (same twr); vis: 057°-R-073°-G-078°-196°-R-216°; *Horn (3) 60s*; FR Lts shown between 2·4M and 5·2M WNW when firing taking place. QR on radio mast 1·2M NW.

DUNGENESS TO NORTH FORELAND

FOLKESTONE

Hythe Flats Outfall ⚲ Fl Y 5s; 51°02'·52N 01°05'·32E.
Breakwater Head ☆ Fl (2) 10s 14m **22M**; vis: 210°-W-090°; 51°04'·56N 01°11'·69E.

DOVER

Admiralty Pier Extension Head ☆ 51°06'·69N 01°19'·66E;
Fl 7·5s 21m **20M**; W twr; vis: 096°-090°, obsc in The Downs
by S Foreland inshore of 226°; *Horn 10s;* Int Port Tfc sigs.
S Bkwtr W Hd ☆ 51°06'·78N 01°19'·80E;Oc R 30s 21m
18M; W twr.
Knuckle ☆ 51°07'·04N 01°20'·49E; Fl (4) WR 10s 15m
W15M, R13M; W twr; vis: 059°-R-239°-W-059°.
N Head ⚶ Fl R 2·5s 11m 5M; 51°07'·20N 01°20'·61E.
EasternArmHd⚶FlG5s12m5M;*Horn(2)30s;*Intporttfcsigs;
51°07'·31N 01°20'·59E.

DOVER STRAIT

Bullock Bank ⚐ VQ; 50°46'·94N 01°07'·60E.
Ridens SE ⚐ VQ (3) 5s; 50°43'·47N 01°18'·87E.
Colbart SW ⚐ VQ (6) + L Fl 10s; 50°48'·86N 01°16'·30E.
South Varne ⚐ Q (6) + L Fl 15s; 50°55'·64N 01°17'·30E.
Mid Varne ⚐ VQ(9)10s; 50°58'·94N 01°19'·88E.
East Varne ⚐ VQ(3)5s; 50°58'·22N 01°20'·90E.
Colbart N ⚐ VQ; 50°57'·45N 01°23'·29E.
Varne NW ⚐ Q; 51°00'·80N 01°22'·70E.
Varne NE ⚐ Q (3) 10s; 50°59'·80N 01°22'·70E.
VARNE ⊐ 51°01'·29N 01°23'·90E; Fl R 5s 12m **15M**;
Racon **(T) 10M**; *Horn 30s;* 992351038.
CS 4 ⚐ Fl (4) Y 15s; 51°08'·62N 01°33'·92E.
MPC ⚐ Fl Y 2·5s; *Racon (O) 10M*; 51°06'·12N 01°38'·20E;
992351122.
SW Goodwin ⚐ Q (6) + LFl 15s; 51°08'·50N 01°28'·88E;
992351036.
S Goodwin ⚑ Fl (4) R 15s; 51°10'·60N 01°32'·26E.
SE Goodwin ⚑ Fl (3) R 10s; 51°12'·99N 01°34'·45E.
E GOODWIN ⚑ 51°13'·26N 01°36'·37E; Fl 15s 12m **23M**;
R hull with lt twr amidships; *Racon (T) 10M*; *Horn 30s;*
992351035.
E Goodwin ⚐ Q (3) 10s; 51°15'·67N 01°35'·69E.
NE Goodwin ⚐ Q(3) 10s; *Racon (M) 10M*. 51°20'·31N
01°34'·16E.

DEAL and THE DOWNS

Trinity Bay VQ (9) 10s; 51°11'·60N 01°29'·00E.
Deal Bank 0 QR; 51°12'·92N 01°25'·57E.
Goodwin Fork ⚐ Q (6) + L Fl 15s; *Bell;* 51°14'·38N 01°26'·70E.
Downs ⚑ Fl (2) R 5s; *Bell;* 51°14'·50N 01°26'·22E.

GULL STREAM

W Goodwin ⚑ Fl G 5s; 51°15'·61N 01°27'·38E.
S Brake ⚑ Fl (3) R 10s; 51°15'·77N 01°26'·82E.
NW Goodwin ⚐ Q (9) 15s; 51°16'·72N 01°28'·47E.
Brake ⚑ Fl (4) R 15s; 51°16'·98N 01°28'·19E.
N Goodwin ⚑ Fl G 2·5s; 51°16'·74N 01°28'·40E.
Gull Stream ⚑ QR; 51°18'·26N 01°29'·69E.
Gull ⚐ VQ (3) 5s; 51°19'·57N 01°31'·30E.
Goodwin Knoll ⚑ Fl (2) G 5s; 51°19'·57N 01°32'·20E.

RAMSGATE CHANNEL

B2 ⚑ Fl (2) G 5s; 51°18'·26N 01°23'·93E.
W Quern ⚐ Q (9) 15s; 51°18'·98N 01°25'·39E.

RAMSGATE

RA ⚐ Q(6) + L Fl 15s; 51°19'·60N 01°30'·13E.
E Brake ⚑ Fl R 5s; 51°19'·47N 01°29'·20E.
No 1 ⚑QG; 51°19'·56N 01°27'·29E.
No 2 ⚑ Fl (4) R 10s; 51°19'·46N 01°27'·28E.
No 3 ⚑ Fl G 2·5s; 51°19'·56N 01°26'·61E.
No 4 ⚑ QR; 51°19'·46N 01°26'·60E.
N Quern ⚐ Q; 51°19'·41N 01°26'·11E.
No 5 ⚐ Q (6) + L Fl 15s; 51°19'·56N 01°25'·91E.
No 6 ⚑ Fl (2) R 5s; 51°19'·46N 01°25'·91E.
South Bkwtr Hd ⚑ VQ R 10m 5M; 51°19'·46N 01°25'·41E.
N Bkwtr Hd ⚑ QG 10m 5M; 51°19'·56N 01°25'·47E.
W Marine Terminal Dir lt 270°, Oc WRG 10s 10m 5M; B
△ Or stripe; vis: 259°-G-269°-W-271°-R-281°; 51°19'·51N
01°24'·85E. Rear 493m fm front Oc 5s 17m 5M; B ▽ Or
stripe; vis: 263°-278°.

BROADSTAIRS and NORTH FORELAND

Broadstairs Knoll ⚑ Fl R 2·5s; 51°20'·88N 01°29'·48E.
Pier SE End ⚶ 2 FR (vert) 7m 4M; 51°21'·50N 01°26'·74E.
Elbow ⚐ Q; 51°23'·23N 01°31'·59E.
North Foreland ☆ 51°22'·49N 01°26'·70E; Fl (5) WR
20s 57m **W19M, R16M, R15M**; W 8-sided twr; vis:
shore-W-150°-R(**16M**)-181°-R(**15M**)-200°-W-011°; H24;
992351020.

		1	2	3	4	5	6	7	8	9	10	11	12	13	14	15	16	17
1	Nab Tower	**1**																
2	Boulder Lt Buoy	5	**2**															
3	Owers Lt Buoy	10	6	**3**														
4	Littlehampton	19	13	12	**4**													
5	Shoreham	32	24	21	13	**5**												
6	Brighton	35	28	24	17	5	**6**											
7	Newhaven	40	34	29	24	12	7	**7**										
8	Beachy Head Lt	46	41	36	30	20	14	8	**8**									
9	Eastbourne	51	45	40	34	24	19	12	7	**9**								
10	Rye	72	67	62	56	46	41	34	25	23	**10**							
11	Dungeness Lt	76	71	66	60	50	44	38	30	26	9	**11**						
12	Folkestone	92	84	81	76	65	60	53	43	40	23	13	**12**					
13	Dover	97	89	86	81	70	65	58	48	45	28	18	5	**13**				
14	Ramsgate	112	104	101	96	85	80	73	63	60	43	33	20	15	**14**			
15	N Foreland Lt	115	107	104	99	88	83	76	66	63	46	36	23	18	3	**15**		
16	Sheerness	146	139	135	132	119	114	107	97	96	79	67	54	49	34	31	**16**	
17	London Bridge	188	184	177	177	161	156	149	139	141	124	109	96	91	76	73	45	**17**

DISTANCE TABLES
Approx distances in nautical miles are by the most direct route allowing for dangers and TSS.

OFFSHORE MARKS

SANDETTIE ⌐ 51°09'·36N 01°47'·12E; Fl 5s 12m **15M**; R hull with lt twr amidships; *Racon; Horn 30s*; 992351029.

F1 ⚓ Fl (4) Y 15s; 51°11'·21N 01°44'·91E.

South Falls ⚓ Q (6) + L Fl 15s; 51°13'·84N 01°43'·93E.
Sandettie W ⚓ Fl (3) G 12s; 51°15'·09N 01°54'·47E.
Mid Falls ⚓ Fl (3) R 10s; 51°18'·63N 01°46'·99E.
Inter Bank ⚓ Fl Y 5s; *Bell; Racon (M) 10M*; 51°16'·47N 01°52'·23E. F2 ⚓ Fl (4) Y 15s; 51°20'·41N 01°56'·19E.

AREA 4 *East England – North Foreland to Berwick-upon-Tweed*

SELECTED LIGHTS, BUOYS & WAYPOINTS

THAMES ESTUARY – SOUTHERN

(Direction of buoyage generally East to West)

APPROACHES to THAMES ESTUARY

Foxtrot 3 ⌐ 51°24'·15N 02°00'·38E; Fl 10s 12m **15M**; *Racon (T) 10M; Horn 10s*; 992351033.
Falls Hd ⚓ Q; 51°28'·23N 01°49'·89E.
Drill Stone ⚓ Q (3) 10s; 51°25'·88N 01°42'·89E.
Thanet N ⚓ VQ 15s; 51°28'·28N 01°38'·06E.
NE Spit ⚓ VQ (3) *Racon (T) 10M*; 51°27'·93N 01°29'·89E; 992351037
East Margate ⚓ Fl R 2·5s; 51°27'·03N 01°26'·40E.
Elbow ⚓ Q; 51°23'·23N 01°31'·59E.
Foreness Pt Outfall ⚓ Fl R 5s; 51°24'·58N 01°26'·12E.
Longnose ⚓ 51°24'·15N 01°26'·08E.
Longnose Spit ⚓ Fl R 2·5s 5m 2M; 51°23'·93N 01°25'·68E.

MARGATE and GORE CHANNEL

SE Margate ⚓ Q (3) 10s; 51°24'·05N 01°20'·40E.
S Margate ⚓ Fl G 2·5s; 51°23'·83N 01°16'·65E.
Copperas ⚓ QG; 51°23'·81N 01°11'·18E.
Reculver ⚓ QR; 51°23'·63N 01°12'·56E.

HERNE BAY

Beltinge Bay Bn ⚓ Fl Y 5s; 51°22'·73N 01°08'·63E.
Landing Stage ⚓ Q 18m 4M, (isolated); 51°22'·91N 01°06'·89E.
N Pier Hd ⚓ 2 FR (vert); 51°22'·43N 01°07'·27E.

WHITSTABLE

Whitstable Street ⚓ ; 51°24'·00N 01°01'·54E.
Oyster ⚓ Fl (2) R 10s; 51°22'·14N 01°01'·16E.
W Quay Dn ⚓ Fl G 5s 2m.

THE SWALE

Whitstable Street ⚓ Fl R 2s; 51°24'·00N 01°01'·54E.
Columbine ⚓ Fl G 2s; 51°24'·26N 01°01'·34E.
Columbine Spit ⚓ Fl (3) G 10s; 51°23'·86N 01°00'·03E.
Ham Gat ⚓ Q G; 51°23'·08N 00°58'·32E.
Pollard Spit ⚓ Q R; 51°22'·98N 00°58'·57E.
Sand End ⚓ Fl G 5s; 51°21'·43N 00°55'·90E.
Receptive Point ⚓ Fl G 10s; 51°20'·86N 00°54'·41E.
Queenborough Spit ⚓ Q (3) 10s; 51°25'·81N 00°43'·93E.
South Oaze ⚓ Fl R 2s; 51°21'·34N 00°56'·01E.

QUEENS CHANNEL and FOUR FATHOMS CHANNEL

E Margate ⚓ Fl R 2·5s; 51°27'·03N 01°26'·40E.
Spaniard ⚓ Q (3) 10s; 51°26'·23N 01°04'·00E.
Spile ⚓ Fl G 2·5s; 51°26'·43N 00°55'·70E.

PRINCES CHANNEL

Tongue Sand E ⚓ VQ (3) 5s; 51°29'·48N 01°22'·21E.
Tongue Sand N ⚓ Q; 51°29'·68N 01°22'·03E.
Princes Outer ⚓ VQ (6) + L Fl 10s; 51°28'·79N 01°19'·87E.

Princes North ⚓ Q G; 51°29'·25N 01°18'·35E.
Princes South ⚓ Q R; 51°28'·74N 01°18'·26E.
Princes No 1 ⚓ Fl (4) G 15s; 51°29'·23N 01°16'·02E.
Princes No 2 ⚓ Fl (2) R 5s; 51°28'·81N 01°13'·08E.
Princes No 3 ⚓ Fl (2) G 5s; 51°29'·33N 01°13'·10E.
Princes No 4 ⚓ Fl (3) R 10s; 51°28'·83N 01°09'·90E.
Princes No 5 ⚓ Fl (3) G 10s; 51°29'·39N 01°10'·00E.
Princes Mid ⚓ Fl Y 5s; 51°29'·19N 01°09'·00E.
Shivering Sand Twr N ⚓ Q; 51°30'·01N 01°04'·76E.
Shivering Sand Twr S ⚓ Q (6)+L Fl 15s; *Bell*; 51°29'·75N 01°04'·83E.
Princes No 8 ⚓ Fl (2) R 5s; 51°29'·14N 01°03'·00E.
Princes Inner ⚓ Fl Y 2·5s; 51°29'·59N 01°03'·47E.

FOULGER'S GAT and KNOB CHANNEL

N Edinburgh Channel is not buoyed. Foulger's Gat, lies within the boundary of the London Array Wind Farm.
Long Sand Outer ⚓ Iso 2s; 51°34'·61N 01°28'·34E.
Long Sand Middle ⚓ Iso 5s; 51°35'·60N 01°26'·45E.
Long Sand Inner ⚓ Iso 2s; 51°38'·78N 01°25'·44E.
SE Knob ⚓ Fl G 5s; 51°30'·89N 01°06'·41E.
Knob ⚓ Iso 5s; *Whis*; 51°30'·69N 01°04'·28E.

OAZE DEEP

Oaze Deep ⚓ Fl (2) G 5s; 51°29'·18N 00°56'·77E.
Red Sand Trs N ⚓ Fl (3) R 10s; *Bell*; 51°28'·73N 00°59'·32E.
N Oaze ⚓ QR; 51°30'·03N 00°57'·65E.
Oaze ⚓ Fl (4) Y 10s; 51°29'·06N 00°56'·93E.
W Oaze ⚓ Iso 5s; 51°29'·06N 00°55'·43E.
Oaze Bank ⚓ Q G 5s; 51°29'·18N 00°56'·77E.
Cant ⚓ (unlit); 51°27'·77N 00°53'·36E.
East Cant ⚓ QR; 51°28'·53N 00°55'·60E.

MEDWAY, SHEERNESS

Medway ⚓ Mo (A) 6s; 51°28'·83N 00°52'·81E.
No 1 ⚓ Fl G 2·5s; 51°28'·55N 00°50'·50E.
No 2 ⚓ Q; 51°28'·33N 00°50'·52E.
No 7 ⚓ Fl G 10s; 51°27'·91N 00°47'·52E.
No 9 ⚓ Fl G 5s; 51°27'·74N 00°46'·61E.
No 11 ⚓ Fl (3) G 10s; 51°27'·51N 00°45'·80E.
Grain Hard ⚓ Fl G 5s; 51°26'·98N 00°44'·17E.
Isle of Grain ⚓ Q 20m 13M; RW ◇ on R twr; 51°26'·70N 00°43'·38E.
Queenborough Spit ⚓ Q (3) 10s; 51°25'·81N 00°43'·93E.

RIVER THAMES

SEA REACH, NORE and YANTLET

Sea Reach 1 (N) ⚓ Fl Y 2·5s; *Racon (T) 10M*; 51°29'·59N 00°52'·71E.
Sea Reach 1 (S) ⚓ Fl R 2·5s; 51°29'·39N 00°52'·45E.
Sea Reach 2 (N) ⚓ Fl R 2·5s; 51°29'·49N 00°49'·73E.
Sea Reach 2 (S) ⚓ Fl R 2·5s; 51°29'·30N 00°49'·75E.
Sea Reach 3 (N) ⚓ Q G (sync); 51°29'·41N 00°46'·80E.

Sea Reach 3 (S) ⚲ Q R (sync); 51°29'·22N 00°46'·71E.
Sea Reach 4 (N) ▲ Fl (2) G 5s; 51°29'·69N 00°44'·19E.
Sea Reach 4 (S) ⚲ Fl (2) R 5s; 51°29'·50N 00°44'·12E.
Sea Reach 5 (N) ▲ VQ G; 51°30'·04N 00°41'·47E.
Sea Reach 5 (S) ⚲ VQ R; 51°29'·85N 00°41'·43E.
Sea Reach 6 (N) ▲ Fl G 5s; 51°30'·13N 00°39'·87E.
Sea Reach 6 (S) ⚲ Fl R 5s; 51°29'·93N 00°39'·84E.
Sea Reach 7 (N) ⚑ Fl Y 2·5s; 51°30'·21N 00°36'·94E.
Sea Reach 7 (S) ⚲ Fl R 2·5s; *Racon (T) 10M*; 51°30'·01N 00°36'·91E.

Nore Swatch ⚲ Fl (4) R 15s; 51°28'·28N 00°45'·55E.
Mid Swatch ▲ Fl G 5s; 51°28'·68N 00°44'·16E.
W Nore Sand ⚲ Fl (3) R 10s; 51°29'·48N 00°40'·87E.
East Blyth ⚑ Q; 51°29'·73N 00°37'·81E.
Mid Blyth ⚑ Q; 51°30'·08N 00°32'·38E.

LEIGH-ON-SEA and SOUTHEND-ON-SEA

Leigh ▲; 51°31'·09N 00°42'·72E.
Southend Pier E End ⚑ 2 FG (vert) 7m; *Horn Mo (N) 30s, Bell (1)*.

LOWER HOPE REACH

West Blyth ⚲ Q R; 51°29'·57N 00°28'·39E.
Mucking 1 ▲ Q G; 51°29'·70N 00°37'·28E.
Lower Hope ⚲ Fl R 5s; 51°29'·32N 00°28'·02E.
Mucking 3 ▲ Fl G 2·5s; 51°29'·33N 00°27'·68E.
Mucking 5 ▲ Fl (3) G 10s; 51°28'·76N 00°27'·19E.
Mucking 7 ▲ Fl G 5s; 51°28'·03N 00°26'·77E.
Bell Ovens ▲ Q G; 51°27'·50N 00°26'·35E.
Higham ⚲ Fl (2) R 5s; 51°27'·40N 00°26'·85E.
Tilbury ⚑ Q(6) + L Fl 15s; 51°27'·16N 00°25'·50E.

GRAVESEND

Shornmead ⚑ Fl (2) WR 10s 12m, W11/7M, R11M; vis 070°-W-084°-R(Intens)-089°-W(Intens)-094°-W-250°; 51°26'·92N 00°26'·24E.

Northfleet Upper ⚑ Oc WRG 10s 30m W10M, R7M, G7M; vis:126°-R-149°-W-159°-G-268°-W-279°; 51°26'·93N 00°20'·06E.

THAMES TIDAL BARRIER

Spans B, C, D, E, F, G are navigable. Spans C – F are for large ships. Eastbound small craft/yachts use Span B (51°29'·73N 00°02'·23E) Westbound small craft/yachts use Span G (51°29'·91N 00°02'·21E). **Red X** indicates span closed **Green** indicates span open. W lights show either side of open spans in poor visibility.

KENTISH KNOCK

Kentish Knock ⚑ Q (3) 10s; 51°38'·08N 01°40·43E.
S Knock ⚑ Q (6) + L Fl 15s; *Bell*; 51°34'·13N 01°34'·29E.

KNOCK JOHN CHANNEL

No 7 ▲ Fl (4) G 15s; 51°32'·03N 01°06'·40E.
No 5 ▲ Fl (3) G 10s; 51°32'·49N 01°07'·75E.
No 4 ⚲ QR 10s; 51°32'·40 N 01°08'·08E.
No 2 ⚲ Fl (3) R 10s; 51°33'·03N 01°09'·63E.
No 3 ⚑ Q (6) + L Fl 15s; 51°33'·29N 01°09'·83E.
No 1 ▲ Fl G 5s; 51°33'·75N 01°10'·72E.
Knock John ⚲ Fl (2) R 5s; 51°33'·61N 01°11'·37E.

BLACK DEEP

No 12 ⚲ Fl (4) R 15s; 51°33'·83N 01°13'·50E.
No 11 ▲ Fl (3) G 10s; 51°34'·33N 01°13'·40E.
No 10 ⚲ Fl (3) R 10s; 51°34'·74N 01°15'·60E.
No 9 ⚑ Q (6) + L Fl 15s; 51°35'·13N 01°15'·09E.
No 8 ⚑ Q (9) 15s; 51°36'·36N 01°20'·43E.

No 7 ▲ QG. 51°37'·08N 01°17'·69E.
No 6 ⚑ Fl R 2·5s; 51°38'·53N 01°24'·40E.
No 5 ⚑ VQ (3) 5s; 51°39'·53N 01°23'·00E.
No 4 ⚲ Fl (2) R 5s; 51°41'·42N 01°28'·49E.
Long Sand Bcn ⚑ ; 51°41'·48N 01°29'·49E.
No 3 ⚑ Fl (3) G 15s; 51°42'·39N 01°26'·65E.
No 1 ▲ Fl G 5s, 51°44'·03N 01°28'·09E.
No 2 ⚲ Fl (4) R 15s; 51°45'·63N 01°32'·20E.
SHM ⚑ Fl Y 2·5s; *Racon (T) 10M*; 51°29'·59N 00°52'·71E.

SUNK

Sunk Head Tower ⚑ Q; *Bell*; 51°46'·63N 01°30'·51E.
Black Deep ⚲ QR; 51°48'·32N 01°36'·96E.
Long Sand Head ⚑ VQ; *Bell*; 51°48'·12N 01°39'·39E.
SUNK CENTRE ⚓ 51°50'·11N 01°46'·02E; Fl (2) 20s 12m **16M**; *Racon (C) 10M*; *Horn (2) 60s*; 992351094.
Dynamo ⚑ Fl Y 2·5s; 51°29'·59N 00°52'·71E.
Trinity ⚑ Q (6) + L Fl 15s; 51°49'·03N 01°36'·39E.
SUNK INNER ⚓ 51°51'·17N 01°34'·40E; Fl(5) 15s 11m 12M; *Racon (C) 10M*; *Horn 30s*; 992351027.

FISHERMANS GAT

Outer Fisherman ⚑ Q (3) 10s; 51°34'·02N 01°25'·10E.
Fisherman No 1 ▲ Fl G 2·5s (sync); 51°34'·50N 01°23'·52E.
Fisherman No 2 ⚲ Fl R 2·5s (sync); 51°34'·30N 01°23'·50E.
Fisherman No 3 ▲ Fl G 5s; 51°34'·78N 01°22'·65E.
Fisherman No 4 ⚲ Fl (2) R 5s; 51°34'·77N 01°22'·08E.
Fisherman No 5 ▲ Fl (2) G 5s; 51°35'·25N 01°21'·84E.
Fisherman No 6 ⚲ Fl (3) R 10s; 51°35'·08N 01°21'·56E.
Inner Fisherman ⚲ Q R; 51°36'·15N 01°20'·08E.

BARROW DEEP

SW Barrow ⚑ Q(9) 15s; 51°32'·12N 01°00'·12E.
Alice Wk ⚑ Fl (2) 5s; 51°32'·33N 01°04'·22E.
Barrow No 14 ⚲ Fl R 2·5s; 51°31'·83N 01°00'·43E.
Barrow No 13 ▲ Fl (2) G 5s; 51°32'·82N 01°03'·07E.
Barrow No 12 ⚲ Fl (2) R 5s; 51°33'·24N 01°05'·94E.
Barrow No 11 ▲ Fl (3) G 10s; 51°34'·08N 01°06'·70E.
Barrow No 9 ⚑ VQ (3) 5s; 51°35'·34N 01°10'·30E.
Barrow No 8 ⚑ Fl (2) R 5s; 51°35'·05N 01°11'·36E.
Barrow No 7 ⚑ Fl G 2·5s; 51°37'·49N 01°13'·47E.
Barrow No 6 ⚑ Fl (4) R 15s; 51°37'·30N 01°14'·68E.
Barrow No 5 ▲ Fl G 10s; 51°40'·03N 01°16'·20E.
Barrow No 4 ⚑ VQ (9) 10s; 51°39'·88N 01°17'·48E.
Barrow No 3 ⚑ Q (3) 10s; *Racon (M)10M*; 51°42'·02N 01°20'·24E.
Barrow No 2 ⚲ Fl (2) R 5s; 51°41'·98N 01°22'·89E.

WEST SWIN and MIDDLE DEEP

Blacktail Spit ▲ Fl (3) G 10s; 51°31'·47N 00°56'·75E.
Maplin ▲ Q G (sync W Swin); *Bell*; 51°33'·66N 01°01'·40E.
W Swin ⚲ Q R (sync Maplin); 51°33'·40N 01°01'·97E.
Maplin Edge ▲ Fl G 2.5s; 51°35'·33N 01°03'·64E.
Maplin Bank ⚲ Fl (3) R 10s; 51°35'·50N 01°04'·70E.
Maplin Middle ▲ Fl G 5s; *Bell*; 51°36'·78N 01°05'·50E.
E Maplin ⚲ 51°38'·29N 01°08'·86E.
Maplin Approach ▲ Fl (2) G 10s; 51°39'·54N 01°09'·39E.

EAST SWIN and KING'S CHANNEL

N Middle ⚑ Q; 51°41'·35N 01°12'·61E.
W Sunk ⚑ Q (9) 15s; 51°44'·33N 01°25'·80E.
Gunfleet Spit ⚑ Q (6) + L Fl 15s; *Bell*; 51°45'·33N 01°21'·70E.

WHITAKER CHANNEL and RIVER CROUCH

Whitaker ⚑ Q (3) 10s; *Bell*; 51°41'·43N 01°10'·51E.
Inner Whitaker ⚑ VQ (6) + L Fl 10s; 51°40'·76N 01°08'·40E.

Swin Spitway ⚓ Iso 10s; *Bell;* 51°41'·95N 01°08'·35E.
Whitaker 1 ▲ FlG 5s (sync Whit 2), 51° 40'·69N 01° 06'·67E.
Whitaker 2 ▱ FlR 5s (sync Whit 1), 51° 40'·41N 01° 06'·78E.
Whitaker 3 ▲ Fl(2) G 5s (sync Whit 4) 51° 40'·41N 01° 04'·74E.
Whitaker 4 ▱ Fl(2) R 5s (sync Whit 4) 51° 40'·16N 01° 04'·91E.
Whitaker 5 ▲ Fl(3) G 10s (sync Whit 6) 51° 40'·03N 01° 03'·22E.
Whitaker 6 ▱ Fl(3) R 10s(sync Whit 5) 51° 39'·77N 01° 03'·43E.
Whitaker 7 ▲ Fl(4) G 10s(sync Whit 8) 51° 39'·54N 01° 02'·00E.
Whitaker 8 ▱ Fl(4) R 10s(sync Whit 7), 51° 39'·35N 01° 02'·00E.
Swallowtail 1 ◯ Fl Y 5s, 51° 41'·38N 01° 08'·20E.
Swallowtail 2 ◯ Fl Y 10s, 51° 41'·19N 01° 06'·28E.
Swallowtail 3 ◯ Fl Y 15s, 51° 40.84N 01° 04.39E.
Swallowtail 4 ◯ (2) Y 10s, 51° 40'·52N 01° 03'·47E.
Buxey Edge ▲ Fl G 10s, 51° 40'·65N 01° 03'·48E.
Swallowtail ⚓ VQ (9) 10s, 51° 40'·04N 01° 02'·65E.
Sunken Buxey ⚓ VQ; 51°39'·59N 01°00'·77E.
Buxey No 1 ⚓ VQ (6) + L Fl 10s; 51°39'·18N 01°01'·13E.
Buxey No 2 ◯ Q; 51°39'·08N 01°00'·23E.
Outer Crouch 1 ▲ Fl G 5s (sync Cro 2) 51° 38'·71N 00° 59'·00E.
Outer Crouch 2 ▱ Fl R 5s (sync Cro 1) 51° 38'·62N 00° 59'·20E.
Outer Crouch 3 ▲ Fl G 10s (sync Cro 4) 51° 38'·10N 00° 57'·83E.
Outer Crouch 4 ▱ Fl R 10s (sync Cro 3) 51° 38'·00N 00° 58'·00E.
Crouch ⚓ Q.Fl, 51° 37.650N 00° 56.582E.
Inner Crouch ⚓ L Fl 10s, 51° 37'·19N 00° 55'·09E.
Branklet (RGR) **Pref Chan to Stbd,** Comp grp Fl (R) 2+1
10s, 51° 36'·99N 00° 52'·10E.

GOLDMER GAT and WALLET
NE Gunfleet ⚓ Q (3) 10s; 51°49'·93N 01°27'·79E.
Wallet No 2 ▱ Fl R 5s; 51°48'·88N 01°22'·99E.
Wallet No 4 ▱ Fl (4) R 10s; 51°46'·53N 01°17'·23E.
Wallet Spitway ◯ L Fl 10s; *Bell,* 51°42'·86N 01°07'·30E.
Knoll ⚓ Q; 51°43'·88N 01°05'·07E.
Eagle ▲ QG; 51°44'·10N 01°03'·63E.
N Eagle ⚓ Q; 51°44'·71N 01°04'·32E.
NW Knoll ▱ Fl (2) R 5s; 51°44'·29N 01°02'·14E.
Colne Bar ▲ Fl (2) G 5s; 51°44'·61N 01°02'·57E.
Bench Head ▲ Fl (3) G 10s; 51°44'·56N 01°01'·18E.

RIVER BLACKWATER
The Nass ⚓ VQ (3) 5s 6m 2M; 51°45'·83N 00°54'·83E.
Thirslet ▲ Fl (3) G 10s; 51°43'·73N 00°50'·39E.
No 1 ▲ ; 51°43'·44N 00°48'·02E.

RIVER COLNE and BRIGHTLINGSEA
Inner Bench Hd No 2 ▱ Fl (2) R 5s; 51°45'·96N 01°01'·74E.
Colne Pt No 1 ▲ Fl G 3s; 51°46'·01N 01°01'·92E.
No 8 ▱ Fl R 3s; 51°46'·90N 01°01'·30E.
No 9 ▲ Fl G 3s; 51°47'·36N 01°01'·07E.

Ldg lts 041°. Front, FR 7m 4M; W ☐, R stripe on post; vis:
020°-080°; 51°48'·39N 01°01'·20E. Rear, 50m from front,
FR 10m 4M; W ☐, R stripe on post. FR lts are shown on 7
masts between 1·5M and 3M NW when firing occurs.

WALTON BACKWATERS
Pye End ◯ L Fl 10s; 51°55'·03N 01°17'·90E.
No 2 ▱ Fl (2) 5s; 51°54'·62N 01°16'·80E.
Crab Knoll No 3 ▲ Fl G 5s; 51°54'·41N 01°16'·41E.
No 16 ▱ 51°53'·17N 01°15'·52E.

HARWICH APPROACHES
(Direction of buoyage is North to South)
MEDUSA CHANNEL
Medusa ▲ Fl G 5s; 51°51'·23N 01°20'·35E.

Stone Banks ▱ FlR 5s; 51°53'·19N 01°19'·23E.
Pennyhole ◬ ; 51°53'·55N 01°18'·00E (Mar–Sep).

CORK SAND and ROUGH SHOALS
S Cork ⚓ Q (6) + L Fl 15s; 51°51'·33N 01°24'·09E.
SE Roughs Tower ⚓ Q (3) 10s; 51°53'·64N 01°28'·94E.
NW Roughs Tower ⚓ VQ (9) 10s; 51°53'·81N 01°28'·77E.
Cork Sand ⚓ Fl (3) R 10s; 51°55'·51N 01°25'·42E.

HARWICH CHANNEL
S Threshold ⚓ Fl (4) Y 10s; 51°52'·20N 01°33'·14E.
S Shipwash ⚓⚓ 2 By(s) Q (6) + L Fl 15s; 51°52'·71N
01°33'·97E.
Outer Tidal Bn ⚓ Mo (U) 15s 2m 3M; 51°52'·85N 01°32'·34E.
E Fort Massac ⚓ VQ (3) 5s; 51°53'·36N 01°32'·79E.
W Fort Massac ⚓ VQ (9) 10s; 51°53'·36N 01°32'·49E.
Walker ⚓ Q (9)15s; 51°53'·79N 01°33'·90E.
N Threshold ⚓ Fl Y 5s; 51°54'·49N 01°33'·47E.
SW Shipwash ⚓ Fl Y 2·5s; 51°54'·75N 01°34'·21E.
Haven ⚓ Mo (A) 5s; 51°55'·76N 01°32'·56E.
W Shipwash ▱ Fl (2) R 10s; 51°57'·13N 01°35'·89E.
NW Shipwash ▱ Fl R 5s; 51°58'·98N 01°37'·01E.
Harwich App (HA) ⚓ Iso 5s; 51°56'·75N 01°30'·66E.
Cross ⚓ Fl (3) Y 10s; 51°56'·23N 01°30'·48E.
Harwich Chan No 1 ▱ Fl Y 2·5s; *Racon (T) 10M;* 51°56'·13N
01°27'·06E.
Harwich Chan No 3 ▱ Fl (3) Y 10s; 51°56'·04N 01°25'·54E.
Harwich Chan No 5 ▱ Fl (5) Y 10s; 51°55'·96N 01°24'·01E.
Harwich Chan No 7 ▱ Fl (3) Y 10s; 51°55'·87N 01°22'·49E.
S Bawdsey ⚓ Q (6) + L Fl 15s; *Whis;* 51°57'·23N 01°30'·19E.
Washington ▲ QG; 51°56'·52N 01°26'·59E.
Felixstowe Ledge ▲ Fl (3) G 10s; 51°56'·30N 01°23'·72E.
Wadgate Ledge ⚓ Fl (4) G 15s; 51°56'·16N 01°21'·99E.
Platters ⚓ Q (6) + L Fl 15s; 51°55'·64N 01°20'·97E.
Rolling Ground ▲ QG; 51°55'·55N 01°19'·75E.
Beach End ▲ Fl (2) G 5s; 51°55'·62N 01°19'·21E.
Cork Sand Yacht Bn ⚓ VQ 2M; 51°55'·21N 01°25'·20E.
Rough ⚓ VQ; 51°55'·19N 01°31'·00E.
Pitching Ground ▱ Fl (4) R 15s; 51°55'·43N 01°21'·05E.
Inner Ridge ▱ QR; 51°55'·38N 01°20'·20E.
Deane ▱ L Fl R 6s; 51°55'·36N 01°19'·28E.
Landguard ⚓ Q; 51°55'·45N 01°18'·84E.

RIVERS STOUR AND ORWELL
RIVER STOUR and HARWICH
Shotley Spit ⚓ Q (6) + L Fl 15s; 51°57'·21N 01°17'·69E.
Shotley Marina Lock E side Dir lt 339·5° 3m 1M (uses
Moiré pattern); Or structure; 51°57'·46N 01°16'·60E.
Guard ▱ Fl R 5s; *Bell;* 51°57'·07N 01°17'·86E.

RIVER ORWELL and IPSWICH
Suffolk Yacht Harbour. Ldg lts Front Iso Y 1M; 51°59'·73N
01°16'·09E. Rear Oc Y 4s 1M.

HARWICH TO ORFORD NESS
FELIXSTOWE, R DEBEN and WOODBRIDGE HAVEN
Woodbridge Haven ◯ Mo(A)15s; 51°57'·99N 01°23'·63E.
Deben ◬ ; 51°59'·30N 01°23'·53E.

RIVERS ORE and ALDE
Orford Haven ◯ L Fl 10s; *Bell.* 52°02'·00N 01°28'·20E.

OFFSHORE MARKS
S Galloper ⚓ Q (6) L Fl 15s; *Racon (T) 10M;* 51°43'·98N
01°56'·43E.

N Galloper ⚓ Q; 51°49'·84N 01°59'·99E.
S Inner Gabbard ⚓ Q (6) + L Fl 15s. 51°49'·92N 01°51'·89E.
N Inner Gabbard ⚓ Q; 51°59'·20N 01°56'·00E.
NHR-SE ⚓ Fl G 5s; 51°45'·39N 02°39'·89E.

SHIPWASH and BAWDSEY BANK
E Shipwash ⚓ VQ (3) 5s; 51°57'·08N 01°37'·89E.
NW Shipwash ⚓ Fl R 5s; 51°58'·98N 01°37'·01E.
N Shipwash ⚓ Q 7M; *Racon (M) 10M*; *Whis*; 52°01'·73N 01°38'·27E; 992351069.
S Bawdsey ⚓ Q (6) + L Fl 15s; *Bell*; 51°57'·23N 01°30'·19E.
Mid Bawdsey ⚓ Fl (3) G 10s; 51°58'·88N 01°33'·59E.
NE Bawdsey ⚓ Fl G 10s; 52°01'·73N 01°36'·09E.

CUTLER and WHITING BANKS
Cutler ⚓ QG; 51°58'·51N 01°27'·48E.
SW Whiting ⚓ Q (6) + L Fl 10s; 52°00'·96N 01°30'·69E.
Whiting Hook ⚓ Fl R 10s; 52°02'·98N 01°31'·82E.
NE Whiting ⚓ Q (3) 10s; 52°03'·61N 01°33'·32E.

ORFORD NESS TO WINTERTON

(Direction of buoyage is South to North)
Orford Ness Lt Ho (dis) 52°05'·04N 01°34'·45E; W ○ twr, R bands.
Aldeburgh Ridge ⚓ QR; 52°06'·49N 01°36'·95E.

SOUTHWOLD
Southwold ☆ 52°19'·63N 01°40'·89E; Fl 10s 37m **W24M**; vis 204°-W-032·5°, 992351019.

LOWESTOFT and APPR VIA STANFORD CHANNEL
E Barnard ⚓ Q (3) 10s; 52°25'·14N 01°46'·38E.
Newcome Sand ⚓ QR; 52°26'·33N 01°47'·16E.
S Holm ⚓ VQ (6) + L Fl 10s; 52°26'·63N 01°47'·11E.
Stanford ⚓ Fl R 2·5s; 52°27'·35N 01°46'·67E.
SW Holm ⚓ Fl (2) G 5s; 52°27'·87N 01°46'·99E.
Kirkley ⚓ Dir WRG 17m 10M, vis: 222°-OcG 10s -225°-FlG 2·5s-226°-FlW 2·5s-227°-OcW 10s-229°-FlW 2·5s-230°-FlR 2·5s-231°-OcR 10s-232°; 52°27'·71N 01°44'·54E.
Outer Hbr S Pier Hd ⚓ Oc R 5s 12m 6M; *Horn (4) 60s*; tfc sigs; 52°28'·29N 01°45'·36E.
N Newcome ⚓ Fl (4) R 15s; 52°28'·39N 01°46'·37E.
Lowestoft ☆ 52°29'·22N 01°45'·35; Fl 15s 37m **23M**; W twr; part obscd 347°- shore.

LOWESTOFT NORTH ROAD and CORTON ROAD
Lowestoft Ness SE ⚓ Q (6) + L Fl 15s; 52°28'·84N 01°46'·25E.
Lowestoft Ness N ⚓ VQ (3) 5s; *Bell*; 52°28'·89N 01°46'·23E.
W Holm ⚓ Fl (3) G 10s; 52°29'·50N 01°46'·99E.
NW Holm ⚓ Fl (4) G 15s; 52°30'·90N 01°46'·50E.

GREAT YARMOUTH APPROACH via HOLM CHANNEL
E Newcome ⚓ Fl (2) R 5s; 52°28'·51N 01°49'·21E.
Holm Approach ⚓ Q (3) 10s; 52°30'·88N 01°50'·22E.
Holm Sand ⚓ Q (9) 15s; 52°33'·28N 01°46'·62E.
S Corton ⚓ Q (6) + L Fl 15s; *Bell*; 52°33'·32N 01°48'·41E.
NE Holm ⚓ Fl R 2·5s; 52°33'·06N 01°48'·43E.
Mid Corton ⚓ Fl G 2·5s; 52°33'·61N 01°47'·98E.
N Holm ⚓ Q 52°33'·73N 01°47'·29E.
W Corton ⚓ Fl (3) G 10s; 52°34'·12N 01°47'·50E.

GREAT YARMOUTH and GORLESTON
Gorleston South Pier Hd ⚓ Fl R 3s 11m 11M; vis: 235°-340°; 52°34'·33N 01°44'·28E.
N Pier Hd ⚓ QG 8m 6M; vis: 176°-078°; *Horn(3) 60s*; 52°34'·38N 01°44'·38E.

Outer Hbr S Pier ⚓ Q R 17m 3M; 52°34'·61N 01°44'·73E.
Outer Hbr N Pier ⚓ Q G 17m 3M; 52°34'·70N 01°44'·74E.

GREAT YARMOUTH TO THE WASH

(Direction of buoyage ⚓ South to North)
YARMOUTH and CAISTER ROADS/COCKLE GATEWAY
SW Scroby ⚓ Fl G 2·5s; 52°35'·13N 01°46'·69E.
Scroby Elbow ⚓ Fl (2) G 5s; *Bell*; 52°36'·55N 01°46'·26E.
Yarmouth Outfall ⚓ Q R; 52°37'·58N 01°45'·70E.
Mid Caister ⚓ Fl (2) R 5s; *Bell*; 52°38'·99N 01°45'·66E.
NW Scroby ⚓ Fl (3) G 10s; 52°40'·36N 01°46'·31E.
N Caister ⚓ Fl (3) R 10s; 52°40'·77N 01°45'·65E.
Hemsby ⚓ Fl R 2·5s; 52°41'·80N 01°46'·00E.
N Scroby ⚓ VQ; 52°41'·39N 01°46'·47E.
Cockle ⚓ VQ (3) 5s; *Bell*; 52°44'·03N 01°43'·59E.

OFFSHORE ROUTE
Cross Sand ⚓ L Fl 10s 5M; *Racon (T) 10M*; 52°40'·33N 01°53'·70E.
Barley ⚓ Q (6) + L Fl 15s 6M; 52°38'·76N 01°52'·90E.
E Cross Sand ⚓ Fl (4) R 15s; 52°40'·33N 01°53'·70E.
NE Cross Sand ⚓ VQ (3) 5s; 52°44'·22N 01° 53'·80E.
Smith's Knoll ⚓ Q (6) + L Fl 15s 7M; *Racon (T) 10M*; 52°43'·52N 02°17'·89E.
S Winterton Ridge ⚓ Q (6) + L Fl 15s; 52°47'·21N 02°03'·44E.
E Hammond Knoll ⚓ Q (3) 10s; 52°52'·32N 01°58'·64E.
Hammond Knoll ⚓ Q (9) 15s; 52°49'·68N 01°57'·54E.
Newarp ⚓ L Fl 10s 7M; *Racon (O) 10M*; 52°48'·37N 01°55'·69E; 992351118.
S Haisbro ⚓ Q (6) + L Fl 15s; *Bell*; 52°50'·82N 01°48'·29E.
Mid Haisbro ⚓ Fl (2) G 5s; *Bell*; 52°54'·22N 01°41'·59E.
N Haisbro ⚓ Q; *Racon (T) 10M*; 53°00'·22N 01°32'·29E; 992351031.
Happisburgh ☆ Fl (3) 30s 41m 14M; 52°49'·21N 01°32'·18E.

(Direction of buoyage ⚓ East to West)
CROMER
Cromer ☆ 52°55'·45N 01°19'·01E; Fl 5s 84m **21M**; W 8-sided twr; vis: 102°-307° H24; *Racon (O) 25M*; 992351015.
Tayjack Wk ⚓ Fl R 2·5s; 52°57'·61N 01°15'·37E.
E Sheringham ⚓ Q (3) 10s; 53°02'·21N 01°14'·84E.
W Sheringham ⚓ Q (9) 15s; 53°02'·95N 01°06'·72E.

BLAKENEY
Blakeney Fairway ⚓; 52°59'·22N 00°58'·53E.
Blakeney Overfalls ⚓ Fl (2) R 5s; *Bell*; 53°03'·01N 01°01'·37E.

WELLS-NEXT-THE-SEA/BRANCASTER STAITHE
Wells WCM ⚓ Q(9) 15s; 52°59'·68N 00°50'·24E.
Bridgirdle ⚓ Fl R 2·5s; 53°01'·73N 00°43'·95E.

APPROACHES TO THE WASH
S Race ⚓ Q (6) + L Fl 15s; *Bell*; 53°07'·81N 00°57'·34E.
E Docking ⚓ Fl R 2·5s; 53°09'·82N 00°50'·39E.
N Race ⚓ Fl G 5s; *Bell*; 53°14'·98N 00°43'·87E.
N Docking ⚓ Q; 53°14'·82N 00°41'·49E.
Scott Patch ⚓ VQ (3) 5s; 53°11'·12N 00°36'·39E.
S Inner Dowsing ⚓ Q (6) + L Fl 15s; *Bell*; 53°12'·12N 00°33'·69E.
Boygrift Tower ⚓ Fl (2) 10s 12m 5M; 53°17'·63N 00°19'·24E.
Burnham Flats ⚓ Q (9) 15s; *Bell*; 53°07'·53N 00°34'·89E.
Lincs WF E ⚓ Q (3) 10s; 53°07'·61N 00°31'·06E.

THE WASH

West Ridge ⚓ Q (9) 15s; 53°19'·06N 00°44'·47E.
N Well ⚓ L Fl 10s; *Whistle*; **Racon (T) 10M**; 53°03'·02N 00°27'·87E.
⚓ Fl(2) 10s; 53°01'·53N 00°25'·63E.
Z9 ⚓ Fl(2) 6s; 52°59'·73N 00°22'·75E.
ROARING MIDDLE ⚓ L Fl 10s 7m 8M; 52°58'·64N 00°21'·08E.
Z6 ⚓ Fl(2) 6s; 52°57'·52N 00°19'·17E.

KING'S LYNN

No 1 ▲ Fl G 3s; 52°56'·00N 00°21'·50E.
No 2 ▱ Fl (2)R 6s; 52°55'·00N 00°21'·90E.

WISBECH CHANNEL/RIVER NENE

W2 ⚓ Fl Y 6s; 52°54'·93N 00°16'·00E.
Nene Roads ⚓ Mo(A) 6s; 52°53'·85N 01°15'·51E
East Knock ⚓ VQ (3) 5s; 52°52'·14N 00°14'·69E.
Bob ▱ LFl R 5s; 52°52'·05N 00°14'·74E.
Wisbech No 1 ▲ Fl G 3s; 52°53'·33N 00°13'·60E.
Tide Gauge DZ6 ⚓; 52°52'·57N 00°13'·10E.
Beacons are moved as required.

FREEMAN CHANNEL

Boston No 1 ▲ Fl G 3s; 52°57'·84N 00°15'·03E.
Alpha ▱ Fl R 3s; 52°57'·69N 00°15'·06E.
No 3 ▲ Fl G 6s; 52°57'·93N 00°15'·42E.
No 5 ▲ Fl G 3s; 52°58'·51N 00°12'·72E.
No 7 ▲ Fl G 6s; 52°58'·63N 00°11'·40E.
Delta ▱ Fl R 6s; 52°58'·38N 00°11'·25E.

BOSTON LOWER ROAD

Echo ▱ Fl R 3s; 52°58'·38N 00°10'·13E.
Foxtrot ▱ Fl R 3s; 52°57'·60N 00°08'·94E.
Boston No 9 ▲ Fl G 3s; 52°57'·58N 00°08'·36E.
Black Buoy ▱ Fl (2) R 6s; 52°56'·82N 00°07'·74E.
Tabs Head ⚓ Q WG 4m 1M; R☐ on W mast; vis: W shore-251°- G-shore; 52°56'·00N 00°04'·91E.

BOSTON, NEW CUT AND RIVER WITHAM

Ent N side, Dollypeg ⚓ QG 4m 1M; B △; 52°56'·13N 00°05'·03E.
New Cut ⚓ Fl G 3s; △ on pile; 52°55'·98N 00°04'·67E.
New Cut Ldg Lts 240°. Front, No 1, F 5m 5M; 52°55'·85N 00°04'·40E. Rear, 90m from front, F 8m 5M.

WELLAND CUT/RIVER WELLAND

SE side ⚡ Iso R 2s; NW side Iso G 2s. Lts QR (to port) and QG (to stbd) mark the chan upstream; 52°55'·72E 00°04'·68E.

THE WASH TO THE RIVER HUMBER

(Direction of buoyage ⬆ South to North)
Dudgeon ⚓ Q (9) 15s 7M; *Racon (O) 10M*; 53°16'·62N 01°16'·90E.
E Dudgeon ⚓ Q (3) 10s; 53°19'·72N 00°58'·69E.
W Ridge ⚓ Q (9) 15s; 53°19'·04N 00°44'·50E.
Inner Dowsing ⚓ Q (3) 10s 7M, **Racon (T) 10M**; Horn 60s; 53°19'·10N 00°34'·80E.
Mid Outer Dowsing ▲ Fl (3) G 10s; 53°24'·82N 01°07'·79E.
N Outer Dowsing ⚓ Q; 53°33'·52N 00°59'·59E; *Racon (T) 10M*; 992351031.
B.1D Platform Dowsing ⌀ 53°33'·68N 00°52'·63E; Fl (2) 10s 28m **22M**; Morse (U) R 15s 28m 3M; *Horn (2) 60s*.

RIVER HUMBER APPROACHES

Protector ▱ Fl R 2·5s; 53°24'·84N 00°25'·12E.

DZ No 4 ⚓ Fl Y 5s; 53°27'·15N 00°19'·06E.
DZ No 3 ⚓ Fl Y 2·5s 53°29'·30N 00°19'·21E.
Rosse Spit ▱ Fl (2) R 5s 53°30'·56N 00°16'·60E.
Outer Sand ⚓ Q (3) 10s; 53°36'·41N 00°29'·39E; 992351119.
Haile Sand No 2 ▱ Fl (3) R 10s; 53°32'·42N 00°13'·18E.
HUMBER LT FLOAT ⚓ L Fl G 10s 5M; **Racon (T) 7M**; 53°38'·70N 00°21'·24E; AIS.
N Binks ▲ Fl G 4s; 53°36'·01N 00°18'·28E.
S Binks ▲ Fl G 2s 53°34'·74N 00°16'·55E.
SPURN ⚓ Q (3) 10s 10m 8M; **Racon (M) 5M;** ; 53°33'·42N 00°14'·15E.
SE CHEQUER ⚓ VQ (6)+L Fl 10s 6m 6M; 53°33'·36N 00°12'·86E.
Chequer No 3 ⚓ Q (6) + L Fl 15s; 53°33'·07N 00°10'·63E.
No 2B ▱ Fl R 4s; 53°32'·33N 00°09'·10E.
TETNEY ⚓ 2 VQ Y (vert); *Horn Mo (A)60s*; QY on 290m floating hose; 53°32'·35N 00°06'·76E.

RIVER HUMBER/GRIMSBY/HULL

Binks No 3A ▲ Fl G 4s; 53°33'·92N 00°07'·43E.
Spurn Pt ⚓ Fl G 3s 11m 5M; 53°34'·37N 00°06'·47E.
BULL ⚓ VQ 8m 6M; 53°33'·54N 00°05'·70E.
Bull Sand ▱ Q R ; 53°34'·45N 00°03'·69E.
North Fort ⚓ Q; 53°33'·80N 00°04'·19E.
South Fort ⚓ Q (6) + L Fl 15s; 53°33'·65N 00°03'·96E.
Haile Sand Fort ⚡ Fl R 5s 21m 3M; 53°32'·07N 00°01'·99E.
Haile Chan No 4 ▱ Fl R 4s; 53°33'·64N 00°02'·84E.
Middle No 7 VQ (6) + L Fl 10s; 53°35'·80N 00°01'·50E.
Sunk S8 ▲ Fl G 1·5s; 53°37'·10N 00°02'·16E (992351275).
Grimsby Royal Dock ent E side ⚡ Fl (2) R 6s 10m 8M; Dn; 53°35'·08N 00°04'·04W.
Immingham Bulk Terminal ⚡ Dir Lt 291° Dir WRG 1s 17m 3M; vis: 288·5°-FG-289·5°-IsoG-290·5-FW-291·5-IsoR-292·5°-FR-295·5; on bldg; 53°38'·41N 00°11'·97W (992351276).

RIVER HUMBER TO WHITBY

Canada & Giorgios Wreck ⚓ VQ (3) 5s; 53°42'·37N 00°07'·16E.
Albrough intake ⚡ Q R 17m 2M; 53°49'·01N 00°03'·38W.

BRIDLINGTON

SW Smithic ⚓ Q (9) 15s; 54°02'·41N 00°09'·21W.
N Pier Hd ⚡ Fl 2s 12m 9M; *Horn 60s*; (Tidal Lts) Fl R or Fl G; 54°04'·77N 00°11'·19W.
N Smithic ⚓ VQ; *Bell*; 54°06'·22N 00°03'·90W.
Flamborough Hd ☆ 54°06'·98N 00°04'·96W; Fl (4) 15s 65m **24M**; W ○ twr; *Horn (2) 90s*.

FILEY/SCARBOROUGH/WHITBY

Filey Brigg ⚓ Q (3) 10s; *Bell*; 54°12'·74N 00°14'·60W.
Scarborough E Pier Hd ⚡ QG 8m 3M; 54°16'·88N 00°23'·36W.
Scarborough Pier ⚡ Iso 5s 17m 9M; W ○ twr; vis: 219°-039° (tide sigs); *Dia 60s*; 54°16'·91N 00°23'·40W.
Whitby ⚓ Q; *Bell*; 54°30'·33N 00°36'·58W.
Whitby High ☆ 54°28'·67N 00°34'·10W; Fl WR 5s 73m **18M**, R16M; W 8-sided twr & dwellings; vis:128°-R-143°-W- 319°.
Whitby E Pier ⚡ Fl(2) R 4s 16m 5M; 54°29'·57N 00°36'·71W; Twr.

Whitby E Pier Ext Hd ⚡ Q R 12m 5M; 54°29'·65N 00°36'·74W.

Whitby W Pier ⚡ Fl(2) G 4s 24m 5M; 54°29'·57N 00°36'·78W; Twr.

Whitby W Pier Ext Hd ⚡ Q G 12m 5M; 54°29'·65N 00°36'·80W.

WHITBY TO THE RIVER TYNE

RUNSWICK/REDCAR

Salt Scar ⚓ 54°38'·12N 01°00'·12W VQ; *Bell*.

Luff Way Ldg Lts 197°. Front, on Esplanade, FR 8m 7M; vis: 182°-212°; 54°37'·10N 01°03'·71W. Rear, 115m from front, FR 12m 7M; vis: 182°-212°.

High Stone. Lade Way Ldg Lts 247°. Front, Oc R 2·5s 9m 7M; 54°37'·15N 01°03'·92W. Rear, 43m from front, Oc R 2·5s 11m 7M; vis: 232°-262°.

TEES APPROACHES/HARTLEPOOL

Tees Approach ⚓ Mo(A) 5s 8M; *Racon (B)*; *Horn*; 54°40'·60N 01°04'·00W; AIS.

Bkwtr Hd S Gare ⚡ 54°38'·85N 01°08'·25W; Fl WR 12s 16m 10M; W ○ twr; vis: 020°-W-240°-R-357°; Sig Stn.

Ldg Lts 210·1° Front, FR 18m 13M; 54°37'·22N 01°10'·20W. **Rear**, 560m from front, FR 20m **16M**.

Longscar ⚓ Q (3) 10s; *Bell*; 54°40'·86N 01°09'·89W.

The Heugh ☆ 54°41'·79N 01°10'·56W; Fl (2) **WR** 10s 19m **19M**; vis: 309°-R-319°-W-190°; W twr.

Hartlepool Marina Lock Dir Lt 308° Dir Iso WRG2s 6m 3M; vis: 305·5°-G-307°-W-309°-R-310·5°; 54°41'·45N 01°11'·92W.

SEAHAM/SUNDERLAND

Seaham N Pier Hd ⚡ Fl G 10s 12m 5M; W col, B bands; 54°50'·26N 01°19'·26W.

Sunderland Roker Pier Hd ☆ 54°55'·28N 01°21'·15W; Fl 5s 25m **18M**; W □ twr, 3 R bands and cupola: vis: 211°-357°; *Siren 20s*.

Old N Pier Hd ⚡ QG 12m 8M; metal column; 54°55'·13N 01°21'·61W.

DZ ⚓ 54°57'·04N 01°18'·90W and ⚓ 54°58'·61N 01°19'·90W; both Fl Y 2·5s.

TYNE ENTRANCE/NORTH SHIELDS

Ent North Pier Hd ☆ 55°00'·88N 01°24'·18W; Fl (3) 10s 26m **26M**; Gy □ twr, W lantern; *Horn 10s*.

Herd Groyne Hd Dir Ldg Lt 249°, Oc 10s 14m **19M**; vis: 246·5°-W-251·5°; R pile structure, R&W lantern. Same structure Oc RG 10s 13m, 11M; vis:224°-G-246·5°, 251·5°-R-277°; sync with Dir lt FR (unintens) 080°-224°. *Bell (1) 5s*; 55°00'·49N 01°25'·44W.

RIVER TYNE TO BERWICK-UPON-TWEED

CULLERCOATS and BLYTH

Cullercoats Ldg Lts 256°. Front, FR 27m 3M; 55°02'·06N 01°25'·91W. Rear, 38m from front, FR 35m 3M.

Blyth Ldg Lts 324°. Front ⚓, F Bu 11m 10M; 55°07'·42N 01°29'·82W. Rear ⚓, 180m from front, F Bu 17m 10M. Both Or ⚓ on twr.

Blyth E Pier Hd ☆ 55°06'·98N 01°29'·21W; Fl (4) 10s 19m **21M**, W twr; same structure FR 13m 13M, vis:152°-249°; Horn (3) 30s.

Met Mast ⚡; Mo(U)15s 17m 10M; 55°08'·78N 01°25'·25W; Aero 3 FR (107m), *Horn 30s*.

COQUET ISLAND, AMBLE and WARKWORTH

Coquet ☆ 55°20'·03N 01°32'·39W; Fl (3) WR 20s 25m **W19M, R15M**; W □ twr, turreted parapet, lower half Gy; vis: 330°-R-140°-W-163°-R-180°-W-330°; sector boundaries are indeter-minate and may appear as Alt WR; *Horn 30s*.

Amble N Pier Head ⚡ Fl G 6s 12m 6M; 55°20'·39N 01°34'·25W.

SEAHOUSES, BAMBURGH and FARNE ISLANDS

N Sunderland ⚓ Fl R 2·5s; 55°34'·62N 01°37'·12W.

Bamburgh Black Rocks Point ☆ 55°36'·99N 01°43'·45W; Oc(2) WRG 8s 12m **W14M**, R11M, G11M; W bldg; vis: 122°-G-165°-W- 175°-R-191°-W- 238°-R- 275°-W- 289°-G-300°.

Inner Farne ⚡ Fl (2) WR 15s 27m W10M, R7M; W ○ twr; vis: 119°- R - 280° - W -119°; 55°36'·92N 01°39'·35W.

Longstone ☆ **W side** 55°38'·62N 01°36'·65W; Fl 20s 23m **18M**; R twr, W band; 992351127.

Swedman ⚓ Fl G 2·5s; 55°37'·65N 01°41'·63W.

HOLY ISLAND

Ridge ⚓ Q (3) 10s; 55°39'·70N 01°45'·97W.

Plough Rock ⚓ Q (9) 15s; 55°40'·24N 01°46'·00W.

Old Law E Bn ⚡ (Guile Pt) Oc WRG 6s 9m 4M; vis: 180·5°-G-258·5°-W-261·5°-R-300°, 55°39'·49N 01°47'·59W; stone obelisk.

Heugh ⚡ Oc WRG 6s 24m 5M; vis: 135°-G-308°-W-311-R-shore; 55°40'·09N 01°47'·99W.

Plough Seat ⚓ QR; 55°40'·37N 01°44'·97W.

Goldstone ⚓ QG; 55°40'·25N 01°43'·64W.

BERWICK-UPON-TWEED

Bkwtr Hd ⚡ Fl 5s 15m 6M; vis: 201°-009°, (obscured 155°-201°); W ○ twr, R cupola and base; FG (same twr) 8m 1M; vis 009°-G-155°; 55°45'·88N 01°59'·06W.

1	Ramsgate	**1**			**11**	31	61	78	91	107	126	189	205	205	232	Berwick-upon-Tweed	**11**
2	Sheerness	34	**2**			**10**	27	42	65	81	102	157	176	185	203	Amble	**10**
3	Gravesend	56	22	**3**			**9**	16	36	51	70	138	149	156	180	Sunderland	**9**
4	London Bridge	76	45	23	**4**			**8**	24	39	58	122	137	140	169	Hartlepool	**8**
5	Burnham-on-Crouch	44	34	54	77	**5**			**7**	16	35	88	114	121	143	Whitby	**7**
6	Brightlingsea	41	28	48	71	21	**6**			**6**	20	81	98	105	130	Scarborough	**6**
7	Harwich	40	50	66	93	31	20	**7**			**5**	58	83	87	114	Bridlington	**5**
8	River Deben (ent)	45	55	75	98	36	25	6	**8**			**4**	79	75	113	Hull	**4**
9	Southwold	62	72	92	115	53	42	25	23	**9**			**3**	34	83	Boston	**3**
10	Lowestoft	72	82	102	125	63	52	35	33	10	**10**			**2**	85	King's Lynn	**2**
11	Great Yarmouth	79	87	105	132	70	59	42	40	18	7	**11**			**1**	Great Yarmouth	**1**

AREA 5 *E Scotland – Berwick-upon-Tweed to C Wrath & N Isles*

SELECTED LIGHTS, BUOYS & WAYPOINTS

BERWICK-UPON-TWEED TO BASS ROCK

BURNMOUTH
Ldg lts 241°. Front, FR 29m 4M; 55°50'·53N 02°04'·25W. Rear, 45m from front, FR 35m 4M. Both on W posts (unclear by day).

EYEMOUTH
Blind Buss ⚓ Q; 55°52'·80N 02°05'·25E.
Ldg Lts 174°. Front, W Bkwtr Hd ⚡, FG 9m 6M; 55°52'·47N 02°05'·29W. Rear, elbow 55m from front, FG 10m 6M.

ST ABBS to DUNBAR and BASS ROCK
St Abbs Hd ☆ 55°54'·96N 02°08'·29W; Fl 10s 68m **18M**; W twr; *Racon (T) 18M*.
Barns Ness Tower (Lt ho disused 36m); 55°59'·22N 02°26'·76W.
Torness Pwr Stn Ldg Lts 215°. Front, Iso G 4s 6m 6M; W □ with B vert stripe on plinth; 55°58'·27N 02°24'·86W. Rear, Iso G 4s 22m 3M; W □ with B vert stripe on post; sync with front.
Dunbar Hbr Ldg Lts (Bayswell Hill) 198°. Front, Oc G 6s 15m 3M;3 Or △ on col; 56°00'·26N 02°31'·21W. Rear, Oc G 6s 22m 3M; 3 Or ▽; sync with front; both lts 188°-G(intens)-208°.
S Carr ⚓ Q; 56°03'·60N 02°37'·65W.
Bass Rock, S side, ⚡ Fl (3) 20s 46m 10M; W twr; vis: 241°-107°; 56°04'·61N 02°38'·48W.

FIRTH OF FORTH AND SOUTH SHORE

(Direction of buoyage East to West)

NORTH BERWICK
Outfall ⚓ Fl Y; 56°04'·29N 02°40'·89W.

Fidra ☆ 56°04'·39N 02°47'·13W; Fl(4) 30s 34m **15M**; W twr; obsc by Bass Rock, Craig Leith and Lamb Island.

PORT SETON, COCKENZIE, FISHERROW and S CHANNEL
Port Seton, E Pier Hd ⚡ Iso WR 4s 10m W9M, R6M; vis: shore-R-105°-W-225°-R-shore; *Bell (occas)*; 55°58'·40N 02°57'·23W.
Fisherrow E Pier Hd ⚡ Oc 6s 5m 6M; 55°56'·79N 03°04'·11W.
Narrow Deep ⚓ Fl(2) R 10s; 56°01'·46N 03°04'·59W.
Herwit ⚓ Fl(3) G 10s; 56°01'·05N 03°06'·52W.
North Craig ⚓ Q(3) 10s; 56°01'·02N 03°03'·52W.
Craigh Waugh ⚓ Fl(2) 10s; 56°00'·26N 03°04'·47W.
Diffuser Hds (Outer) ⚓ Q; 55°59'·81N 03°07'·84W.
Diffuser Hds (Inner) ⚓ Q(6) + LFl 15s; 55°59'·38N 03°08'·02W.

LEITH and GRANTON
Leith Approach ⚓ Fl R 3s; 55°59'·95N 03°11'·51W.
East Bkwtr Hd ⚡ Iso R 4s 7m 9M; 55°59'·48N 03°10'·94W.
Granton E Pier Hd ⚡ Fl R 2s 5m 6M; 55°59'·28N 03°13'·27W.

NORTH CHANNEL and MIDDLE BANK
Inchkeith Fairway ⚓ Iso 2s; *Racon (T) 5M*; 56°03'·49N 03°00'·10W.
No 1 ⚓ Fl G 9s; 56°03'·22N 03°03'·71W.
No 2 ⚓ Fl R 9s; 56°02'·90N 03°03'·72W.
No 3 ⚓ Fl G 6s; 56°03'·22N 03°06'·10W.
No 4 ⚓ Fl R 6s; 56°02'·89N 03°06'·11W.
No 5 ⚓ Fl G 3s; 56°03'·18N 03°07'·88W.
No 6 ⚓ Fl R 3s; 56°03'·05N 03°08'·44W.

No 8 ⚓ Fl R 9s 56°02'·95N 03°09'·62W.
Inchkeith ⚡ 56°02'·01N 03°08'·17W; Fl 15s 67m 14M; stone twr.
Pallas Rock ⚓ VQ (9) 10s 56°01'·50N 03°09'·30W.
East Gunnet ⚓ Q (3) 10s; 56°01'·41N 03°10'·38W.
West Gunnet ⚓ Q (9) 15s 56°01'·34N 03°11'·06W.
No 7 ⚓ QG; *Racon (T) 5M*; 56°02'·80N 03°10'·97W.
No 9 ⚓ Fl G 6s; 56°02'·32N 03°13'·48W.
No 10 ⚓ Fl R 6s; 56°02'·07N 03°13'·32W.
No 11 ⚓ Fl G 3s 56°02'·08N 03°15'·26W.
No 12 ⚓ Fl R 3s; 56°01'·78N 03°15'·15W.
No 13 ⚓ Fl G 9s; 56°01'·77N 03°16'·94W.
No 14 ⚓ Q R; 56°01'·51N 03°16'·90W.
Oxcars ⚡ Fl (2) WR 7s 16m W13M, R12M; W twr, R band; vis: 072°-W-087°- R-196°-W-313°-R-072°; 56°01'·36N 03°16'·84W.
Inchcolm E Pt ⚡ Fl (3) 15s 20m 10M; Gy twr; part obsc by land 075°-145·5°; 56°01'·72N 03°17'·83W.
No 15 ⚓ Fl G 6s; 56°01'·39N 03°18'·95W.

MORTIMER'S DEEP
Hawkcraig Point Ldg Lts 292°. Front, Iso 5s 12m 14M; W twr; vis: 282°-302°; 56°03'·03N 03°17'·07W. Rear, 96m from front, Iso 5s 16m 14M; W twr; vis: 282°-302°.
Inchcolm S Lts in line 066°. Front, 84m from rear, Q 7m 7M; W twr; vis: 062·5°-082·5°; 56°01'·78N 03°18'·28W. Common Rear, Iso 5s 11m 7M; W twr; vis: 062·5°-082·5°; 56°01'·80N 03°18'·13W. N Lts in line 076·7°. Front, 80m from rear, Q 7m 7M; W twr; vis: 062·5°-082·5°.

APPROACHES TO FORTH BRIDGES
No 17 ⚓ Fl G 3s; 56°01'·23N 03°19'·84W.
No 16 ⚓ Fl R 3s; 56°00'·87N 03°19'·60W.
No 19 ⚓ Fl G 9s; 56°00'·71N 03°22'·47W.
Rosyth Chan centreline ⚡ Iso 4s 56m 8M; 56°00'·44N 03°24'·64W.
Central Twr (Beamer Rk) ⚡ Iso 2s 7m 9M; 56°00'·29N 03°24'·75W.
Forth Chan centreline ⚡ Iso 8s 56m 8M; 56°00'·12N 03°24'·85W.

PORT EDGAR
W Bkwtr Hd ⚡ Fl R 4s 4m 8M; 55°59'·86N 03°24'·78W. W blockhouse.

FIRTH OF FORTH – NORTH SHORE (INWARD)

BURNTISLAND
W Pier Outer Hd ⚡ Fl (2) R 6s 7m; W twr; 56°03'·22N 03°14'·26W.
E Pier Outer Hd ⚡ Fl (2) G 6s 7m 5M; 56°03'·24N 03°14'·17W.

ABERDOUR, BRAEFOOT BAY and INCHCOLM
Hawkcraig Pt ⚡ (see **MORTIMER'S DEEP** above).
Braefoot Bay Terminal, W Jetty. Ldg Lts 247·3°. **Front**, Fl 3s 6m **15M**; W △ on E dolphin; vis: 237·2°-257·2°; 56°02'·16N 03°18'·71W; 4 dolphins with 2 FG (vert). **Rear**, 88m from front, Fl 3s 12m **15M**; W ▽ on appr gangway; vis: 237·2°-257·2°; sync with front.

INVERKEITHING BAY
St David's ⚓ Fl G 5s 3m 7M; Or □, on pile; 56°01'·37N 03°22'·29W.
Channel ⚓ QG; 56°01'·43N 03°23'·02W.

ROSYTH

No 2 ⚓ Q (3) 10s; 56°00'·69N 03°25'·18W.
Main Chan Dir lt 323·5°. Bn 'A' Oc WRG 7m 4M; R ☐ on W post with R bands; vis: 318°-G-321°-321°-W-326°-R-328° (H24); 56°01'·19N 03°25'·61W.
Dir lt 115°, Bn 'C' Oc WRG 6s 7m 4M; W ▽ on W Bn; vis: 110°-R -113° W -116·5° - G -120°; 56°00'·61N 03°24'·25W.
S Arm Jetty Hd ⚓ L Fl (2) WR 12s 5m 9M; R6M; vis: 010°-W-280°-R-010°; 56°01'·09N 03°26'·58W.

RIVER FORTH

ROSYTH to GRANGEMOUTH

Dhu Craig ▲ Fl G 5s; 56°00'·74N 03°27'·23W.
Blackness ⚓ QR; 56°01'·06N 03°30'·30W.
Tancred Bank ⚓ Fl (2) R 10s; 56°01'·58N 03°31'·91W.
Dods Bank ⚓ Fl R 3s; 56°02'·03N 03°34'·07W.
Bo'ness ⚓ Fl R 10s; 56°02'·23N 03°35'·38W.
Torry ⚓ Fl G 10s 5m 7M; G ○ structure; 56°02'·46N 03°35'·28W.
Bo'ness Bcns ⚏ 2 QR 3m 2M; 56°01'·85N 03°36'·22W.
Bo'ness Hbr ⚓; 56°01'·26N 03°36'·46W.

GRANGEMOUTH

Grangemouth App No 1 ⚓ Fl (3) 10s 4m 6M;56°02'·12N 03°38'·10W.
Hen & Chickens ▲ Fl (3) G 10s; 56°02'·35N 03°38'·08W.

FIRTH OF FORTH – NORTH SHORE (OUTWARD)

KIRKCALDY and METHIL

Kirkcaldy W Pier Hd ⚓ Fl R 5s 7m 3M; 56°06'·80N 03°08'·97W.
Kirkcaldy E Pier Hd ⚓ Fl G 5s 12m 3M; 56°06'·78N 03°08'·90W.
Methil Outer Pier Hd ⚓ Oc G 6s 8m 5M; W twr; vis: 280°-100°; 56°10'·76N 03°00'·48W.

ELIE and ST MONANS

Elie Ness ☆ 56°11'·04N 02°48'·77W; Fl 6s 15m **17M**; W twr.
St Monans Bwtr Hd ⚓ Fl G 3s 3m 4M; 56°12'·19N 02°45'·94W.
St Monans Inner Lt ⚓ Iso 4s 3m 4M; 56°12'·29N 02°45'·95W.

PITTENWEEM and ANSTRUTHER EASTER

Pittenweem, Ldg Lts 037° Middle Pier Hd. Front, FR 4m 5M. Rear, FR 8m 5M. Both Gy Cols, Or stripes; 56°12'·69N 02°43'·69W.
Pittenweem, E Bkwtr Hd ⚓ Fl (2) RG 5s 9m R9M, G6M; vis: 265°-R-345°-G-055°; 56°12'·63N 02°43'·74W.
Anstruther, Ldg Lts 019°. Front FG 7m 4M; 56°13'·28N 02°41'·76W. Rear, 38m from front, FG 11m 4M (both W masts).

MAY I, CRAIL, ST ANDREWS and FIFE NESS to MONTROSE

Isle of May ☆ 56°11'·12N 02°33'·46W(Summit); Fl (2) 15s 73m **22M**; ☐ twr on stone dwelling.
Crail, Ldg Lts 295°. Front, FR 24m 6M (not lit when hbr closed); 56°15'·46N 02°37'·84W. Rear, 30m from front, FR 30m 6M.
Fife Ness ☆ 56°16'·74N 02°35'·19W; Iso WR 10s 12m **W15M**, R12M; W bldg; vis: 143°-W-197°-R-217°-W-023°; 002320798.
N Carr ⚓ Q (3) 10s 3m 5M; 56°18'·05N 02°32'·94W.
St Andrews ⚓ 56°20'·38N 02°47'·07W; Dir lt 277·5; Iso WRG 2s 17m 9M; vis: 272°-G-276°-AlWG-277°-W-278°-AlWR-279°-R-283°.St Andrews N Bkwtr Bn ⚓ Fl G 3M 56°20'·36N 02°46'·77W.
Bell Rk ☆ 56°26'·08N 02°23'·21W; Fl 5s 28m **18M**; *Racon (M) 18M*.

Met Mast ☆ Mo(U) 15s 22m 10M; Aero FR (116m), *Horn Mo(U) 30s*; 56°26'·40N 02°14'·49W; 992351153.

RIVER TAY, TAYPORT, DUNDEE and PERTH

Tay Fairway ⚓ L Fl 10s; *Bell*; 56°28'·45N 02°36'·60W.
Middle ▲ Fl G 3s; 56°28'·08N 02°38'·47W.
Middle ⚓ Fl (2) R 6s 56°27'·87N 02°37'·95W.
Abertay N ⚓ Q (3) 10s; 56°27'·61N 02°40'·75W.
Abertay S (Elbow) ⚓ Fl R 6s 56°27'·18N 02°39'·63W.
Tayport High Lt ⚓ Dir lt 268·25°; WRG 3s 23m WRG14M; vis: 266°-IsoG-267·5°-VQG-268°-IsoW-268·5°-VQR-269°-IsoR-271°; W twr, 56°27'·17N 02°53'·94W.

ARBROATH

Ldg lts 299·2°. Front , FR 7m 5M; W col; 56°33'·29N 02°35'·16W. Rear, 50m from front, FR 13m 5M; W col.

MONTROSE

Scurdie Ness ☆ 56°42'·10N 02°26'·24W; Fl (3) 20s 38m **20M**; W twr; *Racon (T) 14-16M*.
Outer Ldg Lts 271·5°; Front, FR 11m 5M; W twin pillars, R bands; 56°42'·21N 02°27'·41W; Rear, 272m from front, FR 18m 5M; W twr, R cupola.
Inner Ldg Lts 265°; Front FG 21m 5M; Rear FG 33m 5M.

MONTROSE TO RATTRAY HEAD

JOHNSHAVEN and GOURDON HARBOUR

Johnshaven, Ldg Lts 316°. Front, FR 5m; 56°47'·62N 02°20'·26W. Rear, 85m from front, FG 20m; shows R when unsafe to ent hbr. Gourdon Hbr, Ldg Lts 358°. Front, FR 5m 5M; W twr; shows G when unsafe to enter; *Siren (2) 60s* (occas); 56°49'·69N 02°17'·24W. Rear, 120m from front, FR 30m 5M; W twr.
Gourdon E B'water ⚓ Q 3m 3M; 49°57'·60N 02°17'·19W.
Todhead Lighthouse (disused), white tower, 13m.

STONEHAVEN to GIRDLE NESS

Outer Pier Hd ⚓ Iso WRG 4s 7m 5M; vis: 214°-G-246°-W-268°-R-280°; 56°57'·59N 02°12'·00W.

Girdle Ness ☆ Fl (2) 20s 56m **22M**; obsc by Greg Ness when brg > 020°; *Racon (G) 25M*; 57°08'·34N 02°02'·91W.

ABERDEEN

Fairway ⚓ Mo (A) 5s; *Racon (T) 7M*; 57°09'·31N 02°01'·95W.
Torry Ldg lts 237·2°, Front FR or G 14m 5M; R when ent safe, FG when dangerous to navigate; W twr; 57°08'·38N 02°04'·50W.
Rear, 220m from front, FR or G 19m 5M; R when ent safe, FG when dangerous to navigate; W twr; 57°08'·31N 02°04'·68W.
Aberdeen Harbour Ent ⚓ 57°08'·38N 02°04'·48W; Dir lt 237·2° Fl WRG 1s 7m 9M; metal post; vis: 235·2°-QG-236·2°-AlQGW-236·7°-QW-237·7°-AlQRW-238·2°-QR-239·2°.
S Bkwtr Hd ⚓ Fl (3) R 8s 23m 7M; 57°08'·69N 02°03'·34W.
N Pier Hd ⚓ Iso G 4s 11m 10M; W twr; 57°08'·74N 02°03'·69W.
In fog FY 10m (same twr) vis: 136°-336°; *Bell (3) 12s*.
S Skates Nose Jetty Hd ⚓ Q R 4m 4M; 57°08'·49N 02°04'·06W.
Abercrombie Jetty Hd ⚓ Oc G 4s 5m 4M; 57°08'·53N 02°04'·15W.

BUCHAN NESS TO INVERNESS

PETERHEAD and RATTRAY HEAD

Buchan Ness ☆ Fl 5s 40m **18M**; W twr, R bands; *Racon (O) 14-16M*; 57°28'·23N 01°46'·51W.

Kirktown Ldg lts 314°. Front, Oc R 6s 14m 10M; Or △ on lattice mast; 57°30'·22N 01°47'·21W. Rear, Oc R 6s 21m 10M (sync with front); Or ▽ on lattice mast.

S Bkwtr Hd ⚡ Fl (2) R 12s 24m 7M; 57°29'·79N 01°46'·54W.

N Bkwtr Hd ⚡ Iso RG 6s 19m 11M; W tripod; vis: 171°-R-236°-G-171°; *Horn 30s*; 57°29'·84N 01°46'·32W.

Rattray Hd ☆ 57°36'·61N 01°49'·03W Fl (3) 30s 28m **18M**; W twr; *Racon (M) 15M*; *Horn (2) 45s*.

Smith Bank Met Mast ◰ Mo(U) 15s 17m 10M Mast (101); Horn Mo(U) 30s; 58°10'·93N 02°49'·22W.

FRASERBURGH
Balaclava Bkwtr Head ⚡ Fl (2) G 8s 26m 6M; dome on W twr; vis: 178°-326°; 57°41'·51N 01°59'·70W.

N Pier ⚡ WRG 2s 7m 8M; metal post; 285°-G-287°-WG-289°-W-293°-WR-295°-R-297°; 57°41'·54N 01°59'·99W.

Kinnaird Hd ☆ 57°41'·87N 02°00'·26W Fl 5s 25m **22M**; vis: 092°-297°.

MACDUFF, BANFF and WHITEHILLS
Macduff Pier Hd ⚡ Fl (2) WRG 6s 12m W9M, R7M; W twr; vis: shore-G-115°-W-174°-R-210°; 57°40'·26N 02°30'·01W.

Macduff Ldg Lts 130°, Front FR 28m 3M; 57°40'·18N 02°29'·85W. Rear, 220m from front, FR 55m 3M; both Or △ on mast.

Banff Ldg Lts 295°, Front Fl R 4s; 57°40·30N 02°31·36W. Rear, QR; both vis: 210°-345°.

Whitehills Pier Hd ⚡ 57°40'·80N 02°34'·88W Fl WR 3s 7m W9M, R6M; W twr; vis: 132°-R-212°-W-245°.

PORTSOY and FINDOCHTY
Portsoy Pier Ldg Lts 173°, Front Fl G 4s 20m 3M; post; 57°41'·09N 02°41'·40W; Rear Q G 22m 3M; R △ on BW post.

Findochty Middle Pier Ldg Lts 166°, Front FR 6m 3M; 57°41'·90N 02°54'·20W. Rear FR 10m 3M.

BUCKIE
West Muck ⚡ QR 5m 7M; tripod; 57°41'·06N 02°58'·01W.

N Pier Ldg Lts 096°, Front, FR 6m 9M; 57°40'·83N 02°57'·71W. **Rear** ☆, 60m from front, Oc R 10s 15m 15M; W twr.

LOSSIEMOUTH, HOPEMAN and BURGHEAD
Lossiemouth S Pier Hd ⚡ Fl R 6s 11m 5M; 57°43'·42N 03°16'·69W.

Halliman Skerries ⚓ Q; *Racon M*, 57°44'·33N 03°18'·57W.

Hopeman Ldg Lts 081°, Front, FR 3m; 57°42'·71N 03°26'·18W. Rear, 10m from front, FR, 4m.

Burghead N Bkwtr Hd ⚡ Oc 8s 7m 5M; 57°42'·09N 03°30'·03W.

FINDHORN, NAIRN and INVERNESS FIRTH
Findhorn Landfall ⚓ LF 10s 57°40'·34N 03°38'·77W.

Nairn E Pier Hd ⚡ Oc WRG 4s 6m 5M; 8-sided twr; vis: shore-G-100°-W-207°-R-shore; 57°35'·62N 03°51'·65W.

Riff Bank E ⚓ Fl Y 10s 3m 5M 57°38'·38N 03°58'·18W; AIS.

SOUTH CHANNEL
Riff Bank S ⚓ Q (6) + L Fl 15s; 57°36'·73N 04°00'·97W.

Chanonry ⚡ 57°34'·45N 04°05'·56W Oc 6s 12m 12M; W twr; vis: 148°-073°.

Munlochy ⚓ L Fl 10s; 57°32'·91N 04°07'·65W.

Petty Bank ⚓ Fl R 5s 57°31'·58N 04°08'·98W.

Meikle Mee ▲ Fl G 3s 57°30'·26N 04°12'·02W.

Longman Pt ⚓ Fl WR 2s 7m W5M, R4M; vis: 078°-W-258°-R-078°; 57°29'·99N 04°13'·31W.

Craigton Point ⚡ Fl WRG 4s 6m W11M, R7M, G7M; vis: 312°-W-048°-R-064°-W-085°-G-shore; 57°30'·05N 04°14'·09W.

Bridge Centre, Or △; *Racon (K) 6M*; 57°29'·97N 04°13'·79W.

INVERNESS and CALEDONIAN CANAL
R. Ness Outer ⚓ QR 3m 4M; 57°29'·83N 04°13'·93W.

Carnarc Pt ⚡ Fl G 2s 8m 4M; G lattice twr; 57°29'·72N 04°14'·25W.

Clachnaharry, S Tr'ng Wall Hd ⚓ Iso G 4s 5m 2M; tfc sigs; 57°29'·43N 04°15'·86W.

INVERNESS TO DUNCANSBY HEAD
CROMARTY FIRTH and INVERGORDON
Fairway ⚓ L Fl 10s; *Racon (M) 5M*; 57°39'·96N 03°54'·19W.

Cromarty Bank ▲ Fl (2) G 10s; 57°40'·66N 03°56'·78W.

Buss Bank ⚓ Fl R 3s 57°40'·97N 03°59'·54W.

Cromarty – The Ness (Lt ho disused W tr 13m); 57°40'·98N 04°02'·20W

Nigg Oil Terminal Pier Hd ⚡ Oc G 5s 31m 5M; Gy twr; floodlit; 57°41'·54N 04°02'·60W.

DORNOCH FIRTH to LYBSTER
Tarbat Ness ☆ 57°51'·88N 03°46'·76W Fl (4) 30s 53m **18M**; W twr, R bands; *Racon (T) 14-16M*.

Met Mast ⚡ Mo(U) 15s 17m 10M; FR (101m), *Horn Mo(U) 30s*; 58°10'·93N 00°49'·22W.

Helmsdale ⚡ Dir lt 313° WRG 2s 7m 6M (1M day); post; vis: 308°-Iso G-311°-Al WG-312°-Iso W-313°-Al WR-314°-Iso R-318°; 58°06'·91N 03°39'·04W.

Lybster, S Pier Hd ⚡ Oc R 6s 10m 3M; 58°17'·79N 03°17'·41W.

Clyth Ness Lt Ho (unlit); W twr, R band; 58°18'·64N 03°12'·74W.

WICK
S Pier Hd ⚡ Fl WRG 3s 12m W12M, R9M, G9M; W 8-sided twr; vis: 253°-G-270°-W-286°-R-329°; 58°26'·34N 03°04'·73W.

Dir lt 288·5° F WRG 9m W10M, R7M, G7M; col, N end of bridge; vis: 283·5°-G-287·2°-W-289·7°-R-293·5°; 58°26'·54N 03°05'·34W

Noss Hd ☆ 58°28'·76N 03°03'·09W Fl 20s 53m **W18M**; W twr; vis: 073°-045° (332°).

DUNCANSBY HEAD TO CAPE WRATH
Duncansby Hd ☆ 58°38'·65N 03°01'·58W Fl 12s 67m **21M**; W twr; *Racon (T)*.

Muckle Skerry ☆ 58°41'·41N 02°55'·49W Fl (3) 30s 52m **23M**; W twr; 992351086.

Lother Rock ⚡ Fl 2s 13m 6M; *Racon (M) 10M*; 58°43'·79N 02°58'·69W.

Swona ⚡ Fl 8s 17m 9M; vis: 261°-210°; 58°44'·25N 03°04'·24W.

Swona N Hd ⚡ Fl (3) 10s 16m 10M; 58°45'·11N 03°03'·10W.

Stroma ☆, Swilkie Point 58°41'·75N 03°07'·01W Fl (2) 20s 32m **20M**; W twr; 992351092.

Dunnet Hd ☆ 58°40'·28N 03°22'·60W Fl (4) 30s 105m **23M**.

THURSO, SCRABSTER and CAPE WRATH
Thurso ⚡ FG 5m 4M; Gy post; 58°35'·91N 03°30'·80W.

Scrabster Q. E. Pier Hd ⚡ Fl (2) 4s 8m 8M 58°36'·66N 03°32'·31W.

Strathy Pt Lt Ho (disused) W twr on W dwelling; 58°36'·04N 04°01'·12W.

Sule Skerry ☆ 59°05'·09N 04°24'·38W Fl (2) 15s 34m **21M**; W twr; *Racon (T)*.

Sule Stack ⊙; V-AIS; *ℓ*; 59°01'·45N 04°30'·40W; <u>992356017</u>.
Nun Rock ⊙; V-AIS; *ℓ*; 58°52'·65N 04°58'·30W; <u>992356016</u>.

North Rona ☆ 59°07'·27N 05°48'·91W Fl (3) 20s 114m **22M**.

Sula Sgeir ⚡ Fl 15s 74m 11M; ☐ structure; 59°05'·61N 06°09'·57W.

Loch Eriboll, White Hd ⚡ Fl WR10s 18m W13M, R12M; W twr and bldg; vis: 030°-W-172°-R-191°-W-212°; 58°31'·01N 04°38'·90W.

Cape Wrath ☆ 58°37'·54N 04°59'·99W Fl (4) 30s 122m **22M**; W twr <u>992351087</u>.

ORKNEY ISLANDS

Tor Ness ☆ 58°46'·78N 03°17'·86W Fl 5s 21m **17M**; W twr.
Cantick Hd (S Walls, SE end) ⚡ 58°47'·23N 03°07'·88W Fl 20s 35m 13M; W twr.

SCAPA FLOW and APPROACHES

Long Hope, S Ness Pier Hd ⚡ Fl WRG 3s 6m W7M, R5M, G5M; vis: 082°-G-242°-W-252°-R-082°; 58°48'·05N 03°12'·35W.

Hoxa Head ⚡ Fl WR 3s 15m W9M, R6M; W twr; vis: 026°-W-163°-R-201°-W-215°; 58°49'·31N 03°02'·09W.

Nevi Skerry *ℓ* Fl (2) 6s 7m 6M; 58°50'·67N 03°02'·70W.

Flotta Grinds ⚓ Fl (2) R; 58°50'·97N 03°00'·77W; <u>992351083</u>.

Rose Ness ⚡ 58°52'·33N 02°49'·97W Fl 6s 24m 8M; W twr.

Copinsay ⚡ Fl (5) 30s 79m 14M; W twr; 58°53'·79N 02°40'·33W.

Barrel of Butter ⚡ Fl (2) 10s 6m 7M; 58 53'·40N 03°07'·62W.

Cava ⚡ Fl WR 3s 11m W10M, R8M; W ○ twr; vis: 351°-W-143°-196°-W-251°-R-271°-R-298°; 58°53'·21N 03°10'·70W.

Holm of Houton ⚡ 58°54'·62N 03°10'·97W; Fl R 3s 7m 5M.

Houton Bay Ldg Lts 316°. Front *ℓ* Fl G 3s 8m. Rear *ℓ*, 200m from front, FG 16m; vis: 312°- 320°; 58°54'·97N 03°11'·56W.

CLESTRAN SOUND and HOY SOUND

Graemsay Is Hoy Sound ☆ Ldg Lts 104°. Front Low, Iso 3s 17m 12M; W twr; vis: 070°-255°, 58°56'·42N 03°18'·60W.

High Rear, 1·2M from front, Oc WR 8s 35m **W19M**, R14M; W twr; vis: 097°-R-112°-W-163°-R-178°-W-332°; obsc on Ldg line within 0·5M.

Skerry of Ness ⚡ Fl WG 4s 7m W7M, G4M; vis: shore -W-090°- G-shore; 58°56'·95N 03°17'·83W.

STROMNESS

Ldg Lts 317°. Front FR 29m 11M; W twr; 58°57'·61N 03°18'·15W. Rear, 55m from front, FR 39m 11M; vis: 307°-327°; H24.

AUSKERRY

Auskerry ☆ 59°01'·51N 02°34'·34W Fl 20s 34m **20M**; W twr.

Helliar Holm, S end ⚡ Fl WRG 10s 18m W14M, R11M, G11M; W twr; vis: 256°-G-276°-W-292°-R-098°-W-116°-G-154°; 59°01'·13N 02°54'·09W.

Balfour Pier Shapinsay ⚡ Fl (2) WRG 5s 5m W3M, R2M, G2M; vis: 270°-G-010°-W-020°-R-090°; 59°01'·86N 02°54'·49W.

KIRKWALL

Thieves Holm, ⚡ Q R 8M; 59°01'·09N 02°56'·21W.

Pier N end ☆ 58°59'·29N 02°57'·72W Iso WRG 5s 8m **W15M**, R13M, G13M; W twr; vis: 153°-G-183°-W-192°-R-210°.

WIDE FIRTH

Linga Skerry *ℓ* Q (3) 10s; 59°02'·39N 02°57'·56W.
Boray Skerries *ℓ* Q (6) + L Fl 15s; 59°03'·65N 02°57'·66W.
Skertours *ℓ* Q; 59°04'·11N 02°56'·72W.
Galt Skerry *ℓ* Q; 59°05'·21N 02°54'·20W.
Seal Skerry ⚡ Fl R 3s 5m 3M; platform; 59°05'·21N 02°54'·20W.

Brough of Birsay ☆ 59°08'·19N 03°20'·41W Fl (3) 25s 52m **18M**.

Papa Stronsay NE end, The Ness ⚡ Fl(4)20s 8m 9M; W twr; 59°09'·34N 02°34'·93W.

SANDAY ISLAND and NORTH RONALDSAY

Quiabow ◣ Fl (2) G 12s; 59°09'·82N 02°36'·30W.

Start Pt ☆ 59°16'·69N 02°22'·71W Fl (2) 20s 24m **18M**.

Kettletoft Pier Hd ⚡ Fl WRG 3s 7m W7M, R5M, G5M; vis: 351°-W- 011°-R-180°-G-351°; 59°13'·80N 02°35'·86W.

N Ronaldsay ☆ NE end, 59°23'·34N 02°22'·91W Fl 10s 43m **24M**; R twr, W bands; *Racon (T) 14-17M*.

EDAY and EGILSAY

Calf Sound ⚡ Fl (3) WRG 10s 6m W8M, R6M, G6M; W twr; vis: shore-R-215°-W-222°-G-301°-W-305°; 59°14'·21N 02°45'·82W.

Backaland Pier ⚡ 59°09'·43N 02°44'·88W Fl R 3s 5m 4M; vis: 192°-250°.

Egilsay Graand *ℓ* Q (6) + L Fl 15s; 59°06'·86N 02°54'·42W.

WESTRAY and PIEROWALL

Noup Head ☆ 59°19'·86N 03°04'·23W Fl 30s 79m **20M**; W twr; vis: about 335°-282° but partially obsc 240°-275°.

Pierowall E Pier Head ⚡ Fl WRG 3s 7m W11M, R7M, G7M; vis: 254°-G-276°-W-291°-R-308°-G-215°; 59°19'·35N 02°58'·53W.

Papa Westray, Moclett Bay Pier Head ⚡ Fl WRG 5s 7m W5M, R3M, G3M; vis: 306°-G-341°-W-040°-R-074°; 59°19'·60N 02°53'·52W.

SHETLAND ISLES

FAIR ISLE

Skadan South ☆, 59°30'·84N 01°39'·16W Fl (4) 30s 32m **22M**; W twr; vis: 260°-146°, obsc inshore 260°-282°.

Skroo ☆ N end 59°33'·13N 01°36'·58W Fl (2) 30s 80m **22M**; W twr; vis: 086·7°-358°.

MAINLAND, SOUTH

Sumburgh Head ☆ 59°51'·21N 01°16'·58W Fl (3) 30s 91m **23M**.

Lt Ho disused 59°51'·48N 01°16'·28W; W twr.

Mousa, Perie Bard ⚡ Fl 3s 20m 10M; 59°59'·84N 01°09'·51W.

BRESSAY and LERWICK

Bressay, Kirkabister Ness ⚡ 60°07'·20N 01°07'·31W; Fl (2) 10s 18m 10M. Adjacent Lt Ho disused.

Maryfield Ferry Terminal ⚡ Oc WRG 6s 5m 5M; vis: W008°-R013°-G-111°-008°; 60°09'·43N 01°07'·45W.

North Ness ⚡ Iso WG 4s 4m 5M; vis: shore-W-158°-G-216°-W-301°; 60°09'·57N 01°08'·77W

Loofa Baa *ℓ* Q (6) + L Fl 15s 4m 5M; 60°09'·72N 01°08'·79W.

Soldian Rock ⚓ Q (6) + L Fl 15s 60°12'·51N 01°04'·73W.
N ent Dir lt 215°, Oc WRG 6s 27m 8M; Y △, Or stripe; vis: 211°-R-214°-W-216°-G-221°; 60°10'·47N 01°09'·53W.

Rova Hd ⚮ 60°11'·46N 01°08'·60W; Fl WRG 4s (sync) 12m W12M, R/G9M; W twr; vis: 090°-R-182°-W-191°-G-213°-R-241°-W-261·5°-G-009°-R-040°; same structure: **Dir** ☆ 186·5° Fl WRG 4s (sync) 14m **W16M**, R/G13M; (sync) vis: 176·5°-R-182°-W-191°-G-196·5°.

Dales Voe ⚮ Fl (2) WRG 8s 5m W4M, R3M, G3M; vis: 220°-G-227°-W-233°-R-240°; 60°11'·79N 01°11'·23W.

Hoo Stack ⚮ Fl (4) WRG 12s 40m W7M, R5M, G5M; W pylon; vis: 169°-R-180°-W-184°-G-193°-W-169°. Same structure, Dir lt 182°. Fl (4) WRG 12s 33m W9M, R6M, G6M; vis: 177°- R-180°-W-184°-W-187°; synch with upper lt; 60°14'·96N 01°05'·38W.

Mull (Moul) of Eswick ⚮ Fl WRG 3s 50m W9M, R6M, G6M; W twr; vis: 028°-R-200°-W-207°-G-018°-W-028°; 60°15'·74N 01°05'·90W.

Inner Voder ⚓ Q (9) 15s; 60°16'·44N 01°05'·18W; <u>AIS</u>.

WHALSAY and SKERRIES
Symbister Ness ⚮ Fl (2) WG 12s 11m W8M, G6M; W twr; vis: shore-W-203°-G-shore; 60°20'·43N 01°02'·29W.

Suther Ness ⚮ Fl WRG 3s 10m W10M, R8M, G7M; vis: shore -W-038°-R-173°-W-206°-G-shore; 60°22'·12N 01°00'·20W.

Bound Skerry ☆ 60°25'·47N 00°43'·72W Fl 20s 44m **20M**; W twr.

South Mouth. Ldg Lts 014°. Front, FY3m 2M; 60°25'·33N 00°45'·01W. Rear, FY 12m 2M.

Muckle Skerry ⚮ Fl (2) WRG 10s 15m W7M, R5M, G5M; W twr; vis: 046°-W-192°-R-272°-G-348°-W-353°-R-046°; 60°26'·41N 00°51'·84W.

YELL SOUND
S ent, Lunna Holm ⚮ Fl (3) WRG 15s 19m W10M,R7M,G7M; W ○ twr; vis: shore-R-090°-W-094°-G-209°-W-275°-R-shore; 60°27'·34N 01°02'·52W.

Firths Voe ☆, N shore 60°27'·21N 01°10'·63W Oc WRG 8s 9m **W15M**, R10M, G10M; W twr; vis: 189°-W-194°-G-257°-W-261°-R-339°-W-066°.

Linga Is. Dir lt 150° ⚮ Q (4) WRG 8s 10m W9M, R9M, G9M; vis: 145°-R-148°-W-152°-G-155°. Q (4) WRG 8s 10m W7M, R4M, G4M; same structure; vis: 052°-R-146°, 154°-G-196°-W-312°; synch; 60°26'·80N 01°09'·13W.

The Rumble Bn ⚮ R Bn; Fl 10s 8m 4M; *Racon (O)*; 60°28'·16N 01°07'·26W.

Yell, Ulsta Ferry Term. Bkwtr Hd ⚮ Oc RG 4s 7m R5M, G5M; vis: shore-G-354°, 044°-R-shore. Same structure; Oc WRG 4s 5m W8M, R5M, G5M; vis: shore-G-008°-W-036°-R-shore; 60°29'·74N 01°09'·52W.

Toft Ferry Terminal ☆,Dir lt 241° (H24); Dir Oc WRG 10s 8m **W16M**, R10M, G10M; vis: 236° -G-240°-W-242°-R-246°; by day W2M, R1M, G1M. 60°27'·96N 01°12'·34W.

Ness of Sound, W side ⚮ Fl (3) WRG 12s 18m W9M, R6M, G6M; vis: shore-G-345°-W-350°-R-160°-W-165°-G-shore; 60°31'·34N 01°11'·28W.

Brother Is. Dir lt 329°, Fl (4) WRG 8s 16m W10M, R7M, G7M; vis: 323·5°-G-328°-W-330°-R-333·5°; 60°30'·95N 01°14'·11W.

Mio Ness ⚮ Q (2) WR 10s 12m W7M, R4M; W ○ twr; vis: 282°-W-238°-R-282°; 60°29'·66N 01°13'·68W.

Tinga Skerry ⚮ Q(2)G 10s 9m 5M. W ○ twr; 60°30'·48N 01°14'·86W.

YELL SOUND, NORTH ENTRANCE
Bagi Stack ⚮ Fl (4) 20s 45m 10M; 60°43'·53N 01°07'·54W.

Gruney Is ⚮ Fl WR 5s 53m W8M, R6M; W twr; vis: 064°-R-180°-W-012°; *Racon (T) 14M*; 60°39'·15N 01°18'·17W.

Pt of Fethaland ☆ 60°38'·05N 01°18'·70W Fl (3) WR 15s 65m **W19M, R15M**; vis 080°-R-103°-W-160°-R-206°-W-340°.

Muckle Holm ⚮ Fl (4) 10s 32m 10M 60°34'·83N 01°16'·01W.

Little Holm ⚮ Iso 4s 12m 6M; W twr; 60°33'·42N 01°15'·88W.

Outer Skerry ⚮ Fl 6s 12m 8M; 60°33'·04N 01°18'·32W.

Quey Firth ⚮ Oc WRG 6s 22m W12M, R8M, G8M; W twr; vis: shore (through S & W)-W-290°-G-327°-W-334°-W-shore; 60°31'·43N 01°19'·58W.

Lamba, S side ⚮Fl WRG 3s 30m W8M, R5M, G5M; W twr; vis: shore-G-288°-W-293°-R-327°-W-044°-R-140°-W-shore. Dir lt 290·5° Fl WRG 3s 24m W10M, R7M, G7M; vis: 285·5°-G-288°-W-293°-W-295·5°; 60°30'·73N 01°17'·84W.

SULLOM VOE
Gluss Is ☆ Ldg Lts 194·7° (H24). **Front**, 60°29'·77N 01°19'·44W F 39m **19M**; □ on Gy twr; **Rear**, 0·75M from front, F 69m **19M**; □ on Gy twr; both Lts 9M by day.

Little Roe ⚮ Fl (3) WR 10s 16m W5M, R4M; W structure, Or band; vis: 036°-R-095·5°-W-036°; 60°29'·99N 01°16'·46W.

Skaw Taing ⚮ Ldg Lts 150·5°. Front, Oc WRG 5s 21m W8M, R5M, G5M; Or and W structure; vis: 049°-W-078°-G-147°-W-154°-R-169°-W-288°; 60°29'·10N 01°16'·86W. Rear, 195m from front, Oc 5s 35m 8M; vis: W145°-156°.

Ness of Bardister ⚮ Oc WRG 8s 20m W9M, R6M, G6M; Or &W structure; vis: 180·5°- W-240°-R-310·5°-W-314·5°-G-030·5°; 60°28'·19N 01°19'·63W.

Fugla Ness. Lts in line 212·3°. Rear, Common front 60°27'·45N 01°19'·74W Iso 4s 45m 14M. Common front 60°27'·45N 01°19'·57W Iso 4s 27m 14M; synch with rear Lts. Lts in line 203°. Rear, 60°27'·26N 01°19'·81W Iso 4s 45m 14M.

Sella Ness ☆ Dir lt 133·5°; 60°26'·76N 01°16'·66W Oc WRG 10s 19m **W16M**, R3M, G3M; vis: 123·5°-G-130·5°-Al WG (white phase increasing with brg)-132·5°-W-134·5°-Al WR(R phase inc with brg)-136·5°-R-143·5°; H24. By day Oc WRG 10s 19m W2M, R1M,G1M as above.

EAST YELL, UNST and BALTA SOUND
Whitehill ⚮ Fl WR 3s 24m W9M, R6M; W clad metal frame twr; vis: 147°-W-163°-R-211°-W-352°-R-003°; 60°34'·80N 01°00'·22W.Fetlar. Hamars Ness ⚮ Iso G 6s 5m 3M; 60°37'·78N 00°55'·73W.

Balta Sound ⚮Fl WR 10s 17m 10M, R7M; vis: 249°-W-008°-R-058°-W-154°; 60°44'·43N 00°47'·68W.

Holme of Skaw ⚮ Fl 5s 8m 8M; white metal framework twr; 60°49'·87N 00°46'·30W.

Muckle Flugga ☆ 60°51'·32N 00°53'·13W Fl (2) 20s 66m **22M**.

Yell. Cullivoe Bkwtr Hd ⚮ Fl (2) WRG 10s 3m 4M; vis: 080°-G- 294°-W-355°-R-080°; 60°41'·86N 00°59'·70W.

Unst. Head of Mula ⚮ Fl WRG 5s 48m W10M, G7M, R7M; metal framework twr; vis: 292°-G-357°-W-002°-R-157°-W-161·5; 60°40'·76N 00°57'·58W.

MAINLAND, WEST

Esha Ness ☆ 60°29'·34N 01°37'·65W Fl 12s 61m **25M**.

Ness of Hillswick ⚡ Fl (4) WR 15s 34m W9M, R6M; vis: 217°-W-093°-R-114°; 60°27'·21N 01°29'·80W.

Muckle Roe, Swarbacks Minn ⚡ Fl WR 3s 30m W9M, R6M; vis: 314°-W-041°-R-075°-W-137°; 60°20'·98N 01°27'·07W.

W Burra Firth Outer ⚡ Oc WRG 8s 27m W9M, R7M, G7M; vis: 136°-G-142°-W-150°-R-156°. H24; 60°17'·79N 01°33'·56W.

W Burra Firth Inner ☆ 60°17'·78N 01°32'·17W F WRG 9m **W15M**, R9M, G9M; vis: 095°-G-098°-W-102°-105°; H24.

Ve Skerries ⚡ Fl (2) 20s 17m 11M; W twr; *Racon (T) 15M*; 60°22'·36N 01°48'·78W.

Papa Stour Housa Voe Dir lt 228° ⚡ F WRG 2m W9M, R7M, G7M; vis: 219°- G-226°- W-230°-R-239°; 60°19'·58N 01°40'·47W.

Rams Head ⚡ Fl WRG 8s 16m W9M, R6M; G6M; W house; vis: 265°-G-355°-W-012°-R-090°-W-136°, obsc by Vaila I when brg more than 030°; 60°11'·96N 01°33'·47W.

North Havra ⚡ Fl(3) WRG 12s 24m W11M, R8M, G8M; W twr; vis: 001°-G-053·5°-W-060·5°-R-144°, 274°-G-334°-W-337·5°-R -001°; 60°09'·85N 01°20'·29W.

SCALLOWAY

Bullia Skerry ⚡ Fl 5s 5m 5M; stainless steel pillar & platform 60°06'·55N 01°21'·57W.

Point of the Pund ⚡ Fl WRG 5s 20m W7M, R5M, G5M; W GRP twr; vis: 267°-W-350°-R-090°-G-111°-R-135°-W-140°-G-177°; 60°07'·99N 01°18'·31W.

Whaleback Skerry ⚓ Q; 60°07'·95N 01°18'·90W.

Blacks Ness Pier SW corner ⚡ Oc WRG 10s 10m W11M, G8M, R8M; vis: 052°-G-063·5°-W-065·5°-R-077°; 60°08'·02N 01°16'·59W.

Fugla Ness ⚡ Fl (2) WRG 10s 20m W10M, R7M, G7M; W twr; vis: 014°-G-032°-W-082°-R-134°-W-shore; 60°06'·38N 01°20'·85W.

FOULA

South Ness ☆ 60°06'·75N 02°03'·86W Fl WR (3) 15s 36m **W18M** R14M; W twr; vis: 221°-W-255°-R-277°-W-123°-obscured-221°.

1	Berwick-upon-Tweed	**1**		11	155	79	47	76	104	144	126	120	125	145	Cape Wrath **11**
2	Eyemouth	10	**2**		10	95	124	120	148	190	170	162	156	160	Lerwick **10**
3	Dunbar	26	17	**3**		9	50	46	74	114	104	90	95	115	Kirkwall **9**
4	Port Edgar	58	50	34	**4**		8	31	59	99	89	75	80	100	Scrabster **8**
5	Methil	45	36	20	20	**5**		7	29	69	58	44	50	72	Wick **7**
6	Fife Ness	38	29	17	34	16	**6**		6	43	32	26	44	74	Helmsdale **6**
7	Dundee	58	49	37	54	36	20	**7**		5	13	34	59	90	Inverness **5**
8	Montrose	59	51	43	61	43	27	27	**8**		4	23	48	79	Nairn **4**
9	Stonehaven	72	66	60	78	60	44	45	20	**9**		3	25	56	Lossiemouth **3**
10	Aberdeen	82	78	73	90	72	56	57	32	13	**10**		2	33	Banff/Macduff **2**
11	Peterhead	105	98	93	108	94	78	80	54	35	25	**11**		1	Peterhead **1**

AREA 6 *NW Scotland – C Wrath to Oban including The Western Isles*

SELECTED LIGHTS, BUOYS & WAYPOINTS

CAPE WRATH TO LOCH TORRIDON

Cape Wrath ☆ 58°37'·54N 04°59'·99W Fl (4) 30s 122m **22M**; W twr; 992351087.

LOCH INCHARD and LOCH LAXFORD

Kinlochbervie Dir lt 327° ☆ 58°27'·49N 05°03'·08W WRG 15m **16M** vis: 326°-FG-326·5°-AlGW-326·8°-FW-327·3°-AlRW-327·5°-FR-328°.

Creag Mhòr Dir lt 147°; Iso WRG 2s 16m 4M; vis: 136·5°-R -146·5°-W-147·5°-G-157·5°; 58°26'·99N 05°02'·45W.

Stoer Head ☆ 58°14'·43N 05°24'·07W Fl 15s 59m **24M**; W twr.

LOCH INVER, SUMMER ISLES and ULLAPOOL

Soyea I ⚡ Fl (2) 10s 34m 6M; 58°08'·56N 05°19'·67W.

Glas Leac ⚡ Fl WRG 3s 7m 5M; vis: 071°- W-078°-R-090°-G-103°- W-111°, 243°-W-247°-G-071°; 58°08'·68N 05°16'·36W.

Rubha Cadail ⚡ Fl WRG 6s 11m W9M, R6M, G6M; W twr; vis: 311°-G-320°-W-325°-R-103°-W-111°-G-118°-W-127°-R-157°-W-199°; 57°55'·51N 05°13'·40W.

Ullapool Pt ⚡ Iso R 4s 8m 6M; W twr; vis: 258°-108°; 57°53'·59N 05°09'·93W.

Cailleach Head ⚡ Fl (2) 12s 60m 9M; W twr; vis: 015°-236°; 57°55'·81N 05°24'·23W.

LOCH EWE and LOCH GAIRLOCH

Fairway ⚓ L Fl 10s; 57°51'·98N 05°40'·09W.

Rubha Reidh ☆ 57°51'·52N 05°48'·72W Fl (4) 15s 37m **18M**.

Glas Eilean ⚡ Fl WRG 6s 9m W6M, R4M; vis: 080°-W-102°-R-296°-W-333°-G-080°; 57°42'·79N 05°42'·42W.

Sgeir Dhubh Mhór ⚓; 57°42'·02N 05°42'·72W.

OUTER HEBRIDES – EAST SIDE

LEWIS

Butt of Lewis ☆ 58°30'·92N 06°15'·72W Fl 5s 52m **25M**; R twr; vis: 056°-320°.

Tiumpan Hd ☆ 58°15'·66N 06°08'·29W Fl (2)15s 55m **18M**; W twr.

Broad Bay Tong ⚓ Ldg Lts 320°, Oc R 8s 8m 4M; 58°14'·48N 06°19'·98W. Rear, 70m from front, Oc R 8s 9m 4M.

STORNOWAY

Arnish Point ⚡ Fl WR 10s 17m W9M, R7M; W ○ twr; vis: 088°-W-198°-R-302°-W-013°; 58°11'·50N 06°22'·16W.

Sandwick Bay, NW side ⚡ Oc WRG 6s 10m 9M; vis: 334°-G-341°-W-347°-R-354°; 58°12'·20N 06°22'·11W.

No 1 Pier SW corner ⚡ Q WRG 5m 11M; vis: shore-G-335°-W-352°-R-shore; 58°12'·36N 06°23'·43W.

Creed Estuary ⚓ Iso WRG 10s 24m 5M; vis: 277°-IsoG-282°-Al WG-287°-IsoW-290°-Al WR-292°-R-295°; 58°12'·00N 06°23'·54W.

No 3 Pier ⚓ Q (2) G 10s 7m 2M 58°12'·31N 06°23'·28W.

Glumaig Hbr ⚓ Iso WRG 3s 8m 3M; 58°11'·29N 06°22'·83W; grey framework twr; vis: 150°-G-174°-W-185°-R-205°.

LOCH ERISORT, LOCH SHELL and EAST LOCH TARBERT

Shiants ⬟ QG; 57°54'·57N 06°25'·70W.

Sgeir Inoe ⬟ Fl G 6s; *Racon (M) 5M*; 57°50'·93N 06°33'·93W.

Eilean Glas (Scalpay) ☆ 57°51'·41N 06°38'·55W Fl (3) 20s 43m **18M**; W twr, R bands; *Racon (T) 16-18M*; 992356014.

Sgeir Graidach ⬙ Q (6) + L Fl 15s; 57°50'·36N 06°41'·37W.

Sgeir Ghlas ⚓ Iso WRG 4s 9m W9M, R6M, G6M; W ○ twr; vis: 282°-G-319°-W-329°-R-153°-W-164°-G-171°; 57°52'·36N 06°45'·24W.

Tarbert ⚓ Dir Iso WRG 4s 9m 4M; vis : 290°-Iso G-297°-Al WG-300°-Iso W-303°-Al WR-306°-Iso R306°-313°; 57°53'·82N 06°47'·93W.

SOUND OF HARRIS, LEVERBURGH and BERNERAY

No 1 ⬟ QG; 57°41'·20N 07°02'·67W.

No 3 ⬟ Fl G 5s; 57°41'·86N 07°03'·44W.

No 4 ⬕ Fl R 5s; 57°41'·76N 07°03'·63W.

Suilven ⬕ Fl (3)R 10s; 57°41'·68N 07°04'·36W.

Cabbage ⬕ Fl (2) R 6s; *Racon (T) 5M (3cm)*; 57°42'·13N 07°03'·96W.

Leverburgh Ldg Lts 014·7°. Front, Q 10m 4M 57°46'·23N 07°02'·04W. Rear, Oc 3s 12m 4M.

Jane's Tower ⬙ Q (2) G 5s 6m 4M; vis: obscured 273°-318°; 57°45'·76N 07°02'·11W.

Leverburgh Reef ⬙ Fl R 2s 4m 57°45'·97N 07°01'·86W.

Laimhrig Mhor ⚓ Q G; 57°45'·92N 07°01'·65W.

Leverburg Dir Lt 064·5°; Dir G 4m 6M metal twr; vis: 060°-QG-063°-F G-066°-OcG 2·25s-069°; 57° 46'·00 N 07° 01'·55 W.

NORTH UIST

Fairway ⬕ L Fl 10s; 57°40'·23N 07°01'·39W.

Vallay Island ⚓ Fl WRG 3s 4m 8M; vis: 206°-W-085°-G-140°-W-145°-R-206°; 57°39'·69N 07°26'·42W.

Griminish Hbr Dir lt 183° ⚓ metal post; vis: WRG 4s 6m WRG2M 178°-IsoG-182°-AlWG-182·5°-IsoW-183·5°-AlWR-184°-IsoR-188°; 57°39'·39N 07°26'·72W.

LOCH MADDY and GRIMSAY

Weaver's Pt ⚓ Fl 3s 24m 7M; W hut; 57°36'·49N 07°06'·00W.

Glas Eilean Mòr ⚓ Fl (2) G 4s 8m 5M; 57°35'·95N 07°06'·70W.

Vallaquie Is Dir lt 207·5° / 255·5° ⚓ W pillar; vis: Fl (3) WRG 8s 11m W5M, R5M, G5M; shore-G-205°-W-210°-R-240°; Fl (3) WRG 8s 11m W8M, R8M, G8M; 249°-G-254°-W-257°-R-262° 57°35'·49N 07°09'·32W.

Lochmaddy Ro-Ro Pier, Dir lt 300° ⚓ post; Iso WRG 2s W6M, R4M, G4M; vis: 288°-G-295°-WG-298°-W-302°-WR-305°-R-311° 57°35'·79N 07°09'·46W.

Grimsay No 1 ⬕ Fl (2) R 8s; 57°28'·26N 07°11'·82W.

SOUTH UIST and LOCH CARNAN

Landfall ⬙ L Fl 10s.; 57°22'·27N 07°11'·52W.

Ldg Lts 222°. Front Fl R 2s 7m 5M; W ◇ on post; 57°22'·00N 07°16'·34W. Rear, 58m from front, Iso R 10s 11m 5M; W ◇ on post.

Ushenish ☆ (S Uist) 57°17'·90N 07°11'·57W Fl W 20s 54m **W19M**; W twr; vis: 193°- 018°.

LOCH BOISDALE

MacKenzie Rk ⬕ Fl (3) R 15s 3m 4M; 57°08'·24N 07°13'·71W.

Calvay E End ⚓ Fl (2) WRG 10s 16m W7M, R7M, G7M; W twr; vis: 111°-W-190°-G-202°-W-286°-R-111°; 57°08'·53N 07°15'·38W; 992351139.

Gasay I ⚓ Fl WR 5s 10m W7M, R7M; W twr; vis: 120°-W-284°-R-120°; 57°08'·93N 07°17'·39W.

LochBoisdaleDirlt⚓,292·5°;WRG4s4m5M;vis:287·5°-IsoG-290·5°-AlWG-292°-IsoW-293°-AlWR-294·5°-IsoR-298·5°; 57°09'·19N 07°18'·24W.

2 FG 8m 3M on dn; 57°09'·13N 07°18'·18W.

LUDAIG and ERISKAY

Ludaig Bwtr ⚓ 2 FR (vert) 6m 3M; 57°06'·17N 07°19'·49W.

Acairseid Mhor Ldg Lts 285°. Front, Oc R 6s 9m 4M; 57°03'·89N 07°17'·25W. Rear, 24m from front, Oc R 6s 10m 4M.

BARRA, CASTLEBAY and VATERSAY SOUND

Drover Rocks ⬙ Q (6) + L Fl 15s; 57°04'·08N 07°23'·54W.

Binch Rock ⬙ Q (6) + L Fl 15s; 57°01'·60N 07°17'·12W.

Curachan ⬙ Q (3) 10s; 56°58'·56N 07°20'·51W.

Ardveenish ⚓ Oc WRG 6m 9/6M; vis: 300°-G-304°-W-306°-R-310°; 57°00'·21N 07°24'·43W.

Vich Chuan ⬙ Q(6)+LFl 15s; *Racon (M) 5M*; 56°56'·15N 07°23'·31W.

Channel Rk ⚓ Fl WR 6s 4m W6M, R4M; vis: 121·5°-W-277°-R-121·5°; 56°56'·24N 07°28'·94W.

Sgeir a Scape ⬟ Fl (2) G 8s; 56°56'·25N 07°27'·21W.

Rubha Glas. Ldg Lts 295°. Front ⬙ FBu 9m 6M; Or △ on W twr; 56°56'·77N 07°30'·64W. Rear ⬙, 457m from front, FBu 15m 6M; Or ▽ on W twr; vis: 15° and 8° respectively either side of ldg line.

Barra Hd ☆ 56°47'·12N 07°39'·21W Fl 15s 208m **18M**; W twr; obsc by islands to NE; 992351095.

OUTER HEBRIDES – WEST SIDE

Flannan I ☆, Eilean Mór Fl (2) 30s 101m **20M**; W twr; 58°17'·29N 07°35'·29W, obsc in places by ls to W of Eilean Mór.

Rockall ⚓ Fl 15s 19m 8M (unreliable); 57°35'·76N 13°41'·27W.

Gasker Lt ⚓ Fl (3) 10s 38m 10M; 57°59'·05N 07°17'·20W.

Whale Rock ⬙ Q (3) 10s 5m 5M; *Racon (T)*; 57°54'·40N 07°59·91W.

Haskeir I ☆ 57°41'·96N 07°41·31W Fl 20s 44m **24M**; W twr; *Racon (M) 17–15M*; 992351140.

Monach Is ☆ Fl (2)15s 47m **18M**; red brick twr; 57°31'·55N 07°41'·68W.

EAST LOCH ROAG

Aird Laimishader Carloway ⚓ Fl 6s 63m 8M; W hut; obsc on some brgs; 58°17'·06N 06°49'·50W.

Ardvanich Pt ⚓ Fl G 3s 4m 2M; 58°13'·48N 06°47'·68W.

Tidal Rk ⚓ Fl R 3s 2m 2M (sync with Ardvanich Pt above); 58°13'·45N 06°47'·57W.

Grèinam ⚓ Fl WR 6s 8m W8M, R7M; W bn; vis: R143°-169°, W169°-143°; 58°13'·30N 06°46'·16W.

LOCH ROAG

Rubha Domhain ⚓ Fl G 5s 9m 1M; post; 58°12'·96N 06°45'·40W.

Bogha na Muilne ⬙ Fl (2) 10s; 58°12'·70N 06°54'·23W.

Mia Vaig Bay ⬙ Fl G 2s 2m 1M; bn; 58°11'·83N 06°56'·60W.

NORTH UIST and SOUTH UIST

Vallay I ⚡ Fl WRG 3s 8M; vis: 206°-W-085°-G-140°-W-145°-R-206°; 57°39'·70N 07°26'·34W.

Falconet twr ⚡ FR 25m 8M (3M by day); shown 1hr before firing, changes to Iso R 2s 15 min before firing until completion; 57°22'·04N 07°23'·58W.

ST KILDA

Ldg Lts 270°. Front, Oc 5s 26m 3M; 57°48'·32N 08°34'·31W. Rear, 100m from front, Oc 5s 38m 3M; sync.

LOCH TORRIDON TO MALLAIG
LITTLE MINCH and W SKYE

Eugenie Rock ⚓ Q 6 + LF 15s; 57°46'·47N 06°27'·28W.

Eilean Trodday ⚡ Fl (2) WRG 10s 52m W12M, R9M, G9M; W Bn; vis: W062°-R088°-130°-W-322°-G-062°; 57°43'·63N 06°17'·93W; 992351084.

Uig, Edward Pier Hd ⚡ 57°35'·09N 06°22'·29W Iso WRG 4s 9m W7M, R4M, G4M; vis: 180-W-006°-G-050°-W-073°-R-180°.

Waternish Pt ⚡ Fl 20s 21m 8M; W twr; 57°36'·48N 06°37'·99W.

Loch Dunvegan, Uiginish Pt ⚡ Fl WRG 3s 16m W7M,R5M,G5M; W lattice twr; vis: 041°-G-132°-W-145°-R-148°-W-253°-R- 263°-W-273°-G-306°, (>148° obsc by Fiadhairt Pt); 57°26'·84N 06°36'·53W.

Neist Point ☆ 57°25'·41N 06°47'·30W Fl 5s 43m **16M**; W twr.

Loch Harport, Ardtreck Pt ⚡ 57°20'·38N 06°25'·80W Fl 6s 18m 9M; small W twr.

RONA, LOCH A'BHRAIGE and INNER SOUND

Na Gamhnachain ⚓ Q; 57°35'·89N 05°57'·71W.

Rona NE Point ⚡ 57°34'·69N 05°57'·54W Fl 12s 69m 12M; W twr; vis: 050°-358°; 992351045.

Loch A'Bhraige, Sgeir Shuas ⚡ Fl R 2s 6m 3M; vis: 070°-199°; 57°35'·02N 05°58'·61W.

Ldg Lts 136·5°. Front, ⚓ Q WRG 3m W4M, R3M; vis: 135°-W- 138°-R-318°-G-135°; 57°34'·41N 05°58'·09W. Rear, ⚓ Iso 6s 28m 5M.

Rubha Ard Ghlaisen ⚓ Fl R 3s; 57°29'·67N 05°58'·71W.

Screapadal ⚓ Fl R (2) 5s; 57°25'·54N 06°01'·90W.

SOUND OF RAASAY, PORTREE and CROWLIN ISLANDS

Sgeir Mhór ⚓ Fl G 5s; 57°24'·57N 06°10'·53W.

Eilean Beag ⚡ Fl 6s 32m 6M; W Bn; 57°21'·21N 05°51'·42W.

Eyre Pt ⚡ Fl WR 3s 6m W9M R6M; W clad framework twr; vis: 215°-W-267°-R-288°-W-063°; 57°20'·01N 06°01'·28W.

Sgeir Thraid ⚡ Q 12m 3M; metal twr; 57°19'·82N 05°56'·50W.

Sgeir Ghobhlach ⚡ Fl(3)10s 10m 3M; metal twr; 57°15'·69N 05°52'·25W.

LOCH CARRON

Sgeir Golach ⚡ Fl 10s 5m 3M; 57°21'·20N 05°39'·01W.

Eilean a Chait Lt ho (dis) 13M; 57°20'·96N 05°38'·87W.

Bogha Dubh Sgeir ⚓ Fl (2)R 6s 4m 2M; 57°20'·92N 05°37'·85W.

RAASAY and LOCH SLIGACHAN

Suisnish ⚡ 2 FG (vert) 8m 2M; 57°19'·87N 06°03'·91W.

Eyre Point ⚡ Fl WR 3s 6m W9M, R6M; W twr; vis: 215°-W-266°-R- 288°-W-063°; 57°20'·01N 06°01'·29W.

KYLEAKIN and KYLE OF LOCH ALSH

Carragh Rk ⚓ Fl (2) G 12s; *Racon (T) 5M*; 57°17'·18N 05°45'·36W.

Bow Rk ⚓ Fl (2) R 12s; 57°16'·71N 05°45'·85W.

Fork Rks ⚓ Fl G 6s; 57°16'·85N 05°44'·93W.

Black Eye Rk ⚓ Fl R 6s; 57°16'·68N 05°45'·20W.

Eileanan Dubha East ⚡ Fl (2) 10s 9m 8M; vis: obscured 104°-146°; 57°16'·56N 05°42'·32W.

8 Metre Rock ⚡ Fl G 6s 5m 4M; 57°16'·60N 05°42'·69W.

String Rock ⚓ Fl R 6s; 57°16'·50N 05°42'·89W.

Sgeir-na-Caillich ⚡ Fl (2) R 6s 3m 4M; 57°15'·59N 05°38'·90W.

SOUND OF SLEAT

Kyle Rhea ⚡ Fl WRG 3s 7m W8M, R5M, G5M; W Bn; vis: shore-R-219°-W-228°-G-338°-W-346°-R-shore; 57°14'·22N 05°39'·93W.

Sandaig I, NW point ⚡ Fl 6s 13m 8M; W twr; 57°10'·05N 05°42'·29W.

Ornsay ⚡ Oc 8s 18m 12M; vis: 157°-030°; 57°08'·60N 05°46'·85W.

Pt. of Sleat ⚡ Fl 3s 20m9M; W twr; 57°01'·08N 06°01'·08W.

MALLAIG and LOCH NEVIS ENTRANCE

Sgeir Dhearg ⚓ QG; 57°00'·74N 05°49'·50W.

Northern Pier E end ⚡ Iso WRG 4s 6m W9M, R6M, G6M; Gy twr; vis: 181°-G-185°-W-197°-R-201°. Fl G 3s 14m 6M; same structure; 57°00'·47N 05°49'·50W.

Sgeir Dhearg ⚡ 57°00'·63N 05°49'·61W Fl (2) WG 8s 6m 5M; Gy Bn; vis: 190°-G-055°-W-190°.

SMALL ISLES AND WEST OF MULL
CANNA and RUM

Sanday ⚡ Fl 10s 32m 9M; vis: 152°-061°; 57°02'·82N 06°28'·02W.

Loch Scresort ⚓ Q; 57°00'·79N 06°14'·61W.

HYSKEIR, EIGG, MUCK and ARISAIG

Humla ⚓ Fl G 6s 3m 4M 57°00'·46N 06°37'·39W.

Hyskeir ☆ 56°58'·16N 06°40'·83W Fl (3) 30s 41m **24M**; W twr. *Racon (T) 14-17M*; 992351094.

SE point Eigg (Eilean Chathastail) ⚡ Fl 6s 24m 8M; W twr; vis: 181°-shore; 56°52'·25N 06°07'·28W.

Eigg, Sgeir nam Bagh (Ferry Terminal) ⚡ Dir 245°; Fl WRG 3s 9m W14, R11, G11; H24; steel pole; vis: 242·5°-G-244°-W-246°-R-247·5°. 2FR(vert) on same structure; 56°52'·79N 06°07'·56W.

Isle of Muck ⚡ Dir 322° Fl WRG 3s 7m W14 RG11, by day WRG1; twr; vis: 319·5°-G-321°-W-323°-R-324·5°; 56°49'·96N 06°13'·64W.

Bogha Ruadh ⚡ Fl G 5s 4m 3M; 56°49'·56N 06°13'·05W.

Bo Faskadale ⚓ Fl (3) G 18s; 56°48'·18N 06°06'·37W.

Ardnamurchan ☆ 56°43'·63N 06°13'·58W Fl (2) 20s 55m **18M**; Gy twr; vis: 002°-217°.

Suil Ghorm ⚡ Fl 12s 23m 10M; W twr; 56°42'·26N 06°26'·75W.

TIREE, COLL and ARINAGOUR

Loch Eatharna, Pier Head ⚡ Dir 325°; Oc WRG 7s 6m 2M; vis: 316°-G-322°-W-328°-R-334°; 56°36'·86N 06°31'·29W.

Loch Eatharna, Bogha Mór ⚓ Fl G 6s; 56°36'·65N 06°30'·90W.

Roan Bogha ⚓ Q (6) + L Fl 15s 3m 5M; 56°32'·23N 06°40'·18W.

Placaid Bogha ⚓ Fl G 4s; 56°33'·22N 06°44'·06W.

Scarinish ⚡ Fl 3s 11m 12M; W ☐ twr; vis: 210°-030°; S side of ent, 56°30'·02N 06°48'·26W.

Cairn na Burgh More (Treshnish Is), Fl (3) 15s 36m 8M; solar panels on framework tr; 56°31'·05N 06°22'·95W.

Gott Bay Ldg Lts 286·5°. Front FR 8m; 56°30'·61N 06°47'·82W. Rear 30m from front FR 11m.

Skerryvore ☆ Fl 10s 46m **23M**; Gy twr; *Racon (M) 18M*. 56°19'·36N 07°06'·88W; 992351091.

LOCH NA KEAL, LOCH NA LÀTHAICH and IONA
Sgeir a Charraigein ⚓ Q(6) + LFl 15s; 56°28'·29N 06°07'·71W.

Eileanan na Liathanaich, SE end ⚓ Fl WR 6s 12m W8M, R6M; vis: R088°- W108°-088°; 56°20'·56N 06°16'·38W.

Bo na Sliganach ⚓ Q(6) + LFl 15s; 56°19'·45N 06°23'·12W.

Bogha hun a Chuhoil ⚓ Q(6) + LFl 15s; 56°16'·57N 06°24'·86W.

DUBH ARTACH
Dubh Artach ☆ 56°07'·94N 06°38'·08W Fl (2) 30s 44m **20M**; Gy twr, R band; 992351088.

SOUND OF MULL

LOCH SUNART, TOBERMORY and LOCH ALINE
Ardmore Pt ⚓ Fl (2) 10s 18m 13M; 56°39'·37N 06°07'·70W.

Salen Bay ⚓ 56°42'·67N 05°46'·57W.

New Rks ⚓ Q (9) 15s; 56°39'·07N 06°03'·55W; AIS.

Little Stirk ⚓ Q(6)+L Fl 15s; 56°38'·50N 06°01'·50W.

Rubha nan Gall ☆ 56°38'·33N 06°04'·00W Fl 3s 17m **15M**; W twr.

Tobermory Slip ⚓ Iso WRG 3s 5m 4M; vis: 220°-G-232°-W-244°-R-256° (sectors± 2°); metal column; 56°37'·41N 06°03'·77W.

Dearg Sgeir ⚓ Fl 6s 7m 8M; W ○ twr; 56°32'·25N 05°54'·80W.

Fiunary Spit ⚓ Fl G 6s; 56°32'·66N 05°53'·17W.

Fishnish Ferry Slip ⚓ Iso WRG 3s 5m 4M; vis: 158°-G-170°-W-195°-R-230° (sectors± 4°); metal column; 56°30'·89N 05°48'·61W.

Loch Aline, ⚓ Dir 357°; Oc WRG 6s 2m 4M; vis: 353°-G-356°-W-358°-R-002°; Or concrete plinth; 56°32'·38N 05°46'·47W.

Ardtornish Pt ⚓ Fl (2) WRG 10s 8m W8M, R6M, G6M; W twr; vis: G shore- 301°-W-308°-R-342°-W-057°-R-095°-W-108°-G-shore; 56°31'·09N 05°45'·21W.

Craignure Ldg Lts 240·9°. Front, FR 10m; 56°28'·26N 05°42'·28N. Rear, 150m from front, FR 12m; vis: 225·8°-255·8°.

MULL TO CALEDONIAN CANAL AND OBAN

Lismore ☆, SW end 56°27'·34N 05°36'·45W Fl 10s 31m **17M**; W twr; vis: 237°-208°.

Lady's Rk ⚓ Fl 6s 12m 5M; Red clad lattice tower on W base 56°26'·92N 05°37'·05W; 992351093.

Duart Pt ⚓ Fl (3) WR 18s 14m W5M, R3M; vis: 162°-W-261°-R- 275°-W-353°-R-shore; 56°26'·84N 05°38'·77W.

LOCH LINNHE
Corran Shoal ⚓ QR 56°43'·69N 05°14'·39W.

Corran Pt ⚓ Iso WRG 4s 12m W10M, R7M, G7M; W twr; vis: shore-R-195°-W-215°-G-020-W-030°-R-shore; 56°43'·25N 05°14'·54W.

Corran Narrows NE ⚓ Fl 5s 4m 4M; W twr; vis: S shore-214°; Dir lt 033° Iso WRG 2s 4m 4M (1M day), vis: 028·5°- Iso G -030·5° - Alt W/G -031·5°- Iso W -032·5°- Alt W/R - 033·5°-Iso R -035·5°; co-located 56°43'·62N 05°13'·90W.

Clovullin Spit ⚓ Fl (2) R 15s; 56°42'·29N 05°15'·56W.

Cuil-cheanna Spit ⚓ Fl G 6s; 56°41'·17N 05°15'·72W.

Mc Lean Rk ⚓ QR 56°49'·80N 05°07'·04W.

Eilean na Creiche ⚓ Fl (2) 5s; 56°50'·25N 05°07'·02W.

Eilean na Craobh ⚓ Fl (2) R 6s 4m 2M; 56°50'·43N 05°07'·95W.

FORT WILLIAM and CALEDONIAN CANAL
Corpach, Caledonian Canal Lock ent ⚓ Iso WRG 4s 6m 5M; W twr; vis: G287°- W310°- R335°-030°; 56°50'·52N 05°07'·44W.

LYNN OF LORN
Sgeir Bhuidhe Appin ⚓ Fl (2) WR 7s 8m W9M R6M; W Bn; vis: W013·5°- R184°-220°; 56°33'·63N 05°24'·65W.

Appin Point ⚓ Fl G 6s; 56°32'·69N 05°25'·97W.

Dearg Sgeir, off Aird's Point ⚓ Fl WRG 2s 2m W3M, R1M, G1M; vis: 196°-R-246°-W-258°-G-041°-W-058°-R-093°-W-139°; 56°32'·20N 05°25'·22W.

Rubha nam Faoileann (Eriska) ⚓ QG 2m 2M; G col; vis 128°-329°; 56°32'·20N 05°24'·11W.

Branra Rk ⚓ Fl(2) 10s 4m 5M; metal frame on W twr; 56°32'·02N 05°26'·60W.

OBAN
N spit of Kerrera ⚓ Fl R 3s 9m 5M; W col; 56°25'·49N 05°29'·56W.

Dunollie ⚓ Fl (2) WRG 6s 6m W8M, R6M, G6M; vis: 351°-G-020°- W-047°-R-120°-W-138°-G-143°; twr; 56°25'·37N 05°29'·05W.

Rubh'a'Chruidh ⚓ Q R 3m 2M; W post; 56°25'·32N 05°29'·29W.

Transit Marina ⚓ Fl G 2m 2M; post; 56°25'·00N 05°28'·57W.

Oban Bay ⚓ Q; 56°24'·92N 05°29'·23W.

Sgeir Rathaid ⚓ Q(6)+L Fl 15s; 56°24'·75N 05°29'·37W.

North Pier ⚓ 2 F G (vert); metal post; 56°24'·89N 05°28'·49W.

Ro-Ro Jetty ⚓ 2 F G (vert); post on dn; 56°24'·69N 05°28'·65W.

North'n Lt Pier ⚓ 2 FG (vert); metal post; 56°24'·71N 05°28'·91W.

OBAN TO LOCH CRAIGNISH

Heather Is ⚓ Fl R 2·5s 11m 2M; 56°24'·41N 05°30'·24W.

Ferry Rks NW ⚓ Q G; 56°24'·11N 05°30'·69W.

Kerrera ⚓ Q R; 56°24'·15N 05°30'·81W.

1	Cape Wrath	**1**															
2	Ullapool	54	**2**														
3	Stornoway	53	45	**3**													
4	East Loch Tarbert	75	56	33	**4**												
5	Portree	83	57	53	42	**5**											
6	Kyle of Lochalsh	91	63	62	63	21	**6**										
7	Mallaig	112	82	83	84	42	21	**7**									
8	Eigg	123	98	97	75	54	35	14	**8**								
9	Castlebay (Barra)	133	105	92	69	97	76	59	46	**9**							
10	Tobermory	144	114	115	87	74	53	32	20	53	**10**						
11	Loch Aline	157	127	128	100	87	66	45	33	66	13	**11**					
12	Fort William	198	161	162	134	121	98	75	63	96	43	34	**12**				
13	Oban	169	138	139	111	100	77	56	44	77	24	13	29	**13**			
14	Loch Melfort	184	154	155	117	114	93	69	61	92	40	27	45	18	**14**		
15	Craobh Haven	184	155	155	117	114	92	70	60	93	40	27	50	21	5	**15**	
16	Crinan	187	157	158	129	112	95	74	63	97	42	30	54	25	14	9	**16**	
17	Mull of Kintyre	232	203	189	175	159	143	121	105	120	89	87	98	72	62	57	51	**17**

DISTANCE TABLES
Approx distances in nautical miles are by the most direct route allowing for dangers and TSS.

Ferry Rks SE ⚓ Q (3) 10s; 56°23'·99N 05°30'·53W.
Ferry Pier ⚡ 2 FL (vert); 56 23'.92N 005 31'.02W.
Little Horseshoe ⚓ Fl R 12 s; 56 23'.22N 005 31'.83W.
Sgeirean Dubha ⚡ Fl (2) 12s 7m 5M; W ○ twr; 56°22'·81N 05°32'·27W.
Sgeir an Fheuran ▲ Fl G 3s; 56°22'·80N 05°31'·94W.
Bogha Nuadh ⚓ Q(6)+LFl 15s; 56°21'·69N 05°37'·87W; 992351090.
Bogha Ghair ⚓ Q (3) 10s; 56°16'·50N 05°40'·44W.
Bono Rock ⚓ Q (9) 15s; 56°16'·21N 05°41'·22W.
Fladda ⚡ Fl (2) WRG 9s 13m W11M, R9M, G9M; W twr; vis: 169°-R-186°-W-337°-G-344°-W-356°-R-026°; 56°14'·89N 05°40'·83W.

Dubh Sgeir (Luing) ⚡ Fl WRG 6s 9m W6M, R4M. G4M; W twr; vis: W000°-R010°-W025°-G199°-000°; *Racon (M) 5M*; 56°14'·76N 05°40'·20W.
The Garvellachs, Eileach an Naoimh, SW end ⚡ Fl 6s 21m 9M; W Bn; vis: 240°-215°; 56°13'·04N 05°49'·06W.

LOCH MELFORT and CRAOBH HAVEN
Melfort Pier ⚡ Dir FR 6m 3M; (Apr -Nov); 56°16'·14N 05°30'·19W.
⚓ 56°12'·88N 05°33'·59W.
Craobh Marina Bkwtr Hd ⚡ Iso WRG 5s 10m, W5M, R3M, G3M; vis:114°-G-162°-W-183°-R-200°; 56°12'·78N 05°33'·52W.

AREA 7 *SW Scotland – Colonsay to Kirkcudbright*

SELECTED LIGHTS, BUOYS & WAYPOINTS

COLONSAY TO ISLAY

COLONSAY
Scalasaig, Rubha Dubh ⚡ Fl (2) WR 10s 8m W8M, R6M; W bldg; vis: shore-R- 230°-W-337°-R-354°; 56°04'·01N 06°10'·90W.

SOUND OF ISLAY
Rhubh' a Mháil (Ruvaal) ☆ 55°56'·18N 06°07'·46W Fl (3) 15s 45m **19M**; W twr.
Carragh an t'Struith ⚡ Fl 3s 8m 9M; W twr; vis: 354°-180°; 55°52'·30N 06°05'·78W.
Carraig Mòr ⚡ Fl (2) WR 6s 7m W8M, R6M; W twr; vis: shore-R- 175°-W-347°-R-shore; 55°50'·42N 06°06'·13W.
McArthur's Hd ⚡ Fl (2) WR 10s 39m W13M, R10M; W twr; W in Sound of Islay from NE coast,159°-R-244°-W-E coast of Islay; 55°45'·84N 06°02'·90W.
Orsay Is, **Rhinns of Islay** ☆ 55°40'·40N 06°30'·80W Fl 5s 46m **18M**; W twr; vis: 256°-184°.

PORT ELLEN and LOCH INDAAL
Carraig Fhada ⚡ Fl WRG 3s 20m W8M, R6M, G6M; W □ twr; vis: W shore- 248°-G-311°-W-340°-R-shore; 55°37'·22N 06°12'·71W.
Otter Gander ⚓ VQ (3) 5s; 55°36'·60N 06°12'·34W.
Fhada ⚓ Q (3) 10s; 55°37'·21N 06°12'·41W.
Sgeir nan Ron ⚓ Q R; 55°45'·53N 06°17'·32W.
Hbr entrance ▲ Q G; 55°37'·55N 06°11'·45W.
Rubh'an Dùin ⚡ Fl (2) WR 7s 15m W11M, R8M; W twr; vis: shore-R-218°-W-249°-R-350°-W-shore; 55°44'·70N 06°22'·28 W.
L Indaal, Dir lt 168·5°; Iso WRG 3m 4s WRG 5M, vis: 343°-G-347°-Al WG-348°-Iso W-349°-Al WR-350°-R-354°; 55°46'·01N 06°21'·63W.

JURA TO MULL OF KINTYRE

SOUND OF JURA, CRAIGHOUSE, L SWEEN and GIGHA
Skervuile ⚡ Fl 15s 22m 9M; 55°36'·60N 06°12'·34W; W twr.
Nine Foot Rk ⚓ Q (3) 10s; 55°52'·44N 05°52'·91W.
Goat Rock ⚓ VQ (3) 5s; 55°50'·12N 05°55'·67W.
Eilean nan Gabhar ⚡ Fl 5s 9m 8M; 55°50'·01N 05°56'·25W.
Craighouse ⚡ Fl R 6s 3m 5M; 55°49'·98N 05°56'·43W.
Na Cùiltean ⚡ Fl 10s 9m 9M; 55°48'·64N 05°54'·90W.
Gamhna Gigha ⚡ Fl (2) 6s 7m 5M; 55°43'·78N 05°41'·08W.
Bhanarach Rocks ⚓ Q (3) 5s; 55°40'·73N 05°43'·32W.
Ardminish Bay, ⚡ Q(3) 10s 3m 2M; 55°40'·56N 05°43'·99W.

WEST LOCH TARBERT
Dunskeig Bay ⚡ Q (2) 10s 11m 8M; 55°45'·22N 05°35'·00W.
Eileen Tráighe (S side) ⚓ Fl (2) R 5s 5m 3M; R post; 55°45'·37N 05°35'·75W.

MULL OF KINTYRE
Mull of Kintyre ☆ 55°18'·64N 05°48'·25W Fl (2) 20s 91m **18M**; W twr on W bldg; vis: 347°-178°.

CRINAN CANAL and ARDRISHAIG
Crinan, E of lock ent ⚡ Fl WG 3s 8m 4M; W twr, R band; vis: shore-W-146°-G-shore; 56°05'·48N 05°33'·37W.
Ardrishaig Bkwtr Hd ⚡ L Fl WRG 6s 9m 4M; vis: 287°-G-339°-W- 350°-R-035°; 56°00'·76N 05°26'·59W.

LOCH FYNE TO SANDA ISLAND

EAST LOCH TARBERT
Eilean na Beithe ⚡ Fl WRG 3s 7m 5M; vis: G036°- W065°-R078°-106°; 55°52'·68N 05°19'·62W.

KILBRANNAN SOUND, CRANNAICH and CARRADALE BAY
Port Crannaich Bkwtr Hd ⚡ Fl R 10s 5m 6M; vis: 099°-279°; 55°35'·60N 05°27'·84W.
Claonaig Ferry Terminal ⚡ Iso WRG 3s 5m 2M (Apr-Oct); vis: 305°-G-350° -W-020°-R-040°; metal column; 55°45'·04N 05°23'·28W.

CAMPBELTOWN LOCH to SANDA ISLAND
Davaar N Pt ☆ 55°25'·69N 05°32'·42W Fl (2) 10s 37m **15M**; W twr; vis: 073°-330°.
Sanda Island ☆ 55°16'·50N 05°35'·01W Fl 10s 50m **15M**; W twr; vis: 242°-121°; 992351116.
Patersons Rock ⚓ Fl (3) R 18s; 55°16'·90N 05°32'·48W.

KYLES OF BUTE TO RIVER CLYDE

WEST KYLE
Ardlamont Point No 47 ⚓ Fl R 4s; 55°49'·59N 05°11'·76.
Carry Rk No 46 ⚓ Fl R 4s; 55°51'·40N 05°12'·14W.

BURNT ISLAND CHANNEL
⚓ Fl R 4s; 55°55'·80N 05°10'·46W.
▲ Fl G 3s; 55°55'·79N 05°10'·48W.
⚓ Fl R 2s; 55°55'·76N 05°10'·39W.
▲ Fl G 5s; 55°55'·74N 05°10'·38W.
Creyke Rk No 45 ⚓ ; 55°55'·68N 05°10'·89W.
Beere Rk No 44 ▲ ; 55°55'·10N 05°10'·63W.
Wood Fm Rk ⚓ ; 55°55'·42N 05°10'·31W.

EAST KYLE

Colintrave Pt ⚡ Fl R 3s 7m 2M; metal post; 55°55'·39N 05°09'·22W.

Ardmaleish Point No 41 ⌇ Q; 55°53'·02N 05°04'·70W.

ROTHESAY SOUND

Ardyne ▲ Fl G 3s; 55°52'·10N 05°03'·20W.

Bogany Point No 36 ⌇ Fl R 4s; 55°50'·78N 05°01'·41W.

FIRTH OF CLYDE

Toward Pt ☆ 55°51'·73N 04°58'·78W Fl 10s 21m **22M**; W twr.

No 34 ⌇ Q (3) 10s; 55°51'·44N 04°59'·11W.

Skelmorlie ⌇ Iso 5s; 55°51'·65N 04°56'·34W.

WEMYSS and INVERKIP

Cowal ⌇ L Fl 10s; 55°56'·00N 04°54'·83W.

The Gantocks ⌇ Fl R 6s 12m 6M; ◯ twr; 55°56'·45N 04°55'·08W.

The Gantocks No 31 ⌇ Q; 55°56'·56N 04°55'·13W.

DUNOON

Cloch Point ⚡ Fl 3s 24m 8M; W ◯ twr, B band, W dwellings; 55°56'·55N 04°52'·74W.

LOCH LONG and LOCH GOIL

Loch Long ⌇ Oc 6s; 55°59'·15N 04°52'·42W.

Baron's Pt No 3 ⚡ Oc (2) Y 10s 5m 3M; 55°59'·18N 04°51'·12W.

Ravenrock Pt ⚡ Fl 4s 12m 10M; W twr on W col. Dir lt 204°, WRG 9m (same twr); vis: 201·5°-F R-203°-Al WR(W phase incr with brg)-203·5°-FW-204·5°-Al WG(G phase incr with brg)-205°-FG-206·5°; 56°02'·14N 04°54'·39W.

Port Dornaige ⚡ Fl 6s 8m 11M; W col; vis: 026°-206°; 56°03·75N 04°53'·65W.

Rubha Ardnahein ⚡ Fl R 5s 3m 3M; vis: 132°-312°; 56°06'·15N 04°53'·60W.

The Perch, Dir lt 318°; WRG 3m W8M RG 6M, by day WRG 3M; vis: 314·5°-G-316·5°-Al WG-317·5°-W-318·5°-AlWR-319·5°-R-324·5°; ⚡ Fl R 3s 3m 3M (occas); vis: 187°-322°; 56°06'·91N 04°54'·29W.

Cnap Pt Dir lt 024°; WRG 10m W8M RG 6M, by day WRG 3M; vis: 020·5°-G-022·5°-AlWG-023·5°-W-024·5°-AlWR-025·5°-R-027·5°; 56°07'·38N 04°50'·19W.

GOUROCK

Ashton ⌇ Iso 5s; 55°58'·10N 04°50'·65W.

Rosneath Patch ⌇ Fl (2) 10s 5m 10M; 55°58'·52N 04°47'·45W.

ROSNEATH, RHU NARROWS and GARELOCH

Ldg Lts 356°. **Front, No 7N** ⌇ 56°00'·05N 04°45'·36W Dir lt 356°. WRG 5m **W16M**, R13M, G13M; vis: 353°-Al WG- 355°-FW-357°-Al WR-000°-FR-002°.

Dir lt 115° WRG 5m **W16M**, R13M, G13M; vis: 111°-Al WG-114°-FW- 116°-Al WR-119°-FR-121°. Passing lt Oc 6s 6m 3M; G △ on G pile. Rear, Ardencaple Castle Centre ⚡ 56°00'·54N 04°45'·43W 2 FG (vert) 26m 12M; twr on Castle NW corner; vis: 335°-020°.

No 8N Lt Bn ⌇ 55°59'·09N 04°44'·21W Dir lt 080° WRG 4m; **W16M**, R13M,G13M;vis: 075°-FG-077·5°-Al WG-079·5°-FW-080·5°-AltWR-082·5°-FR-085°. **Dir lt 138°** WRG 4m **W16M**, R13M, G13M; vis: 132°-FG-134°-Al WG-FW137°-139°-Al WR-142°. Passing lt Fl Y 3s 6m 3M.

Gareloch No 1 Lt Bn ⚡ VQ (4) Y 5s 9m; Y 'X' on Y structure; 55°59'·12N 04°43'·89W.

No 3N Lt Bn ⌇ 56°00'·07N 04°46'·72W Dir lt 149° WRG 9m **W16M**, R13M, G13M F & Al; vis: 144°-FG-145°-Al WG-148°-FW-150°-Al WR-153°-FR-154°. Passing lt Oc R 8s 9m 3M.

Rosneath DG Jetty ⚡ 2 FR (vert) 5M; W col; vis: 150°-330°; 56°00'·39N 04°47'·51W.

Rhu Pt ⌇ Dir lt 318° WRG **W16M**, R13M, G13M; vis: 315°-Al WG-317°-F-319°-Al WR-321°-FR-325°; Dir W; vis: 325°-QW-340°-FW-345°-OcW-350°; 56°00'·95N 04°47'·20W.

Limekiln No 2N Lt Bn ⌇ 56°00'·67N 04°47'·64W Dir lt 295° WRG 5m **W16M**, R13M, G13M F & Al; R □ on R Bn; vis: 291°-Al WG- 294°-FW- 296°-Al WR-299°-FR-301°.

Carraig an Roin ⚡ Fl Y 5s 2m 2M; Y post with 'x' topmark; 56°00'·99N 04°48'·40W.

Mambeg Dir lt 331°, Q (4) WRG 8s 10m 14M; vis: 328·5°-G-330°-W-332°-R-333°; H24; 56°03'·74N 04°50'·47W.

GREENOCK and PORT GLASGOW

Anchorage Lts in line 196°. Front, FG 7m 12M; Y col; 55°57'·62N 04°46'·58W. Rear, 32m from front, FG 9m 12M. Y col.

Lts in line 194·5°. Front, FG 18m; 55°57'·45N 04°45'·91W. Rear, 360m from front, FG 33m.

Steamboat Quay, W end ⚡ FG 12m 12M; B&W chequered col; vis 210°-290°; 55°56'·25N 04°41'·44W.

CLYDE TO MULL OF GALLOWAY

HUNTERSTON CHANNEL

'C' ▲ Fl G 5s; 55°48'·10N 05°55'·30W.

Hun 1 ⌇ (Y) Fl (4) Y 15s; 55°48'·10N 04°54'·21W.

Hun 3 ⌇ Fl R 2s; 55°47'·60N 04°53'·52W.

LARGS and FAIRLIE

Approach ⊙ L Fl 10s; 55°46'·40N 04°51'·85W.

Fairlie Patch ▲ Fl G 1·5s; 55°45'·38N 04°52'·34W.

MILLPORT and GREAT CUMBRAE

Tomont End Daymark 55°47'·56N 04°54'·10W.

Tattie Pier ⚡ WRG 3s 5m 4M; vis: 222°-G-234°-W-246°-R-258°; metal column; 55°47'·20N 04°53'·89W.

Ldg Lts 333°. Pier Head front, 55°45'·04N 04°55'·85W FR 7m 5M. Rear, 137m from front, FR 9m 5M.

		1	2	3	4	5	6	7	8	9	10	11	12	13	14
1	Loch Craignish	1													
2	Crinan	5	2												
3	Ardrishaig	14	9	3											
6	East Loch Tarbert	24	19	10	4										
5	Campbeltown	55	50	39	31	5									
6	Lamlash	48	43	34	25	24	6								
7	Largs	48	43	34	24	39	17	7							
8	Kip Marina	53	48	39	28	50	25	10	8						
9	Greenock	59	54	45	36	53	31	16	6	9					
10	Rhu (Helensburgh)	62	57	48	37	59	33	19	9	4	10				
11	Troon	54	49	40	33	33	16	20	29	34	38	11			
12	Girvan	67	62	53	43	29	20	33	46	49	51	21	12		
13	Stranraer	89	84	75	65	34	39	56	69	65	74	44	23	13	
14	Kirkcudbright	136	131	122	114	88	92	110	116	124	125	97	94	71	14

DISTANCE TABLES

Approx distances in nautical miles are by the most direct route allowing for dangers and TSS.

Mountstuart 💡 L Fl 10s; 55°48'·00N 04°57'·57W.

Runnaneun Pt (Rubha'n Eun) ⚡ Fl R 6s 8m 12M; W twr; 55°43'·79N 05°00'·23W.

Little Cumbrae Is, Cumbrae Elbow ⚡ Fl 6s 28m 14M; W twr; vis: 334°-193°; 55°43'·22N 04°58'·06W.

ARDROSSAN

Approach Dir lt 055°, WRG 15mW14M, R11M, G11M; vis: 050°-F G-051·2°-Alt WG(W phase inc with Brg)-053·8°-FW-056·2°-Alt WR(R phase inc with brg)-058·8°-FR-060°; 55°38'·66N 04°49'·22W. Same structure FR 13m 6M; vis: 325°-145°.

Lt ho Pier Hd ⚡ Iso WG 4s 11m 9M; W twr; vis: 035°-W-317°-G-035°; 55°38'·47N 04°49'·57W.

IRVINE

Ldg Lts 051°. Front, FG 10m 5M; 55°36'·40N 04°41'·57W. Rear, 101m from front, FR 15m 5M; G masts, both vis: 019°-120°.

TROON

Troon Approach ⚓ Fl G 4s; 55°33'·08N 04°41'·42W.

W Pier Hd ⚡ Fl (2) WG 5s 11m 9M; W twr; vis: 036°-G-090°-W-036°; 55°33'·07N 04°41'·02W.

Lady I ⚡ Fl 2s 19m 11M; W Tr R vert stripes; *Racon (T) 13-11M*; 55°31'·63N 04°44'·05W.

ARRAN, RANZA, LAMLASH and BRODICK

Pillar Rk Pt ☆ (Holy Island), 55°31'·04N 05°03'·65W Fl (2) 20s 38m **18M**; W ☐ twr.

Holy Is SW end ⚡ Fl G 3s 14m 6M; W twr; vis: 282°-147°; 55°30'·73N 05°04'·21W.

Pladda ☆ 55°25'·50N 05°07'·12W Fl (3) 30s 40m **17M**; W twr.

AYR and AILSA CRAIG

S Pier Hd ⚡ Q 7m 7M; R twr; vis: 012°-161°. Also Fl G 4s 5m 5M; vis: 012°-082°; 55°28'·17N 04°38'·74W.

Ldg Lts 098°. Front, FR 10m 5M; Tfc sigs; 55°28'·15N 04°38'·38W. Rear, 130m from front Oc R 10s 18m 9M.

Maidens Hbr, E side ⚡ Fl G 5s 4m 3M; 55°20'·24N 04°49'·20W. Maidens Hbr, W side ⚡ Fl R 3s 4m 2M; 55°20'·23N 04°49'·19W.

Turnberry Point ⚡, near castle ruins 55°19'·57N 04°50'·69W Fl 15s 29m 12M; W twr.

Ailsa Craig ☆ 55°15'·12N 05°06'·52W Fl 4s 18m **17M**; W twr; vis: 145°-028°.

GIRVAN

S Pier Hd ⚡2 FG (vert) 8m 4M; W twr; 55°14'·72N 04°51'·90W.

LOCH RYAN and STRANRAER

Milleur Point 💡 Q; 55°01'·28N 05°05'·66W.

Fairway ⊛ Iso 4s; 54°59'·77N 05°03'·82W.

Forbes Shoal ⊜ QR; 54°59'·47N 05°02'·96W.

Loch Ryan W ⚓QG; 54°59'·23N 05°03'·24W.

Cairn Pt ⚡ Fl (2) R 10s 14m 12M; W twr; 54°58'·46N 05°01'·85W.

Cairnryan ⚡ Fl R 5s 5m 5M; 54°57'·77N 05°00'·99W. Stranraer No 1 💡 Oc G 6s; 54°56'·67N 05°01'·32W.

No 3 💡 QG; 54°55'·87N 05°01'·60W.

No 5 💡 Fl G 3s; 54°55'·08N 05°01'·86W.

E Pier Hd ⚡ 2 FR (vert) 9m; 54°54'·61N 05°01'·60W.

Corsewall Point ☆ 55°00'·41N 05°09'·58W Fl (5) 30s 34m **22M**; W twr; vis: 027°-257°.

Black Hd Old Lt Ho; W tower, 22m; 54°51'·70N 05°08'·80W.

PORTPATRICK

Ldg Lts 050·5°. Front, FG (occas); 54°50'·50N 05°07'·02W. Rear, 68m from front, FG 8m (occas).

Crammag Hd ☆ 54°39'·90N 04°57'·92W Fl 10s 35m **18M**; W twr.

Mull of Galloway ☆, SE end 54°38'·11N 04°51'·45W Fl 20s 99m **18M**; W twr; vis: 182°-105°.

MULL OF GALLOWAY and WIGTOWN BAY

Port William Ldg Lts 105°. Front, Pier Hd Fl G 3s 7m 3M; 54°45'·66N 04°35'·28W. Rear, 130m from front, FG 10m 2M.

Isle of Whithorn ⚡ Fl WR 3s 20m 6/4M; vis: 310°-W-005°-R-040°; 54°41'·79N 04°21'·54W.

Whithorn Ldg Lts 335°. Front, Oc R 8s 7m 7M; Or ♦; 54°42'·01N 04°22'·05W. Rear, 35m from front, Oc R 8s 9m 7M; Or ♦, synch.

Little Ross ⚡ Fl 5s 50m 12M; W twr; obsc in Wigtown B when brg more than 103°; 54°45'·93N 04°05'·10W.

KIRKCUDBRIGHT BAY and KIPPFORD

Little Ross NNE end of Is ⚡ Fl (2) 5s 21m 5M; Stone bcn; 54°46'·06N 04°05'·02W.

Hestan I, E end ⚡ Fl (2) 10s 42m 9M; 54°49'·95N 03°48'·53W.

AREA 8 *NW England, Isle of Man & N Wales – Solway Firth to Bardsey I*

SELECTED LIGHTS, BUOYS & WAYPOINTS

SOLWAY FIRTH TO BARROW-IN-FURNESS

SILLOTH and MARYPORT

Lees Scar ⚡ Fl G 5s 11m 4M; W piles; 54°51'·78N 03°24'·79W.

Groyne Hd ⚡2 FG (vert) 4m 4M; Fl Bu tfc signals close by; 54°52'·14N 03°23'·93W.

Maryport S Pier Hd ⚡.Fl 1·5s 10m 6M; 54°43'·07N 03°30'·64W.

WORKINGTON and HARRINGTON

N Workington 💡 Q; 54°40'·10N 03°38'·18W.

S Workington 💡 VQ (6) + L Fl 10s; 54°37'·01N 03°38'·58W.

South Pier ⚡ Fl 5s 11m 5M; R bldg; 54°39'·12N 03°34'·67W.

Ldg Lts 131·8°. Front, FR 10m 3M; 54°38'·92N 03°34'·19W. Rear, 134m from front, FR 12m 3M.

WHITEHAVEN

W Pier Hd ⚡ Fl G 5s 16m 8M; W ○ twr; 54°33'·17N 03°35'·92W.

N Pier Hd ⚡ Fl R 5s 8m 10M; W ○ twr; 54°33'·17N 03°35'·75W.

Saint Bees Hd ☆ 54°30'·81N 03°38'·23W Fl (2) 20s 102m **18M**; W○ twr; obsc shore-340°.

RAVENGLASS

Blockhouse ⚡FG; (Eskdale Range); 54°20'·16N 03°25'·34W.

Selker ⚓ Fl (3) G 10s; *Bell;* 54°16'·14N 03°29'·58W.

BARROW-IN-FURNESS

Lightning Knoll ⊛ L Fl 10s; 53°59'·83N 03°14'·28W.

Halfway Shoal 💡 QR 19m 10s; R&W chequer Bn; 54°01'·46N 03°11'·88W.

Isle of Walney ⚡ Fl 15s 21m 10M; stone twr; obsc 122°-127° within 3M of shore; 54°02'·92N 03°10'·64W.

Walney Chan Ldg Lts 040·7°. No 1 Front 💡, Q 7m 10M; vis: 035·2°-W-046·2°; Or ☐; 54°03'·19N 03°09'·22W. No 2 Rear 💡, 0·61M from front, Iso 2s 13m 10M; Or ☐ on Pile.

Rampside Sands Ldg Lts 005·1°. No 3 Front ⤵, Q 9m10M; W ◯ twr; 54°04'·41N 03°09'·79W. No 4 Rear ⤵, 0·77M from front, Iso 2s 14m 6M; R col, W face.

ISLE OF MAN

Ballacash Bank ⤜ VQ (9) 10s; 54°26'·50N 04°16'·70W.

Whitestone Bank ⤜ Q (9) 15s; 54°24'·58N 04°20'·41W.

Point of Ayre ☆ 54°24'·94N 04°22'·13W Fl (4) 20s 32m **19M**; W twr, two R bands, *Racon (M) 13-15M*.

Low Lt Ho (unlit), RW twr, B base, 54°25'·03N 04°21'·86W.

PEEL

Peel Bkwtr Hd ⚲ Oc 7s 11m 6M; W twr; 54°13'·67N 04°41'·69W.

PORT ERIN and PORT ST MARY

Ldg Lts 099·1°. Front, 54°05'·23N 04°45'·57W FR 10m 5M; W twr, R band. Rear, 39m from front, FR 19m 5M; W col, R band.

Calf of Man Lighthouse (disused), white 8-sided tower.

Chicken Rk ☆ Fl 5s 38m **20M**; *Racon (C)* 54°02'·27N 04°50'·32W

Alfred Pier Hd ⚲ Oc R 10s 8m 6M; 54°04'·33N 04°43'·82W.

CASTLETOWN and DERBY HAVEN

Dreswick Pt ⚲ Fl (2) 30s 23m 12M; W twr; 54°03'·29N 04°37'·45W.

New Pier Hd ⚲ Oc R 15s 8m 5M; 54°04'·33N 04°38'·97W.

Derby Haven, Bkwtr SW end ⚲Iso G 2s 5m 5M; W twr, G band; 54°04'·58N 04°37'·06W.

DOUGLAS

Douglas Head ☆ 54°08'·60N 04°27'·95W Fl 10s 32m **15M**; W twr; obsc brg more than 037°. FR Lts on radio masts 1 and 3M West.

No 1 ⬣ Q (3) G 5s; 54°09'·04N 04°27'·68W.

Princess Alexandra Pier Hd ⚲ Fl R 5s 16m 8M; R mast; *Whis (2) 40s*; 54°08'·84N 04°27'·85W.

Ldg Lts 229·3°, Front ⤵, Oc Bu 10s 9m 5M; W △ R border on mast; 54°08'·72N 04°28'·25W. Rear ⤵, 62m from front, Oc Bu 10s 12m 5M; W ▽ on R border; synch with front.

Victoria Pier Hd ⚲ Iso G 10s 6m 10M; Post; Intl Port Tfc Signals; 54°08'·84N 04°28'·08W.

Conister Rk Refuge ⤵ Q 3M; vis: 234°-312°; 54°09'·03N 04°28'·12W.

LAXEY to RAMSEY

Laxey Pier Hd ⚲ Oc R 3s 7m 5M; W twr, R band; obsc when brg less than 318°; 54°13'·50N 04°23'·43W.

Maughold Head ☆ 54°17'·72N 04°18'·58W Fl (3) 30s 65m **15M**.

Bahama ⤜ VQ (6) + L Fl 10s; 54°20'·01N 04°08'·57W.

Queens Pier Dn ⚲ Fl R 5s; 54°19'·28N 04°21'·95W.

King William Bank ⤜ Q (3) 10s; 54°26'·01N 04°00'·08W.

BARROW TO RIVERS MERSEY AND DEE

MORECAMBE

Met Mast ⚲ Fl Y 5s 20m 5M; 54°00'·13N 03°33'·38W; Aero FR (80m), *Horn 30s.*

Lightning Knoll ⌕ L Fl 10s; 53°59'·84N 03°14'·28W.

Morecambe ⤜ Q (9) 15s; 53°52'·00N 03°22'·00W.

Lune Deep ⤜ Q (6) + L Fl 15s; *Racon (T)*; 53°56'·07N 03°12·90W.

Lts in line about 090°. Front, FR 10m 2M; G mast; 54°04'·41N 02°52'·63W. Rear, 140m from front, FR 14m 2M; G mast.

HEYSHAM

SW Quay Ldg Lts 102·2°. Front ⤵, both F Bu 11/14m 2M; Or & B ◆ on masts; 54°01'·91N 02°55'·22W.

RIVER LUNE, GLASSON DOCK and FLEETWOOD

R Lune ⤜ Q (9) 15s; 53°58'·63N 03°00'·03W.

Fairway No 1(Fleetwood) ⤜ 53°57'·67N 03°02'·03W Q; *Bell.*

Fleetwood Esplanade Ldg Lts 156°. Front, Iso G 2s 14m 9M; 53°55'·71N 03°00'·56W. Rear, 320m from front, Iso G 4s 28m 9M. Both vis on Ldg line only. (H24) (chan liable to change).

RIVER RIBBLE

Gut ⌕ L Fl 10s; 53°41'·74N 03°08'·98W.

Perches show Fl R on N side, and Fl G on S side of chan. S side, 14¼M Perch ⚲ Fl G 5s 6m 3M; 53°42'·75N 03°04'·90W.

Jordan's Spit ⤜ Q (9) 15s; 53°35'·76N 03°19'·28W.

FT ⤜ Q; 53°34'·56N 03°13'·20W.

RIVER MERSEY and LIVERPOOL

Bar ⤜ Fl.5s 12M; *Racon (T) 10M*; 53°32'·02N 03°20'·98W, AIS.

Q1 ⤜ VQ; 53°31'·01N 03°16'·70W.

Q2 ⤜ VQ R; 53°31'·48N 03°14'·94W.

Q3 ⬣ Fl G 3s; 53°30'·97N 03°15'·08W.

Formby ⤜ Iso 4s; 53°31'·14N 03°13'·48W.

C4 ⌕ Fl R 3s; 53°31'·83N 03°08'·50W.

CROSBY ⌁ Oc 5s; 53°30'·74N 03°06'·30W.

C14 ⌕ Fl R 3s; 53°29'·93N 03°05'·35W.

Brazil ⬣ QG; G hull,53°26'·85N 03°02'·23W.

RIVER DEE, MOSTYN and CONNAH'S QUAY

HE1 ⤜ Q (9) 15s; 53°26'·33N 03°18'·08W.

HE2 ⬣ Fl G 2·5s; 53°24'·90N 03°12'·88W.

HE3 ⬣ Q G; 53°24'·55N 03°12'·74W.

		1	2	3	4	5	6	7	8	9	10	11	12	13	14	15	16	17
1.	Portpatrick	**1**																
2.	Mull of Galloway	16	**2**															
3.	Kirkcudbright	48	32	**3**														
4.	Maryport	65	49	26	**4**													
5.	Workington	63	47	25	6	**5**												
6.	Ravenglass	70	54	40	30	23	**6**											
7.	Point of Ayre	38	22	28	37	31	34	**7**										
8.	Peel	41	26	46	55	49	52	18	**8**									
9.	Douglas	60	42	46	50	44	39	19	30	**9**								
10.	Glasson Dock	101	85	74	66	60	37	64	85	63	**10**							
11.	Fleetwood	95	79	68	59	53	30	58	80	57	10	**11**						
12.	Liverpool	118	102	97	89	83	60	80	86	70	52	46	**12**					
13.	Conwy	111	95	95	92	86	58	72	72	59	62	56	46	**13**				
14.	Beaumaris	109	93	94	95	89	72	71	73	58	66	60	49	12	**14**			
15.	Caernarfon	117	103	104	105	99	82	81	73	68	76	70	59	22	10	**15**		
16.	Holyhead	93	81	94	96	90	69	68	62	50	79	73	68	36	32	26	**16**	
17.	Fishguard	171	158	175	175	169	160	153	140	134	153	147	136	100	88	78	89	**17**

DISTANCE TABLES

Approx distances in nautical miles are by the most direct route allowing for dangers and TSS.

Mostyn Dir Lt ⚓ 194·5°; Iso WRG 2s 11m W 10M R,G 7M, by day W 3M R,G 2M; vis: 192°-G-194°-W-195°-R-197°; H24; Y framework twr; 53°19'·55N 03°15'·69W.
Dee No1 ⚓ L Fl 10s; 53°20'·70N 03°12'·46W.
Dee ⚓ Q (6) + L Fl 15s; 53°21'·90N 03°18·20W.
West Hoyle Spit (Earwig) Dir Lt 090. ⚓ 53°21'·21N 03°24'·07W; Iso WRG 2s W10M, R7M, G7M (day W3M, R2M, G2M); vis: 087·5°-G-089·5°-W-090·5°-R-092·5°; occasional.
S Hoyle Outer ⚓ Fl R 2·5s; 53°21'·26N 03°26'·95W.

WALES – NORTH COAST AND INNER PASSAGE

South Hoyle Outer ⚓ Fl R 2·5s; 53°21'·47N 03°24'·70W.
Prestatyn ⚓ Q; 53°21'·37N 03°29'·00W.
Inner Passage ⚓ Fl R 5s; 53°21'·91N 03°31'·95W.
Mid Patch Spit ⚓ QR; 53°22'·25N 03°32'·67W.
Mast ⚓ Fl Y 5s 18m 5M; Mast (80); 53°28'·84N 03°30'·50W.
W Constable ⚓ Q (9) 15s; **Racon (M) 10M**; 53°23'·14N 03°49'·26W.

RHYL, LLANDUDNO and CONWY

River Clwyd Outfall ⚓ Q R 7m 2M; 53°19'·45N 03°30'·34W.
Llandudno Pier Hd ⚓ 2 FG (vert) 8m 4M; 53°19'·90N 03°49'·51W.
Great Ormes Hd Lt Ho, (unlit); 53°20'·56N 03°52'·17W.
Conwy Fairway ⚓ L Fl 10s; 53°17'·95N 03°55'·58W.
C1 ⚓ Fl G 10s; 53°17'·83N 03°54'·58W.
C2 ⚓ Fl (2) R 10s; 53°17'·94N 03°54'·52W.
River Conwy ent, ⚓ L Fl G 15s 5m 2M; 53°18'·03N 03°50'·86W.

ANGLESEY

Point Lynas ☆ 53°24'·98N 04°17'·35W Oc 10s 39m **18M**; W castellated twr; vis: 109°-315°; H24.

AMLWCH to HOLYHEAD BAY

Main Bkwtr ⚓ Fl G 15s 11m 3M; W mast; vis: 141°-271°; 53°25'·02N 04°19'·91W.
Furlong ⚓ Fl G 2·5s; 53°25'·41N 04°30'·47W.
Archdeacon Rock ⚓ Q; 53°26'·71N 04°30'·87W.
Victoria Bank ⚓ VQ; 53°25'·61N 04°31'·37W.
Coal Rk ⚓ Q (6) + L Fl 15s; 53°25'·91N 04°32'·79W.
Ethel Rk ⚓ VQ; 53°26'·64N 04°33'·67W.
The Skerries ☆ 53°25'·27N 04°36'·50W Fl (2) 15s 36m **20M**; W ○ twr, R band; **Racon (T) 25M**. Iso R 4s 26m 10M; same twr; vis: 233°-252°, sector unreliable > 4M; Horn

(2) 60s. H24 in periods of reduced visibility; 992351084.
Langdon ⚓ Q (9) 15s; 53°22'·74N 04°38'·74W.
Bolivar ⚓ Fl G 2·5s; 53°21'·51N 04°35'·33W.
Wk ⚓ Fl (2) R 10s; 53°20'·43N 04°36'·60W.

HOLYHEAD to SOUTH STACK

Bkwtr Head ⚓ Fl (3) G 10s 21m 14M; W ☐ twr, B band; Fl Y vis: 174°-226°; *Siren 20s*; 53°19'·86N 04°37'·16W.
Spit ⚓ Fl G 3s; 53°19'·79N 04°37'·15W.
South Stack ☆ 53°18'·41N 04°41'·98W Fl 10s 60m **24M**; (H24); W ○ twr; obsc to N by N Stack and part obsc in Penrhos bay; *Horn 30s*. Fog Det lt vis: 145°-325°.
Holyhead Deep Tidal Array ⚓ Fl Y(4) 15s 53°17'.80N 04°47'.76W.

MENAI STRAIT TO BARDSEY ISLAND

Ten Feet Bank ⚓ QR; 53°19'·47N 04°02'·82W.
Dinmor ⚓ QG; 53°19'·34N 04°03'·32W.
Trwyn-Du ⚓ Fl 5s 19m 12M; W ○ castellated twr, B bands; vis: 101°-023°; *Horn (3) 30s*, sounded continuously; 53°18'·77N 04°02'·45W.

MENAI STRAIT

(Direction of buoyage ⬒ NE to SW)
Perch Rock ⚓ Fl R 5s; 53°18'·73N 04°02'·09W.
Port Dinorwic Pier Hd ⚓ 53°11'·21N 04°12'·60W F WR 5m 2M; vis: 225°-R-357°-W-225°.
(Direction of buoyage ⬒ SW to NE)
Caernarfon N Pier ⚓ 2 FG(vert) 5m 2M; 53°08'·72N 04°16'·56W.
Abermenai Point ⚓ Fl WR 3·5s 6m 3M; W mast; vis: 065°-R-245°-W-065°; 53°07'·62N 04°19'·72W.
C1 ⚓ Fl G 5s; 53°07'·18N 04°24'·60W.
C2 ⚓ Fl R 10s; 53°07'·38N 04°24'·33W.
Caernarfon Bar ⚓ L Fl 10s; 53°07'·00N 04°25'·00W.
Llanddwyn I ⚓Fl WR 2·5s 12m W7M, R4M; W twr; vis: 280°-R- 015°-W-120°; 53°08'·05N 04°24'·79W.

PORTH DINLLÄEN

CG Stn ⚓ FR when firing 10M N; 52°56'·82N 04°33'·89W.
Careg y Chwislen ⚓ Fl(2) 10s 2M 52°56'·99N 04°33'·51W.
Bardsey I ☆ 52°44'·97N 04°48'·02W Fl R 10s 39m **18M**; W ☐ twr, R bands; obsc by Bardsey Is 198°-250° and in Tremadoc B when brg < 260°.

AREA 9 *S Wales & SW England – Cardigan Bay to St Ives*

SELECTED LIGHTS, BUOYS & WAYPOINTS

CARDIGAN BAY (SEE AREA 8)

Bardsey I ☆ 52°44'·98N 04°48'·01W Fl R 10s 39m **18M**; W ☐ twr, R bands; obsc by Bardsey I 198°-250° and in Tremadoc B when brg less than 260°.
St Tudwal's ⚓ Fl WR 15s 46m W14, R10M; vis: 349°-W-169°-R- 221°-W-243°-R-259°-W-293°-R-349°; obsc by East I 211°-231°; 52°47'·92N 04°28'·30W.

PWLLHELI and PORTHMADOG

Pwllheli App ⚓ Iso 2s; 52°53'·03N 04°22'·90W.
Porthmadog Fairway ⚓ L Fl 10s; 52°52'·97N 04°11'·20W.

BARMOUTH and ABERDOVEY

Diffuser ⚓ Fl Y 5s; 52°43'·19N 04°05'·38W.

Barmouth Outer ⚓ L Fl 10s; 52°42'·81N 04°04'·89W.
Aberdovey Outer ⚓ Iso 4s; 52°32'·00N 04°05'·55W.
Cynfelyn Patches, Patches ⚓ Q(9) 15s; 52°25'·83N 04°16'·41W.

ABERYSTWYTH, ABERAERON and NEW QUAY

Aberystwyth S Bkwtr Hd ⚓ Fl (2) WG 10s 12m 10M; vis: 030°-G- 053°-W-210°; 52°24'·40N 04°05'·52W.
Ldg Lts 133°. Front, FR 4m 5M; 52°24'·37N 04°05'·39W. Rear, 52m from front, FR 7m 6M.
Aberaeron N Pier ⚓ Fl (4) WRG 15s 10m 6M; vis: 050°-G-104°-W-178°-R-232°; 52°14'·61N 04°15'·87W.
Carreg Ina ⚓ Q; 52°13'·19N 04°20'·70W.
New Quay Pier Hd ⚓ Fl WG 3s 12m W8M, G5M; G △ vis: 135°-W- 252°-G-295; 52°12'·95N 04°21'·35W.

CARDIGAN and FISHGUARD
Cardigan Channel ⚓ Fl (2) 5s; 52°06'·44N 04°41'·43W.
Cardigan Cliff Base Bn 1 ⚑ Fl R 4s 3M; 52°07'·05N 04°41'·39W.
Cardigan Cliff Base Bn 2 ⚑ Fl R 2s 3M; 52°06'·91N 04°41'·34W.
Fishguard N Bkwtr Hd ⚑ Fl G 4·5s 18m 13M; *Bell (1) 8s*; 52°00'·76N 04°58'·23W.
Strumble Head ☆ 52°01'·79N 05°04'·43W Fl (4) 15s 45m **26M**; vis: 038°-257°; (H24).

BISHOPS and SMALLS
South Bishop ☆ 51°51'·14N 05°24'·74W Fl 5s 44m **16M**; W ○ twr; *Horn (3) 45s; Racon (O)10M*; (H24).
The Smalls ☆ 51°43'·27N 05°40'·19W Fl (3) 15s 36m **18M**; *Racon (T); Horn (2) 60s*. Same twr, Iso R 4s 33m 13M; vis: 253°-285° over Hats & Barrels Rk; both Lts shown H24 in periods of reduced visibility; 992351123.
Skokholm I ⚑, 51°41'·64N 05°17'·22W Fl WR 10s 54m W8M, R8M; vis: 301°-W-154°-R-301°; partially obsc 226°-258°.

WALES – SOUTH COAST – BRISTOL CHANNEL
MILFORD HAVEN
St Ann's Head ☆ 51°40'·87N 05°10'·42W Fl WR 5s 48m **W18M, R17M**, R14M; W 8-sided twr; vis: 233°-W-247°-R-332°-W131°, partially obscured 124°-129°; *Horn (2) 60s*.
W Blockhouse Point ⚓ Ldg Lts 022·5°. Front, F 54m 13M (day 10M); B stripe on W twr; vis: 004·5°-040·5°; intens on lead line. vis: 004·5°-040·5°; *Racon (Q)*; 51°41'·31N 05°09'·56W.
Watwick Point Common Rear ☆, 0·5M from front, F 80m **15M** (day 10M); vis: 013·5°-031·5°; *Racon (Y)*.
W Blockhouse Point ⚓ Q WR 21m W9M, R7M; R lantern on W base: vis: 220°-W-250°-R-020°-W-036°-R-049°; 51°41'·31N 05°09'·56W.
Dale Fort ⚑ Fl (2) WR 5s 20m W5M, R3M; vis: 222°-R-276°-W-019°; 51°42'·16N 05°09'·01W.
Gt Castle Hd ⚓ F WRG 27m W5M, R3M, G3M; vis: 243°-R-281°-G- 299°-W-029°; 51°42'·68N 05°07'·06W. Co-located Dir WRG (040°); vis: 038·25°-G-039°-AlWG-039·5°-W-040·5°-AlWR-041°-R-041·75° (**not** used in conjunction with the front ldg light below) Ldg Lts ≠ 039·7° **Front**, Oc 4s 27m **15M**; vis: 031·2°-048·2°. **Rear**, 890m from front. Oc 8s 53m **15M** (day 10M); vis: 031·2°-048·2°.
St Ann's ⌇ Fl R 2·5s; 51°40'·25N 05°10'·51W.
Mid Channel Rks ⚓ Q (9) 15s; 51°40'·18N 05°10'·14W.
Mid Channel Rk ⚑ Fl(3) G 7s 18m 8M; 51°40'·31N 05°09'·83W.
Rows Rks ⌇ Q R; 51°40'·22N 05°09'·02W.
Sheep ▲ QG; 51°40'·06N 05°08'·31W.
Millbay ⌇ Fl (2) R 5s; 51°41'·05N 05°09'·45W.
W Chapel ▲ Fl G 10s; 51°40'·98N 05°08'·67W.
E Chapel ⌇ Fl R 5s; 51°40'·87N 05°08'·15W.
Rat ▲ Fl G 5s; 51°40'·80N 05°07'·86W.
Angle ⚓ VQ; 51°41'·63N 05°08'·27W.
Thorn Rock ⚓ Q (9) 15s; 51°41'·53N 05°07'·76W.
Turbot Bank ⚓ VQ (9) 10s; 51°37'·41N 05°10'·08W.
St Gowan ⚓ Q (6) + L Fl 15s, *Racon (T) 10M*; 51°31'·93N 04°59'·77W; 992351126.

TENBY to SWANSEA BAY
Caldey I ⚑ Fl (3) WR 20s 65m W13M, R9M; vis: R173°-W212°- R088°-102°; 51°37'·90N 04°41'·08W.

Woolhouse ⚓ Q (6) + L Fl 15s; 51°39'·35N 04°39'·69W.
Burry Port Inlet ⚑ Fl 5s 7m 6½M; 51°40'·62N 04°15'·06W.
W. Helwick ⚓ (9) 15s; *Racon (T) 10M*; 51°31'·40N 04°23'·65W.
E. Helwick ⚓ VQ (3) 5s; Bell; 51°31'·80N 04°12'·68W.

SWANSEA BAY and SWANSEA
Ledge ⚓ VQ (6) + L Fl 10s; 51°29'·93N 03°58'·77W.
Mixon ⌇ Fl (2) R 5s; *Bell*; 51°33'·12N 03°58'·78W.
Outer Spoil Gnd ⌇ Fl Y 2·5s; 51°32'·11N 03°55'·73W.
Grounds ⚓ VQ (3) 5s; 51°32'·81N 03°53'·47W.
Mumbles ☆ 51°34'·01N 03°58'·27W Fl (4) 20s 35m **15M**; W twr; *Horn 3s*.
SW Inner Green Grounds ⚓ Q(3) 10s; 51°34'·21N 03°57'·12W.
Swansea Lts in line 020°. Front: E Breakwater head, Oc G 4s 5m 2M & 2FG(vert) 10m 6M; 51°36'·38N 03°55'·62W. Rear, 3·1ca from front: FG 6M.

SWANSEA BAY, RIVER NEATH and PORT TALBOT
Neath App Chan ▲ Fl G 5s; 51°35'·71N 03°52'·83W.
Cabenda ⚓ Q (6) + L Fl 15s; *Racon (Q)*; 51°33'·36N 03°52'·23W.
Ldg Lts 059·8° (occas). Front, Oc R 3s 12m 6M; 51°34'·92N 03°48'·10W. Rear, 400m from front, Oc R 6s 32m 6M.

BRISTOL CHANNEL – NORTH SHORE (E PART)
W Scar ⚓ Q (9) 15s, *Bell*, *Racon (T) 10M*; 51°28'·31N 03°55'·57W.
South Scar (S SCAR) ⚓ Q (6) + L Fl 15s; 51°27'·61N 03°51'·58W.
E. Scarweather ⚓ Q (3) 10s; *Bell*; 51°27'·98N 03°46'·76W.

PORTHCAWL
Fairy ⚓ Q (9) 15s; *Bell*; 51°27'·86N 03°42'·07W.
Bkwtr Hd ⚑ 51°28'·39N 03°41'·98W F WRG 10m W6M, R4M, G4M; vis: 302°-G-036°-W-082°-R-116°.
W Nash ⚓ VQ (9) 10s ; *Bell*; 51°25'·99N 03°45'·95W.
Nash ☆ 51°24'·03N 03°33'·06W Fl (2) W 15s 56m **W21M, R16M**; vis: 280°-R-290°-W-100°-R-120°-W-128°.
Breaksea ⚓ L Fl 10s; *Racon (T) 10M*; 51°19'·88N 03°19'·08W; 992351124.

BARRY
W Bkwtr Hd ⚑ Fl 2·5s 12m 10M; 51°23'·46N 03°15'·52W.
N. One Fathom ⚓ Q; 51°20'·94N 03°12'·17W.
Mackenzie ⌇ QR; 51°21'·75N 03°08'·24W.

CARDIFF and PENARTH ROADS
Lavernock Outfall ⌇ Fl Y 5s; 51°23'·95N 03°09'·50W.
Ranie ⌇ Fl (2) R 5s; 51°24'·23N 03°09'·39W.
S Cardiff ⚓ Q (6) + L Fl 15s; *Bell*; 51°24'·18N 03°08'·57W.
Mid Cardiff ▲ Fl (3) G 10s; 51°25'·60N 03°08'·09W.
Cardiff Spit ⌇ QR; 51°24'·57N 03°07'·12W.
N Cardiff ▲ QG; 51°26'·52N 03°07'·19W.
Wrach Chan Dir lt 348·5°. Oc WRG 10s 5m; W3M, R3M, G3M; vis: 344·5°-G-347°-W-350°-R-352°; H24; 51°27'·16N 03°09'·75W.
Outer Wrach ⚓ Q (9) 15s; 51°26'·20N 03°09'·46W.

FLATHOLM to THE BRIDGE
Flat Holm ☆, SE Pt 51°22'·54N 03°07'·14W Fl (3) WR 10s 50m **W15M**, R12M; W ○ twr; vis: 106°-R-140°-W-151°-R-203°-W-106°; (H24).
Monkstone ⚑ Fl 5s 13m 12M; R column on W ○ twr; 51°24'·89N 03°06'·01W.

Tail Patch ◣ QG; 51°23'·53N 03°03'·65W.

Hope ⨳ Q (3) 10s; 51°24'·84N 03°02'·68W.

NW Elbow ⨳ VQ (9) 10s; *Bell;* 51°26'·28N 02°59'·93W.

EW Grounds ⨳ L Fl 10s 7M; *Whis; Racon (T) 7M;* 51°27'·12N 02°59'·95W.

NEWPORT DEEP, RIVER USK and NEWPORT

Newport Deep ◣ Fl (3) G 10s; *Bell;* 51°29'·36N 02°59'·12W.

East Usk ☆ 51°32'·40N 02°58'·01W; Oc WRG 10s 10m W11M, R9M, G9M; vis: 011°-G-015°-W- 017°-R-021°.

Julians Pill Ldg Lts 062°. Front, F Bu 5m 5M; 51°33'·32N 02°57'·94W. Rear, `44m from front, F Bu 8m 5M.

BRISTOL CHANNEL – SOUTH SHORE (E PART)

BRISTOL DEEP

N Elbow ◣ QG; *Bell;* 51°26'·97N 02°58'·65W.

S Mid Grounds ⨳ VQ(6) + L Fl 10s; 51°27'·62N 02°58'·68W.

E Mid Grounds ⊚ Fl R 5s; 51°27'·75N 02°54'·98W.

Clevedon ⨳ VQ; 51°27'·39N 02°54'·93W.

Welsh Hook ⨳ Q(6) + L Fl 15s; 51°28'·53N 02°51'·86W.

Avon ◣ Fl G 2·5s; 51°27'·92N 02°51'·73W.

Black Nore Pt Lt Ho; W ○ twr on frame; 51°29'·09N 02°48'·05W.

Newcome ⊚ 51°30'·01N 02°46'·71W Fl (3) R 10s.

Denny Shoal ⨳ VQ(6) + L Fl 10s; 51°30'·15N 02°45'·45W.

Cockburn ⊚ 51°30'·45N 02°44'·10W Fl R 2·5s.

W Dock Middle ◣ 51°29.95'N 02°44'·20W Q G.

W Dock Outer ◣ 51°30'·00N 02°44'·85W Fl G 5s.

Firefly ◣ Fl(2) G 5s; 51°29'·96N 02°45'·35W.

Portishead Point ☆ 51°29'·68N 02°46'·42W Q (3) 10s 9m **16M**; B twr, W base; vis: 060°-262°; *Horn 20s.*

PORTISHEAD

Pier Hd ⚡ Iso G 2s 5m 3M; 51°29'·69N 02°45'·27W.

Seabank. Dir WG 6m 5M; vis: 085·8°-FG-086·7°-AltWG-086·9°-FW-089·7°. 5M; vis: 070·3°-103·3°; by day 1M, vis: 076·8°-096·8°.

Lts in line 086·8°. Q(8) 5M 10/16m; vis: 070·3°-103·3°; day 1M vis: 076·8°-096·8° Front 51°30'·07N 02°43'·80W; Rear, 500m behind.

Knuckle Lts in line 099·6°. Oc G 5s 6m 6M; 51°29'·94N 02°43'·67W. Rear, 165m from front, FG 13m 6M; vis: 044°-134°.

AVONMOUTH

Royal Edward Dock N Pier Hd ⚡ Fl 4s 15m 10M; vis: 060°-228·5°; 51°30'·49N 02°43'·09W.

King Road Ldg Lts 072·4°. N Pier Hd ⚡ Front, Oc R 5s 5m 9M; W obelisk, R bands; vis: 062°-082°; 51°30'·49N 02°43'·09W. Rear ⚡, 546m from front, QR 15m 10M; vis: 066°-078°.

RIVER AVON, CUMBERLAND BASIN and AVON BRIDGE

S Pier Hd ⚡ Oc RG 30s 9m 10M and FBu 4m 1M; vis: 294°-R-036°-G-194°; 51°30'·37N 02°43'·10W. *Bell(1) 10s.*

Ldg Lts 127·2°. Front ⚓, Iso R 2s 6m 3M, vis: 010°-160°; 51°30'·10N 02°42'·59W. Rear⚓ , Iso R 2s10m 3M, vis: 048°-138°.

BRISTOL CHANNEL (SOUTH SHORE)

WESTON-SUPER-MARE

Pier Hd ⚡ 2 FG (vert) 6m; 51°20'·88N 02°59'·26W.

E Culver ⨳ Q (3) 10s; 51°18'·00N 03°15'·44W.

W Culver ⨳ VQ (9) 10s; 51°17'·47N 03°19'·00W.

E Hinkley ◣ 51°13.50'N 03°09'·26W Fl(4) G 10s.

W Hinkley ⊚ 51°13'·67N 03°10'·76W Fl(3) R 10s.

BURNHAM-ON-SEA and RIVER PARRETT

Ent ⚡ Fl 7·5s 7m 12M; vis: 074°-164°; 51°14'·89N 03°00'·36W; Dir lt 080°. F WRG 4m W12M, R10M, G10M; vis: 071°-G- 075°-W-085- R-095°.

DZ No 1 ◿ Fl Y 2·5s; 51°15'·28N 03°09'·49W.

DZ No 2 ◿ Fl Y 10s; 51°13'·77N 03°19'·86W.

DZ No 3 ◿ Fl Y 5s; 51°16'·34N 03°14'·98W.

WATCHET, MINEHEAD and PORLOCK WEIR

Watchet W Bkwtr Hd ⚡ Oc G 3s 9m 9M; 51°11'·03N 03°19'·74W.

Watchet E Pier ⚡ 2 FR (vert) 3M; 51°11'·01N 03°19'·71W.

Minehead Bkwtr Hd ⚡ Fl(2) G 5s 4M; 51°12'·81N 03°28'·35W.

Lynmouth Foreland ☆ 51°14'·73N 03°47'·21W Fl (4) 15s 67m **18M**; W ○ twr; vis: 083°-275°; (H24).

LYNMOUTH and WATERMOUTH

River Training Arm ⚡ 2 FR (vert) 6m 5M; 51°13'·90N 03°49'·83W.

Harbour Arm ⚡ 2 FG (vert) 6m 5M; 51°13'·92N 03°49'·84W.

Sand Ridge ◣ Q G; 51°15'·01N 03°49'·77W.

Copperas Rock ◣ Fl G 2·5s; 51°13'·78N 04°00'·60W.

Watermouth ⚡ Oc WRG 5s 1m 3M; W △; vis: 149·5°-G-151·5°-W-   154·5°-R-156·5°;   51°12'·93N 04°04'·60W.

ILFRACOMBE to BAGGY POINT

Ldg Lts 188°. Front, Oc 10s 8m 3M; 51°12'·53N 04°06'·65W. Rear, Oc 10s 6m 3M.

Horseshoe ⨳ Q; 51°15'·03N 04°12'·96W; AIS.

Bull Point ☆ 51°11'·94N 04°12'·09W Fl (3) 10s 54m **20M**; W ○ twr, obscd shore-056°. Same twr; FR 48m 12M; vis: 058°-096°.

Morte Stone ◣ Fl G 5s; 51°11'·30N 04°14'·95W.

Baggy Leap ◣ Fl(2) G 10s; 51°08'·92N 04°16'·97W.

		1		12	64	66	122	164	192	224	254	286	299	318	361	Kilrush	12
1	Aberystwyth	1			11	13	69	111	139	171	201	233	246	265	308	Dingle	11
2	Fishguard	40	2			10	56	102	131	165	188	227	242	252	295	Valentia	10
3	Milford Haven	84	48	3			9	42	70	102	132	164	177	196	239	Baltimore	9
4	Tenby	107	71	28	4			8	35	69	95	135	150	168	202	Kinsale	8
5	Swansea	130	94	55	36	5			7	34	65	100	115	133	172	Youghal	7
6	Cardiff	161	125	86	66	46	6			6	32	69	84	102	139	Dunmore East	6
7	Sharpness	192	156	117	106	75	33	7			5	34	47	66	108	Rosslare	5
8	Avonmouth	175	139	100	89	58	20	18	8			4	15	36	75	Arklow	4
9	Burnham-on-Sea	169	133	94	70	48	53	50	33	9			3	21	63	Wicklow	3
10	Ilfracombe	128	92	53	35	25	44	74	57	45	10			2	48	Dun Laoghaire	2
11	Padstow	142	106	70	70	76	97	127	110	98	55	11			1	Carlingford Lough	1
12	Longships	169	133	105	110	120	139	169	152	140	95	50	12				

BIDEFORD, RIVERS TAW and TORRIDGE
Bideford Fairway ⚓ L Fl 10s; *Bell;* 51°05'·25N 04°16'·25W.
Bideford Bar ⚓ Q G; 51°04'·89N 04°14'·62W.
Instow ☆ Ldg Lts 118°. **Front,** 51°03'·62N 04°10'·66W Oc
6s 22m **15M**; vis: 103·5°-132°. **Rear,** 427m from front, Oc
10s 38m **15M**; vis: 103°-132·5°; (H24).

Crow Pt ⚡ Fl WR 2. 5s 8m W6M R5M; vis: 225°-R-232°-
W-237°-R-358°-W- 015°-R-045°; 51°03'·96N 04°11'·39W.

LUNDY
North Pt ☆ 51°12'·10N 04°40'·65W Fl 15s 48m **18M**; vis:
009°-285°.
South East Pt ☆ 51°09'·72N 04°39'·37W Fl 5s 53m **15M**;
vis: 170°-073°.
Hartland Point ⚡ Fl (6) 15s 30m 8M;
adjacent to Hartland Point Light House (disused).

NORTH CORNWALL
BUDE, PADSTOW and NEWQUAY
Compass Pt twr 50°49'·71N 04°33'·42W.

Stepper Pt (Padstow) ⚡ LFl 10s 12m 4M; 50°34'·12N
04°56'·72W.
Middle Gnd (Padstow) ⚑ Fl(2+1)R 10s; 50°32'·84N
04°55'·96W.
Trevose Head ☆ 50°32'·94N 05°02'·13W Fl 7·5s 62m **21M**.
North Pier Hd (Newquay) ⚡ 2 FG (vert) 5m 2M; 50°25'·07N
05°05'·19W.

HAYLE and ST IVES
The Stones ⚓ Q; 50°15'·64N 05°25'·51W.
Godrevy I ⚡ Fl WR 10s 28m 8M; metal post; vis:
022°-W-101°-R-145°-W-272°; 50°14'·56N 05°24'·01W;
adjacent to Godrevy Light House (disused).
Hayle App ⚑ QR; 50°12'·26N 05°26'·30W.
St Ives App ▲ 50°12'·85N 05°28'·42W.
Bann Shoal ⚓ Fl G 2.5s; *Racon (B) 10M;* 50°20'·03N
05°51'·11W; 992501053.
Pendeen ☆ 50°09'·90N 05°40'·30W Fl (4) 15s 59m **16M**;
vis: 042°-240°; between Gurnard Hd and Pendeen it
shows to coast.

AREA 10 *Ireland – Clockwise from Lambay Island*
SELECTED LIGHTS, BUOYS & WAYPOINTS

LAMBAY ISLAND TO TUSKAR ROCK
MALAHIDE and LAMBAY ISLAND
Taylor Rks ⚓ Q; 53°30'·21N 06°01'·87W.
Burren Rocks ▲ Fl G 5s; 53°29'·33N 06°02'·37W.
Malahide approach ⚑ L Fl 10s; 53°27'·12N 06°06'·87W.

HOWTH
Rowan Rocks ⚓ Q (3) 10s; 53°23'·88N 06°03'·27W.
Howth ▲ 53°23.727'N 006°03.593'W; 992501250.
E Pier Hd ⚡ Fl (2) WR 7.5s 13m W12M, R9M; W twr; vis:
W256°- R295°-256°; 53°23'·64N 06°04'·02W.
Baily ☆ 53°21'·69N 06°03'·16W Fl 15s 41m **18M**; twr. Fog
Det Lt VQ; 992501010.
Rosbeg E ⚓ Q (3) 10s; 53°21'·02N 06°03'·45W.
Rosbeg S ⚓ Q (6) + L Fl 15s; 53°20'·22N 06°04'·17W.

PORT OF DUBLIN
Dublin Bay ⚓ Iso 4s; *Racon (M);* 53°19'·92N 06°04'·65W;
992351301.
No 1 ▲ Fl (3) G 5s; 53°20'·30N 06°05'·56W.
No 3 ▲ Q G; 53°20'·59N 06°06'·78W.
No 4 ⚑ Q R; 53°20'·39N 06°06'·81W.
No 5 ▲ Fl G 2s; 53°20'·64N 06°08'·60W.
No 6 ⚑ Fl R 2s; 53°20'·56N 06°08'·75W.
Great S Wall Hd Poolbeg ⚡ Fl R 4s 20m 10M (*sync with
N.Bull*); R ○ twr; 53°20'·52N 06°09'·08W.
N Bull ⚡ Fl G 4s 15m 10M; G ○ twr; 53°20'·70N
06°08'·98W.
N Bank ☆ 53°20'·69N 06°10'·59W Oc G 8s 10m **16M**;
G □ twr.

DUN LAOGHAIRE
E Bkwtr Hd ⚡ Fl (2) R 8s 16m **17M**; granite twr, R lantern
7M; 53°18'·14N 06°07'·62W. Fog Det Lt VQ.
Outfall ⚑ Fl Y 5s; 53°18'·41N 06°08'·35W.
Muglins ⚡ Fl R 5s 14m 11M; 53°16'·52N 06°04'·58W;
992501019.

OFFSHORE MARKS
Bennett Bank ⚓ Q(6)+ L Fl 15s; 53°20'·17N 05°55'·11W;
992501012.
Kish Bank ☆ 53°18'·65N 05°55'·54W Fl (2) 20s 29m **21M**
(H24); W twr, R band; *Racon (T) 15M;* 992501017.
N Kish ⚓ VQ; 53°18'·56N 05°56'·44W.
E Kish ⚑ Fl (2) R 10s; 53°14'·35N 05°53'·56W; 992501020.
N Burford ⚓ Q 53°20.51'N 06° 01'.49W; 992501016.
S Burford ⚓ VQ(6)+L Fl 10s; 53°18'.06N 06° 01.30'W;
992501018.
E Codling ⚑ Fl (4) R 10s; 53°08'·54N 05°46'·07W;
992501024.
W Codling ▲ Fl G 10s; 53°06'·97N 05°54'·51W.
Moulditch ⚑ Fl R 10s; 53°08'·43N 06°01'·23W; 992501022.
S Codling ⚓ VQ (6) + L Fl 10s; 53°04'·54N 05°49'·13W.
Codling ⚓ Q(3) 10s; 53°04.19'N 005°37.36'W, *Racon (G)
10M,* 992501028.
Breaches Shoal ⚑ Fl (2) R 6s; 53°05'·67N 05°59'·81W.
North India ⚓ Q; 53°03'·12N 05°53'·46W.
S India ⚓ Q (6) + L Fl 15s; 53°00'·36N 05°53'·31W;
992501030.

WICKLOW to ARKLOW
Wicklow ⚑ Fl (4) Y 10s; 52°59'·54N 06°01'·29W.
E Pier Hd ⚡ Fl WR 5s 11m 6M; W twr, R base and cupola;
vis: 136°-R-293°-W-136°; 52°58'·99N 06°02'·07W.
W Packet Quay Hd ⚡ Fl WG 10s 5m 6M; vis:
076°-G-256°-W-076°; 52°58'·88N 06°02'·08W.
Wicklow Hd ☆ 52°57'·93N 05°59'·93W Fl (3) 15s 37m
18M; W twr; 992501031.
Horseshoe ⚑ Fl R 3s; 52°56'·84N 05°58'·47W; 992501032.
N Arklow ⚓ Q; 52°53'·86N 05°55'·21W; 992501034.
Arklow Bank Wind Farm from 52°48'·47N 05°56'·57W
to 52°46'·47N 05°57'·11W, N and S Turbines Fl Y 5s14m
10M. No 7 Turbine 992501302. Other turbines Fl Y 5s.

ARKLOW to WEXFORD

S Pier Hd ☆ Fl WR 6s 11m 13M; twr; vis: R shore- W223°-R350°-shore; 52°47'·61N 06°08'·22W.

Roadstone Bkwtr Hd ☆ QY; 52°46'·65N 06°08'·23W.

S Arklow ⚓ Q (6) + LFl 15s; *Racon (O) 10M*; 52°40'·20N 05°58'·89W; 992501040.

2 Glassgorman ⚓ Fl (4)R 10s; 52°45'·35N 06°05'·34W; 992501038

1 Glassgorman ⚓ Fl (2) R 6s; 52°37'·69N 06°07'·46W.

Courtown ☆ Fl R 5s 2m 3M; twr; 52°38'·61N 06°13'·45W.

Courtown ☆ Fl G 5s 2m 3M; twr; 52°38'·61N 06°13'·45W.

Blackwater ⚓ Q; 52°32'·22N 06°09'·51W; 992501046.

No 6 Rusk ⚓ Fl R 3s; 52°32'·65N 06°10'·41W.

No 4 Rusk ⚓ Fl (2) R 5s; 52°31'·07N 06°10'·86W.

No 2 Rusk ⚓ Fl (2) R 5s (sync); 52°28'·61N 06°12'·66W.

No 1 Rusk ▲ Fl (2) G 5s (sync); 52°28'·56N 06°11'·78W; AIS.

W Blackwater ▲ Fl G 6s; 52°25'·87N 06°13'·56W.

SE Blackwater ⚓ Q (3) 10s, 52°25'·64N 06°08'·42W; *Racon (M) 6M*; 992501050.

S Blackwater ⚓ Q (6) + L Fl 15s; 52°22'·76N 06°12'·87W.

North Long ⚓ Q; 52°21'·44N 06°17'·04W.

West Long ▲ QG; 52°18'·18N 06°17'·96W.

Lucifer ⚓ VQ (3) 5s; 52°17'·02N 06°12'·67W; 992501054.

ROSSLARE

S Long ▲ Fl G 6s (sync with Splaugh); 52°14'·74N 06°15'·80W.

Splaugh ⚓ Fl R 6s (sync with S Long); 52°14'·36N 06°16'·78W; 992501062.

S Holdens ▲ Fl G 3s; 52°15'·15N 06°17'·25W. (sync Calmines).

Calmines ⚓ Fl R 3s; 52°15'·00N 06°17'·78W. (sync S Holdens).

W Holdens ▲ Fl (3) G 9s; 52°15'·76N 06°18'·75W.

Rosslare Pier Hd ☆ Oc WRG 5s 15m W13M, R10M, G10M; R twr; vis:098°-G-188°-W-208°-R-246°-G-283°-W-286°-R-320°; 52°15'·43N 06°20'·29W.

Ballygeary ☆ Oc WR 1·7s 7m 4M; vis: shore-R-152°-W-200°-W(unintens)-205°; 52°15'·25N 06°20'·48W.

TUSKAR ROCK TO OLD HEAD OF KINSALE

Tuskar ☆ 52°12'·17N 06°12'·44W Q (2) 7·5s 33m **24M**; W twr; *Racon (T) 18M*; 992501065.

S Rock ⚓ Q (6)+L Fl 15s; 52°10'·80N 06°12'·84W.

Fundale ⚓ Fl (2) R 10s; 52°11'·04N 06°19'·78W.

Barrels ⚓ Q (3) 10s; 52°08'·32N 06°22'·05W; 992501070.

KILMORE

Kilmore Quay SWM ⚓ Iso 10s; (Apr-Sep); 52°09'·20N 06°35'·30W.

Kilmore Bkwtr Hd ☆ Q RG 7m 5M; vis: 269°-R-354°-G-003°-R-077°; 52°10'·20N 06°35'·15W.

Ldg lts 007·9°, Front 52°10'·37N 06°35'·08W Oc 4s 3m 6M. Rear, 100m from front, Oc 4s 6m 6M; sync with front.

Bore Rks ⚓ Q (3) 10s; 52°06.07'N 006°31.87'W; 992501072.

Coningbeg ⚓ Q(6)+LFl 15s; 52°03'·20N 06°38'·57W; *Racon (G) 9M*; 992501074.

Red Bank ⚓ VQ (9) 10s; 52°04.499'N 006°41.652'W; 992501076.

'M5' ODAS 35 ⬡ 51°41'·40N 06°42'·24W; Fl (5) Y 20s.

WATERFORD

Hook Hd ☆ 52°07'·42N 06°55'·76W Fl 3s 46m **18M**; W twr, two B bands; *Racon (K) 10M*. Fog Det Lt VQ. 992501079.

Waterford ⚓ Fl R 3s. Fl (3) R 10s; 52°08'·95N 06°57'·00W.

Duncannon Dir lt ☆ F WRG 13m 10M, white tower on fort, 359·5°-FG-001·2°-Alt GW-001·7°-FW-002·4°-Alt WR-002·9°-FR-004·5°; 52°13'·23N 06°56'·25W; Oc WR 4s 13m W 9M R 7M on same tower, 119°-R-149°-W-172°.

Passage Pt ☆ Fl WR 5s 7m W6M, R5M; R pile structure; vis: 114°-W-127°-R-180°-W-302°-R-021° (shore); 52°14'·26N 06°57'·77W.

Cheek Pt ☆ Q WR 6m 5M; W mast; vis: W007°-R289°-007°; 52°16'·12N 06°59'·38W.

Sheagh ☆ Fl R 3s 29m 3M; Gy twr; vis: 090°-318°; 52°16'·29N 06°59'·34W.

Snowhill Point Ldg lts 255°. Front, Fl WR 2·5s 5m 3M; vis: W222°- R020°- W057°-107°; 52°16'·39N 07°00'·91W. Rear, Flour Mill, 750m from front, Q 12m 5M.

Queen's Chan Ldg lts 098°. Front, QR 8m 5M; B twr, W band; vis: 030°-210°;52°15'·32N 07°02'·38W. Rear, 550m from front, Q 15m 5M; W mast.

Beacon Quay ☆ Fl G 3s 9m; vis: 255°-086°; 52°15'·50N 07°04'·21W.

Cove ☆ Fl WRG 6s 6m 2M; W twr; vis: R111°-G161°-W234°-111°; 52°15'·05N 07°05'·16W.

Smelting Ho Pt ☆ Q 8m 3M; W mast; 52°15'·15N 07°05'·27W.

Ballycar ☆ Fl RG 3s 5m; vis: G127°-R212°-284°; 52°15'·06N 07°05'·51W.

DUNMORE EAST

East Pier Head ☆ 52°08'·93N 06°59'·34W Fl WR 8s 13m **W17M**, R13M; Gy twr, vis: W225°- R310°-004°.

Dunmore East 1 ▲ Q G; 52°09'·06N 06°59'·38W.

Dunmore East 2 ▲ Fl G 2s; 52°09'·00N 06°59'·47W.

W Wharf ☆ Fl G 2s 6m 4M; vis: 165°-246°; 52°08'·97N 06°59'·45W.

DUNGARVAN

Ballinacourty Pt ☆ Fl (2) WRG 10s 16m W10M, R8M, G8M; W twr; vis: G245°- W274°- R302°- W325°-117°; 52°04'·69N 07°33'·18W.

Helvick ⚓ Q (3) 10s; 52°03'·61N 07°32'·25W.

Mine Head ☆ 51°59'·56N 07°35'·23W Fl (4) 30s 87m 12M; W twr, B band; vis: 228°-052°; 992501085.

YOUGHAL

Bar Rocks ⚓ Q (6) + L Fl 15s; 51°54'·85N 07°50'·05W.

Blackball Ledge ⚓ Q (3) 10s, 51°55'·34N 07°48'·53W.

W side of ent ☆ 51°56'·57N 07°50'·53W Fl WR 2·5s 24m **W17M**, R13M; W twr; vis: W183°- R273°- W295°- R307°-W351°-003°.

BALLYCOTTON

Ballycotton ☆ 51°49'·50N 07° 59'·13W; Fl WR 10s 59m **W18M**, R14M; B twr, within W walls, B lantern; vis: 238°-W-041°-R-238°; 992501093.

The Smiths ⚓ Fl (3) R 10s; 51°48'·43N 08°00'·60W.

Power ⚓ Q (6) + L Fl 15s; 51°45'·59N 08°06'·67W; 992501098.

CORK

Cork ⚓ L Fl 10s; 51°42'·92N 08°15'·60W; *Racon (T) 7M*; 992501100.

Daunt Rock ⚓ Fl (2) R 6s; 51°43'·53N 08°17'·50W; 992501102.

Fort Davis Ldg lts 354·5°. **Front**, 51°48'·83N 08°15'·79W, H24 Dir WRG 25m **17M**; vis: 351·5°-FG-352·5°-QG-353·5°-FW-355·5°-QR-356·5°-FR-357·5°. Rear, Dognose Quay, 203m from front, Oc 5s 37m 10M; Or 3, sync with front.

Roche's Pt ☆ 51°47'·58N 08°15'·29W Fl WR 3s 30m **W18M**, R12M; vis: shore-R-292°-W-016°-R-033°, 033°- W (unintens)-159°-R-shore; 992501099.

Outer Hbr Rk E2 ⌐ Fl R 2·5s; 51°47'·52N 08°15'·67W.

Chicago Knoll E1 ▲ Fl G 5s; 51°47'·66N 08°15'·54W.

W1 ▲ Fl G 10s; 51°47'·69N 08°16'·05W.

W2 ⌐ Fl R 10s; 51°47'·69N 08°16'·34W.

White Bay Ldg lts 034·6°. Front, Oc R 5s 11m 5M; W hut; 51°48'·53N 08°15'·22W. Rear, 113m from front, Oc R 5s 21m 5M; W hut; synch with front.

Spit Bank Pile ⚡ Iso WR 4s 10m W10M, R7M; W house on R piles; vis: R087°- W196°- R221°- 358°; 51°50'·72N 08°16'·45W.

KINSALE and OYSTER HAVEN

Bulman ⚓ Q (6) + L Fl 15s; 51°40'·14N 08°29'·74W; 992501104.

Charlesfort ⚡ Fl WRG 5s 18m W9M, R6M, G7M; vis: G348°- W358°- R004°-168°; H24; 51°41'·75N 08°29'·84W.

OLD HEAD OF KINSALE TO MIZEN HEAD

Old Head of Kinsale ☆, S point 51°36'·29N 08°32'·02W Fl (2) 10s 72m **20M**; B twr, two W bands; 992501107.

COURTMACSHERRY

Barrel Rock ⌓ 51°37'·01N 08°37'·30W.

Black Tom ▲ Fl G 5s; 51°36'·41N 08°37'·95W; 992501110.

Wood Pt (Land Pt) ⚡ Fl (2) WR 5s 15m 5M; vis: W315°-R332°-315°; 51°38'·16N 08°41'·00W.

Galley Head ☆ summit 51°31'·80N 08°57'·21W Fl (5) 20s 53m **23M**; W twr; vis: 256°-065°.

GLANDORE and CASTLETOWNSHEND

Glandore Dir lt ⚡ Oc WRG 37m 7M, metal tower, vis: 294°-G-304°-W-312°-R-342°; 51°33'·33N 09°07'·08W.

Reen Point ⚡ Fl WRG 10s 9m W5M, R3M, G3M; W twr; vis: shore-G-338°-W-001°-R-shore; 51°30'·98N 09°10'·50W.

Kowloon Bridge ⚓ Q(6)+LFl 15s; 51°27'·58N 09°13'·75W; 992501118.

BALTIMORE and FASTNET

Barrack Pt ⚡ Fl (2) WR 6s 40m W6M, R3M; vis: R168°-W294°-038°; 51°28'·33N 09°23'·65W.

Loo Rock ▲ Fl G 3s; 51°28'·44N 09°23'·46W; 992501119.

Lousy Rks ⌓ Q(6)+LFl 15s; 51°28'·93N 09°23'·39W.

Wallis Rk ⌐ Fl (3) R 10s; 51°28'·93N 09°22'·99W.

Lettuce Pt ⚓ VQ (3) 5s; 51°29'·32N 09°23'·81W.

Mealbeg ⚓ Q(6) + LFl 15s; 51°29'·68N 09°24'·69W.

Inane Pt ⚓ Q(6) + LFl 15s; 51°30'·02N 09°23'·66W.

Hare Is ⚓ Q; 51°30'·17N 09°25'·38W.

Fastnet ☆, W end 51°23'·36N 09°36'·18W Fl 5s 53m **18M**; Gy twr, **Racon (G) 18M**. Fog Det Lt VQ; 992501123.

SCHULL and LONG ISLAND CHANNEL

Amelia ▲; 51°29.979'N 009°31.461'W; 992501120.

Copper Point ⚡ Fl 51°30'·25N 09°32'·06W Q (3) 10s 16m 8M.

Ldg lts 346° Front, Oc 5s 5m 11M, W mast; 51°31'·68N 09°32'·43W. Rear, 91m from front, Oc 5s 8m11M; W mast.

CROOKHAVEN

Rock Is Pt ⚡ L Fl WR 8s 20m W13M, R11M; W twr; vis: W over Long Is B to 281°-R-340°; inside harbour 281°-R-348°-towards N shore; 51°28'·59N 09°42'·27W; 992501124.

MIZEN HEAD TO DINGLE BAY

Mizen Head ⚡ Iso 4s 55m 12M; vis: 313°-133°; 51°26'·99N 09°49'·23W; 992501127.

Sheep's Hd ☆ 51°32'·59N 09°50'·92W Fl (3) WR 15s 83m **W15M** R9M; W bldg; vis: 011·3°-R-016·6°-W-212·5°-(partially obs) 233° (shore); 992501129.

BANTRY BAY, CASTLETOWN BEARHAVEN, WHIDDY IS

Carrigavaddra ⚓ VQ (3) 5s, 51°38'·72N 09°45'·91W.

Roancarrigmore ⚡ Fl WR 5s 13m W11M, R9M, R5M; s/steel twr; vis: 312°-W-050°-R-122°-R(unintens)-207°-obsc-246°-R-312°; 51°39'·18N 09°44'·82W. Old Lt ho W twr, B band; 992501130.

Ardnakinna Pt ⚡ 51°37'·10N 09°55'·09W Fl (2) WR 10s 62m W14M, R9M; W ○ twr; vis: 319°-R-348°-W-066°-R-shore; 992501131.

Walter Scott Rk ⚓ Q (6) + L Fl 15s; 51°38'·52N 09°54'·20W; 992501128.

Castletownbere Dir lt 023·25° ⚡ Oc WRG 5s 5·7m WRG15M; Twr; vis: 020·5°-G-023°-W-023·5°-R-025·5°; 51°38'·73N 09°54'·35W; 992501125.

Castletown Ldg lts 008°. Front, Oc Bu 6s 4m 6M; W col, R stripe; vis: 005°-013°; 51°39'·16N 09°54'·40W. Rear, 80m from front, Oc Bu 6s 7m 6M; W with R stripe; vis: 005°-013°.

Bull Rock ☆ 51°35'·52N 10°18'·07W Fl 15s 91m **18M**; W twr; 992501131.

KENMARE RIVER, DARRYNANE and BALLYCROVANE

Illaunnameanla (Ballycrovane) ⚡ Fl R 3s; 51°42'·60N 09°57'·50W.

Book Rks ⌐ Fl(2) R 10s; 51°46'·54N 09°49'·74W.

Cuskeal ⌐ Fl R 5s; 51°46'·45N 09°48'·85W.

Bunaw Ldg Lts 041°. Front, Oc R 3s 9m 2M; B col, Y bands; 51°46'·80N 09°48'·40W. Rear, 200m from front Iso R 2s 11m 2M.

Maiden Rk ▲ Fl G 5s; 51°49'·00N 09°47'·99W; 992501134.

Bat Rk ▲ Fl G 5s; 51°50'·89N 09°40'·89W.

Carrignaronebeg ⌐ Fl R 5s; 51°50'·99N 09°41'·39W.

No1 ▲ Fl G 5s; 51°52'·09N 09°36'·35W.

Carrignarone (Seal Rk) Fl 5s 2m 2M; 51°48'·58N 09°52'·65W.

Castlecove Ldg Lts 045°. Front, Oc 2s 5m 6M; concrete post W front; 51°46'·29N 10°02'·04W. Rear, 400m from front Oc 2s 18m 6M.

West Cove Hbr ⚡ Fl R 3s; post W front; 51°46'·00N 10°02'·93W.

West Cove Hbr Ldg Lts 312°. Front, Fl 2s 6M; concrete post; 51°46'·11N 10°03'·08W. Rear, 200m from front Fl 2s 4m 6M.

Darrynane Ldg lts 034°. Front, Oc 3s 10m 4M; 51°45'·90N 10°09'·20W. Rear, Oc 3s 16m 4M.

SKELLIG ISLANDS

Skelligs Rock ⚡ Fl (3) 15s 53m 12M; W twr; vis: 262°-115°; part obsc within 6M 110°-115°; 51°46'·11N 10°32'·52W; 992501137.

VALENTIA and PORTMAGEE

Fort (Cromwell) Point ☆ 51°56'·02N 10°19'·27W Fl WR 2s 16m **W17M, R10M**; W twr; vis: 304°-R-351°,104°-W-304°; obsc from seaward by Doulus Head when brg more than 180°; 992501141.

Dir lt 141° ⚡ Oc WRG 4s 25m W11M, R8M, G8M (by day: W3M, R2M, G2M); W twr, R stripe; vis:136°-G-140°-W-142°-R-146°; 51°55'·51N 10°18'·42W.

The Foot ⬨ VQ (3) 5s; 51°55'·72N 10°17'·07W; 992501140.

DINGLE BAY TO LOOP HEAD

DINGLE BAY, VENTRY and DINGLE

Lt Twr ⚡ Fl WRG 3s 20m WRG 6M; W metal twr; vis: 310°-G-328°-W-000°-R-024°; 52°07'·30N 10°15'·51W.

Dingle Hbr ⚡ Fl (2) 3s 6m 3M, 52 07·24 N 10 15·71 W.

Foheragh Dir Lt ⚡ 182° Oc WRG 5s 8 2 Pole; vis:177°-Oc R-181°-Oc W-183°-Oc G-187°, 52 07·43 N 10 16·59 W.

Dingle Dir Lt ⚡ 002° Oc WRG 5s 14 3 Mast; vis: 354°-Oc G-001°-Oc W-003°-Oc R-009°, 52 08·34 N 10 16·52 W.

Inishtearaght ☆, W end Blasket Islands 52°04'·54N 10°39'·67W Fl (2) 20s 84m **18M**; W twr; vis: 318°-221°; *Racon (O)*; 992501143.

BRANDON BAY, TRALEE BAY and FENIT HARBOUR

Lit Samphire Is ⚡ Fl WRG 5s 17m W14M, RG11M; Bu ○ twr; vis: 262°-R-275°, 280°-R-090°-G-140°-W-152°-R-172°; 52°16'·26N 09°52'·91W.

Gt Samphire Is ⚡ QR 15m 3M; vis: 242°-097°; 52°16'·15N 09°51'·81W.

Fenit Hbr Pier Hd ⚡ 2 FR (vert) 12m 3M; vis: 148°-058°; 52°16'·24N 09°51'·55W.

SHANNON ESTUARY

Ballybunnion ⬨ VQ; *Racon (M) 6M*; 52°32'·52N 09°46'·93W; 992501146.

Kilstiffin ⌁ Fl R 3s; 52°33'·80N 09°43'·83W; 992501148.

Kilcredaun ⌁ Q R (sync); 52°34'·42N 09°41'·16W.

Tail of Beal ▲ Q G (sync); 52°34'·37N 09°40'·71W; 992501150.

Kilcredaun Head ◻, W twr; 52°34'·78N 09°42'·58W.

Carrigaholt ⌁ Fl (2) R 6s (sync); 52°34'·90N 09°40'·47W.

Beal Spit ▲ Fl (2) G 6s (sync); 52°34'·80N 09°39'·94W.

Beal Bar ▲ Fl G 3s (sync); 52°35'·18N 09°39'·05W.

Doonaha ⌁ Fl R 3s (sync); 52°35'·54N 09°39'·01W; 992501154.

Corlis Pt (Ldg lts 046·4° H24) ⚡ Front, Iso 4s 9m 7M(day) 10M; hut; 52°37'·10N 09°36'·36W; 992501156.

Querrin Pt ⚡ Rear, Iso 4s 28m 7M(day) 10M; lattice mast; 52°37'·69N 09°35'·34W.

Letter Point ⌁ Fl R 7s; 52°35'·44N 09°35'·89W.

Asdee ⌁ Fl R 5s; 52°35'·09N 09°34'·55W.

Rineanna ⌁ QR; 52°35'·59N 09°31'·24W.

North Carraig ⬨ Q; 52°35'·60N 09°29'·76W.

Scattery Is, Rineanna Pt ⚡ Fl (2) 8s 15m 10M; W twr; vis: 208°-092°; 52°36'·35N 09°31'·07W.

KILRUSH

Marina Ent Chan Ldg lts 355°. Front, Oc 3s; 52°37'·99N 09°30'·27W. Rear, 75m from front, Oc 3s.

Tarbert Is N Point ⚡ Q WR 4s 18m W14M, R10M; W ○ twr; vis: W069°-R277°-W287°-339°; 52°35'·52N 09°21'·83W.

Tarbert (Ballyhoolahan Pt) Ldg lts 128·2° ⬩. Front, Iso 3s 13m 3M; △ on W twr; vis: 123·2°-133·2°; 52°34'·35N 09°18'·80W. Rear, 400m from front, Iso 5s 18m 3M; G stripe on W Bn.

Garraunbaun Pt ⚡ Fl (3) WR 10s 16m W8M, R5M; W ◻ col, vis: R shore - W072°- R242°- shore; 52°35'·62N 09°13'·94W.

Rinealon Pt ⚡ Fl 2·5s 4m 7M; B col, W bands; vis: 234°-088°; 52°37'·12N 09°09'·82W.

FOYNES

W Chan Ldg lts 107·9° (may be moved for changes in chan). Front, Oc 4s 34m 12M; 52°36'·91N 09°06'·59W . Rear, Oc 4s 39m 12M.

RIVER SHANNON

Beeves Rock ⚡ Fl WR 5s 12m W12M, R9M; vis: 064·5°-W-091°-R-238°-W-265°-W(unintens)-064·5°; 52°39'·01N 09°01'·35W .

N Channel Ldg lts 093°. Front, Tradree Rock Fl R 2s 6m 5M; W Trs; vis: 246°-110°; 52°41'·00N 08°49'·87W. Rear 0·65M from front, Iso 6s 14m 5M; W twr, R bands; vis: 327°-190°.

N side, Ldg lts 061°. Front, 52°40'·72N 08°45'·27W, Crawford Rock 490m from rear, Fl R 3s 6m 5M. Crawford No 2, Common Rear, Iso 6s 10m 5M; 52°40'·85N 08°44'·88W.

Ldg lts 302·1°, Flagstaff Rock, 670m from rear, Fl R 7s 7m 5M; 52°40'·66N 08°44'·40W.

Ldg lts 106·5°. Meelick Rk, Front Iso R 4s 6m 5M; 52°40'·24N 08°42'·32W. Meelick No 2, rear 275m from front Iso R 4s 9m 5M; both W beacons.

LOOP HEAD

Loop Head ☆ 52°33'·67N 09°55'·92W Fl (4) 20s 84m **23M**; vis: 280°-218°; 992501161.

Mal Bay ⬨ Fl(5) Y 20s 52°46.42'N 009°35.15'W; *AIS*.

LISCANNOR BAY TO SLYNE HEAD

GALWAY BAY and INISHMORE

Eeragh, Rock Is ☆ 53°08'·91N 09°51'·39W Fl 15s 35m **18M**; W twr, two B bands; vis: 297°-262°; 992501172.

Straw Is ⚡ Fl (2) 5s 11m 12M; W twr; 53°07'·08N 09°37'·82W.

Killeany Ldg lts 192°. Front, Oc 5s 6m 3M; W col on W ◻ base; vis: 142°-197°, 53°06'·25N 09°39'·74W. Rear, 43m from front, Oc 5s 8m 2M; W col on W ◻ base; vis: 142°-197°.

Inishmaan, Ldg lts 199°, Oc 6s 8M; 53°06'·08N 09°34'·77W.

Killeaney ▲ Fl G 3s; 53°07.33'N 009°38.37'W; 992501166.

Inisheer ☆ 53°02'·76N 09°31'·61W Iso WR 12s 34m **W16M**, R11M; vis: 225°-W(partially vis >7M)-231°, 231°-W-245°-R-269°-W-115°; *Racon (K) 13M*; 992501165.

Finnis ⬨ Q (3) 10s; 53°02'·82N 09°29'·14W, 992501164.

Black Hd ⚡ Fl WR 5s 20m W11M, R8M, W ◻ twr; vis: 045°- R268°-276°; 53°09'·25N 09°15'·83W.

GALWAY

Margaretta Shoal ▲ Fl G 3s (sync); *Whis*; 53°13'·68N 09°05'·99W, 992501170.

Black Rk ⌁ Fl R 3s (sync); 53°14'·00N 09°06'·55W.

Leverets ⚡ Q WRG 9m 10M; B ◻ twr, W bands; vis: 015°-G-058°-W-065°-R-103°-G-143·5°-W-146·5°-R-015°; 53°15'·33N 09°01'·90W.

Rinmore ⚡ Iso WRG 4s 7m 5M; W ◻ twr; vis: 359°-G-008°-W-018°-R-027°; 53°16'·12N 09°01'·97W.

Appr Chan Dir lt 325°, WRG 7m 3M; vis: 322·25°-FG-323·75°-AlGW-324·75°-FW-325·25°-AlRW-326·25°-FR-331·25°-FlR-332·25°; 53°16'·12N 09°02'·83W.

GALWAY to SLYNE HEAD

Barna Quay Hd ⚡ Fl 2 WRG 5s 6m W8M, R5M, G5M; vis:250°-G-344·5°-W-355·5°-R-090°; 53°14'·93N 09°08'·90W.

Spiddle Pier Hd ⚡ Fl WRG 3·5s 11m W8M, R8M, G8M; Y col; vis: 265°-G-308°-W-024°-R-066°; 53°14'·42N 09°18'·54M.

Cashla Bay Ent, W side ⚡ Fl (3) WR 10s 8m W6M, R3M; W col on concrete twr; vis: 216°-W-000°-R-069°; 53°14'·23N 09°35'·20W.

Cannon Rk ▲ Fl G 5s; 53°14'·08N 09°34'·35W, 992501173.

Lion Pt Dir lt 010°, Iso WRG 5s 6m (H24), G6M, W8M, R6M,(night), G2M, W3M, R2M(day); vis: 005°-G-008·5°-W-011·5°-R-015°; 53°15'·83N 09°33'·98W; 992501171.

45

Rossaveel Pier Ldg lts 116°. Front, 53°16'·02N 09°33'·38W Oc 3s 7m 3M; W mast. Rear, 90m from front, Oc 3s 8m 3M.

Kiggaul Bay ⚓ Fl WRG 3s 5m W5M, R3M, G3M; vis: 310°-G-329°-W-349°-R-059°; 53°14'·03N 09°43'·02W.

Croaghnakeela Is ⚓ Fl 3·7s 7m 5M; W col; vis: 034°-045°, 218°-286°, 311°-325°; 53°19'·40N 09°58'·21W.

Inishnee ⚓ Fl (2) WRG 10s 9m W5M, R3M, G3M; W col on W □ base; vis: 314°-G-017°-W-030°-R-080°-W-194°; 53°22'·75N 09°54'·53W.

Slyne Head, North twr, Illaunamid ☆ 53°23'·99N 10°14'·05W Fl (2) 15s 35m **19M**; B twr; *Racon (T)*; 992501175.

SLYNE HEAD TO EAGLE ISLAND

CLIFDEN BAY and INISHBOFIN

Carrickrana Rocks Bn, large W Bn; 53°29'·24N 10°09'·48W.

Cleggan Point ⚓ Fl (3) WRG 15s 20m W6M, R3M, G3M; W col on W hut; vis: shore-G-091°-W-124°-R-221°; 53°34'·48N 10°07'·69W.

Inishlyon Lyon Head ⚓ Fl WR 7·5s 13m W7M, R4M; W post; vis: 036°-W-058°-R-184°-W-325°-R-036°; 53°36'·74N 10°09'·56W.

Gun Rk ⚓ Fl (2)6s 8m 4M; W col on W hut; vis: 296°-253°; 53°36'·59N 10°13'·22W.

Inishbofin Dir lt 021°, Oc WRG 6s 10m 11M; W pole; vis: 015·75°-G-020·75°-W-021·25°-R-026·25°; 53°36'·78N 10°13'·16W.

CLEW BAY and WESTPORT

Roonagh Quay Ldg lts 144°. Front 53°45'·75N 09°54'·23W. Rear, 54m from front, both Iso Bu 10s 9/15m.

Inishgort ⚓ L Fl 10s 10M; 53°49.59'N 009°40.25'W; 992501179.

Cloughcormick ⚓ Q (9) 15s; 53°50'·56N 09°43'·20W.

Achillbeg I, S Point ☆ 53°51'·51N 09°56'·84W Fl WR 5s 56m **W16M, R18M,** R11M; W ○ twr on □ building; vis: 262°-R-281°-W-342°-R-060°-W-092°-R(intens)-099°-W-118°; 992501181.

ACHILL SOUND

Ldg lts 330°, 53°52'·50N 09°56'·89W Whitestone Point. Front and rear both Oc 4s 5/6m; W ◊, B stripe.

Achill I Ldg lts 310°, Purteen, Oc 8s 5m; 53°57'·81N 10°05'·96W. Rear, 46m from front Oc 8s 6m.

BLACKSOD BAY

Blacksod ⚓ Q (3) 10s; 54°05'·89N 10°03'·01W.

Blacksod Pier Root ⚓ Fl (2) WR 7·5s 13m W12M, R9M; W twr on bldg; vis: 189°-R-210°-W-018°; 54°05'·92N 10°03'·63W; 992501186.

Carrigeenmore ⚓ VQ(3) 5s 3M; 54°06'·56N 10°03'·4W.

Black Rock ☆ 54°04'·06N 10°19'·23W Fl WR 12s 86m **W20M, R16M;** W twr; vis: 276°-W-212°-R-276°; 992501183.

Eagle Is, W end ☆ 54°17'·02N 10°05'·56W Fl (3) 15s 67m **18M**; W twr; 992501189.

EAGLE ISLAND TO RATHLIN O'BIRNE

BROAD HAVEN BAY

Rinroe Pt ⚓ Fl (2) 10s 5m 3M; 54°17'·83N 09°50'·59W.

Gubacashel Point ⚓ Iso WR 4s 27m **W17M**, R12M; 110°-R-133°-W-355°-R-021° W twr; 54°16'·06N 09°53'·33W.

KILLALA

Carrickpatrick ⚓ Q (3) 10s; 54°15'·56N 09°09'·17W; 992501192.

Inishcrone Pier Root ⚓ Fl WRG 1·5s 8m 2M; vis: 098°-W-116°-G- 136°-R-187°; 54°13'·21N 09°05'·79W.

Ldg lts 230°. Rinnaun Point. Front No 1, Oc 10s 7m 5M; □ twr; 54°13'·21N 09°05'·79W. Rear, 150m from front, No 2 Oc 10s 12m 5M; □ twr.

Inch Is Dir lt 215°, Fl WRG 2s 6m 3M; □ twr; vis: 205°-G-213°-W- 217°-R-225°; 54°13'·29N 09°12'·30W.

Ldg lts 196°. Kilroe. Front, 54°12'·63N 09°12'·33W Oc 4s 5m 2M; □ twr. Rear,120m from front, Oc 10s 4m 2M; □ twr.

Pier Ldg lts 236° Front, Iso Bu 2s 5m 2M; W ◊ on twr; 54°13'·02N 09°12'·84W. Rear, 200m fm front, Iso Bu 2s 7m 2M; W ◊ on pole.

SLIGO

Black Rock ⚓ Fl WR 5s 24m 10/8M; vis: 130°-W-107°-R-130° (R over Wheat + Seal Rks); W twr, B band; 54°18'·46N 08°37'·06W.

Lower Rosses ⚓ Fl (2) WRG 10s 8m 10M; W hut on piles; vis: 061°-G-066°-W-070°-R-075°; shown H24; 54°19'·73N 08°34'·41W.

Ldg lts 125° Fl (3) 6s 7M (sync). Front, Metal Man; 54°18'·24N 08°34'·55W, 3m. Rear, Oyster Is, 365m from front, 13m; H24.

Wheat Rk ⚓ Q (6) + LFl 15s; 54°18'·84N 08°39'·10W; 992501196.

DONEGAL BAY and KILLYBEGS

St John's Pt ⚓ Fl 6s 30m 14M; W twr; 54°34'·16N 08°27'·66W; 992501197.

Bullockmore ⚓ Q (9) 15s; 54°33'·98N 08°30'·14W; 992501198.

Rotten I ☆ 54°36'·97N 08°26'·41W Fl WR 4s 20m **W15M**, R11M; W twr; vis: W255°- R008°- W039°-208°.

New Landing Dir lt 338°, Oc WRG 8s 17m; vis: 328°-G-334°-Al WG-336°-W-340°-Al WR-342°-R-348°; 54°38'·14N 08°26'·38W.

Killybegs Outer ⚓ VQ (6) + L Fl 10s; 54°37'·92N 08°29'·15W.

RATHLIN O'BIRNE TO BLOODY FORELAND

S of ARAN and RUTLAND S CHANNEL

Rathlin O'Birne ⚓ Fl WR 15s 35m W12M, R10M; W twr; vis: 195°-R-307°-W-195°; *Racon (O) 13M*, vis 284°-203°. 54°39'·82N 08°49'·95W; 992501203.

Dawros Head ☆ L Fl 10s 39m 4M; 54°49'·63N 08°33'·64W.

Wyon Point ⚓ Fl (2) WRG 10s 8m W6M, R3M; W □ twr; vis: shore-G-021°-W-042°-R-121°-W-150°-R-shore; 54°56'·51N 08°27'·54W.

BURTONPORT

Ldg lts 068·1°. Front , FG 17m 1M; Gy Bn, W band; 54°58'·95N 08°26'·40W. Rear, 355m from front, FG 23m 1M; Gy Bn, Y band.

N SOUND OF ARAN and RUTLAND N CHANNEL

Rutland I Ldg lts 137·6°. Front, 54°58'·97N 08°27'·68W Oc 6s 8m 1M; W Bn, B band. Rear, 330m from front, Oc 6s 14m 1M.

Inishcoo Ldg lts 119·3°. Front, Iso 6s 6m 1M; W Bn, B band; 54°59'·43N 08°29'·63W. Rear, 248m from front, Iso 6s 11m 1M.

Ldg lts 186°. Front, Oc 8s 8m 3M; B Bn, W band; 54°58'·94N 08°29'·27W. Rear, 395m from front, Oc 8s 17m 3M; B Bn.
Aranmore, Rinrawros Pt ☆ 55°00'·90N 08°33'·69W Fl (2) 20s 71m **18M**; W twr; obsc by land about 234°-007° and about 013°. Auxiliary lt Fl R 3s 61m 13M, same twr; vis: 203°-234°; 992501205.

OWEY SOUND to INISHSIRRER

Cruit Is. Owey Sound Ldg lts 068·3°. Oc 10s. Front, 55°03'·06N 08°25'·85W. Rear, 107m from front.
Rinnalea Point ⚓ 55°02'·59N 08°23'·72W Fl 7·5s 19m 9M; ☐ twr; vis: 132°-167°.
Gola Is Ldg lts 171·2°. Oc 3s 2M (sync). Front, 9m; W Bn, B band; 55°05'·11N 08°21'·07W. Rear, 86m from front, 13m; B Bn, W band.
Glassagh. Ldg lts 137·4°. Front, Oc 8s 12m 3M; 55°06'·83N 08°18'·97W. Rear, 46m from front, Oc 8s 17m 3M; synch.
Inishsirrer, NW end ⚓ Fl 3·7s 20m 4M; W ☐ twr vis: 083°-263°; 55°07'·40N 08°20'·93W.

BLOODY FORELAND TO INISHTRAHULL

BLOODY FORELAND to SHEEPHAVEN

Bloody Foreland ⚓ Fl WG 7·5s 14m W6M, G4M; vis: 062°-W-232°-G-062°; 55°09'·51N 08°17'·03W.
Tory Island ☆ 55°16'·36N 08°14'·96W Fl (4) 30s 40m **18M**; B twr, W band; vis: 302°-277°; *Racon (M) 12-23M;* 992501211.
West Town Ldg lts 001° ⚓ Iso 2s 9m 7M △ on Y structure R stripe; 55°15'·79N 08°13'·50W. Rear Iso 2s 11m 7M ▽ ditto (sync).
Inishbofin Pier ⚓ Fl 8s 3m 3M; 55°10'·14N 08°10'·01W.
Ballyness Hbr. Ldg lts 119·5°. Front, Iso 4s 25m 1M; 55°09'·06N 08°06'·98W. Rear, 61m from front, Iso 4s 26m 1M.
Portnablahy Ldg lts 125·3°. Front Oc 6s 7m 2M; B col, W bands; 55°10'·79N 07°55'·65W. Rear, 81m from front, Oc 6s 12m 2M; B col, W bands.

MULROY BAY

Limeburner ⚓ Q Fl; 55°18'·54N 07°48'·40W; 992501214.
Ravedy Is ⚓ Fl 3s 9m 3M; vis 177°-357°; 55°15'·14N 07°46'·90W.

LOUGH SWILLY, BUNCRANA and RATHMULLAN

Fanad Head ☆ 55°16'·57N 07°37'·92W Fl (5) WR 20s 39m **W18M**, R14M; W twr; vis 100°-R-110°-W-313°-R-345°-W-100°; 992501215.
Swillymore ▲ Fl G 3s; 55°15'·12N 07°35'·79W; 992501216.
Dunree ⚓ Fl (2) WR 5s 49m W12M, R9M; vis: 320°-R-328°-W-183°-R-196°; 55°11'·89N 07°33'·24W; 992501217.
Buncrana Pier near Hd ⚓ Iso WR 4s 11m W13M, R10M; R twr, W band; vis: R shore- over Inch spit, 052°-W-139°-R-shore over White Strand Rock; 55°07'·60N 07°27'·88W.
Rathmullan Pier Hd ⚓ Fl G 3s 5M; vis: 206°-345°; 55°05'·70N 07°31'·66W.
Inishtrahull ☆ 55°25'·89N 07°14'·63W Fl (3) 15s 59m **19M**; W twr; obscd 256°-261° within 3M; *Racon (T) 24M 060°-310°.* Fog Det Lt VQ; 992501229.

INISHTRAHULL TO RATHLIN ISLAND

LOUGH FOYLE

Foyle ⚓ L Fl 10s; 55°15'·32N 06°52'·62W; *Racon (M)*; 992501230.

Tuns ⚓ Fl R 3s; 55°14'·00N 06°53'·46W; 992501232.
Inishowen Dunagree ☆ 55°13'·60N 06°55'·70W Fl (2) WRG 10s 28m **W18M**, R14M, G14M; W twr, 2 B bands; vis: 197°-G-211°-W-249°-R-000°. Fog Det lt VQ 16m vis: 270°.
Greencastle S Bkwtr Dir lt 042·5°. Fl (2) WRG 3s 4m W11M, R9M, G9M; vis 307°-G- 040°-W-045°-R-055°; 55°12'·17N 06°59'·13W.
McKinney's ⚓ Fl R 5s; 55°10'·9N 07°00'·5W.
Moville ⚓ Fl WR 2·5s 11m 4M; W house on G piles vis: 240°-W-064°-R-240°; 55°10'·99N 07°02'·12W.

RIVER BANN, COLERAINE and PORTRUSH

River Bann Ldg lts 165°. Front, Oc 5s 6m 2M; W twr; 55°09'·96N 06°46'·23W. Rear, 245m from front, Oc 5s 14m 2M; W ☐ twr.
W Mole ⚓ Fl G 5s 4m 2M; vis: 170°-000°; 55°10'·25N 06°46'·45W.
Portstewart Point ⚓ Oc R 10s 21m 5M; R ☐ hut; vis: 040°-220°; 55°11'·33N 06°43'·26W.
N Pier Hd ⚓ Fl R 3s 6m 3M; vis: 220°-160°; 55°12'·34N 06°39'·58W.
Skerries ⚓ Fl R 5s; 53°13'·90N 06°36'·90W; 992351096.

RATHLIN ISLAND

Rathlin W ☆ (½M NE of Bull Pt) 55°18'·05N 06°16'·82W; Fl R 5s 62m **18M**; W twr, lantern at base; vis: 015°-225°; H24. Fog Det Lt VQ; 992351000.
Drake Wreck ⚓ 55°17'·00N 06°12'·48W Q (6) + L Fl 15s.
Manor House ⚓ Oc WRG 4s 5M; vis: 020°-G-023°-W-026°-R-029°; 55°17'·52N 06°11'·73W.
Rue Pt ⚓ Fl(2) 5s 16m 14M; W twr B bands; 55°15'·52N 06°11'·46W; 992351131.
Altacarry Head ☆ 55°18'·11N 06°10'·31W Fl (4) 20s 74m **18M**; W twr, B band; vis: 110°-006° and 036°-058°; *Racon (G) 15-27M;* 992320707.

FAIR HEAD TO LAMBAY ISLAND

RED BAY, CARNLOUGH and LARNE

Red Bay Pier ⚓ Fl 3s 10m 5M; 55°03'·93N 06°03'·19W.
Carnlough Hbr N Pier ⚓ Fl G 3s 4m 5M; 54°59'·59N 05°59'·29W.
East Maiden ☆ Fl (3) 15s 32m **18M**; *Racon (M) 11-21M;* W twr, B band; 54°55'·74N 05°43'·65W. Aux lt Fl R 5s 15m 8M; same twr vis:142°-182° over Russel and Highland Rks, H24; 992351110.
N Hunter Rock ⚓ Q; 54°53'·04N 05°45'·13W.
S Hunter Rock ⚓ VQ(6) + LFl 10s; 54°52'·69N 05°45'·22W; 992351007.
Larne No 1 ▲ QG; 54°51'·68N 05°47'·67W; *AIS.*
Chaine Twr ☆ Iso WR 5s 23m **W16M**, R12M; Gy twr; vis: 232°-W-240°-R-000° (shore); 54°51'·27N 05°47'·90W.
Larne Ldg lts 184°, No 11 Front, 54°49'·60N 05°47'·81W Oc 4s 6m 12M; W 2 with R stripe on R pile structure; vis: 179°-189°. No 12 Rear, 610m from front, Oc 4s 14m 12M; W 2 with R stripe on R ☐ twr; synch with front, vis: 5° either side of Ldg line.

CARRICKFERGUS

Black Hd ☆ 54°46'·02N 05°41'·34W Fl 3s 45m **27M**; W 8-sided twr; 992351002.
Marina Ent Appr ⚓ Dir Oc WRG 3s 5m 3M; vis: G308°-W317·5°- R322·5°-332°; 54°42'·58N 05°48'·78W.

BELFAST LOUGH and BANGOR

Mew Is ☆ NE end 54°41'·92N 05°30'·82W F Fl (4) 30s 35m **18M**; B twr, W band; *Racon (O) 14M*; 992351109.

Belfast Fairway ⚓ Iso 4s; 54°42'·32N 05°42'·30W; *Racon (G)*; *AIS*.

Kilroot ⬣ Fl QG (sync); 54°42'·85N 05°42'·85W.

Helen's Bay ⬣ QR (sync); 54°41'·86N 05°42'·85W.

No 1 ⬣ Fl G 2s (sync); 54°41'·67N 05°46'·51W.

No 2 ⬣ Fl R 2s (sync); 54°41'·55N 05°46'·43W.

Briggs ⚓ Q; 54°41'·18N 05°53'·73W; 992351133.

DONAGHADEE

Merandoragh ⬣ Fl (2) G 6s (sync); 54°39'·84N 05°32'·24W.

Foreland Spit ⬣ Fl (2) R 6s (sync); 54°39'·64N 05°32'·31W.

Governor's ⬣ Fl G 3s (sync); 54°39'·36N 05°31'·99W; 992351134.

Riggs Bank ⊙ V–AIS PHM; 54°38'·63N 05°27'·10W; 992356011.

Donaghadee ☆, S Pier Hd 54°38'·71N 05°31'·86W Iso WR 4s 17m **W17M**, R12M; twr; vis: shore-W-326°-R-shore; 002320792.

BALLYWATER and PORTAVOGIE

Ballywater, Bkwtr Hd Fl WRG 3s 4m 9M; vis: 240°-G-267°-W-277°-R-314°; 54°32'·68N 05°28'·83W.

Skulmartin ⬣ Fl (2) R 6s 10s; 54°32'·39N 05°24'·91W; 992351022.

Portavogie Bkwtr Hd ⚓ Iso WRG 5s 6m WRG 5M; ☐ twr; vis: shore-G-262°-W-272°-R-350°; 54°27'·44N 05°26'·14W.

Plough Rock ⬣ 54°27'·40N 05°25'·12W Fl R 3s.

South Rock ⬣ Fl (3) R 30s 9M 54°24'·48N 05°21'·99W; *Racon (T)*; 992351004.

STRANGFORD LOUGH

Strangford ⬣ L Fl 10s; 54°18'·63N 05°28'·69W; 992351028.
Butter Pladdy ⚓ Q (3) 10s; 54°22'·45N 05°25'·74W.

Bar ⚓ Q (6) + L Fl 15s; 54°19'·34N 05°30'·51W; 992351135.
Dogtail Pt Ldg lts 341°. Front, Iso 4s 2m 5M; G Bn; 54°20'·79N 05°31'·84W. Rear, Gowlands Rk, 0·8M fm front, Iso 4s 6m 5M; W twr, G top, B base.

Swan Is ⚓ Q (3) 5m; BYB brick twr; 54°22'·38N 05°33'·16W.

Strangford East Ldg lts 256°. Front, Oc WRG 5s 6m W9M, R6M, G6M: vis: 190°-R-244°-G-252°-W- 260°-R-294°; 54°22'·29N 05°33'·27W. Rear, 46m from front, Oc R 5s 10m 6M; vis: 250°-264°.

Portaferry Pier Hd ⚓ Oc WR 10s 9m W9M, R6M; Or mast; vis: W335°-R005°-W017°-128°; 54°22'·82N 05°33'·03W.

ARDGLASS

Inner Pier Hd ⚓ Iso WRG 4s 10m W8M, R7M, G5M; twr; vis: shore-G-308°-W-314°-R-shore; 54°15'·79N 05°36'·33W.

DUNDRUM BAY

St John's Point ☆ 54°13'·61N 05°39'·61W Q (2) 7·5s 37m **25M**; B twr, Y bands. **Auxiliary Light** ☆ Fl WR 3s 14m **W15M**, R11M; same twr, vis: 064°-W-078°-R-shore; Fog Det lt VQ 14m vis: 270°; 992351005.

DZ East ⚐ Fl (2) Y 10s; 54°12'·05N 05°45'·30W.

DZ West ⚐ Fl Y 5s; 54°11'·84N 05°50'·82W.

ANNALONG

E Bkwtr Hd ⚓ Oc WRG 5s 8m 9M; twr; vis: 204°-G-249°-W-309°-R-024°; 54°06'·51N 05°53'·73W.

KILKEEL

Pier Hd ⚓ Fl WR 2s 8m 8M; vis: R296°-W313°-017°; 54°03'·46N 05°59'·30W; 992356010 (emergency AIS 992356008).

CARLINGFORD LOUGH and NEWRY RIVER

Hellyhunter ⚓ Q(6) + LFl 15s; 54°00'·35N 06°02'·10W; 992351009.

Haulbowline ⚓ 54°01'·19N 06°04'·74W Fl (3) 10s 32m 10M; Grey twr; 992501235.

Ldg lts 310·4° Front, Oc 3s 7m 11M; R △ on twr; vis: 295°-325°; 54°01'·80N 06°05'·43W; 992501237. Rear, 457m from front, Oc 3s 12m 11M; R ▽ on twr; vis: 295°-325°; both H24.

Newry River Ldg lts 310·4°. Front, 54°06'·37N 06°16'·51W. Rear, 274m from front. Both Iso 4s 5/15m 2M; stone cols.

DUNDALK

Imogene ⬣ Fl (2) R 10s; 53°57'·41N 06°07'·02W; 992501238.

Pile Light ⚓ 53°58'·56N 06°17'·71W Fl WR 15s 10m 10M; W Ho.

Dunany ⬣ Fl R 3s; 53°53'·56N 06°09'·47W; 992501243.

SKERRIES BAY

Skerries Pier Hd ⚓ Oc R 6s 7m 7M; W col; vis: 103°-R-154°; 53°35'·09N 06°06'·49W

DROGHEDA to LAMBAY ISLAND

Port Approach Dir lt 53°43'·30N 06°14'·73W WRG 10m **W19M, R15M**, G15M; vis: 268°-FG-269°-Al WG-269·5°-FW-270·5°-Al WR-271°-FR-272°; H24.

Balbriggan ⚓ Fl (3) WRG 10s 12m W13M, R10M, G10M; W twr; vis: 159°-G-193°-W-288°-R-305°; 53°36'·76N 06°10'·80W.

Rockabill ☆ 53°35'·81N 06°00'·30W Fl WR 12s 45m **W17M, R13M**; W twr, B band; vis: 178°-W-329°-R-178°; 992501246.

Skerries Bay Pier Hd ⚓ Oc R 6s 7m 7M; W col; vis: 103°-154°; 53°35'·09N 06°06'·49W.

		1	2	3	4	5	6	7	8	9	10	11	12	13	14	15
1	Strangford Lough	**1**														
2	Bangor	34	**2**													
3	Carrickfergus	39	6	**3**												
4	Larne	45	16	16	**4**											
5	Carnlough	50	25	26	11	**5**										
6	Portrush	87	58	60	48	35	**6**									
7	Lough Foyle	92	72	73	55	47	11	**7**								
8	L Swilly (Fahan)	138	109	104	96	81	48	42	**8**							
9	Burtonport	153	130	130	116	108	74	68	49	**9**						
10	Killybegs	204	175	171	163	148	115	109	93	43	**10**					
11	Sligo	218	189	179	177	156	123	117	107	51	30	**11**				
12	Eagle Island	234	205	198	193	175	147	136	123	72	62	59	**12**			
13	Westport	295	266	249	240	226	193	187	168	120	108	100	57	**13**		
14	Galway	338	309	307	297	284	253	245	227	178	166	163	104	94	**14**	
15	Kilrush	364	335	332	323	309	276	270	251	203	191	183	142	119	76	**15**

DISTANCE TABLES
Approx distances in nautical miles are by the most direct route allowing for dangers and TSS.

AREA 11 *West Denmark – Skagen to Rømø*

SELECTED LIGHTS, BUOYS & WAYPOINTS

SKAGEN TO THYBORØN

SKAGEN

Skagen W ☆ Fl (3) WR 10s 31m **W17M**/R12M; 053°-W-248°-R-323°; W ○ twr; 57°44′·94N 10°35·70E.

Skagen ☆ Fl 4s 44m **23M**; Gy ○ twr; *Racon G, 20M*; 57°44′·14N 10°37′·81E.

Skagen No 1A ⚓ L Fl 10s; *Racon N*; 57°43′·46N 10°53′·55E. (Route T)

Skagen No 2 ⚓ L Fl 10s; 57°37′·61N 11°05′·51E. (Route T)

Skagens Rev ⚓ Q; 57°45′·97N 10°43′·74E.

⚓ Q (3) 10s; 57°43′·87N 10°42′·31E.

Skagen Harbour S bkwtr root, Dir ⚡ Oc WRG 5s 20m W11/RG10M, 263·3°-G-266·3°-W°-270·3°-R-273·3°; Gy lattice twr; 57°42′·77N 10°34′·99E.

S bkwtr head ⚡ Fl R 3s 4m 5M; 57°42′·72N 10°35′·99E.

N bkwtr head ⚡ Fl G 3s 4m 5M; 57°42′·92N 10°35′·91E.

Inner hbr ent SW side⚡ Fl R 5s

Inner hbr ent NE side ⚡ Fl G 5s

HIRTSHALS

Hirtshals ☆ F Fl 30s 57m **F 18M; Fl 25M**; W ○ twr, approx 1M SSW of hbr ent; 57°35′·10N 09°56′·55E.

Ldg lts 166°, both 156°-176°. Front, Iso R 2s 10m 11M; R △ on twr; 57°35′·69N 09°57′·64E; marina ent is close N of this lt. Rear, Iso R 4s 18m 11M; R ▽ on twr; 330m from front.

Approach chan ⬣ Fl (3) G 10s; 57°36′·18N 09°56·94E.

⬣ Fl R 3s; 57°36′·44N 09°57′·67E.

⬣ Fl (5) Y 20s; 57°36′·43N 09°57′·72E.

⬣ Fl G 5s; 57°36′·11N 09°57·14E.

Outer W mole ⚡ Fl G 3s 14m 6M; G mast; *Horn 15s*; 57°35′·97N 09°57′·37E.

W mole spur ⚡ Fl G 5s 9m 4M; G mast; 57°35′·77N 09°57′·51E.

E mole ⚡ Fl R 5s 9m 6M; G mast; 57°35′·85N 09°57′·61E.

LØKKEN

Lee bkwtr ⚡ Fl 5s 5m 5M; 57°22′·39N 09°42′·11E.

TRANUM STRAND (Firing ranges)

Tranum No 1 ☆ Al Fl WR 4s 19m W7M, R7M; twr; by day Q 4M; shown when firing in progress; 57°12′·43N 09°30′·34E.

Tranum No 2 ☆ light as per No 1; 57°10′·57N 09°26′·22E.

LILD STRAND

Bragerne ⬣ Fl G 5s; 57°10′·67N 08°56′·35E.

Ldg lts 138°, three ⚡: F 12/22m 7/8M; 127°-149°; 3 masts. Front 57°09′·22N 08°57′·75E.

HANSTHOLM

Hanstholm ☆ Fl (3) 20s 65m **24M**; shown by day in poor vis; W 8-sided twr; 57°06′·77N 08°35′·92E, approx 1M S of the hbr ent.

Hanstholm ⚓ LFl 10s; 57°08′·24N 08°36′·09E.

Outer bkwtr, W head ⚡ Fl G 3s 11m 9M; G post; 57°07′·70N 08° 35′·48E.

Outer bkwtr, E head ⚡, Fl R 3s11m 9M, R pillar; 57°07′·61N 08° 35′·57E.

Inner W mole, ldg lts, Oc WRG 5s 13m 13M; 197°-G-205°-W-210°-R-218°; mast; 57°07′·53N 08°35′·42E

Roshage ⚡ Fl 5s 7m 5M; 57°07′·75N 08°37′·25E (1M E of hbr).

NØRRE VORUPØR

Mole ⚡ Fl G 5s 6m 5M; 56°57′·75N 08°21′·679E.

Ldg lts, both Iso R 4s 20/30m 9M, indicate safest landing place for FVs; vis 22·5° either side of ldg line; synch. Front 57°57′·46N 08°22′·10E. Rear, 80m from front.

Lodbjerg ☆ Fl (2) 20s 48m **23M**; ○ twr; 56°49′·40N 08°15′·76E.

THYBORØN

Landfall ⚓ L Fl 10s; *Racon T, 10m*; 56°42′·54N 08°08′·69E.

Agger Tange ldg lts 082°: Front, Iso WRG 4s 8m W11M, R/G8M; 074·5°-G-079·5°-W-084·5°-R-089·5°; R △ on bcn; 56°42′·97N 08°14′·14E. Rear, Iso 4s 17m 11M; 075°-089°; synch; R ▽ on Gy twr; 804m from front.

Off Havmolen ⌑ 56°43′·25N 08°12′·52E.

Approach ☆ Fl (3) 10s 24m 12M; intens 023·5°-203·5°; also lit by day in poor vis; lattice twr; 56°42′·49N 08°12′·91E (S side of ent).

Langholm ldg lts 120°, both Iso 2s 7/13m 11M; synch; 113°-127°. Front, R △ on R hut, 56°42′·45N 08°14′·54E. Rear, R ▽ on Gy twr.

Thyborøn Havn ⚡ Oc (2) WRG 12s 6m W11M, R/G8M; 122·5°-G-146·5°- W-150°- R-211·3°-G-337·5°-W-340°-R-344°; W twr R band; 56°42′·35N 08°13′·39E (680m N of ent to Yderhavn and Basins).

Yderhavn approach ⚡ Dir Iso WRG 2s 21m 5M (0.5M by day); 213°-G-218°-W-223°-R-228°; 56°41′·85N 08°13′·32E

N mole ⚡ Fl G 3s 6m 4M; G pedestal; 56°42′·02N 08°13′·52E.

S mole ⚡ Fl R 3s 6m 4M; R pedestal; 56°41′·97N 08°13′·53E.

LIMFJORD (Limited coverage E, only to 08°42′E)

Sælhundeholm Løb, into Nissum Bredning ('Broad').

No 1 ⬣ Fl (2) G 5s; 56°41′·14N 08°14′·17E.

No 3 ⬣ Fl G 3s; 56°40′·75N 08°13′·79E.

No 7 ⬣ Fl G 3s; 56°40′·31N 08°13′·52E.

No 11 ⚓ Fl G 3s; 56°39′·83N 08°13′·59E.

No 16 ⚓ Fl R 3s; 56°38′·51N 08°13′·89E.

No 18 ⌑ Fl (2) R 5s; 56°38′·20N 08°14′·34E.

No 21 ⬣ Fl G 3s; 56°38′·98N 08°14′·71E.

No 26 ⌑ Fl R 3s; 56°38′·71N 08°15′·38E.

No 29 ⬣ Fl G 3s; 56°38′·40N 08°15′·94E.

APPROACHES TO LEMVIG (Marina and Havn)

Toftum Dir ⚡ 120°, Iso WRG 4s 24m, W12M, R/G 8M; 110°-G-120°-W-137°-R-144°; hut; 56°33′·09N 08°18′·33E.

Rønnen ⬣ Fl G 3s; 56°36′·71N 08°21′·74E.

Søgard Mark ldg lts 243·5°: both FR 20/30m 5M; vis 90° either side of ldg line. Front, ⚓ R △ on W bcn; 56°34′·39N 08°17′·29E. Rear, R ▽ on W post; 235m from front.

Chan ⬣ 56°33′·27N 08°18′·31E.

Ldg lts, W of hbr 177·7°, both FR 8/20m 5M; 153°-203°. Front ⚓ R △ on twr; 56°33′·04N 08°18′·16E. Rear, R ▽ on W post; 184m from front.

Vinkel Hage Marina, N mole ⚡ FG 3m 5M; 56°33′·09N 08°18′·33E.

S mole, FR 3m 4M. Marina is 9ca N of the Havn on the W side.

Ostre Havn ⚓ 56°33′·17N 08°18′·40E. Havn ent, FG/FR 4m 5M.

THISTED HAVN (Marina)
Outer W mole ✫ Fl R 3s 4m 2M; 56°57'·10N 08°41'·90E.
Outer E mole ✫ Fl G 3s 4m 2M; 56°57'·10N 08°41'·95E.
Thisted Bredning ✫ Aero 3 Fl R 1·5s (vert; 45m apart) 183m 10M; TV mast; 56°58'·52N 08°41'·15E, 1·55M NNW of hbr ent.

THYBORØN TO BLÅVANDS HUK

Bovbjerg ☆ Fl (2) 15s 62m 16M; 56°30'·79N 08°07'·18E.

THORSMINDE HAVN
(All Lat/Longs for this harbour are approximate)
Lt ho ✫ F 30m 13M; Gy twr; 56°22'·34N 08°06'·99E.
Groyne, N ✫ Fl 5s 8m 5M; Gy hut; 56°22'·46N 08°06'·82E.
N mole ✫ Iso R 2s 9m 4M; R hut; 56°22'·36N 08°06'·62E.
S mole ✫ Iso G 2s 9m 4M; G hut; 56°22'·26N 08°06'·92E.
West hbr, W mole ✫ FG 5m 2M; Gy post; 56°22'·36N 08°07'·12E.
E mole ✫ FR 5m 2M; Gy post; 56°22'·26N 08°07'·18E.
NW dolphin ✫ FG 5m 4M; Gy post; 56°22'·26N 08°07'·22E.
SE dolphin ✫ FG 5m 4M; Gy post; 56°22' 26N 08°07' 26E.
Lock, E side ✫ Iso 4s 12m 4M; Gy mast; 020°-160°; 56°22'·36N 08°07'·22E.
Road bridge ✫ Iso 4s 5m 4M; 200°-340°; 56°22'·36N 08°07'·26E.

HVIDE SANDE
Lyngvig ☆ Fl 5s 53m **23M** W ○ twr; 56°02'·99N 08°06'·22E.
N outer bkwtr ✫ Fl R 3s 7m 8M; R hut; 55°59'·94N 08°06'·55E.
Ent, 2 pairs converging Ldg lts: 2Iso 2s 063·2°, 2IsoR 4s 077·8°.
N mole ✫ Fl R 5s 10m 6·5M; R floodlit,55°59'·98N 08°06'·84E.
S mole ✫ Fl G 5s 10m 6M; 55°59'·96N 08°06'·98E.
Lt ho ✫ F 27m 14M; Gy twr; 56°00'·00N 08°07'·35E.
Nordhavn, E pier ✫ FG 4m 4M; 56°00'·16N 08°07'·42E.
W pier ✫ 2 FR 3m 2M; W posts; 060°-035°; 56°00'·07N 08°07'·12E.
Sydhavn, W pier ✫ FG 4m 2M; 56°00'·06N 08°07'·52E.
E Pier ✫ FR 4m 2M; Gy post; 56°00'·06N 08°07'·53E.
Lock entrance ldg lts 293·5°: both FR 11/14m 2M; 201·6°-021·6°. Front, R △ on Gy tr, 56°00'·0N 08°07'·8E. Rear, R ▽ on Gy twr, 72m from front.
Fjordhavn ldg lts 246·6° (both vis 7·5° either side of ldg line): Front, Iso G 2s 4m 4M; Or △ on mast; 56°00'·5N 08°07'·9E. Rear, Iso G 4s 6m 4M, Or ▽ on mast, 128m from front.

HORNS REV (marks westward from coast)
Oskbøl firing range. Two lights (4M apart) both AlFl WR 4s 35m **16M**, R13M, (by day Q 10M) are shown when firing is in progress: North ☆ 55°37'·24N 08°07'·04E. South ☆ 55°33'·53N 08°04'·67E.
Range safety buoys: ⚓ Fl Y 5s; 55°42'·32N 08°06'·92E.⚓ Fl Y 3s; 55°38'·63N 07°50'·91E.⚓ Fl Y 3s; 55°37'·35N 07°56'·98E.⚐ 55°36'·02N 08°02'·49E.
Blåvands Huk ☆ Fl (3) 20s 55m **23M**; W □ twr; 55°33'·46N 08°04'·95E.
Horns Rev is encircled by:

Tuxen ⚓ Q; 55°34'·22N 07°41'·92E on the N side.
Vyl ⚓ Q (6) + L Fl 15s; 55°26'·22N 07°49'·99E on the S side.
No 2 ⚓ L Fl 10s; 55°28'·74N 07°36'·49E on the SW side.
Horns Rev W ⚓ Q (9) 15s; 55°34'·47N 07°26'·05E, off the W end.

Slugen Channel (crosses Horns Rev ESE/WNW)
▲ L Fl G 10s; 55°33'·99N 07°49'·38E.
▲ Fl G 3s; 55°32'·26N 07°53'·65E.
◣ Fl (2) R 5s; 55°31'·46N 07°52'·88E.
▲ Fl (2) G 5s; 55°30'·52N 07°59'·20E.
◣ Fl (3) R 10s; 55°29'·42N 08°02'·56E.

Søren Bovbjergs Dyb (unlit N/S side channel off Slugen Chan)
⚓ 55°33'·57N 07°55'·55E.
⚑ 55°32'·80N 07°55'·30E.
⚓ 55°32'·19N 07°56'·29E.
⚓ 55°31'·24N 07°57'·46E.

BLÅVANDS HUK TO RØMØ
APPROACHES TO ESBJERG
Grådyb ⚓ L Fl 10s; *Racon G, 10M*; 55°24'·63N 08°11'·59E.
Sædding Strand 053·8° triple ldg lts: valid to buoys 7/8; H24: **Front** Iso 2s 14m **19M**; 052·3°-055·3°; Gy twr, copper roof; 55°29'·74N 08°23'·86E.
Middle Iso 4s 27m **19M**; 052·3°-055·3°; R metal twr, W bands; 55°29'·94N 08°24'·35E, 740m from front.
Rear F 37m **20M**; 052·3°-055·3°; R framework twr; 55°30'·18N 08°24'·92E, 0·75M from front.
No 1 ⚓ Q; 55°25'·49N 08°13'·89E.
No 2 ◣ Fl (3) R 10s; 55°25'·62N 08°13'·73E.
No 3 ▲ Fl G 3s; 55°25'·93N 08°14'·84E.
No 4 ◣ Fl R 3s; 55°26'·02N 08°14'·72E.
Tide Gauge ✫ Fl (5) Y 20s 8m 4M; 55°26'·05N 08°15'·93E.
No 5 ▲ Fl G 5s; 55°26'·32N 08°15'·83E.
No 6 ◣ Fl R 5s; 55°26'·44N 08°15'·70E.
No 7 ⚓ Q; 55°26'·76N 08°16'·91E.
No 8 ◣ Fl (2) R 5s; 55°26'·89N 08°16'·81E.
Ldg lts 067°, valid up to Nos 9/10 buoys. Both FG 10/25m **16M**, H24. Front, Gy tripod; rear, Gy twr, 55°28'·76N 08°24'·70E.
No 9 ▲ Fl (2) G 10s; 55°27'·04N 08°18'·21E.
No 10 ◣ Fl (2) R 10s; 55°27'·20N 08°18'·04E.
Ldg lts 049°, valid up to No 16 buoy/Jerg. Both FR 16/27m **16M**, H24. Front, W twr; rear, Gy twr, 55°29'·92N 08°23'·75E.
No 11 ▲ Fl G 3s; 55°27'·71N 08°19'·59E.
No 12 ◣ Fl R 3s; 55°27'·88N 08°19'·39E.
No 13 ▲ Fl G 5s; 55°28'·40N 08°20'·99E.
No 14 ◣ Fl R 5s; 55°28'·57N 08°20'·73E.
Jerg ✫ Fl G 3s 7m 5M; G twr, Y base; 55°28'·88N 08°22'·00E.
No 16 ⚓ Q (6) + L Fl 15s; 55°29'·04N 08°21'·80E.
No 15A ▲ Fl (2) G 5s; 55°29'·01N 08°22'·47E.
No 18 ◣ Fl (2) R 5s; 55°29'·19N 08°22'·71E.
Fovrfelt N ✫ Oc(2) WRG 6s 7m W6M, R/G4M; 066·5°-G-073°-W-077°-R-085·5°; 327°-G-331°- W-333·5°-R-342°; Y twr; 55°29'·29N 08°23'·79E.
Fovrfelt ✫ Fl (2) R 10s 11m 6M; R twr; 55°29'·03N 08°23'·75E.
No 15B ▲ Fl (2) G 10s; 55°28'·83N 08°23'·65E.

ESBJERG HAVN

Marina, N mole head ⚡ Fl R 3s, 7m 2·5M, R post, 55°28'·83N 08° 24'·44E

Marina, S mole head ⚡ Fl G 3s, 7m 2·5M, G post, 55°28'·82N 08° 24'·46E

Marina, inner entrance, storm gate, 3FR(vert) 11m 2.5M, Gy post, 55°28'·88N 08°24'·52E. SS(Traffic), if lit = gate closed.

Strandby, shelter mole, NW corner ⚡ Oc WRG 5s 6m W7·5M, R6M,G6·5M 102·1°-G-105·9°-W-109·7°-R-111·9°; W bldg, R band; 55°28'·76N 08°24'·63E (just south of marina).

Industrifiskerihavn, W mole ⚡ Fl R 5s 6m 4M; R structure; 55°28'·57N 08°24'·89E.

E mole ⚡ Fl G 5s 7m 4M; G structure; 55°28'·52N 08°25'·03E.

Nordsøkai ⚑ Q (9) 15s 5m; Y twr, B band; 55°28'·45N 08°25'·04E.

Konsumfiskerihavn, W mole ⚡ FlR 3s 6m; 203°-119°; R twr; 55°28'·31N 08°25'·33E.

E mole ⚡ Fl G 3s 6m; 023°-256°; G tr; 55°28·31N 08°25·40E.

Trafikhavn, NW corner, ⚡ Oc (2) WRG 12s 6m W11M, R/G8M; 118°-G-124·5°-W-129°-R-131°; W bldg, R band; 55°28·22N 08°25·43E.

N mole ⚡ FR 8m 5M; 232°-135°; R bldg; 55°28'·13N 08°25'·46E.

S mole ⚡ FG 8m 4M; 045°-276°; G bldg; 55°28'·08N 08°25'·51E.

No 22 ⚬ Fl (2) R 5s; 55°27'·62N 08°25'·50E.

Sønderhavn (industrial) W mole ⚡ FR 9m 4M; 55°27'·49N 08°26'·12E. E mole ⚡ FG 9m 4M; 55°27'·43N 08°26'·31E. Aero ⚡ 3 x Fl 1·5s (vert, 82m apart) 251m 12M, H24; on chimney; 55°27'·27N 08°27'·32E (1200m ESE of Sønderhavn ent).

FANØ

Slunden outer ldg lts 242°, both Iso 2s 5/8m 3M; 227°-257°. Front, twr; 55°27'·20N 08°24'·53E. Rear, twr, 106m from front.

E shore, reciprocal ldg lts 062°, both FR 10/13m 3M; 047°-077°. Front, twr; 55°27'·65N 08°26'·01E. Rear, twr, 140m from front.

No 1 ⚡ Fl (2) G l0s 5m 2M; G pile; 55°27'·45N 08°25'·28E.

No 2 ⚡ Fl (2+1) Y 5s 5m 2M; Y pile; 55°27'·42N 08°25'·32E.

No 3 ⚡ Fl G 3s 5m 2M; G pile; 55°27'·39N 08°25'·07E.

No 4 ⚡ Fl R 3s 5m 2M; R pile; 55°27'·35N 08°25'·10E.

Nordby ldg lts 214°, both FR 7/9m 4M; 123·7°-303·7°. Front, W mast;55°26'·94N 08°24'·44E. Rear, Gy twr, 84m from front.-Kremer Sand ⚡ FG 5m 3M; G dolphin; 55°27'·3N 08°24'·9E.

Næs Søjord ⚡ FR 5m 3M; R pile; 55°27'·27N 08°24'·86E.

Nordby marina 55°26'·65N 08°24'·53E.

KNUDEDYB

G ⚑ 55°20'·50N 08°24'·28E.

K ⚑ 55°18'·92N 08°20'·06E.

No 2 ⚑ 55°18'·82N 08°21'·33E.

No 4 ⚑ 55°18'·81N 08°22'·21E.

No 6 ⚑ 55°18'·38N 08°24'·63E.

No 10 ⚑ 55°18'·68N 08°28'·50E.

Knoben ⚑ 55°18'·71N 08°30'·60E.

JUVRE DYB

No 4 ⚑ 55°13'·76N 08°24'·73E.

No 6 ⚑ 55°13'·41N 08°26'·60E.

No 8 ⚑ 55°12'·69N 08°26'·83E.

No 10 ⚑ 55°12'·55N 08°28'·72E.

Rejsby Stjært ⚑ 55°13'·15N 08°30'·55E.

OUTER APPROACH (Lister Tief) TO RØMØ

See also Area 15 for details of lights on Sylt.

Rode Klit Sand, ⚑ Fl (Y) 15s, 55°08'·40N 08°07'·25E.

Lister Tief ⚑ Iso 8s, *Whis;* 55°05'·32N 08°16'·80E.

No 1 ⚑ 55°05'·48N 08°18'·50E.

No 3 ⚡ Fl G 4s; 55°05'·36E 08°20'·14E.

No 2 ⚬ Fl (3) R 10s; 55°03'·92N 08°21'·22E.

No 9 ⚑ Fl (2) G 9s; 55°03'·76N 08°23'·05E.

Lister Landtief No 5 ⚑ 55°03'·68N 08°24'·73E.

No 4 ⚬ FL (2) R 5s; 55°03'·84N 08°25'·29E.

G1 ⚑ Fl Y 4s; 55°03'·27N 08°28'·32E.

RØMØ DYB and HAVN

No 1 ⚑ Fl (2) G 10s; 55°03'·23N 08°30'·30E.

No 10 ⚡ Fl (2) R 10s 5m 3M; R pole; 55°03'·50N 08°31'·10E.

No 14 ⚡ Fl R 3s 6m 2M; R pole; 55°03'·85N 08°32'·55E.

No 20 ⚡ Fl R 5s 5m 2M; R pole; 55°04'·79N 08°34'·13E.

No 9 ⚑ 55°04'·79N 08°34'·63E.

No 11 ⚑ 55°05'·17N 08°34'·69E.

Rømø Havn, S mole ⚡ Fl R 3s 7m 2M; Gy twr; 55°05'·19N 08°34'·31E.

N mole ⚡ Fl G 3s 7m 2M; Gy twr; 55°05'·23N 08°34'·30E.

Inner S mole ⚡ FR 4m 1M; 55°05'·2N 08°34'·2E.

		1	2	3	4	5	6	7	8	9	10	11	12	13	14	15	16	17	18
1	Skagen	1																	
2	Hirtshals	33	2																
3	Hanstholm	85	52	3															
4	Thyborøn	114	84	32	4														
5	Torsminde	141	108	56	24	5													
6	Hvide Sande	162	179	77	45	24	6												
7	Esbjerg	200	174	122	90	76	54	7											
8	Fanø	210	177	125	93	79	57	3	8										
9	Rømø	233	200	148	116	94	73	30	33	9									
10	Hörnum	248	215	163	131	108	86	70	73	29	10								
11	Husum	275	247	195	163	152	131	95	98	68	45	11							
12	Kiel/Holtenau	261	233	281	249	232	208	180	183	189	126	129	12						
13	Bremerhaven	306	285	233	201	185	163	127	129	107	83	82	123	13					
14	Wilhelmshaven	414	296	242	310	184	162	125	128	106	82	82	123	45	14				
15	Helgoland	259	238	186	154	141	119	83	85	63	39	47	104	44	43	15			
16	Cuxhaven	304	284	232	200	162	138	110	113	85	56	66	70	58	56	38	16		
17	Wangerooge	283	262	210	178	168	147	109	112	94	68	52	108	38	27	24	42	17	
18	Hamburg	338	317	265	233	216	192	163	167	139	99	113	90	81	110	88	54	61	18

DISTANCE TABLES
Approx distances in nautical miles by the most direct route allowing for dangers and TSS.

51

AREA 12 *Germany (North Sea coast) – List to Emden*
SELECTED LIGHTS, BUOYS & WAYPOINTS

DANISH BORDER TO BÜSUM
SYLT
Lister Tief ⁜ Iso 8s; *Whis;* 55°05'·33N 08°16'·79E.
List West (Ellenbogen) ⚡ Oc WRG 6s 19m W14M, R11M, G10M; 040°-R-133°-W-227°-R-266·4°-W-268°-G-285°-W-310°- W(unintens)-040°; W twr, R lantern; 55°03'·15N 08°24'·00E.
List Hafen, S mole ⚡ FR 5m 4M; 218°-353°; R mast; 55°01'·01N 08°26'·51E.
Hörnum ☆ Fl (2) 9s 48m **20M;** 54°45'·23N 08°17'·47E.
Vortrapptief ⁜ Iso 4s; 54°34'·80N 08°14'·36E, toward Hörnum.
S mole ⚡ FR 7m 4M; 54°45'·57N 08°17'·97E.

AMRUM ISLAND
Rütergat ⁜ Iso 8s; 54°30'·08N 08°12'·32E.
Amrum ☆ Fl 7·5s 63m **23M;** R twr, W bands; 54°37'·84N 08°21'·23E.
Wriakhorn Cross ⚡ L Fl (2) WR 15s 26m W9M, R7M; 297·5°-W-319·5°-R-330°-W-005·5°-R-034°; 54°37'·62N 08°21'·22E.

FÖHR ISLAND
Nieblum Dir lt showing over Rütergat. ☆ Oc (2) WRG 10s 11m **W19M, R/G15M;** 028°-G-031°-W-032·5°-R-035·5°; R twr, W band; 54°41'·10N 08°29'·20E.
Ohlörn ⚡ Oc (4) WR 15s 10m 13/10M, 208°-W-237·5°-R-298°- W-353°- R-080°; R twr, Gy lantern; 54°40'·85N 08°34'·00E (SE Föhr).
Wyk Hbr outer ent, FR 54°41'·55N 08°34'·69E; and FG.

DAGEBÜLL
Dagebüll Iso WRG 8s 23m **W18M, R/G15M;** 042° -G-043°-W-044·5°- R-047°; 54°43'·82N 08°41'·43E. FW lts on ent moles.

LANGENESS ISLAND
Nordmarsch ⚡ L Fl (3) WR 20s 13m W14M, R11M; 268°-W-279°-R-306°-W-045°-R-070°-W-218°; dark brown twr; 54°37'·58N 08°31'·85E.

SCHLÜTTSIEL
No 2/SA 26 ⁜ 54°36'·84N 08°38'·95E. Hbr ent ⚑ 54°40'·89N 08°45'·10E.

RIVER HEVER
Hever ⁜ Iso 4s; *Whis;* 54°20'·41N 08°18'·82E.
Westerheversand ☆ Oc (3) WRG 15s 41m **W21M, R17M, G16M;** 012·2°-W-069°-G-079·5°-W-081°(ldg sector for Hever) -R-107°-W-150°-R-207°-W-233°-R-248°; R twr, W bands; 54°22'·40N 08°38'·39E.
Norderhever No 1 ⁜ Fl (2+1) R 15s; 54°22'·46N 08°30'·83E.

PELLWORM ISLAND
Pellworm ☆ Oc WRG 5s 38m **20M, R 16M, G 15M;** 037·5°-G-040°-W-042·5°-R-045°; R twr, W band; 54°29'·78N 08°39'·98E.

NORDSTRAND
Suderhafen, S mole ⁘ 54°28'·07N 08°55'·62E.

HUSUM
⁜ Fl G 4s, 54°28'·80N 08°58'·60E, start of access chan. Ldg lts 090°, both Iso G 8s 7/9m 3M.

RIVER EIDER
Eider ⁜ Iso 4s; 54°15'·70N 08° 29'·20E.
St Peter ☆ L Fl (2) WR 15s 23m **W16M,** R13M; 280°-R-282°-W-334°-R-052°-W-080°-R-091°-W-120°; 54°17'·24N 08°39'·13E.
Eiderdamm lock, N mole, W end ⚡ Oc (2) R 12s 8m 5M; W twr.

BÜSUM
Süderpiep ⁜ Iso 8s; *Whis;* 54°05'·82N 08°25'·70E.
Büsum ☆ Iso WR 6s 22m **W19M,** R12M; 248°-W-317°-R-024°-W-148°; 54°07'·61N 08°51'·49E.
E mole ⚡ Oc (3) G 12s 10m 4M; vis 260°-168°; G twr; 54°07'·19N 08°51'·65E.

GERMAN BIGHT TO RIVER ELBE
GB Light V ⛴ Iso 8s 12m **17M;** R hull marked G-B; *Horn Mo (R) 30s;* 54°09'·89N 06°20'·84E.

HELGOLAND
Helgoland ☆ Fl 5s 82m **28M;** brown ⬜ twr, B lantern, W balcony; 54°10'·91N 07°52'·93E.
Vorhafen. Ostmole, S elbow ⚡ Oc WG 6s 5m W6M, G3M; 203°-W-250°-G-109°; G post; fog det lt; 54°10'·31N 07°53'·94E.

RIVER ELBE (LOWER)
APPROACHES
Nordergründe N ⁜ VQ; 53°57'·06N 08°00'·12E.
Elbe ⁜ Iso 10s; 53°59'·96N 08°06'·51E.
No 1 ⁜ QG; 53°59'·21N 08°13'·20E.
No 25 ⁜ QG; 53°56'·62N 08°38'·25E.
Neuwerk ☆ S side, L Fl (3) WRG 20s 38m **W16M,** R12M, G11M; 165·3°-G-215·3°-W-238·8°-R-321°; 343°-R-100°; 53°54'·92N 08°29'·73E.

CUXHAVEN
No 31 ⁜ Fl G 4s; 53°53'·93N 08°41'·21E.
Yacht hbr ent, F WR and F WG lts; 53°52'·43N 08°42'·49E.

OTTERNDORF
No 43 ⁜ Oc (2) G 9s; 53°50'·23N 08°52'·24E.
Otterndorf 3 ⚑ Fl (3) G 12s; 53°50'·22N 08°53'·94E.

BRUNSBÜTTEL
No 57a ⁜ Fl G 4s; 53°52'·62N 09°07'·93E, 030°/ 8 cables to lock.
Neuer Vorhafen ent, mole 3 head ⁜ VQ (6) + L Fl 10s and ⚡ Iso 3s 17m, 9M, 53°53'·25N 09°08'·07E.
Alter Vorhafen ent, mole 1 head ⚡ F WG 14m W10M, G6M; 266·3°-W-273·9°-G-088·8° (FW in fog), floodlit; 53°53'·27N 09°08'·59E. Mole 2 ⚡ F.RG14m10M 277°-R-022°-G-090°. *Horn (1) 10s.* 53°53'·25N 09° 08'·24E.

RIVER ELBE (BRUNSBÜTTEL TO HAMBURG)
FREIBURG
Reede 1 ⚬ Oc (2) Y 9s; 53°50'·41N 09°19'·45E, off ent.

STÖRLOCH
Stör ldg lts 093·8°, both Fl 3s 7/12m 6M; synch. Front, 53°49'·29N 09°23'·91E; △ on R ○ twr. Rear, 200m east; ▽ on white mast.

GLÜCKSTADT
Glückstadt ldg lts 131·8°, both Iso 8s, front,15m/**19M**, rear 40m/**21M**; intens on ldg line; W twrs, R bands. **Front** ☆, 53°48'·31N 09°24'·24E. **Rear** ☆, 0·68M from front.
Rhinplatte Nord ☆ Oc WRG 6s 11m W6M, R4M, G3M; 122°-G-144°-W-150°-R-177°-W-122°; 53°48'·09N 09°23'·36E.
N mole ☆ Dir Oc WRG 6s 9m W9M R7M, G6M; 330°-R-343°-W-346°-G-008°; 123°-G-145°-W-150°-R-170°; W twr with gallery; 53°47'·12N 09°24'·53E.
N pier hd ☆ FR 5m 5M; 53°47'·10N 09°24'·50E. (S mole hd, FG).

KRUCKAU
S mole Oc WRG 6s 8m, W6M, R4M, G3M; 116·3°-W-120·7° (ldg sector)-R-225°-G-315°-R-331·9°-W-335·4° (ldg sector)-335·4°-G-116·3°; B dolphin; 53°42'·85N 09°30'·72E.

PINNAU
Ldg lts 112·7°, both Iso 4s 8/13m 6M. Front, 53°40'·08N 09°34'·02E.

STADE
Stadersand ☆ Iso 8s 20m 14M; 53°37'·69N 09°31'·64E (at ent).

HAMBURG YACHT HARBOUR, WEDEL
Both entrances show FR & FG, May to Oct; 53°34'·25N 09°40'·77E.

CITY SPORTHAFEN
Brandenburger Hafen Ent ☆ Iso Or 2s; 53°32'·52N 09°58'·81E.

WESER ESTUARY

ALTE WESER
Alte Weser Dir ☆ F WRG 33m **W23M, R19M, G18M**; 288°-FW-352°-FR-003°-FW-017°(ldg sector for Alte Weser) 017°-FG-045°-FW-074°-FG-121°-FW-126°-FR-140°-FG-175°-FW-183°-FR-196°-FW-238°; R ○ twr, 2 W bands, G lantern, B base, floodlit; *Horn Mo (AL) 60s;* 53°51'·80N 08°07'·65E.
16/A15 ⊠ Fl (2+1) R 15s; 53°49'·66N 08°06'·44E (junction with Neuwe Weser).

NEUE WESER
Tegeler Plate, N end, Dir ☆ Occ (3) WRG 12s 21m **W21M, G17M R18M R17M**; 329°-W-340°-R-014°-W-100°-G-116°-W-119° (ldg sector for Neue Weser).119°-R-123°-G-148·3°-W-150° (ldg sector for Alte Weser)150°-R-264°; R ○ twr, gallery; W lantern, R roof; Fog det lt; Ra refl; 53°47'·87N 08°11'·46E.

1	Esbjerg	1																
2	Hörnum Lt (Sylt)	47	2															
3	Husum	95	48	3														
4	Hamburg	163	112	113	4													
5	Kiel/Holtenau	179	128	129	90	5												
6	Brunsbüttel	126	75	76	37	53	6											
7	Cuxhaven	110	63	66	54	70	17	7										
8	Bremerhaven	127	80	82	81	131	78	58	8									
9	Wilhelmshaven	125	78	82	110	123	70	56	45	9								
10	Hooksiel	116	69	73	101	117	64	47	36	9	10							
11	Helgoland	83	38	47	88	104	51	38	44	43	35	11						
12	Wangerooge	109	60	52	61	108	55	42	38	27	19	24	12					
13	Langeoog	119	72	77	114	130	77	60	47	43	34	35	21	13				
14	Norderney	123	77	85	81	137	84	69	62	53	44	44	29	18	14			
15	Emden	165	129	137	174	190	137	120	115	106	97	85	80	63	47	15		
16	Borkum	133	97	105	104	163	110	95	88	80	71	67	55	46	31	32	16	
17	Delfzijl	155	119	127	159	173	120	105	100	89	83	81	65	56	41	10	22	17
18	Den Helder	187	192	198	229	245	192	175	180	159	150	153	148	130	115	125	95	115	18

BREMERHAVEN
No 61 ⚓ QG; 53°32'·26N 08°33'·93E (Km 66·0).
Vorhafen N pier ☆ FR 15m 5M; 245°-166°; F in fog; 53°32'·15N 08°34'·50E.

RIVER JADE

1b/Jade1⚓ Oc G 4s; 53°52'·40N 07°44'·02E.
Mellumplate ☆ FW 28m **24M**; 116·1°-116·4° (ldg sector for outer part of Wangerooger Fahrwasser); R ☐ twr, W band; 53°46'·28N 08°05'·51E.
No 19 ⚓ QG; 53°47'·10N 08°01'·83E.
No 31/P-Reede/W Siel 1 ⚓ Oc (3) G 12s; 53°41'·59N 08°04'·51E.

HOOKSIEL
No 37/Hooksiel 1 ⚓ IQ G 13s; 53°39'·37N 08°06'·58E.
Vorhafen ent ☆ L Fl R 6s 9m 3M; 53°38'·63N 08°05'·25E.

WILHELMSHAVEN
Fluthafen N mole ☆ F WG 9m,W6M, G3M; 216°-W-280°-G-010°-W-020°-G-130°; G twr; 53°30'·86N 08°09'·32E.

EAST FRISIAN ISLANDS

NORTH EDGE OF INSHORE TRAFFIC ZONE
TG9/Weser 2 ⚓ Fl (2+1) G 15s; 53°55'·0N 07°44'·60E.
TG13 ⚓ Oc (3) G 12s; 53°50'·85N 07°15'·43E.
TG7 ⚓ Fl (2) G 9s; 53°47'·24N 06°49'·65E.
TG1 ⚓ Oc (3) G 12s; 53°44'·90N 06°33'·20E.

WANGEROOGE
Harle ⚓ Iso 8s; 53°49'·38N 07°46'·40E.
Wangerooge, W end ☆ Fl R 5s 60m **23M**; R ○ twr, 2 W bands; 53°47'·40N 07°51'·37E.
Dir lt 145·5°, Dir WRG 24m W22M G18M R17M; 119·4°-G-138·8°-W-152·2°-R-159·9°.
Buhne H ☆ VQ (9) 10s; 53°46'·86N 07°49'·65E.
W2 ⚓ ; 53°46'·25N 07°51'·89E, off hbr ent.

SPIEKEROOG
Otzumer Balje ⚓ Iso 4s; 53°48'·26N 07°36'·17E (often moved).
Spiekeroog ☆ FR 6m 4M; 197°-114°; R mast; 53°45'·0N 07°41'·3E.

LANGEOOG
Accumer Ee ⚓ Iso 8s; 53°46'·62N 07° 24'·02E (often moved).
W mole head ☆ Oc WRG 6s 8m W7M, R5M, G4M; 064°-G-070°-W-074°-R-326°-W-330°-G-335°-R-064°; R basket on R mast; *Horn Mo (L) 30s* (0730-1800LT); 53°43'·42N 07°30'·13E.

BALTRUM
Groyne hd ☆ Oc WRG 6s 6m; W6M, R4M, G3M; 074·5°-G-090°-W-095°-R-074·5°; 53°43'·3N 07°21'·7E.

DISTANCE TABLES
Approx distances in nautical miles are by the most direct route allowing for dangers and TSS.

NORDERNEY
Norderney ☆ Fl (3) 12s 59m **23M**; unintens 067°-077° and 270°-280°; R 8-sided twr; 53°42'·54N 07°13'·79E.
Dovetief ⚓ Iso 4s; 53°45'·47N 07°12'·70E.
Schluchter ⚓ Iso 8s; 53°44'·50N 07°02'·13E.
W mole head ☆ Oc (2) R 9s 13m 4M; 53°41'·9N 07°09'·9E.

JUIST
Juist-N ⚓ VQ; 53°43'·82N 06°55'·42E.
Training wall, S end ☆ Oc (2) R 9s 7m 3M; 53°39'·65N 06°59'·81E.

MAINLAND HARBOURS: R JADE TO R EMS

HARLESIEL
Carolinensieler Balje, Leitdamm ☆ L Fl 8s 7m 6M; G mast; 53°44'·13N 07°50'·10E.
Ldg lts 138°, both Iso 6s 12/18m 9M, intens on ldg line; Front 53°40'·70N 07°34'·50E. Rear 167m from front.
N mole head ☆ Iso R 4s 6m 7M; 53°42'·58N 07°48'·64E.

NEUHARLINGERSIEL
Training wall head ☆ Oc 6s 6m 5M; 53°43'·22N 07°42'·30E.

BENSERSIEL
E training wall head ☆ Oc WRG 6s 6m W5M, R3M, G2M; 110°-G-119°-W-121°-R-110°; R post & platform; 53°41'·80N 07°32'·84E.

DORNUMER-ACCUMERSIEL
W bkwtr head, approx 53°41'·04N 07°29'·30E.

NESSMERSIEL
N mole head ☆ Oc 4s 6m 5M; G mast; 53°41'·9N 07°21'·7E.

NORDDEICH
W trng wall head ☆ FG 8m 4M, 021°-327°; G framework twr; 53°38'·62N 07°09'·0E.

GREETSIEL
Meßstation lt bcn, Fl Y 4s 15m 3M; 53°32'·94N 07°02'·18E.

R EMS

APPROACHES
GW/EMS ⚓ Iso 8s 14m **17M** (H24); Emergency Lt, FR, occas. 2 FR vert; R Lt vessel, floodlit; *Horn Mo (R) 30s (H24);* 54°09'·96N 06°20'·72E.
Borkumriff ⚓ Oc 4s; 53°47'·48N 06°22'·27E.
Osterems ⚓ Iso 4s; 53°41'·91N 06°36'·17E.
Riffgat ⚓ Iso 8s; 53°38'·96N 06°27'·10E.
Westerems ⚓ Iso 4s; 53°36'·95N 06°17'·74E. 992111104. H1⊺ 53°34'·91N 06°17'·97E.

BORKUM
Borkum Grosser ☆ Fl (2) 12s 63m **24M**; brown ○ twr; 53°35'·32N 06°39'·64E. Same twr, ☆ F WRG 46m **W19M, R/G15M**; 107·4°-G-109°-W-111·2°- R-112·6°.
Fischerbalje ☆ Oc (2) 16s 15m 3M; 260°-W-123°. Fog det lt; R/W ○ twr on tripod; 53°33'·18N 06°42'·90E.
Schutzhafen, E mole hd ☆ FG10m 4M; 53°33'·48N 06°45'·02E. W mole hd, FR 8m 4M.

RIVER EMS (LOWER)
No 27 ⚓ Fl G 4s; 53°30'·24N 06°47'·52E.
No 35 ⚓ Fl G 4s; 53°27'·03N 06°52'·80E.
No 37 ⚓ QG; 53°26'·01N 06°54'·85E.
No 41 ⚓ Fl (2) G 9s; 53°24'·25N 06°56'·68E.
No 49 ⚓ Oc (2) G 9s; 53°19'·95N 06°59'·71E.

KNOCK
Knock ☆ F WRG 28m W12M,R9M, G8M; 270°-W-299°-R-008·3°-G-023°-W-026·8°-R-039°-W-073°-R-119°-W-154°; fog det lt; Gy twr, white conical radar antenna; 53°20'·32N 07°01'·40E.

EMDEN
No 59 ⚓ Oc (2) G 9s; 53°19'·41N 07°03'·86E.
No 65 ⚓ Fl (2) G 9s; 53°19'·82N 07°06'·56E.
Outer hbr, W pier ☆ FR 10m 4M; R 8-sided twr; 53°20'·06N 07°10'·49E.
E pier ☆ FG 7m 5M; G mast on pedestal; 53°20'·05N 07°10'·84E.

AREA 13 *Netherlands & Belgium – Delfzijl to Nieuwpoort*

SELECTED LIGHTS, BUOYS & WAYPOINTS

TSS OFF NORTHERN NETHERLANDS

TERSCHELLING-GERMAN BIGHT TSS
TG1/Ems ⚓ IQ G 13s; 53°43'·33N 06°22'·24E.
TE5 ⚓ Fl (3) G 10s; 53°37'·79N 05°53'·69E.
TE1 ⚓ Fl (3) G 10s; 53°29'·58N 05°11'·31E.

OFF VLIELAND TSS
VL-CENTER ⚓ Fl 5s 12M; *Racon C, 12–15M*; 53°26'·93N 04°39'·88E. VL7 ⚓ L Fl G 10s; 53°26'·40N 04°57'·60E.
VL1 ⚓ Fl (2) G 10s; 53°10'·96N 04°35'·31E.

DELFZIJL TO HARLINGEN

DELFZIJL
PS3/BW26 ⚓ Fl (2+1) G 12s; 53°19'·25N 07°00'·32E.
W mole ☆ FG; 53°19'·01N 07°00'·27E.
Ldg lts 203° both Iso 4s. Front, 53°18'·63N 07°00'·17E.

SCHIERMONNIKOOG AND LAUWERSOOG
WG (Westgat) ⚓ Iso 8s; *Racon N*; 53°31'·96N 06°01'·84E .
WRG ⚓ Q; 53°32'·87N 06°03'·24E.

AM ⚓ VQ; 53°30'·95N 05°44'·72E.
Schiermonnikoog ☆ Fl (4) 20s 43m **28M**; dark R ○ twr. Same twr: F WR 29m **W15M**, R12M; 210°-W-221°-R-230°. 53°29'·20N 06°08'·79E.
Lauwersoog W mole ☆ FG; *Horn (2) 30s;* 53°24'·68N 06°12'·00E.

ZEEGAT VAN AMELAND
BR ⚓ Q; 53°30'·66N 05°33'·52E.
TS ⚓ VQ; 53°28'·15N 05°21'·53E.
WA ⚓ 53°28'·35N 05°28'·64E. (Westgat buoys are all unlit)
Ameland, W end ☆ Fl (3) 15s 57m **30M**; 53°26'·89N 05°37'·42E.

NES
VA2-R1 ⚓ VQ(6) + L Fl 10s; 53°25'·71N 05°45'·88E.
Reegeul R3 ☆ Iso G 4s; 53°25'·80N 05°45'·93E.
R7 ☆ QG; 53°25'·91N 05°46'·21E.

HET VLIE (ZEEGAT VAN TERSCHELLING)
ZS ⚓ Iso 4s; *Racon T*; 53°18'·28N 04°56'·23E.

ZS1 ◣ VQ G; 53°18'·58N 04°57'·54E.

ZS3 ◣ QG; 53° 19'·29N 04° 59'·49E

ZS5 ◣ L Fl G 8s; 53°18'·55N 05°00'·83E.

ZS11-VS2 ⚓ Q (9) 15s; 53°18'·63N 05°05'·94E.

NOORD MEEP/SLENK TO WEST TERSCHELLING
WM3 ◣ Iso G 2s; 53°17'·45N 05°12'·28E.

NM 4-S 21 ⚓ VQ (3) 5s; 53°19'·02N 05°15'·47E.

SG1 ⚓ Q (9) 15s; 53°20'·44N 05°11'·70E.

Brandaris Twr ☆ Fl 5s 54m **29M**; Y ☐ twr partly obscured by dunes; 53°21'·62N 05°12'·86E.

W Terschelling W hbr mole ⚡ FR 5m 5M; R post, W bands; *Horn 15s*; 53°21'·26N 05°13'·09E. E pier hd ⚡ FG 4m 4M.

VLIELAND
VS3 (Vliesloot) ◣ VQ G; 53°18'·27N 05°06'·25E.

VS14 ◿ Iso R 4s; 53°17'·58N 05°05'62E.

VS16-VB1 ◿ Fl (2+1) R 10s; 53°17'·62N 05°05'·19E.

E/W mole hds ⚡ FG and ⚡ FR; 53°17'·68N 05°05'·51E.

Ldg lts 282° ⚡ Iso 4s 10/16m 1M, synch; 53°17'·75N 05°04'·47W (100m apart); mainly for the ferry terminal at E Vlieland.

E Vlieland (Vuurduin) ☆ Iso 4s 54m **20M**; 53°17'·75N 05°03'·49E.

APPROACHES TO HARLINGEN (selected marks):
VLIESTROOM buoys are frequently moved.

VL1 ◣ QG; 53°18'·99N 05°08'·82E. VL 2 ◿ QR; 53°19'·40N 05°09'·19E.

VL 11 ◣ Iso G 8s; 53°16'·42N 05°09'·70E.

BLAUWE SLENK
BS1-IN2 ⚓ VQ (3) 5s; 53°15'·41N 05°09'·41E.

BS13 ◣ QG; 53°13'·31N 05°17'·13E. BS19 ◣ VQ G; 53°11'·90N 05°18'·28E.

BS23 ◣ L Fl G 8s; 53°11'·42N 05°19'·60E.

POLLENDAM
Ldg lts 112°, both Iso 6s 8/19m 13M (H24); B masts, W bands. Front, 53°10'·52N 05°24'·19E. Use only between P2 and P6. P2 ⚓; 53°11'·47N 05°20'·38E on the training wall.

P4, Iso R 8s; P6, Iso R 4s; P8, Iso R 8s; and P10, Iso R 2s. Yachts should keep outboard of P1 thru 7 SHM buoys. P1 ◣ Iso G 2s; 53°11'·39N 05°20'·32E. P7 ◣ VQ G; 53°10'·68N 05°23'·45E.

HARLINGEN
S mole hd ⚡ FG 9m; 53°10'·56N 05°24'·18E.

N mole hd ⚡ FR 9m 4M; R/W pedestal; 53°10'·59N 05°24'·32E.

TEXEL AND THE WADDENZEE

TEXEL (from NW and W)
Eierland ☆ Fl (2) 10s 52m **29M**; R ◯ twr; 53°10'·93N 04°51'·31E.

TX ⚓ Q(9) 15s; 53°06'·81N 04°41'·19E

MOLENGAT (from the N)
Note: Positions/depths unreliable, see: Pl Terschelling to Texel and Den Helder.

Zinker-MG ⚓ VQ(9) 10s; 53°02'·27N 04°40'·95E

MG-A,Y ◰ ; 53°02'·61N 04°40'·28E.

MG-B, Y ⚓; 53°01'·99N 04°42'·00E

MG-D, Y ⚓ ; 53°00'·90N 04°42'·04E;

MG-G, Y ⚓; 52°59'·30N 04°42'·56E;

MG-H, Y ◰ ; 52°58'·91N 04°43'·10E.

OUDESCHILD
T12 ◿ Iso R 8s; 53°02'·23N 04°51'·52E.

Oudeschild Dir ⚡ Oc 6s; intens 291°; 53°02'·40N 04°50'·94E; leads 291° into hbr between N mole head FG 6m; and S mole head ⚡ FR 6m; 53°02'·33N 04°51'·17E.

APPROACHES TO KORNWERDERZAND SEALOCK

DOOVE BALG (From Texelstroom eastward)
T23 ◣ VQ G; 53°03'·60N 04°55'·85E, 066°/3M from Oudeschild.

T29 ◣ 53°03'·25N 05°00'·05E.

D1 ◿ Iso G 4s; 53°02'·18N 05°03'·42E.

D21 ◿ Iso G 8s; 53°03'·55N 05°15'·71E.

BO2-WG1 ⚓ Q (6) + L Fl 10s; 53°05'·00N 05°17'·91E.

KORNWERDERZAND SEALOCK
W mole ⚡ FG 9m 7M; *Horn Mo(N) 30s*; 53°04'·78N 05°20'·03E.

E mole ⚡ FR 9m 7M; 53°04'·70N 05°20'·08E.

W mole elbow ⚡ Iso G 6s 6m 7M; 53°04'·61N 05°19'·90E.

APPROACHES TO DEN OEVER SEALOCK

MALZWIN and VISJAGERSGAATJE CHANS TO DEN OEVER
MH4-M1 ⚓ VQ (9) 10s; 52°58'·14N 04°47'·49E, close N Den Helder.

M15 ◣ QG; 52°59'·39N 04°55'·48E (thence use DYC 1811.3).

VG1-W2 ◿ Fl (2+1) G 10s; 52°59'·00N 04°56'·85E.

O9 ◣ Iso G 8s; 52°56'·63N 05°02'·38E.

DEN OEVER SEALOCK
Ldg lts 131°, both Oc 10s 6m 7M; 127°-137°. Front, 52°56'·32N 05°02'·98E. Rear, 280m from front.

E end of swing bridge, ⚡ Iso WRG 5s 14m 10/7M; 226°-G-231°-W-235°-R-290°-G-327°-W-335°-R-345°; 52°56'·12N 05°02'·52E.

ZEEGAT VAN TEXEL AND DEN HELDER

OFFSHORE MARKS W and SW OF DEN HELDER
NH (Noorderhaaks) ⚓ VQ; 53°00'·24N 04°35'·37E.

MR ⚓ Q (9) 15s; 52°56'·77N 04°33'·82E.

ZH (Zuiderhaaks) ⚓ VQ (6) + L Fl 10s; 52°54'·65N 04°34'·72E.

Vinca G wreck ⚓ Q (9) 15s; 52°45'·93N 04°12'·31E.

SCHULPENGAT (from the SSW)
Schulpengat Dir ☆ 026·5°, Dir WRG, Al WR, Al WG, **W22M R/G18M**, church spire; 025.1°-FG- 025.6°-AlWG-026.3°-FW-026.7°-Al WR- 027.4° -F R- 027.9°; shown H24.

Licht van Troost ☆, delete entry in toto, substitute: Licht van Troost Dir ⚡ FWRG 27m W3M (Green post on Texel), W8M 21m, R8M, G5M; 333°-W-026°-G-033°-W-038°-R-070°; 53°00'·50N 04°45'·70E.

SG ⚓ Mo (A) 8s; *Racon Z*; 52°52'·90N 04°37'·90E.

S1 ◣ Iso G 4s; 52°53'·53N 04°38'·82E.

S7 ◣ QG; 52°56'·25N 04°40'·92E. S6A ◿ QR; 52°56'·52N 04°40'·51E.

S10 ◿ Iso R 8s; 52°57'·59N 04°41'·57E. S14-MG17 ⚓, see Molengat.

S11 ◣ Iso G 8s; 52°57'·55N 04°43'·25E.

Kijkduin ☆ Fl (4) 20s 56m **30M**; vis 360°, except where obsc'd by dunes on Texel; brown twr; 52°57'·33N 04°43'·58E (mainland).

MARSDIEP and DEN HELDER

T1 ⬦ Fl (3) G 10s; 52°57'·99N 04°44'·62E.

T3 ⬦ Iso G 8s; 52°58'·07N 04°46'·42E.

Den Helder ldg lts 191°, both Oc G 5s 16/25m 3M; synch. Front, vis 183·5°-198·5°; B ▽ on bldg; 52°57'·37N 04°47'·08E.

Marinehaven, W bkwtr head ✦ QG 11m 8M; *Horn 20s*; 52°57'·95N 04°47'·07E (Harssens Island).

W side, ✦ Fl G 5s 9m 4M (H24); 180°-067°; 52°57'·78N 04°47'·08E.

Yacht hbr (KMYC) ent ✦ FR & FG; 165m SW of ✦ Fl G 5s, above.

E side, MH6 ⬳ Iso R 4s; 52°57'·99N 04°47'·41E.

Ent E side, ✦ QR 9m 4M (H24); 52°57'·77N 04°47'·37E.

DEN HELDER TO AMSTERDAM

Zanddijk Grote Kaap ✦ Oc WRG 10s 30m 8M; 041°-G-088°-W-094°-R-120°; brown twr; 52°52'·86N 04°42'·88E.

Petten ⬳ VQ (9) 10s; 52°47'·33N 04°36'·78E (Power stn outfall).

Egmond-aan-Zee ☆ Iso WR 10s 36m **W18M**, R14M; 010°-W-175°-R-188°; W ◯ twr; 52°36'·99N 04°37'·16E.

IJMUIDEN

Baloeran ↙ Q (9) 15s; 52°29'·21N 04°32'·00E.

IJmuiden ⬳ Mo (A) 8s; *Racon Y, 10M*; 52°28'·45N 04°23'·92E.

Ldg lts 100·5° (FW 5M by day; 090·5°-110·5°). **Front** ☆ F WR 30m **W16M**, R13M; 050°-W-122°-R-145°-W-160°; (Tidal and traffic sigs); dark R ◯ twrs; 52°27'·70N 04°34'·47E. **Rear** ☆ Fl 5s 52m **29M**; 019°-199° (FW 5M by day; 090·5°-110·5°); 560m from front.

S bkwtr hd ✦ FG 14m 10M (in fog Fl 3s); W twr, G bands; 52°27'·82N 04°31'·93E.

N bkwtr hd ✦ FR 15m 10M; 52°28'·05N 04°32'·55E.

IJM1 ⬦ Iso G 4s; 52°27'·75N 04°33'·59E.

S outer chan ✦ Iso G 6s, 52°27'·75N 04°33'·81E. ✦ Iso R 6s, 52°27'·84N 04°34'·39E (Forteiland). Kleine Sluis 52°27'·84N 04°35'·43E.

AMSTERDAM

IJ8 ⬳ Iso R 8s (for Sixhaven marina); 52°22'·86N 04°54'·37E.

Oranjesluizen, N lock 52°22'·93N 04°57'·60E (for IJsselmeer).

AMSTERDAM TO ROTTERDAM

Noordwijk-aan-Zee ☆ Oc (3) 20s 32m **18M**; W ☐ twr; 52°14'·88N 04°26'·02E.

SCHEVENINGEN

Lighthouse ☆ Fl (2) 10s 48m **29M**; 014°-244°; brown twr; 52°06'·23N 04°16'·13E, 5ca E of hbr ent.

Ldg lts 156°, both Iso 4s 14M, H24; synch; Gy masts. Front 52°05'·99N 04°15'·44E; rear 250m from front. Intens at night.

SCH ⬳ Iso 4s; 52°07'·76N 04°14'·12E.

KNS ↙ Q (9)15s; 52°06'·48N 04°15'·27E.

W mole ✦ FG 12m 9M; G twr, W bands; 52°06'·23N 04°15'·16E.

E mole ✦ , FR 12m 9M; R twr, W bands; 52°06'·24N 04°15'·37E.

Inner ldg lts 131°: both Iso G 4s synch; Gy posts. Front 52°05'·81N 04°15'·89E. Rear, 34m from front.

NOORD HINDER N & S TSS and JUNCTION

NHR-N ⬳ L Fl 8s; *Racon K, 10M*; 52°10'·91N 03°04'·76E.

Noord Hinder ⬳ Fl (2) 10s; *Horn (2) 30s*; *Racon T, 12-15M*; 52°00'·10N 02° 51'·11E.

NHR-S ⬳ Fl Y 10s; 51°49'·53N 02°25'·95E.

NHR-SE ⬦ Fl G 5s; 51°43'·43N 02°37'·18E.

Birkenfels ↙ Q (9) 15s; 51°38'·96N 02°32'·03E.

Twin ⬳ Fl (3) Y 9s; 51°32'·05N 02°22'·62E.

Garden City ↙ Q (9) 15s; 51°29'·12N 02°17'·92E.

APPROACHES TO HOEK VAN HOLLAND

Europlatform ⬒ Mo (U) 15s; W structure, R bands; helicopter platform; *Horn Mo(U) 30s*; 51°55'·50N 03°40'·10E.

Goeree ☆ Mo(U)15s 32m **28M**; R/W chequered twr on platform; helicopter platform; *Horn Mo(U) 30s*; *Racon T, 12-15M*; 51°55'·42N 03°40'·03E.

Maasvlakte ☆ Fl (5) 20s 67m **28M**, H24; 340°-267°; W twr, B bands; 51°58'·20N 04°00'·84E, 1·5M SSW of Maas ent.

Maas Center ⬳ Iso 4s; *Racon M, 10M*; 52°00'·92N 03°48'·79E.

MO ⬳ Mo (A) 8s; 52°01'·10N 03°58'·19E.

MN3 ⬦ Fl (3) G 10s; 52°07'·04N 04°00'·00E.

MN1 ⬦ Fl G 5s; 52°02'·23N 04°01'·91E.

HOEK VAN HOLLAND

Maasmond ldg lts 112° (for deep draught vessels): both Iso 4s 30/46m **21M**; 101°-123°, synch; W twr, B bands. **Front**, 51°58'·88N 04°04'·88E (NW end of Splitsingsdam). **Rear**, 0·6M from front.

Indusbank N ↙ Q, 52°01'·82N 04°03'·60E.

MVN ↙ VQ; 51°59'·61N 04°00'·23E.

NETW ↙ Q (9) 15s; 51°59'·32N 04°01'·24E.

Maas 1 ⬦ L Fl G 5s; 51°59'·35N 04°01'·68E.

Nieuwe Waterweg ldg lts 107°: both Iso R 6s 29/43m **18M**; 099.5°-114.5°; R twr, W bands. Front, 51°58'·55N 04°07'·52E. Rear, 450m from front.

Noorderdam Head ✦ FR 25m 10M (In fog Al Fl WR 6s; 278°-255°); R twr, W bands; 51°59'·67N 04°02'·80E.

Nieuwe Zuiderdam ✦ FG 25m 10M, 330°-307°; (In fog Al Fl WG 6s); G twr, W bands; 51°59'·14N 04°02'·49E.

ROTTERDAM

Maassluis ✦ FG 6m; 51°54'·94N 04°14'·81E; and FR.

Vlaardingen ✦ FG; 51°53'·99N 04°20'·95E; and FR.

Spuihaven, W ent ✦ FR; 51°53'·98N 04°23'·97E.

Veerhaven, E ent ✦ FG; 51°54'·42N 04°28'·75E; and FR.

City marina ent, 51°54'·64N 04°29'·76E.

APPROACHES TO HARINGVLIET

Buitenbank , Iso 4s; 51°51'·16N 03°25'·71E.

Hinder ↙ Q (9) 15s; 51°54'·55N 03°55'·42E.

SH ↙ VQ (9) 10s; 51°49'·49N 03°45'·79E.

Westhoofd ☆ Fl (3) 15s 55m **30M**; R ☐ tr; 51°48'·79N 03°51'·85E.

Ooster ↙ Q (9) 15s; 51°47'·90N 03°41'·27E.

SLIJKGAT

SG ⬳ Iso 4s; 51°51'·95N 03°51'·42E.

SG 2 ⬳ Iso R 4s; 51°51'·71N 03°53'·45E.

SG 5 ⬦ Iso G 4s; 51°50'·00N 03°55'·56E.

SG 11 ⬦ Iso G 4s; 51°50'·81N 03°58'·52E.

P1 ⬦ Iso G 4s; 51°51'·30N 04°01'·12E.

P3 ▲ Iso G 8s; 51°51'·12N 04°01'·45E.
P9 ▲ Iso G 8s; 51°49'·98N 04°02'·15E.

STELLENDAM
N mole ⚓ FG; *Horn (2) 15s*; 51°49'·88N 04°02'·03E.
Buitenhaven ⚓ Oc 6s; 51°49'·73N 04°01'·75E.

APPROACHES TO OOSTERSCHELDE

OUTER APPROACHES
Schouwenbank ⚓ Mo (A) 8s; *Racon O, 10M*; 51°44'·94N 03°14'·32E.
Middelbank ⚓ Iso 8s; 51°40'·86N 03°18'·20E.
MW ⚓ Q (9) 15s; 51°44'·55N 03°24'·04E (Schouwendiep).
MD 3 ▲ Fl G 5s; 51°42'·70N 03°26'·98E.
Rabsbank ⚓ Iso 4s; 51°38'·25N 03°09'·93E.
Westpit ⚓ Iso 8s; 51°33'·65N 03°09'·92E.
ZSB ⚓ VQ (9) 10s; 51°36'·57N 03°15'·62E.
OG1 ▲ QG; 51°36'·14N 03°20'·08E.

WESTGAT, OUDE ROOMPOT and ROOMPOTSLUIS
West Schouwen ☆ Fl (2+1)15s 57m **30M**; Gy twr, R diagonals on upper part; 51°42'·52N 03°41'·50E, 5·8M N of Roompotsluis.
OG-WG ⚓ VQ (9) 10s; 51°37'·18N 03°23'·82E.
WG1 ▲ Iso G 8s; 51°38'·00N 03°26'·24E.
WG4 ⚓ L Fl R 8s; 51°38'·62N 03°28'·78E.
WG7 ▲ Iso G 4s 51°39'·40N 03°32'·67E.
WG-GB (Geul van de Banjaard) ⚓ 51°39'·72N 03°32'·69E.
OR1 ▲ 51°39'·15N 03°33'·59E.
OR5 ▲ Iso G 8s; 51°38'·71N 03°35'·53E.
OR11 ▲ Iso G 4s; 51°36'·98N 03°38'·40E.
R11A ⚓ QG 51°36'·74N 03°39'·29E.
R11B ⚓ Iso G 4s 51°37'·00N 03°39'·82E.
OR12 ⚓ Iso R 4s; 51°37'·27N 03°39'·25E.
OR13 R14; ⚓ VQ (3) 5s 51°36'·61N 03°38'·67E.
Roompotsluis ldg lts 073·5°, both Oc G 5s; synch. Front, 51°37'·33N 03°40'·75E. Rear, 280m from front.
N bkwtr ⚓ FR 7m; 51°37'·31N 03°40'·09E.

WESTKAPELLE TO VLISSINGEN

OOSTGAT
Ldg lts 149·5°: Front, Noorderhoofd Oc WRG 10s 20m; W13M, R/G10M; 353°-R-008°-G-029°-W-169°; R ○ twr, W band; 51°32'·40N 03°26'·21E, 0·73M from rear (Westkapelle).
Westkapelle ☆, rear, Fl 3s 50m **28M**; obsc'd by land on certain brgs; ☐ twr, R top; 51°31'·75N 03°26'·83E.
Kaloo ⚓ Iso 8s; 51°35'·55N 03°23'·24E. Chan is well buoyed/lit.
OG5 ▲ Iso G 8s; 51°34'·10N 03°23'·88E.
OG 7 ▲ VQ G , 51°32'·76N 03° 24'·87E.
Molenhoofd ⚓ Oc WRG 6s 10m; 311·5°-R-330·5°-W-348·5°-R-008°-G-034·5°-W-036·5°-G-147.5°-W-168.5°-R-198°; W mast R bands; 51°31'·58N 03°26'·05E.
Zoutelande F 22m 12M; 321°-352°; R ☐ twr; 51°30'·28N 03°28'·41E.
Kaapduinen, ldg lts 130°: both Oc 5s 25/34m 13M; synch; Y h twrs, R bands. Front, 122·5° - 137·5°; 51°28'·47N 03°30'·99E. Rear, 122·5° - 137·5°; 220m from front.
Fort de Nolle ⚓ Oc WRG 9s 11m W6M, R/G4M; 293°-R-309°-W-324·5°-G-336·5°-R-014°-G-064°-R-099·5°-W-110·5°-G-117°-R-130°; W col, R bands; 51°26'·94N 03°33'·12E.
Ldg lts 117°: Front, Leugenaar, Oc R 5s 6m 5M; intens 108°-126°; W&R pile; 51°26'·43N 03°34'·14E.

Rear, Sardijngeul ⚓ Oc WR 5s 10m 5M, synch; 245°-R-273°-W-123.5°-R-147°; R △, W bands on R & W mast; Koopmanshaven W Head, 550m from front; 51°26'·30N 03°34'·55E.

OFFSHORE: W HINDER TSS TO SCHEUR CHANNEL
West Hinder ☆ Fl (4) 30s 23m 13M; *Horn Mo (U) 30s*; *Racon W*; 51°23'·30N 02°26'·27E.
WH Zuid ⚓ Q (6) + L Fl 15s; 51°22'·78N 02°26'·25E.
OostdyckBk ⚓ Q; 51°21'·38N 02°31'·12E.
BerguesBk-N ⚓ Q; 51°19'·95N 02°24'·50E.
Oost-Dyck West ⚓ Q (9) 15s; 51°17'·15N 02°26'·32E.
Oostdyck radar twr; ⚓ Mo (U) 15s 15m 12M on 4 corners; *Horn Mo (U) 30s*; *Racon O*. R twr, 3 W bands, with adjacent red twr/helipad; 51°16'·49N 02°26'·85E.
A-N ⚓ Fl (4) R 20s; 51°23'·45N 02°36'·90E.
AS ▲ Fl (3) G 10s; 51°21'·15N 02°36'·92E.
KB2 ⚓ VQ; 51°21'·04N 02°42'·22E.
KB ⚓ Q; *Racon K*; 51°21'·03N 02°42'·83E.
MBN ⚓ Q; 51°20'·82N 02°46'·29E.
Akkaert-SW ⚓ Q (9) 15s; 51°22'·28N 02°46'·34E.
VG ⚓ Q ; 51°23'·38N 02°46'·21E, Vaargeul 1.
VG1 ▲ VQ G; 51°25'·03N 02°49'·04E.
VG2 ⚓ Q (6) + L Fl R 15s; *Racon V*; 51°25'·96N 02°48'·16E.
VG3 ▲ QG; 51°25'·05N 02°52'·92E.
VG5 ▲ Fl G 5s; 51°24'·63N 02°57'·92E.
SVG ⚓ Q ; 51°24'·53N 02°59'·92E.
Goote Bank ⚓ Q (3) 10s; 51°26'·95N 02°52'·72E.
A1 ⚓ Iso 8s; 51°22'·36N 02°53'·33E.
A1bis ⚓ L Fl 10s; 51°21'·68N 02°58'·02E.

WESTERSCHELDE APPROACHES

SCHEUR CHANNEL
S1 ▲ Fl G 5s; 51°23'·14N 03°00'·12E.
S3 ⚓ Q; 51°24'·30N 03°02'·92E.
MOW 0 ☉ Fl (5) Y 20s; *Racon S, 10M*; 51°23'·67N 03°02'·75E.
S5 ▲ Fl G 5s; 51°23'·70N 03°06'·30E.
S7 ▲ Fl G 5s; 51°23'·98N 03°10'·42E.
S9 ▲ QG; 51°24'·42N 03°14'·99E.
S12 ⚓ Fl (4) R 10s; 51°24'·67N 03°18'·22E.
S-W ⚓ Q; 51°24'·13N 03°18'·22E, here Wielingen chan merges.
S14 ⚓ Fl R 5s; 51°24'·58N 03°19'·67E.

WIELINGEN CHANNEL
BVH ⚓ Q (6) + L Fl R 15s; 51°23'·15N 03°12'·04E.
MOW3 tide gauge ⚓ Fl (5) Y 20s; *Racon H, 10M*; 51°23'·38N 03°11'·92E.
W ▲ Fl (3) G 15s; 51°23'·26N 03°14'·90E.
W1 ▲ Fl G 5s; 51°23'·46N 03°18'·21E.
Fort Maisonneuve ⚓ VQ (9) 10s; wreck; 51°24'·20N 03°21'·50E.
W3 ▲ Iso G 4s; 51°23'·95N 03°21'·48E.
W5 ▲ Iso G 8s; 51°24'·30N 03°24'·50E.
W7 ▲ Iso G 8s; 51°24'·59N 03°27'·27E.
W9 ▲ Q G; 51°24'·94N 03°30'·43E.
Nieuwe Sluis ⚓ Oc WRG 10s 26m W14M, R11M, G10M; 055°-R-089°-W-093°-G-105°-R-134°-W-136·5°-G-156·5°-W-236·5°-G-243°-W-254°-R-292°-W-055°; B 8-sided twr, W bands; 51°24'·41N 03°31'·29E.
Songa ▲ QG; 51°25'·26N 03°33'·66E.
W10 ⚓ QR; 51°25'·85N 03°33'·28E.

VLISSINGEN

Koopmanshaven, W mole root, ⚡ Iso WRG 3s 16m 8M; 253°-R-277°-W-284°-R-297°-W-306·5°-G-013°-W-024°-G-033°-W-035°-G-039°-W-055°-G-084·5°-R-092°-G-111°-W-114°; R pylon; 51°26'·37N 03°34'·52E.

Sardijngeul ⚡ Oc WR 5s; 51°26'·30N 03°34'·55E: see OOSTGAT last 3 lines. E mole head, ⚡ FG 7m; W mast; 51°26'·32N 03°34'·67E.

Buitenhaven ent, W side ⚡ FR 10m 5M; also Iso WRG 4s 6M: W073°-324°, G324°-352°, W352°-017°, G017°-042°, W042°-056°, R056°-073°; W post, R bands; tfc sigs; 51°26'·38N 03°36'·06E.

Buitenhaven ent, E side ⚡ FG 7m 4M; 51°26'·41N 03°36'·38E.

Schone Waardin ⚡ Oc WRG 9s 10m W13M, R10M, G9M; 235°-R-271°-W-283°-G-335°-R-341°-G-026°-W-079°-R-091°; R mast, W bands; 51°26'·54N 03°37'·91E (1M E of Buitenhaven ent).

BRESKENS TO CADZAND-BAD

Nieuwe Sluis ⚡ Oc 10s 28m 14M (priv); B/W banded 8 sided tr; 51°24'·43N 03°31'·26E.

ARV-VH ⚷ Q; 51°24'·71N 03°33'·89E.

VH2 (Vaarwaterlangs Hoofdplaat) ⚷ Iso R 2s; 51°24'·34N 03°33'·90E.

Yacht hbr, W mole ⚡ FG 7m; in fog FY; Gy post; 51°24'·03N 03°34'·06E. E mole ⚡ FR 6m; Gy mast; 51°23'·95N 03°34'·09E.

Cadzand-Bad, marina approach, CZ ⚹ Mo (A) 8s; 51°23'·08N 03°23'·07E.

WESTERSCHELDE: TERNEUZEN TO PAAL

TERNEUZEN

Nieuw Neuzenpolder ldg lts 125°, both Oc 5s 6/16m 9/13M; intens 117°-133°; synch. Front, W col, B bands; 51°20'·97N 03°47'·24E. Rear, B & W twr; 365m from front. Oost Buitenhaven E mole ⚡ FR 5M; 51°20'·56N 03°49'·19E. Veerhaven (former ferry hbr, W part) & marinas (E part) W mole head ⚡ FG, Gy mast; 51°20'·57N 03°49'·64E. E mole, FR.

W mole ⚡ Oc WRG 5s 15m W9M, R7M, G6M; 090°-R-115°-W-120°-G-130°-W-245°-G-249°-W-279°-R-004°; B & W post; 51°20'·54N 03°49'·58E, close SW of ⚡ FG.

HANSWEERT

W mole ⚡ Oc WRG 10s 9m W6M, R6M, G6M; (in fog FY); 288°-R-311°-G-320°-W-332·5°-R-348·5°-W-042·5°-R-061·5°-W-078°-G-099°-W-114·5°-R-127·5°-W-288°; R twr, W bands; 51°26'·42N 04°00'·53E.

BELGIUM
ZANDVLIET TO ANTWERPEN

ZANDVLIET

Dir ⚡ 118·3°,WRG 20m W4M, R/ G3M; 116·63°-Oc G-117·17°- FG-117·58°-Alt GW-118·63°-F-118·63°-Alt RW-119·18°-FR-119·58°- Oc R-120·13°; 51°20'·61N 04°16'·47E, near Zandvliet locks.

ANTWERPEN

No 107 ⚓ Iso G 8s, 51°14'·12N 04°23'·80E (Kattendijksluis for Willemdok ④).

Royerssluis, ldg lts 091°, both FR. Ent FR/FG.

No 109 ⚓ Iso G 8s; 51°13'·88N 04°23'·87E, (off Linkeroever ④).

Linkeroever marina ⚓ F WR 9m W3M, R2M; shore-W-283°- R-shore; B ☉, R lantern; 51°13'·91N 04°23'·70E. Marina ent, FR/FG.

COASTAL MARKS

AW2 ⚬ Fl (4) R 20s; 51°21'·95N 03°00'·94E; Wandelaar.

AW1 ⚓ QG; 51°21'·50N 03°02'·59E; Wandelaar.

Oostende Bank N ⚷ Q; 51°21'·20N 02°52'·93E.

Wenduine Bank E ⚬ QR; 51°18'·83N 03°01'·64E.

Wenduine Bank W ⚷ Q (9) 15s; 51°17'·23N 02°52'·76E.

Nautica Ena wreck ⚷ Q; 51°18'·08N 02°52'·79E.

Oostendebank E ⚓ Fl G 5s; 51°17'·35N 02°51'·92E.

Oostendebank W ⚷ Q (9)15s; 51°16'·20N 02°44'·74E.

LST 420 ⚷ Q (9)15s; 51°15'·45N 02°40'·67E.

MBN ⚷ Q; 51°20'·82N 02°46'·29E.

Middelkerke Bank ⚓ Fl G 5s; 51°18'·19N 02°42'·75E.

Middelkerke Bank S ⚷ Q (9) R 15s; 51°14'·73N 02°41'·89E.

D1 ⚷ Q (3) 10s; 51°13'·95N 02°38'·59E.

BT Ratel ⚬ Fl (4) R 15s; 51°11'·63N 02°27'·92E; Buiten Ratel.

ZEEBRUGGE TO THE FRENCH BORDER
ZEEBRUGGE

AW ⚷ Iso 8s; 51°22'·41N 03°07'·05E.

Ldg lts 136°, both Oc 5s 22/45m 8M; 131°-141°; H24, synch; W cols, R bands. Front, 51°20'·71N 03°13'·11E. Rear, 890m SE.

SZ ⚷ Q (3) 10s; 51°23'·30N 03°08'·65E (Scheur Channel).

Z ⚓ QG; 51°22'·48N 03°09'·95E.

WZ ⚷ Q (9) 15s; 51°22'·57N 03°10'·72E.

W outer mole ⚡ Oc G 7s 31m 7M; G vert strip lts visible from seaward; 057°-267°; *Horn (3) 30s;* IPTS; 51°21'·74N 03°11'·17E.

E outer mole ⚡ Oc R 7s 31m 7M; R vert strip lts visible from seaward; 087°-281°; *Bell 25s;* 51°21'·78N 03°11'·86E.

Ldg lts 154°: Front, Oc WR 6s 20m 3M, 135°-W-160°-R-169°; W pylon, R bands; 51°20'·33N 03°12'·89E. Rear, Oc 6s 38m 3M, H24, synch; 520m from front.

Leopold II mole ☆ Oc WR 15s 22m, **W20M, R18M**; 068°-W-145°-R-212°-W-296°; IPTS; 51°20'·85N 03°12'·17E. Entrance to Marina and FV hbr 51°19'·88N 03°11'·85E.

BLANKENBERGE

Promenade pier Fl (3) Y 20s, 8m 4M; 51°19'·28N 03°08'·18E.

Lt ho ☆ Fl (2) 8s 30m **20M**; 065°-245°; W twr, B top; 51°18'·76N 03°06'·87E.

Ldg lts 134°, both FR 5/9m 3/10M; R cross (X) topmarks on masts; front 51°18'·70N 03°08'·82E; rear 81m from front.

E pier ⚡ FR 12m 11M; R290°-245°(315°); W ◯ twr; 51°18'·91N 03°06'·56E.

W pier ⚡ FG 14m 11M; intens 065°-290°, unintens 290°-335°; W ◯ twr; 51°18'·89N 03°06'·42E.

OBST 4 – OBST 14 are eleven ⚷s Q approx 3ca offshore, marking Spoil Ground between Blankenberge and Oostende.

OOSTENDE

Wenduinebank West ⚷ Q (9) 15s; 51°17'·23N 02°52'·76E.

Buitenstroombank ⚷ Q; 51°15'·17N 02°51'·71E.

Binnenstroombank ⚷ Q (3) 10s; 51°14'·47N 02°53'·65E.

Ldg lts 143°: both Iso 4s (triple vert) 36/46m 4M, 068°-218°; X on metal mast, R/W bands. Front, 51°13'·80N 02°55'·89E.

Oostende lt ho ☆ Fl (3) 10s 65m **27M**; obsc 069·5°-071°; Gy twr, 2 sinusoidal Bu bands; 51°14'·18N 02°55'·84E.
W bkwtr hd ⚓ FG 9m 3M G mast; 51°14'·44N 02° 54'·97E.
E bkwtr hd ⚓ FR 9m 3M + QY; R mast; 51°14'·51N 02° 55'·18E and Radar tr, 50m, vert R/W stripes, R top, 51°14'·51N 02°55'·19E.

NIEUWPOORT
Zuidstroombank ⚲ Fl R 5s; 51°12'·28N 02°47'·37E.
Weststroombank ⚲ Fl (4) R 20s; 51°11'·34N 02°43'·03E.
Wreck 4 ⚓ Q (6) + L Fl 15s; 51°10'·98N 02°40'·10E.
Nieuwpoort Bank ⚓ Q (9) 15s; 51°10'·16N 02°36'·09E.
Whitley ⚓ Q; 51°09'·15N 02°39'·44E.
Lt ho ☆ Fl (2) R 14s 28m **16M**; R/W twr; 51°09'·28N 02°43'·80E.
E pier ⚓ FR 10m 10M; R025°-250°(225°) R307°-347°(40°); W ○ twr; 51°09'·41N 02°43'·08E.
W pier ⚓ FG 10m 9M; G025°-250°(225°) G284°-324°(40°); W ○ twr; 51°09'·35N 02°43'·00E.

⚓ QG 51°08'·65N 02°44'·31E marks the Y-junction where the channel forks stbd for KYCN and port for WSKLM and VVW-N.

WESTDIEP and PASSE DE ZUYDCOOTE
Den Oever wreck 2 ⚓ Q; 51°08'·11N 02°37'·43E.
Wreck 1 ⚓ Q; 51°08'·32N 02°35'·03E (adjacent to ⚲ next line).
Wave recorder ⚲ Fl (5) Y 20s; 51°08'·25N 02°34'·98E.
Trapegeer ▲ Fl G 10s; 51°08'·41N 02°34'·36E.
E12 ⚓ VQ (6) + L Fl 10s; 51°07'·92N 02°30'·61E.

French waters, for continuity (see also Area 17):
CME ⚓ Q (3) 10s; 51°07'·30N 02°30'·00E.
E11 ⚓ Fl G 4s; 51°06'·85N 02°30'·83E.
E10 ⚓ Fl (2) R 6s; 51°06'·26N 02°30'·40E.
E9 ⚓ Fl (2) G 6s; 51°05'·61N 02°29'·60E.
E8 ⚓ Fl (3) R 12s; 51°05'·12N 02°28'·60E.

1	Delfzijl	1															
2	Terschelling	85	2														
3	Harlingen	102	19	3													
4	Den Oever	110	34	21	4												
5	Den Helder	115	39	30	11	5											
6	Amsterdam	159	83	81	62	51	6										
7	IJmuiden	146	70	68	49	38	13	7									
8	Scheveningen	171	95	93	74	63	38	25	8								
9	Rotterdam	205	129	127	108	97	72	59	34	9							
10	Hook of Holland	185	109	107	88	77	52	39	14	20	10						
11	Stellendam	201	125	123	104	93	68	55	30	36	16	11					
12	Roompotsluis	233	157	155	136	125	100	87	50	68	48	32	12				
13	Vlissingen	228	152	150	131	120	99	86	61	67	47	45	24	13			
14	Zeebrugge	239	163	161	142	131	106	93	68	74	54	50	28	16	14		
15	Blankenberge	244	168	166	147	136	111	98	73	79	59	55	33	21	5	15	
16	Oostende	239	163	161	142	131	110	106	81	87	67	72	40	29	13	9	16
17	Nieuwpoort	262	186	184	165	154	129	116	91	97	77	83	51	39	23	18	9	17

DISTANCE TABLES
Approx distances in nautical miles are by the most direct route allowing for dangers and TSS.

AREA 14 *North France – Dunkerque to Cap de la Hague*

SELECTED LIGHTS, BUOYS & WAYPOINTS

OFFSHORE MARKS: W Hinder to Dover Strait
Fairy South ⚓ VQ (6) + L Fl 10s; 51°21'·20N 02°17'·31E.
Fairy West ⚓ VQ (9) 10s 6M; 51°23'·89N 02°09'·27E.
992271127. Hinder 1 ⚓ Fl (2) 6s; 51°20'·80N 02°10'·93E.
Bergues ⚓ Fl G 4s 7m 4M; 51°17'·14N 02°18'·63E.
Bergues S ⚓ Q (6) + L Fl 15s; 51°15'·09N 02°19'·42E.
Ruytingen E ⚓ VQ; 51°14'·55N 02°17'·93E.
Ruytingen N ⚓ VQ 4M; 51°13'·16N 02°10'·28E.
Ruytingen SE ⚓ VQ (3) 15s; 51°09'·20N 02°08'·94E.992271126.
Ruytingen NW ⚓ Fl G 4s 3M; 51°09'·11N 01°57'·30E.
Ruytingen W ⚓ VQ 4M; 51°06'·93N 01°50'·45E.
Ruytingen SW ⚓ Fl (3) G 12s 3M; 51°04'·33N 01°45'·84E.
Sandettié N ⚓ VQ 6M; 51°18'·35N 02°04'·73E.
Sandettié E ⚓ Fl R 4s 7m 3M;51°14'·88N 02°02'·65E.992271119.

DUNKERQUE TO BOULOGNE
PASSE DE ZUYDCOOTE
E12 ⚓ VQ (6) + L Fl 10s; 51°07'·92N 02°30'·61E. (Belgium)

CME ⚓ Q (3) 10s; 51°07'·30N 02°30'·00E.
E11 ⚓ Fl G 4s; 51°06'·85N 02°30'·83E.
E10 ⚓ Fl (2) R 6s; 51°06'·26N 02°30'·40E.
E9 ⚓ Fl (2) G 6s; 51°05'·61N 02°29'·60E.
E8 ⚓ Fl (3) R 12s; 51°05'·12N 02°28'·60E. (E7 does not exist)

PASSE DE L'EST
E6 ⚓ QR; 51°04'·86N 02°27'·08E.
E4 ⚓ Fl R 4s; 51°04'·58N 02°24'·52E.
E1 ⚓ Fl (2) G 6s; 51°04'·12N 02°23'·04E.
E2 ⚓ Fl (2) R 6s; 51°04'·35N 02°22'·31E.
⚓ Q (6) + L Fl 15s; 51°04'·28N 02°21'·73E.

DUNKERQUE PORT EST
E jetty ☆ Fl (2) R 6s 12m 10M; R ☐, W pylon; 51°03'·59N 02°21'·20E.
W jetty ☆ Fl (2) G 6s 35m 11M; W twr, brown top; 51°03'·63N 02°20'·95E.
Ldg lts 137·5°, front Q7m11M 51°02'·98N 02°22'·05E, rear, Q10m11M, 114m from front, both W cols, R tops, synched.

Inner W jetty ⚓ Q 11m 9M; 51°03'·33N 02°21'·43E.
Dunkerque lt ho ☆ Fl (2) 10s 59m **26M**; 51°02'·93N 02°21'·86E.

DUNKERQUE INTERMEDIATE CHANNEL
DW30 ⚓ QR; 51°04'·14N 02°20'·16E.
DW29 ⚓ QG; 51°03'·85N 02°20'·21E.
DW16 ⚓ Fl (2) R 6s; 51°03'·52N 02°08'·62E.
DKB ⚓ VQ (9) 10s; 51°02'·95N 02°09'·26E.
DW12 ⚓ Fl (3) R 12s; 51°03'·38N 02°05'·36E.
DW11 ⚓ Fl (3) G 12s; 51°02'·79N 02°05'·53E. (DW10-7 omitted)

GRAVELINES
W jetty ⚓ Fl (2) WG 6s 9m W/G4M; 085°-W-224°-G-085°; Y ○ twr, G top; 51°00'·94N 02°05'·49E.

PASSE DE L'OUEST
DW6 ⚓ VQ R; 51°02'·81N 02°00'·80E.
DW5 ⚓ QG; 51°02'·20N 02°00'·92E.
DKA ⚓ L Fl 10s; 51°02'·55N 01°56'·96E.
RCE (Ridens de Calais East) ⚓ Fl G 4s; 51°02'·29N 01°52'·98E.
Dyck ⚓ Fl R 4s; *Racon B*; 51° 02'·90N 01°51'·80E.
RCA (Ridens de Calais Approach) ⚓ Q; 51°01'·00N 01°48'·53E. 992271125.

CALAIS
E jetty ⚓ Fl (2) R 6s 12m **17M**; (in fog two Fl (2) 6s (vert) on request); Gy twr, R top; *Horn (2) 40s*; 50°58'·39N 01°50'·45E.
E Jetty root, Dir ⚓ WG 12m 1M; 089·4°-FG-093·7°-Al WG-094°·3- FW-098·6°; metal structure; 50°58'·25N 01°51'·20E.
W jetty ⚓ Iso G 3s 12m 9M; (in fog Fl 5s on request); W twr, G top; *Bell 5s*; 50°58'·24N 01°50'·40E.
Calais ☆ Fl (4) 15s 59m **22M**; vis 073°-260°; W 8-sided twr, B top; 50°57'·68N 01°51'·21E (440m E of marina entry gate).

CALAIS, WESTERN APPROACH
CA6 ⚓ Fl (3) R 12s; 50°58'·63N 01°49'·92E.
CA4 ⚓ Fl (2)R 6s; 50°58'·38N 01°48'·65E.
CA1 ⚓ Fl G 4s; 50°57'·64N 01°46'·14E (0.5M NNW of Sangatte).
Sangatte ⚓ Oc WG 4s 13m W8M, G5M; 065°-G-089°-W-152°-G-245°; W pylon, B top; 50°57'·19N 01°46'·50E.
Les Quénocs ⚓ VQ; 50°56'·85N 01°41'·12E.
Abbeville wreck ⚓ VQ (9) 10s; 50°56'·08N 01°37'·58E.
Cap Gris-Nez ☆ Fl 5s 72m **29M**; 005°-232°; W twr, B top; 50°52'·09N 01°34'·96E.

OFFSHORE MARKS: DOVER STRAIT TSS, French side
Colbart N ⚓ Q 6M; 50°57'·50N 01°23'·30E. 992271121.
Colbart SW ⚓ VQ (6) + L Fl 10s 8m; 50°48'·87N 01°16'·32E.
ZC2 (Zone Cotière) ⚓ Fl (2+1) Y 15s 5M; 50°53'·54N 01°30'·89E.
ZC1 ⚓ Fl (4) Y 15s 4MN; 50°44'·99N 01°27'·21E.
Ridens SE ⚓ VQ (3) 5s 6M; 50°43'·48N 01°18'·87E.
Bassurelle ⚓ Fl (4) R 15s 6M; *Racon B, 5-8M*; 50°32'·74N 00°57'·69E.
Vergoyer N ⚓ VQ 5M; 50°39'·67N 01°22'·21E.
Vergoyer NW ⚓ Fl (2) G 6s 4M; 50°37'·16N 01°17'·85E.
Vergoyer E ⚓ VQ (3) 5s 6M; 50°35'·80N 01°19'·70E. 992271132
Vergoyer W ⚓ Fl G 4s 4M; 50°34'·66N 01°13'·57E.
Vergoyer SW ⚓ VQ (9) 10s 6M; 50°27'·01N 01°00'·03E.

BOULOGNE TO DIEPPE
BOULOGNE
Bassure de Baas ⚓ VQ; 50°48'·53N 01°33'·05E.
Approches Boulogne ⚓ VQ (6) + L Fl 10s 8m 6M; 50°45'·31N 01°31'·07E.
Digue N (detached) ⚓ Fl (2) R 6s 10m 7M; 50°44'·71N 01°34'·18E.
Digue S (Carnot) ☆ Fl (2+1) 15s 25m **19M**; W twr, G top; 50°44'·44N 01°34'·05E.
Clearing brg 122·4° : Front, FG in a neon ▽ 4m 5M; 50°43'·71N 01°35'·66E. Rear, FR 44m 11M; intens 113°-133°; 560m from front.
Inner NE jetty ⚓ FR 11m 7M; 50°43'·91N 01°35'·24E.
Inner SW jetty ⚓ FG 17m 5M; W col, G top; *Horn 30s*; 50°43'·90N 01°35'·11E.
Cap d'Alprech ☆ Fl (3) 15s 62m **23M**; W twr, B top; 50°41'·91N 01°33'·75E, 2·5M S of hbr ent.

LE TOUQUET/ÉTAPLES
Pte de Lornel ⚓ VQ (9) 10s 6m 3M; 50°33'·24N 01°35'·12E.
Mérida wreck ⚓ 50°32'·85N 01°33'·44E.
Camiers lt ho ⚓ Oc (2) WRG 6s 17m W10M, R/G7M; 015°-G-090°-W-105°-R-141°; R pylon; 50°32'·86N 01°36'·28E.
Canche Est groyne ⚓ Fl R 4s 8m; 50°32'·57N 01°35'·66E.
Le Touquet ☆ Fl (2) 10s 54m **25M**; Or twr, brown band, W&G top; 50°31'·43N 01°35'·52E.
Pointe du Haut-Blanc ☆ Fl 5s 44m **23M**; W twr, R bands, G top; 50°23'·90N 01°33'·67E (Berck).

BAIE DE LA SOMME
ATSO ⚓ Mo (A) 12s; 50°14'·00N 01°28'·08E.
Pte du Hourdel ⚓ Oc (3) WG 12s 19m, W12M, G9M; 053°-W-248°-G-323°; tidal sigs; *Horn (3) 30s*; W twr, G top; 50°12'·90N 01°33'·98E.
Cayeux-sur-Mer ☆ Fl R 5s 32m **22M**; W twr, R top; 50°11'·65N 01°30'·72E.
Le Crotoy ⚓ Oc (2) R 6s 19m 8M; 285°-135°; W pylon; 50°12'·91N 01°37'·40E. Marina ⚓ Fl R & Fl G 2s 4m 2M; 50°12'·98N 01°38'·20E.

ST VALÉRY-SUR-SOMME
Trng wall hd ⚓ Fl G 2.5s 2m 1M; 50°12'·25N 01°35'·85E.
Embankment head ⚓ Iso G 4s 9m 9M; 347°-222°; W pylon, G top; 50°12'·25N 01°36'·02E.
La Ferté môle ⚓ Fl R 4s 9m 9M; 000°-250°; W pylon, R top; 50°11'·18N 01°38'·14E (ent to marina inlet).

LE TRÉPORT
Ault ☆ Oc (3) WR 12s 95m **W15M**, R11M; 040°-W-175°-R-220°; W twr, R top; 50°06'·28N 01°27'·23E (4M NE of Le Tréport).
W jetty ☆ Fl (2) G 10s 15m **20M**; W twr, G top; 50°03'·88N 01°22'·14E.

DIEPPE
W jetty ⚓ Iso G 4s 11m 8M; W twr, G top; *Horn 30s*; 49°56'·27N 01°04'·97E.
Quai de la Marne ⚓ QR 12m 3M; 49°55'·93N 01°05'·20E, E quay.
Pointe d'Ailly ☆ Fl (3) 20s 95m **31M**; W □ twr, G top; *Horn (3) 60s*; 49°54'·96N 00°57'·50E.

DIEPPE TO LE HAVRE
SAINT VALÉRY-EN-CAUX
W jetty ⚓ Fl (2) G 6s 13m 11M; W twr, G top; 49°52'·40N 00°42'·54E.

Paluel power station, restricted area, Paluel 2 ⟨ Fl Y 4s; 49°52'·33N 00°38'·45E; Wave recorder ⟨ Fl(5) Y 20s; 49°52'·30N 00°37'·87E; Paluel 1 ⟨ Fl Y 4s; 49°52'·33N 00°37'·53E.

FÉCAMP
N jetty ☆ Fl (2) 10s 15m **16M**; Gy twr, R top; 49°45'·94N 00°21'·80E.

Fécamp NW, Met Mast FECO1-YO2 ⚡ Mo(U) W 15s 13m 10M, Aero F R 36m, Aero UQ R 60m, Aero UQ W 60m(day) Gy pylon,Y platform; Horn Mo(U) 30s; 49°50'·85N 00°13'·14E. <u>992271122.</u>

PORT DU HAVRE-ANTIFER
Cap d'Antifer ☆ Fl 20s 128m **29M**; 021°-222°; Gy 8-sided twr, G top, on 90m cliffs; 49°41'·01N 00°09'·93E.
A17 ⟨ Iso G 4s; 49°41'·53N 00°01·75E.
A18 ⟨ QR; 49°42'·02N 00°02'·18E. Cross the chan W of A17/18.
Ldg lts 127·5°, both Dir Oc 4s 113/135m **22M**; 127°-128°; by day F **33M** 126·5°-128·5° occas. Front ☆, 49°38'·31N 00°09'·12E.

LE HAVRE, APPROACH CHANNEL
Cap de la Hève ☆ Fl 5s 123m **24M**; 225°-196°; W 8-sided twr, R top; 49°30'·74N 00°04'·16E.
LHA 🔲 Mo (A) 12s 10m 6M; R&W; *Racon, 8-10M* (a series of 8 dots, or 8 groups of dots; distance between each dot or group represents 0·3M); 49°31'·38N 00°09'·86W. Reserve lt Mo (A).
Ldg lts 106·8°, both Dir F 36/78m **25M** (H24); intens 106°-108°; Gy twrs, G tops. Front, 49°28'·91N 00°06'·50E; rear, 0·73M from front.
LH3 ⟨ QG; 49°30'·84N 00°04'·02W. (LH1 & 2 buoys do not exist)
LH4 ⟨ QR; 49°31'·11N 00°03'·90W.
LH7 ⟨ Iso G 4s; 49°30'·25N 00°00'·82W.
LH8 ⟨ Fl (2) R 6s; 49°30'·44N 00°00'·70W.
Note the W-E longitude change. (LH9 buoy does not exist)
LH13 ⟨ Fl G 4s; 49°29'·32N 00°03'·62E (Ent to Port 2000).
LH14 ⟨ Fl R 4s; 49°29'·67N 00°03'·43E; 1m shoal depth close W.
LH16 ⟨ Fl (2) R 6s; 49°29'·45N 00°04'·28E.
LH 2000 ⟨ VQ (9) 10s; 49°29'·14N 00°04'·78E (Ent to Port 2000).

LE HAVRE
Digue N ⚡ Fl R 4s 15m 8M; IPTS; W ○ twr, R top; 49°29'·19N 00°05'·44E.
Digue S ⚡ Fl G 4s 15m 8M; W twr, G top; 49°29'·05N 00°05'·38E.
Marina ent, W spur ⚡ Fl (2) R 6s 3M; 49°29'·22N 00°05'·53E.

THE SEINE ESTUARY UP TO HONFLEUR

CHENAL DE ROUEN
Nord du Mouillage ⟨ Fl (4) Y 15s; 49°28'·80N 00°00'·22E.
No 2 ⟨ QR; *Racon T;* 49°27'·70N 00°00'·60E.
No 4 ⟨ Fl R 2·5s; 49°27'·19N 00°01'·97E. Yachts keep N of chan.
Amfard SW ⟨ QR; 49°26'·30N 00°04'·82E.
No 10 ⟨ Fl R 4s; 49°26'·10N 00°06'·39E.
Digue du Ratier ⟨ VQ 10m 4M; 49°25'·94N 00°06'·59E.
Falaise des Fonds ☆ Fl (3) WRG 12s 15m, **W17M**, R/G13M; 040°-G-080°-R-084°-G-100°- W-109°-R-162°-G-260°; W twr, G top; 49°25'·47N 00°12'·85E.
No 20 ⟨ Fl (2) R 6s; 49°25'·85N 00°13'·71E. (over to Honfleur)

HONFLEUR
Digue Ouest ⚡ QG 10m 6M; 49°25'·67N 00°13'·83E.
Digue Est ⚡ Q 9m 8M; *Horn (5) 40s;* 49°25'·67N 00°13'·95E.
Inner E jetty head, ⚡ Fl R 2M; 49°25'·40N 00°14'·10E.
No 22 ⟨ Fl R 4s; 49°25'·85N 00°15'·37E.

TROUVILLE TO COURSEULLES

CHENAL DE ROUEN TO DEAUVILLE and TROUVILLE
Ratelets ⟨ Q (9) 15s; 49°25'·29N 00°01'·71E.
Semoy ⟨ VQ (3) 5s; 49°24'·15N 00°02'·35E, close to 148° ldg line.
Trouville SW ⟨ VQ (9) 10s; 49°22'·54N 00°02'·56E.

DEAUVILLE and TROUVILLE
Ldg lts 145°, both Oc R 4s 11/17m 12/10M: Front, East inner jetty (*estacade*); 330°-150°; W twr, R top; 49°22'·03N 00°04'·48E.
Rear, Pte de la Cahotte; synch; 120°-170°; 49°21'·93N 00°04'·58E.
W trng wall ⚡ FlWG 4s 10m W9M, G6M; 005°-W-176°-G-005°; B pylon, G top; 49°22'·37N 00°04'·11E. Also 4 unlit SHM bcns.
E trng wall ☆ Fl (4) WR 12s 8m W7M, R4M; 131°-W-175°-R-131°; W pylon, R top; 49°22'·22N 00°04'·33E. Also 3 unlit PHM bcns.
W outer bkwtr ⚡ Iso G 4s 9m 5M; 49°22'·11N 00°04'·33E.
West inner jetty (*estacade*) ⚡ QG 11m 9M; 49°22'·03N 00°04'·43E.

DIVES-SUR-MER *Note the E–W longitude change.*
DI ⟨ Iso 4s; 49°19'·17N 00°05'·86W.
No 1 ⟨ VQ G; 49°18'·50N 00°05'·67W. Ch bys freq moved.
No 2 ⟨ VQ R; 49°18'·51N 00°05'·56W.
No 3 ⟨ QG 7m 4M; W pylon, G top; 49°18'·30N 00°05'·55W.
No 5 ⟨ Fl G 4s 8m 4M; W pylon, G top; 49°18'·09N 00°05'·50W.
Bcns 3 & 5, if damaged, may be temporarily replaced by buoys.
No 7 ⟨ Fl G 4s; 49°17'·65N 00°05'·31W.

OUISTREHAM and CAEN
Merville ⟨ VQ; 49°19'·65N 00°13'·39W; spoil ground buoy.
Ouistreham ⟨ VQ (3) 5s; wreck buoy; 49°20'·42N 00°14'·81W.
Ldg lts 185°, both Dir Oc (3+1) R 12s 10/30m **17M**; intens 183·5°-186·5°, synch. **Front** ☆, E jetty, W mast, R top; 49°16'·99N 00°14'·81W. **Rear** ☆, 610m from front, tripod, R top.
No 1 ⟨ QG; 49°19'·19N 00°14'·67W.
No 2 ⟨ QR; 49°19'·17N 00°14'·43W.
Barnabé ⚡ QG 7m 5M; W pylon, G top; 49°18'·02N 00°14'·76W.
St-Médard ⚡ QR 7m 5M; 49°18'·02N 00°14'·62W.
Riva ⚡ Fl G 4s 9m 3M; W pylon, G top; 49°17'·73N 00°14'·79W.
Quilbé ⚡ Fl R 4s 9m 3M; W pylon, R top; 49°17'·72N 00°14'·67W.
Ouistreham lt ho ☆ Oc WR 4s 37m **W17M**, R13M; 115°-R-151°-W-115°; W twr, R top; 49°16'·79N 00°14'·87W.

COURSEULLES-SUR-MER
Courseulles ⟨ Iso 4s; 49°21'·28N 00°27'·68W.

W jetty ⚓ Iso WG 4s 7m; W9M, G6M; 135°-W-235°-G-135°; brown pylon on dolphin, G top; 49°20'·41N 00°27'·37W.
E jetty ⚓ Oc (2) R 6s 9m 7M; 49°20'·26N 00°27'·39W.

COURSEULLES TO ST VAAST

Ver ☆ Fl (3)15s 42m **26M**; obsc'd by cliffs of St Aubin when brg >275°; conspic lt ho, W twr, Gy top; 49°20'·41N 00°31'·13W.

ARROMANCHES

Ent buoys: ⬙ 49°21'·35N 00°37'·26W; ⬙ 49°21'·25N 00°37'·30W.
Bombardons ⬙ wreck buoys; 49°21'·66N 00°38'·97W.

PORT-EN-BESSIN

Ldg lts 204°, both Oc (3) 12s 25/42m 10/11M; synch. Front, 069°-339°, W pylon, G top; 49°20'·96N 00°45'·53W. Rear, 114°-294°, W and Gy ho; 93m from front.
E mole ⚓ Oc R 4s 14m 7M; R pylon; 49°21'·12N 00°45'·38W.
W mole ⚓ Fl WG 4s 14m, W10M, G7M; G065°-114·5°, W114·5°-065°; G pylon; 49°21'·17N 00°45'·43W.

COASTAL MARKS

Omaha Beach, 1M off : ⬙ 49°22'·66N 00°50'·28W; ⬙ 49°23'·17N 00°51'·93W; ⬙ 49°23'·66N 00°53'·74W.
Broadsword ⬙ Q (3) 10s, wreck buoy; 49°25'·34N 00°52'·96W.
Est du Cardonnet ⬙ VQ (3) 5s; 49°26'·83N 01°01'·10W.

GRANDCAMP

Les Roches de Grandcamp: No 1 ⬙ 49°24'·72N 01°01'·75W; No 3 ⬙ 49°24'·92N 01°03'·70W; No 5 ⬙ 49°24'·78N 01°04'·98W.
Ldg lts 146°, both Dir Q 9/12m **15M**, 144·5°-147·5°. **Front** ☆, 49°23'·42N 01°02'·90W. **Rear** ☆,102m from front.
Jetée Est ⚓ Oc (2) R 6s 9m 9M; *Horn Mo(N) 30s;* 49°23'·53N 01°02'·96W.
Jetée Ouest ⚓ Fl G 4s 9m 6M; 49°23'·47N 01°02'·96W.

ISIGNY-SUR-MER

IS, small B/Y ⬙, no topmark (⬙ on AC2135); 49°24'·28N 01°06'·37W.
No 1 ⬙, Fl R 4s; 49°23'·60N 01°07·27W
Dir lts 173°, both Dir Q WRG 7m 9M; 49°19'·57N 01°06·78W.
Training wall heads ⬙ Fl G 4s; 49°21'·40N 01°07'·20W; ⬙ Fl R 4s, 49°21'·40N 01°07'·10W, off Pte du Grouin.

CARENTAN

C-I ⬙ Iso 4s; 49°25'·44N 01°07'·08W; 210°/1·76M to 1 & 2 bys.
No 1 ⬙ Fl G 4s; 49°24'·29N 01°08'·57W.
No 2 ⬙ Fl R 4s; 49°23'·93N 01°08'·32W.
Trng wall ⬙ Fl (4) G 15s; G △ on G bcn;49°21'·96N 01°09'·95W.
Trng wall ⬙ Fl (4) R 15s; R ☐ on R bcn;49°21'·93N 01°09'·878W.

ÎLES SAINT-MARCOUF

Iles St-Marcouf ⚓ VQ (3) 5s 18m 8M; ☐ Gy twr, G top; 49°29'·86N 01°08'·81W.
Ouest-Saint-Marcouf ⬙ Q (9) 15s; 49°29'·73N 01°11'·97W.
Saint Floxel ⬙ 49°30'·64N 01°13'·94W.
Quineville ⬙ Q (9) 10s, wreck buoy; 49°31'·79N 01°12'·38W.

ST VAAST TO POINTE DE BARFLEUR

ST VAAST-LA-HOUGUE

Ldg lts 267°: Front, La Hougue Oc 4s 9m 10M; W pylon, G top; 49°34'·25N 01°16'·37W. Rear, Morsalines Oc (4) WRG 12s 90m, W11M, R/G8M; 171°-W-316°-G-321°-R-342°-W-355°; W 8-sided twr, G top; 49°34'·16N 01°19'·10W, 1·8M from front.
Le Manquet ⬙ 49°34'·26N 01°15'·56W.
Le Bout du Roc ⬙ 49°34'·68N 01°15'·27W.
La Dent ⬙ 49°34'·57N 01°14'·20W.
Le Gavendest ⬙ Q (6) + L Fl 15s; 49°34'·36N 01°13'·89W.
Jetty ⚓ Dir Oc (2) WRG 6s 12m W10M, R/G7M; 219°-R-237°-G-310°-W-350°-R-040°; W 8-sided twr, R top; 49°35'·17N 01°15'·41W.
Pte de Saire ⚓ Iso 4s 11m 10M; squat W twr, G top; 49°36'·36N 01°13'·78W.

BARFLEUR

Ldg lts 219·5°, both Oc (3) 12s 7/13m 10M; synch. Front, W☐ twr;49°40'·18N 01°15'·61W. Rear, 085°-355°; Gy and W☐ twr, G top; 288m from front.
La Grotte ⬙ 49°41'·06N 01°14'·86W.
Roche-à-l'Anglais ⬙ 49°40'·78N 01°14'·93W.
La Vimberge ⬙ 49°40'·54N 01°15'·25W.
W jetty ⚓ Fl G 4s 8m 6M; 49°40'·32N 01°15'·57W.
E jetty ⚓ Fl R 4s 5m 6M; 49°40'·32N 01°15'·46W.
La Jamette ⬙ 49°41'·87N 01°15'·59W.
Pte de Barfleur ☆ Fl (2) 10s 72m **25M**; obsc when brg less than 088°; Gy twr, B top; 49°41'·79N 01°15'·95W.

POINTE DE BARFLEUR TO CAP DE LA HAGUE

Les Équets ⬙ Q 8m 3M; 49°43'·62N 01°18'·36W.
Basse du Rénier ⬙ VQ 8m 4M; 49°44'·84N 01°22'·09W.
Les Trois Pierres ⬙ 49°42'·90N 01°21'·80W.
Anse de Vicq, 158° ldg lts; both Iso R 4s 8/14m 6M; front 49°42'·20N 01°23'·95W.
La Pierre Noire ⬙ Q (9) 15s 8m 4M;49°43'·54N 01°29'·07W.

PORT DU LÉVI

Cap Lévi ☆ Fl R 5s 36m **17M**; Gy ☐ twr; 49°41'·75N 01°28'·39W.
Port Lévi ⚓ Oc (2) WRG 6s 7m 7M; 055°-G-083°-W-105°-R-163°; W & Gy hut, W lantern; 49°41'·24N 01°28'·34W.

PORT DU BECQUET

Ldg lts 186·3°, both intens 183°-189·3°; synch. Front, Dir Oc (3) 12s 8m 10M; W 8-sided twr; 49°39'·23N 01°32'·84W. Rear, Dir Oc (3) 12s 13m 7M. W 8-sided twr, R top; 49m from front.

CHERBOURG, EASTERN ENTRANCES

Passe Collignon ⚓ Fl (2) R 6s 5m 4M; 49°39'·59N 01°34'·24W.
Passe de l'Est, Jetée des Flamands ldg lts 189°, both 9/16m 13M. Front, 49°39'·33N 01°35'·94W . Rear, 516m from front.
Roches du Nord-Ouest ⬙ Fl R 2·5s; 49°40'·64N 01°35'·28W.
La Truite ⬙ Fl (4) R 15s; 49°40'·33N 01°35'·49W.
Fort d'Île Pelée ⚓ Oc (2) WR 6s 19m; W10M, R7M; 055°-W-120°-R-055°; W and R pedestal; 49°40'·21N 01°35'·08W.
Fort de l'Est ⚓ 49°40'·28N 01°35'·92W, Iso G 4s 19m 9M.

Fort Central ⚓ VQ (6) + L Fl 10s 5m 4M; 322°-032°; 49°40'·40N 01°37'·04W.

CHERBOURG, PASSE DE L'OUEST

CH1 ◎; V-AIS; 49°43'·24N 01°42'·09W.

Passe de l'Ouest, Dir Q , lights in line140·3°; Front, Jetée du Homet 5m **17M**; W △; 49° 39'·54N 01°37'·97W. Rear, Gare Maritime, 0.99M from front; 35m **17M**; intens 138·8°-141·8°, shows 24H, sync with front; W △ on Gy pylon; 49°38'·78N 01°37'·00W.

Fort de l'Ouest ☆ Fl (3) WR 15s 19m **W24M, R20M**; 122°-W-355°-R-122°; Gy tr, R top; 49°40'·46N 01°38'·87W.

Fort de l'Ouest ⚓ Fl R 4s; 49°40'·39N 01°38'·89W.

⚓ Q (6) + L Fl 15s; 49°40'·34N 01°38'·65W.

Digue de Querqueville ⚓ Fl (2) G 6s 8m 6M; W col, G top; 49°40'·30N 01°39'·80W.

Inner ldg lts 124·3°; both intens 114·3°-134·3°: Front, Digue du Homet head, QG 10m 6M; 49°39'·48N 01°36'·96W. Rear, Dir Iso G 4s 16m 10M; W col, B bands, 397m from front.

La Ténarde ⚓ VQ 8m 4M; 49°39'·74N 01°37'·75W.

CHERBOURG, PETITE RADE and MARINA

Entrance, W side, Digue du Homet ⚓ QG 10m 8M; intens 114·3°-134·3°; W pylon, G top; 49°39'·48N 01°36'·96W.

E side, ⚓ Q R, off Jetée des Flamands; 49°39'·44N 01°36'·60W.

Marina ent, E side, ⚓ Fl (3) R 12s 6m 6M; W col, R lantern; 49°38'·91N 01°37'·08W.

W mole ⚓ Fl (3) G 12s 7m 6M; G pylon; 49°38'·87N 01°37'·15W.

E quay⚓ Fl (4) R 15s 3m 3M; R bcn; 49°38'·79N 01°37'·12W.

Wavescreen pontoon, N end ⚓ Fl (4) G 15s 4m 2M; W post, G top.

CHERBOURG TO CAP DE LA HAGUE

Raz de Bannes ⚓ 49°41'·32N 01°44'·53W.

Omonville Dir lt 257°: Iso WRG 4s13m; W10M, R/G7M; 180°-G-252°-W-262°-R-287°; W pylon, G top; 49°42'·24N 01°50'·15W.

L'Étonnard ⚓ 49°42'·33N 01°49'·84W.

Basse Bréfort ⚓ VQ 8m 4M; 49°43'·93N 01°51'·18W.

Jobourg Nuclear plant chimney, R lts; 49°40'·80N 01°52'·91W.

La Plate ⚓ Fl (2+1) WR 10s 11m; W9M, R6M; 115°-W-272°-R-115°; Y 8-sided twr, with B top; 49°43'·97N 01°55'·74W.

Cap de la Hague (Gros du Raz) ☆ Fl 5s 48m **23M**; Gy twr, W top; *Horn 30s;* 49°43'·31N 01° 57'·26W.

La Foraine ⚓ VQ (9) 10s, 12m 6M; 49°42'·90N 01°58'·31W.

1.	Dunkerque-Est	**1**																	
2.	**Calais**	28	**2**																
3.	**Boulogne**	49	21	**3**															
4.	St Valéry-sur-Somme	86	58	37	**4**														
5.	Le Tréport	90	62	41	16	**5**													
6.	**Dieppe**	100	74	53	30	15	**6**												
7.	St Valéry-en-Caux	109	81	62	42	28	16	**7**											
8.	**Fécamp**	121	93	76	57	44	32	17	**8**										
9.	**Le Havre**	148	121	103	84	71	61	47	27	**9**									
10.	**Honfleur**	157	129	108	92	80	67	51	35	13	**10**								
11.	**Deauville/Trouville**	152	125	108	91	79	61	53	34	9	13	**11**							
12.	Dives-sur-Mer	155	129	110	94	83	66	55	38	16	19	9	**12**						
13.	**Ouistreham**	160	138	115	97	85	73	59	41	20	24	15	9	**13**					
14.	Courseulles	162	136	115	100	87	75	60	44	24	30	23	18	14	**14**				
15.	Grandcamp	177	150	130	118	104	94	80	62	47	52	45	41	37	27	**15**			
16.	Carentan	187	159	139	126	112	100	85	69	56	61	55	50	45	36	13	**16**		
17.	**St Vaast**	179	151	131	120	107	96	80	65	54	61	54	50	46	35	16	20	**17**	
18.	Barfleur	175	147	128	118	105	94	78	64	56	62	57	53	48	39	21	26	10	**18**
19.	**Cherbourg**	188	160	142	131	120	108	94	80	71	77	73	69	66	57	40	44	28	21	**19**

DISTANCE TABLES

Approx distances in nautical miles are by the most direct route allowing for dangers and TSS.

AREA 15 *N Central France (Cap de la Hague to St Quay) & Channel Is*

SELECTED LIGHTS, BUOYS & WAYPOINTS

CAP DE LA HAGUE TO ST MALO

GOURY

La Foraine ⚓ VQ (9) 10s 12m 6M; 49°42'·90 N 01°58'·32W.

Ldg lts 065·2°: Front, QR 5m 7M; R □ in W □ on pier, 49°42'·89N 01°56'·70W. Rear, 116m from front, Q 11m 7M; W pylon/hut.

Hervieu ⚓ 49°42'·77N 01°56'·92W.

DIELETTE

W bkwtr Dir lt 140°, Iso WRG 4s 12m W10M, R/G7M; 070°-G-135°-W-145°-R-180°; W twr, G top ;49°33'·18N 01°51'·81W.

E bkwtr ⚓ Fl R 4s 6m 2M; 49°33'·21N 01°51'·78W.

Inner N jetty, Fl R 6s. Inner S jetty, Fl (2) G 6s; bth 6m 1M.

Banc des Dious ⚓ Q (9) 15s; 49°32'·58N 01°54'·02W.

CARTERET

Cap de Carteret ☆ Fl (2+1) 15s 81m **26M**; Gy twr, G top; 49°22'·41N 01°48'·41W. .

W bkwtr ⚓ Oc R 4s 7m 7M; W post, R top; 49°22'·07N 01°47'·32W.

E training wall ⚓ Fl G 2·5s 4m 2M; W post, G top; 49°22'·17N 01°47'·30W.

Outer sill ⚓ Fl (2) R 6s 5m 1M; R pylon; 49°22'·58N 01°47'·23W. ⚓ Fl (2) G 6s 5m 1M; G pylon; 49°22'·55N 01°47'·20W.

Marina entry sill: ⚓ Fl (3) R 12s and Fl (3) G 12s; R & G pylons.

PORTBAIL

PB ⚓ 49°18'·37N 01°44'·75W.
Ldg lts 042°: Front, Q 14m 10M; W pylon, R top, 49°19'·75N 01°42'·50W. Rear, 870m frm front, Oc 4s 20m 10M; ch belfry.
⚓ 49°19'·32N 01°43'·16W.
⚓ 49°19'·20N 01°43'·00W.
Training wall head ⚓ Fl (2) R 5s 5m 4M; W mast, R top; 49°19'·43N 01°42'·99W.

REGNÉVILLE

La Catheue ⚓ Q (6) + L Fl 15s, 48°57'·67N 01°42'·23W.
Le Ronquet ⚓ Fl (2) WR 6s, W6M, R4M; 100°-R-293°-W-100°; 49°00'·11N 01°38'·07W.
Pte d'Agon ⚓ Oc (2) WR 6s 12m, W10M, R7M; 063°-R-110°-W-063°; W twr, R top, W dwelling; 49°00'·18N 01°34'·63W.
Dir lt 028°, Oc WRG 4s 9m, W12M, R/G9M; 024°-G-027°-W-029°-R-033°; house; 49°00'·63N 01°33'·36W.

PASSAGE DE LA DÉROUTE

Les Trois-Grunes ⚓ Q (9) 15s, 49°21'·84N 01°55'·21W.
Écrévière ⚓ Q (6) + L Fl 15s; *Bell;* 49°15'·27N 01°52'·16W.
Basse Jourdan ⚓ Q (3) 10s; 49°06'·85N 01°43'·96W.
Le Boeuf ⚓ 49°06'·56N 01°47'·17W.
Les Boeuftins ⚓ 49°07'·03N 01°45'·96W.
La Basse du Sénéquet ⚓ 49°05'·96N 01°41'·11W.
Le Sénéquet ⚓ Fl (3) WR 12s 18m W13M, R10M; 083·5°-R-116·5°-W-083·5°; W twr; 49°05'·48N 01°39'·73W.
Les Nattes ⚓ 49°03'·46N 01°41'·81W.
International F ⚓ 49°02'·16N 01°42'·98W.
International E ⚓ 49°02'·08N 01°47'·21W.
Basse le Marié ⚓ Q (9) 15s; 49°01'·79N 01°48'·57W.
NE Minquiers ⚓ VQ (3) 5s; *Bell;* 49°00'·85N 01°55'·30W.
Les Ardentes ⚓ Q (3) 10s; 48°57'·89N 01°51'·53W.
SE Minquiers ⚓ Q (3) 10s; *Bell;* 48°53'·42N 02°00'·09W.
S Minquiers ⚓ Q (6) + L Fl 15s; 48°53'·09N 02°10'·10W.

ÎLES CHAUSEY

La Pointue ⚓ 48°54'·44N 01°50'·92W.
L'Enseigne, W twr, B top; 48°53'·67N 01°50'·37W.
L'Etat, BW ⚓, 48°54'·67N 01°46'·21W.
Anvers wreck ⚓ 48°53'·91N 01°41'·07W.
Le Founet ⚓ Q (3) 10s; 48°53'·25N 01°42'·34W.
Le Pignon ⚓ Fl (2) WR 6s 10m, W9M, R6M; 005°-R-150°-W-005°; B twr, W band; 48°53'·49N 01°43'·36 W.
La Haute Foraine ⚓ 48°52'·89N 01°43'·66W.
Grande Île ☆ Fl 5s 39m **23M;** Gy □ twr, G top; *Horn 30s;* 48°52'·17N 01°49'·34W.
Channel ⚓ Fl G 2s; 48°52'·07N 01°49'·08W.
La Crabière Est ⚓ Dir Oc(3)WRG 12s 5m, W9M, R/G6M; 079°-W-291°-G-329°-W-335°-R-079°; B beacon, Y top; 48°52'·46N 01°49'·39W.
La Cancalaise ⚓ 48°51'·90N 01°51'·11W.

GRANVILLE

Le Videcoq ⚓ VQ (9) 10s; 48°49'·66N 01°42'·06W.
La Fourchie ⚓ 48°50'·15N 01°37'·00W.
Pointe du Roc ☆ Fl (4) 15s 49m **23M;** 48°50'·06N 01°36'·78W.
Le Loup ⚓ Fl (2) 6s 8m 11M; 48°49'·57N 01°36'·24W.
Avant Port, E jetty ⚓ Fl G 2·5s 11m 4M; 48°49'·93N 01°36'·19W.
W jetty ⚓ Fl R 2·5s 12m 4M; 48°49'·86N 01°36'·23W.

Marina S bkwtr ⚓ Fl (2) R 6s 12m 5M; W post, R top; *Horn (2) 40s;* 48°49'·89N 01°35'·90W.
N bkwtr ⚓ Fl (2) G 6s 4m 5M; 48°49'·93N 01°35'·90W.
Sill, W side, QR 2M; E side QG 2M; Gy pylons topped R (W) and G (E).

CANCALE

La Fille ⚓ 48°44'·16N 01°48'·46W.
Pierre-de-Herpin ☆ Oc (2) 6s 20m 13M; W twr, B top and base; 48°43'·77N 01°48'·92W.
Ruet ⚓ *Bell;* 48°43'·44N 01°50'·11W.
Grande Bunouze ⚓ 48°43'·17N 01°50'·95W.
Barbe Brûlée ⚓ 48°42'·11N 01°50'·57W.
Jetty hd ⚓ Oc (3) G 12s 9m 3M; W pylon B top; 48°40'·10N 01°51'·11W.

ST MALO AND RIVER RANCE

CHENAL DE LA BIGNE

Basse Rochefort (aka Basse aux Chiens) ⚓ 48°42'·69N 01°57'·31W.
La Petite Bigne ⚓ 48°41'·66N 01°58'·72W.
La Crolante ⚓; 48°41'·01N 01°59'·51W, off Pte de la Varde.
Les Létruns ⚓; *Bell;* 48°40'·71N 02°00'·61W.
Roches-aux-Anglais ⚓ Fl G 4s; 48°39'·65N 02°02'·27W.
Les Crapauds-du-Bey ⚓ Fl R 4s; 48°39'·37N 02°02'·57W.

CHENAL DES PETITS POINTUS

Dinard ch spire (74m) brg 203° to right of Le Petit Bé rocks.
La Saint-Servantine ⚓ Fl G 2·5s; *Bell;* 48°41'·93N 02°00'·94W.
Les Petits Pontus ⚓ 48°41'·30N 02°00'·86W.

CHENAL DE LA GRANDE CONCHÉE

Villa Brisemoulin 181·5°, on with LH edge of Le Petit Bé rocks.
La Plate ⚓ Q WRG 11m, W10M, R/G7M; 140°-W-203°-210°-W-225°-G-140°; 48°40'·78N 02°01'·91W.
Le Bouton ⚓ 48°40'·59N 02°01'·85W.

CHENAL DU BUNEL

St Énogat ldg lts 158·2°; both Iso 4s 3/85m 7/10M, sync. Front 48°38'·29N 02°04'·11W, vis 126°-236°. Rear, on white water twr, Dinard, vis 143°-210°; 48°36'·97N 02°03'·31W.
Bunel ⚓ Q (9) 15s; 48°40'·84N 02°05'·38W.

CHENAL DE LA PETITE PORTE

Outer ldg lts 129·7°: **Front, Le Grand Jardin** ☆ Fl (2) R 10s 24m **15M,** 48°40'·20N 02°04'·97W. Rear, **La Balue** ☆ FG 20m **22M;** 3·1M from front; intens 128°-129·5°; Gy □ twr; 48°38'·16N 02°01'·30W.
Vieux-Banc E ⚓ Q; 48°42'·38N 02°09'·12W.
Vieux-Banc W ⚓ VQ (9) 10s; 48°41'·84N 02°10'·20W.
St Malo Atterrisage (Fairway) ⚓ Iso 4s; 48°41'·39N 02°07'·28W.
Les Courtis ⚓ Fl G 4s 14m 7M; 48°40'·46N 02°05'·80W.

Nearing Le Grand Jardin, move stbd briefly onto Ch du Bunel 152·8° ldg lts to pick up: Inner ldg lts 128·6°, both Dir FG 20/69m **22/25M;** H24. Front, **Les Bas Sablons** ☆, intens 127·2°-130·2°; W □ twr, B top; 48°38'·16N 02°01'·30W. Rear, **La Balue** ☆, 0·9M from front; intens 128°-129·5°; Gy □ twr; 48°37'·60N 02°00'·24W.
Basse du Nord No 5 ⚓ 48°39'·98N 02°05'·04W.

Les Pierres-Garnier No 8 ⚓ 48°39'·98N 02°04'·41W.

Les Patouillets ⚓ Fl (3) G 12s, 48°39'·68N 02°04'·30W.

Clef d'Aval No 10 ⚓ 48°39'·72N 02°03'·91W.

Basse du Buron No 12 ⚓ Fl (4) R 15s, 48°39'·42N 02°03'·51W.

Le Buron ⚓ Fl (4) G 15s 15m 7M; G twr, 48°39'·32N 02°03'·66W.

Les Grelots ⚓ VQ (6) + L Fl 10s, 48°39'·16N 02°03'·03W.

CHENAL DE LA GRANDE PORTE

Banchenou ⚓ VQ, 48°40'·44N 02°11'·48W.

Outer ldg lts 089·1°: **Front, Le Grand Jardin** ☆ Fl (2) R 10s 24m **15M**, 48°40'·20N 02°04'·97W.

Rear, **Rochebonne** ☆ Dir FR 40m **24M**; intens 088·2°-089·7°; Gy ☐ twr, R top, 4·2M from front; 48°40'·26N 01°58'·71W. .

Buharats W No 2 ⚓ Fl R 2·5s, 48°40'·22N 02°07'·50W.

Buharats E No 4 ⚓ Bell; 48°40'·24N 02°07'·20W.

Bas du Boujaron No 1 ⚓ Fl (2) G 6s, 48°40'·17N 02°05'·97W.

Le Sou ⚓ VQ (3) 5s; 48°40'·11N 02°05'·30W.

Continue on inner 128·6° ldg line: see Chenal de la Petite Porte.

RADE DE ST MALO

Plateau Rance Nord ⚓ VQ, 48°38'·64N 02°02'·35W.

Plateau Rance Sud ⚓ Q (6) + L Fl 15s, 48°38'·43N 02°02'·28W.

Crapaud de la Cité ⚓ QG, 48°38'·34N 02°02'·01W.

ST MALO

Môle des Noires hd ⚓ VQ R 11m 6M; W twr, R top; *Horn (2) 20s*; 48°38'·52N 02°01'·91W.

Écluse du Naye ldg lts 070·4°, both FR 7/23m 3/7M. Front, 48°38'·58N 02°01'·48W. Rear, 030°-120°.

Ferry jetty hd, ⚓ VQ G 6M; 48°38'·44N 02°01'·82W (128·6° ldg line). Ferry jetty, ⚓ Fl R 4s 3m 1M; 260°-080°; 48°38'·44N 02°01'·76W.

Bas-Sablons marina, mole head ⚓ Fl G 4s 7m 5M; Gy mast; 48°38'·42N 02°01'·70W.

LA RANCE BARRAGE

La Jument ⚓ Fl G 4s 6m 4M; G twr, 48°37'·44N 02°01'·76W.

ZI 12 ⚓ Fl R 4s, 48°37'·47N 02°01'·62W.

NE dolphin ⚓ Fl (2) R 6s 6m 5M; 040°-200°, 48°37'·09N 02°01'·71W.

Barrage lock, NW wall ⚓ Fl (2) G 6s 6m 5M, 191°-291°; G pylon, 48°37'·06N 02°01'·73W.

Barrage lock, SW wall, ⚓ Fl (3) G 12s, 48°37'·00N 02°01'·70W.

SE dolphin ⚓ Fl (3) R 12s, 48°36'·97N 02°01'·66W.

ZI 24 ⚓ Fl (2) R 6s, 48°36'·63N 02°01'·33W.

ST MALO TO ST QUAY-PORTRIEUX

ST BRIAC

R. Frémur mouth. Dir lt 125° Iso WRG 4s 10m 12M; 121·5°-G-124·5°-W-125·5°-R-129·5°; W mast on hut, 48°37'·07N 02°08'·20W.

ST CAST

Les Bourdinots *l* 48°39'·01N 02°13'·48W.

St Cast môle ⚓ Iso WG 4s 12m, W9M, G6M; 180°-G-206°-W-217°-G-235°-W-245°-G-340°; G&W structure; 48°38'·41N 02°14'·61W.

Laplace *l*, 48°39'·73N 2°16'·45W; 5ca SE of Pte de la Latte.

Cap Fréhel ☆ Fl (2) 10s 85m **29M**; Gy ☐ twr, G lantern; 48°41'·05N 02°19'·13W. Reserve lt range **15M**.

CHENAL and PORT D'ERQUY

Les Justières ⚓ Q (6) + L Fl 15s; 48°40'·56N 02°26'·48W.

Basses du Courant ⚓ VQ (6) + L Fl 10s; 48°39'·21N 02°29'·16W.

L'Evette ⚓ 48°38'·51N 02°31'·45W.

S môle ⚓ Fl (2) WRG 6s 11m W10M, R/G7M; 055°-R-081°-W-094°-G-111°-W-120°-R-134°; W twr; 48°38'·06N 02°28'·68W.

Inner jetty ⚓ Fl (3) R 12s 10m 3M; R/W twr; 48°38'·09N 02°28'·39W.

DAHOUET

Petit Bignon ⚓ 48°36'·82N 02°35'·06W.

Le Dahouet ⚓ 48°35'·15N 02°35'·43W.

La Petite Muette ⚓ Fl WRG 4s 10m W9M, R/G6M; 055°-G-114°-W-146°-R-196°; W twr, G band; 48°34'·82N 02°34'·30W.

Entry chan, Fl (2) G 6s 5m 1M; 156°-286°; 48°34'·71N 02°34'·19W.

BAIE DE ST BRIEUC

Grand Léjon ☆ Fl (5) WR 20s 17m **W18M**, R14M; 015°-R-058°-W-283°-R-350°-W-015°; R twr, W bands; 48°44'·91N 02°39'·87W.

Petit Léjon *l* ; 48°41'·80N 02°37'·55W.

Les Landas ⚓ Q, 48°41'·43N 02°31'·29W.

Le Rohein ⚓ Q (9) WRG 15s 13m, W8M, R/G5M; 072°-R-105°-W-180°-G-193°-W-237°-G-282°-W-301°-G-330°-W-072°; Y twr, B band; 48°38'·80N 02°37'·77W.

SAINT-BRIEUC LE LÉGUÉ

Tra-Hillion ⚓ 48°33'·38N 02°38'·50W.

Le Légué ⚓ Mo (A)10s; 48°34'·32N 02°41'·15W.

No 1 ⚓ Fl G 2·5s; 48°32'·42N 02°42'·51W.

No 2 ⚓ Fl R 2·5s; 48°32'·37N 02°42'·40W.

No 3 ⚓ Fl (2) G 6s; 48°32'·27N 02°42'·78W.

No 4 ⚓ Fl (2) R 6s; 48°32'·23N 02°42'·70W.

No 5 ⚓ Fl (3) G 12s; 48°32'·18N 02°42'·92W.

No 6 ⚓ Fl (3) R 12s; 48°32'·14N 02°42'·90W.

NE jetty ⚓ VQ R 4M; 48°32'·12N 02°42'·88W.

Pte à l'Aigle jetty ⚓ VQ G 13m 8M; 160°-070°; W twr, G top; 48°32'·12N 02°43'·11W.

No 7 ⚓ Fl (4) G 15s; 48°32'·11N 02°43'·08W.

No 8 ⚓ Fl R 2·5s; 48°32'·01N 02°43'·16W.

No 9 ⚓ Fl (2) G 6s; 48°31'·96N 02°43'·29W.

No 10 ⚓ Fl (2) R 6s; 48°31'·91N 02°43'·31W.

Jetty⚓ Iso G 4s 6m 2M; W cols, G top; 48°31'·90N 02°43'·43W.

No 11 ⚓ Fl (3) G 12s; 48°31'·90N 02°43'·43W.

No 13 ⚓ Fl (4) G 15s; 48°31'·76N 02°43'·56W.

No 14 ⚓ Fl (4) R 15s; 48°31'·70N 02°43'·61W.

BINIC

N Môle hd ⚓ Fl (4) G 15s12m 6M; unintens 020°-110°; W twr, G lantern; 48°36'·07N 02°48'·92W.

ST QUAY-PORTRIEUX

Les Hors *l* 48°39'·60N 02°44'·04W.

Caffa ⚓ Q (3) 10s; 48°37'·82N 02°43'·08W.

La Longue ⚓ 48°37'·88N 02°44'·68W.

La Roselière ⚓ VQ (6) + L Fl 10s; 48°37'·31N 02°46'·19W.

Herflux ⚓ Dir ⚡ 130°, Fl (2) WRG 6s 10m, W 8M, R/G 5M; 115°-G-125°-W-135°-R-145°; 48°39'·07N 02°47'·95W.

Île Harbour (Roches de Saint-Quay) ⚡ Fl WRG 4s 16m, W9M, R/G 6M; 011°-R-133°-G-270°-R-306°-G-358°-W-011°; W twr and dwelling, R top; 48°39'·99N 02°48'·49W.

Madeux ⚓ 48°40'·41N 02°48'·81W.

Grandes Moulières de St Quay ⚓ 48°39'·76N 02°49'·91W.

Moulières de Portrieux ⚓ 48°39'·26N 02°49'·21W.

Les Noirs ⚓ 48°39'·09N 02°48·46W.

Marina, **NE mole elbow,** Dir lt 318·2°: Iso WRG 4s 16m **W15M**, R/G11M; W159°-179°, G179°-316°, W316°-320·5°, R320·5° -159°; Reserve lt ranges 11/8M; 48°38'·99N 02°49'·09W.

NE môle hd ⚡ Fl (3) G 12s 10m 2M; 48°38'·84N 02°48'·91W.

S môle hd ⚡ Fl (3) R 12s 10m 2M; 48°38'·83N 02°49'·03W.

Old hbr ent: N side, Fl G 2.5s 11m 2M; 48°38'·71N 02°49'·36W.

S side, Fl R 2.5s 8m 2M; 48°38'·67N 02°49'·35W.

MID-CHANNEL MARK

Channel ⚓ L Fl 10s, 10M, RW vert stripes, R topmark, *Racon O,10M;* 49°54'·45N 02°53'·74W; <u>992351028</u> .

COTENTIN PENINSULA (NW COAST)

La Plate ⚓ Fl (2+1) WR 10s 11m; W9M, R6M; 115°-W-272°-R-115°; Y 8-sided twr, with B top; 49°43'·98N 01°55'·76W.

Cap de la Hague (Gros du Raz) ☆ Fl 5s 48m **23M**; Gy twr, W top; *Horn 30s;* 49°43'·31N 01° 57'·27W.

La Foraine ⚓ VQ (9) 10s 12m 6M; 49°42'·90 01°58'·32W.

Cap de Carteret ☆ Fl (2+1) 15s 81m **26M**; Gy twr, G top; 49°22'·41N 01°48'·41W.

THE CASQUETS AND ALDERNEY

Casquets ☆ Fl (5) 30s 37m **18M**, H24; W twr, 2 R bands; NW'most of three; *Racon T, 25M;* 49°43'·32N 02°22'·63W. <u>992351121.</u>

Ortac rock, unlit; 49°43'·40N 02°17'·44W.

Pierre au Vraic, unmarked rk <u>1</u>·2m ☼; 49°41'·61N 02°16'·94W.

Quenard Pt (Alderney) ⚡ Fl (4) 15s 37m 12M; 085°-027°; W ○ twr, B band; 49°43'·75N 02°09'·86W.

Château à L'Étoc Pt ⚡ Iso WR 4s 20m W10M, R7M; 071·1°-R- 111·1°-W-151·1°; 49°43'·94N 02°10'·63W.

BRAYE

Ldg bns 142° (to clear the submerged Adm'ty bkwtr). Front, W ⚓, 49°43'·90N 02°10'·97W. Rear, BW ⚓; 720m from front.

Ldg lts 215°: both Q 8/17m 9/12M, synch; 210°-220°; orange △s. Front, old pier elbow, 49°43'·40N 02°11'·91W. Rear, 215°/335m.

Admiralty bkwtr head ⚡ L Fl 10s 7m 5M; 49°43'·82N 02°11'·67W.

Fairway No 1 ⚓ QG; 49°43'·72N 02°11'·72W.

No 2 ⚓ QR; 49°43'·60N 02°11'·75W.

Inner fairway ⚓ Q (2) G 5s; 49°43'·58N 02°11'·98W.

Braye quay ⚡ 2 FR (vert) 8m 5M; 49°43'·53N 02°12'·00W.

Little Crabby hbr ent ⚡ FG & FR 5m 2M; 49°43'·45N 02°12'·12W.

GUERNSEY, NORTHERN APPROACHES

LITTLE RUSSEL CHANNEL

Grande Amfroque, two unlit bcn twrs: larger, BW-banded; smaller, white; 49°30'·57N 02°24'·62W.

Tautenay ⚡ Q (3) WR 6s 7m W7M, R6M; 050°-W-215°-R-050°; B & W striped bcn 49°30'·11N 02°26'·84W.

Platte Fougère ☆ Fl WR 10s 15m **16M**; 155°-W-085°-R-155°; W 8-sided twr, B band. *Horn 45s* **TD 2021**; 49°30'·83N 02°29'·14W.

Corbette d'Amont ⚓ Y bcn twr, topmark; 49°29'·64N 02°29'·38W.

Roustel ⚡ Q 8m 7M; BW chequered base, W framework col; 49°29'·23N 02°28'·79W.

Rousse, Y bcn twr, topmark ⊞; 49°28'·98N 02°28'·36W.

Platte, ⚡ Fl WR 3s 6m, W7M, R5M; 024°-R-219°-W-024°; G conical twr; 49°29'·08N 02°29'·57W.

Vivian bcn twr, BW bands, 49°28'·45N 02°30'·66W.

Brehon ⚡ Iso 4s 19m 9M; bcn on ○ twr, 49°28'·28N 02°29'·28W.

Demie Flieroque, Y bcn twr, topmark F; 49°28'·13N 02°31'·38W.

BIG RUSSEL

Noire Pute ⚡ Fl (2) WR 15s 8m 6M; 220°-W-040°-R-220°; on 2m high rock; 49°28'·21N 02°25'·02W; unreliable.

Fourquies ⚓ Q; 49°27'·34N 02°26'·47W.

Lower Heads ⚓ Q (6) + L Fl 15s; *Bell;* 49°25'·85N 02°28'·55W.

GUERNSEY, HERM AND SARK

BEAUCETTE MARINA

Petite Canupe ⚓ Q (6) + L Fl 15s; 49°30'·20N 02°29'·14W.

Ldg lts 277°: Both FR. Front, W □, R stripe; 49°30'·19N 02°30'·23W. Rear, R □, W stripe; 185m from front.

Appr chan buoys: SWM L Fl 10s 49°30'·15N 02°29'·66W. SHM Fl G 5s, PHM Fl R 5s & Fl (3) R 5s. NCM perch Q 49°30'·165N 02°30'·06W. SHM perch Q (3) G 5s at ent; 49°30'·18N 02°30'·24W.

ST SAMPSON

Ldg lts 286°: Front, FR 3m 5M; 230°-340°; tfc sigs; 49°28'·90N 02°30'·74W. Rear, FG 13m; clock twr, 390m from front.

N Pier ⚡ FG 3m 5M; 230°-340°; 49°28'·92N 02°30'·71W.

Crocq pier ⚡ FR 11m 5M; 250°-340°; 49°28'·98N 02°31'·00W.

ST PETER PORT

Outer ldg lts 220°: **Front**, Castle bkwtr, Al WR 10s 14m **16M**; 187°-007°; dark ○ twr, W on NE side; *Horn 15s;* 49°27'·31N 02°31'·45W.

Rear 220° ldg lt, Belvedere, Oc 10s 61m 14M; 179°-269°; intens 217°-223°; W □ on W twr; 980m from front. The lts are synchronised so that the rear lt is on when the front is W, and the off when the front is R.

Queen Elizabeth II marina, 270° Dir Oc ⚡ WRG 3s 5m 6M; 258°-G-268°-W-272°-R-282°; 49°27'·73N 02°31'·87W.

Reffée ⚓ Q (6) + L Fl 15s; 49°27'·74N 02°31'·27W.

Appr buoys: outer pair ⚓ QG; 49°27'·83N 02°31'·54W. ⚓ QR; 49°27'·71N 02°31'·52W. Inner pair: ⚓ QG; 49°27'·76N 02°31'·74W. ⚓ QR; 49°27'·72N 02°31'·74W.

The Pool ldg lts 265° (*not* into moorings): Front, Victoria marina, S Pier, ⚡ Oc R 5s 10m 14M; 49°27'·32N 02°32'·03W.

Rear, ⚡ Iso R 2s 22m 3M; 260°-270°; on Creasey's bldg, 160m from front.

White Rock pier ⚡ Oc G 5s 11m 14M; intens 174°-354°; ○ twr; tfc sigs; 49°27'·38N 02°31'·59W.

S Fairway ▲ QG; 49°27'·30N 02°31'·76W; N of fuel pontoon W of buoy 3 x ⚏ Fl R; 49°27'·28N 02°31'·74W. 49°27'·27N 02°31'·80W. 49°27'·27N 02°31'·86W.

HAVELET BAY
Oyster Rock ⚑ Y bcn, topmark 'O'; 49°27'·09N 02°31'·46W.
Oyster Rock ▲ QG; 49°27'·04N 02°31'·47W.
Moulinet ⚏ QR; 49°26'·97N 02°31'·54W.
Moulinet ⚑ Y bcn, topmark 'M'; 49°26'·95N 02°31'·58W.

GUERNSEY, SOUTH-EAST and SOUTH COASTS
Anfré, Y bcn, topmark 'A'; 49°26'·45N 02°31'·48W.
Longue Pierre, Y bcn, topmark 'LP'; 49°25'·36N 02°31'·48W.
St Martin's Pt ⚡ Fl (3) WR 10s 15m 14M; 185°-R-191°-W-011°-R-061·5°; flat-topped, W bldg. *Horn (3) 30s*; 49°25'·30N 02°31'·70W.

GUERNSEY, NORTH-WEST COAST
Les Hanois ☆ Fl (2) 13s 33m **20M**; 294°-237°; Gy ○ twr, B lantern, helicopter platform; *Horn (2) 60s*; 49°26'·10N 02°42'·15W.
4 FR on mast 1·3M ESE of Les Hanois lt ho.
Portelet Hbr, bkwtr bcn, 49°26'·16N 02°39'·84W.
Cobo Bay, Grosse Rock, B bcn 11m; 49°29'·02N 02°36'·19W.
Grand Havre, Rousse Point bkwtr, B bcn; 49°29'·92N 02°33'·05W.

HERM
Corbette de la Mare, Wh disc (W side) and R disc (E side) on Y pole, 49°28'·48N 02°28'·72W.
Petit Creux ⚡ QR; red 'C' on red pole; 49°28'·09N 02°28'·72W.
Alligande ⚡ Fl (3) G 5s; B pole, Or 'A'; 49°27'·86N 02°28'·78W.
Épec ⚡ Fl G 3s; black 'E' on G mast; 49°27'·98N 02°27'·89W.
Vermerette ⚡ Fl (2) Y 5s; Or 'V' on bcn; 49°28'·12N 02°27'·75W.
Gate Rock (Percée Pass) ⚑ Q (9) 15s; 49°27'·88N 02°27'·54W.
Hbr ldg lts 078°: White drums. ⚡ 2F occas; 49°28'·25N 02°27'·11W.
Hbr pier, N end ⚡ 2 FG; G ☐ on G bcn; 49°28'·21N 02°27'·26W.

SARK
Courbée du Nez ⚡ Fl (4) WR 15s 14m 8M; 057°-W-230°-R-057°; W structure on rock; 49°27'·09N 02°22'·17W.
Noir Pierre ⚑, Y bcn, topmark radar refl, 49°26'·67N 02°20'·92W. **Point Robert** ☆ Fl 15s 65m **18M**; vis 138°-353°; W 8-sided twr; *Horn (1) 30s*; 49°26'·19N 02°20'·75W.
Founiais ⚑, topmark 'F'; 49°26'·02N 02°20'·36W.
Blanchard ⚑ Q (3) 10s; *Bell*; 49°25'·36N 02°17'·42W.
Pilcher monument (070° appr brg); 49°25'·71N 02°22'·44W.

JERSEY, WEST AND SOUTH COASTS
Desormes ⚑ Q (9) 15s; 49°18'·94N 02°17'·98W.
Grosnez Point ☆ Fl (2) WR 15s 50m **W19M, R17M**;

081°-W-188°-R-241°; W hut; 49°15'·50N 02°14'·80W.
L a Rocco twr (conspic) 15m; 49°11'·90N 02°14'·05W.
La Frouquie ⚑ (seasonal); 49°11'·30N 02°15'·38W.
La Corbière ☆ Iso WR 10s 36m **W18M**, R14M; shore-W-294°-R-328°-W-148°-R-shore; W ○ twr; *Horn Mo (C) 60s*; 49°10'·79N 02°15'·01W.
Pt Corbière ⚡ FR; R ☐, W stripe; 49°10'·87N 02°14'·38W.

WESTERN PASSAGE
Ldg lts 082°. Front, La Gréve d'Azette Oc 5s 23m 14M; 034°-129°; 49°10'·16N 02°05'·09W. Rear, Mont Ubé, Oc R 5s 46m 12M; 250°-095°; 1M from front.
Passage Rock ⚑ VQ; 49°09'·54N 02°12'·26W.
Les Fours ⚑ Q; 49°09'·59N 02°10'·16W.
Noirmont Pt ⚡ Fl (4) 12s 18m 10M; B twr, W band; 49°09'·91N 02°10'·08W.
Pignonet ⚑ 49°09'·88N 02°09'·70W.
Ruaudière Rock ▲ Fl G 3s; *Bell*; 49°09'·74N 02°08'·62W.

ST AUBIN'S BAY and HARBOUR
Les Grunes du Port ⚏ 49°10'·02N 02°09'·14W.
Diamond Rock ⚏ Fl (2) R 6s; 49°10'·12N 02°08'·64W.
Castle pier ⚡ Fl R 4s 8m 1M; 49°11'·13N 02°09'·634W.
North pier, Dir lt 254° ⚡ F WRG 5m, 248°-G-253°-W-255°-R-260°; 49°11'·22N 02°10'·03W. Same col, Iso R 4s 12m 10M.
Beach Rock ⚏ 49°11'·29N 02°08'·42W, (Apr-Oct).
Rocquemin ⚑ 49°10'·64N 02°07'·95W.
Baleine ▲ 49°10'·41N 02°08'·23W.

ST HELIER
Elizabeth marina, west appr: Dir ⚡ 106°: F WRG 4m 1M; 096°-G-104°-W-108°-R-119°; R dayglo ☐, B stripe; 49°10'·76N 02°07'·12W.
La Vrachière ⚑ 49°10'·90N 02°07'·59W, Fl (2) 5s 1M.
Fort Charles North ⚑ 49°10'·81N 02°07'·50W.
Marina ent ⚡ Oc G & Oc R, both 4s 2M; 49°10'·83N 02°07'·13W.
Red & Green Passage, ldg lts 022° on dayglo R dolphins: Front, Elizabeth E berth Dn ⚡ Oc G 5s 10m 11M; 49°10'·63N 02°06'·94W. Rear, Albert Pier root ⚡ Oc R 5s 18m 12M; synch; 230m SSW.
East Rock ▲ QG; 49°09'·96N 02°07'·28W.
Dog's Nest Rk ⚑ Fl Y 3s 3M; Y cross on bcn; 49°09'·99N 02°06'·95W.
Oyster Rocks, R/W bcn, topmark 'O'; 49°10'·10N 02°07'·49W.
Platte Rock ⚑ Fl R 1·5s 6m 5M; R col; 49°10'·16N 02°07'·34W.
Small Road No 2 ⚏ QR; 49°10'·39N 02°07'·24W.
No 4 ⚏ QR; 49°10'·53N 02°07'·12W.
Elizabeth marina, S appr: E1 ▲ Fl G 3s; 49°10'·59N 02°07'·09W.
E2 ⚏ Fl R 2s; 49°10'·58N 02°07'·13W.
E5 ▲ Fl G 5s; 49°10'·70N 02°07'·17W.
E6 ⚏ Fl R 2s; 49°10'·69N 02°07'·21W.
Fort Charles East ⚑ Q (3) 5s 2m 1M; 49°10'·74N 02°07'·04W.
La Collette basin ⚏ QR; 49°10'·54N 02°06'·91W. ⚏ 49°10'·52N 02°06'·90W.
St Helier Hbr, ldg lts 078°, both FG on W cols. Front, 49°10'·62N 02°06'·66W. Rear, 80m from front.

Victoria pier hd, Port control twr; IPTS; 49°10'·57N 02°06'·88W.

JERSEY, SOUTH-EAST AND EAST COASTS

Hinguette ⚓ QR; 49°09'·33N 02°07'·32W.

Hettich ⌀ Fl Y 5s; 49°08'·10N 02°09'·00W.

South Pier Marine ⌀ Fl Y 5s; 49°09'·10N 02°06'·30W.

Demie de Pas ⚓ Mo (D) WR 12s 11m, WR 8M; 130°-R-303°-W-130°; *Horn (3) 60s; Racon T, 10M*; B bn twr, Y top; 49°09'·01N 02°06'·15W. Icho Tower (conspic, 14m) 49°08'·89N 02°02'·90W.

Canger Rock ⌀ Q (9) 15s; 49°07'·35N 02°00'·38W.

La Conchière ⌀ Q (6) + L Fl 15s 2M; 49°08'·22N 02°00'·17W.

Frouquier Aubert ⌀ Q (6) + L Fl 15s; 49°06'·08N 01°58'·84W.

Violet ⌀ L Fl 10s; 49°07'·81N 01°57'·14W.

Petite Anquette; SCM ⌀; 49°08'·47N 01°56'·29W.

Grande Anquette ⌀ VQ(9) 10s; 49°08'·32N 01°55'·20W.

Le Cochon ⚓ 49°09'·77N 01°58'·80W.

La Noire ⌀ 49°10'·13N 01°59'·23W.

Le Giffard ⚓ Fl R 3s 49°10'·59N 01°58'·99W.

GOREY

Pier Hd ⚓ Occ WRG 5s 8m 8M; 228°-G-296·5°-W-299·5°-R-299·5°-008°; W twr on pierhead; 49°11'·81N 02°01'·33W.

Horn Rock ⌀, topmark 'H'; 49°10'·96N 01°59'·85W.

Les Burons, R bcn, topmark 'B'; 49°11'·33N 02°00'·81W.

Fairway ⚓ QG; 49°11'·50N 02°00'·34W.

Écureuil Rock ⌀ 49°11'·67N 02°00'·78W.

Equerrière Rk, bcn 'fishtail' topmark; 49°11'·80N 02°00'·67W.

Les Arch ⌀, BW bcn, 'A' topmark; 49°12'·02N 02°00'·60W.

ST CATHERINE BAY

St Catherine Bay, Le Fara ⌀ Q (3) 10s 3M; 49°12'·85N 02°00'·48W.

Archirondel Tower (conspic, 16m) 49°12'·72N 02°01'·42W.

Verclut bkwtr ⚓ Fl 1·5s 18m 13M; 49°13'·34N 02°00'·64W. In line 315° with unlit turret, 49°13'·96N 02°01'·57W, on La Coupe Pt.

JERSEY, NORTH COAST

Rozel Bay Dir lt 245°, F WRG 11m 5M; 240°-G-244°-W-246°-R-250°; W col; 49°14'·21N 02°02'·76W.

Bonne Nuit Bay ldg lts 223°: both FG 7/34m 6M. Front, Pier 49°15'·10N 02°07'·17W. Rear, 170m from front.

Demie Rock ⚓ 49°15'·56N 02°07'·36W.

Sorel Point ☆ L Fl WR 7·5s 50m **15M**; 095°-W-112°-R-173°-W-230°-R-269°-W-273°; W ◯ twr, only 3m high; 49°15'·60N 02°09'·54W.

OFFLYING ISLANDS

LES ÉCREHOU

Écrevière ⌀ Q (6) + L Fl 15s; 49°15'·26N 01°52'·15W.

Mâitre Ile ⌀ 49°17'·08N 01°55'·60W.

PLATEAU DES MINQUIERS

N Minquiers ⌀ Q; 49°01'·64N 02°00'·58W.

NE Minquiers ⌀ VQ (3) 5s; *Bell;* 49°00'·85N 01°55'·30W.

SE Minquiers ⌀ Q (3) 10s; *Bell;* 48°53'·42N 02°00'·09W.

S Minquiers ⌀ Q (6) + L Fl 15s; 48°53'·09N 02°10'·10W.

SW Minquiers ⌀ Q (9) 15s 5M; *Bell;* 48°54'·34N 02°19'·38W.

NW Minquiers ⌀ Q 5M; *Whis;* 48°59'·63N 02°20'·59W.

Refuge ⌀; B/W bcn; 49°00'·13N 02°10'·16W.

Demie de Vascelin ⚓ Fl G 3s, 49°00'·81N 02°05'·17W.

Grand Vascelin, BW bcn ⚓ 48°59'·97N 02°07'·26W.

Maitresse Ile, Puffin B&W bcn twr ⌀ 48°58'·33N 02°03'·65W.

Le Coq Reef, ⌀ Q (3) 10s 6m 3M; 48°57'·88N 02°01'·29W.

FRENCH MARKS NORTH OF ILE DE BRÉHAT

Roches Douvres ☆ Fl 5s 60m **24M**; pink twr on dwelling with G roof; 49°06'·30N 02°48'·87W. (16M NNE of Ile de Bréhat).

Barnouic ⌀ VQ (3) 5s 15m 7M; 49°01'·64N 02°48'·41W.

Roche Gautier ⌀ VQ (9) 10s; 49°02'·013N 02°54'·36W.

Les Héaux de Bréhat ☆ Fl (4) WRG 15s 48m, **W15M**, R/G11M; 227°-R-247°-W-270°-G-302°-W-227°; Gy twr; 48°54'·50N 03°05'·18W (4·7M WNW of Ile de Bréhat).

		1	2	3	4	5	6	7	8	9	10	11	12	13	14	15	16	17
1	Cherbourg	1																
2	Omonville	10	2															
3	Braye (Alderney)	25	15	3														
4	St Peter Port	44	34	23	4													
5	Creux (Sark)	37	29	22	10	5												
6	St Helier	64	51	46	29	24	6											
7	Carteret	41	29	28	31	23	26	7										
8	Portbail	49	33	32	35	27	25	5	8									
9	Iles Chausey	69	61	58	48	43	25	33	30	9								
10	Granville	75	67	66	55	50	30	38	35	9	10							
11	Dinan	102	91	85	64	64	50	62	59	29	35	11						
12	St Malo	90	79	73	54	52	38	50	47	17	23	12	12					
13	Dahouet	88	80	72	54	52	41	60	59	37	45	41	29	13				
14	Le Légué/St Brieuc	96	86	76	57	56	46	69	69	41	49	45	33	8	14			
15	Binic	95	84	75	56	55	46	70	70	43	51	45	33	10	8	15		
16	St Quay-Portrieux	88	80	73	56	51	46	64	64	47	54	47	35	11	7	4	16	
17	Lézardrieux	88	80	68	48	38	47	68	71	53	54	61	49	33	32	30	21	17

DISTANCE TABLES

Approx distances in nautical miles are by the most direct route allowing for dangers and TSS.

SELECTED LIGHTS, BUOYS & WAYPOINTS

OFFSHORE MARKS

Roches Douvres ☆ Fl 5s 60m **24M**; pink twr on dwelling with G roof; 49°06'·30N 02°48'·87W.

Barnouic ⚓ VQ (3) 5s 15m 7M; 49°01'·63N 02°48'·41W.

Roche Gautier ⚓ VQ (9) 10s; 49°02'·00N 02°54'·73W.

PAIMPOL TO ÎLE DE BRÉHAT

PAIMPOL
Les Calemarguiers ⌁ 48°46'·98N 02°54'·84W.

L'Ost Pic ⚑ Fl(4)WR 15s 20m, W9M, R6M; 105°-W-116°-R-221°-W-253°- R-291°-W-329°; obsc by islets near Bréhat when brg < 162°; W twr/turret, R top; 48°46'·77N 02°56'·42W.

Les Charpentiers ⚓ 48°47'·89N 02°56'·01W.

Pte de Porz-Don ☆ Oc (2) WR 6s 13m **W15M**, R11M; 269°-W-272°-R-279°; W house; 48°47'·48N 03°01'·55W.

El Bras ⚑ Fl G 2·5s; 48°47'·21N 03°01'·50W.

⚑ Fl R 2·5s; 48°47'·17N 03°01'·49W.

Ldg lts 262·2°, both QR 5/12m 7/10M. Front, Kernoa jetty; W & R hut; 48°47'·09N 03°02'·44W. Rear, Dir QR, intens 260·2°-264·2°; W pylon, R top; 360m from front. ⚑ QG 48°47'·12N 03°02'·47W.

CHENAL DU FERLAS (277°-257°-271°)

Lel Ar Serive ⌁ 48°49'·98N 02°58'·76W.

Loguivy Dir lt 257°: Q WRG 12m 10/8M; 254°-G-257°-W-257·7°-R-260·7°; Gy twr; 48°49'·37N 03°03'·67W.

Les Piliers ⚓ 48°49'·77N 02°59'·99W.

Kermouster Dir ⚑ 271°: Fl WRG 2s 16m, W 10M, R/G 8M; 267°-G-270°-W-272°- R-274°; W col; 48°49'·55N 03°05'·19W (R. Trieux).

ÎLE DE BRÉHAT

Le Paon ⚑ Oc WRG 4s 22m W10M, R/G6M; 033°-W-078°-G-181°-W-196°- R-307°-W-316°-R-348°; Y twr; 48°51'·92N 02°59'·15W.

Roche Guarine ⌁ 48°51'·63N 02°57'·63W, Chenal de Bréhat.

Rosédo ☆ Fl 5s 29m **20M**; W twr; vis 006°-340° (334°); 48°51'·45N 03°00'·29W.

La Chambre ⌁ 48°50'·16N 02°59'·58W.

Men-Joliguet ⚓ Fl (2) WRG 6s 6m W11M, R/G8M; 255°-R-279°-W-283°-G-175°; 48°50'·12N 03°00'·20W.

LÉZARDRIEUX TO TRÉGUIER

LE TRIEUX RIVER to LÉZARDRIEUX
Nord Horaine ⌁ VQ, 7M; 48°54'·53N 02°55'·42W.

La Horaine ⚑ Fl (3) 12s 13m 7M; Gy 8-sided twr on B hut; 48°53'·50N 02°55'·22W.

Men-Marc'h ⌁ 48°53'·17N 02°51'·82W.

Ldg lts 224·8°: Front, **La Croix** ☆ Q 15m **18M**; intens 215°-235°; two Gy ○ twrs joined, W on NE side, R tops; 48°50'·23N 03°03'·25W. Rear **Bodic** ☆ Dir Q 55m **22M**; intens 221°-229°; W ho with G gable; 2·1M from front.

Les Sirlots ⚑ *Whis;* 48°52'·95N 02°59'·58W.

Coatmer ldg lts 218·7°. Front, Q RG 16m R/G7M; 200°-R-250°-G-053°; W gable; 48°48'·26N 03°05'·75W. Rear, QR 50m 7M; vis 197°-242°; W gable; 660m from front.

Les Perdrix ⚑ Fl (2) WG 6s 5m, W6M, G3M; 165°-G-197°-W-202·5°-G-040°; G twr; 48°47'·74N 03°05'·79W.

CHENAL DE LA MOISIE (339·4°); PASSE DE LA GAINE (241·5°)

La Vieille du Tréou ⚓ 48°52'·00N 03°01'·09W.

An Ogejou Bihan ⌁ 48°53'·37N 03°01'·91W.

La Moisie ⚓ 48°53'·83N 03°02'·22W.

Les Héaux de Bréhat ☆ Fl (4) WRG 15s 48m, **W15M**, R/G11M; 227°-R-247°-W-270°-G-302°-W-227°; Gy ○ twr; 48°54'·50N 03°05'·17W.

Basse des Héaux ⌁ 48°54'·07N 03°05'·28W.

Pont de la Gaine ⌁ 48°53'·12N 03°07'·40W.

JAUDY RIVER TO TRÉGUIER

La Jument des Héaux ⚓ VQ 7m 4M; 48°55'·42N 03°08'·04W.

Grande Passe ldg lts 137°. Front, Port de la Chaine, Oc 4s 12m 11M; 042°-232°; W house; 48°51'·55N 03°07'·89W.

Rear, **St Antoine** ☆ Dir Oc R 4s 34m **15M**; intens 134°-140°; R & W house; 0·75M from front. (Both marks are hard to see by day.)

Basse Crublent ⚓ QR; 3m 2M; *Whis;* 48°54'·29N 03°11'·16W.

Le Corbeau ⚑ Fl R 4s; 48°53'·35N 03°10'·26W.

Pierre à l'Anglais ⚑ Fl G 4s; 48°53'·21N 03°10'·46W.

Petit Pen ar Guézec ⚑ Fl (2) G 6s 1M; 48°52'·52N 03°09'·44W.

La Corne ⚑ Fl (3) WRG 12s 14m W8M, R/G6M; 052°-W-059°-R-173°-G-213°-W-220°-R-052°; W twr, R base; 48°51'·35N 03°10'·62W.

TRÉGUIER TO TRÉBEURDEN

PORT BLANC
Le Voleur Dir ⚑ 150°: Fl WRG 4s 17m, W14M, R/G 11M; 140°-G-148°-W-152°-R-160°; W twr; 48°50'·20N 03°18'·52W.

Basse Guazer ⚑ ; 48°51'·58N 03°20'·96W.

PERROS-GUIREC
Passe de l'Est, ldg lts 224·8°. Front, Le Colombier ⚑ Dir Q 28m 14M; intens 214·5°-234·5°; W house; 48°47'·87N 03°26'·66W. Rear, **Kerprigent** ☆, Dir Q 79m **21M**; intens 221°-228°; W twr, 1·5M from front.

Pierre du Chenal ⚓ 48°49'·29N 03°24'·67W.

Passe de l'Ouest. Kerjean ⚑ Dir lt 143·6°, Oc (2+1) WRG 12s 78m, W10M, R/G 8M; 133·7°-G-143·2°-W-144·8°-R-154·3°; W twr, B top; 48°47'·79N 03°23'·40W.

Les Couillons de Tomé ⌁ 48°50'·90N 03°25'·75W.

La Horaine ⌁ 48°49'·89N 03°27'·26W.

Roche Bernard ⚑ 48°49'·43N 03°25'·46W.

Gommonénou ⚓ VQ R 1M; 48°48'·27N 03°25'·83W.

Jetée du Linkin ⚑ Fl (2) G 6s 4m 6M; W pile, G top; 48°48'·20N 03°26'·31W.

PLOUMANAC'H
Mean-Ruz ⚑ Oc WR 4s 26m W12M, R9M; 226°-W-242°-R-226°; obsc by Pte de Trégastel when brg <080°; partly obsc by Les Sept-Îles 156°-207° and partly by Île Tomé 264°-278°; pink ☐ twr; 48°50'·25N 03°29'·00W.

LES SEPT ÎLES

Île-aux-Moines ☆ Fl (3) 20s 59m **24M**; obsc by Îliot Rouzic and E end of Île Bono 237°-241°, and in Baie de Lannion when brg <039°; Gy twr/dwelling; 48°52'·72N 03°29'·40W.

Les Dervinis ⚓ 48°52'·35N 03°27'·32W.

TRÉGASTEL-PLAGE
Île Dhu ⚓ 48°50'·37N 03°31'·24W.
Les Triagoz ☆ Fl (2) WR 6s 31m W14M, R11M;
010°-W-339°-R-010°; obsc in places 258°-268° by Les Sept-
Îles; Gy◻twr, R lantern; 48°52'·28N 03°38'·80W. 992271324.
Bar-ar-Gall ⚓ VQ (9) 10s; 48°49'·79N 03°36'·22W.
Le Crapaud ⚓ Q (9) 15s; 48°46'·67N 03°40'·59W.

TRÉBEURDEN
Pte de Lan Kerellec ☆ Iso WRG 4s; W8M, R/G5M; 058°-G-064°-
W-069°-R-130°; Gy twr; 48°46'·74N 03°35'·06W.
Ar Gouredec ⚓ VQ (6) + L Fl 10s 3M; 48°46'·41N 03°36'·59W.
An Ervennou ⚓ Fl (2) R 6s 1m 1M; 48°46'·48N 03°35'·96W.
NW bkwtr ☆ Fl G 2·5s 8m 2M; IPTS; 48°46'·33N 03°35'·21W.

TRÉBEURDEN TO MORLAIX

LÉGUER RIVER
An Taro Braz ⚓ Q (6)+L Fl 15s 1M 48° 44'·70N 03°39'· 64W.
Beg-Léguer ☆ Oc (4) WRG 12s 60m W12M, R/G9M;
007°-G-084°-W-098°-R-129°; W face of W house, R
lantern; 48°44'·31N 03°32'·91W.
Kinierbel ⚓; *Bell;* 48°44'·15N 03°35'·18W.

LOCQUÉMEAU
Locquémeau Dir Lt 121° Q, WRG, 39m W12M, R/G 8M;
QG115·5°-120·5QW-121°5-R27·5°; White gabled house;
48°43'·28N 03°34'·11W.
Ldg lts 121°: Front, ☆ QR 21m 7M; 068°-228°; W pylon, R
top; 48°43'·41N 03°34'·44W. Rear, ☆ QR 39m 7M; 016°-
232°; W gabled house; 484m from front.
Locquémeau ⚓ *Whis;* 48°43'·86N 03°35'·93W.
Locquémeau approach ⚓ Fl G 2.5s; 48°43'·62N 03°34'·96W.

LOCQUIREC
Gouliat ⚓ 48°42'·57N 03°38'·97W.

PRIMEL-TRÉGASTEL
Méloine ⚓ 48°45'·56N 03°50'·68W.
Ldg lts 152°, both ☆ QR 35/56m 7M. Front, 134°-168°; W
◻, R stripe, on pylon; 48°42'·45N 03°49'·19W. Rear, ·R
vert stripe on W wall; 172m from front.
W bkwtr ☆ Fl G 4s 6m 7M; 48°42'·77N 03°49'·52W.

BAIE DE MORLAIX
Chenal de Tréguier ldg lts 190·5°: Front, ☆ Île Noire
Oc (2) WRG 6s 15m, W11M, R/G8M; 051°-G-135°-R-
211°-W-051°; obsc in places; W ◻ twr, R top; 48°40'·35N
03°52'·54W. Common Rear, **La Lande** ☆ Fl 5s 85m **23M;**
obsc by Pte Annelouesten when brg >204°; W ◻ twr, B
top; 48°38'·20N 03°53'·14W.
La Pierre Noire ⚓ 48°42'·56N 03°52'·20W.
La Chambre ⚓ 48°40'·74N 03°52'·51W.
Grande Chenal ldg lts 176·4°: Front, Île Louet ☆ Oc (3)
WG 12s 17m W12M,G8M; 305°-W (except where obsc
by islands)-244°-G-305°; W ◻ twr, B top; 48°40'·41N
03°53'·34W. Common Rear, **La Lande** as above.
Pot de Fer ⚓ *Bell;* 48°44'·23N 03°54'·02W.
Stolvezen ⚓ 48°42'·64N 03°53'·41W.
Ricard ⚓ 48°41'·54N 03°53'·51W.
Vieille ⚓ 48°42'·60N 03°54'·11W. (Ch Ouest de Ricard 188·8°)
La Noire ⚓ 48°41'·65N 03°54'·06W.
Corbeau ⚓ 48°40'·63N 03°53'·33W.

MORLAIX RIVER
Barre de-Flot No 1 ⚓ 48°40'·18N 03°52'·95W.
No 2 ⚓ Fl R 2·5s; 1m 2M; 48°39'·88N 03°52'·53W.
No 3 ⚓ Fl G 2·5s; 1m 2M; 48°39'·25N 03°52'·32W.

No 4 ⚓ Fl R 2·5s; 1m 2M 48°38'·62N 03°51'·62W.
No 5 ⚓ Fl G 2·5s; 1m 2M 48°38'·04N 03°51'·34W.
No 7 ⚓ 48°37'·68N 03°51'·03W.

PENZÉ RIVER
Cordonnier ⚓ 48°42'·93N 03°56'·59W.
Guerhéon ⚓ 48°42'·73N 03°57'·18W.
Trousken ⚓ 48°42'·26N 03°56'·54W.
Pte Fourche ⚓ 48°42'·14N 03°56'·76W.
Ar Tourtu ⚓ 48°41'·99N 03°56'·57W.
An Nehou (Caspari) ⚓ 48°41'·56N 03°56'·45W.
Le Figuier ⚓ 48°40'·46N 03°56'·16W.

ROSCOFF TO ÎLE VIERGE

BLOSCON/ROSCOFF
Astan ⚓ VQ (3) 5s 4m 4M; 48°44'·91N 03°57'·66W.
Le Menk ⚓ Q (9) WR 15s 6m W6M, R4M;
160°-W-188°-R-160°; 48°43'·28N 03°56'·71W.
Basse de Bloscon ⚓ VQ 3m 4M   48°43'·71N 03°57'·55W.
Bloscon pier ☆ Fl WG 4s 9m W10M, G7M (in fog Fl 2s);
200°-W-210°-G-200°; W twr, G top; 48°43'·21N 03°57'·69W.
Roscoff Marina ent, E side, ☆ Fl (2) R 6s 4M; 48°43'·11N
03°57'·89W. Ent W side ☆ Fl (2) G 6s 4M; 48°43'·11N 03°57'·94.
Ar Pourven ⚓ Q 2m 3M; 48°43'·04N 03°57'·70W.
Ar-Chaden ⚓ Q (6) + L Fl WR 15s 14m, W8M, R6M;
262°-R-289·5°-W-293°-R-326°-   W-110°;   YB   twr;
48°43'·94N 03°58'·26W.
Men-Guen-Bras ⚓ Q WRG 14m, W9M, R/ G6M;
068°-W-073°-R-197°-W-257°-G-068°; BY twr; 48°43'·76N
03°58'·07W.
Roscoff ldg lts 209°: Front, N môle ☆ Oc (3) G 12s 7m 7M;
synch; 078°-318°; W col, G top; 48°43'·56N 03°58'·67W.
Rear ☆ Oc (3) 12s 24m **15M**; 062°-242°; Gy ◻ twr, W on
NE side; 430m from front.

CANAL DE L'ÎLE DE BATZ
Roc'h Zu ⚓ 48°43'·88N 03°58'·59W.
Jetty hd (LW landing) ☆ Q 5m 1M; BY col; 48°43'·92N
03°58'·97W.
Run Oan ⚓ 48°44'·10N 03°59'·30W.
Perroch ⚓ 48°44'·10N 03°59'·71W.
Tec'hit Bihan ⚓ 48°44'·02N 04°00'·88W.
La Croix ⚓ 48°44'·19N 04°01'·30W.
L'Oignon ⚓ 48°44'·04N 04°01'·35W.
Basse Plate ⚓ 48°44'·25N 04°02'·53W.

ÎLE DE BATZ
Île aux Moutons ⚓ VQ (6)+ L Fl 10s 3m 7M; 48°44'·25N
04°00'·52W; landing stage, S end and ent to hbr.
Malvoch⚓ 48°44'·26N 04°00'·67W, W side of ent.
Lt ho ☆ Fl (4) 25s 69m **23M**; Gy twr; 48°44'·71N
04°01'·62W. Same twr, auxiliary lt, FR 65m 7M; 024°-059°.

MOGUÉRIEC
Ldg lts 162°: Front ☆ Iso WG 4s 9m W11M, G6M;
158°-W-166°-G-158°; W twr, G top; jetty 48°41'·34N
04°04'·47W. Rear ☆ Iso G 4s 25m 9M, synch; 142°-182°;
W col, G top; 440m from front.

PONTUSVAL
Pointe de Pontusval ⚓ 48°41'·42N 04°19'·32W.
Ar Peich ⚓ 48°41'·90N 04°19'·16W.
Pte de Beg-Pol ☆ Oc (3) WR 12s 15m W10M, R7M; Shore-
W-056°-R-096°-W-shore; W twr, B top, W dwelling;
48°40'·67N 04°20'·76W. QY and FR lts on towers 2·4M S.
Aman-ar-Ross ⚓ Q 5m 4M; 48°41'·88N 04°27'·03W.

Lizen Ven ⚓ VQ (9) 10s 6m 4M; 48°40'·53N 04°33'·63W.
Île-Vierge ☆ Fl 5s 77m **27M**; 337°-325°; Gy twr; 48°38'·33N 04°34'·05W.

ÎLE VIERGE TO L'ABER-ILDUT

L'ABER WRAC'H
Libenter ⚓ Q (9) 15s 5m 4M; 48°37'·45N 04°38'·46W.
Outer ldg lts 100·1°: Front, Île Wrac'h ⚓ QR 20m 7M; W □ twr, Or top; 48°36'·88N 04°34'·56W. Rear, Lanvaon ⚓ Q 55m 12M; intens 090°-110°; W □ twr, Or △ on top; 1·63M from front.
Grand Pot de Beurre ⚓ 48°37'·21N 04°36'·48W.
Petit Pot de Beurre ⚓ 48°37'·12N 04°36'·23W.
Basse de la Croix ⚓ Fl (3) G 12s 3M; 48°36'·92N 04°35'·99W.
Breac'h Ver ⚓ Fl (2) G 2·5s 6m 3M; △ on twr; 48°36'·63N 04°35'·38W. Île Enez Terc'h ⚓ Fl (2) R 6s 1m 2M; 48°36'·20N 04°34'·40W.
Dir ⚓ 128°, Oc (2) WRG 6s 5m W13M, R/G11M; 125·7°-G-127·2°-W-128·7°-R-130·2°; 48°35'·89N 04°33'·82W, root of W bkwtr.
Marina ent: QG 3m 2M; vis 186°-167° (341°); 48°35'·97N 04°33'·64W. QR 3m 2M; vis 244°-226° (342°).

L'ABER BENOÎT
Petite Fourche ⚓ 48°36'·99N 04°38'·75W.
Rusven Est ⚓ 48°36'·30N 04°38'·63W.
Rusven Ouest ⚓ Bell; 48°36'·07N 04°39'·43W.
Basse du Chenal Abers ⚓ 48°35'·81N 04°38'·53W.
Poul Orvil ⚓ 48°35'·52N 04°38'·29W.
La Jument ⚓ 48°35'·10N 04°37'·41W.
Ar Gazel ⚓ 48°34'·90N 04°37'·27W.
Le Chien ⚓ 48°34'·67N 04°36'·88W.

ROCHES DE PORTSALL
Le Relec ⚓ 48°35'·99N 04°40'·84W.
Corn-Carhai ⚓ Fl (3) 12s 19m 9M; W 8-sided twr, B top; 48°35'·19N 04°43'·94W.
Grande Basse de Portsall ⚓ VQ (9) 10s 6m 4M; 48°36'·70N 04°46'·13W.
Basse Paupian ⚓ 48°35'·31N 04°46'·27W.
Bosven Aval ⚓ 48°33'·82N 04°44'·27W.
Men ar Pic ⚓ 48°33'·65N 04°44'·03W.
Portsall ⚓ Oc (4) WRG 12s 9m W13M, R/G10M; 058°-G-084°-W-088°-R-058°; W col, R top; 48°33'·84N 04°42'·26W.

ARGENTON to L'ABER-ILDUT
Le Taureau ⚓ 48°31'·46N 04°47'·34W.
Argenton, Île Dolvez, front ldg bcn 086° ⚓ 48°31'·25N 04°46'·23W.
Le Four ☆ Fl (5) 15s 28m **22M**; Gy ○ twr; 48°31'·38N 04°48'·32W.
L'Aber-Ildut ☆ Dir Oc (2) WRG 6s 12m W10M, R10M, G10M; 078°-G-081°-W-085°-R-088°; W bldg; 48°28'·26N 04°45'·56W.
Le Lieu ⚓ 5m, R twr, 48°28'·25N 04°46'·66W, and associated ⚓ Fl R 2·5s 4M, 48°28'·22N 04°46'·74W
Beg ar Groaz ⚓ FL G 2·5s 1M; 48°28'·22N 04°45'·3W.

CHENAL DU FOUR AND CHENAL DE LA HELLE

Ldg lts 158·5°. Front, **Kermorvan** ☆ Fl 5s 20m **22M**; obsc'd by Pte de St Mathieu when brg <341°; W □ twr; *Horn 60s*; 48°21'·72N 04°47'·40W. 992271316.
Rear, **Pte de St Mathieu** ☆ Fl 15s 56m **24M**; W twr, R top; 48°19'·79N 04°46'·26W. Same twr: Dir F 54m **28M**; intens 157·5°-159·5°.

⚓ Q WRG 26m, W12M, R/G 8M; 085°-G-107°-W-116°-R-134°; W twr 54 m WNW of previous entry; 48°19'·80N 04°46'·30W.
Plâtresses N ⚓ Fl G 2·5s 3m 4M; 48°26'·46N 04°50'·71W.
Valbelle ⚓ Fl (2) R 2·5s 8m 4M; 48°26'·43N 04°50'·03W.
Plâtresses SE ⚓ Fl (2) G 6s 7m 2M; 48°25'·96N 04°50'·52W.
Saint Paul ⚓ Fl (2) R 6s 7m 4M; 48°24'·82N 04°49'·16W.
Pte de Corsen ⚓ Dir Q WRG 33m W12M, R/G8M; 008°-R-012°-W-015° (ldg sector)- G-021°; W hut; 48°24'·89N 04°47'·61W.

CHENAL DE LA HELLE
Ldg lts 137·9°: Front, **Kermorvan** ☆ see above. Rear, **Lochrist** ☆ Dir Oc (3) 12s 49m **22M**; intens 135°-140°; W 8-sided twr, R top; 48°20'·55N 04°45'·82W.
Luronne ⚓; 48°26'·61N 04°53'·78W.
Ldg lts 293·5° astern (to join Ch du Four S of St Paul ⚓): Front, Le Faix ⚓ VQ 16m 8M; 48°25'·73N 04°53'·91W. Rear, **Le Stiff** ☆ (below at Ouessant); 6·9M from front.
Ldg line 142·5°, optional day only (to join Chenal du Four SE of St Pierre ⚓): Front, **Kermorvan** ☆ see above. Rear, two W gables (Les Pignons de Kéraval, 48m) 48°20'·10N 04°45'·55W
Pourceaux ⚓ Q 7m 4M; 48°24'·00N 04°51'·31W.
Saint-Pierre ⚓ Fl (3) G 12s; 48°23'·09N 04°49'·09W.
Rouget ⚓ Fl G 4s 7m 4M; 48°22'·04N 04°48'·88W (Ch du Four).
Grande Vinotière ⚓ Fl R 4s 12m 5M; R 8-sided twr; 48°21'·94N 04°48'·42W.
Le Conquet, Môle Ste Barbe ⚓ Fl G 2·5s 5m 6M; 48°21'·57N 04°46'·98W.
Les Renards ⚓ 48°21'·00N 04°47'·48W.
Tournant et Lochrist ⚓ Fl (2) R 6s 7m 4M; 48°20'·64N 04°48'·12W,
Ar Christian Braz ⚓ 48°20'·68N 04°50'·14W, E of Ile de Béniguet.
Ldg line 325°: Front, Grand Courleau ⚓; rear, La Faix (above).
Ldg lts 007°: Front, **Kermorvan** ☆ above. Rear, **Trézien** ☆ Dir Oc (2) 6s 84m **20M**; intens 003°-011°; Gy twr, W on S side; 48°25'·41N 04°46'·74W.
Les Vieux-Moines ⚓ Fl R 4s 16m 5M; 280°-133°; R 8-sided twr; 48°19'·33N 04°46'·63W, 5ca SSW of Pte de St Mathieu.
La Fourmi ⚓ Fl G 4s; 48°19'·25N 04°47'·96W.

OUESSANT AND ÎLE MOLÉNE

OFF USHANT TSS
Ouessant NE ⊙; V-AIS; 48°59'·51N 05°24'·00W.
Ouessant SW ⊙; V-AIS 48°30'·00N 05°45'·00W.

ÎLE D'OUESSANT
Le Stiff ☆ Fl (2) R 20s 85m **22M**; two adjoining W twrs; 48°28'·47N 05°03'·41W. Radar twr, conspic, 340m NE, ⚓ Q (day); ⚓ FR (night).
Port du Stiff, E môle ⚓ Dir Q WRG 11m W10M, R/G7M; 251°-G-254°-W-264°-R-267°; W twr, G top; 48°28'·12N 05°03'·25W.
Baie du Stiff: Gorle Vihan ⚓ 48°28'·32N 05°02'·60W.
Men-Korn ⚓ VQ (3) WR 5s 21m 8M; 145°-W-040°-R-145°; BYB twr; 48°27'·96N 05°01'·32W.
Men ar Froud ⚓ 48°26'·62N 05°03'·67W.
La Jument ⚓ Fl (3) R 12s 36m 10M; 241°-199°; Gy 8-sided twr, R top; 48°25'·33N 05°08'·04W.

Nividic ⚓ VQ (9) 10s 28m 10M; 290°-225°; Gy 8-sided twr, helicopter platform; 48°26'·74N 05°09'·06W.

Créac'h ☆ Fl (2) 10s 70m **30M**; obsc 247°-255°; W twr, B bands; 48°27'·55N 05°07'·76W.

ÎLE MOLÈNE and ARCHIPELAGO

Kéréon ⚓ Oc (3) WR 12s 38m 10M; 019°-W-248°-R-019°; Gy twr; 48°26'·24N 05°01'·59W; unreliable.

Les Trois-Pierres ⚓ Iso WRG 4s 15m W9M, R/G6M; 070°-G-147°-W-185°-R-191°-G-197°-W-213°-R-070°; W col; 48°24'·70N 04°56'·84W.

Molène, Old môle Dir ⚓ 191°, Fl (3) WRG 12s 6m W9M, R/G7M; 183°-G-190°-W-192°-R-203°; 48°23'·85N 04°57'·29W.

Same structure: Chenal des Laz , Dir ⚓ 261°: Fl (2) WRG 6s 9m W9M, R/G7M ; 252·5°-G-259·5°-W-262·5°-R-269·5°.

Pierres-Vertes ⚓ VQ (9) 10s 9m 4M; 48°22'·19N 05°04'·76W.

Pierres Noires ⚓ ; 48°18'·47N 04°58'·15W.

Les Pierres Noires ☆ Fl R 5s 27m **19M**; W twr, R top; 48°18'·67N 04°54'·88W.

BREST AND APPROACHES

Basse Royale ⚓ Q (6) + L Fl 15s; 48°17'·45N 04°49'·61W.

Vandrée ⚓ VQ (9) 10s 7m 4M; *Whis;* 48°15'·21N 04°48'·24W.

Goëmant ⚓ ; 48°15'·12N 04°46'·34W.

La Parquette ⚓ Fl RG 4s 17m R6M, G6M; 244°-R-285°-G-244°; W 8-sided twr, B diagonal stripes; 48°15'·90N 04°44'·29W.

Coq Iroise ⚓ 48°19'·07N 04°43'·99W.

Charles Martel ⚓ Fl (4) R 15s 7m 4M; 48°18'·95N 04°41'·92W.

Trépied ⚓ 48°16'·73N 04°41'·50W.

GOULET DE BREST

Le Chat ⚓ 48°20'·29N 04°41'·72W (Anse de Bertheaume).

Pte du Petit-Minou ☆ Fl (2) WR 6s 32m **W17M**, R13M; Shore-R-252°-W-260°-R-307°-W(unintens)-015°-W-065·5°; 036·5°-R(intens)- 039·5°; 70·5°-W-shore; Gy twr, R top; 48°20'·19N 04°36'·86W.

Ldg lts 068°, both Dir Q 30/54m **22M. Front, Pte du Petit-Minou**, intens 067·3°-068·8°. **Rear, Pte du Portzic** ☆, Aux Dir Q 54m; intens 065°-071° (see below).

Fillettes ⚓ VQ (9) 10s 7m 4M; 48°19'·75N 04°35'·66W.

Kerviniou ⚓ Fl R 2·5s 7m 4M; 48°19'·77N 04°35'·25W.

Basse Goudron ⚓ Fl (2) R 6s 7m 3M; 48°20'·03N 04°34'·86W.

Mengam ⚓ Fl (3) WR 12s 10m W9M, R6M; 034°-R-054°-W-034°; R twr, B bands; 48°20'·32N 04°34'·56W.

Pte du Portzic ☆ Oc (2) WR 12s 56m **W19M, R15M**; 219°-R-259°-W-338°-R-000°-W-065·5° (vis 041°-069° west of Goulet)-W-219°; Gy twr; 48°21'·49N 04°32'·05W. Same lt ho, Aux Dir Q, rear 068° ldg lt. Aux ☆ Dir Q (6) + L Fl 15s 54m **23M**; intens 045°-050°.

BREST

Pénoupèle ⚓ Fl R 2·5s 4m 4M; 48°21'·45N 04°30'·53W.

S jetty ⚓ QR 10m 6M; 094°-048°; W/R twr; 48°22'·10N 04°29'·46W.

E jetty ⚓ QG 10m 6M; W/G twr; 48°22'·15N 04°29'·22W.

Ldg lts 343.5°: Front ⚓ Dir Q WRG 24m W9M, R/G6M; 334°-G-342°-W-346°-R-024°; 48°22'·80N 04°29'·62W. Rear ⚓ Dir Q 32m 9M; intens 342°-346°; 115m from front.

Le Château Marina, S Jetty hd, ⚓ Fl G 2·5s 8m 4M; 48°22'·66N 04°29'·49W.

Le Château Marina, N Jetty hd, ⚓ Fl R 2·5s 8m 4M; 48°22'·67N 04°29'·45W.

Port de Commerce, E ent: N jetty ⚓ Oc (2) G 6s 8m 6M; W/G pylon; 48°22'·76N 04°28'·53W. S jetty ⚓ Oc (2) R 6s 8m 6M; W pylon, R top; 48°22'·69N 04°28'·48W.

R2 ⚓ Fl (2) R 6s 3m 3M; 48°22'·01N 04°28'·75W.

R1 ⚓ Fl (2) G 6s 3m 3M; 48°21'·83N 04°28'·29W.

R4 ⚓ Fl (3) R 12s 3m 4M; 48°22'·22N 04°28'·06W.

R6 ⚓ Fl R 4s 3m 3M; 48°22'·48N 04°27'·36W.

LE MOULIN BLANC MARINA

Moulin Blanc ⚓ Fl (2) R 6s 3m 3M; 48°22'·80N 04°25'·91W

MBA ⚓ Q(3) 10s 3m 2M; pontoon elbow; 48°23'·54N 04°25'·74W.

CAMARET

N môle ⚓ Iso WG 4s 7m W12M, G9M; 135°-W-182°-G-027°; W pylon, G top; 48°16'·85N 04°35'·31W.

Port Vauban wavebreak, S end, ⚓ Fl (2) G 6s 2m 2M; 48°16'·74N 04° 35'·33W.

S môle ⚓ Fl (2) R 6s 9m 5M; R pylon; 48°16'·63N 04°35'·33W.

Styvel ⚓ QR 2M; 46°16'·73N 04°35'·74W.

POINTE DU TOULINGUET TO RAZ DE SEIN

Pte du Toulinguet ☆ Oc (3) WR 12s 49m **W15M**, R11M; Shore-W-028°-R-090°-W-shore; W □ twr; 48°16'·81N 04°37'·72W.

La Louve ⚓ 48°16'·76N 04°38'·03W.

Mendufa ⚓ 48°16'·05N 04°39'·43W.

Basse du Lis ⚓ Q (6) + L Fl 15s 6m 4M; 48°12'·99N 04°44'·53W.

Le Chevreau ⚓ 48°13'·30N 04°36'·98W.

Le Bouc ⚓ Q (9) 15s 5m 4M; 48°11'·51N 04°37'·37W.

Basse Vieille ⚓ Fl (2) 6s 8m 4M; 48°08'·22N 04°35'·75W.

DISTANCE TABLES

Approx distances in nautical miles are by the most direct route allowing for dangers and TSS.

1	Lézardrieux	1	12	16	18	24	42	43	45	72	97	100	105	124	Pornic	12
2	Tréguier	22	2	11	12	24	39	40	41	66	87	90	95	113	St Nazaire	11
3	Perros-Guirec	28	21	3	10	13	30	30	34	55	78	80	85	106	La Baule/Pornichet	10
4	Trébeurden	40	32	17	4	9	18	22	27	48	73	75	79	100	Le Croisic	9
5	Morlaix	60	46	36	23	5	8	28	36	57	78	80	84	105	Arzal/Camöel	8
6	Roscoff	54	41	28	17	12	6	7	16	37	58	60	64	85	Crouesty	7
7	L'Aberwrac'h	84	72	60	49	48	32	7	6	26	47	48	54	74	Le Palais (Belle Ile)	6
8	Le Conquet	106	98	83	72	68	55	29	8	5	32	33	38	61	Lorient	5
9	Brest (marina)	114	107	92	83	79	67	42	18	9	4	4	12	37	Concarneau	4
10	Morgat	126	118	103	92	88	75	49	20	24	10	3	12	36	Port-la-Forêt	3
11	Douarnenez	131	123	108	97	93	80	54	25	29	11	11	2	30	Loctudy	2
12	Audierne	135	128	113	102	98	86	55	30	34	27	30	12	1	Audierne	1

MORGAT
Pointe de Morgat ☆ Oc (4) WRG 12s 77m **W15M**, R11M, G10M; Shore-W-281°-G-301°-W-021°-R-043°; W ☐ twr, R top, W dwelling; 48°13'·17N 04°29'·80W.
Hbr approach ⚓ Q R 1·2s 3m 2M; 48°13'·60N 04°29'·55W.
Hbr ent, E side, ⚓ Fl R 2·5s 4s 2M; 48°13'·58N 04°29'·72W'.
Hbr ent, W side, ☆ Fl G 2·5s 4s 2M; 48°13'·57N 04°29'·79W'.

DOUARNENEZ to RAZ DE SEIN
Île Tristan ⚓ Fl (3) WR 12s 35m, W6M, R6M; Shore-W-138°-R-153°-W-shore; Gy twr, W band, B top; 48°06'·14N 04°20'·24W.
Pointe du Millier ☆ Oc (2) WRG 6s 34m **W16M**, R12M, G11M; 080°-G-087°-W-113°-R-120°-W-129°-G-148°-W-251°-R-258°; W house; 48°05'·92N 04°27'·93W.
Basse Jaune ⚓ 48°04'·70N 04°42'·45W.

RAZ DE SEIN TO POINTE DE PENMARC'H
Tévennec ⚓ Q WR 28m W9M R6M; 090°-W-345°-R-090°; W ☐ twr and dwelling; 48°04'·28N 04°47'·73W. Same twr, Dir ⚓ Fl 4s 24m 12M; intens 324°-332° (through Raz de Sein).
La Vieille ⚓ Iso WRG 4s 33m WRG10M; 290°-W-298°-R-325°-W-355°-G-017°-W-035°-G-105°-W-123°-R-158°-W-205°; Gy ☐ twr; 48°02'·44N 04°45'·40W.
La Plate ⚓ VQ (9) 15s 10m 8M; 48°02'·37N 04°45'·58W.
Le Chat ⚓ Fl (2) WRG 6s 20m W9M RG6M; 096°-G-215°-W-230°-R-271°-G-286°-R-096°; YB twr; 48°01'·43N 04°48'·86W.

CHAUSSÉE DE SEIN and ÎLE DE SEIN
Cornoc-An-Ar-Braden ⚓ Fl G 4s 7m 4M; 48°03'·23N 04°50'·84W.
Men-Brial ⚓ Oc (2) WRG 6s 16m, W12M, R9M, G7M;

149°-G-186°-W-192°-R-221°-W-227°-G-254°; G&W twr; 48°02'·28N 04°50'·97W.
Île de Sein ☆ Fl (4) 25s 49m **28M**; W twr, B top; 48°02'·62N 04°52'·02W. Same twr, Dir Q WRG, W8M, R/G 6M; 267°-G-269°-W-271°-R-275°. **Ar-Men** ☆ Fl (3) 20s 29m **21M**; W twr, B top; 48°03'·01N 04°59'·87W.
Chaussée de Sein ⚓ VQ (9) 10s 9m 4M; *Whis*; *Racon O (3cm)*, *10M*; 48°03'·75N 05°08'·13W.

AUDIERNE
Pointe de Lervily ⚓ Fl WR 4s 20m W14M, R11M; 236°-W-269°-R-294°-W-087°-R-109°; W twr, R top; 48°00'·04N 04°33'·94W. Gamelle W ⚓, VQ (9) 10s 6m 4M; 47°59'·46N 04°32'·85W.
Jetée de Ste-Évette ⚓ Fl (2) R 6s 2m 7M; R lantern; 090°-000° (270°); 48°00'·31N 04°33'·07W.
Passe de l'Est ldg lts 331°: Front, Jetée de Raoulic ⚓ Fl (3) RG 12s 11m, R/G6M; 034°-G-085°-R-034°; 48°00'·55N 04°32'·46W.
Kergadec ⚓ 006°: Dir Q WRG 43m W12M, R/G9M; 000°-G-005·3°-W-006·7°-R-017°; W 8-sided twr, R top; 48°00'·96N 04°32'·78W.
Gamelle E ⚓; 47°59'·46N 04°32'·05W.

POINTE DE PENMARC'H
Eckmühl ☆ Fl 5s 60m **23M**; Gy 8-sided twr; 47°47'·89N 04°22'·36W.
Men-Hir ⚓ Fl (2) WG 6s 19m, W7M, G4M; G135°-315°, W315°-135°; W twr, B band; 47°47'·74N 04°23'·99W.
Cap Caval ⚓ Q (9) 15s 6m 4M; 47°46'·47N 04°22'·68W.
Locarec ⚓ Iso WRG 4s 11m, W9M, R/G6M; 063°-G-068°-R-271°-W-285°-R-298°-G-340°-R-063°; iron col on rk; 47°47'·29N 04°20'·31W.

AREA 17 *South Biscay – River Loire to Bordeaux*
SELECTED LIGHTS, BUOYS & WAYPOINTS

PTE DE PENMARC'H TO CONCARNEAU GUILVINEC
LE GUILVINEC
Névez ⚓ Fl G 2·5s 7m 4M; 47°45'·84N 04°20'·08W.
Ldg lts (triple Q) 053°, synch: **Front**, ⚓ Q 7m 8M; 233°-066°; W pylon; Môle de Léchiagat, spur; 47°47'·43N 04°17'·07W. Middle, ⚓ Q WG 12m W14M, G11M; 006°-W-293°-G-006°; synch; R ☐ on R col; Rocher Le Faoutés, 210m from front. Rear, ⚓ Q 26m 8M, 051·5°-054·5°, R h on W twr; 0·58M from front.
Spineg ⚓ Q (6) + L Fl 15s 7m 4M; 47°45'·19N 04°18'·90W.

LESCONIL
Karek Greis ⚓ Q (3) 10s; 47°46'·03N 04°11'·36W.
⚓ Q (6) + LFl 15s 47°46'·53N 04°10'·63W
Men-ar-Groas ⚓ Fl (3) WRG 12s 14m, W10M, R/G7M; 268°-G-313°-W-333°-R-050°; W lt ho, G top; 47°47'·79N 04°12'·68W. Rostolou ⚓ 47°46'·64N 04°07'·29W.
Boulanger ⚓ VQ (6) + L Fl 10s;47°47'·38N 04°09'·13W.
Chenal de Bénodet ⚓ 47°48'·53N 04°07'·04W.
Bilien ⚓ VQ (3) 5s; 47°49'·10N 04°08'·09W.

LOCTUDY
Pte de Langoz ☆ Fl (4) WRG 15s 12m, **W15M**, R11M G12M; 115°-G-243°-W-257°-G-284°-W-295°-R-318°-W-328°-R-025°; W twr, R top; 47°49'·88N 04°09'·55W.

Karek-Saoz ⚓ Fl R 2·5s 3m 1M; R twr; 47°50'·02N 04°09'·38W.
Men Audierne ⚓ 47°50'·22N 04°09'·05W.
No 2 (Karek-Croisic) ⚓ Fl (2) R 6s; 47°50'·19N 04°09'·49W.
No 1 ⚓ Fl (2) G 6s; 47°50'·22N 04°09'·73W.
No 3 ⚓ Fl (3) G 12s; 47°50'·22N 04°09'·99W.
Groyne head ⚓ Q 3m 10M; 47°50'·21N 04°10'·34W.
Le Blas ⚓ Fl (4) G 15s 5m 1M; 47°50'·28N 04°10'·23W.

BENODET
Ldg lts 345·5°: Front, Pte du Coq ⚓ Dir Oc (3) G 12s 11m 10M; intens 345°-347°; W ○ twr, G stripe; 47°52'·31N 04°06'·70W. Pyramide ⚓ Oc (3) 12s 48m 14M; 338°-016°, synch; W twr, G top; common rear, 348m from front.
Lts in line 000·5°: Front, Pte de Combrit ⚓ Oc (2) WR 6s 19m, W12M, R9M; 325°-W-017°-R-325°; W ☐ twr, Gy corners 47°51'·86N 04°06'·78W. Common rear, Pyramide; see above.
Rousse ⚓ 47°51'·55N 04°06'·47W. La Potée ⚓ 47°51'·78N 04°06'·55W.
Pte du Toulgoët ⚓ Fl R 2·5s 2m 1M; 47°52'·30N 04°06'·86W.
Le Taro ⚓ 47°50'·51N 04°04'·83W.
La Voleuse ⚓ Q (6) + L Fl 15s; 47°48'·76N 04°02'·49W.

ILE AUX MOUTONS and LES POURCEAUX
Île-aux-Moutons ☆ Iso WRG 2s 18m, **W15M**, R/G11M;

035°-W-050°-G-063°-W-081°-R-141°-W-292°-R-035°; W ☐ twr and dwelling; 47°46'·48N 04°01'·66W.

Rouge de Glénan ⚓ VQ (9) 10s 8m 8M; 47°45'·48N 04°03'·95W.

Grand Pourceaux ⚓ Q; 47°45'·98N 04°00'·80W.

ÎLES DE GLÉNAN

Penfret ☆ Fl R 6s 36m **19M**; W ☐ twr, R top; 47°43'·26N 03°57'·18W. Same twr: auxiliary ⚓ Dir Q 34m 11M; 295°-315°.

La Pie ⚓ Fl (2) 6s 9m 3M; 47°43'·75N 03°59'·76W.

Pte de la Baleine ⚓ VQ (3) 5s 2M; 47°43'·26N 03°59'·20W.

Les Bluiniers ⚓ 47°43'·35N 04°03'·81W.

Offlying marks, anticlockwise from the west:

Basse Pérennès ⚓ Q (9) 15s 8m 4M; 47°41'·06N 04°06'·14W.

Jument de Glénan ⚓ Q (6) + L Fl 15s 10m 4M; 47°38'·76N 04°01'·41W.

Laoennou ⚓ 47°39'·65N 03°54'·70W.

Jaune de Glénan ⚓ Q (3) 10s 4M; 47°42'·56N 03°49'·83W.

PORT-LA-FORÊT

Linuen ⚓ Q (3) 10s; 47°50'·76N 03°57'·31W.

Laouen Pod ⚓ 47°51'·23N 03°58'·00W.

Cap Coz mole ⚓ Fl (2) WRG 6s 5m, W7M, R/G5M; Shore-R-335°-G-340°-W-346°-R-shore; 47°53'·49N 03°58'·28W.

Le Scoré ⚓ 47°52'·75N 03°57'·56W.

Les Ormeaux ⚓ 47°53'·27N 03°58'·34W.

Entry channel ⚓ Fl G 2·5s; 47°53'·39N 03°58'·12W.

⚓ Fl R 2·5s; 47°53'·39N 03°58'·22W.

Kerleven mole ⚓ Fl G 4s 8m 6M; 47°53'·60N 03°58'·37W.

CONCARNEAU

Ldg lts 028·5°: Front, La Croix ⚓ Q 14m 13M; 006·5°-093°; R&W twr; 47°52'·16N 03°55'·08W. **Rear, Beuzec** ☆ Dir Q 87m **23M**; synch, intens 026·5°-030·5°; spire, 1·34M from front.

⚓ QR; 47°51'·40N 03°55'·75W.

Le Cochon ⚓ Fl (3) WRG 12s 5m W9M, R/G6M; 230°-R-352°-W-048°-G-207°-Obsc'd-230°; G twr; 47°51'·47N 03°55'·55W.

Basse du Chenal ⚓ Fl R 4s; 47°51'·54N 03°55'·66W.

Men Fall ⚓ Fl (2) G 6s; 47°51'·76N 03°55'·28W.

Kersos ⚓ 47°51'·80N 03°54'·93W (Anse de Kersos).

Lanriec ⚓ QG 13m 8M; 063°-078°; G window on W gable end; 47°52'·01N 03°54'·64W.

La Medée ⚓ Fl (3) R 12s 9m 4M; 47°52'·07N 03°54'·80W.

Ville-Close ⚓ Q WR, W9M, R6M; 209°-R-354°-W-007°-R-018°; R turret; 47°52'·27N 03°54'·76W.

No 1 ⚓ Fl (4) G 15s 4m 5M; G turret; 47°52'·16N 03°54'·72W.

Marina wavescreen ⚓ Fl (4) R 15s 3m 1M; 47°52'·23N 03°54'·79W. No 2 ⚓ Fl R 4s 4m 5M; G turret; 47°52'·31N 03°54'·71W.

Ville-Close (NE end) ⚓ Fl (2) R 6s; R twr; 47°52'·37N 03°54'·68W.

Ent to FV basin ⚓ Fl (2) G 6s; G twr; 47°52'·36N 03°54'·63W.

Pouldohan ⚓ Fl G 4s 6m 8M; 053°-065°; W ☐ twr, G top; 47°50'·97N 03°53'·69W.

Roché Tudy ⚓ 47°50'·52N 03°54'·49W.

CONCARNEAU TO ÎLE DE GROIX

PTE DE TRÉVIGNON TO PORT MANEC'H

Les Soldats ⚓ VQ (9) 10s 6M; 47°47'·86N 03°53'·42W.

Trévignon mole ⚓ Fl G 4s 5m 6M; 47°47'·69N 03°51'·30W.

Trévignon bkwtr root ⚓ Fl (2) WRG 6s 11m, W10/7M, R/G7M; 004°-W-051°-G-085°-W-092°-R-127°; 322°-R-351°; W ☐ twr, G top; 47°47'·59N 03°51'·33W.

Men Du ⚓ 47°46'·41N 03°50'·50W.

Men an Tréas ⚓ 47°45'·77N 03°49'·66W.

PORT MANEC'H (Aven and Bélon rivers)

Port Manech ⚓ Oc (4) WRG 12s 38m, W10M, R/G7M; obscd by Pte de Beg-Morg when brg <299°; 050°-W-(unintens)-140°-W-296°-G-303°-W-311°-R (over Les Verrès)-328°-W-050°; W & R twr; 47°47'·99N 03°44'·34W.

Les Verrès ⚓ 47°46'·65N 03°42'·71W.

BRIGNEAU

Brigneau ⚓ 47°46'·11N 03°40'·10W.

W mole, ⚓ Oc (2) WRG 6s 7m, W12M, R/G9M; R col, W top; 280°-G-329°-W-339°-R-034°; 47°46'·86N 03°40'·18W. In line 331° with W ☐ daymark behind, Hard to see, rear beacon unlit.

MERRIEN

⚓ Dir QR 26m 7M; 004°-009°; W ☐ twr, R top; 47°47'·04N 03°38'·97W.

Ent, W side ⚓. E side ⚓ 47°46'·45N 03°38'·89W.

DOËLAN

Ldg lts 013·8°: Front ⚓ Oc (3) WG 12s 20m, W13M, G10M; W shore-305°, G305°-314°, W314°-shore; W lt ho, G band and top; 47°46'·32N 03°36'·51W. Rear ⚓ Oc (3)R 12s 27m 9M; W lt ho, R band & top; 326m from front.

LE POULDU

Ent ⚓ 47°45'·74N 03°32'·25W.

Grand Cochon ⚓ 47°43'·03N 03°30'·81W.

Pte de Kerroc'h ⚓ Oc (2) WRG 6s 22m W11M, R/G8M; 096·5°-R-112°·5-G-132°-R-302°-W-096·5°; W twr, R top; 47°41'·97N 03°27'·66W.

ÎLE DE GROIX

Pen Men ☆ Fl (4) 25s 60m **29M**; 309°-275°; W ☐ twr, B top; 47°38'·84N 03°30'·56W.

Speerbrecker, ⚓ 47°39'·10N 03°26'·33W.

Port Tudy, N môle ⚓ Fl (2) G 6s 12m 7M; W twr, G top; 47°38'·72N 03°26'·73W.

E môle ⚓ Fl (2) R 6s 11m 6M; 112°-226°; W twr R top; 47°38'·68N 03°26'·78W.

Basse Melité ⚓ 47°38'·84N 03°25'·54W.

Pte de la Croix ⚓ Oc WR 4s 16m, W12M, R9M; 169°-W-336°-R-345°-W-353°; W pedestal, R lantern; 47°38'·05N 03°25'·02W.

Edouard de Cougy ⚓ 47°37'·93N 03°23'·90W.

Pointe des Chats ☆ Fl R 5s 16m **19M**; W ☐ twr and dwelling; 47°37'·24N 03°25'·30W.

Les Chats ⚓ Q (6) + L Fl 15s; 47°35'·70N 03°23'·57W.

LORIENT AND RIVER ÉTEL

LORIENT, PASSE DE L'OUEST

Passe de l'Ouest ldg lts 057°: both Dir Q 11/22m 13/**18M**. Front, Les Sœurs; (intens 042·5°-058·5°, 058·5°-042·5°, 4M range only); R twr, W bands; 47°42'·13N 03°21'·84W. Rear **Port Louis** ☆, W pylon, R bands; 47°42'·35N 03°21'·34W.

Banc des Truies ⚓ Q (9) 15s; 47°40'·76N 03°24'·48W.

Loméner, Anse de Stole, Dir ⚓ 357·2°: Q WRG 13m, W10M, R/G8M; 349·2°-G-355·2°-W-359·2°-R-005·2°; W twr, R top; 47°42'·30N 03°25'·54W.

A2 ⚓ Fl R 2·5s; 47°40'·94N 03°24'·98W.

Les Trois Pierres ⚓ Q RG 11m R/G6M; 060°-G-196°-R-002°; B twr, W bands; 47°41'·53N 03°22'·47W.
A8 ⚓ Fl R 2·5s; 47°41'·90N 03°22'·52W.

PASSE DU SUD
Bastresses Sud ⚓ QG; 47°40'·77N 03°22'·09W.
Les Errants ⚓ Fl (2) R 6s; 47°41'·10N 03°22'·38W.
Bastresses Nord ⚓ Fl (2) G 6s; 47°41'·11N 03°22'·20W.
Locmalo ⚓ Fl (3) G 12s; 47°41'·67N 03°22'·13W.

SOUTH OF PORT LOUIS
La Paix ⚓; 47°41'·97N 03°21'·84W.
Île aux Souris ☆ Dir Q WG 6m, W3M, G2M; 041·5°-W-043·5°-G-041·5°; G twr; 47°42'·15N 03°21'·52W.
⚓ Fl G 2·5s; 47°42'·13N 03°21'·21W.
Ban-Gâvres FV/yacht hbr, W jetty ☆ Fl (2) G 6s 3M; 47°42'·06N 03°21'·11W. E jetty ☆ Fl (2) R 6s 3M; 47°42'·06N 03°21'·06W.

ENTRANCE CHANNEL
Ldg lts 016·5°, both Dir QG 8/14m 13M; intens 014·5°-017·5°; synch; W twrs, G tops. Front ☆, 47°43'·47N 03°21'·63W (Île St Michel). Rear ☆, 306m from front.
La Citadelle ⚓ Oc G 4s 6m 6M; 012°-192°; 47°42'·59N 03°21'·94W.
Secondary yacht chan, ⬛ RGR, 47°42'·49N 03°22'·12W.
La Petite Jument ⚓ Oc R 4s 5m 6M; 182°-024°; R twr; 47°42'·58N 03°22'·07W.
Le Cochon ⚓ Fl R 4s 5m 5M; RGR twr; 47°42'·80N 03°22'·00W.
No 1 ⚓ 47°42'·80N 03°21'·84W.

PORT LOUIS (Port de la Pointe)
D 1 ⚓ 47°42'·76N 03°21'·52W.
Jetty ⚓ Fl G 2·5s 7m 6M; W twr, G top; 47°42'·71N 03°21'·37W.
Anse du Driasker Stage Head Fl R 2·5s 2M, metal mast.

KERNEVEL
Kéroman ldg lts 350°, both Dir Oc (2) R 6s 25/31m **15M**; synch; intens 349°-351°: **Front** ☆, 47°43'·60N 03°22'·02W, R ho, W bands. **Rear** ☆ R&W topmark on Gy pylon, R top; 91m from front.
Banc du Turc ⚓ Fl G 2·5s; 47°43'·33N 03°21'·85W.
Kernével marina, entrance: ⚓ QR 1M; 47°43'·39N 03°22'·10W.
Ldg lts 217°, both Dir QR 10/18m **15M**; intens 215°-219°; synch: **Front, Kernével** ☆ R&W twr; 47°43'·02N 03°22'·32W. **Rear** ☆ W ⬜ twr, R top; 290m from front.
⚓ Q (3) 10s; marks wreck; 47°43'·49N 03°22'·05W.

NORTHERN PART OF LORIENT HARBOUR
Grand Bassin (FV hbr) E side of ent, ⚓ Fl RG 4s 7m 6M; 000°-G-235°-R-000°; W twr, G top; 47°43'·63N 03°21'·87W.
Ste Catherine marina ent ⚓ QG 5m 3M; 47°43'·52N 03°21'·12W.
N side of marina ent ⚓ QR 2m 2M 47°43'·53N 03°21'·10W.
Pengarne ⚓ Fl G 2·5s 3m 3M; G twr; 47°43'·88N 03°21'·23W.
No 9 ⚓ Fl (2) G 6s; 47°43'·95N 03°21'·16W.
No 11 ⚓ Fl (3) G 12s; 47°44'·04N 03°21'·01W.
Pen-Mané marina, bkwtr elbow ⚓ Fl (2) G 6s 4M; 47°44'·11N 03°20'·86W.
Blavet River, No 1 ⚓ Fl (2+1)G 10s; 47°44'·20N 03°20'·78W.
No 2 ⚓ Fl R 2·5s; 47°44'·26N 03°20'·74W.
Pointe de l'Espérance, Dir ⚓ 037°, Q WRG 8m W10M, R/G8M; 034·2°-G-036·7°-W-037·2°-R-047·2°; W twr, G top; 47°44'·51N 03°20'·66W.

Ro-Ro jetty ⚓ QR 7m 2M; 47°44'·42N 03°20'·96W.
No 8 ⚓ Fl R 2·5s; 47°44'·56N 03°20'·98W, ent to Lorient marina.

RIVIÈRE D'ÉTEL
Roheu ⚓ 47°38'·54N 03°14'·70W.
Épi de Plouhinec ⚓ Fl R 2·5s 7m 2M; 47°38'·59N 03°12'·86W.
W side ent ⚓ Oc (2) WRG 6s 13m W9M, R/G6M; 022°-W-064°-R-123°-W-330°-G-022°; R twr; 47°38'·69N 03°12'·83W.
Conspic R/W radio mast (CROSS Étel) 47°39'·73N 03°12'·11W.
Les Pierres Noires ⚓ 47°35'·53N 03°13'·29W.

BELLE ÎLE AND QUIBERON BAY (W OF 2° 50'W)
PLATEAU DES BIRVIDEAUX (6M NNW of Belle Île)
⚓ Fl (2) 6s 24m 10M; BRB twr; 47°29'·15N 03°17'·46W.

BELLE ÎLE
Pte des Poulains ☆ Fl 5s 34m **23M**; 023°-291°; W ⬜ twr and dwelling; 47°23'·31N 03°15'·11W.
Les Poulains ⚓ 47°23'·44N 03°16'·68W.
N Poulains ⚓ 47°23'·68N 03°14'·88W.
Sauzon, NW jetty ⚓ Fl G 4s 8m 8M; 47°22'·49N 03°13'·04W.
SE jetty ⚓ Fl R 4s 8m 8M; 315°-272°; W twr, R top; 47°22'·45N 03°13'·00W. Inner hbr, W jetty ⚓, QG 9m 5M; 194°-045°; W twr, G top; 47°22'·37N 03°13'·13W.
Le Palais, N jetty ⚓ QG 11m 7M; obsc 298°-170° by Ptes de Kerdonis and Taillefer; W twr, G top; 47°20'·84N 03°09'·04W.
No 1 ⚓ Fl (2) G 6s; 47°20'·82N 03°08'·96W;
No 2 ⚓ Fl R 4s; 47°20'·71N 03°08'·89W;
No 4 ⚓ Fl (2) R 6s; 47°20'·78N 03°09'·01W.
S jetty ⚓ QR 11m 7M; obsc'd 298°-170° (see N jetty); W twr, R lantern; 47°20'·82N 03°09'·07W.
Pointe de Kerdonis ☆ Fl (3) R 15s 49m **15M**; obsc'd 225°-320°
(095°) by vegetation, 004°-155° (151°) by land. W ⬜ twr, R top and W dwelling; 47°18'·60N 03°03'·58W.
Les Galères ⚓ VQ(3)5s; 47°18'·77N 03°02'·76W.
SW coast of Belle Île: La Truie ⚓ 47°17'·11N 03°11'·79W.
Goulphar ☆ Fl (2) 10s 87m **27M**; Gy twr; 47°18'·65N 03°13'·63W.

PORT MARIA (Quiberon ferry port)
Light ho ⚓ Q WRG 28m W14M, R/ G10M; 246°-W-252°-W-297°-G-340°-W-017°-R-051°-W-081°-G-098°-W-143°; W twr, G lantern; 47°28'·78N 03°07'·45W.
Le Pouilloux ⚓ 47°27'·88N 03°08'·01W.
An Tréac'h ⚓ Fl (2)10s; 47°27'·92N 03°07'·20W.
Ldg lts 006·5°, both Dir QG 5/13m **16/17M**; intens 005°-008°; W twrs, B bands: **Front**, 47°28'·63N 03°07'·18W. **Rear**, 230m north.
Les Deux Frères ⚓ Fl R 2·5s; 175°-047°;47°28'·34N 03°07'·29W.
S bkwtr ⚓ Oc (2) R 6s 9m 7M; W twr, R top; 47°28'·54N 03°07'·31W.

CHAUSSÉE and PASSAGE DE LA TEIGNOUSE
Le Four ⚓ 47°27'·78N 03°06'·54W.
Les Trois Pierres ⚓ 47°27'·46N 03°05'·24W.
Roc er Vy ⚓ 47°27'·70N 03°04'·40W; Chenal en Toull Bras.
Roc er Vy ⚓ 47°27'·86N 03°04'·35W.

Basse Cariou ⚓ 47°26'·94N 03°06'·38W.

Basse du Chenal ⚓ 47°26'·66N 03°05'·77W.

Goué Vaz S ⚓ Q (6) + L Fl 15s; 47°25'·76N 03°04'·93W.

La Teignouse ☆ Fl WR 4s 20m **W15M**, R11M; 033°-W-039°-R-033°; W ○ twr, R top; 47°27'·44N 03°02'·75W.

Basse du Milieu ⚓ Fl (2) G 6s 9m 2M; 47°25'·91N 03°04'·12W.

Goué Vaz E ⚓ Fl (3) R 12s; 47°26'·23N 03°04'·28W.

NE Teignouse ⚓ Fl (3) G 12s; 47°26'·55N 03°01'·87W.

Basse Nouvelle ⚓ Fl R 2·5s; 47°26'·98N 03°01'·99W.

CHAUSSÉE and PASSAGE DU BÉNIGUET

Les Esclassiers ⚓ 47°25'·68N 03°03'·05W.

Le Grand Coin ⚓ 47°24'·45N 03°00'·26W.

Bonen Bras ⚓ 47°24'·26N 02°59'·88W.

ÎLE DE HOUAT

Le Rouleau ⚓ 47°23'·67N 03°00'·31W.

Port St-Gildas N môle ⚓ Fl (2) WG 6s 8m W9M, G6M; 168°-W-198°-G-210°-W-240°-G-168°; W twr, G top; 47°23'·57N 02°57'·34W.

Mussel beds, 1 -1.5M NNE of above ⚓ and in its G sector (198°-210°) marked by 2 ⚓ at S end, and ⚓ VQ (3) 5s & ⚓ VQ at N end.

Bcns SE and S of Houat: Men Groise ⚓ 47°22'·77N 02°55'·00W.

Er Spernec Bras ⚓ 47°22'·09N 02°55'·23W.

Men er Houteliguet ⚓ 47°22'·54N 02°56'·38W.

ÎLE DE HOËDIC

Les Sœurs ⚓ 47°21'·14N 02°54'·74W.

La Chèvre ⚓ 47°21'·08N 02°52'·55W.

Port de l'Argol bkwtr ⚓ Fl WG 4s 10m W9M, G6M; 143°-W-163°-G-183°-W-194°-G-143°; W twr, G top; 47°20'·66N 02°52'·48W.

Er Gurranic'h ⚓ 47°20'·51N 02°50'·44W.

Cohfournik ⚓ 47°19'·49N 02°49'·69W.

Grands Cardinaux ⚓ Fl (4) 15s 28m 13M; R and W twr; 47°19'·27N 02°50'·10W. 2·1M SE of Argol.

Le Chariot ⚓ 47°18'·76N 02°52'·95W.

Er Palaire ⚓ 47°20'·16N 02°55'·01W.

PORT HALIGUEN

Banc de Quiberon S ⚓ Q (6) + L Fl 15s; 47°28'·04N 03°02'·34W.

Banc de Quiberon N ⚓ 47°29'·65N 03°02'·58W.

E bkwtr hd ⚓ Fl (2) WR 6s 10m, W10M, R7M; 233°-W-240·5°-R-299°-W-306°-R-233°; W twr, R top; 47°29'·36N 03°05'·94W.

Port Haliguen ⚓ 47°29'·38N 03°05'·55W; marks 1·7m patch.

NW bkwtr hd ⚓ Fl (2) G 6s 10m 6M; 47°29'·34N 03°06'·02W.

Bugalet wreck ⚓ 47°31'·19N 03°05'·45W.

Men er Roué ⚓ 47°32'·25N 03°06'·06W.

LA TRINITÉ-SUR-MER

Rivière de Crac'h ⚓ Q WRG 11m W10M, R/G7M; 321°-G-345°-W-013·5°-R-080°; W twr, G top; 47°34'·09N 03°00'·37W.

Buissons de Méaban ⚓ 47°31'·66N 02°58'·49W.

Le Petit Buisson ⚓ 47°32'·14N 02°58'·57W.

Roche Révision ⚓ 47°32'·63N 02°59'·36W.

Petit Trého ⚓ Fl R 2·5s; 47°33'·47N 03°00'·71W.

R. de Crac'h Dir ⚓ 347°: Oc WRG 4s 9m W13M, R/G 11M; 345°-G-346°-W-348°-R-349°; W twr; 47°35'·03N 03°00'·98W.

S pier ⚓ Q WR 6s 6m, W9M, R6M; 090°-R-293·5°-W-300·5°-R-329°; W twr, R top; 47°35'·09N 03°01'·50W.

Marina wavebreak/pier ⚓ Iso R 4s 8m 5M; 47°35'·28N 03°01'·46W.

GOLFE DU MORBIHAN

Méaban ⚓ 47°30'·77N 02°56'·23W.

Outer ldg marks 001°: Front, Petit Vezid ⚓ ; W obelisk; 47°34'·17N 02°55'·23W. Rear, Baden ch spire (83m) 47°37'·20N 02°55'·14W.

Pointe de Port-Navalo ☆ Oc (3) WRG 12s 32m, **W15M**, R/G11M; 155°-W-220°; 317°-G-359°-W-015°-R-105°; W twr and dwelling; 47°32'·87N 02°55'·11W.

Ldg marks 359°: Front, Grégan ⚓ Q (6) + L Fl 15s 3m 8M; 47°33'·91N 02°55'·05W. Rear, Baden ch spire (5 lines above).

Auray river: Catis ⚓ 47°36'·14N 02°57'·23W.

César ⚓ 47°38'·36N 02°58'·22W.

No 13 ⚓ 47°39'·48N 02°58'·64W (last bcn before 14m bridge).

Morbihan: Grand Mouton ⚓ QG; 47°33'·71N 02°54'·85W.

Gavrinis ⚓ 47°34'·21N 02°54'·05W.

Jument ⚓ 47°34'·29N 02°53'·43W.

Creizic S ⚓ 47°34'·63N 02°52'·84W.

Creizic N ⚓ 47°34'·93N 02°52'·20W.

Les Rechauds, two ⚓ 47°36'·18N 02°51'·30W.

Truie d'Arradon ⚓ 47°36'·58N 02°50'·27W.

Logoden ⚓ 47°36'·70N 02°49'·91W.

Drenec ⚓ 47°36'·84N 02°48'·39W.

Bœdic ⚓ 47°36'·85N 02°47'·59W.

Roguédas ⚓ Fl G 2·5s 4m 4M; G twr; 47°37'·12N 02°47'·28W.

CROUESTY

Ldg lts 058°, both Dir Q 10/27m 8M; intens 056·5°-059·5°: Front ⚓ R panel, W stripe; 47°32'·53N 02°53'·95W. Rear ⚓, W twr; 315m from front.

No 1 ⚓ QG; 47°32'·26N 02°54'·76W.

No 2 ⚓ 47°32'·26N 02°54'·76W.

N jetty ⚓ Fl R 4s 9m 7M; R&W □ twr; 47°32'·47N 02°54'·14W.

S jetty ⚓ Fl G 4s 9m 7M; G&W □ twr; 47°32'·45N 02°54'·10W.

PLATEAU DU GRAND MONT

Chimère ⚓ 47°28'·83N 02°53'·98W.

L'Epieu ⚓ 47°29'·51N 02°52'·91W.

St Gildas ⚓ 47°29'·78N 02°52'·87W.

Grand Mont ⚓ 47°28'·98N 02°51'·12W.

QUIBERON BAY (E OF 2° 50'W) TO PTE DU CROISIC

PLATEAU DE SAINT JACQUES

Le Bauzec ⚓ 47°28'·90N 02°49'·40W.

St Jacques ⚓ 47°28'·17N 02°47'·52W.

Port St Jacques, jetty ⚓ Oc (2) R 6s 5m 6M; W 8-sided twr, R top; 47°29'·24N 02°47'·41W.

PLATEAU DE LA RECHERCHE

Recherche ⚓ Q (9) 15s; 47°25'·56N 02°50'·39W.

Locmariaquer ⚓ 47°25'·82N 02°47'·36W.

PÉNERF

Outer Rade ⚓ Fl (5) Y 20s; 47°27'·58N 02°39'·56W.

Penvins ⚑ 47°28'·93N 02°40'·09W.

Borenis ⚑ 47°29'·21N 02°38'·35W.

Tour des Anglais ⚏ W bcn; 47°30'·21N 02°37'·94W; appr brg 031·4°.

Pignon ⚐ Fl (3) WR 12s 6m W9M, R6M; 028·5°-R-167°-W-175°-R-349·5°-W-028·5°; R twr; 47°30'·03N 02°38'·89W.

VILAINE RIVER

Pte de Penlan ☆ Oc (2) WRG 6s 26m, **W15M**, R/G11M; 292·5°-R-025°-G-052°-W-060°-R-138°-G-180°; W sector defines Passe de la Grande Accroche; W twr, R bands; 47°30'·97N 02°30'·11W.

Bertrand ⚑ Iso WG 4s 6m, W9M, G6M; 040°-W-054°-G-227°-W-234°-G-040°; G twr; 47°31'·06N 02°30'·72W.

Basse de Kervoyal ⚐ Dir Q WR W8M, R5M; 269°-W-271°-R-269°; W sector leads to/from Nos 1 & 2 buoys; 47°30'·37N 02°32'·62W.

No 1 ⚑ Fl G 2·5s; 47°30'·32N 02°28'·73W.

No 2 ⚐ Fl R 2·5s; 47°30'·41N 02°28'·71W.

Pointe du Scal ⚐ QG 8m 4M; 47°29'·67N 02°26'·87W.

ÎLE DUMET

Fort ⚐ Fl (3) WRG 15s 14m, W7M, R/G4M; 090°-G-272°-W-285°-R-335°-W-090°; W sector, G top; 47°24'·69N 02°37'·21W.

Basse-Est Île Dumet ⚑ Q (3) 10s; 47°25'·20N 02°34'·93W.

Île Dumet ⚑ Q; 47°25'·90N 02°36'·05W.

MESQUER

Laronesse ⚑ 47°25'·96N 02°29'·50W.

Basse Normande ⚑ 47°25'·47N 02°29'·80W.

Jetty ⚐ Oc WRG 4s 7m W10M, R/G7M; 067°-W-072°-R-102°-W-118°-R-293°-W-325°-G-067°; W col & bldg; 47°25'·31N 02°28'·05W.

PIRIAC-SUR-MER

Grand Norven ⚑ Q; 47°23'·55N 02°32'·89W.

Inner mole ⚐ Oc (2) WRG 6s 8m, W10M, R/G7M; 066°-R-148°-G-194°-W-201°-R-221°; W col; 47°22'·93N 02°32'·71W. *Siren 120s (occas), 35m SW.* E bkwtr ⚐ Fl R 4s 4m 5M; W pylon, R top; 47°23'·00N 02°32'·67W.

Les Bayonnelles ⚑ Q (9) 15s; 47°22'·56N 02°35'·23W.

LA TURBALLE

Ldg Its 006·5°, both Dir Iso R 4s 11/19m 3M; intens 004°-009°: Front, 47°20'·70N 02°30'·87W. Rear, 275m N of the front lt.

Ouest Jetée de Garlahy ⚐ Fl (4) WR 12s 13m, W10M, R7M; 060°-R-315°-W-060°; W pylon, R top; 47°20'·70N 02°30'·93W.

Digue Tourlandroux ⚐ Fl G 4s 4m 2M; G post, E side of access chan; 47°20'·75N 02°30'·88W.

LE CROISIC

Basse Hergo ⚑ Fl G 2·5s 5m 3M; 47°18'·62N 02°31'·69W.

Jetée du Tréhic ⚐ Iso WG 4s 12m W14M, G11M; 042°-G-093°-W-137°-G-345°; Gy twr, G top; 47°18'·49N 02°31'·42W. F Bu fog det lt, 100m SE.

Outer ldg lts 155·5°, both Dir Q 10/14m 13M; intens 154°-158°: Front ☆ 47°17'·96N 02°30'·99W . Rear ☆, 116m from front.

Middle ldg lts 174°, both QG 5/8m 11M; 170·5°-177·5°: Front 47°18'·06N 02°31'·07W. Rear, 48m from front.

Le Grand Mabon ⚐ Fl (3) R 12s 6m 2M; 47°18'·05N 02°31'·03W.

Inner ldg lts 134·7°, both QR 6/10m 8M; intens 132·5°-143·5°; synch.

Basse Castouillet ⚑ Q (9) 15s; 47°18'·12N 02°34'·37W.

Basse Lovre ⚑ 47°15'·87N 02°29'·58W, Chenal du Nord.

PLATEAU DU FOUR/BANC DE GUÉRANDE

Bonen du Four ⚑ Q; 47°18'·53N 02°39'·29W.

Le Four ☆ Fl 5s 23m **18M**; W twr, B diagonal stripes; 47°17'·87N 02°38'·05W. 992271016.

Ouest Basse Capella ⚑ Q (9) 15s; *Whis;* 47°15'·66N 02°42'·78W.

Goué-Vas-du-Four ⚑ Q (6) + L Fl 15s; 47°14'·91N 02°38'·20W.

Sud Banc Guérande ⚑ VQ (6) + L Fl 10s; 47°08'·80N 02°42'·81W.

Le Croisic ⬥, Mo(U)15s R Lt 14m 5M, and Wavegem electricity generator) Oc(3)Y 10s, (both floating), 2x SPM Fl (5) Y 20s 4x SPM Fl Y 4s centred on 47°14'·37N 02°46'·61W. 992271051.

PLATEAU DE LA BANCHE

NW Banche ⚑ Q 8m 4M; 47°12'·86N 02°31'·02W.

W Banche ⚑ VQ (9) 10s; 47°11'·64N 02°32'·41W.

La Banche ☆ Fl (2) WR 6s 22m **W15M**, R11M; 266°-R-280°-W-266°; B twr, W bands; 47°10'·62N 02°28'·08W. 992271020.

SE Banche ⚑ 47°10'·40N 02°26'·10W.

PLATEAU DE LA LAMBARDE

NW Lambarde ⚑ 47°10'·84N 02°22'·93W.

SE Lambarde ⚑ Q (6) + L Fl 15s; 47°10'·04N 02°20·80W.

BAIE DU POULIGUEN (or Baie de la Baule)

Penchateau ⚑ Fl R 2·5s; 47°15'·24N 02°24'·35W.

Les Guérandaises ⚑ Fl G 2·5s; 47°15'·03N 02°24'·29W.

⚑ 47°15'·24N 02°23'·50W.

Les Evens ⚑ 47°14'·32N 02°22'·55W.

Les Troves ⚑ 47°14'·23N 02°22'·41W.

NNW Pierre Percée ⚑ 47°13'·63N 02°20'·63W.

La Vieille ⚑ 47°14'·03N 02°19'·51W.

Sud de la Vieille ⚑ 47°13'·75N 02°19'·54W.

Le Caillou ⚑ 47°13'·65N 02°19'·18W.

Le Petit Charpentier ⚑ 47°13'·34N 02°18'·95W.

Le Grand Charpentier ⚐ Q WRG 22m, W14M, R/G10M; 020°-G-054°-W-062°-R-092°-W-111°-R-310°-W-020°; Gy lt ho, G lantern; 47°12'·83N 02°19'·13W. 992271026.

LE POULIGUEN

Basse Martineau ⚏ 47°15'·54N 02°24'·34W.

La Vieille ⚑, Fl (2) G 6s 2M, 47°15'· 83N 02°24'·43W.

Petits Impairs ⚑ Fl (3) G 12s 6m 2M; 47°15'·99N 02°24'·61W.

SW jetty ⚐ QR 13m 9M; 171°-081°; W col; 47°16'·39N 02°25'·39W.

PORNICHET (La Baule)

S bkwtr ⚐ Iso WRG 4s 11m, W10M, R/G7M; 303°-G-081°-W-084°-R-180°; W twr, G top; 47°15'·49N 02°21'·14W.

Ent,W side ⚐ QG 3m 1M; B perch, G top; 47°15'·51N 02°21'·10W.

E side ⚐ QR 4m 1M; B perch, R top; 47°15'·50N 02°21'·10W.

ST NAZAIRE APPROACH (Chenal du Sud)

S-N1 ⚑ L Fl 10s 8m 5M; *Racon Z (3cm), 3–8M;* 47°00'·07N 02°39'·84W.

S-N2 ⚑ Iso 4s 8m 5M; 47°02'·08N 02°33'·47W.

Les Chevaux ⚑ Fl G 2·5s; 47°03'·53N 02°26'·37W.

Thérèsia ⚓ Fl R 2·5s; 47°04'·84N 02°27'·27W.

La Couronnée ⚓ Fl (2) G 6s; *Racon T, 3–5M*; 47°07'·60N 02°20'·05W. 992271001.

Lancastria ⚓ Fl (2) R 6s;47°08'·88N 02°20'·37W.

PASSE DES CHARPENTIERS

Portcé ☆ ldg lts 025·5°, both Dir Q 6/36m **22/24M**: **Front**, intens 024·7°-026·2°; synch; W col; 47°14'·57N 02°15'·44W. 992271021. **Rear** ☆ (H24); intens 024°-027°; W twr; 0·75M from front.

Wreck (Y) ⚓ Fl (3) R 12s; 47°09'·87N 02°19'·46W.

No 1 ⚓ VQ G; 47°09'·94N 02°18'·40W.

No 2 ⚓ VQ R; 47°10'·06N 02°18'·72W.

No 6 ⚓ Fl (3) R 12s; 47°12'·05N 02°17'·31W.

No 5 ⚓ Fl (4) G 15s; 47°12'·65N 02°16'·57W.

No 8 ⚓ Fl (4) R 15s; 47°12'·75N 02°16'·86W.

No 7 ⚓ VQ G; 47°13'·30N 02°16'·11W.

No 10 ⚓ VQ R; 47°13'·62N 02°16'·16W. (Buoys 9–18 not listed).

Pointe d'Aiguillon ☆ Oc (3) WR 12s 27m, W13M, R10M; 207°-R-233°-W-293°; 297°-W-300°-R-327°-W-023°; 027°-R-089°; W lt ho, conspic; 47°14'·54N 02°15'·79W.

Ville-ès-Martin jetty ⚡ Fl (2) 6s 10m 10M; W twr, R top; 47°15'·33N 02°13'·66W.

Morées ⚓ Fl (3) WR 12s 12m, W6M, R4M; W058°-224°, R300°-058°; G twr; 47°15'·00N 02°13'·02W.

SAINT NAZAIRE

W jetty ⚡ Oc (4) R 12s 11m 8M; W twr, R top; 47°15'·97N 02°12'·25W.

E jetty ⚡ Oc (4) G 12s 11m 11M; W twr, G top; 47°15'·99N 02°12'·14W. (Ent lock for big ships into Bassin St Nazaire)

No 20 ⚓ QR; 47°16'·19N 02°11'·37W.

Sud Basse Nazaire ⚓ Q (6) + L Fl 15s; 47°16'·21N 02°11'·51W.

Basse Nazaire ⚓ Fl G 2·5s; 47°16'·24N 02°11'·63W.

Old Môle ⚡ Q (3) 10s 18m 11M; 153·5°-063·5°; W twr, R top; weather signals; 47°16'·27N 02°11'·82W.

⚓ Fl (2) R 6s 5m 1M; R dolphin ; 47°16'·37N 02°11'·80W.

Entrée Est ⚡ Fl (3) R 9s 9M; R pylon; 47°16'·47N 02°11'·85W.

Ldg lts 280° (into E lock) 2 VQ Vi; front 47°16'·49N 02°11'·92W.

EAST SIDE OF RIVER, SOUTH TO PTE DE ST GILDAS

Le Pointeau, Digue S ⚡ Fl WG 4s 4m, W10M, G7M; 050°-G-074°-W-149°-G-345°-W-050°; G&W ○ hut; 47°14'·02N 02°10'·96W.

Port de Comberge La Truie ⚓ 47°12'·06N 00°13'·36W.

S jetty ⚡ Oc WG 4s 7m W9M, G6M; 123°-W-140°-G-123°; W twr, G top; 47°10'·70N 02°09'·90W.

La Gravette ⚓ 47°09'·81N 02°13'·06W.

La Gravette bkwtr ⚡ Fl (3) WG 12s 7m, W8M, G5M; 183°-W-188°-G-124°-W-138°-G-183°; W/G top; 47°09'·64N 02°12'·70W.

Anse du Boucau bkwtr ⚡ Fl (2) G 6s 3M; 47°08'·41N 02°14'·80W.

Pte de Saint Gildas ⚡ Q WRG 20m, W14M, R/G10M; 264°-R-308°-G-078°-W-088°-R-174°-W-180°-G-264°; W house, G top; 47°08'·02N 02°14'·74W. 992271017.

RIVER LOIRE TO NANTES

Buoyed/lit to Île de Bois, then G lts, S side; R lts N side.

No 21 ⚓ VQ G; 47°16'·96N 02°10'·25W.

Suspension bridge, ⚡ Iso 4s 55m, 47°17'·10N 02°10'·24W.

MA ⚓ Fl (2) G 6s; 47°17'·50N 02°09'·22W.

MB ⚓ Fl (3) G 12s; 47°17'·95N 02°07'·53W.

Fernais-25 ⚓ Fl (4) G 15s; 47°18'·10N 02°06'·60W.

Paimbœuf, môle root ⚡ Oc (3) WG 12s 9m, W10M, G7M; Shore-G-123°-W-shore; W twr, G top; 47°17'·42N 02°01'·95W.

Île de Bois (upstream) Fl (2) G 6s; 47°12'·79N 01°48'·27W.

Ldg lts 064° Rear Dir VQ R; 47°12'·00N 01°34'·35W, Y-junction with Bras de la Madeleine.

POINTE DE SAINT GILDAS TO FROMENTINE

Pte de Saint Gildas ⚡ Q WRG 20m, W14M, R/G10M; 264°-R-308°-G-078°-W-088°-R-174°-W-180°-G-264°; 47°08'·02N 02°14'·75W. 992271017.

Nord Couronnée ⚓ Q; 47°07'·34N 02°17'·78W.

Notre Dame ⚓ VQ (9) 10s 7m 3M; 47°05'·42N 02°08'·26W.

PORNIC

Approaches ⚓ Fl G 4s; 47°06'·39N 02°06'·60W; ⚓ Fl R 4s; 47°06'·40N 02°06'·64W

Marina ent, S side ⚡ Fl (2) R 6s 4m 2M; 47°06'·47N 02°06'·67W.

Pte de Noëveillard ⚡ Oc (4) WRG 12s 22m W13M, R/G10M; Shore-G-051°-W-079°-R-shore; W □ twr, G top, W house; 47°06'·62N 02°06'·92W.

ÎLE DE NOIRMOUTIER anti-clockwise from the East

Pte des Dames ☆ Oc (3) WRG 12s 34m, **W19M, R/G15M**; 016·5°-G-057°-R-124°-G-165°-W-191°-R191°-267°-W-357°-R-016·5°; W □ twr; 47°00'·67N 02°13'·26W. La Chaise ⚓ 47°01'·21N 02°12'·64W.

L'Herbaudière, ldg lts 187·5°, both Q 5/21m 7M, Gy masts. Front, 47°01'·59N 02°17'·84W. Rear, 310m from front.

Martroger ⚓, Q WRG 11m W9M, R/G6M; 033°-G-055°-W-060°-R-095°-G-124°-W-153°-R-201°-W-240°-R-033°; 47°02'·61N 02°17'·11W.

W jetty ⚡ Oc (2+1) WG 12s 9m W10M, G7M; 187·5°-W-190°-G-187·5°; W col and hut, G top; 47°01'·63N 02°17'·84W.

E jetty ⚡ Fl (2) R 6s 8m 4M; 47°01'·61N 02°17'·81W.

Île du Pilier ☆ Fl (3) 20s 33m **29M**; Gy twr; 47°02'·55N 02°21'·60W. Same twr, aux ⚡ QR 10m 11M, 321°-034°.

Passe de la Grise ⚓ Q (6) + L Fl 15s; 47°01'·66N 02°19'·97W.

Les Bœufs ⚓ VQ (9) 10s; 46°55'·04N 02°27'·99W.

Réaumur ⚓ Q (9) 15s; 46°57'·46N 02°24'·22W.

Le Bavard ⚓ VQ (6) + L Fl 10s; 46°56'·79N 02°23'·34W.

Pte du Devin (Morin) ⚡ Oc (4) WRG 12s 10m W11M, R/G8M; 314°-G-028°-W-035°-R-134°; W col & hut, G top; 46°59'·15N 02°17'·60W.

GOULET DE FROMENTINE

Fromentine ⚓ L Fl 10s 3m 6M; 46°53'·38N 02°11'·90W.

Milieu ⚓ Fl (2) R 6s 6m 2M; 46°53'·59N 02°09'·63W.

Pte de Notre Dame-de-Monts ⚡ Dir Oc (2) WRG 6s 21m, W13M, R/G10M; 000°-G-043°-W-063°-R-073°-W-094°-G-113°-W-116°-R-175°-G-196°-R-230°; W twr, B top; 46°53'·33N 02°08'·54W.

ÎLE D'YEU TO BOURGENAY

ÎLE D'YEU

Petite Foule (main lt) ☆ Fl 5s 56m **24M**; W ☐ twr, G lantern; 46°43'·04N 02°22'·91W. 992271031.
Les Chiens Perrins ⚓ Q (9) WG 15s 16m W7M, G4M; 330°-G-350°-W-200°; 46°43'·60N 02°24'·58W.
Pont d'Yeu ⚓ 46°45'·81N 02°13'·81W.
La Sablaire ⚓ Q (6) + L Fl 15s; 46°43'·62N 02°19'·49W.
Port Joinville ldg lts 219°, both QR 11/16m 6M, 169°-269°: Front, Quai du Canada 46°43'·61N 02°20'·94W. Rear, 85m from front.
NW jetty ⚡ Oc (3) WG 12s 7m, W11M, G8M; Shore-G-150°-W-232°-G-279°-W-285°-G-shore; W 8-sided twr, G top; 46°43'·77N 02°20'·82W. La Galiote ⚓ 46°43'·73N 02°20'·71W.
Pte des Corbeaux ☆ Fl (2+1) R 15s 25m **20M**; 083°-143° obsc by Île de Yeu; W ☐ twr, R top; 46°41'·41N 02°17'·08W.
Port de la Meule ⚡ Oc WRG 4s 9m, W9M, R/G6M; 007·5°-G-018°-W-027·5°-R-041·5°; Gy twr, R top; 46°41'·62N 02°20'·72W.

SAINT GILLES-CROIX-DE-VIE

Pte de Grosse Terre ☆ Fl (4) WR 12s 25m, **W18M, R15M**; 290°- R-339°-W-125°-R-145°; W truncated twr; 46°41'·54N 01°57'·92W.
Ldg lts 043·7°, both Q 7/28m **15M**; 033·5°-053·5°; synch; W ☐ twrs, R tops: Front, 46°41'·86N 01°56'·75W. Rear, 260m NE.
Pilours ⚓ Q (6) + L Fl 15s; 46°40'·99N 01°58'·09W.
Jetée de la Garenne ⚡ Fl G 4s 8m 6M; 46°41'·46N 01°57'·25W.
Jetée de Boisvinet ⚡ Fl R 4s 8m 6M; 46°41'·62N 01°57'·16W.

LES SABLES D'OLONNE

Les Barges ⚡ Fl (2) R 10s 25m 13M; Gy twr; 46°29'·70N 01°50'·50W.
Petite Barge ⚓ Q (6) + L Fl 15s 3M; 46°28'·90N 01°50'·61W.
L'Armandèche ☆ Fl (2+1) 15s 42m **24M**; 295°-130°; W 6-sided twr, R top; 46°29'·39N 01°48'·29W.
Nouch Sud ⚓ Q (6) + L Fl 15s; 46°28'·55N 01°47'·41W.
Nouch Nord ⚓ 46°28'·88N 01°47'·36W.
SW Pass, ldg lts 032·5°, Iso 4s 12/33m **16M, Front** ☆, 46°29'·42N 01°46'·37W. 992271024. **Rear** ☆, **La Potence**, W ☐ twr.
SE Pass, ldg lts 320°: Front, E jetty ⚡ QG 11m 8M; W twr, G top; 46°29'·44N 01°47'·51W. 992271032. Rear, Tour d'Arundel ⚡ Q 33m 13M, synch; large Gy ☐ twr; 46°29'·63N 01°47'·74W.
Jetée St Nicolas (W jetty) ⚡ QR 1·2s 16m 8M; 143°-094°; W twr, R top; 46°29'·23N 01°47'·52W.

BOURGENAY

Ldg lts 040°, both QG 9/19m 7M. Front, 020°-060°; on S bkwtr; 46°26'·34N 01°40'·62W. Rear, 010°-070°; 162m from front.
Landfall ⚓ L Fl 10s; 46°25'·26N 01°41'·93W.
Ent ⚡ Fl R 4s 8m 9M & ⚡ Iso G 4s 6m 5M; 46°26'·29N 01°40'·75W.

PLATEAU DE ROCHEBONNE (Shoal 32M offshore)

NW ⚓ Q (9) 15s; *Whis;* 46°12'·92N 02°31'·58W.
NE ⚓ Iso G 4s; 46°12'·73N 02°24'·83W.
SE ⚓ Q (3) 10s; *Bell;* 46°09'·20N 02°21'·13W.
SW ⚓ Fl (2) R 6s; 46°10'·11N 02°27'·04W.

PERTUIS BRETON

JARD-SUR-MER and LA TRANCHE-SUR-MER

Ldg marks 036°, two unlit W bcns; 46°24'·47N 01°34'·16W.
Pte du Grouin du Cou ☆ Fl WRG 5s 29m, **W20M, R/G16M**; 034°-R-061°-W-117°-G-138°-W-034°; W 8-sided twr, B top; 46°20'·67N 01°27'·83W.
La Tranche pier ⚡ Fl (2) R 6s 6m 6M; R col; 46°20'·55N 01°25'·63W.
Mussel farm, No entry, marked by: ⚓ Q, 46°17'·17N 01°22'·19W.
⚓ Q (3) 10s, 46°15'·73N 01°18'·42W. ⚓ Q (6) + L Fl 15s, 46°15'·16N 01°19'·98W. ⚓ Q (9) 15s, 46°16'·28N 01°22'·88W.

L'AIGUILLON and LA FAUTE-SUR-MER

Le Lay ⚓ Q (6) + L Fl 15s; 46°16'·10N 01°16'·53W.
No 1 ⚓ 46°16'·65N 01°16'·25W. Many mussel beds.

ANSE DE L'AIGUILLON (for La Sèvre Niortaise & Marans)

ATT de L'Aiguillon ⚓ L Fl 10s; 46°15'·33N 01°11'·50W.
Inner fairway ⚓ 46°17'·19N 01°09'·65W.
Port du Pavé ⚡ Fl G 4s 9m 7M; W col, G top; 01°08'·01W.

ÎLE DE RÉ

Les Baleineaux ⚡ VQ 23m 7M; pink twr, R top; 46°15'·81N 01°35'·22W.
Les Baleines ☆ Fl (4) 15s 53m **27M**; conspic Gy 8-sided twr, R lantern; 46°14'·64N 01°33'·69W.

ARS-EN-RÉ

Dir ⚡ 268° Oc WRG 4s, W10M, R/G 7M, 275·5°-G-267·5°-W-268·5°-R-274·5°; W hut with W ☐ topmark; 46°14'·05N 01°28'·60W.
Les Islattes ⚓ Q 13m 3M; NCM bcn twr 46°14'·03N 01°23'·32W.
Bûcheron No 1 ⚓ Fl G 2·5s; 46°14'·21N 01°25'·98W.
Bûcheron No 3 ⚓ Fl (2) G 6s; 46°14'·14N 01°26'·94W.
Le Fier d'Ars, inner ldg lts 232·5°, both Q 5/13m 9/11M: Front ⚡ R/W frame on W col; 46°12'·75N 01°30'·59W. Rear ⚡ 142°-322°; B vert rectangle on W mast, 370m from front.

ST MARTIN DE RÉ

Lt ho, E of ent ⚡ Oc (2) WR 6s 18m W10M, R7M; Shore-W-245°-R-281°-W-shore; W twr, R top; 46°12'·44N 01°21'·89W.
W mole ⚡ Fl G 2·5s 10m 5M; obsc'd by Pte du Grouin when brg <124°; W post, G top; 46°12'·49N 01°21'·91W.

LA FLOTTE

N bkwtr ⚡ Fl WG 4s 10m W12M, G9M; 130°-G-205°-W-220°-G-257°; W ○ twr, G top; 46°11'·33N 01°19'·30W.
Dir lt 212·5°, Moiré effect, is next to the main lt twr.
ÎLE DE RÉ (South coast, from the W, inc bridge)

Chanchardon ⚓ Fl WR 4s 15m W11M, R8M; 118°-R-290°-W-118°; B 8-sided twr, W base; 46°09'·71N 01°28'·41W.

Chauveau ☆ Oc (3) WR 12s 27m **W15M**, R11M; 057°-W-094°-R-104°-W-342°-R-057°; W ○ twr, R top; 46°08'·03N 01°16'·42W.

Bridge span (30m cl'nce) for SE-bound vessels, ⚓ Iso 4s 34m 8M; 46°10'·18N 01°14'·75W . Span (30m cl'nce) for NW-bound vessels, ⚓ Iso 4s 34m 8M; 46°10'·26N 01°14'·52W.

La Pallice, W mole, ⚓ Fl G 4s 5m 6M; 46°09'·78N 01°14'·45W.　　　　S end, ⚓ Q (6) + L Fl 15s 6m 9M; 46°09'·36N 01°14'·52W.

LA ROCHELLE AND LA CHARENTE TO ROCHEFORT

LA ROCHELLE

Chauveau ⚓ VQ (6) + L Fl 10s; 46°06'·56N 01°16'·06W. Roche du Sud ⚓ Q (9) 15s; 46°06'·37N 01°15'·22W.

La Rochelle ldg lts 059°, both Dir Q 15/25m 13/14M; synch; by day Fl 4s. Front; intens 056°-062°; R ○ twr, W bands; 46°09'·35N 01°09'·16W. Rear, 044°-074°, obsc'd 061°-065°; W 8-sided twr, G top, 235m from front.

Lavardin ⚓ Fl (2) 6s 14m 7M; BRB IDM twr; 46°08'·09N 01°14'·52W.

Les Minimes ⚓ Q (9) 15s; 46°08'·01N 01°11'·60W.

Pte des Minimes ⚓ Fl (3) WG 12s 8m; W8M, G5M; 059°-W-213°; 313°-G-059°; 8-sided twr on piles; 46°08'·27N 01°10'·76W.

Chan buoy ⚓ QG; 46°08'·53N 01°10'·87W; marking hbr limit.

Tour Richelieu ⚓ Fl (2)R 6s 0m 6M; R twr; 46°08'·90N 01°10'·34W.

Port des Minimes, W bkwtr ⚓ Fl G 2·5s; W twr, G top; 46°08'·88N 01°10'·18W.

E bkwtr ⚓ VQ(9) 10s 3M; ⚓Y/B band, 46°08'·92N 01°10'·09W.

LA CHARENTE

Fort Boyard twr ⚓ Q (9) 15s; 45°59'·97N 01°12'·86W.

Ldg lts 115°, both Dir QR 8/21m **19/20M**; intens 113°-117°; W ☐ twr, R top: **Front** ☆, 45°57'·96N 01°04'·38W. **Rear, Soumard** ☆, 600m from front. Same twr: ⚓ QR 21m 8M; vis 322°-067°.

Île d'Aix ☆ Fl WR 5s 24m **W24M, R20M**; 103°-R-118°-W-103°; two conspic W ○ twrs, R top; 46°00'·60N 01°10'·67W.

Pte Ste Catherine, jetty hd ⚓ Q (6) + L Fl 15s 5m 4M; 45°59'·05N 01°07'·85W. Les Palles ⚓ Q; 45°59'·54N 01°09'·56W.

Fouras, Port Sud bkwtr ⚓ Fl WR 4s 6m 9/6M; 115°-R-177°-W-115°; 45°58'·97N 01°05'·72W.

ROCHEFORT

Night passage by yachts is not advised.

⚓ Fl (2) G 6s; bcn 45°55'·21N 00°56'·98W, 1·4M S of Rochefort.

ÎLE D'OLÉRON

Pte de Chassiron ☆ Fl 10s 50m, **28M**; conspic W twr, B bands; 46°02'·80N 01°24'·62W, NW tip of island.

Antioche ⚓ Q 20m 11M; 46°03'·94N 01°23'·71W.

ST DENIS

Dir ⚓ 205°, Iso WRG 4s 14m, W11M, R/G8M; 190°-G-204°-W-206°-R-220°; 46°01'·61N 01°21'·92W.

E jetty ⚓ Fl (2) WG 6s 6m, W9M, G6M; 205°-G-277°-W-292°-G-165°; ☐ hut; 46°02'·10N 01°22'·06W.

PORT DU DOUHET and PASSAGE DE L'OUEST

Seaweed farm ⚓ VQ; 46°00'·65N 01°17'·38W.

N ent ⚓ 46°00'·10N 01°19'·20W.

Fish farm ⚓ Q; 46°00'·24N 01°15'·34W. ⚓ Q (3) 10s; 45°59'·84N 01°14'·79W.

BOYARDVILLE

Mole ⚓ Fl (2) R 6s 8m 5M; obsc'd by Pte des Saumonards when brg <150°; W twr, R top; 45°58'·24N 01°13'·83W.

COUREAU D'OLÉRON and LE CHÂTEAU D'OLÉRON

Juliar ⚓ Q (3) WG 10s 12m, W11M; G8M; 147°-W-336°-G-147°; 45°54'·11N 01°09'·48W.

Chateau d'Oléron, ldg lts 318·5°, both QR 11/24m 7M; synch. Front, 191°-087°; R line on W twr; 45°53'·03N 01°11'·45W. Rear, W twr, R top; 240m from front.

St Trojan-les-Bains bridge (limits of nav width, 18m clearance) Fl G 4s 4M, 45°51'·42N 01°11'·20W; Fl R 4s 4M, 45°51'·40N 01°11'·7W.

LA SEUDRE RIVER

Pte du Mus de Loup ⚓ Oc G 4s 8m 6M; 118°-147°; 45°47'·70N 01°08'·60W.

Pertuis de Maumusson. Depths & buoys subject to change.

ATT Maumusson ⚓ L Fl 10s; 45°44'·47N 01°17'·80W. La Barre ⚓ 45°46'·59N 01°16'·25W. Tabouret ⚓ 45°46'·93N 01°16'·15W. Mattes ⚓ 45°46'·93N 01°15'·29W. Gatseau ⚓ 45°47'·36N 01°14'·70W.

LA COTINIÈRE (SW side of island)

Ent ldg lts 339°, both ⚓ Dir Oc (2) 6s 6/14m 13/12M; synch: Front, 329°-349°; W twr, R top; 45°54'·72N 01°19'·79W. Rear, intens 329°-349°; W twr, R bands; 425m from front on W bkwtr.

W bkwtr head ⚓ Fl R 4s 10m 6M, 45°54'·58N 01°19'·66W.

GIRONDE APPROACHES AND TO BORDEAUX

GRANDE PASSE DE L'OUEST

Pte de la Coubre ☆ Fl (2) 10s 64m **28M**; W twr, R top; 45°41'·78N 01°13'·99W. Same twr, Q R 42m10M; 030°-R-110°.

BXA ⚓ Iso 4s 8m 7M; *Racon B*; 45°34'·10N 01°26'·63W. 992271005.

La Palmyre Wtr Twr Dir ☆ 056·7°, WRG 54m **W25M R/G20M**; 055·25°-FG-055·95°-AlWG-056·58°-FW-057·42°-AlWR-058·02-FR-058·72°; Gy Wtr Twr; 45°41'·65N 01°10'·18W.

Duc d'Albe ⚓ Fl(2) 6s 10m 2M; W pylon on dolphin; 45°39'·56N 01°08'·77W.

No 1 ⚓ QG; 45°36'·17N 01°21'·70W; 992271036.

No 6 ⚓ VQ (6) + L Fl 10s; 45°38'·27N 01°17'·91W.

No 7a ⚓ Fl G 4s; 45°38'·96N 01°14'·85W.

No 9 ⚓ Q; 45°39'·43N 01°12'·79W.

No 11 ⚓ Iso G 4s; 45°39'·06N 01°10'·60W.

No 11A Ⓘ Fl G 2·5s; 45°38'·37N 01°07'·90W.

No 13 Ⓘ Fl (2) 6s; 45°37'·34N 01°06'·41W.

No 13A Ⓘ Fl (3) G 12s; 45°35'·68N 01°04'·19W.

No 13B Ⓘ QG; 45°34'·65N 01°02'·99W.

Ldg lts 327° (down-river): Front, Terre-Nègre ⚓, Oc (3) WRG 12s 39m W14M, R/G11M; 304°-R-319°-W-327°-G-000°-W-004°-G-097°-W-104°-R-116°; W twr, R top on W side; 45°38'·77N 01°06'·39W. Rear, **La Palmyre** Oc (3) R 12s 57m 17M; W radar Twr; 45°39'·72N 01° 07'·25W. 1.1M from front (Terre Nègre) above.

Cordouan ☆ Oc (2+1) WRG 12s 60m, **W19M, R16M, G15M**; 014°-W-126°-G-178·5°-W-250°-W (unintens) -267°-R (unintens)-294·5°-R-014°; obsc'd in estuary when brg >285°; W twr, Gy band; 45°35'·18N 01°10'·40W.

PASSE SUD (or DE GRAVE)

Ldg lts 063°: **Front, St Nicolas** ☆ Dir QG 22m **16M**; intens 061·5°-064·5°; W ☐ twr; 45°33'·73N 01°05'·01W.

Rear, Pte de Grave ☆ Oc WRG 4s 26m, **W17M, R/G13M**; 033°-W(unintens)-054°-W-233·5°-R-303°-W-312°-G-330°-W-341°- W(unintens)-025°; W ☐ twr, B corners and top, 0·84M from front.

G ⚓ 45°30'·33N 01°15'·55W. G3 ⚓ 45°32'·79N 01°07'·72W.

Ldg lts 041°, both Dir QR 33/61m **18M**. **Front, Le Chay** ☆ 45°37'·31N 01°02'·43W. **Rear, St Pierre** ☆, 0·97M from front.

G4 ⚓ 45°34'·70N 01°05'·80W. G6 ⚓ 45°34'·88N 01°04'·80W.

ROYAN

R1 Ⓘ Iso G 4s; 45°36'·56N 01°01'·96W.

S jetty ⚹ Fl (2) R 10s 11m 9M; 45°37'·00N 01°01'·81W.

Hbr ent, W jetty ⚹ Fl (3) R 12s 8m 6M; 45°37'·12N 01°01'·53W.

PORT BLOC and PORT-MÉDOC

Pte de Grave, jetty Ⓘ Q 6m 2M; 45°34'·42N 01°03'·68W.

Port Bloc, ent N side ⚹ Fl G 4s 9m 4M; 45°34'·14N 01°03'·74W.

Port-Médoc, N bkwtr head ⚹ QG 4M; 45°33'·40N 01°03'·39W.

MESCHERS, MORTAGNE, PORT MAUBERT, PAUILLAC and BLAYE

Meschers ldg lts 354·4°: QG (privately maintained). Front 45°33'·20N 00°56'·63W, on E bkwtr head. Rear, 130m from front.

Mortagne ent Ⓘ VQ (9) 10s; 45°28'·24N 00°49'·02W.

Port Maubert, ldg lts 024·5°, both QR 5/9m 5M; 45°25'·56N 00°45'·47W.

Pauillac, No 43 Ⓘ Fl (2) G 6s; 45°12'·44N 00°44'·27W.

NE elbow ⚹ Fl G 4s 7m 5M; 45°11'·95N 00°44'·59W.

Ent E side ⚹ QG 7m 4M; 45°11'·83N 00°44'·59W.

Blaye, No S9 ▲ 45°09'·35N 00°40'·27W; 1·8M N of Blaye.

N quay ⚹ Q (3) R 5s 6m 3M; 45°07'·49N 00°39'·99W.

D6 Ⓘ Fl (2) R 6s; 45°06'·91N 00°39'·93W, 0.6M S of Blaye.

Bec d'Ambés Ⓘ QG 5m 5M; 45°02'·53N 00°36'·47W (here Rivers Dordogne and Garonne flow into River Gironde).

BORDEAUX

Pont d'Aquitaine ⚹ 4 F Vi; 44°52'·82N 00°32'·28W.

No 73 Ⓘ Iso G 4s; 44°52'·72N 00°32'·24W.

Lormont Iso R 4s, S end of ❶ pontoon; 44°52'·62N 00°32'·12W.

Lock ent to Bassins Nos 1 and 2, 44°51'·72N 00°33'·07W.

Pont de Pierre, 44°50'·30N 00°33'·78W, Km 0.

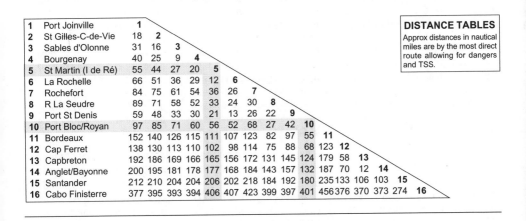

		1	2	3	4	5	6	7	8	9	10	11	12	13	14	15	16
1	Port Joinville	1															
2	St Gilles-C-de-Vie	18	2														
3	Sables d'Olonne	31	16	3													
4	Bourgenay	40	25	9	4												
5	St Martin (I de Ré)	55	44	27	20	5											
6	La Rochelle	66	51	36	29	12	6										
7	Rochefort	84	75	61	54	36	26	7									
8	R La Seudre	89	71	58	52	33	24	30	8								
9	Port St Denis	59	48	33	30	21	13	26	22	9							
10	Port Bloc/Royan	97	85	71	60	56	52	68	27	42	10						
11	Bordeaux	152	140	126	115	111	107	123	82	97	55	11					
12	Cap Ferret	138	130	113	110	102	98	114	75	88	68	123	12				
13	Capbreton	192	186	169	166	165	156	172	131	145	124	179	58	13			
14	Anglet/Bayonne	200	195	181	178	177	168	184	143	157	132	187	70	12	14		
15	Santander	212	210	204	204	206	202	218	184	192	180	235	133	106	103	15	
16	Cabo Finisterre	377	395	393	394	406	407	423	399	397	401	456	376	370	373	274	16

DISTANCE TABLES

Approx distances in nautical miles are by the most direct route allowing for dangers and TSS.

Times are UT - add 1 hour in non-shaded months to convert to Summer Time

SUN RISE/SET LATITUDE 56°N – 2022

	Rise Set JANUARY	Rise Set FEBRUARY	Rise Set MARCH	Rise Set APRIL	Rise Set MAY	Rise Set JUNE
1	0831 1536	0755 1633	0652 1734	0531 1838	0416 1939	0322 2034
4	0830 1540	0749 1639	0644 1740	0523 1844	0410 1945	0319 2038
7	0828 1544	0743 1646	0636 1747	0515 1850	0403 1951	0317 2042
10	0826 1549	0737 1653	0629 1753	0507 1856	0357 1957	0315 2045
13	0823 1554	0730 1659	0621 1759	0500 1903	0351 2003	0314 2047
16	0820 1600	0723 1706	0613 1805	0452 1909	0346 2008	0313 2049
19	0816 1606	0716 1712	0605 1812	0445 1915	0340 2014	0313 2050
22	0812 1612	0709 1719	0557 1818	0437 1921	0335 2019	0313 2051
25	0807 1618	0702 1725	0549 1824	0430 1927	0331 2024	0314 2051
28	0802 1624	0654 1732	0541 1830	0423 1933	0327 2029	0316 2050
31	0757 1631		0534 1836		0323 2033	

	JULY	AUGUST	SEPTEMBER	OCTOBER	NOVEMBER	DECEMBER
1	0318 2049	0404 2008	0504 1855	0603 1735	0707 1620	0807 1531
4	0321 2047	0409 2002	0510 1847	0609 1728	0713 1613	0811 1529
7	0324 2045	0415 1955	0516 1839	0615 1720	0720 1607	0816 1527
10	0328 2042	0421 1948	0522 1831	0621 1712	0726 1601	0820 1526
13	0332 2039	0427 1942	0527 1823	0627 1705	0732 1556	0823 1525
16	0336 2035	0433 1935	0533 1815	0633 1657	0738 1550	0826 1525
19	0341 2031	0439 1927	0539 1807	0639 1650	0744 1546	0828 1526
22	0346 2026	0444 1920	0545 1759	0646 1642	0750 1541	0830 1527
25	0351 2021	0450 1913	0551 1751	0652 1635	0756 1537	0831 1529
28	0356 2015	0456 1905	0557 1743	0658 1628	0802 1534	0832 1532
31	0402 2010	0502 1857		0705 1622		0831 1535

SUN RISE/SET LATITUDE 48°N – 2022

	Rise Set JANUARY	Rise Set FEBRUARY	Rise Set MARCH	Rise Set APRIL	Rise Set MAY	Rise Set JUNE
1	0750 1617	0728 1700	0641 1744	0539 1830	0442 1913	0405 1951
4	0750 1620	0724 1705	0635 1749	0533 1834	0437 1917	0403 1954
7	0749 1624	0719 1709	0630 1753	0527 1839	0433 1921	0402 1956
10	0748 1628	0715 1714	0624 1758	0521 1843	0428 1925	0401 1959
13	0746 1631	0710 1719	0618 1802	0515 1847	0424 1929	0400 2000
16	0744 1636	0705 1724	0611 1807	0509 1852	0420 1933	0400 2002
19	0742 1640	0700 1729	0605 1811	0503 1856	0417 1937	0400 2003
22	0739 1644	0654 1733	0559 1815	0458 1900	0413 1941	0401 2003
25	0736 1649	0649 1738	0553 1820	0452 1904	0410 1944	0402 2004
28	0733 1654	0643 1743	0547 1824	0447 1909	0408 1947	0403 2004
31	0729 1658		0541 1829		0406 1950	

	JULY	AUGUST	SEPTEMBER	OCTOBER	NOVEMBER	DECEMBER
1	0404 2003	0436 1936	0518 1841	0559 1740	0645 1642	0729 1609
4	0406 2002	0440 1931	0522 1835	0603 1733	0649 1637	0732 1608
7	0409 2001	0444 1927	0526 1829	0607 1727	0654 1633	0735 1607
10	0411 1959	0448 1922	0530 1823	0612 1721	0659 1629	0739 1607
13	0414 1957	0452 1917	0534 1817	0616 1716	0703 1625	0741 1607
16	0417 1955	0456 1912	0538 1811	0621 1710	0708 1621	0744 1607
19	0420 1952	0500 1906	0542 1804	0625 1704	0712 1618	0746 1608
22	0424 1949	0504 1901	0546 1758	0629 1659	0716 1615	0747 1610
25	0427 1945	0508 1855	0551 1752	0634 1653	0721 1613	0749 1611
28	0431 1941	0512 1849	0555 1746	0639 1648	0725 1611	0749 1614
31	0435 1937	0516 1843		0643 1643		0750 1616

SUN RISE/SET LATITUDE 40°N – 2022

	Rise Set JANUARY	Rise Set FEBRUARY	Rise Set MARCH	Rise Set APRIL	Rise Set MAY	Rise Set JUNE
1	0722 1645	0709 1719	0634 1752	0544 1824	0500 1855	0433 1923
4	0722 1648	0706 1723	0629 1755	0539 1827	0457 1858	0432 1925
7	0722 1651	0702 1726	0624 1758	0535 1830	0453 1901	0431 1927
10	0721 1654	0659 1730	0620 1801	0530 1833	0450 1904	0431 1928
13	0721 1657	0656 1733	0615 1805	0525 1836	0447 1906	0431 1930
16	0720 1700	0652 1737	0610 1808	0521 1839	0444 1909	0431 1931
19	0718 1704	0648 1740	0605 1811	0517 1842	0441 1912	0431 1932
22	0716 1707	0644 1744	0600 1814	0512 1845	0439 1915	0432 1933
25	0714 1711	0639 1747	0556 1817	0508 1848	0437 1917	0432 1933
28	0712 1714	0635 1751	0551 1820	0504 1852	0435 1920	0433 1933
31	0710 1718		0546 1823		0434 1922	

	Rise Set JULY	Rise Set AUGUST	Rise Set SEPTEMBER	Rise Set OCTOBER	Rise Set NOVEMBER	Rise Set DECEMBER
1	0435 1933	0458 1914	0528 1832	0556 1743	0629 1658	0702 1635
4	0436 1932	0501 1911	0530 1827	0559 1738	0632 1654	0705 1635
7	0438 1931	0504 1907	0533 1822	0602 1733	0636 1651	0708 1635
10	0440 1930	0507 1903	0536 1817	0605 1728	0639 1648	0711 1635
13	0442 1929	0510 1900	0539 1812	0608 1724	0643 1645	0713 1635
16	0444 1927	0512 1856	0542 1807	0611 1719	0646 1643	0715 1636
19	0447 1925	0515 1851	0545 1802	0615 1715	0649 1641	0717 1637
22	0449 1923	0518 1847	0547 1757	0618 1711	0653 1639	0719 1638
25	0452 1921	0521 1843	0550 1752	0621 1707	0656 1637	0720 1640
28	0455 1918	0524 1838	0553 1747	0624 1703	0659 1636	0721 1642
31	0457 1915	0527 1833		0628 1659		0722 1644

MOON RISE/SET LATITUDE 56°N – 2022

	Rise Set JANUARY	Rise Set FEBRUARY	Rise Set MARCH	Rise Set APRIL	Rise Set MAY	Rise Set JUNE
1	0727 1349	0849 1634	0711 1535	0602 1857	0437 2041	0407 2311
4	1026 1737	0930 2104	0745 1959	0629 2300	0532 ****	0708 0023
7	1115 2207	0956 ****	0812 ****	0734 0131	0808 0154	1106 0107
10	1140 0046	1040 0337	0905 0236	1027 0352	1205 0249	1518 0131
13	1217 0436	1244 0643	1134 0520	1432 0441	1620 0315	2009 0210
16	1357 0759	1634 0802	1535 0622	1853 0507	2109 0349	2330 0437
19	1729 0939	2044 0834	1951 0651	2342 0546	0005 0544	0012 0921
22	2134 1017	**** 0903	**** 0724	0216 0800	0151 1010	0039 1335
25	0021 1044	0409 1016	0318 0903	0343 1226	0222 1427	0105 1733
28	0457 1141	0650 1400	0518 1311	0412 1639	0246 1826	0208 2106
31	0820 1458		0554 1735		0334 2213	

	Rise Set JULY	Rise Set AUGUST	Rise Set SEPTEMBER	Rise Set OCTOBER	Rise Set NOVEMBER	Rise Set DECEMBER
1	0457 2249	0800 2141	1119 2023	1340 1934	1454 2229	1338 ****
4	0852 2324	1204 2204	1550 2136	1625 2311	1528 0134	1359 0336
7	1254 2348	1639 2301	1821 ****	1710 0222	1550 0552	1438 0746
10	1731 0012	1953 0058	1901 0451	1733 0649	1634 1004	1641 1102
13	2122 0208	2045 0551	1925 0917	1810 1105	1853 1306	2025 1215
16	2229 0651	2110 1019	2008 1327	2003 1429	2243 1408	**** 1240
19	2255 1119	2146 1426	2218 1633	2345 1549	0122 1432	0305 1302
22	2325 1521	2330 1751	0047 1741	0227 1616	0539 1456	0751 1359
25	0009 1901	0148 1919	0451 1807	0640 1638	1027 1609	1100 1742
28	0247 2055	0548 1950	0904 1830	1123 1733	1300 2012	1146 2233
31	0641 2133	0952 2012		1431 2054		1208 0124

MOON RISE/SET LATITUDE 48°N – 2022

	Rise JANUARY	Set	Rise FEBRUARY	Set	Rise MARCH	Set	Rise APRIL	Set	Rise MAY	Set	Rise JUNE	Set
1	0635	1443	0809	1711	0638	1606	0604	1850	0502	2008	0505	2211
4	0940	1820	0922	2108	0742	1958	0659	2223	0626	2324	0756	****
7	1101	2217	1014	****	0836	2331	0830	0036	0901	0100	1123	0047
10	1153	0037	1126	0253	0956	0145	1116	0301	1228	0224	1504	0139
13	1256	0359	1340	0546	1227	0426	1450	0420	1612	0318	1918	0250
16	1454	0702	1704	0730	1558	0556	1840	0515	2024	0423	2239	0536
19	1805	0901	2043	0830	1944	0653	2251	0626	****	0646	****	0945
22	2140	1006	****	0928	2346	0756	0115	0900	0117	1042	0041	1328
25	0008	1101	0314	1113	0218	1003	0312	1254	0218	1427	0134	1657
28	0409	1231	0605	1443	0440	1347	0410	1636	0308	1756	0304	2007
31	0729	1547			0547	1738			0425	2116		

	Rise JULY	Set	Rise AUGUST	Set	Rise SEPTEMBER	Set	Rise OCTOBER	Set	Rise NOVEMBER	Set	Rise DECEMBER	Set
1	0547	2207	0813	2133	1054	2050	1242	2032	1413	2308	1326	****
4	0912	2311	1148	2224	1451	2237	1536	2358	1519	0149	1416	0323
7	1245	****	1547	2354	1736	0054	1655	0244	1610	0535	1526	0700
10	1647	0046	1902	0158	1851	0508	1747	0638	1726	0914	1741	1001
13	2026	0309	2030	0614	1944	0902	1855	1022	1951	1207	2057	1140
16	2208	0720	2124	1009	2058	1239	2104	1327	2312	1337	****	1233
19	2303	1115	2229	1345	2317	1533	****	1511	0131	1428	0248	1322
22	****	1448	****	1650	0128	1708	0241	1608	0516	1522	0655	1455
25	0103	1802	0234	1841	0500	1803	0623	1659	0926	1710	1010	1830
28	0339	2010	0604	1940	0843	1855	1029	1829	1215	2054	1132	2243
31	0704	2117	0939	2030			1337	2146			1223	0113

MOON RISE/SET LATITUDE 40°N – 2022

	Rise JANUARY	Set	Rise FEBRUARY	Set	Rise MARCH	Set	Rise APRIL	Set	Rise MAY	Set	Rise JUNE	Set
1	0601	1518	0742	1736	0614	1627	0605	1845	0521	1945	0542	2134
4	0910	1848	0916	2110	0740	1957	0719	2158	0701	2247	0827	2337
7	1052	2223	1027	****	0853	2309	0906	0000	0936	0025	1135	0033
10	1202	0030	1156	0224	1030	0113	1148	0228	1244	0205	1455	0144
13	1323	0333	1416	0510	1302	0351	1503	0405	1606	0319	1845	0318
16	1530	0626	1724	0707	1615	0537	1830	0520	1955	0447	2206	0614
19	1830	0835	2043	0827	1939	0654	2218	0654	2326	0724	2354	1002
22	2144	0959	****	0945	2317	0819	0037	0938	0053	1104	0042	1323
25	****	1114	0239	1149	0140	1041	0251	1313	0215	1426	0155	1632
28	0338	1304	0534	1512	0413	1411	0409	1634	0324	1736	0340	1929
31	0656	1620			0541	1740			0459	2040		

	Rise JULY	Set	Rise AUGUST	Set	Rise SEPTEMBER	Set	Rise OCTOBER	Set	Rise NOVEMBER	Set	Rise DECEMBER	Set
1	0620	2138	0822	2128	1037	2110	1205	2110	1345	2334	1318	****
4	0926	2300	1136	2239	1413	2315	1503	****	1513	0159	1428	0313
7	1238	****	1513	****	1706	0129	1645	0300	1625	0523	1557	0630
10	1617	0110	1828	0235	1844	0519	1758	0631	1800	0842	1819	0923
13	1950	0348	2019	0630	1958	0850	1926	0952	2028	1129	2120	1115
16	2153	0740	2133	1002	2131	1208	2143	1249	2332	1315	****	1228
19	2309	1112	2258	1318	2354	1455	****	1446	0138	1426	0236	1337
22	****	1424	0018	1612	0155	1645	0251	1602	0500	1540	0620	1531
25	0138	1724	0305	1814	0507	1759	0612	1714	0849	1749	0936	1902
28	0413	1940	0615	1933	0828	1913	0954	1905	1145	2123	1121	2250
31	0720	2105	0929	2042			1303	2219			1233	0106

SPEED, TIME AND DISTANCE (NAUTICAL MILES)

Speed in knots

Time in minutes	1	2	3	4	5	6	7	8	9	10	15	20
1	0.0	0.0	0.1	0.1	0.1	0.1	0.1	0.1	0.2	0.2	0.3	0.3
2	0.0	0.1	0.1	0.1	0.2	0.2	0.2	0.3	0.3	0.3	0.5	0.7
3	0.1	0.1	0.2	0.2	0.3	0.3	0.4	0.4	0.5	0.5	0.8	1.0
4	0.1	0.1	0.2	0.3	0.3	0.4	0.5	0.5	0.6	0.7	1.0	1.3
5	0.1	0.2	0.3	0.3	0.4	0.5	0.6	0.7	0.8	0.8	1.3	1.7
6	0.1	0.2	0.3	0.4	0.5	0.6	0.7	0.8	0.9	1.0	1.5	2.0
7	0.1	0.2	0.4	0.5	0.6	0.7	0.8	0.9	1.1	1.2	1.8	2.3
8	0.1	0.3	0.4	0.5	0.7	0.8	0.9	1.1	1.2	1.3	2.0	2.7
9	0.2	0.3	0.5	0.6	0.8	0.9	1.1	1.2	1.4	1.5	2.3	3.0
10	0.2	0.3	0.5	0.7	0.8	1.0	1.2	1.3	1.5	1.7	2.5	3.3
11	0.2	0.4	0.6	0.7	0.9	1.1	1.3	1.5	1.7	1.8	2.8	3.7
12	0.2	0.4	0.6	0.8	1.0	1.2	1.4	1.6	1.8	2.0	3.0	4.0
13	0.2	0.4	0.7	0.9	1.1	1.3	1.5	1.7	2.0	2.2	3.3	4.3
14	0.2	0.5	0.7	0.9	1.2	1.4	1.6	1.9	2.1	2.3	3.5	4.7
15	0.3	0.5	0.8	1.0	1.3	1.5	1.8	2.0	2.3	2.5	3.8	5.0
16	0.3	0.5	0.8	1.1	1.3	1.6	1.9	2.1	2.4	2.7	4.0	5.3
17	0.3	0.6	0.9	1.1	1.4	1.7	2.0	2.3	2.6	2.8	4.3	5.7
18	0.3	0.6	0.9	1.2	1.5	1.8	2.1	2.4	2.7	3.0	4.5	6.0
19	0.3	0.6	1.0	1.3	1.6	1.9	2.2	2.5	2.9	3.2	4.8	6.3
20	0.3	0.7	1.0	1.3	1.7	2.0	2.3	2.7	3.0	3.3	5.0	6.7
21	0.4	0.7	1.1	1.4	1.8	2.1	2.5	2.8	3.2	3.5	5.3	7.0
22	0.4	0.7	1.1	1.5	1.8	2.2	2.6	2.9	3.3	3.7	5.5	7.3
23	0.4	0.8	1.2	1.5	1.9	2.3	2.7	3.1	3.5	3.8	5.8	7.7
24	0.4	0.8	1.2	1.6	2.0	2.4	2.8	3.2	3.6	4.0	6.0	8.0
25	0.4	0.8	1.3	1.7	2.1	2.5	2.9	3.3	3.8	4.2	6.3	8.3
30	0.5	1.0	1.5	2.0	2.5	3.0	3.5	4.0	4.5	5.0	7.5	10.0
35	0.6	1.2	1.8	2.3	2.9	3.5	4.1	4.7	5.3	5.8	8.8	11.7
40	0.7	1.3	2.0	2.7	3.3	4.0	4.7	5.3	6.0	6.7	10.0	13.3
45	0.8	1.5	2.3	3.0	3.8	4.5	5.3	6.0	6.8	7.5	11.3	15.0
50	0.8	1.7	2.5	3.3	4.2	5.0	5.8	6.7	7.5	8.3	12.5	16.7

DISTANCE (NAUTICAL MILES) OFF RISING/DIPPING LIGHTS

Height of eye in feet

Height of light in metres	2	3	4	5	6	7	8	9	10	20	30	40	50
2	4.6	4.9	5.2	5.5	5.7	6.0	6.2	6.4	6.6	8.1	9.2	10.2	11.0
3	5.2	5.6	5.9	6.2	6.4	6.6	6.8	7.0	7.2	8.7	9.9	10.8	11.7
4	5.8	6.1	6.4	6.7	6.9	7.2	7.4	7.6	7.8	9.3	10.4	11.4	12.2
5	6.3	6.6	6.9	7.2	7.4	7.7	7.9	8.1	8.3	9.8	10.9	11.9	12.7
6	6.7	7.1	7.4	7.6	7.9	8.1	8.3	8.5	8.7	10.2	11.3	12.3	13.2
7	7.1	7.5	7.8	8.0	8.3	8.5	8.7	8.9	9.1	10.6	11.8	12.7	13.6
8	7.5	7.8	8.2	8.4	8.7	8.9	9.1	9.3	9.5	11.0	12.1	13.1	14.0
9	7.8	8.2	8.5	8.8	9.0	9.2	9.5	9.7	9.8	11.3	12.5	13.5	14.3
10	8.2	8.5	8.8	9.1	9.4	9.6	9.8	10.0	10.2	11.7	12.8	13.8	14.6
11	8.5	8.9	9.2	9.4	9.7	9.9	10.1	10.3	10.5	12.0	13.1	14.1	15.0
12	8.8	9.2	9.5	9.7	10.0	10.2	10.4	10.6	10.8	12.3	13.4	14.4	15.3
13	9.1	9.5	9.8	10.0	10.3	10.5	10.7	10.9	11.1	12.6	13.7	14.7	15.6
14	9.4	9.7	10.0	10.3	10.6	10.8	11.0	11.2	11.4	12.9	14.0	15.0	15.8
15	9.6	10.0	10.3	10.6	10.8	11.1	11.3	11.5	11.6	13.1	14.3	15.3	16.1
16	9.9	10.3	10.6	10.8	11.1	11.3	11.5	11.7	11.9	13.4	14.6	15.5	16.4
17	10.2	10.5	10.8	11.1	11.3	11.6	11.8	12.0	12.2	13.7	14.8	15.8	16.6
18	10.4	10.8	11.1	11.4	11.6	11.8	12.0	12.2	12.4	13.9	15.1	16.0	16.9
19	10.7	11.0	11.3	11.6	11.8	12.1	12.3	12.5	12.7	14.2	15.3	16.3	17.1
20	10.9	11.3	11.6	11.8	12.1	12.3	12.5	12.7	12.9	14.4	15.5	16.5	17.3
25	12.0	12.3	12.6	12.9	13.2	13.4	13.6	13.8	14.0	15.5	16.6	17.6	18.4
30	13.0	13.3	13.6	13.9	14.1	14.4	14.6	14.8	15.0	16.5	17.6	18.6	19.4
40	14.7	15.1	15.4	15.7	15.9	16.1	16.3	16.5	16.7	18.2	19.4	20.3	21.2
50	16.3	16.6	16.9	17.2	17.4	17.7	17.9	18.1	18.3	19.8	20.9	21.9	22.7
60	17.7	18.0	18.3	18.6	18.8	19.1	19.3	19.5	19.7	21.2	22.3	23.3	24.1

CONVERSION TABLE

Sq inches to sq millimetres *multiply by* **645.20**	**Sq millimetres to sq inches** *multiply by* **0.0016**
Inches to millimetres *multiply by* **25.40**	**Millimetres to inches** *multiply by* **0.0394**
Sq feet to square metres *multiply by* **0.093**	**Sq metres to sq feet** *multiply by* **10.7640**
Inches to centimetres *multiply by* **2.54**	**Centimetres to inches** *multiply by* **0.3937**
Feet to metres *multiply by* **0.305**	**Metres to feet** *multiply by* **3.2810**
Nautical miles to kilometres *multiply by* **1.852**	**Kilometres to nautical miles** *multiply by* **0.5400**
Statute miles to kilometres *multiply by* **1.609**	**Kilometres to statute miles** *multiply by* **0.6214**
Statute miles to nautical miles *multiply by* **0.8684**	**Nautical miles to statute miles** *multiply by* **1.1515**
HP to metric HP *multiply by* **1.014**	**Metric HP to HP** *multiply by* **0.9862**
Pounds per sq inch to **kg per sq centimetre** *multiply by* **0.0703**	**Kg per sq centimetre** **to pounds per sq inch** *multiply by* **14.2200**
HP to kilowatts *multiply by* **0.746**	**Kilowatts to HP** *multiply by* **1.341**
Cu inches to cu centimetres *multiply by* **16.39**	**Cu centimetres to cu inches** *multiply by* **0.0610**
Imperial gallons to litres *multiply by* **4.540**	**Litres to imperial gallons** *multiply by* **0.2200**
Pints to litres *multiply by* **0.5680**	**Litres to pints** *multiply by* **1.7600**
Pounds to kilogrammes *multiply by* **0.4536**	**Kilogrammes to pounds** *multiply by* **2.2050**

LIGHT CHARACTERISTICS

CLASS OF LIGHT	International abbreviations	National abbreviations	Illustration Period shown ⊢————⊣
FIXED	F		
OCCULTING (total duration of light longer than dark)			
Single-occulting		Oc Occ	
Group-occulting	eg Oc(2)	Gp Occ(2)	
Composite group-occulting eg	Oc(2+3)	Gp Occ(2+3)	
ISOPHASE (light and dark equal)		Iso	
FLASHING (total duration of light shorter than dark)			
Single-flashing	Fl		
Long-flashing (flash 2s or longer)	L Fl		
Group-flashing	eg Fl(3)	Gp Fl(3)	
Composite group-flashing eg	Fl(2+1)	Gp Fl(2+1)	
QUICK (50 to 79, usually either 50 or 60, flashes per min.)			
Continuous quick	Q	Qk Fl	
Group quick	eg Q(3)	Qk Fl(3)	
Interrupted quick	IQ	Int Qk Fl	
VERY QUICK (80 to 159, usually either 100 or 120, flashes per min.)			
Continuous very quick	VQ	V Qk Fl	
Group very quick	eg VQ(3)	V Qk Fl(3)	
Interrupted very quick	IVQ	Int V Qk Fl	
ULTRA QUICK (160 or more, usually 240 to 300, flashes per min.)			
Continuous ultra quick	UQ		
Interrupted ultra quick	IUQ		
MORSE CODE	eg Mo(K)		
FIXED AND FLASHING	F Fl		
ALTERNATING	eg Al. WR	Alt. WR	

COLOUR	International abbreviations	NOMINAL RANGE in miles	International abbreviations
White	W (may be omitted)	Light with single range	eg 15M
Red	R	Light with two different ranges	eg 15/10M
Green	G	Light with three or more ranges	eg 15-7M
Blue	Bu	**PERIOD** is given in seconds	eg 90s
Violet	Vi	**DISPOSITION** horizontally disposed	(hor)
Yellow	Y	**VERTICALLY DISPOSED**	(vert)
Orange	Y	**SYNCHRONISED** with (an)other light(s)	(sync)
Amber	Y	**ELEVATION** is given in metres (m) or feet (ft) above MHWS	

Chapter 2 – Weather

Beaufort scale

Force	Wind speed (knots)	(km/h)	(m/sec)	Description	State of sea	Probable wave ht(m)
0	0–1	0–2	0–0·5	Calm	Like a mirror	0
1	1–3	2–6	0·5–1·5	Light airs	Ripples like scales are formed	0
2	4–6	7–11	2–3	Light breeze	Small wavelets, still short but more pronounced, not breaking	0·1
3	7–10	13–19	4–5	Gentle breeze	Large wavelets, crests begin to break; a few white horses	0·4
4	11–16	20–30	6–8	Moderate breeze	Small waves growing longer; fairly frequent white horses	1
5	17–21	31–39	8–11	Fresh breeze	Moderate waves, taking more pronounced form; many white horses, perhaps some spray	2
6	22–27	41–50	11–14	Strong breeze	Large waves forming; white foam crests more extensive; probably some spray	3
7	28–33	52–61	14–17	Near gale	Sea heaps up; white foam from breaking waves begins to blow in streaks	4
8	34–40	63–74	17–21	Gale	Moderately high waves of greater length; edge of crests break into spindrift; foam blown in well-marked streaks	5·5

WEATHER

Terminology used in forecasts
Pressure systems' speed of movement

Slowly	< 15 knots
Steadily	15–25 knots
Rather quickly	25–35 knots
Rapidly	35–45 knots
Very rapidly	> 45 knots

Visibility

Good	> 5 miles
Moderate	2–5 miles
Poor	1000 metres–2 miles
Fog	< 1000 metres

Barometric pressure tendency

Rising/falling slowly: Change of 0·1 to 1·5 hPa/mb in the preceding 3 hours.
Rising/falling: Change of 1·6 to 3·5 hPa/mb in the preceding 3 hours.
Rising/falling quickly: Change of 3·6 to 6 hPa/mb in the preceding 3 hours.
Rising/falling very rapidly: Change of > 6 hPa/mb in the preceding 3 hours.
Now rising/falling: Pressure has been falling (rising) or steady in the preceding 3 hours, but was definitely rising (falling) at the time of observation.

Gale warnings

A *Gale* warning means that winds of at least F8 (34-40kn) or gusts up to 43-51kn are expected somewhere within the area, but not necessarily over the whole area

Severe Gale means winds of at least F9 (41-47kn) or gusts reaching 52-60kn

Storm means winds of F10 (48-55kn) or gusts of 61-68kn

Violent Storm means winds of F11 (56-63kn) or gusts of 69+ kn

Hurricane Force means winds of F12 (64+ kn)

Gale warnings remain in force until amended or cancelled. If a gale persists for >24 hours the warning is re-issued.

Timing of gale warnings from time of issue

Imminent	<6 hrs
Soon	6–12 hrs
Later	>12 hrs

Strong wind warnings

Issued, if possible 6 hrs in advance, when winds F6 or more are expected up to 5M offshore; valid for 12 hrs.

MAP OF UK SHIPPING FORECAST AREAS

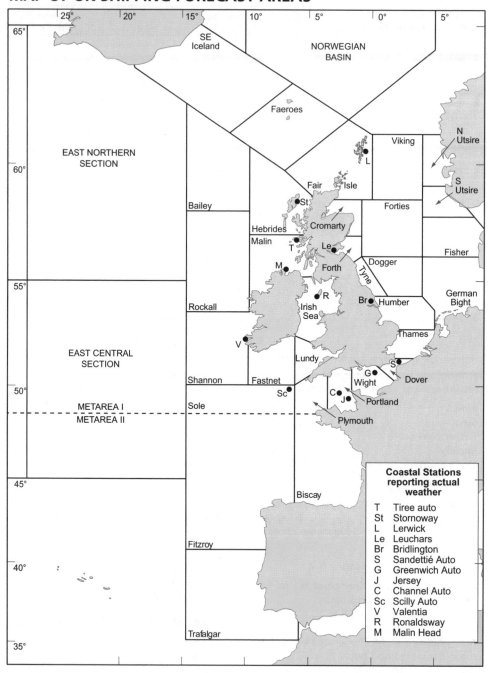

SHIPPING FORECAST RECORD TIME/DAY/DATE ....

GENERAL SYNOPSIS   At 0048, 0520, 1203, 1754 LT

System	Present position	Movement	Forecast position	At

Gales	SEA AREA FORECAST	Wind (At first)	(Later)	Weather	Visibility
	VIKING				
	NORTH UTSIRE				
	SOUTH UTSIRE				
	FORTIES				
	CROMARTY				
	FORTH				
	TYNE				
	DOGGER				
	FISHER				
	GERMAN BIGHT				
	HUMBER				
	THAMES				
	DOVER				
	WIGHT				
	PORTLAND				
	PLYMOUTH				
	BISCAY				
	TRAFALGAR (0048)				
	FITZROY				
	SOLE				
	LUNDY				
	FASTNET				
	IRISH SEA				
	SHANNON				
	ROCKALL				
	MALIN				
	HEBRIDES				
	BAILEY				
	FAIR ISLE				
	FAEROES				
	S E ICELAND				

COASTAL REPORTS at ....UT BST	Wind Direction	Force	Weather	Visibility	Pressure	Change
Tiree auto (T)						
Stornoway (St)						
Lerwick (L)						
Leuchars (Le)						
Bridlington (Br)						
Sandettié auto (S)						

COASTAL REPORTS	Wind Direction	Force	Weather	Visibility	Pressure	Change
Greenwich auto (G)						
Jersey (J)						
Channel auto (C)						
Scilly auto (Sc)						
Valentia (V)						
Ronaldsway (R)						
Malin Head (M)						

SOURCES OF WEATHER INFORMATION IN THE UK

BBC Radio 4 Shipping forecasts are at:

0048 LT[1]	LW FM
0520 LT[1]	LW FM
1203 LT	weekdays only, LW FM
1754 LT	weekdays LW only
0048, 0520,1754 LT	Sat/Sun, LW, FM

[1]includes weather reports from coastal stations

Frequencies

LW		198 kHz
FM	England	92·4–94·6 MHz
	Scotland	91·3–96·1 MHz
		103·5–104·9 MHz
	Wales	92·8–96·1 MHz
		103·5–104·9 MHz
	N Ireland	93·2–96·0 MHz
		103·5–104·6 MHz
	Channel Islands	94·8 MHz

The Shipping forecast contains:

Time of issue; summary of gale warnings in force at that time; a general synopsis of weather systems and their expected development and movement over the next 24 hours; sea area forecasts for the same 24 hours, including wind direction/force, weather and visibility in each; and an outlook for the following 24 hours.

Gale warnings for all affected areas are broadcast at the earliest break in Radio 4 programmes after receipt, as well as after the next news bulletin.

Shipping forecasts cover large sea areas, and rarely include the detailed variations that may occur near land. The inshore waters forecast can be more helpful on coastal passages.

Weather reports from coastal stations follow the 0048 and 0520 shipping forecasts. They include wind direction and force, present weather, visibility, and sea-level pressure and tendency, if available. The stations are shown on the previous page.

BBC Radio 4 Inshore waters forecast

A forecast for inshore waters (up to 12M offshore) in 17 areas around the UK and N Ireland, valid for 24 hrs, is broadcast after the 0048 and 0520 coastal station reports.

It includes forecasts of wind direction and force, weather, visibility and sea state. The 17 inshore areas are defined by the following well-known places and headlands, clockwise around the UK: Cape Wrath, Orkney, Rattray Hd, Berwick-upon-Tweed, Whitby, Gibraltar Point, N Foreland, Selsey Bill, Lyme Regis, Land's End, St David's Head, Great Ormes Head, Isle of Man, Mull of Galloway, Carlingford Lough, Lough Foyle, Mull of Kintyre, Ardnamurchan Pt and Shetland.

Strong wind warnings are issued by the Met Office whenever winds of Force 6 or more are expected over coastal waters up to 5M offshore.

Reports of actual weather are broadcast from all the coastal stations below after the 0048 inshore waters forecast and also after the 0520 forecast, except those in italics: Tiree*, Stornoway, Lerwick, *Wick*, Aberdeen,* Leuchars, *Boulmer,* Bridlington, Sandettie LV*, Greenwich LV*, *St Catherines Point*,* Jersey, Channel LV*, Scilly*, *Milford Haven, Aberporth, Valley, Liverpool (Crosby),* Valentia, Ronaldsway, Malin Head, *Macrihanish*.* An asterix* denotes an automatic station.

BBC general (land) forecasts

Land area forecasts may include an outlook up to 48 hours beyond the shipping forecast, plus more details of frontal systems and weather along the coasts. The most comprehensive land area forecasts are broadcast by Radio 4 on the frequencies above.

Land area forecasts – Wind strength

Wind descriptions used in land forecasts, with their Beaufort scale equivalents, are:

Calm	0	Fresh	5
Light	1–3	Strong	6–7
Moderate	4	Gale	8

Land area forecasts – Visibility

The following visibility definitions are used in land forecasts:

Mist	2000m–1000m
Fog	<1000m
Dense fog	< 50m

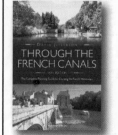

NAVTEX

NAVTEX is the prime method of disseminating MSI to at least 200 miles offshore. A dedicated aerial and receiver with an LCD screen (or integrated printer) are required. The user selects which stations and message categories are recorded for automatic display or printing.

Two frequencies are used. On the international frequency, 518kHz, messages are always available in English with excellent coverage of Europe. Interference between stations is minimised by scheduling time slots and and by limiting transmission power; see Fig 6(3). NAVTEX information applies only to the geographical area for which each station is responsible.

490 kHz (for clarity shown in italics throughout this chapter) is used abroad for transmissions in the national language. In the UK it is used for inshore waters forecasts in English. Identification letters for 490 kHz stations differ from 518 kHz stations.

NAVTEX is convenient and particularly useful when preoccupied handling your vessel as you will not miss potentially important information.

Messages

Each message is prefixed by a four-character group:

The first character is the code letter of the transmitting station (eg E for Niton).

The second character is the message category, see below.

The third and fourth are message serial numbers, running from 01 to 99 and then re-starting at 01.

The serial number 00 denotes urgent messages which are always printed.

Messages which are corrupt or have already been printed are rejected. Weather messages, and certain other message types, are dated and timed.

Message categories

A*	Navigational warnings
B*	Meteorological warnings
C	Ice reports
D*	SAR info and piracy warnings
E	Weather forecasts
F	Pilot service
H	Loran-C
J	Satellite navigation
K	Other electronic navaids
L	Subfacts and Gunfacts (UK)
V	Amplifies Navwarnings initially sent under A; plus weekly oil/gas rig moves.
W-Y	Special service, trials
Z	No messages on hand at scheduled time

Missing category letters are unallocated.

*The receiver cannot reject these categories.

NAVTEX stations/areas – UK & W Europe

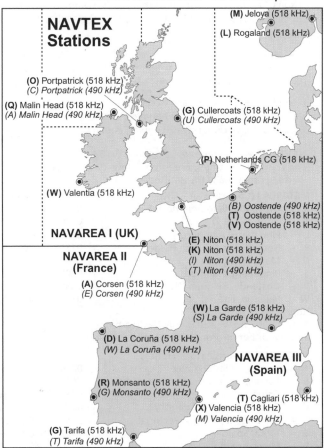

NAVTEX Stations

(M) Jeloya (518 kHz)
(L) Rogaland (518 kHz)

(O) Portpatrick (518 kHz)
(C) Portpatrick (490 kHz)

(Q) Malin Head (518 kHz)
(A) Malin Head (490 kHz)

(G) Cullercoats (518 kHz)
(U) Cullercoats (490 kHz)

(P) Netherlands CG (518 kHz)

(W) Valentia (518 kHz)

(B) Oostende (490 kHz)
(T) Oostende (518 kHz)
(V) Oostende (518 kHz)

NAVAREA I (UK)

NAVAREA II (France)

(E) Niton (518 kHz)
(K) Niton (518 kHz)
(I) Niton (490 kHz)
(T) Niton (490 kHz)

(A) Corsen (518 kHz)
(E) Corsen (490 kHz)

(W) La Garde (518 kHz)
(S) La Garde (490 kHz)

(D) La Coruña (518 kHz)
(W) La Coruña (490 kHz)

NAVAREA III (Spain)

(R) Monsanto (518 kHz)
(G) Monsanto (490 kHz)

(T) Cagliari (518 kHz)
(X) Valencia (518 kHz)
(M) Valencia (490 kHz)

(G) Tarifa (518 kHz)
(T) Tarifa (490 kHz)

UK Sea area forecasts on 518 kHz
The times (UT) of weather messages are in bold; the times of an extended outlook (a further 2 or 3 days beyond the shipping forecast period) are in italics.

G –	**Cullercoats**	*0100*	0500	**0900**	1300	1700	**2100**

Viking, Forties, Cromarty, Forth, Tyne, Dogger, Humber, Thames, Fair Isle .

O –	**Portpatrick**	*0220*	**0620**	1020	1420	**1820**	2220

Lundy clockwise to SE Iceland, excluding Shannon.

E –	**Niton**	*0040*	0440	**0840**	1240	1640	**2040**

Thames clockwise to Fastnet, excluding Trafalgar.

Q –	**Malin Head** Shannon, Rockall, Malin, Hebrides	**0640**	**1840**

T –	**Oostende** Thames, Dover	0710, 1910

UK490 kHz broadcasts (in italic) provide forecasts for UK inshore waters, a national 3 day outlook for inshore waters and, at times in bold, reports of actual weather at some or all of the places listed below. To receive these reports select message category 'V' on the receiver. Times (UT) are listed in chronological order. Reports include some or all of: Sea level pressure (hPa/mb), wind direction and speed (kn), weather, visibility (M), air and sea temperatures (°C), dewpoint temperature (°C) and mean wave height (m).

A –	**Malin Head**	0000	0400	0800	**1200**	**1600**	2000

Lough Foyle to Carlingford Lough, Mull of Galloway to Cape Wrath, the Minch.
Note times of forecasts and actuals not known at time of going to press.

C –	**Portpatrick** Land's End to Shetland	0020	0420	0820	**1220**	**1620**	2020

N Rona, Stornoway, S Uist, Lusa (Skye), Tiree, Campbeltown Airport, Macrihanish, Belfast, Malin Hd, Belmullet, St Bees Hd, Ronaldsway, Crosby, Valley, Aberporth, Milford Haven, Roches Pt, Valentia, St Mawgan .

I –	**Niton** The Wash to St David's Head	0120	0520	**0920**	**1320**	1720	**2120**

Sandettie Lt V, Greenwich Lt V, Bournmouth Airport, Guernsey airport, Jersey airport, Plymouth (Mountbatten), Culdrose, Seven Stones Lt V, Roches Point(Cork).

U –	**Cullercoats** Cape Wrath to N Foreland	0320	0720	**1120**	**1520**	1920	**2320**

Sandettie Lt V, Manston, Shoeburyness, Weybourne, Donna Nook, Boulmer, Leuchars, Aberdeen, Lossiemouth, Wick, Kirkwall, Lerwick, Foula, K7 Met buoy, Sule Skerry.

NAVTEX coverage abroad: Selected NAVTEX stations in Metareas I and II, with identity codes and transmission times, are listed below. Times of weather messages are shown in **bold**. Gale warnings are usually transmitted 4 hourly.

METAREA I (Co-ordinator – UK)

		Transmission times (UT)					
B –	**Oostende**, *Belgium (mostly Dutch)*	*0010*	*0410*	*0810*	*1210*	*1610*	*2010*
K –	**Niton** (Note 1)	0140	0540	0940	1340	1740	2140
L –	**Pinneberg**, *Hamburg*	*0150*	*0550*	*0950*	*1350*	*1750*	*2150*
P –	**Netherlands CG**, Den Helder	0230	0630	1030	**1430**	1830	2230
Q –	**Malin Head**, Eire	0240	**0640**	**1040**	1440	**1840**	2240
S –	**Pinneberg**, Hamburg	**0300**	**0700**	**1100**	**1500**	**1900**	**2300**
V –	**Oostende**, Belgium (Note 2)	0330	0730	1130	1530	1930	2330
W –	**Valentia**, Eire	0340	**0740**	**1140**	1540	**1940**	2340

Notes:
1 In English, no weather; only Nav warnings for waters from Cap Gris Nez to Île de Bréhat.
2 No weather information, only Nav warnings.

METAREA II (Co-ordinator – France)

A –	**Corsen**, Le Stiff, France	0000	0400	0800	**1200**	1600	2000
E –	**Corsen**, *Le Stiff, France (In French)*	*0040*	*0440*	**0840**	*1240*	*1640*	*2040*
D –	**Coruña**, Spain	0030	0430	0830	1230	1630	2030
W –	**Coruña**, *Spain (in Spanish)*	*0340*	*0740*	*1140*	*1540*	*1940*	*2340*
F –	**São Miguel** , Açores, Portugal	0050	0450	0850	1250	1650	2050
G –	**Tarifa**, Spain	0100	0500	**0900**	1300	1700	**2100**
R –	**Monsanto**, Portugal	0250	0650	1050	1450	1850	2250

INTERNET WEATHER SOURCES

The Internet provides a useful back-up for GMDSS services, and information not available by conventional means. www.metoffice.gov.uk/weather/marine/ has texts of all marine forecasts, warnings and weather from coastal stations, light vessels and data buoys. www.bbc.co.uk/weather/coast/ has texts of NAVTEX broadcasts.

Other websites include: www.metmarine.com
www.weatheronline.com / www.mailasail.com
www.grib.us / www.saildocs.com
www.passageweather.com
www.windfinder.com / www.xcweather.co.uk/
www.windguru.com / www.theyr.com /
www.wetterzentrale.de/topkarten/tknf.html
www.weatherweb.net/marine
www.weather.mailasail.com/Franks-Weather

Broadcasts of shipping and inshore waters forecasts by HM Coastguard

HM CGOC broadcast MSI every 3 hours at the times shown below* (LT). The VHF working channel, either 10,62,63, or 64, is announced on VHF Ch 16 prior to each broadcast which will use one of 3 closer Groups of MSI: **Group A**, the full broadcast, contains the Shipping forecast, a new Inshore waters forecast and 24 hrs outlook, Gale warnings, a 3 day forecast for Fishermen in the winter months, Navigational (WZ) warnings and Subfacts & Gunfacts where relevant ‡.

'A' broadcast times are in **bold type**.

Group B contains a new Inshore waters forecast, plus the previous outlook, and Gale warnings. 'B' broadcast times are in plain type.

Group C is a repeat of the Inshore forecast and Gale warnings (as per the previous Group A or B) plus new Strong wind warnings. 'C' broadcast times are *italicised*.

Note: ‡ indicates Subfacts & Gunfacts.

Coastguard	Shipping forecast areas	Inshore areas	Broadcast times, LT*							
East Coast			B	C	A	C	B	C	A	C
Aberdeen‡	Cromarty, Forties, Forth, Fair Isle, Tyne	1,2	0130	*0430*	**0730**	*1030*	1330	*1630*	**1930**	*2230*
Humber	Tyne Dogger Fisher, Humber, German Bight	3,4,5	0150	*0450*	**0750**	*1050*	1350	*1650*	**1950**	*2250*
South Coast			B	C	A	C	B	C	A	C
Dover	Humber, Thames, Dover, Wight	5,6	0110	*0410*	**0710**	*1010*	1310	*1610*	**1910**	*2210*
Solent	Dover, Wight, Portland, Plymouth	5, 6,7	0130	*0430*	**0730**	*1030*	1330	*1630*	**1930**	*2230*
Falmouth‡	Portland, Plymouth, Sole, Lundy, Fastnet.	8,9	0110	*0410*	**0710**	*1010*	1310	*1610*	**1910**	*2210*
West Coast			B	C	A	C	B	C	A	C
Milford Haven	Lundy, Fastnet, Irish Sea	9, 10	0150	*0450*	**0750**	*1050*	1350	*1650*	**1950**	*2250*
Holyhead A	Irish Sea	10,11	0150	*0450*	**0750**	*1050*	1350	*1650*	**1950**	*2250*
Holyhead B	Irish Sea	11,12	0130	*0430*	**0730**	*1030*	1330	*1630*	**1930**	*2230*
Belfast‡	Irish Sea, Rockall, Malin, Hebrides	12,13,14	0210	*0510*	**0810**	*1110*	1410	*1710*	**2010**	*2310*
Stornoway‡	Rockall, Malin, Hebrides, Bailey, Fair Is, Faeroes, SE Iceland	15,16,17	0110	*0410*	**0710**	*1010*	1310	*1610*	**1910**	*2210*
Shetland	Cromarty, Viking, Fair Isle	18	0110	*0410*	**0710**	*1010*	1310	*1610*	**1910**	*2210*

*HMCG endeavour to broadcast at the times shown but this can vary depending on the level of operational activity during busy times and emergencies.

NOTE: Readers are advised to check for changes in the MCA Maritime safety leaflet information (MCA/064) available at www.mcga.gov.uk. See also our free monthly updates from January to June available for download www.reedsnauticalalmanac.co.uk/update.

Remote CG transmitters and their VHF working channels

MSI broadcasts are transmitted every 3 hours from the start times (LT) shown via remote aerial sites giving optimum coverage at the positions listed below. The VHF broadcast channel, either 10, 62, 63 or 64 is usually announced first on Ch 16.

To avoid missing a broadcast, pre-select Ch 16 on Dual watch with the relevant (clearest) channel. **MF frequencies** (*kHz*), as quoted below, are also used for the broadcasts, primarily for fishermen.

INSHORE WATER FORECAST AREAS, MSI TRANSMITTERS, WORKING CHANNELS AND START TIMES

1 Cape Wrath to Rattray Head inc Orkney, 0130

Durness (Loch Eriboll)	63	58°34'N 04°44'W
Noss Head (Wick)	62	58°29'N 03°03'W
Rosemarkie (Cromarty)	64	57°38'N 04°05'W
Windyheads Hill	63	57°39'N 02°14'W

2 Rattray Head to Berwick-upon-Tweed, 0130

Gregness	*2226kHz*, 64	57°08'N 02°03'W
Inverbervie	63	56°51'N 02°16'W
Fife Ness	62	56°17'N 02°35'W
Craigkelly (Burntisland)	63	56°04'N 03°14'W
St Abbs Head/Cross Law	64	55°54'N 02°12'W

3 Berwick-upon-Tweed to Whitby, 0150

Newton	63	55°31'N 01°37'W
Cullercoats(Blyth)*1925kHz*,	64	55°04'N 01°28'W
Boulby	63	54°34'N 00°51'W

4 Whitby to Gibraltar Point, 0150

Ravenscar	64	54°24'N 00°30'W
Flamborough	63	54°07'N 00°05'W
Easington (Spurn Hd)	64	53°39'N 00°06'E
Mablethorpe	62	53°21'N 00°16'E

5 Gibraltar Point to North Foreland, 0110

Guy's Head (Wisbech)	63	52°48'N 00°13'E
Langham (Blakeney)	64	52°57'N 00°58'E
Trimingham (Cromer)	63	52°54'N 01°21'E
Caister (Great Yarmouth)	64	52°36N 01°43E
Lowestoft	63	52°29'N 01°46'E
Bawdsey (R Deben)	62	52°00'N 01°25'E
Walton-on-the-Naze	63	51°51'N 01°17'E
Bradwell (R Blackwater)	64	51°44'N 00°53'E
Shoeburyness	63	51°31'N 00°47'E

6 North Foreland to Selsey Bill, 0110

Langdon (Dover)	64	51°08'N 01°21'E
Fairlight (Hastings)	62	50°52'N 00°39'E

7 Selsey Bill to Lyme Regis, 0130

Newhaven (in Area 6)	62	50°47'N 00°03'E
Boniface (Ventnor, IoW)	63	50°36'N 01°12'W
Needles	62	50°39'N 01°35'W
Portland Bill	63	50°33'N 02°25'W
Beer Head (E Lyme Bay)	62	50°41'N 03°05'W

8 Lyme Regis to Land's End inc Isles of Scilly, 0110

Berry Head	63	50°24'N 03°29'W
Dartmouth	10	50°21'N 03°35'W
Prawle (Salcombe)	62	50°13'N 03°42'W
Rame Head	64	50°19'N 04°13'W
Fowey	10	50°20'N 04°38'W
Falmouth	62	50°09'N 05°03'W
Lizard	63	49°58'N 05°12'W
St Marys, Scilly *1880kHz*,	64	49°56'N 06°18'W
Trevose Head (in Area 9)	62	50°33'N 05°02'W

9 Land's End to St David's Head inc the Bristol Channel, 0150

Hartland Point	64	51°01'N 04°31'W
Combe Martin	63	51°12'N 04°03'W
Severn Bridges	64	51°36'N 02°38'W
St Hilary (Barry)	63	51°27'N 03°25'W
Mumbles (Swansea)	64	51°42'N 04°41'W
Tenby	62	51°41'N 05°10'W
St Ann's Head	62	51°40'N 05°11'W

10 St David's Head to Great Orme Head, inc St George's Channel, 0150

Dinas Hd (Fishguard)	64	52°00'N 04°54'W
Blaenplwyf (Aberystwyth)	62	52°22'N 04°06'W
South Stack (Holyhead)	63	53°19'N 04°41'W
Great Orme Head	64	53°20'N 03°51'W

11 Great Orme Head to the Mull of Galloway, 0130

Moel-y-Parc (NE Wales)	63	53°13'N 04°28'W
Langthwaite (Lancaster)	62	54°02'N 02°46'W
Caldbeck (Carlisle)	63	54°46'N 03°07'W

12 Isle of Man, 0130

Snaefell (Isle of Man)	64	54°16'N 04°28'W

13 Lough Foyle to Carlingford Lough, 0210

Slievemartin (Rostrevor)	64	54°06'N 06°10'W
Orlock Head (Bangor)	62	54°40'N 05°35'W
Black Mountain (Belfast)	63	54°35'N 06°01'W
West Torr (Fair Head)	64	55°12'N 06°06'W
Limavady (Lough Foyle)	10	55°06'N 06°53'W
Navar (Lower L Erne)	64	54°28'N 07°54'W

14 Mull of Galloway to Mull of Kintyre inc the Firth of Clyde and North Channel, 0210

Rhu Staffnish (Kintyre)	10	55°22'N 05°32'W
Lawhill (Ardrossan)	64	55°42'N 04°50'W
Clyde (Greenock)	62	55°58'N 04°48'W

15 Mull of Kintyre to Ardnamurchan Point, 0210

Kilchiaran (W Islay)	62	55°46'N 06°27'W
S Knapdale (Loch Fyne)	63	55°55'N 05°28'W

16 The Minch, 0110

Torosay (E Mull)	10	56°27'N 05°43'W
Glengorm (N Mull)	62	56°38'N 06°08'W
Tiree	*1883kHz*, 63	56°31'N 06°57'W
Arisaig (S of Mallaig)	64	56°55'N 06°50'W
Drumfearn (SE Skye)	63	57°12'N 05°48'W
Skriag (Portree, Skye)	10	57°23'N 06°15'W
Rodel (S Harris)	62	57°45'N 06°57'W
Melvaig (Loch Ewe)	64	5°50'N 05°47'W
Portnaguran (Stornoway)	63	58°15'N 06°10'W

17 Ardnamurchan Point to Cape Wrath, 0110

Barra	10	57°01'N 07°30'W
Clettreval (N Uist)	63	57°37'N 07°26'W
Forsnaval (W Lewis)	62	58°13'N 07°00'W
Butt of Lewis *1743kHz*,	10	58°28'N 06°14'W

18 Shetland Isles and 60 NM radius, 0110

Fitful Head (Sumburgh)	63	59°54'N 01°23'W
Saxavord (Unst)	63	60°42'N 00°51'W
Lerwick (Shetland)	62	60°10'N 01°08'W
Collafirth *1770kHz*,	64	60°32'N 01°23'W
Wideford Hill (Kirkwall)	64	58°59'N 03°01'W

NOTE: This Information can change. Check MCGA MSI leaflet (MCA/064) at www.mcga.gov.uk, and download our free monthly pdf updates from January to June at www.reedsnauticalalmanac.co.uk

Inshore waters forecast area boundaries used by the UK Coastguard

WEATHER

CHANNEL ISLANDS

Jersey Meteorological department

From the CI and UK call ☎ 0900 669 0022 (60p per min) for the Channel Islands recorded shipping forecast. From Guernsey only, call ☎ 12080; it is chargeable. For more detailed info call ☎ +44 1534 448770, www.gov.je/weather.

Forecasts include: general situation, 24hr forecast for wind, weather, vis, sea state, swell, sea temperature, plus 2 & 4 day outlooks and St Helier tide times/heights. The area is bounded by 50°N, 03°W and the mainland from Cap de la Hague to Ile de Bréhat.

Weather by public service radio

BBC Radio Guernsey 93·2 MHz, 99.0 MHz 1116 kHz broadcasts a weather bulletin for the waters around Guernsey, Herm and Sark at 0630 LT. It contains a synopsis, warnings, coastal forecast and coastal reports from Jersey, Guernsey, Alderney, Cap de la Hague, Cherbourg and Portland. ☎ 01481 200600. www.bbc.co.uk/guernseyguernsey@bbc.co.uk.

BBC Radio Jersey 1026 kHz, 88·8 MHz. Storm warnings on receipt. Wind info for Jersey waters: Mon-Fri 0725, 0825, 1325, 1725 LT; Sat/Sun 0725, 0825. ☎ 01534 870000

Shipping forecast for local waters: Mon-Fri @ H+00 (0600-1900, after the news) and 0625 & 1625 LT; Sat/Sun @ H+00 (0700-1300, after the news) and 0725 LT.

Jersey Coastguard broadcasts gale warnings, synopsis, 24h forecast, outlook for next 24 hrs and reports from observation stations on VHF Ch 82 (after prior announcement on Ch 16) at 0645 LT, 0745 LT, 0845 LT 1245 UT 1845 UT 2245 UT and on request on VHF Ch's 25 and 82. Gale warnings are also broadcast at 0307, 0907, 1507 and 2107 UT. Jersey Coastguard is part of CG and SAR services at St Helier. www.jersey-harbours.com ☎ 01534 447705.

REPUBLIC OF IRELAND (ROI)

Met Éireann (Irish Met Office) is at Glasnevin Hill, Dublin 9, Ireland. ☎ +353 1806 4200, 📠 +353 1 806 4247, www.met.ie. General forecasting division: ☎ 1806 4255, 📠 1806 4275 (H24, charges may apply).

Irish Coast radio stations

CRS and their VHF channels are listed below and shown opposite, (see: also www.malinheadcoastguardradio.com/index.htm). Weather bulletins for 30M offshore and the Irish Sea are broadcast on VHF at 0103, 0403, 0703, 1003, 1303, 1603, 1903 and 2203UT after an announcement on Ch 16. Broadcasts are made 1 hour earlier when DST is in force. Bulletins include gale warnings, synopsis and a 24-hour forecast.

MF Valentia Radio broadcasts forecasts for sea areas Shannon and Fastnet on 1752 kHz at 0833 & 2033 UT, and on request.

Gale warnings are broadcast on 1752 kHz on receipt and at 0303, 0903, 1503 and 2103 (UT) after an announcement on 2182 kHz.

Malin Head does not broadcast weather information on 1677 kHz. At Dublin there is no MF transmitter.

Malin Head	01,05	Carlingford	04
Glen Head	03	Dublin	03
Donegal Bay	02	Wicklow Head	02
Belmullet	63	Rosslare	05
Clew Bay	05	Mine Head	03
Clifden	03	Cork	02
Galway	04	Galley Head	16
Shannon	64	Mizen Head	04
Valentia	62	Bantry	05

Gale warnings are broadcast on these VHF channels on receipt and at 0033, 0633, 1233 and 1833 LT, after an announcement Ch 16.

Radio Telefís Éireann (RTE) Radio 1

RTE Radio 1 broadcasts weather bulletins daily at 0602, 1253 & 2355LT on 252kHz (LW) Summerhill (15M W ofDublin airport) and FM (88·2-95·2MHz).

Bulletins contain a situation, forecast and coastal reports. Forecasts include: wind, weather, vis, swell (if higher than 4m) and a 24 hrs outlook.

Gale warnings are included in hourly news bulletins on FM & MF.

Coastal reports include wind, weather, visibility, pressure and pressure tendency. The change over the last 3 hrs is described as:

Steady	=	0–0·4hPa
Rising/falling slowly	=	0·5–1·9
Rising/falling	=	2·0–3·4
Rising/falling rapidly	=	3·5–5·9
Rising/falling very rapidly	=	> 6·0

Weather by telephone

The latest sea area forecast and gale warnings are available as recorded messages H24 from Weatherdial. but only from Republic of Ireland landline or mobile numbers.

Dial ☎ 1550 123 plus the suffixes below:

850	Munster
851	Leinster
852	Connaught
853	Ulster
854	Dublin (plus winds in Dublin Bay and HW times)
855	Coastal waters and Irish Sea.

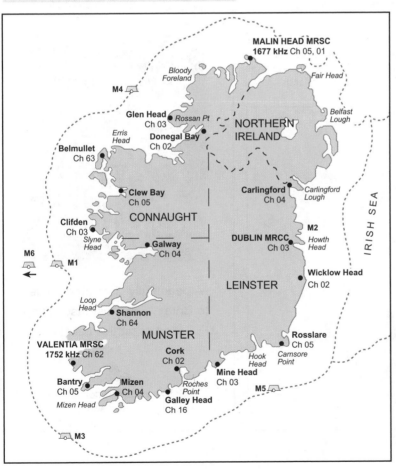

Provinces, headlands, sea areas and coastal stations referred to in weather broadcasts are shown here. Forecasts for coastal waters cover areas within 30M of the shore.

DENMARK

Lyngby Radio broadcasts, in Danish and English on MF/SSB1,734 kHz (Blåvand), 2,586 kHz (Rønne) and on VHF Blåvand, Ch 07. Gale warnings for Skagerrak, Fisher and German Bight are issued on receipt after announcement on 2187.5 kHz and Ch 16 with repeats on 2 182 kHz and Ch16. Forecasts will be provided on request.

Danish sea area forecasts in English are at: http://www.dmi.dk/products-in-english/

Weather bulletins and gale/storm warnings for Danish coastal waters and sea areas 2 to 6, 8 and 9 are broadcast in Danish on 243kHz AM, at 0545, 0845,1145 (plus 5 day forecast) and 1745 (plus 7 day forecast for coastal waters). Navigational warnings are broadcast at 1803 and Firing practice warnings at 1745 after the weather forecast. All LT.

Danmarks Meteorologiske Institut (DM)

Provides marine forecasts in **English** on www.dmi.dk/products-in-english/

'Wetter und warnfunk', a www.bsh/de/DE PDF document in German gives useful, clear information on GMDSS, and other forecasts from Denmark, Germany and the Netherlands.

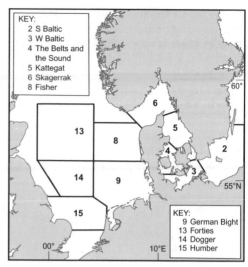

KEY:
- 2 S Baltic
- 3 W Baltic
- 4 The Belts and the Sound
- 5 Kattegat
- 6 Skagerrak
- 8 Fisher

KEY:
- 9 German Bight
- 13 Forties
- 14 Dogger
- 15 Humber

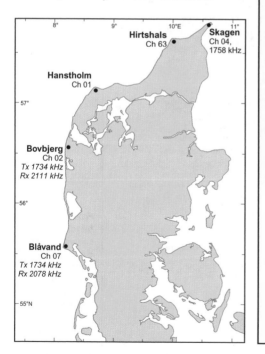

Hirtshals Ch 63
Skagen Ch 04, 1758 kHz
Hanstholm Ch 01
Bovbjerg Ch 02 Tx 1734 kHz Rx 2111 kHz
Blåvand Ch 07 Tx 1734 kHz Rx 2078 kHz

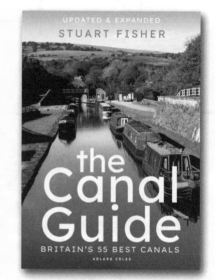

GERMANY
Deutscher Wetterdienst (DWD)

DWD provides a weather service for leisure and commercial sailors, SEEWIS and KUESTE. Current weather data and forecasts can be obtained by telephone/modem/DSL/WLAN and displayed on a PC or tablet. Users choose from an extensive range of information. Details, ☎ (+49) (0)69 8062 6190, ☎ (+49) (0)69 8062 6193, or seewis-online@dwd.de. Find English texts of marine forecasts on the dwd/de site at Wetter und Klima - Deutscher Wetterdienst - North and Baltic Sea.

Traffic Centres

Broadcast local storm/navigational warnings, weather, and visibility in German or **English.** North Sea Traffic also provides them on request.

Traffic Centre	VHF Ch	Every
Westcoast Traffic	15	H+20
North Sea Traffic	11	H+20
German Bight Traffic	79 (West) 80 (East)	H+00
Cuxhaven-Elbe Traffic	71 (outer Elbe)	H+35
Brunsbüttel-Elbe Traffic	68 (lower Elbe)	H+05
Kiel Kanal I+II (W part)	02,13	H+15 & H+45
Kiel Kanal III+IV (E part)	03,12	H+20 & H+50
Bremerhaven-Weser Traffic	02, 04, 05, 07, 21, 22, 82	H+20
Bremen-Weser Traffic	19, 78, 81	H+30
Hunte Traffic	63	H+30
Jade Traffic	20, 63	H+10
Ems Traffic	15, 18, 20, 21	H+50

Coast Radio Stations
DP07 (Seefunk) commercial CRS, below, at:
Nordfriesland (Sylt) Ch 26. **Elbe-Weser** Ch 24. **Hamburg** (Control centre) Ch 83. **Bremen** Ch 25. **Borkum** Ch 28. For Fisher, German Bight and Humber DPO7 broadcasts from late March to early October, in German. Gale and strong wind warnings on receipt. Forecasts for 12 hour with 12 hour outlook at 0745, 0945, 1245, 1645 and 1945 LT, 4–5 day outlook at 0945, 1645 and 1945. Hamburg Ch 83, Accumersiel Ch 28, Borkum Ch 61, Bremen Ch 25, Elbe-Weser Ch 24, Nordfriesland Ch 26.

Public Service Radio
Deutschlandfunk (DLF)
Gale and strong wind warnings, weather situation, forecast for 12 hours, 12 hour outlook, 3-day outlook and weather actuals for the North Sea after the news.

DAB+ Bremerhaven; Kiel; At 0105 0640 1810 LT. Also telephone +49 (0) 221 34 52 99 18.

Norddeutscher Rundfunk (NDR)
Gale and strong wind warnings, weather situation, forecast for 12 hours, 12 hour outlook, 3-day outlook and weather actuals for the North Sea.

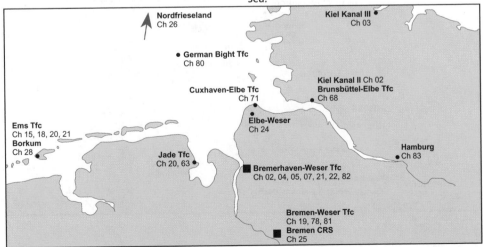

WEATHER

WEATHER

On FM at 0005 LT. **Eutin** 101·9 MHz; **Flensburg/ Eckernförde** 103·3 MHz; **Hamburg/Pinneberg** 88·7 MHz; **Heide** 104·4 MHz; **Helgoland** 107·4 MHz; **Itzehoe** 102·2MHz; **St Peter-Ording** 102·3 MHz; **Westerland** 90·3 MHz; **Aurich** 101·8 MHz; **Bremen**107·1 MHz; **Bremerhaven** 103·4 MHz; **Cuxhaven** 101·6 MHz. Also at 0005 0830 2205 LT on **NDR Info Spezial**.

Digital radio DAB+, satellite DVB-S radio, the **NDR radio app** and as livestream.

Recorded Telephone forecasts

Call ☎+49(0)69 8062 5799 (standard rates); after voice prompt select from the following table:

1	for the general situation report.
2	for the SW North Sea, German Bight and Fisher.
3	for the Skagerrak and Kattegat.
4	for the Baltic Sea (South and West).
5	for the German N Sea coast.
6	for the German Baltic coast.

NETHERLANDS

VHF MSI broadcasts

For coastal waters 30M out to sea and inland waters, in English and Dutch. Wind warnings (F6+) at 0333, 0733, 1133, 1533, 1933, 2333. Weather forecasts at 0805,1305, 1905, 2305, after prior announcement on Chs 16/70.

VHF Ch 23: Schiermonnikoog, Kornwerderzand, Wezep, Huisduinen (Den Helder), IJmuiden, Renesse, Woensdrecht.

VHF Ch 83: Appingedam, West Terschelling, Hoorn, Schoorl, Westkapelle. All stations monitor Ch 16.

Weather bulletins for specifically for the Westerschelde are also broadcast by **Vlissingen Traffic Centre** VHF Ch 14 every H+50 UTC. and **Terneuzen Traffic Centre** VHF Ch 11, every H+00 All times UTC.

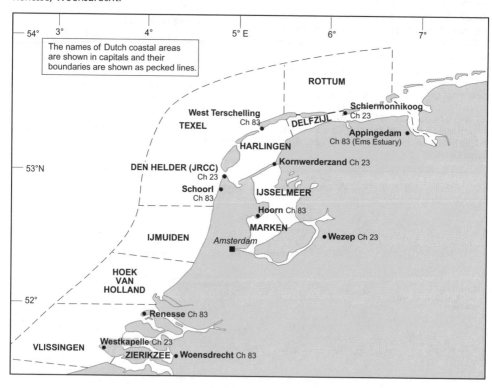

The names of Dutch coastal areas are shown in capitals and their boundaries are shown as pecked lines.

MF/SSB weather broadcasts in English

On 1890 kHz (Appingedam) and 3673 kHz (Scheveningen) after call on 2187·5 kHz. Wind warnings (F7+) for Dogger, Humber, Thames and German Bight at 0333, 7333, 1533, 1933, 2333. Forecasts at 0940, 2140, all UTC.

Radio Noord-Holland (FM)

Northern coastal area, gale warnings/wind strength in Dutch, Mon-Fri at 0730, 0838, 1005, 1230 and 1705LT; Sat/Sun 1005, by: **Haarlem** 97.6 MHz and **Wieringermeer** 93.9 MHz.

Omroep Zeeland (FM)

Southern coastal areas, synopsis, gale warnings / wind strength broadcast in Dutch, Mon-Fri at 0715, 0915, 1215 and 1715LT; Sat/Sun 1015, by:

Philippine 97.8 MHz and **Goes** 101.9 MHz.

BELGIUM, Coast radio stations

Oostende Radio, after prior notice on VHF 16, 24, DSC 70 and 2182kHz, broadcasts in **English** and Dutch on VHF 27, MF 2256, 2376 and 2761 kHz: Strong wind warnings on receipt and after the next 2 silent periods. Forecasts for Thames, Dover and the Belgian coast at 0720 LT and 0820, 1720 UT.

Oostende Radio broadcasts in **English** and Dutch on VHF Ch 24 for the Schelde estuary: Gale warnings on receipt and at every H+48 LT. Also strong wind warnings (F6+) on receipt and at every H+48 LT.

Zeebrugge Traffic Centre broadcasts weather for the Westerschelde on VHF Ch 69 every H+10 LT.

FRANCE

Le Guide Marine a free annual booklet which summarises French weather forecasts, warnings and broadcasts is usually available from marinas or from www.meteofrance.fr/publications/nos-collections/guides-pratiques/guide-marine.

CROSS VHF and MF broadcasts

CROSS broadcasts Met bulletins in French, after an announcement on Ch 16. In the English Channel broadcasts can be given in English, on request Ch 16. Broadcasts include: Any gale warnings, general situation, 24 hrs forecast (actual weather, wind, sea state and vis) and further trends for coastal waters, which extend 20M offshore. VHF channels, remote stations and local times are shown below. A useful source of texts for all Météo France marine forecasts is www.meteo-marine.com/meteo-marine

Gale warnings feature in Special Met Bulletins (*Bulletins Météorologique Spéciaux* or BMS). They are broadcast in French by all CROSS on VHF at H+03 and at other times on MF frequencies as shown below.

CROSS GRIS-NEZ Ch 79
Belgian border to Baie de la Somme

Dunkerque	0720, 1603, 1920
St Frieux	0710, 1545, 1910

Baie de la Somme to Cap de la Hague

St Valéry-en-Caux
0703, 1533, 1903
Gale warnings for areas 12-13 are broadcast in French on MF 1650 & 2677 kHz at 0833 & 2033LT

CROSS JOBOURG Ch 80
Baie de la Somme to Cap de la Hague

Antifer	0803, 1633, 2003
Port-en-Bessin	0745, 1615, 1945
Jobourg	0733, 1603, 1933

Cap de la Hague to Pointe de Penmarc'h

Jobourg	0715, 1545, 1915
Granville	0703, 1533, 1903

Gale warnings for areas 13-14 in **English** on receipt and at H+20 and H+50. No gale warnings on MF.

French forecast areas

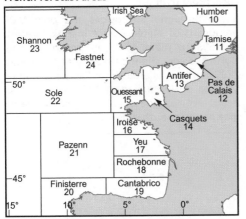

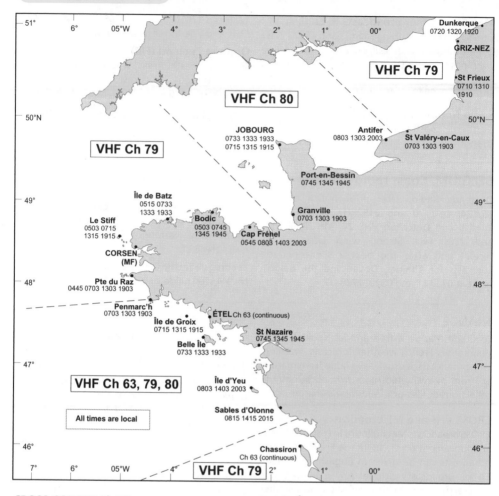

CROSS CORSEN Ch 79
Cap de la Hague to Pte de Penmarc'h (Times in bold = 1 May to 30 Sep only).
Cap Fréhel 0545, 0803, **1203**, 1633, 2003 **Bodic**
0533, 0745, **1145**, 1615, 1945

Ile de Batz	0515, 0733, **1133**, 1603, 1933
Le Stiff	0503, 0715, **1115**, 1545, 1915
Pte du Raz	0445, 0703, **1103**, 1533, 1903

Corsen broadcasts gale warnings for areas 13-22 in French at 0815 and 2015LT on MF 1650 & 2677 kHz.

CROSS ÉTEL Chs 63, 80
Pte de Penmarc'h to l'Anse de l'Aiguillon
(46° 15'N 01°10'W). Étel has no MF freqs

Penmarc'h	0703, 1533, 1903
Ile de Groix	0715, 1545, 1915
Belle Ile	0733, 1603, 1933
Saint-Nazaire	0745, 1615, 1945
Ile d'Yeu	0803, 1633, 2003
Les Sables d'Olonne	0815, 1645, 2015

CROSS ÉTEL Ch 79 L'Anse de l'Aiguillon to Spanish border
Chassiron every 20 minutes

Local radio (FM)

Radio Bretagne 5 provides the only MW broadcasts of Météo France marine forecast on 1593kHz/188m. All LT, in French. For the North Sea and Atlantic sea areas at 0740, and 2205. For coastal areas from Cap de la Hague to Anse de l'Aiguillon at 1330. This can be heard over a wide area but signal strength may be poor south of Brest.

Forecasts by telephone

Automatic service ☎ 08·99·71·08·08 (€2·99 plus call charge). The menu provides:

Bulletin Rivage, (2 miles out to sea) Nine day forecasts updated 3 times daily.

Bulletin Côtier, (20 miles out to sea) Seven day forecast updated 3 times daily.

Bulletin Large, (Offshore sea area) Seven day forecast updated twice daily.

	30°		20°		10° W		9° W
	FARADAY		ROMEO		PAZENN		
45° — 45°N						FINISTERRE	7° W
	ALTAIR		CHARCOT		41°50'N		
					PORTO		
40° — 40°N					39°N		
	AÇORES		JOSEPHINE		SAO VICENTE	CADIZ	
35° — 35°N	35°W		22°W		CASABLANCA		

Forecast areas for the Eastern Atlantic and Coastal/Offshore Areas off France, Spain, Portugal and North West Africa

WEATHER VOCABULARY

ENGLISH	GERMAN	FRENCH	DUTCH
Air mass	Luftmasse	Masse d'air	Luchtmassa
Anticyclone	Antizyklonisch	Anticyclone	Hogedrukgebied
Area	Gebiet	Zone	Gebied
Backing wind	Rückdrehender Wind	Vent reculant	Krimpende wind
Barometer	Barometer	Baromètre	Barometer
Breeze	Brise	Brise	Bries
Calm	Flaute	Calme	Kalmte
Centre	Zentrum	Centre	Centum
Clouds	Wolken	Nuages	Wolken
Cold	Kalt	Froid	Koud
Cold front	Kaltfront	Front froid	Kou front
Cyclonic	Zyklonisch	Cyclonique	Cycloonachtig
Decrease	Abnahme	Affaiblissement	Afnemen
Deep	Tief	Profond	Diep
Deepening	Vertiefend	Approfondissant	Verdiepend
Depression	Sturmtief	Dépression	Depressie
Direction	Richtung	Direction	Richting
Dispersing	Auflösend	Se dispersant	Oplossend
Disturbance	Störung	Perturbation	Verstoving
Drizzle	Niesel	Bruine	Motregen
East	Ost	Est	Oosten
Extending	Ausdehnung	S'étendant	Uitstrekkend
Extensive	Ausgedehnt	Etendu	Uitgebreid
Falling	Fallend	Descendant	Dalen
Filling	Auffüllend	Secomblant	Vullend
Fog	Nebel	Brouillard	Nevel
Fog bank	Nebelbank	Ligne de brouillard	Mist bank
Forecast	Vorhersage	Prévision	Vooruitzicht
Frequent	Häufig	Fréquent	Veelvuldig
Fresh	Frisch	Frais	Fris
Front	Front	Front	Front
Gale	Sturm	Coup de vent	Storm
Gale warning	Sturmwarnung	Avis de coup de vent	Stormwaarschuwing
Good	Gut	Bon	Goed
Gradient	Druckunterschied	Gradient	Gradiatie
Gust, squall	Bö	Rafalle	Windvlaag
Hail	Hagel	Grêle	Hagel
Haze	Diesig	Brume	Nevel
Heavy	Schwer	Abondant	Zwaar
High	Hoch	Anticyclone	Hoog
Increasing	Zunehmend	Augmentant	Toenemend
Isobar	Isobar	Isobare	Isobar
Isolated	Vereinzelt	Isolé	Verspreid
Lightning	Blitze	Eclair de foudre	Bliksem
Local	Örtlich	Locale	Plaatselijk
Low	Tief	Dépression	Laag
Mist	Dunst	Brume légere	Mist
Moderate	Mäßig	Modéré	Matig
Moderating	Abnehmend	Se modérant	Matigend
Moving	Bewegend	Se déplacant	Bewegend
North	Nord	Nord	Noorden
Occluded	Okklusion	Couvert	Bewolkt
Poor	Schlecht	Mauvais	Slecht
Precipitation	Niederschlag	Précipitation	Neerslag
Pressure	Druck	Pression	Druk
Rain	Regen	Pluie	Regen
Ridge	Hochdruckbrücke	Crête	Rug
Rising	Ansteigend	Montant	Stijgen
Rough	Rauh	Agitée	Ruw
Sea	See	Mer	Zee
Seaway	Seegang	Haute mer	Zee

ENGLISH	GERMAN	FRENCH	DUTCH
Scattered	Vereinzelt	Sporadiques	Verspreid
Shower	Schauer	Averse	Bui
Slight	Leicht	Un peu	Licht
Slow	Langsam	Lent	Langzaam
Snow	Schnee	Neige	Sneeuw
South	Süd	Sud	Zuiden
Storm	Sturm	Tempête	Storm
Sun	Sonne	Soleil	Zon
Swell	Schwell	Houle	Deining
Thunder	Donner	Tonnerre	Donder
Thunderstorm	Gewitter	Orage	Onweer
Trough	Trog, Tiefausläufer	Creux	Trog
Variable	Umlaufend	Variable	Veranderlijk
Veering	Rechtdrehend	Virement de vent	Ruimende wind
Warm front	Warmfront	Front chaud	Warm front
Weather	Wetter	Temps	Weer
Wind	Wind	Vent	Wind
Weather report	Wetterbericht	Météo	Weer bericht
			meteorologica

WEATHER

A step-by-step handbook with tried and tested solutions
for handling the most common sailing situations

 Visit **www.adlardcoles.com** to buy at discount

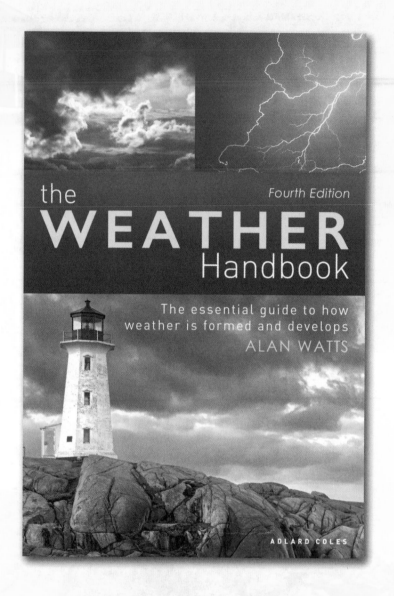

the
WEATHER
Handbook

Fourth Edition

The essential guide to how
weather is formed and develops
ALAN WATTS

ADLARD COLES

'The perfect introduction
to understanding weather'
– *Practical Boat Owner*

Chapter 3 – Communications

COMMUNICATIONS

RADIO OPERATION

Avoiding interference

Before transmitting, first listen on the VHF channel. If occupied, wait for a break before transmitting, or choose another channel. If you cause interference you must comply immediately with any request from a Coastguard or Coast radio station to stop transmitting.

Control of communications

Ship-to-Shore: Communications between ship and shore stations are controlled by the latter, except in distress, urgency or safety cases.

Intership: The ship *called* controls communication. If you call another ship, then it has control. If you are called by a ship, you assume control. If a shore-based station breaks in, both ships must comply with instructions given.

Radio confidentiality

Private conversations heard on the radio must not be reproduced, passed on or otherwise used.

Making yourself understood

Clear R/T speech is vital. If a message cannot be understood by the receiver it is useless. Messages which have to be written down at the receiving station should be spoken slowly. This gives time for it to be written down by the receiving operator. If the transmitting operator himself writes it down all should be well. The average reading speed is 250 words a minute, whilst average writing speed is only 20.

When speaking, consider the following:

- **What** to say, ie *voice Procedure*
- **How** to say it, ie *voice Technique*

Voice Procedure is discussed below and overleaf. It includes procedural words, callsigns, making contact etc.

Voice Technique depends on a few simple rules:

Hold the microphone a few inches in front of the mouth and speak directly into it at a normal level. Speak clearly so that there can be no confusion. The voice should be pitched up at a higher level than normal. Do not drop the voice pitch at the end of a phrase or sentence. Emphasise words with weak syllables; 'Tower', if badly pronounced, could sound like 'tar'. Non Anglophones, or people with strong regional accents must try to pronounce words as clearly as possible.

Difficult words may be spelled phonetically, preceded with 'I spell'. If the word can be pronounced, include it before and after it has been spelt. For example, the message 'I will berth on the yacht *Coila*' would be sent as: 'I will berth on the yacht *Coila* – I spell – Charlie Oscar India Lima Alfa – *Coila*'.

The phonetic alphabet (ITU)

The syllables to emphasise are underlined

Letter	Morse	Phonetic	Spoken as
A	• –	Alfa	AL-fah
B	– • • •	Bravo	BRAH-voh
C	– • – •	Charlie	CHAR-lee
D	– • •	Delta	DELL-tah
E	•	Echo	ECK-oh
F	• • – •	Foxtrot	FOKS-trot
G	– – •	Golf	GOLF
H	• • • •	Hotel	hoh-TELL
I	• •	India	IN-dee-ah
J	• – – –	Juliett	JEW-lee-ett
K	– • –	Kilo	KEY-loh
L	• – • •	Lima	LEE-mah
M	– –	Mike	MIKE
N	– •	November	no-VEM-ber
O	– – –	Oscar	OSS-car
P	• – – •	Papa	pa-PAH
Q	– – • –	Quebec	keh-BECK
R	• – •	Romeo	ROW-me-oh
S	• • •	Sierra	see-AIR-rah
T	–	Tango	TANG-go
U	• • –	Uniform	OO-nee-form
V	• • • –	Victor	VIK-tah
W	• – –	Whiskey	WISS-key
X	– • • –	X-ray	ECKS-ray
Y	– • – –	Yankee	YANG-key
Z	– – • •	Zulu	ZOO-loo

Phonetic numerals

When numerals are transmitted, the following pronunciations make them easier to understand.

No	Morse	Spoken	No	Morse	Spoken
1	• – – – –	WUN	6	– • • • •	SIX
2	• • – – –	TOO	7	– – • • •	SEV-EN
3	• • • – –	TREE	8	– – – • •	AIT
4	• • • • –	FOW-ER	9	– – – – •	NIN-ER
5	• • • • •	FIFE	0	– – – – –	ZERO

Numerals are transmitted digit by digit except that multiples of thousands may be spoken as follows:

Numeral	Spoken as
44	FOW-ER FOW-ER
90	NIN-ER ZERO
136	WUN TREE SIX
500	FIFE ZERO ZERO
1478	WUN FOW-ER SEV-EN AIT
7000	SEV-EN THOU-SAND

Punctuation

Punctuation marks should be used only where their omission would cause confusion.

Mark	Word	Spoken as
.	Decimal	DAY-SEE-MAL
,	Comma	COMMA
.	Stop	STOP

Procedural words or 'prowords'

These are used to shorten transmissions

All after and **All before.** Used after proword *'say again'* to request repetition of a part of a message

Correct Reply to repeat of message that was preceded by prowords *'read back for check'* when it has been correctly repeated. Often said twice

Correction Cancel the last word or group of words. The correct word or group follows. Spoken when an error has been made in a transmission.

I say again I repeat the transmission or the part indicated (see 'All after' and 'All before').

I spell I shall spell the next word or group of letters phonetically

Out This is the end of working to you

Over Invitation to reply

Read back If the receiver is doubtful about accuracy of all or part of message he may repeat it back to the sending station, preceding the repetition with prowords *'I read back'*

Station calling Used when a station is uncertain of the calling station's identification/callsign

This is This transmission is from the station whose callsign or name immediately follows

Wait If a called station cannot accept traffic immediately, it will reply **'WAIT.......MINUTES'**, with reason if delay may exceed 10 minutes

Word after or Word before Used after the proword *'say again'* to request repetition

Wrong Reply to repetition of message preceded by prowords *'read back'* when it has been incorrectly repeated

Calls, calling and callsigns

Shore stations normally use a callsign of their geographic name followed by Coastguard or Radio, eg Solent Coastguard, Dublin Radio etc. Vessels usually identify themselves by the ship's name but the International callsign may be used in certain cases. If two yachts have the same or confusingly similar names, give your International callsign when starting communications, and thereafter use your ship's name as callsign.

'All ships' broadcast

Address used by Coastguard Radio where broadcast information is to be received or used by all who intercept it, eg gale warnings etc. No reply is needed.

Communicating with a coast radio station

Call initially on a working channel or very briefly on channel 16 to establish a working channel.

- Pause to check the working channel is clear before transmitting
- Use low power *(1 watt)* if close enough, ie up to 10 miles away. High power *(25 watts)* drains more from the battery
- The callsign of calling station up to three times only, and prowords 'This is'
- Say how many R/T calls you have to make
- Proword 'Over'

Using high power decreases battery state and the range your VHF will achieve. Continued calling also clutters up the channel and denies access to other users.

Aerial faults commonly reduce your transmitting range. Possibly the station aerial for the channel chosen is directionally orientated and you are on the wrong side. Try another channel or station. Call again when closer.

RADIO DATA

SHORT, MEDIUM and LONG RANGE RADIO COMMUNICATIONS

A suitable radio receiver on board will provide weather forecasts and time signals at scheduled times on a number of frequencies in various wavebands. With a maritime receiver you are not limited to the familiar BBC and commercial broadcasts. HM Coastguard transmit navigation warnings, storm warnings and weather messages for shipping in their respective sea areas.

Short range radiotelephony (RT) transmits and receives on VHF channels in the marine VHF (Very High Frequency) band. The equipment and procedures are simple, but range is normally limited to about 20 miles from ship to shore, rather less from ship to ship. Interconnection with national telephone systems is possible on certain VHF/RT channels when a yacht is within range of a Coast Radio Station, although there are now no such stations on the mainland of the UK, France or the Netherlands. Mobile telephones are now by far the most common form of ship to shore communication.

Medium range two-way communication operate in the marine MF (medium frequency) RT band, the 2MHz 'trawler band'. Single sideband techniques are employed on these medium frequencies and SSB equipment is essential. The effective range depends on the power of the transmitter and the sensitivity of the associated receiver; in general this might be up to 200 miles from certain (but not all) Coast Radio Stations.

THE MARINE VHF BAND

VHF is used by most vessels, Coast Radio Stations, CG centres and other rescue services. Its range is slightly better than the line of sight between the transmitting and receiving aerials. A good aerial, as high as possible, is most important.

In the Marine VHF band (156·00–174·00 MHz) the individual frequencies are separated from their neighbours by exactly 25kHz 'elbow-room' to eliminate mutual interference. Each frequency is given a channel number, not necessarily consecutive. Thus 55 channels are available, plus some with special purposes (see below).

VHF Channel Grouping

Channels are grouped for three main purposes, but some can be used for more than one purpose. They are listed below in their preferred order of usage:

- **Public correspondence** (ie link calls via CRS into the shore telephone system): Ch 26, 27, 25, 24, 23, 28, 04, 01, 03, 02, 07, 05, 84, 87, 86, 83, 85, 88, 61, 64, 65, 62, 66, 63, 60, 82, 78, 81.

- **Inter-ship:** Ch 06, 08, 10, 13, 09, 72, 73, 67, 69, 77, 15, 17. Remember these, so that if another vessel calls you, you can swiftly nominate a working channel from within this group.

- **Port Operations:**
Ch 12, 14, 11, 13, 09, 68, 71, 74, 69, 73, 17, 15, 20, 22, 18, 19, 21, 05, 07, 02, 03, 01, 04, 78, 82, 79, 81, 80, 60, 63, 66, 62, 65, 64, 61, 84.

Special purposes. The following channels have one specific purpose only:

Ch 0 (156·00 MHz): SAR ops, not available to yachts.

Ch's 10 (156·50 MHz), **62** (160·725 MHz), **63** (160·775 MHz) and **64** (160·825 MHz): HMCG MSI broadcasts, (after prior announcement Ch 16).

Ch 13 (156·650 MHz): Intership safety of navigation (sometimes referred to as bridge-to-bridge); a possible channel for calling a merchant ship if no contact on Ch 16.

Ch 16 (156·80 MHz): Distress, Safety and calling. See Chapter 4 for Distress and Safety. Ch 16 is monitored by UK and Irish CG rescue centres (speaker based listening watch) along with DSC Ch 70. Commercial vessels are required to monitor

DSC Ch 70. Although vessels are no longer required to monitor Ch 16 it is always advised and good seamanship too. After an initial call, the stations concerned **must** switch to a working channel, except for Distress and Safety matters.

Ch 67 (156·375 MHz): the Small Craft Safety channel in the UK, accessed via Ch 16.

Ch 70 (156·525 MHz): exclusively for digital selective calling for Distress and Safety purposes.

Ch 80 (157·025 MHz): the primary working channel between yachts and UK marinas.

Ch M (157·85 MHz): the secondary working channel between yachts and UK marinas. For use in UK territorial waters only.

Ch M2 (161·425 MHz): for race control, with Ch M as stand-by. YCs often use Ch M2. For use in UK territorial waters only.

SILENCE PERIODS

The periods are the 3 minutes immediately after the whole and half hours, ie H to H+03 and H+30 to H+33, when no transmissions should be made.

MEDIUM RANGE MF RADIO

Single sideband MF/RT provides communications in the offshore waters of the UK and Western Europe where small craft may be out of VHF contact. A receiver alone gives the ability to hear weather bulletins, storm and navigation warnings for local sea areas broadcast from CRS in the 1.6 to 4.0MHz maritime band, ie on frequencies from 1605 to 4200 kHz.

MF transmissions tend to follow the curvature of the earth, which makes them suitable for direction-finding. For this reason, and because of their good range, the marine Distress R/T frequency (2182 kHz) is in the MF band.

TRAFFIC LISTS

If a Coast Radio station has messages for a vessel, but is unable to contact her, that vessel's name will be added to the Traffic List broadcast at (usually) two hour intervals. This is not a system much used by yachts and small craft.

LONG RANGE HF RADIO

HF radios use short wave frequencies in the 4, 8, 12, 16 and 22 MHz bands, as chosen to suit propagation conditions. HF is more expensive than MF and requires more power, but can provide worldwide coverage. A good installation and skilled operating techniques are essential for satisfactory results.

GLOBAL COMMUNICATIONS

Once out of range of VHF/MF or wireless telephony/broadband service, the yachtsman's communications options are limited to MF/HF radio and satellite systems (Satcoms).

A yachtsman embarking on an extended offshore venture would usually choose a mix of equipment for sensible reasons of redundancy, this will allow a choice of listening and transmitting, via terrestrial and satellite radio systems, to meet his needs at various times and in different circumstances. A typical setup might include a fixed or handheld satcoms transceiver, a HF SSB transceiver and receiver. For data capability, these would be interfaced to an on-board PC.

HF/single sideband radio (HF-SSB)

HF SSB radios use frequencies in the 4, 8, 12, 16 and 22 MHz bands (short wave), provide worldwide coverage and usually include MF frequencies as well.

Despite rapid growth in marine satellite communications, HF SSB remains a popular choice amongst long-distance cruisers, providing a cost-free voice (and limited email) capability for cruisers, sometimes operating over vast distances. Operators have the Long Range Certificate (LRC) or General Operators Certificate (GOC). To use Amateur (ham) bands (giving more frequencies and higher power, therefore range) operators must take the ham examination.

Using HF SSB radio for email requires a radio modem, often proprietary to the supplier. Though slow and requiring some skill to operate effectively, the almost-nil operating costs appeal to many and SSB radio has a strong following amongst blue-water cruisers. Established suppliers include Sailmail and Globe Wireless.

HF SSB radio is also extensively used for receipt of weatherfax images, although a receive-only SSB radio (with an adequate, grounded antenna installation) may be used rather than a full transceiver. Though declining in popularity, several useful weatherfax transmitting stations remain, including Northwood, UK and Offenbach, Germany.

Satellite Communications (Satcoms)

Satellite communications systems operate over **Ultra High Frequency (UHF)** radio using digital technology that makes them simpler-to-operate and more reliable for voice (and data) communications than HF SSB radio; they operate with either a dedicated ship installation or a standalone handheld terminal. Apart from the equipment purchase (and installation if necessary), ongoing costs usually include a monthly service fee and usage charges that will be related to either the amount of satellite time used, or the volume of data transmitted and received.

For two-way voice communications, the 'Ship Station' (aka 'Mobile Earth Station') transmits to a visible satellite that is simultaneously in sight of a 'Land Earth Station', eg Goonhilly, Cornwall. From there, the call is routed to its destination through the normal terrestrial telephone network.

The satellite 'constellations' have different architectures. Inmarsat for example has four geostationary (GEO) satellites, one each positioned over the Pacific and Indian oceans and two over the Atlantic. Because they are comparatively high up 19,400M (36,000km), each satellite has a large signal 'footprint', overlapping the next one and thus world-wide coverage is provided (although not in the polar regions above about 70°N and 70°S).

Other systems employ many more Low Earth Orbit (LEO) satellites orbiting the Earth about 540M (1,000km) above the surface.

The smaller, low-data rate, handheld voice terminals incorporate an omni-directional antenna that works best with an unobstructed view of the satellite. Fixed installations use an external gyro-stabilised antenna (to keep it pointing at the satellite as the boat moves); more powerful systems that support higher data rates employ antenna radomes that are really too large for installation aboard a 10–15m yacht.

The GMDSS provides automatic distress, urgency and safety communications, with some satcom systems (eg Inmarsat C) providing a red button that alerts a Maritime Rescue Coordination Centre (MRCC) when pressed.

There are several service providers, each offering an array of capabilities. The table opposite provides a useful summary of systems that might be used aboard a 10–20m yacht.

This is a fast moving market place and you should check with manufacturers/retailers for up-to-date specifications and prices.

COMMUNICATIONS

[1] typical, if in coverage area [2] using VOIP [3] Likely to be expensive	Wired Broadband	Wi-Fi	Cellular GSM	Cellular GPRS	Cellular 3G	Wi-Max
Range offshore[1] (NM)	0	0-1	0-15	0-15	0-15	0-30
Voice communication	Y[2]	Y[2]	Y	Y	Y	Y[2]
Text messages	Y	Y	Y	Y	Y	Y
Light email traffic	Y	Y	Y[3]	Y	Y	Y
Text weather forecasts	Y	Y	Y[3]	Y	Y	Y
Heavy email traffic	Y	Y	✗	Y[3]	Y	Y
Graphical weather forecasts	Y	Y	✗	Y[3]	Y	Y
Full web browsing	Y	Y	✗	Y[3]	Y	Y

SATELLITE COMMUNICATION SERVICES

System	Antenna	Satellites	Coverage	GMDSS	Phone (voice)	Fax	SMS text	Position tracking	Data rate
INMARSAT C	Omni-directional	4 GEO	Global excepting polar regions	Yes	No	Yes	Yes	Yes (GPS)	Very low, uneconomic for email
Iridium Certus	Omni-directional	66 LEO	Global	Yes	Yes	Yes	Yes	No	352kpbs to 704kbps (1408kbps planned)
Globalstar	Omni-directional	40 LEO	Global excepting polar regions	No	Yes	Yes	Yes	To 10km	9.6kbps uncompressed, 38.6kbps compressed, 56k with data kit
Fleet Broadband	Gyro-stabilised 40cms diameter	GEO	Global excepting polar regions	Yes	Yes	Yes	Yes	No	To 284kpbs
Thuraya	Omni-directional	2 GEO	Europe, N Africa & Middle East	No	Yes	Yes	Yes	Yes (GPS)	Satphone 60kbps download 15kbps upload or 384kbps-444kbpsvia high speed IP+ data terminal

PORT AND/OR MARINA VHF CHANNELS AND TELEPHONE DETAILS

In larger ports it is sensible to monitor the VTS channel (if any) or the primary port channel (in bold) before changing to a marina channel. Times are local, unless marked UT. Abbreviations are at the front of the book. Telephone codes are shown only once unless more than one applies.

ENGLAND – SOUTH COAST

ISLES OF SCILLY, St Mary's HM Ch 14 (0800-1700); ☎ 01720 422768. *Falmouth CG* covers Scilly and the TSS off Land's End on Ch 23. **Tresco** HM ☎ 07778 601237.

NEWLYN HM Ch 09, **12** (M-F: 0800-1700, Sat: 0800-1200). ☎ 01736 362523.

PENZANCE HM Ch 09, **12** (M-F: 0830-1730 and HW –2 to +1). ☎ 01736 366113.

FALMOUTH *Falmouth Hbr Radio* Ch 11, **12**, 14 (M-F 0800-1700). ☎ 01326 310991.

Ch 80: Falmouth ☎ 316620 and Port Pendennis marinas ☎ 311113. **Ch 12**: Falmouth Haven ☎ 310991; St Mawes HM ☎ 270553. **Ch M (HO)**: Mylor Yacht Hbr ☎ 372121.

TRURO HM *Carrick One* Ch 12. ☎ 01872 272130. **Ch M (HO)**: Malpas Marine ☎ 271260.

MEVAGISSEY HM Ch 14 (Summer: 0900-2100, Winter: 0900-1700). ☎ 01726 842496.

CHARLESTOWN HM Ch 14, HW –2 to +1, only when a vessel is expected. ☎ 01726 70241.

FOWEY HM Ch 12 (0900-1700); also Hbr Patrol (0900-2000). ☎ 01726 832471. Water taxi: Ch 06.

LOOE. HM Ch 16, occas. ☎ 01503 262839.

PLYMOUTH *Long Room Port Control* Ch 14 H24, ☎ 01752 836528. **QAB** Ch 80, ☎ 671142. **Sutton Hbr lock**: Ch 12 H24, ☎ 204702. **Cattewater HM** Ch 14 (M-F 0900-1700), ☎ 836528. **Plymouth Yacht Haven**, Ch 80, M; ☎ 404231. **King Point Marina** ☎ 424297. **Mayflower Marina**, Ch 80; ☎ 556633.

SALCOMBE HM & launch: Ch 14, May to mid-Sep: 7/7, 0600-2100; otherwise: M-F 0900-1600; ☎ 01548 843791. *Hbr Taxi* Ch 12. Fuel barge Ch 06, ☎ 07801 798862. **Island CC** ☎ 531776.

DARTMOUTH HM *Dartnav* Ch 11, 7/7 0730-dusk; ☎ 01803 832337. Darthaven marina Ch 80, ☎ 752242. Dart marina Ch 80, ☎ 837161. Noss marina ☎ 839087. Fuel barge Ch 06. Yacht taxi Ch 69.

TORBAY HBRS Brixham Marina Ch 80, ☎ 01803 882929; YC, ☎ 853332, & Water taxi *Shuttle* Ch M. Torquay Marina Ch 80, ☎ 200210. Fuel Ch M.

EXETER Exmouth Marina Ch 14, ☎ 01395 269314. Retreat BY: Ch M, ☎ 01392 874720. **Port of Exeter** HM Ch 12, M-F: 0730-1730 and when vessel due; ☎ 07864 958658.

LYME REGIS HM Ch 14. Summer 0800-2000, winter 1000-1500. ☎ 01297 442137.

BRIDPORT HM Ch 11. ☎ 01308 423222.

PORTLAND PORT Port Control Ch 74 (H24). ☎ 01305 824044. **Marina** ☎ 03454 302012.

WEYMOUTH HM & Town Bridge: Ch 12, M-F 0800-2000 summer & when vessel due; ☎ 01305 838423. **Marina** Ch 80, ☎ 767576. **Fuel** Ch 60.

POOLE
HM Ch 14 (H24); Code 01202 ☎ 440233.
Poole Bridge Ch12.
Marinas Ch 80 M: Salterns ☎ 709971. Parkstone YC ☎ 743610. Poole Quay ☎ 649488. Cobbs Quay ☎ 674299.

YARMOUTH (IoW)
HM & Yar bridge **Ch 68** H24. ☎ 01983 760321. Water taxi **Ch 15**.

LYMINGTON
Marinas Ch 80, M: Yacht Haven ☎ 01590 677071. Berthon Marina ☎ 01590 673312.

COWES
Harbour Radio, Chain Ferry & Folly Inn Ch 69 Mon-Fri: 0800-1700. Marinas **Ch 80, M**. Tel code 01983: Yacht Haven ☎ 299975. Shepards ☎ 297821. East Cowes ☎ 293983. Island Hbr **Ch 80**, ☎ 822999. Water Taxi **Ch 06**.

NEWPORT HM & Yacht Hbr Ch 69 0800-1600. ☎ 01983 823885.

RYDE HM Ch 80. Summer 0900-2000, Winter HX. ☎ 01983 613903. Access HW±2.

BEMBRIDGE Marina **Ch 80**, ☎ 01983 872828. Water Taxi **Ch 80**.

SOUTHAMPTON
Port Ops and VTS Ch 12 14. Marinas **Ch 80, M**. Tel code 02380: Hythe ☎ 207073. Ocean Village ☎ 229385. Shamrock Quay ☎ 229461. Kemp's ☎ 632323. Town Quay ☎ 234397.

HAMBLE
Hbr Radio Ch 68 Apr-Sep daily 0600-2200; Oct-Mar 0700-1830. Marinas **Ch 80, M**. Tel code 02380: Hamble Pt ☎ 452464. Port Hamble ☎ 452741. Mercury ☎ 455994. Water Taxi **Ch 77**, ☎ 454512. Tel code 01489: Universal ☎ 574272. Swanwick ☎ 884081.

PORTSMOUTH
VTS **Ch 11** (& *QHM* if essential). Marinas **80**. Tel code 02392: Haslar ☎ 601201. Gosport ☎ 524811. Royal Clarence ☎ 523810. Port Solent ☎ 210765. **THE CAMBER** (Commercial Hbr): *Portsmouth Hbr Radio* **Ch 11** 14 (H24).

LANGSTONE HBR
HM **Ch 12**. Summer, daily 0830-1700; Winter, M-F 0830-1700; Sat/Sun 0830-1300. Southsea Marina **Ch 80, M, ☎** 02392 822719.

CHICHESTER
HM *Chichester Hbr Radio* **Ch 14**. 1 Apr-Sep: M-Fri: 0830-1700. Sat: 0900-1300. 1 Oct - 31 Mar: 0900-1300, 1400-1700. Marinas **Ch 80, M**. Sparkes ☎ 02392 463572. Tel code 01243: Northney ☎ 466321. Emsworth Yacht Hbr ☎ 377727. Thornham ☎ 375335. Birdham Pool ☎ 512310. Chichester ☎ 512731. Water taxi **Ch 08** 0900-1800, mobile 07970 378350

LITTLEHAMPTON HM/Bridge **Ch 71** 0900-1700. Marina **Ch 80, M;** ☎ 01903 241663.

SHOREHAM HM & lock *Shoreham Hbr Radio* **Ch 14** (H24). Marina ☎ 01273 593801.

BRIGHTON
Marina *Brighton Control* **Ch M 80;** ☎ 01273 819919.

NEWHAVEN HM & Bridge *Newhaven Radio* **Ch 12**. HM / Port Control 612926 (H24). Marina **Ch 80, M;** ☎ 01273 513881.

EASTBOURNE
Sovereign Hbr, inc lock/berthing: **Ch 17.** ☎ 01323 470099.

RYE *Hbr Radio,* **Ch 14** 0900-1700 or when ship due. ☎ 01797 225225.

FOLKESTONE
Port Control **Ch 15** for entry; ☎ 01303 254597.

DOVER
Port Control **Ch 74** for entry. Marina Ch 80; ☎ 01304 241663.

RAMSGATE
Port Control **Ch 14**. Marina **Ch 80;** ☎ 01843 572110.

ENGLAND – EAST COAST

WHITSTABLE
Hbr Radio Ch 09 12, Mon-Fri: 0830-1700 and −3HW+1. ☎ 01227 274086.

MEDWAY
Medway VTS **Ch 74**. Kingsferry Bridge (W Swale) **Ch 10** H24. Marinas **Ch 80, M**. Tel code 01634: Gillingham ☎ 280022. Hoo ☎ 250311. Chatham ☎ 899200.

PORT OF LONDON
LONDON VTS: Ch 69 from sea to Sea Reach No 4 buoy. **Ch 68** Sea Reach No 4 to Crayford Ness. **Ch 14**, 22, W of Crayford Ness.
Thames Barrier Ch 14. ☎ 020 8855 0315.

RIVER THAMES
Patrol Launches *Thames Patrol* **Ch 06, 13, 14, 68**
King George V Dock lock *KG Control* **Ch 13.**
West India Dock lock **Ch 13**
Greenwich Yacht Club **Ch M**

Thames lock (Brentford) **Ch 74** Summer 0800-1800; Winter 0800-1630.
Cadogan Pier **Ch 14** 0900-1700.
Marinas Ch 80, M; Tel code 0207: Gallions Point ☎ 4767054. Poplar Dock ☎ 5151046. South Dock ☎ 2522244. Limehouse Basin ☎ 3089930. St Katherine Haven ☎ 2645312. Chelsea Hbr ☎ 2259100. Brentford Dock ☎ 0208 2328941.

RIVER ROACH Havengore Bridge **Ch 72** *Shoe Bridge* HW±2. ☎ 01702 383436.

BURNHAM-ON-CROUCH
Ch 80: HM Launch 0900-1700. Yacht Hbr ☎ 01621 782150. Essex Marina ☎ 01702 258531.

RIVER BLACKWATER
Marinas **Ch 80, M;** Tel code 01621: Tollesbury ☎ 869202. Bradwell ☎ 776235. **Ch M:** Blackwater ☎ 740264. Heybridge Lock, **Ch 80** ☎ 853506.

RIVER COLNE
Brightlingsea Hbr **Ch 68** 0800-2000. Tel code 01206 ☎ 302200. Waterside Marina Ch 68 ☎ 308709.

WALTON BACKWATERS
Titchmarsh Marina **Ch 80,** ☎ 01255 672185.

RIVERS STOUR AND ORWELL
HARWICH VTS **Ch 71**, 11, 20, H24
SUNK VTS **Ch 14**, H24
Orwell Navigation Service **Ch 68,** H24, ☎ 211066.
Marinas **Ch 80, M**. Tel code 01473: Shotley ☎ 788982. Suffolk Hbr ☎ 659240. Woolverstone ☎ 780206. Fox's ☎ 689111. Neptune ☎ 215204. Ipswich Haven ☎ 236644.

RIVER DEBEN HM ☎ 07803 476621.
Tidemill Yacht Hbr ☎ 01394 385745.

SOUTHWOLD *Port Radio* **Ch 09 12**. HM ☎ 01502 724712.

LOWESTOFT
Hbr Control **Ch 11**, **14**. HM ☎ 01502 572286.
Royal Norfolk & Suffolk YC **Ch 80.** ☎ 566726.
Haven Marina **Ch 80** ☎ 580300.
Mutford Bridge & Lock Ch 73 ☎ 531778.

GREAT YARMOUTH
Yarmouth Radio **Ch 12**. HM ☎ 01493 335511.
Haven & Breydon bridges **Ch 12**.

WELLS-NEXT-THE-SEA
Wells Hbr **Ch 12**, HJ, HW±2 and when vessel expected. HM ☎ 01328 711646.

WISBECH Ch 09 HW−3 when vessel expected. HM 01945 588059. Sutton Bridge **Ch 09**

KING'S LYNN
Harbour Radio **Ch 14** 11 Mon-Fri: 0800-1700 and −3HW+1. HM ☎ 01553 773411.

BOSTON
Port Control **Ch 12** Mon-Fri 0800-1700 and HW HW -2½ to HW + 1½. HM ☎ 01205 362328.
Grand Sluice **Ch 74** only when lock operates.
Marina ☎ 07480 525230.

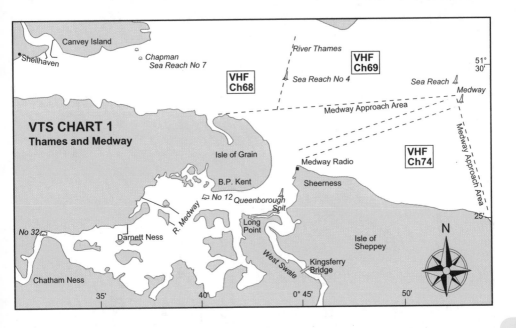

VTS CHART 1
Thames and Medway

Canvey Island
Shellhaven
Chapman
Sea Reach No 7
River Thames
VHF Ch69
Sea Reach No 4
Sea Reach
Medway
51° 30'
VHF Ch68
Medway Approach Area
Isle of Grain
Medway Radio
VHF Ch74
Sheerness
B.P. Kent
No 12 Queenborough Spit
Medway Approach Area
No 32
Darnett Ness
R. Medway
Long Point
Isle of Sheppey
25'
N
West Swale
Kingsferry Bridge
Chatham Ness
35'   40'   0° 45'   50'

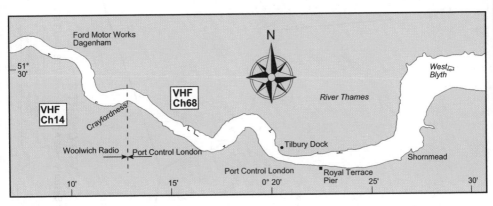

Ford Motor Works Dagenham
N
West Blyth
51° 30'
VHF Ch68
River Thames
VHF Ch14
Crayfordness
Woolwich Radio   Port Control London
Tilbury Dock
Shornmead
Port Control London   Royal Terrace Pier
10'   15'   0° 20'   25'   30'

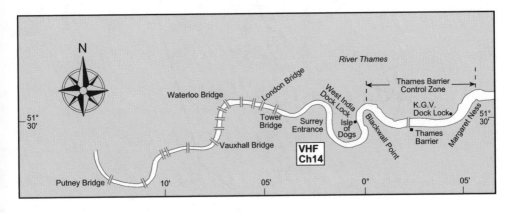

N
River Thames
Waterloo Bridge
London Bridge
West India Dock Lock
Thames Barrier Control Zone
K.G.V. Dock Lock
Margaret Ness
51° 30'
Tower Bridge
Surrey Entrance
Isle of Dogs
Blackwall Point
51° 30'
Thames Barrier
Vauxhall Bridge
VHF Ch14
Putney Bridge
10'   05'   0°   05'

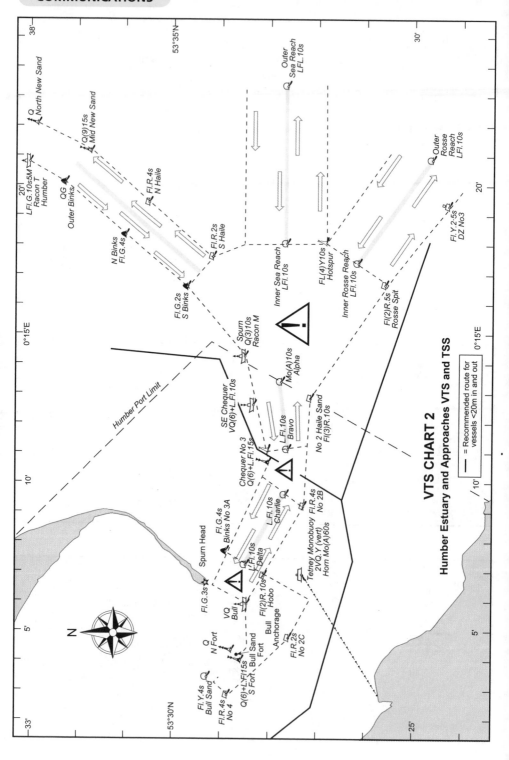

VTS CHART 2

Humber Estuary and Approaches VTS and TSS

RIVER HUMBER
VTS 1, Ch 14 to seaward of Clee Ness Lt F
VTS 2, Ch 12 Clee Ness–Gainsborough (R Trent) & Goole (R Ouse). MSI broadcasts Ch 12 & 14 every 2 hrs from 0103LT.
Grimsby Docks Radio **Ch 74**; 18 79 H24
Marinas: Grimsby, Meridian Quay **Ch 74, ☎** 01472 268424. **Hull, Ch 80, ☎** 01482 330508.
South Ferriby, Sluice **Ch 74. Brough,** Humber Yawl club ☎ 01482 667224. **Goole** Boathouse ☎ 01405 763985.

BRIDLINGTON
HM, call Ch 16; work **Ch 12. ☎** 01262 670148.

SCARBOROUGH
HM *Scarborough Port Control* **Ch 12** H24. **☎** 01723 373530.

WHITBY HM, Bridge & Marina **Ch 11,** 12 H24. ☎ 01947 602354.

RIVER TEES and HARTLEPOOL
Monitor *Tees Port control* **Ch 14**, 08, 11, 12, 22. Hartlepool Marina **Ch 80, M** H24. ☎ 01429 865744.

SEAHAM
HM **Ch 12,** M-F 0800-1700. ☎ 0191 5161700.

SUNDERLAND
Hbr Radio **Ch 14** (H24). Marina **Ch 80, M.** ☎ 0191 5144721.

RIVER TYNE
Tyne VTS **Ch 12,** 08, 11, inc Info service.
Royal Quays Marina **Ch 80** ☎ 0191 2728282.
St Peter's Marina **Ch 80** ☎ 0191 2654472.
Newcastle City Marina ☎ 0191 2211348.

BLYTH
Port control **Ch 12,** 11. ☎ 01670 357025. Marina ☎ 01670 353636 (R Northumberland YC).

WARKWORTH HARBOUR (Amble)
HM Ch 16, work **Ch 14.** ☎ 01665 710306. Marina **Ch 80,** ☎ 01665 712168.

BERWICK-UPON-TWEED
HM **Ch 12,** M-F 0800-1700. ☎ 01289 307404.

SCOTLAND

EYEMOUTH HM **Ch 12,** 06 HO. ☎ 01890 750223.

FIRTH OF FORTH
Forth and Tay Navigation **Ch 71**; may work 12, 20.
PORT EDGAR Marina **Ch 80, M.** ☎ 0131 313330.
GRANTON, Royal Forth YC, Call *Boswell* **Ch M.** ☎ 0131 5523006.
GRANGEMOUTH Docks **Ch 14.** ☎ 01324 498566.
FORTH & CLYDE CANAL *Carron Sea Lock* **Ch 74.** ☎ 01324 483034.
METHIL Docks **Ch 14.** ☎ 01324 4426725.
ANSTRUTHER Ch 11. ☎ 01333 312591.
DUNDEE *Harbour Radio* **Ch 12.** ☎ 01382 224121. **Royal Tay YC Ch M.** ☎ 01382 477516.

PERTH *Perth Harbour* **Ch 09.** ☎ 01738 624056.
ARBROATH *Port Control* **Ch 11.** ☎ 01241 872166.
MONTROSE *Port Control* **Ch 12.** ☎ 01674 672302.
STONEHAVEN HM **Ch 11.** ☎ 01569 762741.
ABERDEEN VTS **Ch 12,** ☎ 01224 597000.
PETERHEAD *Peterhead Hbrs* **Ch 14** for cl'nce to enter/exit. Marina ☎ 01779 477868.
FRASERBURGH Ch 12 H24, ☎ 01346 515858.
MACDUFF Ch 12 H24, ☎ 01261 832236.
BANFF Ch 12, ☎ 01261 815544.
WHITEHILLS *Whitehills Hbr Radio* **Ch 14,** ☎ 01261 861291.
BUCKIE Ch 12, 16 (H24), ☎ 01542 831700.

LOSSIEMOUTH
HM **Ch 12** 0700-1700. Marina, ☎ 01343 813066.

HOPEMAN and BURGHEAD
Same HM: *Burghead Radio* **Ch 14** HX, ☎ 01343 835337.

NAIRN HM/Marina ☎ 01667 454330. No VHF.

INVERNESS
HM **Ch 12,** M-Fri 0900-1700; Tel code 01463: ☎ 715715.
Clachnaharry Sealock **Ch 74,** ☎ 713896. HW ±4.
Inverness Marina **Ch 12.**
Seaport Marina ☎ 239745.
Caley Marina ☎ 236539.

HELMSDALE Ch 13, ☎ 01431 821692.

WICK Ch 14 HM, ☎ 01955 602030.

SCRABSTER HM **Ch 12** H24, Call on arr/dep. ☎ 01847 892779.

ORKNEY HARBOURS NAVIGATION SERVICE
Orkney Harbour Radio **Ch 09 11** 12
Stromness HM **Ch 14** M-Fri 0900-1700; ☎ 07810 465825. Marina, ☎ 465825.
Kirkwall *Hbr Radio* **Ch 14,** ☎ 872292. M-Fri, 0800-1700. Marina, ☎ 871313.
Westray Pier, *Pierowall Hbr* **Ch 14** expected, ☎ 01857 677216. Marina, ☎ 07787 364934.

SHETLAND
Lerwick Hbr Radio **Ch 12** ☎ 01595 692991.
Scalloway Hbr Radio **Ch 09,** 12, M-F 0700-1800, Sat 0900-1230. Piermaster ☎ 01595 744221.
Sullom Voe VTS **Ch 14** for tfc info, weather & radar assistance on request. ☎ 01806 242551.
Balta Sound Harbour **Ch 16, 20** HO

OUTER HEBRIDES
STORNOWAY HM **Ch 12** H24, ☎ 01851 702688.
Loch Maddy, N Uist Ch 12, ☎ 01876 500337.
St Kilda, *Kilda Radio* **Ch 16,** ☎ 01870 604406.

MAINLAND
Kinlochbervie Ch 14 HX, ☎ 01971 521235.
Loch Inver Ch 09 HX, ☎ 01571 844247.

ULLAPOOL Ch 14, ☎ 01854 612724.

Loch Gairloch Hbr Ch 16, ☎ 01445 712140.

ISLE OF SKYE
Portree Ch 12 (occas), **☎ 01478 612926.**

Kyle Akin Ch 11, ☎ 01599 534167.

KYLE OF LOCH ALSH Ch 11, ☎ 01599 534589.

Mallaig Ch 09 HO, **☎ 01687 462154.**

Tiree, Gott Bay Pier, **Ch 31, ☎ 01879 230337.**

Coll, Arinagour Pier, **Ch 31, ☎ 01879 230347.**

L Sunart, Salen Bay, **Ch 16, ☎ 01967 431510.**

ISLAND OF MULL
Tobermory, Ch 12, M HJ, **☎ 01688 302876.**

Loch Lathaich; Sound of Iona; Craignure Pier.

Corpach basin & lock/Caledonian Canal Ch 74, ☎ 01397 772249, mob 07917 348025.

DUNSTAFFNAGE Marina, Ch M, ☎ 01631 566555.

Oban *North Bay* **Ch 12. Marina, ☎ 01631 565333.**

L Melfort, Kilmelford Haven, **Ch M, ☎ 01852 200248.**

L Shuna, Craobh Marina, **Ch M, ☎ 01852 500222.**

L Craignish, Ardfern **Ch 80, M, ☎ 01852 500247.**

CRINAN CANAL, Ch 74. BWB, **☎ 01546 603210.**

Islay, Port Ellen, Marina **☎ 07464 151200;** no VHF.

Tarbert, Loch Fyne Ch 14, ☎ 01880 820344.

Portavadie Marina Ch 80, ☎ 01700 811075.

CAMPBELTOWN Ch 12, 13, **☎ 07798 524821.**

ROTHESAY, Bute Ch 12, ☎ 07799 724225.

LARGS Yacht Haven **Ch 80, M, ☎ 01475 675333.**

KIP Marina **Ch 80, M, ☎ 01475 521485.**

HOLY LOCH Marina **Ch 80, M, ☎ 01369 701800.**

RHU Marina **Ch 80, M, ☎ 01436 820238.**

ARDROSSAN Marina **Ch 80, M, ☎ 01294 607077.**

IRVINE HM/Bridge **Ch 12, ☎ 01292 487286.**

TROON Ch 14. Marina **Ch 80, M, ☎ 01294 315553.**

GIRVAN HM **Ch 12, ☎ 01465 713648.**

STRANRAER Ch 14, ☎ 01776 707500.

KIRKCUDBRIGHT HM **Ch 12, ☎ 01557 331135.**

ENGLAND W COAST AND WALES

MARYPORT Marina **Ch 80, ☎ 01900 814431.**

WORKINGTON HM **Ch 14, ☎ 01900 602301.**

WHITEHAVEN Marina **Ch 12, ☎ 01946 692435.**

ISLE OF MAN (Tel code 01624) If unable to contact IoM hbrs below, call Douglas.

Douglas *Hbr Control* **Ch 12** H24.

Port St Mary HM **Ch 12** HJ, **☎ 833205.**

Peel HM **Ch 12** HJ, **☎ 842338.**

Ramsey HM **Ch 12** 0800-1600. HO, **☎ 812245.**

MAINLAND
GLASSON DOCK Marina **Ch 69, ☎ 01524 751491.**

FLEETWOOD *Fleetwood Dock Radio* (HW±2) **Ch 12** for Marina, **☎ 01253 879062.**

PRESTON Lock *Riversway* **Ch 14.** Marina **Ch 80, ☎** 01772 733595.

LIVERPOOL *Mersey Radio* **Ch 12.** Info **Ch 09.** Radar **Ch 18.** Liverpool Marina (Brunswick Dock) **Ch M, ☎** 0151 7076777. Albert Dock **Ch M, ☎ 0151 7096558;** access via Canning Dock lock.

CONWY HM **Ch 14.** Marinas, both **Ch 80:** Conwy, **☎ 01492 593000.** Deganwy 576888.

MENAI STRAIT and ANGLESEY
Beaumaris/Menai HM **Ch 69, ☎ 01248 712312.**

Caernarfon, HM & Victoria Dock **Ch 80, ☎ 01286** 672118. Mon-Fri: 0900-1700 Sat: 0900-1200

HOLYHEAD *Port Control* **Ch 14, ☎ 01407 606700.** Marina 764242.

MAINLAND
PWLLHELI, HM **Ch 12, ☎ 701219 .** Marina **Ch 80, M, ☎ 01758 704081.**

PORTHMADOG *Hbr* **Ch 12, ☎ 01766 512927.**

BARMOUTH HM *Barmouth Hbr* **Ch 12, ☎ 01341** 280671.

ABERDOVEY *Aberdovey Hbr* **Ch 12, ☎ 01654** 767626.

ABERYSTWYTH HM **Ch 14.** Marina **Ch 80, ☎ 01970** 611422.

FISHGUARD HM **Ch 14.**

MILFORD HAVEN Monitor *Port Control* (and *Patrol launch*) **Ch 12,** whilst under way. **Milford Docks** *Pierhead* **Ch 18.** Milford Dock Marina **Ch 14, ☎** 01646 696312. Neyland Yacht Haven **Ch 80, M, ☎** 01646 601601.

Tenby Ch 80, ☎ 01834 842717.

Saundersfoot Ch 11

SWANSEA Tawe Lock Ch 18. Marina **Ch 80, ☎** 01792 470310.

BARRY *Barry Radio* **Ch 11.** HM **☎ 01446 732665.**

CARDIFF *Cardiff Radio* **Ch 14.** Barrage control **Ch 18.** Penarth Marina **Ch 80, ☎ 02920 705021.**

NEWPORT HM **Ch 71, ☎ 0870 6096699.**

SHARPNESS *Sharpness Radio* **Ch 13** for lock. Marina, **☎ 01453 811476.** Canal **Ch 74**

BRISTOL *Bristol VTS* **Ch 12** ☎ 0117 980 2638. *City Docks Radio* **Ch 14** (low power) to confirm. *Bristol Floating Hbr* **Ch 73.** Bristol Marina **Ch 80, ☎ 0117 9213198.**

PORTISHEAD Marina **Ch 80, ☎ 0198 4631264.**

BURNHAM-ON-SEA HM **Ch 08, ☎ 01938 822666.**

WATCHET Marina **Ch 80**, ☎ 01984 631264.

ILFRACOMBE HM **Ch 80**, ☎ 01271 862108.

APPLEDORE-BIDEFORD HM *Two Rivers* **Ch 12**, Appledore ☎ 01237 428700.

BUDE HM **Ch 12**, ☎ 01288 353111.

PADSTOW HM **Ch 12**, ☎ 01841 532239.

ST IVES HM **Ch 12**, ☎ 07816 077755.

IRELAND

ROSSAVEEL Ch 12, ☎ 091 572108.

GALWAY, HM **Ch 12**, ☎ 091 561874.

SHANNON ESTUARY *Shannon Ports Radio* **Ch 11** (HO), ☎ 087 2560427.

KILRUSH Marina **Ch 80**, ☎ 06590 52072.

LIMERICK HBR Ch 12 13, ☎ 061 315377.

MFENIT HM **Ch 14, M**, ☎ 066 7136231.

DINGLE HM **Ch 14** (no calls req'd), ☎ 087 9254115.

CAHERSIVEEN (Valentia) Marina **Ch 80**, ☎ 066 9472777.

BANTRY BAY, Lawrence Cove Marina **Ch M**, ☎ 027 75044.

CASTLETOWN BEARHAVEN ⚓, ☎ 027 70220.

CROOKHAVEN ⚓, ☎ 028 35319.

SCHULL ⚓, mobile ☎ 086 1039105.

BALTIMORE Ch 09, mobile 087 2351485.

GLANDORE HM **Ch 06**, ☎ 028 34737.

COURTMACSHERRY HM ☎ 08610 40812.

KINSALE HM **Ch 14** ☎ 021 4772503. Marinas **Ch M:** KYC ☎ 4772196. Castlepark ☎ 4774959.

CORK *Cork Hbr Radio* **Ch 12**, 14 H24. HM ☎ 021 4273125. Marinas **Ch M:** Crosshaven ☎ 4831161. Salve ☎ 4831145. Royal Cork YC ☎ 4831023. East Ferry ☎ 4813390. Cork Hbr ☎ (087) 3669009.

YOUGHAL HM/Pilots **Ch 14** Mon-Fri 0900-1700 and when ships expected. ☎ 024 92577.

DUNMORE EAST HM/Pilots **Ch 14** ☎ 051 383166.

WATERFORD & NEW ROSS Ch 12, 14. ☎ 051 873501.

KILMORE QUAY Ch 09. Marina, ☎ 053 29955.

ROSSLARE HM **Ch 12** H24, ☎ 053 33114.

WEXFORD Hbr Boat club. **Ch 16**, ☎ 053 22039.

ARKLOW HM **Ch 12**, ☎ 0402 32466. Marina 39901.

WICKLOW HM **Ch 14** 12, ☎ 0404 67455.

DUN LAOGHAIRE HM **Ch 14**, ☎ 01 2801130. Marina **Ch M**, ☎ 2020040. YCs: National 2805725; R. St George 2801811; R. Irish 2809452; DL Motor 2801371.

Greystones Marina, ☎ 353 (086) 2718161

DUBLIN HM and VTS *Dublin VTS* **Ch 12**, 13. Poolbeg Marina **Ch M**, ☎ 01 6689983. Lifting bridge *Eastlink* **Ch 12, 13.** City moorings, ☎ 01 8183300.

HOWTH HM **Ch 11.** Marina Ch M, 80, ☎ 01 8392777.

MALAHIDE Marina **Ch 80, M**, ☎ 01 8454129.

CARLINGFORDFORD LOUGH
Carlingford Marina Ch M, ☎ 042 9373072.

Warrenpoint Ch 12, ☎ 028 41752878.

Kilkeel Ch 12, ☎ 028 41762287.

ARDGLASS (Phennick Cove) HM **Ch 12**. Marina **Ch M, 80**, ☎ 028 44842332.

STRANGFORD LOUGH
HM **Ch 12 14**, ☎ 028 44881637.

Portaferry Marina Ch 80, M, ☎ 07703 209780.

Donaghadee Copelands Marina, ☎ 028 91882184.

BELFAST VTS *Belfast Hbr Radio* **Ch 12. Marinas Ch 80, M:** Carrickfergus, ☎ 028 93366666. Bangor, ☎ 028 91453217.

LARNE *Port Control* **Ch 14**, 11.

Glenarm HM/Marina, mobile ☎ 07703 606763.

Ballycastle HM/Marina, mob ☎ 07803 505084.

PORTRUSH HM **Ch 12**, ☎ 028 70822307.

COLERAINE HM **Ch 12**. Marina, ☎ 028 70832086.

LONDONDERRY *Hbr radio* **Ch 14**, ☎ 028 71860313.

L SWILLY Fahan Marina, ☎ 074 9360008.

KILLYBEGS HM **Ch 14**, ☎ 07497 31032.

Burton Port HM **Ch 06, 12, 14**, ☎ 075 42155.

SLIGO HM **Ch 12**, 14, ☎ 071 9153819.

DENMARK

Skagen HM **Ch 12** 13 HX, ☎ 98 941346.

Hirtshals HM **Ch 12** 13 HX, ☎ 98 941422.

Torup Strand HM **Ch 12** 13 HX.

Hanstholm HM **Ch 12** 13 HX, ☎ 97 961833/ 96550710.

THYBORØN HM **Ch 12** 13 H24, ☎ 97 831188.

Thisted (Limfjord) Ch 12 13 HX, ☎ 97 911400.

Torsminde HM **Ch 13** 16, ☎ 97 497044.

Hvide Sande HM **Ch 12** (0700-1700), ☎ 97 311633 H24.

ESBJERG *Hbr Control* **Ch 12** 13 14 H24, ☎ 75 124000. **Fanø** HM, ☎ 75 163100.

Rømø HM **Ch 10, 12, 13** HX, ☎ 74 755245.

GERMANY

HELGOLAND HM **Ch 67**, ☎ 04725 81593583. **May-Aug** Mon-Thu 0700-1200, 1300-2000. Fri-Sun 0700-1200.

Sep-Apr Mon-Thu 0700-1200, 1300-1600. Fri 0700-1200.

List HM **Ch 11**, ☎ 046 51870374.

Hörnum HM **67**, ☎ 046 51881027.

Wyk HM **Ch 11**, ☎ 046 81500430.

Pellworm HM **Ch 11**, ☎ 048 44726.

Husum HM **Ch 11**, ☎ 048 16670.

R. Eider sealock **Ch 14**, ☎ 04833 4535211.

Büsum HM **Ch 11**, ☎ 048 413607.

INNER DEUTSCHE BUCHT (GERMAN BIGHT) VTS, Eastern part **Ch 80**, ☎ 04421 489282. VTS, Western part **Ch 79**

BRUNSBÜTTEL WSA (hbr info) ☎ 04852 8850.

NORD-OSTSEE KANAL (KIEL CANAL)

VTS Canal I	**Ch 13**,	☎ 04852 885371.
VTS Canal II	**Ch 02**,	☎ 04852 885369.
VTS Canal III	**Ch 03**,	☎ 0431 3603456.
VTS Canal IV	**Ch 12**,	☎ 0431 3603465.

Brieholz, **Ch 73**. Ostermoor, **Ch 73**. Kiel-Holtenau, HM ☎ 0431 363830.

RIVER ELBE

CUXHAVEN HM **Ch 69** HX, ☎ 04721 500150. **Lock Ch 69**, ☎ 500120. **Cuxhaven** Marina, ☎ 175 90 20015. **YC** Marina, ☎ 34111. **R. Stör Lock Ch 09** Bridge opens on request. **Glückstadt** HM **Ch 08**, ☎ 04124 913200.

HAMBURG Port HM **Ch 12**, ☎ 040 7411540. **VTS** Hamburg Port Traffic **Ch 13, 14, 74**. Wedel Yacht Hbr, ☎ 040 1034438. City Sporthafen, ☎ 040 364297.Lloyd & R Geeste Marinas ☎

BREMERHAVEN Weser VTS **Ch 22**. Port **Ch 12**, ☎ 0471 59613401. **HM**, ☎ 59613416. **Locks Ch 69, 10**. Marinas Weser YC, ☎ 23531. NYC, ☎ 77555. WVW, ☎ 73268.Lloyds/Geeste ☎1428690

BREMEN Port Radio **Ch 03**, ☎ 0421 3618504.

JADE VTS Jade Traffic **Ch 63, 20**.

WILHEMSHAVEN

Port **Ch 11**, ☎ 04421 154580. **Sealock Ch 13**. **Bridges Ch 11**. Marinas Nassauhafen, ☎ 41439. Wiking Sportsbootshafen, ☎ 41301.

HOOKSIEL Ch 63. Alterhafen Marina.

WANGEROOGE HM **Ch 17**, ☎ 04469 1322.

SPIEKEROOG HM No VHF, ☎ 04976 9193133.

DORNUMER-ACCUMERSIEL HM No VHF, ☎ 04933 2510. YC ☎ 2240.

LANGEOOG HM **Ch 17**, ☎ 04972 301.

NORDERNEY HM **Ch 17**, ☎ 04932 82826.

NORDDEICH HM **Ch 17**, ☎ 04931 81317.

BORKUM HM **Ch 14**, ☎ 04922 81317.

EMS VTS Ems Traffic **Ch 15, 18, 20, 21**

EMDEN HM & locks **Ch 13**, ☎ 04921 897260. YC Marina, ☎ 997147. Mariners' Club, ☎ 953795. City Marina, ☎ 8907211.

NETHERLANDS

DELFZIJL/EEMSHAVEN VTS is not compulsory for leisure craft. **Delfzijl Radar** Ch 03 gives radar assistance when visibility falls below 2000m. **Eemshaven Radar** Ch 01. **Port Control** Ch 66 broadcasts info every even H+10.

DELFZIJL HBR. HM Ch 14; ☎ 0596 640400. **Locks** Ch 26, M-Sat H24, Sun & hols on request; ☎ 693293. **Bridges**: Weiwerder Ch 11. Heemskes & Handelshaven Ch 14. **Farmsumerhaven**, Ch 66, ☎ 640494.

EEMSHAVEN HM Ch 14; ☎ 516142. Radar Ch 19.

LAUWERSOOG. HM, Havendienst, Ch 09; ☎ 0519 39023. Mon 0000-1700; Tu-Wed 0800-1700; Th-Sat 0700-1500.

TERSCHELLING VTS Call/monitor Brandaris Ch 02; ☎ 0562 443100. **Marina**, Ch 31; ☎ 443337.

VLIELAND. HM Ch 12. **Marina**, Ch 31; ☎ 0562 451729.

HARLINGEN HM Ch 11 (not on Sun); ☎ 0517 723300. **Locks** Ch 22.

OUDESCHILD HM Ch 12; ☎ 0222 312710. **Marina**, Ch 31; ☎ 0222 321227. See Den Helder VTS.

DEN HELDER VTS. Monitor Tfc Centre Ch 62, H24; broadcasts info and gives radar surveillance. **PORT CONTROL** Ch 14; ☎ 0223 62770. **Marina** ☎ 652645. **Bridge**: Moormanbrug Ch 18. **Lock**: Koopvaarders Ch 22.

IJSSELMEER Den Oever lock Ch 20, ☎ 0227 511789. **Port** Ch 11, ☎ 511303. **Marina** ☎ 511789. **Kornwerderzand lock** Ch 18, ☎ 0517 57441.

ENKHUIZEN Naviduct (also Krabbersgat) Ch 22.

IJMUIDEN VTS. Traffic Centre Ch 07, Roads (W of IJmuiden buoy). Thence **Port Control** Ch 61 to Noordzeesluizen (locks).

Seaport Marina Ch 75, ☎ 0255 560300.

NORDZEEKANAAL VTS

Noordzeesluizen. Sluis IJmuiden Ch 22. Noordzeekanaal. Ch 03, from locks to km 11·2.

AMSTERDAM Port Control Ch 68 (Km 11·2 to Oranjesluisen). **Port Info** Ch 14. Access to Standing Mast route: **Westerkeersluis** Ch 22. **Haarlem hbr** Ch 18. **Westerdoksbrug** ☎ 6241457, Ch 22. **Marinas:** Amsterdam Marina ☎ 6310767. **City Marina** IJdock ☎ 0687478290. **Marina Het Realeneiland,** ☎ 6238855. **Sixhaven,** ☎ 020 6329429. **WV Aeolus,** ☎ 6360791. **Aquadam,** ☎ 6320616. Access to Markermeer: **Oranjesluisen** Ch 18.

SCHEVENINGEN. Traffic Centre & Port Ch 21; ☎ 070 3527711. **Marina** Ch 31; ☎ 070 3520017.

HOEK VAN HOLLAND ROADSTEAD

To cross the mouth of the Maas, call Maas Entrance **Ch 03**, with vessel's name, position and course. Track close W of a line joining buoys MV, MVN and Indusbank N. See VTS Chart No 4. Maintain continuous listening watch and lookout.

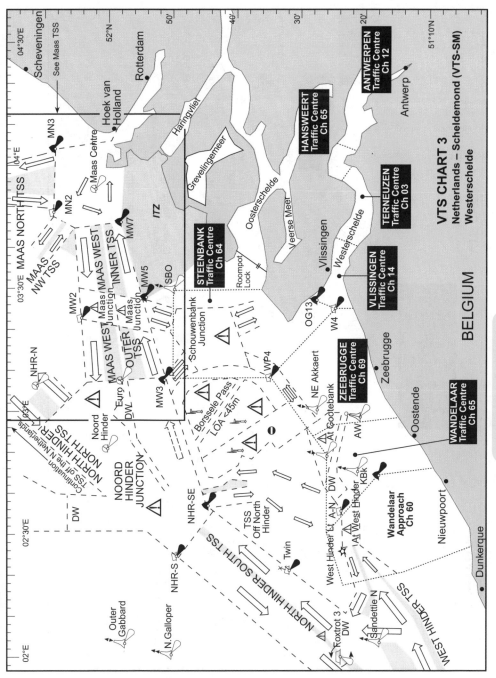

VTS CHART 3
Netherlands – Scheldemond (VTS-SM)
Westerschelde

COMMUNICATIONS

123

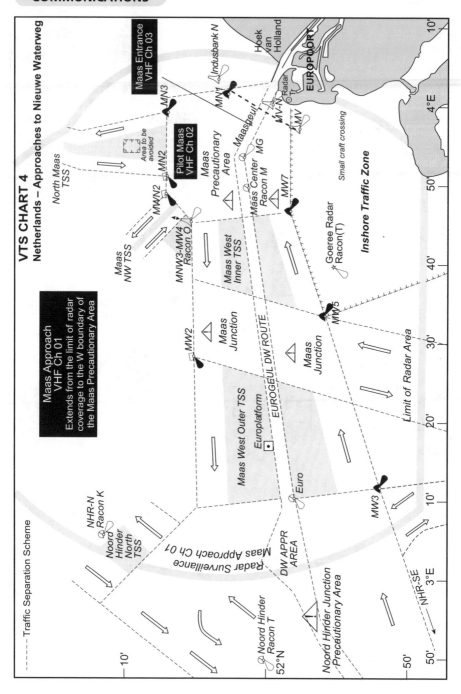

VTS CHART 4
Netherlands – Approaches to Nieuwe Waterweg

Traffic Separation Scheme

Maas Approach VHF Ch 01
Extends from the limit of radar coverage to the W boundary of the Maas Precautionary Area

Maas Entrance VHF Ch 03

Pilot Maas VHF Ch 02

Hoek van Holland

EUROPOORT

Radar T

MN1

Indusbank N

MN3

Maasgeul

MV-N

MV

MN2

Area to be avoided

Maas Precautionary Area

North Maas TSS

Maas Center Racon M

MG

MW7

Small craft crossing

Inshore Traffic Zone

Maas NW TSS

MNW2

MNW3-MW4 Racon O

Maas West Inner TSS

Maas Junction

Goeree Radar Racon(T)

MW5

Maas Junction

Limit of Radar Area

MW2

Maas Junction

EUROGEUL DW ROUTE

Maas West Outer TSS

Europlatform

Euro

MW3

NHR-N Racon K

Noord Hinder North TSS

Radar Surveillance Maas Approach Ch 01

DW APPR AREA

Noord Hinder Junction Precautionary Area

Noord Hinder Racon T

52°N

NHR-SE

10'

NIEUWE WATERWEG VTS. Outer areas as shown on VTS Charts 3 & 4: **Maas Approach** Ch 01. **Pilot Maas** Ch 02. **Maas Entrance** Ch 03. **HCC** *Central Traffic Control* Ch 14 19. Report to/ monitor continuously the relevant Tfc Centre, as listed from seaward to City Marina: Rozenburg Ch 65; Maassluis Ch 80; Botlek Ch 61; Eemhaven Ch 63; Waalhaven Ch 60; Maasbruggen Ch 81.

ROTTERDAM Rotterdam Tfc Centre Ch 11. **Hbr Coordination Centre (HCC)** Ch 19. **Marinas/ Yacht hbrs: Vlaardingen** ☎ 010 2484333; **Lock** Ch 20. **Spuihaven** ☎ 4667765, mob 0644326722. **Coolhaven** ☎ 4764146. **Veerhaven** ☎ 4365446, mob 0653536107. **City Marina** ☎ 48540986, via Erasmus bridge Ch 18.

STELLENDAM Haringvliet lock & lifting bridge: *Goereese Sluis* Ch 20, ☎ 0187 497350. Opening hrs: M-F 0000-2200. 1 Nov - 1 Apr: Sat 0800-2200; Sun 0800-1000, 1600-1800. 1 Apr - 1 Nov: Sat & Sun 0800-2000. **Marina** Ch 31, ☎ 493769.

OOSTERSCHELDE Lock *Roompotsluis* Ch 18, ☎ 0111 659265. Opening hours: Mon & Thu, 0000-2200; Tue & Sun, 0600-0000; Wed H24; Fri & Sat: 0600-2200. **Roompot Marina** Ch 31.

WESTERSCHELDE VTS See VTS Chart No 3. Reporting not compulsory for leisure craft, but monitor the VHF channel for appropriate Traffic Area. Each Traffic Area is controlled by a Traffic Centre and bounded by buoys. *In emergency call the relevant Traffic Centre: Ch 67.*
Tfc Centre Steenbank & Radar Ch 64.
Tfc Centre Vlissingen Ch 14. **Radar** Ch 21. **Info broadcast** Ch 14 H+55.
Tfc Centre Terneuzen & Radar Ch 03. **Info broadcast** Ch 11 H+00.
Tfc Centre Hansweert Ch 65.
Antwerpen, Zeebrugge and Wandelaar Traffic Areas are listed under Belgium.

VLISSINGEN De Ruyter Marina no VHF, ☎ 0118 414498, mobile 06 5353 7181. *Flushing Port Control* Ch 09. **Sealocks & canal bridge** Ch 22. **VVW Schelde Marina** Ch 14, ☎ 465912 / 0615538515.

BRESKENS Marina, Ch 31, ☎ 0117 381902.

TERNEUZEN Port control Ch 11. **Marina,** ☎ 0115 697089. **Oostsluis** (E lock, small craft) Ch 18.

CADZAND-BAD, Jachthaven Cadzand, Ch 31 ☎ +31 611410975.

BELGIUM

ANTWERPEN, Tfc Centre Zandvliet Ch 12. **Info broadcast** Ch 12 H+35.

ANTWERPEN PORT Calling and safety Ch 74. **Kattendijksluis** Ch 69. **Siberia & Londen bridges** Ch 62. **Willemdok Marina** Ch 23, ☎ 03 2315066. **Linkeroever Marina** Ch 09, ☎ 03 2190895.

ZEEBRUGGE Tfc Centre Zeebrugge Ch 69. **Info** broadcasts Ch 69 H+15.

ZEEBRUGGE Port Control Ch 71 H24, ☎ 050 546867/550801. **Marinas VZW** ☎ 544903; **BZYC** ☎, 734738. **E lock** Ch 68.

BLANKENBERGE Marinas: VNZ, ☎ 050 429150, & **SYCB,** ☎ 411420, Ch 31. **VVW** ☎ 417536, Ch 23.

WANDELAAR Tfc Centre Wandelaar Ch 65. **Wandelaar Approach** Ch 60.

OOSTENDE Port Control Ch 09 H24, ☎ 059 340711. **Mercator lock,** ☎ 321669, & **marina,** ☎ 705762: Ch 14 H24. **Marinas: RNSYC,** ☎ 505912. **RYCO,** ☎ +32 59702754 .

NIEUWPOORT Port HM Ch 60 H24, ☎ 058 233000. **Marinas: KYCN,** Ch 23, ☎ 234413. **WSKLuM,** Ch 72, ☎ 5233641. **VVW-N,** Ch 08, ☎ 235232.

NORTH FRANCE

DUNKERQUE Port & VTS Ch 73, H24. The VTS does not affect leisure craft, but monitor Ch 73. **Marinas** Ch 09: Grande Large ☎ 03.28.63.23.00. YCMN ☎ 03.28.66.79.90. **Trystram lock** Ch 14.

GRAVELINES HM/Marina, Ch 09, ☎ 03·59·73·42·42.

CALAIS VTS, Port Control & Marina Ch 17 H24, ☎ 03.21.34.55.23.

BOULOGNE Boulogne Port, ☎ 03.21.31.52.43, Ch 12, H24. **Marina** Ch 09, ☎ 06.76.98.74.98 / 03.21.99.66.50.

LE TOUQUET/ÉTAPLES-SUR-MER Ch 09, 77. **Étaples Marina,** ☎ 03.21.84.54.03.

LE TRÉPORT Marina/lock Ch 12, 72, ☎ 02.35.50.63.06

DIEPPE Port HM Ch 12, HO. **Marina** Ch 09, ☎ 02.35.40.19.79.

ST VALÉRY-EN-CAUX Entry gate & marina Ch 09, ☎ 02.35.97.01.30.

FÉCAMP Port HM, Ch 10, **12,** ☎ 02.35.28.25.53. **Marina & Bérigny lock,** Ch 09, ☎ 02.35.28.13.58.

LE HAVRE Control Tower Ch **12,** 20. **Port Ops** Ch 67, 69. **Marina,** Ch 09, ☎ 02.35.21.23.95.

LA SEINE VTS Rouen Port Control Ch 73 (Estuary), 68 (River). **Honfleur radar** Ch 15, 19, **73.**

HONFLEUR HM Ch **17,** 73 HX, ☎ 02.31.14.61.09. **Lock,** ☎ 02.31.98.72.82, & **Bridge** Ch 17 H24.

ROUEN Port HM Ch **73,** 68 H24. **Halte Nautique,** ☎ 02.35.07.33.94. **Marina** ☎ 02.35.08.30.59.

ROUEN – PARIS, LOCKS Amfreville Ch 18. **Notre-Dame-de-la-Garenne** Ch 22. **Mericourt** Ch 18. **Andrésy** Ch 22. **Bougival** Ch 22. **Chatou** Ch 18. **Suresnes** Ch 22. **PARIS-ARSENAL Marina** Ch 09, ☎ 01.43.41.39.32.

DEAUVILLE Port Deauville lock, ☎ 02.31.88.95.66; **Marina** ☎ 02.31.98.30.01, Ch 09 0800-1730. **Port Morny** gate ☎ 02.31.88.57.89; Marina, Ch 09, ☎ 02.31.98.50.40.

COMMUNICATIONS

COMMUNICATIONS

DIVES-SUR-MER. Marina Ch 09, ☎ 02.31.24.48.00.

OUISTREHAM Port Ch74; **lock** Ch74, ☎02.31.36.22.00. **Marina** Ch 09, ☎ 02.31.96.91.37. **Canal** Ch 68. **CAEN** HM/Marina Ch 74, ☎ 02.31.95.24.47.

COURSEULLES-SUR-MER Marina Ch 09, ☎ 02.31.37.51.69.

PORT-EN-BESSIN HM, ☎ 02.31.21.70.49. **Gate/bridge** Ch 18, ☎ 02.31.21.71.77.

GRANDCAMP Marina Ch 09, ☎ 02.31.22.63.16.

CARENTAN Lock Ch 09, ☎ 02.33.71.10.85. **Marina** Ch 09, ☎ 02.33.42.24.44.

ST VAAST-LA-HOUGUE Marina Ch 09, ☎ 02.33.21.61.00.

BARFLEUR HM, ☎ 02.33.54.08.29. No VHF.

CHERBOURG VTS (yachts to monitor) *Vigie du Homet* Ch 12 H24. **Marina** *Chantereyne* Ch 09, ☎ 02.33.87.65.70. **Gate** (B du Commerce) Ch 12

OMONVILLE-LA-ROGUE No VHF/Tel. 6 W ⚓s.

DIÉLETTE Marina Ch 09, ☎ 02.33.53.68.78.

CARTERET Marina Ch 09, ☎ 02.33.04.70.84.

PORTBAIL Yacht hbr Ch 09, ☎ 02.33.04.83.48.

GRANVILLE Port HM Ch 12. **Marina** Ch 09, ☎ 02.33.50.20.06.

ST MALO Port HM Ch 12 H24. **Marinas** Ch 09: **Bas Sablons**, ☎ 02.99.81.71.34. **Bassin Vauban**, ☎ 02.99.56.51.91. **DINARD**, ☎ 02.99.46.65.55.

R RANCE barrage lock Ch 13, ☎ 02.99.46.21.87. **Chatelier lock** Ch 14, ☎ 02.99.39.55.66.

ST CAST-LE-GUILDO Marina ☎ 02 96 81 04 43

DAHOUËT Marina Ch 09, ☎ 02.96.72.82.85.

LE LÉGUÉ HM/Marina Ch 12, ☎ 02.96.77.49.85.

BINIC Marina Ch 09, ☎ 02.96.73.61.86.

ST QUAY-PORTRIEUX Marina ☎ 02.96.70.81.30. Ch 09.

PAIMPOL Lock/Marina Ch 09, ☎ 02.96.20.47.65.

LÉZARDRIEUX Marina Ch 09, ☎ 02.96.20.14.22.

PONTRIEUX Lock/Marina Ch 12, ☎ 02.96.95.34.87.

TRÉGUIER Marina Ch 09, ☎ 02.96.92.42.37.

PERROS-GUIREC Marina Ch 09, ☎ 02.96.49.80.50.

PLOUMANAC'H Marina Ch 09, ☎ 02.96.91.44.31.

TRÉBEURDEN Marina Ch 09, ☎ 02.96.23.64.00.

MORLAIX Lock, ☎ 06.77.50.15.90 / 02.98.88.15.10. **Marina** Ch 09, ☎ 02.98.62.13.14.

ROSCOFF HM/S Basin Ch 09, ☎ 02.98.69.76.37.

ROSCOFF Marina *Plaisance Roscoff* Ch 09, ☎ 02.98.79.79.49. **Ferry Port** Ch 12, ☎ 02.98.61.27.84.

L'ABERWRACH Marina Ch 09, ☎ 02.98.04.91.62.

CHANNEL ISLANDS

ALDERNEY, Braye Hbr, *Alderney Coastguard* Ch 67, ☎ 01481 822620, or *Guernsey Coastguard. Alderney Port Control* Ch 74.

GUERNSEY Beaucette Marina, Ch 80, ☎ 01481 245000. **St Sampson** Ch 12 H24 via **St Peter Port** Control Ch 12 H24, ☎ 720229. **Victoria Marina** Ch 80 HO, ☎ 725987. *Guernsey Coastguard* Ch 20 H24 (Ch 62 for emergecy link calls).

JERSEY St Helier Port Control Ch 14 H24; 8M max range. **St Helier Marina,** ☎ 01534 447730/447708, has no VHF; call Ch 14 only if essential. **Gorey** Ch 74, ☎ 853616.

WEST FRANCE

BREST VTS *Brest Port* Ch 08 H24. **Marinas** Ch 09. **Marina du Chateau,** ☎ 02·98·33·12·50. **Port du Moulin Blanc,** ☎ 02·98·33·12·50.

CAMARET Marina Ch 09, ☎ 02.98.27.95.99.

MORGAT Marina Ch 09, ☎ 02.98.27.01.97.

DOUARNENEZ HM Ch 12. **Marinas** Ch 09: Tréboul ☎ 02.98.74.02.56; Port Rhu ☎ 02.98.92.00.67.

AUDIERNE HM Ch 09. **Marina** ☎ 02.98.74.04.93. **Ste Evette** ☎ 02.98.70.00.28.

LOCTUDY Marina Ch 09, ☎ 02.98.87.51.36.

BENODÉT Marinas Ch 09: Penfoul ☎ 02.98.57.05.78. Ste Marine ☎ 02.98.56.38.72.

PORT-LA-FORÊT Marina Ch 09, ☎ 02.98.56.98.45.

CONCARNEAU Marina Ch 09, ☎ 02.98.97.57.96.

LORIENT Port Ch 12. **Marinas** Ch 09: Ban-Gâvres ☎ 02.97.65.48.25. Kernével ☎ 02.97.65.48.25. Port Louis ☎ 02.97.83.59.55. Locmiquélic ☎ 02.97.33.59.51. Lorient ☎ 02.97.21.10.14.

PORT TUDY Marina Ch 09, ☎ 02.97.86.54.62.

RIVER ÉTEL Marina Ch 13, ☎ 02.97.55.46.62.

BELLE ILE Sauzon HM Ch 09, ☎ 02.97.31.63.40. **Le Palais** HM Ch 09, ☎ 02.97.31.42.90.

PORT HALIGUEN Marina Ch 09, ☎ 02.97.50.20.56.

LA TRINITÉ Marina Ch 09, ☎ 02.97.55.71.49.

VANNES Marina Ch 09 (0800-1200, 1500-1900 July-Aug), ☎ 02.97.01.55.20.

CROUESTY Marina Ch 09, ☎ 02.97.53.73.33.

LA VILAINE Arzal Marina Ch 09, ☎ 02.97.45.02.97.

PIRIAC Marina Ch 09, ☎ 02.40.23.52.32.

LA TURBALLE Marina Ch 09, ☎ 02.40.23.41.65.

LE CROISIC Marina Ch 09, ☎ 09.81.12.75.92.

LE POULIGUEN Marina Ch 09, ☎ 02.40.11.97.97.

PORNICHET Marina Ch 09, ☎ 02.40.61.03.20.

ST-NAZAIRE VTS *Loire Ports Control* Ch 14. **Port** HM Ch 14, ☎ 02.40.00.45.89.

PORNIC Marina Ch 09, ☎ 02.40.82.05.40.

L'HERBAUDIÈRE Marina Ch 09, ☎ 02.51.39.05.05.

PORT JOINVILLE Marina Ch 09, ☎ 02.51.58.38.11.

ST GILLES CROIX DE VIE Marina Ch 09, ☎ 02.51.55.30.83.

LES SABLES D'OLONNE Port HM Ch 12, ☎ 02.51.95.11.79. **Marina** Ch 09, ☎ 02.51.32.51.16.

BOURGENAY Marina Ch 09, ☎ 02.51.22.20.36.

ILE DE RÉ Ars-en-Ré Ch 09, ☎ 05.46.29.08.52. **St Martin** Ch 09, ☎ 05.46.09.26.69.

LA ROCHELLE Marinas Ch 09: **Port des Minimes** ☎ 05.46.44.41.20. **Vieux Port** ☎ 05.46.41.32.05.

ROCHEFORT Marina Ch 09, ☎ 05.46.83.99.06.

ILE D'OLÉRON St Denis Ch 09, ☎ 05.46.47.97.97. **Boyardville** Ch 09, ☎ 05.46.76.48.56.

LA GIRONDE VTS Ch 12 (yachts to monitor). *Radar Bordeaux Port Control* Ch 12 on request. Depths in Gironde broadcast Ch 17 every 5 mins.

ROYAN Marina Ch 09, ☎ 05.46.38.72.22.

COAST RADIO STATIONS

Coast Radio Stations (CRS) deal with public correspondence (and a few other things). They enable a yachtsman to be linked by radio into the public telephone system to converse with a subscriber ashore, to make or receive a Link call.

However the mobile 'phone has to a great extent rendered Link calls obsolete. Thus there are no longer any CRS in the UK, France and Netherlands. In Germany a limited service is provided by a commercial company (see below).

CRS still operate in the Channel Islands, Ireland*, Denmark, Belgium, Spain and Portugal; see below. But they too may gradually be withdrawn. *In Ireland CRS no longer handle commercial link calls, but Medico link calls are still available on both VHF and MF.

The CG does **not** handle Link calls, except in Denmark and Belgium where the functions of CG and CRS have always been co-located.

CHANNEL ISLANDS

GUERNSEY COASTGUARD 49°27'·00N 02°32'00W ☎ 01481 720672 🖷 01534 714177 VHF **Ch 20** (primary working Ch for pilotage/ navigation). Link calls, Ch 62.

JERSEY COAST GUARD 49°10'·85N 02°14'30W ☎ 01534 447705 🖷 01534 499089 VHF **Ch 82** (primary working Ch for pilotage/ navigation). Emergency link calls **Ch 25.**

REPUBLIC OF IRELAND

A Coast Radio service is provided by the Dept of the Marine, Leeson Lane, Dublin 2, Eire. ☎ +353 (0)1 662 0922; ext 670 for enquiries. Broadcasts are made on a working channel/frequency following a prior announcement on Ch 16 and 2182 kHz. Ch 67 is used for Safety messages only.

VHF calls to an Irish Coast Radio Station should be made on a working channel. Only use Ch 16 in case of difficulty or in emergency.

NW, NE and SE Ireland

Weather broadcasts are at 0103, 0403, 0703, 1003, 1303, 1603, 1903, 2203 LT and at 0033, 0633, 1233, 1833 LT on the VHF Channels below. Nav warnings are broadcast at 0033, 0433, 0833, 1233, 1633 and 2033 LT.

Clifden CG	53°30'N 09°56'W	Ch 03
Clew Bay CG	53°46'·N 09°32'W	Ch 05
Belmullet CG	54°16'N 10°03'W	Ch 63
Donegal Bay CG	54°22'N 08°31'W	Ch 02
Glen Head CG	54°44'N 08°43'W	Ch 03
MALIN HEAD CG and 05.	55°22'N 07°21'W	Chs 01

MF 1677 kHz, ☎ +353 (0) 77 70103
MMSI 002500100 DSC: 2187·5 kHz

Carlingford CG	54°05'N 06°19'W	Ch 04
DUBLIN CG	53°23'N 06°04'W	Ch 03
Wicklow Hd CG	52°58'N 06°00'W	Ch 02
Rosslare CG	52°15'N 06°20'W	Ch 05
Mine Hd CG	52°00'N 07°35'W	Ch 03

SW and W Ireland

Broadcasts at 0103, 0403, 0703, 1003, 1303, 1603, 1903, 2203 and at 0033, 0633, 1233, 1833 LT on VHF Channels listed. below Nav warnings are at 0033, 0633,1233,1833 LT.

Cork CG	51°51'N 08°29'W	Ch 02
Galley Hd CG	51°31'N 08°57'W	Ch 16
Mizen Hd CG	51°34'N 09°33'W	Ch 04
Bantry CG	51°38'N 10°00'W	Ch 05
VALENTIA CG	51°56'N 10°21'W	Ch 62

MF 1752 kHz, ☎ + 353 (0) 66947 6109
MMSI 002500200, DSC: 2187·5 kHz

Shannon CG	52°31'N 09°36'W	Ch 64
Galway Bay CG	53°18'N 09°07'W	Ch 04

DENMARK

All VHF/MF CRS are remotely controlled from Lyngby Radio (55°50N 11°25'E) (MMSI 002191000). Use callsign *Lyngby Radio* on working frequencies The stations listed below monitor Ch 16 H24 and Ch 70 DSC. The MF stations do not monitor 2182 kHz. Traffic lists are broadcast on all VHF channels every odd H+05. Blåvand, Skagen and Lyngby monitor MF 2187·5 kHz DSC.

Skagen	57°44'N 10°35'E	Ch 04,
	MF: Tx 1758, Rx 2102	
Hirtshals	57°31'N 09°57'E	Ch 63
Hanstholm	57°07'N 08°39'E	Ch 01
Bovbjerg	56°32'N 08°10'E	Ch 02
	MF: Tx 1734, Rx 2111	
Blåvand	55°33'N 08°07'E	Ch 07
	MF: Tx 1734, Rx 2078	

GERMANY

CRS: DPO7 – Seefunk (Hamburg) *(MMSI 002113100).* All stns monitor DSC Ch 70 and 16. Traffic lists are broadcast (LT): 0745, 0945, 1245, 1645, 1945 and H & H+30 on request Ch 16.

Nordfriesland	54°31'N 08°41'E	Ch 26
Elbe-Weser	53°50'N 08°39'E	Ch 24
Hamburg	53°33'N 09°58'E	Ch 83
Bremen	53°05'N 08°48'E	Ch 25
Accumersiel	53°40'N 07°29'E	Ch 28
Borkum	53°35'N 06°40'E	Ch 61

SHAPES

◆	Towing vessel - length of tow > 200m	**Rule 24**
▼	Yacht under sail *and* power	**Rule 25**
⧓	Vessel fishing or trawling	**Rule 26**
⧓+▲	Vessel fishing with outlying gear >150m long	**Rule 26**
● ◆ ●	Vessel restricted in her ability to manoeuvre	**Rule 27**
● ●	Vessel not under command	**Rule 27**
▮	Vessel constrained by her draught	**Rule 28**
●	Vessel at anchor	**Rule 30**

SOUND SIGNALS

MANOEUVRING AND WARNING Rule 34

•	A short blast = about 1 second.
—	A prolonged blast = 4 – 6 seconds.
•	I am altering course to **Starboard**
••	I am altering course to **Port**
•••	My engines are going **Astern**
•••••	I do not understand your intentions/ actions

Note: The above sound signals may be supplemented by light signals flashed on an all-round white light with least range of 5 miles.

In a narrow channel

— — •	I intend to overtake on your starboard side.
— — ••	I intend to overtake on your port side.
— • — •	I agree with your overtaking signal
—	Warning by vessel nearing a bend where other vessels may not be seen
—	Approaching vessel acknowledges.

VESSELS IN RESTRICTED VISIBILITY Rule 35

—	Power-driven vessel making way.
— —	Power-driven vessel underway, but stopped and not making way.
— ••	**A sailing vessel**; vessels not under command; restricted in ability to manoeuvre; constrained by draught; engaged in fishing, towing or pushing.
— •••	Vessel being towed or, if more than one vessel is towed, the last vessel in the tow.

VESSELS AT ANCHOR

🔔	Bell, ring for 5 seconds every minute
🔔	Vessel >100m: Bell forward, ring for 5 seconds every minute; plus
⊙	Gong aft, for 5 seconds every minute.
• — •	Optional extra to warn any approaching vessel

Sailing vessels < 12m at ⚓ do not have to sound the above fog signals. But if they do not, they *must* make an efficient noise every 2 minutes.

INTERNATIONAL PORT TRAFFIC SIGNALS (IPTS)

IPTS are widely used on the Continent, but less so around the UK. They may also be used to control traffic at locks and bridges.

- The main movement signal is always 3 lights in a vertical column, to which no extra light shall be added. Thus it is always recognisable as IPTS, as distinct from some kind of navigational lights.

- Red lights ⓡ indicate **Do not proceed.**

- Green lights ⓖ indicate **Proceed, subject to the conditions stipulated**. To avoid confusion ⓡ and ⓖ lights are never displayed together.

- Signals may be omni-directional ie seen by all vessels simultaneously; or directional, ie seen only from outside or from inside the harbour.

- Some ports may only use signals 2 and 4, or only Signal 1 when necessary

- Signal 1 **Serious Emergency** must show at least 60 flashes/minute.

- All other signals may be fixed or slow occulting, eg every 10s (helpful when background glare poses a problem), but never a mixture of both.

- Signal 5 assumes that VHF, signal lamp, loud-hailer, auxiliary signal or other means of communication will specifically inform a vessel that she may proceed.

- Exemption signals. A single ⓨ light, shown to the left of signals 2 or 5 and level with the upper light, means **Vessels which can safely navigate outside the main channel need not comply with the main message.** This signal is obviously important to small craft, which nevertheless have a clear duty to keep clear of manoeuvring vessels.

- Auxiliary signals (only ⓦ and/or ⓨ lights) may be locally authorised and displayed to the right of the main signal. Their meanings must be promulgated.

No	Lights		Main message
1	ⓇⓇⓇ	Flashing	Serious emergency – all vessels to stop or divert according to instructions
2	Ⓡ Ⓡ Ⓡ	Fixed or Slow Occulting	Vessels shall not proceed (*Note:* Some ports may use an exemption signal, as in 2a below)
3	Ⓖ Ⓖ Ⓖ		Vessels may proceed. One-way traffic
4	Ⓖ Ⓖ Ⓦ		Vessels may proceed. Two-way traffic
5	Ⓖ Ⓦ Ⓖ		A vessel may proceed only when she has received specific orders to do so. (*Note:* Some ports may use an exemption signal, as in 5a below)
Exemption signals and messages			
2a	Ⓨ Ⓡ Ⓡ Ⓡ	Fixed or Slow Occulting	Vessels shall not proceed, except that vessels which navigate outside the main channel need not comply with the main message
5a	Ⓨ Ⓖ Ⓦ Ⓖ	Fixed or Slow Occulting	A vessel may proceed when she has received specific orders to do so, except that vessels which navigate outside the main channel need not comply with the main message
Auxiliary signals and messages			
White and/or yellow lights, displayed with the main lights			

COMMUNICATIONS

Chapter 4 – Safety

DISTRESS, URGENCY, SAFETY

MAYDAY (Distress) must only be used if a ship or person is in *grave and imminent danger and requires immediate assistance*. The initial call may be made by voice or DSC, but only with the skipper's authority. It is appropriate for a man overboard if not quickly recovered.

PAN-PAN (Urgency) is used for *very urgent messages concerning the safety* of a vessel or person.

SÉCURITÉ (Safety) is usually used by coast stations to transmit navigational or weather warnings. It may also be used by vessels to report a hazard.

MAYDAY call by voice

A voice MAYDAY call is usually sent on VHF Ch 16 – the calling and distress channel. A distress call has priority over all other transmissions. The MAYDAY format below should be displayed by the radio.

Check the radio is ON, that HIGH POWER (25 watts) and Ch 16 are selected.

Press and hold down the transmit button, and say slowly and distinctly:

> **MAYDAY MAYDAY MAYDAY**
>
> **THIS IS** ....
> (name of boat, spoken three times)
>
> **MAYDAY** ....
> (name of boat spoken once & MMSI No)
>
> **MY POSITION IS** ....
> (latitude and longitude or true bearing and distance *from* a known point)
>
> **Nature of distress** ....
> (sinking, on fire etc)
>
> **Help required** ....
> (immediate assistance)
>
> **Number of persons on board** ....
> **Any other important, helpful information** ..
> (you are taking to the liferaft; distress rockets are being fired etc)
>
> **OVER**

Release the transmit button and listen. If an acknowledgement is not received, check the set and repeat the distress call.

False alerts

If a distress alert is inadvertently transmitted, an All Stations voice message on VHF Ch 16 cancelling the false alert must be sent at once: 'Cancel my Distress Alert of (date/time (GMT/UT)'.

Distress alert by DSC

A distress alert is typically sent as follows:

> Briefly press the red, guarded Distress button. The set will automatically switch to Ch 70. Press *again* for 5 seconds to transmit a basic distress alert* with position and time. The set then reverts to Ch 16.
>
> *If time permits, select the nature of the distress from the menu (eg Collision, Fire, Flooding) then press the Distress button for 5 seconds to send a full distress alert.

CG/CRS automatically send acknowledgements on Ch 70 before replying on Ch 16. Ships in range should reply directly on Ch 16. If a distress acknowledgement is not received from a CG/CRS, the distress alert will automatically be repeated by the radio every four minutes.

> When a DSC distress acknowledgement has been received, or after about 15 seconds, the vessel in distress should transmit a MAYDAY message by voice on Ch 16, including its MMSI and callsign.

MAYDAY acknowledgement

An acknowledgement should be expected:

> **MAYDAY** ....
> (name of vessel sending the distress message, spoken three times)
>
> **THIS IS** ....
> (name of station acknowledging, spoken three times)
>
> **RECEIVED MAYDAY**

On hearing a MAYDAY call, immediately cease all transmissions, listen on the frequency concerned and note down the details. If you can help, acknowledge accordingly but only after giving an opportunity for the nearest Coastguard Station or more suitable vessel to do so.

MAYDAY relay

If you hear a distress message from a vessel which is not acknowledged, you should pass on the message as follows:

> **MAYDAY RELAY** ....
> (spoken three times)
>
> **THIS IS** ....
> (name of vessel re-transmitting the distress message, spoken three times), followed by the intercepted message.

HELICOPTER RESCUE

- **COMMUNICATE ON CHANNEL 16**
- Use flares or smoke when helicopter is seen or heard
- Helicopter may ask you to drop sails and motor on a specific course
- You may be asked to stream the casualty astern in the dinghy
- Brief your crew early (too noisy when helicopter is close)
- **MAINTAIN YOUR COURSE** and do not get distracted
- Weighted line lowered
- Let it touch boat or water first (to earth any static charge)
- Take in slack line only
- **PULL LINE IN AS DIRECTED**
- **DO NOT SECURE IT TO THE BOAT**
- **DO EXACTLY AS YOU ARE TOLD**

    Note: The text and sketch relate to a Hi-line transfer, one of several techniques which may be used

URGENT MEDICAL HELP - PAN PAN

- **Send an URGENCY call by DSC**, if possible, and/or...
- **Make a PAN PAN voice call:**
- **CHANNEL 16, HIGH POWER (25W)** (if necessary, turn off dual watch)
- **PAN PAN** .... (repeat 3 times)
- **ALL STATIONS** .... (repeat 3 times)
- **THIS IS** .... (vessel's name; repeat 3 times)
- **OVER**
    Next message should include:
    Yacht's name, callsign, nationality
    Yacht's position and nearest harbour
    Patient's details, symptoms and advice wanted
    The medication you have on board

FIRST AID

The objectives of First Aid at sea are to:

- **Preserve life** • **Prevent further damage**
- **Relieve pain and distress**
- **Deliver a live casualty ashore**

With any casualty be calm, reassuring and methodical. First ensure your own safety and that of the vessel. If in doubt call for advice and assistance.

Completion of a First Aid Course is strongly recommended. In the UK, RYA approved, one-day, basic training is available through sailing clubs and schools. The St Johns Ambulance and British Red Cross provide a variety of recognised courses.

MEDICAL ADVICE can be obtained almost anywhere in European waters by making an All Stations 'PAN PAN' call or a DSC Urgency Alert to the Coastguard or to a Coast Radio Station. You will then be connected to a doctor or to the nearest hospital.

The Urgency signal 'PAN PAN' is always advised, especially abroad, because it is internationally understood and eliminates most language problems; it is also free.

If you are not qualified to judge how serious the casualty's condition is, get the best possible advice and/or help as quickly as possible. **Urgent help needed** is shown against the more serious medical problems.

Be ready to describe the patient's symptoms, eg consciousness, pulse rate, breathing rate, temperature, skin colour, site and type of injury, any pain, amount of blood lost etc. If a doctor needs to come aboard, or a casualty has to be landed, the Coastguard will arrange.

If non-urgent, wait until in harbour. Consider calling the port authority before arrival so that a doctor or paramedic can meet you on arrival.

MEDICAL CARE ABROAD It is advisable for each person on board to carry the European Health Insurance Card (EHIC) which entitles you to medical treatment on a reciprocal basis, although it may not cover the full charge. See *www.dh.gov.uk* for full details.

EMERGENCY RESUSCITATION (ABC)

The immediate procedure for any collapsed or apparently unconscious person is: Assess whether or not the casualty is conscious. Carefully shake his/her shoulders and ask loudly 'What's happened?' or 'Are you all right?' or give a command such as 'Open your eyes'. An unconscious casualty will not respond.

A = Airway

Remove any visible obstruction from the casualty's mouth (leave well-fitting dentures in place). Listen at the mouth for breathing. Tilt the head backwards, using head tilt and chin lift to maintain a clear airway.

Look, listen and feel for *no more than 10 seconds* to determine if the casualty is breathing normally. If in any doubt, act as if it is *not* normal.

If breathing, place casualty in recovery position. Check the area is clear of danger.

B = Breathing and C = Circulation

If not breathing and the airway is clear, start chest compressions. This situation is called **cardiac arrest**. The casualty will be unconscious and may appear very pale, grey or bluish in colour. An artificial circulation will have to be provided by chest compression. If the circulation stops, the breathing will also stop. Casualties with cardiac arrest will need both rescue breathing and chest compression, a combination known as Cardio Pulmonary Resuscitation (**CPR**).

External chest compression

To start external chest compression, lay the casualty face up on a hard, flat surface. Kneel beside casualty. Place the heel of your hand on top of the other hand and interlock your fingers. Apply pressure at the centre of the chest.

Depress breastbone 5–6cm (2–2½in) then release.

With either one or two operators give 30 chest compressions and continue cycles of 2 breaths to 30 compressions. Use a compression rate of 100 per minute. Chest compression should be combined with rescue breaths; after 30 compressions, give 2 effective rescue breaths (2 breaths should not take more than 5 seconds). *Do not stop.*

Action plan for the resuscitation of adults

Casualty unconscious but is breathing normally:

- *Urgent help needed*
- Turn casualty into the recovery position
- Check for continued breathing

Casualty is unconscious and not breathing:

- *Urgent help needed*
- Start chest compressions
- After 30 compressions, give 2 rescue breaths

Continue with chest compressions and rescue breaths in a ratio of 30:2. If you are untrained, or are unwilling to give rescue breaths, give chest compressions only. Stop to re-check casualty only if he/she starts to show signs of regaining consciousness; coughing, opening eyes, speaking or moving purposefully *and* starts to breath normally. If so place the casualty in the recovery position. Otherwise, *do not interrupt resuscitation*.

BITES AND STINGS Injected poison from bites and stings usually only causes local swelling and discomfort, but some people may react severely. For insect stings, resuscitate if collapse occurs; otherwise give rest, painkillers, antihistamines (eg chlorpheniramine).

BLEEDING – OPEN WOUND Bleeding is often very dramatic, but is virtually always controllable.

* Apply firm continuous direct pressure; bandage on a large pad. If bleeding continues, bandage more pads on top of initial pads; then press directly over wound for at least 10 minutes (blood takes this long to clot).
* Elevate if wound is on a limb.
* Do *not* apply a tourniquet. This practice is out of date due to the danger of losing a limb.

BLEEDING – INTERNAL (CLOSED INJURY)
Follows fractured bones, crush injuries, or rupture of organs such as the liver or spleen. Treat for shock which may appear rapidly. ***Urgent help needed.***

BURNS AND SCALDS Move the victim into fresh air to avoid inhaling smoke.

ABC – Airway, Breathing, Circulation

* Stop further injury: dip the whole of the burnt part into cold water for 10–15 minutes. Seawater is excellent but may be very painful.
* Remove only loose clothing. Do not pull off clothing stuck to the skin.
* Cover with sterile dressing. If skin is broken or blistered, use sterile paraffin gauze beneath the dressing. Separate burnt fingers with paraffin gauze. Never use adhesive dressings.
* Do not prick blisters or apply ointments.
* Elevate burnt limb and immobilise.
* Give strong painkillers.
* Treat for shock: give frequent and copious drinks of water.
* Start giving antibiotics for major burns. If burns extensive or deep, ***urgent help needed.***

CHOKING If blockage by some object (eg a peanut) is suspected, turn the casualty on his side and give up to 5 sharp back slaps with the flat of the hand between the shoulder blades. Check mouth and remove any obstruction.

If unsuccessful, wrap both arms around the victim's waist from behind, and give 5 sharp upward thrusts with both fists into the abdomen above the navel but below the ribs so as to cause coughing. Clear object from mouth.

CUTS AND WOUNDS Often dramatic but only potentially serious if nerves, tendons or blood vessels are severed.

Clean thoroughly with antiseptic. Remove dirt or other foreign bodies. Small clean cuts can be closed using as many Steristrips as necessary to keep the skin edges together. Skin must be dry. Leave for 5 days at least. Larger deep cuts may require stitches; apply a dressing and seek help. Do not try amateur surgery at sea.

Ragged lacerations or very dirty wounds – do not attempt to close these. Clean as well as possible, sprinkle antibiotic powder in wound and apply a dressing. Seek help. If in doubt a wound is best left open and lightly covered to keep it clean and dry.

Fingers and toes Blood may collect under the nail following an injury. Release the blood by piercing the nail with a red hot needle or paper clip. It will not hurt!

DENTAL PAIN seems worse at sea; prevention is better than cure. Dentanurse is an emergency treatment pack which enables an amateur to make temporary repairs, eg replacing crowns, lost fillings. It contains zinc oxide and Eugenol.

Throbbing toothache made worse by hot or cold or when bitten on. Clean out any cavity and apply temporary filling. Take painkiller.

Dull toothache tender to bite on; gum swollen or red with possible discharge. Treat as above but also take an antibiotic.

Broken tooth or filling Cover exposed surfaces with zinc oxide paste. Teeth knocked out should be put in a clean container with milk or moist gauze for a dentist to re-implant asap. This can be attempted onboard - ideally within 1 hour

Bleeding gums Clean teeth more thoroughly. Use regular hot salt water rinses and antibiotics.

Pain round wisdom tooth Clean area with toothbrush; use hot salt water rinses; take antibiotics and painkillers.

Mouth ulcers Hot salt water rinses.

DIARRHOEA Can become serious, especially in young children if much fluid is lost. Stop food, give plenty of fluid. Plain water is usually sufficient, or add salt (1 teaspoonful/litre) and sugar (4–5 teaspoons/litre). Lomotil or Imodium tablets are very effective in adults.

DROWNING ABC Clear seaweed, dentures. If not breathing start mouth to mouth ventilation as soon as possible and in the water if practicable. If no pulse, start chest compression as soon as on board. Keep the head low so that vomit is not inhaled and water can drain.

If stomach is bulging, turn casualty on to side to empty water and avoid inhaling it. Prevent cooling. Remove wet clothes; wrap casualty in blankets to warm him/her.

Continue resuscitation until the casualty revives or death is certain. Hypothermia may mimic death. Do not abandon resuscitation until the casualty has been warmed or signs of death persist despite attempts at warming.

Once revived, put in the recovery position.

Any person rescued from drowning may collapse in the next 24 hours as the lungs react to inhaled water. *Urgent help needed*.

EYE INJURIES are potentially serious. Never put old or previously opened ointment or drops into an eye; serious infection could result.

Foreign object Flush with clean water, pull the lower lid out to inspect, remove object with a clean tissue. For objects under upper eyelid, ask casualty to grasp lashes and pull the upper lid over the lower lid. An eye-bath is very effective. Blinking under water may help. After removal of object, insert sterile antibiotic ointment inside pulled out lower lid. Cover with pad.

Corrosive fluid Flush continuously with water for 15 minutes. Give painkillers and chloramphenicol ointment; cover with pad. *Seek help asap*.

Conjunctivitis Sticky, weeping eye with yellow discharge. Chloramphenicol 4 times a day.

FISH HOOKS Push the hook round until the point and barb can be cut off; withdraw the hook. Dress the holes and give an antibiotic.

FRACTURES AND DISLOCATIONS Fracture is a broken bone. Dislocation is a displaced joint. Both produce pain (aggravated by attempted movement), localised swelling, abnormal shape, and a grating feeling on movement (if it is a fracture). Blood vessels or nerves around the fracture or dislocation may also be damaged causing a cold, pale, or numb limb below the site of the injury.

Fractures of large bones such as the femur (upper leg) will result in major internal bleeding and may cause shock. When complications occur *urgent help is needed*.

Early application of a splint and raising the injured limb where possible will reduce pain and complications. Treat for shock and pain.

Specific fractures and dislocations
Cheek Caused by a direct blow. Rarely serious but requires specialist care.
Jaw Beware of associated brain or spinal injury. Remove blood and teeth fragments; leave loose teeth in place; protect broken teeth. Ensure airway is clear. Start regular antiseptic mouth washes and antibiotics. Support jaw with bandage over top of the head. Give only fluids by mouth.
Neck May result from a direct blow, a fall or a whiplash type injury. If conscious, casualty may complain of pain, tingling, numbness or weakness in limbs below the injury. *Mishandling may damage the spinal cord, causing paralysis or death*. Avoid movement and support the head. Immobilise by wrapping a folded towel around the neck. If movement is necessary then lift the victim as one rigid piece, never allowing the neck to bend. *Urgent help needed.*

Nose Control bleeding by pinching.
Ribs Very painful. Strapping is not advised.
Spine Fracture of the spine below the neck, may cause *paralysis or death*. Mishandling of the victim may greatly worsen the damage. Avoid movement if possible. Lift the casualty without allowing the spine to sag. *Urgent help needed.*
Collar bone Support arm in sling.
Dislocated shoulder If this has happened before, the casualty may remedy the dislocation himself; otherwise do not attempt to remedy it in case a fracture exists.
Upper arm Support the arm with a collar and cuff inside the shirt, ie tie a clove hitch around the wrist and loop the ends behind the neck.
Forearm and wrist Splint (eg with battens or wood). Do not bandage tightly. Elevate or support in a sling.
Fingers Elevate hand and, unless badly crushed, leave unbandaged; keep moving. If very wobbly, bandage to adjacent finger.
Lower limb
Thigh Shock may be considerable. Strap to other leg with padding between. Gently straighten the lower leg. If necessary apply traction at the ankle to help straighten the leg. Do not bandage too tightly.
Knee Twisting injuries or falls damage the ligaments and cartilages of the knee. Very painful and swollen. Treat as for fracture.
Lower leg Pad very well. Splint using oar, broom handle or similar pieces of wood.
Ankle Fracture or severe sprain may be indistinguishable. Immobilise in neutral position with foot at right angles. Raise the limb.

HEART ATTACK Severe 'crushing' chest pain; may spread to shoulders, neck or arms. Sweating, then bluish lips, then collapse. Breathing and heart may stop. Give one 300mg aspirin tablet (to chew) *Urgent help needed*.

Rest, reassure. If unconscious: recovery position; observe breathing and pulse. If breathing stops or no pulse, start mouth to mouth ventilation and chest compression immediately; do not stop.

STROKE Symptoms: if a person develops **sudden** onset weakness on one side of the body, problems with speech &/or visual problems: *think of stroke*.

SAFETY

135

Recognise a stroke using the FAST test:
- Face – Has side of face fallen; can they smile?
- Arms – Can both arms be raised and kept up?
- Speech – Is it slurred or muddled?
- Time – To call for help.

Place in recovery position and check airway. *Urgent help needed* – specialist treatment within 4½ hours can reverse the effects of a stroke. If you are more than 4½ hours from help, and the casualty is conscious and able to swallow, give 300mg of asprin even if he/she is improving.

HEAT STROKE Cool casualty by spraying with cold water or wrap the casualty in a cold wet sheet until their temperature under the tongue falls to 38°C. Encourage drinking (1 teaspoon of salt/ half litre of water). If casualty stops sweating, has a rapid pounding pulse and is becoming unconscious: *Urgent help needed.*

HYPOTHERMIA Symptoms: unreasonable behaviour, apathy and confusion; unsteady gait, stumbling; slurring of speech; pale, cold skin; slow, weak pulse; slow breathing; shivering. It leads to collapse, unconsciousness and ultimately death.

ABC Put in recovery position. If not breathing, start mouth to mouth ventilation. Be prepared to use chest compressions.

Remove wet clothing. Avoid wind chill. Dry and wrap in blankets or sleeping bag plus warm hat and cover, if available, in foil survival bag. *Urgent help needed.*

Give hot sweet drinks if conscious. Do not give alcohol, rub or place very hot objects against skin.

SEASICKNESS is aggravated by anxiety, fatigue and boredom. Symptoms: lethargy, dizziness, headache and nausea/vomiting. Help prevent with anti-seasickness pills, avoiding rich foods and alcohol. Take frequent small amounts of fluid and food. Keep warm; keep busy. Prolonged seasickness may cause serious loss of fluid – seek advice.

SHOCK can result from almost any accident or medical emergency; it can lead to collapse.

Signs and symptoms Thirst, apathy, nausea, restlessness. Pale, cold, clammy skin, sweating. Rapid, weak pulse. Rapid, shallow breathing. Dull, sunken eyes, bluish lips.

ABC Control any bleeding. Lay the casualty flat or in recovery position; raise legs 20°. Splint any fractures; avoid movement. Avoid chilling, keep warm. Give pain killers. Reassure the casualty. Do not let the casualty eat, drink, smoke or move unnecessarily. If complaining of thirst, moisten the lips with a little water. Note: Fluids may be life saving in cases of dehydration (eg diarrhoea, vomiting, severe burns).

FIRST AID KIT

Stow the following items in a waterproof container, readily accessible and clearly marked:

Triangular bandage x 2 (doubles as a sling)
Crepe bandage 75mm x 2
Gauze bandage 50mm x 2
Elastoplast 75mm x 1
Band Aids (or similar) various shapes and sizes
Wound dressings, 1 large, 1 medium
Sterile non-adhesive dressing (Melolin) x 5
Steristrips x 5 packs
Cotton wool. Safety pins. Thermometer.
Scissors and forceps, good quality stainless steel
Disposable gloves
Antiseptic solution (eg Savlon)
Sunscreen with high protection factor
Antifungal powder or cream (athlete's foot)
Insect repellent (DEET, diethyltoluamide)
Individual choice of anti-seasick tablets
Antibiotic eye ointment (prescription only)

Additional items for extended cruising

Vaccinations – a course may need to start as much as 6 months before departure.

Syringes 2ml x 2 (if carrying injections)

Dental kit – see Dental pain.

DRUGS AND MEDICATION

Paracetamol, painkiller. 1-2 500mg tablets 4 hrly.

Asprin, blood thiner. 300mg single dose for heart attack or stroke.

Ibuprofen, anti-inflammatory. 400mg every 8 hours (avoid if history of asthma or stomach ulcer).

*Dihydrocodeine, strong painkiller. 1-2 30mg tablets 4 hourly.

Certirizine, antihistamine. 10mg once a day.

Aludrox, indigestion. 1-2 before meals.

Loperamide, diarrhoea. 2 x 2mg capsules initially, then 1 after each loose stool; max 8 day.

Senokot, constipation. 2-4 tablets per day.

*Amoxycillin, antibiotic. 2 x 250mg capsules 8 hourly (beware penicillin allergy)

*Erythromycin, antibiotic for penicillin-allergic adults. 4 x 250mg tablets daily.

Cinnarizine, seasickness. 2 x 15mg tablets before sailing, then 1 every 8 hours.

*Scopolamine patches, seasickness. 1 patch behind ear 5-6 hours before voyage; replace after 72 hrs if necessary.

Chloramphenicol ointment 1%, eye infection, apply 3-4 times/day

* Only available on prescription.

OBSERVATION FORM

The information recorded by you on this form will be invaluable in helping doctors and/or paramedics ashore to diagnose the problem and arrange the best possible treatment for your casualty.

This is particularly important if there may be a considerable time lapse between requesting medical help and the casualty reaching hospital.

- Keep photocopies of this form in your First Aid kit so as to preserve the original.
  Whilst awaiting help, record your careful observations by ticking or annotating the various boxes at 10 minute intervals. This will help doctors detect any improvement or deterioration in the casualty's condition.

- If within radio range of shore attempt to pass the observations via the Coastguard to a medical authority; or ask a ship to relay.

- Before the casualty is taken off the yacht ensure that this form and personal documents (money, passport, EHIC and mobile 'phone) are securely tied to him/her.

DATE .... CASUALTY'S NAME .... AGE .... M/F ....

Times of observations @ 10 minute intervals:		10	20	30	40	50	60
EYES Observe for reactions whilst testing other responses	Open spontaneously						
	Open when spoken to						
	Open to painful stimulus						
	Nil response						
MOVEMENT Apply painful stimulus: Pinch ear lobe or skin on back of hand	Obeys commands						
	Responds						
	Nil response						
SPEECH Speak clearly and directly, close to the casualty's ear	Responds sensibly to queries						
	Seems confused						
	Uses inappropriate words						
	Incomprehensible sounds						
	Nil response						
PULSE (Beats per minute) Take adult's pulse at wrist or neck. Note rate and whether beats are: weak (w); strong (s); regular (reg) or irregular (irreg)	Over 110						
	101-110						
	91-100						
	81-90						
	71-80						
	61-70						
	Below 61						
BREATHING (Breaths per minute) Note rate and whether breathing is: quiet (q); noisy (n); easy (e); or difficult (d)	Over 40						
	31-40						
	21-30						
	11-20						
	Below 11						

GMDSS

The Global Maritime Distress and Safety System (GMDSS) is a sophisticated, but complex, semi-automatic, third-generation communications system. Although not compulsory for yachts, its potential for saving life, particularly when far offshore and out of VHF range, is so great that every yachtsman should seriously consider it. Equipment costs continue to fall. Training courses, leading to the award of the Short Range Certificate (SRC) of Competence, are widely available. The Long Range Certificate covers MF, HF, SatCom, EPIRBs and SART.

Recommended reading:

- *ALRS, Vol 5* (UK Hydrographic Office)
- *GMDSS: a User's Handbook* (Bréhaut/ACN)
- *GMDSS for small craft* (Clemmetsen/ Fernhurst)
- *Reeds VHF/DSC Handbook* (Fletcher/ACN)

Purpose

GMDSS enables a coordinated SAR operation to be mounted rapidly and reliably anywhere at sea. To this end, terrestrial and satellite communications and navigation equipment is used to alert SAR authorities ashore and ships in the vicinity to a Distress incident or Urgency situation. GMDSS also promulgates Maritime Safety Information.

Sea areas

For the purposes of GMDSS, the world's sea areas are divided into 4 categories (A1-4), defined mainly by the range of radio communications. These are:

A1 An area within R/T coverage of at least one VHF Coastguard or Coast radio station in which continuous VHF alerting is available via DSC. Range: 20–50M from the CG/CRS.

A2 An area, excluding sea area A1, within R/T coverage of at least one MF CG/ CRS in which continuous DSC alerting is available. Range: approx 50–250M from the CG/CRS.

A3 An area between 76°N and 76°S, excluding sea areas A1 and A2, within coverage of HF or an Inmarsat satellite in which continuous alerting is available.

A4 An area outside sea areas A1, A2 and A3, ie the polar regions, within coverage of HF.

The radio equipment to be carried by GMDSS vessels for each sea area category is specified: in

- A1 – VHF DSC;
- A2 – VHF and MF DSC;
- A3 – VHF, MF + HF/SatCom;
- A4 VHF, MF and HF.

Most UK yachtsmen will operate in A1 areas (the English Channel, for example, is an A1 area) where a simple VHF radio and a NAVTEX receiver will initially meet GMDSS requirements. As equipment becomes more affordable, yachtsmen may decide to fit GMDSS. This will become increasingly necessary as the present system for sending and receiving Distress calls is run down. The CG will continue a loudspeaker watch on VHF Ch 16 until further notice.

Functions

Regardless of the sea areas in which they operate, vessels complying with GMDSS must be able to perform certain functions:

- transmit ship-to-shore Distress alerts by two independent means
- receive shore-to-ship Distress alerts
- transmit & receive ship-to-ship Distress alerts
- transmit signals for locating incidents
- transmit and receive communications for SAR co-ordination
- transmit/receive maritime safety info, eg navigation and weather warnings

Distress alerts

A Distress alert is simply a Distress call using DSC. It is transmitted on Ch 70 and is automatically repeated five times. Whenever possible, a Distress alert should always include the last known position and time in UT. The position is normally entered automatically from an interfaced GPS, but can be entered manually if required. The nature of the distress can also be selected from the receiver's menu. The vessel's identity (MMSI number) is automatically included.

GMDSS requires participating ships to be able to send Distress alerts by two out of three independent means. These are:

- Digital Selective Calling (DSC) using terrestrial communications, ie VHF Ch 70, MF 2187·5 kHz, or HF distress and alerting frequencies in the 4, 6, 8,12 and 16 MHz bands.
- Emergency Position Indicating Radio Beacons (EPIRBs). See below.
- Inmarsat, via ship terminals.

Digital Selective Calling

DSC is an essential component of GMDSS.

Information is sent by a burst of digital code, which can be selectively addressed to a specific DSC-equipped vessel or group of vessels.

Every vessel and relevant shore station has a 9-digit identification number, or MMSI (Maritime Mobile Service Identity), which is in effect an automatic, electronic callsign.

DSC is used to transmit Distress alerts from ships, to receive Distress acknowledgements from ships or shore stations; to send Urgency and Safety alerts; to relay Distress alerts; and for routine calling & answering.

Maritime Safety Information (MSI)

MSI consists of the vital navigational, weather and safety messages sent to vessels at sea by R/T on VHF, MF broadcasts and GMDSS. For navigation and weather warnings see this and Chapter 2 respectively.

GMDSS transmits MSI in English by two independent but complementary means, NAVTEX and SafetyNet.

- NAVTEX on MF (518 kHz and 490 kHz) which can be received out to about 300 miles offshore, see Chapter 2.

- SafetyNet uses Inmarsat-C satellites to cover beyond MF range, except Area A4. Enhanced Group Calling (EGC) is a part of SafetyNet which enables MSI to be sent to selected groups of users in any of the four oceans.

Personal Locator Beacons (PLB) operate on the same principle. They must also be registered but they do not have a vessel-specific MMSI.

Emergency Position Indicating Radio Beacons (EPIRB) may be hand-held or float-free, they transmit on 406 MHz. Most EPIRBs have a built in GPS and about 48 hours of battery life. They communicate via the Cospas-Sarsat (C/S) network of geostationary and polar orbit satellites. Although C/S will relay an EPIRB signal to earth with no delay, the position of a non-GPS EPIRB may take several hours to determine.

An EPIRB transmits uniquely coded data to identify the individual beacon and it must be registered. It is important that any changes are immediately notified. The UK registration centre is:-

The EPIRB Registry, The Maritime and Coastguard Agency, CGOC Falmouth, Pendennis Point, Castle Drive, Falmouth, Cornwall TR11 4WZ; ☎ 01326 211569; email: epirb@mcga.gov.uk.

False alerts caused by inadvertent or incorrect use of EPIRBs put a significant burden on SAR Centres and may coincide with an actual distress situation. If an EPIRB is activated accidentally, advise the nearest CG/CRS as soon as possible.

All crew members should be aware of the proper use of the EPIRB onboard. Ensure that testing is adequately supervised; that the EPIRB is correctly installed and maintained; and that it is not activated if assistance is already available.

Search And Rescue Transponders (SART) are radar transceivers which operate on 9 GHz and respond to 3 cm (X-band) radars, like a small portable Racon (see Chapter 3). They are primarily intended for use in liferafts to help searching ships and aircraft find survivors. The transmitted signal shows on a radar screen as 12 dots radiating out from the SART's position.

SAFETY

HM COASTGUARD – CONTACT DETAILS

SCOTLAND & NORTHERN IRELAND

†SHETLAND COASTGUARD
60°09'N 01°08'W. MMSI 002320001
Knab Road, Lerwick ZE1 0AX.
☎ 01595 692976. 📠 01595 694810.
Area: Orkney, Fair Isle and Shetland and mainland from C Wrath to S of Brora, incl Pentland Firth

†ABERDEEN COASTGUARD
57°08'N 02°05'W. MMSI 002320004
Marine House, Blaikies Quay, Aberdeen AB11 5PB.
☎ 01224 592334. 📠 01224 212862.
Area: English border to Cape Wrath, incl Pentland Firth. .

†*STORNOWAY COASTGUARD
58°12'N 06°22'W. MMSI 002320024
Battery Pt, Stornoway, Isle of Lewis H51 2RT.
☎ 01851 702013. 📠 01851 704387.
Area: Cape Wrath to Mull, Western Isles and St Kilda.

†*BELFAST COASTGUARD
54°40'N 05°40'W. MMSI 002320021
Bregenz House, Quay St, Bangor, Co Down BT20 5ED.
☎ 02891 463933. 📠 02891 465886.
Area: Carlingford Lough to Lough Foyle and Firth of Clyde, incl islands.

EASTERN REGION

†HUMBER COASTGUARD
54°06'N 00°11'W. MMSI 002320007
Lime Kiln Lane, Bridlington,
N Humberside YO15 2LX.
☎ 01262 672317. 📠 01262 606915.
Area: Southwold to the Scottish border.

LONDON COASTGUARD
51°30'N 00°03'E   MMSI 002320063   ☎ 0208 3127380 📠 0208 3098196. Thames Barrier Navigation Centre, Unit 28, 34 Bowater Road, Woolwich, London SE18 5TF.
Area: River Thames from Shell Haven Pt (N bank) and Egypt Bay (S bank), up-river to Teddington Lock.

DOVER COASTGUARD
50°08'N 01°20'E   DSC MMSI 002320010
☎ 01304 210008   📠 01304 225762
Langdon Battery, Swingate, Dover CT15 5NA.
Area: Beachy Head to Southwold Note: In this area, use call signs *Thames Coastguard* or *Dover Coastguard*, both VHF Ch 16. Also operates Channel Navigation Information Service (CNIS)

NATIONAL MARITIME OPERATIONS CENTRE FAREHAM, (NMOC)
50°51'·50N 01°14'·90W   DSC MMSI, 002320011
☎ 02392 552100   📠 02392 554131/01305 760451. Kites Croft, Fareham PO14 4LW.
Area: South Coast: Topsham (River Exe) to Beachy Head (Note: in this area make initial calls to *Solent Coastguard* on Ch 67 (H24) to avoid congestion on Ch 16).

WESTERN REGION

†*FALMOUTH COASTGUARD
50°09'N 05°03'W. MMSI 002320014
Pendennis Point, Castle Drive,
Falmouth TR11 4WZ.
☎ 01326 317575. 📠 01326 318342.
Area: Marsland Mouth to Topsham (R. Exe).
NOTES: †Monitors DSC MF 2187.5 kHz.
*Broadcasts Gunfacts/Subfacts.

†MILFORD HAVEN COASTGUARD
51°42'N 05°03'W. MMSI 002320017
Gorsewood Drive, Hakin,
Milford Haven, SA73 2HD.
☎ 01646 690909. 📠 01646 692176.
Area: Friog to Marsland Mouth (nr Bude).

†HOLYHEAD COASTGUARD
53°19'N 04°38'W. MMSI 002320018
Prince of Wales Rd, Holyhead,
Anglesey LL65 1ET.
☎ 01407 762051. 📠 01407 764373.
Area: Area: Mull of Galloway to Friog (1·6M S of Barmouth) inc Isle of Man.

THE SEA SAFETY GROUP – www.seasafetygroup.org – a charity, is an association of independent coastal watch stations, each authorised by HM CG (MCA) to provide additional lookout and communications cover around the UK. They are similar in ethos but separate from the NCI. Stations are:

Pakefield	07367 096492
Happisburgh	07500 628299
Winterton	01493 393989
Sheringham	01263 821200
Hartlepool	07946 036793
Redcar	01642 491606
Sunderland	01915 672579
Berwick	07738 269071
St Monans	07706 664839
Tay	07849 184354
Irvine	01294 271855

NATIONAL COASTWATCH INSTITUTION (NCI)

www.nci.org.uk, a national charity, is a voluntary organisation keeping visual watch along the coast of England and Wales, assisting the preservation and protection of life at sea. The National Office is 17 Dean St, Liskeard, Cornwall, PL14 4AB ☎(01579) 347392. There are 56 operational stations (2021) manned by over 2600 volunteers. They are marked on the Area maps by the symbol © and maintain direct contact with HM CG.

Stations monitor VHF Ch **65** 16, HM CG channels and local operational VHF channels. **65** is the NCI dedicated channel. Seafarers can call directly for radio/AIS checks, actual weather, sea state, hazards and local info.

South West and South Coast

St Mary's, Scilly	01720 422641
Gwennap Head	01736 871351
Penzance	01736 367063
Bass Point (Lizard)	01326 290212
Nare Point (Helford)	01326 231113
Portscatho (w/ends only)	01872 580180
Charlestown	01726 817068
Polruan (Fowey)	01726 870291
Rame Head (Plymouth)	01752 823706
Prawle Point (Salcombe)	01548 511259
Froward Pt (Dartmouth)	07976 505649
Torbay	01803 411145
Teignmouth	01626 772377
Exmouth	01395 222492
Lyme Bay	07745 756872
Charmouth	01308 897778
Portland Bill	01305 860178
St Alban's Head	01929 439220
Swanage	01929 422596

South West and South Coast

Peveril Pt (Swanage)	01929 422596
Hengistbury Hd	07851 672540
Needles	01983 754321

Calshot	02380 893562
Lee on Solent	02392 556758
Gosport	02392 765194
Shoreham	01273 463292
Newhaven	01273 516464
Folkestone (Copt Pt)	01303 227132
Herne Bay (w/ends only)	01227 744454
Whitstable (w/ends only)	07864 646209

East Anglia

Holehaven (Canvey Is)	01268 696971
Southend (w/ends only)	0781 5945210
Felixstowe	01394 670808
Gorleston (Gt Yarmouth)	01493 440384
Caister	07527 977613
Mundesley	01263 722399
Runton	01263 513725
Wells-next-the-Sea	01328 710587

East Coast

Skegness	07902 076605
Mablethorpe	07958 038564
Hornsea	01964 668248

North West Coast

Rossall Pt (Fleetwood)	01253 681378

Wales

Point Lynas	No landline
Rhoscolyn	07887 955496
Porth Dinllean	07773 362005
Wooltack Point (St Brides)	01646 636802
Worms Head (Gower)	01792 390167
Porthcawl	01656 782936
St Donat's Bay	07747 410135
Nells Point (Barry)	01446 420746

South West, North Coast

Boscastle	01840 250965
Stepper Point (Padstow)	01841 530039
St Agnes Head	01872 552073
St Ives	01736 799398
Cape Cornwall	01736 787890

ROYAL NATIONAL LIFEBOAT INSTITUTION

The RNLI is a registered charity which saves life at sea providing a lifeboat service H24 up to 50M off the UK and Irish coasts. There are 237 lifeboat stations, and a combined fleet of over 340 all-weather boats (ALB's) and inshore craft (ILB's). On active service, lifeboats >10m keep watch on VHF and MF DSC as well as VHF Ch 16. They use alternative frequencies to contact shore agencies, SAR aircraft, and HMCG. All show a quick-flashing blue light.

The RNLI actively promotes safety at sea by providing a free safety service both to members and the general public including help, advice, publications and demonstrations, to prevent accidents by helping people to be better prepared through water safety awareness.

If you wish to help support the RNLI financially, ☎ 0300 300 9990, visit www.rnli.org.uk or supporter_care@rnli.gov.uk for details of membership options.

Their website page 'Safety' covers emergencies, first aid, seamanship, navigation, weather, and engines, with contact details for safety checks. Their headquarters are at: RNLI, West Quay Road, Poole, Dorset BH15 1HZ.

THE CHANNEL ISLANDS

Guernsey and Jersey Coastguard stations direct SAR operations in the North and South of the CI area respectively, they also provide communications on VHF and DSC.

Close liaison is maintained with adjacent French SAR authorities. A distress situation may be controlled by the Channel Islands or France, whichever is more appropriate. For example a British yacht in difficulty in French waters may be handled by St Peter Port or Jersey so as to avoid language problems; and vice versa for a French yacht.

GUERNSEY CG 49°27'·00N 02°32'00W. DSC MMSI 002320064. ☎ 01481 720672. ⛵ 714177. Area: Channel Islands North.

JERSEY CG 49°10'·85N 02°14'30W. DSC MMSI 002320060. ☎: 01534 447705. ⛵: 499089. Area: Channel Islands South.

SEARCH AND RESCUE ABROAD
THE IRISH REPUBLIC

The Irish CG co-ordinates SAR operations around the coast of Ireland via Dublin MRCC, Malin Head and Valentia MRSCs and remote sites. It may liaise with the UK and France during any rescue operation within 100M of the Irish coast.

It is part of the Dept of Marine, Leeson Lane, Dublin 2. ☎ (01) 678 3454; ⛵ (01) 662 0795. The Irish EPIRB Registry is co-located; ☎ (01) 6199280; ⛵ (01) 6621571.

The MRCC/MRSCs are co-located with the Coast radio stations of the same name and manned by the same staff. All stations keep watch H24 on VHF Ch 16 and DSC Ch 70. If ashore dial 999 or 112 in an emergency and ask for Marine Rescue.

Details of the MRCC/MRSCs are as follows:

DUBLIN (MRCC)
53°20'N 06°15W. DSC MMSI 002500300 (+2187·5 kHz).
☎ +353 1 662 0922/3; ⛵ +353 1 662 0795.
Area: Carlingford Lough to Youghal.

VALENTIA (MRSC)
51°56'N 10°21'W. DSC MMSI 002500200 (+2187·5 kHz).
☎ +353 669 476 109; ⛵ +353 669 476 289.
Area: Youghal to Slyne Head.

MALIN HEAD (MRSC)
55°22'N 07°20W. DSC MMSI 002500100 (+2187·5 kHz).
☎ +353 749 370103; ⛵ +353 749 370221.
Area: Slyne Head to Lough Foyle.

SAR resources

The Irish CG provides some 50 units around the coast and is on call H24. The RNLI maintains 4 stations around the coast and operates 42 lifeboats; six community-run inshore rescue boats are also available.

Sikorsky S-61 helicopters, based at Dublin, Waterford, Shannon and Sligo, can respond within 15 to 45 minutes and operate to a radius of 200M. They are equipped with infrared search equipment and can uplift 30 survivors.

Military and civilian aircraft and vessels, together with the Garda and lighthouse service, can also be called upon.

Some stations provide specialist cliff climbing services. They are manned by volunteers, who are trained in first aid and equipped with inflatables, breeches buoys, cliff ladders, etc. Their ☎ numbers (the Leader's residence) are given, where appropriate, under each port.

Irish Coastguard centres

DENMARK

The national SAR agency is: JRCC Defence Command Denmark, Defence Command Denmark, JOC Herningvej 30, Karup J, Denmark. ☎ +45 72850380 (switchboard) ⛵ +45 72850384.

The SAR coordinator for Denmark is: **JRCC Denmark**, ☎+45 72850450 switchboard; ⛵+45 72850384; jrcc@sok.dk MMSI 002191000

JRCC Denmark has no direct communications with vessels in distress, but operates via two Maritime Operations Centres (MOC's) and

Coast Radio Station (CRS) Lyngby Radio. **MOC North (MRSC)** ☎ +45 992 21520; 🖷 +45 992 21538, mocn-orum@mil.dk, covers the W coast of Denmark.

Lyngby Radio

This is the main Danish CRS and is DSC VHF/MF/HF equipped. ☎ +45 72198410; 🖷 +45 458 82485, vfk-ktp-joc-lyngbyradio@fiin.dk MMSI 002191000.

Its remote sites at Skagen, Hirtshals, Hantsholm, Bovbjerg and Blavand, all monitor Ch 16 H24 and use callsign *Lyngby Radio*. Their VHF and MF frequencies are shown in the chartlet below.

Firing practice areas

There are four such areas on the W coast as in the chartlet and listed below. Firing times are broadcast daily by Danmarks Radio 1 (243 kHz LW) after the weather at 1745LT. Times can also be obtained from the Range office Ch 16 or ☎.

Ⓐ Tranum & Blokhus ☎+45 728 39699 or call *Tranum.*

Ⓑ Nymindegab ☎+45 728 39550 or call *Nymindegab.*

Ⓒ Oksbøl ☎+45 728 39550 call *Oksbøl,* or see:www.forsvaret.dk/oksbol

Ⓓ Rømø E ☎+45 728 39550 (☎+45 737 55219/2148290 during firing) or call *Fly Rømø.* Rømø W ☎ +45 728 48121 .

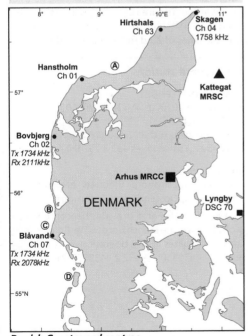

Danish Coastguard centres

GERMANY

The national SAR agency is: *Deutsche Gesellschaft zur Rettung Schiffbrüchiger* (DGzRS), the German Sea Rescue Service. Werderstrasse 2, Hermann-Helms-Haus, D-28199 Bremen. info@seenotretter.de. ☎ +49 421 536870 (emergency), 421 53707-0 (ops); 🖷 421 537 07690.

DGzRS is responsible for coordinating SAR operations, supported by ships and SAR helicopters of the German Navy.

Bremen MRCC (☎ +49 421 536870; mail@mrcc-bremen.de, MMSI 002111240), using call sign *Bremen Rescue Radio,* maintains an H24 watch on Ch 16 and DSC Ch 70 via remote Coast radio stations at: Blumenthal / Borkum / Cuxhaven / Helgoland / kampen / Norderney / Stade / Wangerooge / Westerhever.

DGzRS has a total of 20 offshore lifeboats 20-26m LOA and 40 <11m LOA along the German seaboard with 12 large and 16 small based on their North Sea coast at: List, Amrum, Helgoland, Cuxhaven, Bremerhaven, Wilhelmshaven, Langeoog, Norderney and Borkum. There are also many inshore lifeboats.

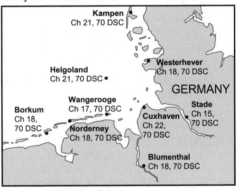

German Coastguard stations

THE NETHERLANDS

The national SAR agency is: SAR Commission, Directorate Transport Safety (DGG), PO Box 20904, 2500 EX The Hague, Netherlands.

The Netherlands CG at Den Helder, co-located with the Navy HQ, coordinates SAR operations as the Dutch JRCC for A1 and A2 Sea Areas. (JRCC = Joint Rescue Coordination Centre – marine & aeronautical.) Callsign is *Netherlands Coastguard,* but *Den Helder Rescue* during SAR operations.

The JRCC keeps a listening watch H24 on DSC Ch 70, and MF DSC 2187·5 kHz (but not on 2182 kHz); MMSI 002442000.

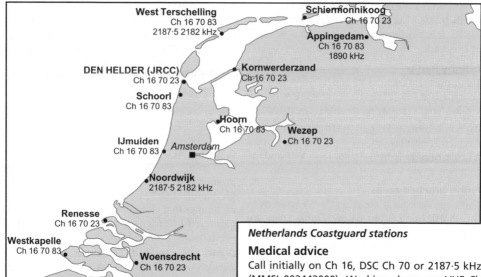

West Terschelling
Ch 16 70 83
2187·5 2182 kHz

Schiermonnikoog
Ch 16 70 23

Appingedam
Ch 16 70 83
1890 kHz

DEN HELDER (JRCC)
Ch 16 70 23

Kornwerderzand
Ch 16 70 23

Schoorl
Ch 16 70 83

Hoorn
Ch 16 70 83

Wezep
Ch 16 70 23

IJmuiden
Ch 16 70 83

Amsterdam

Noordwijk
2187·5 2182 kHz

Renesse
Ch 16 70 23

Westkapelle
Ch 16 70 83

Woensdrecht
Ch 16 70 23

Coastguard Operations can be contacted H24 via:

Emergency and Operations contact details:
☎ + 31 223 542300. 🖷 + 31 223 658358; ccc@kustwacht.nl

Admin/info (HO)
☎+ 31 223 658300. 🖷+31 223 658303. www.kustwacht.nl   info@kustwacht.nl
PO Box 10000, 1780 CA Den Helder.

Remote CG stations are shown above. Working chans are VHF 23 and 83.

Netherlands Coastguard stations
Medical advice
Call initially on Ch 16, DSC Ch 70 or 2187·5 kHz (MMSI 002442000). Working chans are VHF Ch 23 & 83 or MF 2824 kHz (transmit), 2520 kHz (receive).

Resources
The Dutch Lifeboat Ass'n (KNRM) manages 26 lifeboat stations and 13 inshore lifeboat stations along the coast. The 60 lifeboats include 13m LOA water-jet, rigid inflatables capable of 36 kn. Helicopters, fixed wing aircraft and ships of the RNLN can be called upon; also Air Force helos at Leeuwarden. The area of activity is from the Dutch Continental Shelf into the Waddenzee, IJsselmeer and estuaries of Zuid Holland and Zeeland.

BELGIUM
The Belgian CG coordinates SAR operations from Oostende MRCC, callsign *Coastguard Oostende*. The MRCC and *Oostende Radio* (Coast radio station) both keep listening watch H24 on Ch 16, 67, 2182 kHz and DSC Ch 70 and 2187·5 kHz.

Coast Radio stations

OOSTENDE RADIO
☎ +32 59 255493   🖷 +32 59 255467   rmd@mil.be
MMSI 002050480 Ch 16, MF 2182 kHz, DSC Ch 70 and 2187·5 kHz (H24)
MF: Tx 2484, Rx 3178 kHz. VHF Ch 07, 24, 27, 63, 78, 81 85
Zeebrugge Ch 27, 63
Middelkerke (Oostende)Ch 27
De Panne (French border) Ch 78
Antwerp Ch 07, 27
Ghent Ch 81
Rest of Belgium Ch 24.

Coastguard stations

MRCC OOSTENDE
☎ +32 59 701000; 🖷 +32 59 703605. MMSI 002059981.
RCC Brussels (COSPAS/SARSAT agency)
☎ +32 2 751 4615; 🖷 +32 2 7524201.

Resources
Offshore and inshore lifeboats are based at Nieuwpoort, Oostende and Zeebrugge.

The Belgian Air Force provides helicopters from Koksijde near the French border. The Belgian Navy also participates in SAR operations as required, ☎ +32 2 4430350; 🖷 +32 2 4439658; mik@mil.be

FRANCE – CROSS

Four CROSS (Centres Régionaux Opérationnels de Surveillance et de Sauvetage, ie an MRCC) provide a permanent, H24, all weather operational presence along the N and W coasts and liaise with foreign CGs.

CROSS' main functions include:

- Co-ordinating SAR operations.
- Navigational surveillance.
- Broadcasting navigational warnings.
- Broadcasting weather information.
- Anti-pollution control.
- Marine and fishery surveillance.

All centres keep watch on VHF Ch 16 as well as Ch 70 (DSC) and co-ordinate SAR on Ch 15, 67, 68, 73. They also broadcast gale warnings, weather forecasts and local navigational warnings.

CROSS Étel specialises in medical advice and responds to alerts from Cospas/Sarsat satellites.

CROSS can be contacted by R/T, by ☎ dial 112, through Coast Radio Stations, via the National Gendarmerie or Affaires Maritimes, or via a Semaphore station. Call *Semaphore* stations on Ch 16 (working Ch 10) or by ☎ as listed later in this section. If a nautical emergency *is witnessed from the land*, ☎ dial196.

CROSS also monitor TSS in the Dover Strait, off Casquets and off Ouessant using, for example, the callsign *Corsen Traffic*.

For medical advice call CROSS which will contact a doctor or SAMU (Service d'Aide Médicale Urgente). In harbour/marina SAMU responds faster in emergency than calling a doctor. Simply dial 15.

CROSS stations (Emergency ☎ 112).

CROSS Gris-Nez
50°52'N 01°35'E   MMSI 002275100
☎ 03 21 87 21 87; 📠 03 21 87 78 55
Belgian border to Cap d'Antifer.

NavWarnings Ch 79 at every H+10 via Dunkerque, Saint-Frieux and L'Ailly. CROSS Gris-Nez responds to COSPAS/SARSAT alerts.

CROSS Jobourg
49°41'N 01°54'W   MMSI 002275200
☎ 02 33 52 16 16; 📠 02 33 52 71 72
Cap de la Hague to Mont St Michel

NavWarnings Ch 80 every H+20 and H+50 via Antifer, Ver-sur-Mer, Gatteville, Jobourg, Granville and Roche Douvres.

CROSS Corsen
48°24'N 04°47'W   MMSI 002275300
☎ 02 98 89 31 31; 📠 02 98 89 65 75
Mont St Michel to Pointe de Penmarc'h.

NavWarnings Ch 79 every H+10 and H+40 via Cap Fréhel, Bodic, Ile de Batz, Le Stiff and Pte du Raz.

CROSS Étel
47°39'N 03°12'W   MMSI 002275000
☎ 02 97 55 35 35; 📠 02 97 55 49 34
Pte de Penmarc'h to the Spanish border

NavWarnings Ch 79 for Landes range activity via Chassiron 1903.

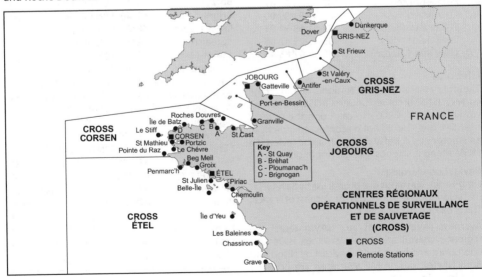

CROSS locations and areas of responsibility

Semaphore stations keep visual, radar and radio watch (Ch 16); are equipped with VHF DF; relay emergency calls to CROSS; show gale warning signals, repeat forecasts and offer local weather reports. Hours sunrise-sunset, but * H24.

* Dunkerque	03·28·66·86·18
* Boulogne	03·21·31·32·10
* Ault	03·22·60·47·33
* Dieppe	02·35·84·23·82
* Fécamp	02·35·28·00·91
* La Hève	02·35·46·07·81
* Villerville	02·31·88·11·13
* Port-en-Bessin	02·31·21·81·51
* St-Vaast	02·33·54·44·50
* Barfleur	02·33·54·04·37
* Le Homet	02·33·92·60·08
* La Hague	02·33·52·71·07
* Barneville-Carteret	02·33·53·85·08
* Granville Le Roc	02·33·50·05·85
St-Cast	02·96·41·85·30
* St Quay-Portrieux	02·96.70.42.18
Bréhat	02·96·20·00·12
* Ploumanac'h	02·96·91·46·51
Batz	02·98·61·76·06
* Brignogan	02·98·83·50·84
* Ouessant Stiff	02·98·48·81·50
* St-Mathieu	02·98·89·01·59
* Portzic (Ch 08)	02·98·22·21·47
Toulinguet	02·98·27·90·02
Cap-de-la-Chèvre	02·98·27·09·55
* Pointe-du-Raz	02·98·70·66·57
* Penmarc'h	02·98·58·61·00
Beg Meil	02·98·94·98·92
Étel Mât Fenoux	02·97·55·35·39
* Beg Melen (Groix)	02·97·86·80·13
Talut (Belle-Île)	02·97·31·85·07
* St-Julien	02·97·50·09·35
Piriac-sur-Mer	02·40·23·59·87
* Chemoulin	02·40·91·99·00
* St-Sauveur (Yeu)	02·51·58·31·01
Les Baleines (Ré)	05·46·29·42·06
* Chassiron (Oléron)	05·46·47·85·43

Lifeboats

The lifeboat service Société National de Sauvetage en Mer (SNSM) comes under CROSS, At sea all vessels must call CROSS to call upon the services of SNSM, they should not be contacted directly in an emergency. A hefty charge may be levied if a SNSM lifeboat attends a vessel not in distress.

Navigation warnings

Long-range warnings are broadcast by SafetyNet for Navarea II, which includes the W coast of France. The N coast is in Navarea I.

Avurnavs (AVis URgents aux NAVigateurs) are regional, coastal and local warnings issued by Cherbourg and Brest and broadcast by Niton and Brest Navtex and on MF. Warnings are prefixed by 'Sécurité Avurnav'.

EMERGENCY VHF DF SERVICE

A yacht in emergency can call CROSS on VHF Ch 16, 11 or 67 to obtain a true bearing of the yacht *from* the DF station. These monitor Ch 16 and other continuously scanned frequencies, which include Ch 1-29, 36, 39, 48, 50, 52, 55, 56 and 60-88. The Semaphore stations overleaf are also equipped with VHF DF.

HJ = Day service only.

VHF DF stations, are listed below geographically from NE to W then S:

Station	Lat/Long	Hrs
Dunkerque	51°03'.40N 02°20'.40E	H24
*Gris-Nez	50°52'.20N 01°35'.01E	H24
Boulogne	50°44'.00N 01°36'.00E	H24
Ault	50°06'.50N 01°27'.50E	H24
Dieppe	49°56'.00N 01°05'.20E	H24
Fécamp	49°46'.10N 00°22'.20E	H24
La Hève	49°30'.60N 00°04'.20E	H24
Villerville	49°23'.20N 00°06'.50E	H24
Port-en-Bessin	49°21'.10N 00°46'.30W	H24
Saint-Vaast	49°34'.50N 01°16'.50W	H24
Barfleur	49°41'.90N 01°15'.90W	H24
Levy	49°41'.70N 01°28'.20W	H24
†Homet	49°39'.50N 01°37'.90W	H24
*Jobourg	49°41'.50N 01°54'.50W	H24
La Hague	49°43'.60N 01°56'.30W	H24
Carteret	49°22'.40N 01°48'.30W	H24
Le Roc	48°50'.10N 01°36'.90W	H24
Grouin/Cancale	48°42'.60N 01°50'.60W	HJ
Saint-Cast	48°38'.60N 02°14'.70W	H24
St-Quay-Port'x	48°39'.30N 02°49'.50W	HJ
Bréhat	48°51'.30N 03°00'.10W	H24
Ploumanac'h	48°49'.50N 03°28'.20W	HJ
Batz	48°44'.80N 04°00'.60W	H24
Brignogan	48°40'.60N 04°19'.70W	HJ
Creac'h (Ushant)	48°27'.60N 05°07'.70W	H24
*Creac'h	48°27'.60N 05°07'.80W	H24
†Saint-Mathieu	48°19'.80N 04°46'.20W	H24
Toulinguet	48°16'.80N 04°37'.50W	HJ
Cap de la Chèvre	48°10'.20N 04°33'.00W	HJ
Pointe du Raz	48°02'.30N 04°43'.80W	H24
Penmarc'h	47°47'.90N 04°22'.40W	H24
Beg-Meil	47°51'.30N 03°58'.40W	HJ
Beg Melen	47°39'.20N 03°30'.10W	H24
*Etel	47°39'.80N 03°12'.00W	H24
Saint-Julien	47°29'.70N 03°07'.50W	HJ
Taillefer	47°21'.80N 03°09'.00W	H24
Le Talut	47°17'.70N 03°13'.00W	H24
Piriac	47°22'.50N 02°33'.40W	H24
Chemoulin	47°14'.10N 02°17'.80W	H24
Saint-Sauveur	46°41'.70N 02°18'.80W	H24
Les Baleines	46°14'.60N 01°33'.70W	HJ
Chassiron	46°02'.80N 01°24'.50W	H24

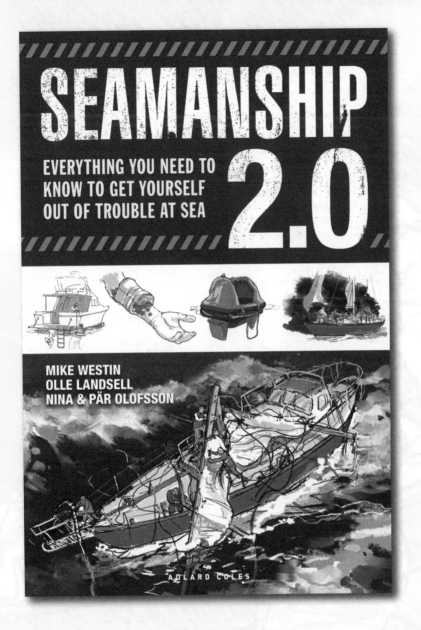

Chapter 5 – Tides

2022 TIDAL COEFFICIENTS

Date	Jan am	Jan pm	Feb am	Feb pm	Mar am	Mar pm	Apr am	Apr pm	May am	May pm	June am	June pm	July am	July pm	Aug am	Aug pm	Sept am	Sept pm	Oct am	Oct pm	Nov am	Nov pm	Dec am	Dec pm
1	81	86	94	98	82	88	97	98	88	87	74	72	70	69	--	77	83	79	78	72	52	47	54	53
2	91	94	101	102	94	98	98	97	86	84	70	67	68	67	76	75	75	70	65	58	45	45	53	55
3	97	99	102	100	101	103	95	92	81	78	64	--	--	66	73	70	65	59	51	44	48	53	57	60
4	99	99	98	94	103	102	88	84	74	70	61	58	64	62	67	64	53	47	40	40	59	65	63	67
5	97	95	89	--	100	96	--	79	--	65	55	51	60	58	60	56	43	41	42	49	71	77	70	72
6	91	87	84	77	92	87	73	67	60	54	48	45	56	54	53	50	42	47	56	65	82	86	75	76
7	--	81	71	64	80	--	60	53	49	44	43	41	52	50	48	47	53	62	73	80	88	90	78	78
8	76	70	57	50	74	67	46	40	39	34	41	42	49	49	48	52	70	79	87	93	91	91	79	78
9	64	58	44	38	60	52	33	28	31	30	44	47	50	52	56	63	86	93	97	100	90	89	78	77
10	53	48	33	31	45	38	24	24	31	34	51	56	56	60	69	77	98	102	101	101	87	84	75	73
11	44	42	30	32	31	26	26	31	39	45	61	67	64	69	83	90	104	105	100	98	80	76	71	68
12	41	41	36	41	24	24	38	45	51	58	72	78	75	80	95	99	105	103	95	91	71	66	65	61
13	42	45	46	51	28	34	52	60	65	72	83	87	85	89	102	103	100	95	86	80	61	55	58	--
14	48	52	57	63	40	47	67	75	78	84	91	93	93	95	103	102	--	90	--	74	50	--	54	51
15	55	59	68	73	54	61	81	87	90	94	95	96	97	98	--	99	84	77	67	61	44	39	47	44
16	62	66	77	81	68	75	92	97	97	99	96	94	97	--	95	90	69	62	53	46	35	31	42	40
17	69	72	85	88	80	86	100	102	100	100	92	--	96	93	84	77	54	46	39	33	30	30	40	40
18	74	76	90	91	91	95	103	102	98	95	89	85	89	85	70	63	39	32	27	24	32	36	42	45
19	78	79	92	92	98	100	101	97	--	91	81	76	79	74	55	48	27	24	24	26	42	48	49	53
20	80	80	90	88	100	100	--	93	86	80	71	66	67	62	41	36	25	28	31	37	54	60	59	64
21	79	78	85	--	99	96	86	80	74	68	62	58	56	51	32	30	34	40	45	51	67	73	70	75
22	77	75	81	76	92	86	72	64	62	57	55	52	46	43	31	34	47	54	59	65	79	84	80	85
23	--	72	70	64	--	80	57	50	53	51	51	51	41	41	39	44	60	67	72	78	88	92	89	92
24	69	66	58	52	72	65	45	43	51	52	52	53	42	44	49	55	73	78	83	88	94	96	95	96
25	62	59	47	44	57	50	45	48	54	57	55	56	47	50	60	65	83	87	92	95	97	96	97	96
26	55	52	43	46	44	40	54	60	61	64	59	61	54	57	70	74	90	93	97	98	94	91	95	92
27	50	50	52	59	41	45	66	71	67	69	63	65	61	64	78	81	95	95	98	97	88	83	89	--
28	51	54	67	74	51	59	76	80	72	74	66	67	67	69	84	86	95	94	94	90	78	--	84	80
29	59	65			67	74	84	86	75	76	69	69	72	74	87	88	92	88	85	--	72	66	75	69
30	71	77			81	86	87	88	76	76	70	70	75	76	88	87	--	84	80	73	62	57	64	60
31	84	89			91	95			76	75			77	77	--	85			66	59			56	53

Tidal coefficients indicate the magnitude of the tide on any particular day without having to look up and calculate the range, and thus determine whether it is springs, neaps or somewhere in between. This table, which is based on Cherbourg, is valid for all areas covered by this Almanac. Typical values are:

120	Very big spring tide
95	**Mean spring tide**
70	Average tide
45	**Mean neap tide**
20	Very small neap tide

TIDAL CALCULATIONS

Find the height at a given time (STANDARD PORT)

1. On Standard Curve diagram, plot heights of HW and LW occuring either side of required time and join by sloping line.
2. Enter HW Time and sufficient others to bracket required time.
3. From required time, proceed vertically to curves, using heights plotted in (1) to help interpolation between Spring and Neaps. Do NOT extrapolate.
4. Proceed horizontally to sloping line, thence vertically to Height scale.
5. Read off height.

EXAMPLE:

Find the height of tide at ULLAPOOL at 1900 on 6th January

Find the time for a given height (STANDARD PORT)

From tables	JANUARY	
ULLAPOOL	**6** 0420	4.6
	1033	1.6
	1641	4.6
	F 2308	1.2

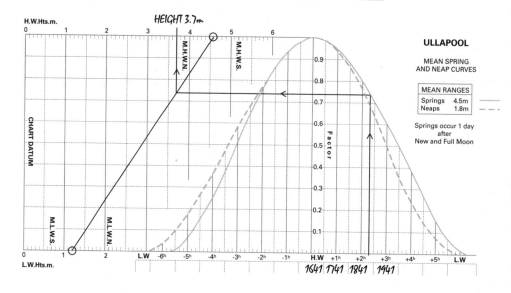

H.W.Hts.m.

HEIGHT 3.7m

ULLAPOOL

MEAN SPRING
AND NEAP CURVES

MEAN RANGES
Springs 4.5m
Neaps 1.8m

Springs occur 1 day
after
New and Full Moon

CHART DATUM

Factor

L.W.Hts.m.

1641 1741 1841 1941

1. On Standard Curve diagram, plot heights of HW and LW occurring either side of required event and join by sloping line.
2. Enter HW time and those for half-tidal cycle covering required event.
3. From required height, proceed vertically to sloping line, thence horizontally to curves, using heights plotted in (1) to assist interpolation between Spring and Neaps. Do NOT extrapolate.
4. Proceed vertically to Time scale.
5. Read off time.

EXAMPLE:

Find the time at which the afternoon tide at ULLAPOOL falls to 3.7m on 6 January

From tables	JANUARY		
ULLAPOOL	**6** 0420	4.6	
	1033	1.6	
	1641	4.6	
	F 2308	1.2	

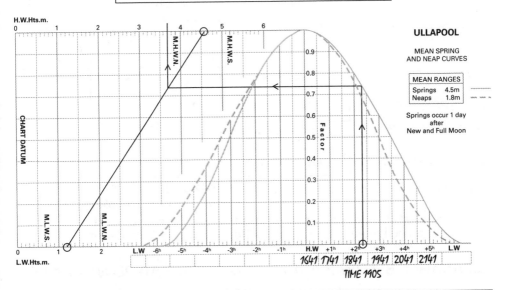

ULLAPOOL

MEAN SPRING
AND NEAP CURVES

MEAN RANGES	
Springs	4.5m
Neaps	1.8m

Springs occur 1 day
after
New and Full Moon

1641 1741 1841 1941 2041 2141

TIME 1905

Find the time and height of HW and LW at a Secondary Port

EXAMPLE:

Find the time and height of the afternoon HW and LW at ST MARY's (Isles of Scilly) on 14th July (BST)

Note: *The data used in this example do not refer to the year of these tables.*

From tables	JULY		
PLYMOUTH (DEVONPORT)	**14** 0309	1.0	
	0927	5.3	
	1532	1.1	
	SA 2149	5.0	

From tables										
Location	Lat	Long	High Water		Low Water		MHWS	MHWN	MLWN	MLWS
DEVONPORT *Standard port*	50°22'N	4°11'W	0000 and 1200	0600 and 1800	0000 and 1200	0600 and 1800	5.5	4.4	2.2	0.8
St Mary's, *Scilly*	49° 55'N	6°19'W	−0035	−0100	−0040	−0025	+0.2	−0.1	−0.2	−0.1

TIDAL PREDICTION FORM (NP 204)

STANDARD PORT ....*Devonport*.... TIME/HEIGHT REQUIRED .....*pm*.....

SECONDARY PORT ...*St Mary's*... DATE *14 July* ... TIME ZONE ...*B.S.T*...

	TIME		HEIGHT		
STANDARD PORT	HW	LW	HW	LW	RANGE
	1 2149	2 1532	3 5·0	4 1·1	5 3·9
Seasonal change	Standard Ports -		6 0·0	6 0·0	
DIFFERENCES	7* -0044	8 -0032	9 0·1	10 -0·1	
Seasonal change *	Secondary Ports +		11 0·0	11 0·0	
SECONDARY PORT	12 2105	13 1500	14 5·1	15 1·0	
Duration	16 0605		LW 1500 UT = 1600 BST		
			HW 2105 UT = 2205 BST		

* The seasonal changes are generally less than ± 0.1m and for most purposes can be ignored. See Admiraly Tide Tables Vol 1. for details

CLEARANCE BELOW BRIDGES AND OVERHEAD POWER LINES

Vertical clearance heights are above the level of HAT (Highest Astronomical Tide) instead of MHWS as in the past. HAT is always a higher level than MHWS, as shown in the diagram on the back cover flap. It helps to draw such a diagram and insert the relevant dimensions when calculating overhead clearances. The Height of HAT above Chart Datum is stated at the foot of each page of Standard port tide tables. New editions of Admiralty charts are referenced to HAT; earlier editions to MHWS. Check the title block under **Heights**.

INTERMEDIATE TIMES/HEIGHTS (SECONDARY PORT)

These are the same as the appropriate calculations for a Standard Port except that the Standard Curve diagram for the Standard Port must be entered with HW and LW heights and times for the Secondary Port obtained on Form N.P. 204. When interpolating between the Spring and Neap curves the Range at the Standard Port must be used.

EXAMPLE:

Find the height of the tide at PADSTOW at 1100 on 28th February. Find the time at which the morning tide at PADSTOW falls to 4.9m on 28th February.

Note: The data in these examples do not refer to the year of these tables.

From tables	FEBRUARY	
MILFORD HAVEN		
	28 0315	1.1
	0922	6.6
	1538	1.3
	TU 2145	6.3

From tables

Location	Lat	Long	High Water		Low Water		MHWS	MHWN	MLWN	MLWS
MILFORD HAVEN Standard port	51°42′N	5°03′W	0100 and 1300	0700 and 1900	0100 and 1300	0700 and 1900	7.0	5.2	2.5	0.7
River Camel										
Padstow	50°33′N	4°56′W	−0055	−0050	−0040	−0050	+0.3	+0.4	+0.1	+0.1
Wadebridge	50°31′N	4°50′W	−0052	−0052	+0235	+0245	−3.8	−3.8	−2.5	−0.4

TIDAL PREDICTION FORM (NP 204)

STANDARD PORT ___*Milford Haven*___ TIME/HEIGHT REQUIRED ___*1100 : 4.9*___

SECONDARY PORT ___*Padstow*___ DATE ___*28 Feb*___ TIME ZONE ___*UT*___

	TIME		HEIGHT		
STANDARD PORT	HW	LW	HW	LW	RANGE
	1 0922	2 1538	3 6.6	4 1.3	5 5.3
Seasonal change	Standard Ports +		6 0.0	6 0.0	
DIFFERENCES	7* −0052	8 –	9 +0.3	10 +0.1	
Seasonal change *	Secondary Ports -		11 0.0	11 0.0	
SECONDARY PORT	12 0830	13 –	14 6.9	15 1.4	
Duration	16 –				

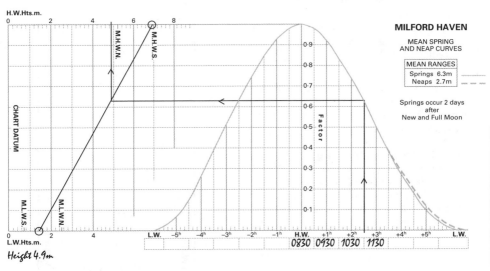

H.W.Hts.m.

CHART DATUM

M.H.W.N.   M.H.W.S.

M.L.W.S.   M.L.W.N.

L.W.Hts.m.

Height 4.9m

MILFORD HAVEN

MEAN SPRING AND NEAP CURVES

MEAN RANGES
Springs 6.3m
Neaps 2.7m

Springs occur 2 days after New and Full Moon

L.W. −5ʰ −4ʰ −3ʰ −2ʰ −1ʰ H.W. +1ʰ +2ʰ +3ʰ +4ʰ +5ʰ L.W.

0830 0930 1030 1130

Factor

TIDES

SPECIAL INSTRUCTIONS FOR PLACES BETWEEN BOURNEMOUTH AND SELSEY BILL

• Owing to the rapid change of tidal characteristics and distortion of the tidal curve in this area, curves are shown for individual ports. It is a characteristic of the tide here that Low Water is more sharply defined than High Water and these curves have therefore been drawn with their times relative to that of Low Water.

• Apart from differences caused by referring the times to Low Water the procedure for obtaining intermediate heights at places whose curves are shown is identical to that used for normal Secondary Ports.

• The **height** differences for ports between Bournemouth and Yarmouth always refer to the higher High Water, i.e. that which is shown as reaching a factor of 1.0 on the curves. Note that the **time** differences, which are not required for this calculation, also refer to the higher High Water.

• The tide at ports between Bournemouth and Christchurch shows considerable change of shape and duration between Springs and Neaps and it is not practical to define the tide with only two curves. A third curve has therefore been drawn for the range at Portsmouth at which the two High Waters are equal at the port concerned – this range being marked on the body of the graph. Interpolation here should be between this 'critical' curve and either the Spring or Neap curve as appropriate.

Note that while the critical curve extends throughout the tidal cycle the Spring and Neap curves stop at the higher High Water. Thus for a range at Portsmouth of 3.5m the factor for 7 hours after LW at Bournemouth should be referred to the following Low Water, whereas had the range at Portsmouth been 2.5, it should be referred to the preceding Low Water.

NOTES

1. NEWPORT. Owing to the constriction of the River Medina, Newport requires slightly different treatment since the harbour dries out at 1.4m. The calculation should be performed using the Low Water Time and Height Differences for Cowes and the High Water Height Differences for Newport. Any calculated heights which fall below 1.4m should be treated as 1.4m

2. CHRISTCHURCH (Tuckton). Low Waters do not fall below 0.7m except under very low river flow conditions.

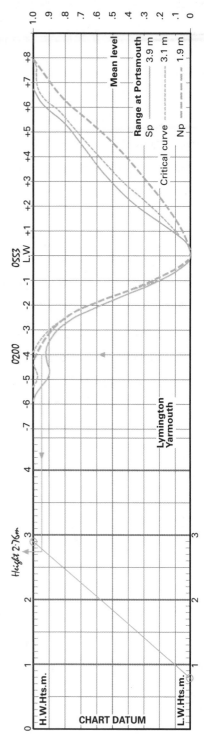

To find the Height of tide at a given time at any Secondary Port between Bournemouth and Selsey Bill

1. Complete top section of N.P. 204 (as below). Omit HW time column (Boxes 1,7,12)
2. On Standard Curve diagram (previous page), plot Secondary Port HW and LW heights and join by sloping line.
3. From the time required, using Secondary Port LW time, proceed vertically to curve, interpolating as necessary using Range at Portsmouth. Do NOT extrapolate.
4. Proceed horizontally to sloping line, thence vertically to Height Scale.
5. Read off height.

EXAMPLE:

Find the height of tide at LYMINGTON at 0200 UT on 18th November

From tables		NOVEMBER	
		0110	4.6
PORTSMOUTH	**18**	0613	1.1
		1318	4.6
		SA 1833	1.0

From tables Location	Lat	Long	High Water		Low Water		MHWS	MHWN	MLWN	MLWS
			0000	0600	0500	1100				
PORTSMOUTH	50°48'N	1°07'W	and	and	and	and	4.7	3.8	1.9	0.8
Standard port			1200	1800	1700	2300				
Lymington	50°46'N	1°32'W	–0110	+0005	–0020	–0020	–1.7	–1.2	–0.5	–0.1

STANDARD PORT ..... *Portsmouth* ..... TIME/HEIGHT REQUIRED *0200*

SECONDARY PORT ..... *Lymington* ..... DATE *18 Nov* ..... TIME ZONE ..... *UT*

	TIME		HEIGHT		
STANDARD PORT	HW	LW	HW	LW	RANGE
	1 —	2 0613	3 4.6	4 1.1	5 3.5
Seasonal change	Standard Ports –		6 0.0	6 0.0	
DIFFERENCES	7* —	8 –0020	9 –1.7	10 –0.2	
Seasonal change *	Secondary Ports +		11 0.0	11 0.0	
SECONDARY PORT	12 —	13 0553	14 2.9	15 0.9	
Duration	16 —				

* The Seasonal changes are generally less than ± 0.1m and for most purposes can be ignored. See Admiralty Tide Tables Vol 1 for full details.

TIDAL CURVES -
BOURNEMOUTH TO FRESHWATER

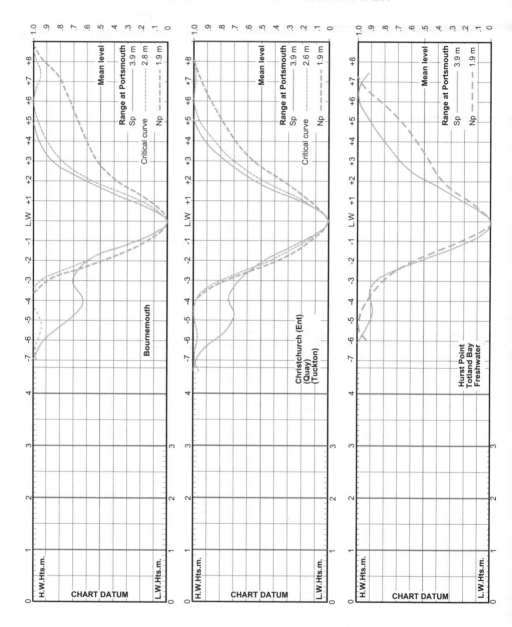

Note: The curves for Lymington and Yarmouth are on page 154, together with a worked example.

TIDAL CURVES -
BUCKLERS HARD TO SELSEY BILL

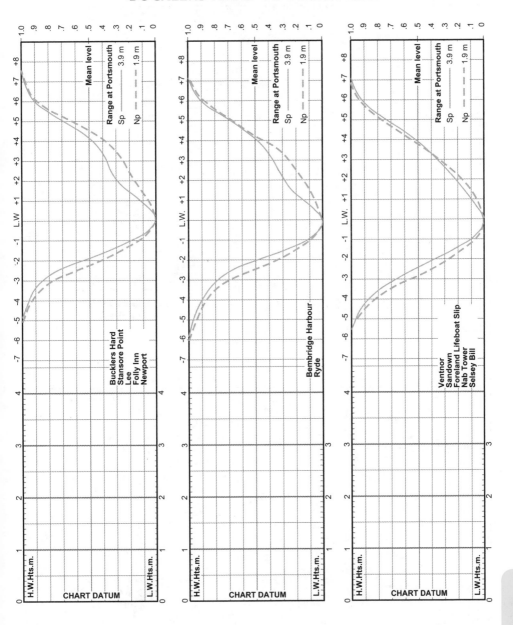

ENGLISH CHANNEL AND SOUTH BRITTANY

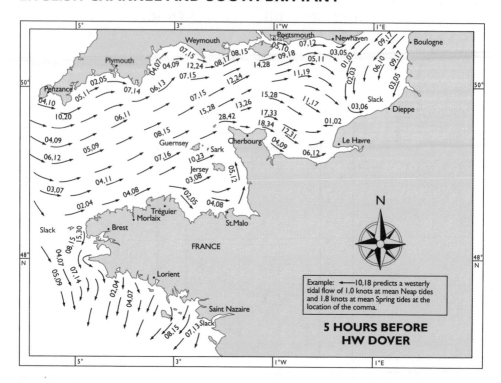

5 HOURS BEFORE HW DOVER

Example: ◄——10,18 predicts a westerly tidal flow of 1.0 knots at mean Neap tides and 1.8 knots at mean Spring tides at the location of the comma.

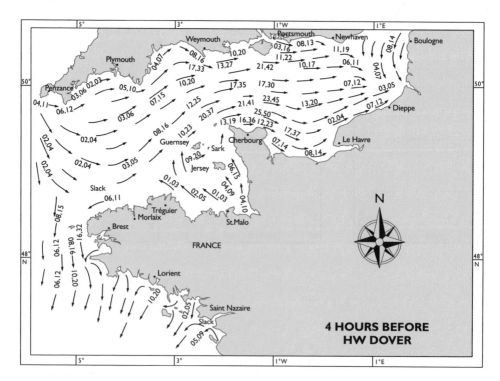

4 HOURS BEFORE HW DOVER

ENGLISH CHANNEL AND SOUTH BRITTANY

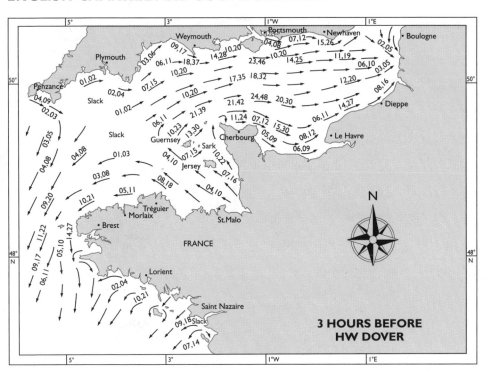

3 HOURS BEFORE HW DOVER

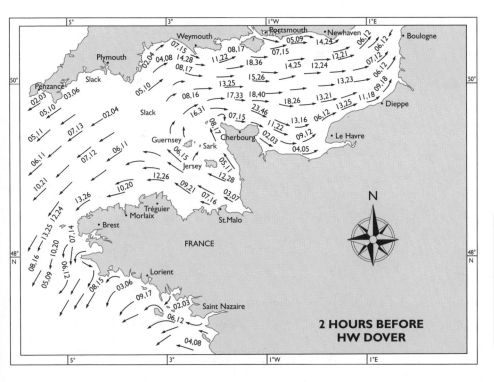

2 HOURS BEFORE HW DOVER

ENGLISH CHANNEL AND SOUTH BRITTANY

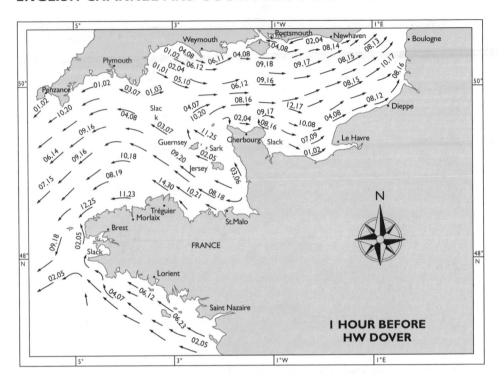

1 HOUR BEFORE
HW DOVER

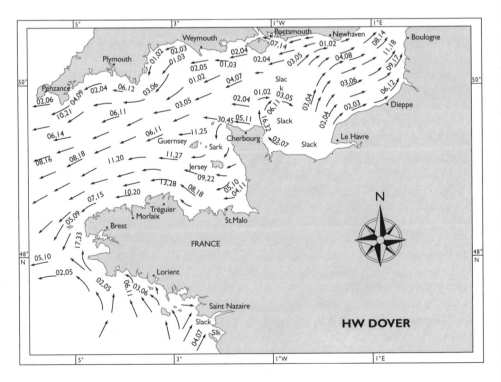

HW DOVER

ENGLISH CHANNEL AND SOUTH BRITTANY

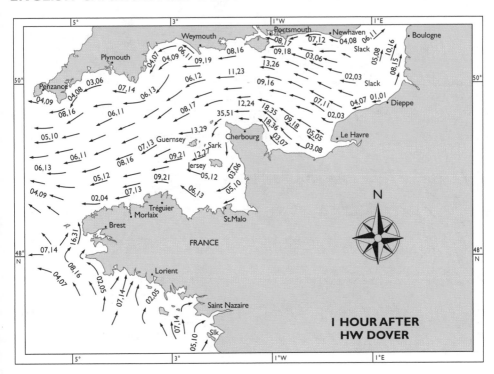

1 HOUR AFTER HW DOVER

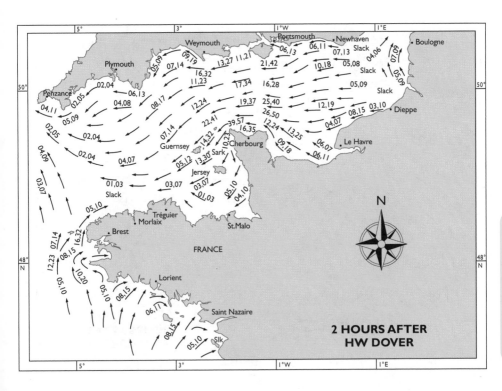

2 HOURS AFTER HW DOVER

ENGLISH CHANNEL AND SOUTH BRITTANY

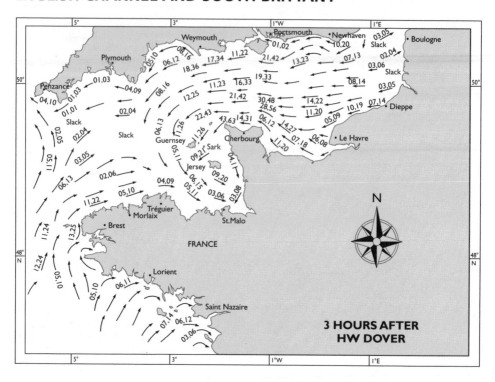

3 HOURS AFTER HW DOVER

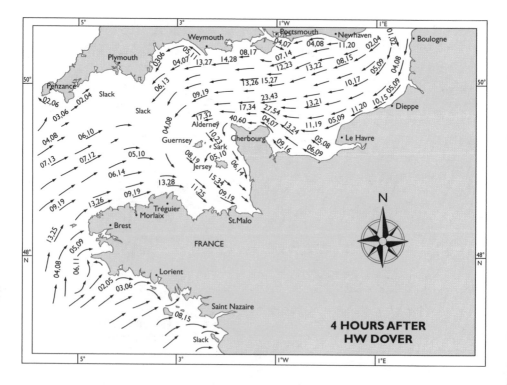

4 HOURS AFTER HW DOVER

ENGLISH CHANNEL AND SOUTH BRITTANY

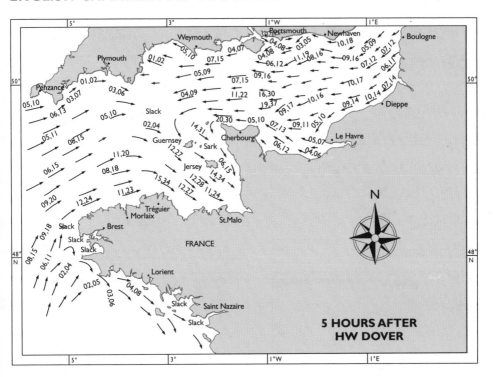

5 HOURS AFTER HW DOVER

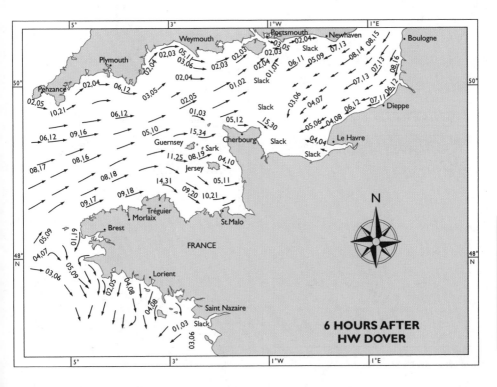

6 HOURS AFTER HW DOVER

PORTLAND

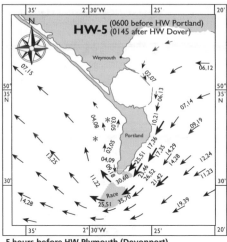

HW-5 (0600 before HW Portland)
(0145 after HW Dover)

5 hours before HW Plymouth (Devonport)

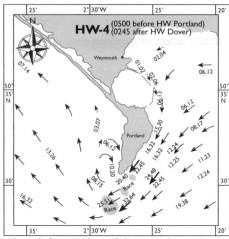

HW-4 (0500 before HW Portland)
(0245 after HW Dover)

4 hours before HW Plymouth (Devonport)

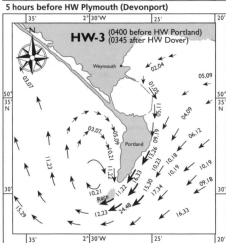

HW-3 (0400 before HW Portland)
(0345 after HW Dover)

3 hours before HW Plymouth (Devonport)

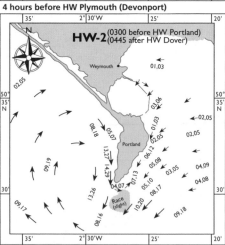

HW-2 (0300 before HW Portland)
(0445 after HW Dover)

2 hours before HW Plymouth (Devonport)

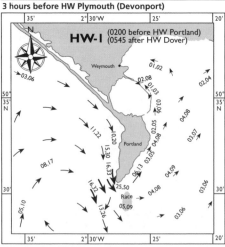

HW-1 (0200 before HW Portland)
(0545 after HW Dover)

1 hour before HW Plymouth (Devonport)

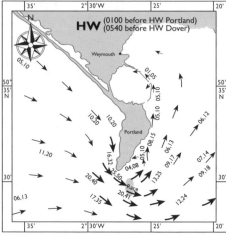

HW (0100 before HW Portland)
(0540 before HW Dover)

HW Plymouth (Devonport)

PORTLAND

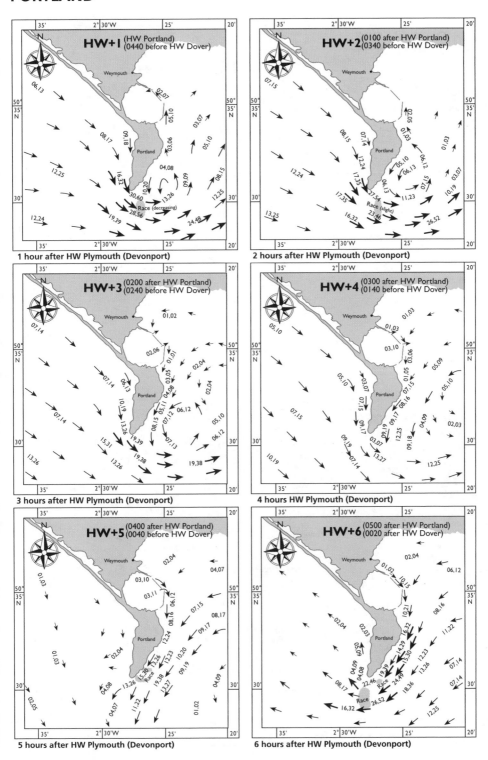

1 hour after HW Plymouth (Devonport)

2 hours after HW Plymouth (Devonport)

3 hours after HW Plymouth (Devonport)

4 hours HW Plymouth (Devonport)

5 hours after HW Plymouth (Devonport)

6 hours after HW Plymouth (Devonport)

ISLE OF WIGHT

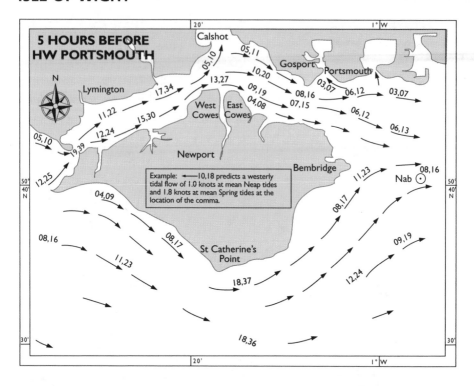

5 HOURS BEFORE HW PORTSMOUTH

Example: ←10,18 predicts a westerly tidal flow of 1.0 knots at mean Neap tides and 1.8 knots at mean Spring tides at the location of the comma.

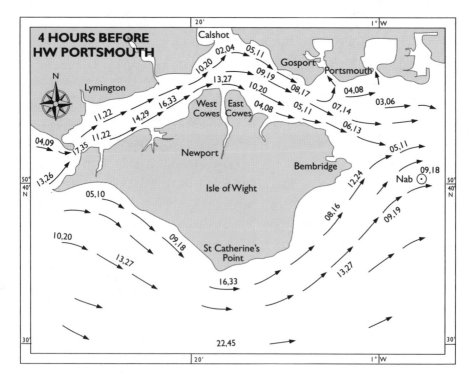

4 HOURS BEFORE HW PORTSMOUTH

ISLE OF WIGHT

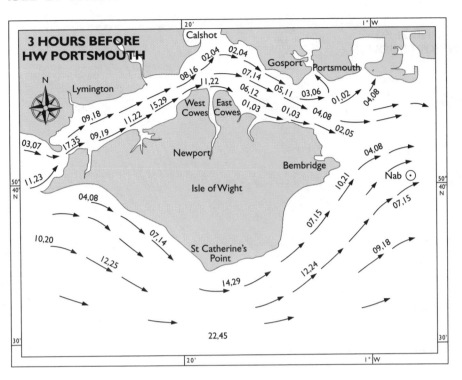

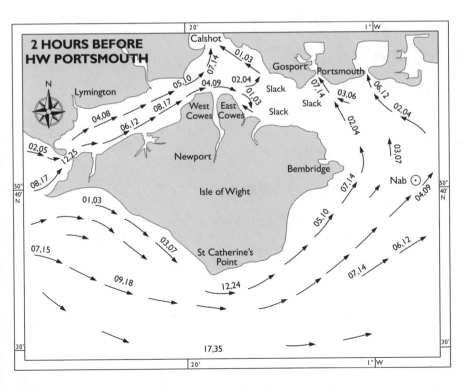

TIDES

ISLE OF WIGHT

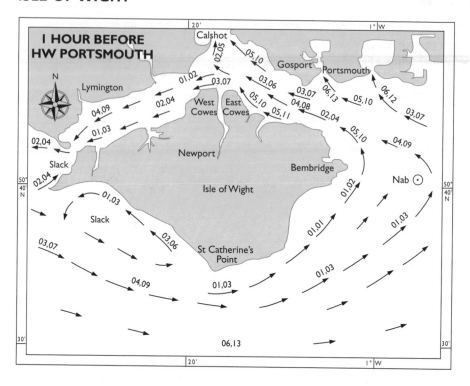

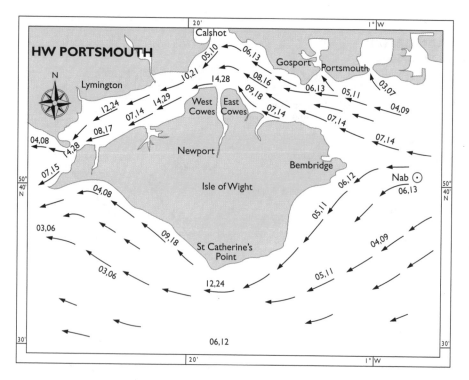

ISLE OF WIGHT

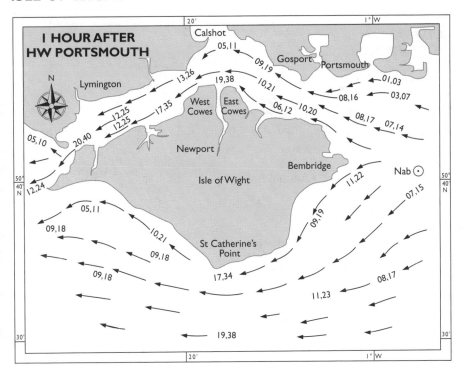

1 HOUR AFTER HW PORTSMOUTH

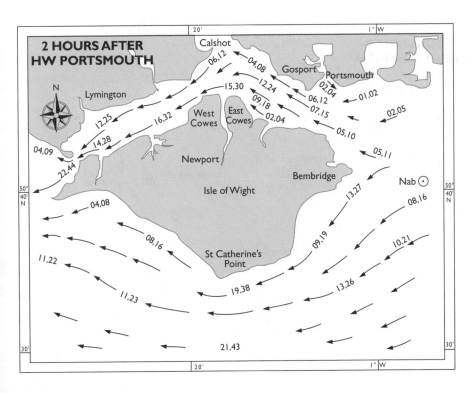

2 HOURS AFTER HW PORTSMOUTH

ISLE OF WIGHT

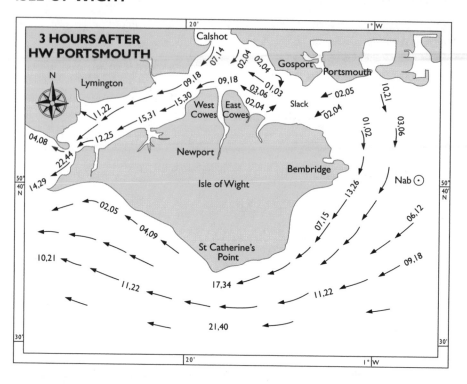

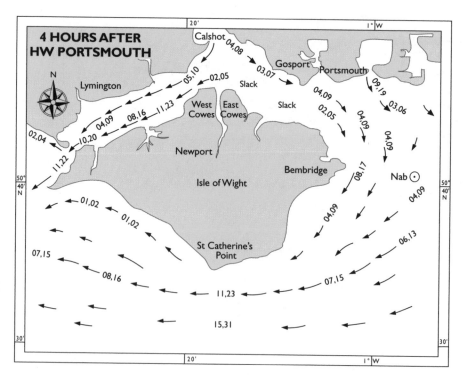

ISLE OF WIGHT

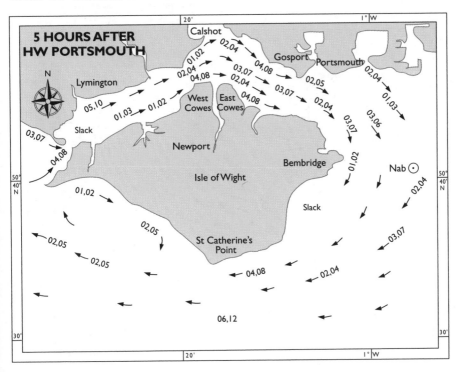

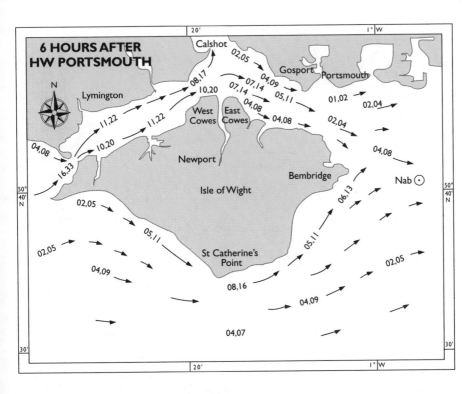

CHANNEL ISLANDS

Example: ◄—10,18 predicts a westerly tidal flow of 1.0 knots at mean
Neap tides and 1.8 knots at mean Spring tides at the location of the comma.

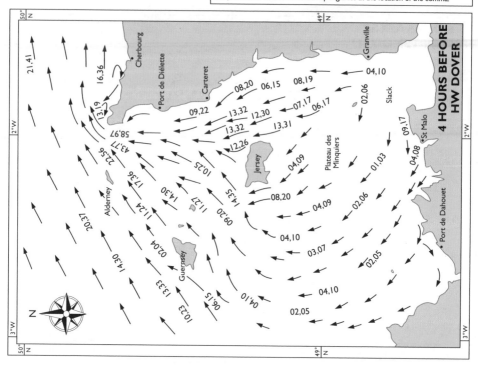

4 HOURS BEFORE HW DOVER

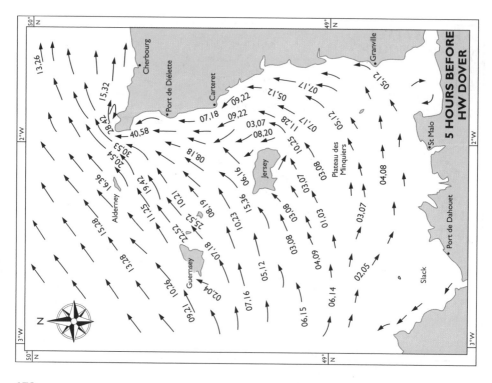

5 HOURS BEFORE HW DOVER

CHANNEL ISLANDS

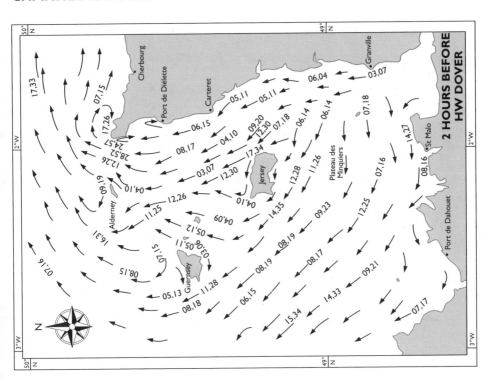

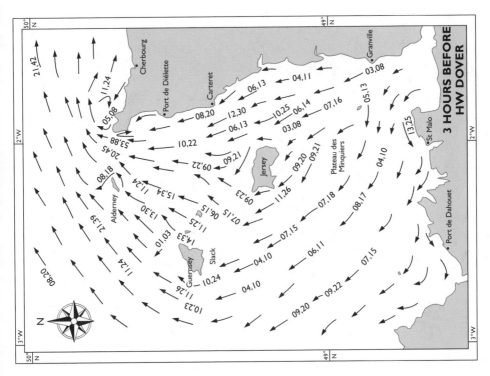

CHANNEL ISLANDS

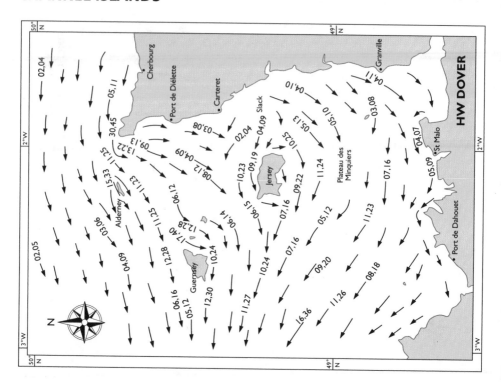

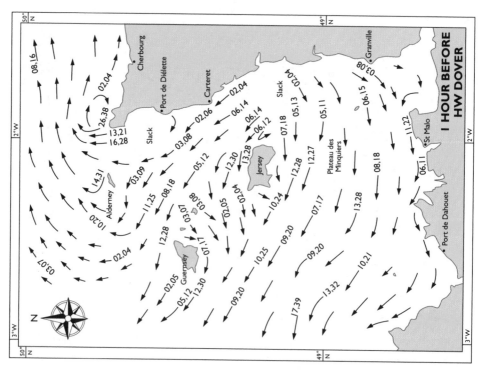

CHANNEL ISLANDS

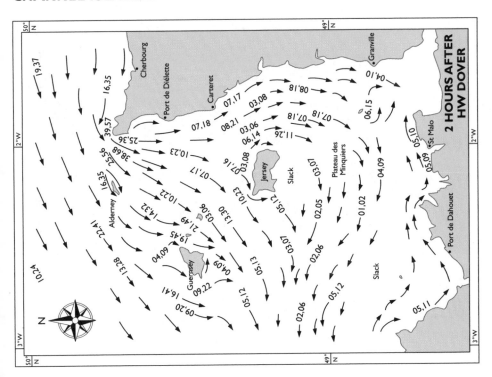

2 HOURS AFTER HW DOVER

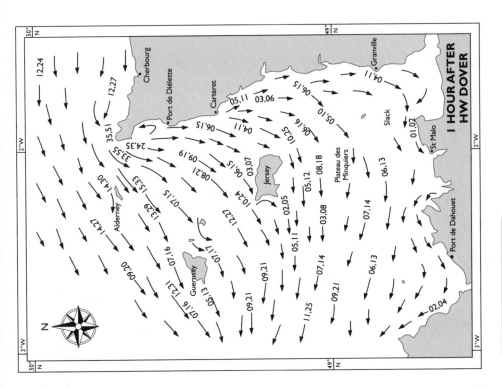

1 HOUR AFTER HW DOVER

CHANNEL ISLANDS

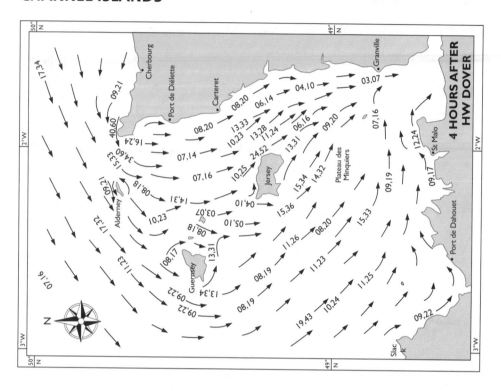

4 HOURS AFTER HW DOVER

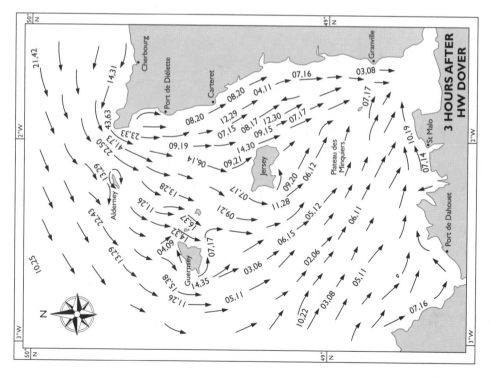

3 HOURS AFTER HW DOVER

CHANNEL ISLANDS

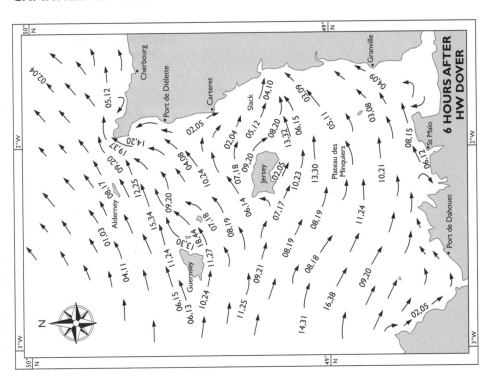

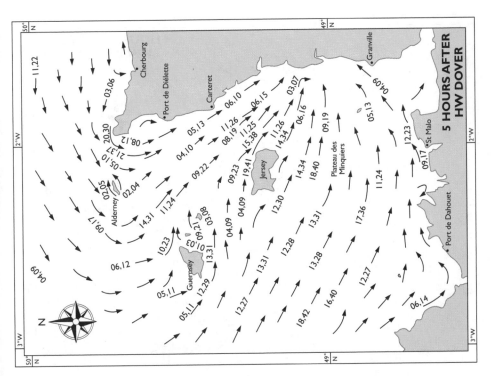

NORTH SEA

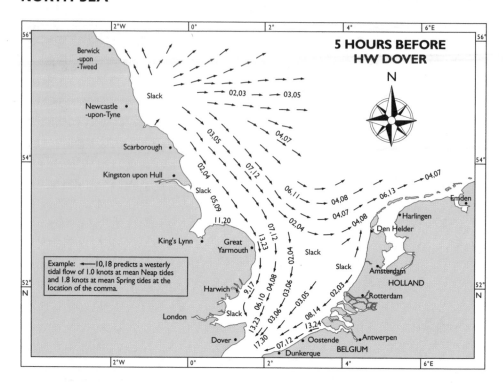

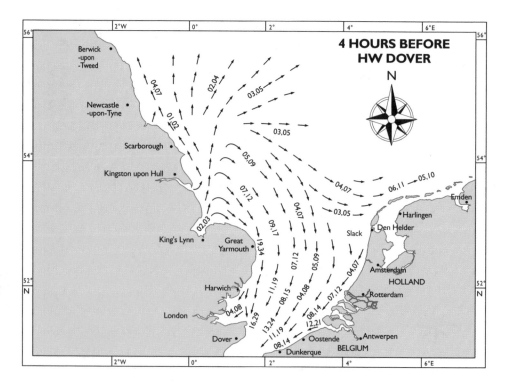

NORTH SEA

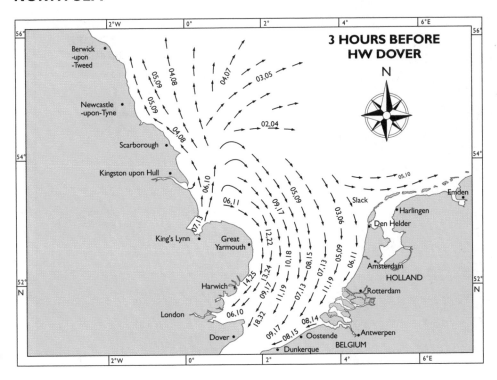

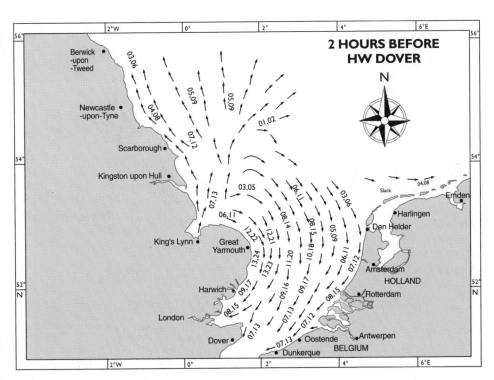

NORTH SEA

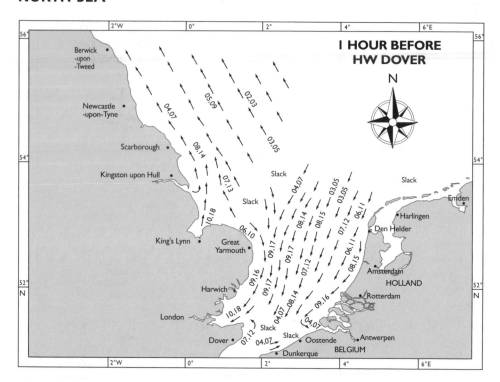

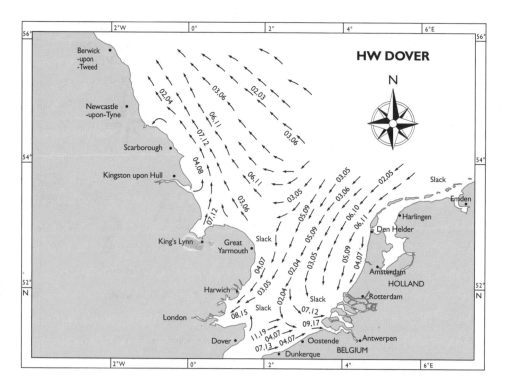

NORTH SEA

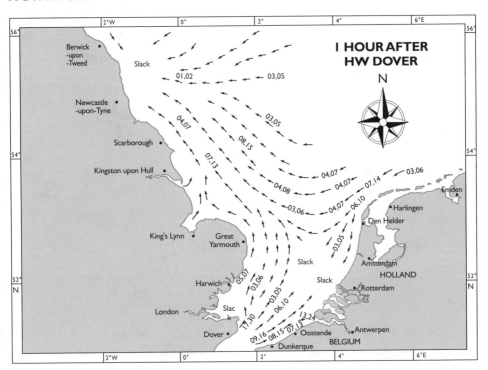

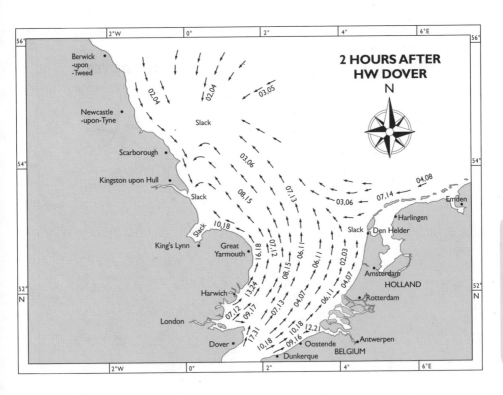

NORTH SEA

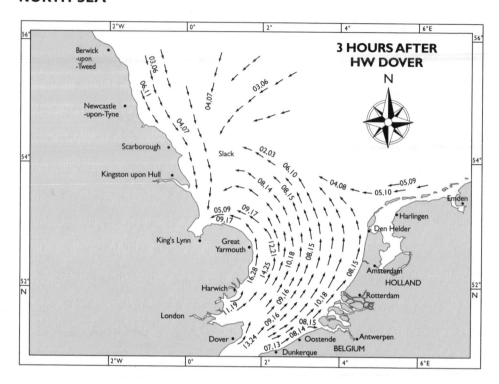

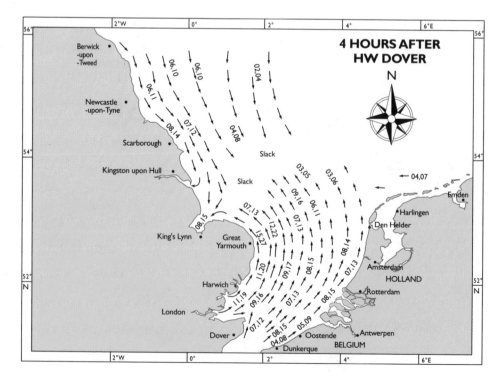

NORTH SEA

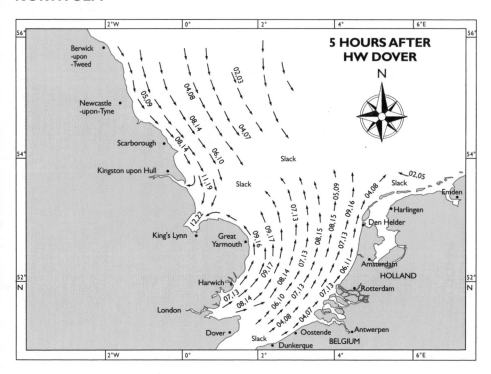

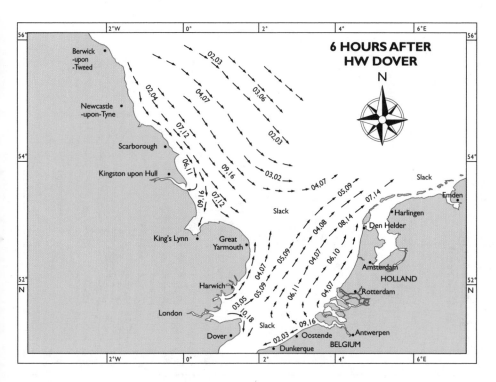

SCOTLAND

Example: ←10,18 predicts a westerly tidal flow of 1.0 knots at mean Neap tides and 1.8 knots at mean Spring tides at the location of the comma.

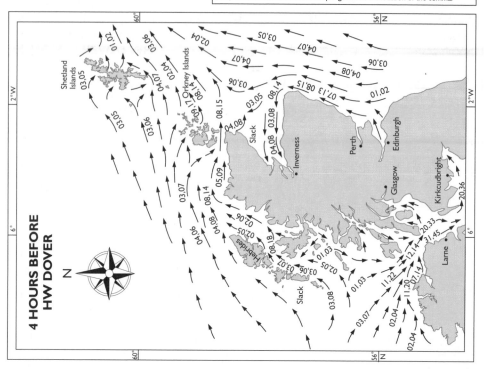

4 HOURS BEFORE HW DOVER

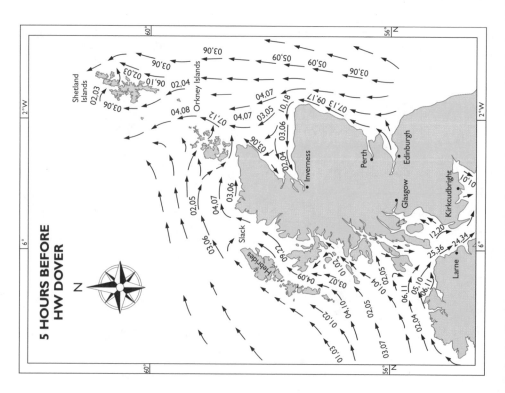

5 HOURS BEFORE HW DOVER

SCOTLAND

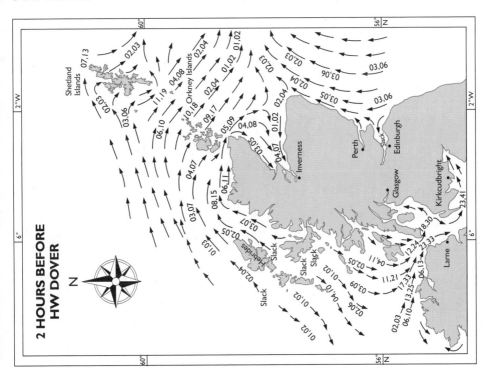

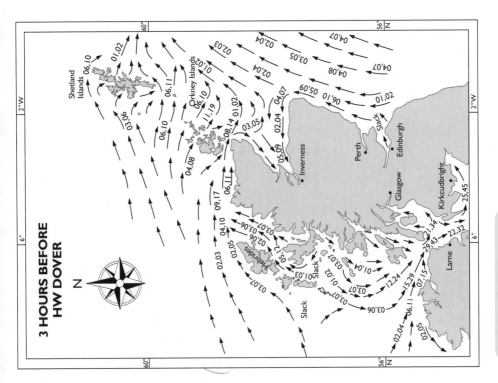

SCOTLAND

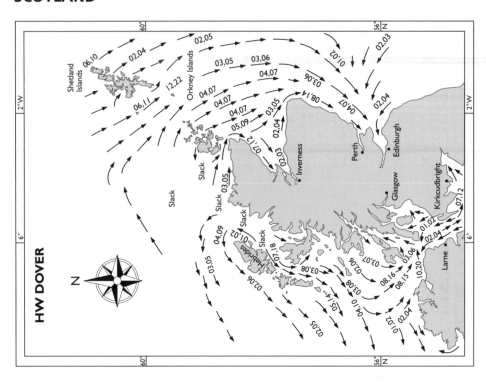

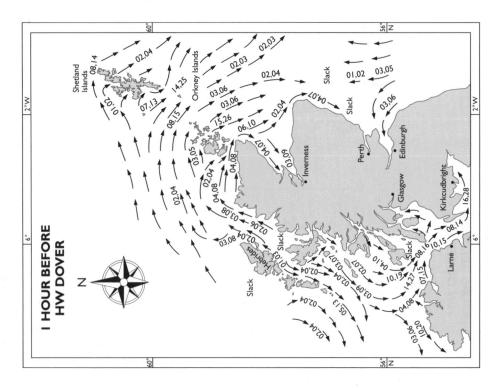

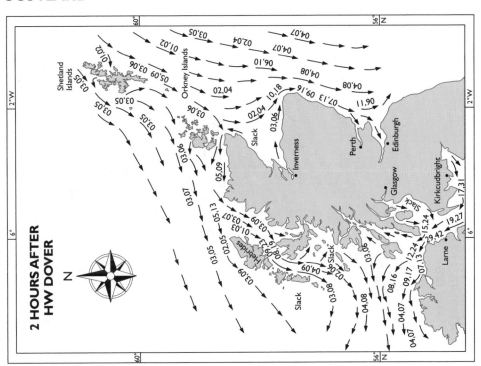

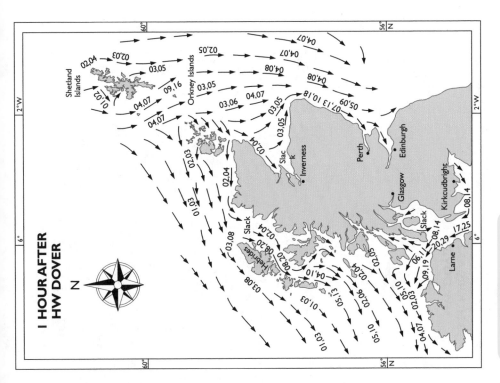

SCOTLAND

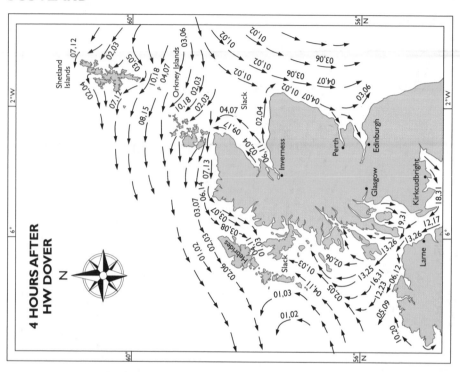

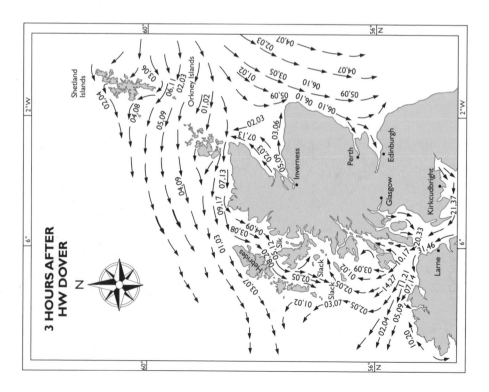

SCOTLAND

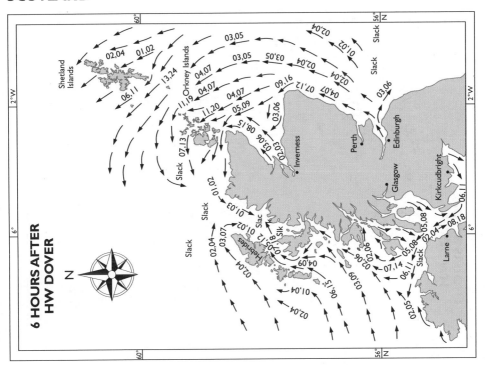

6 HOURS AFTER HW DOVER

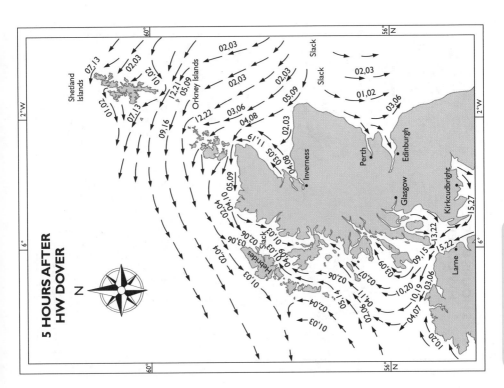

5 HOURS AFTER HW DOVER

WEST UK AND IRELAND

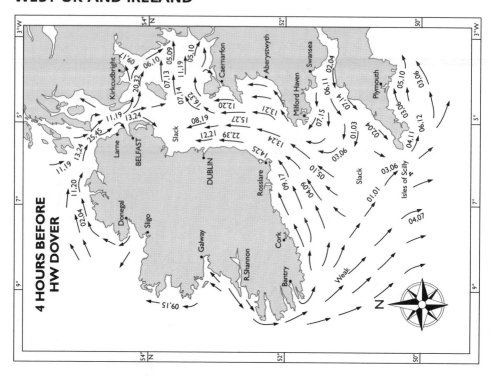

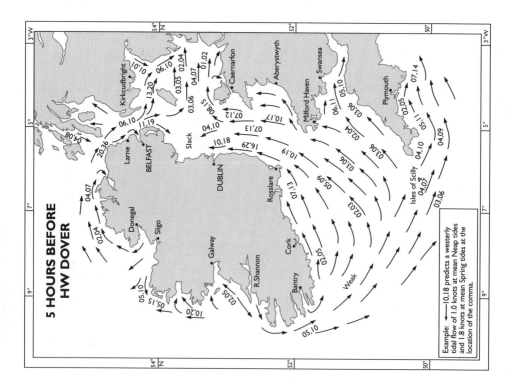

WEST UK AND IRELAND

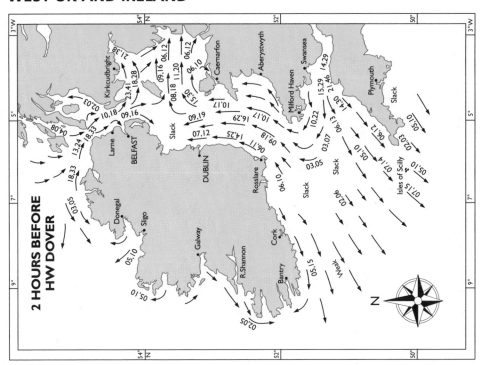

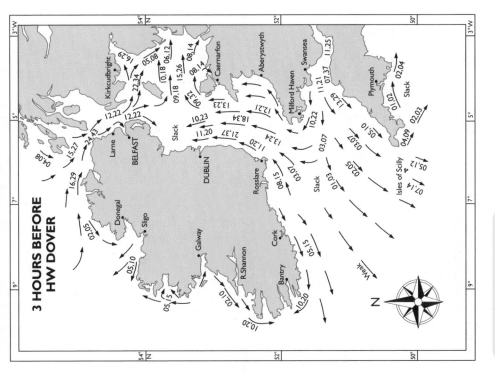

WEST UK AND IRELAND

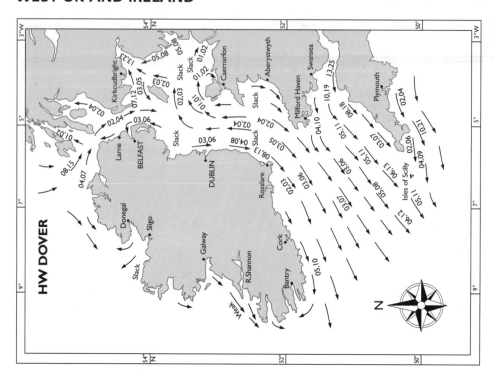

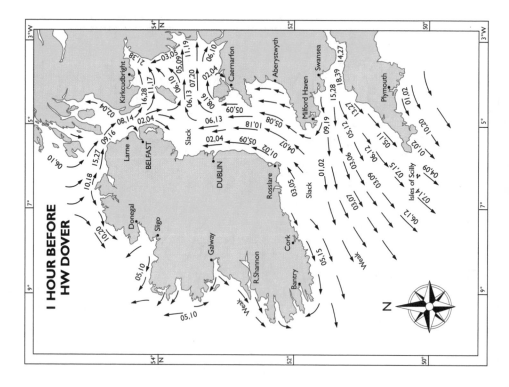

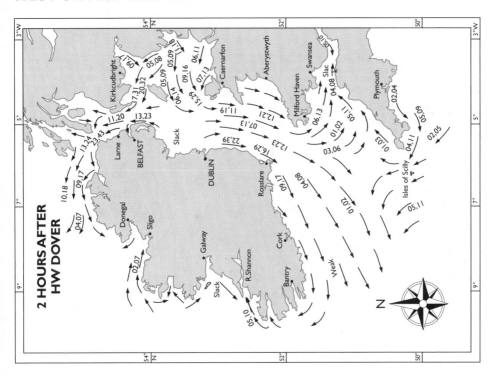

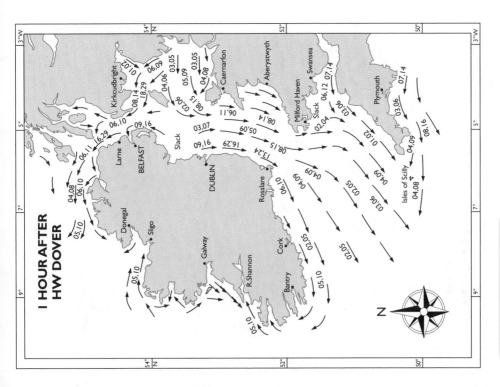

WEST UK AND IRELAND

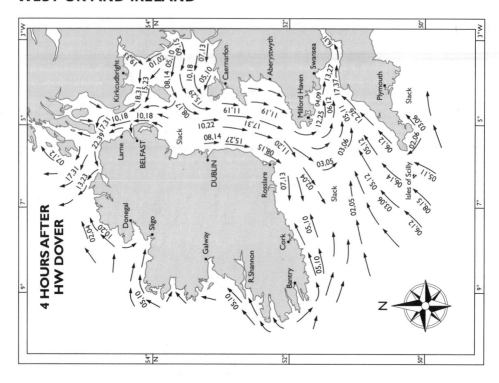

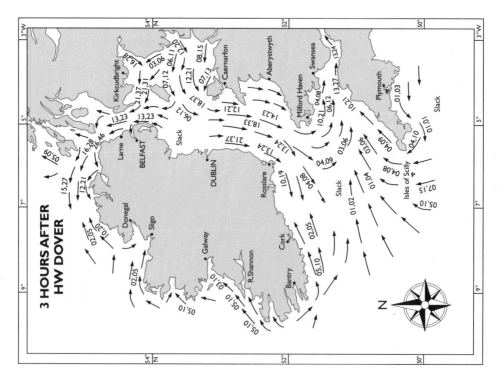

WEST UK AND IRELAND

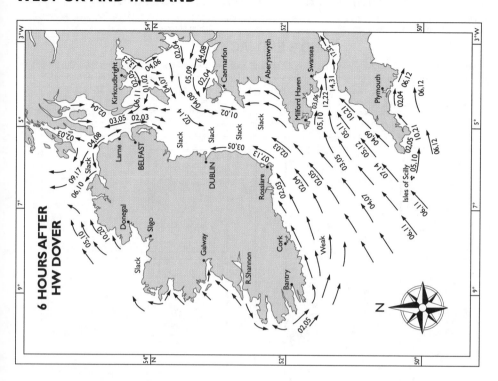

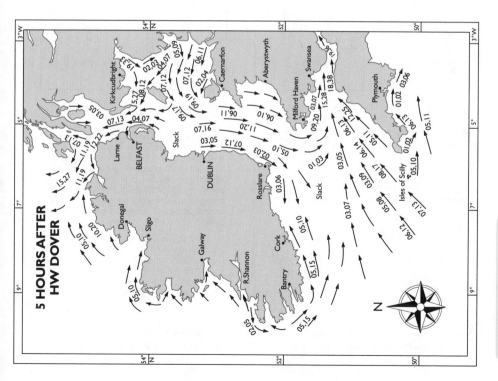

TIDAL GATES – SOUTHERN ENGLAND

A guide to the time of tide turn at tidal gates, the approximate maximum strength of the tidal flow (spring rates shown - neaps are approximately 60% of these), and the position and timing of races, counter tides, etc.

LAND'S END (AC 1148)

Tidal streams set hard north/south round Land's End, and east/west around Gwennap and Pendeen. But the inshore currents run counter to the tidal streams. By staying close inshore, this tidal gate favours a N-bound passage. With careful timing nearly 9½hrs of fair tide can be carried, from HWD–3 to HWD+5. The chartlets, referenced to HW Dover, depict both tidal streams and inshore currents.

FLOOD	EBB

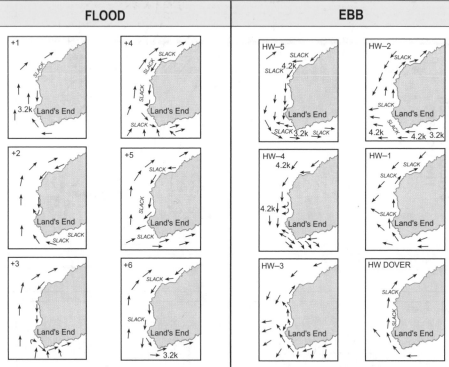

Example N-bound: At HWD+1 the N-going flood starts off Gwennap and does not turn NE along the N Cornish coast until HWD+3. But as early as HWD–3 an inshore current is beginning to set north. Utilise this by arriving off Runnel Stone at HWD–2 and then keeping within ¼M of the shore. If abeam the Brisons at HWD, the tide and current should serve for the next 6 or 7 hours to make good St Ives, or even Newquay and Padstow.

Example S-bound: If S-bound from St Ives to Newlyn, aim to reach the Runnel Stone by HWD+5, ie with 2hrs of E-going tide in hand for the remaining 9M to Newlyn. To achieve this 20M passage, leave St Ives 5 hours earlier, ie at HWD. Buck a foul tide for the first 3 hours, then use the S-going inshore current, keeping as close inshore as is prudent, only moving seaward to clear the Wra and the Brisons. This timing would also suit a passage from S Wales or the Bristol Channel, going inshore of Longships if conditions allow.

From Ireland, ie Cork or further W, the inshore passage would not benefit. But aim to be off the Runnel Stone at HWD+5 if bound for Newlyn; or at HWD+3 if bound for Helford/Falmouth, with the W-going stream slackening and 5hrs of fair tide to cover the remaining 20M past the Lizard.

With acknowledgements to the Royal Cruising Club Pilotage Foundation for their kind permission to use the tidal stream chartlets and text written by Hugh Davies, as first published in Yachting Monthly *magazine.*

TIDAL GATES – SOUTHERN ENGLAND

A guide to the time of tide turn at tidal gates, the approximate maximum strength of the tidal flow (spring rates shown - neaps are approximately 60% of these), and the position and timing of races, counter tides, etc.

FLOOD	EBB

THE LIZARD (AC 777, 2345)

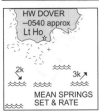

HW DOVER
−0540 approx
Lt Ho

2k   3k

MEAN SPRINGS
SET & RATE

Drying rocks lie approx 5 cables S of the Lizard lt ho and extend westwards. 49°57'N is about as far N as yachts may safely pass inshore of the Race, which extends 2-3M to seaward of these rocks. Race conditions may also exist SE of the Lizard with short, heavy seas in westerlies. If passing S of the Race, route via 49°55'N 05°13'W to clear the worst of the Race.

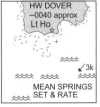

HW DOVER
−0040 approx
Lt Ho

3k

MEAN SPRINGS
SET & RATE

Inshore the E-going Channel flood, 2kn max @ springs, begins at HW Dover +0145; and outside the Race at approx HWD +0300.	Inshore the W-going Channel ebb, 3kn max @ springs, begins at HW Dover −0345; and outside the Race at HWD −0240.

START POINT (AC 1634)

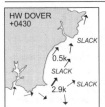

HW DOVER
+0430

SLACK

0.5k

SLACK

2.9k SLACK

Start Pt, and to a lesser extent Prawle Pt (3.3M WSW), can be slow to round when W-bound with a fair tide against a W'ly wind raising a bad sea. Drying rocks extend 3 cables SSE of the lt ho and a Race may extend up to 1.7M ESE and 1.0M S of the lt ho. It is safe to pass between the Race and the rocks, but in bad weather wiser to go outside the Race. The Skerries Bank (least depth 2.1m) lies 8 cables NE of Start Pt. On both the flood and the ebb back eddies form between Start Pt and Hallsands, 1M NW.

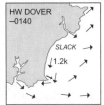

HW DOVER
−0140

SLACK

1.2k

The NE-going Channel flood, 3.1kn max @ springs, begins at HW Dover +0430.	The SW-going Channel ebb, 2.2kn max @ springs, begins at HW Dover −0140, but an hour earlier it is possible to round Start Pt close inshore using the back eddy.

PORTLAND (AC 2255)

Tidal streams off Portland Bill run very strongly. The notorious Portland Race is caused by the almost constant strong southerly flow down both sides of the Bill meeting the main E and W-going streams in the English Channel. The violence of the race is increased by the sudden decrease in depth on Portland Ledge. The tidal stream chartlets on Pages 158–159 show that the race shifts to the E on the flood, and to the W on the ebb. Even in calm weather the race can be dangerous for small craft; in heavy weather or with wind against tide the whole area should be given a wide berth. In such conditions, pass at least 3 miles S of the Bill and do not pass between Portland and The Shambles bank.

In settled weather, with winds <F4/5, but not at springs nor with wind against tide, passage may be made very close S of the Bill in the narrow stretch of relatively smooth water N of the race. Night passage should not be attempted due to numerous fishing floats which may be semi-submerged.

Seaward of the race the Channel flood sets east from HW Plymouth -1 to HW +5; the ebb sets west from HW Plymouth +5 to HW -1.

Inshore passage

E-bound across Lyme Bay timing is critical to be close inshore about 2M north of the Bill by HW Plymouth −2 to achieve passage around the Bill between HW Plymouth −2 to HW+1.	W-bound timing is easier if starting from Portland Hbr, Weymouth or Lulworth Cove. Aim to be close inshore about 2M north of the Bill at HW Plymouth +4, and make the passage between HW Plymouth +5 and HW−5.

When using the inshore passage be particularly wary of being set S into the race itself.

ST ALBAN'S HEAD (AC 2610)

A sometimes vicious Race forms over St Alban's Ledge, a rocky dorsal ridge (least depth 8.5m) which extends approx 4M SW from St Alban's Head. Three yellow naval target buoys (DZ A, B and C) straddle the middle and outer sections, but are only occasionally used. In settled weather and at neaps the Race may be barely perceptible in which case it can be crossed with impunity. Avoid it either by keeping to seaward via 50°31'.40N 02°07'.80W; or by using the narrow inshore passage at the foot of St Alban's Head.

Based on a position 1M S of St Alban's Head, the tidal stream windows are:

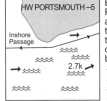

HW PORTSMOUTH −5

Inshore
Passage

2.7k

ESE-going stream starts at HW Portsmouth +0530. Spring rates are the same, max 4kn. Along the W side of St Alban's Head the stream runs almost continuously SE due to a back eddy.

The inshore passage lies as close to the foot of St Alban's Head as feels comfortable. It may be hard to see the width of clear water in the inshore passage until committed to it, but except in onshore gales when it is better to stay offshore, the passage will be swiftly made

WNW-going stream starts at HW Portsmouth. Overfalls extend 2.5M further SW than on the E-going stream and are more dangerous to small craft. Slack water lasts barely half an hour.

HW PORTSMOUTH +2

Inshore
Passage

3.0k

with only a few, if any, overfalls. The NCI station on the Head (☎ 01929 439220) may advise on conditions.

TIDES

TIDAL GATES – SOUTHERN ENGLAND

A guide to the time of tide turn at tidal gates, the approximate maximum strength of the tidal flow (spring rates shown - neaps are approximately 60% of these), and the position and timing of races, counter tides, etc.

FLOOD	EBB

THE NEEDLES CHANNEL (AC 2035)

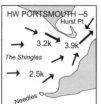

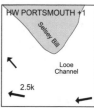

The Needles Channel lies between the SW Shingles PHM buoy and the Bridge WCM buoy. Once through this narrow section the channel widens with the Island shore to starboard and the long, drying 1.2m, Shingles bank to port. Abeam Hurst Castle the channel again narrows (assisted by The Trap, a shoal spit south of Hurst Castle) before opening out into the west Solent.

Study carefully the hourly tidal stream chartlets for the Isle of Wight on pp.186-191 and the values shown on AC 2035 at tidal diamonds B, C, D and E.

The ENE-going flood runs from HW Portsmouth +5 until HW P –1½, at springs reaching 3.1kn at The Bridge and 3.9kn at Hurst.	The WSW-going ebb runs from HW P –1 until HW P +4½, reaching 4.4kn at Hurst and 3.4kn at The Bridge, both spring rates. The ebb sets strongly WSW across the Shingles which with adequate rise is routinely crossed by racing yachts; but cruisers should stay clear even in calm conditions when any swell causes the sea to break heavily.

Prevailing W/SW winds, even if only F4, against the ebb raise dangerous breaking seas in the Needles Channel and at The Bridge. Worst conditions are often found just after LW slack. In such conditions it is safer to go via the North Channel to Hurst. In W/SW gales avoid the Needles altogether by sheltering at Poole or going east-about via Nab Tower.

ON PASSAGE UP CHANNEL

The following 3 tidal gates (Looe Channel, Beachy Head and Dungeness) are components in the tidal conveyor belt which, if stepped onto at the outset, can enable a fastish yacht to carry a fair tide for 88M from Selsey Bill to Dover. Go through the Looe at slackish water, HW Portsmouth +4½ (HW Dover +5). Based on a mean SOG of 7 knots, Beachy Head will be passed at HW D –1, Dungeness at HW D +3 and Dover at HW +5½, only bucking the first of the ebb in the last hour. A faster boat could make Ramsgate. The down-Channel passage is less rewarding and many yachts will pause at Brighton.

LOOE CHANNEL (AC 2045, 1652)

This channel is little shorter than the detour south of the Owers, but is much used by yachts on passage from/to points east of the Solent. Although adequately lit, it is best not attempted at night due to many lobster floats; nor in onshore gales as searoom is limited by extensive shoals on which the sea breaks.

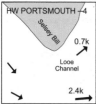

The E-going flood runs from HW Portsmouth +4½ (HW Dover +5) until HW P –1½ (HW D –1), at springs reaching 2.4kn near the Boulder and Street light buoys which marks its narrow western end; they may be hard to see in other than good visibility. Max neap rate is 1.2kn.	The W-going ebb runs from HW P –1½ (HW D –1) until HW P +4½ (HW D +5), at springs reaching 2.6kn near Boulder and Street. Max neap rate is 1.3kn.

At the wider eastern end of the channel (near E Borough Head buoy) rates are greatly reduced.

BEACHY HEAD (AC 1652, 536)

Stay at least 5 cables to seaward of the towering chalk cliffs to avoid isolated boulders and rocky, part-drying ridges such as Head Ledge. The lt ho stands on a drying rock ledge. Close inshore many fishing floats are a trap for the unwary. In bad weather stay 2M offshore to avoid overfalls caused by a ridge of uneven ground which extends 1M SSE from Beachy Head.

2M south of Beachy Head the E-going flood starts at HW Dover -0530, max spring rate 2.6kn.	The W-going ebb starts at HW Dover +0030, max spring rate 2.0kn.

Between 5M and 7M east of Beachy Head avoid breakers and eddies caused by the Horse of Willingdon, Royal Sovereign and other shoals.

DUNGENESS (AC 536, 1892)

Tidal stream atlases: Dungeness is on the east and west edges respectively of NP 250 (English Channel) and NP 233 (Dover Strait). The nearest tidal stream diamond (2.2M SE of Dungeness) is 'H' on AC 536 and 'B' on AC 1892; their positions and values are the same.

The NE-going flood starts at HW Dover –0100, max spring rate 1.9kn.	The SW-going ebb starts at HW Dover +0430, max spring rate 2.1kn.

TIDAL GATES – NORTH EAST SCOTLAND

A guide to the time of tide turn at tidal gates, and in straits and estuaries, showing the approximate strength of the tidal flow (spring rates shown - neaps are approximately 60% of these), and the pos ition and timing of races, counter tides etc.

FLOOD	EBB

FIRTHS of FORTH (AC 175) & TAY (AC 1481)

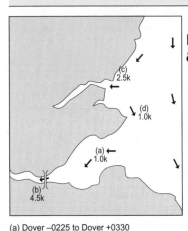

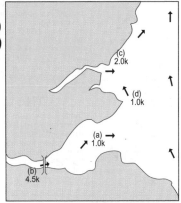

Tidal streams are quite weak in the outer part of the Firth, increasing as the narrows at islands and the bridges are approached. Apart from the stream of the Tay, which attains 5 knots in most places, the coastwise tidal streams between Fife Ness and Arbroath are weak.

(a) Dover –0225 to Dover +0330
(b) Dover –0200 to Dover +0400
(c) Dover –0210 to Dover +0420
(d) Dover –0110 to Dover +0520

(a) Dover +0330 to Dover –0225
(b) Dover +0400 to Dover –0200
(c) Dover +0420 to Dover –0210
(d) Dover +0520 to Dover –0110

PASSAGES FROM FORTH & TAY

Northbound. Leave before HW (Dover +0400) to be at N Carr at Dover +0600. Bound from Forth to Tay aim to arrive at Abertay By at LW slack (Dover –0200).
Southbound. Leave before LW (Dover -0200) to be at Bass Rk at HW Dover. Similar timings if bound from Tay to Forth, leave late in ebb to pick up early flood off St Andrews to N Carr and into Forth.

INVERNESS & CROMARTY FIRTHS (AC 1077)

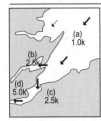

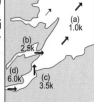

Tidal streams in the Inverness Firth and approaches are not strong, except in the Cromarty Firth Narrows, the Fort George Narrows and the Kessock Road, including off the entrance to the Caledonian Canal.

(a) Dover –0555 to Dover +0030	(a) Dover +0030 to Dover –0555
(b) Dover –0400 to Dover +0115	(b) Dover +0115 to Dover –0400
(c) Dover –0400 to Dover HW	(c) Dover +0115 to Dover –0525
(d) Dover –0430 to Dover +0100	(d) Dover +0130 to Dover +0545

PENTLAND FIRTH & ORKNEYS (AC 1954)

The tide flows strongly around and through the Orkney Islands. The Pentland Firth is a dangerous area for all craft, tidal flows reach 12 knots between Duncansby Head and S Ronaldsay. W of Dunnet Hd & Hoy is less violent. There is little tide within Scapa Flow.

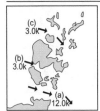

(a) Dover –0500 to Dover +0100	(a) Dover +0115 to Dover –0535
(b) Dover +0530 to Dover –0110	(b) Dover –0110 to Dover +0530
(c) Dover –0530 to Dover +0040	(c) Dover +0040 to Dover –0530

SHETLAND ISLANDS (AC 219)

The tidal flow around the Shetland Islands rotates as the cycle progresses. When the flood begins, at –0400 HW Dover, the tidal flow is to the E, at HW Dover it is S, at Dover +0300 it is W, and at –0600 Dover it is N.

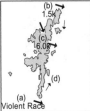

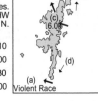

(a) Dover –0410 to Dover +0020	(a) Dover +0050 to Dover –0410
(b) Dover –0400 to Dover +0030	(b) Dover +0130 to Dover –0500
(c) Dover –0530 to Dover +0100	(c) Dover +0100 to Dover –0530
(d) Dover –0400 to Dover –0200	(d) Dover +0200 to Dover +0500

TIDAL GATES – NORTH WEST SCOTLAND

A guide to the time of tide turn at tidal gates, the approximate maximum strength of the tidal flow (spring rates shown – neaps are approximately 60% of these), and the position and timing of races, counter tides, etc.

FLOOD	EBB

SOUND OF HARRIS (AC 2802)

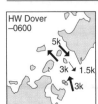

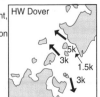

The behaviour of tidal streams in the Sd of Harris varies from day to night, springs to neaps, and winter to summer. The following data applies to daylight, in summer at spring tides in the Cope Channel. Further information can be sought in the Admiralty West of Scotland Pilot.
HW Dover - HW D +0200: SE stream.
HW D +0300 - HW D +0600: Incoming stream from both ends.
HW D −0600 - HW D −0500: NW stream.
HW D −0500 - HW Dover: Outgoing stream from both ends.
At neaps in summer the stream will run SE for most of the day.
Tide rates shown are the maxima likely to be encountered at any time.

THE LITTLE MINCH (AC 1795)

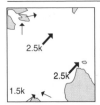

The N going stream on both shores begins at HW Dover +0430 (HW Ullapool -0345), with the strongest flow from mid channel to the Skye coast. There is a W going counter tide E of Vaternish Point.

The S going stream on both shores begins at HW Dover −0130 (HW Ullapool +0240), with the strongest flow from mid channel to the Skye coast. The E going stream in Sound of Scalpay runs at up to 2k.The E going flood and W going ebb in Sound of Scalpay run at up to 2k.

KYLE OF LOCHALSH & KYLERHEA (AC 2540)

NOTE: THESE STREAMS ARE SUBJECT TO VARIATION

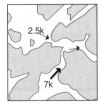

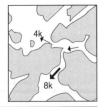

N going stream in Kyle Rhea begins HW Dover +0140 (HW Ullapool +0555) and runs for 6 hours. The E going stream in Kyle Akin begins (Sp) HW Dover +0350 (HW Ullapool −0415). (Nps) HW Dover −0415 (HW Ullapool).

S going stream in Kyle Rhea begins HW Dover -0415 (HW Ullapool) and runs for 6 hours. The W going stream in Kyle Akin begins (Sp) HW Dover −0015 (HW Ullapool +0400). (Nps) HW Dover +0140 (HW Ullapool +0555).

ARDNAMURCHAN POINT (AC 2171)

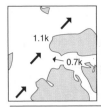

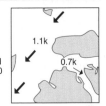

The N going stream off Ardnamurchan begins at HW Dover +0130 (HW Oban −0525). The E going stream in the Sound of Mull begins at HW Dover +0555 (HW Oban −0100).

The S going stream off Ardnamurchan begins at HW Dover −0430 (HW Oban +0100). The W going stream in the Sound of Mull begins at HW Dover −0130 (HW Oban +0400).

SOUND OF MULL – EAST (AC 2171)

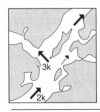

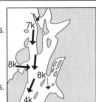

The N going stream in the Firth of Lorne begins at HW Dover −0100 (HW Oban +0430). The W going stream in the Sound of Mull begins at HW Dover +0105 (HW Oban −0550). The ingoing tides at Lochs Feochan, Etive and Creran begin at HW Dover +0300, −0100 & +0030.

The S going stream in the Firth of Lorne begins at HW Dover +0500 (HW Oban −0155). The E going stream in the Sound of Mull begins at HW Dover +0555 (HW Oban −0025). The outgoing tides at Lochs Feochan, Etive and Creran begin at HW Dover −0500, −0520 & −0505.

SOUND OF LUING & DORUS MOR (AC 2343)

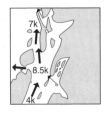

The N or W going stream begins as follows:
Dorus Mor: HW Dover −0200 (HW Oban +0330). Springs: 8 knots.
Corryvreckan: HW D −0120 (HW O +0410). Sp: 8.5 knots.
Cuan Sound: HW D −0110 (HW O +0420). Sp: 6 knots.
Sound of Jura: HW D −0130 (HW O +0400). Sp: 4 knots.
Sound of Luing: HW D −0100 (HW O +0430). Sp: 7 knots.
The S or E going stream begins as follows:
Dorus Mor: HW Dover +0440 (HW Oban −0215). Springs: 8 knots.
Corryvreckan: HW D +0445 (HW O −0210). Sp: 8.5 knots.
Cuan Sound: HW D +0455 (HW O −0200). Sp: 6 knots.
Sound of Jura: HW D +0450 (HW O −0205). Sp: 4 knots.
Sound of Luing: HW D +0500 (HW O −0155). Sp: 7 knots.

TIDAL GATES – SOUTH WEST SCOTLAND

A guide to the time of tide turn at tidal gates, the approximate maximum strength of the tidal flow (spring rates shown - neaps are approximately 60% of these), and the position and timing of races, counter tides, etc.

FLOOD	EBB

SOUNDS OF ISLAY AND GIGHA (AC 2168)

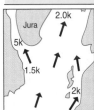

Main flood begins +0015 HW Dover (HW Oban +0545). Streams turn approx 1 hr earlier in Gigha Sd & at Kintyre & Jura shores. S going stream for 9hrs close inshore between Gigha and Machrihanish starting HW Dover (HW Oban –0530).

Main ebb begins HW Dover –0545 (HW Oban –0015). Streams turn 1 hr earlier in Gigha Sd, Kintyre & Jura shores. Overfalls off McArthur's Hd.

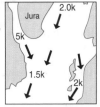

NORTH CHANNEL – NORTH (AC 2798)

Main flood begins HW Dover –0600 (HW Greenock +0505). Races off Mull of Kintyre, Altacarry Hd & Fair Hd. Counter tides in bays of Antrim coast. W-going streams in Rathlin Sd, counter tide from Sanda Sd to Machrihanish last 1h30 - 2 hrs.

Main ebb begins HW Dover (HW Greenock –0120). Races off Mull of Kintyre & Altacarry Hd. Counter tides in bays of Antrim coast, counter tide from Macrihanish to Sanda Sd last 1h30 - 2 hrs.

NORTH CHANNEL – SOUTH (AC 2198)

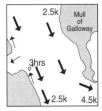

Irish coast - flood begins HW Dover +0610 (HW Belfast –0600). Scottish coast - HW Dover +0430 (HW Greenock +0310). Races off Copeland Is. & Mull of Galloway. Counter tide off Donaghadee and Island Magee last 3 hrs of flood.

Irish coast - ebb begins HW Dover –0015 (HW Belfast). Scottish coast - HW Dover –0130 (HW Greenock –0250). Races off Copeland Is. & Mull of Galloway. Flood begins 2 hrs early close inshore N of Mull of Galloway.

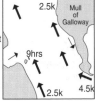

APPROACHES TO STRANGFORD LOUGH (AC 2156)

The tide cycle is approx 3 hours later than in the N Channel

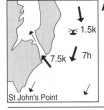

Flood runs for 6 hours from HW Dover –0345 (HW Belfast –0330), with a maximum rate of 7.5 knots at Rue Point. The strong flow flattens the sea in onshore winds and entrance can be made in strong winds.

Ebb runs for 6 hours from HW Dover +0215 (HW Belfast +0230), max rate 7.5k, E of Angus Rk. If entering against ebb use West Channel with care. Smoothest water near Bar Pladdy Buoy when leaving.

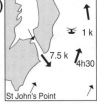

ISLE OF MAN – NORTH (AC 2094)

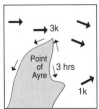

E going stream at Point of Ayre begins HW Dover –0545 (HW Liverpool –0600). Counter tide inside banks E of Point. In Ramsey Bay the S Going tide runs for 3h from +0530 Dover (+0515 Liverpool).

W going stream at Point of Ayre begins HW Dover +0015 (HW Liverpool). Counter tide inside banks W of Point. In Ramsey Bay the N going tide runs for 9h from –0330 Dover (–0345 Liverpool).

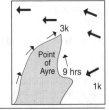

ISLE OF MAN – SOUTH (AC 2094)

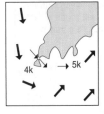

E going stream begins –0600 Dover (Liverpool +0610). Overfalls and race E of Chicken Rock. Calf Sound: The E going stream begins earlier, at approximately Dover +0400 (Liverpool +0345).

W going stream begins +0015 Dover (HW Liverpool). Overfalls and race N of Chicken Rock. Calf Sound: The W going stream begins earlier, at approximately –0130 Dover (–0145 Liverpool). Note: all times may vary due to weather conditions.

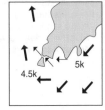

TIDES

MENAI STRAIT (AC 1464) – TIDAL GATES

FLOOD

(T): turning → : < 2k ➡ : 2-4k ‖➡ : 4k +

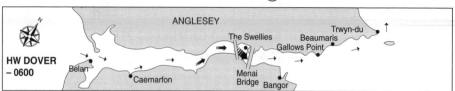

LOCAL LW: Caernarfon: HW Dover –0555. Port Dinorwic: –0620. Menai: –0540. Beaumaris: –0605.

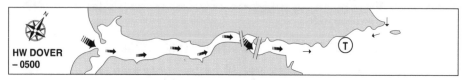

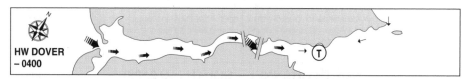

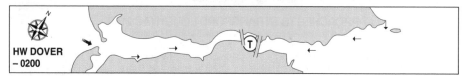

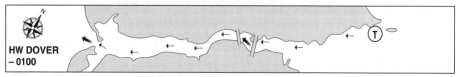

SLACK WATER IN THE SWELLIES: HW Dover –0200 to –0230.

LOCAL HW: Belan: HW Dover –0115. Caernarfon: –0105. Port Dinorwic: –0050.

THE SWELLIES

WESTBOUND: Leave or pass Beaumaris in time to arrive at the Swellies by HW Dover –0230 to –0200. If in doubt about passage speed, leave early; the adverse tide will check your progress. For a first time passage this is useful, as the yacht's speed over the ground is reduced. Late arrival will mean a faster passage, but with perhaps less control.

EASTBOUND: Leave or pass Port Dinorwic in time to arrive at Menai Bridge by HW Dover –0230 to –0200. Progress towards the Swellies should be closely monitored, as you are travelling with the last of the flood. Early arrival will mean a fast, perhaps dangerous passage, being late may make it impossible.

MENAI STRAIT (AC 1464) – TIDAL GATES *contd*

EBB

(T) : turning   → : < 2k   ➡ : 2-4k   ⧑➡ : 4k +

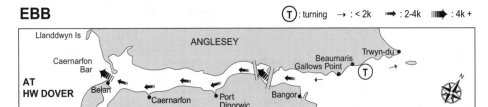

LOCAL HW TIMES: Menai: Dover – 0005.   Beaumaris: Dover – 0010

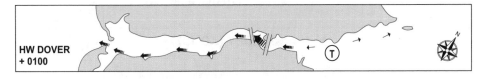

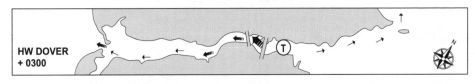

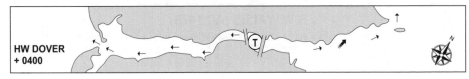

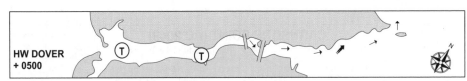

LOCAL LW TIMES: Belan: Dover + 0520.

CAERNARFON BAR

CAERNARFON BAR is without question highly dangerous in certain conditions. Buoys are located to suit changing channel; positions obtainable from Caernarfon Port Radio - VHF Ch 16; 06, 12: 2h–HW, or when vessel expected. Beware cross track tides near high water. Bar impassable during or after fresh or strong onshore weather. Keep strictly in channel.

OUTWARD BOUND: Do not leave Belan Narrows after half tide, better as soon as possible after the ebb commences, which gives maximum depth and duration of fair tide if bound S & W.	INWARD BOUND: Locating the bar buoys may be difficult; head for Llanddwyn I. until they are located. Only cross after half tide (HW Dover –0400), which inevitably limits onward passage to max of 3 hours.

TIDAL GATES – IRISH SEA

A guide to the time of tide turn at tidal gates, the approximate strength of the tidal flow (spring rates shown – neaps are approximately 60% of these), and the position and timing of races, counter tides, etc.

FLOOD	EBB

DUBLIN BAY (AC 1415)

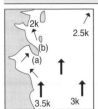

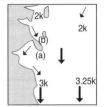

Tide between Rosbeg bank and Howth Hd (a) runs NE from HW Dublin +0300 for 9h30. In Howth Sd (b) the stream is NW going from +0430 to –0130.
New flood and ebb tides begin close to the S shore and N of Baily up to 1h before HW Dublin .

The tide between Rosbeg bank and Howth Hd (a) runs SW from HW Dublin for 3h. In Howth Sd (b) the stream is SE going from –0130 to +0430.
Strengths of streams increase S of Dublin Bay, and decrease N of it.

N W ANGLESEY (AC 1977)

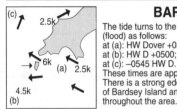

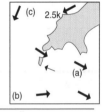

Flood tide close to the coast runs at over 5k springs, and at about 2.5k 7 miles offshore. The brief period of slack water offshore is 1h before HW Dover (1h15 before HW L'pool). Slack water lasts longer in Holyhead Bay.

Ebb tide close to the coast runs at over 5k springs, and at about 2.5k 7 miles offshore. Slack water is 5h after HW Dover (4h45 after HW L'pool). There is no significant counter tide in Holyhead Bay, but the ebb starts first there, giving about 9h W-going tide N of the harbour (a).

BARDSEY SOUND (AC 1971)

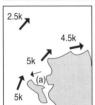

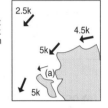

The tide turns to the NW or NE (flood) as follows:
at (a): HW Dover +0300;
at (b): HW D +0500;
at (c): –0545 HW D.
These times are approximate.
There is a strong eddy down tide of Bardsey Island and overfalls throughout the area.

The tide turns to the SW or SE (ebb) as follows:
at (a): HW Dover –0300;
at (b): HW D –0100 ;
at (c): at HW D –0030.
These times are approximate.
There is a strong eddy down tide of Bardsey Island and overfalls throughout the area.

S W WALES (AC 1478)

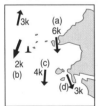

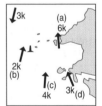

The tide turns to the S or SE (Bristol Channel flood) as follows:
at (a): HW Dover –0200;
at (b) & (c): HW D –0100 ;
at (d): –0300 HW D

The tide turns to the N or NW (Bristol Channel ebb) as follows:
at (a): HW Dover +0400;
at (b) & (c): HW D +0500 ;
at (d): +0300 HW D

CARNSORE POINT (AC 2049)

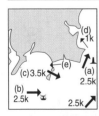

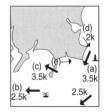

The tide turns to the NE or N (Irish Sea flood) as follows:
at (a): HW Dover +0500; at (b): HW D +0520; at (c): HW D +0600; at (d): –0600 HW D. NE going streams are shorter in duration and weaker than SE going - careful passage planning is essential.

The tide turns to the SW or S as follows:
at (a): –0200 HW D ; at (b): HW D –0020; at (c): –0015 HW D; at (d): –0300 HW Dover. Leaving Rosslare at –0300 HW D a yacht can carry a fair tide for about 8h until HW D +0515 off Hook Head.

NOTE: The tide turns on St Patrick's Bridge (e) up to 2 hours earlier than in Saltee Sound

CORK COAST (AC 2049)

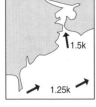

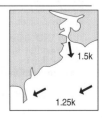

The tide, which flows coastwise, turns to the NE at HW Dover +0045. There is an eddy 5 miles ESE of Old Head of Kinsale at HW Dover +0400. The ingoing Cork Harbour tide begins at HW Dover +0055.

The tide turns SW at HW Dover +0500. The outgoing Cork Harbour tide begins at HW Dover –0540.

SECONDARY PORTS: TIME & HEIGHT DIFFERENCES
SOUTH COAST OF ENGLAND *Time zone UT*

Location	Lat	Long	High Water		Low Water		MHWS	MHWN	MLWN	MLWS
			0000	0600	0000	0600				
PLYMOUTH (DEVONPORT)	50 22N	4 11W	and	and	and	and	5.5	4.4	2.2	0.8
Standard port			1200	1800	1200	1800				
Isles of Scilly, St Mary's	49 55N	6 19W	−0052	−0103	−0048	−0045	+0.2	−0.1	−0.2	−0.1
Penzance & Newlyn	50 06N	5 33W	−0053	−0108	−0035	−0036	0.0	−0.1	−0.2	0.0
Porthleven	50 05N	5 19W	−0045	−0105	−0030	−0025	0.0	−0.1	−0.2	0.0
Lizard Point	49 57N	5 12W	−0045	−0100	−0030	−0030	−0.2	−0.2	−0.3	−0.2
Coverack	50 01N	5 05W	−0030	−0050	−0020	−0015	−0.2	−0.2	−0.3	−0.2
Helford River Entrance	50 05N	5 05W	−0030	−0035	−0015	−0010	−0.2	−0.2	−0.3	−0.2
FALMOUTH	50 09N	5 03W	*Standard port (no Secondaries)*							
River Fal, Truro	50 16N	5 03W	−0020	−0025	*Dries*	*Dries*	−2.0	−2.0	*Dries*	
Mevagissey	50 16N	4 47W	−0015	−0020	−0010	−0005	−0.1	−0.1	−0.2	−0.1
Par	50 21N	4 42W	−0010	−0015	−0010	−0005	−0.4	−0.4	−0.4	−0.2
River Fowey, Fowey	50 20N	4 38W	−0010	−0015	−0010	−0005	−0.1	−0.1	−0.2	−0.2
Lostwithiel	50 24N	4 40W	+0005	−0010	*Dries*	*Dries*	−4.1	−4.1	*Dries*	
Looe	50 21N	4 27W	−0010	−0010	−0005	−0005	−0.1	−0.2	−0.2	−0.2
Whitsand Bay	50 20N	4 15W	0000	0000	0000	0000	0.0	+0.1	−0.1	+0.2
River Tamar										
Saltash	50 24N	4 12W	0000	+0010	0000	−0005	+0.1	+0.1	+0.1	+0.1
Cargreen	50 26N	4 12W	0000	+0010	+0020	+0020	0.0	0.0	−0.1	0.0
Cotehele Quay	50 29N	4 13W	0000	+0020	+0045	+0045	−0.9	−0.9	−0.8	−0.4
River Tavy, Lopwell	50 28N	4 09W	*No data*	*No data*	*Dries*	*Dries*	−2.6	−2.7	*Dries*	
River Lynher, Jupiter Point	50 23N	4 14W	+0010	+0005	0000	−0005	0.0	0.0	+0.1	0.0
St Germans	50 23N	4 18W	0000	0000	+0020	+0020	−0.3	−0.1	0.0	+0.2
Turnchapel	50 22N	4 07W	0000	0000	+0010	−0015	0.0	+0.1	+0.2	+0.1
Bovisand Pier	50 20N	4 08W	−0010	−0010	−0008	−0009	−0.1	0.0	+0.2	+0.2
River Yealm, Entrance	50 18N	4 04W	+0006	+0006	+0002	+0002	−0.1	−0.1	−0.1	−0.1
			0100	0600	0100	0600				
PLYMOUTH (DEVONPORT)	50 22N	4 11W	and	and	and	and	5.5	4.4	2.2	0.8
Standard port			1300	1800	1300	1800				
Salcombe	50 13N	3 47W	0000	+0010	+0005	−0005	−0.2	−0.3	−0.1	−0.1
Start Point	50 13N	3 39W	+0015	+0015	+0005	+0010	−0.1	−0.2	+0.1	+0.2
River Dart										
DARTMOUTH	50 21N	3 34W	*Standard port (no Secondaries)*							
Greenway Quay	50 23N	3 35W	+0030	+0045	+0025	+0005	−0.6	−0.6	−0.2	−0.2
Totnes	50 26N	3 41W	+0030	+0040	+0115	+0030	−2.0	−2.1	*Dries*	
Torquay	50 28N	3 31W	+0025	+0045	+0010	0000	−0.6	−0.7	−0.2	−0.1
Teignmouth, Approaches	50 33N	3 29W	+0020	+0050	+0025	0000	−0.9	−0.8	−0.2	−0.1
Teignmouth, New Quay	50 33N	3 30W	+0025	+0055	+0040	+0005	−0.8	−0.8	−0.2	+0.1
Exmouth Approaches	50 36N	3 23W	+0030	+0050	+0015	+0005	−0.9	−1.0	−0.5	−0.3
River Exe										
Exmouth Dock	50 37N	3 25W	+0035	+0055	+0050	+0020	−1.5	−1.6	−0.9	−0.5
Starcross	50 38N	3 27W	+0040	+0100	+0055	+0025	−1.4	−1.5	−0.8	−0.1
Turf Lock	50 40N	3 28W	+0045	+0100	+0034	*No data*	−1.6	−1.6	−1.2	−0.4
Topsham	50 41N	3 28W	+0045	+0105	*No data*	*No data*	−1.5	−1.6	*No data*	
Lyme Regis	50 43N	2 56W	+0040	+0100	+0005	−0005	−1.2	−1.3	−0.5	−0.2
Bridport (West Bay)	50 42N	2 45W	+0025	+0040	0000	0000	−1.4	−1.4	−0.6	−0.1
Chesil Beach	50 37N	2 33W	+0040	+0055	−0005	+0010	−1.6	−1.5	−0.5	0.0
Chesil Cove	50 34N	2 28W	+0035	+0050	−0010	+0005	−1.5	−1.6	−0.5	−0.2
			0100	0700	0100	0700				
PORTLAND	50 34N	2 26W	and	and	and	and	2.1	1.4	0.8	0.1
Standard port			1300	1900	1300	1900				
Lulworth Cove, Mupe Bay	50 37N	2 14W	+0005	+0015	−0005	0000	+0.1	+0.1	+0.2	+0.1
			—	—	0500	1100				
POOLE HARBOUR	50 42N	1 59W			and	and	2.2	1.7	1.2	0.6
Standard port			—	—	1700	2300				
Swanage	50 37N	1 57W	—	—	−0045	+0050	−0.1	+0.1	+0.2	+0.2
Poole Harbour Entrance	50 41N	1 57W	—	—	−0025	−0010	0.0	0.0	0.0	0.0
Ro-Ro terminal	50 42N	1 59W	*Standard port*							
Pottery Pier	50 42N	1 59W	—	—	+0010	+0010	−0.2	0.0	+0.1	+0.2
Wareham, River Frome	50 41N	2 06W	—	—	+0130	+0045	0.0	0.0	0.0	+0.3
Cleavel Point	50 40N	2 00W	—	—	−0005	−0005	−0.1	−0.2	0.0	−0.1
			0000	0600	0500	1100				
PORTSMOUTH	50 48N	1 07W	and	and	and	and	4.7	3.8	1.9	0.8
Standard port			1200	1800	1700	2300				
Bournemouth	50 43N	1 52W	−0240	+0055	−0050	−0030	−2.6	−2.0	−0.6	−0.2
Christchurch Entrance	50 43N	1 45W	−0230	+0030	−0035	−0035	−2.9	−2.4	−1.2	−0.2

Location	Lat	Long	High Water		Low Water		MHWS	MHWN	MLWN	MLWS
Christchurch Quay	50 44N	1 47W	−0210	+0100	+0105	+0055	−2.9	−2.4	−1.0	0.0
Christchurch, Tuckton	50 44N	1 47W	−0205	+0110	+0110	+0105	−3.0	−2.5	−1.0	+0.1
Hurst Point	50 42N	1 33W	−0115	−0005	−0030	−0025	−2.0	−1.5	−0.5	−0.1
Lymington	50 46N	1 32W	−0110	+0005	−0020	−0020	−1.6	−1.2	−0.4	−0.1
Bucklers Hard	50 48N	1 25W	−0040	−0010	+0010	−0010	−1.0	−0.8	−0.2	−0.3
Stansore Point	50 47N	1 20W	−0030	−0010	−0005	−0015	−0.8	−0.5	−0.3	−0.3
Isle of Wight										
Yarmouth	50 42N	1 30W	−0105	+0005	−0025	−0030	−1.7	−1.2	−0.3	0.0
Totland Bay	50 41N	1 33W	−0130	−0045	−0035	−0045	−2.2	−1.7	−0.4	−0.1
Freshwater	50 40N	1 31W	−0210	+0025	−0040	−0020	−2.1	−1.5	−0.4	0.0
Ventnor	50 36N	1 12W	−0025	−0030	−0025	−0030	−0.8	−0.6	−0.2	+0.2
Sandown	50 39N	1 09W	0000	+0005	+0010	+0025	−0.6	−0.5	−0.2	0.0
Foreland Lifeboat Slip	50 41N	1 04W	−0005	0000	+0005	+0010	+0.1	+0.1	0.0	+0.1
Bembridge Harbour	50 42N	1 07W	+0020	0000	+0100	+0020	−1.5	−1.4	−1.3	−1.0
Ryde	50 44N	1 10W	−0010	−0010	−0005	−0005	−0.1	0.0	0.0	0.0
Medina River										
Cowes	50 46N	1 18W	−0015	+0015	0000	−0020	−0.5	−0.3	−0.1	0.0
Folly Inn	50 44N	1 17W	−0015	+0015	0000	−0020	−0.6	−0.4	−0.1	+0.2
Newport	50 42N	1 17W	*No data*	*No data*	*No data*	*No data*	−0.6	−0.4	+0.1	+0.8
			0400	**1100**	**0000**	**0600**				
SOUTHAMPTON	50 53N	1 24W	and	and	and	and	**4.5**	**3.7**	**1.8**	**0.5**
Standard port			**1600**	**2300**	**1200**	**1800**				
Calshot Castle	50 49N	1 18W	0000	+0025	0000	0000	0.0	0.0	+0.2	+0.3
Redbridge	50 55N	1 28W	−0020	+0005	0000	−0005	−0.1	−0.1	−0.1	−0.1
River Hamble										
Warsash	50 51N	1 18W	+0020	+0010	+0010	0000	0.0	+0.1	+0.1	+0.3
Bursledon	50 53N	1 18W	+0020	+0020	+0010	+0010	+0.1	+0.1	+0.2	+0.2
			0500	**1000**	**0000**	**0600**				
PORTSMOUTH	50 48N	1 07W	and	and	and	and	**4.7**	**3.8**	**1.9**	**0.8**
Standard port			**1700**	**2200**	**1200**	**1800**				
Lee-on-the-Solent	50 48N	1 12W	−0005	+0005	−0015	−0010	−0.2	−0.1	+0.1	+0.2
Chichester Harbour Entrance	50 47N	0 56W	−0010	+0005	+0015	+0020	+0.2	+0.2	0.0	+0.1
Northney	50 50N	0 58W	+0020	+0010	0000	+0005	0.0	−0.2	−0.2	−0.4
Bosham	50 50N	0 52W	+0010	+0005	*No data*	*No data*	0.0	−0.1	*No data*	
Itchenor	50 48N	0 52W	+0005	0000	−0010	+0005	−0.1	−0.2	−0.2	−0.3
Dell Quay	50 49N	0 49W	+0015	+0010	*no data*	*No data*	0.0	−0.1	*No data*	
Selsey Bill	50 43N	0 47W	+0010	−0010	+0035	+0020	+0.5	+0.3	−0.1	−0.2
Nab Tower	50 40N	0 57W	+0015	0000	+0015	+0015	−0.2	0.0	+0.2	0.0
			0500	**1000**	**0000**	**0600**				
SHOREHAM	50 50N	0 15W	and	and	and	and	**6.3**	**4.8**	**1.9**	**0.6**
Standard port			**1700**	**2200**	**1200**	**1800**				
Pagham	50 46N	0 43W	+0015	0000	−0015	−0025	−0.7	−0.5	−0.1	−0.1
Bognor Regis	50 47N	0 40W	+0010	−0005	−0005	−0020	−0.6	−0.5	−0.2	−0.1
River Arun										
Littlehampton Entrance	50 48N	0 33W	+0010	0000	−0005	−0010	−0.4	−0.4	−0.2	−0.2
Littlehampton UMA wharf	50 49N	0 33W	+0015	+0005	0000	+0045	−0.7	−0.7	−0.3	+0.2
Arundel	50 51N	0 33W	*No data*	+0120	*No data*	*No data*	−3.1	−2.8	*No data*	
Worthing	50 48N	0 22W	+0010	0000	−0005	−0010	−0.1	−0.2	0.0	0.0
Brighton	50 49N	0 08W	−0002	−0002	0000	0000	+0.2	+0.2	+0.1	+0.1
Newhaven	50 47N	0 04E	−0003	−0005	0000	+0005	+0.5	+0.4	+0.2	+0.2
Eastbourne	50 46N	0 17E	−0010	−0005	+0015	+0020	+1.1	+0.6	+0.2	+0.1
			0000	**0600**	**0100**	**0700**				
DOVER	51 07N	1 19E	and	and	and	and	**6.8**	**5.3**	**2.1**	**0.8**
Standard port			**1200**	**1800**	**1300**	**1900**				
Hastings	50 51N	0 36E	0000	−0010	−0030	−0030	+0.8	+0.5	+0.1	−0.1
Rye Approaches	50 55N	0 47E	+0005	−0010	*No data*	*No data*	+1.0	+0.7	*No data*	
Rye Harbour	50 56N	0 48E	+0005	−0010	*Dries*	*Dries*	−1.4	−1.7	*Dries*	
Dungeness	50 55N	0 58E	−0010	−0015	−0020	−0010	+1.0	+0.6	+0.4	+0.1
Folkestone	51 05N	1 12E	−0020	−0005	−0010	−0010	+0.4	+0.4	0.0	−0.1
Deal	51 13N	1 25E	+0012	+0010	+0004	+0002	−0.5	−0.3	0.0	+0.1
Richborough	51 18N	1 21E	+0015	+0015	+0030	+0030	−3.4	−2.6	−1.7	−0.7
Ramsgate	51 20N	1 25E	+0030	+0030	+0017	+0007	−1.6	−1.3	−0.7	−0.2

EAST COAST ENGLAND *Time Zone UT*

Location	Lat	Long	High Water		Low Water		MHWS	MHWN	MLWN	MLWS
			0100	**0700**	**0100**	**0700**				
MARGATE	51 23N	1 23E	and	and	and	and	**4.8**	**3.9**	**1.4**	**0.5**
Standard port			**1300**	**1900**	**1300**	**1900**				
Herne Bay	51 23N	1 07E	+0022	+0020	+0019	+0017	+0.6	+0.3	+0.2	+0.1
Whitstable approaches	51 22N	1 02E	+0042	+0029	+0025	+0050	+0.6	+0.6	+0.1	0.0

Location	Lat	Long	High Water		Low Water		MHWS	MHWN	MLWN	MLWS
			0200	0800	0200	0700				
SHEERNESS	51 27N	0 45E	and	and	and	and	5.8	4.7	1.5	0.6
Standard port			1400	2000	1400	1900				
River Swale										
Grovehurst Jetty	51 22N	0 46E	−0007	0000	0000	+0016	0.0	0.0	0.0	−0.1
Faversham	51 19N	0 54E	No data	No data	No data	No data	−0.2	−0.2	No data	
River Medway										
Bee Ness	51 25N	0 39E	+0002	+0002	0000	+0005	+0.2	+0.1	0.0	0.0
Bartlett Creek	51 23N	0 38E	+0016	+0008	No data	No data	+0.1	0.0	No data	
Darnett Ness	51 24N	0 36E	+0004	+0004	0000	+0010	+0.2	+0.1	0.0	−0.1
Chatham, Lock approaches	51 24N	0 33E	+0010	+0012	+0012	+0018	+0.3	+0.1	−0.1	−0.2
Upnor	51 25N	0 32E	+0015	+0015	+0015	+0025	+0.2	+0.2	−0.1	−0.1
Rochester, Strood Pier	51 24N	0 30E	+0018	+0018	+0018	+0028	+0.2	+0.2	−0.2	−0.3
Wouldham	51 21N	0 27E	+0030	+0025	+0035	+0120	−0.2	−0.3	−1.0	−0.3
New Hythe	51 19N	0 28E	+0035	+0035	+0220	+0240	−1.6	−1.7	−1.2	−0.3
Allington Lock	51 17N	0 30E	+0050	+0035	No data	No data	−2.1	−2.2	−1.3	−0.4
River Thames										
Southend–on–Sea	51 31N	0 43E	−0005	−0005	−0005	−0005	+0.1	0.0	−0.1	−0.1
Coryton	51 30N	0 31E	+0005	+0010	+0010	+0010	+0.4	+0.3	0.0	0.0
			0300	0900	0400	1100				
LONDON BRIDGE	51 30N	0 05W	and	and	and	and	7.1	5.9	1.3	0.5
Standard port			1500	2100	1600	2300				
Tilbury	51 27N	0 22E	−0055	−0040	−0050	−0115	−0.7	−0.5	+0.1	0.0
North Woolwich	51 30N	0 05E	−0020	−0020	−0035	−0045	−0.1	0.0	+0.2	0.0
Albert bridge	51 29N	0 10W	+0025	+0020	+0105	+0110	−0.9	−0.8	−0.7	−0.4
Hammersmith bridge	51 29N	0 14W	+0040	+0035	+0205	+0155	−1.4	−1.3	−1.0	−0.5
Kew bridge	51 29N	0 17W	+0055	+0050	+0255	+0235	−1.8	−1.8	−1.2	−0.5
Richmond lock	51 28N	0 19W	+0105	+0055	+0325	+0305	−2.2	−2.7	−0.9	−0.5
			0200	0700	0100	0700				
SHEERNESS	51 27N	0 45E	and	and	and	and	5.8	4.7	1.5	0.6
Standard port			1400	1900	1300	1900				
Thames Estuary Shivering Sand	51 30N	1 05E	−0025	−0019	−0008	−0026	−0.6	−0.6	−0.1	−0.1
			0000	0600	0500	1100				
WALTON-ON-THE-NAZE	51 51N	1 17E	and	and	and	and	4.2	3.4	1.1	0.4
Standard port			1200	1800	1700	2300				
Whitaker Beacon	51 40N	1 06E	+0022	+0024	+0033	+0027	+0.6	+0.5	+0.2	+0.1
Holliwell Point	51 38N	0 56E	+0034	+0037	+0100	+0037	+1.1	+0.9	+0.3	+0.1
River Roach Rochford	51 35N	0 43E	+0050	+0040	Dries	Dries	−0.8	−1.1	Dries	
River Crouch										
Burnham-on-Crouch	51 37N	0 48E	+0050	+0035	+0115	+0050	+1.0	+0.8	−0.1	−0.2
North Fambridge	51 38N	0 41E	+0115	+0050	+0130	+0100	+1.1	+0.8	0.0	−0.1
Hullbridge	51 38N	0 38E	+0115	+0050	+0135	+0105	+1.1	+0.8	0.0	−0.1
Battlesbridge	51 37N	0 34E	+0120	+0110	Dries	Dries	−1.8	−2.0	Dries	
River Blackwater										
Bradwell Waterside	51 45N	0 54E	+0035	+0023	+0047	+0004	+1.0	+0.8	+0.2	0.0
Osea Island	51 43N	0 46E	+0057	+0045	+0050	+0007	+1.1	+0.9	+0.1	0.0
Maldon	51 44N	0 42E	+0107	+0055	No data	No data	−1.3	−1.1	No data	
West Mersea	51 47N	0 54E	+0035	+0015	+0055	+0010	+0.9	+0.4	+0.1	+0.1
River Colne										
Brightlingsea	51 48N	1 00E	+0025	+0021	+0046	+0004	+0.8	+0.4	+0.1	0.0
Colchester	51 53N	0 56E	+0035	+0025	Dries	Dries	0.0	−0.3	Dries	
Clacton–on–Sea	51 47N	1 10E	+0012	+0010	+0025	+0008	+0.3	+0.1	+0.1	+0.1
Bramble Creek	51 53N	1 14E	+0010	−0007	−0005	+0010	+0.3	+0.3	+0.3	+0.3
Sunk Head	51 47N	1 30E	0000	+0002	−0002	+0002	−0.3	−0.3	−0.1	−0.1
Harwich	51 57N	1 17E	+0007	+0002	−0010	−0012	−0.2	0.0	0.0	0.0
Mistley	51 57N	1 05E	+0032	+0027	−0010	−0012	0.0	0.0	−0.1	−0.1
Ipswich	52 03N	1 10E	+0022	+0027	0000	−0012	0.0	0.0	−0.1	−0.1
			0100	0700	0100	0700				
WALTON–ON–THE–NAZE	51 51N	1 17E	and	and	and	and	4.2	3.4	1.1	0.4
Standard port			1300	1900	1300	1900				
Felixstowe Pier	51 57N	1 21E	−0005	−0007	−0018	−0020	−0.5	−0.4	0.0	0.0
River Deben										
Woodbridge Haven	51 59N	1 24E	0000	−0005	−0020	−0025	−0.5	−0.5	−0.1	+0.1
Woodbridge	52 05N	1 19E	+0045	+0025	+0025	−0020	−0.2	−0.3	−0.2	0.0
Bawdsey	52 01N	1 26E	−0016	−0020	−0030	−0032	−0.8	−0.6	−0.1	−0.1
Orford Haven										
Bar	52 02N	1 28E	−0026	−0030	−0036	−0038	−1.0	−0.8	−0.1	0.0
Orford Quay	52 05N	1 32E	+0040	+0040	+0055	+0055	−1.4	−1.1	0.0	+0.2
Slaughden Quay	52 08N	1 36E	+0105	+0105	+0125	+0125	−1.3	−0.8	−0.1	+0.2
Iken Cliffs	52 09N	1 31E	+0130	+0130	+0155	+0155	−1.3	−1.0	0.0	+0.2

TIDES

Location	Lat	Long	High Water		Low Water		MHWS	MHWN	MLWN	MLWS
			0300	0900	0200	0800				
LOWESTOFT	52 28N	1 45E	and	and	and	and	2.4	2.1	1.0	0.5
Standard port			1500	2100	1400	2000				
Orford Ness	52 05N	1 35E	+0135	+0135	+0135	+0125	+0.4	+0.6	−0.1	0.0
Aldeburgh	52 09N	1 36E	+0130	+0130	+0115	+0120	+0.3	+0.2	−0.1	−0.2
Minsmere Sluice	52 14N	1 38E	+0110	+0110	+0110	+0110	0.0	−0.1	−0.2	−0.2
Southwold	52 19N	1 40E	+0105	+0105	+0055	+0055	0.0	0.0	−0.1	0.0
Great Yarmouth										
Gorleston-on-Sea	52 34N	1 44E	−0035	−0035	−0030	−0030	0.0	0.0	0.0	0.0
Britannia Pier	52 36N	1 45E	−0105	−0100	−0040	−0055	+0.1	+0.1	0.0	0.0
Caister-on-Sea	52 39N	1 44E	−0120	−0120	−0100	−0100	0.0	−0.1	0.0	0.0
Winterton-on-Sea	52 43N	1 42E	−0225	−0215	−0135	−0135	+0.8	+0.5	+0.2	+0.1
			0100	0700	0100	0700				
IMMINGHAM	53 38N	0 11W	and	and	and	and	7.3	5.8	2.6	0.9
Standard port			1300	1900	1300	1900				
Cromer	52 56N	1 18E	+0044	+0032	+0108	+0059	−2.3	−1.8	−0.7	0.0
Blakeney Bar	52 59N	0 59E	+0035	+0025	+0030	+0040	−1.6	−1.3	No data	
Blakeney	52 57N	1 01E	+0115	+0055	No data	No data	−3.9	−3.8	No data	
Wells Bar	52 59N	0 49E	+0020	+0020	+0020	+0020	−1.3	−1.0	No data	
Wells	52 57N	0 51E	+0035	+0045	+0340	+0310	−3.8	−3.8	Not below CD	
Burnham Overy Staithe	52 58N	0 48E	+0045	+0055	No data	No data	−5.0	−4.9	No data	
The Wash										
Hunstanton	52 56N	0 29E	+0010	+0020	+0105	+0025	+0.1	−0.2	−0.1	0.0
West Stones	52 50N	0 21E	+0025	+0025	+0115	+0040	−0.3	−0.4	−0.3	+0.2
King's Lynn	52 45N	0 24E	+0030	+0030	+0305	+0140	−0.5	−0.8	−0.8	+0.1
Outer Westmark Knock	52 53N	0 13E	+0010	+0015	+0040	+0020	−0.2	−0.5	−0.6	−0.4
Wisbech Cut	52 48N	0 13E	+0020	+0010	+0120	+0055	−0.3	−0.7	−0.4	No data
Port Sutton bridge	52 46N	0 12E	+0030	+0020	+0130	+0105	−0.3	−0.6	−0.6	+0.3
Wisbech	52 40N	0 09E	+0055	+0040	Dries	Dries	−0.2	−0.6	Dries	Dries
Lawyer's Creek	52 53N	0 05E	+0010	+0020	No data	No data	−0.3	−0.6	No data	
Tabs Head	52 56N	0 05E	0000	+0005	+0125	+0020	+0.2	−0.2	−0.2	−0.2
Boston	52 58N	0 01W	0000	+0010	+0140	+0050	−0.5	−1.0	−0.9	−0.5
Skegness	53 09N	0 21E	+0010	+0015	+0030	+0020	−0.4	−0.5	−0.1	0.0
Inner Dowsing Light Tower	53 19N	0 35E	0000	0000	+0010	+0010	−0.9	−0.7	−0.1	+0.3
River Humber										
Bull Sand Fort	53 34N	0 04E	−0020	−0030	−0035	−0015	−0.4	−0.3	+0.1	+0.2
Grimsby	53 35N	0 04W	−0012	−0012	−0015	−0013	−0.3	−0.2	+0.1	+0.4
Hull, King George Dock	53 44N	0 16W	+0010	+0010	+0021	+0017	+0.3	+0.2	−0.1	−0.2
Hull, Albert Dock	53 44N	0 21W	+0019	+0019	+0033	+0027	+0.3	+0.1	−0.1	−0.2
Humber Bridge	53 43N	0 27W	+0027	+0022	+0049	+0039	−0.1	−0.4	−0.7	−0.6
River Trent										
Burton Stather	53 39N	0 42W	+0105	+0050	+0240	+0205	−2.0	−2.7	−2.2	−1.1
Flixborough Wharf	53 37N	0 42W	+0100	+0115	+0305	+0220	−2.1	−2.8	−2.2	−0.9
Keadby	53 36N	0 44W	+0130	+0115	+0320	+0235	−2.8	−3.3	−2.3	−0.9
Owston Ferry	53 29N	0 46W	+0155	+0145	Dries	Dries	−3.5	−3.9	Dries	
River Ouse										
Blacktoft	53 42N	0 43W	+0100	+0055	+0325	+0255	−1.6	−1.8	−2.2	−1.1
Goole	53 42N	0 52W	+0130	+0115	+0355	+0350	−1.6	−2.1	−1.9	−0.6
			0000	0600	0000	0600				
R TEES ENTRANCE	54 38N	1 09W	and	and	and	and	5. 5	4.3	2.0	0.9
Standard port			1200	1800	1200	1800				
Bridlington	54 05N	0 11W	+0100	+0050	+0055	+0050	+0.6	+0.4	+0.3	+0.2
Filey Bay	54 13N	0 16W	+0042	+0042	+0047	+0034	+0.3	+0.6	+0.4	+0.1
Scarborough	54 17N	0 23W	+0040	+0040	+0030	+0030	+0.2	+0.3	+0.3	0.0
Whitby	54 29N	0 37W	+0020	+0020	+0018	+0017	+0.1	+0.1	+0.2	+0.1
Middlesborough Dock ent	54 35N	1 13W	0000	+0002	0000	−0003	+0.1	+0.2	+0.1	−0.1
Tees (Newport) Bridge	54 34N	1 16W	−0002	+0004	+0005	−0003	+0.1	+0.2	0.0	−0.1
Hartlepool	54 42N	1 12W	−0004	−0004	−0006	−0006	−0.1	−0.1	−0.2	−0.1
Seaham	54 50N	1 19W	−0015	−0015	−0015	−0015	−0.3	−0.2	0.0	−0.2
Sunderland	54 55N	1 22W	−0017	−0017	−0016	−0016	−0.2	−0.1	0.0	0.0
			0200	0800	0100	0800				
R TYNE, NORTH SHIELDS	55 00N	1 26W	and	and	and	and	5. 0	3.9	1.8	0.7
Standard port			1400	2000	1300	2000				
Newcastle-upon-Tyne	54 58N	1 36W	+0003	+0003	+0008	+0008	+0.3	+0.2	+0.1	+0.1
Blyth	55 07N	1 29W	+0005	−0007	−0001	+0009	0.0	0.0	−0.1	+0.1
Coquet Island	55 20N	1 32W	−0010	−0010	−0020	−0020	+0.1	+0.1	0.0	+0.1
Amble	55 20N	1 34W	−0013	−0013	−0016	−0020	0.0	0.0	+0.1	+0.1

Location	Lat	Long	High Water		Low Water		MHWS	MHWN	MLWN	MLWS
North Sunderland	55 35N	1 39W	−0048	−0044	−0058	−0102	−0.2	−0.2	−0.2	0.0
Holy Island	55 40N	1 48W	−0043	−0039	−0105	−0110	−0.2	−0.2	−0.3	−0.1
Berwick	55 46N	1 59W	−0053	−0053	−0109	−0109	−0.3	−0.1	−0.5	−0.1

SCOTLAND *Time Zone UT*

Location	Lat	Long	High Water		Low Water		MHWS	MHWN	MLWN	MLWS
LEITH	55 59N	3 11W	0300 and 1500	0900 and 2100	0300 and 1500	0900 and 2100	5.6	4.4	2.0	0.8
Standard port										
Eyemouth	55 52N	2 05W	−0005	+0007	+0012	+0008	−0.4	−0.3	0.0	+0.1
Dunbar	56 00N	2 31W	−0005	+0003	+0003	−0003	−0.3	−0.3	0.0	+0.1
Fidra	56 04N	2 47W	−0001	0000	−0002	+0001	−0.2	−0.2	0.0	0.0
Cockenzie	55 58N	2 57W	−0007	−0015	−0013	−0005	−0.2	0.0	No data	
Granton	55 59N	3 13W	0000	0000	0000	0000	0.0	0.0	0.0	0.0
River Forth Grangemouth	56 02N	3 41W	+0015	+0010	−0050	−0045	0.0	−0.1	−0.2	−0.2
Kincardine	56 04N	3 43W	+0015	+0030	−0030	−0030	0.0	−0.2	−0.5	−0.3
Alloa	56 06N	3 48W	+0040	+0040	+0025	+0025	−0.2	−0.5	No data	−0.7
Stirling	56 07N	3 56W	+0100	+0100	No data		−2.9	−3.1	−2.3	−0.7
Firth of Forth										
Burntisland	56 03N	3 14W	+0013	+0004	−0002	+0007	+0.1	0.0	+0.1	+0.2
Kirkcaldy	56 09N	3 09W	+0005	0000	−0004	−0001	−0.3	−0.3	−0.2	−0.2
Methil	56 11N	3 00W	−0005	−0001	−0001	−0001	−0.1	−0.1	−0.1	−0.1
Anstruther Easter	56 13N	2 42W	−0018	−0012	−0006	−0008	−0.3	−0.2	0.0	0.0
ABERDEEN	57 09N	2 04W	0000 and 1200	0600 and 1800	0100 and 1300	0700 and 1900	4.3	3.4	1.6	0.6
Standard port										
River Tay										
Bar	56 28N	2 38W	+0100	+0100	+0050	+0110	+0.9	+0.8	+0.3	+0.1
Dundee	56 27N	2 58W	+0140	+0120	+0055	+0145	+1.2	+1.0	+0.5	+0.4
Newburgh	56 21N	3 14W	+0215	+0200	+0250	+0335	−0.2	−0.4	−1.1	−0.5
Perth	56 24N	3 25W	+0220	+0225	+0510	+0530	−0.9	−1.4	−1.2	−0.3
Arbroath	56 33N	2 35W	+0056	+0037	+0034	+0055	+1.0	+0.8	+0.4	+0.2
Montrose	56 42N	2 28W	+0050	+0045	+0035	+0030	+0.6	+0.4	+0.3	+0.2
Stonehaven	56 58N	2 12W	+0013	+0008	+0013	+0009	+0.2	+0.2	+0.1	0.0
Peterhead	57 30N	1 46W	−0035	−0045	−0035	−0040	−0.3	−0.2	0.0	+0.1
Fraserburgh	57 41N	2 00W	−0122	−0118	−0115	−0115	−0.5	−0.4	−0.1	+0.2
ABERDEEN	57 09N	2 04W	0200 and 1400	0900 and 2100	0400 and 1600	0900 and 2100	4.3	3.4	1.6	0.6
Standard port										
Banff	57 40N	2 31W	−0100	−0150	−0150	−0050	−0.4	−0.2	−0.1	+0.2
Whitehills	57 41N	2 35W	−0122	−0137	−0117	−0127	−0.4	−0.3	+0.1	+0.1
Buckie	57 41N	2 57W	−0130	−0145	−0125	−0140	−0.2	−0.2	0.0	+0.1
Lossiemouth	57 43N	3 18W	−0125	−0200	−0130	−0130	−0.2	−0.2	0.0	0.0
Burghead	57 42N	3 29W	−0120	−0150	−0135	−0120	−0.2	−0.2	0.0	0.0
Nairn	57 36N	3 52W	−0120	−0150	−0135	−0130	0.0	−0.1	0.0	+0.1
McDermott Base	57 36N	3 59W	−0110	−0140	−0120	−0115	−0.1	−0.1	+0.1	+0.3
ABERDEEN	57 09N	2 04W	0300 and 1500	1000 and 2200	0000 and 1200	0700 and 1900	4.3	3.4	1.6	0.6
Standard port										
Inverness Firth										
Fortrose	57 35N	4 08W	−0125	−0125	−0125	−0125	0.0	0.0	No data	
Inverness	57 30N	4 15W	−0050	−0150	−0200	−0150	+0.5	+0.3	+0.2	+0.1
Cromarty Firth										
Cromarty	57 42N	4 03W	−0120	−0155	−0155	−0120	0.0	0.0	+0.1	+0.2
Invergordon	57 41N	4 10W	−0105	−0200	−0200	−0110	+0.1	+0.1	+0.1	+0.1
Dingwall	57 36N	4 25W	−0045	−0145	No data	No data	+0.1	+0.2	No data	
ABERDEEN	57 09N	2 04W	0300 and 1500	0800 and 2000	0200 and 1400	0800 and 2000	4.3	3.4	1.6	0.6
Standard port										
Dornoch Firth										
Portmahomack	57 50N	3 50W	−0120	−0210	−0140	−0110	−0.2	−0.1	+0.1	+0.1
Meikle Ferry	57 51N	4 08W	−0100	−0140	−0120	−0055	+0.1	0.0	−0.1	0.0
Golspie	57 58N	3 59W	−0130	−0215	−0215	−0130	−0.3	−0.3	−0.1	0.0
WICK	58 26N	3 05W	0000 and 1200	0700 and 1900	0200 and 1400	0700 and 1900	3.5	2.8	1.4	0.7
Standard port										
Helmsdale	58 07N	3 39W	+0025	+0015	+0035	+0030	+0.5	+0.3	+0.1	−0.1
Duncansby Head	58 39N	3 02W	−0115	−0115	−0110	−0110	−0.4	−0.4	No data	
Orkney Islands										
Muckle Skerry	58 41N	2 55W	−0025	−0025	−0020	−0020	−0.9	−0.8	−0.4	−0.3

Location	Lat	Long	High Water		Low Water		MHWS	MHWN	MLWN	MLWS
Burray Ness	58 51N	2 52W	+0005	+0005	+0015	+0015	-0.2	-0.3	-0.1	-0.1
Deer Sound	58 58N	2 50W	-0040	-0040	-0035	-0035	-0.3	-0.3	-0.1	-0.1
Kirkwall	58 59N	2 58W	-0042	-0042	-0041	-0041	-0.5	-0.4	-0.1	-0.1
Egilsay	59 09N	2 57W	-0125	-0125	-0125	-0125	-0.1	0.0	+0.2	+0.1
Whitehall	58 09N	2 36W	-0030	-0030	-0025	-0030	-0.1	0.0	+0.2	+0.2
Loth	59 11N	2 42W	-0045	-0045	-0055	-0105	-0.4	-0.3	+0.1	+0.2
Kettletoft Pier	59 14N	2 36W	-0030	-0025	-0025	-0025	0.0	0.0	+0.2	+0.2
Rapness	59 15N	2 52W	-0205	-0205	-0205	-0200	+0.1	+0.1	+0.2	0.0
Pierowall	59 19N	2 59W	-0150	-0150	-0145	-0145	+0.2	0.0	0.0	-0.1
Tingwall	59 05N	3 03W	-0200	-0125	-0145	-0125	-0.4	-0.4	-0.1	-0.1
Stromness	58 58N	3 18W	-0225	-0135	-0205	-0205	+0.1	-0.1	0.0	0.0
St Mary's	58 54N	2 55W	-0140	-0140	-0140	-0140	-0.2	-0.2	0.0	-0.1
Widewall Bay	58 49N	3 01W	-0155	-0155	-0150	-0150	+0.1	-0.1	-0.1	-0.3
Bur Wick	58 44N	2 58W	-0100	-0100	-0150	-0150	-0.1	-0.1	+0.2	+0.1
LERWICK	60 09N	1 08W	0000 and 1200	0600 and 1800	0100 and 1300	0800 and 2000	2.1	1.7	0.9	0.5
Standard port										
Fair Isle	59 32N	1 36W	-0006	-0015	-0031	-0037	+0.1	0.0	+0.1	+0.1
Shetland Islands										
Sumburgh (Grutness Voe)	59 53N	1 17W	+0006	+0008	+0004	-0002	-0.3	-0.3	-0.2	-0.1
Dury Voe	60 21N	1 10W	-0015	-0015	-0010	-0010	0.0	-0.1	0.0	-0.2
Out Skerries	60 25N	0 45W	-0025	-0025	-0010	-0010	+0.1	0.0	0.0	-0.1
Toft Pier	60 28N	1 12W	-0105	-0100	-0125	-0115	+0.2	+0.1	-0.1	-0.1
Burra Voe (Yell Sound)	60 30N	1 03W	-0025	-0025	-0025	-0025	+0.2	+0.1	0.0	-0.1
Mid Yell	60 36N	1 03W	-0030	-0020	-0035	-0025	+0.3	+0.2	+0.2	+0.1
Balta Sound	60 46N	0 50W	-0040	-0045	-0040	-0045	+0.3	+0.2	+0.1	0.0
Burra Firth	60 48N	0 52W	-0110	-0110	-0115	-0115	+0.4	+0.2	0.0	0.0
Bluemull Sound	60 42N	1 00W	-0135	-0135	-0155	-0155	+0.5	+0.2	+0.1	0.0
Sullom Voe	60 27N	1 18W	-0135	-0125	-0135	-0120	0.0	0.0	-0.2	-0.2
Hillswick	60 29N	1 29W	-0220	-0220	-0200	-0200	-0.1	-0.1	-0.1	-0.1
Scalloway	60 08N	1 16W	-0150	-0150	-0150	-0150	-0.5	-0.4	-0.3	0.0
Bay of Quendale	59 54N	1 21W	-0025	-0025	-0030	-0030	-0.4	-0.3	0.0	+0.1
Foula	60 07N	2 03W	-0140	-0140	-0130	-0130	-0.1	-0.1	0.0	0.0
WICK	58 26N	3 05W	0200 and 1400	0700 and 1900	0100 and 1300	0700 and 1900	3.5	2.8	1.4	0.7
Standard port										
Stroma	58 40N	3 08W	-0115	-0115	-0110	-0110	-0.4	-0.5	-0.1	-0.2
Gills Bay	58 38N	3 10W	-0150	-0150	-0202	-0202	+0.7	+0.7	+0.6	+0.3
Scrabster	58 37N	3 33W	-0255	-0225	-0240	-0230	+1.5	+1.2	+0.8	+0.3
Sule Skerry	59 05N	4 24W	-0320	-0255	-0315	-0250	+0.4	+0.3	+0.2	+0.1
Loch Eriboll Portnancon	58 30N	4 42W	-0340	-0255	-0315	-0255	+1.6	+1.3	+0.8	+0.4
Kyle of Durness	58 36N	4 47W	-0350	-0350	-0315	-0315	+1.1	+0.7	+0.4	-0.1
Rona	59 08N	5 49W	-0350	-0350	-0350	-0340	-0.3	-0.4	-0.2	-0.4
STORNOWAY	58 12N	6 23W	0100 and 1300	0700 and 1900	0300 and 1500	0900 and 2100	4.8	3.7	2.0	0.7
Standard port										
Outer Hebrides										
Loch Shell	58 00N	6 25W	-0013	0000	0000	-0017	0.0	-0.1	-0.1	0.0
E Loch Tarbert	57 54N	6 48W	-0025	-0010	-0010	-0020	+0.2	0.0	+0.1	+0.1
Leverburgh	57 46N	7 02W	-0041	-0020	-0015	-0025	-0.2	-0.2	-0.2	-0.1
Bays Loch	57 43N	7 10W	-0038	-0013	-0014	-0027	-0.1	-0.2	-0.2	-0.1
Loch Maddy	57 36N	7 09W	-0044	-0014	-0016	-0030	0.0	-0.1	-0.1	0.0
Loch Carnan	57 22N	7 16W	-0050	-0010	-0020	-0040	-0.3	-0.5	-0.1	-0.1
Loch Skiport	57 20N	7 16W	-0100	-0025	-0024	-0024	-0.2	-0.4	-0.3	-0.2
Loch Boisdale	57 09N	7 16W	-0055	-0030	-0020	-0040	-0.7	-0.7	-0.3	-0.2
Barra (North Bay)	57 00N	7 24W	-0103	-0031	-0034	-0048	-0.6	-0.5	-0.2	-0.1
Castle Bay	56 57N	7 29W	-0115	-0040	-0045	-0100	-0.5	-0.6	-0.3	-0.1
Barra Head	56 47N	7 38W	-0115	-0040	-0045	-0055	-0.8	-0.7	-0.2	+0.1
Shillay	57 32N	7 42W	-0103	-0043	-0047	-0107	-0.6	-0.7	-0.7	-0.3
Balivanich	57 29N	7 23W	-0103	-0017	-0031	-0045	-0.7	-0.6	-0.5	-0.2
Scolpaig	57 39N	7 29W	-0033	-0033	-0040	-0040	-1.0	-0.9	-0.5	0.0
W Loch Tarbert	57 55N	6 55W	-0015	-0015	-0046	-0046	-1.1	-0.9	-0.5	0.0
Little Bernera	58 16N	6 52W	-0021	-0011	-0017	-0027	-0.5	-0.6	-0.4	-0.2
Carloway	58 17N	6 47W	-0040	+0020	-0035	-0015	-0.7	-0.5	0.0	0.0
St Kilda Village Bay	57 48N	8 34W	-0040	-0040	-0045	-0045	-1.4	-1.1	-0.8	-0.3
Flannan Isles	58 17N	7 35W	-0026	-0016	-0016	-0026	-0.9	-0.7	-0.6	-0.2
Rockall	57 36N	13 41W	-0055	-0055	-0105	-0105	-1.8	-1.5	-0.9	-0.2

Location	Lat	Long	High Water		Low Water		MHWS	MHWN	MLWN	MLWS
			0000	0600	0300	0900				
ULLAPOOL	57 54N	5 09W	and	and	and	and	5.2	3.9	2.1	0.7
Standard port			1200	1800	1500	2100				
Loch Bervie	58 27N	5 03W	+0017	+0020	+0015	+0015	−0.4	−0.2	−0.1	+0.1
Loch Laxford	58 24N	5 05W	+0015	+0015	+0005	+0005	−0.3	−0.4	−0.2	0.0
Eddrachillis Bay										
Badcall Bay	58 19N	5 08W	+0005	+0005	+0005	+0005	−0.7	−0.5	−0.5	+0.2
Loch Nedd	58 14N	5 10W	0000	0000	0000	0000	−0.3	−0.2	−0.2	0.0
Loch Inver	58 09N	5 18W	−0005	−0005	−0005	−0005	−0.2	0.0	0.0	+0.1
Summer Isles Tanera Mor	58 01N	5 24W	−0005	−0005	−0010	−0010	−0.1	+0.1	0.0	+0.1
Loch Ewe Mellon Charles	57 51N	5 38W	−0005	−0010	−0005	−0005	−0.1	−0.1	−0.1	+0.1
Loch Gairloch Gairloch	57 43N	5 41W	−0012	−0011	−0011	−0011	−0.2	+0.1	−0.2	+0.2
Loch Torridon Shieldaig	57 31N	5 39W	−0020	−0020	−0015	−0015	+0.4	+0.3	+0.1	0.0
Inner Sound Applecross	57 26N	5 49W	−0010	−0015	−0010	−0010	0.0	0.0	0.0	+0.1
Loch Carron Plockton	57 21N	5 39W	+0005	−0025	−0005	−0010	+0.5	+0.5	+0.5	+0.2
Rona Loch a' Bhraige	57 35N	5 58W	−0020	0000	−0010	0000	−0.1	−0.1	−0.1	−0.2
Skye										
Broadford Bay	57 15N	5 54W	−0015	−0015	−0010	−0015	+0.2	+0.1	+0.1	0.0
Portree	57 24N	6 11W	−0025	−0025	−0025	−0025	+0.1	−0.2	−0.2	0.0
Loch Snizort (Uig Bay)	57 35N	6 22W	−0045	−0020	−0005	−0025	+0.1	−0.4	−0.2	0.0
Loch Dunvegan	57 27N	6 38W	−0105	−0030	−0020	−0040	0.0	−0.1	0.0	0.0
Loch Harport	57 20N	6 25W	−0115	−0035	−0020	−0100	−0.1	−0.1	0.0	+0.1
Soay Camus nan Gall	57 09N	6 13W	−0055	−0025	−0025	−0045	−0.4	−0.2	No data	
Loch Alsh										
Kyle of Lochalsh	57 17N	5 43W	−0040	−0020	−0005	−0025	+0.1	0.0	0.0	−0.1
Dornie Bridge	57 17N	5 31W	−0040	−0010	−0005	−0020	+0.1	−0.1	0.0	0.0
Kyle Rhea Glenelg Bay	57 13N	5 38W	−0105	−0035	−0035	−0055	−0.4	−0.4	−0.9	−0.1
Loch Hourn	57 06N	5 34W	−0125	−0050	−0040	−0110	−0.2	−0.1	−0.1	+0.1
			0000	0600	0100	0700				
OBAN	56 25N	5 29W	and	and	and	and	4.0	2.9	1.8	0.7
Standard port			1200	1800	1300	1900				
Loch Nevis										
Inverie Bay	57 02N	5 41W	+0030	+0020	+0035	+0020	+1.0	+0.9	+0.2	0.0
Mallaig	57 00N	5 50W	+0017	+0017	+0030	+0024	+1.0	+0.7	+0.3	+0.1
Eigg Bay of Laig	56 55N	6 10W	+0015	+0030	+0040	+0005	+0.7	+0.6	−0.2	− 0.2
Loch Moidart	56 47N	5 53W	+0015	+0015	+0040	+0020	+0.8	+0.6	− 0.2	−0.2
Coll Loch Eatharna	56 37N	6 31W	+0025	+0010	+0015	+0025	+0.4	+0.3	No data	
Tiree Gott Bay	56 31N	6 48W	0000	+0010	+0005	+0010	0.0	+0.1	0.0	0.0
			0100	0700	0100	0800				
OBAN	56 25N	5 29W	and	and	and	and	4.0	2.9	1.8	0.7
Standard port			1300	1900	1300	2000				
Mull										
Carsaig Bay	56 19N	5 58W	−0015	−0005	−0030	+0020	+0.1	+0.2	0.0	−0.1
Iona	56 20N	6 23W	−0010	−0005	−0020	+0015	0.0	+0.1	−0.3	−0.2
Bunessan	56 19N	6 14W	−0015	−0015	−0010	−0015	+0.3	+0.1	0.0	−0.1
Ulva Sound	56 29N	6 08W	−0010	−0015	0000	−0005	+0.4	+0.3	0.0	−0.1
Loch Sunart Salen	56 43N	5 47W	−0015	+0015	+0010	+0005	+0.6	+0.5	−0.1	−0.1
Sound of Mull										
Tobermory	56 37N	6 04W	+0025	+0010	+0015	+0025	+0.5	+0.6	+0.1	+0.2
Salen	56 31N	5 57W	+0045	+0015	+0020	+0030	+0.2	+0.2	−0.1	0.0
Loch Aline	56 32N	5 46W	+0012	+0012	No data	No data	+0.5	+0.3	No data	
Craignure	56 28N	5 42W	+0030	+0005	+0010	+0015	0.0	+0.1	−0.1	−0.1
Loch Linnhe										
Corran	56 43N	5 14W	+0007	+0007	+0004	+0004	+0.4	+0.4	−0.1	0.0
Corpach	56 51N	5 07W	0000	+0020	+0040	0000	0.0	0.0	−0.2	−0.2
Loch Eil Head	56 51N	5 20W	+0025	+0045	+0105	+0025	No data		No data	
Loch Leven Head	56 43N	5 00W	+0045	+0045	+0045	+0045	No data		No data	
Loch Linnhe Port Appin	56 33N	5 25W	−0005	−0005	−0030	0000	+0.2	+0.2	+0.1	+0.1
Loch Creran										
Barcaldine Pier	56 32N	5 19W	+0010	+0020	+0040	+0015	+0.1	+0.1	0.0	+0.1
Loch Creran Head	56 33N	5 16W	+0015	+0025	+0120	+0020	−0.3	−0.3	−0.4	−0.3
Loch Etive										
Dunstaffnage Bay	56 27N	5 26W	+0005	0000	0000	+0005	+0.1	+0.1	+0.1	+0.1
Connel	56 27N	5 24W	+0020	+0005	+0010	+0015	−0.3	−0.2	−0.1	+0.1
Bonawe	56 27N	5 13W	+0150	+0205	+0240	+0210	−2.0	−1.7	−1.3	−0.5
Seil Sound	56 18N	5 35W	−0035	−0015	−0040	−0015	−1.3	−0.9	−0.7	−0.3
Colonsay Scalasaig	56 04N	6 11W	−0020	−0005	−0015	+0005	−0.3	−0.2	−0.3	0.0
Jura Glengarrisdale Bay	56 07N	5 47W	−0020	0000	−0010	0000	−0.4	−0.2	0.0	−0.2

Location	Lat	Long	High Water		Low Water		MHWS	MHWN	MLWN	MLWS
Islay										
Rubha A'Mhail	55 56N	6 07W	−0020	0000	+0005	−0015	−0.3	−0.1	−0.3	−0.1
Ardnave Point	55 52N	6 20W	−0035	+0010	0000	−0025	−0.4	−0.2	−0.3	−0.1
Orsay	55 41N	6 31W	−0110	−0110	−0040	−0040	−1.4	−0.6	−0.5	−0.2
Bruichladdich	55 46N	6 22W	−0105	−0035	−0110	−0110	−1.8	−1.3	−0.4	+0.3
Port Ellen	55 38N	6 11W	−0530	−0050	−0045	−0530	−3.1	−2.1	−1.3	−0.4
Port Askaig	55 51N	6 06W	−0030	−0035	−0015	−0025	−1.8	−1.3	−0.7	−0.2
Sound of Jura										
Craighouse	55 50N	5 57W	−0230	−0250	−0150	−0230	−3.0	−2.4	−1.3	−0.6
Loch Melfort	56 15N	5 29W	−0055	−0025	−0040	−0035	−1.2	−0.8	−0.5	−0.1
Loch Beag	56 09N	5 36W	−0110	−0045	−0035	−0045	−1.6	−1.2	−0.8	−0.4
Carsaig Bay	56 02N	5 38W	−0105	−0040	−0050	−0050	−2.1	−1.6	−1.0	−0.4
Sound of Gigha	55 41N	5 44W	−0450	−0210	−0130	−0410	−2.5	−1.6	−1.0	−0.1
Machrihanish	55 25N	5 45W	−0520	−0350	−0340	−0540	Mean range 0.5 metres			
			0000	**0600**	**0000**	**0600**				
GREENOCK	**55 57N**	**4 46W**	**and**	**and**	**and**	**and**	**3.4**	**2.8**	**1.0**	**0.3**
Standard port			**1200**	**1800**	**1200**	**1800**				
Firth of Clyde										
Southend, Kintyre	55 19N	5 38W	−0030	−0010	+0005	+0035	−1.3	−1.2	−0.5	−0.2
Campbeltown	55 25N	5 36W	−0025	−0005	−0015	+0005	−0.5	−0.3	+0.1	+0.2
Carradale	55 36N	5 28W	−0015	−0005	−0005	+0005	−0.3	−0.2	+0.1	+0.1
Loch Ranza	55 43N	5 18W	−0015	−0005	−0010	−0005	−0.4	−0.3	−0.1	0.0
Loch Fyne										
East Loch Tarbert	55 52N	5 24W	−0005	−0005	0000	−0005	+0.2	+0.1	0.0	0.0
Inveraray	56 14N	5 04W	+0011	+0011	+0034	+0034	−0.1	+0.1	−0.5	−0.2
Kyles of Bute										
Rubha a'Bhodaich	55 55N	5 09W	−0020	−0010	−0007	−0007	−0.2	−0.1	+0.2	+0.2
Tighnabruich	55 55N	5 13W	+0007	−0010	−0002	−0015	0.0	+0.2	+0.4	+0.5
Firth of Clyde – continued										
Millport	55 45N	4 56W	−0005	−0025	−0025	−0005	0.0	−0.1	0.0	+0.1
Rothesay Bay	55 50N	5 03W	−0020	−0015	−0010	−0002	+0.2	+0.2	+0.2	+0.2
Wemyss Bay	55 53N	4 53W	−0005	−0005	−0005	−0005	0.0	0.0	+0.1	+0.1
Loch Long										
Coulport	56 03N	4 53W	−0011	−0011	−0008	−0008	0.0	0.0	0.0	0.0
Lochgoilhead	56 10N	4 54W	+0015	0000	−0005	−0005	−0.2	−0.3	−0.3	−0.3
Arrochar	56 12N	4 45W	−0005	−0005	−0005	−0005	0.0	0.0	−0.1	−0.1
Gare Loch										
Rhu Marina	56 01N	4 46W	−0007	−0007	−0007	−0007	−0.1	−0.1	−0.1	−0.2
Faslane	56 04N	4 49W	+0003	+0003	+0003	+0003	+0.1	+0.1	+0.1	0.0
Garelochhead	56 05N	4 50W	0000	0000	0000	0000	0.0	0.0	0.0	−0.1
River Clyde										
Helensburgh	56 00N	4 44W	0000	0000	0000	0000	0.0	0.0	0.0	0.0
Port Glasgow	55 56N	4 41W	+0010	+0005	+0010	+0020	+0.2	+0.1	0.0	0.0
Bowling	55 56N	4 29W	+0020	+0010	+0030	+0055	+0.6	+0.5	+0.3	+0.1
Clydebank (Rothesay Dock)	55 54N	4 24W	+0025	+0015	+0035	+0100	+1.1	+0.9	+0.6	+0.3
Glasgow	55 51N	4 16W	+0025	+0015	+0035	+0105	+1.4	+1.1	+0.8	+0.4
Firth of Clyde – continued										
Brodick Bay	55 35N	5 08W	−0013	−0013	−0008	−0008	−0.2	−0.1	0.0	+0.1
Lamlash	55 32N	5 07W	−0016	−0036	−0024	−0004	−0.2	−0.2	No data	
Ardrossan	55 38N	4 49W	−0020	−0010	−0010	−0010	−0.2	−0.2	+0.1	+0.1
Irvine	55 36N	4 42W	−0020	−0020	−0030	−0010	−0.3	−0.3	−0.1	0.0
Troon	55 33N	4 41W	−0025	−0025	−0020	−0020	−0.2	−0.2	0.0	0.0
Ayr	55 28N	4 39W	−0025	−0025	−0030	−0015	−0.4	−0.3	+0.1	+0.1
Girvan	55 15N	4 52W	−0025	−0040	−0035	−0010	−0.3	−0.3	−0.1	0.0
Loch Ryan Stranraer	54 55N	5 02W	−0030	−0025	−0010	−0010	−0.2	−0.1	0.0	+0.1
			0000	**0600**	**0200**	**0800**				
LIVERPOOL	**53 27N**	**3 01W**	**and**	**and**	**and**	**and**	**9.4**	**7.5**	**3.2**	**1.1**
Standard port			**1200**	**1800**	**1400**	**2000**				
Portpatrick	54 51N	5 07W	+0038	+0032	+0009	−0008	−5.5	−4.4	−2.0	−0.6
Luce Bay										
Drummore	54 42N	4 53W	+0035	+0045	+0010	+0015	−3.5	−2.6	−1.2	−0.5
Port William	54 46N	4 35W	+0035	+0035	+0020	−0005	−3.0	−2.3	−1.1	*No data*
Wigtown Bay										
Isle of Whithorn	54 42N	4 22W	+0025	+0030	+0020	0000	−2.5	−2.1	−1.1	−0.4
Garlieston	54 47N	4 22W	+0030	+0040	+0025	0000	−2.4	−1.8	−0.8	*No data*
Solway Firth										
Kirkcudbright Bay	54 48N	4 04W	+0020	+0020	+0005	−0005	−1.9	−1.6	−0.8	−0.3
Hestan Islet	54 50N	3 48W	+0030	+0030	+0015	+0020	−1.1	−1.2	−0.8	−0.2
Southerness Point	54 52N	3 36W	+0035	+0035	+0025	+0005	−0.8	−0.8	*No data*	

Location	Lat	Long	High Water		Low Water		MHWS	MHWN	MLWN	MLWS
Annan Waterfoot	54 58N	3 16W	+0055	+0110	+0215	+0305	−2.3	−2.7	−3.0	
Torduff Point	54 58N	3 09W	+0110	+0145	+0515	+0405	−4.2	−5.0	Not below CD	
Redkirk	54 59N	3 06W	+0115	+0220	+0710	+0440	−5.6	−6.3	Not below CD	
WEST COAST OF ENGLAND										
Silloth	54 52N	3 24W	+0035	+0045	+0040	+0050	−0.2	−0.4	−0.9	−0.3
Maryport	54 43N	3 30W	+0021	+0036	+0017	+0002	−0.8	−0.9	−0.7	−0.2
Workington	54 39N	3 34W	+0029	+0027	+0014	+0004	−1.1	−1.1	−0.5	−0.1
Whitehaven	54 33N	3 36W	+0010	+0020	+0005	0000	−1.4	−1.2	−0.8	−0.2
Tarn Point	54 17N	3 25W	+0010	+0010	+0005	−0005	−1.1	−1.1	−0.7	−0.2
Duddon Bar	54 09N	3 20W	+0007	+0007	+0005	−0001	−0.9	−0.9	−0.6	−0.2
			0000	**0600**	**0200**	**0700**				
LIVERPOOL	53 27N	3 01W	and	and	and	and	9.4	7.5	3.2	1.1
Standard port			**1200**	**1800**	**1400**	**1900**				
Barrow-in-Furness	54 06N	3 12W	+0020	+0020	+0010	+0010	+0.1	−0.2	−0.2	0.0
Ulverston	54 11N	3 04W	+0025	+0045	No data	no data	−0.1	−0.2	No data	
Arnside	54 12N	2 51W	+0105	+0140	No data	no data	+0.4	+0.1	No data	
Morecambe	54 04N	2 53W	+0010	+0015	+0025	+0010	+0.1	−0.1	−0.3	0.0
Heysham	54 02N	2 55W	+0014	+0012	+0002	−0003	+0.2	−0.1	−0.2	0.0
River Lune Glasson Dock	54 00N	2 51W	+0025	+0035	+0215	+0235	−2.8	−3.1	No data	
Lancaster	54 03N	2 49W	+0115	+0035	Dries	Dries	−5.1	−5.0	Dries	
River Wyre										
Wyre Lighthouse	53 57N	3 02W	−0005	−0005	0000	−0005	−0.2	−0.2	No data	
Fleetwood	53 56N	3 00W	−0004	−0004	−0006	−0006	−0.2	−0.2	−0.1	+0.1
Blackpool	53 49N	3 04W	−0010	0000	−0010	−0020	−0.5	−0.5	−0.4	−0.1
River Ribble Preston	53 45N	2 45W	+0015	+0015	+0330	+0305	−4.1	−4.2	−3.1	−1.0
Liverpool Bay										
Southport	53 39N	3 01W	−0015	−0005	No data	No data	−0.4	−0.4	No data	
Formby	53 32N	3 07W	−0010	−0005	−0025	−0025	−0.4	−0.2	−0.3	−0.1
River Mersey										
Alfred Dock	53 24N	3 01W	+0007	+0007	0000	0000	−0.1	−0.1	−0.3	−0.2
Eastham	53 19N	2 57W	+0014	+0014	+0006	+0006	+0.2	0.0	−0.4	−0.5
Hale Head	53 19N	2 48W	+0035	+0030	No data	No data	−2.5	−2.6	No data	
Widnes	53 21N	2 44W	+0045	+0050	+0355	+0340	−4.3	−4.5	−2.8	−0.6
Fiddler's Ferry	53 22N	2 40W	+0105	+0120	+0535	+0445	−6.0	−6.4	−2.7	−0.6
River Dee										
Hilbre Island	53 23N	3 14W	−0011	−0008	−0013	−0018	−0.4	−0.3	−0.1	+0.2
Chester	53 12N	2 54W	+0110	+0110	+0455	+0455	−5.4	−5.5	Dries	
Connah's Quay (Wales)	53 13N	3 03W	+0005	+0020	+0350	+0335	−4.7	−4.5	Dries	
Mostyn Docks (Wales)	53 19N	3 16W	−0015	−0010	−0025	−0025	−0.9	−0.8	No data	
Isle of Man Peel	54 14N	4 42W	+0010	+0010	−0020	−0030	−4.2	−3.2	−1.7	−0.7
Ramsey	54 19N	4 22W	+0010	+0020	−0010	−0020	−2.0	−1.6	−0.9	−0.2
Douglas	54 09N	4 28W	+0010	+0020	−0020	−0030	−2.5	−2.1	−0.8	−0.3
Port St Mary	54 04N	4 44W	+0010	+0020	−0015	−0035	−3.5	−2.7	−1.6	−0.6
Calf Sound	54 04N	4 48W	+0010	+0010	−0020	−0030	−3.3	−2.7	−1.2	−0.5
Port Erin	54 05N	4 46W	+0018	+0010	−0013	−0028	−4.1	−3.3	−1.6	−0.6
WALES										
Colwyn Bay	53 18N	3 43W	−0015	−0015	No data	No data	−1.6	−1.4	No data	
Llandudno	53 20N	3 50W	−0019	−0021	−0031	−0038	−1.7	−1.6	−0.9	−0.6
			0000	**0600**	**0500**	**1100**				
HOLYHEAD	53 19N	4 37W	and	and	and	and	5.6	4.4	2.0	0.7
Standard port			**1200**	**1800**	**1700**	**2300**				
Conwy	53 17N	3 50W	+0025	+0035	+0120	+0105	+2.3	+1.8	+0.6	+0.4
Menai Strait										
Beaumaris	53 16N	4 05W	+0025	+0010	+0055	+0035	+2.0	+1.6	+0.5	+0.1
Menai Bridge	53 13N	4 10W	+0030	+0010	+0100	+0035	+1.7	+1.4	+0.3	0.0
Port Dinorwic	53 11N	4 13W	−0015	−0025	+0030	0000	0.0	0.0	0.0	+0.1
Caernarfon	53 09N	4 16W	−0030	−0030	+0015	−0005	−0.4	−0.4	−0.1	−0.1
Fort Belan	53 07N	4 20W	−0040	−0015	−0025	−0005	−1.0	−0.9	−0.2	−0.1
Trwyn Dinmor	53 19N	4 03W	+0025	+0015	+0050	+0035	+1.9	+1.5	+0.5	+0.2
Moelfre	53 20N	4 14W	+0025	+0020	+0050	+0035	+1.9	+1.4	+0.5	+0.2
Amlwch	53 25N	4 20W	+0020	+0010	+0035	+0025	+1.6	+ 1.3	+0.5	+0.2
Cemaes Bay	53 25N	4 27W	+0020	+0025	+0040	+0035	+1.0	+0.7	+0.3	+0.1
Trearddur Bay	53 16N	4 37W	−0045	−0025	−0015	−0015	−0.4	−0.4	0.0	+0.1
Porth Trecastell	53 12N	4 30W	−0045	−0025	−0005	−0015	−0.6	−0.6	0.0	0.0
Llanddwyn Island	53 08N	4 25W	−0115	−0055	−0030	−0020	−0.7	−0.5	−0.1	0.0
Trefor	53 00N	4 25W	−0115	−0100	−0030	−0020	−0.8	−0.9	−0.2	−0.1
Porth Dinllaen	52 57N	4 34W	−0120	−0105	−0035	−0025	−1.0	−1.0	−0.2	−0.2
Porth Ysgaden	52 54N	4 39W	−0125	−0110	−0040	−0035	−1.1	−1.0	−0.1	−0.1
Bardsey Island	52 46N	4 47W	−0220	−0240	−0145	−0140	−1.2	−1.2	−0.5	−0.1

TIDES

Location	Lat	Long	High Water		Low Water		MHWS	MHWN	MLWN	MLWS
			0100 and 1300	0800 and 2000	0100 and 1300	0700 and 1900				
MILFORD HAVEN Standard port	51 42N	5 03W					7.0	5.2	2.5	0.7
Cardigan Bay										
Aberdaron	52 48N	4 43W	+0210	+0200	+0240	+0310	−2.4	−1.9	−0.6	−0.2
St Tudwal's Roads	52 49N	4 29W	+0155	+0145	+0240	+0310	−2.2	−1.9	−0.7	−0.2
Pwllheli	52 53N	4 24W	+0210	+0150	+0245	+0320	−1.9	−1.6	−0.6	−0.1
Criccieth	52 55N	4 14W	+0210	+0155	+0255	+0320	−2.0	−1.8	−0.7	−0.3
Porthmadog	52 55N	4 08W	+0235	+0210	No data	No data	−1.9	−1.8	No data	
Barmouth	52 43N	4 03W	+0207	+0200	+0300	+0233	−2.0	−1.5	−0.6	0.0
Aberdovey	52 33N	4 03W	+0215	+0200	+0230	+0305	−2.0	−1.7	−0.5	0.0
Aberystwyth	52 24N	4 05W	+0145	+0130	+0210	+0245	−2.0	−1.7	−0.7	0.0
New Quay	52 13N	4 21W	+0150	+0125	+0155	+0230	−2.1	−1.8	−0.6	−0.1
Aberporth	52 08N	4 33W	+0135	+0120	+0150	+0220	−2.1	−1.8	−0.6	−0.1
Port Cardigan	52 07N	4 41W	+0140	+0120	+0220	+0130	−2.3	−1.8	−0.5	0.0
Cardigan (Town)	52 05N	4 40W	+0220	+0150	No data	No data	−2.2	−1.6	No data	
Fishguard	52 01N	4 59W	+0115	+0100	+0110	+0135	−2.2	−1.8	−0.5	+0.1
Porthgain	51 57N	5 11W	+0055	+0045	+0045	+0100	−2.5	−1.8	−0.6	0.0
Ramsey Sound	51 53N	5 19W	+0030	+0030	+0030	+0030	−1.9	−1.3	−0.3	0.0
Solva	51 52N	5 12W	+0015	+0010	+0035	+0015	−1.5	−1.0	−0.2	0.0
Little Haven	51 46N	5 07W	+0010	+0010	+0025	+0015	−1.1	−0.8	−0.2	0.0
Martin's Haven	51 44N	5 15W	+0010	+0010	+0015	+0015	−0.8	−0.5	+0.1	+0.1
Skomer Island	51 44N	5 17W	−0005	−0005	+0005	+0005	−0.4	−0.1	0.0	0.0
Dale Roads	51 42N	5 09W	−0005	−0005	−0008	−0008	0.0	0.0	0.0	−0.1
Cleddau River										
Neyland	51 42N	4 57W	+0002	+0010	0000	0000	0.0	0.0	0.0	0.0
Black Tar	51 45N	4 54W	+0010	+0020	+0005	0000	+0.1	+0.1	0.0	−0.1
Haverfordwest	51 48N	4 58W	+0010	+0025	Dries	Dries	−4.8	−4.9	Dries	
Stackpole Quay	51 37N	4 54W	−0005	+0025	−0010	−0010	+0.9	+0.7	+0.2	+0.3
Tenby	51 40N	4 42W	−0015	−0010	−0015	−0020	+1.4	+1.1	+0.5	+0.2
Towy River										
Ferryside	51 46N	4 22W	0000	−0010	+0220	0000	−0.3	−0.7	−1.7	−0.6
Carmarthen	51 51N	4 18W	+0010	0000	Dries	Dries	−4.4	−4.8	Dries	
Burry Inlet										
Burry Port	51 41N	4 15W	+0003	+0003	+0007	+0007	+1.6	+1.4	+0.5	+0.4
Llanelli	51 40N	4 10W	−0003	−0003	+0150	+0020	+0.8	+0.6	No data	
Mumbles	51 34N	3 58W	+0001	+0003	−0012	−0005	+2.5	+2.0	+0.8	+0.4
River Neath Entrance	51 37N	3 51W	+0002	+0011	Dries	Dries	+2.7	+2.2	Dries	
Port Talbot	51 35N	3 49W	0000	+0005	−0010	−0005	+2.7	+2.1	+1.0	+0.4
Porthcawl	51 28N	3 42W	+0005	+0010	−0010	−0005	+2.9	+2.3	+0.8	+0.3
			0600 and 1800	1100 and 2300	0300 and 1500	0800 and 2000				
BRISTOL, AVONMOUTH Standard port	51 30N	2 44W					13.2	9.8	3.8	1.0
Barry	51 23N	3 16W	−0025	−0025	−0130	−0045	−1.5	−1.1	0.0	+0.2
Flat Holm	51 23N	3 07W	−0015	−0015	−0035	−0035	−1.4	−1.0	−0.5	0.0
Steep Holm	51 20N	3 06W	−0020	−0020	−0040	−0040	−1.7	−1.1	−0.5	−0.4
Cardiff	51 27N	3 10W	−0015	−0015	−0035	−0030	−0.9	−0.7	+0.2	+0.2
Newport	51 33N	2 59W	−0005	−0010	−0015	−0015	−0.9	−0.9	−0.2	−0.2
River Wye Chepstow	51 39N	2 40W	+0020	+0020	No data	No data	No data		No data	
			0000 and 1200	0600 and 1800	0000 and 1200	0700 and 1900				
BRISTOL, AVONMOUTH Standard port	51 30N	2 44W					13.2	9.8	3.8	1.0

WEST COAST OF ENGLAND

Location	Lat	Long	High Water		Low Water		MHWS	MHWN	MLWN	MLWS
River Severn										
Sudbrook	51 35N	2 43W	+0010	+0010	+0025	+0015	+0.2	+0.1	−0.1	+0.1
Beachley (Aust)	51 36N	2 38W	+0010	+0015	+0040	+0025	−0.2	−0.2	−0.5	−0.3
Inward Rocks	51 39N	2 37W	+0020	+0020	+0105	+0045	−1.0	−1.1	−1.4	−0.6
Narlwood Rocks	51 39N	2 36W	+0025	+0025	+0120	+0100	−1.9	−2.0	−2.3	−0.8
White House	51 40N	2 33W	+0025	+0025	+0145	+0120	−3.0	−3.1	−3.6	−1.0
Berkeley	51 42N	2 30W	+0030	+0045	+0245	+0220	−3.8	−3.9	−3.4	−0.5
Sharpness Dock	51 43N	2 29W	+0035	+0050	+0305	+0245	−3.9	−4.2	−3.3	−0.4
Wellhouse Rock	51 44N	2 29W	+0040	+0055	+0320	+0305	−4.1	−4.4	−3.1	−0.2
Epney	51 42N	2 24W	+0130	No data	No data	No data	−9.4	No data	No data	
Minsterworth	51 50N	2 23W	+0140	No data	No data	No data	−10.1	No data	No data	
Llanthony	51 51N	2 21W	+0215	No data	No data	No data	−10.7	No data	No data	
			0200 and 1400	0800 and 2000	0300 and 1500	0800 and 2000				
BRISTOL, AVONMOUTH Standard port	51 30N	2 44W					13.2	9.8	3.8	1.0
River Avon										
Shirehampton	51 29N	2 41W	0000	0000	+0035	+0010	−0.7	−0.7	−0.8	0.0
Sea Mills	51 29N	2 39W	+0005	+0005	+0105	+0030	−1.4	−1.5	−1.7	−0.1
Cumberland Basin Entrance	51 27N	2 37W	+0010	+0010	Dries	Dries	−2.9	−3.0	Dries	
Portishead	51 30N	2 45W	−0002	0000	No data	No data	−0.1	−0.1	No data	

Location	Lat	Long	High Water		Low Water		MHWS	MHWN	MLWN	MLWS
Clevedon	51 27N	2 52W	−0010	−0020	−0025	−0015	−0.4	−0.2	+0.2	0.0
St Thomas Head	51 24N	2 56W	0000	0000	−0030	−0030	−0.4	−0.2	+0.1	+0.1
English & Welsh Grounds	51 28N	2 59W	−0008	−0008	−0030	−0030	−0.5	−0.8	−0.3	0.0
Weston-super-Mare	51 21N	2 59W	−0020	−0030	−0130	−0030	−1.2	−1.0	−0.8	−0.2
River Parrett										
Burnham-on-Sea	51 14N	3 00W	−0020	−0025	−0030	0000	−2.3	−1.9	−1.4	−1.1
Bridgwater	51 08N	3 00W	−0015	−0030	+0305	+0455	−8.6	−8.1	Dries	
Hinkley Point	51 13N	3 08W	−0032	−0028	−0055	−0049	−1.4	−1.1	−0.1	0.0
Minehead	51 13N	3 28W	−0037	−0052	−0155	−0045	−2.6	−1.9	−0.2	0.0
Porlock Bay	51 13N	3 38W	−0045	−0055	−0205	−0050	−3.0	−2.2	−0.1	−0.1
Lynmouth	51 14N	3 50W	−0055	−0115	No data	No data	−3.6	−2.7	No data	
			0100	**0700**	**0100**	**0700**				
MILFORD HAVEN	51 42N	5 03W	and	and	and	and	**7.0**	**5.2**	**2.5**	**0.7**
Standard port			**1300**	**1900**	**1300**	**1900**				
Ilfracombe	51 13N	4 07W	−0016	−0016	−0041	−0031	+2.3	+1.8	+0.6	+0.3
Rivers Taw & Torridge										
Appledore	51 03N	4 12W	−0020	−0025	+0015	−0045	+0.5	0.0	−0.9	−0.5
Yelland Marsh	51 04N	4 10W	−0010	−0015	+0100	−0015	+0.1	−0.4	−1.2	−0.6
Fremington	51 05N	4 07W	−0010	−0015	+0030	−0030	−1.1	−1.8	−2.2	−0.5
Barnstaple	51 05N	4 04W	0000	−0015	−0155	−0245	−2.9	−3.8	−2.2	−0.4
Bideford	51 01N	4 12W	−0020	−0025	0000	0000	−1.1	−1.6	−2.5	−0.7
Clovelly	51 00N	4 24W	−0030	−0030	−0020	−0040	+1.3	+1.1	+0.2	+0.2
Lundy	51 10N	4 39W	−0025	−0025	−0035	−0030	+1.0	+0.8	+0.2	+0.1
Bude	50 50N	4 33W	−0040	−0040	−0035	−0045	+0.7	+0.6	No data	
Boscastle	50 41N	4 42W	−0045	−0010	−0110	−0100	+0.3	+0.4	+0.2	+0.2
Port Isaac	50 35N	4 50W	−0100	−0100	−0100	−0100	+0.5	+0.6	0.0	+0.2
River Camel										
Padstow	50 33N	4 56W	−0055	−0050	−0040	−0050	+0.3	+0.4	+0.1	+0.1
Wadebridge	50 31N	4 50W	−0052	−0052	+0235	+0245	−3.8	−3.8	−2.5	−0.4
Newquay	50 25N	5 05W	−0100	−0110	−0105	−0050	0.0	+0.1	0.0	−0.1
Perranporth	50 21N	5 09W	−0100	−0110	−0110	−0050	−0.1	0.0	0.0	+0.1
St Ives	50 13N	5 29W	−0050	−0115	−0105	−0040	−0.4	−0.3	−0.1	+0.1
Cape Cornwall	50 08N	5 42 W	−0130	−0145	−0120	−0120	−1.0	−0.9	−0.5	−0.1
Sennen Cove	50 05N	5 42W	−0130	−0145	−0125	−0125	−0.9	−0.4	No data	

IRELAND

Location	Lat	Long	High Water		Low Water		MHWS	MHWN	MLWN	MLWS
			0000	**0700**	**0000**	**0500**				
DUBLIN, NORTH WALL	53 21N	6 13W	and	and	and	and	**4.1**	**3.4**	**1.5**	**0.7**
Standard port			**1200**	**1900**	**1200**	**1700**				
Courtown	52 39N	6 13W	−0328	−0242	−0158	−0138	−2.8	−2.4	−0.5	0.0
Arklow	52 48N	6 08W	−0315	−0201	−0140	−0134	−2.7	−2.2	−0.6	−0.1
Wicklow	52 59N	6 02W	−0019	−0019	−0024	−0026	−1.4	−1.1	−0.4	0.0
Greystones	53 09N	6 04W	−0008	−0008	−0008	−0008	−0.5	−0.4	No data	
Dun Laoghaire	53 18N	6 08W	0000	0000	+0002	+0003	0.0	+0.1	0.0	0.0
Dublin Bar	53 21N	6 09W	−0006	−0001	−0002	−0003	0.0	0.0	0.0	0.0
Howth	53 23N	6 04W	−0007	−0005	+0001	+0005	0.0	−0.1	−0.2	−0.2
Malahide	53 27N	6 09W	+0002	+0003	+0009	+0009	+0.1	−0.2	−0.4	−0.2
Balbriggan	53 37N	6 11W	−0021	−0015	+0010	+0002	+0.3	+0.2	No data	
River Boyne Bar	53 43N	6 14W	−0005	0000	+0020	+0030	+0.4	+0.3	−0.1	−0.2
Dunany Point	53 52N	6 14W	−0028	−0018	−0008	−0006	+0.7	+0.9	No data	
Dundalk Soldiers Point	54 00N	6 21W	−0010	−0010	0000	+0045	+1.0	+0.8	+0.1	−0.1

NORTHERN IRELAND

Location	Lat	Long	High Water		Low Water		MHWS	MHWN	MLWN	MLWS
Carlingford Lough										
Cranfield Point	54 01N	6 04W	−0027	−0011	+0005	−0010	+0.7	+0.9	+0.3	+0.2
Warrenpoint	54 06N	6 15W	−0020	−0010	+0025	+0035	+1.0	+0.7	+0.2	+0.0
Newry (Victoria Lock)	54 09N	6 19W	+0005	+0015	+0045	Dries	+1.2	+0.9	+0.1	Dries
			0100	**0700**	**0000**	**0600**				
BELFAST	54 36N	5 55W	and	and	and	and	**3.5**	**3.0**	**1.1**	**0.4**
Standard port			**1300**	**1900**	**1200**	**1800**				
Kilkeel	54 03N	5 59W	+0040	+0030	+0010	+0010	+1.2	+1.1	+0.4	+0.4
Newcastle	54 12N	5 53W	+0025	+0035	+0020	+0040	+1.6	+1.1	+0.4	+0.1
Killough Harbour	54 15N	5 38W	0000	+0020	No data	No data	+1.8	+1.6	No data	
Ardglass	54 16N	5 36W	+0010	+0015	+0005	+0010	+1.7	+1.2	+0.6	+0.3
Strangford Lough										
Killard Point	54 19N	5 31W	+0011	+0021	+0005	+0025	+1.0	+0.8	+0.1	+0.1
Strangford	54 22N	5 33W	+0147	+0157	+0148	+0208	+0.1	+0.1	−0.2	0.0
Quoile Barrier	54 22N	5 41W	+0150	+0200	+0150	+0300	+0.2	+0.2	−0.3	−0.1
Killyleagh	54 24N	5 39W	+0157	+0207	+0211	+0231	+0.3	+0.3	No data	
South Rock	54 24N	5 25W	+0023	+0023	+0025	+0025	+1.0	+0.8	+0.1	+0.1
Portavogie	54 27N	5 26W	+0010	+0020	+0010	+0020	+1.2	+0.9	+0.3	+0.2
Donaghadee	54 39N	5 32W	+0020	+0020	+0023	+0023	+0.5	+0.4	0.0	+0.1
Carrickfergus	54 43N	5 48W	+0005	+0005	+0005	+0005	−0.3	−0.3	−0.2	−0.1
Larne	54 51N	5 48W	+0005	0000	+0010	−0005	−0.7	−0.5	−0.3	0.0
Red Bay	55 04N	6 03W	+0022	−0010	+0007	−0017	−1.9	−1.5	−0.8	−0.2

TIDES

Location	Lat	Long	High Water		Low Water		MHWS	MHWN	MLWN	MLWS
Cushendun	55 08N	6 02W	+0010	−0030	0000	−0025	−1.7	−1.5	−0.6	−0.2
Portrush	55 12N	6 40W	−0433	−0433	−0433	−0433	−1.6	−1.6	−0.3	0.0
Coleraine	55 08N	6 40W	−0403	−0403	−0403	−0403	−1.3	−1.2	−0.2	0.0
			0200	0900	0200	0800				
GALWAY	53 16N	9 03W	and	and	and	and	5.1	3.9	2.0	0.8
Standard port			1400	2100	1400	2000				
Londonderry	55 00N	7 19W	+0254	+0319	+0322	+0321	−2.4	−1.8	−0.8	−0.1

IRELAND

Location	Lat	Long	High Water		Low Water		MHWS	MHWN	MLWN	MLWS
Inishtrahull	55 26N	7 14W	+0100	+0100	+0115	+0200	−1.8	−1.4	−0.4	−0.4
Bulbinbeg	55 22N	7 20W	+0120	+0120	+0135	+0135	−1.3	−1.1	−0.4	−0.3
Trawbreaga Bay	55 19N	7 23W	+0115	+0059	+0109	+0125	−1.1	−0.8	No data	
Lough Swilly										
Rathmullan	55 06N	7 32W	+0125	+0050	+0126	+0118	−0.8	−0.7	−0.1	−0.3
Fanad Head	55 17N	7 38W	+0115	+0040	+0125	+0120	−1.1	−0.9	−0.5	−0.3
Mulroy Bay Bar	55 15N	7 46W	+0108	+0052	+0102	+0118	−1.2	−1.0	No data	
Fanny's Bay	55 12N	7 49W	+0145	+0129	+0151	+0207	−2.2	−1.7	No data	
Seamount Bay	55 11N	7 44W	+0210	+0154	+0226	+0242	−3.1	−2.3	No data	
Cranford Bay	55 09N	7 42W	+0329	+0313	+0351	+0407	−3.7	−2.8		
No data										
Sheephaven Downies Bay	55 11N	7 50W	+0057	+0043	+0053	+0107	−1.1	−0.9	No data	
Inishbofin Bay	55 10N	8 10W	+0040	+0026	+0032	+0046	−1.2	−0.9	No data	
			0600	1100	0000	0700				
GALWAY	53 16N	9 03W	and	and	and	and	5.1	3.9	2.0	0.8
Standard port			1800	2300	1200	1900				
Gweedore Harbour	55 04N	8 19W	+0048	+0100	+0055	+0107	−1.3	−1.0	−0.5	−0.3
Burtonport	54 59N	8 26W	+0042	+0055	+0115	+0055	−1.2	−1.0	−0.6	−0.3
Loughros More Bay	54 47N	8 30W	+0042	+0054	+0046	+0058	−1.1	−0.9	No data	
Donegal Bay										
Killybegs	54 38N	8 26W	+0040	+0050	+0055	+0035	−1.0	−0.9	−0.5	−0.2
Donegal Hbr, Salt Hill Quay	54 38N	8 12W	+0038	+0050	+0052	+0104	−1.2	−0.9	No data	
Mullaghmore	54 28N	8 27W	+0036	+0048	+0047	+0059	−1.4	−1.0	−0.4	−0.4
Sligo Hbr (Oyster Island)	54 18N	8 34W	+0043	+0055	+0042	+0054	−1.0	−0.9	−0.5	−0.3
Ballysadare Bay, Culleenamore	54 16N	8 36W	+0059	+0111	+0111	+0123	−1.2	−0.9	No data	
Killala Bay (Inishcrone)	54 13N	9 06W	+0035	+0055	+0030	+0050	−1.3	−1.2	−0.7	−0.4
Broadhaven	54 16N	9 53W	+0035	+0035	+0040	+0040	−1.4	−1.0	−0.6	−0.2
Blacksod Bay										
Blacksod Quay	54 06N	10 04W	+0025	+0035	+0040	+0040	−1.2	−1.0	−0.6	−0.4
Inishbiggle	54 00N	9 53W	+0055	+0100	+0125	+0110	−1.3	−0.9	−0.5	−0.2
Clare Island	53 48N	9 57W	+0015	+0021	+0039	+0027	−0.6	−0.4	−0.1	0.0
Clew Bay Inishgort	53 50N	9 40W	+0035	+0045	+0115	+0100	−0.7	−0.5	−0.2	0.0
Killary Harbour	53 38N	9 53W	+0021	+0015	+0035	+0029	−1.0	−0.8	−0.4	−0.3
Inishbofin Bofin Harbour	53 37N	10 12W	+0013	+0009	+0021	+0017	−1.0	−0.8	−0.4	−0.3
Clifden Bay	53 29N	10 04W	+0005	+0005	+0016	+0016	−0.7	−0.5	No data	
Slyne Head	53 24N	10 14W	+0002	+0002	+0010	+0010	−0.7	−0.5	No data	
Roundstone Bay	53 23N	9 55W	+0003	+0003	+0008	+0008	−0.7	−0.5	−0.3	−0.3
Kilkieran Cove	53 19N	9 44W	+0005	+0005	+0016	+0016	−0.3	−0.2	−0.1	−0.2
Aran Islands Killeany Bay	53 07N	9 40W	0000	0000	+0001	−0001	−0.1	+0.1	+0.1	+0.2
Liscannor	52 56N	9 23W	−0003	−0007	+0006	+0002	−0.4	−0.3	No data	
Seafield Point	52 48N	9 30W	−0006	−0014	+0004	−0004	−0.5	−0.4	No data	
Kilrush	52 38N	9 30W	−0006	+0027	+0057	−0016	−0.1	−0.2	−0.3	−0.1
Limerick Dock	52 40N	8 38W	+0135	+0141	+0141	+0219	+1.0	+0.7	−0.8	−0.2
			0500	1100	0500	1100				
COBH	51 51N	8 18W	and	and	and	and	4.1	3.2	1.3	0.4
Standard port			1700	2300	1700	2300				
Tralee Bay Fenit Pier	52 16N	9 52W	−0057	−0017	−0029	−0109	+0.5	+0.2	+0.3	+0.1
Smerwick Harbour	52 12N	10 24W	−0107	−0027	−0041	−0121	−0.3	−0.4	No data	
Dingle Harbour	52 07N	10 15W	−0111	−0041	−0049	−0119	−0.1	0.0	+0.3	+0.4
Castlemaine Hbr Cromane Pt	52 08N	9 54W	−0026	−0006	−0017	−0037	+0.4	+0.2	+0.4	+0.2
Valentia Harbour										
Knights Town	51 56N	10 18W	−0118	−0038	−0056	−0136	−0.6	−0.4	−0.1	0.0
Ballinskelligs Bay Castle	51 49N	10 16W	−0119	−0039	−0054	−0134	−0.5	−0.5	−0.1	0.0
Kenmare River										
West Cove	51 46N	10 03W	−0113	−0033	−0049	−0129	−0.6	−0.5	−0.1	0.0
Dunkerron Harbour	51 52N	9 39W	−0117	−0027	−0050	−0140	−0.2	−0.3	+0.1	0.0
Coulagh Bay										
Ballycrovane Hbr	51 43N	9 57W	−0116	−0036	−0053	−0133	−0.6	−0.5	−0.1	0.0
Black Ball Harbour	51 36N	10 02W	−0115	−0035	−0047	−0127	−0.7	−0.6	−0.1	+0.1
Bantry Bay										
Castletown Bearhaven	51 39N	9 54W	−0048	−0012	−0025	−0101	−0.8	−0.6	−0.2	0.0
Bantry	51 41N	9 28W	−0045	−0025	−0040	−0105	−0.7	−0.6	−0.2	+0.1

Location	Lat	Long	High Water		Low Water		MHWS	MHWN	MLWN	MLWS
Dunmanus Bay										
Dunbeacon Harbour	51 37N	9 33W	−0057	−0025	−0032	−0104	−0.8	−0.7	−0.3	−0.1
Dunmanus Harbour	51 32N	9 40W	−0107	−0031	−0044	−0120	−0.7	−0.6	−0.2	0.0
Crookhaven	51 28N	9 44W	−0057	−0033	−0048	−0112	−0.8	−0.6	−0.4	−0.1
Skull	51 31N	9 32W	−0040	−0015	−0015	−0110	−0.9	−0.6	−0.2	0.0
Baltimore	51 29N	9 23W	−0025	−0005	−0010	−0050	−0.6	−0.3	+0.1	+0.2
Castletownshend	51 32N	9 10W	−0020	−0030	−0020	−0050	−0.4	−0.2	+0.1	+0.3
Clonakilty Bay	51 35N	8 50W	−0033	−0011	−0019	−0041	−0.3	−0.2	No data	
Courtmacsherry	51 38N	8 43W	−0025	−0008	−0008	−0015	−0.1	−0.1	−0.0	+0.1
Kinsale	51 42N	8 31W	−0019	−0005	−0009	−0023	−0.2	0.0	+0.1	+0.2
Roberts Cove	51 45N	8 19W	−0005	−0005	−0005	−0005	−0.1	0.0	0.0	+0.1
Cork Harbour										
Ringaskiddy	51 50N	8 19W	+0005	+0020	+0007	+0013	+0.1	+0.1	+0.1	+0.1
Marino Point	51 53N	8 20W	0000	+0010	0000	+0010	+0.1	+0.1	0.0	0.0
Cork City	51 54N	8 27W	+0005	+0010	+0020	+0010	+0.4	+0.4	+0.3	+0.2
Ballycotton	51 50N	8 01W	−0011	+0001	+0003	−0009	0.0	0.0	−0.1	0.0
Youghal	51 57N	7 51W	0000	+0010	+0010	0000	−0.2	−0.1	−0.1	−0.1
Dungarvan Harbour	52 05N	7 34W	+0004	+0012	+0007	−0001	0.0	+0.1	−0.2	0.0
Waterford Harbour										
Dunmore East	52 09N	6 59W	+0008	+0003	0000	0000	+0.1	0.0	+0.1	+0.2
Cheekpoint	52 16N	7 00W	+0026	+0021	+0019	+0022	+0.5	+0.4	+0.3	+0.2
Kilmokea Point	52 17N	7 00W	+0026	+0022	+0020	+0020	+0.2	+0.1	+0.1	+0.1
Waterford	52 16N	7 07W	+0053	+0032	+0015	+0100	+0.6	+0.6	+0.4	+0.2
New Ross	52 24N	6 57W	+0100	+0030	+0055	+0130	+0.3	+0.4	+0.3	+0.4
Baginbun Head	52 10N	6 50W	+0003	+0003	−0008	−0008	−0.2	−0.1	+0.2	+0.2
Great Saltee	52 07N	6 37W	+0019	+0009	−0004	+0006	−0.3	−0.4	No data	
Carnsore Point	52 10N	6 22W	+0029	+0019	−0002	+0008	−1.1	−1.0	No data	
Rosslare Europort	52 15N	6 21W	+0045	+0035	+0015	−0005	−2.2	−1.8	−0.5	−0.1
Wexford Harbour	52 20N	6 27W	+0126	+0126	+0118	+0108	−2.1	−1.7	−0.3	+0.1

DENMARK *Time zone −0100*

			0300	0700	0100	0800				
ESBJERG	55 28N	8 27E	and	and	and	and	2.0	1.6	0.6	0.2
Standard port			1500	1900	1300	2000				
Hirtshals	57 36N	9 58E	+0055	+0320	+0340	+0100	−1.7	−1.4	−0.5	−0.2
Hanstholm	57 07N	8 36E	+0100	+0340	+0340	+0130	−1.7	−1.3	−0.5	−0.2
Thyborøn	56 42N	8 13E	+0120	+0230	+0410	+0210	−1.6	−1.3	−0.5	−0.2
Thorsminde	56 22N	8 07E	+0045	+0050	+0040	+0010	−1.4	−1.1	−0.5	−0.2
Hvide Sande	56 00N	8 08E	0000	+0010	−0015	−0025	−1.2	−0.9	−0.4	−0.2
Blavands Huk	55 33N	8 05E	−0120	−0110	−0050	−0100	−0.2	−0.2	−0.3	−0.2
Esbjerg, Gradyb Bar	55 26N	8 15E	−0130	−0115	No data	No data	−0.5	−0.4	−0.3	−0.2
Havneby (Rømø)	55 05N	8 34E	−0040	−0005	0000	−0020	−0.1	0.0	−0.3	−0.3
Hojer	54 58N	8 40E	−0020	+0015	No data	No data	+0.4	+0.5	−0.2	−0.2

GERMANY *Time zone −0100*

			0100	0600	0100	0800				
HELGOLAND	54 11N	7 53E	and	and	and	and	3.1	2.8	0.8	0.4
Standard port			1300	1800	1300	2000				
Lister Tief, List	55 01N	8 26E	+0252	+0240	+0201	+0210	−0.7	−0.6	−0.1	0.0
Hörnum	54 45N	8 18E	+0223	+0218	+0131	+0137	−0.4	−0.3	−0.1	−0.1
Amrum - Hafen	54 38N	8 23E	+0138	+0137	+0128	+0134	+0.3	+0.3	0.0	0.0
Dagebüll	54 44N	8 41E	+0226	+0217	+0211	+0225	+0.7	+0.8	+0.1	+0.1
Suderoogsand	54 25N	8 30E	+0116	+0102	+0038	+0122	+0.6	+0.5	+0.1	+0.1
River Hever, Husum	54 28N	9 01E	+0205	+0152	+0118	+0200	+1.2	+1.2	+0.1	+0.1
Suederhoeft	54 16N	8 42E	+0103	+0056	+0051	+0112	+0.7	+0.6	−0.2	0.0
Eidersperrwerk	54 16N	8 51E	+0120	+0115	+0130	+0155	+0.6	+0.5	−0.1	0.0
Linnenplate	54 13N	8 40E	+0047	+0046	+0034	+0046	+0.7	+0.6	0.0	0.0
Büsum	54 07N	8 52E	+0054	+0049	−0001	+0027	+0.9	+0.9	−0.1	0.0

			0200	0800	0200	0900				
CUXHAVEN	53 52N	8 43E	and	and	and	and	3.7	3.3	0.8	0.4
Standard port			1400	2000	1400	2100				
River Elbe Großer Vogelsand	54 00N	8 29E	−0044	−0046	−0101	−0103	+0.1	0.0	+0.1	+0.1
Scharhörn	53 58N	8 28E	−0045	−0047	−0101	−0103	0.0	0.0	0.0	0.0
Otterndorf	53 50N	8 52E	+0029	+0029	+0027	+0027	0.0	−0.1	0.0	+0.1
Brunsbüttel	53 53N	9 08E	+0057	+0105	+0121	+0112	−0.1	−0.2	−0.1	+0.1
Glückstadt	53 47N	9 25E	+0205	+0214	+0220	+0213	−0.1	0.0	0.0	+0.1
Stadersand	53 38N	9 32E	+0241	+0245	+0300	+0254	+0.1	+0.2	−0.1	+0.1
Schulau	53 34N	9 42E	+0304	+0315	+0337	+0321	+0.3	+0.3	−0.2	0.0
Seemannshoeft	53 32N	9 53E	+0324	+0332	+0403	+0347	+0.4	+0.5	−0.3	−0.1
Hamburg	53 33N	9 58E	+0338	+0346	+0422	+0406	+0.5	+0.5	−0.3	−0.2

TIDES

Location	Lat	Long	High Water		Low Water		MHWS	MHWN	MLWN	MLWS
			0200	0800	0200	0900				
WILHELMSHAVEN	53 31N	8 09E	and	and	and	and	4.8	4.3	1.1	0.5
Standard port			1400	2000	1400	2100				
River Weser										
Alte Weser lt ho	53 32N	8 08E	−0055	−0048	−0015	−0029	−1.1	−1.0	−0.2	0.0
Dwarsgat	53 43N	8 18E	−0015	+0002	−0006	−0001	−0.6	−0.5	−0.2	0.0
Bremerhaven	53 33N	8 34E	+0029	+0046	+0033	+0038	−0.1	0.0	−0.1	0.0
Nordenham	53 28N	8 29E	+0051	+0109	+0055	+0058	0.0	0.1	−0.2	−0.1
Brake	53 19N	8 29E	+0120	+0119	+0143	+0155	−0.2	−0.1	−0.4	−0.2
Elsfleth	53 16N	8 29E	+0137	+0137	+0206	+0216	−0.2	−0.1	−0.4	−0.2
Vegesack	53 10N	8 37E	+0208	+0204	+0250	+0254	−0.1	−0.1	−0.4	−0.1
Bremen	53 07N	8 43E	+0216	+0211	+0311	+0314	0.0	0.0	−0.5	−0.2
River Jade										
Wangerooge East	53 46N	7 59E	−0058	−0053	−0024	−0034	−1.0	−0.9	−0.2	−0.1
Wangerooge West	53 47N	7 52E	−0101	−0058	−0035	−0045	−1.1	−1.0	−0.2	−0.1
Schillig	53 42N	8 03E	−0031	−0025	−0006	−0014	−0.7	−0.6	−0.1	0.0
Hooksiel	53 39N	8 05E	−0023	−0022	−0008	−0012	−0.5	−0.4	−0.1	0.0
			0200	0700	0200	0800				
HELGOLAND	54 11N	7 53E	and	and	and	and	3.1	2.8	0.8	0.4
Standard port			1400	1900	1400	2000				
East Frisian Islands and coast										
Spiekeroog	53 45N	7 41E	+0003	−0003	−0031	−0012	+0.4	+0.4	+0.1	+0.1
Neuharlingersiel	53 42N	7 42E	+0014	+0008	−0024	−0013	+0.6	+0.5	+0.1	+0.1
Langeoog	53 43N	7 30E	+0003	−0001	−0034	−0018	+0.4	+0.3	+0.1	0.0
Norderney (Riffgat)	53 42N	7 09E	−0024	−0030	−0056	−0045	+0.1	+0.1	0.0	0.0
Norddeich Hafen	53 39N	7 09E	−0018	−0017	−0029	−0012	+0.2	+0.2	+0.1	0.0
Juist	53 40N	7 00E	−0026	−0032	−0019	−0008	+0.1	+0.1	0.0	0.0
River Ems										
Memmert	53 38N	6 54E	−0032	−0038	−0114	−0103	+0.2	+0.2	+0.1	0.0
Borkum (Fischerbalje)	53 33N	6 45E	−0048	−0052	−0124	−0105	0.0	0.0	0.0	0.0
Emshorn	53 30N	6 50E	−0037	−0041	−0108	−0047	+0.2	+0.2	0.0	0.0
Knock	53 20N	7 02E	+0018	+0005	−0028	+0004	+0.7	+0.7	+0.1	0.0
Emden	53 20N	7 11E	+0041	+0028	−0011	+0022	+0.8	+0.8	−0.1	−0.1

NETHERLANDS *Time zone −0100*

Location	Lat	Long	High Water		Low Water		MHWS	MHWN	MLWN	MLWS
			0200	0700	0200	0800				
HELGOLAND	54 11N	7 53E	and	and	and	and	3.1	2.8	0.8	0.4
Standard port			1400	1900	1400	2000				
Delfzijl	53 20N	6 56E	+0020	−0005	−0040	0000	+0.6	+0.6	0.0	0.0
Eemshaven	53 27N	6 50E	−0025	−0045	−0115	−0045	0.0	+0.1	−0.1	−0.1
Huibertgat	53 35N	6 24E	−0150	−0150	−0210	−0210	−0.5	−0.4	−0.2	−0.2
Schiermonnikoog	53 28N	6 12E	−0120	−0130	−0240	−0220	−0.2	−0.3	−0.1	−0.1
Waddenzee										
Lauwersoog	53 25N	6 12E	−0130	−0145	−0235	−0220	−0.3	−0.2	−0.2	0.0
Nes	53 26N	5 47E	−0135	−0150	−0245	−0225	−0.3	−0.2	−0.2	0.0
West Terschelling	53 22N	5 13E	−0220	−0250	−0335	−0310	−0.7	−0.7	−0.2	−0.1
Vlieland-Haven	53 18N	5 06E	−0250	−0320	−0355	−0330	−0.7	−0.7	−0.2	−0.1
Harlingen	53 10N	5 25E	−0155	−0245	−0210	−0130	−0.8	−0.7	−0.4	−0.1
Kornwerderzand	53 04N	5 20E	−0210	−0315	−0300	−0215	−1.0	−0.8	−0.4	−0.2
Den Oever	52 56N	5 02E	−0245	−0410	−0400	−0305	−1.2	−1.0	−0.5	−0.2
Oudeschild	53 02N	4 51E	−0310	−0420	−0445	−0400	−1.4	−1.1	−0.4	−0.2
Den Helder	52 58N	4 45E	−0410	−0520	−0520	−0430	−1.3	−1.1	−0.4	−0.2
Noordwinning (Platform K13–A)	53 13N	3 13E	−0420	−0430	−0520	−0530	−1.3	−1.4	−0.1	−0.1
			0300	0900	0400	1000				
VLISSINGEN	51 27N	3 36E	and	and	and	and	5.0	4.1	1.1	0.5
Standard port			1500	2100	1600	2200				
IJmuiden	52 28N	4 33E	+0145	+0140	+0305	+0325	−2.8	−2.4	−0.7	−0.3
Scheveningen	52 06N	4 16E	+0105	+0100	+0220	+0245	−2.7	−2.3	−0.7	−0.2
Europlatform	52 00N	3 17E	+0005	−0005	−0030	−0055	−2.8	−2.3	−0.6	−0.2
Nieuwe Waterweg										
HOEK VAN HOLLAND			*Standard port, no Secondaries*							
Maassluis	51 55N	4 15E	+0155	+0115	+0100	+0310	−2.9	−2.4	−0.8	−0.3
Nieuwe Maas, Vlaardingen	51 54N	4 21E	+0150	+0120	+0130	+0330	−2.9	−2.4	−0.9	−0.3
Haringvlietsluizen	51 50N	4 03E	+0015	+0015	+0015	−0020	−2.1	−1.9	−0.7	−0.3
Ooster Schelde										
Roompot Buiten	51 37N	3 40E	−0015	+0005	+0005	−0020	−1.3	−1.1	−0.4	−0.1
Walcheren, Westkapelle	51 32N	3 26E	−0025	−0015	−0010	−0025	−0.7	−0.6	−0.2	−0.1
Westerschelde										
Terneuzen	51 20N	3 50E	+0020	+0020	+0020	+0030	+0.4	+0.3	+0.1	0.0
Hansweert	51 27N	4 00E	+0100	+0050	+0040	+0100	+0.6	+0.6	0.0	0.0
Bath	51 24N	4 13E	+0125	+0115	+0115	+0140	+1.1	+1.0	0.0	0.0

Location	Lat	Long	High Water		Low Water		MHWS	MHWN	MLWN	MLWS

BELGIUM *Time zone –0100*

Location	Lat	Long	High Water		Low Water		MHWS	MHWN	MLWN	MLWS
Antwerpen	51 21N	4 14E	+0128	+0116	+0121	+0144	+1.2	+1.0	+0.1	+0.1
			0300	0900	0300	0900				
ZEEBRUGGE	51 21N	3 12E	and	and	and	and	4.8	4.0	1.2	0.5
Standard port			1500	2100	1500	2100				
Cadzand	51 23N	3 23E	+0005	–0010	+0000	+0010	0.0	0.0	–0.1	0.0
Blankenberge	51 19N	3 07E	No data	No data	No data	No data	+0.1	0.0	–0.1	0.0
Oostende	51 14N	2 56E	–0019	–0019	–0008	–0008	+0.4	+0.2	+0.2	+0.1
Nieuwpoort	51 09N	2 43E	–0031	–0031	–0010	–0010	+0.7	+0.5	+0.2	+0.1

FRANCE *Time zone –0100*

Location	Lat	Long	High Water		Low Water		MHWS	MHWN	MLWN	MLWS
			0200	0800	0200	0900				
DUNKERQUE	51 03N	2 22E	and	and	and	and	6.0	5.0	1.5	0.6
Standard port			1400	2000	1400	2100				
Gravelines	51 01N	2 06E	–0010	–0015	–0010	–0005	+0.5	+0.3	+0.1	0.0
Sandettie Bank	51 15N	2 03E	–0010	–0015	–0015	–0010	–0.6	–0.6	–0.2	–0.1
Calais	50 58N	1 51E	–0020	–0030	–0015	–0005	+1.2	+0.9	+0.6	+0.3
Wissant	50 53N	1 40E	–0035	–0050	–0030	–0010	+2.0	+1.5	+0.9	+0.4
Boulogne	50 44N	1 35E	–0045	–0100	–0045	–0025	+2.8	+2.2	+1.1	+0.5
			0100	0600	0100	0700				
DIEPPE	49 56N	1 05E	and	and	and	and	9.3	7.4	2.5	0.8
Standard port			1300	1800	1300	1900				
Le Touquet, Étaples	50 31N	1 35E	+0010	+0015	+0030	+0030	+0.2	+0.2	+0.3	+0.4
Berck	50 24N	1 34E	+0005	+0015	+0025	+0030	+0.4	+0.5	+0.3	+0.4
La Somme										
Le Hourdel	50 13N	1 34E	+0020	+0020	No data	No data	+0.8	+0.6	No data	
St Valéry	50 11N	1 37E	+0035	+0035	No data	No data	+0.9	+0.7	No data	
Cayeux	50 11N	1 29E	0000	+0005	+0015	+0010	+0.5	+0.6	+0.4	+0.4
Le Tréport	50 04N	1 22E	+0005	0000	+0005	+0015	+0.3	+0.2	+0.1	+0.1
St Valéry–en–Caux	49 52N	0 42E	–0005	–0005	–0015	–0015	–0.5	–0.4	–0.1	–0.1
Fécamp	49 46N	0 22E	–0015	–0010	–0030	–0040	–1.0	–0.6	+0.3	+0.4
Etretat	49 42N	0 12E	–0020	–0015	–0050	–0050	–1.2	–0.8	+0.3	+0.4
			0000	0500	0000	0700				
LE HAVRE	49 29N	0 07E	and	and	and	and	7.9	6.6	2.8	1.2
Standard port			1200	1700	1200	1900				
Antifer (Le Havre)	49 39N	0 09E	+0025	+0015	+0005	–0005	+0.1	0.0	0.0	0.0
La Seine										
Chenal du Rouen	49 26N	0 07E	0000	0000	0000	+0015	+0.1	0.0	+0.1	–0.1
Honfleur	49 25N	0 14E	–0150	–0135	+0025	+0040	+0.1	+0.1	+0.1	+0.3
Tancarville	49 28N	0 28E	–0135	–0120	+0030	+0145	+0.2	+0.2	+0.4	+1.0
Quilleboeuf	49 28N	0 32E	–0055	–0110	+0105	+0210	+0.2	+0.2	+0.6	+1.4
Vatteville	49 29N	0 40E	+0015	–0040	+0205	+0240	0.0	0.0	+0.1	+2.2
Caudebec	49 32N	0 44E	–0005	–0030	+0220	+0300	0.0	0.0	+1.1	+2.3
Heurteauville	49 27N	0 49E	+0055	+0005	+0250	+0330	–0.1	0.0	+1.3	+2.6
Duclair	49 29N	0 53E	+0210	+0145	+0350	+0410	–0.1	+0.1	+1.6	+3.2
Rouen	49 27N	1 06E	+0305	+0240	+0505	+0515	0.0	+0.3	+1.7	+3.3
Trouville	49 22N	0 05E	–0100	–0010	0000	+0005	+0.4	+0.3	+0.3	+0.1
Dives	49 18N	0 05W	–0100	–0010	0000	0000	+0.3	+0.2	+0.2	+0.1
Ouistreham	49 17N	0 15W	–0045	–0010	–0005	0000	–0.3	–0.3	–0.2	–0.3
Courseulles-sur-Mer	49 20N	0 27W	–0100	–0005	–0015	–0025	–0.5	–0.5	–0.1	–0.1
Arromanches	49 21N	0 37W	–0055	–0025	–0025	–0035	–0.5	–0.5	–0.1	–0.2
Port-en-Bessin	49 21N	0 45W	–0055	–0030	–0030	–0035	–0.7	–0.7	–0.2	–0.1
Alpha-Baie de Seine	49 49N	0 20W	+0030	+0020	–0005	–0020	–0.9	–0.8	–0.3	–0.2
			0300	1000	0400	1000				
CHERBOURG	49 39N	1 38W	and	and	and	and	6.4	5.1	2.6	1.1
Standard port			1500	2200	1600	2200				
Rade de la Capelle	49 25N	1 05W	+0125	+0055	+0125	+0110	+0.8	+0.8	+0.1	+0.2
Iles Saint Marcouf	49 30N	1 08W	+0130	+0055	+0120	+0110	+0.5	+0.5	+0.2	0.0
Vaast-la-Hougue	49 34N	1 16W	+0115	+0045	+0120	+0110	+0.4	+0.4	–0.1	–0.1
Barfleur	49 40N	1 15W	+0115	+0050	+0045	+0050	+0.1	+0.3	0.0	+0.1
Omonville	49 42N	1 50W	–0015	–0010	–0015	–0015	–0.3	–0.3	–0.3	–0.1
Goury	49 43N	1 57W	–0100	–0040	–0105	–0120	+1.7	+1.6	+0.9	+0.3

CHANNEL ISLANDS *Time zone UT*

Location	Lat	Long	High Water		Low Water		MHWS	MHWN	MLWN	MLWS
			0300	0900	0200	0900				
ST HELIER	49 11N	2 07W	and	and	and	and	11.0	8.1	4.0	1.4
Standard port			1500	2100	1400	2100				
Alderney, Braye	49 43N	2 12W	+0050	+0040	+0025	+0105	–4.8	–3.4	–1.5	–0.5
Sark, Maseline Pier	49 26N	2 21W	+0005	+0015	+0005	+0010	–2.1	–1.5	–0.6	–0.3
Guernsey, ST PETER PORT	49 27N	2 31W	*Standard port (no Secondaries)*							

Location	Lat	Long	High Water		Low Water		MHWS	MHWN	MLWN	MLWS
Jersey										
St Catherine Bay	49 13N	2 01W	0000	+0010	+0010	+0010	0.0	−0.1	0.0	+0.1
Bouley Bay	49 15N	2 05W	+0002	+0002	+0004	+0004	−0.3	−0.3	−0.1	−0.1
Les Ecrehou	49 17N	1 56W	+0005	+0009	+0011	+0009	−0.2	+0.1	−0.2	0.0
Les Minquiers	48 57N	2 08W	−0014	−0018	−0001	−0008	+0.5	+0.6	+0.1	+0.1

FRANCE *Time zone −0100*

			0100	0800	0300	0800				
ST MALO	48 38N	2 02W	and	and	and	and	**12.2**	9.2	4.4	1.5
Standard port			1300	2000	1500	2000				
Les Ardentes	48 58N	1 52W	+0010	+0010	+0020	+0010	0.0	0.0	−0.2	−0.1
Iles Chausey	48 52N	1 49W	+0005	+0005	+0015	+0015	+0.8	+0.8	+0.5	+0.3
Diélette	49 33N	1 52W	+0045	+0035	+0020	+0035	−2.5	−1.8	−0.7	−0.3
Carteret	49 22N	1 47W	+0030	+0020	+0015	+0030	−1.6	−1.1	−0.9	−0.3
Portbail	49 18N	1 45W	+0030	+0025	+0025	+0030	−0.8	−0.5	−0.4	−0.1
St Germain sur Ay	49 14N	1 36W	+0025	+0025	+0035	+0035	−0.7	−0.4	−0.2	+0.1
Le Sénéquet	49 05N	1 40W	+0015	+0015	+0025	+0025	−0.3	−0.2	−0.1	+0.1
Regnéville sur Mer	49 01N	1 33W	+0010	+0010	+0030	+0020	+0.5	+0.5	0.0	0.0
Granville	48 50N	1 36W	+0010	+0005	+0025	+0015	+0.7	+0.5	+0.1	0.0
Cancale	48 40N	1 51W	0000	0000	+0010	+0010	+0.8	+0.7	+0.1	+0.1
Ile des Hebihens	48 37N	2 11W	0000	0000	−0005	−0005	−0.2	−0.1	−0.3	−0.1
St Cast	48 38N	2 15W	0000	0000	−0005	−0005	−0.2	−0.1	−0.3	−0.1
Erquy	48 38N	2 28W	0000	−0005	−0020	−0010	−0.6	−0.4	−0.2	0.0
Dahouët	48 35N	2 34W	−0005	0000	−0025	−0010	−0.9	−0.6	−0.4	−0.2
Le Légué (Buoy)	48 34N	2 41W	−0010	−0005	−0020	−0015	−0.8	−0.4	−0.4	−0.1
Binic	48 36N	2 49W	−0005	−0005	−0025	−0015	−0.8	−0.6	−0.4	−0.2
St Quay-Portrieux	48 38N	2 49W	−0010	−0010	−0030	−0010	−1.0	−0.6	−0.4	−0.1
Paimpol	48 47N	3 02W	−0010	−0005	−0035	−0025	−1.4	−0.8	−0.6	−0.1
Ile de Bréhat	48 50N	3 00W	−0015	−0005	−0040	−0030	−1.8	−1.2	−0.6	−0.2
Les Héaux de Bréhat	48 55N	3 05W	−0015	−0010	−0010	−0045	−2.4	−1.6	−0.8	−0.2
Lézardrieux	48 47N	3 06W	−0020	−0015	−0055	−0045	−1.7	−1.2	−0.7	−0.2
Port-Béni	48 51N	3 10W	−0020	−0020	−0105	−0050	−2.4	−1.5	−0.7	−0.1
Tréguier	48 47N	3 13W	−0020	−0020	−0100	−0045	−2.3	−1.5	−0.8	−0.2
Perros-Guirec	48 49N	3 28W	−0035	−0035	−0115	−0100	−2.9	−1.8	−1.0	−0.2
Ploumanac'h	48 50N	3 29W	−0035	−0040	−0120	−0100	−2.9	−1.8	−0.8	−0.1

			0000	0600	0000	0600				
BREST	48 23N	4 30W	and	and	and	and	**7.0**	5.5	2.7	1.1
Standard port			1200	1800	1200	1800				
Trébeurden	48 46N	3 35W	+0100	+0110	+0120	+0100	+2.2	+1.8	+0.8	+0.3
Locquirec	48 42N	3 38W	+0100	+0110	+0125	+0100	+2.2	+1.8	+0.7	+0.4
Anse de Primel	48 43N	3 50W	+0100	+0110	+0120	+0100	+2.0	+1.6	+0.8	+0.2
Chateau du Taureau (Morlaix)	48 41N	3 53W	+0055	+0105	+0115	+0055	+1.9	+1.6	+0.7	+0.2
Roscoff	48 43N	3 58W	+0055	+0105	+0115	+0055	+1.9	+1.6	+0.7	+0.2
Ile de Batz	48 44N	4 00W	+0045	+0100	+0105	+0055	+1.9	+1.5	+0.8	+0.3
Brignogan	48 40N	4 19W	+0040	+0045	+0100	+0040	+1.4	+1.1	+0.5	+0.1
L'Aber Wrac'h	48 36N	4 34W	+0030	+0030	+0040	+0035	+0.9	+0.6	+0.2	0.0
Aber Benoit	48 35N	4 37W	+0022	+0025	+0035	+0020	+1.1	+0.9	+0.3	0.0
Portsall	48 34N	4 43W	+0015	+0020	+0025	+0015	+0.6	+0.4	+0.1	− 0.1
L'Aber-Ildut	48 28N	4 45W	+0010	+0010	+0020	+0010	+0.3	+0.2	+0.1	−0.1
Ouessant, Baie de Lampaul	48 27N	5 06W	+0010	+0010	−0005	+0005	− 0.1	−0.2	−0.2	− 0.1
Molene	48 24N	4 58W	+0015	+0010	+0020	+0020	+0.3	+0.2	+0.1	0.0
Le Conquet	48 22N	4 47W	0000	0000	+0005	+0005	−0.2	−0.2	−0.2	−0.1
Le Trez Hir	48 21N	4 42W	−0005	−0005	−0015	−0010	−0.4	−0.4	−0.2	0.0
Camaret	48 17N	4 35W	−0010	−0010	−0015	−0010	−0.4	−0.4	−0.2	−0.1
Morgat	48 13N	4 30W	−0005	−0010	−0020	−0005	−0.5	−0.4	−0.2	0.0
Douarnenez	48 06N	4 19W	−0010	−0010	−0020	−0010	−0.4	−0.4	−0.2	−0.1
Ile de Sein	48 02N	4 51W	−0005	−0005	−0015	−0010	−0.9	−0.7	−0.4	−0.2
Anse de Feunteun Aod	48 02N	4 42W	−0030	−0040	−0035	−0025	−1.4	−1.2	−0.6	−0.2
Audierne	48 01N	4 33W	−0035	−0030	−0035	−0030	−1.8	−1.4	−0.7	−0.3
Le Guilvinec	47 48N	4 17W	−0010	−0025	−0025	−0015	−1.9	−1.5	−0.7	−0.2
Lesconil	47 48N	4 13W	−0010	−0030	−0030	−0020	−2.0	−1.5	−0.7	−0.2
Pont l'Abbe River, Loctudy	47 50N	4 10W	−0010	−0030	−0035	−0020	−2.1	−1.7	−0.9	−0.4
Odet River										
Bénodet	47 53N	4 07W	−0010	−0025	−0030	−0020	−1.7	−1.4	−0.6	−0.1
Corniguel	47 58N	4 06W	+0015	+0010	−0015	−0010	−2.1	−1.7	−1.1	−0.8

Location	Lat	Long	High Water		Low Water		MHWS	MHWN	MLWN	MLWS
Concarneau	47 52N	3 55W	−0010	−0030	−0030	−0020	−1.9	−1.5	−0.7	−0.2
Iles de Glenan, Ile de Penfret	47 44N	3 57W	−0005	−0030	−0030	−0020	−2.0	−1.5	−0.8	−0.3
Port Louis	47 42N	3 21W	+0005	−0020	−0020	−0010	−1.8	−1.5	−0.6	−0.2
Lorient	47 45N	3 21W	+0005	−0020	−0020	−0010	−1.9	−1.5	−0.7	−0.3
Hennebont	47 48N	3 17W	+0015	−0015	+0005	+0005	−2.0	−1.6	−0.9	−0.3
Ile de Groix, Port Tudy	47 39N	3 27W	0000	−0025	−0025	−0015	−1.9	−1.5	−0.6	−0.2
Port d'Etel	47 39N	3 12W	+0020	−0010	+0030	+0010	−2.1	−1.4	−0.5	+0.4
Port Haliguen	47 29N	3 06W	+0010	−0020	−0015	−0010	−1.7	−1.3	−0.7	−0.3
Port Maria	47 29N	3 08W	+0010	−0025	−0025	−0015	−1.7	−1.4	−0.7	−0.2
Belle Ile, Le Palais	47 21N	3 09W	−0005	−0025	−0025	−0010	−1.8	−1.4	−0.7	−0.3
Crac'h River, La Trinité	47 35N	3 01W	+0025	−0020	−0015	−0010	−1.6	−1.2	−0.6	−0.3
Golfe du Morbihan										
Port Navalo	47 33N	2 55W	+0030	−0005	−0010	−0005	−2.0	−1.5	−0.8	−0.4
Auray	47 40N	2 59W	+0035	0000	+0015	−0005	−2.3	−1.9	−1.2	−0.5
Arradon	47 37N	2 50W	+0135	+0145	+0140	+0115	−3.9	−3.1	−1.9	−0.8
Vannes	47 39N	2 46W	+0200	+0150	+0140	+0120	−3.8	−3.0	−2.1	−0.9
St Armel (Le Passage)	47 36N	2 43W	+0200	+0200	+0210	+0135	−3.8	−3.0	−2.0	−0.9
Le Logeo	47 33N	2 51W	+0140	+0140	+0145	+0115	−4.1	−3.2	−2.1	−0.9
Port du Crouesty	47 32N	2 54W	+0010	−0025	−0015	−0010	−1.6	−1.2	−0.7	−0.3
Ile de Houat	47 24N	2 57W	+0005	−0025	−0025	−0010	−1.8	−1.4	−0.7	−0.4
Ile de Hoëdic	47 20N	2 52W	+0010	−0035	−0025	−0020	−1.9	−1.5	−0.8	−0.4
Pénerf	47 31N	2 37W	+0015	−0025	−0015	−0015	−1.6	−1.2	−0.7	−0.4
Tréhiguier	47 30N	2 27W	+0035	−0020	−0005	−0010	−1.5	−1.1	−0.6	−0.4
Le Croisic	47 18N	2 31W	+0015	−0040	−0020	−0015	−1.6	−1.3	−0.7	−0.4
Le Pouliguen	47 17N	2 25W	+0020	−0025	−0020	−0025	−1.6	−1.2	−0.7	−0.4
Le Grand-Charpentier	47 13N	2 19W	+0015	−0045	−0025	−0020	−1.6	−1.2	−0.7	−0.4
Pornichet	47 16N	2 21W	+0020	−0045	−0022	−0022	−1.5	−1.1	−0.6	−0.3
La Loire										
St Nazaire	47 16N	2 12W	+0030	−0040	−0010	−0010	−1.2	−0.9	−0.5	−0.3
Donges	47 18N	2 05W	+0035	−0040	+0005	+0005	−1.1	−0.8	−0.6	−0.5
Cordemais	47 17N	1 54W	+0055	−0005	+0105	+0030	−0.8	−0.6	−0.8	−0.5
Le Pellerin	47 12N	1 46W	+0110	+0010	+0145	+0100	−0.8	−0.6	−1.0	−0.5
Nantes (Chantenay)	47 12N	1 35W	+0135	+0055	+0215	+0125	−0.7	−0.4	−0.9	−0.2

Location	Lat	Long	High Water		Low Water		MHWS	MHWN	MLWN	MLWS
BREST	48 23N	4 30W	0500 and 1700	1100 and 2300	0500 and 1700	1100 and 2300	7.0	5.5	2.7	1.1
Standard port										
Pointe de Saint–Gildas	47 08N	2 15W	−0030	+0025	−0005	−0020	−1.4	−1.1	−0.6	−0.3
Pornic	47 06N	2 07W	−0050	+0030	−0010	−0010	−1.2	−0.9	−0.5	−0.3
Ile de Noirmoutier, L'Herbaudière	47 02N	2 18W	−0045	+0025	−0020	−0020	−1.5	−1.1	−0.6	−0.3
Fromentine	46 54N	2 10W	−0045	+0020	−0015	+0005	−1.8	−1.3	−0.8	−0.1
Ile de Yeu, Port Joinville	46 44N	2 21W	−0040	+0015	−0030	−0035	−2.0	−1.5	−0.8	−0.4
St Gilles-Croix-de-Vie	46 41N	1 56W	−0030	+0015	−0030	−0030	−1.9	−1.4	−0.7	−0.4
Les Sables d'Olonne	46 30N	1 48W	−0030	+0015	−0035	−0035	−1.8	−1.4	−0.7	−0.4

Location	Lat	Long	High Water		Low Water		MHWS	MHWN	MLWN	MLWS
POINTE DE GRAVE	45 34N	1 04W	0000 and 1200	0600 and 1800	0000 and 1200	0500 and 1700	5.3	4.4	2.1	1.0
Standard port										
Ile de Ré, St Martin	46 12N	1 22W	+0005	−0030	−0025	−0030	+0.7	+0.6	+0.3	−0.1
La Pallice	46 10N	1 13W	+0015	−0030	−0020	−0025	+0.7	+0.6	+0.3	−0.1
La Rochelle	46 09N	1 09W	+0015	−0030	−0020	−0025	+0.7	+0.6	+0.3	−0.2
Ile d'Aix	46 01N	1 10W	+0015	−0040	−0025	−0030	+0.9	+0.7	+0.3	0.0
La Charente, Rochefort	45 57N	0 58W	+0035	−0015	+0125	+0030	+1.2	+1.0	+0.1	−0.2
Le Chapus	45 51N	1 11W	+0015	−0040	−0015	−0025	+0.7	+0.7	+0.4	+0.1
La Cayenne	45 47N	1 08W	+0030	−0015	−0005	−0010	+0.3	+0.3	+0.3	0.0
Pointe de Gatseau	45 48N	1 14W	+0015	0000	−0020	−0015	0.0	0.0	+0.2	0.0
Cordouan	45 35N	1 10W	−0010	−0010	−0025	−0015	−0.3	−0.3	−0.3	−0.1
La Gironde										
Royan	45 37N	1 01W	0000	−0005	0000	0000	+0.1	+0.1	+0.1	0.0
Richard	45 27N	0 56W	+0020	+0020	+0035	+0030	0.0	0.0	−0.4	−0.5
Lamena	45 20N	0 48W	+0035	+0045	+0125	+0100	+0.3	+0.2	−0.5	−0.3
Pauillac	45 12N	0 45W	+0100	+0100	+0205	+0135	+0.2	+0.1	−1.0	−0.4
La Reuille	45 03N	0 36W	+0135	+0145	+0305	+0230	−0.1	−0.2	−1.3	−0.7
La Garonne										
Le Marquis	45 00N	0 33W	+0145	+0150	+0320	+0245	−0.2	−0.3	−1.5	−0.9
Bordeaux	44 52N	0 33W	+0200	+0225	+0405	+0330	0.0	−0.1	−1.7	−1.0

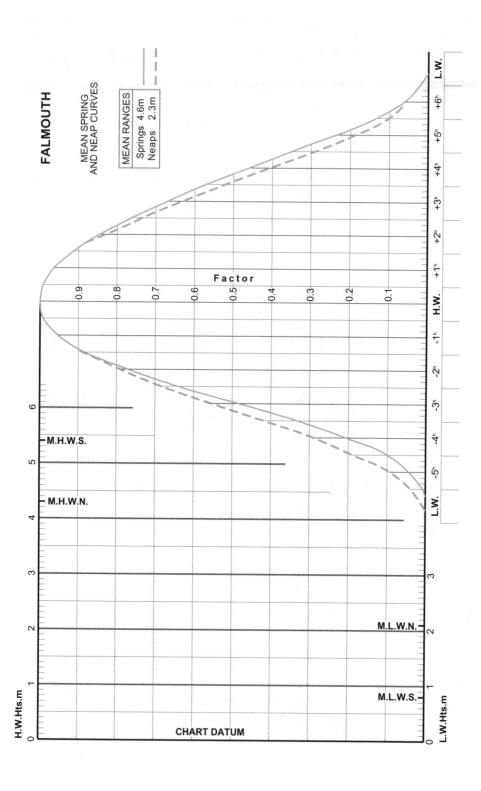

FALMOUTH

MEAN SPRING
AND NEAP CURVES

MEAN RANGES	
Springs	4.6m
Neaps	2.3m

Factor

0.9 0.8 0.7 0.6 0.5 0.4 0.3 0.2 0.1

H.W.Hts.m

M.H.W.S.

M.H.W.N.

CHART DATUM

L.W.Hts.m

M.L.W.N.

M.L.W.S.

FALMOUTH

LAT 50°09′N   LONG 5°03′W

TIMES AND HEIGHTS OF HIGH AND LOW WATERS

Dates in amber are **SPRINGS**
Dates in grey are **NEAPS**

2022

JANUARY

	Time	m		Time	m
1 SA	0331 1013 1557 2241	4.8 0.9 4.9 0.7	**16** SU	0413 1042 1633 2258	4.7 1.2 4.5 1.1
2 SU ●	0425 1111 1653 2336	5.0 0.6 5.0 0.6	**17** O	0453 1124 1713 2338	4.8 1.0 4.7 1.0
3 M	0518 1205 1746	5.2 0.4 5.0	**18** TU	0532 1202 1751	4.9 0.9 4.7
4 TU ○	0026 0608 1254 1837	0.5 5.3 0.3 5.0	**19** W	0013 0608 1237 1827	0.9 5.0 0.9 4.7
5 W	0114 0656 1341 1924	0.4 5.3 0.3 4.9	**20** TH	0048 0641 1310 1901	0.9 5.1 0.8 4.7
6 TH	0158 0740 1425 2008	0.5 5.3 0.5 4.8	**21** F	0121 0713 1344 1934	0.9 5.0 0.8 4.6
7 F	0240 0823 1508 2050	0.7 5.1 0.7 4.6	**22** SA	0155 0745 1419 2005	0.9 4.9 1.0 4.6
8 SA	0322 0905 1550 2134	0.9 4.9 1.0 4.4	**23** SU	0230 0819 1456 2037	1.0 4.8 1.1 4.5
9 SU ☽	0405 0950 1635 2222	1.2 4.6 1.3 4.2	**24** M	0309 0857 1537 2119	1.1 4.7 1.4 4.4
10 M	0453 1040 1726 2319	1.5 4.3 1.5 4.0	**25** TU ☽	0354 0946 1627 2218	1.3 4.6 1.3 4.2
11 TU	0548 1139 1824	1.7 4.1 1.7	**26** W	0451 1050 1731 2331	1.5 4.4 1.5 4.2
12 W	0026 0652 1251 1929	3.9 1.8 4.0 1.7	**27** TH	0601 1205 1847	1.6 4.2 1.5
13 TH	0139 0759 1404 2033	4.0 1.8 4.1 1.7	**28** F	0051 0725 1326 2010	4.2 1.6 4.3 1.3
14 F	0240 0902 1502 2128	4.2 1.6 4.2 1.4	**29** SA	0211 0849 1444 2127	4.4 1.4 4.4 1.2
15 SA	0329 0955 1550 2216	4.4 1.4 4.4 1.2	**30** SU	0318 1002 1549 2232	4.6 1.0 4.6 0.9
			31 M	0415 1104 1646 2329	4.9 0.7 4.8 0.6

FEBRUARY

	Time	m		Time	m
1 TU ●	0507 1159 1737	5.1 0.4 4.9	**16** W O	0512 1143 1733 2357	4.9 0.8 4.7 0.8
2 W	0019 0556 1245 1824	0.4 5.3 0.3 5.0	**17** TH	0547 1220 1809	5.0 0.7 4.8
3 TH	0105 0640 1330 1906	0.3 5.4 0.2 5.0	**18** F	0032 0621 1254 1843	0.7 5.1 0.5 4.8
4 F	0145 0721 1409 1944	0.3 5.3 0.3 4.9	**19** SA	0106 0654 1328 1914	0.6 5.1 0.5 4.8
5 SA	0221 0759 1444 2019	0.5 5.2 0.5 4.8	**20** SU	0140 0725 1401 1941	0.6 5.1 0.6 4.8
6 SU	0255 0834 1517 2054	0.7 5.0 0.8 4.6	**21** M	0213 0755 1435 2006	0.7 5.0 0.7 4.7
7 M	0329 0908 1550 2131	1.0 4.7 1.1 4.4	**22** TU	0248 0826 1511 2040	0.8 4.8 0.9 4.6
8 TU ☾	0405 0946 1627 2214	1.4 4.4 1.5 4.1	**23** W ☾	0328 0906 1554 2131	1.0 4.6 1.2 4.4
9 W	0448 1032 1715 2310	1.7 4.1 1.8 3.9	**24** TH	0418 1008 1651 2249	1.3 4.3 1.5 4.1
10 TH	0550 1133 1823	2.0 3.9 2.0	**25** F	0527 1137 1811	1.6 4.0 1.7
11 F	0025 0706 1301 1940	3.8 2.0 3.8 2.0	**26** SA	0028 0701 1317 1954	4.0 1.7 4.0 1.7
12 SA	0202 0821 1437 2050	3.8 1.9 3.9 1.7	**27** SU	0200 0846 1442 2124	4.0 1.5 4.2 1.4
13 SU	0306 0925 1532 2147	4.2 1.6 4.2 1.5	**28** M	0310 1000 1545 2227	4.2 1.1 4.5 1.0
14 M	0353 1017 1616 2235	4.5 1.3 4.4 1.2			
15 TU	0434 1103 1656 2318	4.7 1.0 4.6 1.0			

MARCH

	Time	m		Time	m
1 TU	0405 1057 1637 2320	4.9 0.6 4.7 0.6	**16** W	0407 1036 1631 2253	4.7 1.0 4.6 0.9
2 W ●	0453 1147 1722	5.1 0.3 4.9	**17** TH	0443 1117 1706 2333	4.9 0.7 4.8 0.7
3 TH	0006 0538 1230 1804	0.3 5.3 0.1 5.1	**18** F O	0519 1156 1742	5.1 0.5 4.9
4 F	0047 0619 1310 1841	0.2 5.4 0.1 5.1	**19** SA	0011 0555 1232 1817	0.5 5.2 0.4 5.0
5 SA	0124 0656 1344 1915	0.2 5.3 0.2 5.1	**20** SU	0046 0630 1307 1849	0.4 5.2 0.3 5.0
6 SU	0156 0731 1414 1947	0.3 5.2 0.4 5.0	**21** M	0120 0704 1340 1918	0.4 5.2 0.4 5.0
7 M	0225 0802 1440 2018	0.5 5.0 0.7 4.8	**22** TU	0154 0736 1413 1946	0.4 5.1 0.6 4.9
8 TU	0251 0831 1503 2049	0.9 4.7 1.1 4.5	**23** W	0229 0807 1449 2021	0.6 4.8 0.8 4.7
9 W	0316 0903 1527 2125	1.3 4.4 1.5 4.3	**24** TH	0308 0848 1531 2112	1.0 4.5 1.2 4.4
10 TH ☾	0343 0944 1600 2214	1.6 4.1 1.8 4.0	**25** F ☾	0359 0953 1629 2233	1.3 4.1 1.6 4.1
11 F	0431 1042 1706 2322	2.0 3.8 2.1 3.8	**26** SA	0511 1134 1754	1.7 3.8 1.9
12 SA	0611 1200 1850	2.2 3.6 2.2	**27** SU	0020 0659 1319 1955	4.0 1.8 3.9 1.8
13 SU	0100 0742 1408 2013	3.8 2.0 3.8 2.0	**28** M	0152 0847 1438 2118	4.2 1.4 4.1 1.3
14 M	0237 0853 1510 2117	4.1 1.7 4.1 1.6	**29** TU	0258 0950 1535 2214	4.5 0.9 4.4 0.9
15 TU	0327 0949 1553 2208	4.4 1.3 4.4 1.3	**30** W	0349 1041 1620 2302	4.9 0.5 4.6 0.5
			31 TH	0433 1126 1659 2345	5.1 0.3 5.0 0.3

APRIL

	Time	m		Time	m
1 F ●	0514 1207 1736	5.2 0.1 5.1	**16** SA O	0444 1126 1708 2345	5.1 0.4 5.0 0.4
2 SA	0023 0553 1243 1812	0.2 5.3 0.2 5.1	**17** SU	0524 1206 1746	5.2 0.3 5.1
3 SU	0057 0629 1314 1845	0.3 5.2 0.3 5.1	**18** M	0024 0606 1244 1825	0.3 5.2 0.3 5.1
4 M	0127 0702 1341 1917	0.4 5.1 0.5 5.0	**19** TU	0101 0646 1321 1901	0.3 5.2 0.3 5.1
5 TU	0154 0732 1404 1946	0.7 4.9 0.8 4.8	**20** W	0138 0724 1357 1937	0.4 5.0 0.6 5.0
6 W	0217 0800 1423 2015	0.9 4.7 1.1 4.6	**21** TH	0216 0804 1435 2019	0.6 4.8 0.9 4.8
7 TH	0236 0830 1444 2047	1.2 4.4 1.4 4.4	**22** F	0259 0852 1522 2115	1.0 4.4 1.3 4.4
8 F	0301 0909 1514 2134	1.6 4.1 1.8 4.1	**23** SA ☾	0355 1002 1625 2235	1.3 4.0 1.6 4.2
9 SA ☾	0344 1007 1606 2239	1.9 3.8 2.1 3.9	**24** SU	0513 1140 1753	1.6 3.8 1.8
10 SU	0514 1134 1759 2358	2.1 3.7 2.2 3.8	**25** M	0013 0659 1311 1940	4.1 1.6 3.9 1.7
11 M	0657 1300 1929	2.0 3.7 2.0	**26** TU	0135 0827 1421 2054	4.3 1.4 4.2 1.3
12 TU	0137 0813 1430 2037	4.0 1.7 4.0 1.7	**27** W	0237 0926 1512 2148	4.5 0.9 4.5 0.9
13 W	0243 0911 1515 2132	4.3 1.3 4.3 1.3	**28** TH	0325 1014 1554 2235	4.8 0.6 4.7 0.6
14 TH	0326 1000 1553 2219	4.7 1.0 4.6 0.8	**29** F	0408 1058 1631 2317	5.0 0.4 4.9 0.4
15 F	0405 1044 1630 2303	4.9 0.7 4.8 0.7	**30** SA ●	0447 1137 1707 2354	5.0 0.4 5.0 0.4

Chart Datum: 2·91 metres below Ordnance Datum (Newlyn)
HAT is 5·7 metres above Chart Datum

TIDES

223

TIDES

TIME ZONE (UT)
For Summer Time add ONE hour in **non-shaded areas**

FALMOUTH
LAT 50°09'N   LONG 5°03'W
TIMES AND HEIGHTS OF HIGH AND LOW WATERS

Dates in amber are **SPRINGS**
Dates in grey are **NEAPS**

2022

MAY

Day	Time	m	Time	m	Time	m	Time	m
1 SU	0525	5.0	1213	0.4	1742	5.0		
2 M	0028	0.5	0601	5.0	1243	0.6	1816	5.0
3 TU	0058	0.6	0635	4.9	1311	0.7	1849	4.9
4 W	0126	0.8	0706	4.7	1334	1.0	1920	4.8
5 TH	0149	1.0	0735	4.6	1355	1.2	1949	4.7
6 F	0212	1.3	0807	4.4	1420	1.4	2022	4.5
7 SA	0241	1.5	0847	4.1	1453	1.7	2107	4.2
8 SU	0324	1.7	0941	3.9	1544	1.9	2206	4.1
9 M ◐	0438	1.9	1049	3.8	1713	2.1	2315	4.0
10 TU	0607	1.9	1203	3.8	1839	2.0		
11 W	0026	4.1	0722	1.7	1317	4.0	1948	1.7
12 TH	0136	4.3	0824	1.3	1418	4.3	2047	1.3
13 F	0233	4.6	0918	1.0	1506	4.6	2140	1.0
14 SA	0322	4.9	1008	0.7	1550	4.8	2230	0.7
15 SU	0409	5.0	1055	0.5	1634	5.0	2317	0.5
16 M ○	0456	5.1	1141	0.4	1719	5.1		
17 TU	0002	0.3	0545	5.2	1224	0.3	1805	5.2
18 W	0046	0.3	0635	5.1	1306	0.4	1851	5.2
19 TH	0129	0.4	0720	4.9	1349	0.6	1936	5.1
20 F	0213	0.6	0808	4.7	1433	0.9	2024	4.9
21 SA	0302	0.9	0901	4.4	1525	1.2	2121	4.6
22 SU ◐	0401	1.2	1008	4.2	1627	1.4	2232	4.4
23 M	0511	1.4	1129	4.0	1740	1.6	2353	4.3
24 TU	0630	1.4	1246	4.0	1859	1.5		
25 W	0105	4.3	0746	1.3	1349	4.2	2012	1.3
26 TH	0205	4.5	0848	1.1	1440	4.4	2110	1.1
27 F	0255	4.6	0939	0.9	1523	4.6	2159	0.9
28 SA	0339	4.7	1023	0.8	1601	4.7	2243	0.8
29 SU	0420	4.8	1104	0.7	1638	4.8	2323	0.8
30 M ●	0458	4.8	1141	0.8	1715	4.9	2359	0.8
31 TU	0536	4.8	1215	0.8	1751	4.9		

JUNE

Day	Time	m	Time	m	Time	m	Time	m
1 W	0032	0.9	0612	4.7	1245	1.0	1827	4.9
2 TH	0103	1.0	0646	4.6	1312	1.1	1859	4.8
3 F	0131	1.1	0718	4.5	1339	1.2	1931	4.7
4 SA	0159	1.3	0752	4.4	1408	1.4	2005	4.6
5 SU	0232	1.4	0830	4.2	1444	1.6	2046	4.4
6 M	0315	1.5	0917	4.1	1532	1.7	2136	4.3
7 TU	0411	1.7	1015	4.0	1635	1.8	2236	4.3
8 W	0520	1.7	1118	4.0	1747	1.8	2339	4.3
9 TH	0629	1.6	1221	4.1	1856	1.6		
10 F	0042	4.4	0734	1.4	1323	4.3	2000	1.4
11 SA	0145	4.6	0835	1.1	1421	4.6	2101	1.1
12 SU	0245	4.8	0932	0.9	1516	4.8	2158	0.9
13 M	0341	4.9	1027	0.7	1608	5.0	2253	0.6
14 TU ○	0436	5.0	1120	0.6	1700	5.0	2346	0.5
15 W	0531	5.1	1211	0.5	1752	5.2		
16 TH	0037	0.4	0625	5.0	1300	0.5	1844	5.2
17 F	0127	0.4	0717	4.9	1347	0.6	1933	5.2
18 SA	0215	0.5	0807	4.8	1435	0.7	2022	5.0
19 SU	0305	0.7	0859	4.6	1524	0.9	2114	4.9
20 M	0356	0.9	0954	4.4	1616	1.1	2211	4.6
21 TU ◐	0451	1.1	1056	4.2	1721	1.3	2314	4.4
22 W	0548	1.3	1201	4.1	1811	1.4		
23 TH	0020	4.3	0650	1.4	1304	4.1	1915	1.5
24 F	0123	4.3	0754	1.4	1400	4.2	2019	1.4
25 SA	0220	4.3	0853	1.3	1450	4.4	2117	1.3
26 SU	0310	4.4	0944	1.2	1533	4.5	2207	1.2
27 M	0355	4.5	1030	1.1	1614	4.7	2252	1.1
28 TU	0437	4.6	1111	1.1	1654	4.8	2334	1.1
29 W ●	0517	4.6	1149	1.1	1732	4.8		
30 TH	0011	1.0	0555	4.6	1224	1.1	1810	4.9

JULY

Day	Time	m	Time	m	Time	m	Time	m
1 F	0046	1.1	0632	4.6	1256	1.1	1844	4.8
2 SA	0117	1.1	0706	4.6	1327	1.2	1916	4.8
3 SU	0148	1.1	0739	4.5	1358	1.2	1948	4.7
4 M	0222	1.2	0813	4.4	1433	1.3	2024	4.7
5 TU	0300	1.3	0851	4.3	1514	1.4	2105	4.6
6 W	0344	1.4	0936	4.3	1601	1.5	2155	4.5
7 TH ◐	0437	1.4	1031	4.2	1659	1.6	2255	4.5
8 F	0539	1.5	1133	4.2	1806	1.6	2359	4.4
9 SA	0646	1.5	1240	4.3	1916	1.5		
10 SU	0108	4.5	0756	1.3	1348	4.5	2027	1.3
11 M	0219	4.6	0903	1.2	1454	4.7	2135	1.1
12 TU	0325	4.7	1007	1.0	1553	4.9	2239	0.8
13 W ○	0425	4.9	1108	0.9	1649	5.1	2339	0.6
14 TH	0522	5.0	1204	0.6	1743	5.3		
15 F	0033	0.4	0617	5.0	1255	0.5	1835	5.4
16 SA	0123	0.3	0709	5.0	1343	0.4	1923	5.4
17 SU	0210	0.3	0756	5.0	1427	0.5	2009	5.3
18 M	0253	0.4	0840	4.8	1509	0.7	2052	5.1
19 TU	0336	0.7	0922	4.6	1551	0.9	2136	4.8
20 W ◐	0418	1.0	1006	4.4	1635	1.2	2221	4.5
21 TH	0504	1.3	1055	4.2	1725	1.5	2314	4.3
22 F	0555	1.5	1155	4.1	1822	1.7		
23 SA	0021	4.1	0655	1.7	1309	4.0	1927	1.8
24 SU	0141	4.0	0801	1.7	1417	4.2	2035	1.7
25 M	0245	4.1	0904	1.6	1511	4.4	2136	1.6
26 TU	0336	4.3	0959	1.4	1556	4.6	2228	1.4
27 W	0420	4.4	1047	1.3	1637	4.8	2313	1.2
28 TH ●	0501	4.6	1129	1.2	1716	4.9	2354	1.1
29 F	0540	4.7	1207	1.1	1753	4.9		
30 SA	0029	1.0	0618	4.7	1240	1.0	1828	5.0
31 SU	0102	1.0	0652	4.7	1312	1.0	1859	5.0

AUGUST

Day	Time	m	Time	m	Time	m	Time	m
1 M	0133	0.9	0723	4.7	1343	1.0	1929	4.9
2 TU	0205	0.9	0752	4.7	1416	1.1	1959	4.9
3 W	0239	1.0	0820	4.6	1451	1.1	2032	4.8
4 TH	0316	1.1	0853	4.5	1530	1.3	2112	4.7
5 F ◐	0359	1.3	0940	4.4	1619	1.5	2208	4.5
6 SA	0454	1.5	1047	4.3	1723	1.6	2322	4.3
7 SU	0604	1.6	1207	4.2	1841	1.7		
8 M	0045	4.3	0726	1.6	1330	4.3	2008	1.6
9 TU	0209	4.4	0848	1.4	1445	4.6	2127	1.3
10 W	0320	4.6	1000	1.2	1546	4.9	2235	0.9
11 TH	0420	4.8	1103	0.8	1641	5.2	2334	0.6
12 F ○	0514	5.0	1157	0.5	1731	5.4		
13 SA	0025	0.3	0605	5.1	1245	0.3	1820	5.5
14 SU	0111	0.1	0651	5.2	1329	0.3	1904	5.5
15 M	0153	0.1	0732	5.1	1408	0.3	1945	5.4
16 TU	0230	0.3	0808	5.0	1444	0.5	2021	5.2
17 W	0305	0.6	0842	4.8	1518	0.9	2055	4.9
18 TH	0339	1.0	0917	4.6	1554	1.3	2130	4.6
19 F ◐	0415	1.4	0956	4.3	1637	1.6	2212	4.2
20 SA	0500	1.8	1047	4.1	1732	2.0	2309	3.9
21 SU	0601	2.0	1158	3.9	1843	2.1		
22 M	0045	3.8	0715	2.1	1346	4.0	2000	2.0
23 TU	0226	3.9	0831	1.9	1451	4.3	2112	1.8
24 W	0320	4.2	0934	1.7	1538	4.6	2207	1.3
25 TH	0403	4.4	1025	1.4	1619	4.8	2253	1.2
26 F	0443	4.7	1108	1.2	1657	5.0	2332	1.0
27 SA ●	0520	4.8	1146	1.0	1732	5.1		
28 SU	0007	0.9	0557	4.9	1220	0.9	1806	5.1
29 M	0040	0.9	0630	4.9	1252	0.8	1837	5.1
30 TU	0111	0.8	0701	4.9	1323	0.8	1906	5.1
31 W	0142	0.7	0727	4.9	1354	0.8	1934	5.0

Chart Datum: 2·91 metres below Ordnance Datum (Newlyn)
HAT is 5·7 metres above Chart Datum

FALMOUTH

LAT 50°09′N   LONG 5°03′W

TIMES AND HEIGHTS OF HIGH AND LOW WATERS

Dates in amber are **SPRINGS**
Dates in grey are **NEAPS**

2022

SEPTEMBER

Day	Time m	Time m	Time m	Time m		Day	Time m	Time m	Time m	Time m
1 TH	0215 0.8	0750 4.8	1427 1.0	2002 4.9		**16** F	0257 1.1	0836 4.7	1512 1.3	2048 4.5
2 F	0248 1.0	0818 4.7	1503 1.2	2037 4.7		**17** SA	0323 1.5	0911 4.4	1543 1.7	2127 4.2 ☽
3 SA	0327 1.3	0902 4.5	1548 1.4	2132 4.4 ☽		**18** SU	0356 1.9	1008 4.3	1632 2.1	2222 3.9
4 SU	0418 1.6	1015 4.3	1651 1.7	2302 4.1		**19** M	0459 2.3	1103 3.9	1800 2.3	2343 3.7
5 M	0532 1.9	1151 4.2	1822 1.9			**20** TU	0633 2.4	1257 3.9	1928 2.2	
6 TU	0041 4.0	0713 1.9	1325 4.3	2009 1.7		**21** W	0203 3.8	0758 2.2	1425 4.2	2045 1.9
7 W	0212 4.2	0850 1.6	1441 4.6	2130 1.3		**22** TH	0258 4.2	0907 1.8	1514 4.5	2140 1.5
8 TH	0321 4.5	0958 1.2	1539 5.0	2230 0.8		**23** F	0340 4.5	0957 1.4	1553 4.8	2224 1.2
9 F	0414 4.9	1054 0.8	1629 5.3	2322 0.4		**24** SA	0418 4.7	1039 1.1	1629 5.0	2303 0.9
10 SA	0501 5.1	1143 0.4	1715 5.5 ○			**25** SU	0453 4.9	1118 0.9	1703 5.2	2339 0.7 ●
11 SU	0008 0.2	0545 5.2	1227 0.2	1758 5.5		**26** M	0527 5.0	1154 0.7	1736 5.2	
12 M	0050 0.1	0625 5.3	1306 0.2	1838 5.5		**27** TU	0013 0.6	0601 5.1	1228 0.6	1810 5.3
13 TU	0127 0.2	0701 5.2	1341 0.4	1915 5.4		**28** W	0046 0.6	0633 5.1	1301 0.6	1843 5.2
14 W	0200 0.4	0733 5.1	1413 0.7	1947 5.2		**29** TH	0119 0.6	0702 5.1	1333 0.7	1913 5.1
15 TH	0229 0.7	0804 5.0	1442 0.9	2017 4.9		**30** F	0152 0.8	0728 5.0	1407 0.8	1943 4.9

OCTOBER

Day	Time m	Time m	Time m	Time m		Day	Time m	Time m	Time m	Time m
1 SA	0225 1.0	0800 4.8	1443 1.1	2022 4.6		**16** SU	0239 1.6	0836 4.5	1457 1.7	2055 4.2
2 SU	0304 1.3	0849 4.5	1529 1.5	2126 4.3		**17** M	0305 1.9	0921 4.3	1534 2.1	2150 3.9 ☽
3 M	0357 1.7	1008 4.3	1637 1.8	2304 4.0 ☽		**18** TU	0353 2.3	1023 4.0	1708 2.3	2305 3.7
4 TU	0519 2.0	1147 4.1	1825 1.9			**19** W	0546 2.4	1144 3.9	1846 2.2	
5 W	0047 4.0	0717 2.0	1320 4.3	2014 1.6		**20** TH	0118 3.8	0716 2.2	1337 4.1	2003 1.9
6 TH	0213 4.2	0846 1.6	1432 4.6	2122 1.1		**21** F	0223 4.1	0825 1.9	1435 4.4	2100 1.5
7 F	0313 4.6	0946 1.1	1526 5.0	2214 0.7		**22** SA	0307 4.4	0918 1.5	1517 4.7	2145 1.2
8 SA	0359 4.9	1036 0.7	1611 5.3	2301 0.4		**23** SU	0343 4.7	1003 1.2	1553 5.0	2227 0.9
9 SU	0440 5.1	1125 0.3	1652 5.4	2344 0.2 ○		**24** M	0418 4.9	1045 0.9	1628 5.1	2306 0.7
10 M	0518 5.2	1202 0.3	1732 5.4			**25** TU	0453 5.1	1125 0.7	1705 5.2	2345 0.5 ●
11 TU	0022 0.2	0554 5.3	1239 0.3	1810 5.4		**26** W	0529 5.2	1203 0.6	1743 5.3	
12 W	0057 0.4	0628 5.2	1312 0.5	1844 5.2		**27** TH	0022 0.5	0606 5.2	1240 0.5	1823 5.2
13 TH	0127 0.6	0700 5.2	1342 0.7	1915 5.0		**28** F	0058 0.6	0642 5.2	1316 0.6	1901 5.1
14 F	0154 0.9	0731 5.0	1409 1.0	1944 4.8		**29** SA	0134 0.7	0719 5.1	1353 0.8	1942 4.8
15 SA	0218 1.2	0802 4.8	1434 1.4	2015 4.5		**30** SU	0211 1.0	0801 4.9	1435 1.1	2030 4.5
						31 M	0255 1.4	0856 4.6	1526 1.4	2138 4.2

NOVEMBER

Day	Time m	Time m	Time m	Time m		Day	Time m	Time m	Time m	Time m
1 TU	0354 1.7	1009 4.3	1641 1.7	2307 4.0 ☽		**16** W	0328 2.1	0950 4.2	1618 2.1	2231 3.8 ☽
2 W	0519 1.9	1138 4.2	1823 1.8			**17** TH	0449 2.2	1057 4.1	1748 2.1	2349 3.8
3 TH	0041 4.0	0702 1.8	1303 4.4	1954 1.5		**18** F	0618 2.2	1211 4.1	1904 1.9	
4 F	0156 4.3	0822 1.5	1410 4.6	2057 1.1		**19** SA	0111 4.0	0730 1.9	1323 4.3	2008 1.6
5 SA	0252 4.6	0920 1.1	1503 4.9	2148 0.7		**20** SU	0211 4.3	0830 1.6	1420 4.6	2101 1.3
6 SU	0335 4.8	1009 0.8	1547 5.1	2233 0.5		**21** M	0256 4.6	0922 1.3	1508 4.8	2148 1.0
7 M	0414 5.0	1053 0.6	1627 5.2	2315 0.5		**22** TU	0337 4.8	1010 1.0	1552 5.0	2234 0.7
8 TU	0449 5.1	1133 0.5	1705 5.2	2353 0.5 ○		**23** W	0418 5.0	1056 0.7	1636 5.1	2318 0.6 ●
9 W	0524 5.2	1210 0.5	1742 5.1			**24** TH	0501 5.1	1140 0.6	1722 5.2	
10 TH	0026 0.6	0559 5.2	1243 0.7	1817 5.0		**25** F	0000 0.5	0545 5.2	1223 0.5	1809 5.1
11 F	0057 0.8	0632 5.1	1314 0.8	1849 4.9		**26** SA	0043 0.6	0630 5.2	1306 0.6	1856 5.0
12 SA	0124 1.0	0705 5.0	1343 1.1	1920 4.7		**27** SU	0125 0.7	0716 5.2	1350 0.7	1944 4.8
13 SU	0149 1.3	0737 4.8	1408 1.4	1953 4.5		**28** M	0208 0.9	0804 5.0	1438 0.9	2036 4.5
14 M	0213 1.5	0812 4.6	1435 1.6	2033 4.2		**29** TU	0257 1.2	0857 4.8	1533 1.2	2138 4.3
15 TU	0243 1.8	0855 4.4	1512 1.9	2125 4.0		**30** W	0356 1.5	1001 4.6	1639 1.4	2253 4.1 ☽

DECEMBER

Day	Time m	Time m	Time m	Time m		Day	Time m	Time m	Time m	Time m
1 TH	0505 1.6	1114 4.4	1754 1.5			**16** F	0403 1.9	1013 4.3	1646 1.8	2255 4.0 ☽
2 F	0011 4.1	0622 1.6	1228 4.4	1911 1.4		**17** SA	0511 1.9	1114 4.2	1757 1.8	2359 4.0
3 SA	0120 4.2	0737 1.5	1335 4.5	2018 1.2		**18** SU	0624 1.9	1218 4.3	1907 1.6	
4 SU	0218 4.4	0842 1.3	1431 4.6	2113 1.0		**19** M	0102 4.2	0735 1.7	1321 4.4	2012 1.4
5 M	0305 4.6	0935 1.1	1519 4.7	2201 0.9		**20** TU	0203 4.4	0838 1.4	1423 4.6	2110 1.2
6 TU	0345 4.7	1022 0.9	1601 4.8	2244 0.8		**21** W	0258 4.6	0936 1.1	1520 4.8	2204 0.9
7 W	0423 4.9	1104 0.8	1641 4.8	2323 0.8		**22** TH	0350 4.9	1031 0.9	1614 4.9	2256 0.7
8 TH	0459 5.0	1144 0.8	1719 4.8	2359 0.8		**23** F	0441 5.1	1123 0.6	1707 5.0	2346 0.6 ●
9 F	0536 5.0	1220 0.9	1756 4.8			**24** SA	0531 5.2	1214 0.5	1759 5.0	
10 SA	0032 0.9	0612 5.0	1253 1.0	1831 4.7		**25** SU	0035 0.5	0621 5.3	1303 0.4	1851 5.0
11 SU	0103 1.1	0647 4.9	1324 1.1	1905 4.6		**26** M	0123 0.6	0710 5.3	1351 0.5	1940 5.0
12 M	0131 1.2	0721 4.8	1353 1.2	1939 4.5		**27** TU	0209 0.6	0758 5.2	1439 0.6	2030 4.7
13 TU	0159 1.4	0755 4.7	1422 1.4	2016 4.3		**28** W	0256 0.8	0847 5.1	1527 0.8	2121 4.5
14 W	0231 1.5	0833 4.6	1458 1.6	2100 4.2		**29** TH	0344 1.0	0939 4.8	1619 1.0	2216 4.3
15 TH	0311 1.7	0918 4.4	1545 1.7	2153 4.0		**30** F	0437 1.2	1035 4.6	1714 1.2	2318 4.2 ☽
						31 SA	0534 1.4	1137 4.4	1814 1.4	

Chart Datum: 2·91 metres below Ordnance Datum (Newlyn)
HAT is 5·7 metres above Chart Datum

TIDES

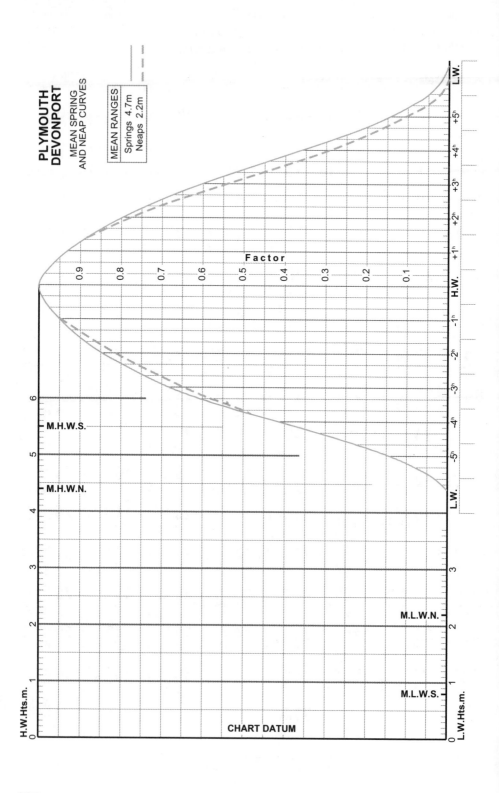

PLYMOUTH (DEVONPORT)
LAT 50°22'N   LONG 4°11'W
TIMES AND HEIGHTS OF HIGH AND LOW WATERS

Dates in amber are **SPRINGS**
Dates in grey are **NEAPS**

2022

JANUARY

#	Time	m	#	Time	m
1 SA	0403 / 1025 / 1630 / 2253	5.2 / 1.3 / 5.2 / 1.1	**16** SU	0435 / 1056 / 1659 / 2311	5.0 / 1.6 / 4.9 / 1.5
2 SU ●	0459 / 1121 / 1727 / 2346	5.4 / 1.0 / 5.4 / 1.0	**17** M	0517 / 1137 / 1741 / 2350	5.2 / 1.5 / 5.0 / 1.4
3 M	0551 / 1214 / 1820	5.6 / 0.8 / 5.4	**18** TU	0557 / 1215 / 1820	5.3 / 1.3 / 5.0
4 TU	0035 / 0642 / 1303 / 1912	0.9 / 5.7 / 0.7 / 5.4	**19** W	0026 / 0635 / 1250 / 1859	1.3 / 5.3 / 1.3 / 5.1
5 W	0123 / 0731 / 1350 / 2001	0.8 / 5.7 / 0.7 / 5.3	**20** TH	0101 / 0712 / 1324 / 1936	1.3 / 5.3 / 1.2 / 5.0
6 TH	0208 / 0818 / 1435 / 2048	0.9 / 5.6 / 0.8 / 5.2	**21** F	0135 / 0746 / 1358 / 2010	1.3 / 5.3 / 1.2 / 5.0
7 F	0251 / 0903 / 1519 / 2132	1.1 / 5.4 / 1.1 / 5.0	**22** SA	0208 / 0820 / 1432 / 2043	1.3 / 5.2 / 1.3 / 4.9
8 SA	0333 / 0945 / 1601 / 2214	1.4 / 5.2 / 1.3 / 4.8	**23** SU	0242 / 0855 / 1507 / 2118	1.4 / 5.2 / 1.4 / 4.8
9 SU ☽	0414 / 1028 / 1644 / 2257	1.6 / 5.0 / 1.6 / 4.6	**24** M	0319 / 0934 / 1546 / 2200	1.5 / 5.1 / 1.5 / 4.7
10 M	0459 / 1113 / 1732 / 2347	1.9 / 4.7 / 1.9 / 4.4	**25** TU ☽	0403 / 1020 / 1633 / 2251	1.7 / 4.9 / 1.7 / 4.6
11 TU	0552 / 1209 / 1828	2.1 / 4.5 / 2.1	**26** W	0457 / 1117 / 1734 / 2356	1.9 / 4.7 / 1.9 / 4.5
12 W	0048 / 0658 / 1315 / 1934	4.4 / 2.3 / 4.4 / 2.2	**27** TH	0609 / 1229 / 1855	2.0 / 4.6 / 2.0
13 TH	0154 / 0810 / 1423 / 2041	4.4 / 2.2 / 4.5 / 2.0	**28** F	0115 / 0740 / 1353 / 2025	4.5 / 2.0 / 4.6 / 1.9
14 F	0255 / 0916 / 1522 / 2139	4.6 / 2.1 / 4.6 / 1.8	**29** SA	0237 / 0905 / 1514 / 2141	4.7 / 1.8 / 4.7 / 1.7
15 SA	0348 / 1010 / 1613 / 2228	4.8 / 1.8 / 4.7 / 1.7	**30** SU	0347 / 1015 / 1622 / 2244	5.0 / 1.4 / 5.0 / 1.3
			31 M	0448 / 1115 / 1720 / 2339	5.3 / 1.1 / 5.2 / 1.0

FEBRUARY

#	Time	m	#	Time	m
1 TU ●	0541 / 1207 / 1813	5.5 / 0.7 / 5.3	**16** W ○	0539 / 1159 / 1805	5.2 / 1.2 / 5.0
2 W	0028 / 0631 / 1255 / 1902	0.8 / 5.7 / 0.5 / 5.4	**17** TH	0012 / 0619 / 1236 / 1844	1.1 / 5.3 / 1.0 / 5.1
3 TH	0113 / 0718 / 1338 / 1947	0.6 / 5.7 / 0.5 / 5.4	**18** F	0048 / 0657 / 1311 / 1921	1.0 / 5.4 / 0.9 / 5.2
4 F	0154 / 0801 / 1419 / 2027	0.6 / 5.7 / 0.6 / 5.3	**19** SA	0122 / 0732 / 1345 / 1954	0.9 / 5.4 / 0.9 / 5.2
5 SA	0232 / 0839 / 1456 / 2101	0.8 / 5.5 / 0.8 / 5.1	**20** SU	0155 / 0806 / 1417 / 2026	0.9 / 5.4 / 0.9 / 5.1
6 SU	0307 / 0913 / 1529 / 2130	1.0 / 5.3 / 1.1 / 4.9	**21** M	0228 / 0840 / 1449 / 2058	1.0 / 5.3 / 1.0 / 5.0
7 M	0340 / 0942 / 1602 / 2158	1.3 / 5.0 / 1.4 / 4.7	**22** TU	0302 / 0915 / 1524 / 2134	1.1 / 5.1 / 1.2 / 4.9
8 TU ☽	0413 / 1014 / 1637 / 2234	1.7 / 4.7 / 1.8 / 4.5	**23** W ☽	0340 / 0956 / 1605 / 2218	1.4 / 4.9 / 1.5 / 4.7
9 W	0452 / 1054 / 1721 / 2323	2.0 / 4.5 / 2.1 / 4.3	**24** TH	0428 / 1049 / 1658 / 2322	1.7 / 4.6 / 1.9 / 4.5
10 TH	0549 / 1152 / 1824	2.3 / 4.2 / 2.4	**25** F	0535 / 1205 / 1818	2.0 / 4.4 / 2.2
11 F	0035 / 0704 / 1323 / 1939	4.2 / 2.4 / 4.1 / 2.4	**26** SA	0051 / 0717 / 1343 / 2010	4.4 / 2.2 / 4.3 / 2.2
12 SA	0209 / 0826 / 1451 / 2056	4.3 / 2.3 / 4.2 / 2.2	**27** SU	0225 / 0901 / 1511 / 2137	4.5 / 1.9 / 4.5 / 1.8
13 SU	0319 / 0940 / 1552 / 2200	4.5 / 2.0 / 4.5 / 1.9	**28** M	0340 / 1012 / 1620 / 2239	4.8 / 1.4 / 4.8 / 1.3
14 M	0412 / 1035 / 1640 / 2250	4.8 / 1.7 / 4.7 / 1.6			
15 TU	0457 / 1119 / 1724 / 2333	5.0 / 1.4 / 4.9 / 1.4			

MARCH

#	Time	m	#	Time	m
1 TU	0439 / 1108 / 1714 / 2330	5.2 / 0.9 / 5.1 / 0.9	**16** W	0431 / 1052 / 1659 / 2308	5.0 / 1.3 / 4.9 / 1.3
2 W ●	0530 / 1156 / 1802	5.5 / 0.6 / 5.3	**17** TH	0513 / 1134 / 1740 / 2349	5.2 / 1.0 / 5.1 / 1.0
3 TH	0014 / 0616 / 1239 / 1845	0.6 / 5.6 / 0.3 / 5.4	**18** F ○	0554 / 1213 / 1820	5.3 / 0.8 / 5.2
4 F	0056 / 0658 / 1318 / 1923	0.4 / 5.7 / 0.3 / 5.4	**19** SA	0027 / 0634 / 1249 / 1857	0.8 / 5.4 / 0.6 / 5.3
5 SA	0133 / 0736 / 1354 / 1956	0.4 / 5.6 / 0.4 / 5.3	**20** SU	0103 / 0711 / 1324 / 1932	0.7 / 5.5 / 0.6 / 5.3
6 SU	0207 / 0808 / 1427 / 2023	0.6 / 5.5 / 0.6 / 5.2	**21** M	0137 / 0747 / 1358 / 2005	0.6 / 5.5 / 0.7 / 5.3
7 M	0237 / 0835 / 1455 / 2047	0.8 / 5.3 / 1.0 / 5.1	**22** TU	0211 / 0823 / 1430 / 2038	0.7 / 5.4 / 0.9 / 5.2
8 TU	0303 / 0901 / 1520 / 2113	1.2 / 5.0 / 1.4 / 4.9	**23** W	0245 / 0859 / 1505 / 2114	0.9 / 5.1 / 1.2 / 5.0
9 W	0329 / 0930 / 1545 / 2145	1.5 / 4.7 / 1.7 / 4.6	**24** TH	0324 / 0941 / 1546 / 2158	1.3 / 4.8 / 1.6 / 4.7
10 TH ☽	0356 / 1005 / 1615 / 2227	1.9 / 4.4 / 2.1 / 4.4	**25** F ☽	0412 / 1035 / 1640 / 2302	1.7 / 4.5 / 2.0 / 4.4
11 F	0441 / 1057 / 1717 / 2329	2.3 / 4.1 / 2.4 / 4.2	**26** SA	0523 / 1159 / 1805	2.1 / 4.2 / 2.3
12 SA	0611 / 1218 / 1851	2.5 / 3.9 / 2.6	**27** SU	0041 / 0715 / 1346 / 2009	4.3 / 2.2 / 4.2 / 2.2
13 SU	0110 / 0741 / 1421 / 2014	4.1 / 2.4 / 4.0 / 2.4	**28** M	0219 / 0858 / 1509 / 2128	4.5 / 1.8 / 4.5 / 1.8
14 M	0247 / 0904 / 1527 / 2128	4.3 / 2.1 / 4.3 / 2.0	**29** TU	0330 / 1001 / 1610 / 2224	4.9 / 1.3 / 4.8 / 1.3
15 TU	0344 / 1006 / 1616 / 2223	4.7 / 1.7 / 4.6 / 1.6	**30** W	0424 / 1051 / 1658 / 2311	5.2 / 0.8 / 5.1 / 0.8
			31 TH	0510 / 1135 / 1740 / 2353	5.4 / 0.5 / 5.3 / 0.6

APRIL

#	Time	m	#	Time	m
1 F	0552 / 1215 / 1817	5.6 / 0.4 / 5.4	**16** SA	0523 / 1143 / 1749	5.3 / 0.7 / 5.3
2 SA	0031 / 0631 / 1252 / 1851	0.4 / 5.6 / 0.4 / 5.4	**17** SU	0000 / 0606 / 1222 / 1829	0.7 / 5.5 / 0.6 / 5.4
3 SU ○	0107 / 0704 / 1325 / 1920	0.5 / 5.5 / 0.5 / 5.4	**18** M	0039 / 0647 / 1301 / 1907	0.6 / 5.5 / 0.5 / 5.5
4 M	0138 / 0734 / 1354 / 1945	0.6 / 5.4 / 0.7 / 5.3	**19** TU	0118 / 0727 / 1338 / 1944	0.5 / 5.5 / 0.6 / 5.4
5 TU	0205 / 0800 / 1419 / 2010	0.9 / 5.2 / 1.1 / 5.1	**20** W	0155 / 0807 / 1415 / 2022	0.7 / 5.3 / 0.9 / 5.3
6 W	0229 / 0826 / 1441 / 2037	1.2 / 5.0 / 1.4 / 5.0	**21** TH	0234 / 0849 / 1453 / 2102	0.9 / 5.1 / 1.2 / 5.1
7 TH	0250 / 0856 / 1500 / 2109	1.5 / 4.7 / 1.7 / 4.7	**22** F	0317 / 0935 / 1539 / 2150	1.3 / 4.8 / 1.6 / 4.8
8 F	0312 / 0931 / 1524 / 2149	1.9 / 4.4 / 2.1 / 4.5	**23** SA	0411 / 1036 / 1638 / 2258	1.7 / 4.4 / 2.0 / 4.5
9 SA ☽	0348 / 1021 / 1611 / 2246	2.2 / 4.1 / 2.4 / 4.2	**24** SU	0525 / 1206 / 1805	2.0 / 4.2 / 2.0
10 SU	0523 / 1134 / 1808	2.5 / 3.9 / 2.6	**25** M	0036 / 0710 / 1338 / 1951	4.4 / 2.0 / 4.3 / 2.1
11 M	0006 / 0701 / 1336 / 1934	4.1 / 2.4 / 4.0 / 2.4	**26** TU	0202 / 0836 / 1450 / 2103	4.6 / 1.7 / 4.6 / 1.7
12 TU	0200 / 0819 / 1451 / 2046	4.3 / 2.1 / 4.3 / 2.1	**27** W	0306 / 0934 / 1544 / 2156	4.9 / 1.3 / 4.8 / 1.3
13 W	0306 / 0923 / 1542 / 2144	4.6 / 1.7 / 4.6 / 1.6	**28** TH	0358 / 1023 / 1629 / 2243	5.1 / 0.9 / 5.1 / 1.0
14 TH	0355 / 1014 / 1626 / 2234	4.9 / 1.3 / 4.9 / 1.2	**29** F	0442 / 1106 / 1709 / 2325	5.3 / 0.7 / 5.2 / 0.8
15 F	0440 / 1100 / 1708 / 2318	5.2 / 0.9 / 5.1 / 0.9	**30** SA ●	0522 / 1146 / 1744	5.4 / 0.6 / 5.3

Chart Datum: 3·22 metres below Ordnance Datum (Newlyn)
HAT is 5·9 metres above Chart Datum

TIDES

TIME ZONE (UT)	PLYMOUTH (DEVONPORT)	Dates in amber are SPRINGS
For Summer Time add ONE hour in non-shaded areas	LAT 50°22'N LONG 4°11'W	Dates in grey are NEAPS

PLYMOUTH (DEVONPORT)
LAT 50°22'N   LONG 4°11'W
TIMES AND HEIGHTS OF HIGH AND LOW WATERS

2022

MAY

Day	DoW	Time	m	Time	m	Time	m	Time	m
1	SU	0002	0.7	0600	5.4	1221	0.6	1817	5.3
2	M	0037	0.7	0632	5.3	1254	0.8	1845	5.3
3	TU	0108	0.9	0702	5.2	1322	1.0	1913	5.3
4	W	0135	1.1	0731	5.1	1347	1.2	1941	5.2
5	TH	0200	1.3	0800	4.9	1410	1.5	2011	5.0
6	F	0223	1.6	0832	4.7	1432	1.7	2043	4.8
7	SA	0249	1.8	0910	4.4	1501	2.0	2123	4.6
8	SU	0328	2.1	0958	4.2	1549	2.3	2216	4.4
9	M	0443	2.3	1103	4.1	1722	2.4	◑ 2323	4.3
10	TU	0617	2.3	1230	4.1	1849	2.3		
11	W	0047	4.4	0732	2.0	1357	4.3	2000	2.0
12	TH	0210	4.6	0836	1.7	1455	4.6	2101	1.7
13	F	0309	4.9	0932	1.3	1545	4.9	2155	1.3
14	SA	0401	5.1	1023	1.0	1631	5.1	2245	1.0
15	SU	0450	5.3	1111	0.8	1717	5.3	2332	0.7
16	M	0537	5.4	1156	0.6	1801	5.5	○	
17	TU	0017	0.6	0625	5.5	1239	0.6	1845	5.5
18	W	0100	0.6	0711	5.4	1322	0.7	1928	5.5
19	TH	0144	0.7	0757	5.3	1405	0.9	2012	5.4
20	F	0229	0.9	0845	5.1	1450	1.2	2058	5.2
21	SA	0318	1.2	0938	4.8	1540	1.5	2150	5.0
22	SU	0414	1.5	1041	4.5	1639	1.8	◑ 2257	4.7
23	M	0521	1.7	1157	4.4	1751	2.0		
24	TU	0017	4.6	0640	1.8	1310	4.4	1912	2.0
25	W	0130	4.7	0755	1.7	1412	4.6	2022	1.8
26	TH	0230	4.8	0856	1.4	1505	4.8	2119	1.5
27	F	0322	4.9	0947	1.2	1551	4.9	2208	1.3
28	SA	0409	5.0	1032	1.1	1633	5.1	2252	1.1
29	SU	0450	5.1	1113	1.0	1710	5.2	2333	1.1
30	M	0529	5.1	1151	1.0	1744	5.2		
31	TU	0008	1.1	0604	5.1	1224	1.1	1817	5.2

JUNE

Day	DoW	Time	m	Time	m	Time	m	Time	m
1	W	0041	1.1	0638	5.0	1254	1.2	1849	5.2
2	TH	0111	1.3	0711	5.0	1323	1.4	1921	5.1
3	F	0140	1.4	0744	4.8	1350	1.5	1953	5.0
4	SA	0208	1.6	0819	4.7	1419	1.7	2027	4.9
5	SU	0240	1.7	0857	4.5	1453	1.9	2105	4.8
6	M	0320	1.9	0941	4.4	1538	2.0	2152	4.6
7	TU	0414	2.0	1035	4.3	1640	2.2	◑ 2248	4.5
8	W	0525	2.0	1139	4.3	1756	2.2	2353	4.5
9	TH	0639	1.9	1250	4.4	1909	2.0		
10	F	0105	4.6	0748	1.7	1358	4.6	2016	1.8
11	SA	0217	4.8	0850	1.5	1459	4.8	2117	1.5
12	SU	0321	5.0	0948	1.2	1555	5.1	2214	1.2
13	M	0419	5.2	1042	1.0	1647	5.3	2308	0.9
14	TU	0514	5.3	1134	0.8	1738	5.4	○ 2359	0.7
15	W	0607	5.4	1224	0.8	1827	5.5		
16	TH	0049	0.7	0659	5.3	1312	0.8	1917	5.6
17	F	0138	0.7	0751	5.3	1400	0.9	2006	5.5
18	SA	0226	0.8	0843	5.1	1447	1.1	2055	5.4
19	SU	0316	1.0	0936	4.9	1536	1.3	2146	5.2
20	M	0406	1.2	1030	4.8	1626	1.5	2241	5.0
21	TU	0459	1.4	1127	4.6	1720	1.7	◑ 2341	4.8
22	W	0557	1.6	1226	4.5	1821	1.9		
23	TH	0044	4.6	0701	1.7	1324	4.5	1928	1.9
24	F	0145	4.6	0805	1.7	1419	4.6	2032	1.8
25	SA	0241	4.6	0904	1.7	1510	4.7	2130	1.7
26	SU	0333	4.7	0955	1.6	1557	4.8	2220	1.5
27	M	0420	4.8	1041	1.4	1639	5.0	2304	1.4
28	TU	0503	4.9	1122	1.4	1719	5.1	2345	1.3
29	W	0542	4.9	1200	1.3	1756	5.2	●	
30	TH	0021	1.3	0621	4.9	1234	1.3	1833	5.2

JULY

Day	DoW	Time	m	Time	m	Time	m	Time	m
1	F	0055	1.3	0658	4.9	1307	1.4	1908	5.2
2	SA	0127	1.4	0735	4.8	1338	1.5	1942	5.1
3	SU	0158	1.4	0811	4.8	1410	1.5	2016	5.0
4	M	0231	1.5	0847	4.6	1444	1.6	2051	4.9
5	TU	0307	1.6	0924	4.6	1521	1.7	2130	4.9
6	W	0348	1.6	1007	4.5	1606	1.8	2216	4.8
7	TH	0438	1.7	1058	4.5	1702	1.9	◑ 2311	4.7
8	F	0541	1.8	1159	4.5	1813	2.0		
9	SA	0017	4.6	0656	1.8	1308	4.5	1932	1.9
10	SU	0133	4.7	0811	1.7	1420	4.7	2045	1.7
11	M	0250	4.8	0919	1.5	1527	4.9	2151	1.4
12	TU	0358	5.0	1022	1.3	1627	5.2	2252	1.1
13	W	0459	5.1	1120	1.0	1722	5.4	○ 2349	0.8
14	TH	0556	5.3	1214	0.8	1815	5.6		
15	F	0041	0.6	0651	5.3	1304	0.7	1907	5.6
16	SA	0131	0.5	0743	5.3	1352	0.7	1956	5.6
17	SU	0218	0.5	0833	5.3	1437	0.8	2043	5.5
18	M	0302	0.7	0919	5.1	1519	1.0	2127	5.4
19	TU	0344	0.9	1002	5.0	1600	1.2	2209	5.1
20	W	0426	1.3	1043	4.7	1642	1.5	◑ 2251	4.8
21	TH	0510	1.6	1128	4.5	1729	1.8	2338	4.6
22	F	0600	1.9	1221	4.4	1826	2.1		
23	SA	0042	4.4	0701	2.1	1325	4.4	1935	2.2
24	SU	0155	4.3	0810	2.1	1429	4.4	2047	2.1
25	M	0301	4.4	0917	2.0	1526	4.6	2150	1.9
26	TU	0356	4.5	1013	1.8	1615	4.8	2242	1.7
27	W	0443	4.7	1100	1.6	1658	5.0	2326	1.5
28	TH	0526	4.8	1141	1.4	1739	5.1	●	
29	F	0005	1.3	0606	4.9	1218	1.3	1818	5.2
30	SA	0041	1.2	0646	5.0	1253	1.3	1855	5.2
31	SU	0114	1.2	0723	5.0	1325	1.3	1930	5.2

AUGUST

Day	DoW	Time	m	Time	m	Time	m	Time	m
1	M	0145	1.2	0758	4.9	1356	1.3	2003	5.2
2	TU	0215	1.2	0831	4.9	1427	1.3	2035	5.1
3	W	0247	1.3	0902	4.8	1500	1.4	2108	5.0
4	TH	0321	1.4	0938	4.7	1537	1.6	2147	4.9
5	F	0402	1.6	1021	4.6	1623	1.8	2236	4.7
6	SA	0453	1.8	1119	4.5	1726	2.0	2342	4.6
7	SU	0606	2.0	1232	4.5	1853	2.1		
8	M	0105	4.5	0740	2.0	1355	4.6	2024	1.9
9	TU	0235	4.6	0904	1.8	1512	4.8	2141	1.6
10	W	0350	4.8	1013	1.4	1616	5.2	2245	1.2
11	TH	0452	5.1	1113	1.1	1712	5.4	2341	0.8
12	F	0548	5.3	1205	0.8	1804	5.6	○	
13	SA	0031	0.5	0639	5.4	1252	0.6	1853	5.7
14	SU	0117	0.3	0727	5.4	1336	0.5	1939	5.7
15	M	0159	0.4	0810	5.4	1416	0.6	2020	5.6
16	TU	0238	0.5	0848	5.3	1453	0.8	2056	5.4
17	W	0314	0.8	0921	5.1	1527	1.1	2127	5.2
18	TH	0347	1.2	0950	4.9	1601	1.5	2155	4.8
19	F	0421	1.7	1021	4.6	1639	1.9	◑ 2229	4.5
20	SA	0502	2.1	1103	4.4	1730	2.3	2319	4.2
21	SU	0601	2.3	1210	4.2	1841	2.5		
22	M	0051	4.1	0717	2.4	1348	4.3	2006	2.4
23	TU	0235	4.2	0841	2.3	1501	4.5	2128	2.1
24	W	0336	4.4	0950	2.0	1554	4.8	2223	1.8
25	TH	0424	4.7	1040	1.7	1638	5.0	2307	1.5
26	F	0506	4.9	1122	1.4	1719	5.2	2345	1.2
27	SA	0547	5.0	1159	1.2	1758	5.3	●	
28	SU	0020	1.1	0626	5.1	1233	1.1	1836	5.3
29	M	0053	1.0	0703	5.1	1306	1.0	1911	5.4
30	TU	0124	1.0	0737	5.2	1336	1.0	1944	5.3
31	W	0154	1.0	0808	5.2	1406	1.1	2015	5.3

Chart Datum: 3·22 metres below Ordnance Datum (Newlyn)
HAT is 5·9 metres above Chart Datum

PLYMOUTH (DEVONPORT)

LAT 50°22'N   LONG 4°11'W

TIMES AND HEIGHTS OF HIGH AND LOW WATERS

Dates in amber are SPRINGS
Dates in grey are NEAPS

2022

SEPTEMBER

Day	Time	m	Time	m	Time	m	Time	m
1 TH	0224	1.1	0838	5.0	1437	1.2	2047	5.1
2 F	0255	1.3	0910	4.9	1512	1.4	2124	4.9
3 SA ◑	0332	1.6	0951	4.7	1555	1.7	2211	4.7
4 SU	0420	1.9	1049	4.5	1655	2.1	2320	4.4
5 M	0533	2.2	1209	4.4	1833	2.3		
6 TU	0056	4.3	0728	2.3	1346	4.5	2022	2.1
7 W	0237	4.5	0903	1.9	1507	4.8	2140	1.6
8 TH	0351	4.8	1009	1.5	1609	5.2	2238	1.1
9 F	0447	5.1	1102	1.0	1701	5.5	2329	0.7
10 SA ○	0535	5.4	1150	0.7	1748	5.7		
11 SU	0013	0.4	0620	5.5	1233	0.5	1832	5.8
12 M	0055	0.3	0701	5.6	1313	0.4	1912	5.8
13 TU	0133	0.4	0738	5.5	1349	0.5	1948	5.6
14 W	0208	0.6	0809	5.4	1421	0.8	2018	5.4
15 TH	0238	0.9	0835	5.2	1451	1.2	2043	5.1
16 F	0306	1.4	0900	5.0	1519	1.6	2110	4.8
17 SA ◑	0332	1.8	0930	4.7	1548	2.0	2143	4.5
18 SU	0402	2.2	1010	4.5	1632	2.4	2230	4.2
19 M	0500	2.6	1109	4.2	1756	2.7	2345	4.0
20 TU	0633	2.7	1256	4.2	1928	2.6		
21 W	0210	4.1	0805	2.5	1433	4.4	2100	2.3
22 TH	0313	4.4	0921	2.1	1528	4.7	2155	1.8
23 F	0400	4.7	1011	1.7	1612	5.0	2237	1.5
24 SA	0441	5.0	1052	1.4	1653	5.2	2315	1.2
25 SU ●	0521	5.1	1131	1.2	1732	5.4	2351	1.0
26 M	0559	5.3	1207	1.0	1810	5.5		
27 TU	0026	0.9	0636	5.3	1241	0.9	1847	5.5
28 W	0059	0.8	0710	5.3	1313	0.9	1921	5.5
29 TH	0130	0.9	0742	5.3	1345	1.0	1955	5.4
30 F	0202	1.2	0815	5.1	1418	1.2	2030	5.2

OCTOBER

Day	Time	m	Time	m	Time	m	Time	m
1 SA	0234	1.3	0850	5.1	1454	1.4	2109	4.9
2 SU	0312	1.7	0933	4.8	1539	1.8	2200	4.6
3 M ◑	0402	2.1	1032	4.6	1645	2.2	2313	4.3
4 TU	0523	2.4	1159	4.4	1835	2.4		
5 W	0103	4.2	0732	2.4	1343	4.6	2022	2.0
6 TH	0240	4.5	0857	1.9	1500	4.9	2129	1.5
7 F	0343	4.9	0954	1.4	1556	5.3	2221	1.0
8 SA	0432	5.2	1043	1.0	1643	5.6	2307	0.7
9 SU ○	0514	5.5	1127	0.7	1726	5.7	2349	0.5
10 M	0554	5.6	1208	0.5	1806	5.8		
11 TU	0028	0.4	0630	5.6	1245	0.6	1842	5.7
12 W	0103	0.6	0702	5.5	1319	0.7	1914	5.5
13 TH	0135	0.8	0730	5.4	1349	1.0	1941	5.3
14 F	0202	1.2	0755	5.3	1416	1.3	2007	5.1
15 SA	0226	1.5	0822	5.1	1441	1.7	2036	4.8
16 SU	0247	1.9	0854	4.8	1504	2.1	2110	4.5
17 M ◑	0308	2.2	0934	4.6	1537	2.4	2158	4.2
18 TU	0347	2.6	1030	4.3	1710	2.7	2307	4.0
19 W	0550	2.8	1151	4.2	1846	2.6		
20 TH	0124	4.1	0721	2.6	1348	4.4	2009	2.3
21 F	0237	4.4	0834	2.3	1450	4.7	2109	1.9
22 SA	0326	4.7	0929	1.9	1537	5.0	2156	1.5
23 SU	0408	5.0	1015	1.5	1620	5.2	2238	1.2
24 M	0449	5.2	1057	1.2	1701	5.4	2318	1.0
25 TU	0528	5.4	1136	1.0	1742	5.5	2356	0.9
26 W	0606	5.5	1215	0.9	1821	5.5		
27 TH	0033	0.8	0644	5.5	1252	0.9	1900	5.5
28 F	0109	0.9	0720	5.5	1328	0.9	1939	5.4
29 SA	0145	1.1	0758	5.4	1406	1.2	2019	5.2
30 SU	0222	1.4	0838	5.2	1448	1.5	2104	4.9
31 M	0305	1.8	0926	5.0	1539	1.8	2200	4.6

NOVEMBER

Day	Time	m	Time	m	Time	m	Time	m
1 TU ◑	0402	2.1	1028	4.7	1650	2.1	2318	4.4
2 W	0526	2.4	1156	4.6	1831	2.2		
3 TH	0100	4.4	0716	2.3	1328	4.7	2001	1.9
4 F	0221	4.6	0832	1.9	1437	5.0	2104	1.5
5 SA	0319	4.9	0928	1.5	1531	5.3	2154	1.2
6 SU	0405	5.2	1016	1.2	1617	5.4	2239	0.9
7 M	0446	5.4	1059	0.9	1659	5.5	2320	0.8
8 TU ○	0524	5.5	1140	0.8	1738	5.6	2358	0.8
9 W	0558	5.5	1217	0.9	1813	5.5		
10 TH	0033	0.9	0629	5.5	1250	1.0	1844	5.4
11 F	0103	1.1	0658	5.4	1321	1.2	1913	5.2
12 SA	0131	1.4	0726	5.3	1348	1.5	1942	5.0
13 SU	0156	1.6	0756	5.2	1415	1.7	2014	4.8
14 M	0219	1.9	0830	5.0	1441	2.0	2051	4.6
15 TU	0245	2.2	0910	4.7	1517	2.3	2137	4.3
16 W ◑	0327	2.5	1001	4.5	1623	2.5	2239	4.2
17 TH	0453	2.7	1106	4.4	1754	2.5		
18 F	0002	4.2	0626	2.6	1229	4.4	1911	2.3
19 SA	0135	4.3	0739	2.4	1350	4.6	2015	2.0
20 SU	0237	4.6	0840	2.0	1449	4.9	2109	1.7
21 M	0326	4.9	0933	1.7	1540	5.1	2158	1.4
22 TU	0411	5.1	1021	1.3	1627	5.3	2244	1.1
23 W ●	0455	5.4	1107	1.1	1713	5.4	2329	1.0
24 TH	0538	5.5	1151	0.9	1759	5.5		
25 F	0011	0.9	0621	5.6	1235	0.9	1844	5.5
26 SA	0053	1.0	0704	5.6	1318	0.9	1930	5.4
27 SU	0136	1.1	0748	5.5	1403	1.1	2016	5.2
28 M	0220	1.3	0835	5.4	1451	1.3	2107	5.0
29 TU	0309	1.6	0926	5.2	1545	1.6	2204	4.7
30 W ◑	0406	1.9	1027	5.0	1648	1.8	2314	4.6

DECEMBER

Day	Time	m	Time	m	Time	m	Time	m
1 TH	0515	2.1	1139	4.8	1802	1.9		
2 F	0030	4.5	0635	2.1	1254	4.8	1919	1.9
3 SA	0140	4.6	0750	2.0	1400	4.9	2025	1.7
4 SU	0239	4.8	0851	1.7	1456	5.0	2120	1.5
5 M	0329	5.0	0944	1.5	1546	5.1	2208	1.3
6 TU	0414	5.2	1030	1.3	1631	5.2	2251	1.2
7 W	0454	5.3	1113	1.2	1712	5.2	2331	1.2
8 TH ○	0531	5.4	1152	1.2	1749	5.2		
9 F	0006	1.2	0605	5.4	1228	1.3	1823	5.2
10 SA	0039	1.3	0637	5.4	1301	1.4	1856	5.1
11 SU	0109	1.5	0709	5.3	1331	1.5	1929	5.0
12 M	0138	1.6	0742	5.2	1401	1.7	2004	4.8
13 TU	0207	1.8	0817	5.1	1432	1.8	2040	4.7
14 W	0238	2.0	0855	4.9	1507	2.0	2121	4.5
15 TH	0316	2.1	0937	4.7	1551	2.1	2210	4.4
16 F ◑	0406	2.3	1028	4.6	1650	2.2	2308	4.3
17 SA	0515	2.4	1127	4.6	1803	2.2		
18 SU	0014	4.4	0634	2.3	1235	4.6	1916	2.1
19 M	0126	4.5	0746	2.1	1346	4.7	2021	1.9
20 TU	0233	4.7	0850	1.9	1454	4.9	2120	1.6
21 W	0331	5.0	0948	1.5	1554	5.1	2215	1.3
22 TH	0425	5.2	1043	1.3	1650	5.2	2307	1.1
23 F ●	0516	5.4	1135	1.0	1742	5.4	2357	1.0
24 SA	0605	5.6	1225	0.9	1833	5.4		
25 SU	0046	0.9	0654	5.7	1314	0.8	1925	5.4
26 M	0134	1.0	0743	5.7	1403	0.8	2015	5.3
27 TU	0221	1.1	0833	5.6	1451	1.0	2105	5.2
28 W	0308	1.2	0923	5.4	1539	1.2	2156	5.0
29 TH	0356	1.5	1014	5.2	1629	1.4	2249	4.8
30 F ◑	0447	1.7	1108	5.0	1722	1.7	2346	4.6
31 SA	0544	1.9	1208	4.8	1822	1.7		

Chart Datum: 3·22 metres below Ordnance Datum (Newlyn)
HAT is 5·9 metres above Chart Datum

TIDES

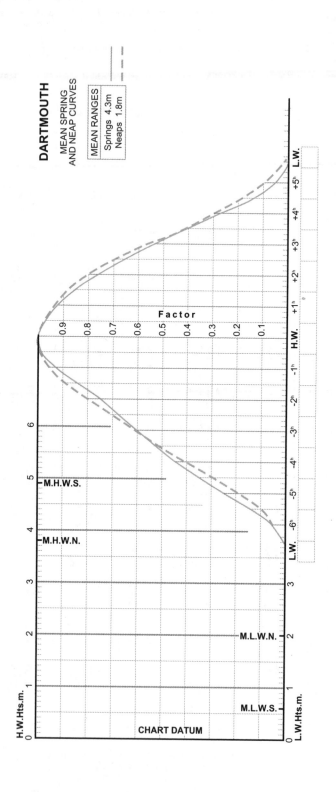

DARTMOUTH
MEAN SPRING
AND NEAP CURVES

MEAN RANGES
Springs 4.3m
Neaps 1.8m

DARTMOUTH

LAT 50°21'N LONG 3°35'W

TIMES AND HEIGHTS OF HIGH AND LOW WATERS

TIME ZONE (UT) — For Summer Time add ONE hour in **non-shaded areas**

Dates in amber are **SPRINGS**
Dates in grey are **NEAPS**

2022

JANUARY

Day	Time m	Day	Time m
1 SA	0424 4.6 / 1023 1.1 / 1652 4.6 / 2251 0.9	**16** SU	0457 4.4 / 1054 1.4 / 1721 4.2 / 2309 1.3
2 SU	0521 4.8 / 1119 0.8 / 1750 4.8 / ● 2345 0.8	**17** M	0540 4.6 / 1136 1.3 / 1805 4.4 / ○ 2349 1.2
3 M	0615 5.0 / 1213 0.6 / 1844 4.8	**18** TU	0621 4.7 / 1214 1.1 / 1844 4.4
4 TU	0034 0.7 / 0705 5.1 / 1302 0.5 / 1935 4.8	**19** W	0025 1.1 / 0659 4.7 / 1249 1.1 / 1922 4.5
5 W	0122 0.6 / 0753 5.1 / 1349 0.5 / 2023 4.7	**20** TH	0100 1.1 / 0735 4.7 / 1323 1.0 / 1958 4.4
6 TH	0206 0.7 / 0839 5.0 / 1433 0.6 / 2108 4.6	**21** F	0134 1.1 / 0808 4.7 / 1357 1.0 / 2031 4.4
7 F	0249 0.9 / 0923 4.8 / 1516 0.9 / 2151 4.4	**22** SA	0206 1.1 / 0841 4.6 / 1430 1.1 / 2104 4.3
8 SA	0330 1.2 / 1004 4.6 / 1557 1.1 / 2232 4.2	**23** SU	0240 1.2 / 0915 4.6 / 1504 1.2 / 2138 4.2
9 SU	0410 1.4 / 1046 4.4 / 1641 1.5 / ◐ 2314 4.0	**24** M	0316 1.3 / 0953 4.5 / 1543 1.3 / 2219 4.1
10 M	0455 1.7 / 1130 4.1 / 1727 1.7	**25** TU	0359 1.5 / 1038 4.3 / 1629 1.5 / ◑ 2309 4.0
11 TU	0003 3.8 / 0547 1.9 / 1225 3.9 / 1823 1.9	**26** W	0453 1.7 / 1134 4.1 / 1729 1.7
12 W	0103 3.8 / 0653 2.1 / 1330 3.8 / 1930 2.0	**27** TH	0012 3.9 / 0604 1.8 / 1244 4.0 / 1850 1.8
13 TH	0210 3.8 / 0806 2.0 / 1440 3.9 / 2037 1.9	**28** F	0130 3.9 / 0736 1.8 / 1409 4.0 / 2021 1.7
14 F	0313 4.0 / 0913 1.9 / 1541 4.0 / 2136 1.7	**29** SA	0255 4.1 / 0902 1.6 / 1533 4.1 / 2138 1.5
15 SA	0408 4.2 / 1007 1.6 / 1634 4.1 / 2226 1.5	**30** SU	0407 4.4 / 1013 1.2 / 1643 4.4 / 2242 1.1
		31 M	0510 4.7 / 1113 0.9 / 1743 4.6 / 2338 0.8

FEBRUARY

Day	Time m	Day	Time m
1 TU	0605 4.9 / 1206 0.5 / 1837 4.7 ●	**16** W	0603 4.6 / 1158 1.0 / 1829 4.4 ○
2 W	0027 0.6 / 0655 5.1 / 1254 0.3 / 1925 4.8	**17** TH	0011 0.9 / 0643 4.7 / 1235 0.8 / 1907 4.5
3 TH	0112 0.4 / 0741 5.1 / 1337 0.3 / 2009 4.8	**18** F	0047 0.8 / 0720 4.8 / 1310 0.7 / 1944 4.6
4 F	0153 0.4 / 0823 5.1 / 1417 0.3 / 2048 4.7	**19** SA	0121 0.7 / 0754 4.8 / 1344 0.7 / 2016 4.6
5 SA	0230 0.6 / 0900 4.9 / 1454 0.4 / 2121 4.5	**20** SU	0154 0.7 / 0827 4.8 / 1415 0.7 / 2047 4.5
6 SU	0304 0.8 / 0933 4.7 / 1526 0.9 / 2149 4.3	**21** M	0226 0.8 / 0901 4.7 / 1447 0.8 / 2118 4.4
7 M	0337 1.1 / 1001 4.4 / 1558 1.2 / 2218 4.1	**22** TU	0259 0.9 / 0935 4.5 / 1521 1.0 / 2153 4.3
8 TU	0409 1.5 / 1032 4.1 / 1633 1.6 / ◑ 2252 3.9	**23** W	0337 1.2 / 1015 4.3 / 1601 1.3 / ◑ 2236 4.1
9 W	0448 1.8 / 1111 3.9 / 1716 1.9 / 2340 3.7	**24** TH	0424 1.5 / 1107 4.0 / 1654 1.7 / 2339 3.9
10 TH	0544 2.1 / 1208 3.6 / 1819 2.2	**25** F	0530 1.8 / 1221 3.8 / 1813 2.0
11 F	0050 3.6 / 0659 2.2 / 1338 3.5 / 1935 2.2	**26** SA	0106 3.8 / 0712 2.0 / 1359 3.7 / 2006 2.0
12 SA	0226 3.7 / 0822 2.1 / 1509 3.6 / 2053 2.0	**27** SU	0242 3.9 / 0858 1.7 / 1530 3.9 / 2134 1.6
13 SU	0338 3.9 / 0937 1.8 / 1612 3.9 / 2157 1.7	**28** M	0400 4.3 / 1010 1.2 / 1641 4.2 / 2237 1.1
14 M	0433 4.2 / 1033 1.5 / 1702 4.1 / 2248 1.4		
15 TU	0519 4.4 / 1117 1.2 / 1747 4.3 / 2331 1.2		

MARCH

Day	Time m	Day	Time m
1 TU	0501 4.6 / 1106 0.7 / 1737 4.5 / 2328 0.7	**16** W	0453 4.4 / 1050 1.1 / 1721 4.3 / 2306 1.1
2 W	0554 4.9 / 1155 0.4 / 1826 4.7 ●	**17** TH	0536 4.6 / 1132 0.8 / 1804 4.5 / 2348 0.8
3 TH	0013 0.4 / 0640 5.0 / 1238 0.1 / 1908 4.8	**18** F	0618 4.7 / 1212 0.6 / 1844 4.6 ○
4 F	0055 0.2 / 0721 5.1 / 1317 0.1 / 1946 4.8	**19** SA	0026 0.6 / 0658 4.8 / 1248 0.4 / 1920 4.7
5 SA	0132 0.2 / 0758 5.0 / 1353 0.2 / 2018 4.8	**20** SU	0102 0.5 / 0734 4.9 / 1323 0.4 / 1954 4.7
6 SU	0205 0.4 / 0829 4.9 / 1425 0.4 / 2044 4.6	**21** M	0136 0.4 / 0809 4.9 / 1357 0.5 / 2027 4.7
7 M	0235 0.6 / 0856 4.7 / 1453 0.8 / 2108 4.5	**22** TU	0209 0.5 / 0844 4.8 / 1428 0.7 / 2059 4.6
8 TU	0300 1.0 / 0921 4.4 / 1517 1.2 / 2133 4.3	**23** W	0243 0.7 / 0919 4.5 / 1502 1.0 / 2134 4.4
9 W	0326 1.3 / 0949 4.1 / 1542 1.5 / 2204 4.0	**24** TH	0321 1.1 / 1000 4.2 / 1543 1.4 / 2217 4.1
10 TH	0353 1.7 / 1024 3.8 / 1611 1.9 / ◑ 2245 3.8	**25** F	0408 1.5 / 1053 3.9 / 1636 1.8 / ◑ 2319 3.8
11 F	0437 2.1 / 1114 3.5 / 1712 2.2 / 2346 3.6	**26** SA	0518 1.9 / 1215 3.6 / 1800 2.1
12 SA	0606 2.3 / 1233 3.3 / 1846 2.4	**27** SU	0056 3.7 / 0710 2.0 / 1402 3.6 / 2005 2.0
13 SU	0125 3.5 / 0737 2.2 / 1438 3.4 / 2010 2.2	**28** M	0236 3.9 / 0855 1.6 / 1528 3.9 / 2125 1.6
14 M	0305 3.7 / 0901 1.9 / 1546 3.7 / 2125 1.8	**29** TU	0350 4.3 / 0958 1.1 / 1631 4.2 / 2222 1.1
15 TU	0404 4.1 / 1003 1.5 / 1637 4.0 / 2221 1.4	**30** W	0445 4.6 / 1049 0.6 / 1720 4.5 / 2309 0.6
		31 TH	0533 4.8 / 1134 0.3 / 1804 4.7 / 2352 0.4

APRIL

Day	Time m	Day	Time m
1 F	0616 5.0 / 1214 0.2 / 1841 4.8	**16** SA	0546 4.7 / 1142 0.5 / 1813 4.7 / ○ 2359 0.5
2 SA	0030 0.2 / 0655 5.0 / 1251 0.2 / 1914 4.8	**17** SU	0630 4.9 / 1221 0.4 / 1853 4.8
3 SU	0106 0.3 / 0727 4.9 / 1324 0.3 / 1943 4.8	**18** M	0038 0.4 / 0710 4.9 / 1300 0.3 / 1930 4.9
4 M	0137 0.4 / 0756 4.8 / 1353 0.5 / 2007 4.7	**19** TU	0117 0.3 / 0749 4.9 / 1337 0.4 / 2006 4.8
5 TU	0203 0.7 / 0822 4.6 / 1417 0.9 / 2031 4.5	**20** W	0154 0.5 / 0828 4.7 / 1413 0.7 / 2043 4.7
6 W	0227 1.0 / 0847 4.4 / 1439 1.2 / 2058 4.4	**21** TH	0232 0.7 / 0909 4.5 / 1451 1.0 / 2122 4.5
7 TH	0248 1.3 / 0916 4.1 / 1458 1.5 / 2129 4.1	**22** F	0314 1.1 / 0954 4.2 / 1536 1.4 / 2209 4.2
8 F	0309 1.7 / 0950 3.8 / 1521 1.9 / 2208 3.9	**23** SA	0407 1.5 / 1054 3.8 / 1634 1.8 / ◑ 2315 3.9
9 SA	0345 2.0 / 1039 3.5 / 1607 2.2 / ◑ 2304 3.6	**24** SU	0520 1.8 / 1222 3.6 / 1800 2.0
10 SU	0518 2.3 / 1151 3.3 / 1803 2.4	**25** M	0051 3.8 / 0705 1.8 / 1354 3.7 / 1947 1.9
11 M	0022 3.5 / 0656 2.2 / 1352 3.4 / 1930 2.2	**26** TU	0219 4.0 / 0832 1.5 / 1508 4.0 / 2100 1.5
12 TU	0217 3.7 / 0815 1.9 / 1509 3.7 / 2042 1.9	**27** W	0325 4.3 / 0931 1.1 / 1604 4.2 / 2153 1.1
13 W	0325 4.0 / 0920 1.5 / 1602 4.0 / 2141 1.4	**28** TH	0418 4.5 / 1021 0.7 / 1650 4.5 / 2241 0.8
14 TH	0415 4.3 / 1012 1.1 / 1647 4.3 / 2232 1.1	**29** F	0504 4.7 / 1104 0.5 / 1732 4.6 / 2323 0.6
15 F	0502 4.6 / 1058 0.7 / 1731 4.5 / 2316 0.7	**30** SA	0545 4.8 / 1145 0.4 / 1808 4.7 ●

Chart Datum: 2·62 metres below Ordnance Datum (Newlyn)
HAT is 5·3 metres above Chart Datum

TIDES

TIDES

TIME ZONE (UT)
For Summer Time add ONE hour in **non-shaded areas**

DARTMOUTH
LAT 50°21'N   LONG 3°35'W
TIMES AND HEIGHTS OF HIGH AND LOW WATERS

Dates in amber are **SPRINGS**
Dates in grey are **NEAPS**

2022

MAY

Day	Time m	Time m	Time m	Time m
1 SU	0001 0.5	0625 4.8	1220 0.4	1841 4.7
16 M	0601 4.8	1155 0.4	1825 4.9 ○	
2 M	0036 0.5	0656 4.7	1253 0.6	1908 4.7
17 TU	0016 0.4	0649 4.9	1238 0.4	1908 4.9
3 TU	0107 0.7	0725 4.6	1321 0.8	1936 4.7
18 W	0100 0.4	0734 4.8	1321 0.5	1950 4.9
4 W	0134 0.9	0753 4.5	1346 1.0	2003 4.6
19 TH	0143 0.5	0819 4.7	1403 0.7	2033 4.8
5 TH	0159 1.1	0822 4.3	1408 1.3	2032 4.4
20 F	0227 0.7	0906 4.5	1448 1.0	2118 4.6
6 F	0221 1.4	0853 4.1	1430 1.5	2104 4.2
21 SA	0315 1.0	0957 4.2	1537 1.3	2209 4.4
7 SA	0247 1.6	0930 3.8	1458 1.8	2143 4.0
22 SU	0410 1.3	1059 3.9	1635 1.6	2314 4.1 ◑
8 SU	0325 1.9	1017 3.6	1546 2.1	2234 3.8
23 M	0516 1.5	1213 3.8	1746 1.8	
9 M	0439 2.1	1120 3.5	1717 2.2	2340 3.7 ◑
24 TU	0033 4.0	0635 1.6	1325 3.8	1907 1.8
10 TU	0612 2.1	1245 3.5	1844 2.1	
25 W	0146 4.1	0751 1.5	1429 4.0	2018 1.6
11 W	0102 3.8	0728 1.8	1413 3.7	1956 1.8
26 TH	0248 4.2	0853 1.2	1524 4.2	2116 1.3
12 TH	0227 4.0	0832 1.5	1513 4.0	2058 1.5
27 F	0341 4.3	0944 1.0	1611 4.3	2205 1.1
13 F	0328 4.3	0929 1.1	1605 4.3	2152 1.1
28 SA	0430 4.4	1030 0.9	1655 4.5	2250 0.9
14 SA	0422 4.5	1021 0.8	1653 4.5	2243 0.8
29 SU	0512 4.5	1111 0.8	1733 4.6	2331 0.8
15 SU	0512 4.7	1109 0.6	1740 4.7	2330 0.5
30 M	0552 4.5	1150 0.8	1808 4.6 ●	
31 TU	0007 0.9	0628 4.5	1223 0.9	1841 4.6

JUNE

Day	Time m	Time m	Time m	Time m
1 W	0040 0.9	0702 4.4	1253 1.0	1912 4.6
16 TH	0048 0.5	0722 4.7	1311 0.5	1940 5.0
2 TH	0110 1.1	0734 4.4	1322 1.2	1944 4.5
17 F	0137 0.5	0813 4.7	1359 0.7	2027 4.9
3 F	0139 1.2	0806 4.2	1349 1.3	2015 4.4
18 SA	0224 0.6	0904 4.5	1445 0.9	2115 4.8
4 SA	0206 1.4	0840 4.1	1417 1.5	2048 4.3
19 SU	0313 0.8	0955 4.3	1533 1.1	2205 4.6
5 SU	0238 1.5	0917 3.9	1451 1.7	2125 4.2
20 M	0402 1.0	1048 4.2	1622 1.3	2259 4.4
6 M	0317 1.7	1000 3.8	1535 1.8	2211 4.0
21 TU	0455 1.2	1144 4.0	1715 1.5	2357 4.2 ◑
7 TU	0410 1.8	1053 3.7	1636 2.0	2306 3.9
22 W	0552 1.4	1241 3.9	1816 1.7	
8 W	0520 1.8	1155 3.7	1751 2.0	
23 TH	0059 4.0	0656 1.5	1339 3.9	1924 1.7
9 TH	0009 3.9	0634 1.7	1305 3.8	1904 1.8
24 F	0201 4.0	0801 1.5	1436 4.0	2028 1.6
10 F	0120 4.0	0744 1.5	1414 4.0	2012 1.6
25 SA	0259 4.0	0901 1.5	1529 4.1	2127 1.5
11 SA	0234 4.2	0847 1.3	1517 4.2	2114 1.3
26 SU	0353 4.1	0952 1.4	1617 4.2	2218 1.3
12 SU	0340 4.4	0945 1.0	1615 4.5	2212 1.0
27 M	0441 4.2	1039 1.2	1701 4.4	2302 1.2
13 M	0440 4.6	1040 0.8	1709 4.7	2306 0.7
28 TU	0526 4.3	1120 1.2	1742 4.5	2344 1.1
14 TU	0537 4.7	1132 0.6	1802 4.8	2358 0.5 ○
29 W	0606 4.3	1159 1.1	1820 4.6	
15 W	0631 4.8	1223 0.6	1851 4.9	
30 TH	0020 1.1	0645 4.3	1233 1.1	1857 4.6

JULY

Day	Time m	Time m	Time m	Time m
1 F	0054 1.1	0721 4.3	1306 1.2	1931 4.6
16 SA	0130 0.3	0805 4.7	1351 0.5	2018 5.0
2 SA	0126 1.2	0757 4.2	1337 1.3	2004 4.5
17 SU	0216 0.3	0854 4.7	1435 0.6	2104 4.9
3 SU	0157 1.2	0832 4.2	1408 1.3	2037 4.4
18 M	0259 0.5	0939 4.5	1516 0.8	2147 4.8
4 M	0229 1.3	0908 4.1	1442 1.4	2111 4.3
19 TU	0341 0.7	1021 4.4	1557 1.0	2228 4.5
5 TU	0304 1.4	0944 4.0	1518 1.5	2149 4.3
20 W	0422 1.1	1101 4.1	1638 1.3	2309 4.2 ◑
6 W	0345 1.4	1026 3.9	1602 1.6	2234 4.2
21 TH	0505 1.4	1145 3.9	1724 1.6	2354 4.0
7 TH	0434 1.5	1115 3.9	1657 1.7	2328 4.1 ◑
22 F	0555 1.7	1236 3.8	1821 1.9	
8 F	0536 1.6	1215 3.9	1808 1.8	
23 SA	0057 3.8	0656 1.9	1340 3.8	1931 2.0
9 SA	0033 4.0	0651 1.6	1323 3.9	1928 1.7
24 SU	0211 3.7	0806 1.9	1446 3.8	2043 1.9
10 SU	0149 4.1	0807 1.5	1437 4.1	2041 1.5
25 M	0320 3.8	0914 1.8	1545 4.0	2147 1.7
11 M	0308 4.2	0916 1.3	1546 4.3	2148 1.2
26 TU	0416 3.9	1011 1.6	1636 4.2	2240 1.5
12 TU	0418 4.4	1020 1.1	1648 4.6	2250 0.9
27 W	0505 4.1	1058 1.4	1720 4.4	2324 1.3
13 W	0521 4.5	1118 0.8	1745 4.8	2348 0.6 ○
28 TH	0549 4.2	1140 1.2	1803 4.5 ●	
14 TH	0620 4.7	1213 0.6	1839 5.0	
29 F	0004 1.1	0630 4.3	1217 1.1	1842 4.6
15 F	0040 0.4	0714 4.7	1303 0.5	1930 5.0
30 SA	0040 1.0	0709 4.4	1252 1.1	1918 4.6
31 SU	0113 1.0	0746 4.4	1324 1.1	1952 4.6

AUGUST

Day	Time m	Time m	Time m	Time m
1 M	0144 1.0	0820 4.3	1355 1.1	2025 4.6
16 TU	0236 0.3	0908 4.7	1451 0.6	2116 4.8
2 TU	0213 1.0	0852 4.3	1425 1.1	2056 4.5
17 W	0311 0.6	0941 4.5	1524 0.9	2147 4.6
3 W	0245 1.1	0922 4.2	1458 1.2	2128 4.4
18 TH	0344 1.0	1009 4.3	1557 1.3	2214 4.2
4 TH	0318 1.2	0957 4.1	1534 1.4	2206 4.3
19 F	0417 1.5	1039 4.0	1635 1.7	2247 3.9 ◑
5 F	0358 1.4	1039 4.0	1619 1.6	2254 4.1 ◑
20 SA	0457 1.9	1120 3.8	1725 2.1	2336 3.6
6 SA	0449 1.6	1136 3.9	1721 1.8	2358 4.0
21 SU	0556 2.1	1226 3.6	1836 2.3	
7 SU	0601 1.8	1247 3.9	1848 1.9	
22 M	0106 3.5	0712 2.2	1404 3.7	2002 2.2
8 M	0120 3.9	0736 1.8	1411 4.0	2020 1.7
23 TU	0253 3.6	0837 2.1	1520 3.9	2125 1.9
9 TU	0253 4.0	0901 1.6	1531 4.2	2138 1.4
24 W	0356 3.8	0947 1.8	1614 4.2	2221 1.6
10 W	0410 4.2	1011 1.2	1637 4.6	2243 1.0
25 TH	0445 4.1	1038 1.5	1700 4.4	2305 1.3
11 TH	0514 4.5	1111 0.9	1735 4.8	2340 0.6
26 F	0529 4.3	1120 1.2	1742 4.6	2344 1.0
12 F	0612 4.7	1204 0.6	1828 5.0 ○	
27 SA	0611 4.4	1158 1.0	1822 4.7 ●	
13 SA	0030 0.3	0703 4.8	1251 0.4	1916 5.1
28 SU	0019 0.9	0650 4.5	1232 0.9	1900 4.7
14 SU	0116 0.1	0749 4.8	1335 0.3	2001 5.1
29 M	0052 0.8	0726 4.5	1305 0.8	1934 4.8
15 M	0158 0.2	0831 4.8	1414 0.4	2041 5.0
30 TU	0123 0.8	0759 4.5	1335 0.8	2006 4.7
31 W	0153 0.8	0829 4.5	1404 0.9	2036 4.7

Chart Datum: 2·62 metres below Ordnance Datum (Newlyn)
HAT is 5·3 metres above Chart Datum

DARTMOUTH

LAT 50°21'N LONG 3°35'W

TIMES AND HEIGHTS OF HIGH AND LOW WATERS

Dates in amber are SPRINGS
Dates in grey are NEAPS

2022

SEPTEMBER

Day	Time m	Time m	Time m	Time m	Day	Time m	Time m	Time m	Time m
1 TH	0222 0.9	0859 4.4	1435 1.0	2108 4.5	16 F	0303 1.2	0920 4.4	1516 1.4	2130 4.2
2 F	0253 1.1	0930 4.3	1509 1.2	2144 4.3	17 SA	0329 1.6	0949 4.1	1545 1.8	2202 3.9
3 SA	0329 1.4	1010 4.1	1552 1.5	2230 4.1	18 SU	0358 2.0	1029 3.9	1628 2.2	2248 3.6
4 SU	0416 1.7	1107 3.9	1651 1.9	2337 3.8	19 M	0456 2.4	1126 3.6	1751 2.5	
5 M	0528 2.0	1225 3.8	1828 2.1		20 TU	0001 3.4	0628 2.5	1311 3.6	1924 2.4
6 TU	0111 3.7	0724 2.1	1402 3.9	2018 1.9	21 W	0227 3.5	0801 2.3	1451 3.8	2057 2.1
7 W	0255 3.9	0900 1.7	1526 4.2	2137 1.4	22 TH	0332 3.8	0918 1.9	1547 4.1	2152 1.6
8 TH	0411 4.2	1006 1.3	1630 4.6	2236 0.9	23 F	0421 4.1	1008 1.5	1633 4.4	2235 1.3
9 F	0509 4.5	1100 0.8	1724 4.9	2327 0.5	24 SA	0503 4.4	1050 1.2	1715 4.6	2313 1.0
10 SA	0559 4.8	1149 0.5	1812 5.1	○	25 SU	0544 4.5	1129 1.0	1756 4.8	● 2350 0.8
11 SU	0012 0.2	0644 4.8	1232 0.3	1856 5.2	26 M	0623 4.7	1206 0.8	1834 4.9	
12 M	0054 0.1	0724 5.0	1312 0.2	1935 5.2	27 TU	0025 0.7	0700 4.7	1240 0.7	1910 4.9
13 TU	0132 0.2	0800 4.9	1348 0.3	2010 5.0	28 W	0058 0.6	0733 4.7	1312 0.7	1944 4.9
14 W	0206 0.4	0830 4.8	1419 0.6	2039 4.8	29 TH	0129 0.7	0804 4.7	1344 0.8	2017 4.8
15 TH	0236 0.7	0856 4.6	1449 1.0	2104 4.5	30 F	0200 0.9	0836 4.6	1416 1.0	2051 4.6

OCTOBER

Day	Time m	Time m	Time m	Time m	Day	Time m	Time m	Time m	Time m
1 SA	0232 1.1	0910 4.5	1452 1.2	2129 4.3	16 SU	0245 1.7	0914 4.2	1501 1.9	2130 3.9
2 SU	0309 1.5	0952 4.2	1534 1.6	2219 4.0	17 M	0305 2.0	0953 4.0	1534 2.2	2217 3.6
3 M	0358 1.9	1050 4.0	1641 2.0	2330 3.7	18 TU	0344 2.4	1048 3.7	1705 2.5	2324 3.4
4 TU	0518 2.2	1215 3.8	1830 2.2		19 W	0545 2.6	1207 3.6	1841 2.4	
5 W	0118 3.6	0728 2.2	1359 4.0	2018 1.8	20 TH	0139 3.5	0716 2.4	1404 3.8	2005 2.1
6 TH	0258 3.9	0854 1.7	1519 4.3	2126 1.3	21 F	0255 3.8	0830 2.1	1508 4.1	2106 1.7
7 F	0403 4.3	0951 1.2	1616 4.7	2219 0.8	22 SA	0345 4.1	0926 1.7	1557 4.4	2153 1.3
8 SA	0454 4.6	1041 0.8	1705 5.0	2305 0.5	23 SU	0429 4.4	1013 1.3	1641 4.6	2236 1.0
9 SU	0537 4.9	1125 0.5	1754 5.1	○ 2348 0.3	24 M	0511 4.6	1055 1.0	1724 4.8	2316 0.8
10 M	0618 5.0	1207 0.3	1830 5.2		25 TU	0551 4.8	1135 0.8	1806 4.9	● 2355 0.7
11 TU	0027 0.2	0654 5.0	1244 0.4	1905 5.1	26 W	0630 4.9	1214 0.7	1845 4.9	
12 W	0102 0.4	0725 4.9	1318 0.5	1937 4.9	27 TH	0032 0.6	0707 4.9	1251 0.7	1923 4.9
13 TH	0134 0.6	0752 4.8	1348 0.8	2003 4.7	28 F	0108 0.7	0743 4.8	1327 0.7	2001 4.8
14 F	0200 1.0	0817 4.7	1414 1.1	2028 4.4	29 SA	0144 0.9	0820 4.8	1404 1.0	2040 4.6
15 SA	0224 1.3	0843 4.5	1439 1.5	2057 4.2	30 SU	0220 1.2	0859 4.6	1446 1.3	2124 4.3
					31 M	0302 1.6	0946 4.4	1536 1.6	2219 4.0

NOVEMBER

Day	Time m	Time m	Time m	Time m	Day	Time m	Time m	Time m	Time m
1 TU	0358 1.9	1046 4.1	1646 1.9	◑ 2335 3.8	16 W	0324 2.3	1020 3.9	1619 2.3	○ 2257 3.6
2 W	0521 2.2	1212 4.0	1826 2.0		17 TH	0449 2.5	1123 3.8	1749 2.3	
3 TH	0115 3.8	0711 2.1	1343 4.1	1957 1.7	18 F	0018 3.6	0621 2.4	1244 3.8	1906 2.1
4 F	0238 4.0	0828 1.7	1455 4.4	2101 1.3	19 SA	0151 3.7	0735 2.2	1406 4.0	2011 1.7
5 SA	0338 4.3	0925 1.3	1551 4.7	2151 1.0	20 SU	0255 4.0	0836 1.8	1507 4.3	2106 1.5
6 SU	0426 4.6	1014 1.0	1638 4.8	2237 0.7	21 M	0345 4.3	0930 1.5	1600 4.5	2155 1.2
7 M	0508 4.8	1057 0.7	1721 4.9	2318 0.6	22 TU	0432 4.5	1019 1.1	1648 4.7	2242 0.9
8 TU	0547 4.9	1139 0.6	1802 5.0	○ 2357 0.6	23 W	0517 4.8	1105 0.9	1736 4.8	● 2327 0.8
9 W	0622 4.9	1216 0.7	1837 4.9		24 TH	0602 4.9	1150 0.7	1823 4.9	
10 TH	0032 0.7	0653 4.9	1249 0.8	1907 4.8	25 F	0010 0.7	0645 5.0	1234 0.7	1907 4.9
11 F	0102 0.9	0717 4.8	1320 1.0	1936 4.6	26 SA	0052 0.8	0727 5.0	1317 0.7	1952 4.8
12 SA	0130 1.2	0748 4.7	1347 1.3	2004 4.4	27 SU	0135 0.9	0810 4.9	1401 0.9	2037 4.6
13 SU	0155 1.4	0818 4.6	1413 1.5	2035 4.2	28 M	0218 1.1	0856 4.8	1449 1.1	2127 4.4
14 M	0217 1.7	0851 4.4	1439 1.8	2111 4.0	29 TU	0306 1.2	0946 4.6	1542 1.4	2223 4.1
15 TU	0243 2.0	0930 4.1	1514 2.1	2156 3.7	30 W	0402 1.7	1045 4.4	1644 1.6	2331 4.0

DECEMBER

Day	Time m	Time m	Time m	Time m	Day	Time m	Time m	Time m	Time m
1 TH	0510 1.9	1155 4.2	1757 1.7		16 F	0402 2.1	1046 4.0	1646 2.0	○ 2325 3.7
2 F	0045 3.9	0630 1.9	1309 4.2	1914 1.7	17 SA	0510 2.2	1144 4.0	1758 2.0	
3 SA	0156 4.0	0746 1.8	1417 4.3	2021 1.5	18 SU	0030 3.8	0629 2.1	1250 4.0	1911 1.9
4 SU	0257 4.2	0848 1.5	1514 4.4	2117 1.3	19 M	0141 3.9	0742 1.9	1402 4.1	2017 1.7
5 M	0348 4.4	0941 1.1	1606 4.5	2205 1.1	20 TU	0251 4.1	0847 1.7	1512 4.3	2117 1.4
6 TU	0435 4.6	1028 1.1	1653 4.6	2249 1.0	21 W	0351 4.4	0945 1.3	1614 4.5	2213 1.1
7 W	0516 4.7	1111 1.0	1735 4.6	2329 1.0	22 TH	0446 4.6	1041 1.1	1712 4.6	2305 0.9
8 TH	0555 4.8	1151 1.0	1813 4.6	○	23 F	0539 4.8	1134 0.8	1806 4.8	● 2356 0.8
9 F	0005 1.0	0629 4.8	1227 1.1	1847 4.6	24 SA	0629 5.0	1224 0.7	1857 4.8	
10 SA	0038 1.1	0701 4.8	1300 1.2	1919 4.5	25 SU	0045 0.7	0717 5.1	1313 0.6	1947 4.8
11 SU	0108 1.3	0732 4.7	1330 1.3	1951 4.4	26 M	0133 0.8	0805 5.1	1401 0.6	2036 4.7
12 M	0137 1.4	0804 4.6	1359 1.5	2026 4.2	27 TU	0219 0.9	0854 5.0	1449 0.8	2125 4.6
13 TU	0205 1.6	0838 4.5	1430 1.6	2101 4.1	28 W	0305 1.0	0943 4.8	1536 1.0	2215 4.4
14 W	0236 1.8	0915 4.3	1504 1.8	2141 3.9	29 TH	0353 1.3	1032 4.6	1625 1.2	2307 4.2
15 TH	0313 1.9	0956 4.1	1548 1.9	◑ 2229 3.8	30 F	0443 1.5	1125 4.4	1717 1.5	○
					31 SA	0002 4.0	0539 1.7	1224 4.2	1817 1.7

Chart Datum: 2·62 metres below Ordnance Datum (Newlyn)
HAT is 5·3 metres above Chart Datum

TIDES

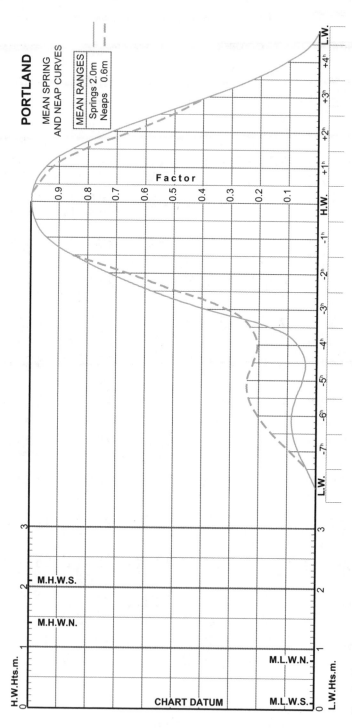

PORTLAND

MEAN SPRING AND NEAP CURVES

MEAN RANGES
Springs 2.0m
Neaps 0.6m

Factor

0.9 0.8 0.7 0.6 0.5 0.4 0.3 0.2 0.1

H.W.Hts.m.

M.H.W.S.

M.H.W.N.

CHART DATUM

L.W.Hts.m.

M.L.W.N.

M.L.W.S.

Note - Double LWs occur at Portland. The predictions are for the first LW. The second LW occurs from 3 to 4 Hrs later and may, at Springs, on occasions be lower than the first.

TIME ZONE (UT)
For Summer Time add ONE hour in **non-shaded areas**

PORTLAND

LAT 50°34'N   LONG 2°26'W

TIMES AND HEIGHTS OF HIGH AND LOW WATERS

Dates in amber are **SPRINGS**
Dates in grey are **NEAPS**

2022

JANUARY

Day				
1 SA	0501 2.0	1003 0.6	1724 1.9	2228 0.4
2 SU	0554 2.1	1100 0.5	1822 2.0	● 2321 0.4
3 M	0645 2.2	1152 0.4	1918 2.1	
4 TU	0008 0.3	0736 2.3	1239 0.3	2014 2.1
5 W	0052 0.3	0827 2.3	1324 0.3	2104 2.0
6 TH	0135 0.4	0916 2.3	1409 0.4	2146 2.0
7 F	0217 0.5	0958 2.1	1455 0.4	2223 1.8
8 SA	0258 0.6	1036 2.0	1541 0.4	2300 1.7
9 SU	0340 0.7	1114 1.8	1629 0.5	◐ 2339 1.5
10 M	0425 0.8	1157 1.6	1721 0.6	
11 TU	0029 1.4	0521 0.9	1253 1.4	1820 0.7
12 W	0143 1.4	0636 0.9	1411 1.4	1921 0.7
13 TH	0258 1.4	0745 0.9	1525 1.4	2018 0.7
14 F	0357 1.6	0844 0.8	1627 1.6	2110 0.6
15 SA	0447 1.7	0939 0.7	1719 1.6	2201 0.6
16 SU	0531 1.9	1032 0.6	1805 1.7	2250 0.5
17 M	0613 2.0	1121 0.5	1847 1.8	○ 2333 0.5
18 TU	0653 2.0	1204 0.5	1928 1.8	
19 W	0011 0.4	0732 2.1	1239 0.4	2006 1.8
20 TH	0045 0.4	0809 2.1	1311 0.4	2040 1.8
21 F	0120 0.4	0841 2.0	1345 0.3	2109 1.8
22 SA	0156 0.4	0911 1.9	1421 0.3	2137 1.7
23 SU	0232 0.4	0943 1.8	1459 0.4	2209 1.6
24 M	0310 0.4	1020 1.6	1540 0.3	2250 1.5
25 TU	0352 0.5	1106 1.6	1628 0.4	◐ 2342 1.5
26 W	0446 0.6	1204 1.5	1725 0.5	
27 TH	0057 1.4	0556 0.7	1325 1.4	1836 0.6
28 F	0226 1.5	0717 0.8	1453 1.4	1959 0.6
29 SA	0339 1.6	0857 0.7	1608 1.5	2123 0.6
30 SU	0444 1.8	1010 0.6	1718 1.7	2224 0.5
31 M	0543 2.0	1103 0.5	1821 1.9	2314 0.4

FEBRUARY

Day				
1 TU	0637 2.2	1149 0.3	1921 2.0	●
2 W	0000 0.3	0731 2.3	1231 0.2	2015 2.1
3 TH	0041 0.2	0822 2.3	1311 0.2	2055 2.1
4 F	0120 0.2	0905 2.3	1351 0.1	2128 2.0
5 SA	0158 0.2	0940 2.2	1429 0.2	2156 1.9
6 SU	0233 0.3	1009 2.0	1506 0.3	2221 1.8
7 M	0305 0.5	1035 1.8	1541 0.4	2247 1.6
8 TU	0331 0.6	1103 1.6	1611 0.6	◐ 2316 1.5
9 W	0356 0.7	1138 1.4	1635 0.7	2356 1.4
10 TH	0437 0.8	1225 1.3	1720 0.8	
11 F	0058 1.3	0555 0.9	1404 1.2	1946 0.8
12 SA	0255 1.3	0825 0.8	1557 1.3	2046 0.7
13 SU	0414 1.5	0922 0.7	1659 1.4	2140 0.6
14 M	0507 1.7	1016 0.6	1748 1.6	2231 0.5
15 TU	0553 1.8	1105 0.5	1834 1.7	2317 0.4
16 W	0638 2.0	1148 0.4	1918 1.8	○ 2357 0.3
17 TH	0720 2.1	1225 0.3	2000 1.9	
18 F	0033 0.2	0801 2.1	1257 0.2	2037 1.9
19 SA	0108 0.2	0834 2.1	1330 0.1	2103 1.9
20 SU	0142 0.2	0900 2.0	1404 0.1	2121 1.8
21 M	0217 0.2	0926 2.0	1439 0.2	2147 1.8
22 TU	0251 0.3	1000 1.8	1515 0.2	2221 1.7
23 W	0326 0.4	1041 1.7	1553 0.4	◐ 2305 1.5
24 TH	0408 0.5	1132 1.5	1643 0.5	
25 F	0006 1.4	0515 0.7	1257 1.3	1757 0.7
26 SA	0204 1.4	0734 0.8	1448 1.3	2015 0.8
27 SU	0327 1.5	1202 0.6	1606 1.4	2126 0.7
28 M	0435 1.7	1019 0.5	1715 1.6	2217 0.5

MARCH

Day				
1 TU	0535 1.9	1056 0.3	1816 1.8	2303 0.3
2 W	0628 2.1	1137 0.2	1908 2.0	● 2346 0.2
3 TH	0719 2.3	1216 0.1	1953 2.1	
4 F	0025 0.1	0805 2.3	1252 0.0	2031 2.2
5 SA	0101 0.1	0844 2.3	1327 0.0	2101 2.1
6 SU	0133 0.1	0913 2.2	1359 0.1	2124 2.0
7 M	0204 0.2	0936 2.0	1429 0.2	2143 1.8
8 TU	0230 0.3	0958 1.8	1453 0.4	2205 1.7
9 W	0252 0.5	1023 1.6	1512 0.5	2231 1.5
10 TH	0314 0.6	1053 1.4	1537 0.6	◐ 2302 1.4
11 F	0350 0.7	1132 1.2	1621 0.7	2346 1.3
12 SA	0454 0.8	1237 1.1	1731 0.8	
13 SU	0113 1.3	0809 0.8	1519 1.1	2024 0.8
14 M	0331 1.4	0902 0.7	1636 1.3	2117 0.6
15 TU	0436 1.6	0952 0.5	1726 1.5	2207 0.5
16 W	0528 1.8	1040 0.4	1812 1.7	2253 0.4
17 TH	0615 1.9	1123 0.3	1857 1.9	2335 0.3
18 F	0701 2.1	1200 0.2	1941 2.0	○
19 SA	0012 0.2	0743 2.2	1234 0.1	2020 2.1
20 SU	0048 0.1	0818 2.2	1308 0.0	2048 2.1
21 M	0122 0.1	0841 2.1	1341 0.1	2102 2.0
22 TU	0156 0.1	0907 2.0	1415 0.1	2126 1.9
23 W	0230 0.2	0942 1.9	1450 0.3	2200 1.8
24 TH	0305 0.3	1024 1.6	1527 0.4	2244 1.6
25 F	0348 0.5	1119 1.4	1614 0.6	◐ 2345 1.4
26 SA	0501 0.7	1307 1.2	1739 0.7	
27 SU	0156 1.3	1001 0.7	1449 1.1	2008 0.8
28 M	0319 1.5	0933 0.6	1601 1.4	2108 0.7
29 TU	0423 1.7	0953 0.4	1701 1.7	2157 0.5
30 W	0519 1.9	1033 0.3	1753 1.9	2243 0.3
31 TH	0609 2.1	1114 0.1	1839 2.0	2326 0.2

APRIL

Day				
1 F	0656 2.2	1153 0.0	1921 2.1	●
2 SA	0003 0.1	0739 2.3	1226 0.0	1959 2.2
3 SU	0035 0.1	0814 2.2	1257 0.0	2028 2.1
4 M	0105 0.1	0840 2.1	1326 0.1	2048 2.0
5 TU	0133 0.2	0901 1.9	1352 0.3	2108 1.9
6 W	0158 0.3	0924 1.7	1413 0.4	2131 1.7
7 TH	0219 0.4	0951 1.5	1431 0.5	2156 1.6
8 F	0242 0.5	1022 1.4	1456 0.6	2226 1.5
9 SA	0316 0.7	1104 1.2	1538 0.7	◐ 2311 1.4
10 SU	0431 0.8	1208 1.1	1659 0.8	
11 M	0027 1.3	0747 0.8	1426 1.1	1955 0.8
12 TU	0240 1.3	0837 0.6	1555 1.3	2047 0.7
13 W	0356 1.5	0924 0.5	1650 1.5	2136 0.5
14 TH	0454 1.7	1008 0.3	1739 1.7	2222 0.4
15 F	0544 1.9	1050 0.2	1826 1.9	2305 0.3
16 SA	0631 2.1	1129 0.1	1910 2.1	○ 2345 0.2
17 SU	0714 2.2	1206 0.1	1950 2.2	
18 M	0022 0.1	0749 2.2	1241 0.0	2023 2.2
19 TU	0059 0.1	0817 2.1	1317 0.1	2042 2.1
20 W	0135 0.1	0850 2.0	1353 0.2	2111 2.0
21 TH	0213 0.2	0931 1.9	1431 0.3	2151 1.8
22 F	0255 0.4	1021 1.6	1513 0.5	2241 1.7
23 SA	0350 0.6	1125 1.4	1611 0.7	◐ 2349 1.5
24 SU	0527 0.7	1314 1.3	1745 0.9	
25 M	0144 1.3	1015 0.6	1438 1.3	1926 0.8
26 TU	0300 1.5	0844 0.6	1541 1.5	2034 0.7
27 W	0400 1.7	0920 0.4	1634 1.7	2127 0.6
28 TH	0453 1.9	1002 0.3	1722 1.9	2215 0.4
29 F	0541 2.0	1044 0.2	1807 2.0	2258 0.3
30 SA	0627 2.1	1122 0.1	1848 2.1	● 2334 0.2

Chart Datum: 0·93 metres below Ordnance Datum (Newlyn)
HAT is 2·5 metres above Chart Datum

TIME ZONE (UT)
For Summer Time add ONE hour in **non-shaded areas**

PORTLAND

LAT 50°34'N   LONG 2°26'W

TIMES AND HEIGHTS OF HIGH AND LOW WATERS

Dates in amber are **SPRINGS**
Dates in grey are **NEAPS**

2022

MAY

Day	Time m	Time m	Time m	Time m
1 SU	0707 2.1	1155 0.1	1924 2.1	
2 M	0006 0.2	0741 2.1	1225 0.1	1952 2.1
3 TU	0037 0.2	0806 2.0	1254 0.2	2016 2.0
4 W	0106 0.3	0831 1.8	1321 0.3	2041 1.9
5 TH	0132 0.4	0859 1.7	1343 0.4	2107 1.8
6 F	0155 0.5	0929 1.5	1404 0.5	2134 1.6
7 SA	0222 0.5	1004 1.4	1432 0.6	2209 1.5
8 SU	0300 0.6	1050 1.3	1517 0.7	2258 1.4
9 M ◖	0406 0.7	1151 1.2	1638 0.8	
10 TU	0004 1.4	0534 0.7	1335 1.2	1806 0.8
11 W	0140 1.4	0805 0.6	1506 1.3	2004 0.7
12 TH	0307 1.5	0848 0.5	1606 1.6	2056 0.6
13 F	0408 1.7	0929 0.4	1659 1.7	2144 0.5
14 SA	0503 1.9	1011 0.3	1748 1.9	2229 0.4
15 SU	0552 2.0	1054 0.2	1834 2.1	2314 0.3
16 M ○	0637 2.1	1136 0.1	1915 2.2	2357 0.2
17 TU	0717 2.2	1217 0.1	1952 2.2	
18 W	0038 0.2	0758 2.1	1257 0.2	2028 2.2
19 TH	0120 0.2	0843 2.0	1338 0.3	2109 2.1
20 F	0205 0.3	0934 1.9	1422 0.4	2156 2.0
21 SA	0256 0.4	1029 1.7	1511 0.6	2247 1.8
22 SU	0359 0.6	1132 1.5	1612 0.7	2350 1.6
23 M	0511 0.6	1255 1.4	1721 0.8	
24 TU	0115 1.6	0626 0.6	1410 1.4	1832 0.8
25 W	0227 1.6	0738 0.6	1509 1.5	1942 0.8
26 TH	0326 1.6	0834 0.5	1600 1.7	2042 0.7
27 F	0419 1.7	0920 0.4	1648 1.8	2133 0.6
28 SA	0509 1.8	1002 0.3	1734 1.9	2219 0.5
29 SU	0555 1.9	1043 0.3	1815 2.0	2301 0.4
30 M ●	0636 1.9	1121 0.3	1851 2.0	2339 0.4
31 TU	0710 1.9	1156 0.3	1922 2.0	

JUNE

Day	Time m	Time m	Time m	Time m
1 W	0015 0.4	0740 1.8	1229 0.3	1952 2.0
2 TH	0047 0.4	0811 1.8	1259 0.4	2023 1.9
3 F	0117 0.4	0843 1.6	1326 0.5	2055 1.8
4 SA	0146 0.5	0917 1.5	1355 0.5	2126 1.7
5 SU	0218 0.5	0954 1.4	1429 0.6	2202 1.6
6 M	0300 0.5	1036 1.3	1516 0.6	2245 1.5
7 TU ◖	0355 0.6	1129 1.3	1619 0.7	2339 1.5
8 W	0500 0.6	1239 1.3	1729 0.7	
9 TH	0047 1.5	0611 0.6	1408 1.4	1841 0.7
10 F	0206 1.5	0727 0.5	1515 1.5	1955 0.6
11 SA	0314 1.6	0833 0.4	1611 1.7	2058 0.5
12 SU	0415 1.8	0928 0.3	1705 1.9	2154 0.5
13 M	0512 1.9	1021 0.3	1755 2.0	2248 0.4
14 TU ○	0606 2.0	1111 0.2	1843 2.2	2339 0.3
15 W	0658 2.0	1159 0.2	1931 2.2	
16 TH	0027 0.3	0752 2.0	1244 0.2	2021 2.3
17 F	0114 0.2	0836 1.9	1329 0.3	2111 2.2
18 SA	0202 0.3	0942 1.9	1415 0.4	2158 2.1
19 SU	0253 0.3	1030 1.8	1503 0.5	2244 2.0
20 M	0346 0.4	1118 1.6	1554 0.6	2331 1.8
21 TU ○	0440 0.5	1215 1.5	1648 0.7	
22 W	0027 1.7	0536 0.6	1321 1.4	1746 0.8
23 TH	0135 1.5	0636 0.6	1425 1.5	1850 0.8
24 F	0240 1.5	0735 0.6	1520 1.5	1952 0.8
25 SA	0339 1.5	0830 0.6	1612 1.6	2050 0.7
26 SU	0435 1.6	0919 0.5	1700 1.8	2143 0.6
27 M	0525 1.6	1008 0.5	1744 1.9	2234 0.6
28 TU	0609 1.7	1054 0.4	1823 2.0	2322 0.5
29 W ●	0649 1.8	1136 0.4	1900 2.0	
30 TH	0004 0.4	0726 1.8	1214 0.4	1937 2.0

JULY

Day	Time m	Time m	Time m	Time m
1 F	0041 0.4	0801 1.7	1248 0.4	2013 1.9
2 SA	0113 0.4	0836 1.7	1320 0.4	2047 1.9
3 SU	0144 0.4	0909 1.6	1353 0.4	2119 1.8
4 M	0218 0.4	0942 1.5	1429 0.5	2150 1.7
5 TU	0255 0.4	1017 1.5	1510 0.5	2226 1.6
6 W	0339 0.4	1100 1.4	1557 0.6	2310 1.6
7 TH ◖	0430 0.4	1153 1.4	1655 0.6	
8 F	0006 1.5	0529 0.5	1305 1.4	1759 0.7
9 SA	0115 1.5	0634 0.5	1422 1.5	1908 0.7
10 SU	0231 1.5	0744 0.5	1529 1.6	2021 0.6
11 M	0342 1.6	0856 0.5	1631 1.8	2133 0.6
12 TU	0450 1.7	1001 0.4	1730 2.0	2238 0.5
13 W ○	0553 1.8	1058 0.3	1825 2.1	2333 0.4
14 TH	0652 2.0	1149 0.3	1918 2.3	
15 F	0023 0.2	0754 2.0	1235 0.2	2013 2.3
16 SA	0108 0.2	0854 2.0	1319 0.2	2105 2.3
17 SU	0153 0.2	0938 2.0	1402 0.3	2148 2.2
18 M	0237 0.2	1015 1.9	1445 0.4	2226 2.1
19 TU	0321 0.3	1050 1.8	1527 0.5	2302 1.9
20 W ◗	0406 0.4	1127 1.6	1610 0.6	2340 1.7
21 TH	0453 0.5	1210 1.5	1657 0.7	
22 F	0024 1.5	0546 0.6	1310 1.4	1758 0.8
23 SA	0131 1.3	0648 0.7	1431 1.4	1912 0.9
24 SU	0256 1.3	0750 0.7	1537 1.5	2020 0.8
25 M	0406 1.4	0847 0.7	1631 1.6	2120 0.7
26 TU	0503 1.5	0941 0.6	1719 1.8	2217 0.6
27 W	0550 1.6	1034 0.5	1802 1.9	2311 0.5
28 TH ●	0634 1.7	1121 0.4	1843 2.0	2357 0.4
29 F	0715 1.8	1203 0.4	1923 2.0	
30 SA	0035 0.3	0754 1.8	1238 0.3	2003 2.0
31 SU	0106 0.3	0831 1.8	1311 0.3	2038 2.0

AUGUST

Day	Time m	Time m	Time m	Time m
1 M	0135 0.3	0902 1.7	1344 0.3	2108 1.9
2 TU	0206 0.3	0927 1.7	1418 0.3	2133 1.8
3 W	0239 0.3	0953 1.6	1453 0.4	2202 1.8
4 TH	0315 0.3	1027 1.6	1531 0.5	2240 1.7
5 F	0356 0.4	1111 1.5	1618 0.5	2329 1.5
6 SA	0448 0.5	1212 1.4	1720 0.7	
7 SU	0034 1.4	0553 0.6	1342 1.4	1835 0.7
8 M	0207 1.4	0712 0.6	1506 1.5	2016 0.7
9 TU	0332 1.5	0849 0.6	1615 1.7	2148 0.6
10 W	0445 1.6	0958 0.5	1717 1.9	2244 0.4
11 TH	0550 1.8	1052 0.4	1814 2.1	2330 0.3
12 F ○	0650 2.0	1140 0.3	1907 2.3	
13 SA	0014 0.1	0751 2.1	1223 0.2	2001 2.4
14 SU	0055 0.1	0841 2.2	1304 0.1	2049 2.4
15 M	0135 0.0	0917 2.1	1343 0.2	2128 2.3
16 TU	0213 0.1	0947 2.0	1419 0.2	2200 2.1
17 W	0250 0.2	1013 1.9	1454 0.4	2227 1.9
18 TH	0325 0.4	1037 1.7	1525 0.5	2252 1.7
19 F ◗	0356 0.5	1104 1.5	1554 0.7	2323 1.5
20 SA	0423 0.7	1141 1.4	1629 0.8	
21 SU	0006 1.3	0459 0.8	1236 1.3	1846 0.9
22 M	0129 1.2	0722 0.8	1500 1.3	2003 0.9
23 TU	0352 1.2	0825 0.8	1610 1.5	2103 0.8
24 W	0449 1.4	0920 0.7	1658 1.7	2158 0.6
25 TH	0534 1.6	1013 0.6	1741 1.8	2250 0.5
26 F	0617 1.7	1101 0.4	1824 2.0	2336 0.3
27 SA ●	0659 1.8	1144 0.3	1906 2.1	
28 SU	0015 0.3	0741 1.9	1221 0.3	1947 2.1
29 M	0046 0.2	0819 2.0	1254 0.2	2023 2.1
30 TU	0115 0.2	0848 1.9	1326 0.2	2049 2.0
31 W	0144 0.2	0904 1.9	1358 0.2	2109 1.9

Chart Datum: 0·93 metres below Ordnance Datum (Newlyn)
HAT is 2·5 metres above Chart Datum

PORTLAND

LAT 50°34'N   LONG 2°26'W

TIMES AND HEIGHTS OF HIGH AND LOW WATERS

Dates in amber are **SPRINGS**
Dates in grey are **NEAPS**

2022

SEPTEMBER

Day	Time m		Day	Time m	
1 TH	0215 0.2 / 0924 1.8	1430 0.3 / 2136 1.8	**16** F	0238 0.4 / 0950 1.8	1443 0.5 / 2210 1.6
2 F	0247 0.3 / 0954 1.7	1503 0.4 / 2213 1.7	**17** SA	0257 0.6 / 1017 1.6	1505 0.7 / 2241 1.4
3 SA	0320 0.4 / 1036 1.6	1541 0.5 / 2300 1.5	**18** SU	0313 0.7 / 1050 1.5	1533 0.8 / 2321 1.3
4 SU	0403 0.6 / 1131 1.5	1644 0.7	**19** M	0344 0.9 / 1136 1.3	1640 1.0
5 M	0008 1.3 / 0514 0.7	1317 1.4 / 1822 0.8	**20** TU	0027 1.1 / 0703 1.0	1306 1.3 / 1947 0.9
6 TU	0211 1.3 / 0711 0.8	1459 1.5 / 2316 0.7	**21** W	0358 1.2 / 0803 0.9	1544 1.4 / 2041 0.7
7 W	0336 1.4 / 0901 0.7	1608 1.7 / 2214 0.5	**22** TH	0436 1.4 / 0856 0.8	1631 1.6 / 2131 0.6
8 TH	0446 1.6 / 0952 0.6	1708 1.9 / 2235 0.4	**23** F	0514 1.6 / 0946 0.6	1715 1.8 / 2220 0.4
9 F	0545 1.9 / 1040 0.4	1802 2.2 / 2316 0.2	**24** SA	0553 1.8 / 1034 0.5	1758 2.0 / 2306 0.3
10 SA	0637 2.0 / 1125 0.2	1852 2.3 / 2357 0.1	**25** SU	0634 2.0 / 1117 0.4	1842 2.1 / 2345 0.2
11 SU	0725 2.2	1940 2.4	**26** M	0715 2.1 / 1155 0.3	1923 2.2
12 M	0035 0.0 / 0808 2.2	1243 0.1 / 2023 2.4	**27** TU	0017 0.2 / 0753 2.1	1229 0.2 / 1959 2.2
13 TU	0110 0.0 / 0843 2.2	1318 0.1 / 2058 2.3	**28** W	0047 0.2 / 0822 2.1	1301 0.2 / 2022 2.1
14 W	0143 0.1 / 0910 2.1	1349 0.2 / 2124 2.1	**29** TH	0117 0.2 / 0834 2.0	1334 0.2 / 2042 2.0
15 TH	0212 0.3 / 0928 1.9	1418 0.4 / 2145 1.9	**30** F	0149 0.3 / 0856 2.0	1406 0.3 / 2114 1.9

OCTOBER

Day	Time m		Day	Time m	
1 SA	0220 0.4 / 0929 1.8	1440 0.4 / 2155 1.7	**16** SU	0213 0.7 / 0940 1.7	1429 0.7 / 2211 1.4
2 SU	0252 0.5 / 1013 1.7	1521 0.6 / 2247 1.5	**17** M	0228 0.8 / 1011 1.5	1456 0.8 / 2254 1.3
3 M	0330 0.7 / 1112 1.5	1634 0.8	**18** TU	0246 0.9 / 1056 1.4	1601 1.0
4 TU	0012 1.3 / 0454 0.9	1319 1.4 / 2100 0.8	**19** W	0000 1.2 / 0303 1.0	1218 1.3 / 1923 0.9
5 W	0221 1.3 / 0748 0.9	1453 1.5 / 2124 0.7	**20** TH	0349 1.2 / 0737 0.6	1434 1.4 / 2014 0.7
6 TH	0337 1.5 / 0845 0.8	1557 1.8 / 2131 0.5	**21** F	0406 1.4 / 0828 0.8	1546 1.6 / 2102 0.6
7 F	0436 1.7 / 0933 0.6	1652 1.9 / 2210 0.3	**22** SA	0439 1.6 / 0916 0.7	1648 1.8 / 2147 0.4
8 SA	0525 2.0 / 1020 0.4	1742 2.2 / 2252 0.2	**23** SU	0519 1.8 / 1001 0.6	1725 2.0 / 2230 0.3
9 SU	0611 2.1	1829 2.3 / 2333 0.1	**24** M	0601 2.0 / 1044 0.4	1810 2.1 / 2308 0.3
10 M	0654 2.3 / 1143 0.2	1913 2.3	**25** TU	0642 2.2 / 1123 0.4	1851 2.2 / 2343 0.2
11 TU	0008 0.1 / 0733 2.3	1217 0.2 / 1952 2.3	**26** W	0719 2.2 / 1200 0.3	1925 2.2
12 W	0039 0.1 / 0805 2.2	1248 0.2 / 2022 2.2	**27** TH	0016 0.2 / 0745 2.2	1235 0.3 / 1951 2.2
13 TH	0108 0.2 / 0826 2.1	1317 0.3 / 2045 2.0	**28** F	0051 0.3 / 0805 2.2	1311 0.3 / 2021 2.1
14 F	0135 0.4 / 0847 2.0	1345 0.4 / 2109 1.8	**29** SA	0126 0.3 / 0836 2.1	1349 0.4 / 2101 1.9
15 SA	0158 0.5 / 0912 1.8	1409 0.5 / 2137 1.6	**30** SU	0201 0.5 / 0912 1.9	1430 0.5 / 2151 1.7
			31 M	0240 0.7 / 1008 1.8	1525 0.7 / 2253 1.5

NOVEMBER

Day	Time m		Day	Time m	
1 TU	0331 0.9 / 1114 1.6	1654 0.8	**16** W	0237 0.9 / 1039 1.5	1550 0.9 / 2335 1.2
2 W	0033 1.4 / 0504 1.0	1309 1.5 / 2122 0.7	**17** TH	0350 1.0 / 1144 1.4	1855 0.8
3 TH	0211 1.4 / 0656 1.0	1433 1.6 / 2018 0.7	**18** F	0112 1.2 / 0533 1.0	1320 1.4 / 1943 0.7
4 F	0318 1.6 / 0811 0.9	1534 1.8 / 2056 0.5	**19** SA	0252 1.4 / 0751 0.9	1448 1.5 / 2028 0.6
5 SA	0409 1.8 / 0905 0.7	1626 1.9 / 2139 0.4	**20** SU	0348 1.6 / 0837 0.8	1549 1.7 / 2108 0.5
6 SU	0457 2.0 / 0953 0.6	1716 2.1 / 2221 0.3	**21** M	0436 1.8 / 0921 0.7	1641 1.8 / 2146 0.4
7 M	0541 2.1 / 1036 0.5	1803 2.1 / 2300 0.2	**22** TU	0522 2.0 / 1003 0.6	1731 2.0 / 2226 0.4
8 TU	0622 2.2 / 1115 0.4	1845 2.2 / 2335 0.2	**23** W	0604 2.1 / 1047 0.5	1815 2.1 / 2308 0.3
9 W	0658 2.3 / 1148 0.4	1921 2.1 / 2350 0.3	**24** TH	0641 2.2 / 1131 0.4	1853 2.1
10 TH	0005 0.3 / 0728 2.2	1219 0.4 / 1949 2.1	**25** F	0713 2.3 / 1214 0.3	1931 2.1
11 F	0036 0.4 / 0752 2.1	1251 0.4 / 2015 1.9	**26** SA	0031 0.3 / 0749 2.3	1257 0.3 / 2014 2.1
12 SA	0104 0.5 / 0819 2.0	1321 0.5 / 2045 1.8	**27** SU	0112 0.4 / 0831 2.2	1342 0.4 / 2103 1.9
13 SU	0128 0.6 / 0848 1.9	1347 0.6 / 2117 1.6	**28** M	0155 0.5 / 0920 2.1	1432 0.5 / 2158 1.8
14 M	0147 0.7 / 0918 1.7	1411 0.7 / 2153 1.5	**29** TU	0242 0.7 / 1015 1.9	1532 0.6 / 2259 1.6
15 TU	0208 0.8 / 0952 1.6	1444 0.8 / 2237 1.3	**30** W	0339 0.8 / 1117 1.8	1641 0.7

DECEMBER

Day	Time m		Day	Time m	
1 TH	0015 1.5 / 0447 0.9	1236 1.7 / 1752 0.7	**16** F	0338 0.8 / 1110 1.5	1629 0.7
2 F	0136 1.5 / 0559 1.0	1355 1.6 / 1905 0.7	**17** SA	0002 1.3 / 0448 1.0	1212 1.5 / 1734 0.7
3 SA	0240 1.6 / 0713 0.9	1458 1.7 / 2007 0.6	**18** SU	0128 1.4 / 0602 0.9	1331 1.5 / 1845 0.6
4 SU	0334 1.7 / 0820 0.8	1553 1.8 / 2056 0.5	**19** M	0244 1.5 / 0717 0.8	1446 1.6 / 1955 0.6
5 M	0423 1.9 / 0913 0.7	1645 1.8 / 2140 0.5	**20** TU	0342 1.7 / 0825 0.7	1549 1.7 / 2055 0.5
6 TU	0509 2.0 / 0959 0.6	1734 1.9 / 2222 0.4	**21** W	0435 1.9 / 0923 0.6	1648 1.8 / 2150 0.5
7 W	0551 2.1 / 1042 0.6	1818 1.9 / 2302 0.4	**22** TH	0525 2.0 / 1019 0.6	1744 1.9 / 2243 0.4
8 TH	0629 2.1 / 1122 0.5	1856 1.9 / 2339 0.4	**23** F	0611 2.2 / 1113 0.5	1836 2.0 / 2334 0.4
9 F	0701 2.1 / 1200 0.5	1928 1.9	**24** SA	0657 2.3 / 1204 0.4	1926 2.1
10 SA	0014 0.5 / 0732 2.0	1236 0.5 / 2000 1.8	**25** SU	0021 0.5 / 0745 2.3	1252 0.3 / 2020 2.1
11 SU	0046 0.5 / 0805 2.0	1310 0.5 / 2033 1.7	**26** M	0107 0.4 / 0836 2.3	1340 0.3 / 2114 2.0
12 M	0115 0.6 / 0838 1.9	1340 0.6 / 2107 1.6	**27** TU	0152 0.4 / 0927 2.2	1429 0.3 / 2203 1.9
13 TU	0142 0.6 / 0912 1.8	1410 0.6 / 2142 1.5	**28** W	0238 0.5 / 1016 2.1	1520 0.4 / 2249 1.8
14 W	0210 0.7 / 0945 1.7	1445 0.6 / 2219 1.4	**29** TH	0326 0.6 / 1103 1.9	1612 0.5 / 2338 1.5
15 TH	0246 0.7 / 1023 1.6	1531 0.7 / 2303 1.4	**30** F	0416 0.7 / 1155 1.8	1705 0.5
			31 SA	0037 1.5 / 0512 0.8	1258 1.6 / 1803 0.6

Chart Datum: 0·93 metres below Ordnance Datum (Newlyn)
HAT is 2·5 metres above Chart Datum

TIDES

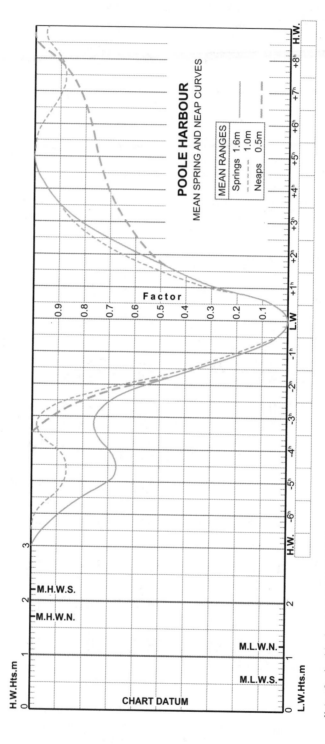

POOLE HARBOUR
MEAN SPRING AND NEAP CURVES

MEAN RANGES	
Springs	1.6m
	1.0m
Neaps	0.5m

Note - Sea level is above mean tide level from 2 hrs after LW to 2 hrs before the next LW. HW occurs between 5 hrs after LW and 3 hrs before the next LW, the time shown is approximate and should be checked for suitability.

POOLE HARBOUR

LAT 50°43′N   LONG 1°59′W

TIMES AND HEIGHTS OF HIGH AND LOW WATERS

TIME ZONE (UT)
For Summer Time add ONE hour in **non-shaded areas**

Dates in amber are **SPRINGS**
Dates in grey are **NEAPS**

2022

JANUARY

Day	Time	m	Time	m	Day	Time	m	Time	m
1 SA	0219 0753 1450 2020	0.6 2.2 0.6 2.1			16 SU	0305 0647 1530 2007	1.1 1.9 0.9 1.8		
2 SU ●	0312 0837 1541 2106	0.6 2.3 0.4 2.2			17 M ○	0345 0735 1608 2054	1.0 2.0 0.8 1.9		
3 M	0402 0922 1629 2151	0.5 2.4 0.3 2.2			18 TU	0422 0835 1642 2138	1.0 2.0 0.7 1.9		
4 TU	0452 1006 1717 2236	0.6 2.4 0.3 2.2			19 W	0457 0931 1717 2221	0.9 2.1 0.6 2.0		
5 W	0541 1047 1804 2318	0.6 2.4 0.3 2.1			20 TH	0534 1014 1753 2302	0.9 2.1 0.6 1.9		
6 TH	0630 1125 1852	0.7 2.2 0.4			21 F	0611 1050 1830 2341	0.9 2.1 0.6 1.9		
7 F	0000 0719 1159 1939	2.0 0.8 2.1 0.6			22 SA	0649 1119 1909 2359	0.9 2.1 0.6 1.8		
8 SA	0039 0810 1219 2029	1.8 1.0 2.0 0.7			23 SU	0730 1048 1951 2308	1.0 1.9 0.6 1.7		
9 SU ☾	0118 0903 1225 2122	1.7 1.1 1.8 0.9			24 M	0815 1120 2037 2348	1.0 1.9 0.7 1.7		
10 M	0151 1003 1302 2223	1.6 1.2 1.7 1.1			25 TU ☽	0905 1208 2132	1.0 1.8 0.8		
11 TU	0239 1109 1402 2332	1.6 1.3 1.6 1.2			26 W	0057 1008 1311 2240	1.6 1.1 1.7 0.9		
12 W	0829 1215 1522	1.9 1.2 1.5			27 TH	0746 1122 1545 2353	1.9 1.1 1.7 0.9		
13 TH	0036 0933 1313 1641	1.2 1.9 1.2 1.5			28 F	0623 1234 1842	1.8 1.0 1.8		
14 F	0132 0748 1404 1959	1.2 1.8 1.1 1.7			29 SA	0101 0701 1340 1930	0.9 1.9 0.8 1.8		
15 SA	0221 0606 1450 2002	1.1 1.8 1.0 1.7			30 SU	0205 0745 1438 2017	0.8 2.0 0.6 2.0		
					31 M	0302 0830 1531 2101	0.7 2.2 0.4 2.1		

FEBRUARY

Day	Time	m	Time	m	Day	Time	m	Time	m
1 TU ●	0354 0912 1619 2142	0.6 2.3 0.3 2.1			16 W ○	0406 0842 1625 2127	0.9 2.0 0.6 2.0		
2 W	0442 0953 1704 2221	0.5 2.4 0.2 2.2			17 TH	0441 0928 1659 2204	0.8 2.1 0.4 2.1		
3 TH	0527 1030 1747 2257	0.5 2.4 0.2 2.1			18 F	0516 1007 1734 2240	0.7 2.2 0.4 2.1		
4 F	0611 1104 1829 2332	0.5 2.3 0.3 2.0			19 SA	0552 1045 1810 2317	0.6 2.2 0.4 2.1		
5 SA	0653 1135 1911 2359	0.7 2.2 0.5 1.9			20 SU	0628 1121 1846 2354	0.6 2.2 0.4 2.0		
6 SU	0736 1156 1952	0.8 2.0 0.7			21 M	0705 1157 1924 2359	0.7 2.1 0.5 1.9		
7 M	0818 1148 2033 2354	1.0 1.8 0.9 1.7			22 TU	0746 1108 2007 2329	0.8 1.9 0.7 1.8		
8 TU ☽	0901 1208 2115	1.1 1.7 1.1			23 W ☽	0831 1147 2056	0.9 1.8 0.9		
9 W	0022 0952 1243 2208	1.6 1.2 1.6 1.3			24 TH	0018 0929 1243 2203	1.7 1.0 1.7 1.0		
10 TH	0106 1113 1337 2350	1.5 1.3 1.5 1.4			25 F	0708 1051 1932 2333	1.8 1.1 1.8 1.1		
11 F	0232 1247 2138	1.5 1.3 1.7			26 SA	0751 1219 2019	1.8 1.0 1.8		
12 SA	0113 0949 1346 2240	1.3 1.8 1.2 1.8			27 SU	0056 0659 1332 1942	1.1 1.9 0.9 1.8		
13 SU	0207 0858 1433 2333	1.3 1.7 1.0 1.8			28 M	0203 0739 1431 2016	0.9 2.0 0.6 1.9		
14 M	0251 0624 1513 2042	1.1 1.8 0.9 1.7							
15 TU	0330 0722 1550 2053	1.0 1.9 0.7 1.9							

MARCH

Day	Time	m	Time	m	Day	Time	m	Time	m
1 TU	0256 0820 1520 2053	0.8 2.1 0.4 2.0			16 W	0306 0743 1523 2033	1.0 1.8 0.7 1.9		
2 W ●	0344 0858 1605 2126	0.6 2.2 0.3 2.1			17 TH	0342 0910 1559 2105	0.8 2.0 0.5 2.1		
3 TH	0428 0933 1646 2159	0.5 2.3 0.2 2.2			18 F ○	0418 0910 1635 2140	0.6 2.2 0.4 2.2		
4 F	0508 1007 1726 2230	0.4 2.4 0.2 2.2			19 SA	0453 0950 1710 2216	0.5 2.3 0.3 2.3		
5 SA	0547 1038 1804 2259	0.5 2.3 0.3 2.1			20 SU	0529 1028 1745 2252	0.5 2.3 0.3 2.2		
6 SU	0625 1108 1840 2327	0.6 2.2 0.5 2.0			21 M	0604 1106 1822 2329	0.5 2.3 0.4 2.1		
7 M	0701 1134 1915 2339	0.7 2.0 0.7 1.8			22 TU	0641 1144 1900	0.5 2.1 0.6		
8 TU	0736 1116 1950 2310	1.0 1.8 0.9 1.7			23 W	0006 0721 1223 1943	2.0 0.7 2.0 0.8		
9 W	0813 1128 2029 2336	1.0 1.7 1.1 1.7			24 TH	0045 0807 1309 2033	1.9 0.8 1.8 1.0		
10 TH ☽	0856 1201 2116	1.1 1.6 1.3			25 F ☽	0016 0904 1420 2147	1.7 1.0 1.7 1.2		
11 F	0011 0949 1243 2216	1.6 1.3 1.5 1.4			26 SA	0254 1039 1911 2335	1.7 1.1 1.9 1.3		
12 SA	0057 1101 1928	1.6 1.3 1.7			27 SU	0615 1212 2005	1.8 1.0 1.9		
13 SU	0108 0748 1326 2212	1.3 1.7 1.2 1.8			28 M	0053 0641 1320 1936	1.1 1.8 0.8 1.9		
14 M	0152 0824 1409 2054	1.3 1.6 1.0 1.7			29 TU	0152 0721 1414 2001	1.0 1.9 0.6 1.9		
15 TU	0230 0659 1447 2015	1.2 1.7 0.9 1.8			30 W	0241 0800 1500 2033	0.8 2.0 0.5 2.0		
					31 TH	0326 0830 1543 2102	0.6 2.1 0.3 2.1		

APRIL

Day	Time	m	Time	m	Day	Time	m	Time	m
1 F	0407 0907 1623 2129	0.5 2.2 0.3 2.2			16 SA ○	0348 0847 1605 2112	0.6 2.2 0.4 2.3		
2 SA	0445 0938 1701 2155	0.5 2.3 0.4 2.2			17 SU	0425 0928 1642 2150	0.4 2.3 0.3 2.4		
3 SU	0522 1008 1737 2224	0.5 2.3 0.5 2.2			18 M	0503 1008 1721 2228	0.4 2.4 0.3 2.4		
4 M	0557 1041 1810 2253	0.6 2.1 0.7 2.1			19 TU	0541 1049 1800 2306	0.4 2.3 0.5 2.3		
5 TU	0629 1111 1842 2249	0.7 2.0 0.9 1.9			20 W	0621 1130 1842 2345	0.5 2.2 0.7 2.1		
6 W	0702 1050 1916 2238	0.8 1.8 1.0 1.8			21 TH	0705 1214 1929	0.7 2.0 0.9		
7 TH	0738 1059 1956 2302	1.0 1.7 1.2 1.8			22 F	0023 0756 1307 2030	2.0 0.8 1.8 1.1		
8 F	0820 1130 2044 2333	1.1 1.6 1.4 1.7			23 SA ☽	0112 0904 1809 2200	1.8 1.0 2.0 1.3		
9 SA ☽	0912 1212 2145	1.2 1.5 1.5			24 SU	0225 1032 1911 2323	1.7 1.0 2.0 1.3		
10 SU	0004 1018 1901 2306	1.6 1.3 1.8 1.5			25 M	0527 1148 2025	1.8 1.0 2.0		
11 M	0141 1159 2012	1.5 1.2 1.8			26 TU	0030 0609 1251 1910	1.1 1.8 0.8 1.9		
12 TU	0117 0614 1324 2006	1.4 1.6 1.1 1.8			27 W	0126 0652 1345 1935	1.0 1.8 0.7 1.9		
13 W	0153 0639 1406 1931	1.2 1.7 0.9 1.8			28 TH	0215 0732 1433 2005	0.9 1.9 0.6 2.0		
14 TH	0231 0720 1446 2001	1.0 1.8 0.7 2.0			29 F	0300 0807 1516 2031	0.7 2.0 0.5 2.1		
15 F	0310 0805 1526 2036	0.8 2.0 0.5 2.2			30 SA ●	0342 0836 1557 2050	0.5 2.1 0.5 2.2		

Chart Datum: 1·40 metres below Ordnance Datum (Newlyn)
HAT is 2·6 metres above Chart Datum

TIME ZONE (UT)
For Summer Time add ONE hour in **non-shaded areas**

POOLE HARBOUR
LAT 50°43'N   LONG 1°59'W
TIMES AND HEIGHTS OF HIGH AND LOW WATERS

Dates in amber are **SPRINGS**
Dates in grey are **NEAPS**

2022

MAY

Date	Time	m	Date	Time	m
1 SU	0420 / 0904 / 1635 / 2115	0.6 / 2.2 / 0.6 / 2.2	16 M	0358 / 0908 / 1616 / 2126	0.5 / 2.3 / 0.4 / 2.4
2 M	0456 / 0938 / 1710 / 2148	0.6 / 2.2 / 0.7 / 2.2	17 TU	0439 / 0952 / 1658 / 2208	0.4 / 2.3 / 0.5 / 2.4
3 TU	0530 / 1014 / 1743 / 2219	0.7 / 2.1 / 0.9 / 2.1	18 W	0522 / 1035 / 1743 / 2249	0.4 / 2.3 / 0.6 / 2.3
4 W	0602 / 1050 / 1815 / 2212	0.8 / 2.0 / 1.0 / 2.0	19 TH	0607 / 1120 / 1831 / 2331	0.5 / 2.2 / 0.8 / 2.2
5 TH	0634 / 1040 / 1850 / 2216	0.8 / 1.8 / 1.1 / 1.9	20 F	0656 / 1207 / 1926	0.6 / 2.0 / 1.0
6 F	0710 / 1042 / 1932 / 2241	0.9 / 1.7 / 1.3 / 1.8	21 SA	0013 / 0753 / 1301 / 2033	2.1 / 0.8 / 1.9 / 1.1
7 SA	0754 / 1113 / 2022 / 2314	1.0 / 1.6 / 1.4 / 1.8	22 SU	0058 / 0858 / 1809 / 2145	1.9 / 0.9 / 2.1 / 1.2
8 SU	0846 / 1156 / 2122 / 2359	1.1 / 1.5 / 1.4 / 1.7	23 M	0148 / 1008 / 1909 / 2253	1.8 / 0.9 / 2.1 / 1.2
9 M	0948 / 1304 / 2231	1.2 / 1.5 / 1.4	24 TU	0240 / 1115 / 2012 / 2356	1.8 / 0.9 / 2.1 / 1.1
10 TU	0111 / 1058 / 1953 / 2348	1.6 / 1.1 / 1.9 / 1.4	25 W	0330 / 1216 / 2116	1.7 / 0.9 / 2.0
11 W	0307 / 1212 / 1836	1.6 / 1.1 / 1.8	26 TH	0052 / 0423 / 1311 / 1910	1.1 / 1.7 / 0.9 / 1.9
12 TH	0054 / 0612 / 1313 / 1856	1.2 / 1.7 / 0.9 / 1.9	27 F	0144 / 0520 / 1402 / 1939	1.0 / 1.8 / 0.8 / 1.9
13 F	0146 / 0652 / 1403 / 1929	1.8 / 1.8 / 0.7 / 2.0	28 SA	0231 / 0742 / 1448 / 1958	0.9 / 1.8 / 0.8 / 2.0
14 SA	0232 / 0739 / 1449 / 2006	0.8 / 2.0 / 0.6 / 2.2	29 SU	0315 / 0804 / 1531 / 1951	0.8 / 1.9 / 0.8 / 2.1
15 SU	0316 / 0824 / 1533 / 2045	0.6 / 2.2 / 0.4 / 2.3	30 M	0356 / 0831 / 1611 / 2031	0.7 / 2.0 / 0.6 / 2.2
			31 TU	0433 / 0910 / 1648 / 2112	0.7 / 2.0 / 0.9 / 2.2

JUNE

Date	Time	m	Date	Time	m
1 W	0508 / 0952 / 1721 / 2148	0.8 / 2.0 / 1.0 / 2.1	16 TH	0508 / 1026 / 1731 / 2239	0.4 / 2.3 / 0.7 / 2.4
2 TH	0540 / 1034 / 1755 / 2156	0.8 / 1.9 / 1.1 / 2.0	17 F	0556 / 1112 / 1823 / 2322	0.4 / 2.2 / 0.8 / 2.3
3 F	0614 / 1116 / 1832 / 2206	0.9 / 1.8 / 1.2 / 1.9	18 SA	0647 / 1157 / 1918	0.5 / 2.1 / 0.9
4 SA	0651 / 1041 / 1915 / 2231	0.9 / 1.7 / 1.2 / 1.9	19 SU	0003 / 0741 / 1243 / 2016	2.2 / 0.6 / 1.9 / 1.0
5 SU	0735 / 1105 / 2003 / 2304	0.9 / 1.7 / 1.3 / 1.8	20 M	0040 / 0837 / 1331 / 2116	2.0 / 0.7 / 1.8 / 1.1
6 M	0824 / 1142 / 2057 / 2346	1.0 / 1.6 / 1.3 / 1.8	21 TU	0107 / 0935 / 1417 / 2216	1.9 / 0.8 / 1.7 / 1.1
7 TU	0919 / 1237 / 2157	1.0 / 1.6 / 1.3	22 W	0143 / 1036 / 1451 / 2317	1.8 / 0.9 / 1.7 / 1.2
8 W	0044 / 1020 / 1930 / 2300	1.7 / 1.0 / 1.9 / 1.3	23 TH	0235 / 1138 / 1533	1.7 / 1.0 / 1.7
9 TH	0204 / 1124 / 1805	1.7 / 1.0 / 1.8	24 F	0017 / 0334 / 1237 / 1900	1.1 / 1.7 / 1.1 / 1.9
10 F	0002 / 0348 / 1226 / 1827	1.2 / 1.7 / 0.9 / 1.9	25 SA	0112 / 0434 / 1332 / 1717	1.1 / 1.7 / 1.1 / 1.8
11 SA	0101 / 0503 / 1322 / 1901	1.0 / 1.8 / 0.8 / 2.0	26 SU	0204 / 0536 / 1422 / 1807	1.0 / 1.7 / 1.1 / 1.9
12 SU	0154 / 0716 / 1415 / 1941	0.8 / 2.0 / 0.7 / 2.2	27 M	0251 / 0644 / 1509 / 1857	0.9 / 1.8 / 1.1 / 2.0
13 M	0245 / 0806 / 1505 / 2024	0.7 / 2.1 / 0.6 / 2.3	28 TU	0335 / 0805 / 1552 / 1949	0.9 / 1.9 / 1.1 / 2.1
14 TU	0333 / 0853 / 1554 / 2109	0.5 / 2.2 / 0.6 / 2.4	29 W	0415 / 0851 / 1631 / 2042	0.8 / 1.9 / 1.1 / 2.1
15 W	0421 / 0940 / 1642 / 2154	0.4 / 2.3 / 0.6 / 2.4	30 TH	0451 / 0938 / 1706 / 2131	0.8 / 2.0 / 1.1 / 2.1

JULY

Date	Time	m	Date	Time	m
1 F	0525 / 1022 / 1741 / 2209	0.8 / 2.0 / 1.1 / 2.1	16 SA	0544 / 1100 / 1810 / 2308	0.3 / 2.3 / 0.7 / 2.4
2 SA	0558 / 1106 / 1817 / 2218	0.8 / 1.9 / 1.1 / 2.0	17 SU	0631 / 1140 / 1859 / 2346	0.3 / 2.2 / 0.8 / 2.3
3 SU	0635 / 1150 / 1857 / 2234	0.8 / 1.9 / 1.1 / 1.9	18 M	0718 / 1218 / 1948	0.5 / 2.0 / 0.9
4 M	0715 / 1232 / 1940 / 2256	0.8 / 1.8 / 1.1 / 1.9	19 TU	0016 / 0807 / 1250 / 2040	2.1 / 0.6 / 1.9 / 1.0
5 TU	0758 / 1134 / 2027 / 2327	0.8 / 1.7 / 1.2 / 1.9	20 W	0033 / 0857 / 1306 / 2135	2.0 / 0.8 / 1.8 / 1.1
6 W	0847 / 1206 / 2120	0.9 / 1.7 / 1.2	21 TH	0055 / 0952 / 1331 / 2237	1.8 / 1.0 / 1.7 / 1.2
7 TH	0013 / 0942 / 1314 / 2219	1.8 / 0.9 / 1.7 / 1.2	22 F	0138 / 1056 / 1426 / 2342	1.7 / 1.2 / 1.7 / 1.2
8 F	0115 / 1043 / 1956 / 2322	1.1 / 1.0 / 1.9 / 1.1	23 SA	0241 / 1204 / 1539	1.6 / 1.3 / 1.7
9 SA	0252 / 1147 / 1806	1.7 / 0.9 / 1.9	24 SU	0044 / 0357 / 1307 / 2158	1.2 / 1.6 / 1.3 / 1.9
10 SU	0024 / 0427 / 1248 / 1841	1.0 / 1.8 / 0.9 / 2.0	25 M	0142 / 0512 / 1404 / 1742	1.1 / 1.6 / 1.3 / 1.8
11 M	0124 / 0704 / 1347 / 1924	0.9 / 1.9 / 0.8 / 2.1	26 TU	0233 / 0833 / 1453 / 1830	1.0 / 1.7 / 1.2 / 1.9
12 TU	0221 / 0756 / 1444 / 2012	0.7 / 2.0 / 0.8 / 2.2	27 W	0319 / 0850 / 1537 / 1923	0.9 / 1.8 / 1.1 / 2.0
13 W	0315 / 0846 / 1539 / 2059	0.6 / 2.1 / 0.7 / 2.4	28 TH	0400 / 0854 / 1617 / 2027	0.8 / 1.8 / 1.1 / 2.1
14 TH	0407 / 0933 / 1631 / 2144	0.4 / 2.2 / 0.6 / 2.4	29 F	0435 / 0930 / 1651 / 2123	0.8 / 2.0 / 1.1 / 2.1
15 F	0456 / 1017 / 1721 / 2228	0.3 / 2.3 / 0.6 / 2.5	30 SA	0509 / 1009 / 1721 / 2206	0.7 / 2.0 / 1.1 / 2.2
			31 SU	0541 / 1047 / 1759 / 2243	0.7 / 2.1 / 0.9 / 2.2

AUGUST

Date	Time	m	Date	Time	m
1 M	0615 / 1123 / 1834 / 2314	0.6 / 2.0 / 0.9 / 2.1	16 TU	0651 / 1147 / 1916 / 2350	0.4 / 2.1 / 0.8 / 2.2
2 TU	0651 / 1158 / 1912 / 2328	0.6 / 2.0 / 0.9 / 2.0	17 W	0733 / 1212 / 2000	0.6 / 2.0 / 1.0
3 W	0729 / 1231 / 1953 / 2306	0.7 / 1.9 / 1.0 / 1.9	18 TH	0005 / 0816 / 1211 / 2048	2.0 / 0.9 / 1.8 / 1.1
4 TH	0812 / 1135 / 2040 / 2343	0.8 / 1.8 / 1.1 / 1.9	19 F	0010 / 0901 / 1222 / 2143	1.8 / 1.1 / 1.7 / 1.3
5 F	0901 / 1219 / 2137	0.9 / 1.8 / 1.1	20 SA	0039 / 0957 / 1258 / 2303	1.7 / 1.3 / 1.7 / 1.3
6 SA	0036 / 1003 / 1457 / 2245	1.8 / 1.0 / 1.8 / 1.1	21 SU	0129 / 1131 / 1405	1.5 / 1.5 / 1.6
7 SU	0202 / 1113 / 1756 / 2356	1.1 / 1.1 / 1.9 / 1.1	22 M	0024 / 0920 / 1253 / 2125	1.3 / 1.8 / 1.4 / 1.9
8 M	0617 / 1224 / 1831	1.8 / 1.1 / 2.0	23 TU	0127 / 1022 / 1352 / 2003	1.2 / 1.9 / 1.4 / 1.8
9 TU	0105 / 0706 / 1333 / 1916	1.0 / 1.8 / 1.0 / 2.1	24 W	0217 / 1116 / 1439 / 1834	1.1 / 1.9 / 1.3 / 1.9
10 W	0209 / 0756 / 1435 / 2004	0.8 / 2.0 / 0.9 / 2.2	25 TH	0300 / 0853 / 1520 / 1921	0.9 / 1.8 / 1.1 / 2.0
11 TH	0305 / 0842 / 1530 / 2050	0.6 / 2.1 / 0.7 / 2.4	26 F	0339 / 0849 / 1557 / 2021	0.8 / 1.9 / 1.0 / 2.1
12 F	0356 / 0924 / 1620 / 2131	0.4 / 2.2 / 0.6 / 2.5	27 SA	0414 / 0912 / 1630 / 2108	0.7 / 2.1 / 0.9 / 2.2
13 SA	0442 / 1004 / 1706 / 2211	0.2 / 2.3 / 0.6 / 2.5	28 SU	0446 / 0947 / 1702 / 2149	0.6 / 2.2 / 0.8 / 2.3
14 SU	0526 / 1041 / 1750 / 2248	0.2 / 2.3 / 0.6 / 2.5	29 M	0518 / 1022 / 1735 / 2226	0.5 / 2.2 / 0.8 / 2.3
15 M	0609 / 1115 / 1833 / 2322	0.3 / 2.3 / 0.6 / 2.4	30 TU	0551 / 1057 / 1808 / 2302	0.5 / 2.2 / 0.8 / 2.3
			31 W	0624 / 1131 / 1843 / 2336	0.5 / 2.1 / 0.8 / 2.2

Chart Datum: 1·40 metres below Ordnance Datum (Newlyn)
HAT is 2·6 metres above Chart Datum

POOLE HARBOUR

TIME ZONE (UT)
For Summer Time add **ONE** hour in **non-shaded** areas

LAT 50°43'N   LONG 1°59'W

TIMES AND HEIGHTS OF HIGH AND LOW WATERS

Dates in amber are **SPRINGS**
Dates in grey are **NEAPS**

2022

SEPTEMBER

Day	Time m	Day	Time m
1 TH	0659 0.6 / 1206 2.0 / 1920 0.9 / 2252 1.8	**16** F	0736 1.0 / 1120 1.9 / 2001 1.1 / 2328 1.8
2 F	0739 0.8 / 1113 1.9 / 2003 1.0 / 2317 1.9	**17** SA	0815 1.2 / 1133 1.8 / 2045 1.3 / ◔2353 1.6
3 SA ●	0824 0.9 / 1148 1.8 / 2057 1.1	**18** SU	0901 1.4 / 1205 1.7 / 2144 1.4
4 SU	0006 1.8 / 0922 1.1 / 1301 1.8 / 2212 1.2	**19** M	0609 1.9 / 1009 1.6 / 1253 1.6
5 M	0705 1.8 / 1049 1.3 / 1922 1.9 / 2343 1.2	**20** TU	0009 1.4 / 0656 1.8 / 1246 1.5 / 1857 1.8
6 TU	0757 1.9 / 1219 1.2 / 1826 2.0	**21** W	0108 1.2 / 0959 1.9 / 1335 1.4 / 1919 1.8
7 W	0100 1.0 / 0719 1.9 / 1332 1.1 / 1908 2.1	**22** TH	0153 1.1 / 0808 1.8 / 1417 1.3 / 1848 1.8
8 TH	0202 0.8 / 0754 2.0 / 1430 0.9 / 1952 2.2	**23** F	0233 0.9 / 0805 1.9 / 1454 1.1 / 1921 2.0
9 F	0254 0.5 / 0832 2.1 / 1519 0.7 / 2034 2.3	**24** SA	0309 0.8 / 0814 2.0 / 1528 1.0 / 2005 2.1
10 SA ○	0340 0.3 / 0907 2.3 / 1604 0.6 / 2112 2.5	**25** SU ●	0343 0.6 / 0844 2.1 / 1602 0.8 / 2047 2.3
11 SU	0423 0.2 / 0942 2.3 / 1646 0.5 / 2148 2.5	**26** M	0417 0.5 / 0918 2.3 / 1635 0.7 / 2127 2.4
12 M	0504 0.2 / 1014 2.4 / 1726 0.5 / 2222 2.5	**27** TU	0450 0.5 / 0953 2.4 / 1708 0.6 / 2205 2.4
13 TU	0543 0.3 / 1045 2.3 / 1805 0.6 / 2254 2.4	**28** W	0523 0.5 / 1029 2.3 / 1741 0.6 / 2242 2.4
14 W	0621 0.5 / 1113 2.2 / 1844 0.8 / 2324 2.2	**29** TH	0557 0.5 / 1104 2.3 / 1816 0.7 / 2321 2.2
15 TH	0658 0.8 / 1135 2.0 / 1922 0.9 / 2341 2.0	**30** F	0633 0.7 / 1141 2.2 / 1853 0.8 / 2359 2.1

OCTOBER

Day	Time m	Day	Time m
1 SA	0713 0.8 / 1218 2.0 / 1937 0.9 / 2305 1.9	**16** SU	0740 1.3 / 1056 1.9 / 2005 1.2 / 2321 1.6
2 SU	0759 1.1 / 1138 1.9 / 2029 1.1	**17** M ●	0827 1.5 / 1129 1.8 / 2058 1.3
3 M	0201 1.8 / 0859 1.3 / 1428 1.8 / ◔2200 1.2	**18** TU	0541 2.0 / 0931 1.6 / 1212 1.7 / 2214 1.4
4 TU	0637 1.9 / 1056 1.4 / 1740 1.9 / 2340 1.1	**19** W	0619 1.9 / 1223 1.6 / 1820 1.8
5 W	0733 1.9 / 1221 1.3 / 1808 2.0	**20** TH	0033 1.3 / 0706 1.9 / 1305 1.4 / 1814 1.8
6 TH	0050 0.9 / 0707 2.0 / 1322 1.1 / 1850 2.0	**21** F	0115 1.1 / 0715 1.9 / 1342 1.3 / 1829 1.8
7 F	0145 0.7 / 0736 2.0 / 1414 0.9 / 1931 2.1	**22** SA	0153 1.0 / 0714 1.9 / 1417 1.1 / 1903 1.9
8 SA	0233 0.5 / 0810 2.1 / 1500 0.7 / 2011 2.3	**23** SU	0229 0.8 / 0739 2.1 / 1452 0.9 / 1942 2.1
9 SU ○	0318 0.4 / 0842 2.2 / 1543 0.6 / 2047 2.4	**24** M	0306 0.6 / 0812 2.2 / 1528 0.7 / 2023 2.2
10 M	0359 0.3 / 0913 2.2 / 1623 0.5 / 2121 2.4	**25** TU ●	0343 0.5 / 0847 2.3 / 1605 0.6 / 2103 2.3
11 TU	0438 0.4 / 0942 2.4 / 1700 0.6 / 2153 2.4	**26** W	0420 0.5 / 0924 2.4 / 1640 0.5 / 2143 2.4
12 W	0516 0.5 / 1009 2.3 / 1737 0.6 / 2226 2.3	**27** TH	0457 0.5 / 1001 2.4 / 1717 0.5 / 2224 2.4
13 TH	0552 0.7 / 1037 2.2 / 1813 0.8 / 2258 2.1	**28** F	0535 0.6 / 1039 2.3 / 1755 0.6 / 2305 2.2
14 F	0627 0.9 / 1057 2.1 / 1847 0.9 / 2321 1.9	**29** SA	0614 0.7 / 1118 2.2 / 1836 0.7 / 2351 2.1
15 SA	0702 1.1 / 1038 1.9 / 1923 1.1 / 2254 1.8	**30** SU	0659 1.0 / 1159 2.1 / 1924 0.9
		31 M	0046 1.9 / 0752 1.2 / 1250 1.9 / 2025 1.0

NOVEMBER

Day	Time m	Day	Time m
1 TU ◔	0538 2.0 / 0915 1.4 / 1402 1.9 / 2158 1.1	**16** W ○	0902 1.5 / 1148 1.7 / 2128 1.2
2 W	0637 2.0 / 1050 1.4 / 1701 1.9 / 2320 1.0	**17** TH	0046 1.5 / 1012 1.5 / 1250 1.6 / 2240 1.2
3 TH	0749 2.0 / 1200 1.2 / 1741 1.9	**18** F	0709 1.9 / 1138 1.5 / 1433 1.6 / 2356 1.1
4 F	0023 0.9 / 0642 2.0 / 1257 1.1 / 1825 1.9	**19** SA	0849 1.9 / 1241 1.3 / 1808 1.7
5 SA	0117 0.8 / 0711 2.0 / 1348 0.9 / 1907 2.0	**20** SU	0054 1.0 / 0644 1.9 / 1327 1.1 / 1841 1.8
6 SU	0206 0.6 / 0744 2.1 / 1434 0.8 / 1946 2.1	**21** M	0142 0.8 / 0710 2.0 / 1411 0.9 / 1918 2.0
7 M	0251 0.6 / 0815 2.1 / 1507 0.7 / 2021 2.2	**22** TU	0227 0.7 / 0742 2.2 / 1453 0.7 / 2000 2.1
8 TU ○	0333 0.6 / 0841 2.2 / 1558 0.6 / 2052 2.2	**23** W ●	0310 0.6 / 0818 2.3 / 1535 0.6 / 2042 2.2
9 W	0413 0.6 / 0903 2.3 / 1636 0.6 / 2124 2.2	**24** TH	0353 0.5 / 0858 2.4 / 1617 0.5 / 2126 2.3
10 TH	0450 0.7 / 0931 2.3 / 1712 0.7 / 2200 2.2	**25** F	0434 0.5 / 0940 2.4 / 1658 0.5 / 2211 2.3
11 F	0526 0.9 / 1002 2.2 / 1747 0.8 / 2236 2.0	**26** SA	0518 0.6 / 1022 2.4 / 1742 0.5 / 2256 2.2
12 SA	0601 1.1 / 1020 2.1 / 1820 0.9 / 2313 1.9	**27** SU	0604 0.8 / 1106 2.3 / 1829 0.6 / 2345 2.1
13 SU	0636 1.2 / 1011 2.0 / 1856 1.0 / 2235 1.7	**28** M	0655 1.0 / 1150 2.2 / 1921 0.7
14 M	0716 1.3 / 1033 1.9 / 1938 1.1 / 2301 1.6	**29** TU	0038 1.9 / 0755 1.1 / 1238 2.0 / 2024 0.9
15 TU	0804 1.4 / 1106 1.8 / 2028 1.2 / 2342 1.5	**30** W	0145 1.8 / 0907 1.2 / 1329 1.9 / ◔2134 0.9

DECEMBER

Day	Time m	Day	Time m
1 TH	0637 2.1 / 1019 1.2 / 1423 1.8 / 2245 0.9	**16** F ◔	0004 1.5 / 0927 1.3 / 1211 1.7 / 2151 1.1
2 F	0738 2.1 / 1125 1.2 / 1516 1.8 / 2348 0.9	**17** SA	0657 2.0 / 1029 1.3 / 1317 1.6 / 2254 1.0
3 SA	0842 2.1 / 1225 1.1 / 1804 1.8	**18** SU	0756 1.9 / 1134 1.2 / 1503 1.6 / 2358 1.0
4 SU	0045 0.9 / 0652 1.9 / 1319 1.0 / 1849 1.8	**19** M	0621 1.9 / 1235 1.2 / 1636 1.7
5 M	0136 0.8 / 0724 2.0 / 1408 0.9 / 1929 1.9	**20** TU	0056 0.9 / 0646 1.9 / 1330 0.9 / 1858 1.9
6 TU	0224 0.8 / 0753 2.0 / 1453 0.8 / 2003 2.0	**21** W	0150 0.8 / 0718 2.1 / 1421 0.8 / 1942 2.0
7 W	0309 0.8 / 0811 2.1 / 1536 0.7 / 2031 2.0	**22** TH	0241 0.7 / 0757 2.2 / 1510 0.6 / 2029 2.1
8 TH	0351 0.8 / 0818 2.1 / 1616 0.7 / 2101 2.0	**23** F ●	0330 0.6 / 0843 2.3 / 1558 0.5 / 2117 2.2
9 F	0431 0.9 / 0854 2.2 / 1654 0.8 / 2139 2.0	**24** SA	0419 0.6 / 0929 2.4 / 1645 0.5 / 2203 2.2
10 SA	0508 1.0 / 0934 2.1 / 1728 0.8 / 2221 2.0	**25** SU	0507 0.6 / 1016 2.4 / 1732 0.6 / 2250 2.2
11 SU	0544 1.1 / 1005 2.1 / 1802 0.8 / 2308 1.9	**26** M	0556 0.7 / 1100 2.3 / 1821 0.6 / 2335 2.1
12 M	0619 1.2 / 1001 2.0 / 1837 0.9 / 2359 1.7	**27** TU	0648 0.8 / 1142 2.2 / 1911 0.5
13 TU	0659 1.2 / 1021 1.9 / 1918 0.9 / 2251 1.6	**28** W	0021 2.0 / 0742 0.9 / 1222 2.1 / 2005 0.6
14 W	0743 1.3 / 1050 1.8 / 2002 1.0 / 2321 1.6	**29** TH	0108 1.8 / 0839 1.0 / 1257 2.0 / 2101 0.8
15 TH	0831 1.3 / 1126 1.8 / 2053 1.0	**30** F	0156 1.7 / 0940 1.1 / 1329 1.8 / ◔2203 1.0
		31 SA	0709 2.1 / 1045 1.4 / 1413 1.7 / 2308 1.0

Chart Datum: 1·40 metres below Ordnance Datum (Newlyn)
HAT is 2·6 metres above Chart Datum

TIDES

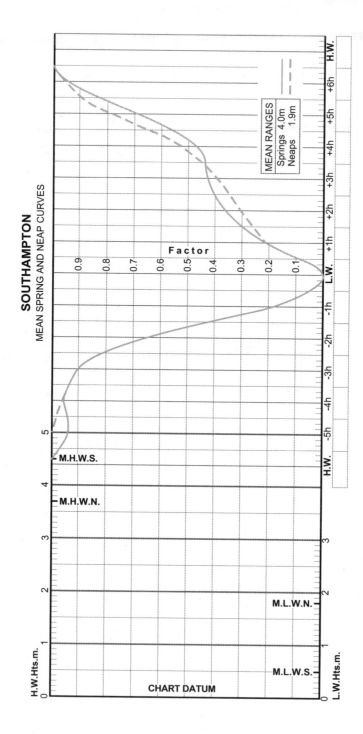

SOUTHAMPTON

MEAN SPRING AND NEAP CURVES

MEAN RANGES
Springs 4.0m
Neaps 1.9m

Factor

0.9 0.8 0.7 0.6 0.5 0.4 0.3 0.2 0.1

H.W. +6h +5h +4h +3h +2h +1h L.W. -1h -2h -3h -4h -5h H.W.

M.H.W.S.
M.H.W.N.
M.L.W.N.
M.L.W.S.
CHART DATUM

H.W.Hts.m.
L.W.Hts.m.

Note - Double HWs occur at Southampton. The predictions are for the first HW.

TIME ZONE (UT)	SOUTHAMPTON	Dates in amber are SPRINGS
For Summer Time add ONE hour in **non-shaded areas**	LAT 50°53'N LONG 1°24'W	Dates in grey are NEAPS
	TIMES AND HEIGHTS OF HIGH AND LOW WATERS	**2022**

JANUARY

Time	m	Time	m
1 SA 0240 / 0854 / 1510 / 2122	1.2 / 4.5 / 0.9 / 4.4	**16** SU 0322 / 0933 / 1547 / 2205	1.6 / 4.1 / 1.3 / 4.1
2 SU 0333 / 0944 / 1601 / ● 2240	1.0 / 4.5 / 0.7 / 4.6	**17** M 0405 / 1020 / 1627 / ○ 2246	1.5 / 4.2 / 1.2 / 4.2
3 M 0423 / 1059 / 1650 / 2328	0.8 / 4.7 / 0.6 / 4.6	**18** TU 0444 / 1055 / 1704 / 2322	1.4 / 4.3 / 1.1 / 4.2
4 TU 0511 / 1145 / 1736	0.8 / 4.7 / 0.5	**19** W 0520 / 1130 / 1739 / 2355	1.3 / 4.3 / 1.0 / 4.3
5 W 0017 / 0559 / 1232 / 1823	4.6 / 0.8 / 4.6 / 0.6	**20** TH 0553 / 1201 / 1810	1.2 / 4.3 / 1.0
6 TH 0108 / 0645 / 1320 / 1908	4.5 / 0.9 / 4.5 / 0.7	**21** F 0026 / 0626 / 1236 / 1843	4.3 / 1.2 / 4.3 / 0.9
7 F 0204 / 0731 / 1412 / 1954	4.4 / 1.1 / 4.4 / 0.9	**22** SA 0127 / 0701 / 1318 / 1919	4.4 / 1.1 / 4.3 / 0.9
8 SA 0219 / 0820 / 1509 / 2042	4.2 / 1.3 / 4.1 / 1.2	**23** SU 0206 / 0740 / 1400 / 1959	4.4 / 1.1 / 4.3 / 1.0
9 SU 0313 / 0911 / 1524 / ◐ 2135	4.1 / 1.4 / 3.8 / 1.5	**24** M 0251 / 0824 / 1443 / 2044	4.4 / 1.1 / 4.2 / 1.1
10 M 0402 / 1007 / 1619 / 2234	4.0 / 1.6 / 3.7 / 1.8	**25** TU 0342 / 0913 / 1533 / ◑ 2137	4.3 / 1.4 / 4.0 / 1.4
11 TU 0456 / 1111 / 1716 / 2338	3.9 / 1.9 / 3.6 / 1.9	**26** W 0410 / 1015 / 1630 / 2244	4.1 / 1.6 / 3.9 / 1.6
12 W 0553 / 1220 / 1818	3.8 / 2.0 / 3.5	**27** TH 0511 / 1130 / 1739	4.0 / 1.7 / 3.8
13 TH 0043 / 0648 / 1323 / 1921	2.0 / 3.8 / 1.9 / 3.6	**28** F 0004 / 0616 / 1254 / 1854	1.7 / 3.9 / 1.7 / 3.8
14 F 0143 / 0747 / 1416 / 2019	1.9 / 3.8 / 1.6 / 3.7	**29** SA 0128 / 0736 / 1408 / 2012	1.6 / 4.1 / 1.4 / 4.0
15 SA 0235 / 0845 / 1504 / 2116	1.8 / 4.0 / 1.5 / 3.9	**30** SU 0235 / 0841 / 1506 / 2117	1.4 / 4.2 / 1.1 / 4.2
		31 M 0329 / 0939 / 1556 / 2239	1.1 / 4.4 / 0.8 / 4.5

FEBRUARY

Time	m	Time	m
1 TU 0418 / 1050 / 1642 / ● 2322	0.9 / 4.6 / 0.5 / 4.5	**16** W 0427 / 1039 / 1645 / ○ 2301	1.2 / 4.3 / 0.9 / 4.3
2 W 0503 / 1132 / 1727	0.7 / 4.6 / 0.4	**17** TH 0502 / 1110 / 1720 / 2333	1.0 / 4.3 / 0.7 / 4.4
3 TH 0005 / 0547 / 1215 / 1809	4.5 / 0.6 / 4.6 / 0.4	**18** F 0536 / 1143 / 1754	0.9 / 4.4 / 0.6
4 F 0050 / 0629 / 1259 / 1849	4.5 / 0.6 / 4.5 / 0.5	**19** SA 0031 / 0608 / 1220 / 1825	4.5 / 0.8 / 4.5 / 0.6
5 SA 0138 / 0710 / 1344 / 1929	4.4 / 0.8 / 4.3 / 0.7	**20** SU 0103 / 0643 / 1316 / 1859	4.5 / 0.7 / 4.6 / 0.6
6 SU 0147 / 0750 / 1451 / 2009	4.2 / 1.0 / 4.2 / 1.0	**21** M 0141 / 0719 / 1357 / 1936	4.5 / 0.7 / 4.5 / 0.7
7 M 0232 / 0831 / 1441 / 2051	4.1 / 1.3 / 3.9 / 1.4	**22** TU 0224 / 0759 / 1418 / 2018	4.5 / 0.9 / 4.3 / 0.9
8 TU 0312 / 0916 / 1528 / ◑ 2140	3.9 / 1.6 / 3.7 / 1.7	**23** W 0248 / 0844 / 1506 / ◑ 2106	4.3 / 1.1 / 4.1 / 1.3
9 W 0401 / 1010 / 1612 / 2241	3.8 / 1.9 / 3.5 / 2.0	**24** TH 0336 / 0938 / 1602 / 2208	4.0 / 1.5 / 3.8 / 1.7
10 TH 0448 / 1120 / 1712 / 2358	3.6 / 2.1 / 3.3 / 2.2	**25** F 0434 / 1057 / 1709 / 2350	3.8 / 1.8 / 3.6 / 2.0
11 F 0552 / 1252 / 1838	3.5 / 2.1 / 3.4	**26** SA 0557 / 1301 / 1846	3.7 / 1.8 / 3.7
12 SA 0122 / 0710 / 1400 / 1954	2.2 / 3.5 / 1.9 / 3.6	**27** SU 0140 / 0726 / 1410 / 2011	1.8 / 3.8 / 1.5 / 3.9
13 SU 0222 / 0820 / 1448 / 2058	2.0 / 3.7 / 1.6 / 3.8	**28** M 0237 / 0835 / 1501 / 2111	1.5 / 4.1 / 1.1 / 4.2
14 M 0308 / 0913 / 1530 / 2145	1.7 / 3.9 / 1.4 / 4.0		
15 TU 0349 / 0959 / 1609 / 2224	1.4 / 4.1 / 1.1 / 4.2		

MARCH

Time	m	Time	m
1 TU 0324 / 0924 / 1546 / 2233	1.1 / 4.2 / 0.7 / 4.4	**16** W 0325 / 0931 / 1542 / 2157	1.4 / 4.1 / 1.0 / 4.2
2 W 0408 / 1038 / 1628 / ● 2311	0.8 / 4.4 / 0.4 / 4.5	**17** TH 0401 / 1009 / 1619 / 2232	1.1 / 4.2 / 0.7 / 4.4
3 TH 0449 / 1117 / 1709 / 2350	0.5 / 4.5 / 0.3 / 4.5	**18** F 0437 / 1045 / 1655 / ○ 2307	0.8 / 4.4 / 0.5 / 4.5
4 F 0529 / 1156 / 1748	0.4 / 4.5 / 0.3	**19** SA 0511 / 1121 / 1729 / 2343	0.6 / 4.5 / 0.4 / 4.6
5 SA 0030 / 0608 / 1236 / 1826	4.5 / 0.5 / 4.4 / 0.4	**20** SU 0546 / 1155 / 1803	0.5 / 4.6 / 0.4
6 SU 0111 / 0645 / 1316 / 1902	4.4 / 0.6 / 4.3 / 0.7	**21** M 0038 / 0620 / 1253 / 1838	4.7 / 0.4 / 4.7 / 0.4
7 M 0151 / 0720 / 1358 / 1936	4.3 / 0.9 / 4.1 / 1.0	**22** TU 0117 / 0657 / 1335 / 1915	4.6 / 0.5 / 4.6 / 0.6
8 TU 0232 / 0752 / 1442 / 2008	4.2 / 1.2 / 4.1 / 1.3	**23** W 0200 / 0735 / 1358 / 1955	4.5 / 0.7 / 4.4 / 0.9
9 W 0225 / 0825 / 1439 / 2043	3.9 / 1.4 / 3.8 / 1.7	**24** TH 0220 / 0820 / 1445 / 2043	4.2 / 1.1 / 4.1 / 1.4
10 TH 0258 / 0904 / 1514 / ◑ 2132	3.7 / 1.8 / 3.5 / 2.0	**25** F 0306 / 0915 / 1541 / ◑ 2150	3.9 / 1.5 / 3.7 / 1.9
11 F 0333 / 1009 / 1550 / 2302	3.4 / 2.1 / 3.2 / 2.3	**26** SA 0412 / 1054 / 1709	3.6 / 1.9 / 3.6
12 SA 0410 / 1155 / 1632	3.1 / 2.2 / 2.9	**27** SU 0024 / 0550 / 1256 / 1846	2.0 / 3.6 / 1.8 / 3.7
13 SU 0118 / 0450 / 1340 / 1928	2.3 / 2.8 / 2.1 / 3.5	**28** M 0132 / 0713 / 1355 / 1957	1.8 / 3.7 / 1.5 / 3.9
14 M 0209 / 0752 / 1425 / 2030	2.1 / 3.6 / 1.7 / 3.8	**29** TU 0222 / 0819 / 1442 / 2151	1.5 / 3.9 / 1.1 / 4.3
15 TU 0248 / 0850 / 1504 / 2121	1.8 / 3.8 / 1.4 / 4.1	**30** W 0306 / 0945 / 1525 / 2221	1.1 / 4.1 / 0.8 / 4.4
		31 TH 0347 / 1020 / 1606 / 2254	0.8 / 4.3 / 0.5 / 4.5

APRIL

Time	m	Time	m
1 F 0427 / 1057 / 1646 / ● 2331	0.5 / 4.4 / 0.4 / 4.5	**16** SA 0406 / 1014 / 1624 / ○ 2235	0.7 / 4.4 / 0.5 / 4.6
2 SA 0506 / 1136 / 1723	0.5 / 4.4 / 0.4	**17** SU 0442 / 1053 / 1701 / 2315	0.4 / 4.6 / 0.3 / 4.7
3 SU 0009 / 0544 / 1213 / 1800	4.4 / 0.5 / 4.3 / 0.6	**18** M 0520 / 1151 / 1738	0.3 / 4.7 / 0.3
4 M 0042 / 0618 / 1250 / 1834	4.4 / 0.7 / 4.3 / 0.8	**19** TU 0013 / 0558 / 1232 / 1816	4.8 / 0.4 / 4.7 / 0.4
5 TU 0112 / 0649 / 1326 / 1903	4.3 / 0.9 / 4.2 / 1.1	**20** W 0054 / 0637 / 1318 / 1857	4.7 / 0.5 / 4.6 / 0.7
6 W 0144 / 0715 / 1403 / 1929	4.2 / 1.1 / 4.1 / 1.4	**21** TH 0116 / 0719 / 1411 / 1941	4.5 / 0.7 / 4.4 / 1.1
7 TH 0145 / 0742 / 1446 / 2000	4.0 / 1.3 / 4.0 / 1.6	**22** F 0201 / 0807 / 1526 / 2035	4.2 / 1.1 / 4.1 / 1.5
8 F 0217 / 0818 / 1439 / 2041	3.8 / 1.6 / 3.6 / 2.0	**23** SA 0253 / 0856 / 1546 / ◑ 2201	3.8 / 1.6 / 3.8 / 1.9
9 SA 0254 / 0909 / 1524 / ◑ 2202	3.5 / 2.0 / 3.4 / 2.3	**24** SU 0415 / 1052 / 1709 / 2346	3.7 / 1.6 / 3.7 / 2.0
10 SU 0336 / 1055 / 1617	3.2 / 2.2 / 3.2	**25** M 0533 / 1218 / 1822	3.6 / 1.7 / 3.8
11 M 0048 / 0423 / 1247 / 1829	2.4 / 2.9 / 2.1 / 3.4	**26** TU 0057 / 0645 / 1321 / 1931	1.8 / 3.7 / 1.5 / 4.0
12 TU 0136 / 0707 / 1344 / 1952	2.1 / 3.4 / 1.8 / 3.8	**27** W 0152 / 0749 / 1412 / 2027	1.5 / 3.8 / 1.2 / 4.1
13 W 0214 / 0813 / 1428 / 2042	1.8 / 3.7 / 1.4 / 4.1	**28** TH 0237 / 0932 / 1456 / 2217	1.2 / 4.1 / 1.0 / 4.4
14 TH 0252 / 0859 / 1508 / 2123	1.4 / 4.0 / 1.0 / 4.3	**29** F 0319 / 1002 / 1537 / 2238	0.9 / 4.2 / 0.7 / 4.4
15 F 0329 / 0936 / 1546 / 2203	1.0 / 4.2 / 0.7 / 4.5	**30** SA 0400 / 1038 / 1618 / ● 2311	0.7 / 4.2 / 0.7 / 4.4

Chart Datum: 2·74 metres below Ordnance Datum (Newlyn)
HAT is 5·0 metres above Chart Datum

TIDES

TIME ZONE (UT)
For Summer Time add ONE hour in **non-shaded areas**

SOUTHAMPTON

LAT 50°53'N   LONG 1°24'W

TIMES AND HEIGHTS OF HIGH AND LOW WATERS

Dates in amber are **SPRINGS**
Dates in grey are **NEAPS**

2022

MAY

Day	Time	m	Day	Time	m
1 SU	0439 / 1117 / 1657 / 2346	0.6 / 4.3 / 0.7 / 4.4	16 M ○	0413 / 1027 / 1633 / 2309	0.5 / 4.6 / 0.5 / 4.8
2 M	0517 / 1156 / 1733	0.7 / 4.2 / 0.8	17 TU	0456 / 1129 / 1716 / 2351	0.4 / 4.7 / 0.5 / 4.8
3 TU	0014 / 0552 / 1232 / 1807	4.3 / 0.8 / 4.2 / 1.0	18 W	0538 / 1216 / 1759	0.4 / 4.7 / 0.6
4 W	0042 / 0621 / 1306 / 1835	4.3 / 1.0 / 4.2 / 1.3	19 TH	0037 / 0622 / 1306 / 1845	4.7 / 0.5 / 4.6 / 0.8
5 TH	0114 / 0645 / 1342 / 1900	4.2 / 1.2 / 4.1 / 1.5	20 F	0128 / 0709 / 1407 / 1935	4.5 / 0.8 / 4.4 / 1.2
6 F	0114 / 0714 / 1423 / 1934	4.0 / 1.3 / 4.0 / 1.7	21 SA	0153 / 0803 / 1433 / 2035	4.2 / 1.1 / 4.1 / 1.5
7 SA	0150 / 0752 / 1518 / 2017	3.8 / 1.5 / 3.9 / 1.9	22 SU ☽	0251 / 0907 / 1542 / 2147	3.9 / 1.4 / 4.0 / 1.7
8 SU	0231 / 0843 / 1508 / 2125	3.6 / 1.8 / 3.6 / 2.2	23 M	0402 / 1020 / 1650 / 2259	3.8 / 1.6 / 3.9 / 1.8
9 M ☽	0322 / 1007 / 1607 / 2257	3.4 / 2.0 / 3.5 / 2.3	24 TU	0606 / 1128 / 1752	3.8 / 1.6 / 3.9
10 TU	0416 / 1130 / 1718	3.2 / 2.0 / 3.5	25 W	0007 / 0611 / 1233 / 1853	1.8 / 3.7 / 1.6 / 4.0
11 W	0012 / 0543 / 1239 / 1848	2.1 / 3.3 / 1.8 / 3.8	26 TH	0109 / 0708 / 1331 / 1950	1.6 / 3.7 / 1.4 / 4.1
12 TH	0115 / 0717 / 1337 / 1955	1.8 / 3.7 / 1.5 / 4.1	27 F	0202 / 0803 / 1421 / 2034	1.4 / 3.8 / 1.3 / 4.1
13 F	0205 / 0814 / 1425 / 2042	1.4 / 4.0 / 1.1 / 4.3	28 SA	0248 / 0947 / 1506 / 2219	1.2 / 4.1 / 1.1 / 4.3
14 SA	0249 / 0902 / 1509 / 2124	1.1 / 4.2 / 0.8 / 4.5	29 SU	0331 / 1026 / 1549 / 2155	1.0 / 4.1 / 1.0 / 4.2
15 SU	0332 / 0943 / 1551 / 2204	0.7 / 4.4 / 0.6 / 4.6	30 M ●	0413 / 1018 / 1630 / 2236	0.9 / 4.1 / 1.1 / 4.2
			31 TU	0452 / 1058 / 1709 / 2309	1.0 / 4.1 / 1.1 / 4.2

JUNE

Day	Time	m	Day	Time	m
1 W	0529 / 1136 / 1745 / 2344	1.0 / 4.3 / 1.3 / 4.1	16 TH	0525 / 1205 / 1748	0.5 / 4.6 / 0.7
2 TH	0601 / 1209 / 1817	1.2 / 4.1 / 1.4	17 F	0023 / 0613 / 1257 / 1838	4.6 / 0.5 / 4.6 / 0.8
3 F	0018 / 0628 / 1247 / 1845	4.1 / 1.3 / 4.1 / 1.5	18 SA	0114 / 0702 / 1356 / 1928	4.5 / 0.7 / 4.4 / 1.0
4 SA	0056 / 0658 / 1412 / 1919	4.0 / 1.3 / 4.1 / 1.6	19 SU	0210 / 0753 / 1422 / 2022	4.3 / 0.9 / 4.2 / 1.3
5 SU	0134 / 0737 / 1451 / 2003	3.9 / 1.4 / 4.1 / 1.8	20 M	0312 / 0847 / 1518 / 2119	4.1 / 1.1 / 4.1 / 1.5
6 M	0214 / 0825 / 1455 / 2059	3.8 / 1.6 / 3.9 / 1.9	21 TU	0420 / 0945 / 1619 / 2219	4.0 / 1.3 / 4.0 / 1.6
7 TU ☽	0306 / 0926 / 1548 / 2205	3.7 / 1.7 / 3.8 / 2.0	22 W	0434 / 1045 / 1713 / 2321	3.8 / 1.5 / 4.0 / 1.7
8 W	0402 / 1035 / 1646 / 2312	3.6 / 1.7 / 3.8 / 1.9	23 TH	0533 / 1147 / 1812	3.7 / 1.6 / 3.9
9 TH	0505 / 1141 / 1745	3.6 / 1.7 / 3.8	24 F	0025 / 0630 / 1248 / 1902	1.7 / 3.6 / 1.7 / 3.9
10 F	0016 / 0616 / 1243 / 1854	1.7 / 3.7 / 1.5 / 4.0	25 SA	0125 / 0728 / 1345 / 1955	1.6 / 3.7 / 1.6 / 3.9
11 SA	0116 / 0725 / 1341 / 1955	1.5 / 3.9 / 1.3 / 4.2	26 SU	0218 / 0821 / 1436 / 2044	1.5 / 3.8 / 1.5 / 4.0
12 SU	0211 / 0820 / 1434 / 2048	1.2 / 4.2 / 1.0 / 4.4	27 M	0306 / 0915 / 1524 / 2132	1.3 / 3.9 / 1.4 / 4.1
13 M	0301 / 0912 / 1523 / 2139	0.9 / 4.4 / 0.8 / 4.6	28 TU	0351 / 0959 / 1609 / 2215	1.2 / 4.0 / 1.4 / 4.1
14 TU ○	0349 / 1002 / 1611 / 2224	0.6 / 4.5 / 0.7 / 4.7	29 W ●	0433 / 1046 / 1652 / 2257	1.2 / 4.1 / 1.4 / 4.2
15 W	0437 / 1115 / 1700 / 2335	0.5 / 4.6 / 0.7 / 4.7	30 TH	0513 / 1123 / 1731 / 2332	1.1 / 4.1 / 1.4 / 4.1

JULY

Day	Time	m	Day	Time	m
1 F	0549 / 1202 / 1805	1.2 / 4.1 / 1.4	16 SA	0009 / 0604 / 1245 / 1827	4.6 / 0.4 / 4.6 / 0.7
2 SA	0006 / 0619 / 1234 / 1835	4.1 / 1.2 / 4.1 / 1.5	17 SU	0056 / 0649 / 1336 / 1913	4.5 / 0.5 / 4.5 / 0.8
3 SU	0038 / 0649 / 1347 / 1907	4.1 / 1.2 / 4.2 / 1.5	18 M	0146 / 0734 / 1400 / 1959	4.4 / 0.7 / 4.3 / 1.0
4 M	0116 / 0723 / 1419 / 1945	4.1 / 1.2 / 4.2 / 1.5	19 TU	0241 / 0821 / 1447 / 2047	4.2 / 0.9 / 4.2 / 1.3
5 TU	0156 / 0804 / 1501 / 2030	4.0 / 1.3 / 4.2 / 1.5	20 W ☽	0346 / 0910 / 1541 / 2140	4.1 / 1.2 / 4.1 / 1.5
6 W	0242 / 0851 / 1519 / 2123	3.9 / 1.3 / 4.1 / 1.6	21 TH	0356 / 1004 / 1637 / 2238	3.8 / 1.5 / 4.0 / 1.7
7 TH ☽	0335 / 0947 / 1609 / 2223	3.9 / 1.5 / 4.0 / 1.7	22 F	0453 / 1103 / 1727 / 2342	3.7 / 1.8 / 3.8 / 1.9
8 F	0429 / 1051 / 1710 / 2329	3.8 / 1.5 / 4.0 / 1.6	23 SA	0551 / 1208 / 1820	3.6 / 1.9 / 3.7
9 SA	0531 / 1158 / 1809	3.8 / 1.5 / 4.0	24 SU	0049 / 0646 / 1313 / 1919	1.9 / 3.5 / 2.0 / 3.7
10 SU	0036 / 0639 / 1304 / 1916	1.5 / 3.8 / 1.5 / 4.1	25 M	0152 / 0757 / 1414 / 2020	1.8 / 3.6 / 1.9 / 3.8
11 M	0141 / 0749 / 1408 / 2020	1.4 / 4.0 / 1.3 / 4.3	26 TU	0247 / 0859 / 1507 / 2114	1.6 / 3.8 / 1.7 / 4.0
12 TU	0241 / 0853 / 1507 / 2121	1.1 / 4.2 / 1.1 / 4.5	27 W	0334 / 0949 / 1554 / 2201	1.4 / 4.0 / 1.5 / 4.1
13 W ○	0336 / 0950 / 1601 / 2212	0.8 / 4.4 / 0.9 / 4.6	28 TH ●	0417 / 1033 / 1637 / 2243	1.2 / 4.1 / 1.4 / 4.2
14 TH	0428 / 1108 / 1652 / 2323	0.6 / 4.6 / 0.8 / 4.6	29 F	0457 / 1111 / 1715 / 2318	1.1 / 4.2 / 1.3 / 4.2
15 F	0517 / 1156 / 1740	0.5 / 4.6 / 0.7	30 SA	0533 / 1144 / 1749 / 2352	1.0 / 4.2 / 1.3 / 4.2
			31 SU	0605 / 1213 / 1819	1.0 / 4.2 / 1.2

AUGUST

Day	Time	m	Day	Time	m
1 M	0024 / 0633 / 1316 / 1848	4.2 / 1.0 / 4.4 / 1.2	16 TU	0120 / 0711 / 1331 / 1933	4.4 / 0.6 / 4.4 / 0.9
2 TU	0056 / 0704 / 1348 / 1923	4.2 / 1.0 / 4.4 / 1.2	17 W	0209 / 0751 / 1413 / 2014	4.3 / 0.9 / 4.4 / 1.2
3 W	0138 / 0739 / 1428 / 2002	4.3 / 1.0 / 4.4 / 1.2	18 TH	0309 / 0833 / 1457 / 2059	4.1 / 1.2 / 4.1 / 1.5
4 TH	0217 / 0820 / 1514 / 2047	4.2 / 1.1 / 4.3 / 1.3	19 F ◐	0308 / 0921 / 1541 / 2152	3.8 / 1.6 / 3.9 / 1.8
5 F ◐	0307 / 0908 / 1536 / 2141	4.1 / 1.3 / 4.1 / 1.5	20 SA	0358 / 1020 / 1634 / 2259	3.6 / 2.0 / 3.7 / 2.1
6 SA	0359 / 1006 / 1632 / 2248	3.9 / 1.5 / 4.0 / 1.7	21 SU	0456 / 1132 / 1732	3.4 / 2.2 / 3.5
7 SU	0501 / 1119 / 1736	3.8 / 1.7 / 3.9	22 M	0020 / 0614 / 1252 / 1847	2.1 / 3.4 / 2.3 / 3.6
8 M	0007 / 0611 / 1243 / 1851	1.8 / 3.7 / 1.8 / 3.9	23 TU	0135 / 0731 / 1401 / 2056	2.0 / 3.5 / 2.1 / 3.8
9 TU	0130 / 0735 / 1403 / 2011	1.6 / 3.9 / 1.6 / 4.1	24 W	0231 / 0839 / 1453 / 2055	1.8 / 3.8 / 1.9 / 3.9
10 W	0239 / 0849 / 1505 / 2112	1.3 / 4.1 / 1.4 / 4.4	25 TH	0316 / 0926 / 1536 / 2141	1.5 / 4.0 / 1.6 / 4.1
11 TH	0333 / 0946 / 1557 / 2203	0.9 / 4.4 / 1.0 / 4.5	26 F	0356 / 1010 / 1616 / 2221	1.2 / 4.2 / 1.3 / 4.2
12 F ○	0421 / 1101 / 1644 / 2310	0.6 / 4.6 / 0.8 / 4.6	27 SA ●	0434 / 1047 / 1652 / 2255	1.0 / 4.3 / 1.1 / 4.3
13 SA	0506 / 1143 / 1728 / 2352	0.4 / 4.6 / 0.6 / 4.6	28 SU	0509 / 1123 / 1725 / 2329	0.9 / 4.4 / 1.0 / 4.4
14 SU	0549 / 1227 / 1810	0.3 / 4.6 / 0.6	29 M	0541 / 1149 / 1755	0.8 / 4.4 / 1.0
15 M	0035 / 0630 / 1313 / 1852	4.5 / 0.4 / 4.6 / 0.7	30 TU	0002 / 0610 / 1246 / 1824	4.4 / 0.8 / 4.5 / 0.9
			31 W	0035 / 0640 / 1319 / 1858	4.5 / 0.8 / 4.6 / 0.9

Chart Datum: 2·74 metres below Ordnance Datum (Newlyn)
HAT is 5·0 metres above Chart Datum

SOUTHAMPTON

LAT 50°53'N   LONG 1°24'W

TIMES AND HEIGHTS OF HIGH AND LOW WATERS

Dates in amber are SPRINGS
Dates in grey are NEAPS

2022

SEPTEMBER

Day	Time	m	Time	m	Day	Time	m	Time	m
1 TH	0132 / 0713 / 1359 / 1934	4.5 / 0.8 / 4.5 / 1.0			16 F	0224 / 0756 / 1406 / 2015	4.1 / 1.4 / 4.0 / 1.6		
2 F	0215 / 0751 / 1418 / 2015	4.4 / 1.0 / 4.4 / 1.2			17 SA	0220 / 0835 / 1439 / 2058 ◑	3.8 / 1.8 / 3.8 / 1.9		
3 SA	0238 / 0836 / 1505 / 2105 ◑	4.2 / 1.3 / 4.2 / 1.5			18 SU	0250 / 0930 / 1508 / 2212	3.5 / 2.2 / 3.5 / 2.2		
4 SU	0327 / 0930 / 1557 / 2214	3.9 / 1.7 / 3.9 / 1.9			19 M	0323 / 1105 / 1526	3.2 / 2.4 / 3.1		
5 M	0526 / 1055 / 1706	3.8 / 2.1 / 3.7			20 TU	0000 / 0346 / 1239 / 1905	2.3 / 2.9 / 2.4 / 2.4		
6 TU	0011 / 0556 / 1302 / 1842	2.0 / 3.6 / 2.0 / 3.8			21 W	0113 / 0700 / 1343 / 2018	2.2 / 3.5 / 2.2 / 3.7		
7 W	0141 / 0739 / 1410 / 2005	1.7 / 3.9 / 1.7 / 4.1			22 TH	0205 / 0806 / 1430 / 2023	1.9 / 3.8 / 1.9 / 3.8		
8 TH	0236 / 0847 / 1500 / 2103	1.3 / 4.2 / 1.4 / 4.3			23 F	0248 / 0858 / 1510 / 2113	1.6 / 4.1 / 1.6 / 4.1		
9 F	0323 / 0936 / 1545 / 2145	0.9 / 4.4 / 1.0 / 4.5			24 SA	0327 / 0943 / 1547 / 2152	1.2 / 4.3 / 1.3 / 4.3		
10 SA	0406 / 1049 / 1627 / 2252 ○	0.6 / 4.6 / 0.7 / 4.6			25 SU	0403 / 1018 / 1622 / 2229 ●	1.0 / 4.5 / 1.0 / 4.4		
11 SU	0447 / 1127 / 1708 / 2333	0.4 / 4.7 / 0.5 / 4.6			26 M	0438 / 1053 / 1654 / 2259	0.8 / 4.6 / 0.9 / 4.5		
12 M	0527 / 1207 / 1748	0.3 / 4.7 / 0.5			27 TU	0511 / 1122 / 1726 / 2335	0.7 / 4.6 / 0.8 / 4.6		
13 TU	0012 / 0606 / 1249 / 1826	4.5 / 0.4 / 4.6 / 0.7			28 W	0542 / 1218 / 1759	0.7 / 4.7 / 0.7		
14 W	0054 / 0644 / 1333 / 1903	4.4 / 0.7 / 4.5 / 0.9			29 TH	0030 / 0614 / 1253 / 1832	4.7 / 0.7 / 4.7 / 0.8		
15 TH	0136 / 0720 / 1329 / 1939	4.3 / 1.0 / 4.2 / 1.2			30 F	0109 / 0649 / 1312 / 1909	4.7 / 0.8 / 4.6 / 0.9		

OCTOBER

Day	Time / m		16–	Time / m
1 SA	0152 / 0727 / 1353 / 1950	4.5 / 1.1 / 4.4 / 1.2	16 SU	0239 / 0749 / 1400 / 2005 = 4.0 / 1.9 / 3.9 / 1.9
2 SU	0213 / 0811 / 1434 / 2040	4.2 / 1.5 / 4.1 / 1.6	17 M	0217 / 0830 / 1429 / 2100 ◑ = 3.7 / 2.2 / 3.6 / 2.2
3 M	0304 / 0909 / 1523 / 2205 ◑	3.9 / 2.0 / 3.7 / 2.1	18 TU	0257 / 1033 / 1500 / 2328 = 3.4 / 2.5 / 3.2 / 2.3
4 TU	0415 / 1142 / 1701	3.6 / 2.2 / 3.6	19 W	0353 / 1216 / 1828 = 3.2 / 2.5 / 3.6
5 W	0026 / 0603 / 1300 / 1835	2.0 / 3.7 / 2.0 / 3.8	20 TH	0035 / 0719 / 1312 / 1842 = 2.2 / 3.7 / 2.3 / 3.5
6 TH	0127 / 0729 / 1354 / 1948	1.7 / 4.0 / 1.7 / 4.0	21 F	0126 / 0728 / 1356 / 1948 = 2.0 / 3.8 / 2.0 / 3.8
7 F	0217 / 0828 / 1441 / 2041	1.3 / 4.3 / 1.3 / 4.3	22 SA	0210 / 0822 / 1434 / 2037 = 1.7 / 4.1 / 1.6 / 4.1
8 SA	0301 / 1008 / 1524 / 2158	1.0 / 4.6 / 1.0 / 4.5	23 SU	0249 / 0903 / 1510 / 2120 = 1.3 / 4.4 / 1.3 / 4.3
9 SU	0343 / 1034 / 1605 / 2234 ○	0.7 / 4.7 / 0.7 / 4.6	24 M	0327 / 0943 / 1546 / 2157 = 1.0 / 4.5 / 1.0 / 4.5
10 M	0423 / 1109 / 1644 / 2312	0.5 / 4.8 / 0.6 / 4.6	25 TU	0403 / 1018 / 1621 / 2229 ● = 0.8 / 4.6 / 0.8 / 4.6
11 TU	0501 / 1146 / 1723 / 2350	0.5 / 4.6 / 0.6 / 4.5	26 W	0438 / 1052 / 1657 / 2309 = 0.7 / 4.7 / 0.7 / 4.7
12 W	0539 / 1223 / 1759	0.6 / 4.6 / 0.8	27 TH	0514 / 1131 / 1733 = 0.6 / 4.8 / 0.6
13 TH	0028 / 0616 / 1256 / 1834	4.4 / 0.9 / 4.5 / 0.8	28 F	0007 / 0551 / 1209 / 1811 = 4.8 / 0.7 / 4.7 / 0.7
14 F	0106 / 0649 / 1330 / 1905	4.3 / 1.2 / 4.4 / 1.3	29 SA	0050 / 0630 / 1252 / 1851 = 4.7 / 0.9 / 4.6 / 0.9
15 SA	0147 / 0720 / 1408 / 1933	4.2 / 1.5 / 4.2 / 1.6	30 SU	0138 / 0712 / 1332 / 1936 = 4.5 / 1.2 / 4.4 / 1.3
			31 M	0238 / 0802 / 1420 / 2033 = 4.3 / 1.6 / 4.0 / 1.7

NOVEMBER

Day	Time / m		16–	Time / m
1 TU	0303 / 0918 / 1531 / 2219 ◑	3.9 / 2.1 / 3.8 / 2.0	16 W	0251 / 0911 / 1456 / 2155 ◑ = 3.7 / 2.4 / 3.5 / 2.2
2 W	0426 / 1115 / 1657 / 2351	3.8 / 2.1 / 3.7 / 1.9	17 TH	0348 / 1051 / 1554 / 2322 = 3.6 / 2.4 / 3.3 / 2.2
3 TH	0546 / 1227 / 1811	3.9 / 2.0 / 3.8	18 F	0456 / 1207 / 1722 = 3.6 / 2.3 / 3.4
4 F	0053 / 0658 / 1323 / 1916	1.7 / 4.0 / 1.7 / 3.9	19 SA	0025 / 0621 / 1300 / 1849 = 2.0 / 3.8 / 2.1 / 3.7
5 SA	0145 / 0800 / 1412 / 2123	1.4 / 4.3 / 1.4 / 4.3	20 SU	0117 / 0732 / 1345 / 1954 = 1.8 / 4.1 / 1.7 / 4.0
6 SU	0231 / 0847 / 1455 / 2141	1.2 / 4.4 / 1.1 / 4.4	21 M	0203 / 0822 / 1427 / 2038 = 1.5 / 4.3 / 1.4 / 4.2
7 M	0313 / 1021 / 1537 / 2216	1.0 / 4.6 / 0.9 / 4.4	22 TU	0246 / 0903 / 1509 / 2121 = 1.2 / 4.5 / 1.0 / 4.4
8 TU	0355 / 1053 / 1617 / 2255 ○	0.8 / 4.6 / 0.8 / 4.4	23 W	0328 / 0946 / 1550 / 2202 ● = 0.9 / 4.7 / 0.8 / 4.6
9 W	0434 / 1128 / 1656 / 2335	0.8 / 4.6 / 0.8 / 4.4	24 TH	0409 / 1023 / 1631 / 2307 = 0.8 / 4.7 / 0.6 / 4.7
10 TH	0513 / 1200 / 1734	1.0 / 4.5 / 0.9	25 F	0451 / 1108 / 1714 / 2351 = 0.7 / 4.8 / 0.6 / 4.8
11 F	0015 / 0550 / 1229 / 1808	4.4 / 1.2 / 4.4 / 1.1	26 SA	0533 / 1152 / 1757 = 0.8 / 4.7 / 0.7
12 SA	0053 / 0623 / 1302 / 1837	4.3 / 1.4 / 4.3 / 1.4	27 SU	0039 / 0619 / 1235 / 1843 = 4.7 / 1.0 / 4.6 / 0.9
13 SU	0133 / 0652 / 1259 / 1904	4.2 / 1.6 / 4.1 / 1.6	28 M	0132 / 0707 / 1353 / 1933 = 4.5 / 1.2 / 4.5 / 1.2
14 M	0124 / 0723 / 1332 / 1938	4.0 / 1.9 / 3.9 / 1.8	29 TU	0237 / 0803 / 1418 / 2035 = 4.4 / 1.5 / 4.1 / 1.5
15 TU	0200 / 0803 / 1409 / 2025	3.8 / 2.1 / 3.7 / 2.0	30 W	0304 / 0912 / 1525 / 2148 ◑ = 4.1 / 1.8 / 3.9 / 1.7

DECEMBER

Day	Time / m		16–	Time / m
1 TH	0414 / 1028 / 1633 / 2301	4.0 / 1.9 / 3.8 / 1.7	16 F	0323 / 0933 / 1534 / 2202 ◑ = 3.9 / 2.1 / 3.6 / 1.9
2 F	0517 / 1139 / 1738	4.0 / 1.9 / 3.8	17 SA	0418 / 1041 / 1635 / 2312 = 3.8 / 2.1 / 3.6 / 1.9
3 SA	0007 / 0623 / 1242 / 1841	1.7 / 4.1 / 1.8 / 3.8	18 SU	0515 / 1148 / 1741 = 3.8 / 2.0 / 3.6
4 SU	0106 / 0721 / 1337 / 1938	1.6 / 4.2 / 1.6 / 3.9	19 M	0016 / 0620 / 1249 / 1849 = 1.8 / 3.9 / 1.8 / 3.8
5 M	0157 / 0810 / 1425 / 2132	1.4 / 4.2 / 1.3 / 4.2	20 TU	0115 / 0727 / 1345 / 1953 = 1.6 / 4.1 / 1.5 / 4.0
6 TU	0243 / 0859 / 1510 / 2211	1.3 / 4.3 / 1.2 / 4.2	21 W	0208 / 0823 / 1437 / 2052 = 1.4 / 4.3 / 1.2 / 4.3
7 W	0327 / 1039 / 1553 / 2306	1.2 / 4.5 / 1.1 / 4.3	22 TH	0259 / 0917 / 1526 / 2139 = 1.1 / 4.5 / 0.9 / 4.4
8 TH	0411 / 1018 / 1635 / 2238	1.2 / 4.3 / 1.0 / 4.2	23 F	0348 / 1004 / 1614 / 2254 ● = 0.9 / 4.7 / 0.7 / 4.6
9 F	0452 / 1054 / 1715 / 2320	1.2 / 4.3 / 1.1 / 4.2	24 SA	0436 / 1049 / 1702 / 2341 = 0.8 / 4.7 / 0.6 / 4.7
10 SA	0532 / 1131 / 1752 / 2358	1.3 / 4.3 / 1.2 / 4.2	25 SU	0524 / 1138 / 1749 = 0.8 / 4.8 / 0.6
11 SU	0608 / 1206 / 1823	1.5 / 4.2 / 1.3	26 M	0030 / 0613 / 1248 / 1838 = 4.7 / 0.9 / 4.7 / 0.6
12 M	0031 / 0639 / 1244 / 1852	4.1 / 1.6 / 4.1 / 1.4	27 TU	0122 / 0702 / 1339 / 1927 = 4.6 / 1.0 / 4.5 / 0.8
13 TU	0107 / 0709 / 1319 / 1924	4.1 / 1.7 / 4.0 / 1.6	28 W	0220 / 0752 / 1435 / 2018 = 4.5 / 1.2 / 4.3 / 1.0
14 W	0148 / 0746 / 1359 / 2005	4.0 / 1.9 / 3.9 / 1.7	29 TH	0247 / 0846 / 1540 / 2113 = 4.3 / 1.4 / 4.2 / 1.3
15 TH	0230 / 0833 / 1442 / 2056	3.9 / 2.0 / 3.8 / 1.8	30 F	0344 / 0945 / 1702 / 2213 ◑ = 4.1 / 1.6 / 4.0 / 1.5
			31 SA	0444 / 1050 / 1702 / 2319 = 4.1 / 1.8 / 3.8 / 1.7

Chart Datum: 2·74 metres below Ordnance Datum (Newlyn)
HAT is 5·0 metres above Chart Datum

TIDES

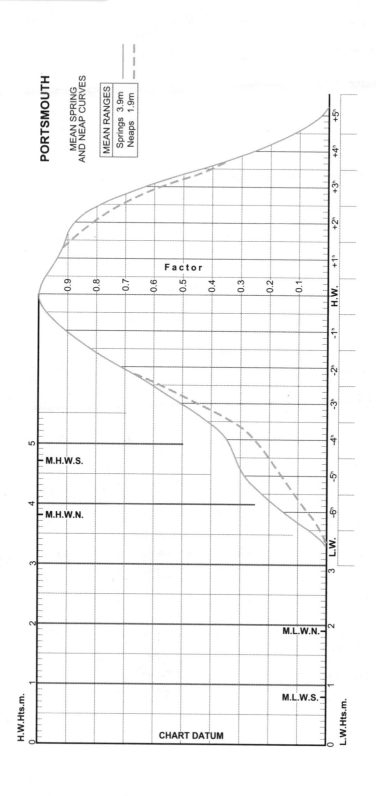

PORTSMOUTH

MEAN SPRING
AND NEAP CURVES

MEAN RANGES

Springs 3.9m
Neaps 1.9m

Factor

0.9 0.8 0.7 0.6 0.5 0.4 0.3 0.2 0.1

H.W.Hts.m.

M.H.W.S.

M.H.W.N.

CHART DATUM

L.W.Hts.m.

M.L.W.N.

M.L.W.S.

H.W.

L.W.

PORTSMOUTH

LAT 50°48'N   LONG 1°07'W

Dates in amber are **SPRINGS**
Dates in grey are **NEAPS**

2022

TIMES AND HEIGHTS OF HIGH AND LOW WATERS

JANUARY

Time	m		Time	m
1 0246	1.2	**16** 0331	1.6
0944	4.7	1037	4.3
SA 1516	1.0	SU 1557	1.1
2212	4.6	2308	4.3
2 0338	1.0	**17** 0413	1.5
1034	4.8	1116	4.4
SU 1607	0.8	M 1636	1.2
● 2305	4.7	○ 2346	4.4
3 0429	0.9	**18** 0452	1.4
1122	4.8	1152	4.4
M 1656	0.7	TU 1712	1.1
2357	4.8		
4 0519	0.9	**19** 0021	4.5
1210	4.8	0528	1.3
TU 1744	0.6	W 1225	4.5
		1746	1.0
5 0051	4.8	**20** 0054	4.5
0607	0.9	0602	1.2
W 1258	4.8	TH 1256	4.4
1831	0.7	1820	1.0
6 0150	4.7	**21** 0127	4.5
0654	1.0	0635	1.2
TH 1349	4.6	F 1328	4.4
1918	0.8	1853	0.9
7 0254	4.7	**22** 0203	4.5
0742	1.2	0710	1.2
F 1444	4.5	SA 1403	4.4
2005	1.0	1928	1.0
8 0345	4.6	**23** 0241	4.4
0833	1.4	0748	1.2
SA 1539	4.3	SU 1442	4.3
2056	1.4	2007	1.0
9 0429	4.4	**24** 0324	4.4
0928	1.6	0831	1.3
SU 1633	4.1	M 1529	4.2
◗ 2154	1.5	2052	1.1
10 0516	4.2	**25** 0415	4.3
1031	1.8	0921	1.4
M 1729	3.9	TU 1627	4.1
2257	1.7	◑ 2146	1.3
11 0608	4.1	**26** 0513	4.2
1138	1.9	1024	1.6
TU 1829	3.8	W 1736	4.0
		2254	1.5
12 0000	1.9	**27** 0618	4.1
0707	4.0	1144	1.6
W 1241	1.9	TH 1850	3.9
1935	3.8		
13 0059	1.9	**28** 0019	1.6
0808	4.0	0728	4.1
TH 1338	1.8	F 1304	1.6
2039	3.8	2004	4.0
14 0154	1.8	**29** 0134	1.6
0904	4.1	0836	4.3
F 1429	1.7	SA 1411	1.4
2137	4.0	2111	4.2
15 0244	1.7	**30** 0238	1.4
0953	4.2	0935	4.4
SA 1515	1.5	SU 1509	1.1
2225	4.2	2210	4.4
		31 0334	1.2
		1026	4.6
		M 1601	0.8
		2302	4.6

FEBRUARY

Time	m		Time	m
1 0424	1.0	**16** 0435	1.2
1113	4.7	1130	4.4
TU 1649	0.6	W 1652	0.9
● 2351	4.7	○ 2357	4.5
2 0511	0.8	**17** 0509	1.0
1158	4.7	1203	4.5
W 1733	0.5	TH 1727	0.8
3 0040	4.7	**18** 0029	4.5
0555	0.7	0544	0.9
TH 1243	4.7	F 1234	4.5
1817	0.5	1801	0.7
4 0132	4.7	**19** 0103	4.6
0638	0.8	0617	0.8
F 1330	4.6	SA 1307	4.5
1858	0.6	1834	0.6
5 0226	4.7	**20** 0137	4.6
0719	0.9	0651	0.8
SA 1419	4.5	SU 1341	4.5
1939	0.8	1908	0.7
6 0308	4.6	**21** 0213	4.5
0800	1.1	0726	0.8
SU 1506	4.3	M 1419	4.5
2019	1.1	1945	0.7
7 0346	4.4	**22** 0253	4.5
0842	1.4	0806	0.9
M 1551	4.1	TU 1503	4.3
2100	1.4	2026	0.9
8 0423	4.2	**23** 0340	4.3
0928	1.6	0852	1.2
TU 1636	3.9	W 1559	4.2
◗ 2148	1.7	◗ 2115	1.3
9 0505	4.0	**24** 0439	4.1
1028	1.9	0949	1.5
W 1723	3.7	TH 1710	4.0
2259	2.0	2219	1.6
10 0600	3.8	**25** 0550	4.0
1153	2.0	1116	1.7
TH 1846	3.6	F 1835	3.8
11 0020	2.1	**26** 0009	1.8
0722	3.7	0713	3.9
F 1308	2.0	SA 1300	1.7
2009	3.6	1959	3.9
12 0131	2.1	**27** 0136	1.7
0835	3.8	0828	4.0
SA 1411	1.9	SU 1410	1.5
2114	3.8	2109	4.1
13 0231	1.9	**28** 0239	1.5
0931	3.9	0927	4.2
SU 1500	1.6	M 1505	1.1
2205	4.0	2205	4.4
14 0318	1.7		
1016	4.1		
M 1540	1.4		
2246	4.2		
15 0358	1.4		
1055	4.3		
TU 1617	1.1		
2323	4.4		

MARCH

Time	m		Time	m
1 0330	1.2	**16** 0333	1.4
1016	4.4	1028	4.2
TU 1552	0.8	W 1548	1.1
2253	4.5	2253	4.4
2 0415	0.9	**17** 0409	1.1
1059	4.6	1102	4.4
W 1635	0.6	TH 1625	0.8
2337	4.7	2326	4.5
3 0457	0.7	**18** 0444	0.9
1142	4.6	1134	4.5
TH 1717	0.5	F 1701	0.6
		○ 2359	4.6
4 0020	4.7	**19** 0519	0.7
0538	0.6	1208	4.6
F 1224	4.6	SA 1736	0.5
1757	0.7		
5 0104	4.7	**20** 0033	4.7
0617	0.6	0554	0.6
SA 1308	4.6	SU 1241	4.6
1834	0.6	1811	0.5
6 0147	4.6	**21** 0107	4.7
0653	0.8	0628	0.6
SU 1351	4.5	M 1318	4.6
1910	0.8	1846	0.5
7 0224	4.5	**22** 0144	4.7
0727	1.0	0705	0.6
M 1431	4.4	TU 1359	4.6
1942	1.0	1923	0.7
8 0257	4.4	**23** 0226	4.6
0759	1.2	0744	0.8
TU 1508	4.2	W 1447	4.4
2014	1.3	2005	1.0
9 0329	4.2	**24** 0316	4.4
0832	1.5	0830	1.1
W 1544	4.0	TH 1547	4.2
2051	1.6	2055	1.4
10 0405	4.0	**25** 0418	4.1
0914	1.8	0929	1.5
TH 1627	3.8	F 1704	4.0
◗ 2139	2.0	◗ 2209	1.8
11 0451	3.7	**26** 0535	3.9
1015	2.0	1121	1.8
F 1725	3.5	SA 1831	3.8
2333	2.2		
12 0556	3.5	**27** 0017	1.9
1233	2.1	0704	3.8
SA 1935	3.5	SU 1253	1.7
		1954	3.9
13 0110	2.2	**28** 0131	1.8
0804	3.5	0818	3.9
SU 1345	2.0	M 1357	1.5
2047	3.7	2102	4.2
14 0215	2.0	**29** 0228	1.5
0905	3.8	0916	4.2
M 1433	1.7	TU 1448	1.0
2139	4.0	2156	4.4
15 0257	1.7	**30** 0314	1.2
0951	4.0	1001	4.4
TU 1512	1.4	W 1533	0.9
2219	4.2	2240	4.6
		31 0356	0.9
		1042	4.5
		TH 1614	0.7
		2318	4.7

APRIL

Time	m		Time	m
1 0436	0.7	**16** 0413	0.8
1122	4.5	1102	4.6
F 1654	0.6	SA 1630	0.6
● 2356	4.7	○ 2325	4.7
2 0515	0.6	**17** 0450	0.6
1203	4.5	1138	4.7
SA 1732	0.6	SU 1708	0.5
3 0033	4.6	**18** 0001	4.8
0552	0.7	0528	0.5
SU 1244	4.5	M 1216	4.7
1808	0.7	1746	0.5
4 0110	4.6	**19** 0039	4.8
0626	0.8	0606	0.5
M 1323	4.5	TU 1258	4.7
1840	0.9	1825	0.6
5 0144	4.5	**20** 0120	4.8
0655	1.0	0645	0.6
TU 1400	4.4	W 1344	4.7
1909	1.1	1906	0.8
6 0215	4.4	**21** 0206	4.6
0724	1.2	0729	0.8
W 1433	4.3	TH 1440	4.5
1939	1.4	1952	1.1
7 0246	4.2	**22** 0301	4.4
0755	1.4	0819	1.2
TH 1509	4.1	F 1549	4.3
2014	1.6	2049	1.5
8 0324	4.0	**23** 0408	4.1
0834	1.7	0928	1.5
F 1552	3.9	SA 1704	4.1
2059	2.0	2228	1.9
9 0411	3.8	**24** 0525	3.9
0927	2.0	1114	1.7
SA 1647	3.7	SU 1823	4.0
◗ 2210	2.3	2358	1.9
10 0510	3.5	**25** 0648	3.8
1140	2.1	1228	1.7
SU 1818	3.5	M 1942	4.1
11 0032	2.2	**26** 0106	1.8
0715	3.4	0803	4.0
M 1258	2.0	TU 1329	1.5
2011	3.7	2053	4.3
12 0135	2.0	**27** 0202	1.5
0830	3.7	0903	4.1
TU 1350	1.7	W 1421	1.3
2104	4.0	2147	4.5
13 0219	1.5	**28** 0249	1.3
0917	3.9	0946	4.3
W 1433	1.4	TH 1506	1.1
2144	4.3	2226	4.6
14 0258	1.2	**29** 0331	1.0
0954	4.2	1022	4.4
TH 1513	1.1	F 1548	0.9
2218	4.5	2254	4.6
15 0335	1.1	**30** 0411	0.9
1027	4.4	1100	4.4
F 1552	0.8	SA 1627	0.9
2251	4.6	● 2327	4.6

Chart Datum: 2·73 metres below Ordnance Datum (Newlyn)
HAT is 5·1 metres above Chart Datum

TIDES

TIME ZONE (UT)
For Summer Time add ONE hour in **non-shaded areas**

PORTSMOUTH
LAT 50°48'N   LONG 1°07'W
TIMES AND HEIGHTS OF HIGH AND LOW WATERS

Dates in amber are **SPRINGS**
Dates in grey are **NEAPS**

2022

MAY

Day					Day				
1 SU	0449 0.8	1141 4.5	1704 0.9		**16** M	0421 0.6	1110 4.7	1640 0.6	○ 2332 4.9
2 M	0002 4.6	0525 0.9	1221 4.5	1740 1.0	**17** TU	0503 0.5	1155 4.8	1723 0.6	
3 TU	0038 4.5	0558 1.0	1300 4.4	1812 1.1	**18** W	0015 4.9	0546 0.5	1242 4.8	1808 0.7
4 W	0112 4.5	0628 1.1	1336 4.4	1843 1.3	**19** TH	0101 4.8	0631 0.7	1337 4.7	1854 0.9
5 TH	0143 4.4	0657 1.2	1410 4.3	1914 1.5	**20** F	0153 4.6	0719 0.9	1442 4.6	1946 1.2
6 F	0216 4.2	0729 1.4	1447 4.2	1950 1.7	**21** SA	0252 4.4	0814 1.2	1552 4.4	2049 1.5
7 SA	0255 4.1	0808 1.6	1531 4.0	2034 1.9	**22** SU	0358 4.2	0924 1.4	1657 4.3	◔ 2209 1.7
8 SU	0343 3.8	0859 1.8	1624 3.9	2138 2.1	**23** M	0508 4.0	1043 1.6	1806 4.2	2323 1.8
9 M	0440 3.6	1018 2.0	1730 3.8	◑ 2332 2.2	**24** TU	0621 3.9	1152 1.6	1918 4.2	
10 TU	0553 3.6	1200 1.9	1905 3.8		**25** W	0028 1.7	0733 4.0	1252 1.5	2025 4.3
11 W	0039 2.0	0732 3.7	1259 1.7	2014 4.0	**26** TH	0127 1.6	0834 4.1	1346 1.4	2117 4.4
12 TH	0130 1.7	0828 3.9	1348 1.4	2057 4.3	**27** F	0217 1.4	0919 4.2	1433 1.3	2151 4.5
13 F	0215 1.4	0909 4.2	1433 1.2	2135 4.5	**28** SA	0301 1.3	0958 4.3	1517 1.2	2223 4.5
14 SA	0257 1.1	0948 4.4	1516 0.9	2212 4.7	**29** SU	0343 1.1	1039 4.3	1558 1.2	2259 4.5
15 SU	0339 0.8	1028 4.6	1558 0.7	2251 4.8	**30** M	0422 1.1	1122 4.4	1638 1.2	● 2337 4.5
					31 TU	0500 1.1	1204 4.4	1715 1.2	

JUNE

Day					Day				
1 W	0014 4.5	0536 1.1	1244 4.4	1751 1.3	**16** TH	0532 0.6	1235 4.8	1756 0.8	
2 TH	0049 4.4	0608 1.2	1321 4.4	1824 1.4	**17** F	0048 4.8	0621 0.7	1334 4.7	1846 1.4
3 F	0122 4.4	0639 1.3	1356 4.3	1857 1.5	**18** SA	0141 4.7	0711 0.8	1444 4.7	1938 1.1
4 SA	0155 4.3	0709 1.4	1432 4.3	1934 1.6	**19** SU	0240 4.5	0804 1.0	1547 4.6	2034 1.4
5 SU	0234 4.1	0751 1.5	1514 4.2	2016 1.8	**20** M	0342 4.3	0902 1.2	1641 4.5	2136 1.5
6 M	0319 4.0	0838 1.6	1602 4.1	2109 1.9	**21** TU	0444 4.2	1005 1.4	1735 4.4	◔ 2240 1.7
7 TU	0412 3.8	0936 1.7	1657 4.0	2214 1.9	**22** W	0545 4.0	1109 1.6	1831 4.3	2344 1.7
8 W	0513 3.8	1046 1.7	1758 4.0	2328 1.9	**23** TH	0646 4.0	1210 1.6	1928 4.2	
9 TH	0621 3.8	1158 1.6	1902 4.1		**24** F	0045 1.7	0746 3.9	1306 1.6	2022 4.2
10 F	0033 1.7	0726 4.0	1258 1.5	2000 4.3	**25** SA	0141 1.6	0843 4.0	1359 1.6	2110 4.3
11 SA	0128 1.4	0822 4.2	1351 1.3	2050 4.5	**26** SU	0231 1.5	0935 4.1	1447 1.5	2154 4.3
12 SU	0219 1.2	0912 4.4	1441 1.1	2137 4.6	**27** M	0317 1.4	1024 4.2	1533 1.5	2236 4.4
13 M	0308 0.9	1001 4.5	1530 0.9	2224 4.7	**28** TU	0400 1.3	1108 4.3	1617 1.4	2317 4.4
14 TU	0356 0.8	1051 4.7	1618 0.8	○ 2311 4.8	**29** W	0441 1.2	1150 4.4	1658 1.4	● 2356 4.4
15 W	0444 0.6	1142 4.7	1707 0.8	2359 4.8	**30** TH	0519 1.2	1230 4.4	1736 1.4	

JULY

Day					Day				
1 F	0032 4.4	0554 1.2	1306 4.4	1812 1.4	**16** SA	0035 4.8	0611 0.6	1325 4.8	1835 0.8
2 SA	0106 4.3	0627 1.2	1334 4.3	1845 1.4	**17** SU	0126 4.7	0657 0.6	1434 4.8	1922 1.0
3 SU	0139 4.3	0700 1.2	1416 4.3	1918 1.4	**18** M	0221 4.6	0744 0.8	1531 4.7	2010 1.1
4 M	0213 4.2	0735 1.3	1454 4.3	1956 1.5	**19** TU	0319 4.4	0833 1.1	1613 4.6	2101 1.4
5 TU	0253 4.1	0814 1.3	1536 4.2	2039 1.5	**20** W	0413 4.3	0926 1.3	1655 4.4	◔ 2158 1.6
6 W	0340 4.1	0900 1.4	1623 4.2	2130 1.6	**21** TH	0506 4.1	1025 1.6	1742 4.2	2300 1.7
7 TH	0434 4.0	0955 1.5	1716 4.2	◔ 2231 1.6	**22** F	0602 3.9	1127 1.8	1835 4.1	
8 F	0536 3.9	1100 1.5	1815 4.2	2339 1.6	**23** SA	0004 1.8	0705 3.8	1229 1.9	1937 4.0
9 SA	0641 4.0	1210 1.5	1916 4.2		**24** SU	0107 1.8	0813 3.8	1329 1.9	2038 4.0
10 SU	0047 1.5	0747 4.1	1315 1.4	2018 4.3	**25** M	0206 1.7	0917 3.9	1426 1.8	2132 4.1
11 M	0149 1.3	0849 4.2	1415 1.3	2115 4.5	**26** TU	0259 1.6	1008 4.1	1518 1.7	2217 4.2
12 TU	0247 1.1	0948 4.4	1512 1.2	2209 4.6	**27** W	0345 1.4	1052 4.2	1604 1.5	2259 4.3
13 W	0342 0.9	1043 4.6	1607 1.0	○ 2259 4.7	**28** TH	0426 1.2	1131 4.4	1645 1.4	● 2337 4.4
14 TH	0434 0.7	1136 4.7	1658 0.9	2348 4.8	**29** F	0503 1.1	1209 4.4	1721 1.3	
15 F	0523 0.6	1229 4.8	1747 0.8		**30** SA	0012 4.4	0538 1.1	1244 4.5	1755 1.2
					31 SU	0046 4.4	0610 1.0	1318 4.5	1827 1.2

AUGUST

Day					Day				
1 M	0117 4.4	0641 1.0	1352 4.5	1858 1.2	**16** TU	0156 4.6	0719 0.7	1456 4.7	1942 1.0
2 TU	0149 4.3	0713 1.0	1426 4.4	1932 1.2	**17** W	0247 4.5	0801 1.0	1533 4.6	2025 1.3
3 W	0223 4.3	0748 1.0	1503 4.4	2010 1.2	**18** TH	0336 4.3	0844 1.3	1610 4.4	2112 1.5
4 TH	0304 4.2	0828 1.1	1546 4.3	2054 1.3	**19** F	0423 4.1	0934 1.7	1650 4.1	◑ 2210 1.8
5 F	0354 4.1	0915 1.3	1636 4.2	◔ 2149 1.5	**20** SA	0514 3.8	1043 2.0	1739 3.9	2326 2.0
6 SA	0456 4.0	1015 1.5	1736 4.1	2257 1.6	**21** SU	0624 3.7	1159 2.1	1853 3.7	
7 SU	0609 3.9	1133 1.7	1846 4.1		**22** M	0039 2.1	0747 3.6	1309 2.2	2011 3.8
8 M	0020 1.7	0729 4.0	1257 1.7	2001 4.2	**23** TU	0148 1.9	0858 3.8	1414 2.0	2111 3.9
9 TU	0136 1.5	0844 4.1	1408 1.6	2108 4.3	**24** W	0243 1.7	0950 4.1	1505 1.8	2158 4.1
10 W	0241 1.3	0947 4.4	1509 1.3	2201 4.5	**25** TH	0326 1.5	1031 4.3	1546 1.6	2238 4.3
11 TH	0337 1.0	1039 4.6	1602 1.1	2249 4.7	**26** F	0404 1.2	1108 4.4	1623 1.3	2314 4.4
12 F	0426 0.7	1127 4.7	1650 0.8	○ 2334 4.7	**27** SA	0439 1.0	1143 4.5	1658 1.2	● 2348 4.5
13 SA	0512 0.5	1216 4.8	1734 0.7		**28** SU	0513 0.9	1216 4.6	1731 1.0	
14 SU	0019 4.8	0556 0.5	1306 4.8	1818 0.7	**29** M	0020 4.5	0546 0.8	1249 4.6	1802 1.0
15 M	0106 4.7	0638 0.5	1404 4.8	1900 0.8	**30** TU	0050 4.5	0617 0.8	1321 4.6	1834 1.0
					31 W	0121 4.5	0648 0.8	1352 4.6	1906 1.0

Chart Datum: 2·73 metres below Ordnance Datum (Newlyn)
HAT is 5·1 metres above Chart Datum

TIME ZONE (UT)
For Summer Time add ONE hour in non-shaded areas

PORTSMOUTH

LAT 50°48'N   LONG 1°07'W

TIMES AND HEIGHTS OF HIGH AND LOW WATERS

Dates in amber are SPRINGS
Dates in grey are NEAPS

2022

SEPTEMBER

Day	Time	m	Time	m	Time	m	Time	m
1 TH	0153	4.5	0721	0.9	1426	4.5	1942	1.0
16 F	0253	4.3	0801	1.4	1517	4.1	2022	1.6
2 F	0233	4.4	0759	1.1	1507	4.4	2023	1.2
17 SA	0334	4.1	0839	1.8	1553	4.1	◐ 2105	1.9
3 SA	0322	4.2	0843	1.3	1600	4.2	◑ 2114	1.5
18 SU	0418	3.9	0933	2.1	1637	3.8	2237	2.2
4 SU	0429	4.0	0940	1.7	1707	4.0	2227	1.8
19 M	0520	3.6	1137	2.3	1741	3.6		
5 M	0554	3.9	1121	2.0	1831	3.9		
20 TU	0014	2.2	0716	3.6	1250	2.3	1941	3.6
6 TU	0020	1.9	0728	3.9	1305	1.9	1957	4.0
21 W	0122	2.1	0834	3.8	1354	2.1	2048	3.8
7 W	0139	1.6	0845	4.1	1412	1.7	2101	4.3
22 TH	0216	1.8	0927	4.1	1441	1.9	2135	4.1
8 TH	0238	1.3	0942	4.4	1506	1.5	2151	4.5
23 F	0256	1.5	1006	4.3	1519	1.6	2212	4.3
9 F	0327	1.0	1029	4.7	1552	1.0	2235	4.7
24 SA	0333	1.3	1040	4.5	1554	1.3	2246	4.4
10 SA	0412	0.7	1113	4.8	1635	0.8	O 2317	4.7
25 SU	0408	1.0	1112	4.6	1628	1.1	● 2319	4.5
11 SU	0454	0.5	1156	4.9	1716	0.7		
26 M	0442	0.8	1144	4.7	1701	0.9	2350	4.6
12 M	0000	4.8	0534	0.5	1241	4.9	1756	0.7
27 TU	0516	0.8	1216	4.7	1734	0.8		
13 TU	0043	4.8	0614	0.6	1325	4.8	1835	0.8
28 W	0020	4.7	0550	0.7	1247	4.7	1807	0.8
14 W	0127	4.6	0651	0.8	1407	4.4	1912	1.0
29 TH	0053	4.7	0622	0.8	1319	4.7	1841	0.8
15 TH	0211	4.5	0726	1.1	1443	4.6	1947	1.3
30 F	0130	4.6	0657	0.9	1355	4.6	1918	1.0

OCTOBER

Day	Time	m	Time	m	Time	m	Time	m
1 SA	0212	4.5	0736	1.1	1439	4.5	2000	1.2
16 SU	0255	4.2	0801	1.9	1510	4.1	2021	1.9
2 SU	0307	4.3	0822	1.5	1538	4.2	2053	1.6
17 M	0339	4.0	0846	2.2	1555	3.9	◐ 2118	2.2
3 M	0424	4.1	0924	1.9	1654	4.0	◑ 2228	1.9
18 TU	0435	3.8	1111	2.4	1653	3.6	2341	2.3
4 TU	0555	3.9	1150	2.1	1826	3.9		
19 W	0618	3.6	1221	2.4	1851	3.5		
5 W	0023	1.9	0725	4.0	1303	2.0	1949	4.0
20 TH	0043	2.1	0756	3.8	1319	2.2	2013	3.7
6 TH	0128	1.6	0838	4.3	1401	1.7	2050	4.3
21 F	0134	1.9	0852	4.1	1404	1.9	2103	4.0
7 F	0221	1.3	0934	4.6	1449	1.3	2137	4.5
22 SA	0216	1.6	0933	4.3	1441	1.6	2141	4.3
8 SA	0308	1.0	1018	4.8	1532	1.0	2218	4.6
23 SU	0254	1.3	1006	4.5	1517	1.3	2213	4.5
9 SU	0350	0.8	1104	4.9	1613	0.8	O 2257	4.7
24 M	0332	1.1	1037	4.7	1553	1.1	2245	4.6
10 M	0431	0.7	1134	4.9	1653	0.7	2338	4.7
25 TU	0409	0.9	1108	4.8	1629	0.9	● 2318	4.7
11 TU	0509	0.7	1211	4.8	1731	0.8		
26 W	0445	0.8	1141	4.9	1705	0.8	2353	4.8
12 W	0018	4.7	0547	0.8	1248	4.8	1807	0.9
27 TH	0522	0.8	1216	4.9	1742	0.7		
13 TH	0100	4.6	0622	0.9	1325	4.7	1841	1.1
28 F	0031	4.8	0559	0.8	1253	4.8	1820	0.8
14 F	0139	4.5	0654	1.3	1359	4.5	1912	1.3
29 SA	0114	4.7	0639	1.0	1335	4.7	1902	1.0
15 SA	0217	4.4	0726	1.5	1433	4.4	1944	1.6
30 SU	0204	4.8	0722	1.3	1426	4.5	1948	1.3
31 M	0309	4.4	0815	1.9	1530	4.2	2049	1.7

NOVEMBER

Day	Time	m	Time	m	Time	m	Time	m
1 TU	0429	4.2	0940	2.0	1648	4.0	◑ 2242	1.9
16 W	0407	4.0	0925	2.3	1620	3.8	◑ 2214	2.2
2 W	0549	4.1	1133	2.0	1812	3.9		
17 TH	0511	3.8	1133	2.3	1729	3.6	2350	2.1
3 TH	0000	1.8	0712	4.2	1239	1.9	1931	4.1
18 F	0644	3.9	1230	2.2	1910	3.7		
4 F	0102	1.6	0826	4.4	1335	1.7	2035	4.3
19 SA	0043	1.9	0800	4.1	1316	2.0	2014	3.9
5 SA	0154	1.4	0923	4.6	1423	1.4	2122	4.4
20 SU	0129	1.7	0846	4.3	1357	1.7	2056	4.2
6 SU	0241	1.2	1006	4.7	1506	1.2	2159	4.5
21 M	0211	1.4	0922	4.5	1437	1.4	2132	4.4
7 M	0323	1.0	1037	4.8	1547	1.0	2237	4.6
22 TU	0253	1.2	0956	4.7	1517	1.1	2210	4.6
8 TU	0404	1.0	1108	4.8	1627	0.9	O 2317	4.6
23 W	0334	1.0	1033	4.8	1558	0.9	● 2249	4.7
9 W	0443	1.0	1142	4.8	1705	0.9	2358	4.6
24 TH	0416	0.9	1112	4.9	1640	0.8	2332	4.8
10 TH	0520	1.1	1219	4.7	1741	1.0		
25 F	0458	0.8	1152	4.9	1722	0.7		
11 F	0039	4.6	0556	1.2	1254	4.6	1815	1.2
26 SA	0016	4.8	0542	0.9	1235	4.9	1806	0.8
12 SA	0118	4.5	0629	1.4	1328	4.5	1846	1.4
27 SU	0106	4.8	0628	1.0	1323	4.7	1853	0.9
13 SU	0154	4.4	0702	1.6	1401	4.4	1918	1.6
28 M	0204	4.7	0717	1.3	1418	4.6	1944	1.2
14 M	0232	4.3	0736	1.9	1439	4.2	1955	1.8
29 TU	0314	4.5	0814	1.6	1523	4.3	2047	1.5
15 TU	0315	4.1	0819	2.1	1525	4.0	2044	2.0
30 W	0424	4.4	0931	1.8	1634	4.2	◐ 2208	1.6

DECEMBER

Day	Time	m	Time	m	Time	m	Time	m
1 TH	0532	4.3	1055	1.9	1746	4.1	2323	1.7
16 F	0432	4.0	0943	2.1	1644	3.8	2211	1.9
2 F	0642	4.3	1203	1.8	1856	4.1		
17 SA	0529	4.0	1057	2.1	1748	3.8	2326	1.9
3 SA	0025	1.6	0751	4.4	1301	1.7	2000	4.1
18 SU	0632	4.0	1209	1.9	1856	3.9		
4 SU	0120	1.5	0849	4.5	1353	1.5	2054	4.2
19 M	0031	1.7	0735	4.2	1305	1.7	1958	4.0
5 M	0209	1.4	0935	4.6	1438	1.4	2138	4.3
20 TU	0126	1.5	0829	4.3	1356	1.5	2051	4.2
6 TU	0254	1.3	1008	4.6	1521	1.2	2221	4.4
21 W	0216	1.3	0918	4.5	1445	1.2	2142	4.4
7 W	0337	1.3	1042	4.6	1603	1.1	2304	4.5
22 TH	0306	1.2	1005	4.7	1534	1.0	2231	4.6
8 TH	0419	1.3	1120	4.6	1644	1.1	O 2346	4.5
23 F	0355	1.0	1051	4.8	1622	0.8	● 2320	4.7
9 F	0459	1.4	1158	4.6	1722	1.1		
24 SA	0443	0.9	1137	4.8	1710	0.7		
10 SA	0026	4.5	0538	1.4	1234	4.5	1758	1.2
25 SU	0010	4.8	0532	0.9	1224	4.8	1758	0.7
11 SU	0105	4.5	0614	1.5	1309	4.5	1831	1.3
26 M	0103	4.8	0621	1.0	1313	4.8	1846	0.7
12 M	0142	4.4	0647	1.6	1342	4.3	1903	1.4
27 TU	0202	4.8	0710	1.1	1407	4.6	1936	0.9
13 TU	0217	4.3	0721	1.7	1418	4.2	1938	1.5
28 W	0308	4.7	0803	1.3	1508	4.5	2029	1.1
14 W	0256	4.2	0759	1.8	1459	4.1	2019	1.7
29 TH	0408	4.6	0901	1.5	1611	4.3	2129	1.3
15 TH	0340	4.1	0845	2.0	1547	3.9	2108	1.8
30 F	0503	4.5	1007	1.7	1712	4.1	2236	1.5
31 SA	0558	4.4	1116	1.8	1812	4.1	2342	1.6

Chart Datum: 2·73 metres below Ordnance Datum (Newlyn)
HAT is 5·1 metres above Chart Datum

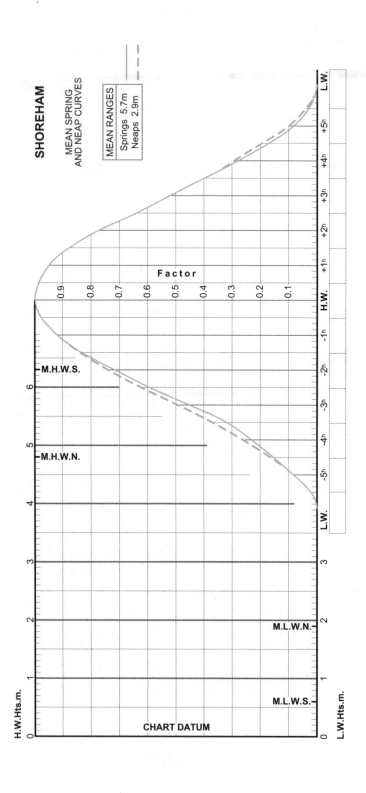

SHOREHAM

MEAN SPRING
AND NEAP CURVES

MEAN RANGES
Springs 5.7m
Neaps 2.9m

Factor

0.9 0.8 0.7 0.6 0.5 0.4 0.3 0.2 0.1

H.W.Hts.m.

M.H.W.S.

M.H.W.N.

CHART DATUM

M.L.W.N.

M.L.W.S.

L.W.Hts.m.

L.W. +5h +4h +3h +2h +1h H.W. -1h -2h -3h -4h -5h L.W.

SHOREHAM
LAT 50°50'N   LONG 0°15'W
TIMES AND HEIGHTS OF HIGH AND LOW WATERS

Dates in amber are **SPRINGS**
Dates in grey are **NEAPS**

2022

JANUARY

Day	Time m	Time m	Day	Time m	Time m
1 SA	0324 1.1	1553 0.9	**16** SU	0413 1.5	1635 1.2
	0935 6.1	2206 6.1		1015 5.6	2244 5.6
2 SU	0417 0.9	1645 0.7	**17** M	0452 1.3	1713 1.1
	1028 6.3	2300 6.3		1052 5.7	2320 5.8
3 M	0509 0.8	1736 0.6	**18** TU	0529 1.2	1749 1.0
	1119 6.4	2353 6.4		1127 5.8	2354 5.9
4 TU	0559 0.7	1826 0.5	**19** W	0604 1.2	1824 1.0
	1209 6.4			1200 5.9	
5 W	0043 6.4	1258 6.4	**20** TH	0026 5.9	1233 5.9
	0649 0.8	1916 0.6		0639 1.1	1859 1.0
6 TH	0132 6.4	1346 6.2	**21** F	0059 5.9	1307 5.9
	0738 0.9	2004 0.7		0712 1.1	1930 1.0
7 F	0219 6.2	1434 5.9	**22** SA	0132 5.9	1343 5.8
	0827 1.0	2052 0.9		0745 1.1	2003 1.0
8 SA	0305 6.0	1521 5.6	**23** SU	0208 5.9	1421 5.8
	0916 1.2	2140 1.2		0821 1.2	2040 1.1
9 SU	0352 5.7	1610 5.3	**24** M	0249 5.8	1505 5.6
	1007 1.5	2230 1.5		0903 1.3	2124 1.2
10 M	0441 5.4	1704 5.0	**25** TU	0335 5.6	1555 5.4
	1101 1.7	2325 1.7		0954 1.4	2218 1.4
11 TU	0535 5.2	1803 4.8	**26** W	0431 5.4	1658 5.2
	1205 1.9			1056 1.6	2324 1.6
12 W	0030 1.9	1314 1.9	**27** TH	0541 5.3	1819 5.0
	0635 5.0	1911 4.8		1213 1.7	
13 TH	0139 2.0	1416 1.8	**28** F	0047 1.7	1333 1.6
	0742 5.0	2021 4.9		0705 5.3	1947 5.2
14 F	0239 1.9	1509 1.6	**29** SA	0207 1.6	1444 1.3
	0844 5.2	2119 5.1		0822 5.5	2101 5.5
15 SA	0330 1.7	1555 1.4	**30** SU	0314 1.3	1545 1.0
	0934 5.4	2204 5.4		0927 5.8	2203 5.8
			31 M	0411 1.0	1638 0.7
				1024 6.1	2258 6.2

FEBRUARY

Day	Time m	Time m	Day	Time m	Time m
1 TU	0502 0.8	1727 0.5	**16** W	0510 1.1	1729 0.9
	1116 6.3	2349 6.4		1108 5.8	2335 5.9
2 W	0550 0.7	1815 0.4	**17** TH	0545 1.0	1804 0.8
	1204 6.4			1143 6.0	
3 TH	0035 6.5	1249 6.4	**18** F	0007 6.1	1216 6.1
	0637 0.6	1900 0.4		0620 0.9	1838 0.7
4 F	0118 6.5	1332 6.3	**19** SA	0040 6.1	1250 6.1
	0721 0.7	1943 0.5		0653 0.8	1910 0.7
5 SA	0158 6.4	1411 6.1	**20** SU	0113 6.2	1325 6.1
	0803 0.8	2023 0.7		0725 0.8	1942 0.7
6 SU	0236 6.1	1449 5.8	**21** M	0148 6.2	1401 6.1
	0842 1.0	2100 1.0		0800 0.8	2018 0.8
7 M	0313 5.8	1527 5.5	**22** TU	0225 6.1	1442 5.9
	0919 1.2	2137 1.3		0839 0.9	2059 1.0
8 TU	0351 5.5	1610 5.1	**23** W	0308 5.8	1528 5.6
	0959 1.6	2219 1.7		0925 1.2	2148 1.3
9 W	0436 5.1	1704 4.7	**24** TH	0359 5.5	1628 5.1
	1047 1.9	2311 2.0		1023 1.5	2254 1.7
10 TH	0534 4.8	1811 4.5	**25** F	0507 5.1	1754 4.8
	1149 2.1			1143 1.8	
11 F	0024 2.2	1332 2.2	**26** SA	0028 1.9	1319 1.8
	0644 4.6	1927 4.5		0645 4.9	1940 4.9
12 SA	0207 2.2	1443 1.9	**27** SU	0201 1.8	1439 1.5
	0759 4.7	2047 4.8		0818 5.1	2101 5.3
13 SU	0308 1.9	1534 1.6	**28** M	0310 1.4	1539 1.1
	0906 5.0	2142 5.2		0926 5.5	2202 5.8
14 M	0354 1.6	1615 1.3			
	0954 5.3	2224 5.5			
15 TU	0433 1.3	1653 1.1			
	1033 5.6	2300 5.8			

MARCH

Day	Time m	Time m	Day	Time m	Time m
1 TU	0404 1.0	1629 0.7	**16** W	0407 1.3	1625 1.0
	1021 5.9	2252 6.2		1006 5.5	2233 5.8
2 W	0451 0.7	1714 0.5	**17** TH	0443 1.0	1701 0.8
	1109 6.2	2337 6.4		1043 5.8	2308 6.1
3 TH	0535 0.6	1757 0.4	**18** F	0518 0.8	1736 0.6
	1153 6.4			1119 6.1	2342 6.2
4 F	0018 6.5	1233 6.4	**19** SA	0553 0.7	1811 0.5
	0618 0.5	1838 0.4		1155 6.2	
5 SA	0056 6.5	1310 6.3	**20** SU	0016 6.3	1230 6.3
	0657 0.5	1915 0.5		0628 0.6	1845 0.5
6 SU	0131 6.4	1344 6.1	**21** M	0050 6.4	1305 6.3
	0732 0.6	1949 0.7		0703 0.5	1921 0.5
7 M	0202 6.2	1415 5.9	**22** TU	0126 6.3	1343 6.2
	0805 0.8	2021 0.9		0740 0.6	1959 0.7
8 TU	0230 5.9	1444 5.6	**23** W	0204 6.2	1424 6.0
	0837 1.1	2053 1.2		0821 0.8	2041 0.9
9 W	0257 5.6	1517 5.2	**24** TH	0246 5.8	1511 5.5
	0911 1.4	2131 1.6		0907 1.1	2132 1.4
10 TH	0330 5.1	1603 4.8	**25** F	0338 5.4	1614 5.1
	0954 1.8	2218 2.0		1007 1.5	2243 1.8
11 F	0422 4.7	1721 4.4	**26** SA	0452 4.9	1752 4.7
	1051 2.1	2327 2.3		1132 1.8	
12 SA	0554 4.4	1844 4.4	**27** SU	0025 2.0	1314 1.8
	1214 2.3			0641 4.7	1940 4.9
13 SU	0121 2.4	1411 2.1	**28** M	0156 1.8	1430 1.5
	0717 4.4	2007 4.6		0814 5.0	2055 5.3
14 M	0242 2.1	1506 1.7	**29** TU	0300 1.4	1526 1.0
	0832 4.7	2112 5.1		0918 5.5	2149 5.8
15 TU	0329 1.7	1548 1.3	**30** W	0351 1.0	1612 0.7
	0926 5.2	2155 5.5		1008 5.9	2235 6.2
			31 TH	0434 0.7	1654 0.5
				1052 6.1	2316 6.4

APRIL

Day	Time m	Time m	Day	Time m	Time m
1 F	0514 0.5	1733 0.5	**16** SA	0446 0.7	1703 0.6
	1133 6.3	2354 6.5		1050 6.1	2312 6.3
2 SA	0552 0.5	1810 0.5	**17** SU	0523 0.6	1741 0.5
	1211 6.3			1129 6.3	2350 6.4
3 SU	0029 6.4	1245 6.2	**18** M	0602 0.5	1820 0.5
	0628 0.6	1844 0.6		1208 6.4	
4 M	0100 6.3	1315 6.1	**19** TU	0027 6.5	1247 6.4
	0701 0.7	1916 0.7		0642 0.4	1902 0.5
5 TU	0126 6.1	1341 5.9	**20** W	0106 6.4	1328 6.2
	0731 0.8	1946 1.0		0725 0.5	1945 0.7
6 W	0149 5.8	1408 5.6	**21** TH	0147 6.1	1414 5.9
	0802 1.0	2018 1.2		0810 0.7	2033 1.0
7 TH	0214 5.5	1439 5.3	**22** F	0234 5.8	1507 5.5
	0835 1.3	2054 1.6		0901 1.1	2130 1.4
8 F	0246 5.1	1519 4.9	**23** SA	0331 5.3	1618 5.1
	0914 1.7	2139 2.0		1004 1.5	2245 1.8
9 SA	0330 4.7	1630 4.5	**24** SU	0452 4.9	1751 4.9
	1007 2.0	2246 2.3		1130 1.7	
10 SU	0501 4.3	1805 4.4	**25** M	0019 1.9	1300 1.7
	1125 2.2			0632 4.8	1924 5.1
11 M	0020 2.4	1311 2.2	**26** TU	0139 1.7	1409 1.4
	0637 4.3	1922 4.6		0756 5.0	2032 5.4
12 TU	0200 2.1	1424 1.8	**27** W	0240 1.3	1502 1.1
	0749 4.7	2027 5.1		0856 5.4	2124 5.8
13 W	0252 1.7	1510 1.4	**28** TH	0328 1.0	1547 0.8
	0845 5.1	2115 5.5		0944 5.7	2208 6.1
14 TH	0332 1.3	1549 1.0	**29** F	0409 0.8	1627 0.7
	0930 5.5	2156 5.9		1027 6.0	2248 6.2
15 F	0409 1.0	1626 0.8	**30** SA	0448 0.7	1705 0.7
	1011 5.9	2234 6.1		1107 6.1	2325 6.3

Chart Datum: 3·27 metres below Ordnance Datum (Newlyn)
HAT is 6·9 metres above Chart Datum

TIDES

TIME ZONE (UT)
For Summer Time add ONE hour in **non-shaded areas**

SHOREHAM
LAT 50°50'N   LONG 0°15'W
TIMES AND HEIGHTS OF HIGH AND LOW WATERS

Dates in amber are **SPRINGS**
Dates in grey are **NEAPS**

2022

MAY

Day	Time	m	Day	Time	m
1 SU	0525 / 1144 / 1741 / 2359	0.7 / 6.1 / 0.7 / 6.2	16 M	0454 / 1104 / 1715 / ○2324	0.5 / 6.3 / 0.6 / 6.5
2 M	0600 / 1218 / 1815	0.7 / 6.0 / 0.8	17 TU	0539 / 1149 / 1800	0.5 / 6.4 / 0.5
3 TU	0028 / 0633 / 1246 / 1848	6.1 / 0.8 / 5.9 / 0.9	18 W	0007 / 0625 / 1234 / 1848	6.5 / 0.4 / 6.4 / 0.6
4 W	0053 / 0704 / 1314 / 1919	5.9 / 0.9 / 5.8 / 1.1	19 TH	0052 / 0713 / 1322 / 1937	6.3 / 0.5 / 6.2 / 0.8
5 TH	0118 / 0736 / 1343 / 1952	5.7 / 1.1 / 5.6 / 1.3	20 F	0139 / 0804 / 1413 / 2029	6.1 / 0.7 / 6.0 / 1.0
6 F	0146 / 0809 / 1415 / 2029	5.5 / 1.3 / 5.4 / 1.6	21 SA	0231 / 0859 / 1511 / 2129	5.8 / 1.0 / 5.7 / 1.3
7 SA	0220 / 0848 / 1455 / 2114	5.2 / 1.6 / 5.1 / 1.9	22 SU	0333 / 1002 / 1618 / ◑2240	5.4 / 1.3 / 5.4 / 1.6
8 SU	0304 / 0938 / 1554 / 2214	4.8 / 1.8 / 4.8 / 2.1	23 M	0446 / 1117 / 1733 / 2359	5.1 / 1.5 / 5.2 / 1.7
9 M	0412 / 1045 / 1723 / ◐2333	4.5 / 2.0 / 4.6 / 2.2	24 TU	0606 / 1232 / 1849	5.0 / 1.5 / 5.3
10 TU	0552 / 1207 / 1836	4.5 / 2.0 / 4.8	25 W	0109 / 0721 / 1335 / 1956	1.6 / 5.1 / 1.4 / 5.4
11 W	0055 / 0703 / 1323 / 1938	2.1 / 4.7 / 1.8 / 5.1	26 TH	0207 / 0822 / 1429 / 2049	1.4 / 5.3 / 1.2 / 5.6
12 TH	0159 / 0801 / 1420 / 2030	1.7 / 5.1 / 1.5 / 5.5	27 F	0257 / 0913 / 1516 / 2136	1.2 / 5.6 / 1.1 / 5.8
13 F	0248 / 0851 / 1506 / 2116	1.3 / 5.5 / 1.1 / 5.9	28 SA	0341 / 0959 / 1558 / 2217	1.0 / 5.7 / 1.0 / 5.9
14 SA	0330 / 0936 / 1548 / 2159	1.0 / 5.8 / 0.9 / 6.2	29 SU	0421 / 1040 / 1638 / 2255	0.9 / 5.8 / 1.0 / 6.0
15 SU	0411 / 1020 / 1631 / 2242	0.7 / 6.1 / 0.7 / 6.4	30 M	0459 / 1117 / 1715 / ○2329	0.9 / 5.8 / 1.0 / 5.9
			31 TU	0535 / 1152 / 1751	0.9 / 5.8 / 1.0

JUNE

Day	Time	m	Day	Time	m
1 W	0000 / 0610 / 1224 / 1826	5.9 / 1.0 / 5.8 / 1.1	16 TH	0613 / 1228 / 1837	0.5 / 6.3 / 0.7
2 TH	0028 / 0644 / 1254 / 1900	5.8 / 1.0 / 5.8 / 1.2	17 F	0045 / 0705 / 1320 / 1930	6.3 / 0.5 / 6.3 / 0.8
3 F	0057 / 0718 / 1326 / 1935	5.7 / 1.1 / 5.6 / 1.3	18 SA	0136 / 0757 / 1412 / 2023	6.1 / 0.7 / 6.1 / 0.9
4 SA	0129 / 0753 / 1359 / 2012	5.5 / 1.3 / 5.4 / 1.5	19 SU	0229 / 0852 / 1506 / 2120	5.9 / 0.8 / 6.0 / 1.1
5 SU	0204 / 0830 / 1438 / 2054	5.3 / 1.4 / 5.3 / 1.7	20 M	0325 / 0949 / 1602 / 2221	5.6 / 1.0 / 5.7 / 1.3
6 M	0246 / 0914 / 1526 / 2145	5.1 / 1.6 / 5.1 / 1.9	21 TU	0423 / 1049 / 1659 / ◑2325	5.4 / 1.2 / 5.5 / 1.5
7 TU	0340 / 1008 / 1627 / ◐2248	4.9 / 1.7 / 5.0 / 1.9	22 W	0525 / 1152 / 1800	5.2 / 1.4 / 5.4
8 W	0450 / 1113 / 1740 / 2357	4.8 / 1.8 / 5.0 / 1.9	23 TH	0028 / 0631 / 1253 / 1905	1.5 / 5.0 / 1.5 / 5.3
9 TH	0608 / 1222 / 1846	4.9 / 1.7 / 5.2	24 F	0128 / 0738 / 1351 / 2006	1.5 / 5.0 / 1.5 / 5.3
10 F	0102 / 0713 / 1325 / 1945	1.7 / 5.1 / 1.5 / 5.5	25 SA	0223 / 0837 / 1444 / 2100	1.5 / 5.1 / 1.5 / 5.4
11 SA	0200 / 0810 / 1422 / 2038	1.4 / 5.4 / 1.3 / 5.8	26 SU	0312 / 0923 / 1532 / 2146	1.4 / 5.3 / 1.4 / 5.5
12 SU	0252 / 0903 / 1515 / 2128	1.1 / 5.7 / 1.0 / 6.1	27 M	0357 / 1014 / 1615 / 2228	1.2 / 5.5 / 1.3 / 5.6
13 M	0342 / 0954 / 1605 / 2216	0.8 / 6.0 / 0.8 / 6.3	28 TU	0438 / 1054 / 1656 / 2305	1.2 / 5.6 / 1.2 / 5.7
14 TU	0432 / 1045 / 1656 / ○2305	0.6 / 6.2 / 0.7 / 6.4	29 W	0516 / 1131 / 1733 / ●2338	1.1 / 5.7 / 1.2 / 5.7
15 W	0522 / 1136 / 1746 / 2355	0.5 / 6.3 / 0.7 / 6.4	30 TH	0553 / 1205 / 1809	1.1 / 5.7 / 1.2

JULY

Day	Time	m	Day	Time	m
1 F	0010 / 0629 / 1238 / 1845	5.7 / 1.1 / 5.8 / 1.2	16 SA	0040 / 0655 / 1314 / 1919	6.3 / 0.5 / 6.4 / 0.7
2 SA	0042 / 0704 / 1310 / 1921	5.7 / 1.1 / 5.7 / 1.3	17 SU	0129 / 0745 / 1402 / 2009	6.3 / 0.5 / 6.4 / 0.8
3 SU	0114 / 0738 / 1343 / 1955	5.6 / 1.2 / 5.7 / 1.3	18 M	0217 / 0834 / 1448 / 2059	6.1 / 0.7 / 6.2 / 0.9
4 M	0149 / 0812 / 1418 / 2032	5.5 / 1.2 / 5.6 / 1.4	19 TU	0304 / 0922 / 1533 / 2148	5.9 / 0.9 / 6.0 / 1.1
5 TU	0227 / 0849 / 1457 / 2113	5.4 / 1.3 / 5.5 / 1.5	20 W	0351 / 1010 / 1619 / ◐2239	5.6 / 1.1 / 5.7 / 1.4
6 W	0310 / 0932 / 1544 / 2203	5.3 / 1.4 / 5.4 / 1.6	21 TH	0440 / 1100 / 1708 / 2336	5.3 / 1.5 / 5.4 / 1.7
7 TH	0402 / 1025 / 1639 / ◐2303	5.2 / 1.5 / 5.3 / 1.7	22 F	0534 / 1159 / 1803	5.0 / 1.7 / 5.1
8 F	0504 / 1127 / 1746	5.1 / 1.6 / 5.3	23 SA	0042 / 0638 / 1308 / 1908	1.8 / 4.8 / 1.9 / 4.9
9 SA	0011 / 0618 / 1237 / 1858	1.6 / 5.1 / 1.6 / 5.4	24 SU	0149 / 0753 / 1414 / 2020	1.8 / 4.8 / 1.9 / 5.0
10 SU	0120 / 0732 / 1348 / 2005	1.5 / 5.2 / 1.5 / 5.6	25 M	0247 / 0901 / 1510 / 2119	1.7 / 5.0 / 1.8 / 5.2
11 M	0225 / 0838 / 1453 / 2105	1.3 / 5.5 / 1.3 / 5.8	26 TU	0337 / 0953 / 1557 / 2206	1.5 / 5.2 / 1.6 / 5.4
12 TU	0324 / 0938 / 1551 / 2202	1.0 / 5.8 / 1.0 / 6.0	27 W	0420 / 1036 / 1639 / 2245	1.3 / 5.5 / 1.4 / 5.6
13 W	0419 / 1036 / 1645 / ○2256	0.8 / 6.1 / 0.8 / 6.3	28 TH	0459 / 1113 / 1716 / ●2321	1.2 / 5.7 / 1.2 / 5.7
14 TH	0512 / 1131 / 1737 / 2349	0.6 / 6.3 / 0.7 / 6.3	29 F	0536 / 1148 / 1752 / 2353	1.0 / 5.8 / 1.2 / 5.8
15 F	0603 / 1224 / 1828	0.5 / 6.4 / 0.7	30 SA	0611 / 1220 / 1828	1.0 / 5.9 / 1.1
			31 SU	0024 / 0647 / 1250 / 1902	5.8 / 1.0 / 5.9 / 1.1

AUGUST

Day	Time	m	Day	Time	m
1 M	0056 / 0719 / 1321 / 1934	5.8 / 1.0 / 5.9 / 1.1	16 TU	0155 / 0806 / 1420 / 2027	6.3 / 0.6 / 6.4 / 0.8
2 TU	0129 / 0749 / 1353 / 2006	5.8 / 1.0 / 5.9 / 1.2	17 W	0234 / 0845 / 1457 / 2106	6.0 / 0.8 / 6.1 / 1.1
3 W	0204 / 0821 / 1429 / 2042	5.7 / 1.1 / 5.8 / 1.2	18 TH	0313 / 0922 / 1535 / 2145	5.7 / 1.2 / 5.7 / 1.4
4 TH	0242 / 0859 / 1510 / 2125	5.6 / 1.2 / 5.7 / 1.4	19 F	0354 / 1002 / 1618 / ◑2229	5.3 / 1.6 / 5.3 / 1.8
5 F	0327 / 0946 / 1559 / 2219	5.5 / 1.4 / 5.5 / 1.5	20 SA	0445 / 1050 / 1712 / 2328	4.9 / 1.9 / 4.9 / 2.1
6 SA	0422 / 1044 / 1700 / 2328	5.2 / 1.6 / 5.3 / 1.7	21 SU	0548 / 1200 / 1818	4.6 / 2.3 / 4.6
7 SU	0534 / 1201 / 1820	5.0 / 1.8 / 5.1	22 M	0111 / 0706 / 1347 / 1939	2.2 / 4.5 / 2.3 / 4.6
8 M	0051 / 0707 / 1328 / 1946	1.7 / 5.0 / 1.8 / 5.3	23 TU	0225 / 0838 / 1451 / 2058	2.0 / 4.7 / 2.0 / 4.9
9 TU	0211 / 0829 / 1444 / 2058	1.5 / 5.3 / 1.5 / 5.6	24 W	0318 / 0935 / 1539 / 2148	1.7 / 5.1 / 1.7 / 5.3
10 W	0317 / 0936 / 1545 / 2158	1.2 / 5.7 / 1.2 / 5.9	25 TH	0400 / 1016 / 1619 / 2226	1.4 / 5.5 / 1.4 / 5.6
11 TH	0413 / 1033 / 1638 / 2252	0.8 / 6.1 / 0.9 / 6.2	26 F	0438 / 1052 / 1655 / 2259	1.1 / 5.8 / 1.2 / 5.8
12 F	0503 / 1126 / 1727 / ○2342	0.6 / 6.4 / 0.7 / 6.4	27 SA	0513 / 1124 / 1730 / ●2331	1.0 / 5.9 / 1.1 / 5.9
13 SA	0551 / 1214 / 1815	0.4 / 6.6 / 0.6	28 SU	0548 / 1156 / 1804	0.9 / 6.0 / 1.0
14 SU	0029 / 0638 / 1258 / 1901	6.5 / 0.4 / 6.6 / 0.6	29 M	0002 / 0622 / 1225 / 1838	6.0 / 0.9 / 6.1 / 0.9
15 M	0114 / 0723 / 1340 / 1945	6.4 / 0.4 / 6.5 / 0.6	30 TU	0033 / 0653 / 1255 / 1908	6.0 / 0.8 / 6.1 / 0.9
			31 W	0106 / 0722 / 1327 / 1939	6.1 / 0.6 / 6.1 / 1.0

Chart Datum: 3·27 metres below Ordnance Datum (Newlyn)
HAT is 6·9 metres above Chart Datum

SHOREHAM
LAT 50°50′N LONG 0°15′W
TIMES AND HEIGHTS OF HIGH AND LOW WATERS

Dates in amber are **SPRINGS**
Dates in grey are **NEAPS**

2022

SEPTEMBER

Day	Time m	Day	Time m
1	0139 6.0 / 0754 0.9 / TH 1402 6.0 / 2014 1.1	**16**	0232 5.7 / 0838 1.3 / F 1448 5.6 / 2057 1.5
2	0216 5.9 / 0832 1.1 / F 1441 5.9 / 2056 1.3	**17**	0307 5.3 / 0914 1.7 / SA 1523 5.2 / ☽ 2138 1.8
3	0259 5.6 / 0918 1.4 / SA 1527 5.5 / ☽ 2149 1.6	**18**	0354 4.9 / 1001 2.1 / SU 1615 4.8 / 2233 2.2
4	0352 5.2 / 1017 1.7 / SU 1628 5.1 / 2301 1.9	**19**	0506 4.5 / 1108 2.4 / M 1737 4.4 / 2357 2.4
5	0511 4.9 / 1143 2.0 / M 1803 4.9	**20**	0627 4.4 / 1312 2.5 / TU 1901 4.4
6	0039 2.0 / 0704 4.8 / TU 1325 2.0 / 1944 5.0	**21**	0157 2.2 / 0803 4.7 / W 1427 2.2 / 2030 4.8
7	0208 1.7 / 0830 5.2 / W 1442 1.6 / 2058 5.5	**22**	0252 1.9 / 0907 5.1 / TH 1514 1.8 / 2121 5.2
8	0313 1.2 / 0934 5.7 / TH 1539 1.2 / 2155 5.9	**23**	0334 1.5 / 0947 5.5 / F 1553 1.4 / 2157 5.6
9	0404 0.8 / 1026 6.2 / F 1627 0.8 / 2244 6.3	**24**	0410 1.2 / 1020 5.9 / SA 1628 1.1 / 2230 5.9
10	0449 0.5 / 1112 6.5 / SA 1711 0.6 / ○ 2329 6.5	**25**	0445 1.0 / 1052 6.1 / SU 1702 1.0 / ● 2302 6.1
11	0533 0.4 / 1155 6.7 / SU 1754 0.5	**26**	0518 0.8 / 1124 6.2 / M 1735 0.9 / 2335 6.2
12	0011 6.5 / 0615 0.4 / M 1235 6.7 / 1836 0.5	**27**	0551 0.8 / 1156 6.2 / TU 1808 0.8
13	0050 6.5 / 0655 0.5 / TU 1312 6.6 / 1915 0.6	**28**	0008 6.2 / 0623 0.8 / W 1228 6.3 / 1841 0.8
14	0127 6.3 / 0731 0.7 / W 1346 6.3 / 1950 0.8	**29**	0042 6.3 / 0656 0.8 / TH 1301 6.3 / 1915 0.8
15	0200 6.0 / 0805 0.9 / TH 1418 6.0 / 2023 1.1	**30**	0117 6.2 / 0732 0.9 / F 1337 6.2 / 1953 1.0

OCTOBER

Day	Time m	Day	Time m
1	0155 6.0 / 0812 1.1 / SA 1417 5.9 / 2038 1.3	**16**	0228 5.4 / 0839 1.7 / SU 1436 5.2 / 2100 1.8
2	0239 5.6 / 0901 1.5 / SU 1505 5.4 / 2133 1.7	**17**	0309 5.0 / 0925 2.1 / M 1521 4.8 / ☽ 2154 2.2
3	0337 5.2 / 1006 1.9 / M 1613 5.0 / ☽ 2252 2.0	**18**	0424 4.6 / 1031 2.4 / TU 1655 4.4 / 2310 2.4
4	0513 4.8 / 1142 2.2 / TU 1805 4.8	**19**	0549 4.5 / 1204 2.6 / W 1821 4.4
5	0037 2.0 / 0705 4.9 / W 1322 2.0 / 1942 5.0	**20**	0104 2.4 / 0708 4.7 / TH 1347 2.3 / 1937 4.7
6	0202 1.7 / 0824 5.4 / TH 1433 1.6 / 2049 5.5	**21**	0212 2.0 / 0816 5.1 / F 1438 1.8 / 2035 5.1
7	0301 1.2 / 0921 5.9 / F 1525 1.1 / 2141 6.0	**22**	0257 1.6 / 0902 5.5 / SA 1518 1.5 / 2116 5.6
8	0347 0.8 / 1008 6.3 / SA 1609 0.8 / 2226 6.3	**23**	0335 1.3 / 0939 5.9 / SU 1553 1.2 / 2154 5.9
9	0429 0.6 / 1050 6.5 / SU 1650 0.6 / ○ 2308 6.5	**24**	0410 1.0 / 1015 6.2 / M 1628 0.9 / 2230 6.1
10	0509 0.5 / 1129 6.6 / M 1729 0.6 / 2347 6.5	**25**	0445 0.9 / 1050 6.3 / TU 1703 0.8 / ● 2307 6.3
11	0547 0.6 / 1206 6.6 / TU 1807 0.6	**26**	0519 0.8 / 1125 6.4 / W 1739 0.7 / 2343 6.4
12	0023 6.4 / 0624 0.7 / W 1240 6.4 / 1843 0.7	**27**	0556 0.8 / 1201 6.4 / TH 1817 0.7
13	0056 6.2 / 0658 0.9 / TH 1310 6.2 / 1915 0.9	**28**	0020 6.4 / 0635 0.8 / F 1238 6.4 / 1857 0.8
14	0126 6.0 / 0730 1.1 / F 1337 5.9 / 1947 1.2	**29**	0059 6.3 / 0717 1.0 / SA 1318 6.2 / 1941 1.0
15	0155 5.7 / 0802 1.4 / SA 1404 5.6 / 2020 1.5	**30**	0143 6.0 / 0803 1.2 / SU 1403 5.8 / 2030 1.3
		31	0233 5.6 / 0858 1.6 / M 1458 5.4 / 2131 1.6

NOVEMBER

Day	Time m	Day	Time m
1	0341 5.2 / 1008 1.9 / TU 1616 5.0 / ☽ 2251 1.9	**16**	0340 4.9 / 0959 2.3 / W 1600 4.6 / ☽ 2230 2.3
2	0516 5.0 / 1139 2.1 / W 1757 4.9	**17**	0504 4.7 / 1113 2.4 / TH 1734 4.5 / 2348 2.3
3	0024 1.9 / 0649 5.1 / TH 1305 1.9 / 1922 5.1	**18**	0616 4.8 / 1234 2.3 / F 1844 4.7
4	0139 1.6 / 0800 5.5 / F 1410 1.5 / 2026 5.5	**19**	0105 2.1 / 0718 5.1 / SA 1341 2.0 / 1942 5.0
5	0236 1.3 / 0855 5.9 / SA 1501 1.1 / 2117 5.9	**20**	0204 1.8 / 0811 5.5 / SU 1431 1.6 / 2032 5.4
6	0322 1.0 / 0941 6.2 / SU 1545 0.9 / 2202 6.1	**21**	0250 1.5 / 0856 5.8 / M 1512 1.3 / 2116 5.8
7	0404 0.8 / 1022 6.4 / M 1625 0.8 / 2243 6.3	**22**	0331 1.2 / 0937 6.1 / TU 1552 1.0 / 2158 6.1
8	0443 0.8 / 1101 6.4 / TU 1704 0.7 / ○ 2321 6.3	**23**	0411 1.0 / 1018 6.3 / W 1632 0.8 / ○ 2240 6.3
9	0521 0.8 / 1137 6.4 / W 1740 0.8 / 2357 6.2	**24**	0452 0.9 / 1058 6.4 / TH 1715 0.7 / 2322 6.4
10	0556 0.9 / 1209 6.3 / TH 1815 0.9	**25**	0535 0.8 / 1140 6.5 / F 1759 0.7
11	0029 6.1 / 0631 1.0 / F 1237 6.1 / 1848 1.0	**26**	0006 6.4 / 0621 0.9 / SA 1223 6.4 / 1846 0.8
12	0059 6.0 / 0703 1.2 / SA 1305 5.9 / 1921 1.2	**27**	0052 6.3 / 0708 1.0 / SU 1309 6.2 / 1935 0.9
13	0130 5.8 / 0737 1.4 / SU 1334 5.6 / 1956 1.6	**28**	0141 6.1 / 0800 1.2 / M 1400 5.9 / 2028 1.1
14	0203 5.5 / 0815 1.7 / M 1408 5.3 / 2035 1.7	**29**	0238 5.8 / 0857 1.4 / TU 1459 5.6 / 2129 1.4
15	0243 5.2 / 0900 2.0 / TU 1451 4.9 / 2125 2.0	**30**	0344 5.5 / 1003 1.6 / W 1611 5.3 / ☽ 2239 1.6

DECEMBER

Day	Time m	Day	Time m
1	0458 5.4 / 1119 1.8 / TH 1730 5.1 / 2355 1.6	**16**	0357 5.1 / 1023 2.1 / F 1618 4.8 / ☽ 2247 2.0
2	0613 5.4 / 1233 1.7 / F 1845 5.2	**17**	0507 5.0 / 1128 2.1 / SA 1737 4.8 / 2353 2.0
3	0103 1.6 / 0722 5.5 / SA 1336 1.5 / 1951 5.4	**18**	0617 5.1 / 1234 2.0 / SU 1846 4.9
4	0201 1.4 / 0819 5.7 / SU 1430 1.3 / 2046 5.6	**19**	0059 1.9 / 0719 5.3 / M 1335 1.7 / 1946 5.2
5	0252 1.3 / 0909 5.9 / M 1517 1.1 / 2134 5.8	**20**	0159 1.7 / 0814 5.6 / TU 1430 1.4 / 2040 5.5
6	0337 1.2 / 0953 6.0 / TU 1601 1.0 / 2218 5.9	**21**	0253 1.4 / 0904 5.9 / W 1521 1.2 / 2131 5.8
7	0420 1.1 / 1034 6.1 / W 1642 1.0 / 2258 6.0	**22**	0343 1.2 / 0952 6.2 / TH 1610 0.9 / 2220 6.1
8	0459 1.1 / 1111 6.1 / TH 1720 1.0 / ○ 2335 6.0	**23**	0433 1.0 / 1040 6.3 / F 1659 0.7 / ○ 2310 6.3
9	0536 1.1 / 1144 6.0 / F 1756 1.0	**24**	0522 0.9 / 1128 6.4 / SA 1748 0.6
10	0009 6.0 / 0612 1.2 / SA 1215 5.9 / 1831 1.1	**25**	0000 6.4 / 0612 0.8 / SU 1216 6.4 / 1839 0.6
11	0041 5.9 / 0646 1.3 / SU 1246 5.8 / 1905 1.2	**26**	0051 6.4 / 0702 0.8 / M 1307 6.3 / 1930 0.7
12	0114 5.8 / 0721 1.4 / M 1317 5.6 / 1940 1.3	**27**	0142 6.3 / 0754 0.9 / TU 1359 6.1 / 2022 0.8
13	0146 5.6 / 0758 1.6 / TU 1351 5.4 / 2018 1.5	**28**	0235 6.1 / 0848 1.1 / W 1453 5.9 / 2117 1.0
14	0222 5.4 / 0838 1.8 / W 1429 5.2 / 2059 1.7	**29**	0329 5.9 / 0945 1.3 / TH 1549 5.6 / 2214 1.2
15	0304 5.2 / 0926 1.9 / TH 1516 5.0 / 2148 1.9	**30**	0425 5.7 / 1047 1.4 / F 1649 5.4 / 2315 1.4
		31	0524 5.5 / 1151 1.6 / SA 1752 5.2

TIDES

Chart Datum: 3·27 metres below Ordnance Datum (Newlyn)
HAT is 6·9 metres above Chart Datum

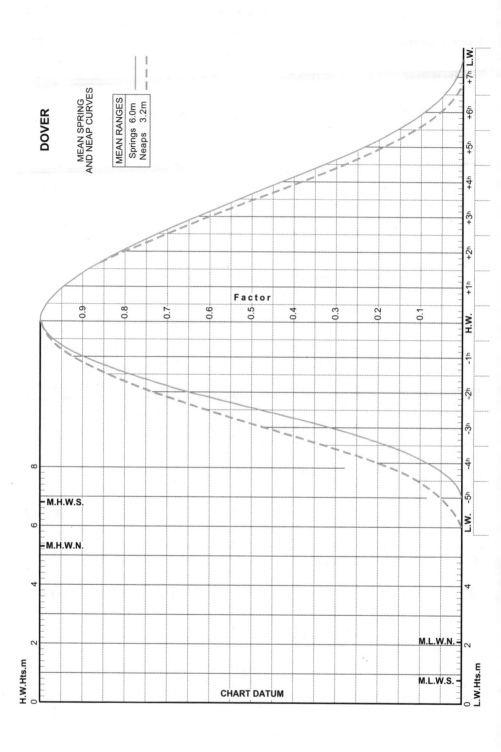

DOVER

MEAN SPRING
AND NEAP CURVES

MEAN RANGES
Springs 6.0m
Neaps 3.2m

Factor

TIME ZONE (UT)	DOVER	Dates in amber are **SPRINGS**
For Summer Time add ONE hour in **non-shaded areas**	LAT 51°07′N LONG 1°19′E	Dates in grey are **NEAPS**

DOVER
LAT 51°07′N   LONG 1°19′E
TIMES AND HEIGHTS OF HIGH AND LOW WATERS

2022

JANUARY

	Time	m		Time	m
1 SA	0414 0922 1647 2154	1.4 6.5 1.1 6.4	**16** SU	0455 1015 1714 2238	1.6 5.9 1.5 6.1
2 SU ●	0515 1016 1748 2245	1.2 6.6 1.0 6.6	**17** M ○	0536 1051 1754 2313	1.4 6.1 1.4 6.2
3 M	0613 1108 1845 2334	1.0 6.7 0.9 6.7	**18** TU	0615 1125 1832 2345	1.3 6.2 1.3 6.3
4 TU	0709 1158 1938	0.8 6.7 0.9	**19** W	0653 1157 1910	1.2 6.2 1.3
5 W	0021 0802 1246 2027	6.8 0.8 6.7 0.9	**20** TH	0015 0732 1228 1948	6.4 1.2 6.2 1.3
6 TH	0108 0850 1334 2111	6.8 0.8 6.5 1.1	**21** F	0046 0810 1259 2023	6.4 1.2 6.2 1.3
7 F	0154 0936 1423 2152	6.7 1.0 6.1 1.3	**22** SA	0118 0847 1332 2058	6.5 1.2 6.3 1.3
8 SA	0242 1020 1514 2233	6.5 1.2 6.0 1.6	**23** SU	0154 0923 1410 2133	6.5 1.3 6.2 1.4
9 SU ◑	0331 1104 1607 2316	6.2 1.4 5.7 1.8	**24** M	0236 1001 1454 2213	6.4 1.4 6.1 1.6
10 M	0424 1151 1705	5.9 1.7 5.5	**25** TU ◑	0323 1045 1546 2301	6.2 1.5 5.9 1.8
11 TU	0006 0524 1244 1812	2.1 5.7 1.9 5.3	**26** W	0420 1140 1651	2.0 1.7 5.6
12 W	0106 0632 1343 1920	2.2 5.5 2.1 5.3	**27** TH	0003 0532 1250 1820	2.0 5.8 1.8 5.5
13 TH	0211 0740 1444 2022	2.2 5.5 2.1 5.4	**28** F	0123 0658 1407 1946	2.0 5.7 1.8 5.6
14 F	0314 0841 1541 2115	2.1 5.6 1.9 5.6	**29** SA	0242 0815 1521 2055	1.9 5.9 1.6 5.8
15 SA	0409 0932 1631 2200	1.9 5.8 1.7 5.9	**30** SU	0357 0922 1637 2154	1.6 6.1 1.4 6.1
			31 M	0509 1022 1748 2246	1.3 6.3 1.1 6.5

FEBRUARY

	Time	m		Time	m
1 TU ●	0613 1113 1846 2332	1.0 6.6 0.9 6.7	**16** W ○	0557 1103 1817 2322	1.2 6.2 1.3 6.4
2 W	0709 1159 1935	0.7 6.7 0.8	**17** TH	0638 1136 1857 2354	1.1 6.3 1.1 6.5
3 TH	0014 0758 1240 2018	6.8 0.6 6.7 0.8	**18** F	0718 1208 1934	1.0 6.4 1.1
4 F	0056 0840 1320 2055	6.9 0.6 6.6 0.8	**19** SA	0025 0756 1239 2009	6.6 0.9 6.5 1.0
5 SA	0136 0918 1400 2128	6.8 0.7 6.4 1.0	**20** SU	0058 0831 1312 2041	6.7 0.9 6.6 1.0
6 SU	0216 0951 1440 2157	6.6 0.9 6.2 1.3	**21** M	0133 0904 1347 2114	6.7 0.9 6.5 1.1
7 M	0256 1023 1522 2225	6.4 1.3 5.9 1.6	**22** TU	0211 0939 1429 2151	6.7 1.1 6.4 1.3
8 TU	0339 1055 1611 2259	6.0 1.6 5.5 1.9	**23** W ◑	0255 1019 1517 2235	6.4 1.3 6.0 1.6
9 W	0428 1136 1710 2349	5.6 1.9 5.2 2.3	**24** TH	0348 1109 1618 2334	6.0 1.7 5.6 1.9
10 TH	0531 1239 1821	5.3 2.3 5.0	**25** F	0501 1220 1756	5.6 2.0 5.3
11 F	0109 0647 1353 1937	2.5 5.1 2.3 5.1	**26** SA	0057 0647 1347 1939	2.2 5.4 2.1 5.3
12 SA	0228 0804 1501 2045	2.4 5.2 2.2 5.3	**27** SU	0226 0819 1513 2054	2.1 5.6 1.9 5.7
13 SU	0334 0908 1600 2137	2.1 5.5 1.9 5.7	**28** M	0354 0930 1642 2153	1.7 5.9 1.5 6.1
14 M	0428 0954 1650 2217	1.7 5.7 1.6 6.0			
15 TU	0514 1030 1735 2250	1.5 6.0 1.4 6.2			

MARCH

	Time	m		Time	m
1 TU	0512 1026 1748 2241	1.2 6.3 1.1 6.5	**16** W	0448 1002 1712 2220	1.4 6.0 1.4 6.2
2 W ●	0611 1112 1838 2323	0.8 6.5 0.9 6.7	**17** TH	0533 1036 1755 2254	1.2 6.3 1.2 6.5
3 TH	0700 1150 1921	0.6 6.7 0.7	**18** F ○	0616 1110 1835 2327	1.0 6.5 1.0 6.7
4 F	0000 0743 1225 1958	6.9 0.5 6.7 0.7	**19** SA	0657 1143 1912	0.8 6.6 0.9
5 SA	0037 0819 1259 2029	6.9 0.5 6.6 0.8	**20** SU	0000 0735 1215 1947	6.8 0.7 6.7 0.8
6 SU	0113 0850 1332 2055	6.8 0.7 6.5 0.9	**21** M	0034 0810 1249 2021	6.9 0.7 6.8 0.8
7 M	0148 0916 1406 2117	6.7 0.9 6.3 1.2	**22** TU	0110 0843 1326 2055	6.9 0.8 6.7 0.9
8 TU	0220 0938 1441 2139	6.4 1.2 6.0 1.4	**23** W	0150 0918 1409 2133	6.8 1.0 6.5 1.2
9 W	0252 1000 1518 2207	6.1 1.5 5.7 1.8	**24** TH	0235 0959 1459 2219	6.4 1.3 6.1 1.6
10 TH	0330 1032 1612 2248	5.6 2.0 5.3 2.2	**25** F	0331 1050 1606 2320	5.9 1.8 5.5 2.0
11 F	0435 1123 1732 2357	5.2 2.4 5.0 2.5	**26** SA	0454 1204 1750	5.4 2.2 5.2
12 SA	0603 1303 1853	2.6 2.6 4.9	**27** SU	0047 0649 1340 1931	2.2 5.3 2.2 5.3
13 SU	0146 0725 1427 2008	2.5 5.0 2.4 5.2	**28** M	0223 0821 1517 2046	2.1 5.5 1.9 5.7
14 M	0301 0836 1531 2105	2.2 5.3 2.0 5.6	**29** TU	0358 0927 1637 2141	1.6 5.9 1.5 6.1
15 TU	0359 0925 1625 2146	1.8 5.7 1.7 5.9	**30** W	0505 1016 1732 2225	1.1 6.3 1.1 6.5
			31 TH	0556 1056 1818 2303	0.7 6.5 0.8 6.7

APRIL

	Time	m		Time	m
1 F ●	0640 1130 1856 2340	0.6 6.6 0.7 6.8	**16** SA ○	0547 1040 1806 2257	0.9 6.6 1.0 6.8
2 SA	0718 1202 1929	0.5 6.6 0.7	**17** SU	0630 1115 1846 2333	0.7 6.7 0.8 6.9
3 SU	0014 0750 1233 1957	6.8 0.6 6.6 0.8	**18** M	0710 1151 1924	0.6 6.8 0.8
4 M	0048 0816 1305 2020	6.8 0.6 6.5 1.0	**19** TU	0010 0748 1228 2001	7.0 0.6 6.8 0.8
5 TU	0119 0837 1336 2039	6.6 0.8 6.3 1.2	**20** W	0050 0825 1310 2040	6.9 0.6 6.7 0.9
6 W	0146 0855 1404 2102	6.3 1.3 6.1 1.4	**21** TH	0134 0903 1357 2122	6.7 1.0 6.4 1.2
7 TH	0210 0919 1431 2133	6.0 1.6 5.8 1.7	**22** F	0225 0948 1454 2212	6.3 1.4 6.0 1.6
8 F	0241 0953 1509 2213	5.7 1.8 5.4 2.1	**23** SA ◑	0330 1044 1608 2319	5.8 1.8 5.6 1.9
9 SA	0336 1038 1647 2310	5.2 2.3 5.1 2.4	**24** SU	0458 1203 1737	5.4 2.2 5.4
10 SU	0526 1157 1810	4.9 2.6 5.0	**25** M	0047 0643 1335 1911	2.1 5.3 2.1 5.4
11 M	0101 0647 1349 1923	2.5 5.0 2.5 5.2	**26** TU	0218 0808 1500 2023	1.8 5.6 1.8 5.8
12 TU	0223 0754 1456 2021	2.2 5.3 2.1 5.5	**27** W	0339 0908 1609 2116	1.4 5.9 1.5 6.1
13 W	0322 0845 1551 2106	1.8 5.7 1.7 5.9	**28** TH	0440 0953 1702 2159	1.1 6.2 1.2 6.4
14 TH	0413 0927 1639 2144	1.4 6.0 1.4 6.3	**29** F	0529 1030 1745 2238	0.8 6.4 1.0 6.6
15 F	0501 1004 1724 2220	1.1 6.3 1.2 6.6	**30** SA ●	0611 1103 1823 2315	0.8 6.5 0.9 6.7

Chart Datum: 3·67 metres below Ordnance Datum (Newlyn)
HAT is 7·4 metres above Chart Datum

DOVER

LAT 51°07'N LONG 1°19'E

TIMES AND HEIGHTS OF HIGH AND LOW WATERS

2022

TIME ZONE (UT)
For Summer Time add ONE hour in **non-shaded areas**

Dates in amber are **SPRINGS**
Dates in grey are **NEAPS**

MAY

Day	Time m	Day	Time m
1 SU	0646 0.8 / 1135 6.5 / 1855 0.9 / 2350 6.6	**16** M	0601 0.8 / 1048 6.7 / 1820 0.9 / ○ 2308 6.9
2 M	0715 0.9 / 1208 6.5 / 1922 1.0	**17** TU	0647 0.7 / 1130 6.8 / 1904 0.8 / 2351 6.9
3 TU	0023 6.5 / 0740 1.0 / 1240 6.4 / 1946 1.1	**18** W	0730 0.7 / 1214 6.8 / 1947 0.8
4 W	0053 6.4 / 0801 1.2 / 1311 6.3 / 2009 1.2	**19** TH	0036 6.8 / 0814 0.8 / 1301 6.7 / 2033 0.9
5 TH	0119 6.2 / 0823 1.4 / 1338 6.1 / 2037 1.4	**20** F	0127 6.6 / 0859 1.1 / 1354 6.4 / 2122 1.1
6 F	0142 5.9 / 0852 1.6 / 1404 5.9 / 2110 1.7	**21** SA	0225 6.2 / 0948 1.4 / 1454 6.2 / 2217 1.4
7 SA	0214 5.7 / 0928 1.9 / 1443 5.6 / 2151 2.0	**22** SU	0332 5.9 / 1048 1.7 / 1559 5.9 / ◐ 2324 1.7
8 SU	0307 5.3 / 1013 2.2 / 1557 5.3 / 2245 2.2	**23** M	0448 5.6 / 1159 1.9 / 1711 5.7
9 M	0448 5.1 / 1115 2.4 / 1722 5.2 ☽	**24** TU	0038 1.7 / 0618 5.5 / 1313 1.9 / 1833 5.6
10 TU	0010 2.3 / 0605 5.1 / 1257 2.4 / 1833 5.3	**25** W	0151 1.6 / 0735 5.6 / 1421 1.8 / 1945 5.8
11 W	0136 2.1 / 0709 5.3 / 1411 2.1 / 1932 5.6	**26** TH	0300 1.4 / 0833 5.8 / 1524 1.6 / 2041 6.0
12 TH	0238 1.8 / 0802 5.7 / 1507 1.8 / 2021 5.9	**27** F	0400 1.3 / 0919 6.0 / 1619 1.4 / 2128 6.2
13 F	0332 1.4 / 0847 6.0 / 1558 1.5 / 2104 6.3	**28** SA	0452 1.1 / 0958 6.1 / 1706 1.3 / 2210 6.3
14 SA	0423 1.1 / 0928 6.3 / 1647 1.2 / 2145 6.6	**29** SU	0534 1.1 / 1034 6.2 / 1746 1.2 / 2249 6.4
15 SU	0513 0.9 / 1008 6.5 / 1734 1.0 / 2226 6.8	**30** M	0610 1.1 / 1109 6.3 / 1820 1.2 / ● 2326 6.4
		31 TU	0640 1.2 / 1145 6.3 / 1851 1.2

JUNE

Day	Time m	Day	Time m
1 W	0001 6.3 / 0707 1.3 / 1219 6.3 / 1919 1.2	**16** TH	0722 0.8 / 1207 6.7 / 1943 0.8
2 TH	0033 6.2 / 0734 1.3 / 1252 6.2 / 1949 1.3	**17** F	0032 6.7 / 0814 0.9 / 1258 6.7 / 2035 0.8
3 F	0102 6.0 / 0803 1.4 / 1322 6.1 / 2021 1.4	**18** SA	0125 6.5 / 0903 1.0 / 1350 6.6 / 2127 0.9
4 SA	0130 5.9 / 0836 1.6 / 1352 6.0 / 2057 1.6	**19** SU	0222 6.3 / 0953 1.2 / 1444 6.4 / 2220 1.1
5 SU	0203 5.7 / 0913 1.8 / 1428 5.8 / 2139 1.8	**20** M	0321 6.1 / 1043 1.4 / 1539 6.2 / 2314 1.3
6 M	0247 5.5 / 0956 1.9 / 1518 5.6 / 2227 1.9	**21** TU	0423 5.8 / 1137 1.6 / 1638 6.0 ☽
7 TU	0351 5.4 / 1047 2.1 / 1622 5.5 / 2328 2.0	**22** W	0010 1.5 / 0532 5.6 / 1234 1.8 / 1743 5.8
8 W	0508 5.3 / 1155 2.2 / 1731 5.5	**23** TH	0109 1.6 / 0642 5.5 / 1333 1.9 / 1853 5.7
9 TH	0042 2.0 / 0616 5.4 / 1313 2.1 / 1836 5.7	**24** F	0209 1.6 / 0745 5.6 / 1433 1.8 / 1958 5.8
10 F	0148 1.8 / 0715 5.6 / 1418 1.9 / 1933 5.9	**25** SA	0308 1.6 / 0838 5.7 / 1531 1.7 / 2054 5.9
11 SA	0247 1.5 / 0806 5.9 / 1516 1.6 / 2024 6.2	**26** SU	0404 1.6 / 0925 5.8 / 1624 1.6 / 2143 6.0
12 SU	0344 1.3 / 0854 6.2 / 1611 1.4 / 2113 6.5	**27** M	0452 1.5 / 1008 5.9 / 1710 1.5 / 2227 6.1
13 M	0440 1.1 / 0941 6.4 / 1706 1.1 / 2201 6.6	**28** TU	0533 1.4 / 1048 6.1 / 1750 1.4 / 2306 6.1
14 TU	0536 0.9 / 1029 6.6 / 1759 1.0 / ○ 2251 6.7	**29** W	0608 1.4 / 1125 6.2 / 1825 1.3 / ● 2342 6.1
15 W	0630 0.8 / 1118 6.7 / 1851 0.8 / 2341 6.8	**30** TH	0642 1.4 / 1200 6.3 / 1859 1.3

JULY

Day	Time m	Day	Time m
1 F	0015 6.1 / 0715 1.4 / 1233 6.3 / 1934 1.3	**16** SA	0031 6.7 / 0813 0.8 / 1251 6.8 / 2035 0.6
2 SA	0046 6.0 / 0750 1.4 / 1304 6.2 / 2011 1.4	**17** SU	0120 6.6 / 0859 0.8 / 1338 6.8 / 2122 0.7
3 SU	0116 6.0 / 0825 1.5 / 1334 6.2 / 2048 1.4	**18** M	0209 6.4 / 0941 1.0 / 1425 6.7 / 2205 0.8
4 M	0146 5.9 / 0902 1.6 / 1407 6.1 / 2126 1.5	**19** TU	0257 6.2 / 1022 1.1 / 1512 6.5 / 2247 1.1
5 TU	0221 5.8 / 0939 1.7 / 1446 6.0 / 2207 1.6	**20** W	0346 6.0 / 1101 1.5 / 1601 6.2 / ◐ 2331 1.4
6 W	0305 5.8 / 1020 1.8 / 1534 5.9 / 2253 1.7	**21** TH	0439 5.7 / 1145 1.8 / 1655 5.9
7 TH	0358 5.7 / 1109 1.9 / 1630 5.8 / ◐ 2349 1.8	**22** F	0019 1.7 / 0539 5.4 / 1239 2.0 / 1757 5.6
8 F	0503 5.6 / 1210 2.0 / 1736 5.8	**23** SA	0116 1.9 / 0647 5.3 / 1342 2.2 / 1908 5.5
9 SA	0055 1.8 / 0619 5.6 / 1325 2.0 / 1847 5.8	**24** SU	0217 2.0 / 0755 5.4 / 1447 2.1 / 2019 5.5
10 SU	0204 1.7 / 0729 5.7 / 1436 1.9 / 1952 6.0	**25** M	0318 2.0 / 0856 5.5 / 1548 1.9 / 2121 5.7
11 M	0311 1.5 / 0831 5.9 / 1542 1.6 / 2053 6.2	**26** TU	0414 1.8 / 0947 5.8 / 1640 1.7 / 2210 5.8
12 TU	0415 1.3 / 0928 6.2 / 1646 1.3 / 2152 6.4	**27** W	0502 1.7 / 1029 6.0 / 1725 1.5 / 2249 6.0
13 W	0520 1.1 / 1023 6.4 / 1748 1.1 / ○ 2322 6.6	**28** TH	0544 1.5 / 1106 6.2 / 1804 1.4 / ● 2322 6.1
14 TH	0623 1.0 / 1115 6.6 / 1847 0.9 / 2341 6.7	**29** F	0622 1.4 / 1140 6.3 / 1842 1.3 / 2354 6.1
15 F	0721 0.9 / 1204 6.8 / 1944 0.7	**30** SA	0659 1.4 / 1211 6.4 / 1920 1.2
		31 SU	0024 6.2 / 0736 1.4 / 1240 6.4 / 1957 1.2

AUGUST

Day	Time m	Day	Time m
1 M	0053 6.2 / 0811 1.3 / 1310 6.4 / 2033 1.2	**16** TU	0144 6.6 / 0915 0.9 / 1359 6.8 / 2137 0.7
2 TU	0121 6.2 / 0845 1.4 / 1341 6.4 / 2108 1.2	**17** W	0224 6.4 / 0946 1.1 / 1440 6.6 / 2210 1.1
3 W	0153 6.2 / 0918 1.4 / 1416 6.4 / 2142 1.3	**18** TH	0306 6.1 / 1016 1.4 / 1523 6.3 / 2243 1.5
4 TH	0231 6.1 / 0952 1.5 / 1458 6.3 / 2220 1.5	**19** F	0353 5.8 / 1048 1.8 / 1611 5.9 / ◐ 2321 1.9
5 F	0316 6.0 / 1033 1.7 / 1548 6.1 / ◐ 2306 1.7	**20** SA	0449 5.4 / 1133 2.2 / 1709 5.5
6 SA	0413 5.7 / 1126 1.9 / 1650 5.8	**21** SU	0018 2.3 / 0557 5.2 / 1247 2.5 / 1822 5.2
7 SU	0008 1.9 / 0531 5.5 / 1240 2.1 / 1813 5.6	**22** M	0133 2.4 / 0714 5.1 / 1409 2.5 / 1945 5.2
8 M	0129 2.0 / 0710 5.5 / 1407 2.1 / 1941 5.7	**23** TU	0244 2.3 / 0829 5.4 / 1519 2.2 / 2103 5.5
9 TU	0249 1.8 / 0825 5.7 / 1525 1.8 / 2054 6.0	**24** W	0346 2.1 / 0927 5.7 / 1616 1.9 / 2154 5.8
10 W	0404 1.6 / 0928 6.1 / 1637 1.4 / 2157 6.3	**25** TH	0439 1.8 / 1008 6.0 / 1703 1.6 / 2228 6.0
11 TH	0517 1.3 / 1023 6.4 / 1745 1.1 / 2252 6.5	**26** F	0523 1.6 / 1042 6.3 / 1744 1.4 / 2257 6.2
12 F	0621 1.0 / 1111 6.7 / 1845 0.8 / ○ 2341 6.7	**27** SA	0603 1.4 / 1113 6.4 / 1822 1.1 / ● 2327 6.4
13 SA	0715 0.8 / 1155 6.9 / 1937 0.6	**28** SU	0640 1.3 / 1143 6.5 / 1900 1.1 / 2356 6.4
14 SU	0024 6.7 / 0801 0.7 / 1237 7.0 / 2023 0.5	**29** M	0715 1.2 / 1212 6.6 / 1936 1.1
15 M	0105 6.7 / 0841 0.7 / 1318 7.0 / 2102 0.5	**30** TU	0024 6.4 / 0749 1.2 / 1241 6.6 / 2011 1.0
		31 W	0053 6.5 / 0821 1.2 / 1313 6.7 / 2043 1.1

Chart Datum: 3·67 metres below Ordnance Datum (Newlyn)
HAT is 7·4 metres above Chart Datum

TIME ZONE (UT)
For Summer Time add ONE hour in **non-shaded areas**

DOVER

LAT 51°07'N LONG 1°19'E

TIMES AND HEIGHTS OF HIGH AND LOW WATERS

Dates in amber are **SPRINGS**
Dates in grey are **NEAPS**

2022

SEPTEMBER

Day	Time	m	Time	m	Time	m	Time	m
1 TH	0124	6.5	0853	1.3	1347	6.6	2115	1.2
2 F	0201	6.4	0926	1.4	1427	6.5	2150	1.4
3 SA	0245	6.1	1006	1.7	1515	6.1	2235	1.8
4 SU	0341	5.7	1057	2.0	1620	5.7	2337	2.1
5 M	0507	5.3	1213	2.3	1807	5.4		
6 TU	0108	2.3	0706	5.3	1352	2.3	1945	5.6
7 W	0243	2.1	0823	5.7	1521	1.9	2059	5.9
8 TH	0407	1.7	0924	6.1	1639	1.4	2159	6.3
9 F	0516	1.3	1015	6.5	1741	1.0	2247	6.6
10 SA	0610	1.0	1058	6.8	1834	0.7	2329	6.8
11 SU	0657	0.8	1138	7.0	1919	0.5		
12 M	0005	6.8	0737	0.7	1216	7.1	1959	0.5
13 TU	0039	6.8	0811	0.8	1253	7.0	2032	0.6
14 W	0114	6.7	0840	0.9	1330	6.9	2101	0.9
15 TH	0150	6.5	0906	1.2	1406	6.6	2126	1.2
16 F	0227	6.2	0929	1.5	1443	6.2	2149	1.6
17 SA	0309	5.8	0954	1.9	1527	5.8	2217	2.1
18 SU	0405	5.4	1031	2.3	1628	5.3	2302	2.5
19 M	0515	5.1	1134	2.7	1745	5.0		
20 TU	0043	2.8	0634	5.1	1332	2.7	1909	5.1
21 W	0214	2.6	0755	5.3	1450	2.4	2034	5.4
22 TH	0320	2.2	0856	5.7	1548	1.9	2123	5.7
23 F	0413	1.9	0936	6.0	1635	1.6	2154	6.1
24 SA	0457	1.6	1008	6.3	1716	1.3	2224	6.3
25 SU	0537	1.4	1110	6.5	1755	1.1	2254	6.5
26 M	0613	1.2	1110	6.7	1833	1.0	2325	6.6
27 TU	0649	1.2	1141	6.8	1910	1.0	2355	6.7
28 W	0723	1.1	1212	6.9	1944	1.0		
29 TH	0025	6.7	0756	1.1	1245	6.9	2017	1.0
30 F	0059	6.7	0829	1.2	1321	6.8	2050	1.2

OCTOBER

Day	Time	m	Time	m	Time	m	Time	m
1 SA	0138	6.5	0905	1.4	1403	6.5	2128	1.5
2 SU	0224	6.2	0947	1.7	1454	6.0	2215	1.9
3 M	0326	5.7	1042	2.1	1614	5.5	2320	2.3
4 TU	0451	5.3	1204	2.4	1814	5.3		
5 W	0103	2.5	0657	5.4	1350	2.3	1945	5.6
6 TH	0245	2.2	0812	5.7	1752	1.8	2055	6.0
7 F	0402	1.7	0910	6.2	1633	1.3	2148	6.4
8 SA	0500	1.2	0957	6.6	1725	0.9	2230	6.7
9 SU	0548	1.0	1037	6.9	1812	0.7	2306	6.8
10 M	0629	0.8	1115	7.0	1852	0.6	2339	6.8
11 TU	0705	0.8	1151	7.0	1927	0.7		
12 W	0011	6.8	0736	0.9	1227	6.9	1957	0.9
13 TH	0044	6.7	0803	1.1	1301	6.8	2021	1.1
14 F	0118	6.5	0826	1.3	1333	6.5	2041	1.4
15 SA	0152	6.2	0848	1.6	1405	6.1	2103	1.7
16 SU	0228	5.9	0916	1.9	1443	5.7	2134	2.1
17 M	0320	5.5	0954	2.2	1552	5.3	2216	2.5
18 TU	0436	5.2	1048	2.6	1712	5.0	2326	2.8
19 W	0552	5.1	1241	2.7	1829	5.0		
20 TH	0133	2.8	0707	5.3	1409	2.4	1942	5.3
21 F	0243	2.4	0807	5.6	1508	2.0	2034	5.7
22 SA	0337	2.0	0851	6.0	1556	1.6	2112	6.0
23 SU	0422	1.6	0927	6.3	1640	1.3	2146	6.3
24 M	0503	1.4	1001	6.6	1722	1.1	2219	6.6
25 TU	0542	1.2	1034	6.8	1803	1.0	2252	6.7
26 W	0620	1.1	1109	6.9	1841	0.9	2326	6.8
27 TH	0657	1.0	1144	7.0	1918	0.9		
28 F	0001	6.9	0734	1.1	1222	6.9	1955	1.0
29 SA	0040	6.8	0811	1.2	1303	6.7	2032	1.2
30 SU	0125	6.5	0852	1.4	1350	6.4	2115	1.6
31 M	0218	6.2	0940	1.7	1452	5.9	2206	2.0

NOVEMBER

Day	Time	m	Time	m	Time	m	Time	m
1 TU	0330	5.7	1041	2.1	1624	5.5	2318	2.3
2 W	0503	5.5	1208	2.2	1805	5.5		
3 TH	0058	2.4	0634	5.6	1342	2.0	1930	5.7
4 F	0227	2.1	0748	5.9	1503	1.6	2035	6.0
5 SA	0336	1.7	0844	6.2	1606	1.2	2124	6.3
6 SU	0430	1.3	0930	6.5	1658	1.0	2204	6.5
7 M	0516	1.1	1011	6.7	1743	0.9	2239	6.6
8 TU	0556	1.0	1049	6.8	1821	0.9	2312	6.7
9 W	0631	1.0	1126	6.8	1853	1.0	2346	6.7
10 TH	0703	1.1	1202	6.7	1920	1.1		
11 F	0019	6.6	0730	1.2	1235	6.5	1944	1.3
12 SA	0054	6.5	0755	1.4	1307	6.3	2007	1.5
13 SU	0127	6.3	0821	1.6	1337	6.0	2034	1.8
14 M	0200	6.0	0853	1.8	1413	5.7	2108	2.0
15 TU	0241	5.7	0933	2.1	1511	5.4	2152	2.3
16 W	0347	5.4	1024	2.4	1632	5.1	2248	2.6
17 TH	0502	5.3	1140	2.5	1745	5.1		
18 F	0022	2.7	0612	5.3	1311	2.4	1850	5.3
19 SA	0148	2.5	0712	5.5	1416	2.1	1944	5.6
20 SU	0247	2.1	0801	5.9	1510	1.7	2028	5.9
21 M	0338	1.8	0842	6.1	1600	1.4	2107	6.2
22 TU	0425	1.5	0922	6.5	1647	1.2	2145	6.5
23 W	0510	1.3	1001	6.7	1733	1.0	2223	6.7
24 TH	0554	1.1	1041	6.9	1817	0.9	2303	6.7
25 F	0636	1.0	1123	6.9	1859	0.9	2346	6.8
26 SA	0719	1.0	1207	6.8	1941	1.0		
27 SU	0031	6.8	0803	1.1	1255	6.6	2026	1.2
28 M	0122	6.6	0851	1.3	1350	6.4	2114	1.5
29 TU	0219	6.3	0945	1.6	1456	6.0	2210	1.8
30 W	0325	6.0	1048	1.8	1614	5.7	2318	2.0

DECEMBER

Day	Time	m	Time	m	Time	m	Time	m
1 TH	0437	5.8	1200	1.8	1738	5.6		
2 F	0033	2.1	0555	5.8	1313	1.8	1856	5.7
3 SA	0145	2.0	0709	5.9	1423	1.6	1959	6.0
4 SU	0250	1.8	0809	6.1	1527	1.4	2050	6.0
5 M	0349	1.6	0859	6.2	1623	1.3	2134	6.2
6 TU	0440	1.4	0944	6.4	1709	1.2	2212	6.3
7 W	0523	1.3	1026	6.4	1748	1.2	2249	6.4
8 TH	0601	1.3	1105	6.5	1821	1.2	2325	6.5
9 F	0635	1.3	1142	6.4	1851	1.4		
10 SA	0001	6.5	0706	1.3	1216	6.3	1919	1.5
11 SU	0036	6.4	0735	1.4	1250	6.2	1947	1.6
12 M	0110	6.3	0806	1.5	1321	6.0	2018	1.7
13 TU	0141	6.1	0841	1.7	1354	5.8	2054	1.8
14 W	0213	5.9	0920	1.8	1432	5.6	2134	2.0
15 TH	0254	5.8	1005	2.0	1522	5.4	2221	2.2
16 F	0349	5.6	1058	2.1	1633	5.3	2317	2.3
17 SA	0456	5.5	1205	2.1	1746	5.3		
18 SU	0031	2.4	0605	5.5	1316	2.0	1849	5.4
19 M	0146	2.2	0706	5.7	1419	1.8	1942	5.7
20 TU	0249	2.0	0759	6.0	1518	1.6	2031	6.0
21 W	0347	1.7	0848	6.3	1614	1.3	2117	6.3
22 TH	0441	1.4	0936	6.5	1708	1.1	2204	6.5
23 F	0533	1.2	1024	6.7	1800	1.0	2252	6.7
24 SA	0623	1.0	1113	6.8	1851	1.0	2340	6.8
25 SU	0715	0.9	1203	6.7	1941	1.0		
26 M	0029	6.8	0807	0.9	1254	6.6	2032	1.0
27 TU	0119	6.7	0859	1.0	1348	6.5	2121	1.2
28 W	0212	6.6	0950	1.1	1445	6.2	2209	1.4
29 TH	0307	6.4	1041	1.2	1546	6.0	2300	1.6
30 F	0404	6.2	1134	1.4	1650	5.7	2354	1.8
31 SA	0506	5.9	1231	1.8	1800	5.6		

Chart Datum: 3·67 metres below Ordnance Datum (Newlyn)
HAT is 7·4 metres above Chart Datum

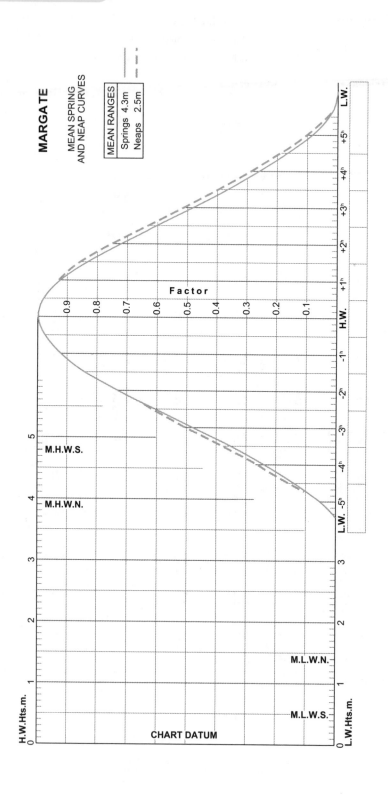

MARGATE

MEAN SPRING
AND NEAP CURVES

MEAN RANGES	
Springs	4.3m
Neaps	2.5m

TIME ZONE (UT)
For Summer Time add ONE hour in **non-shaded areas**

MARGATE

LAT 51°23′N   LONG 1°23′E

TIMES AND HEIGHTS OF HIGH AND LOW WATERS

Dates in amber are **SPRINGS**
Dates in grey are **NEAPS**

2022

JANUARY

Day	Time	m	Day	Time	m
1 SA	0415 / 1018 / 1640 / 2254	1.0 / 4.6 / 0.7 / 4.6	16 SU	0511 / 1111 / 1718 / 2331	1.0 / 4.3 / 1.1 / 4.4
2 SU ●	0513 / 1117 / 1733 / 2344	0.8 / 4.7 / 0.7 / 4.6	17 M ○	0553 / 1151 / 1756	0.9 / 4.4 / 1.1
3 M	0610 / 1213 / 1824	0.6 / 4.8 / 0.7	18 TU	0005 / 0631 / 1226 / 1829	4.5 / 0.8 / 4.6 / 1.0
4 TU	0033 / 0705 / 1305 / 1914	4.7 / 0.5 / 4.9 / 0.8	19 W	0039 / 0704 / 1302 / 1901	4.5 / 0.7 / 4.5 / 1.0
5 W	0121 / 0757 / 1357 / 2000	4.7 / 0.4 / 4.9 / 0.9	20 TH	0115 / 0738 / 1340 / 1935	4.6 / 0.6 / 4.5 / 0.9
6 TH	0208 / 0846 / 1447 / 2043	4.7 / 0.4 / 4.7 / 1.0	21 F	0152 / 0813 / 1419 / 2012	4.6 / 0.6 / 4.5 / 0.9
7 F	0253 / 0932 / 1536 / 2126	4.6 / 0.5 / 4.6 / 1.1	22 SA	0228 / 0850 / 1457 / 2050	4.6 / 0.6 / 4.4 / 1.0
8 SA	0338 / 1017 / 1626 / 2210	4.5 / 0.6 / 4.4 / 1.3	23 SU	0302 / 0928 / 1534 / 2129	4.5 / 0.6 / 4.4 / 1.1
9 SU ☽	0425 / 1105 / 1719 / 2259	4.4 / 0.8 / 4.2 / 1.4	24 M	0337 / 1008 / 1612 / 2212	4.4 / 0.7 / 4.3 / 1.2
10 M	0519 / 1157 / 1817	4.3 / 0.9 / 4.0	25 TU ☽	0419 / 1052 / 1645 / 2301	4.4 / 0.8 / 4.2 / 1.2
11 TU	0000 / 0623 / 1256 / 1917	1.5 / 4.1 / 1.1 / 4.0	26 W	0510 / 1146 / 1752	4.3 / 0.9 / 4.1
12 W	0118 / 0727 / 1356 / 2016	1.6 / 4.0 / 1.2 / 4.0	27 TH	0003 / 0612 / 1255 / 1905	1.3 / 4.2 / 1.0 / 4.0
13 TH	0226 / 0829 / 1453 / 2113	1.5 / 4.0 / 1.2 / 4.0	28 F	0126 / 0731 / 1413 / 2031	1.3 / 4.2 / 1.0 / 4.1
14 F	0327 / 0930 / 1546 / 2206	1.4 / 4.1 / 1.2 / 4.2	29 SA	0249 / 0857 / 1525 / 2144	1.2 / 4.3 / 1.0 / 4.2
15 SA	0422 / 1025 / 1635 / 2252	1.2 / 4.2 / 1.1 / 4.3	30 SU	0403 / 1013 / 1630 / 2246	1.0 / 4.4 / 0.9 / 4.4
			31 M	0512 / 1117 / 1728 / 2340	0.8 / 4.6 / 0.9 / 4.5

FEBRUARY

Day	Time	m	Day	Time	m
1 TU ●	0611 / 1212 / 1820	0.6 / 4.7 / 0.8	16 W ○	0612 / 1212 / 1814	0.7 / 4.4 / 1.0
2 W	0028 / 0703 / 1302 / 1906	4.7 / 0.4 / 4.8 / 0.8	17 TH	0025 / 0646 / 1246 / 1846	4.5 / 0.6 / 4.5 / 0.9
3 TH	0113 / 0749 / 1349 / 1947	4.7 / 0.3 / 4.8 / 0.8	18 F	0059 / 0719 / 1322 / 1920	4.6 / 0.5 / 4.6 / 0.8
4 F	0156 / 0831 / 1433 / 2026	4.8 / 0.3 / 4.7 / 0.9	19 SA	0134 / 0753 / 1400 / 1955	4.7 / 0.4 / 4.6 / 0.8
5 SA	0236 / 0909 / 1513 / 2101	4.8 / 0.4 / 4.6 / 1.0	20 SU	0209 / 0828 / 1436 / 2032	4.7 / 0.4 / 4.6 / 0.8
6 SU	0313 / 0942 / 1550 / 2137	4.7 / 0.6 / 4.4 / 1.1	21 M	0241 / 0902 / 1509 / 2108	4.6 / 0.5 / 4.5 / 0.9
7 M	0349 / 1015 / 1625 / 2215	4.5 / 0.7 / 4.2 / 1.2	22 TU	0314 / 0937 / 1543 / 2146	4.6 / 0.6 / 4.3 / 1.0
8 TU	0427 / 1052 / 1705 / 2259	4.4 / 1.0 / 4.0 / 1.4	23 W ☽	0353 / 1016 / 1625 / 2232	4.5 / 0.7 / 4.2 / 1.1
9 W	0514 / 1141 / 1801	4.1 / 1.2 / 3.8	24 TH	0442 / 1107 / 1719 / 2333	4.4 / 0.9 / 4.0 / 1.2
10 TH	0000 / 0620 / 1250 / 1918	1.6 / 3.9 / 1.4 / 3.7	25 F	0546 / 1222 / 1836	4.2 / 1.2 / 3.9
11 F	0131 / 0741 / 1407 / 2030	1.6 / 3.8 / 1.5 / 3.8	26 SA	0103 / 0717 / 1355 / 2015	1.3 / 4.0 / 1.3 / 3.9
12 SA	0249 / 0857 / 1515 / 2135	1.5 / 3.8 / 1.4 / 3.9	27 SU	0239 / 0856 / 1518 / 2136	1.2 / 4.1 / 1.2 / 4.1
13 SU	0356 / 1004 / 1614 / 2230	1.3 / 4.0 / 1.4 / 4.1	28 M	0406 / 1017 / 1628 / 2243	1.0 / 4.3 / 1.1 / 4.3
14 M	0451 / 1056 / 1702 / 2314	1.0 / 4.2 / 1.2 / 4.3			
15 TU	0535 / 1137 / 1741 / 2351	0.9 / 4.3 / 1.1 / 4.4			

MARCH

Day	Time	m	Day	Time	m
1 TU	0514 / 1118 / 1723 / 2335	0.7 / 4.6 / 0.9 / 4.5	16 W	0505 / 1113 / 1717 / 2327	0.8 / 4.3 / 1.1 / 4.4
2 W ●	0606 / 1208 / 1808	0.5 / 4.7 / 0.9	17 TH	0543 / 1148 / 1751	0.7 / 4.4 / 1.0
3 TH	0019 / 0650 / 1252 / 1848	4.7 / 0.3 / 4.8 / 0.8	18 F ○	0001 / 0619 / 1222 / 1824	4.5 / 0.5 / 4.6 / 0.8
4 F	0058 / 0729 / 1332 / 1926	4.8 / 0.3 / 4.7 / 0.8	19 SA	0035 / 0652 / 1258 / 1859	4.7 / 0.4 / 4.7 / 0.7
5 SA	0135 / 0804 / 1409 / 2001	4.8 / 0.3 / 4.7 / 0.8	20 SU	0109 / 0726 / 1334 / 1935	4.8 / 0.3 / 4.7 / 0.7
6 SU	0210 / 0834 / 1441 / 2034	4.8 / 0.4 / 4.5 / 0.8	21 M	0144 / 0800 / 1410 / 2011	4.8 / 0.4 / 4.6 / 0.7
7 M	0243 / 0900 / 1509 / 2106	4.7 / 0.6 / 4.4 / 0.9	22 TU	0218 / 0833 / 1444 / 2048	4.8 / 0.4 / 4.5 / 0.8
8 TU	0315 / 0928 / 1537 / 2138	4.6 / 0.8 / 4.2 / 1.1	23 W	0253 / 0909 / 1519 / 2128	4.7 / 0.6 / 4.4 / 0.9
9 W	0349 / 0959 / 1611 / 2216	4.4 / 1.0 / 4.1 / 1.2	24 TH	0336 / 0950 / 1603 / 2216	4.6 / 0.8 / 4.2 / 1.0
10 TH ☽	0429 / 1040 / 1654 / 2305	4.1 / 1.2 / 3.8 / 1.4	25 F	0430 / 1045 / 1701 / 2323	4.3 / 1.1 / 4.0 / 1.2
11 F	0521 / 1139 / 1756	3.8 / 1.5 / 3.6	26 SA	0542 / 1208 / 1827	4.1 / 1.4 / 3.8
12 SA	0023 / 0639 / 1311 / 1939	1.6 / 3.6 / 1.7 / 3.6	27 SU	0100 / 0722 / 1349 / 2006	1.3 / 3.9 / 1.4 / 3.8
13 SU	0205 / 0820 / 1442 / 2058	1.6 / 3.6 / 1.6 / 3.7	28 M	0242 / 0900 / 1514 / 2128	1.1 / 4.1 / 1.3 / 4.1
14 M	0322 / 0936 / 1548 / 2159	1.3 / 3.9 / 1.4 / 4.0	29 TU	0403 / 1014 / 1619 / 2231	0.8 / 4.4 / 1.1 / 4.3
15 TU	0421 / 1031 / 1638 / 2247	1.1 / 4.1 / 1.2 / 4.2	30 W	0502 / 1109 / 1708 / 2320	0.6 / 4.6 / 1.0 / 4.5
			31 TH	0548 / 1154 / 1747	0.4 / 4.7 / 0.9

APRIL

Day	Time	m	Day	Time	m
1 F ●	0000 / 0626 / 1232 / 1823	4.6 / 0.4 / 4.7 / 0.8	16 SA ○	0544 / 1150 / 1757	0.5 / 4.6 / 0.8
2 SA	0034 / 0658 / 1305 / 1900	4.7 / 0.4 / 4.6 / 0.7	17 SU	0002 / 0620 / 1227 / 1835	4.7 / 0.4 / 4.7 / 0.7
3 SU	0107 / 0727 / 1335 / 1935	4.8 / 0.4 / 4.6 / 0.7	18 M	0039 / 0656 / 1305 / 1914	4.8 / 0.3 / 4.7 / 0.6
4 M	0140 / 0755 / 1403 / 2009	4.8 / 0.5 / 4.5 / 0.7	19 TU	0118 / 0732 / 1344 / 1953	4.9 / 0.4 / 4.7 / 0.6
5 TU	0213 / 0822 / 1431 / 2040	4.7 / 0.6 / 4.4 / 0.8	20 W	0159 / 0809 / 1423 / 2034	4.8 / 0.4 / 4.6 / 0.7
6 W	0246 / 0849 / 1501 / 2110	4.5 / 0.8 / 4.3 / 1.0	21 TH	0243 / 0849 / 1505 / 2119	4.7 / 0.5 / 4.4 / 0.8
7 TH	0319 / 0919 / 1534 / 2143	4.3 / 1.0 / 4.1 / 1.1	22 F	0332 / 0936 / 1554 / 2214	4.5 / 0.7 / 4.2 / 0.9
8 F	0357 / 0956 / 1614 / 2228	4.1 / 1.2 / 3.9 / 1.3	23 SA	0432 / 1038 / 1656 / 2329	4.3 / 1.2 / 4.0 / 1.1
9 SA	0445 / 1049 / 1707 / 2334	3.8 / 1.5 / 3.7 / 1.5	24 SU ☽	0549 / 1203 / 1821	4.1 / 1.4 / 3.9
10 SU	0551 / 1207 / 1827	3.6 / 1.7 / 3.5	25 M	0102 / 0723 / 1339 / 1950	1.0 / 4.0 / 1.4 / 3.9
11 M	0111 / 0727 / 1353 / 2010	1.5 / 3.6 / 1.7 / 3.6	26 TU	0232 / 0848 / 1456 / 2104	0.9 / 4.2 / 1.2 / 4.1
12 TU	0237 / 0852 / 1508 / 2116	1.3 / 3.8 / 1.5 / 3.9	27 W	0343 / 0954 / 1555 / 2205	0.7 / 4.4 / 1.1 / 4.3
13 W	0338 / 0950 / 1600 / 2207	1.0 / 4.1 / 1.2 / 4.2	28 TH	0437 / 1046 / 1641 / 2253	0.5 / 4.5 / 1.0 / 4.5
14 TH	0426 / 1035 / 1642 / 2249	0.8 / 4.3 / 1.0 / 4.4	29 F	0519 / 1128 / 1720 / 2331	0.5 / 4.5 / 0.9 / 4.6
15 F	0506 / 1113 / 1719 / 2326	0.6 / 4.5 / 0.9 / 4.6	30 SA ●	0552 / 1203 / 1756	0.5 / 4.5 / 0.8

Chart Datum: 2·50 metres below Ordnance Datum (Newlyn)
HAT is 5·2 metres above Chart Datum

TIDES

MARGATE

TIME ZONE (UT)
For Summer Time add ONE hour in **non-shaded areas**

LAT 51°23'N LONG 1°23'E

Dates in amber are **SPRINGS**
Dates in grey are **NEAPS**

2022

TIMES AND HEIGHTS OF HIGH AND LOW WATERS

MAY

Time m	Time m
1 SU 0003 4.7 / 0621 0.5 / 1232 4.5 / 1834 0.7	**16** M 0549 0.4 / 1158 4.6 / 1812 0.7 ○
2 M 0036 4.7 / 0651 0.5 / 1259 4.5 / 1911 0.7	**17** TU 0012 4.8 / 0630 0.4 / 1240 4.7 / 1857 0.6
3 TU 0111 4.7 / 0721 0.6 / 1329 4.5 / 1946 0.7	**18** W 0059 4.9 / 0712 0.5 / 1325 4.7 / 1942 0.6
4 W 0147 4.6 / 0750 0.7 / 1401 4.4 / 2018 0.8	**19** TH 0149 4.9 / 0755 0.6 / 1410 4.6 / 2029 0.6
5 TH 0221 4.5 / 0819 0.9 / 1434 4.3 / 2048 0.9	**20** F 0240 4.8 / 0840 0.8 / 1458 4.5 / 2121 0.6
6 F 0256 4.3 / 0850 1.0 / 1508 4.2 / 2122 1.0	**21** SA 0334 4.6 / 0932 1.0 / 1549 4.3 / 2220 0.7
7 SA 0335 4.1 / 0928 1.2 / 1547 4.0 / 2205 1.1	**22** SU 0434 4.4 / 1034 1.2 / 1650 4.2 / 2332 0.8
8 SU 0421 3.9 / 1017 1.4 / 1636 3.9 / 2304 1.2	**23** M 0547 4.2 / 1150 1.4 / 1806 4.1
9 M 0518 3.8 / 1123 1.6 / 1738 3.7 ☽	**24** TU 0051 0.8 / 0707 4.2 / 1313 1.4 / 1921 4.1
10 TU 0021 1.3 / 0631 3.7 / 1244 1.6 / 1902 3.7	**25** W 0205 0.7 / 0818 4.2 / 1423 1.3 / 2027 4.2
11 W 0142 1.2 / 0755 3.8 / 1410 1.5 / 2020 3.9	**26** TH 0308 0.7 / 0920 4.3 / 1521 1.2 / 2126 4.3
12 TH 0248 0.9 / 0859 4.1 / 1512 1.3 / 2116 4.2	**27** F 0359 0.6 / 1012 4.4 / 1609 1.1 / 2216 4.4
13 F 0341 0.7 / 0949 4.3 / 1601 1.1 / 2204 4.4	**28** SA 0440 0.7 / 1055 4.4 / 1651 0.9 / 2258 4.5
14 SA 0426 0.6 / 1034 4.5 / 1645 0.9 / 2247 4.6	**29** SU 0513 0.7 / 1130 4.4 / 1732 0.8 / 2335 4.5
15 SU 0508 0.5 / 1116 4.6 / 1728 0.8 / 2329 4.7	**30** M 0546 0.7 / 1200 4.5 / 1812 0.7 ●
	31 TU 0011 4.6 / 0621 0.7 / 1230 4.5 / 1851 0.7

JUNE

Time m	Time m
1 W 0048 4.6 / 0654 0.8 / 1303 4.5 / 1927 0.7	**16** TH 0050 4.9 / 0701 0.6 / 1313 4.7 / 1940 0.5
2 TH 0125 4.5 / 0726 0.8 / 1339 4.5 / 2000 0.7	**17** F 0144 4.9 / 0749 0.7 / 1402 4.6 / 2032 0.5
3 F 0202 4.4 / 0757 0.9 / 1414 4.4 / 2033 0.8	**18** SA 0237 4.8 / 0837 0.8 / 1451 4.6 / 2125 0.5
4 SA 0240 4.3 / 0831 1.0 / 1451 4.3 / 2109 0.8	**19** SU 0331 4.7 / 0927 1.0 / 1542 4.5 / 2221 0.5
5 SU 0319 4.2 / 0910 1.1 / 1530 4.2 / 2151 0.9	**20** M 0428 4.5 / 1021 1.1 / 1637 4.4 / 2320 0.6
6 M 0402 4.1 / 0956 1.3 / 1613 4.1 / 2242 1.0	**21** TU 0530 4.3 / 1122 1.3 / 1739 4.3 ☽
7 TU 0451 4.0 / 1050 1.4 / 1703 4.0 / 2342 1.0	**22** W 0022 0.7 / 0636 4.2 / 1231 1.3 / 1843 4.3
8 W 0547 3.9 / 1153 1.5 / 1803 4.0	**23** TH 0124 0.8 / 0738 4.2 / 1339 1.4 / 1944 4.2
9 TH 0048 1.0 / 0654 4.0 / 1305 1.4 / 1913 4.0	**24** F 0222 0.8 / 0836 4.2 / 1440 1.3 / 2042 4.2
10 F 0155 0.9 / 0804 4.1 / 1418 1.3 / 2021 4.2	**25** SA 0313 0.9 / 0931 4.2 / 1535 1.2 / 2138 4.3
11 SA 0255 0.7 / 0905 4.3 / 1520 1.1 / 2119 4.4	**26** SU 0359 0.9 / 1019 4.3 / 1625 1.0 / 2229 4.3
12 SU 0348 0.6 / 0958 4.4 / 1614 0.9 / 2212 4.5	**27** M 0442 0.9 / 1101 4.3 / 1712 0.9 / 2314 4.4
13 M 0437 0.6 / 1048 4.5 / 1705 0.8 / 2304 4.7	**28** TU 0522 0.9 / 1137 4.4 / 1756 0.8 / 2354 4.4
14 TU 0525 0.6 / 1136 4.6 / 1756 0.7 / 2356 4.8 ○	**29** W 0600 0.9 / 1211 4.4 / 1836 0.7
15 W 0612 0.6 / 1224 4.6 / 1848 0.6	**30** TH 0031 4.5 / 0636 0.9 / 1245 4.5 / 1912 0.7

JULY

Time m	Time m
1 F 0108 4.5 / 0709 0.9 / 1321 4.5 / 1946 0.7	**16** SA 0139 4.9 / 0744 0.8 / 1353 4.7 / 2029 0.4
2 SA 0146 4.4 / 0741 0.9 / 1359 4.5 / 2020 0.7	**17** SU 0230 4.8 / 0829 0.8 / 1440 4.8 / 2117 0.4
3 SU 0225 4.4 / 0817 1.0 / 1436 4.4 / 2056 0.7	**18** M 0320 4.7 / 0913 0.9 / 1526 4.7 / 2203 0.5
4 M 0304 4.3 / 0855 1.0 / 1513 4.4 / 2135 0.8	**19** TU 0409 4.6 / 0956 1.1 / 1611 4.6 / 2248 0.6
5 TU 0343 4.2 / 0936 1.1 / 1551 4.3 / 2218 0.8	**20** W 0458 4.4 / 1043 1.2 / 1659 4.5 / 2336 0.8 ☽
6 W 0424 4.1 / 1020 1.2 / 1632 4.2 / 2305 0.9	**21** TH 0551 4.2 / 1137 1.3 / 1754 4.3
7 TH 0509 4.1 / 1111 1.3 / 1721 4.2 ☽	**22** F 0030 1.0 / 0649 4.0 / 1245 1.4 / 1856 4.2
8 F 0000 0.9 / 0603 4.1 / 1212 1.4 / 1818 4.2	**23** SA 0129 1.1 / 0749 4.0 / 1356 1.5 / 2001 4.1
9 SA 0104 0.9 / 0709 4.1 / 1327 1.3 / 1927 4.2	**24** SU 0229 1.2 / 0849 4.0 / 1502 1.4 / 2106 4.1
10 SU 0212 0.9 / 0823 4.1 / 1443 1.2 / 2041 4.4	**25** M 0326 1.2 / 0947 4.1 / 1603 1.2 / 2208 4.2
11 M 0316 0.8 / 0929 4.3 / 1549 1.0 / 2149 4.5	**26** TU 0419 1.2 / 1038 4.2 / 1658 1.0 / 2259 4.3
12 TU 0415 0.8 / 1029 4.4 / 1650 0.9 / 2252 4.6	**27** W 0505 1.1 / 1120 4.3 / 1743 0.9 / 2342 4.4
13 W 0510 0.8 / 1123 4.5 / 1749 0.7 / 2350 4.8 ○	**28** TH 0546 1.1 / 1157 4.4 / 1821 0.8 ●
14 TH 0604 0.7 / 1214 4.6 / 1846 0.5	**29** F 0018 4.4 / 0621 1.0 / 1230 4.5 / 1856 0.7
15 F 0045 4.8 / 0656 0.7 / 1304 4.7 / 1939 0.4	**30** SA 0052 4.5 / 0653 1.0 / 1305 4.6 / 1929 0.6
	31 SU 0128 4.5 / 0726 0.9 / 1341 4.6 / 2002 0.6

AUGUST

Time m	Time m
1 M 0205 4.5 / 0800 0.9 / 1418 4.6 / 2037 0.6	**16** TU 0258 4.7 / 0848 0.9 / 1459 4.8 / 2129 0.5
2 TU 0243 4.5 / 0836 1.0 / 1452 4.5 / 2112 0.7	**17** W 0337 4.6 / 0925 1.0 / 1536 4.7 / 2202 0.7
3 W 0319 4.4 / 0913 1.0 / 1525 4.5 / 2148 0.7	**18** TH 0412 4.3 / 1002 1.1 / 1614 4.6 / 2237 0.9
4 TH 0353 4.3 / 0951 1.1 / 1600 4.4 / 2226 0.8	**19** F 0450 4.1 / 1045 1.3 / 1659 4.3 / 2323 1.2 ☽
5 F 0432 4.2 / 1034 1.2 / 1644 4.4 / 2312 0.9	**20** SA 0541 3.9 / 1143 1.5 / 1759 4.1
6 SA 0520 4.1 / 1128 1.3 / 1739 4.3	**21** SU 0027 1.4 / 0654 3.8 / 1307 1.6 / 1917 3.9
7 SU 0015 1.1 / 0624 4.0 / 1244 1.4 / 1850 4.2	**22** M 0145 1.6 / 0808 3.8 / 1428 1.5 / 2037 3.9
8 M 0137 1.1 / 0749 4.0 / 1416 1.3 / 2018 4.2	**23** TU 0258 1.6 / 0916 3.9 / 1541 1.3 / 2149 4.1
9 TU 0255 1.1 / 0911 4.1 / 1535 1.1 / 2140 4.4	**24** W 0400 1.4 / 1014 4.2 / 1639 1.1 / 2244 4.2
10 W 0404 1.0 / 1018 4.3 / 1645 0.9 / 2250 4.6	**25** TH 0450 1.3 / 1101 4.3 / 1723 0.9 / 2326 4.4
11 TH 0504 0.9 / 1116 4.5 / 1747 0.6 / 2348 4.8	**26** F 0530 1.1 / 1139 4.5 / 1800 0.8
12 F 0557 0.8 / 1207 4.7 / 1840 0.4 ○	**27** SA 0001 4.5 / 0603 1.1 / 1211 4.7 / 1833 0.7 ●
13 SA 0040 4.9 / 0645 0.8 / 1253 4.8 / 1928 0.3	**28** SU 0032 4.5 / 0634 1.0 / 1244 4.7 / 1905 0.6
14 SU 0129 4.9 / 0729 0.8 / 1338 4.9 / 2012 0.3	**29** M 0105 4.6 / 0706 0.9 / 1318 4.7 / 1937 0.6
15 M 0215 4.8 / 0809 0.8 / 1420 4.9 / 2053 0.4	**30** TU 0140 4.6 / 0740 0.9 / 1352 4.7 / 2009 0.6
	31 W 0215 4.6 / 0814 0.9 / 1425 4.7 / 2041 0.6

Chart Datum: 2·50 metres below Ordnance Datum (Newlyn)
HAT is 5·2 metres above Chart Datum

MARGATE

LAT 51°23'N   LONG 1°23'E

TIMES AND HEIGHTS OF HIGH AND LOW WATERS

2022

SEPTEMBER

Day	Time m		Day	Time m
1 TH	0248 4.5 / 0848 1.0 / 1455 4.6 / 2113 0.7		**16** F	0322 4.4 / 0927 1.1 / 1535 4.5 / 2145 1.1
2 F	0319 4.4 / 0924 1.1 / 1529 4.5 / 2148 0.9		**17** SA	0354 4.2 / 1004 1.3 / 1616 4.3 / 2223 1.4
3 SA	0356 4.2 / 1004 1.2 / 1614 4.4 / ☾ 2232 1.1		**18** SU	0437 3.9 / 1052 1.5 / 1708 4.0 / 2320 1.7
4 SU	0445 4.1 / 1059 1.3 / 1713 4.3 / 2339 1.3		**19** M	0538 3.7 / 1210 1.6 / 1824 3.7
5 M	0553 3.9 / 1221 1.4 / 1833 4.1		**20** TU	0053 1.9 / 0719 3.6 / 1348 1.6 / 2004 3.7
6 TU	0117 1.4 / 0732 3.8 / 1404 1.4 / 2015 4.1		**21** W	0227 1.8 / 0841 3.8 / 1507 1.4 / 2121 4.0
7 W	0247 1.4 / 0901 4.0 / 1533 1.1 / 2144 4.4		**22** TH	0336 1.6 / 0942 4.0 / 1607 1.1 / 2216 4.2
8 TH	0359 1.2 / 1012 4.3 / 1643 0.8 / 2250 4.4		**23** F	0426 1.3 / 1031 4.3 / 1651 0.9 / 2258 4.4
9 F	0456 1.0 / 1108 4.5 / 1738 0.5 / 2343 4.8		**24** SA	0504 1.2 / 1110 4.5 / 1728 0.8 / 2332 4.5
10 SA	0543 0.9 / 1154 4.7 / 1824 0.4 / ○		**25** SU	0537 1.1 / 1143 4.6 / 1801 0.7 / ●
11 SU	0028 4.9 / 0625 0.8 / 1235 4.8 / 1906 0.3		**26** M	0002 4.6 / 0609 1.0 / 1214 4.7 / 1834 0.6
12 M	0110 4.9 / 0705 0.8 / 1313 4.9 / 1943 0.4		**27** TU	0034 4.7 / 0642 0.9 / 1247 4.8 / 1905 0.5
13 TU	0148 4.8 / 0743 0.8 / 1351 4.9 / 2017 0.5		**28** W	0108 4.7 / 0716 0.8 / 1321 4.8 / 1937 0.6
14 W	0223 4.7 / 0819 1.0 / 1426 4.9 / 2046 0.6		**29** TH	0143 4.7 / 0750 0.6 / 1354 4.8 / 2009 0.6
15 TH	0254 4.5 / 0854 1.0 / 1500 4.7 / 2114 0.8		**30** F	0215 4.6 / 0826 0.9 / 1428 4.7 / 2042 0.8

OCTOBER

Day	Time m		Day	Time m
1 SA	0248 4.4 / 0903 1.0 / 1507 4.6 / 2120 1.0		**16** SU	0314 4.2 / 0932 1.2 / 1543 4.2 / 2140 1.4
2 SU	0329 4.3 / 0947 1.1 / 1558 4.4 / 2210 1.2		**17** M	0354 4.0 / 1014 1.4 / 1631 4.0 / ☾ 2230 1.7
3 M	0424 4.1 / 1048 1.3 / 1705 4.2 / ☾ 2324 1.5		**18** TU	0447 3.8 / 1118 1.5 / 1735 3.7 / 2346 1.9
4 TU	0540 3.8 / 1220 1.4 / 1838 4.0		**19** W	0604 3.6 / 1254 1.6 / 1913 3.7
5 W	0109 1.6 / 0724 3.8 / 1403 1.2 / 2020 4.2		**20** TH	0137 1.9 / 0751 3.7 / 1420 1.4 / 2037 3.9
6 TH	0240 1.5 / 0850 4.1 / 1526 0.9 / 2140 4.5		**21** F	0255 1.7 / 0857 3.9 / 1521 1.1 / 2133 4.2
7 F	0347 1.2 / 0958 4.4 / 1629 0.6 / 2239 4.7		**22** SA	0346 1.4 / 0948 4.2 / 1608 0.9 / 2216 4.4
8 SA	0439 1.0 / 1050 4.6 / 1719 0.5 / 2326 4.8		**23** SU	0427 1.2 / 1029 4.4 / 1648 0.8 / 2253 4.5
9 SU	0521 0.9 / 1132 4.7 / 1759 0.4 / ○		**24** M	0503 1.1 / 1105 4.6 / 1724 0.7 / 2327 4.7
10 M	0006 4.8 / 0600 0.8 / 1208 4.8 / 1835 0.4		**25** TU	0539 0.9 / 1140 4.7 / 1758 0.6 / ●
11 TU	0041 4.8 / 0638 0.8 / 1243 4.9 / 1906 0.5		**26** W	0000 4.7 / 0615 0.9 / 1214 4.8 / 1832 0.6
12 W	0113 4.7 / 0716 0.7 / 1318 4.9 / 1937 0.6		**27** TH	0036 4.8 / 0652 0.8 / 1251 4.9 / 1906 0.6
13 TH	0142 4.7 / 0753 0.8 / 1354 4.8 / 2006 0.8		**28** F	0112 4.7 / 0730 0.8 / 1330 4.8 / 1942 0.8
14 F	0211 4.6 / 0827 1.0 / 1429 4.7 / 2034 1.0		**29** SA	0149 4.6 / 0809 0.8 / 1413 4.8 / 2021 0.9
15 SA	0241 4.4 / 0858 1.0 / 1504 4.5 / 2103 1.2		**30** SU	0230 4.5 / 0853 0.9 / 1502 4.6 / 2106 1.1
			31 M	0318 4.3 / 0944 1.0 / 1559 4.4 / 2202 1.3

NOVEMBER

Day	Time m		Day	Time m
1 TU	0417 4.1 / 1052 1.1 / 1710 4.2 / ☾ 2320 1.6		**16** W	0412 3.9 / 1044 1.3 / 1659 3.8 / 2258 1.8
2 W	0535 3.9 / 1222 1.1 / 1841 4.1		**17** TH	0511 3.8 / 1155 1.4 / 1807 3.8
3 TH	0057 1.6 / 0708 3.9 / 1352 1.0 / 2010 4.3		**18** F	0013 1.9 / 0630 3.7 / 1316 1.3 / 1932 3.9
4 F	0220 1.5 / 0826 4.1 / 1505 0.8 / 2120 4.5		**19** SA	0144 1.7 / 0756 3.9 / 1425 1.1 / 2037 4.1
5 SA	0323 1.3 / 0930 4.4 / 1603 0.6 / 2215 4.6		**20** SU	0253 1.5 / 0854 4.1 / 1519 0.9 / 2127 4.3
6 SU	0413 1.1 / 1022 4.6 / 1650 0.6 / 2300 4.7		**21** M	0342 1.3 / 0942 4.3 / 1604 0.8 / 2211 4.5
7 M	0455 1.0 / 1103 4.7 / 1727 0.6 / 2338 4.7		**22** TU	0426 1.1 / 1025 4.5 / 1646 0.7 / 2252 4.6
8 TU	0534 0.8 / 1139 4.8 / 1759 0.6 / ○		**23** W	0508 1.0 / 1106 4.7 / 1725 0.7 / ● 2331 4.7
9 W	0008 4.7 / 0613 0.7 / 1214 4.8 / 1831 0.7		**24** TH	0550 0.8 / 1147 4.8 / 1804 0.7
10 TH	0037 4.7 / 0652 0.7 / 1251 4.8 / 1903 0.7		**25** F	0010 4.7 / 0633 0.8 / 1231 4.9 / 1845 0.7
11 F	0107 4.6 / 0730 0.7 / 1328 4.7 / 1934 0.9		**26** SA	0052 4.7 / 0717 0.7 / 1319 4.9 / 1927 0.8
12 SA	0140 4.6 / 0804 0.8 / 1405 4.6 / 2004 1.0		**27** SU	0137 4.7 / 0803 0.7 / 1410 4.8 / 2012 0.9
13 SU	0213 4.4 / 0836 0.9 / 1441 4.4 / 2034 1.2		**28** M	0224 4.6 / 0853 0.7 / 1504 4.7 / 2102 1.1
14 M	0247 4.3 / 0909 1.1 / 1520 4.2 / 2111 1.4		**29** TU	0315 4.4 / 0950 0.8 / 1602 4.5 / 2159 1.3
15 TU	0325 4.1 / 0950 1.2 / 1605 4.0 / 2157 1.6		**30** W	0412 4.3 / 1057 0.8 / 1710 4.3 / ☾ 2308 1.5

DECEMBER

Day	Time m		Day	Time m
1 TH	0523 4.1 / 1212 0.9 / 1827 4.3		**16** F	0435 4.0 / 1112 1.1 / 1718 3.9 / ☾ 2320 1.6
2 F	0030 1.5 / 0642 4.1 / 1326 0.8 / 1942 4.3		**17** SA	0528 4.0 / 1212 1.1 / 1817 3.9
3 SA	0146 1.5 / 0751 4.2 / 1432 0.8 / 2046 4.4		**18** SU	0025 1.6 / 0632 3.9 / 1318 1.1 / 1928 4.0
4 SU	0249 1.3 / 0853 4.3 / 1528 0.8 / 2142 4.4		**19** M	0141 1.5 / 0745 4.0 / 1422 1.0 / 2035 4.1
5 M	0342 1.2 / 0947 4.4 / 1614 0.8 / 2230 4.3		**20** TU	0251 1.4 / 0851 4.2 / 1520 0.9 / 2132 4.3
6 TU	0429 1.0 / 1034 4.5 / 1653 0.8 / 2309 4.3		**21** W	0349 1.2 / 0948 4.4 / 1611 0.8 / 2223 4.5
7 W	0512 0.9 / 1116 4.6 / 1727 0.8 / 2342 4.3		**22** TH	0442 1.0 / 1040 4.6 / 1700 0.8 / 2311 4.6
8 TH	0554 0.8 / 1154 4.6 / 1803 0.9 / ○		**23** F	0533 0.8 / 1132 4.7 / 1747 0.8 / 2357 4.6
9 F	0012 4.6 / 0635 0.7 / 1232 4.6 / 1838 0.9		**24** SA	0624 0.7 / 1224 4.8 / 1834 0.8
10 SA	0045 4.6 / 0713 0.7 / 1310 4.6 / 1911 1.0		**25** SU	0043 4.7 / 0715 0.6 / 1316 4.9 / 1923 0.8
11 SU	0119 4.5 / 0748 0.8 / 1347 4.5 / 1943 1.1		**26** M	0131 4.7 / 0806 0.5 / 1410 4.8 / 2010 0.9
12 M	0155 4.5 / 0820 0.8 / 1424 4.4 / 2015 1.2		**27** TU	0220 4.7 / 0858 0.5 / 1503 4.8 / 2059 1.0
13 TU	0231 4.4 / 0854 0.9 / 1503 4.2 / 2052 1.3		**28** W	0310 4.6 / 0951 0.5 / 1558 4.6 / 2150 1.1
14 W	0308 4.3 / 0933 1.0 / 1543 4.1 / 2134 1.4		**29** TH	0402 4.5 / 1046 0.6 / 1656 4.4 / 2245 1.3
15 TH	0348 4.1 / 1018 1.0 / 1628 4.0 / 2223 1.5		**30** F	0500 4.4 / 1145 0.7 / 1758 4.3 / ☾ 2347 1.4
			31 SA	0604 4.3 / 1246 0.8 / 1901 4.2

Chart Datum: 2·50 metres below Ordnance Datum (Newlyn)
HAT is 5·2 metres above Chart Datum

TIDES

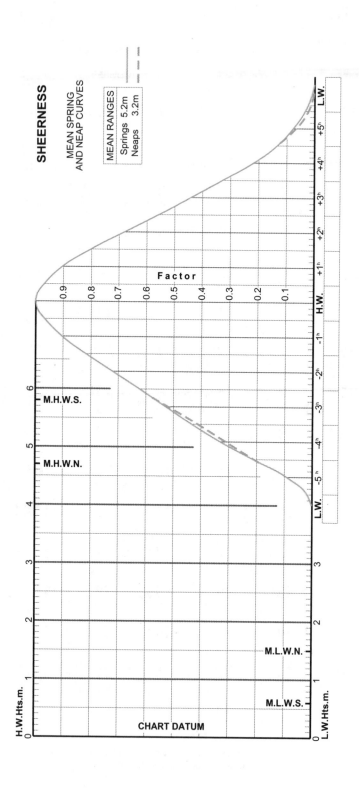

SHEERNESS

MEAN SPRING
AND NEAP CURVES

MEAN RANGES
Springs 5.2m
Neaps   3.2m

TIME ZONE (UT)
For Summer Time add ONE hour in **non-shaded areas**

Dates in amber are SPRINGS
Dates in grey are NEAPS

2022

JANUARY

Time m	Time m	Time m	Time m
1 SA 0435 1.1 / 1051 5.6 / 1715 0.8 / 2325 5.6	**16** SU 0524 1.2 / 1144 5.2 / 1741 1.2		
2 SU 0540 0.9 / 1148 5.7 / 1812 0.8 ●	**17** M 0002 5.3 / 0609 1.0 / 1224 5.3 / ○1819 1.1		
3 M 0017 5.7 / 0641 0.7 / 1242 5.9 / 1904 0.7	**18** TU 0039 5.4 / 0649 0.9 / 1301 5.4 / 1855 1.1		
4 TU 0106 5.7 / 0736 0.6 / 1334 6.0 / 1951 0.8	**19** W 0114 5.4 / 0727 0.8 / 1336 5.5 / 1930 1.0		
5 W 0154 5.7 / 0828 0.5 / 1424 6.0 / 2036 0.9	**20** TH 0148 5.3 / 0805 0.7 / 1411 5.6 / 2006 0.9		
6 TH 0240 5.7 / 0916 0.5 / 1513 5.9 / 2117 1.0	**21** F 0222 5.5 / 0844 0.7 / 1447 5.6 / 2043 1.0		
7 F 0326 5.6 / 1001 0.6 / 1601 5.7 / 2157 1.2	**22** SA 0256 5.5 / 0923 0.7 / 1524 5.5 / 2118 1.0		
8 SA 0411 5.5 / 1044 0.7 / 1650 5.4 / 2236 1.3	**23** SU 0331 5.4 / 0958 0.8 / 1603 5.4 / 2152 1.1		
9 SU 0458 5.3 / 1126 0.9 / 1740 5.2 / ○2320 1.5	**24** M 0409 5.4 / 1031 0.9 / 1646 5.3 / 2228 1.2		
10 M 0549 5.1 / 1214 1.1 / 1833 5.0	**25** TU 0451 5.3 / 1106 0.9 / 1734 5.2 / ○2312 1.3		
11 TU 0013 1.6 / 0646 4.9 / 1310 1.3 / 1933 4.8	**26** W 0542 5.2 / 1153 1.0 / 1832 5.0		
12 W 0119 1.7 / 0750 4.8 / 1413 1.4 / 2036 4.7	**27** TH 0010 1.4 / 0648 5.0 / 1258 1.2 / 1942 4.9		
13 TH 0230 1.7 / 0858 4.7 / 1514 1.4 / 2139 4.8	**28** F 0127 1.5 / 0808 5.0 / 1430 1.3 / 2057 5.0		
14 F 0335 1.5 / 1002 4.9 / 1609 1.1 / 2234 5.0	**29** SA 0300 1.4 / 0927 5.1 / 1552 1.2 / 2209 5.1		
15 SA 0433 1.3 / 1057 5.0 / 1658 1.3 / 2322 5.1	**30** SU 0421 1.2 / 1040 5.3 / 1701 1.0 / 2313 5.3		
	31 M 0536 0.9 / 1144 5.6 / 1803 0.8		

FEBRUARY

Time m	Time m	Time m	Time m
1 TU 0009 5.5 / 0640 0.6 / 1238 5.8 / ●1856 0.8	**16** W 0021 5.3 / 0635 0.8 / 1243 5.5 / ○1840 1.0		
2 W 0058 5.7 / 0734 0.4 / 1328 6.0 / 1942 0.8	**17** TH 0057 5.5 / 0714 0.7 / 1318 5.6 / 1916 0.9		
3 TH 0143 5.8 / 0821 0.3 / 1413 6.0 / 2023 0.8	**18** F 0131 5.6 / 0752 0.6 / 1353 5.7 / 1953 0.8		
4 F 0226 5.8 / 0903 0.3 / 1457 5.9 / 2100 0.9	**19** SA 0204 5.7 / 0831 0.5 / 1428 5.8 / 2030 0.8		
5 SA 0306 5.7 / 0941 0.4 / 1538 5.7 / 2134 1.0	**20** SU 0237 5.7 / 0908 0.5 / 1504 5.7 / 2103 0.8		
6 SU 0344 5.6 / 1013 0.6 / 1617 5.5 / 2205 1.1	**21** M 0311 5.7 / 0940 0.6 / 1541 5.6 / 2133 0.9		
7 M 0422 5.5 / 1042 0.8 / 1657 5.2 / 2237 1.3	**22** TU 0347 5.6 / 1007 0.7 / 1620 5.5 / 2203 1.0		
8 TU 0501 5.2 / 1111 1.1 / 1738 5.0 / ●2316 1.4	**23** W 0427 5.5 / 1036 0.9 / 1703 5.2 / ●2243 1.1		
9 W 0547 4.9 / 1152 1.3 / 1826 4.7	**24** TH 0515 5.3 / 1119 1.1 / 1757 5.0 / 2339 1.3		
10 TH 0007 1.6 / 0645 4.6 / 1252 1.6 / 1928 4.5	**25** F 0620 5.0 / 1226 1.3 / 1909 4.7		
11 F 0125 1.8 / 0801 4.5 / 1418 1.7 / 2043 4.5	**26** SA 0100 1.5 / 0747 4.8 / 1410 1.5 / 2035 4.7		
12 SA 0255 1.7 / 0924 4.5 / 1532 1.6 / 2157 4.6	**27** SU 0251 1.4 / 0919 5.0 / 1541 1.4 / 2158 4.9		
13 SU 0406 1.5 / 1033 4.8 / 1632 1.5 / 2256 4.9	**28** M 0423 1.1 / 1039 5.3 / 1656 1.2 / 2306 5.2		
14 M 0505 1.2 / 1125 5.1 / 1722 1.3 / 2342 5.2			
15 TU 0553 1.0 / 1207 5.3 / 1803 1.1			

MARCH

Time m	Time m	Time m	Time m
1 TU 0539 0.8 / 1141 5.6 / 1756 1.0	**16** W 0528 1.0 / 1140 5.3 / 1739 1.1 / 2355 5.4		
2 W 0000 5.5 / 0636 0.5 / 1231 5.8 / ●1844 0.8	**17** TH 0611 0.8 / 1218 5.6 / 1818 1.0		
3 TH 0045 5.7 / 0722 0.4 / 1315 6.0 / 1925 0.8	**18** F 0031 5.5 / 0651 0.6 / 1253 5.7 / ○1856 0.8		
4 F 0126 5.8 / 0803 0.3 / 1355 6.0 / 2002 0.7	**19** SA 0105 5.7 / 0731 0.5 / 1329 5.8 / 1934 0.7		
5 SA 0204 5.8 / 0839 0.3 / 1433 5.9 / 2036 0.7	**20** SU 0139 5.8 / 0809 0.4 / 1404 5.9 / 2011 0.7		
6 SU 0239 5.7 / 0911 0.4 / 1508 5.7 / 2107 0.8	**21** M 0214 5.8 / 0846 0.4 / 1440 5.9 / 2045 0.7		
7 M 0313 5.7 / 0937 0.6 / 1541 5.5 / 2134 0.9	**22** TU 0249 5.8 / 0918 0.5 / 1517 5.7 / 2116 0.8		
8 TU 0346 5.5 / 1000 0.8 / 1613 5.3 / 2200 1.1	**23** W 0327 5.8 / 0946 0.7 / 1556 5.5 / 2147 0.9		
9 W 0420 5.3 / 1024 1.1 / 1646 5.0 / 2232 1.3	**24** TH 0409 5.6 / 1017 0.9 / 1639 5.2 / 2230 1.0		
10 TH 0459 5.0 / 1058 1.3 / 1726 4.7 / ○2315 1.5	**25** F 0501 5.3 / 1104 1.2 / 1734 4.9 / ○2329 1.3		
11 F 0550 4.6 / 1149 1.7 / 1821 4.4	**26** SA 0611 5.0 / 1218 1.5 / 1851 4.6		
12 SA 0019 1.7 / 0703 4.3 / 1313 1.9 / 1942 4.3	**27** SU 0103 1.4 / 0744 4.8 / 1405 1.6 / 2024 4.6		
13 SU 0208 1.8 / 0840 4.3 / 1455 1.9 / 2115 4.4	**28** M 0256 1.3 / 0918 5.0 / 1533 1.5 / 2149 4.9		
14 M 0335 1.5 / 1002 4.7 / 1603 1.6 / 2224 4.8	**29** TU 0424 1.0 / 1033 5.4 / 1646 1.2 / 2253 5.2		
15 TU 0438 1.2 / 1057 5.0 / 1656 1.3 / 2313 5.1	**30** W 0530 0.6 / 1129 5.7 / 1740 1.0 / 2344 5.5		
	31 TH 0619 0.5 / 1215 5.8 / 1823 0.9		

APRIL

Time m	Time m	Time m	Time m
1 F 0025 5.7 / 0700 0.4 / 1254 5.9 / ●1901 0.8	**16** SA 0621 0.6 / 1223 5.8 / 1828 0.8 ○		
2 SA 0102 5.8 / 0736 0.4 / 1330 5.9 / 1935 0.7	**17** SU 0035 5.7 / 0703 0.5 / 1301 5.9 / 1910 0.7		
3 SU 0137 5.8 / 0807 0.4 / 1404 5.8 / 2008 0.7	**18** M 0112 5.9 / 0743 0.4 / 1338 5.9 / 1950 0.7		
4 M 0210 5.8 / 0836 0.5 / 1435 5.7 / 2039 0.7	**19** TU 0150 6.0 / 0821 0.4 / 1417 5.9 / 2029 0.7		
5 TU 0242 5.7 / 0901 0.6 / 1505 5.5 / 2106 0.9	**20** W 0230 5.9 / 0857 0.6 / 1456 5.7 / 2106 0.7		
6 W 0314 5.5 / 0923 0.9 / 1533 5.4 / 2131 1.0	**21** TH 0313 5.8 / 0931 0.8 / 1537 5.5 / 2145 0.8		
7 TH 0348 5.3 / 0947 1.1 / 1604 5.1 / 2159 1.2	**22** F 0401 5.6 / 1010 1.1 / 1625 5.2 / 2233 1.0		
8 F 0425 5.0 / 1019 1.4 / 1641 4.8 / 2238 1.4	**23** SA 0459 5.3 / 1103 1.4 / 1724 4.9 / ○2339 1.2		
9 SA 0511 4.7 / 1106 1.7 / 1730 4.5 / ○2336 1.6	**24** SU 0613 5.0 / 1219 1.6 / 1843 4.7		
10 SU 0615 4.4 / 1217 2.0 / 1844 4.3	**25** M 0119 1.2 / 0741 5.0 / 1354 1.6 / 2011 4.7		
11 M 0109 1.7 / 0747 4.3 / 1404 2.0 / 2024 4.3	**26** TU 0251 1.1 / 0905 5.2 / 1513 1.4 / 2129 5.0		
12 TU 0253 1.5 / 0914 4.6 / 1522 1.7 / 2139 4.7	**27** W 0408 0.8 / 1013 5.5 / 1620 1.2 / 2230 5.3		
13 W 0358 1.2 / 1015 5.0 / 1618 1.4 / 2234 5.1	**28** TH 0507 0.6 / 1106 5.7 / 1712 1.0 / 2318 5.5		
14 TH 0451 0.9 / 1103 5.4 / 1704 1.1 / 2318 5.4	**29** F 0552 0.6 / 1150 5.7 / 1754 0.9 / 2359 5.6		
15 F 0537 0.7 / 1144 5.6 / 1747 1.0 / 2358 5.6	**30** SA 0629 0.6 / 1228 5.7 / 1830 0.8 ●		

Chart Datum: 2·90 metres below Ordnance Datum (Newlyn)
HAT is 6·3 metres above Chart Datum

TIDES

TIDES

TIME ZONE (UT)
For Summer Time add ONE hour in **non-shaded areas**

SHEERNESS
LAT 51°27'N   LONG 0°45'E
TIMES AND HEIGHTS OF HIGH AND LOW WATERS

Dates in amber are **SPRINGS**
Dates in grey are **NEAPS**

2022

MAY

	Time	m		Time	m
1 SU	0035	5.7	**16** M	0005	5.8
	0701	0.6		0633	0.5
	1302	5.7	○	1233	5.9
	1906	0.7		1846	0.7
2 M	0109	5.7	**17** TU	0048	5.9
	0731	0.6		0717	0.5
	1334	5.7		1315	5.9
	1941	0.7		1933	0.6
3 TU	0143	5.7	**18** W	0132	6.0
	0800	0.7		0800	0.6
	1404	5.6		1357	5.8
	2013	0.7		2018	0.6
4 W	0216	5.6	**19** TH	0217	6.0
	0827	0.9		0841	0.7
	1433	5.5		1440	5.7
	2042	0.9		2103	0.6
5 TH	0249	5.5	**20** F	0306	5.8
	0852	1.0		0922	0.9
	1502	5.4		1527	5.5
	2109	1.0		2151	0.7
6 F	0323	5.3	**21** SA	0359	5.6
	0919	1.2		1008	1.1
	1533	5.2		1619	5.3
	2138	1.1		2244	0.8
7 SA	0401	5.0	**22** SU	0500	5.4
	0952	1.4		1102	1.4
	1610	4.9	◐	1720	5.1
	2217	1.3		2352	0.9
8 SU	0446	4.8	**23** M	0609	5.2
	1037	1.6		1210	1.5
	1657	4.7		1831	4.9
	2311	1.4			
9 M	0543	4.6	**24** TU	0112	1.0
	1139	1.8		0724	5.2
◐	1801	4.5		1327	1.6
				1946	5.0
10 TU	0025	1.5	**25** W	0226	0.9
	0658	4.5		0837	5.2
	1302	1.9		1438	1.5
	1927	4.5		2056	5.1
11 W	0156	1.4	**26** TH	0333	0.8
	0818	4.7		0941	5.4
	1425	1.7		1540	1.3
	2045	4.7		2156	5.2
12 TH	0307	1.2	**27** F	0430	0.8
	0925	5.0		1035	5.5
	1527	1.4		1634	1.0
	2145	5.0		2247	5.4
13 F	0404	0.9	**28** SA	0515	0.8
	1019	5.4		1120	5.5
	1620	1.2		1719	1.1
	2236	5.3		2330	5.4
14 SA	0457	0.7	**29** SU	0552	0.8
	1107	5.6		1200	5.5
	1710	1.0		1800	0.9
	2322	5.6			
15 SU	0546	0.6	**30** M	0009	5.5
	1151	5.8		0625	0.8
	1758	0.9	●	1234	5.6
				1839	0.8
			31 TU	0046	5.5
				0657	0.9
				1307	5.6
				1916	0.8

JUNE

	Time	m		Time	m
1 W	0122	5.5	**16** TH	0120	5.9
	0729	0.9		0745	0.7
	1338	5.5		1344	5.8
	1952	0.8		2014	0.5
2 TH	0157	5.5	**17** F	0211	6.0
	0759	1.0		0831	0.8
	1409	5.4		1432	5.7
	2024	0.9		2105	0.5
3 F	0231	5.4	**18** SA	0303	5.9
	0829	1.1		0916	0.9
	1440	5.3		1520	5.5
	2055	1.0		2155	0.5
4 SA	0307	5.3	**19** SU	0356	5.8
	0900	1.2		1002	1.1
	1513	5.2		1611	5.5
	2129	1.0		2248	0.6
5 SU	0345	5.1	**20** M	0452	5.6
	0936	1.4		1051	1.2
	1551	5.1		1706	5.3
	2208	1.1		2343	0.7
6 M	0428	5.0	**21** TU	0550	5.4
	1018	1.5		1145	1.4
	1635	4.9		1805	5.2
	2256	1.2	◐		
7 TU	0518	4.9	**22** W	0043	0.8
	1109	1.6		0653	5.3
	1729	4.8		1246	1.5
	2353	1.3		1908	5.1
8 W	0617	4.8	**23** TH	0145	0.9
	1212	1.7		0756	5.2
	1834	4.7		1350	1.5
				2013	5.1
9 TH	0100	1.2	**24** F	0245	1.0
	0725	4.9		0859	5.1
	1322	1.6		1453	1.5
	1947	4.8		2116	5.1
10 F	0211	1.1	**25** SA	0341	1.1
	0833	5.1		0957	5.2
	1432	1.5		1551	1.4
	2054	5.0		2213	5.1
11 SA	0316	1.0	**26** SU	0430	1.1
	0935	5.3		1048	5.3
	1535	1.3		1645	1.2
	2154	5.3		2304	5.2
12 SU	0416	0.8	**27** M	0513	1.1
	1031	5.5		1133	5.3
	1634	1.1		1734	1.1
	2248	5.5		2350	5.3
13 M	0512	0.7	**28** TU	0553	1.1
	1122	5.7		1212	5.4
	1732	1.0		1818	1.0
	2340	5.7			
14 TU	0606	0.7	**29** W	0030	5.4
	1211	5.8		0630	1.1
	1828	0.8		1248	5.4
○			●	1859	0.9
15 W	0030	5.8	**30** TH	0108	5.4
	0657	0.7		0704	1.1
	1258	5.8		1321	5.4
	1922	0.6		1936	0.9

JULY

	Time	m		Time	m
1 F	0143	5.4	**16** SA	0206	6.0
	0738	1.1		0822	0.8
	1354	5.4		1423	5.8
	2012	0.9		2102	0.3
2 SA	0218	5.4	**17** SU	0255	6.0
	0812	1.1		0906	0.9
	1427	5.4		1509	5.8
	2047	0.9		2148	0.3
3 SU	0254	5.4	**18** M	0343	5.9
	0847	1.1		0948	1.0
	1501	5.3		1554	5.7
	2124	0.9		2232	0.5
4 M	0330	5.3	**19** TU	0431	5.7
	0923	1.2		1028	1.1
	1537	5.3		1640	5.6
	2202	0.9		2315	0.7
5 TU	0410	5.3	**20** W	0520	5.5
	1001	1.3		1109	1.3
	1616	5.2		1728	5.4
	2240	1.0	◑	2358	0.9
6 W	0453	5.2	**21** TH	0611	5.2
	1041	1.4		1156	1.5
	1659	5.1		1821	5.2
	2322	1.1			
7 TH	0542	5.1	**22** F	0046	1.1
	1128	1.5		0707	5.0
	1750	5.0		1253	1.6
◑				1922	5.0
8 F	0010	1.1	**23** SA	0145	1.3
	0640	5.0		0808	4.9
	1225	1.5		1403	1.6
	1854	5.0		2031	4.8
9 SA	0112	1.1	**24** SU	0248	1.4
	0746	5.0		0914	4.9
	1335	1.5		1512	1.6
	2006	5.0		2141	4.9
10 SU	0228	1.1	**25** M	0348	1.4
	0855	5.1		1016	5.0
	1454	1.4		1617	1.4
	2117	5.2		2243	5.0
11 M	0341	1.1	**26** TU	0442	1.4
	0959	5.3		1109	5.1
	1607	1.2		1715	1.2
	2223	5.4		2334	5.2
12 TU	0447	1.0	**27** W	0530	1.3
	1100	5.5		1153	5.3
	1714	1.0		1804	1.1
	2325	5.6	○	1914	0.5
13 W	0547	0.9	**28** TH	0017	5.3
	1155	5.6		0611	1.2
	1819	0.8		1232	5.4
○				1846	1.0
14 TH	0021	5.8	**29** F	0055	5.4
	0644	0.8		0647	1.2
	1247	5.7		1307	5.5
	1918	0.6		1923	0.9
15 F	0115	6.0	**30** SA	0129	5.5
	0735	0.8		0722	1.1
	1336	5.8		1340	5.5
	2012	0.4		1959	0.8
			31 SU	0203	5.5
				0757	1.0
				1413	5.5
				2036	0.7

AUGUST

	Time	m		Time	m
1 M	0237	5.6	**16** TU	0320	5.9
	0833	1.0		0924	0.9
	1445	5.5		1528	5.9
	2112	0.7		2203	0.5
2 TU	0311	5.6	**17** W	0401	5.7
	0908	1.1		0957	1.1
	1518	5.5		1606	5.7
	2147	0.8		2234	0.8
3 W	0347	5.5	**18** TH	0441	5.5
	0941	1.2		1030	1.2
	1552	5.4		1646	5.5
	2218	0.9		2304	1.0
4 TH	0425	5.4	**19** F	0522	5.2
	1012	1.3		1106	1.4
	1630	5.3		1730	5.3
	2249	1.0	◑	2339	1.3
5 F	0508	5.2	**20** SA	0608	4.9
	1049	1.4		1153	1.6
	1714	5.2		1826	4.8
	2326	1.1			
6 SA	0559	5.1	**21** SU	0033	1.6
	1139	1.5		0707	4.6
	1811	5.1		1304	1.8
				1940	4.6
7 SU	0020	1.3	**22** M	0154	1.8
	0704	5.0		0822	4.6
	1247	1.6		1437	1.8
	1927	5.0		2108	4.6
8 M	0146	1.4	**23** TU	0313	1.7
	0820	4.9		0942	4.7
	1424	1.6		1554	1.5
	2052	5.0		2222	4.9
9 TU	0319	1.3	**24** W	0418	1.6
	0936	5.1		1044	5.0
	1552	1.3		1657	1.3
	2210	5.3		2316	5.2
10 W	0432	1.2	**25** TH	0511	1.4
	1046	5.3		1131	5.2
	1709	1.0		1746	1.1
	2319	5.6		2358	5.4
11 TH	0538	1.0	**26** F	0553	1.3
	1146	5.5		1211	5.4
	1817	0.7		1827	0.9
12 F	0017	5.8	**27** SA	0034	5.5
	0635	0.9		0629	1.2
	1237	5.7		1245	5.6
○	1914	0.5	●	1903	0.8
13 SA	0108	6.0	**28** SU	0107	5.6
	0724	0.8		0703	1.1
	1323	5.9		1318	5.6
	2003	0.3		1939	0.7
14 SU	0154	6.1	**29** M	0140	5.7
	0808	0.8		0738	1.0
	1407	5.9		1350	5.7
	2047	0.2		2015	0.6
15 M	0238	6.1	**30** TU	0213	5.8
	0847	0.8		0814	0.9
	1448	5.9		1421	5.7
	2127	0.3		2051	0.6
			31 W	0247	5.7
				0848	1.0
				1453	5.7
				2124	0.6

Chart Datum: 2·90 metres below Ordnance Datum (Newlyn)
HAT is 6·3 metres above Chart Datum

SHEERNESS

LAT 51°27'N LONG 0°45'E

TIMES AND HEIGHTS OF HIGH AND LOW WATERS

Dates in amber are **SPRINGS**
Dates in grey are **NEAPS**

2022

SEPTEMBER

Day	Time	m	Time	m	Time	m	Time	m
1 TH	0321	5.7	0918	1.1	1527	5.6	2151	0.9
2 F	0357	5.5	0944	1.2	1603	5.5	2215	1.0
3 SA ◑	0437	5.3	1018	1.3	1647	5.3	2250	1.2
4 SU	0525	5.1	1108	1.4	1744	5.1	2349	1.5
5 M	0630	4.8	1221	1.6	1905	4.9		
6 TU	0127	1.7	0755	4.7	1416	1.6	2041	4.9
7 W	0308	1.6	0923	4.9	1550	1.3	2208	5.3
8 TH	0424	1.3	1037	5.2	1709	0.9	2314	5.7
9 F	0529	1.1	1134	5.6	1811	0.6		
10 SA ○	0007	5.9	0621	0.9	1222	5.8	1900	0.4
11 SU	0053	6.1	0705	0.8	1304	5.9	1943	0.3
12 M	0135	6.1	0745	0.8	1343	6.0	2022	0.3
13 TU	0213	6.0	0821	0.8	1420	6.0	2056	0.4
14 W	0250	5.9	0854	0.9	1456	5.9	2126	0.7
15 TH	0325	5.7	0925	1.0	1531	5.7	2150	0.9
16 F	0358	5.4	0952	1.2	1606	5.5	2214	1.2
17 SA ◑	0432	5.2	1022	1.4	1646	5.1	2245	1.5
18 SU	0511	4.9	1102	1.6	1735	4.8	2332	1.8
19 M	0603	4.6	1205	1.8	1847	4.4		
20 TU	0051	2.1	0724	4.4	1356	1.9	2026	4.4
21 W	0238	2.0	0859	4.5	1525	1.6	2150	4.7
22 TH	0349	1.8	1010	4.8	1628	1.3	2245	5.1
23 F	0443	1.5	1100	5.2	1717	1.0	2328	5.4
24 SA	0525	1.3	1140	5.5	1757	0.9		
25 SU ●	0004	5.6	0602	1.1	1215	5.8	1834	0.8
26 M	0038	5.7	0637	1.0	1248	5.7	1911	0.7
27 TU	0111	5.8	0713	0.8	1321	5.8	1947	0.6
28 W	0145	5.9	0750	0.8	1354	5.8	2023	0.6
29 TH	0219	5.9	0824	0.9	1428	5.8	2056	0.9
30 F	0254	5.8	0855	1.0	1504	5.8	2123	0.9

OCTOBER

Day	Time	m	Time	m	Time	m	Time	m
1 SA	0330	5.6	0924	1.1	1544	5.6	2151	1.1
2 SU	0411	5.3	1002	1.2	1632	5.4	2233	1.4
3 M ◑	0501	5.0	1057	1.4	1735	5.1	2339	1.7
4 TU	0610	4.7	1222	1.6	1901	4.9		
5 W	0124	1.8	0742	4.7	1421	1.5	2039	5.0
6 TH	0258	1.6	0912	4.9	1549	1.1	2200	5.4
7 F	0412	1.4	1022	5.3	1700	0.8	2301	5.7
8 SA	0511	1.1	1115	5.6	1753	0.5	2349	5.9
9 SU ○	0558	1.0	1159	5.8	1837	0.5		
10 M	0031	6.0	0639	0.9	1238	5.9	1915	0.5
11 TU	0108	6.0	0715	0.8	1315	5.8	1948	0.5
12 W	0144	5.9	0750	0.8	1350	5.8	2019	0.6
13 TH	0217	5.8	0824	0.9	1425	5.9	2046	0.8
14 F	0249	5.7	0854	1.0	1459	5.7	2109	1.1
15 SA	0319	5.4	0920	1.2	1534	5.4	2132	1.3
16 SU	0350	5.2	0947	1.3	1612	5.1	2202	1.5
17 M ◑	0425	4.9	1023	1.5	1657	4.8	2247	1.8
18 TU	0512	4.6	1119	1.7	1801	4.5	2354	2.1
19 W	0624	4.4	1251	1.9	1931	4.4		
20 TH	0141	2.2	0804	4.4	1441	1.7	2058	4.6
21 F	0305	1.9	0921	4.7	1544	1.3	2159	5.0
22 SA	0401	1.6	1016	5.1	1635	1.1	2246	5.4
23 SU	0446	1.3	1059	5.4	1718	0.9	2326	5.6
24 M	0526	1.1	1138	5.6	1758	0.8		
25 TU ●	0003	5.8	0606	1.0	1215	5.7	1838	0.7
26 W	0040	5.9	0645	0.9	1251	5.9	1917	0.6
27 TH	0116	5.9	0725	0.9	1328	5.9	1954	0.7
28 F	0153	5.9	0803	0.9	1406	5.9	2029	0.8
29 SA	0231	5.8	0840	0.9	1448	5.8	2103	1.0
30 SU	0310	5.6	0918	1.0	1534	5.6	2140	1.2
31 M	0355	5.3	1004	1.1	1628	5.4	2230	1.5

NOVEMBER

Day	Time	m	Time	m	Time	m	Time	m
1 TU ◑	0450	5.0	1106	1.3	1736	5.1	2340	1.7
2 W	0603	4.8	1239	1.4	1900	5.0		
3 TH	0113	1.8	0730	4.8	1415	1.2	2026	5.1
4 F	0236	1.6	0851	5.0	1532	1.0	2139	5.4
5 SA	0344	1.4	0956	5.3	1636	0.7	2237	5.7
6 SU	0441	1.2	1048	5.5	1726	0.6	2324	5.8
7 M	0527	1.1	1132	5.7	1806	0.7		
8 TU ◑	0004	5.8	0607	0.9	1211	5.8	1840	0.7
9 W	0040	5.8	0645	0.9	1248	5.8	1911	0.7
10 TH	0114	5.8	0721	0.8	1324	5.8	1941	0.8
11 F	0147	5.7	0756	0.8	1400	5.7	2009	1.0
12 SA	0217	5.6	0828	1.0	1435	5.6	2035	1.1
13 SU	0247	5.4	0855	1.1	1510	5.3	2101	1.3
14 M	0318	5.2	0923	1.2	1548	5.1	2132	1.5
15 TU	0353	5.0	0959	1.4	1631	4.9	2215	1.7
16 W	0437	4.8	1050	1.5	1725	4.6	2312	1.9
17 TH	0537	4.5	1159	1.6	1835	4.5		
18 F	0027	2.0	0659	4.5	1329	1.6	1952	4.6
19 SA	0155	1.9	0818	4.7	1445	1.4	2100	4.9
20 SU	0302	1.7	0921	5.0	1542	1.1	2155	5.2
21 M	0356	1.4	1013	5.3	1632	0.9	2244	5.5
22 TU	0445	1.2	1059	5.5	1719	0.8	2328	5.7
23 W ●	0532	1.1	1143	5.7	1804	0.8		
24 TH	0010	5.8	0618	0.9	1225	5.8	1848	0.7
25 F	0051	5.8	0704	0.8	1308	5.9	1930	0.7
26 SA	0133	5.8	0750	0.8	1353	5.9	2012	0.8
27 SU	0215	5.7	0836	0.8	1440	5.9	2053	1.0
28 M	0300	5.6	0923	0.8	1531	5.7	2138	1.2
29 TU	0349	5.4	1016	0.9	1628	5.5	2229	1.4
30 W ◑	0446	5.2	1118	1.0	1733	5.3	2332	1.6

DECEMBER

Day	Time	m	Time	m	Time	m	Time	m
1 TH	0552	5.0	1233	1.1	1844	5.2		
2 F	0045	1.6	0705	5.0	1348	1.0	1958	5.2
3 SA	0157	1.6	0817	5.1	1457	1.0	2105	5.3
4 SU	0303	1.5	0921	5.2	1558	0.9	2204	5.4
5 M	0401	1.3	1017	5.3	1649	0.9	2254	5.5
6 TU	0452	1.2	1105	5.4	1729	0.9	2337	5.5
7 W	0537	1.1	1148	5.5	1804	0.9		
8 TH ○	0015	5.5	0619	0.9	1228	5.6	1837	1.0
9 F	0051	5.6	0658	0.9	1306	5.6	1910	1.0
10 SA	0124	5.5	0736	0.9	1343	5.6	1941	1.1
11 SU	0155	5.5	0809	0.9	1419	5.4	2010	1.2
12 M	0226	5.4	0840	1.0	1454	5.3	2041	1.3
13 TU	0258	5.2	0911	1.1	1531	5.2	2114	1.4
14 W	0334	5.1	0948	1.2	1611	5.0	2153	1.5
15 TH	0414	5.0	1031	1.3	1656	4.9	2240	1.6
16 F	0502	4.8	1122	1.3	1749	4.8	2335	1.7
17 SA	0600	4.7	1222	1.4	1851	4.8		
18 SU	0039	1.8	0710	4.7	1331	1.3	1959	4.9
19 M	0152	1.7	0821	4.9	1442	1.2	2104	5.1
20 TU	0302	1.5	0924	5.1	1546	1.1	2203	5.3
21 W	0405	1.3	1022	5.3	1643	1.0	2256	5.5
22 TH	0502	1.1	1116	5.5	1736	0.9	2346	5.6
23 F	0558	0.9	1207	5.7	1826	0.9		
24 SA	0033	5.7	0653	0.8	1257	5.9	1915	0.8
25 SU	0120	5.7	0746	0.6	1346	5.9	2002	0.8
26 M	0206	5.7	0838	0.5	1437	5.9	2049	0.9
27 TU	0254	5.7	0929	0.5	1528	5.9	2134	1.0
28 W	0342	5.6	1019	0.6	1621	5.7	2220	1.2
29 TH	0434	5.4	1110	0.7	1716	5.5	2310	1.3
30 F ◑	0528	5.3	1205	0.8	1815	5.3		
31 SA	0004	1.5	0629	5.2	1304	1.0	1918	5.1

Chart Datum: 2·90 metres below Ordnance Datum (Newlyn)
HAT is 6·3 metres above Chart Datum

TIDES

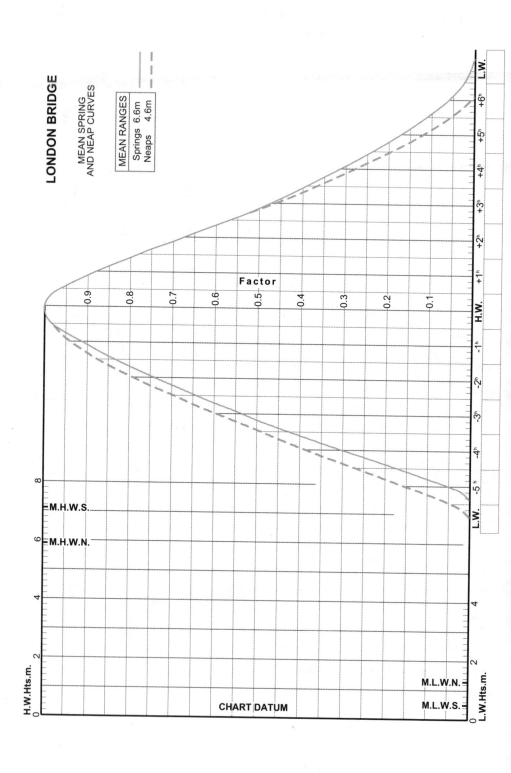

LONDON BRIDGE

MEAN SPRING
AND NEAP CURVES

MEAN RANGES
Springs 6.6m
Neaps 4.6m

LONDON BRIDGE

LAT 51°30'N LONG 0°05'W
TIMES AND HEIGHTS OF HIGH AND LOW WATERS

TIME ZONE (UT)
For Summer Time add ONE hour in **non-shaded areas**

Dates in amber are **SPRINGS**
Dates in grey are **NEAPS**

2022

JANUARY

Day	Time	m	Time	m	Day	Time	m	Time	m
1 SA	0623	1.1	1212	6.9	16 SU	0040	6.3	0700	1.0
	1850	0.8				1300	6.6	1915	1.1
2 SU	0045	6.8	0734	0.8	17 M	0124	6.5	0749	0.8
	1308	7.2	1956	0.7		1342	6.7	2000	1.1
3 M	0140	6.9	0835	0.6	18 TU	0204	6.6	0833	0.7
	1403	7.3	2052	0.7		1421	6.7	2041	1.1
4 TU	0232	6.9	0930	0.4	19 W	0240	6.7	0915	0.6
	1455	7.4	2142	0.6		1456	6.8	2119	1.1
5 W	0321	7.0	1019	0.3	20 TH	0314	6.7	0955	0.6
	1545	7.3	2227	0.8		1530	6.8	2155	1.0
6 TH	0407	6.9	1104	0.3	21 F	0347	6.7	1033	0.5
	1633	7.2	2307	0.9		1604	6.9	2231	1.0
7 F	0452	6.8	1144	0.4	22 SA	0420	6.7	1107	0.5
	1720	7.0	2344	1.1		1640	6.8	2305	1.0
8 SA	0536	6.6	1220	0.5	23 SU	0454	6.6	1136	0.6
	1807	6.7				1718	6.7	2337	1.1
9 SU	0020	1.2	0621	6.4	24 M	0531	6.6	1202	0.7
	1254	0.7	1856	6.4		1759	6.5		
10 M	0059	1.4	0709	6.2	25 TU	0011	1.2	0612	6.5
	1335	0.9	1948	6.2		1234	0.8	1846	6.3
11 TU	0146	1.6	0804	6.1	26 W	0052	1.4	0700	6.4
	1425	1.1	2042	6.0		1317	0.9	1942	6.1
12 W	0248	1.7	0905	6.0	27 TH	0144	1.5	0802	6.3
	1524	1.3	2140	5.9		1418	1.1	2056	6.0
13 TH	0359	1.7	1008	6.0	28 F	0301	1.6	0925	6.2
	1625	1.3	2244	5.9		1552	1.3	2214	6.1
14 F	0504	1.5	1113	6.1	29 SA	0439	1.5	1046	6.4
	1725	1.3	2348	6.1		1716	1.2	2328	6.3
15 SA	0604	1.2	1211	6.3	30 SU	0606	1.2	1158	6.6
	1822	1.2				1838	1.0		
					31 M	0036	6.5	0727	0.8
						1302	6.9	1949	0.9

FEBRUARY

Day	Time	m	Time	m	Day	Time	m	Time	m
1 TU	0134	6.7	0830	0.4	16 W	0146	6.6	0816	0.7
	1358	7.2	2046	0.8		1403	6.7	2030	1.1
2 W	0225	6.9	0924	0.2	17 TH	0223	6.7	0900	0.5
	1448	7.3	2135	0.7		1438	6.8	2112	1.1
3 TH	0310	7.0	1011	0.0	18 F	0258	6.8	0942	0.4
	1534	7.3	2219	0.7		1512	6.9	2151	0.9
4 F	0353	7.1	1052	0.0	19 SA	0330	6.9	1020	0.3
	1617	7.2	2256	0.7		1546	7.0	2227	0.8
5 SA	0432	7.1	1127	0.2	20 SU	0403	6.9	1054	0.3
	1658	7.0	2329	0.9		1621	7.0	2300	0.9
6 SU	0510	6.9	1154	0.4	21 M	0435	6.9	1121	0.4
	1737	6.7	2356	0.9		1657	6.8	2328	1.0
7 M	0546	6.7	1215	0.6	22 TU	0510	6.8	1143	0.6
	1814	6.4				1735	6.6	2357	1.1
8 TU	0021	1.2	0625	6.5	23 W	0550	6.7	1211	0.8
	1238	0.9	1854	6.1		1818	6.3		
9 W	0052	1.4	0708	6.2	24 TH	0032	1.3	0637	6.5
	1311	1.2	1940	5.8		1248	1.0	1911	6.0
10 TH	0135	1.7	0805	5.9	25 F	0119	1.5	0737	6.2
	1402	1.5	2038	5.6		1343	1.4	2024	5.8
11 F	0242	1.8	0915	5.7	26 SA	0234	1.7	0903	6.0
	1530	1.7	2149	5.5		1530	1.6	2153	5.7
12 SA	0418	1.8	1031	5.7	27 SU	0423	1.6	1034	6.1
	1649	1.7	2309	5.7		1705	1.5	2321	6.0
13 SU	0529	1.4	1143	6.0	28 M	0605	1.2	1156	6.4
	1756	1.5				1835	1.2		
14 M	0014	6.1	0633	1.1					
	1239	6.3	1856	1.3					
15 TU	0104	6.4	0728	0.8					
	1324	6.6	1946	1.2					

MARCH

Day	Time	m	Time	m	Day	Time	m	Time	m
1 TU	0033	6.4	0724	0.6	16 W	0034	6.3	0659	0.8
	1259	6.8	1940	0.9		1255	6.5	1921	1.2
2 W	0128	6.7	0821	0.2	17 TH	0117	6.6	0750	0.6
	1351	7.1	2033	0.7		1334	6.7	2008	1.1
3 TH	0213	6.9	0909	0.0	18 F	0155	6.8	0836	0.5
	1435	7.2	2119	0.6		1411	6.9	2052	1.0
4 F	0253	7.1	0952	0.0	19 SA	0230	6.9	0918	0.4
	1516	7.2	2159	0.6		1447	7.0	2133	0.8
5 SA	0330	7.2	1028	0.1	20 SU	0305	7.1	0957	0.3
	1553	7.2	2234	0.7		1523	7.1	2211	0.8
6 SU	0405	7.2	1056	0.3	21 M	0339	7.2	1031	0.3
	1628	7.0	2303	0.8		1559	7.0	2245	0.7
7 M	0439	7.1	1115	0.5	22 TU	0414	7.1	1058	0.4
	1700	6.7	2325	0.9		1635	6.8	2315	0.9
8 TU	0512	6.9	1130	0.7	23 W	0451	7.0	1121	0.6
	1731	6.4	2346	1.1		1713	6.5	2343	1.0
9 W	0545	6.6	1152	0.9	24 TH	0532	6.8	1150	0.9
	1803	6.1				1756	6.2		
10 TH	0013	1.3	0623	6.2	25 F	0018	1.1	0622	6.5
	1221	1.2	1841	5.8		1230	1.2	1851	5.9
11 F	0047	1.5	0708	5.8	26 SA	0106	1.4	0727	6.1
	1259	1.6	1933	5.5		1332	1.6	2008	5.6
12 SA	0137	1.8	0816	5.5	27 SU	0227	1.6	0858	5.9
	1402	2.0	2053	5.3		1520	1.8	2143	5.6
13 SU	0322	1.9	0947	5.4	28 M	0415	1.5	1029	6.1
	1610	2.0	2226	5.4		1658	1.6	2313	5.9
14 M	0453	1.6	1108	5.7	29 TU	0603	1.0	1149	6.5
	1727	1.7	2341	5.8		1821	1.1		
15 TU	0600	1.2	1209	6.2	30 W	0020	6.4	0709	0.4
	1828	1.4				1247	6.9	1921	0.8
					31 TH	0111	6.6	0800	0.2
						1334	7.1	2010	0.7

APRIL

Day	Time	m	Time	m	Day	Time	m	Time	m
1 F	0152	7.0	0844	0.1	16 SA	0119	6.8	0801	0.5
	1414	7.1	2053	0.6		1338	6.9	2023	1.0
2 SA	0228	7.1	0921	0.2	17 SU	0158	7.1	0847	0.6
	1450	7.1	2131	0.6		1418	7.1	2108	0.8
3 SU	0301	7.2	0952	0.3	18 M	0236	7.2	0928	0.4
	1523	7.0	2204	0.6		1457	7.1	2149	0.7
4 M	0334	7.2	1015	0.5	19 TU	0315	7.3	1004	0.4
	1554	6.9	2231	0.7		1537	7.0	2227	0.7
5 TU	0407	7.1	1030	0.6	20 W	0355	7.3	1034	0.5
	1623	6.7	2252	0.8		1617	6.8	2300	0.7
6 W	0439	6.9	1050	0.8	21 TH	0436	7.1	1103	0.7
	1653	6.4	2315	1.0		1658	6.5	2332	0.8
7 TH	0512	6.6	1115	1.0	22 F	0522	6.8	1138	1.0
	1722	6.2	2341	1.1		1745	6.1		
8 F	0546	6.2	1142	1.2	23 SA	0010	0.9	0618	6.5
	1755	5.9				1224	1.3	1844	5.8
9 SA	0009	1.3	0626	5.9	24 SU	0103	1.2	0729	6.2
	1214	1.6	1840	5.5		1334	1.7	2003	5.7
10 SU	0049	1.6	0709	5.5	25 M	0227	1.3	0852	6.1
	1302	2.0	1946	5.2		1507	1.7	2129	5.8
11 M	0201	1.8	0850	5.3	26 TU	0402	1.1	1012	6.3
	1452	2.2	2134	5.2		1634	1.5	2249	6.1
12 TU	0407	1.6	1019	5.6	27 W	0535	0.8	1126	6.6
	1638	1.9	2254	5.7		1751	1.1	2354	6.5
13 W	0515	1.2	1123	6.1	28 TH	0639	0.5	1224	6.8
	1743	1.5	2352	6.1		1849	0.9		
14 TH	0614	0.9	1214	6.5	29 F	0043	6.7	0728	0.4
	1840	1.1				1309	6.9	1938	0.8
15 F	0038	6.5	0711	0.6	30 SA	0123	6.9	0808	0.4
	1257	6.8	1934	1.1		1347	6.9	2021	0.7

Chart Datum: 3·20 metres below Ordnance Datum (Newlyn)
HAT is 7·7 metres above Chart Datum

TIDES

TIME ZONE (UT)
For Summer Time add ONE hour in **non-shaded areas**

LONDON BRIDGE
LAT 51°30′N   LONG 0°05′W
TIMES AND HEIGHTS OF HIGH AND LOW WATERS

Dates in amber are SPRINGS
Dates in grey are NEAPS

2022

MAY

Day	Time m	Time m	Time m	Time m		Day	Time m	Time m	Time m	Time m
1 SU	0158 7.0	0842 0.5	1420 6.9	2058 0.7		16 M	0127 7.2	0812 0.5	1352 7.0	○ 2042 0.8
2 M	0231 7.1	0909 0.6	1451 6.9	2130 0.6		17 TU	0211 7.3	0859 0.5	1436 7.0	2129 0.6
3 TU	0304 7.2	0929 0.7	1521 6.8	2157 0.7		18 W	0256 7.4	0941 0.5	1521 6.9	2212 0.5
4 W	0338 7.1	0951 0.7	1551 6.7	2222 0.8		19 TH	0341 7.3	1019 0.7	1606 6.7	2251 0.5
5 TH	0411 6.8	1018 0.8	1621 6.5	2248 0.9		20 F	0429 7.1	1055 0.8	1653 6.5	2330 0.6
6 F	0444 6.5	1045 1.0	1652 6.2	2316 1.0		21 SA	0520 6.9	1137 1.0	1743 6.2	
7 SA	0518 6.3	1113 1.2	1725 6.0	2344 1.2		22 SU	0012 0.7	0619 6.6	1226 1.3	☽ 1843 6.0
8 SU	0558 6.0	1147 1.4	1808 5.7			23 M	0108 0.9	0725 6.4	1330 1.5	1952 6.0
9 M	0021 1.3	0648 5.7	☽ 1232 1.7	1906 5.5		24 TU	0220 0.9	0834 6.3	1445 1.5	2103 6.0
10 TU	0119 1.5	0756 5.6	1346 1.9	2030 5.4		25 W	0333 0.9	0943 6.4	1559 1.4	2212 6.2
11 W	0305 1.5	0924 5.7	1527 1.8	2159 5.7		26 TH	0444 0.7	1051 6.5	1708 1.2	2315 6.4
12 TH	0421 1.2	1030 6.1	1642 1.5	2301 6.1		27 F	0550 0.7	1151 6.6	1809 1.0	
13 F	0521 0.8	1127 6.5	1747 1.3	2354 6.6		28 SA	0008 6.6	0643 0.7	1238 6.7	1902 0.9
14 SA	0619 0.7	1219 6.8	1850 1.1			29 SU	0051 6.8	0724 0.7	1318 6.7	1946 0.8
15 SU	0041 6.9	0718 0.6	1306 6.9	1950 1.0		30 M	0129 6.9	0758 0.8	1352 6.7	● 2025 0.7
						31 TU	0205 7.0	0827 0.8	1424 6.8	2100 0.7

JUNE

Day	Time m	Time m	Time m	Time m		Day	Time m	Time m	Time m	Time m
1 W	0240 7.0	0855 0.8	1456 6.7	2131 0.7		16 TH	0244 7.4	0928 0.7	1511 6.9	2205 0.4
2 TH	0316 6.9	0924 0.9	1528 6.6	2201 0.7		17 F	0334 7.4	1014 0.7	1600 6.8	2251 0.3
3 F	0350 6.8	0955 0.9	1601 6.5	2232 0.8		18 SA	0425 7.3	1058 0.8	1648 6.7	2335 0.3
4 SA	0425 6.6	1027 1.0	1634 6.3	2304 0.9		19 SU	0516 7.1	1140 0.9	1738 6.6	
5 SU	0501 6.4	1100 1.2	1710 6.1	2336 1.0		20 M	0019 0.4	0611 6.8	1225 1.1	1831 6.4
6 M	0540 6.2	1136 1.3	1752 6.0			21 TU	0106 0.5	0707 6.6	1316 1.2	☽ 1928 6.3
7 TU	0012 1.1	0627 6.1	1220 1.5	☽ 1841 5.8		22 W	0158 0.6	0806 6.4	1414 1.3	2028 6.3
8 W	0101 1.1	0722 6.0	1318 1.6	1942 5.8		23 TH	0254 0.7	0906 6.3	1517 1.4	2129 6.3
9 TH	0206 1.2	0832 6.0	1430 1.6	2101 5.9		24 F	0351 0.8	1007 6.3	1621 1.3	2230 6.3
10 F	0322 1.0	0944 6.1	1546 1.5	2213 6.2		25 SA	0447 0.9	1109 6.3	1722 1.2	2328 6.4
11 SA	0431 0.8	1047 6.4	1700 1.3	2314 6.4		26 SU	0543 1.0	1204 6.4	1821 1.0	
12 SU	0534 0.7	1145 6.7	1812 1.1			27 M	0020 6.6	0636 1.0	1250 6.5	1912 0.8
13 M	0010 6.9	0638 0.6	1240 6.8	1921 0.9		28 TU	0105 6.7	0722 1.0	1330 6.6	1958 0.7
14 TU	0102 7.2	0742 0.6	1332 6.9	○ 2021 0.7		29 W	0147 6.8	0803 1.0	1408 6.6	● 2038 0.7
15 W	0153 7.3	0838 0.6	1422 6.9	2115 0.5		30 TH	0226 6.8	0840 1.0	1443 6.6	2116 0.7

JULY

Day	Time m	Time m	Time m	Time m		Day	Time m	Time m	Time m	Time m
1 F	0302 6.8	0914 1.0	1517 6.6	2153 0.6		16 SA	0326 7.4	1013 0.7	1550 7.0	2250 0.0
2 SA	0337 6.7	0948 1.0	1551 6.6	2228 0.6		17 SU	0415 7.4	1056 0.7	1636 7.0	2332 0.0
3 SU	0411 6.7	1024 1.0	1624 6.5	2303 0.6		18 M	0503 7.2	1136 0.7	1720 6.9	
4 M	0446 6.6	1100 1.1	1659 6.4	2335 0.7		19 TU	0009 0.1	0551 7.0	1212 0.9	1806 6.8
5 TU	0524 6.5	1135 1.2	1736 6.3			20 W	0044 0.3	0639 6.7	1251 1.1	☽ 1852 6.6
6 W	0006 0.8	0605 6.3	1211 1.3	1818 6.2		21 TH	0121 0.6	0728 6.4	1333 1.3	1944 6.4
7 TH	0041 0.9	0651 6.2	1254 1.4	☽ 1906 6.1		22 F	0204 0.9	0820 6.2	1426 1.4	2041 6.2
8 F	0125 0.9	0747 6.1	1348 1.5	2007 6.1		23 SA	0257 1.1	0916 6.0	1530 1.5	2142 6.1
9 SA	0225 1.0	0859 6.1	1458 1.5	2126 6.1		24 SU	0357 1.2	1019 5.9	1637 1.4	2248 6.2
10 SU	0344 1.0	1011 6.2	1624 1.4	2239 6.5		25 M	0459 1.3	1128 6.0	1742 1.2	2352 6.3
11 M	0500 0.9	1118 6.4	1745 1.1	2345 6.8		26 TU	0602 1.2	1226 6.3	1843 0.9	
12 TU	0611 0.8	1221 6.6	1900 0.8			27 W	0046 6.6	0701 1.1	1313 6.5	1937 0.7
13 W	0045 7.0	0724 0.8	1318 6.8	○ 2009 0.6		28 TH	0133 6.7	0750 1.1	1354 6.6	● 2023 0.6
14 TH	0142 7.2	0829 0.7	1412 6.9	2109 0.3		29 F	0213 6.8	0832 1.1	1432 6.7	2104 0.6
15 F	0235 7.4	0924 0.7	1503 7.0	2202 0.1		30 SA	0250 6.8	0911 1.0	1506 6.7	2143 0.5
						31 SU	0323 6.8	0948 1.0	1538 6.7	2221 0.4

AUGUST

Day	Time m	Time m	Time m	Time m		Day	Time m	Time m	Time m	Time m
1 M	0355 6.8	1023 0.9	1609 6.7	2255 0.4		16 TU	0440 7.2	1118 0.7	1653 7.1	2344 0.2
2 TU	0427 6.8	1057 1.0	1641 6.6	2325 0.5		17 W	0521 7.0	1149 0.8	1731 6.9	
3 W	0501 6.7	1127 1.1	1714 6.5	2350 0.7		18 TH	0008 0.5	0600 6.7	1217 1.0	1811 6.7
4 TH	0538 6.5	1157 1.2	1751 6.4			19 F	0031 0.8	0639 6.3	1246 1.3	☽ 1854 6.4
5 F	0015 0.8	0619 6.3	1230 1.4	1834 6.4		20 SA	0100 1.1	0723 5.9	1325 1.5	1946 6.0
6 SA	0049 0.9	0708 6.1	1314 1.5	1928 6.2		21 SU	0145 1.5	0817 5.7	1427 1.7	2053 5.8
7 SU	0137 1.1	0814 5.9	1417 1.6	2043 6.1		22 M	0304 1.7	0927 5.5	1555 1.7	2210 5.8
8 M	0259 1.3	0938 5.9	1557 1.6	2212 6.2		23 TU	0427 1.7	1050 5.7	1710 1.4	2326 6.0
9 TU	0438 1.3	1056 6.1	1727 1.3	2328 6.5		24 W	0539 1.5	1200 6.0	1817 1.0	
10 W	0559 1.1	1209 6.4	1854 0.8			25 TH	0025 6.4	0647 1.3	1250 6.4	1914 0.8
11 TH	0036 6.9	0720 0.9	1310 6.7	2006 0.4		26 F	0112 6.6	0733 1.1	1333 6.6	2002 0.6
12 F	0135 7.2	0823 0.7	1403 6.9	○ 2103 0.1		27 SA	0152 6.8	0817 1.1	1410 6.7	● 2044 0.5
13 SA	0226 7.4	0916 0.6	1450 7.1	2152 -0.1		28 SU	0227 6.8	0857 1.0	1444 6.8	2124 0.4
14 SU	0313 7.4	1002 0.6	1533 7.2	2236 -0.2		29 M	0259 6.9	0935 1.0	1515 6.9	2201 0.4
15 M	0358 7.4	1043 0.6	1614 7.2	2313 -0.1		30 TU	0330 6.9	1011 0.9	1545 6.9	2235 0.4
						31 W	0402 6.9	1044 1.0	1616 6.9	2303 0.5

Chart Datum: 3·20 metres below Ordnance Datum (Newlyn)
HAT is 7·7 metres above Chart Datum

TIME ZONE (UT)	LONDON BRIDGE	Dates in amber are **SPRINGS**
For Summer Time add ONE hour in **non-shaded areas**	LAT 51°30'N LONG 0°05'W	Dates in grey are **NEAPS**

2022

TIMES AND HEIGHTS OF HIGH AND LOW WATERS

SEPTEMBER

Time	m	Time	m
1 0435	6.7	**16** 0516	6.5
1113	1.1	1139	1.1
TH 1649	6.8	F 1731	6.7
2324	0.7	2341	1.0
2 0510	6.5	**17** 0548	6.2
1138	1.2	1203	1.3
F 1725	6.6	SA 1808	6.3
2346	0.9	☽	
3 0549	6.2	**18** 0006	1.3
1208	1.4	0624	5.8
SA 1808	6.5	SU 1235	1.5
☽		1854	5.9
4 0017	1.1	**19** 0042	1.7
0636	6.0	0711	5.5
SU 1247	1.5	M 1322	1.8
1903	6.2	1958	5.5
5 0103	1.4	**20** 0144	2.1
0739	5.7	0827	5.2
M 1349	1.7	TU 1506	2.0
2019	6.0	2128	5.4
6 0231	1.8	**21** 0351	2.2
0913	5.6	1007	5.3
TU 1542	1.7	W 1637	1.6
2157	6.0	2251	5.7
7 0426	1.7	**22** 0512	1.8
1043	5.8	1124	5.7
W 1724	1.3	TH 1743	1.2
2321	6.4	2354	6.2
8 0558	1.3	**23** 0612	1.5
1202	6.2	1218	6.2
TH 1854	0.7	F 1840	0.8
9 0030	6.8	**24** 0041	6.5
0713	0.9	0704	1.2
F 1300	6.7	SA 1301	6.5
1956	0.2	1930	0.7
10 0125	7.2	**25** 0120	6.7
0809	0.2	0749	1.1
SA 1348	7.0	SU 1338	6.7
○ 2047	-0.1	● 2014	0.6
11 0211	7.3	**26** 0154	6.8
0858	0.6	0831	1.1
SU 1430	7.1	M 1412	6.9
2131	-0.1	2055	0.5
12 0254	7.3	**27** 0227	6.9
0941	0.6	0911	1.0
M 1508	7.3	TU 1444	7.0
2210	0.2	2133	0.5
13 0333	7.3	**28** 0300	7.0
1019	0.6	0949	0.9
TU 1545	7.3	W 1517	7.1
2242	0.2	2207	0.5
14 0410	7.1	**29** 0335	6.9
1052	0.9	1024	0.9
W 1620	7.2	TH 1550	7.1
2307	0.5	2234	0.6
15 0444	6.9	**30** 0410	6.8
1118	0.9	1054	1.0
TH 1655	7.0	F 1626	7.0
2322	0.7	2255	0.8

OCTOBER

Time	m	Time	m
1 0445	6.5	**16** 0505	6.2
1120	1.1	1128	1.2
SA 1705	6.8	SU 1731	6.3
2322	1.0	2326	1.4
2 0524	6.2	**17** 0535	5.9
1151	1.2	1155	1.4
SU 1751	6.5	M 1810	5.9
2358	1.3	◑ 2356	1.7
3 0613	5.9	**18** 0615	5.5
1233	1.4	1232	1.7
M 1849	6.2	TU 1902	5.5
◑			
4 0048	1.7	**19** 0040	2.1
0720	5.6	0716	5.2
TU 1339	1.6	W 1342	2.0
2014	5.9	2028	5.3
5 0232	2.0	**20** 0226	2.4
0859	5.5	0907	5.1
W 1536	1.6	TH 1551	1.8
2149	6.1	2200	5.5
6 0416	1.8	**21** 0423	2.1
1032	5.8	1033	5.5
TH 1721	1.1	F 1657	1.4
2311	6.5	2304	6.0
7 0545	1.3	**22** 0526	1.7
1146	6.3	1132	6.0
F 1837	0.5	SA 1753	1.0
		2355	6.4
8 0016	6.9	**23** 0620	1.4
0652	1.0	1219	6.4
SA 1241	6.7	SU 1845	0.7
1933	0.2		
9 0107	7.1	**24** 0037	6.7
0744	0.7	0710	1.3
SU 1325	7.0	M 1258	6.7
○ 2019	0.1	1934	0.7
10 0149	7.2	**25** 0116	6.8
0831	0.4	0757	1.1
M 1404	7.1	TU 1335	6.9
2100	0.2	● 2018	0.6
11 0227	7.2	**26** 0154	7.0
0912	0.6	0842	1.0
TU 1439	7.3	W 1412	7.1
2135	0.3	2059	0.6
12 0302	7.1	**27** 0232	7.0
0949	0.7	0924	0.9
W 1513	7.3	TH 1450	7.2
2202	0.5	2135	0.7
13 0335	7.0	**28** 0311	6.9
1019	0.9	1002	0.9
TH 1548	7.3	F 1529	7.2
2219	0.7	2206	0.8
14 0406	6.8	**29** 0349	6.8
1042	0.9	1036	0.9
F 1622	7.0	SA 1609	7.1
2236	0.9	2234	0.9
15 0436	6.5	**30** 0428	6.5
1103	1.1	1108	0.9
SA 1656	6.7	SU 1653	6.9
2259	1.1	2309	1.1
		31 0511	6.2
		1144	1.1
		M 1744	6.5
		2352	1.4

NOVEMBER

Time	m	Time	m
1 0604	5.9	**16** 0544	5.8
1231	1.2	1203	1.4
TU 1848	6.2	W 1828	5.8
◑		◑	
2 0052	1.8	**17** 0010	1.9
0716	5.6	0636	5.5
W 1346	1.4	TH 1254	1.6
2012	6.1	1928	5.6
3 0226	1.9	**18** 0113	2.1
0847	5.7	0746	5.3
TH 1525	1.3	F 1431	1.7
2133	6.2	2052	5.6
4 0355	1.7	**19** 0250	2.2
1008	6.0	0927	5.5
F 1653	0.9	SA 1547	1.5
2247	6.5	2204	5.9
5 0514	1.4	**20** 0414	1.9
1117	6.3	1035	5.9
SA 1805	0.6	SU 1657	1.1
2351	6.8	2301	6.3
6 0619	1.1	**21** 0522	1.6
1213	6.7	1129	6.3
SU 1859	0.4	M 1752	0.9
		2353	6.6
7 0041	6.9	**22** 0622	1.4
0713	0.9	1217	6.7
M 1257	6.9	TU 1846	0.8
1944	0.4		
8 0123	7.0	**23** 0041	6.8
0759	0.8	0720	1.2
TU 1334	7.0	W 1302	7.0
○ 2022	0.6	● 1939	0.7
9 0159	7.0	**24** 0126	6.8
0840	0.7	0813	1.0
W 1409	7.2	TH 1346	7.2
2053	0.7	2027	0.7
10 0231	6.9	**25** 0211	6.9
0915	0.7	0901	0.9
TH 1444	7.2	F 1430	7.3
2115	0.8	2111	0.8
11 0302	6.8	**26** 0255	6.9
0945	0.8	0946	0.7
F 1519	7.1	SA 1515	7.3
2134	0.9	2151	0.9
12 0333	6.7	**27** 0339	6.7
1010	0.9	1028	0.7
SA 1554	6.9	SU 1602	7.2
2200	1.0	2230	1.0
13 0404	6.5	**28** 0424	6.5
1034	1.0	1108	0.7
SU 1629	6.6	M 1652	7.0
2229	1.2	2312	1.1
14 0434	6.3	**29** 0512	6.3
1101	1.1	1150	0.8
M 1703	6.3	TU 1746	6.7
2258	1.4		
15 0505	6.0	**30** 0000	1.3
1130	1.3	0606	6.1
TU 1741	6.0	W 1242	0.9
2329	1.6	◑ 1849	6.5

DECEMBER

Time	m	Time	m
1 0058	1.5	**16** 0613	5.9
0711	6.0	1235	1.2
TH 1349	1.0	F 1852	6.0
1958	6.4	◑	
2 0209	1.6	**17** 0046	1.7
0824	6.0	0705	5.8
F 1500	0.9	SA 1326	1.3
2107	6.4	1951	5.9
3 0323	1.6	**18** 0146	1.8
0934	6.2	0810	5.7
SA 1608	0.9	SU 1432	1.3
2214	6.5	2104	5.9
4 0433	1.4	**19** 0257	1.8
1039	6.3	0933	5.9
SU 1715	0.8	M 1551	1.2
2317	6.6	2213	6.1
5 0539	1.2	**20** 0420	1.7
1138	6.5	1042	6.2
M 1814	0.8	TU 1701	1.0
		2315	6.4
6 0011	6.6	**21** 0539	1.4
0637	1.0	1141	6.6
TU 1226	6.7	W 1804	0.9
1902	0.8		
7 0056	6.7	**22** 0012	6.7
0726	0.9	0648	1.1
W 1308	6.8	TH 1236	6.9
1942	1.0	1907	0.8
8 0134	6.7	**23** 0106	6.8
0809	0.8	0750	0.9
TH 1346	6.9	F 1328	7.2
○ 2014	1.0	● 2007	0.8
9 0208	6.7	**24** 0157	6.9
0847	0.8	0848	0.7
F 1423	7.0	SA 1419	7.3
2042	1.0	2101	0.8
10 0240	6.7	**25** 0246	6.9
0920	0.8	0941	0.5
SA 1500	6.9	SU 1509	7.3
2109	1.1	2151	0.8
11 0313	6.6	**26** 0335	6.4
0950	0.9	1030	0.4
SU 1535	6.8	M 1559	7.3
2140	1.1	2237	0.9
12 0346	6.5	**27** 0422	6.8
1019	0.9	1116	0.3
M 1610	6.6	TU 1649	7.2
2212	1.2	2320	0.9
13 0418	6.4	**28** 0509	6.5
1050	1.0	1159	0.3
TU 1645	6.4	W 1741	7.0
2246	1.3		
14 0452	6.2	**29** 0003	1.0
1122	1.1	0559	6.6
W 1722	6.3	TH 1243	0.5
2321	1.4	1835	6.8
15 0529	6.1	**30** 0050	1.2
1155	1.1	0652	6.5
TH 1804	6.1	F 1330	0.6
2359	1.6	◑ 1933	6.5
		31 0142	1.3
		0751	6.3
		SA 1422	0.8
		2032	6.4

Chart Datum: 3·20 metres below Ordnance Datum (Newlyn)
HAT is 7·7 metres above Chart Datum

TIDES

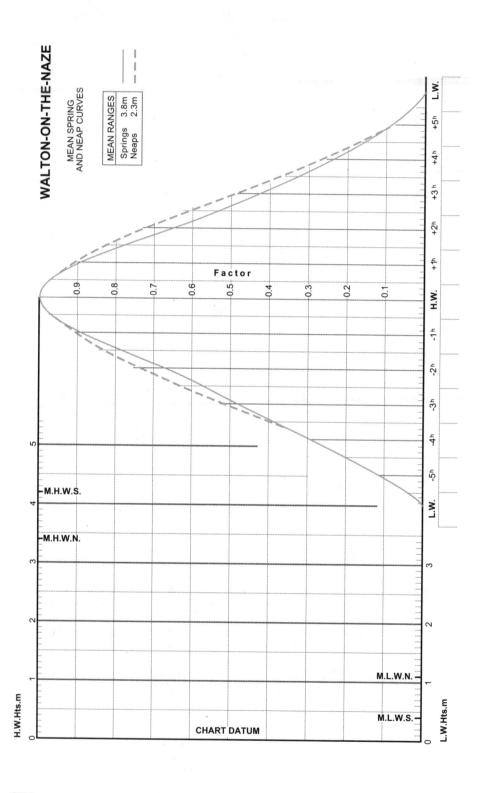

WALTON-ON-THE-NAZE

MEAN SPRING
AND NEAP CURVES

MEAN RANGES	
Springs	3.8m
Neaps	2.3m

WALTON-ON-THE-NAZE

LAT 51°51′N   LONG 1°17′E

TIMES AND HEIGHTS OF HIGH AND LOW WATERS

Dates in amber are **SPRINGS**
Dates in grey are **NEAPS**

2022

JANUARY

Time	m	Time	m
1 SA 0345 0.8 / 0958 4.2 / 1610 0.5 / 2233 4.1		**16** SU 0444 0.8 / 1043 3.8 / 1655 0.9 / 2312 3.9	
2 SU 0443 0.6 / 1053 4.3 / 1705 0.6 / ● 2325 4.2		**17** M 0524 0.7 / 1124 3.9 / 1733 0.9 / ○ 2349 4.0	
3 M 0540 0.5 / 1145 4.4 / 1757 0.6		**18** TU 0601 0.6 / 1202 4.0 / 1806 0.9	
4 TU 0015 4.2 / 0635 0.5 / 1235 4.5 / 1848 0.7		**19** W 0024 4.0 / 0636 0.5 / 1238 4.0 / 1837 0.8	
5 W 0103 4.3 / 0727 0.4 / 1325 4.4 / 1935 0.8		**20** TH 0100 4.1 / 0710 0.4 / 1314 4.1 / 1908 0.8	
6 TH 0151 4.2 / 0816 0.2 / 1415 4.3 / 2019 0.9		**21** F 0135 4.1 / 0746 0.4 / 1351 4.1 / 1941 0.8	
7 F 0237 4.2 / 0903 0.3 / 1505 4.2 / 2102 1.0		**22** SA 0210 4.0 / 0821 0.4 / 1428 4.0 / 2018 0.8	
8 SA 0324 4.0 / 0949 0.4 / 1556 4.0 / 2147 1.1		**23** SU 0246 4.0 / 0857 0.4 / 1507 3.9 / 2057 0.9	
9 SU 0411 3.9 / 1036 0.5 / 1649 3.8 / ◐ 2237 1.2		**24** M 0323 4.0 / 0936 0.5 / 1550 3.9 / 2141 1.0	
10 M 0501 3.8 / 1127 0.7 / 1745 3.6 / 2336 1.3		**25** TU 0405 3.9 / 1022 0.6 / 1638 3.8 / ◑ 2235 1.1	
11 TU 0557 3.6 / 1223 0.8 / 1844 3.5		**26** W 0455 3.8 / 1120 0.6 / 1737 3.7 / 2342 1.1	
12 W 0043 1.3 / 0700 3.5 / 1321 0.9 / 1950 3.5		**27** TH 0559 3.7 / 1231 0.7 / 1847 3.6	
13 TH 0151 1.3 / 0807 3.5 / 1422 1.0 / 2053 3.5		**28** F 0102 1.1 / 0717 3.7 / 1346 0.8 / 2006 3.6	
14 F 0258 1.1 / 0908 3.6 / 1522 1.0 / 2146 3.7		**29** SA 0222 1.0 / 0838 3.8 / 1456 0.8 / 2122 3.7	
15 SA 0357 1.0 / 0959 3.7 / 1612 1.0 / 2231 3.8		**30** SU 0334 0.8 / 0948 3.9 / 1601 0.8 / 2227 3.9	
		31 M 0440 0.6 / 1047 4.1 / 1700 0.7 / 2321 4.0	

FEBRUARY

Time	m	Time	m
1 TU 0539 0.4 / 1140 4.3 / 1752 0.7 / ●		**16** W 0541 0.5 / 1146 3.9 / 1749 0.8 / ○	
2 W 0009 4.2 / 0632 0.2 / 1228 4.4 / 1839 0.7		**17** TH 0007 4.0 / 0615 0.4 / 1222 4.1 / 1820 0.8	
3 TH 0054 4.3 / 0719 0.1 / 1314 4.4 / 1921 0.7		**18** F 0043 4.1 / 0650 0.3 / 1258 4.1 / 1852 0.7	
4 F 0136 4.3 / 0802 0.1 / 1359 4.3 / 2001 0.8		**19** SA 0118 4.2 / 0724 0.2 / 1333 4.2 / 1925 0.7	
5 SA 0217 4.3 / 0841 0.2 / 1442 4.1 / 2038 0.8		**20** SU 0152 4.2 / 0758 0.2 / 1409 4.1 / 2000 0.7	
6 SU 0256 4.2 / 0915 0.3 / 1525 4.0 / 2113 0.9		**21** M 0226 4.2 / 0831 0.3 / 1447 4.0 / 2037 0.8	
7 M 0334 4.0 / 0949 0.5 / 1607 3.7 / 2151 1.0		**22** TU 0301 4.1 / 0905 0.4 / 1526 3.9 / 2118 0.8	
8 TU 0414 3.8 / 1027 0.7 / 1652 3.5 / ◐ 2237 1.1		**23** W 0340 4.1 / 0947 0.5 / 1611 3.8 / ◐ 2207 0.9	
9 W 0501 3.6 / 1116 0.9 / 1743 3.4 / 2338 1.3		**24** TH 0427 3.9 / 1043 0.7 / 1706 3.6 / 2313 1.0	
10 TH 0559 3.4 / 1220 1.1 / 1844 3.3		**25** F 0530 3.7 / 1201 0.9 / 1817 3.4	
11 F 0055 1.3 / 0711 3.3 / 1332 1.2 / 2000 3.3		**26** SA 0038 1.1 / 0656 3.5 / 1329 1.0 / 1950 3.3	
12 SA 0215 1.2 / 0830 3.3 / 1448 1.2 / 2114 3.4		**27** SU 0211 1.0 / 0833 3.6 / 1449 1.0 / 2120 3.5	
13 SU 0331 1.0 / 0935 3.5 / 1552 1.1 / 2208 3.6		**28** M 0334 0.8 / 0948 3.8 / 1559 0.9 / 2223 3.8	
14 M 0425 0.8 / 1025 3.7 / 1639 1.0 / 2252 3.8			
15 TU 0505 0.6 / 1108 3.8 / 1716 0.9 / 2331 3.9			

MARCH

Time	m	Time	m
1 TU 0441 0.5 / 1046 4.1 / 1654 0.8 / 2314 4.0		**16** W 0436 0.6 / 1043 3.8 / 1650 0.9 / 2303 3.9	
2 W 0534 0.3 / 1134 4.2 / 1740 0.7 / ● 2357 4.2		**17** TH 0512 0.4 / 1121 4.0 / 1722 0.8 / 2340 4.0	
3 TH 0619 0.1 / 1216 4.3 / 1821 0.7		**18** F 0546 0.3 / 1157 4.1 / 1754 0.7 / ○	
4 F 0037 4.3 / 0700 0.1 / 1257 4.3 / 1900 0.6		**19** SA 0015 4.1 / 0622 0.2 / 1233 4.2 / 1829 0.6	
5 SA 0114 4.3 / 0736 0.1 / 1336 4.2 / 1937 0.7		**20** SU 0051 4.3 / 0656 0.2 / 1310 4.3 / 1904 0.6	
6 SU 0150 4.3 / 0807 0.2 / 1414 4.1 / 2010 0.7		**21** M 0127 4.3 / 0729 0.2 / 1347 4.2 / 1940 0.6	
7 M 0223 4.2 / 0835 0.4 / 1449 3.9 / 2041 0.8		**22** TU 0203 4.3 / 0802 0.3 / 1425 4.1 / 2018 0.6	
8 TU 0257 4.1 / 0901 0.5 / 1524 3.7 / 2113 0.9		**23** W 0240 4.2 / 0837 0.4 / 1505 3.9 / 2100 0.7	
9 W 0332 3.9 / 0932 0.7 / 1600 3.6 / 2151 1.0		**24** TH 0320 4.1 / 0920 0.6 / 1549 3.7 / 2150 0.8	
10 TH 0414 3.6 / 1013 1.0 / 1645 3.3 / ◐ 2242 1.1		**25** F 0410 3.9 / 1021 0.9 / 1644 3.5 / ◐ 2259 0.9	
11 F 0508 3.4 / 1117 1.2 / 1745 3.2 / 2359 1.3		**26** SA 0517 3.6 / 1147 1.1 / 1802 3.3	
12 SA 0622 3.2 / 1248 1.4 / 1903 3.1		**27** SU 0032 1.0 / 0656 3.5 / 1320 1.2 / 1946 3.2	
13 SU 0130 1.2 / 0752 3.2 / 1414 1.4 / 2030 3.2		**28** M 0209 0.9 / 0832 3.6 / 1442 1.1 / 2110 3.5	
14 M 0254 1.1 / 0906 3.4 / 1525 1.2 / 2136 3.4		**29** TU 0331 0.6 / 0942 3.9 / 1549 1.0 / 2209 3.8	
15 TU 0354 0.8 / 1000 3.6 / 1613 1.0 / 2223 3.7		**30** W 0430 0.4 / 1035 4.1 / 1638 0.8 / 2256 4.0	
		31 TH 0516 0.2 / 1118 4.2 / 1719 0.7 / 2336 4.2	

APRIL

Time	m	Time	m
1 F 0556 0.2 / 1156 4.2 / 1757 0.7 / ●		**16** SA 0512 0.3 / 1126 4.1 / 1725 0.7 / ○ 2343 4.2	
2 SA 0012 4.3 / 0631 0.2 / 1232 4.2 / 1834 0.6		**17** SU 0549 0.2 / 1205 4.2 / 1803 0.6	
3 SU 0045 4.3 / 0702 0.2 / 1308 4.2 / 1910 0.6		**18** M 0022 4.4 / 0626 0.2 / 1244 4.3 / 1843 0.5	
4 M 0118 4.3 / 0730 0.3 / 1342 4.1 / 1943 0.6		**19** TU 0101 4.4 / 0701 0.2 / 1325 4.2 / 1923 0.5	
5 TU 0150 4.2 / 0755 0.5 / 1414 3.9 / 2013 0.7		**20** W 0141 4.4 / 0738 0.3 / 1406 4.1 / 2004 0.5	
6 W 0223 4.1 / 0820 0.6 / 1444 3.8 / 2042 0.7		**21** TH 0223 4.3 / 0818 0.5 / 1449 3.9 / 2051 0.6	
7 TH 0258 3.9 / 0848 0.8 / 1516 3.6 / 2117 0.8		**22** F 0309 4.1 / 0908 0.7 / 1536 3.7 / 2147 0.7	
8 F 0336 3.7 / 0924 1.0 / 1556 3.4 / 2201 1.0		**23** SA 0405 3.9 / 1015 1.0 / 1637 3.5 / ◐ 2300 0.8	
9 SA 0423 3.4 / 1015 1.3 / 1651 3.2 / ◐ 2308 1.1		**24** SU 0520 3.6 / 1139 1.2 / 1758 3.3	
10 SU 0532 3.2 / 1151 1.5 / 1811 3.1		**25** M 0032 0.8 / 0654 3.6 / 1304 1.2 / 1930 3.4	
11 M 0043 1.2 / 0708 3.1 / 1332 1.5 / 1937 3.2		**26** TU 0159 0.7 / 0817 3.7 / 1422 1.2 / 2046 3.6	
12 TU 0206 1.0 / 0824 3.3 / 1443 1.3 / 2048 3.4		**27** W 0313 0.5 / 0922 3.9 / 1525 1.0 / 2143 3.8	
13 W 0308 0.8 / 0921 3.6 / 1534 1.1 / 2141 3.6		**28** TH 0408 0.4 / 1012 4.1 / 1613 0.9 / 2229 4.0	
14 TH 0355 0.6 / 1007 3.8 / 1613 0.9 / 2225 3.9		**29** F 0450 0.3 / 1054 4.1 / 1653 0.8 / 2308 4.1	
15 F 0435 0.4 / 1047 4.0 / 1649 0.8 / 2304 4.1		**30** SA 0526 0.3 / 1131 4.1 / 1730 0.7 / ● 2343 4.2	

TIDES

Chart Datum: 2·16 metres below Ordnance Datum (Newlyn)
HAT is 4·7 metres above Chart Datum

TIDES

TIME ZONE (UT)
For Summer Time add ONE hour in **non-shaded areas**

WALTON-ON-THE-NAZE
LAT 51°51′N   LONG 1°17′E
TIMES AND HEIGHTS OF HIGH AND LOW WATERS

Dates in amber are **SPRINGS**
Dates in grey are **NEAPS**

2022

MAY

Day	Time	m	Time	m	Day	Time	m	Time	m
1 SU	0556	0.4	1205	4.1	16 M	0518	0.3	1138	4.2
	1808	0.6				1741	0.6	○ 2355	4.4
2 M	0015	4.2	0626	0.4	17 TU	0559	0.3	1222	4.3
	1239	4.1	1845	0.5		1826	0.5		
3 TU	0048	4.2	0655	0.5	18 W	0039	4.5	0642	0.4
	1311	4.0	1919	0.6		1307	4.2	1912	0.5
4 W	0121	4.2	0722	0.6	19 TH	0125	4.5	0726	0.5
	1342	4.0	1949	0.6		1353	4.1	2000	0.4
5 TH	0155	4.0	0748	0.7	20 F	0213	4.4	0814	0.7
	1413	3.8	2019	0.7		1441	4.0	2053	0.5
6 F	0230	3.9	0817	0.9	21 SA	0305	4.2	0908	0.9
	1445	3.7	2053	0.9		1533	3.8	2152	0.5
7 SA	0308	3.7	0853	1.0	22 SU	0405	3.9	1011	1.1
	1524	3.5	2135	0.8		1635	3.6	☽ 2303	0.6
8 SU	0352	3.5	0940	1.2	23 M	0517	3.8	1122	1.2
	1614	3.4	2234	1.0		1745	3.6		
9 M	0450	3.3	1050	1.4	24 TU	0020	0.6	0634	3.7
	1724	3.2	☽ 2357	1.0		1237	1.2	1900	3.6
10 TU	0613	3.3	1231	1.4	25 W	0133	0.5	0747	3.8
	1843	3.3				1348	1.2	2010	3.7
11 W	0116	0.9	0730	3.4	26 TH	0241	0.5	0850	3.9
	1349	1.3	1953	3.4		1451	1.1	2108	3.8
12 TH	0218	0.7	0831	3.6	27 F	0336	0.5	0942	4.0
	1444	1.1	2051	3.7		1542	0.9	2156	4.0
13 F	0309	0.5	0922	3.8	28 SA	0419	0.5	1025	4.0
	1530	0.9	2141	3.9		1626	0.8	2237	4.0
14 SA	0354	0.4	1009	4.0	29 SU	0453	0.6	1104	4.0
	1613	0.8	2227	4.1		1706	0.7	2314	4.1
15 SU	0437	0.3	1054	4.1	30 M	0524	0.6	1140	4.0
	1657	0.7	2311	4.3		1745	0.6	2349	4.1
					31 TU	0557	0.6	1214	4.0
						1823	0.6		

JUNE

Day	Time	m	Time	m	Day	Time	m	Time	m
1 W	0023	4.1	0630	0.7	16 TH	0024	4.5	0633	0.6
	1247	4.0	1859	0.6		1255	4.2	1910	0.4
2 TH	0059	4.1	0659	0.8	17 F	0115	4.5	0722	0.7
	1319	4.0	1932	0.6		1344	4.2	2003	0.3
3 F	0134	4.0	0728	0.8	18 SA	0206	4.4	0812	0.8
	1352	3.9	2004	0.6		1434	4.1	2056	0.3
4 SA	0211	3.9	0759	0.9	19 SU	0300	4.3	0903	0.9
	1427	3.8	2040	0.7		1526	4.0	2152	0.4
5 SU	0249	3.8	0836	1.0	20 M	0357	4.1	0956	1.0
	1506	3.7	2121	0.7		1621	3.9	2250	0.4
6 M	0331	3.6	0921	1.1	21 TU	0458	3.9	1055	1.1
	1552	3.6	2211	0.8		1718	3.8	☽ 2352	0.5
7 TU	0421	3.5	1016	1.3	22 W	0600	3.8	1159	1.2
	1647	3.5	☽ 2314	0.8		1820	3.8		
8 W	0522	3.5	1126	1.3	23 TH	0053	0.6	0706	3.7
	1752	3.5				1304	1.2	1925	3.8
9 TH	0023	0.8	0632	3.5	24 F	0155	0.7	0810	3.7
	1242	1.3	1859	3.6		1408	1.1	2027	3.8
10 F	0128	0.7	0738	3.7	25 SA	0253	0.7	0907	3.8
	1351	1.1	2002	3.7		1508	1.0	2121	3.8
11 SA	0224	0.6	0838	3.8	26 SU	0342	0.8	0956	3.8
	1449	1.0	2100	3.9		1601	0.9	2208	3.9
12 SU	0316	0.5	0934	4.0	27 M	0423	0.8	1039	3.9
	1542	0.8	2154	4.1		1647	0.8	2250	4.0
13 M	0406	0.4	1027	4.1	28 TU	0501	0.8	1119	3.9
	1634	0.7	2245	4.3		1729	0.7	2329	4.0
14 TU	0455	0.4	1117	4.2	29 W	0538	0.8	1156	4.0
	1725	0.6	○ 2335	4.4		1808	0.6		
15 W	0543	0.5	1206	4.2	30 TH	0006	4.0	0614	0.8
	1817	0.5				1231	4.0	1845	0.6

JULY

Day	Time	m	Time	m	Day	Time	m	Time	m
1 F	0044	4.0	0646	0.9	16 SA	0106	4.5	0717	0.7
	1306	4.0	1920	0.5		1334	4.3	2000	0.2
2 SA	0121	4.0	0716	0.9	17 SU	0156	4.5	0803	0.8
	1341	4.0	1954	0.5		1421	4.3	2048	0.2
3 SU	0157	4.0	0748	0.9	18 M	0246	4.3	0847	0.9
	1416	3.9	2029	0.5		1508	4.2	2134	0.3
4 M	0234	3.9	0824	0.9	19 TU	0336	4.2	0932	1.0
	1453	3.9	2106	0.6		1554	4.2	2220	0.4
5 TU	0313	3.8	0903	1.0	20 W	0427	4.0	1019	1.1
	1532	3.8	2147	0.6		1642	4.0	☽ 2307	0.6
6 W	0355	3.7	0948	1.1	21 TH	0520	3.8	1113	1.2
	1615	3.8	2234	0.7		1734	3.9	2359	0.7
7 TH	0445	3.7	1042	1.2	22 F	0617	3.6	1214	1.2
	1707	3.7	☽ 2331	0.7		1832	3.7		
8 F	0543	3.7	1147	1.2	23 SA	0055	0.9	0720	3.5
	1808	3.7				1320	1.2	1939	3.6
9 SA	0036	0.7	0650	3.7	24 SU	0157	1.0	0827	3.5
	1302	1.2	1916	3.8		1431	1.2	2046	3.7
10 SU	0144	0.7	0759	3.7	25 M	0304	1.1	0928	3.6
	1415	1.1	2025	3.9		1540	1.0	2143	3.7
11 M	0246	0.7	0906	3.8	26 TU	0401	1.0	1018	3.8
	1519	0.9	2130	4.0		1634	0.8	2231	3.9
12 TU	0345	0.7	1008	3.9	27 W	0446	1.0	1101	3.9
	1619	0.7	2229	4.2		1717	0.7	2314	3.9
13 W	0442	0.7	1104	4.1	28 TH	0524	0.9	1140	4.0
	1718	0.6	○ 2323	4.4		1754	0.6	● 2353	4.0
14 TH	0536	0.7	1157	4.2	29 F	0559	0.9	1217	4.1
	1815	0.4				1829	0.5		
15 F	0015	4.5	0628	0.7	30 SA	0030	4.1	0632	0.9
	1246	4.3	1909	0.3		1252	4.1	1902	0.5
					31 SU	0106	4.1	0702	0.9
						1326	4.1	1936	0.5

AUGUST

Day	Time	m	Time	m	Day	Time	m	Time	m
1 M	0141	4.1	0733	0.9	16 TU	0224	4.3	0824	0.8
	1400	4.1	2009	0.5		1440	4.4	2102	0.3
2 TU	0215	4.0	0807	0.9	17 W	0307	4.1	0902	0.9
	1433	4.1	2042	0.5		1519	4.2	2137	0.5
3 W	0250	4.0	0842	0.9	18 TH	0349	3.9	0941	1.0
	1507	4.0	2115	0.6		1559	4.1	2213	0.7
4 TH	0328	3.9	0921	1.0	19 F	0434	3.7	1025	1.1
	1544	4.0	2153	0.7		1644	3.9	☽ 2258	1.0
5 F	0412	3.8	1006	1.1	20 SA	0523	3.5	1109	1.2
	1629	3.9	☽ 2242	0.8		1740	3.6	2357	1.2
6 SA	0504	3.7	1105	1.2	21 SU	0623	3.4	1231	1.3
	1725	3.8	2350	0.9		1850	3.5		
7 SU	0609	3.6	1224	1.2	22 M	0108	1.3	0740	3.3
	1837	3.7				1352	1.3	2012	3.5
8 M	0111	1.0	0727	3.5	23 TU	0230	1.3	0857	3.5
	1350	1.1	2001	3.8		1518	1.1	2121	3.6
9 TU	0227	0.9	0849	3.6	24 W	0342	1.0	0955	3.7
	1505	0.9	2117	3.9		1616	0.9	2213	3.8
10 W	0335	0.9	1000	3.8	25 TH	0429	1.1	1040	3.8
	1615	0.7	2222	4.1		1657	0.7	2256	3.9
11 TH	0436	0.8	1058	4.0	26 F	0506	1.0	1119	4.0
	1717	0.5	2318	4.3		1732	0.6	2334	4.0
12 F	0530	0.8	1148	4.2	27 SA	0539	0.9	1155	4.1
	1811	0.3	○			1804	0.5	●	
13 SA	0007	4.5	0618	0.7	28 SU	0009	4.1	0610	0.9
	1234	4.3	1900	0.2		1228	4.2	1837	0.4
14 SU	0054	4.5	0703	0.7	29 M	0043	4.2	0640	0.9
	1318	4.4	1944	0.1		1302	4.2	1909	0.4
15 M	0139	4.5	0744	0.8	30 TU	0117	4.2	0711	0.8
	1400	4.4	2025	0.2		1335	4.2	1940	0.4
					31 W	0151	4.1	0744	0.8
						1407	4.2	2010	0.5

Chart Datum: 2·16 metres below Ordnance Datum (Newlyn)
HAT is 4·7 metres above Chart Datum

TIME ZONE (UT)	WALTON-ON-THE-NAZE	Dates in amber are SPRINGS
For Summer Time add ONE hour in non-shaded areas	LAT 51°51′N LONG 1°17′E	Dates in grey are NEAPS
	TIMES AND HEIGHTS OF HIGH AND LOW WATERS	2022

SEPTEMBER

Day	Time m	Time m	Day	Time m	Time m
1 TH	0225 4.1 / 0818 0.9	1439 4.2 / 2040 0.6	**16** F	0308 3.9 / 0904 0.9	1517 4.1 / 2119 0.9
2 F	0301 4.0 / 0855 0.9	1515 4.1 / 2115 0.7	**17** SA	0344 3.7 / 0942 1.0	1558 3.8 / 2158 1.1
3 SA	0341 3.8 / 0938 1.0	1558 4.0 / 2202 0.9	**18** SU	0427 3.5 / 1031 1.2	1651 3.5 / 2259 1.4
4 SU	0430 3.7 / 1036 1.1	1654 3.8 / 2315 1.1	**19** M	0526 3.3 / 1142 1.3	1805 3.3
5 M	0536 3.5 / 1159 1.2	1813 3.6	**20** TU	0024 1.6 / 0646 3.2	1309 1.3 / 1937 3.3
6 TU	0053 1.2 / 0705 3.3	1337 1.1 / 1952 3.6	**21** W	0155 1.6 / 0814 3.2	1439 1.2 / 2052 3.5
7 W	0217 1.2 / 0844 3.5	1501 1.0 / 2116 3.9	**22** TH	0311 1.4 / 0920 3.5	1542 0.9 / 2146 3.7
8 TH	0329 1.1 / 0955 3.8	1612 0.6 / 2218 4.2	**23** F	0400 1.2 / 1008 3.8	1625 0.7 / 2229 3.9
9 F	0428 0.9 / 1048 4.0	1708 0.4 / 2309 4.4	**24** SA	0438 1.0 / 1047 3.9	1659 0.6 / 2305 4.1
10 SA	0516 0.8 / 1133 4.2	1755 0.2 / 2353 4.5	**25** SU	0510 0.9 / 1122 4.1	1731 0.5 / 2340 4.2
11 SU	0559 0.8 / 1214 4.4	1838 0.2	**26** M	0540 0.9 / 1156 4.2	1803 0.4
12 M	0034 4.5 / 0640 0.7	1253 4.5 / 1917 0.2	**27** TU	0013 4.2 / 0612 0.8	1230 4.3 / 1836 0.4
13 TU	0115 4.4 / 0719 0.7	1330 4.5 / 1952 0.3	**28** W	0048 4.3 / 0646 0.7	1304 4.3 / 1906 0.4
14 W	0154 4.3 / 0756 0.7	1406 4.4 / 2022 0.5	**29** TH	0123 4.2 / 0720 0.7	1338 4.3 / 1936 0.5
15 TH	0232 4.1 / 0830 0.8	1441 4.3 / 2050 0.7	**30** F	0159 4.1 / 0755 0.8	1414 4.3 / 2008 0.6

OCTOBER

Day	Time m	Time m	Day	Time m	Time m
1 SA	0236 4.0 / 0834 0.8	1453 4.2 / 2047 0.8	**16** SU	0258 3.7 / 0907 0.9	1520 3.8 / 2108 1.2
2 SU	0316 3.8 / 0920 0.8	1539 4.0 / 2139 1.1	**17** M	0335 3.5 / 0950 1.0	1607 3.5 / 2158 1.5
3 M	0406 3.6 / 1023 1.0	1639 3.8 / 2301 1.3	**18** TU	0427 3.3 / 1054 1.2	1717 3.3 / 2326 1.7
4 TU	0516 3.4 / 1154 1.1	1808 3.6	**19** W	0549 3.2 / 1223 1.3	1851 3.3
5 W	0042 1.4 / 0659 3.3	1332 1.0 / 1952 3.7	**20** TH	0110 1.7 / 0717 3.2	1347 1.1 / 2006 3.4
6 TH	0206 1.3 / 0833 3.5	1453 0.7 / 2109 4.0	**21** F	0226 1.5 / 0828 3.4	1451 0.9 / 2104 3.7
7 F	0316 1.1 / 0938 3.8	1558 0.5 / 2205 4.2	**22** SA	0319 1.3 / 0922 3.7	1539 0.7 / 2149 3.9
8 SA	0409 1.0 / 1028 4.1	1649 0.3 / 2251 4.3	**23** SU	0359 1.1 / 1005 3.9	1617 0.6 / 2227 4.1
9 SU	0453 0.9 / 1110 4.3	1731 0.3 / 2332 4.4	**24** M	0433 0.9 / 1043 4.1	1653 0.5 / 2304 4.2
10 M	0533 0.8 / 1148 4.4	1808 0.3	**25** TU	0507 0.8 / 1120 4.2	1727 0.4 / 2341 4.3
11 TU	0009 4.4 / 0613 0.7	1223 4.4 / 1843 0.3	**26** W	0543 0.7 / 1158 4.4	1801 0.4
12 W	0046 4.3 / 0651 0.6	1257 4.4 / 1913 0.5	**27** TH	0019 4.3 / 0621 0.7	1235 4.4 / 1835 0.5
13 TH	0121 4.2 / 0728 0.7	1331 4.4 / 1941 0.6	**28** F	0058 4.3 / 0700 0.7	1314 4.4 / 1909 0.6
14 F	0155 4.1 / 0802 0.7	1405 4.2 / 2007 0.8	**29** SA	0138 4.2 / 0740 0.7	1355 4.4 / 1947 0.7
15 SA	0227 3.9 / 0833 0.8	1441 4.0 / 2034 1.0	**30** SU	0218 4.0 / 0824 0.7	1440 4.2 / 2034 0.9
			31 M	0303 3.8 / 0917 0.8	1532 4.0 / 2135 1.2

NOVEMBER

Day	Time m	Time m	Day	Time m	Time m
1 TU	0357 3.6 / 1026 0.9	1639 3.8 / ☽ 2258 1.4	**16** W	0348 3.5 / 1017 1.0	1630 3.4 / ☽ 2223 1.6
2 W	0513 3.4 / 1155 0.9	1810 3.7	**17** TH	0453 3.3 / 1130 1.1	1750 3.3 / 2355 1.6
3 TH	0026 1.4 / 0647 3.4	1319 0.8 / 1938 3.8	**18** F	0616 3.3 / 1251 1.0	1906 3.4
4 F	0143 1.3 / 0808 3.6	1433 0.6 / 2048 4.0	**19** SA	0124 1.5 / 0727 3.4	1355 0.9 / 2007 3.6
5 SA	0250 1.2 / 0911 3.9	1534 0.5 / 2142 4.2	**20** SU	0225 1.3 / 0826 3.6	1447 0.7 / 2059 3.8
6 SU	0343 1.0 / 1000 4.1	1622 0.4 / 2227 4.2	**21** M	0312 1.1 / 0917 3.8	1532 0.6 / 2145 4.0
7 M	0427 0.9 / 1042 4.2	1702 0.4 / 2306 4.3	**22** TU	0354 1.0 / 1003 4.0	1613 0.5 / 2229 4.1
8 TU	0508 0.8 / 1119 4.3	1736 0.5 / ○ 2343 4.3	**23** W	0436 0.8 / 1046 4.2	1653 0.5 / ● 2312 4.2
9 W	0547 0.7 / 1154 4.3	1808 0.7	**24** TH	0519 0.7 / 1130 4.4	1733 0.5 / 2356 4.3
10 TH	0017 4.2 / 0627 0.6	1228 4.1 / 1839 0.6	**25** F	0603 0.6 / 1214 4.5	1813 0.6
11 F	0051 4.2 / 0704 0.6	1302 4.3 / 1908 0.8	**26** SA	0040 4.3 / 0648 0.5	1258 4.5 / 1856 0.7
12 SA	0123 4.1 / 0738 0.7	1337 4.1 / 1934 0.9	**27** SU	0125 4.2 / 0735 0.5	1345 4.4 / 1943 0.8
13 SU	0154 3.9 / 0809 0.7	1413 4.0 / 2002 1.1	**28** M	0211 4.1 / 0826 0.5	1435 4.3 / 2036 1.0
14 M	0226 3.8 / 0842 0.8	1452 3.8 / 2036 1.2	**29** TU	0301 3.9 / 0923 0.5	1532 4.1 / 2136 1.2
15 TU	0302 3.6 / 0923 0.9	1535 3.6 / 2121 1.4	**30** W	0358 3.7 / 1030 0.6	1639 3.9 / ☽ 2245 1.3

DECEMBER

Day	Time m	Time m	Day	Time m	Time m
1 TH	0506 3.6 / 1144 0.6	1753 3.8 / 2358 1.3	**16** F	0415 3.5 / 1042 0.9	1651 3.5 / ☽ 2247 1.4
2 F	0619 3.6 / 1255 0.6	1907 3.8	**17** SA	0514 3.5 / 1146 0.9	1756 3.5 / 2359 1.4
3 SA	0109 1.3 / 0732 3.7	1401 0.6 / 2015 3.9	**18** SU	0621 3.5 / 1253 0.9	1903 3.6
4 SU	0215 1.2 / 0836 3.8	1501 0.6 / 2113 4.0	**19** M	0117 1.4 / 0728 3.6	1354 0.8 / 2007 3.7
5 M	0312 1.1 / 0929 4.0	1551 0.6 / 2200 4.0	**20** TU	0223 1.2 / 0830 3.8	1449 0.7 / 2105 3.9
6 TU	0401 0.9 / 1014 4.1	1631 0.7 / 2242 4.1	**21** W	0319 1.0 / 0926 4.0	1540 0.6 / 2200 4.0
7 W	0446 0.8 / 1054 4.1	1707 0.7 / 2320 4.1	**22** TH	0411 0.8 / 1019 4.1	1629 0.6 / 2251 4.1
8 TH	0528 0.7 / 1131 4.1	1741 0.7 / ○ 2356 4.1	**23** F	0502 0.7 / 1110 4.3	1717 0.6 / ● 2341 4.2
9 F	0608 0.6 / 1207 4.2	1814 0.8	**24** SA	0553 0.5 / 1200 4.4	1805 0.6
10 SA	0030 4.1 / 0647 0.6	1242 4.1 / 1847 0.9	**25** SU	0029 4.2 / 0645 0.4	1249 4.5 / 1855 0.7
11 SU	0103 4.0 / 0721 0.6	1319 4.0 / 1916 1.0	**26** M	0118 4.2 / 0737 0.3	1340 4.5 / 1944 0.8
12 M	0135 4.0 / 0754 0.6	1355 3.9 / 1945 1.0	**27** TU	0207 4.2 / 0829 0.3	1431 4.4 / 2034 0.9
13 TU	0209 3.9 / 0827 0.7	1433 3.8 / 2020 1.1	**28** W	0256 4.1 / 0922 0.3	1526 4.2 / 2125 1.0
14 W	0245 3.8 / 0905 0.7	1513 3.7 / 2100 1.2	**29** TH	0348 4.0 / 1018 0.3	1623 4.0 / 2220 1.1
15 TH	0326 3.6 / 0949 0.8	1558 3.6 / 2148 1.3	**30** F	0443 3.9 / 1116 0.4	1724 3.8 / ☽ 2321 1.2
			31 SA	0542 3.8 / 1216 0.5	1827 3.7

Chart Datum: 2·16 metres below Ordnance Datum (Newlyn)
HAT is 4·7 metres above Chart Datum

TIDES

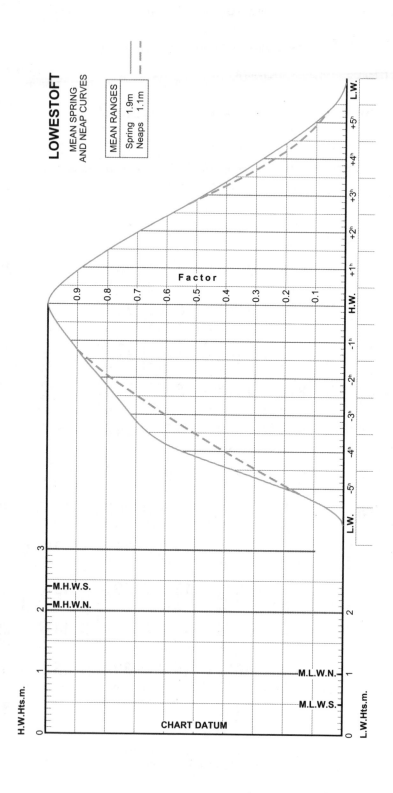

LOWESTOFT
MEAN SPRING
AND NEAP CURVES

MEAN RANGES	
Spring	1.9m
Neaps	1.1m

Factor

0.9
0.8
0.7
0.6
0.5
0.4
0.3
0.2
0.1

L.W.

+5ʰ +4ʰ +3ʰ +2ʰ +1ʰ H.W. -1ʰ -2ʰ -3ʰ -4ʰ -5ʰ L.W.

H.W.Hts.m.

3

M.H.W.S.
M.H.W.N.

2

1

0

CHART DATUM

L.W.Hts.m.

2

M.L.W.N.
M.L.W.S.

1

0

TIME ZONE (UT)

For Summer Time add ONE hour in **non-shaded areas**

LOWESTOFT

LAT 52°28'N LONG 1°45'E

TIMES AND HEIGHTS OF HIGH AND LOW WATERS

Dates in amber are **SPRINGS**
Dates in grey are **NEAPS**

2022

JANUARY

Date	Day	Time	m	Time	m	Time	m	Time	m
1	SA	0129	0.9	0732	2.5	1400	0.7	2015	2.5
2	SU	0228	0.8	0830	2.6	1453	0.7	● 2101	2.5
3	M	0325	0.6	0930	2.6	1543	0.7	2148	2.6
4	TU	0419	0.5	1026	2.6	1631	0.8	2234	2.6
5	W	0510	0.4	1119	2.5	1717	0.8	2320	2.6
6	TH	0559	0.4	1211	2.5	1759	0.9		
7	F	0005	2.6	0647	0.4	1303	2.3	1841	1.0
8	SA	0051	2.6	0736	0.5	1401	2.2	1923	1.1
9	SU	0137	2.5	0829	0.6	1512	2.1	◐ 2008	1.3
10	M	0226	2.4	0927	0.8	1619	2.1	2103	1.3
11	TU	0326	2.3	1030	0.9	1717	2.1	2227	1.4
12	W	0439	2.2	1130	1.0	1813	2.2	2348	1.3
13	TH	0546	2.2	1224	1.0	1904	2.2		
14	F	0049	1.2	0653	2.2	1311	1.0	1947	2.3
15	SA	0141	1.1	0758	2.2	1354	1.0	2023	2.3
16	SU	0226	1.0	0848	2.2	1431	1.0	2054	2.4
17	M	0306	0.9	0927	2.3	1504	1.0	○ 2125	2.4
18	TU	0344	0.8	1001	2.3	1537	1.0	2157	2.5
19	W	0421	0.7	1034	2.3	1613	0.9	2233	2.5
20	TH	0500	0.7	1108	2.3	1649	0.9	2309	2.5
21	F	0538	0.6	1143	2.3	1727	0.9	2347	2.5
22	SA	0616	0.6	1220	2.3	1804	1.0		
23	SU	0024	2.5	0656	0.7	1259	2.2	1844	1.0
24	M	0103	2.5	0737	0.7	1342	2.2	1928	1.1
25	TU	0146	2.5	0823	0.7	1433	2.1	◑ 2018	1.1
26	W	0236	2.4	0920	0.8	1547	2.1	2117	1.2
27	TH	0340	2.4	1034	0.8	1711	2.1	2240	1.2
28	F	0506	2.3	1147	0.9	1810	2.2		
29	SA	0008	1.1	0620	2.4	1249	0.9	1905	2.3
30	SU	0118	0.9	0728	2.4	1348	0.9	1957	2.4
31	M	0222	0.7	0835	2.5	1444	0.8	2047	2.5

FEBRUARY

Date	Day	Time	m	Time	m	Time	m	Time	m
1	TU	0321	0.5	0932	2.5	1535	0.8	● 2134	2.6
2	W	0412	0.4	1021	2.5	1621	0.8	2219	2.6
3	TH	0459	0.3	1106	2.5	1701	0.8	2302	2.7
4	F	0542	0.3	1150	2.4	1739	0.8	2344	2.7
5	SA	0624	0.3	1233	2.3	1815	0.9		
6	SU	0024	2.6	0705	0.5	1315	2.2	1850	1.0
7	M	0105	2.5	0745	0.6	1401	2.1	1928	1.1
8	TU	0149	2.4	0829	0.8	1459	2.0	◐ 2012	1.2
9	W	0240	2.3	0925	1.0	1612	2.0	2111	1.3
10	TH	0355	2.2	1043	1.1	1713	2.0	2302	1.3
11	F	0519	2.1	1152	1.2	1812	2.1		
12	SA	0021	1.2	0641	2.1	1248	1.2	1910	2.2
13	SU	0120	1.1	0757	2.1	1336	1.2	1955	2.2
14	M	0208	0.9	0841	2.2	1416	1.1	2031	2.3
15	TU	0249	0.8	0915	2.2	1450	1.0	2103	2.4
16	W	0326	0.7	0944	2.3	1524	0.9	○ 2137	2.5
17	TH	0404	0.6	1014	2.3	1600	0.8	2212	2.5
18	F	0441	0.5	1046	2.4	1636	0.8	2248	2.6
19	SA	0518	0.5	1120	2.4	1712	0.8	2324	2.6
20	SU	0555	0.5	1155	2.3	1747	0.8		
21	M	0000	2.6	0631	0.5	1231	2.3	1823	0.9
22	TU	0038	2.6	0708	0.6	1312	2.2	1903	0.9
23	W	0121	2.5	0750	0.7	1358	2.2	◑ 1950	1.0
24	TH	0212	2.4	0842	0.8	1457	2.1	2050	1.1
25	F	0322	2.3	0957	1.0	1625	2.1	2221	1.1
26	SA	0502	2.3	1132	1.1	1740	2.1		
27	SU	0001	1.0	0625	2.3	1242	1.0	1843	2.2
28	M	0114	0.8	0742	2.4	1345	1.0	1941	2.3

MARCH

Date	Day	Time	m	Time	m	Time	m	Time	m
1	TU	0219	0.6	0841	2.4	1440	0.9	2031	2.4
2	W	0313	0.4	0926	2.5	1525	0.8	● 2117	2.5
3	TH	0358	0.3	1006	2.5	1605	0.8	2159	2.6
4	F	0440	0.2	1045	2.4	1641	0.7	2240	2.7
5	SA	0518	0.3	1122	2.4	1715	0.7	2320	2.7
6	SU	0554	0.4	1159	2.3	1748	0.8	2358	2.6
7	M	0628	0.5	1233	2.2	1820	0.8		
8	TU	0036	2.5	0701	0.7	1307	2.1	1856	0.9
9	W	0117	2.3	0735	0.9	1345	2.1	1937	1.0
10	TH	0206	2.2	0815	1.1	1433	2.0	◐ 2029	1.1
11	F	0317	2.1	0910	1.3	1547	2.0	2155	1.2
12	SA	0457	2.0	1122	1.4	1708	2.0	2353	1.1
13	SU	0623	2.0	1229	1.3	1814	2.1		
14	M	0051	1.0	0736	2.1	1318	1.2	1912	2.1
15	TU	0139	0.9	0818	2.2	1356	1.1	1956	2.2
16	W	0220	0.7	0849	2.3	1429	1.0	2033	2.3
17	TH	0258	0.6	0918	2.3	1504	0.9	2109	2.4
18	F	0337	0.5	0947	2.4	1540	0.8	○ 2145	2.5
19	SA	0414	0.4	1020	2.4	1616	0.7	2222	2.6
20	SU	0452	0.3	1054	2.4	1653	0.7	2259	2.6
21	M	0528	0.4	1129	2.4	1728	0.7	2337	2.6
22	TU	0604	0.5	1206	2.3	1805	0.7		
23	W	0018	2.6	0642	0.6	1246	2.3	1847	0.8
24	TH	0104	2.5	0724	0.8	1332	2.2	1936	0.8
25	F	0202	2.3	0816	1.0	1429	2.1	◑ 2042	0.9
26	SA	0331	2.2	0937	1.2	1549	2.1	2231	0.9
27	SU	0515	2.2	1125	1.2	1712	2.1	2358	0.8
28	M	0639	2.3	1237	1.2	1820	2.2		
29	TU	0106	0.6	0746	2.4	1338	1.1	1921	2.3
30	W	0206	0.5	0832	2.4	1427	1.0	2011	2.4
31	TH	0255	0.4	0910	2.4	1507	0.8	2055	2.5

APRIL

Date	Day	Time	m	Time	m	Time	m	Time	m
1	F	0336	0.3	0945	2.4	1543	0.7	● 2136	2.6
2	SA	0414	0.3	1019	2.4	1618	0.7	2216	2.6
3	SU	0449	0.4	1053	2.4	1651	0.7	2255	2.6
4	M	0521	0.5	1125	2.3	1723	0.7	2333	2.5
5	TU	0551	0.6	1156	2.3	1755	0.8		
6	W	0010	2.4	0620	0.8	1228	2.2	1830	0.8
7	TH	0051	2.3	0649	1.0	1304	2.2	1909	0.9
8	F	0139	2.1	0725	1.1	1348	2.1	1958	1.0
9	SA	0247	2.0	0812	1.3	1444	2.1	◐ 2108	1.1
10	SU	0433	2.0	0921	1.4	1600	2.0	2313	1.1
11	M	0549	2.0	1153	1.4	1721	2.0		
12	TU	0011	0.9	0654	2.1	1241	1.3	1822	2.1
13	W	0058	0.8	0739	2.2	1319	1.2	1912	2.2
14	TH	0141	0.7	0813	2.3	1356	1.0	1955	2.3
15	F	0222	0.5	0845	2.3	1434	0.9	2035	2.4
16	SA	0303	0.4	0917	2.4	1513	0.7	○ 2114	2.5
17	SU	0343	0.3	0951	2.4	1553	0.7	2154	2.6
18	M	0423	0.3	1027	2.5	1633	0.6	2235	2.6
19	TU	0502	0.4	1105	2.4	1713	0.6	2318	2.6
20	W	0541	0.5	1144	2.4	1754	0.6		
21	TH	0004	2.5	0622	0.7	1226	2.3	1841	0.7
22	F	0059	2.4	0707	0.9	1314	2.3	1937	0.7
23	SA	0209	2.3	0802	1.1	1413	2.2	◑ 2053	0.8
24	SU	0352	2.2	0927	1.3	1526	2.1	2230	0.7
25	M	0518	2.3	1107	1.3	1645	2.1	2342	0.6
26	TU	0632	2.3	1216	1.2	1754	2.2		
27	W	0045	0.5	0730	2.3	1314	1.1	1855	2.3
28	TH	0141	0.5	0813	2.4	1402	1.0	1946	2.4
29	F	0228	0.5	0847	2.4	1442	0.9	2030	2.4
30	SA	0307	0.4	0920	2.4	1518	0.8	● 2112	2.5

Chart Datum: 1·50 metres below Ordnance Datum (Newlyn)
HAT is 2·9 metres above Chart Datum

TIME ZONE (UT)	LOWESTOFT	Dates in amber are SPRINGS
For Summer Time add ONE hour in **non-shaded areas**	LAT 52°28′N LONG 1°45′E	Dates in grey are NEAPS
	TIMES AND HEIGHTS OF HIGH AND LOW WATERS	**2022**

MAY

Time	m	Time	m		Time	m	Time	m
1 0343	0.5	**16** 0312	0.4					
0952	2.4	0924	2.5					
SU 1553	0.7	M 1530	0.7					
2153	2.5	○ 2130	2.6					
2 0417	0.6	**17** 0356	0.4					
1024	2.4	1003	2.5					
M 1628	0.7	TU 1616	0.6					
2233	2.4	2217	2.6					
3 0447	0.7	**18** 0439	0.5					
1055	2.4	1044	2.5					
TU 1701	0.7	W 1702	0.5					
2312	2.3	2307	2.6					
4 0515	0.8	**19** 0523	0.6					
1125	2.3	1127	2.5					
W 1734	0.7	TH 1750	0.5					
2350	2.3							
5 0542	0.9	**20** 0001	2.5					
1157	2.3	0608	0.8					
TH 1809	0.8	F 1213	2.4					
		1843	0.5					
6 0030	2.2	**21** 0102	2.4					
0613	1.0	0656	1.0					
F 1233	2.3	SA 1303	2.4					
1849	0.8	1943	0.5					
7 0117	2.1	**22** 0218	2.3					
0650	1.1	0751	1.2					
SA 1316	2.2	SU 1400	2.3					
1936	0.9	◑ 2055	0.6					
8 0218	2.0	**23** 0348	2.2					
0737	1.3	0904	1.3					
SU 1408	2.2	M 1504	2.3					
2038	1.0	2210	0.6					
9 0358	2.0	**24** 0502	2.3					
0834	1.4	1030	1.3					
M 1509	2.1	TU 1615	2.3					
◑ 2213	1.0	2316	0.6					
10 0508	2.0	**25** 0607	2.3					
1002	1.4	1139	1.3					
TU 1623	2.1	W 1724	2.3					
2322	0.9							
11 0605	2.1	**26** 0014	0.6					
1138	1.3	0702	2.3					
W 1732	2.1	TH 1238	1.2					
		1824	2.3					
12 0012	0.8	**27** 0109	0.6					
0653	2.2	0746	2.3					
TH 1229	1.2	F 1330	1.1					
1827	2.4	1918	2.3					
13 0058	0.6	**28** 0155	0.6					
0733	2.3	0823	2.3					
F 1315	1.1	SA 1414	1.0					
1915	2.4	2007	2.3					
14 0143	0.5	**29** 0236	0.6					
0810	2.4	0856	2.4					
SA 1400	0.9	SU 1454	0.8					
2000	2.4	2053	2.4					
15 0228	0.4	**30** 0312	0.7					
0846	2.4	0928	2.4					
SU 1445	0.8	M 1532	0.8					
2044	2.5	● 2136	2.3					
		31 0345	0.8					
		0959	2.4					
		TU 1609	0.7					
		2218	2.3					

JUNE

Time	m	Time	m
1 0416	0.8	**16** 0423	0.6
1029	2.4	1028	2.5
W 1644	0.7	TH 1656	0.4
2258	2.3	2304	2.5
2 0444	0.9	**17** 0510	0.7
1100	2.4	1114	2.5
TH 1719	0.7	F 1748	0.4
2336	2.2		
3 0513	1.0	**18** 0000	2.5
1134	2.4	0557	0.9
F 1755	0.8	SA 1201	2.5
		1841	0.4
4 0015	2.2	**19** 0058	2.4
0547	1.0	0644	1.0
SA 1211	2.4	SU 1250	2.5
1835	0.8	1936	0.4
5 0058	2.1	**20** 0204	2.3
0626	1.1	0733	1.1
SU 1253	2.3	M 1341	2.5
1920	0.8	2035	0.5
6 0146	2.1	**21** 0323	2.2
0711	1.2	0827	1.2
M 1340	2.3	TU 1436	2.4
2013	0.9	◑ 2138	0.5
7 0248	2.0	**22** 0431	2.2
0803	1.3	0934	1.3
TU 1431	2.2	W 1540	2.4
◑ 2116	0.9	2241	0.6
8 0417	2.1	**23** 0531	2.2
0904	1.3	1050	1.3
W 1528	2.2	TH 1649	2.3
2226	0.8	2340	0.7
9 0517	2.1	**24** 0626	2.2
1020	1.3	1158	1.3
TH 1636	2.2	F 1753	2.3
2325	0.7		
10 0608	2.2	**25** 0034	0.8
1135	1.2	0715	2.3
F 1741	2.3	SA 1257	1.1
		1854	2.2
11 0018	0.6	**26** 0123	0.8
0654	2.3	0757	2.3
SA 1234	1.1	SU 1349	1.0
1837	2.3	1952	2.2
12 0108	0.6	**27** 0206	0.9
0736	2.3	0834	2.3
SU 1328	1.0	M 1435	0.9
1929	2.4	2045	2.4
13 0157	0.5	**28** 0245	0.9
0818	2.4	0907	2.4
M 1420	0.8	TU 1516	0.8
2020	2.5	2131	2.3
14 0246	0.5	**29** 0319	0.9
0900	2.5	0938	2.4
TU 1512	0.7	W 1555	0.8
○ 2113	2.5	⊕ 2212	2.3
15 0335	0.6	**30** 0351	1.0
0943	2.5	1009	2.5
W 1604	0.5	TH 1632	0.7
2208	2.6	2248	2.2

JULY

Time	m	Time	m
1 0421	1.0	**16** 0458	0.8
1041	2.5	1100	2.7
F 1708	0.7	SA 1740	0.3
2323	2.2	2350	2.5
2 0453	1.0	**17** 0542	0.9
1117	2.5	1145	2.7
SA 1744	0.7	SU 1827	0.3
2358	2.2		
3 0529	1.0	**18** 0039	2.4
1154	2.5	0625	0.9
SU 1822	0.7	M 1230	2.7
		1915	0.3
4 0035	2.2	**19** 0132	2.3
0608	1.1	0706	1.0
M 1233	2.4	TU 1316	2.6
1903	0.7	2004	0.5
5 0114	2.1	**20** 0236	2.2
0649	1.1	0749	1.1
TU 1313	2.4	W 1404	2.5
1946	0.8	◑ 2057	0.6
6 0158	2.1	**21** 0347	2.2
0734	1.2	0839	1.2
W 1357	2.4	TH 1500	2.4
2034	0.8	2157	0.8
7 0252	2.1	**22** 0447	2.1
0826	1.2	0948	1.3
TH 1445	2.3	F 1613	2.3
◑ 2131	0.8	2301	0.9
8 0415	2.1	**23** 0543	2.2
0925	1.3	1118	1.3
F 1543	2.3	SA 1726	2.2
2237	0.8		
9 0522	2.2	**24** 0000	1.0
1041	1.2	0638	2.2
SA 1658	2.3	SU 1229	1.2
2341	0.8	1838	2.2
10 0615	2.2	**25** 0055	1.1
1159	1.2	0729	2.3
SU 1806	2.2	M 1330	1.1
		1953	2.2
11 0039	0.7	**26** 0143	1.1
0705	2.3	0811	2.3
M 1303	1.0	TU 1421	1.0
1907	2.4	2046	2.2
12 0134	0.7	**27** 0226	1.1
0752	2.4	0847	2.4
TU 1403	0.8	W 1503	0.9
2008	2.5	2126	2.3
13 0228	0.7	**28** 0302	1.1
0839	2.5	0918	2.4
W 1502	0.7	TH 1541	0.8
○ 2109	2.5	● 2201	2.3
14 0321	0.7	**29** 0333	1.0
0927	2.5	0949	2.5
TH 1558	0.5	F 1617	0.7
2207	2.6	2232	2.3
15 0411	0.8	**30** 0405	1.0
1013	2.6	1022	2.5
F 1650	0.3	SA 1652	0.6
2259	2.4	2302	2.3
		31 0438	0.9
		1057	2.6
		SU 1727	0.6
		2334	2.3

AUGUST

Time	m	Time	m
1 0513	0.9	**16** 0011	2.4
1133	2.6	0559	0.9
M 1802	0.6	TU 1205	2.8
		1845	0.4
2 0007	2.3	**17** 0053	2.3
0550	1.0	0636	1.0
TU 1208	2.6	W 1247	2.7
1838	0.6	1925	0.6
3 0042	2.3	**18** 0138	2.2
0626	1.0	0715	1.1
W 1245	2.5	TH 1331	2.5
1915	0.7	2008	0.8
4 0121	2.2	**19** 0231	2.2
0707	1.1	0758	1.2
TH 1325	2.5	F 1423	2.4
1956	0.7	◑ 2058	1.0
5 0206	2.2	**20** 0342	2.1
0752	1.1	0855	1.3
F 1410	2.5	SA 1538	2.2
◑ 2044	0.8	2211	1.2
6 0304	2.2	**21** 0447	2.1
0847	1.2	1037	1.3
SA 1506	2.4	SU 1705	2.2
2148	0.9	2331	1.3
7 0429	2.2	**22** 0547	2.2
0958	1.2	1207	1.2
SU 1628	2.3	M 1830	2.2
2310	0.9		
8 0538	2.2	**23** 0034	1.3
1136	1.1	0649	2.2
M 1750	2.3	TU 1310	1.1
		1948	2.2
9 0019	1.0	**24** 0128	1.3
0636	2.3	0741	2.3
TU 1249	1.0	W 1401	1.0
1902	2.4	2034	2.3
10 0119	1.0	**25** 0211	1.2
0730	2.4	0809	2.4
W 1354	0.8	TH 1442	0.9
2012	2.5	2109	2.3
11 0217	0.9	**26** 0245	1.1
0821	2.5	0851	2.5
TH 1456	0.6	F 1518	0.7
2110	2.5	2138	2.3
12 0312	0.9	**27** 0315	1.0
0910	2.6	0923	2.5
F 1550	0.4	SA 1553	0.7
○ 2200	2.6	● 2205	2.4
13 0400	0.8	**28** 0347	1.0
0956	2.7	0957	2.6
SA 1638	0.3	SU 1627	0.6
2245	2.6	2234	2.4
14 0442	0.8	**29** 0420	0.9
1040	2.8	1031	2.7
SU 1722	0.2	M 1701	0.5
2328	2.5	2305	2.4
15 0522	0.8	**30** 0454	0.9
1123	2.8	1106	2.7
M 1804	0.3	TU 1735	0.5
		2338	2.4
		31 0528	0.9
		1142	2.6
		W 1809	0.6

Chart Datum: 1·50 metres below Ordnance Datum (Newlyn)
HAT is 2·9 metres above Chart Datum

TIME ZONE (UT)		
For Summer Time add ONE hour in **non-shaded areas**		

LOWESTOFT

LAT 52°28'N   LONG 1°45'E

TIMES AND HEIGHTS OF HIGH AND LOW WATERS

Dates in amber are **SPRINGS**
Dates in grey are **NEAPS**

2022

SEPTEMBER

Day	Time m	Time m	Time m	Time m
1 TH	0012 2.4	0604 0.9	1217 2.6	1844 0.7
16 F	0051 2.3	0645 1.1	1301 2.5	1919 0.9
2 F	0050 2.3	0641 1.1	1257 2.6	1921 0.8
17 SA	0130 2.3	0726 1.1	1352 2.3	1958 1.2
3 SA	0132 2.3	0726 1.1	1344 2.5	2007 0.9
18 SU	0217 2.2	0811 1.0	1508 2.2	2050 1.4
4 SU	0224 2.2	0821 1.1	1447 2.4	2109 1.1
19 M	0325 2.2	0949 1.3	1646 2.1	2301 1.5
5 M	0337 2.2	0937 1.2	1622 2.3	2248 1.2
20 TU	0445 2.2	1140 1.2	1811 2.2	
6 TU	0502 2.2	1128 1.1	1753 2.3	
21 W	0014 1.4	0551 2.2	1239 1.1	1923 2.2
7 W	0008 1.2	0609 2.3	1242 0.9	1912 2.4
22 TH	0106 1.4	0650 2.3	1327 0.9	2007 2.3
8 TH	0112 1.1	0708 2.4	1348 0.7	2015 2.5
23 F	0146 1.3	0736 2.4	1408 0.8	2039 2.4
9 F	0210 1.1	0801 2.5	1446 0.5	2102 2.6
24 SA	0218 1.2	0814 2.5	1444 0.7	2106 2.4
10 SA	0259 1.0	0849 2.6	1534 0.3	2143 2.6
25 SU	0248 1.0	0849 2.6	1519 0.6	2133 2.4
11 SU	0342 0.9	0933 2.8	1617 0.3	2222 2.6
26 M	0320 0.9	0925 2.6	1554 0.5	2202 2.5
12 M	0420 0.8	1016 2.8	1657 0.3	2301 2.6
27 TU	0355 0.9	1001 2.7	1630 0.5	2235 2.5
13 TU	0457 0.8	1058 2.8	1734 0.4	2339 2.4
28 W	0431 0.8	1038 2.7	1705 0.5	2309 2.5
14 W	0532 0.8	1138 2.7	1810 0.5	
29 TH	0507 0.8	1115 2.7	1739 0.6	2344 2.5
15 TH	0015 2.4	0608 0.9	1218 2.6	1845 0.7
30 F	0543 0.9	1154 2.6	1814 0.7	

OCTOBER

Day	Time m	Time m	Time m	Time m
1 SA	0022 2.4	0623 0.9	1238 2.6	1854 0.9
16 SU	0048 2.4	0700 1.0	1327 2.2	1910 1.3
2 SU	0106 2.4	0710 1.0	1331 2.4	1942 1.1
17 M	0131 2.3	0749 1.1	1441 2.1	1954 1.4
3 M	0158 2.3	0811 1.0	1446 2.3	2046 1.3
18 TU	0226 2.2	0902 1.2	1621 2.1	2055 1.6
4 TU	0307 2.2	0945 1.0	1638 2.3	2237 1.4
19 W	0337 2.2	1101 1.1	1734 2.2	2336 1.6
5 W	0430 2.3	1123 0.9	1802 2.4	2358 1.3
20 TH	0455 2.2	1158 1.0	1839 2.2	
6 TH	0542 2.3	1231 0.7	1913 2.5	
21 F	0025 1.4	0558 2.3	1243 0.9	1925 2.3
7 F	0100 1.2	0644 2.4	1333 0.6	2005 2.5
22 SA	0103 1.3	0648 2.4	1324 0.8	1959 2.4
8 SA	0154 1.1	0737 2.6	1426 0.5	2045 2.5
23 SU	0137 1.2	0732 2.5	1403 0.7	2028 2.4
9 SU	0239 1.0	0824 2.7	1510 0.4	2121 2.5
24 M	0212 1.1	0812 2.5	1441 0.6	2058 2.5
10 M	0318 0.9	0908 2.7	1550 0.4	2156 2.5
25 TU	0250 0.9	0851 2.6	1519 0.5	2131 2.5
11 TU	0355 0.8	0951 2.8	1627 0.4	2231 2.5
26 W	0329 0.8	0931 2.7	1557 0.5	2205 2.6
12 W	0432 0.8	1033 2.7	1702 0.6	2306 2.5
27 TH	0408 0.8	1011 2.7	1635 0.5	2242 2.6
13 TH	0507 0.8	1114 2.6	1734 0.7	2340 2.4
28 F	0448 0.8	1053 2.7	1713 0.6	2320 2.6
14 F	0542 0.9	1154 2.5	1804 0.9	
29 SA	0530 0.8	1138 2.6	1753 0.8	
15 SA	0013 2.4	0619 0.9	1236 2.4	1835 1.1
30 SU	0000 2.5	0616 0.8	1229 2.5	1837 1.0
31 M	0047 2.4	0710 0.8	1332 2.4	1928 1.2

NOVEMBER

Day	Time m	Time m	Time m	Time m
1 TU	0142 2.4	0818 0.9	1502 2.3	2034 1.4
16 W	0149 2.3	0826 1.1	1538 2.1	2009 1.5
2 W	0247 2.3	0950 0.9	1642 2.3	2217 1.4
17 TH	0247 2.3	0955 1.1	1649 2.1	2118 1.5
3 TH	0402 2.3	1107 0.7	1755 2.4	2334 1.4
18 F	0355 2.2	1105 1.0	1746 2.2	2306 1.5
4 F	0514 2.4	1210 0.7	1856 2.4	
19 SA	0505 2.3	1154 0.9	1833 2.3	
5 SA	0034 1.2	0616 2.4	1307 0.6	1944 2.5
20 SU	0004 1.4	0602 2.3	1238 0.8	1914 2.3
6 SU	0126 1.2	0710 2.5	1358 0.6	2021 2.5
21 M	0050 1.2	0651 2.4	1321 0.7	1950 2.4
7 M	0212 1.0	0758 2.6	1441 0.5	2056 2.5
22 TU	0135 1.1	0736 2.5	1403 0.6	2025 2.5
8 TU	0253 0.9	0844 2.6	1520 0.6	2129 2.5
23 W	0219 1.0	0820 2.6	1446 0.6	2101 2.5
9 W	0332 0.8	0929 2.6	1556 0.6	2204 2.5
24 TH	0304 0.8	0904 2.6	1528 0.6	2139 2.6
10 TH	0409 0.8	1012 2.6	1629 0.8	2237 2.5
25 F	0350 0.7	0951 2.6	1611 0.6	2219 2.6
11 F	0446 0.8	1054 2.5	1659 0.9	2309 2.5
26 SA	0436 0.7	1040 2.6	1655 0.7	2301 2.6
12 SA	0522 0.8	1135 2.4	1728 1.0	2341 2.4
27 SU	0525 0.6	1133 2.6	1739 0.9	2346 2.6
13 SU	0559 0.9	1218 2.3	1757 1.1	
28 M	0616 0.6	1231 2.5	1826 1.0	
14 M	0016 2.4	0639 1.0	1305 2.2	1832 1.4
29 TU	0035 2.5	0714 0.6	1336 2.4	1918 1.2
15 TU	0058 2.4	0726 1.0	1406 2.1	1916 1.4
30 W	0128 2.5	0820 0.7	1501 2.3	2018 1.3

DECEMBER

Day	Time m	Time m	Time m	Time m
1 TH	0227 2.4	0933 0.7	1626 2.3	2135 1.4
16 F	0208 2.3	0849 1.0	1539 2.1	2031 1.4
2 F	0332 2.4	1041 0.7	1731 2.3	2253 1.4
17 SA	0301 2.3	0954 0.9	1650 2.1	2136 1.4
3 SA	0444 2.4	1141 0.7	1828 2.3	2357 1.3
18 SU	0403 2.3	1058 0.9	1743 2.2	2256 1.4
4 SU	0548 2.4	1237 0.7	1916 2.4	
19 M	0513 2.3	1153 0.9	1830 2.3	
5 M	0054 1.2	0645 2.4	1327 0.7	1956 2.4
20 TU	0005 1.3	0612 2.4	1243 0.7	1913 2.3
6 TU	0145 1.1	0737 2.5	1412 0.7	2032 2.4
21 W	0101 1.1	0704 2.4	1331 0.7	1955 2.4
7 W	0230 1.0	0827 2.5	1451 0.8	2106 2.5
22 TH	0153 1.0	0755 2.5	1419 0.7	2036 2.5
8 TH	0313 0.9	0916 2.4	1527 0.8	2140 2.5
23 F	0245 0.8	0847 2.5	1507 0.7	2118 2.5
9 F	0353 0.8	1001 2.4	1600 0.9	2213 2.5
24 SA	0338 0.7	0942 2.6	1555 0.7	2202 2.6
10 SA	0431 0.8	1044 2.4	1630 1.0	2245 2.5
25 SU	0430 0.6	1037 2.6	1643 0.8	2248 2.6
11 SU	0508 0.8	1124 2.3	1659 1.1	2317 2.5
26 M	0522 0.5	1132 2.5	1730 0.9	2335 2.6
12 M	0545 0.8	1203 2.2	1730 1.1	2353 2.5
27 TU	0614 0.4	1226 2.5	1816 1.0	
13 TU	0623 0.9	1243 2.2	1806 1.2	
28 W	0022 2.6	0708 0.4	1323 2.4	1903 1.1
14 W	0034 2.4	0706 0.9	1327 2.1	1849 1.2
29 TH	0111 2.6	0803 0.5	1432 2.3	1952 1.2
15 TH	0119 2.4	0754 0.9	1419 2.1	1937 1.3
30 F	0202 2.5	0902 0.6	1553 2.2	2047 1.3
31 SA	0259 2.5	1005 0.7	1656 2.2	2158 1.3

Chart Datum: 1·50 metres below Ordnance Datum (Newlyn)
HAT is 2·9 metres above Chart Datum

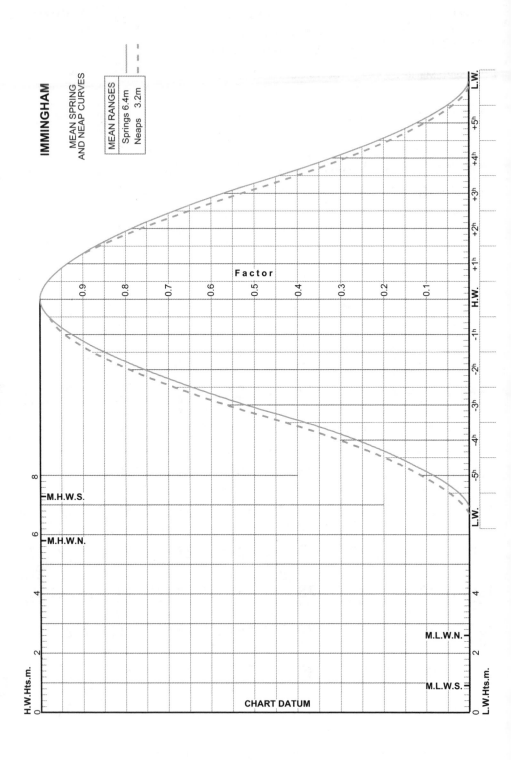

IMMINGHAM

MEAN SPRING
AND NEAP CURVES

MEAN RANGES
Springs 6.4m
Neaps 3.2m

IMMINGHAM

LAT 53°38'N LONG 0°11'W

TIMES AND HEIGHTS OF HIGH AND LOW WATERS

Dates in amber are **SPRINGS**
Dates in grey are **NEAPS**

2022

JANUARY

Date	Time m	Time m	Time m	Time m
1 SA	0403 6.9	1033 1.4	1640 6.9	2300 1.5
16 SU	0451 6.3	1101 2.0	1711 6.6	2334 1.8
2 SU	0502 7.1	1128 1.3	1729 7.1	2357 1.1 ●
17 M	0532 6.4	1143 1.8	1748 6.7 ○	
3 M	0558 7.2	1219 1.2	1816 7.3	
18 TU	0015 1.6	0611 6.6	1221 1.8	1824 6.9
4 TU	0050 0.9	0653 7.3	1307 1.2	1902 7.4
19 W	0055 1.5	0649 6.6	1257 1.7	1859 6.9
5 W	0140 0.8	0744 7.2	1353 1.3	1947 7.4
20 TH	0131 1.4	0726 6.7	1330 1.7	1932 6.9
6 TH	0228 0.8	0833 7.1	1436 1.5	2030 7.3
21 F	0206 1.4	0802 6.7	1402 1.7	2004 6.9
7 F	0314 1.0	0922 6.8	1518 1.7	2115 7.0
22 SA	0239 1.4	0838 6.6	1436 1.7	2036 6.9
8 SA	0400 1.3	1012 6.4	1600 2.1	2203 6.7
23 SU	0313 1.5	0914 6.5	1513 1.8	2113 6.8
9 SU	0445 1.7	1104 6.1	1644 2.4	2257 6.4 ☽
24 M	0351 1.6	0955 6.3	1554 2.0	2157 6.7
10 M	0534 2.0	1159 5.9	1735 2.7	2357 6.1
25 TU	0436 1.7	1043 6.1	1746 2.2	2250 6.5 ☾
11 TU	0627 2.3	1257 5.7	1836 2.8	
26 W	0532 1.9	1144 5.9	1746 2.4	2355 6.3
12 W	0102 5.9	0728 2.5	1355 5.7	1950 2.8
27 TH	0641 2.1	1300 5.9	1903 2.5	
13 TH	0208 5.9	0831 2.5	1453 5.8	2104 2.6
28 F	0116 6.1	0759 2.2	1418 6.0	2028 2.4
14 F	0310 6.0	0928 2.4	1546 6.1	2201 2.3
29 SA	0243 6.2	0914 2.0	1527 6.2	2147 2.0
15 SA	0404 6.1	1017 2.2	1631 6.3	2250 2.0
30 SU	0359 6.5	1019 1.8	1627 6.6	2254 1.6
31 M	0505 6.8	1117 1.5	1720 7.0	2352 1.1

FEBRUARY

Date	Time m	Time m	Time m	Time m
1 TU	0602 7.0	1209 1.3	1807 7.2 ●	
16 W	0000 1.5	0555 6.6	1207 1.7	1804 6.9 ○
2 W	0044 0.8	0653 7.2	1256 1.2	1852 7.4
17 TH	0040 1.3	0632 6.7	1243 1.6	1840 7.0
3 TH	0132 0.6	0738 7.2	1340 1.1	1934 7.5
18 F	0118 1.1	0708 6.8	1317 1.5	1913 7.1
4 F	0215 0.6	0819 7.1	1419 1.2	2014 7.4
19 SA	0152 1.0	0742 6.9	1349 1.4	1946 7.2
5 SA	0255 0.8	0857 6.9	1455 1.4	2052 7.3
20 SU	0223 1.0	0815 6.9	1421 1.4	2018 7.2
6 SU	0330 1.1	0933 6.6	1529 1.7	2130 6.9
21 M	0254 1.1	0849 6.8	1455 1.4	2053 7.1
7 M	0403 1.5	1009 6.2	1602 2.0	2210 6.6
22 TU	0326 1.3	0925 6.6	1531 1.6	2135 6.8
8 TU	0437 2.0	1049 5.9	1641 2.4	2257 6.1 ☾
23 W	0404 1.6	1008 6.3	1614 1.9	2224 6.5
9 W	0518 2.4	1140 5.6	1730 2.7	2359 5.7
24 TH	0454 2.1	1103 6.0	1713 2.3	2330 6.1
10 TH	0613 2.7	1250 5.4	1835 2.9	
25 F	0606 2.4	1220 5.7	1837 2.5	
11 F	0118 5.5	0724 2.9	1404 5.5	2001 2.9
26 SA	0102 5.8	0739 2.6	1354 5.7	2019 2.5
12 SA	0237 5.5	0845 2.8	1511 5.7	2135 2.6
27 SU	0249 5.9	0905 2.4	1515 6.0	2146 2.0
13 SU	0343 5.8	0952 2.5	1605 6.1	2231 2.2
28 M	0408 6.3	1013 2.0	1617 6.5	2251 1.4
14 M	0435 6.1	1043 2.2	1649 6.4	2318 1.8
15 TU	0517 6.3	1127 1.9	1728 6.7	

MARCH

Date	Time m	Time m	Time m	Time m
1 TU	0509 6.7	1108 1.6	1708 6.9	2345 1.0
16 W	0454 6.4	1105 1.9	1700 6.6	2336 1.4
2 W	0558 7.0	1157 1.3	1753 7.2 ●	
17 TH	0532 6.6	1145 1.6	1737 6.9	
3 TH	0032 0.6	0641 7.2	1241 1.1	1836 7.4
18 F	0016 1.1	0608 6.9	1221 1.4	1813 7.1 ○
4 F	0115 0.5	0719 7.2	1321 1.0	1915 7.5
19 SA	0054 0.9	0643 7.0	1257 1.2	1848 7.3
5 SA	0153 0.6	0753 7.1	1357 1.1	1951 7.5
20 SU	0129 0.8	0717 7.1	1331 1.1	1923 7.4
6 SU	0227 0.8	0823 6.9	1429 1.2	2025 7.3
21 M	0201 0.8	0750 7.1	1404 1.1	1958 7.4
7 M	0255 1.1	0851 6.7	1457 1.5	2057 7.0
22 TU	0233 0.9	0823 7.0	1438 1.2	2036 7.3
8 TU	0321 1.5	0916 6.4	1525 1.8	2129 6.6
23 W	0305 1.2	0900 6.8	1515 1.4	2119 6.9
9 W	0349 1.9	0945 6.1	1558 2.1	2207 6.1
24 TH	0342 1.6	0943 6.4	1559 1.8	2211 6.4
10 TH	0424 2.4	1025 5.7	1642 2.5	2259 5.6 ☾
25 F	0432 2.2	1038 6.0	1701 2.2	2323 5.9 ☾
11 F	0515 2.8	1127 5.4	1745 2.9	
26 SA	0549 2.7	1159 5.6	1834 2.5	
12 SA	0026 5.3	0628 3.1	1313 5.3	1908 3.0
27 SU	0117 5.6	0731 2.8	1342 5.6	2022 2.3
13 SU	0207 5.3	0759 3.1	1436 5.5	2103 2.7
28 M	0258 5.9	0858 2.5	1502 6.0	2141 1.8
14 M	0319 5.6	0928 2.7	1536 5.9	2207 2.2
29 TU	0408 6.4	1001 2.0	1601 6.5	2238 1.2
15 TU	0412 6.0	1022 2.3	1621 6.3	2254 1.8
30 W	0459 6.8	1051 1.6	1649 6.9	2326 0.9
31 TH	0541 7.0	1137 1.3	1732 7.2	

APRIL

Date	Time m	Time m	Time m	Time m
1 F	0009 0.7	0618 7.1	1218 1.1	1812 7.3 ●
16 SA	0537 7.0	1152 1.3	1742 7.2 ○	
2 SA	0048 0.6	0651 7.1	1256 1.0	1850 7.4
17 SU	0022 0.8	0614 7.1	1231 1.1	1821 7.4
3 SU	0123 0.8	0721 7.0	1331 0.9	1925 7.3
18 M	0101 0.7	0650 7.2	1310 0.9	1901 7.5
4 M	0154 1.0	0748 6.9	1401 1.2	1958 7.1
19 TU	0137 0.7	0725 7.2	1348 0.9	1942 7.5
5 TU	0220 1.3	0812 6.8	1428 1.4	2027 6.8
20 W	0213 0.9	0802 7.1	1427 1.0	2025 7.2
6 W	0245 1.6	0836 6.5	1456 1.7	2058 6.5
21 TH	0250 1.3	0842 6.9	1509 1.3	2113 6.8
7 TH	0311 1.9	0904 6.3	1527 2.0	2133 6.0
22 F	0331 1.7	0928 6.5	1559 1.7	2211 6.3
8 F	0343 2.3	0939 5.9	1609 2.4	2220 5.6
23 SA	0426 2.3	1026 6.0	1709 2.1	2336 5.8 ☾
9 SA	0430 2.8	1030 5.5	1711 2.7	2341 5.2 ☾
24 SU	0545 2.7	1150 5.7	1840 2.2	
10 SU	0541 3.1	1212 5.2	1831 2.8	
25 M	0124 5.7	0717 2.8	1325 5.8	2010 2.0
11 M	0130 5.2	0712 3.1	1353 5.4	2006 2.6
26 TU	0246 6.0	0836 2.5	1438 6.1	2118 1.6
12 TU	0245 5.5	0844 2.8	1456 5.8	2125 2.2
27 W	0349 6.4	0935 2.1	1536 6.5	2211 1.2
13 W	0339 6.0	0945 2.4	1543 6.2	2216 1.7
28 TH	0435 6.7	1025 1.7	1623 6.8	2257 1.0
14 TH	0422 6.4	1030 2.0	1624 6.6	2301 1.3
29 F	0514 6.9	1109 1.4	1706 7.0	2339 0.9
15 F	0500 6.7	1112 1.6	1703 6.9	2343 1.0
30 SA	0547 6.9	1151 1.2	1746 7.1 ●	

Chart Datum: 3·90 metres below Ordnance Datum (Newlyn)
HAT is 8·0 metres above Chart Datum

TIDES

TIDES

IMMINGHAM
LAT 53°38′N   LONG 0°11′W
TIMES AND HEIGHTS OF HIGH AND LOW WATERS

Dates in amber are **SPRINGS**
Dates in grey are **NEAPS**

2022

MAY

Time	m		Time	m
1 0016	1.0	**16** 0545	7.1
0619	6.9	1206	1.1
SU 1229	1.2	M 1757	7.4
1824	7.1	○	
2 0050	1.1	**17** 0034	0.8
0648	6.9	0626	7.3
M 1304	1.2	TU 1251	0.9
1900	7.0	1844	7.4
3 0121	1.2	**18** 0116	0.8
0716	6.9	0706	7.3
TU 1336	1.3	W 1336	0.8
1933	6.8	1931	7.3
4 0149	1.4	**19** 0158	1.0
0741	6.8	0747	7.2
W 1405	1.4	TH 1421	0.9
2004	6.6	2020	7.1
5 0215	1.7	**20** 0241	1.3
0807	6.6	0831	7.0
TH 1434	1.7	F 1510	1.1
2036	6.3	2114	6.7
6 0243	2.0	**21** 0328	1.8
0837	6.4	0921	6.6
F 1506	1.9	SA 1606	1.6
2113	6.0	2219	6.3
7 0316	2.3	**22** 0423	2.2
0912	6.0	1021	6.3
SA 1549	2.2	SU 1713	1.7
2159	5.6	☽ 2344	6.0
8 0401	2.6	**23** 0532	2.5
0959	5.7	1138	6.1
SU 1647	2.5	M 1827	1.8
2308	5.4		
9 0504	2.9	**24** 0103	5.9
1115	5.4	0649	2.6
M 1800	2.6	TU 1256	6.1
☾		1940	1.7
10 0041	5.3	**25** 0213	6.1
0623	3.0	0800	2.5
TU 1253	5.5	W 1404	6.2
1916	2.4	2042	1.6
11 0156	5.6	**26** 0312	6.3
0742	2.8	0901	2.2
W 1402	5.8	TH 1502	6.4
2028	2.1	2135	1.5
12 0254	6.0	**27** 0400	6.4
0850	2.5	0953	1.9
TH 1456	6.1	F 1553	6.6
2127	1.7	2222	1.4
13 0342	6.3	**28** 0439	6.6
0944	2.1	1040	1.7
F 1543	6.5	SA 1638	6.7
2218	1.3	2304	1.4
14 0425	6.7	**29** 0514	6.7
1033	1.7	1123	1.5
SA 1627	6.9	SU 1720	6.7
2305	1.1	2343	1.4
15 0505	6.9	**30** 0547	6.7
1120	1.3	1204	1.4
SU 1712	7.2	M 1800	6.7
2350	0.9	●	
		31 0019	1.5
		0620	6.8
		TU 1241	1.4
		1838	6.7

JUNE

Time	m		Time	m
1 0053	1.5	**16** 0100	1.0
0650	6.8	0653	7.3
W 1315	1.4	TH 1329	0.8
1914	6.6	1929	7.2
2 0124	1.6	**17** 0147	1.1
0720	6.7	0739	7.3
TH 1348	1.5	F 1419	0.8
1948	6.5	2022	7.1
3 0154	1.8	**18** 0234	1.3
0751	6.6	0825	7.1
F 1421	1.7	SA 1510	0.9
2023	6.3	2117	6.8
4 0224	2.0	**19** 0321	1.6
0823	6.5	0915	6.9
SA 1455	1.8	SU 1604	1.1
2101	6.1	2218	6.5
5 0258	2.2	**20** 0412	1.9
0858	6.2	1010	6.7
SU 1536	2.0	M 1700	1.3
2145	5.9	2322	6.3
6 0340	2.4	**21** 0507	2.2
0941	6.0	1113	6.4
M 1627	2.1	TU 1759	1.6
2241	5.7	☽	
7 0433	2.6	**22** 0024	6.1
1038	5.8	0609	2.4
TU 1727	2.2	W 1218	6.3
☽ 2349	5.6	1859	1.8
8 0536	2.7	**23** 0125	6.0
1149	5.8	0714	2.5
W 1831	2.1	TH 1322	6.2
		1959	1.9
9 0059	5.7	**24** 0222	6.0
0646	2.7	0819	2.4
TH 1300	5.9	F 1423	6.2
1935	2.0	2055	1.9
10 0202	5.9	**25** 0315	6.1
0754	2.5	0919	2.2
F 1404	6.2	SA 1520	6.2
2037	1.7	2145	1.9
11 0258	6.2	**26** 0401	6.2
0858	2.2	1011	2.0
SA 1501	6.5	SU 1612	6.3
2136	1.5	2231	1.9
12 0349	6.5	**27** 0442	6.4
0957	1.8	1058	1.8
SU 1556	6.8	M 1659	6.4
2231	1.3	2314	1.8
13 0436	6.8	**28** 0520	6.6
1052	1.5	1142	1.7
M 1649	7.0	TU 1742	6.4
2323	1.1	2354	1.8
14 0520	6.7	**29** 0556	6.7
1146	1.2	1224	1.6
TU 1742	7.2	W 1821	6.5
○		●	
15 0012	1.0	**30** 0031	1.8
0608	7.2	0631	6.8
W 1238	0.9	TH 1302	1.5
1836	7.3	1859	6.5

JULY

Time	m		Time	m
1 0106	1.8	**16** 0138	1.1
0705	6.8	0731	7.4
F 1339	1.5	SA 1414	0.5
1935	6.5	2021	7.2
2 0139	1.8	**17** 0223	1.2
0739	6.7	0816	7.4
SA 1414	1.6	SU 1501	0.6
2012	6.4	2108	7.0
3 0211	1.9	**18** 0307	1.4
0812	6.6	0901	7.3
SU 1448	1.6	M 1547	0.8
2049	6.3	2156	6.7
4 0244	2.0	**19** 0349	1.7
0846	6.5	0948	7.0
M 1524	1.7	TU 1632	1.2
2128	6.2	2244	6.4
5 0321	2.1	**20** 0432	2.0
0923	6.4	1038	6.7
TU 1605	1.8	W 1718	1.6
2211	6.1	☽ 2335	6.1
6 0404	2.2	**21** 0519	2.3
1007	6.3	1134	6.3
W 1652	1.9	TH 1806	2.0
2302	5.9		
7 0456	2.4	**22** 0029	5.8
1101	6.2	0614	2.6
TH 1746	1.9	F 1236	6.1
☾		1903	2.3
8 0001	5.9	**23** 0127	5.7
0557	2.5	0723	2.7
F 1203	6.2	SA 1342	5.9
1848	2.0	2007	2.5
9 0109	5.9	**24** 0227	5.8
0706	2.5	0842	2.6
SA 1314	6.2	SU 1449	5.8
1955	1.9	2109	2.5
10 0216	6.1	**25** 0324	5.9
0818	2.3	0947	2.4
SU 1427	6.3	M 1550	6.0
2102	1.8	2204	2.3
11 0318	6.3	**26** 0414	6.2
0929	2.0	1040	2.1
M 1535	6.5	TU 1643	6.1
2206	1.6	2251	2.1
12 0414	6.6	**27** 0458	6.5
1034	1.6	1126	1.8
TU 1639	6.8	W 1728	6.3
2304	1.4	2335	2.0
13 0507	6.9	**28** 0536	6.7
1135	1.3	1210	1.6
W 1740	7.0	TH 1807	6.4
○ 2359	1.3	●	
14 0557	7.1	**29** 0016	1.8
1232	0.9	0613	6.8
TH 1837	7.2	F 1250	1.4
		1844	6.5
15 0050	1.1	**30** 0053	1.8
0645	7.3	0649	6.9
F 1324	0.7	SA 1328	1.4
1931	7.3	1919	6.6
		31 0127	1.7
		0723	6.9
		SU 1403	1.3
		1954	6.6

AUGUST

Time	m		Time	m
1 0158	1.7	**16** 0244	1.2
0756	6.9	0838	7.5
M 1435	1.4	TU 1519	0.8
2029	6.6	2120	6.9
2 0228	1.7	**17** 0319	1.5
0828	6.8	0918	7.2
TU 1506	1.4	W 1554	1.3
2103	6.5	2157	6.5
3 0300	1.8	**18** 0353	1.8
0900	6.8	0959	6.8
W 1537	1.5	TH 1627	1.8
2138	6.4	2236	6.1
4 0336	1.9	**19** 0429	2.2
0938	6.7	1046	6.3
TH 1614	1.7	F 1704	2.3
2219	6.2	☽ 2324	5.8
5 0419	2.1	**20** 0514	2.6
1025	6.5	1146	5.8
F 1702	1.9	SA 1753	2.7
☽ 2311	6.0		
6 0514	2.4	**21** 0028	5.5
1123	6.2	0616	2.9
SA 1804	2.2	SU 1301	5.6
		1902	3.0
7 0018	5.8	**22** 0141	5.5
0627	2.5	0752	3.0
SU 1238	6.1	M 1421	5.5
1921	2.3	2034	2.9
8 0141	5.8	**23** 0251	5.7
0751	2.5	0930	2.6
M 1410	6.1	TU 1532	5.7
2041	2.2	2144	2.7
9 0257	6.1	**24** 0349	6.1
0916	2.2	1024	2.2
TU 1534	6.3	W 1627	6.1
2153	2.0	2234	2.3
10 0402	6.5	**25** 0435	6.4
1029	1.7	1109	1.8
W 1643	6.7	TH 1710	6.3
2255	1.7	2318	2.0
11 0457	6.9	**26** 0514	6.7
1131	1.2	1151	1.5
TH 1743	7.0	F 1747	6.6
2349	1.4	2359	1.8
12 0546	7.2	**27** 0550	6.9
1225	0.8	1231	1.3
F 1835	7.2	SA 1822	6.7
○		●	
13 0038	1.2	**28** 0035	1.7
0633	7.5	0626	7.0
SA 1314	0.5	SU 1308	1.2
1922	7.3	1856	6.8
14 0124	1.1	**29** 0108	1.6
0716	7.6	0700	7.1
SU 1359	0.4	M 1342	1.1
2005	7.3	1930	6.9
15 0205	1.1	**30** 0138	1.5
0758	7.6	0732	7.2
M 1441	0.5	TU 1412	1.1
2043	7.1	2002	6.9
		31 0207	1.7
		0803	7.2
		W 1440	1.2
		2033	6.8

Chart Datum: 3·90 metres below Ordnance Datum (Newlyn)
HAT is 8·0 metres above Chart Datum

TIME ZONE (UT)
For Summer Time add ONE hour in **non-shaded areas**

IMMINGHAM
LAT 53°38′N   LONG 0°11′W
TIMES AND HEIGHTS OF HIGH AND LOW WATERS

Dates in amber are **SPRINGS**
Dates in grey are **NEAPS**

2022

SEPTEMBER

Day	Time	m	Day	Time	m
1 TH	0238 / 0835 / 1508 / 2105	1.6 / 7.1 / 1.4 / 6.7	**16** F	0314 / 0920 / 1537 / 2136	1.8 / 6.7 / 1.9 / 6.3
2 F	0310 / 0912 / 1540 / 2143	1.7 / 6.9 / 1.7 / 6.4	**17** SA ☽	0346 / 0959 / 1609 / 2213	2.2 / 6.2 / 2.4 / 5.9
3 SA ☽	0350 / 0958 / 1623 / 2232	2.0 / 6.6 / 2.0 / 6.1	**18** SU	0427 / 1053 / 1656 / 2315	2.6 / 5.7 / 2.9 / 5.5
4 SU	0442 / 1058 / 1727 / 2341	2.3 / 6.1 / 2.5 / 5.8	**19** M	0528 / 1222 / 1806	2.9 / 5.3 / 3.2
5 M	0602 / 1225 / 1900	2.6 / 5.8 / 2.7	**20** TU	0057 / 0656 / 1355 / 1950	5.4 / 3.1 / 5.3 / 3.2
6 TU	0118 / 0742 / 1417 / 2034	5.7 / 2.6 / 5.9 / 2.6	**21** W	0219 / 0907 / 1507 / 2122	5.6 / 2.7 / 5.7 / 2.9
7 W	0246 / 0918 / 1542 / 2148	6.0 / 2.2 / 6.3 / 2.2	**22** TH	0320 / 0959 / 1602 / 2212	6.0 / 2.2 / 6.1 / 2.4
8 TH	0351 / 1027 / 1644 / 2245	6.5 / 1.6 / 6.7 / 1.8	**23** F	0406 / 1042 / 1644 / 2254	6.4 / 1.8 / 6.4 / 2.1
9 F	0444 / 1122 / 1736 / 2335	7.0 / 1.0 / 7.1 / 1.4	**24** SA	0445 / 1122 / 1719 / 2332	6.7 / 1.4 / 6.7 / 1.8
10 SA ○	0529 / 1210 / 1820	7.3 / 0.6 / 7.3	**25** SU ●	0520 / 1201 / 1753	7.0 / 1.2 / 6.9
11 SU	0020 / 0613 / 1255 / 1900	1.1 / 7.6 / 0.4 / 7.4	**26** M	0008 / 0556 / 1238 / 1827	1.6 / 7.1 / 1.0 / 7.0
12 M	0102 / 0653 / 1335 / 1936	1.0 / 7.7 / 0.4 / 7.3	**27** TU	0041 / 0630 / 1312 / 1900	1.5 / 7.3 / 1.0 / 7.1
13 TU	0141 / 0732 / 1411 / 2009	1.0 / 7.7 / 0.7 / 7.2	**28** W	0113 / 0704 / 1343 / 1931	1.4 / 7.4 / 1.0 / 7.1
14 W	0215 / 0809 / 1443 / 2039	1.2 / 7.5 / 1.0 / 6.9	**29** TH	0144 / 0738 / 1412 / 2003	1.4 / 7.4 / 1.2 / 7.0
15 TH	0246 / 0845 / 1510 / 2107	1.4 / 7.2 / 1.5 / 6.6	**30** F	0217 / 0813 / 1441 / 2036	1.4 / 7.2 / 1.4 / 6.8

OCTOBER

Day	Time	m	Day	Time	m
1 SA	0251 / 0854 / 1515 / 2115	1.6 / 6.9 / 1.8 / 6.5	**16** SU	0313 / 0923 / 1527 / 2125	2.1 / 6.2 / 2.5 / 6.1
2 SU	0331 / 0942 / 1559 / 2205	1.9 / 6.5 / 2.3 / 6.1	**17** M ☽	0353 / 1012 / 1611 / 2215	2.5 / 5.7 / 2.9 / 5.7
3 M ☽	0429 / 1050 / 1708 / 2319	2.3 / 6.0 / 2.8 / 5.7	**18** TU	0453 / 1138 / 1718	2.9 / 5.3 / 3.3
4 TU	0558 / 1239 / 1851	2.6 / 5.7 / 3.0	**19** W	0000 / 0617 / 1318 / 1852	5.4 / 3.0 / 5.3 / 3.4
5 W	0105 / 0746 / 1424 / 2026	5.7 / 2.5 / 5.9 / 2.7	**20** TH	0136 / 0810 / 1430 / 2037	5.5 / 2.8 / 5.6 / 3.0
6 TH	0231 / 0912 / 1537 / 2134	6.1 / 1.9 / 6.4 / 2.3	**21** F	0240 / 0917 / 1525 / 2134	5.9 / 2.3 / 6.0 / 2.6
7 F	0333 / 1012 / 1632 / 2226	6.6 / 1.4 / 6.8 / 1.8	**22** SA	0327 / 1002 / 1607 / 2217	6.3 / 1.8 / 6.4 / 2.2
8 SA	0422 / 1101 / 1714 / 2312	7.0 / 0.9 / 7.1 / 1.4	**23** SU	0407 / 1044 / 1644 / 2255	6.6 / 1.5 / 6.7 / 1.9
9 SU ○	0506 / 1146 / 1755 / 2356	7.4 / 0.7 / 7.3 / 1.4	**24** M	0444 / 1124 / 1719 / 2333	6.9 / 1.2 / 7.0 / 1.6
10 M	0547 / 1227 / 1829	7.6 / 0.6 / 7.3	**25** TU ●	0521 / 1202 / 1754	7.2 / 1.1 / 7.1
11 TU	0036 / 0627 / 1304 / 1902	1.1 / 7.6 / 0.7 / 7.3	**26** W	0010 / 0559 / 1238 / 1829	1.4 / 7.4 / 1.0 / 7.2
12 W	0113 / 0705 / 1337 / 1932	1.1 / 7.5 / 1.0 / 7.1	**27** TH	0046 / 0638 / 1313 / 1903	1.3 / 7.4 / 1.0 / 7.3
13 TH	0145 / 0741 / 1405 / 2000	1.2 / 7.3 / 1.3 / 7.0	**28** F	0123 / 0717 / 1347 / 1938	1.2 / 7.4 / 1.2 / 7.2
14 F	0214 / 0814 / 1431 / 2025	1.5 / 7.0 / 1.6 / 6.7	**29** SA	0201 / 0759 / 1423 / 2016	1.3 / 7.2 / 1.4 / 7.0
15 SA	0242 / 0847 / 1456 / 2051	1.7 / 6.6 / 2.0 / 6.4	**30** SU	0241 / 0845 / 1502 / 2059	1.5 / 6.9 / 1.9 / 6.7
			31 M	0329 / 0940 / 1551 / 2152	1.8 / 6.4 / 2.4 / 6.3

NOVEMBER

Day	Time	m	Day	Time	m
1 TU ☽	0434 / 1057 / 1703 / 2308	2.2 / 5.9 / 2.8 / 5.9	**16** W ☽	0426 / 1054 / 1637 / 2253	2.6 / 5.5 / 3.1 / 5.6
2 W	0601 / 1245 / 1836	2.3 / 5.8 / 3.0	**17** TH	0538 / 1222 / 1753	2.7 / 5.4 / 3.2
3 TH	0046 / 0734 / 1408 / 2000	5.9 / 2.2 / 6.0 / 2.7	**18** F	0031 / 0657 / 1335 / 1916	5.6 / 2.6 / 5.6 / 3.1
4 F	0204 / 0847 / 1515 / 2105	6.2 / 1.8 / 6.4 / 2.3	**19** SA	0141 / 0809 / 1433 / 2028	5.8 / 2.3 / 5.9 / 2.8
5 SA	0305 / 0943 / 1606 / 2158	6.6 / 1.4 / 6.8 / 1.9	**20** SU	0236 / 0907 / 1522 / 2123	6.1 / 2.0 / 6.3 / 2.4
6 SU	0355 / 1031 / 1648 / 2244	7.0 / 1.1 / 7.0 / 1.6	**21** M	0322 / 0956 / 1604 / 2211	6.5 / 1.6 / 6.6 / 2.0
7 M	0439 / 1114 / 1724 / 2328	7.2 / 1.0 / 7.1 / 1.4	**22** TU	0406 / 1041 / 1644 / 2256	6.8 / 1.4 / 6.9 / 1.7
8 TU ○	0521 / 1154 / 1757	7.3 / 1.0 / 7.1	**23** W ●	0449 / 1125 / 1723 / 2340	7.1 / 1.2 / 7.1 / 1.4
9 W	0008 / 0602 / 1230 / 1830	1.3 / 7.3 / 1.2 / 7.1	**24** TH	0533 / 1207 / 1802	7.3 / 1.1 / 7.2
10 TH	0045 / 0640 / 1302 / 1900	1.3 / 7.2 / 1.3 / 7.1	**25** F	0024 / 0618 / 1248 / 1842	1.2 / 7.4 / 1.1 / 7.3
11 F	0119 / 0716 / 1332 / 1928	1.4 / 7.0 / 1.5 / 7.0	**26** SA	0108 / 0705 / 1330 / 1922	1.1 / 7.3 / 1.2 / 7.3
12 SA	0149 / 0750 / 1359 / 1955	1.5 / 6.8 / 1.8 / 6.8	**27** SU	0153 / 0753 / 1412 / 2005	1.1 / 7.2 / 1.5 / 7.1
13 SU	0218 / 0824 / 1426 / 2024	1.7 / 6.5 / 2.1 / 6.6	**28** M	0241 / 0844 / 1457 / 2051	1.3 / 6.9 / 1.8 / 6.9
14 M	0250 / 0901 / 1459 / 2057	2.0 / 6.1 / 2.4 / 6.3	**29** TU	0334 / 0944 / 1549 / 2146	1.5 / 6.5 / 2.2 / 6.6
15 TU	0331 / 0947 / 1540 / 2142	2.3 / 5.8 / 2.7 / 5.9	**30** W ☽	0437 / 1100 / 1652 / 2255	1.8 / 6.2 / 2.6 / 6.3

DECEMBER

Day	Time	m	Day	Time	m
1 TH	0549 / 1222 / 1806	1.9 / 6.0 / 2.7	**16** F ☽	0457 / 1118 / 1700 / 2313	2.4 / 5.7 / 2.9 / 5.9
2 F	0015 / 0702 / 1332 / 1921	6.2 / 1.9 / 6.1 / 2.7	**17** SA	0559 / 1227 / 1807	2.4 / 5.7 / 2.9
3 SA	0126 / 0809 / 1435 / 2027	6.3 / 1.8 / 6.3 / 2.4	**18** SU	0025 / 0704 / 1331 / 1918	5.9 / 2.3 / 5.8 / 2.8
4 SU	0229 / 0906 / 1529 / 2125	6.5 / 1.7 / 6.5 / 2.1	**19** M	0132 / 0807 / 1430 / 2025	6.0 / 2.1 / 6.0 / 2.5
5 M	0324 / 0956 / 1613 / 2215	6.7 / 1.6 / 6.6 / 1.9	**20** TU	0233 / 0907 / 1523 / 2126	6.2 / 1.9 / 6.3 / 2.2
6 TU	0413 / 1041 / 1652 / 2301	6.8 / 1.5 / 6.8 / 1.7	**21** W	0329 / 1002 / 1612 / 2223	6.6 / 1.6 / 6.6 / 1.8
7 W	0458 / 1122 / 1728 / 2344	6.9 / 1.5 / 6.9 / 1.5	**22** TH	0423 / 1054 / 1658 / 2317	6.9 / 1.4 / 6.9 / 1.5
8 TH ○	0541 / 1200 / 1802	6.9 / 1.6 / 6.9	**23** F	0516 / 1144 / 1743	7.1 / 1.3 / 7.1
9 F	0023 / 0621 / 1234 / 1836	1.5 / 6.8 / 1.6 / 7.0	**24** SA	0009 / 0609 / 1232 / 1829	1.2 / 7.2 / 1.2 / 7.3
10 SA	0100 / 0659 / 1306 / 1907	1.5 / 6.7 / 1.7 / 6.9	**25** SU	0101 / 0701 / 1319 / 1913	1.0 / 7.3 / 1.2 / 7.4
11 SU	0133 / 0734 / 1337 / 1938	1.6 / 6.6 / 1.9 / 6.8	**26** M	0151 / 0753 / 1405 / 1958	0.9 / 7.2 / 1.3 / 7.3
12 M	0205 / 0809 / 1407 / 2009	1.7 / 6.4 / 2.0 / 6.7	**27** TU	0241 / 0846 / 1451 / 2045	0.9 / 7.0 / 1.5 / 7.2
13 TU	0239 / 0846 / 1440 / 2042	1.9 / 6.2 / 2.2 / 6.4	**28** W	0332 / 0941 / 1539 / 2136	1.0 / 6.7 / 1.8 / 7.0
14 W	0316 / 0927 / 1517 / 2121	2.1 / 6.0 / 2.4 / 6.2	**29** TH	0425 / 1041 / 1630 / 2233	1.3 / 6.4 / 2.1 / 6.7
15 TH	0402 / 1016 / 1603 / 2210	2.2 / 5.8 / 2.7 / 6.0	**30** F ☽	0521 / 1143 / 1727 / 2336	1.6 / 6.2 / 2.4 / 6.5
			31 SA	0620 / 1244 / 1830	1.8 / 6.0 / 2.4

Chart Datum: 3·90 metres below Ordnance Datum (Newlyn)
HAT is 8·0 metres above Chart Datum

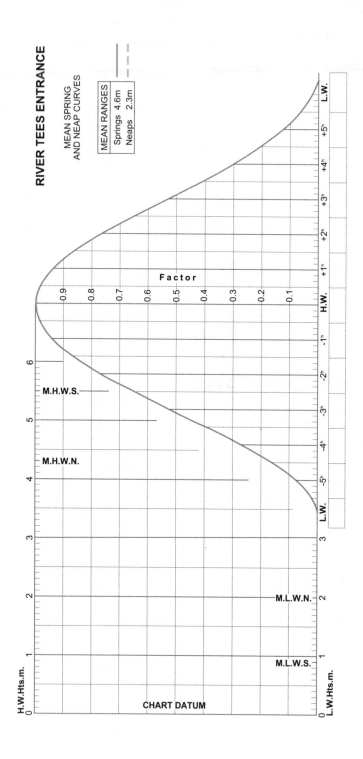

RIVER TEES ENTRANCE

MEAN SPRING
AND NEAP CURVES

MEAN RANGES	
Springs	4.6m
Neaps	2.3m

RIVER TEES

LAT 54°38'N   LONG 1°09'W

TIMES AND HEIGHTS OF HIGH AND LOW WATERS

Dates in amber are SPRINGS
Dates in grey are NEAPS

2022

JANUARY

Day	Time m	Time m	Time m	Time m
1 SA	0142 5.2	0813 1.1	1413 5.2	2039 1.1
16 SU	0239 4.7	0851 1.7	1458 4.9	2116 1.4
2 SU ●	0240 5.3	0907 1.0	1504 5.4	2134 0.9
17 M ○	0320 4.8	0928 1.6	1533 5.0	2154 1.3
3 M	0335 5.5	0958 0.9	1553 5.5	2226 0.7
18 TU	0357 4.9	1002 1.5	1606 5.1	2230 1.1
4 TU	0428 5.5	1047 1.0	1641 5.6	2317 0.6
19 W	0432 5.0	1036 1.4	1638 5.2	2305 1.1
5 W	0520 5.4	1134 1.1	1727 5.6	
20 TH	0507 5.0	1110 1.4	1712 5.2	2341 1.0
6 TH	0005 0.6	0611 5.3	1219 1.2	1814 5.5
21 F	0542 5.0	1145 1.4	1746 5.2	
7 F	0052 0.7	0701 5.1	1304 1.5	1901 5.3
22 SA	0016 1.0	0621 4.9	1221 1.5	1824 5.1
8 SA	0139 0.9	0751 4.8	1350 1.7	1950 5.1
23 SU	0055 1.1	0702 4.9	1258 1.6	1904 5.1
9 SU ◖	0228 1.2	0844 4.6	1440 2.0	2043 4.8
24 M	0137 1.2	0748 4.7	1341 1.7	1950 4.9
10 M	0322 1.5	0940 4.4	1538 2.2	2142 4.6
25 TU ◖	0224 1.3	0840 4.6	1431 1.8	2045 4.8
11 TU	0422 1.8	1040 4.3	1645 2.3	2247 4.4
26 W	0321 1.5	0939 4.5	1536 2.0	2152 4.7
12 W	0530 2.0	1143 4.2	1755 2.2	2355 4.3
27 TH	0428 1.6	1045 4.4	1654 2.0	2307 4.6
13 TH	0634 2.0	1244 4.4	1858 2.1	
28 F	0543 1.7	1154 4.5	1814 1.8	
14 F	0058 4.4	0727 1.9	1335 4.5	1950 1.8
29 SA	0023 4.7	0658 1.6	1301 4.7	1931 1.5
15 SA	0153 4.5	0812 1.8	1419 4.7	2035 1.6
30 SU	0136 4.9	0805 1.4	1403 5.0	2036 1.2
31 M	0239 5.1	0901 1.2	1457 5.2	2132 0.8

FEBRUARY

Day	Time m	Time m	Time m	Time m
1 TU ●	0333 5.3	0952 1.0	1545 5.4	2222 0.6
16 W ○	0341 4.9	0948 1.4	1548 5.1	2213 0.9
2 W	0423 5.4	1038 1.0	1630 5.6	2308 0.4
17 TH	0414 5.0	1021 1.2	1620 5.3	2247 0.8
3 TH	0508 5.4	1120 1.0	1712 5.6	2350 0.4
18 F	0447 5.1	1054 1.1	1651 5.3	2321 0.7
4 F	0552 5.3	1200 1.0	1753 5.6	
19 SA	0520 5.2	1127 1.1	1723 5.4	2355 0.7
5 SA	0029 0.6	0634 5.2	1236 1.2	1834 5.4
20 SU	0555 5.2	1201 1.1	1757 5.4	
6 SU	0107 0.8	0715 4.9	1313 1.4	1915 5.2
21 M	0031 0.7	0634 5.1	1235 1.2	1836 5.3
7 M	0145 1.2	0757 4.7	1351 1.7	2000 4.9
22 TU	0109 0.9	0715 4.9	1313 1.4	1921 5.1
8 TU ◐	0225 1.6	0843 4.4	1435 2.0	2051 4.6
23 W ◐	0153 1.2	0804 4.7	1400 1.6	2016 4.8
9 W	0312 1.9	0935 4.2	1533 2.2	2153 4.3
24 TH	0245 1.5	0902 4.4	1501 1.8	2126 4.5
10 TH	0417 2.2	1039 4.0	1707 2.3	2307 4.1
25 F	0356 1.8	1013 4.3	1628 2.0	2251 4.4
11 F	0542 2.3	1153 4.1	1821 2.2	
26 SA	0524 2.0	1133 4.3	1808 1.9	
12 SA	0025 4.1	0657 2.2	1303 4.2	1927 2.0
27 SU	0022 4.4	0654 1.8	1253 4.5	1934 1.5
13 SU	0132 4.3	0751 2.0	1357 4.5	2017 1.7
28 M	0140 4.7	0802 1.6	1358 4.8	2036 1.1
14 M	0233 4.5	0855 1.8	1439 4.7	2059 1.4
15 TU	0304 4.7	0913 1.6	1515 4.9	2138 1.1

MARCH

Day	Time m	Time m	Time m	Time m
1 TU	0239 5.0	0854 1.3	1449 5.2	2126 0.7
16 W	0239 4.7	0849 1.5	1447 4.9	2112 1.0
2 W ●	0326 5.2	0940 1.1	1534 5.4	2210 0.4
17 TH	0314 5.0	0924 1.3	1520 5.1	2148 0.7
3 TH	0409 5.4	1021 0.9	1613 5.6	2250 0.3
18 F ○	0347 5.1	0958 1.1	1552 5.3	2222 0.5
4 F	0448 5.4	1058 0.9	1651 5.6	2326 0.4
19 SA	0419 5.3	1031 0.9	1624 5.5	2255 0.4
5 SA	0525 5.3	1133 0.9	1726 5.6	2359 0.6
20 SU	0453 5.3	1104 0.8	1657 5.6	2330 0.4
6 SU	0600 5.2	1205 1.0	1803 5.4	
21 M	0528 5.3	1138 0.8	1734 5.5	
7 M	0030 0.8	0635 5.0	1236 1.2	1841 5.2
22 TU	0006 0.6	0606 5.2	1213 0.9	1815 5.4
8 TU	0101 1.2	0710 4.7	1309 1.5	1921 4.9
23 W	0044 0.8	0647 5.0	1254 1.1	1903 5.1
9 W	0132 1.6	0749 4.5	1346 1.8	2007 4.5
24 TH	0128 1.2	0736 4.7	1342 1.4	2002 4.7
10 TH	0209 1.9	0836 4.2	1434 2.1	2105 4.2
25 F	0221 1.7	0835 4.4	1447 1.7	2118 4.4
11 F	0301 2.3	0937 4.0	1556 2.3	2220 3.9
26 SA	0338 2.0	0952 4.2	1625 1.9	2251 4.2
12 SA	0439 2.5	1058 3.9	1742 2.3	2351 3.9
27 SU	0520 2.1	1122 4.2	1814 1.7	
13 SU	0623 2.4	1225 4.0	1858 2.0	
28 M	0028 4.4	0650 1.9	1246 4.5	1930 1.3
14 M	0107 4.1	0725 2.1	1327 4.3	1951 1.7
29 TU	0137 4.7	0750 1.6	1346 4.8	2024 0.9
15 TU	0159 4.4	0811 1.8	1411 4.6	2034 1.3
30 W	0228 5.0	0838 1.3	1433 5.2	2109 0.6
31 TH	0310 5.2	0919 1.1	1514 5.4	2148 0.5

APRIL

Day	Time m	Time m	Time m	Time m
1 F ●	0347 5.3	0956 0.9	1550 5.5	2223 0.5
16 SA ○	0313 5.2	0927 1.0	1519 5.4	2151 0.4
2 SA	0422 5.3	1031 0.9	1624 5.5	2255 0.6
17 SU	0348 5.4	1003 0.8	1555 5.6	2228 0.4
3 SU	0454 5.2	1103 0.9	1658 5.4	2325 0.7
18 M	0424 5.4	1040 0.7	1634 5.6	2305 0.4
4 M	0525 5.1	1134 0.9	1733 5.3	2354 1.0
19 TU	0502 5.4	1118 0.7	1716 5.6	2344 0.6
5 TU	0556 5.0	1205 1.1	1809 5.1	
20 W	0543 5.3	1159 0.8	1804 5.3	
6 W	0021 1.3	0629 4.8	1237 1.3	1849 4.8
21 TH	0025 0.9	0628 5.1	1243 1.0	1858 5.0
7 TH	0051 1.6	0706 4.6	1313 1.6	1934 4.5
22 F	0112 1.3	0719 4.8	1338 1.3	2002 4.6
8 F	0127 1.9	0751 4.4	1359 1.9	2028 4.1
23 SA ◐	0211 1.8	0821 4.5	1452 1.6	2120 4.3
9 SA ◐	0215 2.3	0849 4.0	1509 2.2	2138 3.9
24 SU	0333 2.1	0940 4.3	1628 1.6	2251 4.3
10 SU	0337 2.6	1004 3.9	1655 2.2	2308 3.9
25 M	0508 2.2	1108 4.3	1801 1.4	
11 M	0536 2.5	1132 4.0	1817 1.9	
26 TU	0017 4.4	0628 1.9	1225 4.6	1909 1.2
12 TU	0027 4.1	0646 2.2	1240 4.2	1913 1.6
27 W	0118 4.7	0725 1.7	1323 4.8	2000 0.9
13 W	0121 4.4	0734 1.9	1328 4.6	1958 1.2
28 TH	0205 4.9	0811 1.4	1409 5.1	2043 0.8
14 TH	0202 4.7	0814 1.5	1408 4.9	2037 0.9
29 F	0245 5.1	0852 1.2	1448 5.2	2120 0.7
15 F	0238 5.0	0851 1.2	1444 5.2	2114 0.6
30 SA ●	0320 5.1	0928 1.2	1524 5.3	2153 0.7

Chart Datum: 2·85 metres below Ordnance Datum (Newlyn)
HAT is 6·1 metres above Chart Datum

TIDES

TIME ZONE (UT)	RIVER TEES	Dates in amber are **SPRINGS**
For Summer Time add ONE hour in **non-shaded areas**	LAT 54°38'N LONG 1°09'W	Dates in grey are **NEAPS**
	TIMES AND HEIGHTS OF HIGH AND LOW WATERS	**2022**

MAY

Time	m		Time	m
1 0353	5.2	**16** 0318	5.3
1002	1.0	0937	0.8
SU 1558	5.3	M 1532	5.5
2223	0.8	○ 2203	0.5
2 0423	5.1	**17** 0359	5.4
1035	0.9	1020	0.6
M 1633	5.2	TU 1618	5.6
2253	1.0	2245	0.5
3 0452	5.1	**18** 0442	5.4
1107	1.0	1104	0.6
TU 1708	5.1	W 1708	5.5
2321	1.2	2329	0.7
4 0523	5.0	**19** 0527	5.3
1140	1.1	1152	0.7
W 1744	4.9	TH 1801	5.3
2350	1.4		
5 0556	4.8	**20** 0015	1.0
1214	1.3	0616	5.1
TH 1824	4.7	F 1243	0.9
		1859	5.0
6 0022	1.6	**21** 0107	1.4
0635	4.6	0710	4.9
F 1252	1.5	SA 1343	1.1
1909	4.4	2003	4.7
7 0100	1.9	**22** 0208	1.8
0720	4.4	0812	4.7
SA 1338	1.8	SU 1453	1.3
2001	4.2	◑ 2115	4.5
8 0148	2.2	**23** 0321	2.0
0815	4.2	0924	4.5
SU 1440	2.0	M 1611	1.4
2103	4.0	2231	4.4
9 0257	2.4	**24** 0438	2.1
0920	4.1	1041	4.5
M 1603	2.0	TU 1728	1.3
◑ 2217	4.0	2345	4.5
10 0434	2.4	**25** 0550	2.0
1034	4.1	1152	4.6
TU 1720	1.8	W 1833	1.2
2330	4.1		
11 0548	2.2	**26** 0045	4.6
1142	4.3	0650	1.8
W 1821	1.6	TH 1250	4.8
		1927	1.1
12 0029	4.4	**27** 0134	4.7
0644	1.9	0739	1.6
TH 1236	4.6	F 1339	4.9
1911	1.2	2011	1.1
13 0116	4.7	**28** 0215	4.9
0730	1.6	0822	1.4
F 1323	4.9	SA 1421	5.0
1956	0.9	2049	1.1
14 0157	5.0	**29** 0252	4.9
0813	1.3	0901	1.2
SA 1406	5.2	SU 1500	5.0
2038	0.7	2123	1.1
15 0238	5.2	**30** 0325	5.0
0855	1.0	0937	1.1
SU 1448	5.4	M 1537	5.0
2120	0.5	● 2155	1.2
		31 0357	5.0
		1012	1.1
		TU 1613	5.0
		2226	1.3

JUNE

Time	m		Time	m
1 0427	5.0	**16** 0428	5.4
1047	1.1	1059	0.6
W 1650	4.9	TH 1704	5.4
2256	1.3	2322	0.9
2 0459	5.0	**17** 0517	5.4
1122	1.2	1151	0.6
TH 1727	4.8	F 1759	5.3
2328	1.5		
3 0534	4.9	**18** 0011	1.1
1159	1.3	0607	5.3
F 1807	4.7	SA 1244	0.7
		1855	5.1
4 0003	1.6	**19** 0102	1.3
0613	4.8	0700	5.2
SA 1238	1.4	SU 1339	0.8
1850	4.5	1953	4.9
5 0042	1.8	**20** 0156	1.6
0657	4.6	0756	5.0
SU 1322	1.6	M 1437	1.0
1938	4.4	2053	4.7
6 0128	2.0	**21** 0255	1.8
0746	4.5	0857	4.8
M 1415	1.7	TU 1539	1.2
2032	4.3	◑ 2155	4.5
7 0225	2.2	**22** 0358	2.0
0842	4.4	1002	4.7
TU 1516	1.7	W 1644	1.4
◑ 2132	4.2	2300	4.4
8 0335	2.2	**23** 0504	2.0
0944	4.3	1108	4.6
W 1621	1.7	TH 1749	1.5
2234	4.3		
9 0446	2.1	**24** 0002	4.4
1047	4.4	0608	1.9
TH 1723	1.5	F 1211	4.6
2334	4.4	1848	1.5
10 0548	1.9	**25** 0057	4.5
1146	4.6	0705	1.8
F 1821	1.3	SA 1308	4.7
		1937	1.5
11 0029	4.6	**26** 0144	4.6
0644	1.7	0754	1.6
SA 1241	4.9	SU 1357	4.7
1915	1.1	2020	1.5
12 0119	4.9	**27** 0226	4.8
0736	1.4	0838	1.5
SU 1334	5.1	M 1442	4.8
2006	0.9	2058	1.5
13 0207	5.1	**28** 0303	4.9
0827	1.1	0918	1.3
M 1425	5.3	TU 1522	4.8
2055	0.8	2134	1.5
14 0254	5.3	**29** 0338	4.9
0917	0.9	0956	1.2
TU 1517	5.4	W 1600	4.9
○ 2145	0.7	● 2207	1.5
15 0341	5.4	**30** 0410	5.0
1007	0.7	1033	1.2
W 1610	5.5	TH 1637	4.9
2233	0.8	2240	1.5

JULY

Time	m		Time	m
1 0443	5.0	**16** 0507	5.6
1109	1.2	1146	0.4
F 1713	4.8	SA 1749	5.4
2314	1.5		
2 0517	5.0	**17** 0001	1.0
1146	1.2	0554	5.6
SA 1750	4.8	SU 1233	0.4
2350	1.6	1840	5.3
3 0554	4.9	**18** 0046	1.2
1223	1.3	0641	5.5
SU 1830	4.7	M 1320	0.6
		1929	5.1
4 0027	1.7	**19** 0132	1.4
0634	4.8	0730	5.3
M 1303	1.3	TU 1408	0.9
1913	4.6	2019	4.8
5 0108	1.8	**20** 0219	1.6
0717	4.8	0821	5.0
TU 1347	1.4	W 1458	1.3
2000	4.5	◑ 2111	4.6
6 0153	1.9	**21** 0312	1.9
0804	4.7	0918	4.7
W 1436	1.5	TH 1554	1.6
2051	4.5	2208	4.3
7 0246	2.0	**22** 0413	2.1
0858	4.6	1021	4.5
TH 1532	1.5	F 1657	1.9
◑ 2148	4.4	2310	4.2
8 0349	2.0	**23** 0523	2.1
0959	4.6	1130	4.4
F 1634	1.5	SA 1805	2.0
2248	4.4		
9 0457	2.0	**24** 0015	4.3
1104	4.7	0632	2.0
SA 1738	1.5	SU 1239	4.4
2349	4.5	1907	2.0
10 0604	1.8	**25** 0114	4.4
1209	4.8	0731	1.8
SU 1841	1.4	M 1338	4.5
		1957	1.9
11 0048	4.7	**26** 0204	4.6
0708	1.5	0820	1.6
M 1313	5.0	TU 1427	4.6
1943	1.2	2040	1.8
12 0145	4.9	**27** 0246	4.8
0809	1.2	0903	1.4
TU 1414	5.2	W 1510	4.8
2041	1.1	2118	1.6
13 0239	5.2	**28** 0323	4.9
0908	0.9	0942	1.3
W 1511	5.3	TH 1548	4.9
○ 2135	1.0	● 2154	1.5
14 0330	5.4	**29** 0356	5.1
1003	0.7	1019	1.1
TH 1606	5.5	F 1623	4.9
2226	0.9	2227	1.4
15 0419	5.5	**30** 0428	5.1
1056	0.5	1054	1.1
F 1659	5.5	SA 1657	5.0
2315	0.9	2300	1.4
		31 0500	5.2
		1128	1.0
		SU 1730	5.0
		2334	1.4

AUGUST

Time	m		Time	m
1 0532	5.2	**16** 0020	1.0
1203	1.0	0614	5.6
M 1805	5.0	TU 1251	0.6
		1856	5.2
2 0007	1.4	**17** 0058	1.2
0607	5.1	0657	5.4
TU 1238	1.1	W 1330	1.0
1844	4.9	1938	4.9
3 0043	1.5	**18** 0137	1.5
0644	5.1	0742	5.1
W 1317	1.2	TH 1411	1.4
1925	4.8	2023	4.6
4 0121	1.6	**19** 0221	1.8
0725	5.0	0833	4.7
TH 1400	1.3	F 1457	1.8
2012	4.6	◑ 2114	4.3
5 0205	1.8	**20** 0318	2.1
0816	4.8	0935	4.4
F 1451	1.5	SA 1559	2.2
2106	4.5	2216	4.1
6 0301	1.9	**21** 0437	2.3
0918	4.7	1050	4.2
SA 1553	1.7	SU 1721	2.4
2209	4.4	2331	4.1
7 0415	2.0	**22** 0603	2.2
1032	4.6	1213	4.2
SU 1706	1.8	M 1839	2.3
2318	4.4		
8 0537	1.9	**23** 0045	4.3
1151	4.6	0711	2.0
M 1822	1.7	TU 1321	4.3
		1937	2.1
9 0028	4.6	**24** 0142	4.5
0657	1.6	0803	1.7
TU 1306	4.8	W 1412	4.6
1934	1.5	2022	1.9
10 0133	4.8	**25** 0226	4.8
0806	1.3	0845	1.4
W 1412	5.1	TH 1453	4.8
2035	1.3	2100	1.7
11 0230	5.1	**26** 0303	5.0
0905	0.9	0923	1.1
TH 1509	5.3	F 1529	5.0
2128	1.1	2135	1.5
12 0321	5.4	**27** 0336	5.1
0958	0.6	0959	1.0
F 1559	5.5	SA 1601	5.1
○ 2216	0.9	● 2208	1.3
13 0407	5.6	**28** 0406	5.3
1046	0.3	1032	0.9
SA 1646	5.6	SU 1632	5.2
2300	0.9	2240	1.2
14 0450	5.7	**29** 0435	5.4
1130	0.3	1104	0.8
SU 1730	5.5	M 1703	5.3
2342	0.9	2311	1.2
15 0532	5.7	**30** 0505	5.4
1211	0.4	1136	0.8
M 1813	5.4	TU 1736	5.3
		2343	1.2
		31 0537	5.4
		1210	0.9
		W 1811	5.1

Chart Datum: 2·85 metres below Ordnance Datum (Newlyn)
HAT is 6·1 metres above Chart Datum

TIME ZONE (UT)	RIVER TEES	Dates in amber are SPRINGS
For Summer Time add ONE hour in **non-shaded areas**	LAT 54°38'N LONG 1°09'W	Dates in grey are NEAPS
	TIMES AND HEIGHTS OF HIGH AND LOW WATERS	**2022**

SEPTEMBER

Day				
1 TH	0015 1.3	0612 5.3	1246 1.0	1850 5.0
16 F	0057 1.4	0705 5.0	1321 1.6	1934 4.6
2 F	0051 1.4	0653 5.1	1327 1.3	1935 4.8
17 SA	0136 1.7	0752 4.6	1358 2.0	2019 4.4
3 SA ☾	0133 1.6	0744 4.9	1416 1.6	2029 4.5
18 SU	0226 2.1	0851 4.3	1451 2.0	2120 4.1
4 SU	0229 1.9	0851 4.6	1520 1.9	2137 4.3
19 M	0350 2.3	1011 4.0	1632 2.6	2242 4.0
5 M	0350 2.0	1017 4.4	1647 2.1	2256 4.3
20 TU	0532 2.3	1144 4.0	1810 2.5	
6 TU	0531 2.0	1149 4.5	1818 2.0	
21 W	0010 4.2	0645 2.0	1258 4.3	1911 2.3
7 W	0017 4.5	0700 1.6	1311 4.7	1931 1.7
22 TH	0113 4.4	0737 1.7	1347 4.6	1956 2.0
8 TH	0127 4.8	0805 1.1	1411 5.1	2027 1.4
23 F	0157 4.7	0819 1.4	1427 4.8	2034 1.7
9 F	0221 5.2	0858 0.7	1500 5.4	2115 1.1
24 SA	0234 5.0	0856 1.1	1501 5.1	2108 1.4
10 SA ○	0307 5.5	0944 0.5	1544 5.5	2158 0.9
25 SU	0306 5.2	0930 0.9	1531 5.2	2141 1.2
11 SU	0348 5.7	1026 0.3	1625 5.6	2237 0.8
26 M	0336 5.4	1002 0.7	1601 5.3	2212 1.1
12 M	0427 5.8	1105 0.3	1704 5.5	2314 0.9
27 TU	0405 5.5	1034 0.7	1632 5.4	2244 1.0
13 TU	0505 5.8	1141 0.5	1741 5.4	2349 1.0
28 W	0436 5.6	1107 0.7	1705 5.4	2317 1.0
14 W	0543 5.6	1215 0.8	1817 5.2	
29 TH	0509 5.5	1142 0.8	1741 5.3	2352 1.1
15 TH	0023 1.2	0623 5.4	1247 1.2	1854 4.9
30 F	0548 5.4	1219 1.0	1820 5.1	

OCTOBER

Day				
1 SA	0029 1.3	0634 5.2	1300 1.4	1906 4.9
16 SU	0102 1.7	0719 4.6	1312 2.1	1935 4.5
2 SU	0114 1.5	0730 4.8	1350 1.8	2002 4.6
17 M ☾	0119 2.0	0815 4.2	1400 2.4	2031 4.2
3 M	0214 1.8	0844 4.5	1501 2.1	2115 4.3
18 TU	0304 2.3	0929 4.0	1528 2.7	2147 4.1
4 TU	0347 2.0	1016 4.3	1641 2.3	2243 4.3
19 W	0448 2.3	1102 4.0	1724 2.6	2318 4.1
5 W	0536 1.8	1155 4.5	1814 2.1	
20 TH	0605 2.0	1219 4.2	1832 2.4	
6 TH	0009 4.6	0656 1.4	1308 4.8	1919 1.8
21 F	0027 4.4	0659 1.7	1310 4.5	1919 2.0
7 F	0114 4.9	0753 1.0	1400 5.1	2009 1.4
22 SA	0115 4.7	0742 1.4	1350 4.8	1958 1.7
8 SA	0204 5.3	0840 0.7	1443 5.4	2053 1.2
23 SU	0153 4.9	0820 1.1	1424 5.1	2033 1.5
9 SU ○	0247 5.5	0922 0.6	1523 5.5	2133 1.0
24 M	0228 5.2	0855 0.9	1456 5.3	2108 1.2
10 M	0325 5.7	1000 0.5	1559 5.5	2210 0.9
25 TU ●	0301 5.4	0929 0.7	1528 5.4	2143 1.0
11 TU	0401 5.7	1034 0.6	1634 5.5	2244 0.9
26 W	0335 5.5	1004 0.6	1602 5.5	2218 0.9
12 W	0437 5.6	1108 0.7	1707 5.4	2318 1.0
27 TH	0411 5.6	1040 0.7	1638 5.6	2255 0.9
13 TH	0514 5.5	1138 1.0	1739 5.2	2351 1.2
28 F	0451 5.6	1118 0.8	1717 5.4	2334 1.0
14 F	0552 5.2	1207 1.4	1813 5.0	
29 SA	0535 5.4	1158 1.1	1759 5.2	
15 SA	0025 1.4	0633 4.9	1237 1.7	1851 4.7
30 SU	0017 1.1	0628 5.1	1243 1.5	1849 5.0
31 M	0109 1.4	0730 4.8	1338 1.9	1948 4.7

NOVEMBER

Day				
1 TU ☾	0217 1.6	0846 4.5	1455 2.2	2101 4.5
16 W ☾	0226 2.1	0848 4.1	1434 2.5	2059 4.2
2 W	0349 1.7	1015 4.4	1629 2.3	2226 4.3
17 TH	0346 2.1	1002 4.1	1612 2.6	2212 4.2
3 TH	0523 1.6	1143 4.5	1751 2.1	2347 4.7
18 F	0504 2.0	1116 4.2	1729 2.4	2322 4.3
4 F	0635 1.3	1249 4.8	1853 1.8	
19 SA	0605 1.8	1215 4.4	1826 2.2	
5 SA	0050 4.9	0730 1.0	1338 5.1	1944 1.6
20 SU	0018 4.6	0654 1.5	1300 4.7	1912 1.9
6 SU	0140 5.2	0815 0.8	1420 5.2	2027 1.3
21 M	0105 4.8	0737 1.2	1340 5.0	1954 1.6
7 M	0223 5.4	0855 0.8	1457 5.3	2106 1.1
22 TU	0147 5.1	0817 1.0	1418 5.2	2035 1.3
8 TU ○	0301 5.4	0931 0.8	1532 5.4	2143 1.1
23 W ●	0229 5.3	0857 0.8	1457 5.4	2116 1.1
9 W	0338 5.4	1004 0.9	1605 5.3	2218 1.0
24 TH	0311 5.5	0938 0.8	1536 5.5	2158 0.9
10 TH	0414 5.4	1036 1.1	1636 5.3	2252 1.1
25 F	0355 5.5	1019 0.8	1618 5.5	2241 0.8
11 F	0451 5.2	1105 1.3	1707 5.2	2327 1.2
26 SA	0442 5.5	1102 0.9	1701 5.4	2327 0.8
12 SA	0529 5.0	1135 1.5	1741 5.0	
27 SU	0533 5.3	1148 1.2	1748 5.3	
13 SU	0002 1.4	0610 4.8	1206 1.8	1820 4.8
28 M	0017 0.9	0630 5.1	1237 1.5	1840 5.1
14 M	0041 1.6	0655 4.5	1243 2.0	1904 4.6
29 TU	0113 1.1	0732 4.9	1335 1.8	1938 4.9
15 TU	0126 1.8	0746 4.3	1329 2.3	1956 4.4
30 W ☾	0219 1.3	0840 4.6	1444 2.1	2045 4.8

DECEMBER

Day				
1 TH	0332 1.4	0954 4.5	1559 2.2	2158 4.7
16 F ☾	0248 1.8	0907 4.3	1500 2.4	2115 4.4
2 F	0449 1.4	1109 4.6	1713 2.1	2311 4.7
17 SA	0351 1.9	1008 4.3	1612 2.4	2217 4.4
3 SA	0559 1.3	1215 4.7	1818 1.9	
18 SU	0455 1.8	1109 4.4	1720 2.2	2318 4.5
4 SU	0016 4.8	0658 1.3	1307 4.8	1913 1.7
19 M	0556 1.6	1205 4.5	1819 2.0	
5 M	0112 5.0	0746 1.2	1353 5.0	2001 1.5
20 TU	0016 4.7	0651 1.4	1257 4.8	1914 1.7
6 TU	0159 5.0	0828 1.2	1433 5.1	2043 1.4
21 W	0111 4.9	0743 1.2	1345 5.0	2005 1.4
7 W	0242 5.1	0905 1.2	1509 5.1	2122 1.3
22 TH	0204 5.1	0832 1.1	1432 5.2	2056 1.1
8 TH ○	0321 5.1	0940 1.3	1542 5.4	2159 1.2
23 F ●	0256 5.3	0920 1.0	1518 5.4	2146 0.9
9 F	0359 5.1	1012 1.4	1614 5.2	2235 1.2
24 SA	0347 5.4	1008 1.0	1605 5.5	2236 0.7
10 SA	0437 5.0	1043 1.5	1646 5.1	2312 1.2
25 SU	0440 5.5	1056 1.0	1652 5.5	2327 0.6
11 SU	0514 4.9	1114 1.6	1720 5.1	2348 1.3
26 M	0533 5.4	1145 1.1	1741 5.5	
12 M	0553 4.8	1148 1.7	1758 5.0	
27 TU	0017 0.6	0627 5.3	1233 1.3	1831 5.4
13 TU	0025 1.5	0635 4.6	1224 1.9	1840 4.8
28 W	0109 0.7	0722 5.1	1324 1.5	1924 5.3
14 W	0107 1.6	0720 4.5	1307 2.1	1926 4.6
29 TH	0204 0.9	0819 4.8	1419 1.8	2020 5.1
15 TH	0153 1.7	0811 4.4	1358 2.3	2017 4.5
30 F ☾	0301 1.2	0919 4.6	1519 2.0	2121 4.8
31 SA	0404 1.4	1023 4.5	1625 2.1	2227 4.7

Chart Datum: 2·85 metres below Ordnance Datum (Newlyn)
HAT is 6·1 metres above Chart Datum

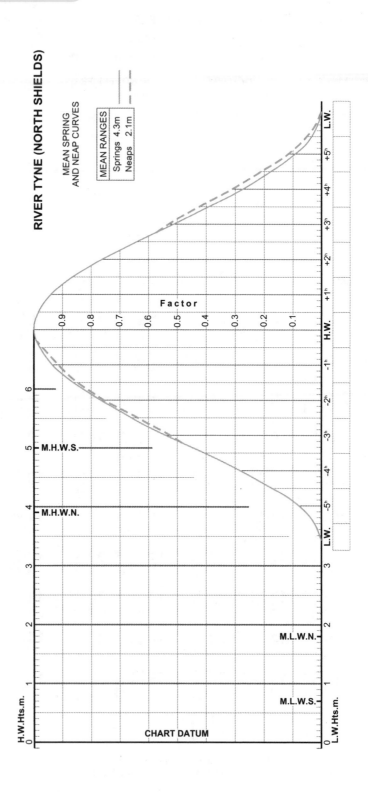

RIVER TYNE (NORTH SHIELDS)

MEAN SPRING
AND NEAP CURVES

MEAN RANGES
Springs 4.3m
Neaps 2.1m

NORTH SHIELDS

LAT 55°00'N   LONG 1°26'W

TIMES AND HEIGHTS OF HIGH AND LOW WATERS

Dates in amber are **SPRINGS**
Dates in grey are **NEAPS**

2022

JANUARY

Time	m		Time	m
1 SA 0130	4.9		**16** SU 0231	4.4
0801	1.0		0841	1.6
1402	4.9		1448	4.6
2027	1.1		2108	1.4
2 SU 0227	5.1		**17** M 0310	4.6
0854	0.9		0917	1.5
1450	5.1		1522	4.7
● 2121	0.8		○ 2145	1.2
3 M 0320	5.2		**18** TU 0345	4.6
0944	0.9		0951	1.0
1537	5.2		1555	4.8
2213	0.6		2220	1.1
4 TU 0413	5.2		**19** W 0420	4.7
1032	1.0		1024	1.3
1623	5.3		1627	4.9
2304	0.5		2255	1.0
5 W 0504	5.2		**20** TH 0454	4.7
1119	1.1		1057	1.3
1709	5.2		1659	4.9
2353	0.6		2330	0.9
6 TH 0555	5.0		**21** F 0529	4.7
1203	1.2		1131	1.3
1757	5.1		1733	4.9
7 F 0041	0.7		**22** SA 0006	0.9
0647	4.8		0606	4.7
1247	1.4		1205	1.4
1846	5.0		1809	4.9
8 SA 0129	0.9		**23** SU 0044	1.0
0739	4.5		0645	4.6
1332	1.7		1241	1.6
1938	4.8		1849	4.8
9 SU 0219	1.2		**24** M 0125	1.1
0832	4.3		0729	4.5
1423	1.9		1322	1.6
☾ 2033	4.6		1934	4.7
10 M 0313	1.5		**25** TU 0211	1.2
0928	4.1		0820	4.3
1522	2.1		1412	1.7
2133	4.3		☾ 2028	4.6
11 TU 0412	1.7		**26** W 0307	1.4
1029	4.0		0920	4.2
1632	2.1		1517	1.9
2239	4.2		2134	4.4
12 W 0516	1.8		**27** TH 0416	1.5
1134	4.0		1029	4.2
1744	2.1		1640	1.9
2349	4.1		2252	4.4
13 TH 0619	1.9		**28** F 0532	1.6
1235	4.1		1143	4.3
1850	2.0		1803	1.8
14 F 0053	4.2		**29** SA 0013	4.4
0715	1.8		0646	1.5
1326	4.3		1252	4.4
1944	1.8		1919	1.5
15 SA 0146	4.3		**30** SU 0126	4.6
0801	1.7		0752	1.3
1410	4.5		1351	4.7
2029	1.6		2024	1.1
			31 M 0226	4.9
			0848	1.2
			1442	4.9
			2119	0.8

FEBRUARY

Time	m		Time	m
1 TU 0319	5.1		**16** W 0328	4.6
0938	1.0		0936	1.3
1528	5.2		1536	4.8
● 2209	0.5		○ 2202	0.9
2 W 0407	5.1		**17** TH 0400	4.8
1023	0.9		1008	1.1
1612	5.4		1607	5.0
2255	0.4		2236	0.7
3 TH 0453	5.1		**18** F 0433	4.9
1104	0.9		1040	1.0
1654	5.3		1638	5.1
2338	0.4		2310	0.6
4 F 0536	5.0		**19** SA 0506	4.9
1143	1.0		1113	1.1
1736	5.3		1710	5.1
			2345	0.6
5 SA 0017	0.6		**20** SU 0540	4.8
0619	4.8		1145	1.0
1219	1.2		1745	5.1
1818	5.1			
6 SU 0056	0.6		**21** M 0020	0.7
0700	4.6		0618	4.8
1255	1.4		1219	1.1
1901	4.9		1824	5.0
7 M 0133	1.1		**22** TU 0057	0.9
0743	4.3		0658	4.6
1333	1.6		1257	1.3
1946	4.6		1908	4.8
8 TU 0214	1.5		**23** W 0139	1.1
0829	4.1		0745	4.4
1418	1.9		1343	1.5
☾ 2038	4.3		☾ 2001	4.6
9 W 0302	1.8		**24** TH 0232	1.4
0924	3.9		0843	4.2
1520	2.1		1445	1.7
2141	4.0		2110	4.3
10 TH 0406	2.0		**25** F 0344	1.7
1030	3.8		0957	4.1
1644	2.2		1616	1.9
2259	3.9		2239	4.2
11 F 0526	2.2		**26** SA 0515	1.8
1149	3.8		1122	4.1
1813	2.1		1756	1.7
12 SA 0023	3.9		**27** SU 0014	4.2
0645	2.2		0642	1.7
1257	4.0		1242	4.3
1923	1.9		1920	1.4
13 SU 0128	4.1		**28** M 0129	4.5
0742	1.9		0749	1.5
1349	4.2		1344	4.6
2012	1.6		2022	1.0
14 M 0216	4.3			
0826	1.7			
1429	4.5			
2052	1.3			
15 TU 0254	4.5			
0903	1.5			
1504	4.7			
2128	1.1			

MARCH

Time	m		Time	m
1 TU 0226	4.8		**16** W 0228	4.4
0842	1.2		0840	1.4
1433	4.9		1436	4.6
2112	0.6		2102	1.0
2 W 0312	5.0		**17** TH 0301	4.7
0926	1.0		0913	1.2
1516	5.1		1508	4.8
● 2157	0.4		2136	0.7
3 TH 0354	5.1		**18** F 0333	4.8
1006	0.9		0945	1.0
1556	5.3		1539	5.0
2237	0.3		○ 2210	0.5
4 F 0432	5.1		**19** SA 0405	5.0
1043	0.8		1017	0.8
1633	5.3		1611	5.2
2313	0.4		2245	0.4
5 SA 0509	5.0		**20** SU 0439	5.0
1117	0.8		1050	0.8
1710	5.2		1645	5.2
2347	0.5		2320	0.4
6 SU 0544	4.8		**21** M 0513	5.0
1149	1.0		1124	0.8
1747	5.1		1722	5.2
			2355	0.6
7 M 0018	0.8		**22** TU 0551	4.9
0620	4.6		1200	0.9
1220	1.1		1803	5.1
1825	4.9			
8 TU 0049	1.1		**23** W 0032	0.8
0655	4.4		0632	4.7
1253	1.4		1239	1.1
1906	4.6		1851	4.8
9 W 0122	1.5		**24** TH 0115	1.2
0735	4.2		0720	4.5
1332	1.7		1329	1.3
1952	4.2		1950	4.5
10 TH 0202	1.8		**25** F 0210	1.6
0823	4.0		0820	4.2
1424	1.9		1437	1.6
☾ 2052	3.9		2107	4.2
11 F 0259	2.1		**26** SA 0330	1.9
0927	3.8		0938	4.0
1544	2.2		1615	1.7
2211	3.7		2244	4.0
12 SA 0430	2.3		**27** SU 0511	2.0
1051	3.7		1111	4.0
1729	2.2		1758	1.5
2347	3.7			
13 SU 0611	2.3		**28** M 0017	4.2
1219	3.8		0638	1.8
1852	1.9		1232	4.2
			1915	1.2
14 M 0102	3.9		**29** TU 0124	4.5
0719	2.0		0739	1.5
1319	4.1		1331	4.6
1946	1.6		2010	0.9
15 TU 0151	4.2		**30** W 0215	4.7
0803	1.7		0826	1.2
1401	4.3		1418	4.8
2026	1.3		2056	0.6
			31 TH 0256	4.9
			0907	1.0
			1457	5.0
			2135	0.4

APRIL

Time	m		Time	m
1 F 0332	5.0		**16** SA 0301	4.9
0943	0.8		0915	0.9
1533	5.2		1507	5.1
2211	0.4		○ 2139	0.4
2 SA 0406	5.0		**17** SU 0335	5.0
1017	0.8		0950	0.7
1609	5.2		1543	5.2
2243	0.5		2217	0.3
3 SU 0438	4.9		**18** M 0411	5.1
1049	0.8		1027	0.6
1644	5.1		1622	5.3
2313	0.7		2254	0.4
4 M 0510	4.8		**19** TU 0448	5.1
1120	0.9		1105	0.6
1719	5.0		1704	5.2
2342	0.9		2333	0.6
5 TU 0542	4.7		**20** W 0528	5.0
1152	1.1		1147	0.7
1755	4.7		1751	5.0
6 W 0010	1.2		**21** TH 0015	0.9
0616	4.5		0613	4.8
1224	1.3		1233	0.9
1835	4.5		1846	4.8
7 TH 0041	1.5		**22** F 0102	1.3
0652	4.3		0705	4.5
1302	1.5		1329	1.2
1920	4.2		1952	4.4
8 F 0118	1.8		**23** SA 0203	1.7
0736	4.0		0808	4.3
1350	1.8		1443	1.4
2017	3.9		☾ 2113	4.2
9 SA 0210	2.1		**24** SU 0327	2.0
0835	3.8		0929	4.1
1500	2.0		1618	1.5
☾ 2131	3.7		2242	4.1
10 SU 0334	2.4		**25** M 0502	2.0
0955	3.7		1056	4.1
1637	2.1		1747	1.3
2259	3.7			
11 M 0523	2.3		**26** TU 0004	4.2
1124	3.8		0619	1.8
1804	1.8		1211	4.3
			1855	1.1
12 TU 0018	3.9		**27** W 0105	4.4
0638	2.1		0716	1.5
1232	4.0		1309	4.6
1904	1.5		1947	0.9
13 W 0111	4.1		**28** TH 0152	4.6
0726	1.7		0801	1.3
1320	4.3		1354	4.8
1947	1.2		2030	0.7
14 TH 0151	4.4		**29** F 0230	4.7
0805	1.4		0841	1.1
1358	4.6		1433	4.9
2026	0.9		2107	0.7
15 F 0226	4.7		**30** SA 0305	4.8
0840	1.2		0916	0.9
1432	4.8		1509	5.0
2103	0.6		● 2140	0.7

Chart Datum: 2·60 metres below Ordnance Datum (Newlyn)
HAT is 5·7 metres above Chart Datum

TIDES

TIME ZONE (UT)	NORTH SHIELDS	Dates in amber are SPRINGS
For Summer Time add ONE hour in non-shaded areas	LAT 55°00'N LONG 1°26'W	Dates in grey are NEAPS
	TIMES AND HEIGHTS OF HIGH AND LOW WATERS	2022

MAY

Time	m		Time	m
1 SU 0337 / 0950 / 1544 / 2211	4.9 / 0.9 / 5.0 / 0.8	**16** 0306 / 0925 / M 1519 / ○ 2151		5.0 / 0.7 / 5.2 / 0.5
2 M 0409 / 1024 / 1620 / 2241	4.8 / 0.9 / 4.9 / 0.9	**17** 0345 / 1008 / TU 1605 / 2234		5.1 / 0.6 / 5.2 / 0.6
3 TU 0440 / 1056 / 1656 / 2310	4.8 / 0.9 / 4.8 / 1.1	**18** 0427 / 1053 / W 1654 / 2318		5.1 / 0.6 / 5.2 / 0.8
4 W 0512 / 1129 / 1733 / 2340	4.7 / 1.1 / 4.6 / 1.3	**19** 0512 / 1141 / TH 1747		5.0 / 0.6 / 5.0
5 TH 0545 / 1204 / 1813	4.5 / 1.2 / 4.4	**20** 0005 / 0601 / F 1233 / 1847		1.0 / 4.9 / 0.8 / 4.7
6 F 0012 / 0623 / 1242 / 1858	1.6 / 4.4 / 1.4 / 4.2	**21** 0057 / 0656 / SA 1333 / 1953		1.4 / 4.7 / 1.0 / 4.5
7 SA 0049 / 0706 / 1329 / 1951	1.8 / 4.2 / 1.6 / 3.9	**22** 0158 / 0800 / SU 1445 / (2106		1.7 / 4.5 / 1.1 / 4.3
8 SU 0138 / 0800 / 1430 / 2055	2.1 / 4.0 / 1.8 / 3.8	**23** 0314 / 0913 / M 1603 / 2221		1.9 / 4.3 / 1.2 / 4.2
9 M 0247 / 0908 / 1547 / (2208	2.3 / 3.8 / 1.8 / 3.8	**24** 0433 / 1028 / TU 1718 / 2333		1.9 / 4.3 / 1.2 / 4.2
10 TU 0419 / 1023 / 1705 / 2320	2.3 / 3.9 / 1.7 / 3.9	**25** 0542 / 1138 / W 1822		1.8 / 4.4 / 1.1
11 W 0538 / 1132 / 1808	2.1 / 4.0 / 1.5	**26** 0032 / 0641 / TH 1237 / 1915		4.3 / 1.6 / 4.5 / 1.1
12 TH 0019 / 0635 / 1227 / 1859	4.1 / 1.8 / 4.3 / 1.2	**27** 0120 / 0730 / F 1326 / 1958		4.5 / 1.4 / 4.6 / 1.0
13 F 0106 / 0720 / 1313 / 1944	4.4 / 1.5 / 4.5 / 0.9	**28** 0201 / 0812 / SA 1408 / 2036		4.6 / 1.3 / 4.7 / 1.0
14 SA 0148 / 0802 / 1355 / 2026	4.7 / 1.2 / 4.8 / 0.7	**29** 0237 / 0851 / SU 1447 / 2110		4.7 / 1.1 / 4.7 / 1.0
15 SU 0227 / 0843 / 1436 / 2108	4.9 / 1.0 / 5.0 / 0.5	**30** 0311 / 0928 / M 1525 / ● 2142		4.7 / 1.1 / 4.7 / 1.1
		31 0345 / 1003 / TU 1602 / 2214		4.8 / 1.0 / 4.7 / 1.2

JUNE

Time	m		Time	m
1 W 0417 / 1038 / 1640 / 2246	4.7 / 1.0 / 4.6 / 1.3	**16** 0413 / 1047 / TH 1649 / 2309		5.1 / 0.5 / 5.1 / 0.9
2 TH 0450 / 1113 / 1717 / 2318	4.7 / 1.1 / 4.5 / 1.4	**17** 0500 / 1139 / F 1744 / 2358		5.1 / 0.5 / 5.0 / 1.1
3 F 0524 / 1149 / 1756 / 2352	4.6 / 1.2 / 4.4 / 1.5	**18** 0551 / 1232 / SA 1842		5.0 / 0.6 / 4.8
4 SA 0601 / 1228 / 1839	4.5 / 1.3 / 4.2	**19** 0048 / 0645 / SU 1328 / 1942		1.3 / 4.9 / 0.7 / 4.6
5 SU 0030 / 0643 / 1312 / 1926	1.7 / 4.4 / 1.4 / 4.1	**20** 0143 / 0744 / M 1428 / 2043		1.5 / 4.7 / 0.9 / 4.4
6 M 0114 / 0731 / 1403 / 2020	1.9 / 4.2 / 1.5 / 4.0	**21** 0243 / 0846 / TU 1531 / (2145		1.7 / 4.6 / 1.1 / 4.2
7 TU 0209 / 0826 / 1503 / (2120	2.0 / 4.1 / 1.6 / 3.9	**22** 0348 / 0951 / W 1635 / 2249		1.8 / 4.4 / 1.3 / 4.2
8 W 0316 / 0928 / 1608 / 2223	2.1 / 4.1 / 1.5 / 4.0	**23** 0455 / 1056 / TH 1737 / 2350		1.9 / 4.3 / 1.4 / 4.2
9 TH 0430 / 1031 / 1712 / 2324	2.0 / 4.2 / 1.4 / 4.1	**24** 0559 / 1200 / F 1834		1.8 / 4.3 / 1.4
10 F 0536 / 1132 / 1809	1.8 / 4.3 / 1.2	**25** 0044 / 0657 / SA 1257 / 1924		4.3 / 1.7 / 4.4 / 1.4
11 SA 0020 / 0633 / 1229 / 1903	4.4 / 1.6 / 4.5 / 1.0	**26** 0131 / 0747 / SU 1346 / 2007		4.4 / 1.5 / 4.4 / 1.4
12 SU 0110 / 0725 / 1322 / 1954	4.6 / 1.3 / 4.8 / 0.8	**27** 0213 / 0831 / M 1431 / 2045		4.5 / 1.4 / 4.5 / 1.4
13 M 0157 / 0816 / 1413 / 2043	4.8 / 1.1 / 5.0 / 0.7	**28** 0251 / 0911 / TU 1512 / 2121		4.6 / 1.2 / 4.5 / 1.3
14 TU 0242 / 0906 / 1504 / ○ 2132	5.0 / 0.8 / 5.1 / 0.7	**29** 0326 / 0948 / W 1550 / ● 2155		4.7 / 1.1 / 4.6 / 1.3
15 W 0327 / 0956 / 1556 / 2220	5.1 / 0.6 / 5.2 / 0.7	**30** 0400 / 1024 / TH 1626 / 2229		4.7 / 1.1 / 4.6 / 1.3

JULY

Time	m		Time	m
1 F 0433 / 1100 / 1702 / 2302	4.7 / 1.0 / 4.6 / 1.4	**16** 0449 / 1132 / SA 1734 / 2345		5.3 / 0.3 / 5.1 / 1.1
2 SA 0507 / 1135 / 1739 / 2336	4.7 / 1.0 / 4.5 / 1.4	**17** 0537 / 1221 / SU 1825		5.2 / 0.4 / 4.9
3 SU 0543 / 1213 / 1817	4.7 / 1.1 / 4.4	**18** 0029 / 0626 / M 1308 / 1916		1.1 / 5.1 / 0.6 / 4.7
4 M 0012 / 0621 / 1252 / 1859	1.5 / 4.6 / 1.2 / 4.3	**19** 0114 / 0716 / TU 1357 / 2007		1.3 / 4.9 / 0.8 / 4.5
5 TU 0051 / 0701 / 1335 / 1943	1.6 / 4.5 / 1.2 / 4.2	**20** 0201 / 0809 / W 1447 / (2100		1.5 / 4.7 / 1.1 / 4.2
6 W 0134 / 0747 / 1422 / 2034	1.7 / 4.4 / 1.3 / 4.2	**21** 0255 / 0907 / TH 1542 / 2158		1.8 / 4.5 / 1.4 / 4.1
7 TH 0225 / 0839 / 1517 / 2131	1.8 / 4.4 / 1.4 / 4.1	**22** 0359 / 1010 / F 1644 / 2301		1.9 / 4.2 / 1.7 / 4.0
8 F 0328 / 0939 / 1620 / 2233	1.9 / 4.3 / 1.4 / 4.2	**23** 0512 / 1120 / SA 1749		2.0 / 4.1 / 1.8
9 SA 0440 / 1045 / 1725 / 2337	1.9 / 4.4 / 1.4 / 4.3	**24** 0006 / 0625 / SU 1230 / 1853		4.1 / 1.9 / 4.1 / 1.8
10 SU 0551 / 1154 / 1829	1.7 / 4.5 / 1.3	**25** 0104 / 0726 / M 1330 / 1945		4.2 / 1.7 / 4.2 / 1.7
11 M 0038 / 0657 / 1301 / 1930	4.5 / 1.5 / 4.6 / 1.1	**26** 0153 / 0816 / TU 1418 / 2028		4.4 / 1.5 / 4.3 / 1.6
12 TU 0134 / 0759 / 1402 / 2027	4.7 / 1.2 / 4.8 / 1.0	**27** 0234 / 0857 / W 1500 / 2106		4.5 / 1.3 / 4.5 / 1.5
13 W 0226 / 0856 / 1458 / ○ 2121	4.9 / 0.9 / 5.0 / 0.9	**28** 0310 / 0935 / TH 1536 / ● 2141		4.7 / 1.1 / 4.6 / 1.4
14 TH 0314 / 0951 / 1551 / 2211	5.1 / 0.6 / 5.2 / 0.9	**29** 0343 / 1009 / F 1610 / 2214		4.8 / 1.0 / 4.6 / 1.3
15 F 0402 / 1042 / 1643 / 2259	5.2 / 0.4 / 5.2 / 0.9	**30** 0415 / 1043 / SA 1643 / 2246		4.8 / 0.9 / 4.7 / 1.3
		31 0447 / 1117 / SU 1716 / 2318		4.9 / 0.9 / 4.7 / 1.2

AUGUST

Time	m		Time	m
1 M 0520 / 1152 / 1751 / 2351	4.9 / 0.9 / 4.6 / 1.3	**16** 0002 / 0558 / TU 1238 / 1841		1.0 / 5.3 / 0.6 / 4.8
2 TU 0553 / 1227 / 1827	4.9 / 0.9 / 4.6	**17** 0040 / 0642 / W 1316 / 1924		1.2 / 5.0 / 0.9 / 4.5
3 W 0024 / 0630 / 1304 / 1907	1.4 / 4.8 / 1.0 / 4.5	**18** 0119 / 0728 / TH 1356 / 2010		1.4 / 4.7 / 1.3 / 4.3
4 TH 0102 / 0711 / 1345 / 1952	1.5 / 4.7 / 1.2 / 4.4	**19** 0203 / 0820 / F 1443 / (2103		1.7 / 4.4 / 1.7 / 4.1
5 F 0146 / 0759 / 1434 / (2046	1.6 / 4.6 / 1.3 / 4.3	**20** 0302 / 0922 / SA 1543 / 2207		2.0 / 4.1 / 2.0 / 3.9
6 SA 0242 / 0859 / 1536 / 2150	1.8 / 4.4 / 1.4 / 4.2	**21** 0422 / 1039 / SU 1702 / 2324		2.1 / 3.9 / 2.2 / 3.9
7 SU 0357 / 1013 / 1652 / 2303	1.9 / 4.3 / 1.6 / 4.2	**22** 0554 / 1206 / M 1825		2.1 / 3.9 / 2.1
8 M 0524 / 1136 / 1809	1.8 / 4.3 / 1.6	**23** 0036 / 0708 / TU 1314 / 1927		4.1 / 1.9 / 4.1 / 2.0
9 TU 0017 / 0645 / 1255 / 1920	4.3 / 1.5 / 4.5 / 1.4	**24** 0132 / 0759 / W 1403 / 2012		4.3 / 1.6 / 4.3 / 1.8
10 W 0121 / 0754 / 1400 / 2021	4.6 / 1.2 / 4.8 / 1.2	**25** 0214 / 0839 / TH 1442 / 2049		4.5 / 1.3 / 4.5 / 1.6
11 TH 0216 / 0853 / 1455 / 2113	4.9 / 0.8 / 5.0 / 1.0	**26** 0250 / 0915 / F 1515 / 2122		4.7 / 1.1 / 4.6 / 1.4
12 F 0304 / 0944 / 1544 / ○ 2200	5.1 / 0.5 / 5.2 / 0.9	**27** 0321 / 0948 / SA 1547 / ● 2153		4.9 / 0.9 / 4.8 / 1.2
13 SA 0348 / 1032 / 1630 / 2243	5.3 / 0.2 / 5.2 / 0.8	**28** 0351 / 1020 / SU 1617 / 2224		5.0 / 0.7 / 4.9 / 1.1
14 SU 0432 / 1116 / 1715 / 2324	5.4 / 0.2 / 5.2 / 0.9	**29** 0421 / 1052 / M 1649 / 2255		5.1 / 0.7 / 4.9 / 1.1
15 M 0515 / 1158 / 1758	5.4 / 0.3 / 5.0	**30** 0452 / 1125 / TU 1721 / 2326		5.1 / 0.7 / 4.9 / 1.1
		31 0524 / 1159 / W 1755 / 2359		5.1 / 0.7 / 4.8 / 1.2

Chart Datum: 2·60 metres below Ordnance Datum (Newlyn)
HAT is 5·7 metres above Chart Datum

TIME ZONE (UT)	NORTH SHIELDS	Dates in amber are SPRINGS
For Summer Time add ONE hour in **non-shaded areas**	LAT 55°00′N LONG 1°26′W TIMES AND HEIGHTS OF HIGH AND LOW WATERS	Dates in grey are NEAPS **2022**

SEPTEMBER

Day	Time m	Time m	Day	Time m	Time m
1 TH	0600 5.0 1233 0.9	1833 4.7	**16** F	0041 1.4 0650 4.7	1307 1.5 1918 4.4
2 F	0034 1.3 0642 4.9	1311 1.1 1916 4.5	**17** SA	0121 1.7 0738 4.3	1346 1.9 2007 4.1 ◑
3 SA	0116 1.5 0731 4.6	1358 1.4 2010 4.3 ◑	**18** SU	0213 2.0 0839 4.0	1442 2.2 2111 3.9
4 SU	0213 1.7 0835 4.4	1504 1.7 2118 4.2	**19** M	0332 2.2 0959 3.8	1611 2.4 2234 3.8
5 M	0335 1.9 1000 4.2	1633 1.9 2242 4.1	**20** TU	0518 2.2 1135 3.8	1756 2.4
6 TU	0517 1.8 1137 4.2	1804 1.9	**21** W	0001 4.0 0641 1.9	1249 4.0 1904 2.1
7 W	0006 4.3 0646 1.5	1258 4.5 1918 1.6	**22** TH	0102 4.2 0732 1.6	1338 4.3 1948 1.8
8 TH	0113 4.6 0752 1.0	1358 4.8 2013 1.3	**23** F	0145 4.5 0811 1.3	1415 4.5 2024 1.6
9 F	0205 4.9 0844 0.7	1446 5.1 2100 1.1	**24** SA	0220 4.7 0846 1.0	1446 4.7 2056 1.3
10 SA	0249 5.2 0927 0.4	1529 5.2 ○ 2142 0.9	**25** SU	0251 4.9 0918 0.8	1517 4.9 ● 2126 1.1
11 SU	0330 5.4 1012 0.2	1609 5.2 2220 0.8	**26** M	0321 5.1 0950 0.7	1547 5.0 2157 1.0
12 M	0409 5.5 1051 0.3	1647 5.2 2257 0.8	**27** TU	0351 5.2 1023 0.6	1618 5.1 2229 0.9
13 TU	0448 5.4 1128 0.4	1724 5.0 2332 0.9	**28** W	0423 5.3 1056 0.6	1651 5.1 2301 0.9
14 W	0527 5.3 1201 0.7	1800 4.8	**29** TH	0458 5.2 1130 0.7	1725 5.0 2336 1.0
15 TH	0005 1.1 0607 5.0	1233 1.1 1838 4.6	**30** F	0537 5.1 1205 0.9	1804 4.8

OCTOBER

Day	Time m	Time m	Day	Time m	Time m
1 SA	0014 1.2 0622 4.9	1245 1.3 1850 4.6	**16** SU	0049 1.6 0706 4.3	1301 2.0 1920 4.2
2 SU	0100 1.4 0717 4.6	1336 1.6 1945 4.4	**17** M	0139 1.9 0804 4.0	1351 2.3 2020 4.0 ◑
3 M	0204 1.7 0830 4.3	1449 2.0 2100 4.2 ◑	**18** TU	0249 2.1 0919 3.8	1514 2.5 2140 3.9
4 TU	0335 1.8 1005 4.1	1630 2.1 2231 4.1	**19** W	0426 2.2 1046 3.8	1707 2.5 2307 3.9
5 W	0520 1.7 1141 4.3	1801 2.0 2357 4.3	**20** TH	0552 2.0 1205 4.0	1822 2.3
6 TH	0641 1.4 1254 4.6	1907 1.7	**21** F	0016 4.1 0649 1.7	1258 4.2 1910 1.9
7 F	0100 4.7 0740 0.9	1346 4.8 1957 1.4	**22** SA	0104 4.4 0732 1.4	1337 4.5 1948 1.7
8 SA	0149 5.0 0827 0.6	1429 5.0 2040 1.1	**23** SU	0142 4.7 0808 1.1	1411 4.8 2022 1.4
9 SU	0230 5.2 0909 0.5	1507 5.2 ○ 2118 0.9	**24** M	0215 4.9 0843 0.8	1443 5.0 2055 1.2
10 M	0308 5.4 0947 0.4	1542 5.2 2154 0.8	**25** TU	0248 5.1 0917 0.7	1515 5.1 ● 2128 1.0
11 TU	0344 5.4 1021 0.5	1616 5.1 2229 0.9	**26** W	0322 5.3 0952 0.6	1548 5.2 2204 0.9
12 W	0421 5.3 1054 0.7	1650 5.0 2303 1.0	**27** TH	0358 5.3 1028 0.6	1623 5.2 2241 0.9
13 TH	0459 5.1 1124 1.0	1723 4.9 2336 1.1	**28** F	0438 5.3 1106 0.8	1701 5.1 2320 1.0
14 F	0538 4.9 1154 1.3	1758 4.7	**29** SA	0523 5.1 1146 1.1	1744 4.9
15 SA	0010 1.4 0619 4.6	1225 1.6 1836 4.5	**30** SU	0005 1.1 0615 4.9	1231 1.4 1833 4.7
			31 M	0059 1.3 0717 4.6	1327 1.8 1933 4.5

NOVEMBER

Day	Time m	Time m	Day	Time m	Time m
1 TU	0208 1.5 0835 4.3	1445 2.1 ◔ 2049 4.3	**16** W	0214 1.9 0838 3.9	1422 2.4 ◑ 2048 4.0
2 W	0339 1.6 1004 4.2	1621 2.2 2216 4.3	**17** TH	0328 2.0 0949 3.8	1553 2.5 2202 4.0
3 TH	0509 1.5 1128 4.3	1742 2.0 2335 4.5	**18** F	0446 1.9 1101 3.9	1716 2.3 2312 4.1
4 F	0621 1.2 1234 4.6	1843 1.7	**19** SA	0550 1.7 1202 4.2	1815 2.1
5 SA	0037 4.7 0717 1.0	1324 4.8 1933 1.5	**20** SU	0009 4.3 0641 1.5	1249 4.4 1902 1.8
6 SU	0126 4.9 0803 0.8	1405 4.9 2015 1.3	**21** M	0055 4.6 0725 1.2	1330 4.7 1943 1.6
7 M	0207 5.1 0843 0.8	1442 5.0 2053 1.1	**22** TU	0136 4.8 0805 1.0	1408 4.9 2022 1.3
8 TU	0246 5.2 0918 0.8	1516 5.1 ○ 2130 1.0	**23** W	0216 5.0 0845 0.8	1445 5.1 ● 2102 1.1
9 W	0323 5.2 0951 0.9	1549 5.1 2205 1.0	**24** TH	0257 5.2 0926 0.8	1523 5.2 2144 0.9
10 TH	0400 5.1 1023 1.0	1621 5.0 2240 1.1	**25** F	0341 5.3 1008 0.8	1603 5.2 2228 0.8
11 F	0438 5.0 1053 1.2	1654 4.9 2315 1.2	**26** SA	0428 5.2 1051 0.9	1645 5.2 2315 0.8
12 SA	0517 4.8 1123 1.5	1728 4.7 2350 1.4	**27** SU	0518 5.1 1136 1.2	1732 5.0
13 SU	0557 4.6 1155 1.7	1805 4.6	**28** M	0005 0.9 0615 4.9	1226 1.5 1824 4.9
14 M	0029 1.6 0643 4.3	1231 2.0 1848 4.4	**29** TU	0103 1.1 0718 4.7	1323 1.8 1924 4.7
15 TU	0115 1.8 0735 4.1	1318 2.2 1941 4.2	**30** W	0209 1.2 0829 4.4	1432 2.0 ◑ 2034 4.5

DECEMBER

Day	Time m	Time m	Day	Time m	Time m
1 TH	0325 1.3 0943 4.3	1551 2.1 2149 4.5	**16** F	0237 1.7 0854 4.0	1441 2.2 2059 4.2
2 F	0440 1.3 1056 4.3	1704 2.0 2301 4.5	**17** SA	0340 1.8 0955 4.0	1554 2.3 2202 4.2
3 SA	0547 1.3 1200 4.4	1808 1.9	**18** SU	0444 1.7 1057 4.1	1706 2.2 2305 4.3
4 SU	0005 4.6 0646 1.2	1253 4.5 1903 1.7	**19** M	0544 1.6 1156 4.3	1808 1.9
5 M	0059 4.7 0734 1.2	1338 4.7 1950 1.5	**20** TU	0004 4.4 0640 1.4	1248 4.5 1903 1.7
6 TU	0146 4.8 0815 1.2	1418 4.8 2032 1.3	**21** W	0100 4.7 0731 1.2	1336 4.7 1954 1.4
7 W	0228 4.9 0852 1.2	1454 4.9 2111 1.2	**22** TH	0152 4.9 0820 1.1	1421 4.9 2043 1.1
8 TH	0308 4.9 0926 1.2	1528 4.9 ○ 2149 1.2	**23** F	0243 5.1 0908 1.0	1505 5.1 ● 2133 0.9
9 F	0347 4.8 0959 1.3	1602 4.9 2225 1.2	**24** SA	0333 5.2 0956 0.9	1550 5.2 2223 0.7
10 SA	0425 4.8 1032 1.4	1635 4.9 2301 1.2	**25** SU	0424 5.2 1043 1.0	1635 5.2 2314 0.6
11 SU	0503 4.7 1103 1.5	1709 4.8 2336 1.3	**26** M	0516 5.2 1131 1.1	1723 5.2
12 M	0541 4.5 1136 1.7	1745 4.7	**27** TU	0005 0.6 0611 5.0	1219 1.3 1814 5.1
13 TU	0014 1.4 0623 4.4	1212 1.8 1825 4.6	**28** W	0058 0.7 0708 4.8	1309 1.5 1909 5.0
14 W	0055 1.5 0707 4.2	1222 2.0 1909 4.4	**29** TH	0154 0.9 0807 4.6	1404 1.7 2008 4.8
15 TH	0142 1.6 0757 4.1	1341 2.1 2001 4.3	**30** F	0254 1.1 0908 4.4	1506 1.9 ◑ 2111 4.6
			31 SA	0357 1.3 1011 4.2	1614 2.0 2218 4.5

Chart Datum: 2·60 metres below Ordnance Datum (Newlyn)
HAT is 5·7 metres above Chart Datum

TIDES

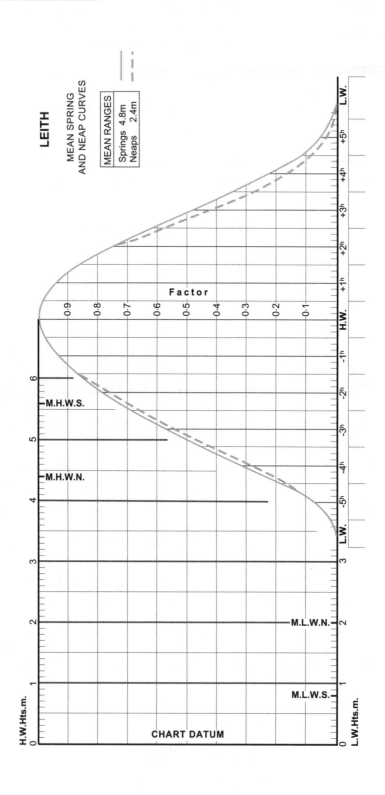

LEITH

MEAN SPRING
AND NEAP CURVES

MEAN RANGES
Springs 4.8m
Neaps 2.4m

TIME ZONE (UT)
For Summer Time add ONE hour in **non-shaded areas**

SCOTLAND – LEITH
LAT 55°59′N LONG 3°11′W
TIMES AND HEIGHTS OF HIGH AND LOW WATERS

Dates in amber are **SPRINGS**
Dates in grey are **NEAPS**

2022

JANUARY

Day	Time	m	Time	m	Day	Time	m	Time	m
1 SA	0041 / 0651 / 1308 / 1913	5.4 / 1.2 / 5.4 / 1.1			**16** SU	0140 / 0719 / 1358 / 1946	4.8 / 1.7 / 5.0 / 1.5		
2 SU	0136 / 0747 / 1357 / ●2013	5.6 / 1.0 / 5.6 / 0.9			**17** M	0218 / 0754 / 1434 / ○2023	5.0 / 1.6 / 5.1 / 1.3		
3 M	0228 / 0840 / 1446 / 2109	5.8 / 0.6 / 5.7 / 0.6			**18** TU	0254 / 0830 / 1508 / 2100	5.1 / 1.4 / 5.2 / 1.1		
4 TU	0319 / 0929 / 1534 / 2202	5.8 / 0.5 / 5.7 / 0.5			**19** W	0328 / 0905 / 1541 / 2137	5.2 / 1.4 / 5.3 / 1.0		
5 W	0410 / 1016 / 1623 / 2251	5.8 / 1.0 / 5.7 / 0.6			**20** TH	0402 / 0941 / 1614 / 2214	5.2 / 1.3 / 5.3 / 1.0		
6 TH	0500 / 1059 / 1712 / 2337	5.6 / 1.2 / 5.6 / 1.0			**21** F	0438 / 1016 / 1648 / 2251	5.2 / 1.3 / 5.3 / 1.0		
7 F	0552 / 1139 / 1803	5.4 / 1.5 / 5.4			**22** SA	0516 / 1047 / 1723 / 2326	5.2 / 1.4 / 5.2 / 1.1		
8 SA	0020 / 0644 / 1215 / 1858	1.0 / 5.1 / 1.7 / 5.2			**23** SU	0556 / 1115 / 1802	5.1 / 1.5 / 5.2		
9 SU	0103 / 0738 / 1257 / ◐1955	1.4 / 4.8 / 2.0 / 4.9			**24** M	0000 / 0640 / 1147 / 1846	1.2 / 5.0 / 1.7 / 5.1		
10 M	0149 / 0834 / 1353 / 2053	1.7 / 4.6 / 2.2 / 4.7			**25** TU	0039 / 0729 / 1234 / ◐1938	1.4 / 4.8 / 1.8 / 4.9		
11 TU	0250 / 0931 / 1507 / 2153	1.9 / 4.5 / 2.3 / 4.6			**26** W	0130 / 0820 / 1343 / 2043	1.6 / 4.7 / 2.0 / 4.8		
12 W	0403 / 1030 / 1621 / 2255	2.1 / 4.4 / 2.3 / 4.5			**27** TH	0243 / 0934 / 1519 / 2204	1.7 / 4.6 / 2.1 / 4.7		
13 TH	0508 / 1133 / 1725 / 2358	2.1 / 4.5 / 2.1 / 4.6			**28** F	0418 / 1046 / 1652 / 2322	1.8 / 4.7 / 1.9 / 4.9		
14 F	0559 / 1231 / 1820	2.0 / 4.7 / 1.9			**29** SA	0538 / 1155 / 1807	1.7 / 4.9 / 1.6		
15 SA	0054 / 0642 / 1318 / 1906	4.7 / 1.9 / 4.9 / 1.7			**30** SU	0032 / 0645 / 1256 / 1915	5.1 / 1.5 / 5.1 / 1.2		
					31 M	0131 / 0742 / 1349 / 2015	5.4 / 1.2 / 5.4 / 0.8		

FEBRUARY

Day	Time / m		**16** W	0236 / 0817 / 1451 / ○2047	5.1 / 1.4 / 5.3 / 1.0
1 TU	0223 / 0833 / 1437 / ●2107	5.6 / 1.0 / 5.6 / 0.5	**16** W	0236 / 0817 / 1451 / ○2047	5.1 / 1.4 / 5.3 / 1.0
2 W	0311 / 0918 / 1523 / 2153	5.7 / 0.9 / 5.8 / 0.4	**17** TH	0309 / 0853 / 1523 / 2124	5.3 / 1.2 / 5.4 / 0.8
3 TH	0357 / 1000 / 1608 / 2235	5.7 / 0.9 / 5.8 / 0.4	**18** F	0342 / 0928 / 1554 / 2200	5.4 / 1.0 / 5.5 / 0.6
4 F	0441 / 1038 / 1652 / 2313	5.6 / 1.0 / 5.7 / 0.6	**19** SA	0416 / 1002 / 1627 / 2235	5.4 / 1.0 / 5.5 / 0.6
5 SA	0525 / 1109 / 1736 / 2345	5.4 / 1.1 / 5.5 / 0.9	**20** SU	0452 / 1030 / 1701 / 2306	5.4 / 1.0 / 5.5 / 0.8
6 SU	0609 / 1134 / 1820	5.1 / 1.4 / 5.3	**21** M	0530 / 1052 / 1739 / 2332	5.3 / 1.2 / 5.4 / 0.9
7 M	0007 / 0653 / 1202 / 1907	1.2 / 4.8 / 1.7 / 5.0	**22** TU	0611 / 1119 / 1822	5.1 / 1.3 / 5.2
8 TU	0034 / 0740 / 1245 / ◐1959	1.6 / 4.6 / 2.0 / 4.6	**23** W	0002 / 0657 / 1201 / ◐1913	1.2 / 4.9 / 1.6 / 5.0
9 W	0117 / 0832 / 1347 / 2058	1.9 / 4.3 / 2.2 / 4.4	**24** TH	0048 / 0751 / 1303 / 2018	1.6 / 4.7 / 1.8 / 4.7
10 TH	0223 / 0930 / 1524 / 2202	2.3 / 4.2 / 2.4 / 4.2	**25** F	0204 / 0900 / 1449 / 2146	1.9 / 4.5 / 2.1 / 4.6
11 F	0411 / 1036 / 1656 / 2316	2.4 / 4.2 / 2.3 / 4.2	**26** SA	0407 / 1023 / 1652 / 2316	2.1 / 4.5 / 1.9 / 4.7
12 SA	0530 / 1152 / 1803	2.3 / 4.4 / 2.0	**27** SU	0537 / 1144 / 1815	1.9 / 4.7 / 1.5
13 SU	0030 / 0624 / 1255 / 1854	4.4 / 2.1 / 4.6 / 1.8	**28** M	0031 / 0643 / 1249 / 1920	5.0 / 1.6 / 5.0 / 1.1
14 M	0122 / 0705 / 1340 / 1935	4.7 / 1.8 / 4.9 / 1.5			
15 TU	0202 / 0742 / 1417 / 2012	4.9 / 1.6 / 5.1 / 1.2			

MARCH

Day	Time / m		Day	Time / m	
1 TU	0128 / 0735 / 1341 / 2011	5.3 / 1.3 / 5.3 / 0.7	**16** W	0135 / 0723 / 1350 / 1951	4.9 / 1.6 / 5.0 / 1.1
2 W	0215 / 0819 / 1425 / ●2055	5.5 / 1.0 / 5.6 / 0.4	**17** TH	0210 / 0757 / 1424 / 2026	5.1 / 1.2 / 5.3 / 0.8
3 TH	0257 / 0900 / 1506 / 2135	5.6 / 0.8 / 5.7 / 0.3	**18** F	0243 / 0832 / 1456 / ○2102	5.3 / 1.0 / 5.5 / 0.5
4 F	0337 / 0947 / 1547 / 2211	5.6 / 0.8 / 5.8 / 0.3	**19** SA	0316 / 0907 / 1528 / 2138	5.5 / 0.8 / 5.6 / 0.4
5 SA	0416 / 1010 / 1627 / 2243	5.5 / 0.8 / 5.7 / 0.5	**20** SU	0350 / 0941 / 1602 / 2212	5.6 / 0.7 / 5.7 / 0.4
6 SU	0454 / 1038 / 1706 / 2306	5.4 / 0.9 / 5.5 / 0.8	**21** M	0426 / 1010 / 1639 / 2243	5.5 / 0.8 / 5.6 / 0.6
7 M	0532 / 1058 / 1744 / 2320	5.1 / 1.2 / 5.2 / 1.2	**22** TU	0505 / 1033 / 1720 / 2308	5.4 / 0.9 / 5.5 / 0.9
8 TU	0610 / 1121 / 1825 / 2343	4.9 / 1.4 / 4.9 / 1.5	**23** W	0546 / 1102 / 1806 / 2338	5.2 / 1.1 / 5.3 / 1.3
9 W	0651 / 1155 / 1911	4.6 / 1.8 / 4.6	**24** TH	0632 / 1146 / 1859	4.9 / 1.4 / 5.0
10 TH	0018 / 0738 / 1245 / ◐2007	1.9 / 4.3 / 2.1 / 4.3	**25** F	0029 / 0727 / 1255 / ◐2010	1.7 / 4.6 / 1.8 / 4.6
11 F	0115 / 0836 / 1413 / 2113	2.3 / 4.1 / 2.4 / 4.1	**26** SA	0203 / 0842 / 1508 / 2143	2.1 / 4.4 / 2.0 / 4.5
12 SA	0302 / 0944 / 1629 / 2227	2.6 / 4.1 / 2.4 / 4.1	**27** SU	0409 / 1012 / 1701 / 2313	2.2 / 4.4 / 1.7 / 4.8
13 SU	0505 / 1103 / 1745 / 2355	2.5 / 4.2 / 2.1 / 4.2	**28** M	0531 / 1135 / 1815	2.0 / 4.6 / 1.3
14 M	0604 / 1222 / 1835	2.2 / 4.4 / 1.7	**29** TU	0025 / 0630 / 1237 / 1911	4.9 / 1.6 / 5.0 / 0.9
15 TU	0055 / 0647 / 1312 / 1916	4.6 / 1.9 / 4.7 / 1.4	**30** W	0117 / 0716 / 1325 / 1955	5.2 / 1.3 / 5.3 / 0.7
			31 TH	0159 / 0756 / 1406 / 2033	5.4 / 1.0 / 5.5 / 0.5

APRIL

Day	Time / m		Day	Time / m	
1 F	0236 / 0834 / 1445 / ●2109	5.5 / 0.8 / 5.6 / 0.4	**16** SA	0210 / 0802 / 1424 / ○2032	5.4 / 0.9 / 5.5 / 0.5
2 SA	0312 / 0909 / 1523 / 2141	5.5 / 0.7 / 5.6 / 0.5	**17** SU	0246 / 0839 / 1500 / 2110	5.6 / 0.7 / 5.7 / 0.4
3 SU	0348 / 0942 / 1600 / 2208	5.4 / 0.7 / 5.5 / 0.7	**18** M	0323 / 0916 / 1538 / 2148	5.6 / 0.6 / 5.8 / 0.4
4 M	0423 / 1009 / 1637 / 2227	5.3 / 0.9 / 5.4 / 1.0	**19** TU	0401 / 0953 / 1620 / 2224	5.6 / 0.6 / 5.7 / 0.7
5 TU	0458 / 1029 / 1714 / 2240	5.1 / 1.1 / 5.1 / 1.3	**20** W	0442 / 1027 / 1706 / 2259	5.5 / 0.8 / 5.6 / 1.0
6 W	0533 / 1050 / 1753 / 2301	4.9 / 1.3 / 4.9 / 1.6	**21** TH	0526 / 1106 / 1756 / 2340	5.3 / 1.0 / 5.3 / 1.4
7 TH	0610 / 1120 / 1836 / 2334	4.7 / 1.6 / 4.6 / 1.9	**22** F	0615 / 1202 / 1856	5.0 / 1.3 / 4.9
8 F	0654 / 1207 / 1928	4.4 / 2.0 / 4.3	**23** SA	0042 / 0716 / 1327 / ◐2012	1.9 / 4.7 / 1.6 / 4.6
9 SA	0025 / 0750 / 1324 / ◐2030	2.3 / 4.2 / 2.3 / 4.1	**24** SU	0217 / 0836 / 1522 / 2137	2.2 / 4.5 / 1.7 / 4.6
10 SU	0202 / 0858 / 1540 / 2140	2.6 / 4.1 / 2.3 / 4.1	**25** M	0355 / 1001 / 1650 / 2258	2.2 / 4.5 / 1.5 / 4.7
11 M	0426 / 1014 / 1710 / 2258	2.5 / 4.1 / 2.0 / 4.2	**26** TU	0505 / 1115 / 1755	1.9 / 4.7 / 1.2
12 TU	0528 / 1131 / 1759	2.2 / 4.3 / 1.7	**27** W	0005 / 0600 / 1215 / 1847	4.9 / 1.7 / 5.0 / 1.0
13 W	0008 / 0612 / 1229 / 1840	4.5 / 1.9 / 4.7 / 1.3	**28** TH	0055 / 0646 / 1302 / 1929	5.1 / 1.4 / 5.2 / 0.8
14 TH	0055 / 0649 / 1312 / 1918	4.8 / 1.5 / 5.0 / 1.0	**29** F	0135 / 0726 / 1343 / 2005	5.3 / 1.1 / 5.3 / 0.7
15 F	0134 / 0725 / 1349 / 1954	5.2 / 1.2 / 5.3 / 0.7	**30** SA	0212 / 0804 / 1421 / ●2037	5.3 / 0.9 / 5.4 / 0.7

Chart Datum: 2·90 metres below Ordnance Datum (Newlyn)
HAT is 6·3 metres above Chart Datum

TIDES

TIME ZONE (UT)
For Summer Time add ONE hour in **non-shaded areas**

SCOTLAND – LEITH
LAT 55°59'N   LONG 3°11'W
TIMES AND HEIGHTS OF HIGH AND LOW WATERS

Dates in amber are **SPRINGS**
Dates in grey are **NEAPS**

2022

MAY

Day	Time m	Time m	Time m	Time m		Day	Time m	Time m	Time m	Time m
1 SU	0247 5.3	0840 0.8	1459 5.4	2107 0.8		16 M	0216 5.5	0811 0.7	1435 5.7	○ 2043 0.5
2 M	0321 5.3	0914 0.8	1536 5.3	2132 0.9		17 TU	0257 5.6	0857 0.6	1519 5.8	2128 0.6
3 TU	0355 5.2	0944 1.0	1613 5.2	2152 1.2		18 W	0340 5.6	0945 0.6	1607 5.7	2213 0.8
4 W	0428 5.1	1009 1.1	1650 5.0	2211 1.4		19 TH	0425 5.5	1034 0.7	1657 5.6	2300 1.1
5 TH	0502 4.9	1034 1.3	1728 4.8	2236 1.6		20 F	0513 5.3	1126 0.9	1752 5.3	2350 1.5
6 F	0539 4.7	1106 1.5	1810 4.6	2310 1.9		21 SA	0607 5.1	1225 1.1	1854 5.0	
7 SA	0621 4.5	1152 1.8	1858 4.4			22 SU	0049 1.8	0711 4.9	1338 1.3	◐ 2005 4.8
8 SU	0000 2.2	0712 4.3	1257 2.0	1953 4.3		23 M	0203 2.0	0826 4.7	1503 1.4	2118 4.7
9 M	0121 2.5	0815 4.2	1421 2.1	◐ 2057 4.2		24 TU	0320 2.1	0939 4.7	1618 1.4	2228 4.7
10 TU	0310 2.5	0926 4.2	1607 1.9	2205 4.3		25 W	0425 1.9	1045 4.8	1721 1.3	2331 4.8
11 W	0432 2.2	1036 4.4	1706 1.6	2311 4.5		26 TH	0519 1.7	1144 4.9	1813 1.2	
12 TH	0523 1.9	1137 4.6	1752 1.3			27 F	0023 4.9	0608 1.5	1234 5.0	1856 1.2
13 F	0007 4.8	0606 1.6	1217 5.0	1834 1.0		28 SA	0107 5.0	0652 1.3	1319 5.1	1930 1.1
14 SA	0054 5.1	0647 1.3	1311 5.3	1916 0.8		29 SU	0146 5.1	0734 1.2	1400 5.2	2002 1.1
15 SU	0136 5.4	0728 1.0	1352 5.5	1959 0.6		30 M	0223 5.2	0813 1.2	1439 5.2	● 2031 1.1
						31 TU	0258 5.2	0849 1.2	1516 5.1	2059 1.2

JUNE

Day	Time m	Time m	Time m	Time m		Day	Time m	Time m	Time m	Time m
1 W	0331 5.1	0922 1.1	1553 5.1	2127 1.3		16 TH	0324 5.6	0943 0.5	1558 5.7	2207 0.9
2 TH	0405 5.1	0953 1.2	1629 5.0	2155 1.5		17 F	0412 5.6	0943 0.5	1650 5.6	2256 1.1
3 F	0439 5.0	1025 1.3	1707 4.9	2226 1.6		18 SA	0503 5.5	1129 0.6	1745 5.4	2344 1.3
4 SA	0516 4.8	1101 1.4	1747 4.8	2302 1.8		19 SU	0558 5.3	1223 0.8	1843 5.2	
5 SU	0557 4.7	1144 1.6	1832 4.6	2347 2.0		20 M	0034 1.6	0658 5.1	1320 1.1	1945 5.0
6 M	0642 4.6	1235 1.7	1921 4.5			21 TU	0130 1.8	0803 5.0	1423 1.3	◐ 2047 4.8
7 TU	0047 2.2	0736 4.5	1336 1.8	◐ 2017 4.4		22 W	0231 2.0	0906 4.9	1530 1.5	2148 4.7
8 W	0203 2.3	0837 4.4	1449 1.8	2119 4.5		23 TH	0335 2.0	1008 4.8	1633 1.6	2248 4.6
9 TH	0323 2.2	0943 4.5	1600 1.6	2222 4.6		24 F	0435 1.9	1107 4.8	1729 1.6	2346 4.7
10 F	0427 2.0	1046 4.7	1659 1.4	2322 4.8		25 SA	0531 1.8	1204 4.8	1815 1.6	
11 SA	0520 1.7	1144 4.9	1750 1.2			26 SU	0037 4.8	0623 1.6	1256 4.8	1854 1.5
12 SU	0015 5.1	0609 1.4	1237 5.2	1841 1.0		27 M	0122 4.9	0709 1.4	1342 4.9	1928 1.5
13 M	0105 5.3	0659 1.1	1327 5.4	1932 0.8		28 TU	0202 5.0	0751 1.3	1423 5.0	2002 1.4
14 TU	0151 5.5	0751 0.8	1417 5.6	○ 2024 0.8		29 W	0239 5.1	0829 1.2	1500 5.0	● 2035 1.4
15 W	0237 5.6	0847 0.6	1507 5.7	2116 0.8		30 TH	0314 5.1	0904 1.1	1535 5.0	2108 1.4

JULY

Day	Time m	Time m	Time m	Time m		Day	Time m	Time m	Time m	Time m
1 F	0347 5.1	0939 1.1	1611 5.0	2142 1.4		16 SA	0401 5.7	1031 0.3	1638 5.7	2242 0.9
2 SA	0422 5.1	1015 1.1	1647 5.0	2217 1.5		17 SU	0450 5.7	1118 0.4	1728 5.5	2325 1.1
3 SU	0457 5.0	1052 1.2	1725 4.9	2253 1.6		18 M	0540 5.6	1203 0.6	1820 5.3	
4 M	0535 4.9	1131 1.3	1806 4.9	2329 1.7		19 TU	0005 1.3	0633 5.4	1245 0.9	1913 5.0
5 TU	0614 4.9	1212 1.4	1850 4.8			20 W	0044 1.6	0728 5.1	1328 1.3	◐ 2007 4.8
6 W	0009 1.9	0659 4.8	1257 1.5	1940 4.7		21 TH	0131 1.9	0826 4.9	1417 1.7	2102 4.6
7 TH	0101 2.0	0750 4.7	1351 1.6	◐ 2035 4.6		22 F	0234 2.1	0925 4.7	1524 1.9	2200 4.5
8 F	0211 2.1	0850 4.7	1455 1.6	2137 4.6		23 SA	0350 2.1	1027 4.5	1637 2.0	2302 4.5
9 SA	0328 2.0	0959 4.7	1608 1.6	2241 4.7		24 SU	0502 2.0	1133 4.5	1737 2.0	
10 SU	0439 1.8	1109 4.8	1717 1.4	2343 4.9		25 M	0005 4.6	0603 1.9	1235 4.6	1825 1.9
11 M	0543 1.6	1213 5.1	1819 1.3			26 TU	0100 4.8	0653 1.6	1327 4.7	1905 1.8
12 TU	0041 5.1	0644 1.2	1312 5.3	1918 1.1		27 W	0145 4.9	0736 1.4	1409 4.9	1941 1.6
13 W	0134 5.4	0746 0.9	1406 5.6	○ 2015 1.0		28 TH	0223 5.1	0814 1.2	1448 5.1	● 2017 1.5
14 TH	0223 5.6	0846 0.6	1458 5.7	2108 0.9		29 F	0258 5.2	0849 1.1	1518 5.1	2052 1.3
15 F	0312 5.7	0940 0.4	1548 5.8	2157 0.9		30 SA	0331 5.2	0925 0.9	1551 5.2	2128 1.3
						31 SU	0403 5.3	1001 0.9	1625 5.2	2203 1.3

AUGUST

Day	Time m	Time m	Time m	Time m		Day	Time m	Time m	Time m	Time m
1 M	0436 5.3	1037 0.9	1701 5.2	2236 1.3		16 TU	0514 5.7	1132 0.6	1748 5.3	2328 1.2
2 TU	0510 5.2	1111 1.0	1739 5.1	2303 1.4		17 W	0600 5.5	1202 1.0	1833 5.0	2356 1.5
3 W	0546 5.1	1143 1.1	1819 5.0	2330 1.6		18 TH	0647 5.1	1226 1.4	1921 4.8	
4 TH	0626 5.0	1215 1.3	1904 4.9			19 F	0032 1.8	0741 4.8	1300 1.8	◐ 2013 4.5
5 F	0007 1.7	0712 4.9	1257 1.5	1955 4.7		20 SA	0129 2.1	0839 4.5	1359 2.2	2110 4.3
6 SA	0104 1.9	0809 4.8	1359 1.7	2056 4.6		21 SU	0300 2.3	0944 4.3	1544 2.4	2214 4.3
7 SU	0229 2.0	0923 4.7	1529 1.8	2208 4.6		22 M	0441 2.3	1057 4.3	1712 2.3	2329 4.4
8 M	0414 2.0	1046 4.7	1702 1.8	2320 4.8		23 TU	0552 2.0	1216 4.4	1808 2.2	
9 TU	0536 1.7	1202 5.0	1813 1.6			24 W	0038 4.6	0644 1.7	1311 4.9	1850 1.9
10 W	0026 5.0	0646 1.3	1306 5.3	1914 1.3		25 TH	0126 4.9	0725 1.4	1351 4.9	1926 1.7
11 TH	0123 5.3	0748 0.8	1359 5.6	2007 1.1		26 F	0203 5.1	0759 1.2	1424 5.1	2000 1.4
12 F	0212 5.6	0842 0.5	1448 5.8	○ 2055 0.8		27 SA	0236 5.3	0832 1.0	1455 5.2	● 2035 1.2
13 SA	0258 5.8	0930 0.2	1533 5.8	2139 0.7		28 SU	0308 5.4	0906 0.8	1527 5.3	2109 1.1
14 SU	0343 5.9	1014 0.1	1618 5.8	2220 0.8		29 M	0339 5.5	0941 0.7	1559 5.4	2143 1.0
15 M	0428 5.9	1055 0.3	1703 5.6	2257 0.9		30 TU	0410 5.5	1014 0.7	1634 5.4	2212 1.1
						31 W	0443 5.5	1044 0.8	1710 5.3	2233 1.2

Chart Datum: 2·90 metres below Ordnance Datum (Newlyn)
HAT is 6·3 metres above Chart Datum

SCOTLAND – LEITH

LAT 55°59′N   LONG 3°11′W

TIMES AND HEIGHTS OF HIGH AND LOW WATERS

Dates in amber are **SPRINGS**
Dates in grey are **NEAPS**

2022

SEPTEMBER

Time	m		Time	m
1 TH 0518	5.4	**16** F 0609	5.1
1108	1.0		1129	1.5
1749	5.2		1836	4.8
2256	1.3		2343	1.8
2 F 0559	5.2	**17** SA 0658	4.7
1133	1.2		1201	2.0
1832	5.0		1924 ○	4.5
2332	1.5			
3 SA 0646	5.0	**18** SU 0033	2.1
1213	1.5		0755	4.4
1921 ☾	4.8		1255	2.4
			2022	4.3
4 SU 0026	1.8	**19** M 0201	2.4
0745	4.8		0904	4.2
1320	1.9		1439	2.7
2024	4.6		2129	4.2
5 M 0202	2.1	**20** TU 0425	2.4
0906	4.6		1014	4.1
1521	2.2		1651	2.6
2145	4.5		2246	4.3
6 TU 0418	2.0	**21** W 0537	2.1
1038	4.6		1144	4.3
1703	2.0		1749	2.3
2308	4.7			
7 W 0544	1.6	**22** TH 0004	4.5
1159	4.9		0625	1.7
1811	1.7		1244	4.6
			1830	2.0
8 TH 0017	5.0	**23** F 0055	4.8
0650	1.1		0702	1.4
1300	5.3		1322	4.9
1905	1.4		1904	1.7
9 F 0111	5.4	**24** SA 0133	5.1
0743	0.7		0735	1.1
1349	5.6		1355	5.2
1952	1.1		1937	1.4
10 SA 0157	5.7	**25** SU 0206	5.3
0829	0.4		0807	0.9
1432	5.8		1426	5.4
2034 ○	0.8		2010 ●	1.1
11 SU 0239	5.9	**26** M 0238	5.5
0911	0.2		0840	0.7
1512	5.8		1457	5.5
2115	0.7		2044	1.0
12 M 0320	5.9	**27** TU 0309	5.6
0950	0.2		0913	0.6
1553	5.7		1530	5.6
2152	0.7		2116	0.9
13 TU 0402	5.7	**28** W 0341	5.6
1025	0.4		0945	0.6
1633	5.6		1605	5.6
2225	0.9		2144	0.9
14 W 0444	5.7	**29** TH 0417	5.6
1054	0.7		1014	0.7
1713	5.3		1641	5.5
2250	1.1		2207	1.0
15 TH 0526	5.4	**30** F 0456	5.5
1112	1.1		1036	1.0
1753	5.0		1721	5.3
2312	1.4		2234	1.2

OCTOBER

Time	m		Time	m
1 SA 0540	5.3	**16** SU 0623	4.7
1103	1.3		1116	2.1
1805	5.0		1840	4.6
2314	1.5		2355	2.1
2 SU 0631	5.0	**17** M 0716	4.4
1148	1.8		1206	2.4
1857 ○	4.8		1936 ○	4.3
3 M 0016	1.8	**18** TU 0110	2.3
0736	4.7		0818	4.2
1317	2.2		1337	2.8
2005 ☾	4.6		2044	4.2
4 TU 0225	2.1	**19** W 0346	2.4
0904	4.6		0926	4.1
1529	2.4		1610	2.7
2134	4.5		2158	4.3
5 W 0427	1.9	**20** TH 0500	2.1
1035	4.7		1043	4.3
1657	2.1		1712	2.4
2258	4.7		2312	4.5
6 TH 0542	1.4	**21** F 0547	1.8
1152	5.0		1154	4.6
1757	1.8		1754	2.1
7 F 0004	5.1	**22** SA 0010	4.8
0640	1.0		0625	1.5
1248	5.3		1239	4.9
1846	1.4		1830	1.7
8 SA 0054	5.4	**23** SU 0053	5.1
0726	0.7		0659	1.2
1332	5.6		1316	5.2
1928	1.1		1905	1.4
9 SU 0137	5.7	**24** M 0129	5.3
0807	0.5		0732	0.9
1410	5.7		1351	5.4
2008 ○	0.9		1939	1.2
10 M 0217	5.8	**25** TU 0204	5.5
0845	0.4		0806	0.7
1447	5.7		1426	5.6
2046	0.8		2014 ●	1.0
11 TU 0256	5.8	**26** W 0239	5.7
0920	0.5		0841	0.6
1525	5.6		1501	5.7
2123	0.8		2048	0.9
12 W 0336	5.7	**27** TH 0316	5.7
0957	0.7		0916	0.7
1602	5.5		1538	5.7
2154	0.9		2123	0.9
13 TH 0416	5.5	**28** F 0356	5.7
1013	1.0		0950	0.8
1640	5.3		1617	5.6
2218	1.2		2156	1.0
14 F 0456	5.3	**29** SA 0440	5.6
1025	1.3		1022	1.1
1716	5.1		1659	5.4
2239	1.4		2234	1.2
15 SA 0538	5.0	**30** SU 0529	5.4
1044	1.7		1100	1.5
1755	4.8		1746	5.1
2308	1.7		2308	1.7
		31 M 0625	5.1
			1202	2.0
			1842	4.9

NOVEMBER

Time	m		Time	m
1 TU 0052	1.7	**16** W 0036	2.1
0735	4.8		0738	4.3
1335	2.3		1250	2.6
1956 ☾	4.7		1958 ○	4.4
2 W 0239	1.8	**17** TH 0157	2.2
0859	4.7		0839	4.3
1515	2.3		1436	2.7
2123	4.7		2107	4.3
3 TH 0414	1.6	**18** F 0351	2.1
1021	4.8		0945	4.3
1631	2.1		1611	2.5
2239	4.9		2214	4.5
4 F 0522	1.3	**19** SA 0450	1.9
1131	5.0		1050	4.5
1728	1.8		1704	2.2
2341	5.1		2315	4.7
5 SA 0616	1.1	**20** SU 0535	1.6
1225	5.2		1146	4.8
1816	1.5		1747	1.9
6 SU 0031	5.4	**21** M 0006	5.0
0702	0.9		0615	1.3
1308	5.4		1233	5.1
1859	1.3		1827	1.6
7 M 0115	5.5	**22** TU 0050	5.2
0740	0.8		0653	1.1
1346	5.5		1316	5.4
1939	1.1		1905	1.3
8 TU 0155	5.6	**23** W 0132	5.5
0815	0.8		0732	0.9
1423	5.5		1355	5.5
2019 ●	1.0		1945	1.1
9 W 0235	5.6	**24** TH 0214	5.6
0847	0.8		0812	0.8
1500	5.5		1435	5.7
2056	1.0		2028	0.9
10 TH 0315	5.5	**25** F 0256	5.7
0915	1.0		0855	0.8
1536	5.4		1515	5.7
2129	1.1		2114	0.8
11 F 0354	5.4	**26** SA 0342	5.7
0936	1.3		0940	1.0
1611	5.3		1559	5.6
2156	1.2		2204	0.9
12 SA 0433	5.2	**27** SU 0430	5.6
0954	1.5		1028	1.2
1646	5.1		1645	5.5
2221	1.4		2257	1.0
13 SU 0513	5.0	**28** M 0523	5.4
1019	1.8		1119	1.6
1722	4.9		1736	5.3
2253	1.7		2355	1.2
14 M 0555	4.7	**29** TU 0621	5.2
1053	2.0		1216	1.9
1804	4.7		1834	5.1
2337	1.9			
15 TU 0643	4.5	**30** W 0102	1.4
1139	2.3		0728	5.0
1856	4.5		1324	2.1
			1946 ○	4.9

DECEMBER

Time	m		Time	m
1 TH 0220	1.5	**16** F 0105	1.9
0842	4.8		0754	4.5
1439	2.2		1318	2.4
2102	4.9		2010 ○	4.5
2 F 0339	1.5	**17** SA 0212	2.0
0952	4.8		0852	4.4
1549	2.1		1441	2.4
2210	4.9		2114	4.5
3 SA 0446	1.4	**18** SU 0327	1.9
1057	4.9		0954	4.5
1649	1.9		1557	2.3
2311	5.0		2219	4.6
4 SU 0544	1.4	**19** M 0433	1.7
1154	5.0		1055	4.7
1742	1.7		1656	2.1
			2319	4.8
5 M 0005	5.1	**20** TU 0527	1.5
0632	1.3		1152	4.9
1242	5.1		1747	1.8
1830	1.5			
6 TU 0054	5.2	**21** W 0015	5.1
0711	1.3		0617	1.3
1324	5.2		1243	5.2
1915	1.3		1836	1.5
7 W 0138	5.3	**22** TH 0107	5.3
0744	1.3		0706	1.2
1403	5.3		1330	5.4
1957	1.2		1927	1.2
8 TH 0220	5.3	**23** F 0156	5.5
0815	1.3		0756	1.1
1440	5.3		1415	5.6
2035	1.2		2020 ●	0.9
9 F 0300	5.3	**24** SA 0244	5.7
0844	1.4		0847	1.0
1516	5.3		1500	5.7
2109	1.2		2115	0.7
10 SA 0338	5.2	**25** SU 0333	5.8
0911	1.5		0938	1.0
1550	5.2		1547	5.7
2140	1.3		2209	0.6
11 SU 0414	5.1	**26** M 0423	5.7
0938	1.6		1028	1.1
1624	5.1		1635	5.7
2211	1.3		2302	0.7
12 M 0452	5.0	**27** TU 0515	5.6
1009	1.7		1116	1.3
1659	5.0		1726	5.5
2245	1.5		2354	0.8
13 TU 0531	4.9	**28** W 0610	5.4
1043	1.9		1204	1.5
1738	4.9		1821	5.4
2324	1.6			
14 W 0614	4.7	**29** TH 0046	1.0
1123	2.1		0709	5.1
1822	4.7		1253	1.8
			1923	5.2
15 TH 0010	1.8	**30** F 0143	1.3
0701	4.6		0811	4.9
1212	2.3		1349	2.0
1913	4.6		2029	4.9
		31 SA 0246	1.5
			0914	4.7
			1454	2.1
			2134	4.9

Chart Datum: 2·90 metres below Ordnance Datum (Newlyn)
HAT is 6·3 metres above Chart Datum

TIDES

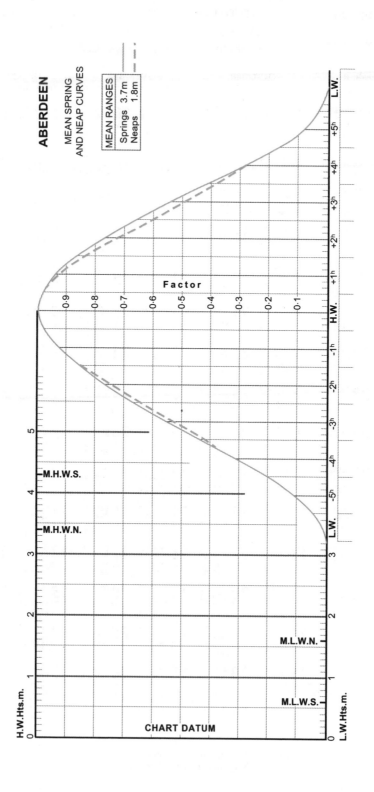

TIME ZONE (UT)
For Summer Time add ONE hour in **non-shaded areas**

SCOTLAND – ABERDEEN
LAT 57°09′N LONG 2°04′W
TIMES AND HEIGHTS OF HIGH AND LOW WATERS

Dates in amber are SPRINGS
Dates in grey are NEAPS

2022

JANUARY
Time m — Time m

	Time	m		Time	m
1 SA	0537 / 1156 / 1804	1.0 / 4.2 / 1.0	**16** SU	0023 / 0620 / 1240 / 1846	3.8 / 1.5 / 3.9 / 1.3
2 SU ●	0021 / 0630 / 1243 / 1857	4.3 / 0.9 / 4.4 / 0.8	**17** M ○	0103 / 0655 / 1314 / 1921	3.9 / 1.4 / 4.0 / 1.1
3 M	0114 / 0719 / 1329 / 1947	4.4 / 0.9 / 4.5 / 0.6	**18** TU	0139 / 0728 / 1347 / 1956	3.9 / 1.3 / 4.1 / 1.0
4 TU	0207 / 0806 / 1416 / 2037	4.5 / 0.9 / 4.5 / 0.5	**19** W	0213 / 0801 / 1419 / 2030	4.0 / 1.2 / 4.2 / 0.9
5 W	0259 / 0853 / 1503 / 2126	4.4 / 1.0 / 4.5 / 0.6	**20** TH	0248 / 0834 / 1451 / 2106	4.0 / 1.2 / 4.2 / 0.9
6 TH	0350 / 0938 / 1551 / 2216	4.3 / 1.2 / 4.4 / 0.7	**21** F	0323 / 0908 / 1525 / 2142	4.0 / 1.2 / 4.2 / 0.9
7 F	0442 / 1024 / 1641 / 2306	4.1 / 1.3 / 4.2 / 0.9	**22** SA	0400 / 0943 / 1601 / 2220	3.9 / 1.3 / 4.1 / 0.9
8 SA	0534 / 1112 / 1733 / 2357	3.9 / 1.5 / 4.1 / 1.1	**23** SU	0440 / 1020 / 1641 / 2301	3.8 / 1.3 / 4.0 / 1.0
9 SU ☾	0627 / 1204 / 1828	3.7 / 1.7 / 3.9	**24** M	0524 / 1103 / 1727 / 2349	3.8 / 1.4 / 3.9 / 1.1
10 M	0050 / 0726 / 1302 / 1927	1.3 / 3.5 / 1.8 / 3.7	**25** TU ☾	0616 / 1155 / 1823	3.7 / 1.6 / 3.9
11 TU	0149 / 0826 / 1409 / 2034	1.5 / 3.4 / 1.9 / 3.5	**26** W	0046 / 0717 / 1302 / 1931	1.3 / 3.6 / 1.7 / 3.7
12 W	0256 / 0932 / 1526 / 2145	1.7 / 3.4 / 1.9 / 3.5	**27** TH	0153 / 0825 / 1420 / 2047	1.4 / 3.6 / 1.7 / 3.7
13 TH	0405 / 1031 / 1634 / 2248	1.7 / 3.5 / 1.8 / 3.6	**28** F	0308 / 0937 / 1543 / 2207	1.4 / 3.6 / 1.6 / 3.8
14 F	0458 / 1121 / 1725 / 2340	1.6 / 3.7 / 1.6 / 3.7	**29** SA	0425 / 1045 / 1659 / 2320	1.4 / 3.8 / 1.3 / 4.0
15 SA	0541 / 1203 / 1807	1.6 / 3.8 / 1.4	**30** SU	0530 / 1144 / 1800	1.2 / 4.0 / 1.0
			31 M	0020 / 0624 / 1234 / 1853	4.2 / 1.1 / 4.2 / 0.7

FEBRUARY
Time m — Time m

	Time	m		Time	m
1 TU ●	0113 / 0712 / 1321 / 1942	4.3 / 1.0 / 4.4 / 0.5	**16** W ○	0122 / 0711 / 1329 / 1937	3.9 / 1.2 / 4.1 / 0.8
2 W	0201 / 0756 / 1405 / 2027	4.4 / 0.9 / 4.5 / 0.4	**17** TH	0155 / 0744 / 1400 / 2011	4.0 / 1.1 / 4.2 / 0.7
3 TH	0247 / 0837 / 1447 / 2111	4.4 / 0.8 / 4.5 / 0.4	**18** F	0227 / 0816 / 1431 / 2045	4.1 / 0.9 / 4.3 / 0.6
4 F	0330 / 0917 / 1529 / 2152	4.2 / 0.8 / 4.5 / 0.5	**19** SA	0300 / 0848 / 1504 / 2119	4.1 / 0.9 / 4.3 / 0.6
5 SA	0412 / 0955 / 1612 / 2232	1.1 / 1.1 / 4.3 / 0.8	**20** SU	0334 / 0921 / 1539 / 2154	4.1 / 1.0 / 4.3 / 0.7
6 SU	0455 / 1033 / 1655 / 2311	3.9 / 1.2 / 4.1 / 1.0	**21** M	0411 / 0956 / 1617 / 2232	4.0 / 1.0 / 4.2 / 0.8
7 M	0538 / 1114 / 1740 / 2354	3.7 / 1.4 / 3.9 / 1.3	**22** TU	0452 / 1035 / 1702 / 2316	3.9 / 1.2 / 4.1 / 1.0
8 TU ☾	0625 / 1202 / 1833	3.5 / 1.7 / 3.6	**23** W ☾	0540 / 1123 / 1756	3.7 / 1.3 / 3.9
9 W	0043 / 0720 / 1304 / 1936	1.6 / 3.3 / 1.9 / 3.4	**24** TH	0010 / 0640 / 1229 / 1908	1.3 / 3.6 / 1.6 / 3.7
10 TH	0145 / 0827 / 1425 / 2054	1.8 / 3.3 / 2.0 / 3.3	**25** F	0123 / 0753 / 1356 / 2034	1.5 / 3.4 / 1.6 / 3.5
11 F	0310 / 0944 / 1603 / 2218	1.9 / 3.3 / 1.9 / 3.3	**26** SA	0252 / 0915 / 1538 / 2207	1.6 / 3.5 / 1.5 / 3.6
12 SA	0433 / 1051 / 1706 / 2322	1.9 / 3.4 / 1.7 / 3.4	**27** SU	0423 / 1034 / 1659 / 2323	1.6 / 3.6 / 1.2 / 3.8
13 SU	0524 / 1141 / 1751	1.7 / 3.6 / 1.5	**28** M	0527 / 1137 / 1757	1.4 / 3.9 / 0.9
14 M	0009 / 0604 / 1221 / 1829	3.6 / 1.6 / 3.8 / 1.2			
15 TU	0048 / 0639 / 1256 / 1903	3.8 / 1.4 / 4.0 / 1.0			

MARCH
Time m — Time m

	Time	m		Time	m
1 TU	0019 / 0617 / 1226 / 1846	4.0 / 1.1 / 4.1 / 0.6	**16** W	0023 / 0615 / 1229 / 1837	3.7 / 1.3 / 3.9 / 0.9
2 W ●	0106 / 0700 / 1309 / 1930	4.2 / 1.0 / 4.3 / 0.4	**17** TH	0056 / 0647 / 1302 / 1910	3.9 / 1.1 / 4.1 / 0.7
3 TH	0147 / 0739 / 1348 / 2009	4.3 / 0.8 / 4.5 / 0.3	**18** F ○	0128 / 0719 / 1333 / 1944	4.1 / 0.9 / 4.2 / 0.5
4 F	0226 / 0816 / 1426 / 2046	4.3 / 0.8 / 4.5 / 0.4	**19** SA	0200 / 0752 / 1406 / 2018	4.2 / 0.8 / 4.4 / 0.4
5 SA	0302 / 0851 / 1504 / 2121	4.2 / 0.8 / 4.4 / 0.5	**20** SU	0233 / 0825 / 1440 / 2053	4.2 / 0.7 / 4.4 / 0.4
6 SU	0338 / 0924 / 1541 / 2154	4.1 / 0.9 / 4.3 / 0.7	**21** M	0308 / 0859 / 1517 / 2128	4.2 / 0.7 / 4.4 / 0.5
7 M	0413 / 0958 / 1618 / 2226	3.9 / 1.0 / 4.1 / 1.0	**22** TU	0345 / 0935 / 1558 / 2207	4.1 / 0.8 / 4.3 / 0.8
8 TU	0449 / 1033 / 1659 / 2301	3.7 / 1.2 / 3.8 / 1.3	**23** W	0425 / 1016 / 1646 / 2251	4.0 / 1.0 / 4.1 / 1.1
9 W	0529 / 1114 / 1747 / 2343	3.5 / 1.5 / 3.5 / 1.6	**24** TH	0513 / 1107 / 1745 / 2350	3.7 / 1.2 / 3.8 / 1.4
10 TH ☾	0619 / 1208 / 1848	3.3 / 1.7 / 3.3	**25** F ☾	0614 / 1219 / 1904	3.5 / 1.4 / 3.5
11 F	0041 / 0724 / 1328 / 2006	1.9 / 3.2 / 1.9 / 3.1	**26** SA	0109 / 0733 / 1355 / 2036	1.7 / 3.4 / 1.5 / 3.4
12 SA	0210 / 0845 / 1521 / 2142	2.1 / 3.1 / 1.9 / 3.1	**27** SU	0251 / 0902 / 1541 / 2213	1.7 / 3.4 / 1.4 / 3.6
13 SU	0404 / 1025 / 1640 / 2257	2.0 / 3.2 / 1.7 / 3.3	**28** M	0418 / 1025 / 1653 / 2320	1.6 / 3.6 / 1.1 / 3.8
14 M	0502 / 1112 / 1726 / 2346	1.8 / 3.4 / 1.4 / 3.5	**29** TU	0516 / 1124 / 1745	1.4 / 3.8 / 0.8
15 TU	0541 / 1155 / 1803	1.6 / 3.7 / 1.1	**30** W	0009 / 0602 / 1210 / 1830	4.0 / 1.1 / 4.1 / 0.6
			31 TH	0049 / 0624 / 1250 / 1909	4.1 / 0.9 / 4.3 / 0.4

APRIL
Time m — Time m

	Time	m		Time	m
1 F ●	0125 / 0717 / 1326 / 1944	4.2 / 0.8 / 4.4 / 0.4	**16** SA ○	0056 / 0650 / 1302 / 1913	4.1 / 0.8 / 4.2 / 0.4
2 SA	0159 / 0751 / 1402 / 2017	4.2 / 0.7 / 4.4 / 0.5	**17** SU	0130 / 0725 / 1339 / 1950	4.2 / 0.7 / 4.4 / 0.3
3 SU	0231 / 0824 / 1437 / 2048	4.1 / 0.7 / 4.3 / 0.6	**18** M	0205 / 0801 / 1418 / 2027	4.3 / 0.6 / 4.4 / 0.4
4 M	0303 / 0856 / 1512 / 2117	4.0 / 0.8 / 4.1 / 0.8	**19** TU	0242 / 0839 / 1500 / 2106	4.3 / 0.6 / 4.4 / 0.6
5 TU	0335 / 0928 / 1549 / 2147	3.9 / 1.0 / 4.0 / 1.1	**20** W	0322 / 0921 / 1546 / 2149	4.2 / 0.7 / 4.2 / 0.8
6 W	0408 / 1002 / 1628 / 2219	3.8 / 1.1 / 3.7 / 1.4	**21** TH	0405 / 1009 / 1640 / 2239	4.0 / 0.8 / 4.0 / 1.2
7 TH	0444 / 1041 / 1714 / 2257	3.6 / 1.4 / 3.5 / 1.6	**22** F	0457 / 1108 / 1748 / 2343	3.8 / 1.1 / 3.7 / 1.5
8 F	0529 / 1131 / 1814 / 2351	3.4 / 1.6 / 3.3 / 1.9	**23** SA ☾	0603 / 1225 / 1907	3.6 / 1.2 / 3.5
9 SA ☾	0632 / 1244 / 1927	3.2 / 1.8 / 3.2	**24** SU	0106 / 0722 / 1358 / 2036	1.8 / 3.4 / 1.3 / 3.5
10 SU	0117 / 0750 / 1422 / 2053	2.1 / 3.1 / 1.8 / 3.1	**25** M	0241 / 0846 / 1529 / 2201	1.8 / 3.5 / 1.2 / 3.6
11 M	0310 / 0915 / 1555 / 2215	2.1 / 3.2 / 1.6 / 3.3	**26** TU	0358 / 1004 / 1634 / 2301	1.6 / 3.6 / 1.0 / 3.7
12 TU	0424 / 1027 / 1647 / 2308	1.8 / 3.3 / 1.3 / 3.5	**27** W	0453 / 1100 / 1723 / 2347	1.4 / 3.8 / 0.8 / 3.9
13 W	0506 / 1115 / 1726 / 2348	1.6 / 3.6 / 1.1 / 3.7	**28** TH	0537 / 1148 / 1805	1.2 / 4.0 / 0.7
14 TH	0542 / 1153 / 1802	1.3 / 3.8 / 0.8	**29** F	0025 / 0616 / 1226 / 1842	4.0 / 1.0 / 4.1 / 0.6
15 F	0022 / 0616 / 1228 / 1837	3.9 / 1.0 / 4.0 / 0.6	**30** SA ●	0058 / 0652 / 1303 / 1915	4.0 / 0.9 / 4.2 / 0.6

Chart Datum: 2·25 metres below Ordnance Datum (Newlyn)
HAT is 4·8 metres above Chart Datum

TIDES

TIME ZONE (UT)
For Summer Time add ONE hour in **non-shaded areas**

SCOTLAND – ABERDEEN
LAT 57°09'N   LONG 2°04'W
TIMES AND HEIGHTS OF HIGH AND LOW WATERS

2022

MAY

Day	Time	m	Time	m	Time	m	Time	m
1 SU	0130	4.1	0726	0.8	SU 1338	4.2	1946	0.7
16 M	0101	4.2	0700	0.7	M 1316	4.4	O 1924	0.4
2 M	0202	4.1	0800	0.8	M 1414	4.1	2017	0.8
17 TU	0140	4.3	0742	0.6	TU 1400	4.4	2007	0.5
3 TU	0233	4.0	0833	0.9	TU 1449	4.0	2047	1.0
18 W	0221	4.3	0827	0.5	W 1449	4.3	2052	0.7
4 W	0304	3.9	0906	1.0	W 1526	3.8	2117	1.2
19 TH	0305	4.2	0916	0.6	TH 1541	4.2	2140	1.0
5 TH	0337	3.8	0941	1.1	TH 1606	3.7	2150	1.4
20 F	0353	4.1	1010	0.7	F 1642	4.0	2235	1.3
6 F	0413	3.7	1020	1.3	F 1652	3.5	2229	1.6
21 SA	0449	3.9	1113	0.9	SA 1749	3.8	2339	1.5
7 SA	0456	3.5	1109	1.4	SA 1748	3.3	2319	1.8
22 SU	0555	3.7	1225	1.0	☽ SU 1900	3.6		
8 SU	0553	3.3	1211	1.6	SU 1853	3.2		
23 M	0052	1.7	0706	3.6	M 1341	1.1	2016	3.5
9 M	0031	2.0	0704	3.2	M 1330	1.6	☽ 2003	3.2
24 TU	0209	1.7	0820	3.6	TU 1457	1.1	2130	3.6
10 TU	0202	2.0	0816	3.2	TU 1448	1.5	2115	3.3
25 W	0321	1.6	0932	3.6	W 1602	1.0	2230	3.6
11 W	0320	1.8	0925	3.3	W 1551	1.3	2217	3.5
26 TH	0420	1.5	1032	3.7	TH 1653	1.0	2317	3.7
12 TH	0416	1.6	1023	3.5	TH 1639	1.1	2304	3.7
27 F	0508	1.3	1120	3.8	F 1735	0.9	2356	3.8
13 F	0459	1.3	1110	3.8	F 1721	0.8	2344	3.9
28 SA	0550	1.1	1203	3.8	SA 1813	0.9		
14 SA	0539	1.1	1152	4.0	SA 1802	0.6		
29 SU	0031	3.9	0629	1.0	SU 1241	3.9	1847	0.9
15 SU	0022	4.1	0620	0.9	SU 1233	4.2	1843	0.5
30 M	0105	4.0	0705	0.9	M 1319	3.9	● 1920	1.0
31 TU	0137	4.0	0741	0.9	TU 1356	3.9	1952	1.0

JUNE

Day	Time	m	Time	m	Time	m	Time	m
1 W	0209	4.0	0816	0.9	W 1433	3.9	2024	0.9
16 TH	0206	4.3	0822	0.5	TH 1444	4.3	2044	0.8
2 TH	0242	3.9	0850	1.0	TH 1511	3.8	2057	1.3
17 F	0253	4.3	0914	0.5	F 1539	4.2	2134	1.0
3 F	0315	3.9	0927	1.1	F 1550	3.7	2132	1.4
18 SA	0344	4.2	1008	0.5	SA 1638	4.1	2226	1.2
4 SA	0352	3.8	1006	1.1	SA 1634	3.5	2211	1.5
19 SU	0439	4.1	1106	0.7	SU 1737	3.9	2322	1.4
5 SU	0433	3.6	1051	1.3	SU 1723	3.4	2256	1.7
20 M	0538	4.0	1206	0.8	M 1837	3.7		
6 M	0523	3.5	1143	1.3	M 1818	3.3	2352	1.8
21 TU	0022	1.5	0639	3.8	TU 1308	1.0	☽ 1940	3.6
7 TU	0621	3.4	1244	1.4	TU 1916	3.3		
22 W	0125	1.6	0743	3.7	W 1412	1.1	2045	3.5
8 W	0101	1.8	0724	3.4	W 1348	1.4	2018	3.4
23 TH	0232	1.7	0850	3.6	TH 1518	1.2	2148	3.5
9 TH	0212	1.8	0826	3.5	TH 1450	1.2	2119	3.5
24 F	0339	1.6	0955	3.6	F 1617	1.3	2241	3.6
10 F	0316	1.6	0927	3.6	F 1547	1.1	2216	3.7
25 SA	0438	1.5	1052	3.6	SA 1705	1.3	2327	3.7
11 SA	0413	1.4	1026	3.8	SA 1640	0.9	2306	3.9
26 SU	0527	1.3	1141	3.7	SU 1747	1.3		
12 SU	0504	1.2	1119	4.0	SU 1730	0.8	2352	4.0
27 M	0007	3.8	0610	1.2	M 1225	3.7	1825	1.2
13 M	0553	1.0	1210	4.2	M 1818	0.7		
28 TU	0044	3.9	0649	1.1	TU 1305	3.8	1901	1.2
14 TU	0036	4.2	0642	0.7	TU 1300	4.3	O 1907	0.7
29 W	0119	3.9	0727	1.0	W 1344	3.8	● 1935	1.2
15 W	0121	4.3	0731	0.6	W 1351	4.4	1955	0.7
30 TH	0153	4.0	0802	1.0	TH 1421	3.8	2008	1.2

JULY

Day	Time	m	Time	m	Time	m	Time	m
1 F	0226	4.0	0837	0.9	F 1457	3.8	2042	1.3
16 SA	0242	4.4	0907	0.3	SA 1530	4.3	2120	0.9
2 SA	0259	4.0	0913	1.0	SA 1534	3.8	2116	1.3
17 SU	0330	4.4	0956	0.4	SU 1620	4.1	2206	1.0
3 SU	0334	3.9	0950	1.0	SU 1613	3.7	2152	1.4
18 M	0419	4.3	1045	0.5	M 1711	4.0	2253	1.2
4 M	0412	3.8	1030	1.0	M 1655	3.6	2232	1.5
19 TU	0510	4.2	1134	0.8	TU 1802	3.8	2342	1.4
5 TU	0453	3.8	1113	1.1	TU 1741	3.5	2316	1.5
20 W	0603	4.0	1225	1.0	W 1855	3.6		
6 W	0541	3.7	1202	1.2	W 1832	3.5		
21 TH	0036	1.6	0701	3.7	TH 1319	1.3	1954	3.4
7 TH	0009	1.6	0636	3.6	TH 1257	1.2	☽ 1929	3.5
22 F	0138	1.7	0804	3.6	F 1421	1.5	2058	3.4
8 F	0114	1.7	0736	3.6	F 1358	1.2	2029	3.5
23 SA	0252	1.8	0916	3.4	SA 1534	1.6	2202	3.4
9 SA	0222	1.6	0842	3.6	SA 1502	1.2	2133	3.6
24 SU	0410	1.7	1026	3.4	SU 1638	1.6	2259	3.6
10 SU	0331	1.5	0950	3.7	SU 1607	1.1	2234	3.8
25 M	0509	1.5	1125	3.5	M 1727	1.6	2346	3.7
11 M	0437	1.3	1057	3.9	M 1709	1.0	2329	3.9
26 TU	0555	1.4	1213	3.6	TU 1808	1.5		
12 TU	0538	1.0	1158	4.1	TU 1805	0.9		
27 W	0027	3.8	0635	1.2	W 1254	3.7	1845	1.4
13 W	0019	4.1	0634	0.8	W 1253	4.2	O 1857	0.9
28 TH	0103	3.9	0712	1.0	TH 1331	3.8	● 1919	1.3
14 TH	0108	4.3	0726	0.5	TH 1346	4.3	1946	0.8
29 F	0137	4.0	0746	0.9	F 1405	3.9	1951	1.2
15 F	0155	4.4	0817	0.4	F 1438	4.4	2034	0.8
30 SA	0209	4.1	0820	0.8	SA 1439	3.9	2024	1.1
31 SU	0241	4.1	0854	0.8	SU 1512	3.9	2056	1.1

AUGUST

Day	Time	m	Time	m	Time	m	Time	m
1 M	0313	4.1	0928	0.8	M 1547	3.9	2129	1.2
16 TU	0352	4.4	1013	0.5	TU 1635	4.0	2217	1.1
2 TU	0347	4.1	1004	0.8	TU 1623	3.8	2204	1.2
17 W	0436	4.2	1054	0.8	W 1719	3.8	2259	1.3
3 W	0424	4.0	1041	0.9	W 1703	3.7	2242	1.3
18 TH	0523	4.0	1136	1.2	TH 1806	3.6	2347	1.5
4 TH	0505	3.9	1122	1.0	TH 1749	3.7	2328	1.5
19 F	0616	3.7	1224	1.5	F 1900	3.4	☾	
5 F	0555	3.8	1213	1.2	☽ F 1844	3.6		
20 SA	0046	1.7	0719	3.5	SA 1323	1.8	2004	3.3
6 SA	0026	1.6	0657	3.7	SA 1315	1.3	1948	3.5
21 SU	0204	1.9	0835	3.3	SU 1444	1.9	2119	3.3
7 SU	0141	1.7	0811	3.6	SU 1428	1.4	2059	3.5
22 M	0346	1.8	1002	3.3	M 1615	1.9	2230	3.5
8 M	0304	1.6	0931	3.6	M 1548	1.4	2211	3.7
23 TU	0453	1.6	1109	3.4	TU 1710	1.8	2324	3.6
9 TU	0427	1.4	1050	3.8	TU 1701	1.3	2315	3.9
24 W	0539	1.4	1158	3.6	W 1751	1.6		
10 W	0534	1.1	1155	4.0	W 1759	1.1		
25 TH	0006	3.8	0617	1.2	TH 1237	3.8	1827	1.4
11 TH	0009	4.1	0629	0.7	TH 1250	4.2	1849	1.0
26 F	0042	4.0	0652	1.0	F 1311	3.9	1859	1.3
12 F	0057	4.3	0719	0.4	F 1339	4.4	O 1935	0.9
27 SA	0115	4.1	0724	0.8	SA 1342	4.0	● 1930	1.1
13 SA	0142	4.5	0805	0.3	SA 1425	4.4	2017	0.8
28 SU	0145	4.2	0756	0.7	SU 1413	4.1	2001	1.0
14 SU	0225	4.6	0850	0.2	SU 1509	4.3	2058	0.8
29 M	0215	4.3	0828	0.6	M 1444	4.1	2032	1.0
15 M	0308	4.6	0932	0.3	M 1552	4.2	2138	0.9
30 TU	0247	4.3	0901	0.6	TU 1516	4.1	2103	1.0
31 W	0320	4.3	0933	0.7	W 1551	4.0	2136	1.1

Chart Datum: 2·25 metres below Ordnance Datum (Newlyn)
HAT is 4·8 metres above Chart Datum

SCOTLAND – ABERDEEN

LAT 57°09'N   LONG 2°04'W

TIMES AND HEIGHTS OF HIGH AND LOW WATERS

Dates in amber are SPRINGS
Dates in grey are NEAPS

2022

SEPTEMBER

#	Time	m	#	Time	m
1 TH	0356 / 1008 / 1628 / 2212	4.2 / 0.8 / 3.9 / 1.2	16 F	0444 / 1046 / 1714 / 2302	3.9 / 1.3 / 3.7 / 1.5
2 F	0437 / 1047 / 1712 / 2256	4.1 / 1.0 / 3.8 / 1.3	17 SA	0534 / 1127 / 1804 / 2358	3.6 / 1.7 / 3.5 / 1.8
3 SA	0527 / 1137 / 1807 / 2355	3.9 / 1.3 / 3.6 / 1.5	18 SU	0637 / 1225 / 1909	3.4 / 2.0 / 3.3
4 SU	0633 / 1244 / 1916	3.7 / 1.6 / 3.5	19 M	0118 / 0756 / 1352 / 2028	1.9 / 3.2 / 2.2 / 3.3
5 M	0119 / 0758 / 1411 / 2036	1.7 / 3.6 / 1.7 / 3.3	20 TU	0313 / 0930 / 1549 / 2153	1.9 / 3.2 / 2.1 / 3.4
6 TU	0259 / 0930 / 1546 / 2158	1.6 / 3.6 / 1.7 / 3.6	21 W	0428 / 1045 / 1647 / 2254	1.7 / 3.4 / 1.9 / 3.6
7 W	0428 / 1053 / 1658 / 2306	1.3 / 3.8 / 1.5 / 3.9	22 TH	0514 / 1133 / 1727 / 2338	1.4 / 3.6 / 1.7 / 3.8
8 TH	0530 / 1153 / 1750 / 2358	1.0 / 4.1 / 1.2 / 4.2	23 F	0550 / 1210 / 1801	1.2 / 3.8 / 1.5
9 F	0620 / 1242 / 1835	0.6 / 4.3 / 1.0	24 SA	0013 / 0623 / 1242 / 1832	4.0 / 1.0 / 4.0 / 1.2
10 SA	0043 / 0705 / 1324 / 1916	4.4 / 0.4 / 4.4 / 0.8	25 SU	0045 / 0654 / 1312 / 1902	4.2 / 0.8 / 4.1 / 1.1
11 SU	0123 / 0746 / 1403 / 1955	4.6 / 0.3 / 4.4 / 0.8	26 M	0115 / 0726 / 1342 / 1933	4.3 / 0.6 / 4.2 / 0.9
12 M	0203 / 0825 / 1441 / 2031	4.6 / 0.3 / 4.4 / 0.8	27 TU	0146 / 0758 / 1413 / 2004	4.4 / 0.6 / 4.3 / 0.9
13 TU	0242 / 0901 / 1518 / 2107	4.6 / 0.4 / 4.4 / 0.9	28 W	0219 / 0830 / 1446 / 2037	4.4 / 0.6 / 4.3 / 0.9
14 W	0321 / 0936 / 1555 / 2142	4.4 / 0.7 / 4.1 / 1.0	29 TH	0255 / 0904 / 1521 / 2111	4.4 / 0.7 / 4.2 / 1.0
15 TH	0401 / 1010 / 1633 / 2220	4.2 / 1.0 / 3.9 / 1.2	30 F	0334 / 0939 / 1559 / 2150	4.3 / 0.9 / 4.1 / 1.1

OCTOBER

#	Time	m	#	Time	m
1 SA	0418 / 1021 / 1644 / 2238	4.1 / 1.2 / 3.9 / 1.3	16 SU	0501 / 1042 / 1714 / 2321	3.6 / 1.8 / 3.6 / 1.7
2 SU	0514 / 1114 / 1740 / 2345	3.9 / 1.6 / 3.7 / 1.5	17 M	0602 / 1134 / 1817	3.4 / 2.1 / 3.4
3 M	0629 / 1230 / 1857	3.7 / 1.8 / 3.5	18 TU	0034 / 0717 / 1259 / 1935	1.9 / 3.2 / 2.3 / 3.3
4 TU	0117 / 0759 / 1408 / 2023	1.6 / 3.5 / 1.9 / 3.5	19 W	0212 / 0841 / 1452 / 2058	1.9 / 3.2 / 2.2 / 3.4
5 W	0303 / 0935 / 1543 / 2148	1.5 / 3.6 / 1.8 / 3.7	20 TH	0344 / 1002 / 1608 / 2209	1.7 / 3.4 / 2.0 / 3.5
6 TH	0422 / 1049 / 1646 / 2253	1.2 / 3.9 / 1.5 / 4.0	21 F	0434 / 1054 / 1651 / 2258	1.5 / 3.6 / 1.8 / 3.7
7 F	0517 / 1142 / 1734 / 2342	0.9 / 4.1 / 1.3 / 4.2	22 SA	0512 / 1133 / 1726 / 2336	1.2 / 3.8 / 1.5 / 4.0
8 SA	0603 / 1224 / 1815	0.6 / 4.3 / 1.1	23 SU	0546 / 1206 / 1758	1.0 / 4.0 / 1.3
9 SU	0023 / 0644 / 1301 / 1854	4.4 / 0.5 / 4.3 / 0.9	24 M	0010 / 0619 / 1238 / 1831	4.2 / 0.8 / 4.2 / 1.1
10 M	0101 / 0721 / 1336 / 1929	4.5 / 0.5 / 4.4 / 0.8	25 TU	0043 / 0652 / 1310 / 1904	4.3 / 0.7 / 4.3 / 0.9
11 TU	0138 / 0756 / 1410 / 2004	4.6 / 0.5 / 4.3 / 0.8	26 W	0118 / 0727 / 1343 / 1939	4.5 / 0.6 / 4.4 / 0.8
12 W	0216 / 0828 / 1443 / 2039	4.5 / 0.7 / 4.2 / 0.9	27 TH	0155 / 0805 / 1418 / 2015	4.5 / 0.7 / 4.4 / 0.8
13 TH	0253 / 0900 / 1517 / 2113	4.3 / 0.9 / 4.1 / 1.1	28 F	0235 / 0839 / 1456 / 2055	4.5 / 0.8 / 4.3 / 0.9
14 F	0332 / 0931 / 1551 / 2149	4.1 / 1.2 / 3.9 / 1.3	29 SA	0319 / 0920 / 1538 / 2141	4.3 / 1.0 / 4.2 / 1.0
15 SA	0413 / 1004 / 1629 / 2229	3.9 / 1.5 / 3.8 / 1.5	30 SU	0410 / 1007 / 1626 / 2237	4.1 / 1.3 / 4.0 / 1.2
			31 M	0514 / 1107 / 1727 / 2350	3.9 / 1.6 / 3.8 / 1.4

NOVEMBER

#	Time	m	#	Time	m
1 TU	0632 / 1226 / 1845	3.7 / 1.9 / 3.7	16 W	0636 / 1207 / 1843	3.3 / 2.2 / 3.4
2 W	0119 / 0757 / 1358 / 2007	1.5 / 3.6 / 2.0 / 3.7	17 TH	0111 / 0744 / 1335 / 1955	1.8 / 3.3 / 2.2 / 3.4
3 TH	0250 / 0924 / 1521 / 2127	1.3 / 3.7 / 1.8 / 3.8	18 F	0229 / 0856 / 1456 / 2104	1.7 / 3.4 / 2.1 / 3.5
4 F	0402 / 1030 / 1622 / 2230	1.1 / 3.9 / 1.6 / 4.0	19 SA	0333 / 0958 / 1556 / 2203	1.5 / 3.5 / 1.9 / 3.7
5 SA	0455 / 1120 / 1710 / 2319	0.9 / 4.0 / 1.4 / 4.2	20 SU	0422 / 1046 / 1641 / 2251	1.3 / 3.8 / 1.6 / 3.9
6 SU	0539 / 1200 / 1751	0.8 / 4.2 / 1.2	21 M	0503 / 1126 / 1720 / 2332	1.1 / 4.0 / 1.4 / 4.1
7 M	0000 / 0619 / 1236 / 1830	4.3 / 0.8 / 4.2 / 1.0	22 TU	0541 / 1203 / 1759	0.9 / 4.2 / 1.2
8 TU	0039 / 0654 / 1309 / 1906	4.4 / 0.8 / 4.3 / 1.0	23 W	0012 / 0621 / 1240 / 1838	4.3 / 0.8 / 4.3 / 1.0
9 W	0117 / 0727 / 1342 / 1942	4.4 / 0.8 / 4.3 / 0.9	24 TH	0054 / 0700 / 1318 / 1919	4.4 / 0.7 / 4.4 / 0.9
10 TH	0154 / 0759 / 1414 / 2017	4.3 / 1.0 / 4.2 / 1.0	25 F	0137 / 0742 / 1357 / 2003	4.5 / 0.8 / 4.4 / 0.8
11 F	0232 / 0830 / 1447 / 2052	4.2 / 1.2 / 4.1 / 1.1	26 SA	0223 / 0825 / 1439 / 2050	4.5 / 0.9 / 4.4 / 0.8
12 SA	0311 / 0901 / 1520 / 2128	4.0 / 1.4 / 4.0 / 1.3	27 SU	0313 / 0911 / 1524 / 2141	4.4 / 1.1 / 4.3 / 0.9
13 SU	0351 / 0935 / 1556 / 2208	3.8 / 1.6 / 3.9 / 1.4	28 M	0410 / 1003 / 1616 / 2240	4.2 / 1.4 / 4.1 / 1.0
14 M	0437 / 1013 / 1639 / 2255	3.6 / 1.8 / 3.7 / 1.6	29 TU	0515 / 1102 / 1718 / 2349	4.0 / 1.6 / 4.0 / 1.1
15 TU	0533 / 1100 / 1734 / 2356	3.5 / 2.0 / 3.5 / 1.7	30 W	0624 / 1212 / 1828	3.8 / 1.8 / 3.9

DECEMBER

#	Time	m	#	Time	m
1 TH	0103 / 0737 / 1327 / 1940	1.2 / 3.7 / 1.9 / 3.8	16 F	0017 / 0651 / 1224 / 1855	1.6 / 3.4 / 2.0 / 3.6
2 F	0217 / 0852 / 1441 / 2053	1.2 / 3.7 / 1.8 / 3.8	17 SA	0120 / 0750 / 1336 / 1957	1.6 / 3.4 / 2.0 / 3.6
3 SA	0327 / 0958 / 1547 / 2159	1.2 / 3.8 / 1.7 / 3.9	18 SU	0222 / 0852 / 1445 / 2059	1.5 / 3.5 / 1.9 / 3.6
4 SU	0425 / 1050 / 1641 / 2253	1.1 / 3.9 / 1.5 / 4.0	19 M	0321 / 0951 / 1546 / 2200	1.4 / 3.6 / 1.8 / 3.8
5 M	0512 / 1134 / 1728 / 2340	1.1 / 4.0 / 1.4 / 4.1	20 TU	0416 / 1044 / 1641 / 2256	1.3 / 3.8 / 1.6 / 3.9
6 TU	0553 / 1212 / 1809	1.0 / 4.1 / 1.2	21 W	0507 / 1131 / 1731 / 2348	1.1 / 4.0 / 1.3 / 4.1
7 W	0022 / 0630 / 1247 / 1849	4.1 / 1.1 / 4.1 / 1.1	22 TH	0555 / 1215 / 1820	1.0 / 4.2 / 1.1
8 TH	0102 / 0704 / 1321 / 1927	4.1 / 1.2 / 4.2 / 1.1	23 F	0038 / 0643 / 1258 / 1908	4.3 / 0.9 / 4.3 / 0.9
9 F	0141 / 0738 / 1354 / 2003	4.1 / 1.2 / 4.2 / 1.1	24 SA	0127 / 0730 / 1342 / 1957	4.4 / 0.9 / 4.4 / 0.7
10 SA	0219 / 0810 / 1427 / 2038	4.0 / 1.3 / 4.1 / 1.1	25 SU	0218 / 0818 / 1428 / 2048	4.4 / 1.0 / 4.5 / 0.6
11 SU	0257 / 0843 / 1500 / 2114	3.9 / 1.4 / 4.1 / 1.2	26 M	0311 / 0906 / 1516 / 2140	4.4 / 1.1 / 4.4 / 0.6
12 M	0336 / 0917 / 1536 / 2152	3.8 / 1.6 / 4.0 / 1.3	27 TU	0406 / 0955 / 1607 / 2235	4.3 / 1.2 / 4.2 / 0.7
13 TU	0417 / 0953 / 1615 / 2234	3.7 / 1.7 / 3.9 / 1.4	28 W	0503 / 1047 / 1702 / 2332	4.1 / 1.4 / 4.2 / 0.9
14 W	0503 / 1034 / 1700 / 2322	3.6 / 1.8 / 3.7 / 1.5	29 TH	0601 / 1144 / 1801	3.9 / 1.6 / 4.1
15 TH	0554 / 1123 / 1754	3.5 / 1.9 / 3.6	30 F	0031 / 0702 / 1244 / 1904	1.0 / 3.7 / 1.7 / 3.9
			31 SA	0133 / 0806 / 1350 / 2011	1.2 / 3.6 / 1.8 / 3.8

Chart Datum: 2·25 metres below Ordnance Datum (Newlyn)
HAT is 4·8 metres above Chart Datum

TIDES

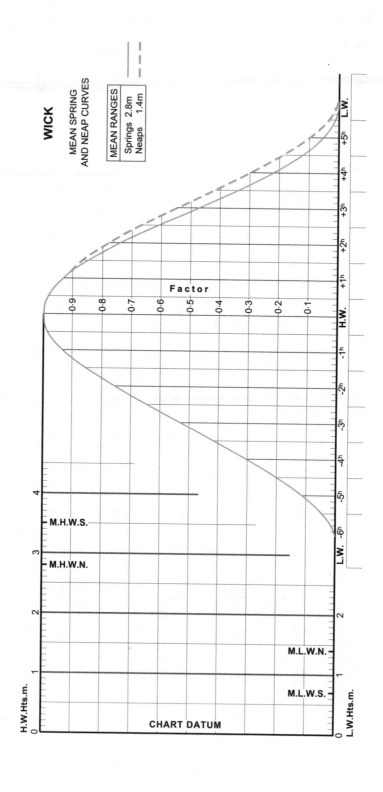

WICK

MEAN SPRING
AND NEAP CURVES

MEAN RANGES
Springs 2.8m
Neaps 1.4m

TIME ZONE (UT)	Dates in amber are SPRINGS
For Summer Time add ONE hour in **non-shaded areas**	Dates in grey are NEAPS

2022

TIMES AND HEIGHTS OF HIGH AND LOW WATERS

JANUARY

Day	Time m	Time m	Time m	Time m	Day	Time m	Time m	Time m	Time m
1 SA	0326 0.9	0947 3.4	1550 0.9	2215 3.5	16 SU	0404 1.3	1030 3.2	1634 1.1	2252 3.1
2 SU ●	0416 0.9	1038 3.6	1642 0.8	2310 3.6	17 M ○	0439 1.2	1106 3.3	1710 1.0	2329 3.2
3 M	0504 0.9	1126 3.7	1733 0.6		18 TU	0512 1.2	1140 3.4	1744 0.9	
4 TU	0002 3.6	0551 0.9	1213 3.7	1824 0.5	19 W	0004 3.2	0544 1.1	1213 3.4	1818 0.8
5 W	0053 3.6	0637 1.0	1259 3.7	1914 0.6	20 TH	0039 3.2	0617 1.1	1247 3.5	1853 0.8
6 TH	0143 3.5	0721 1.1	1346 3.7	2004 0.6	21 F	0115 3.2	0650 1.1	1322 3.4	1929 0.8
7 F	0232 3.3	0805 1.2	1433 3.5	2054 0.8	22 SA	0151 3.2	0725 1.1	1358 3.4	2006 0.8
8 SA	0322 3.1	0850 1.4	1522 3.4	2146 1.0	23 SU	0230 3.1	0802 1.2	1436 3.3	2047 0.9
9 SU ☾	0413 2.9	0940 1.5	1615 3.0	2242 1.2	24 M	0313 3.0	0843 1.3	1520 3.3	2136 1.0
10 M	0508 2.8	1040 1.6	1713 3.0	2344 1.3	25 TU	0403 2.9	0932 1.4	1612 3.2	2237 1.1
11 TU	0607 2.8	1153 1.7	1815 2.9		26 W	0501 2.9	1041 1.5	1717 3.1	2349 1.2
12 W	0052 1.4	0711 2.8	1315 1.6	1923 2.9	27 TH	0609 2.9	1209 1.5	1833 3.0	
13 TH	0155 1.4	0815 2.9	1422 1.5	2030 2.9	28 F	0104 1.2	0721 2.9	1335 1.4	1953 3.1
14 F	0245 1.4	0908 3.0	1513 1.4	2126 3.0	29 SA	0218 1.2	0831 3.1	1450 1.2	2110 3.2
15 SA	0327 1.3	0952 3.1	1556 1.2	2212 3.0	30 SU	0319 1.1	0934 3.3	1550 0.9	2213 3.4
					31 M	0411 1.0	1028 3.5	1642 0.7	2307 3.5

FEBRUARY

Day	Time m	Time m	Time m	Time m	Day	Time m	Time m	Time m	Time m
1 TU ●	0457 0.9	1117 3.6	1729 0.5	2356 3.5	16 W ○	0456 1.1	1121 3.4	1726 0.7	2346 3.2
2 W	0540 0.9	1202 3.7	1814 0.4		17 TH	0527 1.0	1155 3.5	1758 0.6	
3 TH	0041 3.5	0620 0.8	1245 3.8	1857 0.4	18 F	0020 3.3	0559 0.9	1228 3.5	1831 0.5
4 F	0124 3.4	0659 0.9	1327 3.7	1937 0.5	19 SA	0054 3.3	0632 0.8	1302 3.5	1905 0.5
5 SA	0204 3.3	0736 1.0	1407 3.6	2016 0.7	20 SU	0129 3.3	0705 0.8	1337 3.5	1941 0.6
6 SU	0244 3.1	0812 1.2	1448 3.4	2055 0.9	21 M	0205 3.2	0740 0.9	1414 3.4	2018 0.7
7 M	0325 2.9	0850 1.2	1531 3.2	2136 1.1	22 TU	0244 3.1	0818 1.0	1456 3.3	2100 0.9
8 TU ☾	0410 2.8	0935 1.4	1620 3.0	2226 1.4	23 W ◑	0329 3.0	0902 1.2	1547 3.1	2155 1.1
9 W	0504 2.7	1042 1.6	1720 2.8	2333 1.5	24 TH	0424 2.9	1004 1.3	1653 3.0	2315 1.3
10 TH	0608 2.6	1215 1.6	1834 2.7		25 F	0534 2.8	1147 1.4	1819 2.8	
11 F	0102 1.6	0723 2.7	1355 1.6	1959 2.7	26 SA	0049 1.4	0656 2.8	1335 1.3	1954 2.9
12 SA	0221 1.6	0835 2.8	1457 1.4	2108 2.8	27 SU	0216 1.3	0818 2.9	1453 1.1	2114 3.1
13 SU	0312 1.5	0928 3.0	1542 1.2	2156 2.9	28 M	0317 1.2	0925 3.2	1549 0.8	2212 3.2
14 M	0351 1.3	1010 3.1	1619 1.0	2236 3.0					
15 TU	0425 1.2	1046 3.2	1653 0.9	2312 3.1					

MARCH

Day	Time m	Time m	Time m	Time m	Day	Time m	Time m	Time m	Time m
1 TU	0404 1.0	1018 3.4	1635 0.6	2259 3.4	16 W	0401 1.1	1018 3.1	1626 0.7	2247 3.1
2 W ●	0444 0.9	1104 3.6	1716 0.4	2342 3.5	17 TH	0432 1.0	1054 3.3	1658 0.6	2321 3.2
3 TH	0522 0.8	1146 3.7	1754 0.3		18 F ○	0502 0.8	1129 3.4	1730 0.4	2355 3.3
4 F	0021 3.5	0558 0.7	1225 3.7	1830 0.3	19 SA	0535 0.7	1204 3.5	1804 0.3	
5 SA	0057 3.4	0632 0.7	1302 3.6	1905 0.5	20 SU	0029 3.4	0609 0.6	1239 3.6	1839 0.4
6 SU	0132 3.3	0706 0.8	1338 3.5	1937 0.7	21 M	0104 3.4	0644 0.6	1316 3.5	1915 0.5
7 M	0205 3.1	0738 0.9	1414 3.3	2008 0.9	22 TU	0140 3.3	0720 0.7	1356 3.4	1953 0.7
8 TU	0239 3.0	0811 1.0	1451 3.1	2039 1.1	23 W	0219 3.2	0800 0.8	1440 3.3	2035 0.9
9 W	0316 2.8	0849 1.2	1533 2.9	2117 1.4	24 TH	0304 3.0	0846 1.0	1534 3.0	2130 1.2
10 TH ☾	0400 2.7	0942 1.4	1628 2.6	2216 1.6	25 F ◑	0359 2.9	0957 1.2	1647 2.8	2301 1.4
11 F	0502 2.6	1121 1.6	1748 2.5	2358 1.7	26 SA	0513 2.7	1154 1.3	1823 2.7	
12 SA	0625 2.5	1320 1.5	1923 2.5		27 SU	0047 1.5	0642 2.7	1340 1.2	2001 2.8
13 SU	0151 1.7	0751 2.6	1431 1.3	2044 2.6	28 M	0211 1.4	0806 2.9	1447 0.9	2110 3.0
14 M	0250 1.5	0855 2.8	1516 1.1	2133 2.8	29 TU	0306 1.2	0911 3.1	1537 0.6	2159 3.2
15 TU	0329 1.3	0940 3.0	1553 0.9	2212 3.0	30 W	0348 1.0	1001 3.3	1617 0.5	2242 3.3
					31 TH	0424 0.8	1044 3.5	1653 0.4	2319 3.3

APRIL

Day	Time m	Time m	Time m	Time m	Day	Time m	Time m	Time m	Time m
1 F ●	0458 0.7	1124 3.5	1726 0.4	2355 3.4	16 SA ○	0433 0.7	1058 3.4	1659 0.3	2325 3.4
2 SA	0532 0.6	1201 3.6	1759 0.4		17 SU	0508 0.6	1137 3.5	1735 0.3	
3 SU	0027 3.3	0606 0.6	1235 3.5	1830 0.5	18 M	0002 3.4	0546 0.5	1216 3.6	1813 0.3
4 M	0059 3.2	0638 0.7	1309 3.4	1900 0.7	19 TU	0039 3.4	0624 0.5	1258 3.5	1852 0.5
5 TU	0129 3.1	0710 0.8	1343 3.2	1928 0.9	20 W	0118 3.4	0705 0.6	1343 3.4	1934 0.7
6 W	0200 3.0	0743 0.9	1419 3.0	1958 1.1	21 TH	0200 3.2	0751 0.7	1433 3.2	2021 1.0
7 TH	0234 2.9	0819 1.1	1500 2.8	2032 1.3	22 F	0247 3.1	0848 0.9	1534 2.9	2124 1.3
8 F	0314 2.7	0908 1.3	1551 2.6	2119 1.6	23 SA ◑	0346 2.8	1016 1.0	1653 2.8	2258 1.5
9 SA ☾	0408 2.6	1039 1.4	1705 2.4	2301 1.7	24 SU	0502 2.8	1159 1.0	1823 2.7	
10 SU	0527 2.5	1225 1.4	1837 2.4		25 M	0035 1.5	0626 2.8	1326 0.9	1949 2.8
11 M	0056 1.7	0654 2.5	1346 1.3	2000 2.5	26 TU	0151 1.4	0744 2.9	1428 0.8	2050 2.9
12 TU	0209 1.5	0805 2.7	1437 1.1	2055 2.7	27 W	0243 1.2	0847 3.1	1514 0.6	2136 3.1
13 W	0252 1.3	0857 2.9	1516 0.9	2136 2.9	28 TH	0323 1.0	0937 3.2	1552 0.6	2216 3.2
14 TH	0327 1.1	0940 3.1	1550 0.6	2213 3.1	29 F	0359 0.9	1020 3.3	1625 0.5	2252 3.2
15 F	0400 0.9	1019 3.3	1624 0.5	2249 3.3	30 SA ●	0433 0.7	1059 3.4	1656 0.5	2326 3.3

Chart Datum: 1·71 metres below Ordnance Datum (Newlyn)
HAT is 4·0 metres above Chart Datum

TIDES

TIME ZONE (UT)
For Summer Time add ONE hour in **non-shaded areas**

SCOTLAND – WICK
LAT 58°26′N   LONG 3°05′W
TIMES AND HEIGHTS OF HIGH AND LOW WATERS

Dates in amber are **SPRINGS**
Dates in grey are **NEAPS**

2022

MAY

Time	m		Time	m
1 SU 0507	0.7	**16** M 0444	0.6
1135	3.3	1112	3.5
1728	0.6	1710	0.4
2358	3.3	O 2337	3.5
2 M 0541	0.7	**17** TU 0526	0.5
1210	3.3	1159	3.5
1758	0.7	1752	0.5
3 TU 0028	3.2	**18** W 0018	3.5
0616	0.7	0612	0.5
1244	3.2	1246	3.5
1829	0.8	1836	0.6
4 W 0058	3.2	**19** TH 0102	3.4
0649	0.8	0700	0.6
1318	3.1	1337	3.3
1858	1.0	1923	0.9
5 TH 0130	3.1	**20** F 0148	3.3
0723	0.9	0754	0.6
1355	2.9	1432	3.2
1929	1.2	2016	1.1
6 F 0204	3.0	**21** SA 0239	3.2
0802	1.0	0900	0.7
1436	2.8	1536	3.0
2004	1.3	2122	1.3
7 SA 0244	2.8	**22** SU 0338	3.0
0851	1.2	1020	0.8
1526	2.6	1648	2.8
2050	1.5	(2240	1.4
8 SU 0333	2.7	**23** M 0449	2.9
1006	1.3	1140	0.9
1629	2.5	1802	2.7
2209	1.6		
9 M 0438	2.6	**24** TU 0000	1.4
1131	1.4	0601	2.9
1747	2.5	1256	0.8
(2349	1.6	1914	2.8
10 TU 0556	2.6	**25** 0113	1.4
1245	1.2	0710	2.9
1859	2.5	1356	0.8
		2015	2.9
11 W 0105	1.5	**26** TH 0209	1.2
0706	2.7	0814	3.0
1343	1.0	1443	0.8
2000	2.7	2104	3.0
12 TH 0201	1.3	**27** F 0254	1.1
0804	2.8	0907	3.1
1430	0.8	1522	0.8
2050	2.9	2146	3.0
13 F 0244	1.1	**28** SA 0333	1.0
0854	3.0	0953	3.1
1511	0.6	1556	0.8
2133	3.1	2224	3.1
14 SA 0324	0.9	**29** SU 0411	0.9
0941	3.2	1035	3.1
1550	0.5	1629	0.8
2215	3.3	2259	3.2
15 SU 0403	0.7	**30** M 0447	0.8
1027	3.4	1113	3.1
1629	0.4	1701	0.8
2256	3.4	● 2332	3.2
		31 TU 0524	0.8
		1150	3.1
		1733	0.9

JUNE

Time	m		Time	m
1 W 0004	3.2	**16** TH 0003	3.5
0600	0.8	0607	0.4
1225	3.1	1239	3.5
1805	1.0	1828	0.8
2 TH 0036	3.2	**17** F 0050	3.5
0636	0.8	0700	0.4
1301	3.0	1333	3.4
1837	1.1	1917	0.9
3 F 0109	3.1	**18** SA 0139	3.4
0712	0.9	0756	0.5
1338	2.9	1427	3.2
1911	1.2	2009	1.1
4 SA 0144	3.0	**19** SU 0230	3.3
0752	1.0	0857	0.6
1418	2.8	1525	3.0
1948	1.3	2104	1.2
5 SU 0223	2.9	**20** M 0325	3.2
0837	1.0	0959	0.7
1504	2.7	1625	2.9
2031	1.4	2205	1.3
6 M 0308	2.8	**21** TU 0424	3.1
0934	1.1	1104	0.8
1556	2.6	1725	2.8
2128	1.5	(2311	1.4
7 TU 0401	2.8	**22** W 0527	3.0
1040	1.1	1211	0.9
1658	2.6	1827	2.7
(2245	1.5		
8 W 0503	2.7	**23** TH 0020	1.4
1146	1.1	0630	2.9
1803	2.6	1314	1.0
2359	1.5	1929	2.7
9 TH 0609	2.8	**24** F 0128	1.3
1246	1.0	0735	2.9
1904	2.7	1407	1.0
		2026	2.8
10 F 0103	1.4	**25** SA 0225	1.2
0712	2.9	0836	2.9
1341	0.9	1452	1.0
2001	2.9	2115	2.9
11 SA 0159	1.2	**26** SU 0313	1.1
0810	3.0	0929	2.9
1431	0.7	1531	1.1
2053	3.0	2158	3.0
12 SU 0250	1.0	**27** M 0355	1.0
0907	3.2	1015	3.0
1519	0.6	1607	1.0
2143	3.2	2236	3.1
13 M 0338	0.9	**28** TU 0435	0.9
1002	3.3	1057	3.0
1605	0.6	1642	1.0
2230	3.4	2312	3.2
14 TU 0427	0.7	**29** W 0513	0.9
1055	3.4	1135	3.0
1652	0.6	1716	1.1
O 2317	3.5	● 2346	3.2
15 W 0516	0.5	**30** TH 0549	0.8
1148	3.5	1211	3.0
1739	0.6	1749	1.1

JULY

Time	m		Time	m
1 F 0020	3.2	**16** SA 0039	3.6
0625	0.8	0654	0.3
1247	3.0	1323	3.4
1823	1.1	1904	0.8
2 SA 0053	3.2	**17** SU 0126	3.6
0701	0.8	0744	0.3
1323	3.0	1412	3.3
1857	1.1	1948	0.9
3 SU 0128	3.2	**18** M 0213	3.5
0738	0.8	0833	0.5
1400	2.9	1500	3.1
1932	1.2	2033	1.1
4 M 0205	3.1	**19** TU 0301	3.4
0817	0.9	0923	0.7
1440	2.8	1549	3.0
2011	1.2	2120	1.2
5 TU 0244	3.0	**20** W 0352	3.2
0900	0.9	1015	0.9
1524	2.8	1640	2.8
2054	1.3	(2215	1.3
6 W 0328	3.0	**21** TH 0446	3.0
0951	1.0	1112	1.1
1614	2.7	1736	2.7
2146	1.4	2322	1.4
7 TH 0419	2.9	**22** F 0547	2.9
1050	1.0	1216	1.2
1711	2.7	1837	2.7
(2256	1.4		
8 F 0519	2.9	**23** SA 0042	1.5
1154	1.0	0654	2.8
1814	2.8	1326	1.3
		1943	2.7
9 SA 0010	1.4	**24** SU 0200	1.4
0627	2.9	0807	2.7
1257	1.0	1425	1.3
1917	2.9	2045	2.8
10 SU 0120	1.3	**25** M 0258	1.3
0735	3.0	0911	2.8
1359	0.9	1513	1.3
2018	3.0	2134	3.0
11 M 0226	1.1	**26** TU 0345	1.1
0844	3.1	1001	2.9
1458	0.9	1553	1.2
2117	3.1	2217	3.1
12 TU 0326	0.9	**27** W 0424	1.0
0949	3.2	1043	3.0
1552	0.8	1629	1.2
2212	3.3	2254	3.2
13 W 0420	0.7	**28** TH 0501	0.9
1048	3.4	1121	3.0
1642	0.8	1702	1.1
O 2303	3.5	● 2329	3.3
14 TH 0513	0.5	**29** F 0535	0.8
1142	3.5	1156	3.1
1731	0.8	1734	1.1
2352	3.6		
15 F 0604	0.3	**30** SA 0003	3.3
1234	3.5	0609	0.7
1818	0.8	1230	3.1
		1807	1.0
		31 SU 0036	3.3
		0642	0.7
		1303	3.1
		1839	1.0

AUGUST

Time	m		Time	m
1 M 0109	3.3	**16** TU 0149	3.6
0715	0.7	0758	0.5
1338	3.1	1426	3.2
1912	1.0	1957	0.9
2 TU 0143	3.3	**17** W 0230	3.5
0750	0.7	0837	0.7
1413	3.0	1507	3.0
1946	1.0	2035	1.1
3 W 0218	3.2	**18** TH 0314	3.2
0826	0.8	0918	1.0
1452	3.0	1550	2.9
2023	1.1	2120	1.3
4 TH 0258	3.2	**19** F 0402	3.0
0907	0.9	1005	1.3
1536	2.9	1641	2.7
2105	1.2	(2223	1.5
5 F 0344	3.1	**20** SA 0501	2.8
0958	1.0	1108	1.5
1627	2.8	1743	2.7
(2202	1.3	2356	1.6
6 SA 0441	3.0	**21** SU 0615	2.6
1106	1.1	1236	1.6
1730	2.8	1856	2.7
2327	1.4		
7 SU 0554	2.9	**22** M 0140	1.5
1223	1.2	0742	2.6
1841	2.8	1403	1.6
		2013	2.8
8 M 0057	1.4	**23** TU 0244	1.3
0716	2.9	0856	2.7
1341	1.2	1457	1.5
1954	2.9	2111	2.9
9 TU 0220	1.2	**24** W 0329	1.2
0837	3.0	0946	2.9
1451	1.1	1538	1.4
2102	3.1	2155	3.1
10 W 0325	0.9	**25** TH 0407	1.0
0947	3.2	1026	3.0
1547	1.0	1612	1.2
2200	3.3	2232	3.2
11 TH 0418	0.6	**26** F 0440	0.8
1044	3.4	1101	3.1
1635	0.9	1643	1.1
2252	3.5	2307	3.3
12 F 0507	0.4	**27** SA 0512	0.7
1134	3.5	1134	3.2
1719	0.8	1713	1.0
O 2339	3.7	● 2340	3.4
13 SA 0552	0.3	**28** SU 0543	0.6
1220	3.5	1206	3.2
1800	0.7	1743	0.9
14 SU 0023	3.8	**29** M 0012	3.5
0636	0.2	0615	0.5
1304	3.5	1238	3.3
1841	0.7	1815	0.8
15 M 0107	3.8	**30** TU 0045	3.5
0718	0.3	0647	0.5
1346	3.4	1311	3.3
1919	0.8	1847	0.8
		31 W 0118	3.5
		0719	0.6
		1345	3.2
		1920	0.9

Chart Datum: 1·71 metres below Ordnance Datum (Newlyn)
HAT is 4·0 metres above Chart Datum

SCOTLAND – WICK

LAT 58°26'N   LONG 3°05'W

TIMES AND HEIGHTS OF HIGH AND LOW WATERS

Dates in amber are **SPRINGS**
Dates in grey are **NEAPS**

2022

	SEPTEMBER			OCTOBER			NOVEMBER			DECEMBER	
	Time m	Time m		Time m	Time m		Time m	Time m		Time m	Time m

SEPTEMBER

1 0153 3.4 / 0754 0.7 / TH 1421 3.1 / 1956 1.0
16 0236 3.2 / 0824 1.1 / F 1501 3.0 / 2037 1.3

2 0232 3.3 / 0832 0.9 / F 1503 3.0 / 2037 1.1
17 0320 2.9 / 0900 1.4 / SA 1545 2.8 / ◖ 2132 1.5

3 0318 3.1 / 0919 1.1 / SA 1552 2.9 / ◖ 2130 1.3
18 0416 2.7 / 0955 1.7 / SU 1646 2.7 / 2313 1.6

4 0418 3.0 / 1029 1.3 / SU 1656 2.8 / 2306 1.4
19 0537 2.6 / 1138 1.8 / M 1808 2.7

5 0540 2.8 / 1207 1.5 / M 1817 2.8
20 0110 1.6 / 0713 2.6 / TU 1335 1.8 / 1932 2.7

6 0058 1.4 / 0716 2.8 / TU 1341 1.4 / 1940 2.9
21 0218 1.4 / 0833 2.7 / W 1434 1.6 / 2038 2.9

7 0224 1.1 / 0843 3.0 / W 1449 1.3 / 2052 3.1
22 0303 1.2 / 0921 2.9 / TH 1514 1.4 / 2124 3.1

8 0323 0.8 / 0945 3.2 / TH 1539 1.1 / 2149 3.4
23 0339 1.0 / 0959 3.0 / F 1546 1.3 / 2202 3.2

9 0410 0.6 / 1034 3.4 / F 1621 0.9 / 2237 3.6
24 0411 0.8 / 1032 3.2 / SA 1616 1.1 / 2237 3.4

10 0452 0.4 / 1118 3.5 / SA 1659 0.8 / ○ 2321 3.8
25 0441 0.7 / 1105 3.3 / SU 1645 0.9 / ● 2310 3.5

11 0531 0.3 / 1159 3.6 / SU 1736 0.7
26 0512 0.6 / 1137 3.4 / M 1716 0.8 / 2344 3.6

12 0002 3.8 / 0609 0.3 / M 1237 3.5 / 1813 0.7
27 0543 0.5 / 1209 3.4 / TU 1748 0.8

13 0041 3.8 / 0645 0.4 / TU 1313 3.4 / 1848 0.8
28 0018 3.6 / 0616 0.5 / W 1242 3.4 / 1822 0.8

14 0120 3.6 / 0719 0.6 / W 1348 3.3 / 1923 0.9
29 0053 3.6 / 0650 0.6 / TH 1317 3.4 / 1857 0.8

15 0157 3.4 / 0752 0.9 / TH 1423 3.1 / 1958 1.1
30 0131 3.5 / 0726 0.8 / F 1354 3.3 / 1935 1.0

OCTOBER

1 0213 3.3 / 0806 1.0 / SA 1436 3.2 / 2019 1.1
16 0247 2.9 / 0815 1.5 / SU 1500 2.9 / 2059 1.5

2 0305 3.1 / 0855 1.3 / SU 1528 3.0 / 2121 1.3
17 0340 2.7 / 0901 1.7 / M 1555 2.8 / ◖ 2232 1.6

3 0412 2.9 / 1015 1.5 / M 1636 2.9 / ◖ 2317 1.4
18 0456 2.6 / 1040 1.9 / TU 1714 2.7

4 0545 2.8 / 1206 1.6 / TU 1803 2.9
19 0015 1.6 / 0628 2.6 / W 1237 1.9 / 1839 2.7

5 0104 1.2 / 0723 2.9 / W 1337 1.5 / 1928 3.0
20 0134 1.4 / 0749 2.7 / TH 1353 1.7 / 1948 2.9

6 0218 1.0 / 0839 3.1 / TH 1437 1.3 / 2037 3.2
21 0223 1.2 / 0842 2.9 / F 1436 1.5 / 2040 3.0

7 0310 0.7 / 0932 3.3 / F 1522 1.1 / 2131 3.4
22 0301 1.0 / 0921 3.0 / SA 1511 1.3 / 2122 3.2

8 0352 0.6 / 1016 3.4 / SA 1600 1.0 / 2217 3.6
23 0335 0.8 / 0956 3.2 / SU 1542 1.1 / 2200 3.4

9 0429 0.4 / 1056 3.5 / SU 1635 0.8 / ○ 2258 3.7
24 0407 0.7 / 1030 3.4 / M 1614 1.0 / 2237 3.5

10 0504 0.4 / 1132 3.5 / M 1710 0.7 / 2338 3.7
25 0439 0.6 / 1105 3.5 / TU 1647 0.8 / ● 2314 3.6

11 0538 0.5 / 1207 3.5 / TU 1745 0.7
26 0513 0.5 / 1140 3.6 / W 1723 0.8 / 2353 3.7

12 0015 3.7 / 0611 0.6 / W 1240 3.4 / 1821 0.8
27 0548 0.6 / 1216 3.6 / TH 1800 0.7

13 0051 3.5 / 0642 0.8 / TH 1312 3.3 / 1855 0.9
28 0033 3.6 / 0626 0.7 / F 1253 3.5 / 1841 0.8

14 0127 3.4 / 0712 1.0 / F 1344 3.2 / 1929 1.1
29 0116 3.5 / 0706 0.9 / SA 1334 3.4 / 1925 0.9

15 0204 3.1 / 0742 1.3 / SA 1419 3.1 / 2008 1.3
30 0205 3.3 / 0750 1.2 / SU 1420 3.3 / 2018 1.1

31 0302 3.1 / 0846 1.4 / M 1514 3.1 / 2137 1.2

NOVEMBER

1 0416 2.9 / 1014 1.7 / TU 1625 3.0 / ◖ 2320 1.2
16 0414 2.7 / 0941 1.8 / W 1621 2.8 / ◖ 2313 1.5

2 0545 2.9 / 1153 1.7 / W 1749 3.0
17 0531 2.6 / 1121 1.9 / TH 1738 2.8

3 0050 1.1 / 0711 3.0 / TH 1314 1.6 / 1906 3.1
18 0027 1.4 / 0642 2.7 / F 1241 1.8 / 1846 2.9

4 0157 0.9 / 0818 3.1 / F 1413 1.4 / 2013 3.3
19 0127 1.3 / 0743 2.8 / SA 1341 1.6 / 1944 3.0

5 0247 0.8 / 0909 3.2 / SA 1457 1.2 / 2107 3.4
20 0213 1.1 / 0832 3.0 / SU 1426 1.4 / 2034 3.2

6 0328 0.7 / 0951 3.4 / SU 1535 1.1 / 2153 3.5
21 0253 0.9 / 0914 3.2 / M 1505 1.2 / 2120 3.3

7 0403 0.7 / 1029 3.4 / M 1612 0.9 / 2235 3.6
22 0330 0.8 / 0954 3.4 / TU 1543 1.1 / 2204 3.5

8 0436 0.7 / 1105 3.5 / TU 1647 0.9 / ○ 2314 3.6
23 0408 0.7 / 1033 3.5 / W 1622 0.9 / ● 2248 3.6

9 0509 0.8 / 1139 3.5 / W 1723 0.9 / 2351 3.5
24 0446 0.7 / 1113 3.6 / TH 1703 0.8 / 2334 3.7

10 0540 0.9 / 1211 3.5 / TH 1759 0.9
25 0527 0.7 / 1154 3.7 / F 1747 0.7

11 0027 3.4 / 0612 1.0 / F 1242 3.4 / 1835 1.0
26 0020 3.6 / 0610 0.9 / SA 1236 3.6 / 1834 0.7

12 0103 3.3 / 0643 1.2 / SA 1315 3.3 / 1911 1.1
27 0110 3.5 / 0656 1.0 / SU 1321 3.6 / 1926 0.8

13 0141 3.1 / 0713 1.4 / SU 1349 3.2 / 1951 1.2
28 0203 3.4 / 0745 1.2 / M 1411 3.4 / 2027 0.9

14 0223 2.9 / 0748 1.5 / M 1429 3.1 / 2040 1.4
29 0303 3.2 / 0844 1.4 / TU 1507 3.3 / 2142 1.0

15 0312 2.8 / 0832 1.7 / TU 1518 2.9 / 2151 1.5
30 0412 3.0 / 0958 1.6 / W 1613 3.2 / ◖ 2301 1.1

DECEMBER

1 0525 3.0 / 1116 1.6 / TH 1724 3.2
16 0432 2.7 / 1003 1.7 / F 1636 2.9 / ◖ 2318 1.3

2 0018 1.1 / 0636 3.0 / F 1232 1.6 / 1834 3.2
17 0535 2.7 / 1123 1.7 / SA 1740 2.9

3 0125 1.0 / 0742 3.0 / SA 1337 1.5 / 1939 3.2
18 0020 1.3 / 0638 2.8 / SU 1233 1.7 / 1844 3.0

4 0218 1.0 / 0837 3.1 / SU 1429 1.3 / 2038 3.3
19 0117 1.2 / 0736 2.9 / M 1334 1.5 / 1944 3.1

5 0301 1.0 / 0923 3.2 / M 1513 1.2 / 2129 3.3
20 0209 1.1 / 0829 3.1 / TU 1428 1.4 / 2042 3.2

6 0338 1.0 / 1003 3.3 / TU 1553 1.1 / 2214 3.4
21 0257 1.0 / 0919 3.3 / W 1517 1.2 / 2138 3.4

7 0412 1.0 / 1041 3.4 / W 1632 1.0 / 2256 3.4
22 0343 0.9 / 1007 3.4 / TH 1605 1.0 / 2231 3.5

8 0445 1.1 / 1116 3.4 / TH 1710 1.0 / ○ 2335 3.3
23 0429 0.9 / 1053 3.6 / F 1654 0.8 / ● 2323 3.6

9 0518 1.1 / 1150 3.5 / F 1747 1.0
24 0515 0.9 / 1139 3.7 / SA 1743 0.7

10 0011 3.3 / 0552 1.2 / SA 1222 3.4 / 1824 1.0
25 0014 3.6 / 0602 0.9 / SU 1225 3.7 / 1834 0.6

11 0048 3.2 / 0624 1.3 / SU 1255 3.4 / 1901 1.1
26 0106 3.6 / 0650 1.0 / M 1313 3.7 / 1927 0.6

12 0125 3.1 / 0657 1.4 / M 1330 3.3 / 1939 1.1
27 0158 3.5 / 0738 1.1 / TU 1402 3.6 / 2023 0.7

13 0204 3.0 / 0732 1.5 / TU 1408 3.2 / 2022 1.2
28 0253 3.3 / 0829 1.3 / W 1454 3.5 / 2123 0.8

14 0246 2.9 / 0811 1.6 / W 1450 3.1 / 2112 1.3
29 0350 3.1 / 0924 1.4 / TH 1550 3.4 / 2225 0.9

15 0335 2.8 / 0899 1.7 / TH 1539 3.0 / 2213 1.3
30 0449 3.0 / 1027 1.5 / F 1651 3.3 / ◖ 2331 1.1

31 0550 2.9 / 1136 1.6 / SA 1754 3.1

Chart Datum: 1·71 metres below Ordnance Datum (Newlyn)
HAT is 4·0 metres above Chart Datum

TIDES

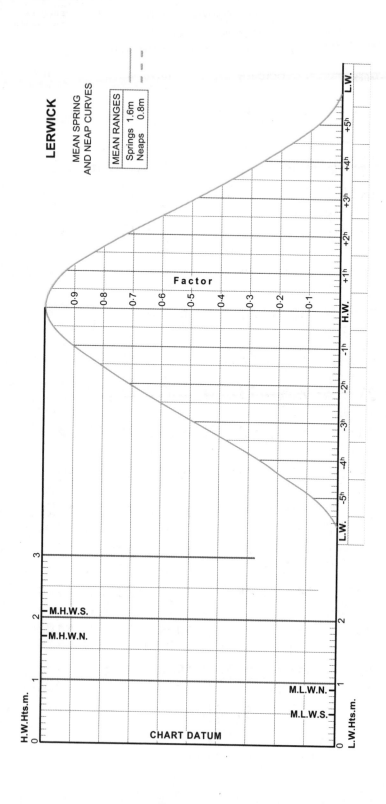

LERWICK

MEAN SPRING
AND NEAP CURVES

MEAN RANGES

Springs 1.6m
Neaps 0.8m

TIME ZONE (UT)	SCOTLAND – LERWICK	Dates in amber are SPRINGS
For Summer Time add ONE hour in non-shaded areas	LAT 60°09′N LONG 1°08′W	Dates in grey are NEAPS
	TIMES AND HEIGHTS OF HIGH AND LOW WATERS	2022

JANUARY

Day	Time m	Time m	Time m	Time m
1 SA	0308 0.7	0922 2.2	1536 0.7	2153 2.2
16 SU	0349 0.9	1003 2.1	1619 0.8	2230 2.0
2 SU ●	0359 0.6	1012 2.3	1627 0.5	2249 2.3
17 M ○	0424 0.9	1040 2.1	1654 0.7	2308 2.0
3 M	0447 0.7	1101 2.3	1717 0.5	2345 2.3
18 TU	0457 0.9	1115 2.2	1728 0.6	2344 2.0
4 TU	0534 0.7	1150 2.4	1806 0.4	
19 W	0530 0.8	1149 2.2	1802 0.6	
5 W	0037 2.2	0621 0.7	1238 2.4	1856 0.4
20 TH	0019 2.0	0604 0.8	1222 2.2	1838 0.6
6 TH	0126 2.2	0706 0.8	1325 2.3	1945 0.4
21 F	0055 2.0	0638 0.8	1256 2.2	1915 0.6
7 F	0214 2.0	0752 0.9	1412 2.2	2035 0.6
22 SA	0131 2.0	0714 0.8	1333 2.1	1954 0.6
8 SA	0300 1.9	0839 0.9	1459 2.1	2127 0.7
23 SU	0210 1.9	0753 0.8	1412 2.1	2036 0.6
9 SU	0349 1.8	0930 1.0	1549 2.0	2225 0.8
24 M	0254 1.9	0836 0.9	1458 2.0	2124 0.7
10 M	0442 1.7	1032 1.1	1646 1.8	2332 0.9
25 TU ☽	0344 1.8	0927 1.0	1552 1.9	2220 0.8
11 TU	0544 1.7	1151 1.1	1756 1.8	
26 W	0442 1.8	1032 1.0	1658 1.9	2331 0.8
12 W	0041 1.0	0651 1.7	1309 1.1	1909 1.8
27 TH	0550 1.8	1200 1.0	1816 1.9	
13 TH	0141 1.0	0750 1.8	1412 1.1	2011 1.8
28 F	0049 0.9	0704 1.8	1326 0.9	1939 1.9
14 F	0231 1.0	0840 1.9	1501 0.9	2103 1.8
29 SA	0159 0.8	0812 1.9	1435 0.8	2050 2.0
15 SA	0313 1.0	0924 2.0	1543 0.9	2149 1.9
30 SU	0300 0.8	0910 2.1	1532 0.6	2153 2.1
31 M	0352 0.7	1004 2.2	1623 0.5	2249 2.2

FEBRUARY

Day	Time m	Time m	Time m	Time m
1 TU	0439 0.7	1054 2.3	1710 0.3	2338 2.2
16 W ○	0442 0.8	1057 2.1	1708 0.5	2325 2.0
2 W	0523 0.6	1141 2.4	1754 0.3	
17 TH	0514 0.7	1131 2.2	1741 0.4	2359 2.0
3 TH	0023 2.2	0605 0.6	1224 2.4	1838 0.3
18 F	0545 0.6	1205 2.2	1815 0.4	
4 F	0105 2.1	0645 0.6	1306 2.3	1919 0.4
19 SA	0033 2.0	0619 0.6	1237 2.2	1850 0.4
5 SA	0145 2.0	0724 0.7	1346 2.2	2000 0.5
20 SU	0107 2.0	0654 0.6	1312 2.2	1927 0.4
6 SU	0223 1.9	0803 0.8	1426 2.1	2041 0.6
21 M	0142 2.0	0731 0.6	1349 2.1	2007 0.5
7 M	0302 1.8	0844 0.9	1507 2.0	2124 0.8
22 TU	0222 1.9	0812 0.7	1432 2.0	2052 0.6
8 TU ☽	0344 1.7	0931 1.0	1553 1.8	2214 1.0
23 W	0307 1.8	0901 0.8	1525 1.9	2145 0.8
9 W	0433 1.7	1040 1.1	1649 1.7	2326 1.1
24 TH	0403 1.7	1004 0.9	1634 1.8	2255 0.9
10 TH	0542 1.6	1220 1.1	1818 1.6	
25 F	0512 1.7	1139 0.9	1803 1.7	
11 F	0053 1.1	0708 1.7	1346 1.0	1946 1.6
26 SA	0035 1.0	0640 1.7	1323 0.8	1942 1.8
12 SA	0206 1.1	0813 1.7	1445 0.9	2047 1.7
27 SU	0156 0.9	0802 1.8	1434 0.7	2055 1.9
13 SU	0257 1.0	0902 1.8	1528 0.8	2134 1.8
28 M	0257 0.8	0904 2.0	1529 0.5	2152 2.0
14 M	0336 0.9	0944 1.9	1603 0.7	2214 1.9
15 TU	0410 0.9	1022 2.0	1636 0.6	2250 1.9

MARCH

Day	Time m	Time m	Time m	Time m
1 TU	0345 0.7	0957 2.1	1615 0.3	2240 2.1
16 W	0345 0.8	0955 1.9	1607 0.5	2223 1.9
2 W ●	0426 0.6	1043 2.2	1656 0.2	2322 2.1
17 TH	0417 0.6	1030 2.0	1640 0.4	2257 2.0
3 TH	0505 0.5	1125 2.3	1734 0.2	
18 F ○	0449 0.5	1105 2.1	1713 0.3	2331 2.0
4 F	0001 2.1	0543 0.5	1204 2.3	1812 0.2
19 SA	0521 0.5	1139 2.2	1748 0.2	
5 SA	0037 2.1	0619 0.5	1241 2.3	1848 0.3
20 SU	0005 2.1	0556 0.4	1214 2.2	1824 0.2
6 SU	0111 2.0	0655 0.5	1316 2.2	1923 0.4
21 M	0039 2.0	0632 0.4	1250 2.2	1901 0.3
7 M	0143 1.9	0730 0.6	1351 2.0	1957 0.6
22 TU	0115 2.0	0712 0.5	1330 2.1	1942 0.4
8 TU	0216 1.8	0805 0.7	1428 1.9	2030 0.8
23 W	0153 1.9	0755 0.6	1416 2.0	2026 0.6
9 W	0251 1.7	0846 0.8	1509 1.7	2108 0.9
24 TH	0237 1.8	0846 0.7	1514 1.8	2120 0.8
10 TH ☽	0333 1.7	0942 1.0	1600 1.6	2204 1.1
25 F	0333 1.7	0954 0.8	1629 1.7	2238 1.0
11 F	0426 1.6	1125 1.0	1712 1.5	2359 1.1
26 SA	0446 1.6	1146 0.8	1810 1.6	
12 SA	0553 1.5	1306 1.0	1922 1.5	
27 SU	0033 1.0	0626 1.6	1321 0.7	1947 1.7
13 SU	0135 1.1	0741 1.6	1414 0.9	2027 1.6
28 M	0150 0.9	0751 1.8	1426 0.5	2050 1.8
14 M	0233 1.0	0835 1.7	1458 0.8	2111 1.7
29 TU	0245 0.8	0851 1.9	1516 0.4	2138 1.9
15 TU	0312 0.9	0917 1.8	1534 0.6	2148 1.8
30 W	0328 0.7	0940 2.0	1557 0.3	2220 2.0
31 TH	0406 0.5	1024 2.1	1634 0.2	2258 2.0

APRIL

Day	Time m	Time m	Time m	Time m
1 F	0442 0.4	1103 2.2	1709 0.2	2333 2.0
16 SA ○	0419 0.5	1033 2.1	1642 0.2	2259 2.0
2 SA	0518 0.4	1139 2.2	1742 0.3	
17 SU	0455 0.4	1112 2.2	1719 0.2	2336 2.1
3 SU	0004 2.0	0553 0.4	1212 2.1	1815 0.4
18 M	0533 0.3	1151 2.2	1758 0.2	
4 M	0034 2.0	0626 0.4	1246 2.1	1847 0.5
19 TU	0012 2.1	0613 0.3	1233 2.1	1838 0.3
5 TU	0104 1.9	0700 0.5	1319 1.9	1917 0.6
20 W	0050 2.0	0657 0.4	1319 2.0	1922 0.5
6 W	0134 1.9	0735 0.6	1356 1.8	1947 0.8
21 TH	0131 2.0	0745 0.4	1413 1.9	2010 0.7
7 TH	0207 1.8	0815 0.7	1437 1.7	2020 0.9
22 F	0219 1.9	0842 0.5	1517 1.7	2109 0.9
8 F	0246 1.7	0907 0.9	1527 1.5	2107 1.1
23 SA ☽	0319 1.7	0959 0.6	1634 1.6	2237 1.0
9 SA	0337 1.6	1035 0.9	1631 1.4	2302 1.1
24 SU	0435 1.7	1145 0.6	1811 1.6	
10 SU	0443 1.5	1211 0.9	1836 1.4	
25 M	0018 1.0	0610 1.6	1304 0.6	1931 1.6
11 M	0046 1.1	0642 1.5	1321 0.8	1951 1.5
26 TU	0127 0.9	0729 1.7	1405 0.5	2026 1.7
12 TU	0150 1.0	0754 1.6	1413 0.7	2034 1.6
27 W	0221 0.8	0827 1.8	1452 0.4	2112 1.8
13 W	0234 0.9	0839 1.7	1453 0.5	2112 1.7
28 TH	0304 0.6	0915 1.9	1532 0.3	2152 1.9
14 TH	0310 0.7	0918 1.8	1530 0.4	2147 1.9
29 F	0342 0.5	0958 2.0	1607 0.3	2228 1.9
15 F	0345 0.6	0956 2.0	1606 0.3	2223 2.0
30 SA ●	0418 0.4	1037 2.0	1640 0.3	2301 2.0

TIDES

Chart Datum: 1·22 metres below Ordnance Datum (Local)
HAT is 2·5 metres above Chart Datum

TIDES

TIME ZONE (UT)
For Summer Time add ONE hour in **non-shaded areas**

SCOTLAND – LERWICK
LAT 60°09′N   LONG 1°08′W
TIMES AND HEIGHTS OF HIGH AND LOW WATERS

Dates in amber are **SPRINGS**
Dates in grey are **NEAPS**

2022

MAY

Day	Time m	Day	Time m
1 SU	0453 0.4 / 1112 2.0 / 1712 0.4 / 2332 2.0	16 M	0431 0.4 / 1047 2.1 / 1654 0.2 / 2309 2.1 ○
2 M	0528 0.4 / 1147 2.0 / 1743 0.5	17 TU	0513 0.3 / 1134 2.1 / 1736 0.3 / 2350 2.1
3 TU	0001 2.0 / 0602 0.4 / 1220 1.9 / 1814 0.6	18 W	0559 0.3 / 1223 2.1 / 1821 0.4
4 W	0031 1.9 / 0637 0.5 / 1255 1.8 / 1844 0.7	19 TH	0033 2.1 / 0648 0.3 / 1317 2.0 / 1909 0.6
5 TH	0102 1.9 / 0713 0.6 / 1332 1.7 / 1915 0.8	20 F	0120 2.0 / 0741 0.4 / 1416 1.9 / 2001 0.7
6 F	0135 1.8 / 0755 0.7 / 1414 1.6 / 1951 0.9	21 SA	0213 1.9 / 0843 0.4 / 1518 1.7 / 2103 0.9
7 SA	0214 1.7 / 0845 0.7 / 1504 1.5 / 2038 1.0	22 SU	0314 1.8 / 0958 0.5 / 1626 1.6 / 2219 0.9 ☽
8 SU	0304 1.6 / 0954 0.8 / 1602 1.5 / 2157 1.1	23 M	0423 1.7 / 1122 0.5 / 1743 1.6 / 2342 0.9
9 M	0405 1.5 / 1118 0.8 / 1715 1.4 / 2347 1.0 ☽	24 TU	0541 1.7 / 1234 0.5 / 1853 1.6
10 TU	0519 1.5 / 1225 0.7 / 1846 1.5	25 W	0051 0.9 / 0655 1.7 / 1334 0.5 / 1950 1.7
11 W	0054 1.0 / 0648 1.6 / 1320 0.6 / 1943 1.6	26 TH	0148 0.8 / 0754 1.8 / 1422 0.5 / 2037 1.7
12 TH	0145 0.8 / 0749 1.7 / 1408 0.6 / 2027 1.7	27 F	0236 0.7 / 0845 1.8 / 1503 0.5 / 2118 1.8
13 F	0229 0.7 / 0835 1.8 / 1451 0.5 / 2108 1.8	28 SA	0318 0.6 / 0930 1.9 / 1539 0.5 / 2156 1.9
14 SA	0310 0.6 / 0919 1.9 / 1532 0.5 / 2148 2.0	29 SU	0357 0.5 / 1011 1.9 / 1613 0.5 / 2231 1.9
15 SU	0350 0.5 / 1003 2.0 / 1612 0.2 / 2228 2.0	30 M	0433 0.5 / 1049 1.9 / 1645 0.6 / 2304 2.0 ●
		31 TU	0509 0.5 / 1126 1.9 / 1717 0.6 / 2336 2.0

JUNE

Day	Time m	Day	Time m
1 W	0544 0.5 / 1203 1.8 / 1749 0.7	16 TH	0551 0.2 / 1220 2.1 / 1810 0.5
2 TH	0008 1.9 / 0621 0.5 / 1239 1.8 / 1822 0.8	17 F	0024 2.1 / 0643 0.2 / 1315 2.0 / 1900 0.6
3 F	0041 1.9 / 0659 0.6 / 1317 1.7 / 1857 0.8	18 SA	0115 2.1 / 0736 0.3 / 1410 1.9 / 1951 0.7
4 SA	0115 1.8 / 0740 0.6 / 1358 1.7 / 1935 0.9	19 SU	0208 2.1 / 0833 0.3 / 1504 1.8 / 2045 0.8
5 SU	0155 1.8 / 0826 0.7 / 1443 1.6 / 2020 0.9	20 M	0302 2.0 / 0935 0.4 / 1600 1.7 / 2144 0.9
6 M	0241 1.7 / 0919 0.7 / 1534 1.5 / 2117 1.0	21 TU	0400 1.9 / 1042 0.5 / 1701 1.6 / 2252 0.9
7 TU	0336 1.6 / 1021 0.7 / 1631 1.5 / 2229 1.0 ☽	22 W	0503 1.8 / 1151 0.6 / 1804 1.6
8 W	0436 1.6 / 1128 0.7 / 1736 1.5 / 2349 0.9	23 TH	0005 0.9 / 0612 1.7 / 1254 0.7 / 1904 1.6
9 TH	0543 1.6 / 1228 0.6 / 1843 1.6	24 F	0112 0.8 / 0717 1.7 / 1348 0.7 / 1958 1.7
10 F	0053 0.9 / 0653 1.7 / 1322 0.6 / 1940 1.7	25 SA	0209 0.8 / 0815 1.7 / 1435 0.7 / 2045 1.8
11 SA	0147 0.8 / 0753 1.8 / 1413 0.5 / 2030 1.8	26 SU	0258 0.7 / 0906 1.8 / 1515 0.7 / 2128 1.8
12 SU	0236 0.6 / 0847 1.9 / 1501 0.4 / 2116 1.9	27 M	0341 0.7 / 0951 1.8 / 1552 0.7 / 2207 1.9
13 M	0324 0.5 / 0938 2.0 / 1548 0.4 / 2202 2.0	28 TU	0420 0.6 / 1033 1.8 / 1627 0.7 / 2244 2.0
14 TU	0412 0.4 / 1030 2.1 / 1635 0.4 / 2248 2.1 ○	29 W	0456 0.6 / 1112 1.8 / 1712 0.7 / 2319 2.0 ●
15 W	0501 0.3 / 1124 2.1 / 1722 0.5 / 2335 2.1	30 TH	0532 0.5 / 1150 1.8 / 1735 0.8 / 2353 2.0

JULY

Day	Time m	Day	Time m
1 F	0608 0.5 / 1227 1.8 / 1808 0.8	16 SA	0016 2.2 / 0633 0.2 / 1305 2.1 / 1846 0.6
2 SA	0027 2.0 / 0645 0.5 / 1302 1.8 / 1843 0.8	17 SU	0104 2.2 / 0721 0.2 / 1352 2.0 / 1931 0.6
3 SU	0101 1.9 / 0722 0.5 / 1339 1.7 / 1920 0.8	18 M	0152 2.2 / 0810 0.3 / 1438 1.9 / 2017 0.7
4 M	0138 1.9 / 0802 0.6 / 1419 1.7 / 1959 0.8	19 TU	0239 2.1 / 0900 0.4 / 1525 1.8 / 2105 0.8
5 TU	0219 1.8 / 0846 0.6 / 1503 1.7 / 2044 0.9	20 W	0327 2.0 / 0953 0.6 / 1613 1.7 / 2200 0.9 ☽
6 W	0306 1.8 / 0934 0.6 / 1553 1.6 / 2136 0.9	21 TH	0420 1.8 / 1054 0.7 / 1709 1.6 / 2312 0.9
7 TH	0358 1.7 / 1030 0.7 / 1648 1.6 / 2239 0.9 ☽	22 F	0523 1.7 / 1204 0.7 / 1813 1.6
8 F	0458 1.7 / 1134 0.7 / 1751 1.6 / 2357 0.9	23 SA	0035 0.9 / 0638 1.6 / 1311 0.9 / 1919 1.7
9 SA	0606 1.7 / 1241 0.7 / 1856 1.6	24 SU	0147 0.9 / 0749 1.6 / 1409 0.9 / 2016 1.7
10 SU	0109 0.8 / 0719 1.8 / 1341 0.6 / 1957 1.8	25 M	0244 0.8 / 0848 1.7 / 1458 0.9 / 2105 1.8
11 M	0211 0.7 / 0824 1.9 / 1438 0.6 / 2052 1.9	26 TU	0330 0.8 / 0937 1.7 / 1539 0.9 / 2148 1.9
12 TU	0308 0.6 / 0925 2.0 / 1532 0.6 / 2144 2.0	27 W	0409 0.7 / 1020 1.8 / 1615 0.8 / 2227 2.0
13 W	0402 0.4 / 1024 2.1 / 1623 0.6 / 2235 2.1 ○	28 TH	0444 0.6 / 1059 1.9 / 1648 0.8 / 2304 2.0 ●
14 TH	0454 0.3 / 1121 2.1 / 1712 0.5 / 2326 2.2	29 F	0517 0.5 / 1135 1.9 / 1721 0.7 / 2338 2.1
15 F	0544 0.2 / 1215 2.1 / 1759 0.6	30 SA	0551 0.5 / 1209 1.9 / 1753 0.7
		31 SU	0011 2.1 / 0624 0.5 / 1242 1.9 / 1825 0.7

AUGUST

Day	Time m	Day	Time m
1 M	0044 2.1 / 0659 0.5 / 1315 1.9 / 1858 0.7	16 TU	0127 2.3 / 0738 0.3 / 1404 2.0 / 1944 0.6
2 TU	0117 2.0 / 0734 0.5 / 1350 1.8 / 1934 0.7	17 W	0208 2.1 / 0820 0.5 / 1443 1.8 / 2026 0.7
3 W	0153 2.0 / 0813 0.5 / 1429 1.8 / 2014 0.8	18 TH	0250 2.0 / 0902 0.7 / 1524 1.8 / 2114 0.9
4 TH	0234 1.9 / 0856 0.6 / 1514 1.8 / 2100 0.8	19 F	0337 1.8 / 0951 0.9 / 1611 1.7 / 2219 1.0 ◔
5 F	0323 1.9 / 0946 0.7 / 1607 1.7 / 2157 0.9	20 SA	0432 1.7 / 1059 1.0 / 1712 1.6
6 SA	0422 1.8 / 1047 0.8 / 1708 1.7 / 2314 0.9	21 SU	0000 1.0 / 0555 1.6 / 1231 1.1 / 1839 1.6
7 SU	0534 1.8 / 1206 0.8 / 1819 1.7	22 M	0127 1.0 / 0730 1.6 / 1348 1.1 / 1951 1.7
8 M	0047 0.9 / 0700 1.8 / 1323 0.8 / 1934 1.8	23 TU	0229 0.9 / 0835 1.7 / 1443 1.0 / 2045 1.8
9 TU	0202 0.8 / 0818 1.9 / 1429 0.8 / 2038 1.9	24 W	0314 0.8 / 0923 1.8 / 1524 1.0 / 2129 1.9
10 W	0304 0.6 / 0924 2.0 / 1526 0.7 / 2135 2.1	25 TH	0351 0.7 / 1002 1.8 / 1558 0.9 / 2207 2.0
11 TH	0358 0.4 / 1022 2.1 / 1615 0.6 / 2227 2.2	26 F	0423 0.6 / 1037 1.9 / 1629 0.8 / 2242 2.1
12 F	0446 0.3 / 1113 2.1 / 1700 0.6 / 2316 2.3 ○	27 SA	0454 0.5 / 1111 2.0 / 1659 0.7 / 2316 2.1 ●
13 SA	0531 0.2 / 1200 2.2 / 1742 0.5	28 SU	0525 0.4 / 1144 2.0 / 1729 0.6 / 2348 2.2
14 SU	0001 2.3 / 0615 0.1 / 1244 2.1 / 1824 0.5	29 M	0557 0.4 / 1215 2.0 / 1800 0.6
15 M	0045 2.3 / 0657 0.2 / 1325 2.1 / 1904 0.6	30 TU	0019 2.2 / 0630 0.4 / 1246 2.0 / 1834 0.6
		31 W	0051 2.2 / 0705 0.4 / 1319 2.0 / 1909 0.6

Chart Datum: 1·22 metres below Ordnance Datum (Local)
HAT is 2·5 metres above Chart Datum

TIME ZONE (UT)	SCOTLAND – LERWICK	Dates in amber are SPRINGS
For Summer Time add ONE hour in **non-shaded areas**	LAT 60°09′N LONG 1°08′W	Dates in grey are NEAPS
		2022

TIMES AND HEIGHTS OF HIGH AND LOW WATERS

SEPTEMBER

Date	Time m		Date	Time m
1 TH	0127 2.1 / 0742 0.5 / 1356 1.9 / 1948 0.7		**16** F	0213 2.0 / 0814 0.8 / 1436 1.8 / 2034 0.9
2 F	0207 2.0 / 0823 0.6 / 1438 1.9 / 2034 0.8		**17** SA	0257 1.8 / 0853 1.0 / 1518 1.8 / 2133 1.0
3 SA ☽	0255 1.9 / 0912 0.8 / 1529 1.8 / 2131 0.9		**18** SU	0350 1.7 / 0948 1.2 / 1611 1.7 / 2320 1.1
4 SU	0359 1.8 / 1014 0.9 / 1633 1.7 / 2255 1.0		**19** M	0506 1.6 / 1148 1.2 / 1738 1.6
5 M	0521 1.7 / 1150 1.0 / 1754 1.7		**20** TU	0056 1.0 / 0712 1.6 / 1321 1.2 / 1923 1.7
6 TU	0046 0.9 / 0703 1.7 / 1321 1.0 / 1924 1.8		**21** W	0201 1.0 / 0816 1.7 / 1419 1.1 / 2019 1.8
7 W	0203 0.7 / 0824 1.8 / 1427 0.9 / 2032 2.0		**22** TH	0246 0.8 / 0858 1.8 / 1458 1.0 / 2101 1.9
8 TH	0301 0.6 / 0923 2.0 / 1518 0.8 / 2126 2.1		**23** F	0320 0.7 / 0934 1.9 / 1530 0.9 / 2138 2.0
9 F	0348 0.4 / 1012 2.1 / 1601 0.7 / 2214 2.3		**24** SA	0352 0.6 / 1007 2.0 / 1600 0.8 / 2213 2.1
10 SA ○	0431 0.3 / 1057 2.2 / 1641 0.6 / 2259 2.3		**25** SU ●	0423 0.5 / 1040 2.0 / 1631 0.7 / 2246 2.2
11 SU	0511 0.2 / 1138 2.2 / 1719 0.5 / 2340 2.4		**26** M	0454 0.4 / 1112 2.1 / 1702 0.6 / 2319 2.2
12 M	0549 0.2 / 1216 2.2 / 1757 0.5		**27** TU	0527 0.4 / 1144 2.1 / 1735 0.6 / 2352 2.3
13 TU	0019 2.4 / 0627 0.3 / 1251 2.1 / 1835 0.6		**28** W	0600 0.4 / 1216 2.1 / 1809 0.6
14 W	0056 2.3 / 0704 0.5 / 1325 2.0 / 1912 0.6		**29** TH	0026 2.3 / 0637 0.5 / 1249 2.1 / 1847 0.6
15 TH	0134 2.1 / 0739 0.6 / 1359 1.9 / 1951 0.7		**30** F	0104 2.2 / 0715 0.6 / 1326 2.1 / 1929 0.7

OCTOBER

Date	Time m		Date	Time m
1 SA	0148 2.1 / 0757 0.7 / 1408 2.0 / 2018 0.8		**16** SU	0225 1.8 / 0805 1.1 / 1434 1.9 / 2100 1.0
2 SU	0242 1.9 / 0848 0.9 / 1500 1.9 / 2122 0.9		**17** M	0317 1.7 / 0852 1.2 / 1525 1.8 / 2233 1.1
3 M	0354 1.8 / 0957 1.1 / 1610 1.8 / 2302 0.9		**18** TU	0424 1.6 / 1055 1.3 / 1633 1.7
4 TU	0526 1.7 / 1153 1.1 / 1742 1.8		**19** W	0004 1.0 / 0630 1.6 / 1233 1.3 / 1833 1.7
5 W	0047 0.8 / 0712 1.8 / 1316 1.1 / 1916 1.9		**20** TH	0112 1.0 / 0738 1.7 / 1336 1.2 / 1940 1.8
6 TH	0155 0.7 / 0819 1.9 / 1415 0.9 / 2019 2.0		**21** F	0201 0.8 / 0821 1.8 / 1418 1.1 / 2024 1.9
7 F	0248 0.5 / 0909 2.0 / 1501 0.8 / 2110 2.2		**22** SA	0239 0.7 / 0856 1.9 / 1453 0.9 / 2102 2.0
8 SA	0331 0.4 / 0953 2.1 / 1541 0.7 / 2155 2.3		**23** SU	0314 0.6 / 0930 2.0 / 1526 0.8 / 2137 2.1
9 SU ○	0409 0.3 / 1032 2.2 / 1618 0.6 / 2236 2.3		**24** M	0347 0.5 / 1004 2.1 / 1600 0.7 / 2213 2.2
10 M	0446 0.3 / 1109 2.2 / 1655 0.5 / 2315 2.3		**25** TU ●	0422 0.4 / 1038 2.2 / 1634 0.6 / 2250 2.3
11 TU	0521 0.4 / 1143 2.2 / 1731 0.5 / 2352 2.3		**26** W	0457 0.4 / 1112 2.2 / 1710 0.5 / 2327 2.3
12 W	0555 0.5 / 1215 2.2 / 1808 0.6		**27** TH	0534 0.4 / 1148 2.3 / 1749 0.5
13 TH	0027 2.2 / 0629 0.6 / 1246 2.1 / 1844 0.6		**28** F	0007 2.3 / 0613 0.5 / 1224 2.2 / 1831 0.6
14 F	0103 2.1 / 0701 0.8 / 1318 2.0 / 1922 0.8		**29** SA	0051 2.2 / 0654 0.7 / 1304 2.2 / 1918 0.6
15 SA	0142 2.0 / 0732 0.9 / 1353 1.9 / 2004 0.9		**30** SU	0142 2.1 / 0741 0.9 / 1350 2.1 / 2013 0.7
			31 M	0245 1.9 / 0836 1.0 / 1447 2.0 / 2124 0.8

NOVEMBER

Date	Time m		Date	Time m
1 TU ☽	0359 1.8 / 0952 1.1 / 1601 1.9 / 2306 0.8		**16** W	0349 1.7 / 0938 1.3 / 1551 1.8 / 2303 1.0
2 W	0528 1.8 / 1139 1.2 / 1729 1.7		**17** TH	0459 1.6 / 1126 1.3 / 1702 1.7
3 TH	0031 0.8 / 0656 1.8 / 1254 1.1 / 1854 1.9		**18** F	0010 1.0 / 0633 1.7 / 1235 1.2 / 1832 1.8
4 F	0135 0.7 / 0756 1.9 / 1351 1.0 / 1956 2.0		**19** SA	0105 0.9 / 0729 1.8 / 1327 1.1 / 1932 1.9
5 SA	0226 0.6 / 0844 2.0 / 1437 0.8 / 2047 2.1		**20** SU	0151 0.8 / 0811 1.9 / 1411 1.0 / 2018 2.0
6 SU	0308 0.5 / 0926 2.1 / 1518 0.7 / 2132 2.2		**21** M	0233 0.7 / 0850 2.0 / 1451 0.9 / 2100 2.1
7 M	0345 0.5 / 1004 2.1 / 1556 0.6 / 2213 2.2		**22** TU	0312 0.6 / 0928 2.1 / 1530 0.7 / 2142 2.2
8 TU	0420 0.5 / 1040 2.2 / 1633 0.6 / 2251 2.2		**23** W ●	0351 0.5 / 1006 2.2 / 1610 0.6 / 2225 2.3
9 W	0454 0.6 / 1112 2.2 / 1710 0.6 / 2328 2.2		**24** TH	0431 0.5 / 1046 2.3 / 1651 0.6 / 2309 2.3
10 TH	0527 0.7 / 1144 2.2 / 1746 0.6		**25** F	0512 0.6 / 1126 2.3 / 1735 0.5 / 2357 2.3
11 F	0004 2.1 / 0559 0.8 / 1216 2.1 / 1824 0.7		**26** SA	0556 0.7 / 1208 2.3 / 1823 0.5
12 SA	0041 2.0 / 0630 0.9 / 1248 2.1 / 1902 0.8		**27** SU	0049 2.2 / 0642 0.8 / 1253 2.3 / 1915 0.6
13 SU	0120 1.9 / 0702 1.0 / 1323 2.0 / 1944 0.9		**28** M	0146 2.1 / 0733 0.9 / 1345 2.2 / 2013 0.6
14 M	0203 1.8 / 0736 1.1 / 1402 1.9 / 2035 1.0		**29** TU	0247 2.0 / 0829 1.0 / 1444 2.1 / 2120 0.7
15 TU	0252 1.7 / 0822 1.2 / 1451 1.8 / 2144 1.0		**30** W	0352 1.9 / 0937 1.1 / 1550 2.0 / 2242 0.7

DECEMBER

Date	Time m		Date	Time m
1 TH	0504 1.8 / 1058 1.1 / 1703 2.0		**16** F ☽	0407 1.7 / 0954 1.2 / 1612 1.8 / 2303 0.9
2 F	0000 0.7 / 0618 1.8 / 1215 1.1 / 1818 2.0		**17** SA	0508 1.7 / 1115 1.2 / 1715 1.8
3 SA	0104 0.7 / 0720 1.9 / 1318 1.0 / 1924 2.0		**18** SU	0005 0.9 / 0616 1.7 / 1228 1.1 / 1825 1.8
4 SU	0158 0.7 / 0811 1.9 / 1411 0.9 / 2019 2.0		**19** M	0101 0.8 / 0717 1.8 / 1326 1.0 / 1929 1.9
5 M	0242 0.7 / 0856 2.0 / 1457 0.8 / 2108 2.1		**20** TU	0152 0.8 / 0809 1.9 / 1417 0.9 / 2025 2.0
6 TU	0321 0.7 / 0937 2.1 / 1539 0.8 / 2153 2.1		**21** W	0240 0.7 / 0855 2.1 / 1504 0.8 / 2117 2.1
7 W	0357 0.7 / 1014 2.1 / 1618 0.7 / 2234 2.1		**22** TH	0326 0.7 / 0941 2.2 / 1552 0.7 / 2208 2.2
8 TH	0432 0.8 / 1049 2.2 / 1656 0.7 / 2313 2.1		**23** F ●	0412 0.7 / 1026 2.3 / 1640 0.6 / 2300 2.3
9 F	0505 0.8 / 1123 2.2 / 1733 0.7 / 2351 2.1		**24** SA	0459 0.7 / 1112 2.3 / 1728 0.5 / 2355 2.3
10 SA	0538 0.9 / 1157 2.2 / 1811 0.7		**25** SU	0546 0.7 / 1200 2.4 / 1819 0.4
11 SU	0028 2.0 / 0612 1.0 / 1230 2.1 / 1849 0.8		**26** M	0049 2.2 / 0635 0.8 / 1249 2.3 / 1910 0.4
12 M	0106 1.9 / 0645 1.0 / 1305 2.1 / 1929 0.8		**27** TU	0142 2.2 / 0723 0.8 / 1341 2.3 / 2004 0.5
13 TU	0145 1.9 / 0721 1.1 / 1342 2.0 / 2012 0.8		**28** W	0235 2.0 / 0813 0.9 / 1433 2.2 / 2100 0.5
14 W	0227 1.8 / 0801 1.1 / 1421 1.9 / 2101 0.9		**29** TH	0329 1.9 / 0907 1.0 / 1528 2.1 / 2202 0.7
15 TH	0314 1.7 / 0851 1.2 / 1515 1.9 / 2158 0.9		**30** F ☽	0425 1.8 / 1008 1.0 / 1627 2.0 / 2313 0.8
			31 SA	0528 1.8 / 1122 1.1 / 1734 1.9

Chart Datum: 1·22 metres below Ordnance Datum (Local)
HAT is 2·5 metres above Chart Datum

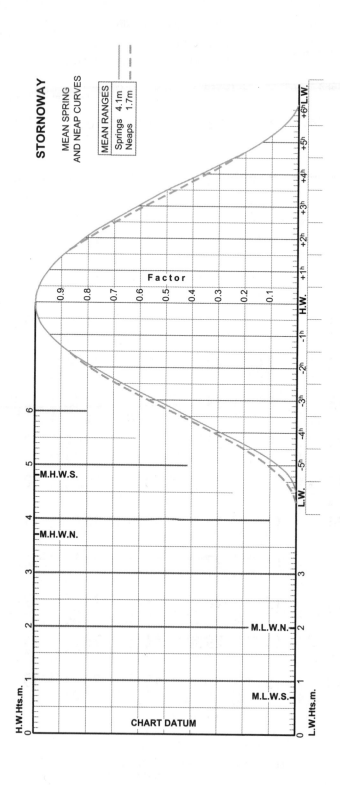

STORNOWAY

MEAN SPRING
AND NEAP CURVES

MEAN RANGES
Springs 4.1m
Neaps 1.7m

SCOTLAND – STORNOWAY

LAT 58°12′N   LONG 6°23′W

TIMES AND HEIGHTS OF HIGH AND LOW WATERS

Dates in amber are SPRINGS
Dates in grey are NEAPS

2022

JANUARY

Day	Time m	Time m	Time m	Time m	Day	Time m	Time m	Time m	Time m
1 SA	0523 4.7	1140 1.2	1744 4.8		16 SU	0000 1.7	0611 4.4	1232 1.6	1826 4.3
2 SU ●	0009 1.0	0610 5.0	1232 1.0	1836 4.9	17 M ○	0035 1.5	0642 4.5	1308 1.4	1900 4.3
3 M	0057 0.9	0656 5.1	1323 0.8	1927 4.9	18 TU	0109 1.4	0711 4.6	1343 1.3	1933 4.4
4 TU	0143 0.9	0742 5.2	1412 0.7	2016 4.8	19 W	0142 1.3	0740 4.7	1417 1.2	2005 4.4
5 W	0228 0.9	0829 5.2	1500 0.7	2105 4.6	20 TH	0215 1.3	0810 4.7	1451 1.2	2039 4.4
6 TH	0313 1.1	0916 5.1	1548 0.9	2155 4.4	21 F	0249 1.2	0843 4.7	1525 1.2	2115 4.4
7 F	0358 1.3	1006 4.8	1635 1.1	2247 4.1	22 SA	0324 1.3	0919 4.7	1602 1.2	2155 4.2
8 SA	0445 1.5	1059 4.6	1723 1.4	2344 3.9	23 SU	0402 1.4	0959 4.6	1642 1.3	2242 4.1
9 SU ☽	0535 1.8	1158 4.3	1815 1.7		24 M	0444 1.5	1046 4.4	1727 1.4	2338 4.0
10 M	0050 3.7	0632 2.0	1304 4.1	1913 1.9	25 TU ☽	0532 1.7	1143 4.2	1820 1.6	
11 TU	0204 3.6	0740 2.2	1414 3.9	2021 2.0	26 W	0047 3.9	0633 1.9	1256 4.1	1928 1.8
12 W	0315 3.7	0859 2.3	1520 3.9	2133 2.0	27 TH	0201 3.9	0750 2.0	1418 4.0	2048 1.8
13 TH	0414 3.8	1011 2.2	1618 3.9	2233 1.9	28 F	0314 4.0	0915 1.9	1539 4.1	2206 1.7
14 F	0500 4.0	1107 2.0	1707 4.0	2320 1.8	29 SA	0419 4.2	1034 1.7	1649 4.3	2310 1.5
15 SA	0538 4.2	1152 1.8	1749 4.1		30 SU	0515 4.5	1137 1.3	1747 4.5	
					31 M	0003 1.2	0604 4.8	1231 1.0	1837 4.7

FEBRUARY

Day	Time m	Time m	Time m	Time m	Day	Time m	Time m	Time m	Time m
1 TU ●	0051 1.0	0648 5.1	1319 0.7	1921 4.8	16 W ○	0054 1.3	0653 4.6	1326 1.1	1914 4.5
2 W	0134 0.8	0730 5.3	1404 0.5	2002 4.8	17 TH	0126 1.1	0720 4.8	1358 0.9	1943 4.6
3 TH	0216 0.8	0811 5.3	1446 0.5	2041 4.7	18 F	0158 1.0	0749 4.9	1430 0.8	2015 4.6
4 F	0256 0.8	0851 5.2	1526 0.6	2120 4.5	19 SA	0231 0.9	0820 4.9	1502 0.7	2048 4.6
5 SA	0335 1.0	0931 4.9	1604 0.9	2158 4.2	20 SU	0304 0.9	0854 4.9	1536 0.8	2125 4.5
6 SU	0414 1.2	1012 4.6	1643 1.2	2238 4.0	21 M	0340 1.0	0932 4.7	1612 0.9	2207 4.3
7 M	0454 1.5	1057 4.3	1722 1.5	2327 3.7	22 TU	0419 1.2	1015 4.5	1653 1.2	2257 4.1
8 TU ☾	0538 1.9	1154 3.9	1807 1.9		23 W ☾	0504 1.4	1109 4.2	1741 1.5	
9 W	0042 3.5	0634 2.2	1313 3.7	1904 2.1	24 TH	0005 3.9	0600 1.8	1227 3.9	1846 1.8
10 TH	0214 3.5	0756 2.4	1437 3.6	2029 2.3	25 F	0132 3.8	0719 2.0	1409 3.8	2022 2.0
11 F	0335 3.6	0941 2.3	1553 3.6	2203 2.2	26 SA	0257 3.8	0908 2.0	1543 3.8	2202 1.9
12 SA	0435 3.8	1052 2.1	1651 3.8	2302 2.0	27 SU	0411 4.1	1038 1.7	1654 4.1	2308 1.6
13 SU	0520 4.0	1140 1.8	1736 3.9	2344 1.8	28 M	0508 4.4	1138 1.2	1746 4.3	2357 1.2
14 M	0555 4.2	1219 1.6	1812 4.1						
15 TU	0020 1.5	0625 4.4	1253 1.3	1844 4.3					

MARCH

Day	Time m	Time m	Time m	Time m	Day	Time m	Time m	Time m	Time m
1 TU	0553 4.8	1226 0.9	1828 4.6		16 W	0556 4.4	1228 1.1	1817 4.3	
2 W ●	0040 1.0	0634 5.0	1308 0.6	1905 4.7	17 TH	0029 1.2	0624 4.6	1259 0.8	1846 4.5
3 TH	0119 0.7	0711 5.2	1346 0.4	1939 4.8	18 F ○	0102 0.9	0651 4.8	1330 0.6	1916 4.7
4 F	0157 0.6	0747 5.2	1422 0.4	2012 4.7	19 SA	0134 0.7	0721 5.0	1402 0.4	1947 4.8
5 SA	0232 0.6	0821 5.1	1456 0.5	2043 4.6	20 SU	0207 0.6	0754 5.0	1435 0.4	2021 4.8
6 SU	0307 0.8	0856 4.8	1530 0.8	2114 4.3	21 M	0242 0.6	0829 4.9	1509 0.5	2057 4.7
7 M	0342 1.0	0930 4.5	1603 1.1	2145 4.1	22 TU	0318 0.7	0909 4.7	1546 0.8	2139 4.4
8 TU	0418 1.3	1007 4.2	1636 1.4	2220 3.8	23 W	0358 1.0	0955 4.4	1626 1.1	2231 4.1
9 W	0456 1.7	1053 3.8	1713 1.8	2308 3.6	24 TH	0444 1.3	1057 4.0	1714 1.6	2344 3.9
10 TH ☾	0541 2.0	1209 3.5	1757 2.1		25 F ☾	0542 1.7	1233 3.7	1821 2.0	
11 F	0058 3.4	0651 2.3	1353 3.4	1910 2.4	26 SA	0117 3.7	0714 1.9	1416 3.6	2015 2.1
12 SA	0243 3.4	0906 2.4	1521 3.4	2126 2.4	27 SU	0245 3.8	0916 1.8	1546 3.7	2156 1.9
13 SU	0359 3.6	1032 2.1	1627 3.6	2239 2.1	28 M	0358 4.1	1035 1.5	1650 4.0	2256 1.6
14 M	0450 3.8	1118 1.8	1713 3.8	2321 1.8	29 TU	0453 4.4	1127 1.1	1735 4.3	2341 1.2
15 TU	0526 4.1	1155 1.5	1748 4.1	2357 1.5	30 W	0535 4.7	1209 0.8	1810 4.5	
					31 TH	0021 0.9	0613 4.9	1247 0.6	1843 4.6

APRIL

Day	Time m	Time m	Time m	Time m	Day	Time m	Time m	Time m	Time m
1 F ●	0058 0.7	0647 5.0	1321 0.5	1912 4.7	16 SA ○	0031 0.8	0619 4.8	1258 0.5	1846 4.8
2 SA	0133 0.6	0720 5.0	1354 0.5	1941 4.7	17 SU	0106 0.6	0653 5.0	1332 0.3	1920 4.9
3 SU	0207 0.6	0752 5.0	1425 0.6	2009 4.5	18 M	0142 0.5	0729 5.0	1408 0.3	1956 4.9
4 M	0240 0.8	0824 4.6	1455 0.8	2037 4.4	19 TU	0220 0.5	0810 4.9	1445 0.5	2036 4.7
5 TU	0313 1.0	0857 4.4	1526 1.1	2106 4.2	20 W	0301 0.6	0856 4.6	1524 0.8	2122 4.5
6 W	0347 1.3	0933 4.0	1558 1.4	2139 3.9	21 TH	0345 0.9	0952 4.2	1608 1.2	2221 4.2
7 TH	0424 1.6	1019 3.7	1632 1.7	2221 3.7	22 F	0436 1.2	1110 3.9	1700 1.6	2340 4.0
8 F	0506 1.9	1131 3.4	1712 2.1	2340 3.5	23 SA ☾	0543 1.6	1244 3.6	1815 2.0	
9 SA ☾	0608 2.2	1311 3.3	1811 2.3		24 SU	0107 3.9	0721 1.8	1413 3.6	2005 2.1
10 SU	0141 3.4	0811 2.3	1437 3.3	2021 2.4	25 M	0226 3.9	0905 1.6	1533 3.7	2133 1.9
11 M	0304 3.5	0952 2.0	1548 3.5	2156 2.2	26 TU	0335 4.1	1013 1.3	1631 3.9	2230 1.6
12 TU	0403 3.7	1040 1.7	1637 3.7	2244 1.9	27 W	0429 4.3	1102 1.1	1713 4.1	2316 1.3
13 W	0444 4.0	1118 1.4	1713 4.0	2322 1.5	28 TH	0511 4.5	1143 0.9	1747 4.3	2357 1.0
14 TH	0517 4.3	1152 1.0	1744 4.3	2357 1.2	29 F	0548 4.6	1219 0.7	1817 4.5	
15 F	0547 4.6	1225 0.7	1814 4.6		30 SA ●	0033 0.9	0622 4.7	1252 0.7	1846 4.5

Chart Datum: 2·71 metres below Ordnance Datum (Local)
HAT is 5·5 metres above Chart Datum

TIDES

TIME ZONE (UT)	SCOTLAND – STORNOWAY	Dates in amber are SPRINGS
For Summer Time add ONE hour in **non-shaded areas**	LAT 58°12'N LONG 6°23'W	Dates in grey are NEAPS

SCOTLAND – STORNOWAY
LAT 58°12'N   LONG 6°23'W

TIMES AND HEIGHTS OF HIGH AND LOW WATERS

2022

MAY

Time	m	Time	m
1 0109 / 0655 / SU 1324 / 1914	0.8 / 4.7 / 0.7 / 4.5	**16** 0039 / 0629 / M 1305 / ○ 1857	0.7 / 4.9 / 0.4 / 4.9
2 0143 / 0727 / M 1355 / 1942	0.8 / 4.6 / 0.8 / 4.5	**17** 0121 / 0712 / TU 1345 / 1938	0.5 / 4.9 / 0.5 / 4.9
3 0216 / 0800 / TU 1425 / 2011	0.9 / 4.4 / 1.0 / 4.4	**18** 0204 / 0800 / W 1427 / 2024	0.5 / 4.7 / 0.6 / 4.8
4 0250 / 0835 / W 1456 / 2041	1.1 / 4.2 / 1.2 / 4.2	**19** 0250 / 0855 / TH 1511 / 2116	0.6 / 4.5 / 0.9 / 4.6
5 0324 / 0915 / TH 1528 / 2116	1.3 / 4.0 / 1.4 / 4.0	**20** 0341 / 1001 / F 1600 / 2219	0.9 / 4.2 / 1.3 / 4.4
6 0402 / 1004 / F 1603 / 2201	1.5 / 3.7 / 1.7 / 3.8	**21** 0438 / 1116 / SA 1657 / 2332	1.1 / 3.9 / 1.6 / 4.2
7 0446 / 1110 / SA 1644 / 2307	1.8 / 3.5 / 2.0 / 3.6	**22** 0546 / 1234 / SU 1809	1.4 / 3.7 / 1.9
8 0543 / 1229 / SU 1740	2.0 / 3.3 / 2.2	**23** 0047 / 0707 / M 1350 / 1934	4.1 / 1.5 / 3.6 / 2.0
9 0039 / 0710 / M 1344 / ◑ 1912	3.5 / 2.1 / 3.3 / 2.3	**24** 0158 / 0828 / TU 1502 / 2052	4.0 / 1.5 / 3.7 / 1.9
10 0159 / 0843 / TU 1452 / 2049	3.5 / 1.9 / 3.4 / 2.2	**25** 0304 / 0935 / W 1601 / 2154	4.1 / 1.4 / 3.8 / 1.7
11 0302 / 0944 / W 1547 / 2150	3.7 / 1.7 / 3.7 / 1.9	**26** 0359 / 1027 / TH 1645 / 2245	4.2 / 1.3 / 4.0 / 1.5
12 0351 / 1029 / TH 1629 / 2237	3.9 / 1.4 / 4.0 / 1.6	**27** 0445 / 1111 / F 1722 / 2330	4.2 / 1.1 / 4.2 / 1.3
13 0432 / 1109 / F 1706 / 2318	4.2 / 1.0 / 4.3 / 1.2	**28** 0524 / 1150 / SA 1754	4.3 / 1.0 / 4.3
14 0510 / 1148 / SA 1742 / 2359	4.5 / 0.7 / 4.6 / 0.9	**29** 0010 / 0601 / SU 1225 / 1825	1.2 / 4.4 / 1.0 / 4.4
15 0548 / 1226 / SU 1818	4.7 / 0.5 / 4.8	**30** 0048 / 0636 / M 1258 / ● 1855	1.1 / 4.3 / 1.0 / 4.4
		31 0124 / 0711 / TU 1330 / 1924	1.1 / 4.3 / 1.1 / 4.4

JUNE

Time	m	Time	m
1 0159 / 0747 / W 1402 / 1955	1.1 / 4.2 / 1.2 / 4.4	**16** 0156 / 0800 / TH 1416 / 2017	0.6 / 4.6 / 0.8 / 4.9
2 0234 / 0824 / TH 1435 / 2027	1.2 / 4.1 / 1.3 / 4.3	**17** 0246 / 0857 / F 1504 / 2110	0.6 / 4.5 / 0.9 / 4.8
3 0310 / 0905 / F 1509 / 2104	1.3 / 3.9 / 1.5 / 4.1	**18** 0339 / 0956 / SA 1554 / 2208	0.7 / 4.3 / 1.2 / 4.6
4 0348 / 0951 / SA 1545 / 2148	1.5 / 3.8 / 1.6 / 4.0	**19** 0433 / 1059 / SU 1647 / 2310	0.9 / 4.0 / 1.4 / 4.4
5 0431 / 1044 / SU 1626 / 2241	1.6 / 3.6 / 1.8 / 3.9	**20** 0531 / 1204 / M 1746	1.1 / 3.8 / 1.6
6 0521 / 1145 / M 1717 / 2345	1.7 / 3.5 / 2.0 / 3.8	**21** 0015 / 0633 / TU 1311 / ◑ 1851	4.2 / 1.3 / 3.7 / 1.8
7 0621 / 1250 / TU 1822	1.8 / 3.5 / 2.1	**22** 0121 / 0737 / W 1419 / 2001	4.1 / 1.5 / 3.6 / 1.9
8 0055 / 0731 / W 1354 / 1939	3.7 / 1.8 / 3.6 / 2.1	**23** 0225 / 0844 / TH 1523 / 2111	4.0 / 1.6 / 3.7 / 1.9
9 0200 / 0838 / TH 1453 / 2049	3.8 / 1.6 / 3.7 / 1.9	**24** 0326 / 0945 / F 1616 / 2213	3.9 / 1.6 / 3.8 / 1.8
10 0257 / 0936 / F 1545 / 2148	3.9 / 1.4 / 3.9 / 1.7	**25** 0419 / 1038 / SA 1659 / 2306	4.0 / 1.5 / 4.0 / 1.6
11 0349 / 1026 / SA 1631 / 2241	4.1 / 1.2 / 4.2 / 1.4	**26** 0506 / 1123 / SU 1737 / 2352	4.0 / 1.5 / 4.1 / 1.5
12 0438 / 1114 / SU 1714 / 2330	4.4 / 1.0 / 4.5 / 1.1	**27** 0547 / 1202 / M 1811	4.1 / 1.4 / 4.3
13 0526 / 1159 / M 1757	4.5 / 0.8 / 4.7	**28** 0033 / 0626 / TU 1238 / 1843	1.4 / 4.1 / 1.3 / 4.3
14 0018 / 0615 / TU 1244 / ○ 1841	0.9 / 4.7 / 0.7 / 4.9	**29** 0111 / 0703 / W 1313 / ● 1914	1.3 / 4.1 / 1.3 / 4.4
15 0107 / 0706 / W 1330 / 1928	0.7 / 4.7 / 0.7 / 4.9	**30** 0147 / 0738 / TH 1347 / 1945	1.2 / 4.1 / 1.3 / 4.4

JULY

Time	m	Time	m
1 0223 / 0814 / F 1420 / 2016	1.2 / 4.1 / 1.3 / 4.4	**16** 0240 / 0845 / SA 1454 / 2054	0.5 / 4.6 / 0.8 / 5.0
2 0258 / 0850 / SA 1454 / 2051	1.2 / 4.1 / 1.4 / 4.3	**17** 0328 / 0934 / SU 1539 / 2143	0.5 / 4.4 / 1.0 / 4.9
3 0334 / 0929 / SU 1530 / 2128	1.3 / 4.0 / 1.4 / 4.3	**18** 0414 / 1024 / M 1625 / 2235	0.7 / 4.2 / 1.2 / 4.6
4 0412 / 1011 / M 1609 / 2210	1.3 / 3.9 / 1.6 / 4.1	**19** 0501 / 1119 / TU 1713 / 2332	1.0 / 3.9 / 1.4 / 4.3
5 0453 / 1100 / TU 1652 / 2259	1.4 / 3.8 / 1.7 / 4.0	**20** 0549 / 1220 / W 1806	1.3 / 3.7 / 1.7
6 0540 / 1157 / W 1742 / 2357	1.5 / 3.7 / 1.8 / 3.9	**21** 0035 / 0642 / TH 1329 / 1908	4.0 / 1.6 / 3.6 / 1.9
7 0634 / 1300 / TH 1843	1.6 / 3.7 / 1.9	**22** 0143 / 0743 / F 1440 / 2023	3.8 / 1.8 / 3.6 / 2.1
8 0102 / 0737 / F 1404 / 1953	3.9 / 1.7 / 3.7 / 1.9	**23** 0253 / 0856 / SA 1546 / 2144	3.7 / 1.9 / 3.7 / 2.1
9 0210 / 0844 / SA 1505 / 2105	3.9 / 1.6 / 3.9 / 1.9	**24** 0358 / 1007 / SU 1639 / 2250	3.7 / 1.9 / 3.8 / 1.9
10 0316 / 0949 / SU 1602 / 2212	4.0 / 1.4 / 4.1 / 1.6	**25** 0452 / 1102 / M 1722 / 2341	3.8 / 1.8 / 4.0 / 1.7
11 0419 / 1049 / M 1655 / 2312	4.2 / 1.3 / 4.4 / 1.3	**26** 0538 / 1146 / TU 1758	3.9 / 1.7 / 4.2
12 0518 / 1143 / TU 1745	4.4 / 1.1 / 4.6	**27** 0022 / 0617 / W 1224 / ○ 1831	1.5 / 4.0 / 1.5 / 4.3
13 0008 / 0614 / W 1233 / ○ 1833	1.0 / 4.5 / 0.9 / 4.9	**28** 0100 / 0652 / TH 1300 / ● 1901	1.3 / 4.2 / 1.4 / 4.5
14 0101 / 0706 / TH 1322 / 1920	0.7 / 4.7 / 0.8 / 5.0	**29** 0135 / 0724 / F 1333 / 1929	1.2 / 4.2 / 1.3 / 4.6
15 0152 / 0756 / F 1408 / 2007	0.5 / 4.7 / 0.8 / 5.1	**30** 0208 / 0755 / SA 1406 / 1958	1.1 / 4.3 / 1.2 / 4.6
		31 0240 / 0826 / SU 1438 / 2028	1.0 / 4.3 / 1.2 / 4.6

AUGUST

Time	m	Time	m
1 0313 / 0900 / M 1511 / 2101	1.0 / 4.2 / 1.2 / 4.5	**16** 0345 / 0940 / TU 1556 / 2153	0.6 / 4.3 / 1.0 / 4.7
2 0346 / 0936 / TU 1546 / 2137	1.1 / 4.2 / 1.3 / 4.4	**17** 0424 / 1023 / W 1637 / 2240	0.9 / 4.1 / 1.3 / 4.3
3 0422 / 1017 / W 1624 / 2219	1.1 / 4.0 / 1.4 / 4.3	**18** 0503 / 1113 / TH 1722 / 2339	1.3 / 3.8 / 1.7 / 3.9
4 0501 / 1107 / TH 1707 / 2309	1.3 / 3.9 / 1.6 / 4.1	**19** 0546 / 1207 / F 1815 / ◐	1.7 / 3.6 / 2.0
5 0547 / 1210 / F 1800	1.5 / 3.8 / 1.8	**20** 0058 / 0639 / SA 1354 / 1933	3.7 / 2.0 / 3.5 / 2.3
6 0014 / 0646 / SA 1323 / 1908	3.9 / 1.7 / 3.8 / 1.9	**21** 0221 / 0757 / SU 1513 / 2123	3.5 / 2.3 / 3.6 / 2.3
7 0137 / 0801 / SU 1437 / 2034	3.8 / 1.8 / 3.8 / 2.0	**22** 0337 / 0940 / M 1617 / 2240	3.5 / 2.3 / 3.8 / 2.1
8 0302 / 0926 / M 1546 / 2200	3.8 / 1.9 / 4.0 / 1.8	**23** 0438 / 1046 / TU 1703 / 2328	3.7 / 2.1 / 4.0 / 1.8
9 0419 / 1039 / TU 1647 / 2310	4.0 / 1.6 / 4.3 / 1.4	**24** 0524 / 1131 / W 1740	3.9 / 1.8 / 4.2
10 0522 / 1137 / W 1738	4.3 / 1.3 / 4.7	**25** 0007 / 0601 / TH 1207 / 1811	1.5 / 4.1 / 1.6 / 4.4
11 0006 / 0614 / TH 1227 / 1824	1.0 / 4.5 / 1.0 / 5.0	**26** 0041 / 0632 / F 1241 / 1838	1.3 / 4.2 / 1.4 / 4.6
12 0056 / 0659 / F 1312 / ○ 1906	0.7 / 4.7 / 0.8 / 5.2	**27** 0113 / 0700 / SA 1313 / ● 1904	1.1 / 4.4 / 1.2 / 4.7
13 0142 / 0741 / SA 1355 / 1948	0.4 / 4.8 / 0.7 / 5.3	**28** 0144 / 0728 / SU 1344 / 1931	0.9 / 4.5 / 1.0 / 4.8
14 0225 / 0821 / SU 1436 / 2029	0.3 / 4.7 / 0.7 / 5.2	**29** 0214 / 0757 / M 1415 / 2000	0.9 / 4.5 / 0.9 / 4.8
15 0305 / 0901 / M 1516 / 2110	0.4 / 4.6 / 0.8 / 5.0	**30** 0245 / 0828 / TU 1446 / 2031	0.8 / 4.5 / 0.9 / 4.8
		31 0316 / 0901 / W 1520 / 2106	0.8 / 4.5 / 1.0 / 4.7

Chart Datum: 2·71 metres below Ordnance Datum (Local)
HAT is 5·5 metres above Chart Datum

TIME ZONE (UT)
For Summer Time add ONE hour in **non-shaded areas**

SCOTLAND – STORNOWAY

LAT 58°12′N   LONG 6°23′W

TIMES AND HEIGHTS OF HIGH AND LOW WATERS

Dates in amber are **SPRINGS**
Dates in grey are **NEAPS**

2022

SEPTEMBER

Day	Time	m	Time	m	Time	m	Time	m
1 TH	0350	1.0	0940	4.3	1557	1.2	2145	4.5
2 F	0427	1.2	1026	4.1	1638	1.4	2234	4.2
3 SA	0510	1.5	1129	3.9	1729	1.7	◔ 2347	3.9
4 SU	0606	1.8	1256	3.8	1839	2.0		
5 M	0132	3.7	0733	2.1	1423	3.8	2026	2.1
6 TU	0309	3.7	0923	2.0	1539	4.0	2206	1.8
7 W	0426	4.0	1038	1.7	1639	4.4	2311	1.3
8 TH	0521	4.3	1131	1.4	1727	4.7		
9 F	0000	0.9	0605	4.6	1215	1.0	1808	5.1
10 SA	0043	0.6	0642	4.8	1256	0.8	○ 1846	5.3
11 SU	0123	0.4	0717	4.9	1334	0.6	1923	5.3
12 M	0201	0.3	0751	4.8	1412	0.6	2000	5.2
13 TU	0236	0.4	0824	4.7	1448	0.7	2036	5.0
14 W	0311	0.7	0857	4.5	1525	1.0	2112	4.6
15 TH	0345	1.0	0930	4.2	1602	1.3	2152	4.3
16 F	0420	1.4	1007	3.9	1642	1.7	2242	3.9
17 SA	0457	1.8	1100	3.7	1730	2.1	◑	
18 SU	0009	3.5	0541	2.2	1259	3.5	1844	2.4
19 M	0148	3.4	0652	2.5	1433	3.5	2101	2.4
20 TU	0311	3.4	0910	2.5	1544	3.7	2221	2.1
21 W	0415	3.6	1024	2.2	1634	3.9	2305	1.8
22 TH	0500	3.9	1107	1.9	1711	4.2	2341	1.5
23 F	0534	4.1	1142	1.6	1741	4.4		
24 SA	0012	1.2	0604	4.3	1214	1.4	1808	4.7
25 SU	0043	1.0	0630	4.6	1245	1.1	● 1834	4.8
26 M	0113	0.8	0658	4.7	1316	0.9	1901	5.0
27 TU	0143	0.6	0726	4.8	1348	0.8	1931	5.0
28 W	0214	0.6	0757	4.8	1421	0.8	2004	5.0
29 TH	0246	0.7	0831	4.7	1456	0.9	2040	4.8
30 F	0321	0.9	0910	4.5	1534	1.1	2123	4.5

OCTOBER

Day	Time	m	Time	m	Time	m	Time	m
1 SA	0359	1.2	0958	4.3	1618	1.4	2220	4.1
2 SU	0443	1.6	1106	4.0	1712	1.8	2353	3.8
3 M	0543	2.0	1244	3.9	1834	2.0	◐	
4 TU	0142	3.7	0727	2.3	1412	3.9	2038	2.0
5 W	0313	3.8	0921	2.1	1527	4.2	2205	1.6
6 TH	0421	4.1	1026	1.8	1624	4.5	2259	1.2
7 F	0509	4.4	1114	1.4	1709	4.8	2343	0.9
8 SA	0547	4.6	1155	1.1	1747	5.1		
9 SU	0021	0.6	0620	4.8	1234	0.9	○ 1823	5.3
10 M	0058	0.5	0651	4.9	1311	0.7	1858	5.2
11 TU	0132	0.5	0722	4.9	1346	0.7	1932	5.1
12 W	0205	0.7	0751	4.8	1421	0.9	2005	4.8
13 TH	0237	0.9	0821	4.6	1457	1.1	2027	4.4
14 F	0309	1.2	0851	4.4	1533	1.4	2118	4.2
15 SA	0342	1.5	0924	4.1	1611	1.7	2206	3.8
16 SU	0417	1.9	1008	3.9	1657	2.1	2326	3.5
17 M	0458	2.2	1139	3.6	1803	2.3	◑	
18 TU	0105	3.4	0600	2.5	1337	3.6	2009	2.4
19 W	0228	3.4	0808	2.6	1454	3.7	2140	2.0
20 TH	0336	3.6	0941	2.4	1551	3.9	2227	1.9
21 F	0424	3.9	1028	2.1	1631	4.1	2303	1.5
22 SA	0459	4.1	1105	1.7	1703	4.4	2336	1.4
23 SU	0529	4.4	1139	1.4	1732	4.7		
24 M	0007	1.0	0558	4.7	1212	1.1	○ 1801	4.9
25 TU	0038	0.8	0627	4.9	1246	0.9	● 1832	5.0
26 W	0111	0.6	0658	5.0	1321	0.8	1906	5.1
27 TH	0145	0.6	0732	5.0	1357	0.8	1944	5.0
28 F	0220	0.7	0810	4.9	1437	0.9	2027	4.8
29 SA	0258	1.0	0853	4.7	1519	1.1	2119	4.4
30 SU	0340	1.3	0947	4.4	1609	1.4	2230	4.1
31 M	0430	1.8	1102	4.2	1711	1.7		

NOVEMBER

Day	Time	m	Time	m	Time	m	Time	m
1 TU	0006	3.8	0538	2.1	1232	4.1	◐ 1841	1.9
2 W	0137	3.7	0721	2.3	1353	4.1	2027	1.8
3 TH	0258	3.9	0856	2.1	1504	4.3	2142	1.5
4 F	0402	4.1	1000	1.8	1601	4.5	2234	1.3
5 SA	0448	4.5	1048	1.5	1646	4.7	2317	1.0
6 SU	0525	4.5	1131	1.3	1725	4.9	2356	0.9
7 M	0557	4.7	1211	1.1	1801	4.9		
8 TU	0031	0.8	0628	4.8	1248	1.0	○ 1836	4.9
9 W	0104	0.9	0658	4.8	1324	1.0	1910	4.8
10 TH	0137	1.0	0727	4.8	1400	1.1	1945	4.6
11 F	0209	1.2	0757	4.6	1435	1.3	2021	4.4
12 SA	0241	1.4	0828	4.5	1511	1.5	2101	4.1
13 SU	0314	1.6	0902	4.3	1550	1.7	2149	3.9
14 M	0350	1.9	0946	4.1	1635	2.0	2252	3.7
15 TU	0431	2.2	1049	3.9	1733	2.2		
16 W	0010	3.5	0525	2.4	1222	3.7	◑ 1856	2.3
17 TH	0127	3.5	0650	2.5	1345	3.8	2026	2.2
18 F	0237	3.6	0827	2.4	1449	3.9	2129	1.9
19 SA	0333	3.8	0921	2.2	1538	4.1	2214	1.7
20 SU	0416	4.1	1018	1.9	1618	4.3	2252	1.4
21 M	0451	4.4	1100	1.6	1654	4.6	2329	1.1
22 TU	0525	4.6	1139	1.3	1730	4.8		
23 W	0005	0.9	0600	4.9	1218	1.1	● 1808	4.9
24 TH	0043	0.8	0636	5.0	1259	0.9	1850	5.0
25 F	0122	0.8	0715	5.1	1341	0.8	1935	4.9
26 SA	0203	0.9	0758	5.0	1426	0.9	2027	4.7
27 SU	0246	1.1	0848	4.9	1515	1.0	2126	4.5
28 M	0333	1.4	0945	4.7	1609	1.3	2236	4.2
29 TU	0426	1.7	1053	4.5	1713	1.5	2353	4.0
30 W	0531	2.0	1209	4.3	1828	1.7	◐	

DECEMBER

Day	Time	m	Time	m	Time	m	Time	m
1 TH	0110	3.9	0651	2.1	1322	4.3	1948	1.7
2 F	0225	3.9	0811	2.1	1431	4.3	2100	1.6
3 SA	0331	4.0	0921	1.9	1531	4.4	2159	1.5
4 SU	0422	4.2	1018	1.7	1622	4.5	2248	1.4
5 M	0503	4.3	1107	1.6	1706	4.5	2330	1.3
6 TU	0539	4.5	1151	1.4	1745	4.6		
7 W	0007	1.3	0612	4.6	1231	1.3	1823	4.6
8 TH	0042	1.2	0644	4.7	1309	1.3	○ 1859	4.5
9 F	0116	1.3	0714	4.7	1346	1.3	1936	4.5
10 SA	0149	1.4	0745	4.6	1422	1.4	2012	4.3
11 SU	0222	1.5	0817	4.6	1459	1.5	2051	4.2
12 M	0256	1.6	0852	4.4	1537	1.6	2132	4.0
13 TU	0332	1.8	0931	4.3	1618	1.8	2219	3.9
14 W	0411	1.9	1017	4.1	1704	1.9	2314	3.7
15 TH	0457	2.1	1114	4.0	1758	2.0		
16 F	0018	3.6	0554	2.3	1222	3.9	◑ 1903	2.0
17 SA	0127	3.6	0705	2.3	1333	3.9	2011	2.0
18 SU	0230	3.8	0819	2.2	1435	4.0	2112	1.8
19 M	0325	4.0	0923	2.1	1529	4.2	2206	1.6
20 TU	0413	4.2	1019	1.8	1619	4.4	2254	1.4
21 W	0457	4.5	1109	1.5	1707	4.6	2339	1.2
22 TH	0539	4.7	1158	1.3	1755	4.7		
23 F	0023	1.0	0622	5.0	1245	1.0	1845	4.8
24 SA	0108	0.9	0707	5.1	1334	0.9	1936	4.9
25 SU	0154	0.9	0753	5.2	1423	0.8	2028	4.8
26 M	0240	1.0	0843	5.1	1513	0.8	2122	4.6
27 TU	0327	1.2	0935	5.0	1605	0.9	2219	4.4
28 W	0417	1.4	1032	4.8	1659	1.2	2320	4.2
29 TH	0511	1.6	1134	4.6	1756	1.4		
30 F	0027	3.9	0611	1.8	1241	4.4	◐ 1858	1.6
31 SA	0138	3.8	0719	2.0	1350	4.2	2005	1.8

Chart Datum: 2·71 metres below Ordnance Datum (Local)
HAT is 5·5 metres above Chart Datum

TIDES

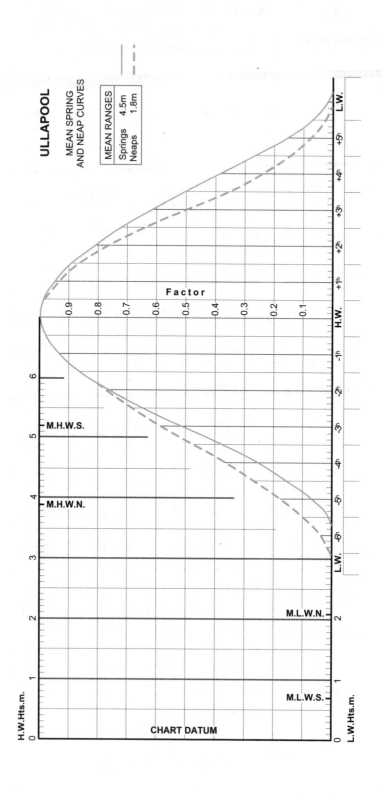

ULLAPOOL

MEAN SPRING
AND NEAP CURVES

MEAN RANGES

Springs 4.5m
Neaps   1.8m

TIME ZONE (UT)	SCOTLAND – ULLAPOOL	Dates in amber are SPRINGS
For Summer Time add ONE hour in non-shaded areas	LAT 57°54'N LONG 5°09'W	Dates in grey are NEAPS
	TIMES AND HEIGHTS OF HIGH AND LOW WATERS	2022

JANUARY

Time	m		Time	m
1 SA	0527 5.1 / 1147 1.3 / 1750 5.1	**16** SU	0006 1.8 / 0616 4.7 / 1237 1.7 / 1834 4.6	
2 SU ●	0015 1.1 / 0615 5.3 / 1239 1.0 / 1843 5.2	**17** M ○	0043 1.6 / 0647 4.8 / 1314 1.5 / 1908 4.7	
3 M	0104 1.0 / 0702 5.5 / 1329 0.8 / 1933 5.2	**18** TU	0117 1.5 / 0717 4.9 / 1348 1.4 / 1940 4.8	
4 TU	0151 0.9 / 0749 5.6 / 1418 0.8 / 2023 5.2	**19** W	0151 1.4 / 0746 5.0 / 1422 1.3 / 2013 4.8	
5 W	0236 1.0 / 0835 5.5 / 1506 0.8 / 2112 5.0	**20** TH	0224 1.3 / 0817 5.1 / 1456 1.2 / 2046 4.8	
6 TH	0322 1.1 / 0923 5.4 / 1553 0.9 / 2201 4.8	**21** F	0257 1.3 / 0849 5.0 / 1530 1.2 / 2122 4.7	
7 F	0407 1.4 / 1012 5.1 / 1640 1.2 / 2252 4.5	**22** SA	0332 1.4 / 0925 5.0 / 1606 1.3 / 2201 4.6	
8 SA	0454 1.6 / 1105 4.8 / 1729 1.5 / 2348 4.2	**23** SU	0410 1.5 / 1005 4.8 / 1646 1.4 / 2247 4.5	
9 SU ☾	0545 1.9 / 1204 4.5 / 1820 1.8	**24** M	0452 1.6 / 1051 4.7 / 1731 1.6 / 2343 4.3	
10 M	0053 4.0 / 0643 2.2 / 1310 4.3 / 1919 2.0	**25** TU ☽	0541 1.8 / 1149 4.5 / 1825 1.7	
11 TU	0206 4.0 / 0752 2.3 / 1421 4.1 / 2027 2.2	**26** W	0051 4.2 / 0643 2.0 / 1303 4.4 / 1932 1.9	
12 W	0318 4.0 / 0908 2.4 / 1529 4.1 / 2138 2.2	**27** TH	0204 4.2 / 0759 2.1 / 1424 4.3 / 2052 1.9	
13 TH	0417 4.1 / 1018 2.3 / 1627 4.2 / 2238 2.1	**28** F	0316 4.3 / 0923 2.1 / 1543 4.4 / 2211 1.8	
14 F	0503 4.3 / 1113 2.1 / 1715 4.3 / 2326 1.9	**29** SA	0423 4.6 / 1040 1.8 / 1655 4.6 / 2316 1.6	
15 SA	0542 4.5 / 1158 1.9 / 1757 4.5	**30** SU	0521 4.9 / 1143 1.4 / 1753 4.8	
		31 M	0010 1.3 / 0610 5.2 / 1237 1.1 / 1843 5.1	

FEBRUARY

Time	m		Time	m
1 TU ●	0058 1.1 / 0655 5.4 / 1325 0.8 / 1927 5.2	**16** W ○	0102 1.4 / 0659 4.9 / 1331 1.1 / 1921 4.9	
2 W	0143 0.9 / 0737 5.6 / 1410 0.6 / 2009 5.2	**17** TH	0135 1.2 / 0726 5.1 / 1403 0.9 / 1951 5.0	
3 TH	0224 0.8 / 0818 5.6 / 1452 0.6 / 2048 5.1	**18** F	0207 1.0 / 0755 5.2 / 1435 0.8 / 2022 5.0	
4 F	0304 0.9 / 0858 5.5 / 1531 0.7 / 2126 4.9	**19** SA	0239 0.9 / 0826 5.3 / 1507 0.8 / 2055 5.0	
5 SA	0343 1.0 / 0937 5.2 / 1610 0.9 / 2205 4.6	**20** SU	0312 0.9 / 0900 5.2 / 1541 0.9 / 2131 4.9	
6 SU	0422 1.3 / 1018 4.9 / 1648 1.3 / 2246 4.4	**21** M	0348 1.1 / 0938 5.0 / 1617 1.1 / 2212 4.7	
7 M	0503 1.6 / 1104 4.5 / 1728 1.6 / 2335 4.1	**22** TU	0427 1.3 / 1021 4.8 / 1658 1.3 / 2303 4.4	
8 TU ☾	0548 2.0 / 1201 4.2 / 1813 2.0	**23** W ☾	0512 1.6 / 1116 4.5 / 1747 1.6	
9 W	0044 3.9 / 0644 2.3 / 1317 3.9 / 1911 2.3	**24** TH	0010 4.2 / 0609 1.9 / 1235 4.2 / 1853 2.0	
10 TH	0213 3.8 / 0805 2.5 / 1443 3.8 / 2036 2.5	**25** F ☽	0135 4.1 / 0728 2.1 / 1412 4.0 / 2028 2.2	
11 F	0338 3.8 / 0944 2.5 / 1601 3.9 / 2208 2.4	**26** SA	0300 4.1 / 0913 2.1 / 1548 4.1 / 2207 2.0	
12 SA	0439 4.0 / 1055 2.3 / 1701 4.1 / 2308 2.2	**27** SU	0417 4.4 / 1042 1.8 / 1701 4.4 / 2314 1.7	
13 SU	0524 4.3 / 1144 2.0 / 1743 4.3 / 2351 1.9	**28** M	0515 4.7 / 1143 1.3 / 1752 4.7	
14 M	0600 4.5 / 1223 1.7 / 1819 4.5			
15 TU	0028 1.6 / 0631 4.7 / 1258 1.4 / 1851 4.7			

MARCH

Time	m		Time	m
1 TU	0005 1.3 / 0601 5.1 / 1231 0.9 / 1835 5.0	**16** W	0004 1.6 / 0603 4.6 / 1232 1.2 / 1824 4.7	
2 W ●	0048 1.0 / 0641 5.4 / 1314 0.6 / 1911 5.1	**17** TH	0037 1.3 / 0630 4.9 / 1304 0.9 / 1853 4.9	
3 TH	0128 0.8 / 0718 5.5 / 1352 0.5 / 1946 5.2	**18** F ○	0110 1.0 / 0658 5.2 / 1336 0.7 / 1922 5.1	
4 F	0205 0.7 / 0754 5.5 / 1428 0.4 / 2018 5.1	**19** SA	0142 0.7 / 0728 5.3 / 1408 0.5 / 1954 5.1	
5 SA	0241 0.7 / 0828 5.4 / 1502 0.6 / 2050 5.0	**20** SU	0215 0.6 / 0800 5.4 / 1440 0.5 / 2027 5.2	
6 SU	0315 0.8 / 0902 5.2 / 1535 0.8 / 2121 4.7	**21** M	0249 0.6 / 0836 5.3 / 1515 0.6 / 2104 5.0	
7 M	0350 1.1 / 0937 4.8 / 1609 1.1 / 2153 4.5	**22** TU	0326 0.8 / 0915 5.1 / 1552 0.8 / 2145 4.8	
8 TU	0425 1.4 / 1014 4.5 / 1643 1.5 / 2229 4.2	**23** W	0406 1.0 / 1002 4.7 / 1633 1.2 / 2237 4.5	
9 W	0504 1.8 / 1101 4.1 / 1720 1.9 / 2317 3.9	**24** TH	0452 1.4 / 1104 4.3 / 1722 1.7 / 2350 4.2	
10 TH ☾	0549 2.2 / 1216 3.8 / 1807 2.3	**25** F	0551 1.8 / 1238 4.0 / 1831 2.1	
11 F	0055 3.7 / 0659 2.5 / 1355 3.6 / 1921 2.6	**26** SA	0121 4.0 / 0721 2.1 / 1419 3.9 / 2023 2.3	
12 SA	0244 3.7 / 0905 2.5 / 1528 3.7 / 2132 2.5	**27** SU	0251 4.1 / 0919 2.0 / 1552 4.0 / 2204 2.0	
13 SU	0405 3.8 / 1033 2.3 / 1634 3.9 / 2245 2.3	**28** M	0406 4.3 / 1039 1.6 / 1655 4.3 / 2304 1.7	
14 M	0456 4.1 / 1121 1.9 / 1719 4.1 / 2328 1.9	**29** TU	0501 4.6 / 1132 1.2 / 1740 4.6 / 2350 1.3	
15 TU	0532 4.4 / 1159 1.6 / 1754 4.4	**30** W	0543 5.0 / 1215 0.9 / 1816 4.9	
		31 TH	0029 1.0 / 0621 5.2 / 1252 0.6 / 1849 5.0	

APRIL

Time	m		Time	m
1 F ●	0107 0.7 / 0655 5.3 / 1327 0.5 / 1919 5.1	**16** SA ○	0039 0.9 / 0626 5.1 / 1304 0.5 / 1852 5.2	
2 SA	0141 0.6 / 0727 5.3 / 1400 0.5 / 1948 5.1	**17** SU	0114 0.6 / 0700 5.3 / 1338 0.4 / 1926 5.3	
3 SU	0215 0.7 / 0759 5.2 / 1431 0.6 / 2016 5.0	**18** M	0150 0.5 / 0736 5.3 / 1414 0.4 / 2002 5.3	
4 M	0248 0.8 / 0831 5.0 / 1502 0.9 / 2045 4.7	**19** TU	0228 0.5 / 0817 5.2 / 1451 0.5 / 2043 5.1	
5 TU	0320 1.1 / 0904 4.7 / 1533 1.1 / 2114 4.5	**20** W	0308 0.7 / 0903 4.9 / 1532 0.9 / 2129 4.8	
6 W	0354 1.4 / 0941 4.4 / 1606 1.5 / 2147 4.2	**21** TH	0353 1.0 / 0959 4.6 / 1616 1.3 / 2228 4.5	
7 TH	0431 1.7 / 1027 4.0 / 1641 1.8 / 2230 4.0	**22** F	0444 1.3 / 1116 4.2 / 1711 1.7 / 2347 4.2	
8 F	0513 2.0 / 1136 3.7 / 1723 2.2 / 2343 3.7	**23** SA ☾	0551 1.7 / 1246 3.9 / 1827 2.1	
9 SA	0614 2.3 / 1312 3.6 / 1826 2.5	**24** SU	0112 4.1 / 0726 1.9 / 1416 3.9 / 2015 2.2	
10 SU	0140 3.6 / 0809 2.4 / 1441 3.6 / 2035 2.6	**25** M	0235 4.1 / 0907 1.7 / 1538 4.0 / 2142 2.0	
11 M	0311 3.7 / 0951 2.2 / 1554 3.8 / 2204 2.3	**26** TU	0345 4.3 / 1017 1.5 / 1636 4.3 / 2239 1.6	
12 TU	0411 3.9 / 1043 1.9 / 1642 4.0 / 2252 1.9	**27** W	0438 4.6 / 1107 1.2 / 1718 4.5 / 2325 1.3	
13 W	0452 4.2 / 1122 1.5 / 1718 4.3 / 2330 1.6	**28** TH	0520 4.8 / 1149 1.0 / 1752 4.7	
14 TH	0524 4.6 / 1157 1.1 / 1750 4.7	**29** F	0005 1.1 / 0557 4.9 / 1225 0.9 / 1824 4.8	
15 F	0004 1.2 / 0555 4.9 / 1230 0.8 / 1821 5.0	**30** SA ●	0042 0.9 / 0630 5.0 / 1259 0.7 / 1853 4.9	

Chart Datum: 2·75 metres below Ordnance Datum (Newlyn)
HAT is 5·9 metres above Chart Datum

TIDES

TIME ZONE (UT)
For Summer Time add ONE hour in **non-shaded areas**

SCOTLAND – ULLAPOOL
LAT 57°54′N   LONG 5°09′W
TIMES AND HEIGHTS OF HIGH AND LOW WATERS

Dates in amber are **SPRINGS**
Dates in grey are **NEAPS**

2022

MAY

Day	Time m	Time m	Time m	Time m
1 SU	0117 0.8	0703 5.0	1331 0.8	1921 4.9
2 M	0150 0.9	0735 4.9	1402 0.7	1949 4.8
3 TU	0223 1.0	0808 4.7	1433 1.0	2018 4.7
4 W	0256 1.2	0843 4.5	1504 1.3	2049 4.5
5 TH	0331 1.4	0923 4.2	1537 1.5	2124 4.3
6 F	0408 1.6	1011 4.0	1613 1.8	2208 4.1
7 SA	0451 1.9	1115 3.8	1656 2.1	2311 3.9
8 SU	0547 2.1	1231 3.6	1754 2.3	
9 M ◑	0042 3.7	0711 2.2	1347 3.6	1926 2.4
10 TU	0204 3.7	0845 2.1	1457 3.7	2101 2.3
11 W	0310 3.9	0948 1.8	1552 4.0	2200 2.0
12 TH	0359 4.2	1034 1.5	1635 4.3	2246 1.6
13 F	0440 4.5	1115 1.1	1712 4.6	2327 1.3
14 SA	0517 4.8	1153 0.8	1747 4.9	
15 SU	0006 0.9	0556 5.0	1232 0.6	1824 5.1
16 M ○	0046 0.7	0636 5.2	1311 0.5	1903 5.3
17 TU	0128 0.5	0720 5.2	1352 0.5	1944 5.3
18 W	0212 0.5	0808 5.1	1434 0.7	2031 5.1
19 TH	0258 0.7	0903 4.8	1520 1.0	2124 4.9
20 F	0348 0.9	1008 4.5	1610 1.3	2227 4.6
21 SA	0445 1.2	1122 4.2	1708 1.7	2340 4.4
22 SU ◔	0552 1.5	1237 4.0	1821 1.9	
23 M	0053 4.3	0712 1.6	1354 4.0	1946 2.0
24 TU	0207 4.2	0832 1.6	1507 4.0	2102 1.9
25 W	0314 4.3	0939 1.5	1605 4.2	2204 1.7
26 TH	0409 4.4	1033 1.4	1650 4.3	2254 1.5
27 F	0454 4.5	1117 1.2	1727 4.5	2338 1.3
28 SA	0533 4.6	1156 1.2	1800 4.6	
29 SU	0018 1.2	0610 4.7	1232 1.1	1831 4.7
30 M ●	0055 1.2	0645 4.7	1305 1.1	1901 4.7
31 TU	0130 1.1	0720 4.6	1338 1.2	1931 4.7

JUNE

Day	Time m	Time m	Time m	Time m
1 W	0205 1.2	0755 4.5	1411 1.3	2002 4.6
2 TH	0240 1.3	0832 4.4	1444 1.4	2034 4.5
3 F	0315 1.4	0913 4.3	1518 1.5	2111 4.4
4 SA	0353 1.5	0958 4.1	1555 1.7	2154 4.2
5 SU	0435 1.7	1049 3.9	1638 1.9	2246 4.1
6 M	0524 1.8	1149 3.8	1729 2.1	2350 4.0
7 TU ◔	0624 1.9	1254 3.8	1834 2.2	
8 W	0101 3.9	0734 1.9	1358 3.8	1950 2.1
9 TH	0207 4.0	0842 1.8	1457 3.9	2059 2.0
10 F	0305 4.2	0940 1.5	1549 4.2	2157 1.7
11 SA	0356 4.4	1032 1.3	1635 4.5	2249 1.4
12 SU	0445 4.6	1119 1.0	1718 4.8	2338 1.1
13 M	0533 4.9	1206 0.8	1802 5.0	
14 TU ○	0025 0.9	0622 5.0	1251 0.7	1847 5.2
15 W	0114 0.7	0714 5.1	1338 0.7	1935 5.3
16 TH	0203 0.6	0807 5.0	1425 0.8	2025 5.2
17 F	0253 0.6	0904 4.8	1513 1.0	2118 5.1
18 SA	0345 0.8	1003 4.6	1604 1.2	2216 4.9
19 SU	0439 1.0	1105 4.4	1658 1.5	2318 4.7
20 M	0537 1.2	1208 4.2	1757 1.7	
21 TU ◔	0022 4.5	0638 1.4	1315 4.0	1903 1.9
22 W	0128 4.3	0743 1.6	1424 4.0	2013 1.9
23 TH	0235 4.2	0849 1.7	1527 4.0	2121 1.9
24 F	0336 4.2	0950 1.7	1619 4.1	2222 1.8
25 SA	0428 4.2	1044 1.6	1703 4.3	2313 1.7
26 SU	0514 4.3	1129 1.6	1741 4.4	2359 1.6
27 M	0556 4.4	1210 1.5	1816 4.5	
28 TU	0039 1.4	0635 4.4	1246 1.4	1849 4.6
29 W	0117 1.4	0711 4.5	1322 1.4	1920 4.7
30 TH	0153 1.3	0747 4.5	1356 1.4	1951 4.7

JULY

Day	Time m	Time m	Time m	Time m
1 F	0228 1.3	0822 4.5	1430 1.4	2023 4.7
2 SA	0303 1.3	0858 4.4	1504 1.4	2057 4.6
3 SU	0339 1.3	0936 4.3	1540 1.5	2134 4.5
4 M	0416 1.4	1017 4.2	1618 1.6	2216 4.4
5 TU ◔	0457 1.5	1105 4.1	1701 1.8	2305 4.3
6 W	0543 1.6	1201 4.0	1752 1.9	
7 TH ●	0003 4.2	0638 1.7	1304 4.0	1853 2.0
8 F	0110 4.1	0740 1.7	1407 4.0	2003 2.0
9 SA	0217 4.2	0848 1.7	1508 4.2	2113 1.9
10 SU	0322 4.3	0954 1.6	1606 4.4	2219 1.6
11 M	0425 4.5	1055 1.4	1659 4.7	2319 1.4
12 TU	0525 4.7	1150 1.2	1750 4.9	
13 W ○	0015 1.0	0621 4.9	1241 1.0	1839 5.2
14 TH	0107 0.8	0713 5.0	1330 0.9	1927 5.3
15 F	0158 0.6	0803 5.1	1417 0.8	2014 5.4
16 SA	0247 0.5	0852 5.0	1503 0.8	2102 5.3
17 SU	0334 0.6	0941 4.8	1549 1.0	2151 5.1
18 M	0420 0.7	1031 4.6	1635 1.2	2242 4.9
19 TU	0506 1.0	1124 4.3	1723 1.5	2339 4.6
20 W ◔	0554 1.4	1224 4.1	1816 1.8	
21 TH	0041 4.3	0648 1.7	1331 3.9	1919 2.0
22 F	0150 4.1	0749 1.9	1443 3.9	2033 2.2
23 SA	0301 4.0	0902 2.1	1549 4.0	2151 2.1
24 SU	0406 4.0	1012 2.1	1643 4.1	2255 2.0
25 M	0500 4.1	1108 1.9	1726 4.3	2345 1.8
26 TU	0545 4.2	1153 1.8	1803 4.5	
27 W	0027 1.6	0624 4.4	1232 1.6	1836 4.6
28 TH	0104 1.4	0659 4.5	1308 1.5	1907 4.7
29 F	0140 1.3	0731 4.6	1342 1.4	1936 4.8
30 SA	0213 1.1	0802 4.6	1414 1.3	2004 4.9
31 SU	0245 1.1	0834 4.6	1447 1.2	2035 4.9

AUGUST

Day	Time m	Time m	Time m	Time m
1 M	0318 1.1	0906 4.6	1519 1.2	2107 4.8
2 TU	0351 1.1	0942 4.5	1554 1.3	2143 4.7
3 W	0426 1.2	1023 4.4	1632 1.5	2225 4.6
4 TH	0506 1.4	1112 4.3	1716 1.6	2316 4.4
5 F	0552 1.6	1214 4.1	1809 1.9	
6 SA	0022 4.2	0651 1.8	1326 4.1	1918 2.0
7 SU	0144 4.1	0806 1.9	1439 4.1	2041 2.0
8 M	0307 4.1	0931 1.9	1549 4.3	2205 1.8
9 TU	0424 4.3	1045 1.7	1651 4.6	2315 1.5
10 W	0528 4.6	1144 1.4	1744 4.9	
11 TH	0012 1.1	0620 4.9	1235 1.1	1830 5.3
12 F ○	0102 0.7	0705 5.1	1320 0.8	1914 5.5
13 SA	0148 0.4	0747 5.2	1403 0.7	1955 5.6
14 SU	0231 0.3	0827 5.1	1445 0.7	2036 5.5
15 M	0311 0.4	0907 5.0	1525 0.8	2117 5.3
16 TU	0350 0.6	0947 4.7	1605 1.0	2200 5.0
17 W	0429 1.0	1030 4.4	1646 1.4	2247 4.6
18 TH	0509 1.4	1120 4.1	1731 1.8	2346 4.2
19 F ◔	0553 1.8	1228 3.9	1825 2.1	
20 SA	0102 3.9	0647 2.2	1352 3.8	1942 2.4
21 SU	0227 3.8	0806 2.4	1516 3.8	2125 2.4
22 M	0345 3.8	0946 2.4	1610 4.0	2242 2.2
23 TU	0445 4.0	1052 2.2	1708 4.2	2331 1.9
24 W	0530 4.2	1138 1.9	1745 4.4	
25 TH	0010 1.6	0607 4.4	1215 1.7	1816 4.7
26 F	0045 1.4	0638 4.6	1249 1.4	1844 4.9
27 SA ●	0118 1.1	0707 4.8	1321 1.2	1911 5.0
28 SU	0149 0.9	0735 4.9	1352 1.1	1938 5.1
29 M	0219 0.8	0804 4.9	1423 1.0	2006 5.1
30 TU	0250 0.8	0834 4.9	1454 1.0	2038 5.1
31 W	0321 0.9	0908 4.8	1527 1.1	2112 5.0

Chart Datum: 2·75 metres below Ordnance Datum (Newlyn)
HAT is 5·9 metres above Chart Datum

TIME ZONE (UT)
For Summer Time add ONE
hour in **non-shaded areas**

SCOTLAND – ULLAPOOL
LAT 57°54′N   LONG 5°09′W
TIMES AND HEIGHTS OF HIGH AND LOW WATERS

Dates in amber are **SPRINGS**
Dates in grey are **NEAPS**

2022

SEPTEMBER

Time	m	Time	m
1 0355	1.0	**16** 0426	1.5
0945	4.7	1015	4.3
TH 1604	1.3	F 1650	1.8
2152	4.8	2249	4.1
2 0432	1.3	**17** 0504	1.9
1031	4.5	1108	4.0
F 1646	1.5	SA 1738	2.2
2241	4.5	◐	
3 0516	1.6	**18** 0012	3.8
1133	4.2	0551	2.3
SA 1738	1.8	SU 1253	3.8
◐ 2354	4.2	1850	2.5
4 0614	1.9	**19** 0150	3.7
1259	4.1	0705	2.6
SU 1848	2.1	M 1435	3.8
		2056	2.5
5 0136	4.0	**20** 0318	3.7
0740	2.2	0917	2.6
M 1425	4.1	TU 1550	3.9
2031	2.2	2221	2.3
6 0312	4.0	**21** 0421	3.9
0929	2.1	1030	2.3
TU 1543	4.3	W 1641	4.2
2209	1.9	2308	1.9
7 0431	4.3	**22** 0506	4.2
1045	1.8	1114	2.0
W 1646	4.6	TH 1717	4.4
2315	1.4	2344	1.6
8 0527	4.6	**23** 0540	4.4
1138	1.4	1149	1.7
TH 1734	5.0	F 1747	4.7
9 0005	1.0	**24** 0017	1.3
0610	4.9	0610	4.7
F 1223	1.1	SA 1221	1.4
1816	5.4	1814	4.9
10 0049	0.6	**25** 0048	1.0
0648	5.2	0637	4.9
SA 1304	0.8	SU 1253	1.1
○ 1854	5.6	● 1841	5.1
11 0129	0.4	**26** 0118	0.8
0723	5.3	0704	5.1
SU 1343	0.6	M 1323	0.9
1930	5.6	1908	5.3
12 0206	0.4	**27** 0148	0.7
0757	5.2	0733	5.2
M 1420	0.6	TU 1355	0.8
2006	5.5	1938	5.3
13 0242	0.5	**28** 0219	0.7
0831	5.1	0803	5.2
TU 1456	0.8	W 1428	0.8
2042	5.3	2010	5.3
14 0317	0.7	**29** 0252	0.7
0904	4.9	0837	5.1
W 1532	1.0	TH 1503	0.9
2119	4.9	2047	5.1
15 0351	1.1	**30** 0326	1.0
0937	4.6	0916	4.9
TH 1610	1.4	F 1541	1.2
2159	4.5	2130	4.8

OCTOBER

Time	m	Time	m
1 0405	1.3	**16** 0426	2.0
1003	4.6	1015	4.1
SA 1625	1.5	SU 1703	2.2
2226	4.4	2329	3.8
2 0451	1.7	**17** 0510	2.4
1111	4.3	1138	3.9
SU 1720	1.9	M 1807	2.5
2358	4.1	◐	
3 0553	2.1	**18** 0104	3.7
1247	4.1	0615	2.7
M 1841	2.2	TU 1336	3.8
◐		2004	2.6
4 0143	4.0	**19** 0233	3.7
0736	2.4	0822	2.7
TU 1417	4.2	W 1502	3.9
2040	2.1	2139	2.3
5 0317	4.1	**20** 0342	3.9
0928	2.2	0949	2.5
W 1534	4.4	TH 1559	4.1
2207	1.8	2229	2.0
6 0426	4.4	**21** 0429	4.2
1034	1.8	1036	2.1
TH 1632	4.7	F 1639	4.4
2303	1.3	2307	1.7
7 0514	4.7	**22** 0505	4.5
1122	1.4	1113	1.8
F 1717	5.1	SA 1710	4.7
2348	1.0	2340	1.3
8 0552	5.0	**23** 0535	4.7
1204	1.1	1147	1.5
SA 1755	5.4	SU 1739	4.9
9 0027	0.7	**24** 0012	1.1
0626	5.2	0604	5.0
SU 1242	0.9	M 1220	1.2
○ 1831	5.5	1808	5.2
10 0104	0.6	**25** 0044	0.8
0657	5.3	0633	5.2
M 1318	0.7	TU 1253	1.0
1905	5.5	● 1839	5.4
11 0138	0.6	**26** 0117	0.7
0728	5.3	0704	5.4
TU 1354	0.8	W 1328	0.8
1939	5.4	1913	5.4
12 0211	0.7	**27** 0151	0.7
0758	5.1	0738	5.4
W 1429	0.9	TH 1404	0.8
2012	5.2	1950	5.3
13 0243	0.9	**28** 0227	0.8
0828	4.9	0815	5.3
TH 1503	1.2	F 1443	0.9
2047	4.8	2033	5.1
14 0316	1.3	**29** 0305	1.1
0858	4.7	0859	5.0
F 1539	1.5	SA 1526	1.2
2125	4.5	2125	4.8
15 0350	1.6	**30** 0348	1.4
0932	4.4	0952	4.7
SA 1618	1.8	SU 1616	1.5
2213	4.1	2236	4.4
		31 0439	1.9
		1108	4.5
		M 1718	1.8

NOVEMBER

Time	m	Time	m
1 0008	4.1	**16** 0011	3.8
0549	2.2	0538	2.5
TU 1237	4.3	W 1222	4.0
◐ 1846	2.0	◐ 1856	2.4
2 0139	4.1	**17** 0129	3.8
0731	2.4	0704	2.7
W 1400	4.3	TH 1348	4.0
2029	2.0	2027	2.3
3 0303	4.2	**18** 0241	3.9
0905	2.2	0839	2.5
TH 1513	4.5	F 1456	4.1
2145	1.7	2131	2.1
4 0406	4.4	**19** 0338	4.1
1008	1.9	0941	2.3
F 1610	4.8	SA 1546	4.3
2239	1.4	2218	1.8
5 0453	4.7	**20** 0421	4.4
1057	1.6	1027	2.0
SA 1655	5.0	SU 1625	4.6
2323	1.1	2257	1.5
6 0530	4.9	**21** 0456	4.7
1140	1.3	1108	1.7
SU 1733	5.2	M 1701	4.9
		2334	1.2
7 0001	0.9	**22** 0530	5.0
0603	5.1	1146	1.4
M 1218	1.1	TU 1737	5.1
1809	5.3		
8 0037	0.9	**23** 0011	1.0
0634	5.2	0605	5.2
TU 1256	1.0	W 1225	1.1
○ 1844	5.3	● 1815	5.3
9 0111	0.9	**24** 0049	0.9
0704	5.2	0641	5.4
W 1331	1.1	TH 1306	0.9
1918	5.2	1856	5.3
10 0144	1.0	**25** 0129	0.8
0733	5.1	0721	5.4
TH 1406	1.2	F 1348	0.9
1952	5.0	1942	5.3
11 0216	1.3	**26** 0210	0.9
0803	5.0	0805	5.4
F 1441	1.3	SA 1433	0.9
2028	4.7	2033	5.1
12 0249	1.5	**27** 0254	1.2
0835	4.8	0854	5.2
SA 1517	1.6	SU 1522	1.1
2108	4.5	2132	4.8
13 0323	1.7	**28** 0342	1.5
0909	4.6	0952	5.0
SU 1556	1.8	M 1616	1.4
2155	4.2	2241	4.5
14 0400	2.0	**29** 0436	1.8
0952	4.3	1100	4.7
M 1640	2.1	TU 1718	1.6
2256	4.0	2356	4.3
15 0442	2.3	**30** 0542	2.1
1052	4.1	1215	4.6
TU 1736	2.3	W 1832	1.8
		◐	

DECEMBER

Time	m	Time	m
1 0113	4.2	**16** 0022	4.0
0702	2.2	0605	2.4
TH 1329	4.5	F 1226	4.1
1952	1.8	◐ 1905	2.2
2 0229	4.2	**17** 0130	4.0
0822	2.2	0715	2.4
F 1439	4.6	SA 1338	4.1
2104	1.7	2013	2.1
3 0335	4.3	**18** 0234	4.1
0930	2.0	0829	2.4
SA 1540	4.6	SU 1441	4.2
2204	1.6	2116	2.0
4 0426	4.5	**19** 0329	4.3
1027	1.8	0932	2.2
SU 1631	4.8	M 1536	4.4
2253	1.5	2210	1.7
5 0508	4.7	**20** 0417	4.5
1115	1.6	1027	1.9
M 1714	4.9	TU 1626	4.7
2336	1.4	2259	1.5
6 0544	4.8	**21** 0501	4.8
1158	1.5	1116	1.6
TU 1753	4.9	W 1714	4.9
		2345	1.3
7 0014	1.3	**22** 0544	5.1
0617	5.0	1204	1.3
W 1238	1.4	TH 1802	5.1
1831	4.9		
8 0050	1.3	**23** 0030	1.1
0649	5.0	0628	5.3
TH 1316	1.4	F 1252	1.1
○ 1907	4.9	○ 1852	5.2
9 0124	1.4	**24** 0116	1.0
0720	5.0	0713	5.5
F 1352	1.4	SA 1340	0.9
1943	4.8	1942	5.2
10 0157	1.5	**25** 0202	1.0
0752	5.0	0800	5.5
SA 1428	1.5	SU 1429	0.8
2020	4.7	2035	5.2
11 0231	1.6	**26** 0248	1.1
0824	4.9	0850	5.4
SU 1504	1.6	M 1519	0.9
2058	4.5	2129	5.0
12 0306	1.7	**27** 0337	1.2
0858	4.7	0942	5.3
M 1542	1.7	TU 1611	1.0
2139	4.4	2225	4.8
13 0342	1.9	**28** 0427	1.5
0937	4.6	1039	5.1
TU 1622	1.9	W 1704	1.2
2225	4.2	2325	4.5
14 0421	2.1	**29** 0521	1.7
1022	4.4	1141	4.9
W 1707	2.0	TH 1801	1.5
2318	4.1		
15 0507	2.2	**30** 0030	4.3
1117	4.2	0622	1.9
TH 1800	2.1	F 1247	4.6
		◐ 1903	1.7
		31 0141	4.3
		0730	2.1
		SA 1357	4.5
		2010	1.9

Chart Datum: 2·75 metres below Ordnance Datum (Newlyn)
HAT is 5·9 metres above Chart Datum

TIDES

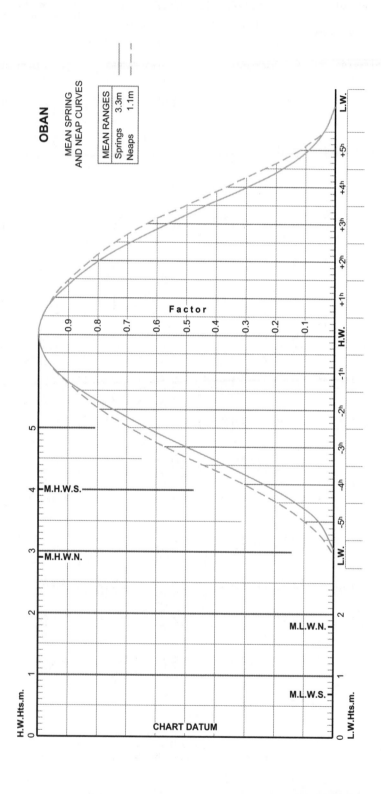

OBAN

MEAN SPRING
AND NEAP CURVES

MEAN RANGES	
Springs	3.3m
Neaps	1.1m

SCOTLAND – OBAN

LAT 56°25′N   LONG 5°29′W

TIMES AND HEIGHTS OF HIGH AND LOW WATERS

Dates in amber are **SPRINGS**
Dates in grey are **NEAPS**

2022

	JANUARY			FEBRUARY			MARCH			APRIL	
	Time m	Time m		Time m	Time m		Time m	Time m		Time m	Time m

JANUARY

	Time m		Time m
1 SA	0416 3.8 / 1024 1.0 / 1636 3.9 / 2257 1.0	**16** SU	0440 3.5 / 1127 1.6 / 1711 3.6 / 2317 1.3
2 SU ●	0503 4.0 / 1120 0.8 / 1723 4.0 / 2345 0.8	**17** ○	0520 3.7 / 1201 1.5 / 1750 3.7 / 2356 1.2
3 M	0548 4.1 / 1212 0.8 / 1809 4.0	**18** TU	0558 3.8 / 1235 1.4 / 1827 3.8
4 TU	0030 0.7 / 0634 4.2 / 1301 0.8 / 1853 3.9	**19** W	0032 1.1 / 0635 3.8 / 1309 1.3 / 1902 3.8
5 W	0116 0.7 / 0719 4.2 / 1350 0.8 / 1936 3.8	**20** TH	0106 1.0 / 0708 3.9 / 1342 1.3 / 1932 3.7
6 TH	0202 0.8 / 0804 4.0 / 1437 1.0 / 2018 3.6	**21** F	0138 1.0 / 0739 3.8 / 1413 1.4 / 2002 3.6
7 F	0248 0.9 / 0849 3.8 / 1524 1.2 / 2100 3.4	**22** SA	0211 1.1 / 0811 3.8 / 1441 1.4 / 2034 3.5
8 SA	0335 1.1 / 0936 3.6 / 1612 1.4 / 2143 3.2	**23** SU	0246 1.1 / 0846 3.7 / 1513 1.5 / 2111 3.4
9 SU ☽	0424 1.3 / 1027 3.4 / 1702 1.6 / 2231 3.0	**24** M	0327 1.2 / 0927 3.6 / 1558 1.6 / 2155 3.3
10 M	0516 1.5 / 1128 3.2 / 1756 1.8 / 2335 2.9	**25** TU ☽	0416 1.3 / 1017 3.4 / 1656 1.7 / 2251 3.1
11 TU	0615 1.7 / 1252 3.1 / 1857 1.9	**26** W	0517 1.5 / 1121 3.3 / 1812 1.8
12 W	0103 2.9 / 0727 1.8 / 1411 3.1 / 2001 1.9	**27** TH	0006 3.0 / 0631 1.5 / 1252 3.2 / 1935 1.7
13 TH	0216 3.0 / 0853 1.8 / 1509 3.2 / 2102 1.8	**28** F	0153 3.1 / 0753 1.5 / 1435 3.3 / 2051 1.6
14 F	0311 3.1 / 1000 1.8 / 1553 3.3 / 2153 1.6	**29** SA	0319 1.3 / 0912 1.4 / 1549 3.4 / 2156 1.3
15 SA	0358 3.3 / 1048 1.7 / 1633 3.4 / 2237 1.5	**30** SU	0417 3.6 / 1022 1.1 / 1644 3.6 / 2251 1.1
		31 M	0505 3.9 / 1120 0.9 / 1728 3.8 / 2339 0.8

FEBRUARY

	Time m		Time m
1 TU ●	0548 4.1 / 1210 0.8 / 1809 3.9	**16** W ○	0547 3.8 / 1224 1.2 / 1814 3.8
2 W	0024 0.6 / 0630 4.2 / 1255 0.7 / 1847 3.9	**17** TH	0013 0.9 / 0621 3.9 / 1253 1.0 / 1845 3.8
3 TH	0106 0.5 / 0709 4.2 / 1337 0.7 / 1923 3.8	**18** F	0045 0.7 / 0651 4.0 / 1322 1.0 / 1912 3.8
4 F	0148 0.6 / 0748 4.1 / 1417 0.8 / 1958 3.7	**19** SA	0116 0.7 / 0720 4.0 / 1349 1.0 / 1938 3.8
5 SA	0228 0.7 / 0824 4.0 / 1455 1.0 / 2030 3.6	**20** SU	0148 0.7 / 0749 3.9 / 1415 1.0 / 2008 3.7
6 SU	0306 0.9 / 0900 3.7 / 1532 1.3 / 2102 3.4	**21** M	0223 0.7 / 0822 3.8 / 1447 1.1 / 2043 3.5
7 M	0345 1.2 / 0937 3.5 / 1612 1.5 / 2135 3.2	**22** TU	0303 0.9 / 0900 3.6 / 1527 1.3 / 2124 3.4
8 TU	0426 1.4 / 1018 3.4 / 1658 1.7 / 2215 3.0	**23** W ☾	0350 1.1 / 0945 3.4 / 1620 1.5 / 2215 3.1
9 W	0515 1.7 / 1112 2.9 / 1753 1.9 / 2311 2.9	**24** TH	0451 1.3 / 1044 3.1 / 1736 1.7 / 2331 3.0
10 TH	0615 1.9 / 1254 2.8 / 1859 2.0	**25** F	0612 1.5 / 1229 2.9 / 1908 1.7
11 F	0111 2.8 / 0739 2.0 / 1500 2.9 / 2015 1.9	**26** SA	0150 3.0 / 0744 1.6 / 1453 3.0 / 2038 1.6
12 SA	0251 2.9 / 1002 1.9 / 1554 3.0 / 2130 1.7	**27** SU	0322 3.2 / 0916 1.4 / 1606 3.2 / 2151 1.3
13 SU	0349 3.1 / 1050 1.7 / 1630 3.2 / 2223 1.5	**28** M	0418 3.6 / 1027 1.1 / 1652 3.4 / 2245 1.0
14 M	0432 3.3 / 1125 1.5 / 1704 3.5 / 2304 1.3		
15 TU	0511 3.6 / 1155 1.3 / 1739 3.6 / 2340 1.0		

MARCH

	Time m		Time m
1 TU	0501 3.9 / 1118 0.9 / 1728 3.6 / 2330 0.7	**16** W	0450 3.5 / 1132 1.2 / 1717 3.6 / 2314 0.9
2 W	0539 4.1 / 1200 0.7 / 1759 3.8	**17** TH	0524 3.8 / 1158 0.9 / 1749 3.8 / 2346 0.7
3 TH	0011 0.5 / 0615 4.2 / 1239 0.6 / 1831 3.9	**18** F ○	0556 3.9 / 1226 0.8 / 1818 3.9
4 F	0050 0.4 / 0650 4.2 / 1315 0.6 / 1901 3.9	**19** SA	0018 0.5 / 0626 4.0 / 1253 0.7 / 1843 3.9
5 SA	0127 0.5 / 0723 4.2 / 1349 0.7 / 1930 3.8	**20** SU	0051 0.4 / 0655 4.1 / 1321 0.7 / 1910 3.9
6 SU	0203 0.6 / 0754 4.0 / 1421 0.9 / 1958 3.7	**21** M	0126 0.4 / 0725 4.0 / 1351 0.7 / 1943 3.8
7 M	0236 0.8 / 0825 3.7 / 1454 1.1 / 2025 3.6	**22** TU	0204 0.5 / 0800 3.8 / 1426 0.9 / 2020 3.6
8 TU	0309 1.1 / 0856 3.5 / 1530 1.4 / 2055 3.4	**23** W	0247 0.7 / 0838 3.6 / 1508 1.1 / 2102 3.4
9 W	0345 1.5 / 0929 3.2 / 1613 1.6 / 2131 3.2	**24** TH	0337 1.0 / 0924 3.2 / 1603 1.4 / 2155 3.1
10 TH	0430 1.8 / 1008 2.9 / 1707 1.8 / 2215 2.9	**25** F	0444 1.3 / 1026 2.9 / 1720 1.6 / 2320 2.9
11 F	0531 2.0 / 1123 2.7 / 1815 2.0 / 2335 2.7	**26** SA	0608 1.5 / 1252 2.7 / 1853 1.7
12 SA	0657 2.2 / 1446 2.7 / 1935 2.0	**27** SU	0153 3.0 / 0746 1.6 / 1500 2.8 / 2028 1.5
13 SU	0241 2.8 / 1001 2.0 / 1540 2.9 / 2101 1.8	**28** M	0311 3.2 / 0922 1.3 / 1601 3.1 / 2139 1.2
14 M	0339 3.0 / 1038 1.7 / 1614 3.1 / 2200 1.5	**29** TU	0402 3.5 / 1020 1.1 / 1640 3.3 / 2229 0.9
15 TU	0416 3.3 / 1106 1.4 / 1645 3.4 / 2240 1.2	**30** W	0442 3.8 / 1102 0.9 / 1708 3.5 / 2311 0.7
		31 TH	0517 4.0 / 1139 0.7 / 1735 3.7 / 2351 0.5

APRIL

	Time m		Time m
1 F ●	0550 4.1 / 1213 0.6 / 1804 3.9	**16** SA ○	0524 4.0 / 1152 0.7 / 1744 3.9 / 2348 0.4
2 SA	0027 0.5 / 0623 4.1 / 1245 0.6 / 1833 3.9	**17** SU	0556 4.1 / 1222 0.5 / 1813 3.9
3 SU	0103 0.5 / 0653 4.1 / 1317 0.7 / 1900 3.9	**18** M	0026 0.3 / 0629 4.1 / 1254 0.5 / 1846 3.9
4 M	0135 0.7 / 0723 3.9 / 1348 0.9 / 1927 3.8	**19** TU	0107 0.3 / 0704 4.0 / 1330 0.6 / 1923 3.9
5 TU	0206 1.0 / 0752 3.7 / 1420 1.1 / 1955 3.7	**20** W	0150 0.5 / 0743 3.8 / 1412 0.8 / 2004 3.7
6 W	0237 1.2 / 0822 3.5 / 1455 1.3 / 2026 3.5	**21** TH	0239 0.7 / 0826 3.5 / 1459 1.0 / 2051 3.4
7 TH	0312 1.6 / 0854 3.2 / 1537 1.6 / 2101 3.2	**22** F	0335 1.0 / 0916 3.1 / 1558 1.2 / 2151 3.2
8 F	0355 1.8 / 0930 2.9 / 1630 1.8 / 2144 3.0	**23** SA ☾	0444 1.3 / 1029 2.8 / 1711 1.5 / 2326 3.0
9 SA	0501 2.1 / 1030 2.6 / 1738 1.9 / 2251 2.8	**24** SU	0606 1.5 / 1303 2.6 / 1837 1.5
10 SU	0634 2.2 / 1406 2.6 / 1854 1.9	**25** M	0135 3.0 / 0743 1.5 / 1442 2.8 / 2006 1.4
11 M	0204 2.8 / 0930 2.0 / 1502 2.8 / 2014 1.8	**26** TU	0246 3.3 / 0904 1.3 / 1538 3.0 / 2114 1.2
12 TU	0305 3.0 / 1001 1.7 / 1540 3.1 / 2116 1.5	**27** W	0336 3.5 / 0956 1.1 / 1612 3.2 / 2204 1.0
13 W	0343 3.3 / 1026 1.4 / 1614 3.3 / 2200 1.2	**28** TH	0414 3.7 / 1036 1.0 / 1636 3.4 / 2247 0.8
14 TH	0417 3.5 / 1054 1.1 / 1646 3.5 / 2237 0.9	**29** F	0449 3.8 / 1110 0.9 / 1704 3.6 / 2326 0.7
15 F	0451 3.8 / 1122 0.9 / 1716 3.7 / 2312 0.6	**30** SA ●	0521 3.9 / 1142 0.7 / 1733 3.8

Chart Datum: 2·10 metres below Ordnance Datum (Newlyn)
HAT is 4·5 metres above Chart Datum

TIDES

SCOTLAND – OBAN
LAT 56°25'N   LONG 5°29'W
TIMES AND HEIGHTS OF HIGH AND LOW WATERS

TIME ZONE (UT) — For Summer Time add ONE hour in **non-shaded areas**

Dates in amber are **SPRINGS** / Dates in grey are **NEAPS**

2022

MAY

Day	Time	m		Day	Time	m
1 SU	0002	0.7		**16** M	0528	4.0
	0554	3.9			1153	0.6
	1213	0.8			1748	3.9 ○
	1803	3.8				
2 M	0036	0.8		**17** TU	0005	0.4
	0624	3.9			0608	4.0
	1245	0.9			1232	0.5
	1831	3.9			1828	4.0
3 TU	0109	1.0		**18** W	0052	0.4
	0655	3.8			0649	3.9
	1318	1.0			1315	0.6
	1901	3.8			1911	3.9
4 W	0141	1.2		**19** TH	0142	0.5
	0727	3.6			0734	3.7
	1352	1.1			1401	0.7
	1932	3.7			1958	3.7
5 TH	0213	1.4		**20** F	0235	0.8
	0800	3.4			0822	3.4
	1428	1.3			1453	0.9
	2006	3.5			2050	3.5
6 F	0250	1.7		**21** SA	0333	1.0
	0834	3.2			0917	3.1
	1509	1.5			1550	1.1
	2043	3.3			2152	3.3
7 SA	0334	1.9		**22** SU	0438	1.2
	0915	2.9			1032	2.8
	1558	1.7			1656	1.3
	2127	3.1			2319 ◑	3.1
8 SU	0438	2.1		**23** M	0553	1.4
	1017	2.7			1230	2.7
	1658	1.8			1811	1.4
	2229	2.9				
9 M	0604	2.1		**24** TU	0100	3.1
	1257	2.7			0716	1.4
	1805	1.9 ◐			1358	2.8
					1930	1.4
10 TU	0018	2.9		**25** W	0210	3.2
	0745	2.0			0828	1.4
	1411	2.8			1456	2.9
	1913	1.8			2039	1.3
11 W	0201	3.0		**26** TH	0302	3.3
	0851	1.7			0921	1.3
	1456	3.0			1533	3.1
	2015	1.5			2134	1.2
12 TH	0253	3.3		**27** F	0343	3.5
	0933	1.5			1002	1.2
	1533	3.2			1559	3.3
	2107	1.2			2219	1.1
13 F	0334	3.5		**28** SA	0419	3.6
	1008	1.2			1037	1.1
	1607	3.4			1631	3.5
	2153	1.0			2300	1.0
14 SA	0413	3.8		**29** SU	0453	3.6
	1042	0.9			1110	1.1
	1639	3.7			1703	3.6
	2237	0.7			2338	1.1
15 SU	0450	3.9		**30** M	0527	3.7
	1117	0.7			1144	1.0
	1712	3.8			1736	3.7
	2321	0.5				
				31 TU	0012	1.1
					0601	3.7
					1218	1.0
					1810	3.8

JUNE

Day	Time	m		Day	Time	m
1 W	0047	1.2		**16** TH	0044	0.5
	0636	3.6			0643	3.8
	1254	1.1			1305	0.6
	1844	3.7			1907	4.0
2 TH	0122	1.4		**17** F	0136	0.6
	0712	3.5			0731	3.6
	1331	1.2			1353	0.6
	1919	3.7			1956	3.9
3 F	0159	1.5		**18** SA	0229	0.7
	0749	3.4			0820	3.4
	1408	1.3			1443	0.8
	1955	3.5			2047	3.7
4 SA	0238	1.7		**19** SU	0324	0.9
	0827	3.2			0912	3.2
	1447	1.4			1536	0.9
	2033	3.4			2143	3.5
5 SU	0321	1.8		**20** M	0422	1.2
	0909	3.1			1012	3.0
	1528	1.6			1633	1.1
	2115	3.3			2247	3.3
6 M	0413	1.9		**21** TU	0523	1.3
	0959	2.9			1126	2.8
	1616	1.7			1734	1.3
	2205	3.2			◑	
7 TU	0518	1.9		**22** W	0004	3.2
	1105	2.8			0628	1.5
	1711	1.7			1245	2.8
	2308 ◑	3.1			1841	1.4
8 W	0630	1.9		**23** TH	0119	3.1
	1239	2.8			0735	1.5
	1811	1.7			1350	2.8
					1952	1.5
9 TH	0026	3.1		**24** F	0221	3.1
	0737	1.7			0834	1.5
	1352	2.9			1441	3.0
	1914	1.5			2058	1.5
10 F	0145	3.3		**25** SA	0312	3.2
	0833	1.5			0923	1.5
	1442	3.1			1523	3.1
	2015	1.3			2153	1.4
11 SA	0245	3.4		**26** SU	0354	3.3
	0921	1.3			1005	1.4
	1526	3.3			1602	3.3
	2113	1.1			2240	1.4
12 SU	0337	3.6		**27** M	0432	3.4
	1006	1.1			1043	1.3
	1608	3.6			1641	3.4
	2208	0.9			2321	1.4
13 M	0424	3.8		**28** TU	0510	3.5
	1049	0.9			1121	1.2
	1651	3.8			1719	3.6
	2301	0.7			2359	1.4
14 TU	0510	3.9		**29** W	0548	3.5
	1133	0.7			1159	1.1
	1735	3.9			1757	3.7
	2353 ○	0.6			●	
15 W	0556	3.9		**30** TH	0035	1.4
	1218	0.6			0627	3.6
	1820	4.0			1237	1.1
					1834	3.7

JULY

Day	Time	m		Day	Time	m
1 F	0112	1.4		**16** SA	0131	0.6
	0705	3.6			0726	3.7
	1314	1.1			1344	0.5
	1911	3.7			1949	4.1
2 SA	0149	1.4		**17** SU	0219	0.7
	0742	3.5			0809	3.6
	1350	1.2			1430	0.6
	1946	3.6			2034	3.9
3 SU	0227	1.5		**18** M	0306	0.9
	0817	3.4			0852	3.4
	1424	1.2			1515	0.8
	2021	3.6			2119	3.7
4 M	0302	1.6		**19** TU	0352	1.1
	0851	3.3			0935	3.2
	1459	1.3			1602	1.0
	2057	3.5			2205	3.4
5 TU	0337	1.7		**20** W	0440	1.3
	0929	3.1			1021	3.0
	1539	1.4			1651	1.2
	2137	3.4			2257 ◑	3.2
6 W	0420	1.7		**21** TH	0531	1.5
	1014	3.0			1117	2.9
	1625	1.5			1745	1.5
	2224	3.3				
7 TH	0517	1.7		**22** F	0003	3.0
	1109	3.0			0628	1.7
	1721	1.5			1234	2.8
	2324 ◑	3.3			1848	1.7
8 F	0626	1.7		**23** SA	0129	2.9
	1220	3.0			0732	1.7
	1825	1.5			1352	2.8
					2010	1.8
9 SA	0038	3.2		**24** SU	0246	2.9
	0736	1.6			0839	1.7
	1345	3.0			1455	2.9
	1935	1.4			2139	1.8
10 SU	0203	3.3		**25** M	0343	3.0
	0841	1.5			0938	1.6
	1456	3.2			1546	3.1
	2045	1.3			2237	1.7
11 M	0315	3.4		**26** TU	0425	3.2
	0940	1.3			1026	1.4
	1553	3.5			1630	3.3
	2152	1.1			2320	1.6
12 TU	0414	3.6		**27** W	0503	3.4
	1034	1.0			1107	1.3
	1644	3.7			1710	3.5
	2253	0.9			2356	1.4
13 W	0506	3.7		**28** TH	0541	3.5
	1123	0.8			1146	1.1
	1732	3.9			1748	3.7
	○ 2349	0.7			●	
14 TH	0555	3.8		**29** F	0028	1.3
	1211	0.6			0619	3.6
	1819	4.1			1222	1.0
					1825	3.8
15 F	0041	0.6		**30** SA	0101	1.3
	0641	3.8			0655	3.7
	1258	0.5			1257	1.0
	1905	4.1			1859	3.8
				31 SU	0135	1.2
					0728	3.7
					1329	1.0
					1931	3.8

AUGUST

Day	Time	m		Day	Time	m
1 M	0206	1.2		**16** TU	0237	0.8
	0756	3.6			0820	3.6
	1359	1.0			1449	0.7
	2000	3.8			2045	3.8
2 TU	0234	1.3		**17** W	0315	1.0
	0823	3.5			0852	3.4
	1430	1.0			1528	1.0
	2031	3.7			2121	3.5
3 W	0259	1.4		**18** TH	0355	1.3
	0855	3.4			0924	3.2
	1506	1.1			1609	1.3
	2105	3.6			2159	3.2
4 TH	0333	1.5		**19** F	0439	1.5
	0933	3.2			1002	3.0
	1549	1.3			1656	1.6
	2146	3.4			2247 ◑	2.9
5 F	0422	1.6		**20** SA	0533	1.7
	1022	3.1			1057	2.8
	1643	1.4			1754	1.9
	2239 ◑	3.3				
6 SA	0530	1.7		**21** SU	0014	2.7
	1127	3.0			0639	1.9
	1751	1.5			1307	2.7
	2353	3.1			1917	2.0
7 SU	0655	1.7		**22** M	0243	2.7
	1312	3.0			0758	1.9
	1911	1.6			1448	2.9
					2149	2.0
8 M	0147	3.1		**23** TU	0348	2.9
	0818	1.6			0920	1.7
	1456	3.2			1544	3.1
	2034	1.5			2239	1.8
9 TU	0322	3.2		**24** W	0422	3.1
	0930	1.4			1014	1.5
	1559	3.5			1623	3.3
	2152	1.2			2314	1.6
10 W	0425	3.4		**25** TH	0453	3.4
	1028	1.1			1055	1.2
	1649	3.8			1658	3.6
	2255	1.0			2345	1.4
11 TH	0513	3.6		**26** F	0526	3.6
	1118	0.8			1130	1.0
	1732	4.0			1733	3.8
	2348	0.7				
12 F	0555	3.8		**27** SA	0012	1.2
	1204	0.6			0601	3.7
	1813	4.2			1202	0.9
	○				● 1807	3.9
13 SA	0034	0.6		**28** SU	0040	1.0
	0634	3.8			0634	3.8
	1247	0.4			1233	0.8
	1853	4.3			1838	4.0
14 SU	0117	0.5		**29** M	0109	1.0
	0711	3.8			0702	3.8
	1329	0.4			1303	0.7
	1931	4.2			1906	4.0
15 M	0158	0.6		**30** TU	0137	1.0
	0746	3.7			0725	3.8
	1409	0.5			1332	0.8
	2009	4.1			1932	3.9
				31 W	0201	1.0
					0751	3.7
					1403	0.8
					2001	3.9

Chart Datum: 2·10 metres below Ordnance Datum (Newlyn)
HAT is 4·5 metres above Chart Datum

TIME ZONE (UT)	SCOTLAND – OBAN	Dates in amber are **SPRINGS**
For Summer Time add ONE hour in **non-shaded areas**	LAT 56°25′N LONG 5°29′W	Dates in grey are **NEAPS**
	TIMES AND HEIGHTS OF HIGH AND LOW WATERS	**2022**

SEPTEMBER

Day	Time	m		Day	Time	m
1 TH	0227 0822 1439 2035	1.1 3.6 1.0 3.7		16 F	0313 0841 1532 2111	1.3 3.4 1.5 3.3
2 F	0301 0900 1522 2114	1.3 3.4 1.2 3.5		17 SA	0357 0917 1617 ☽2150	1.6 3.2 1.8 3.0
3 SA	0347 0946 1617 ☾2204	1.5 3.2 1.4 3.2		18 SU	0452 1003 1719 2259	1.8 2.9 2.1 2.7
4 SU	0457 1054 1734 2327	1.7 3.0 1.6 2.9		19 M	0600 1208 1852	2.0 2.8 2.2
5 M	0634 1331 1907	1.8 3.0 1.7		20 TU	0232 0724 1451 2149	2.7 2.0 2.9 2.0
6 TU	0217 0807 1502 2042	2.9 1.7 3.2 1.6		21 W	0329 0854 1535 2224	2.3 1.8 3.1 1.8
7 W	0339 0925 1557 2159	3.1 1.4 3.6 1.3		22 TH	0401 0950 1605 2252	3.2 1.5 3.4 1.5
8 TH	0429 1021 1641 2252	3.4 1.0 3.9 1.0		23 F	0430 1029 1635 2317	3.4 1.2 3.6 1.3
9 F	0508 1107 1719 2336	3.6 0.7 4.2 0.7		24 SA	0501 1103 1707 2343	3.6 1.0 3.9 1.1
10 SA	0541 1149 1755 O	3.8 0.5 4.3		25 SU	0533 1134 1739 ●	3.8 0.8 4.0
11 SU	0015 0613 1229 1830	0.6 3.9 0.4 4.4		26 M	0009 0603 1203 1808	0.9 3.9 0.7 4.1
12 M	0053 0644 1307 1904	0.6 4.0 0.4 4.3		27 TU	0036 0628 1233 1835	0.8 3.9 0.6 4.1
13 TU	0128 0715 1344 1936	0.6 3.9 0.5 4.1		28 W	0103 0652 1305 1903	0.8 3.9 0.6 4.1
14 W	0202 0744 1419 2007	0.8 3.8 0.8 3.9		29 TH	0130 0721 1340 1934	0.9 3.8 0.7 3.9
15 TH	0236 0811 1454 2038	1.0 3.6 1.1 3.6		30 F	0202 0755 1419 2010	1.0 3.7 0.9 3.7

OCTOBER

Day	Time	m		Day	Time	m
1 SA	0240 0836 1507 2051	1.2 3.5 1.2 3.4		16 SU	0323 0848 1548 2113	1.6 3.4 2.0 3.0
2 SU	0330 0926 1610 2144	1.4 3.3 1.5 3.0		17 M	0417 0935 1654 ☽2214	1.8 3.1 2.2 2.7
3 M	0445 1044 1735 ☾2333	1.7 3.0 1.7 2.8		18 TU	0524 1059 1836	2.0 2.9 2.3
4 TU	0620 1336 1911	1.8 3.1 1.7		19 W	0154 0643 1417 2120	2.7 2.0 3.0 2.1
5 W	0226 0756 1449 2049	2.9 1.6 3.4 1.5		20 TH	0250 0807 1502 2151	2.9 1.9 3.2 1.9
6 TH	0331 0910 1539 2151	3.1 1.3 3.7 1.2		21 F	0326 0907 1534 2214	3.2 1.6 3.4 1.6
7 F	0414 1003 1620 2236	3.4 1.0 4.0 1.0		22 SA	0358 0950 1602 2239	3.4 1.4 3.7 1.3
8 SA	0447 1047 1655 2314	3.6 0.8 4.2 0.8		23 SU	0429 1024 1634 2305	3.6 1.1 3.9 1.1
9 SU	0515 1127 1728 O2349	3.8 0.6 4.3 0.7		24 M	0459 1130 1705 2333	3.8 0.7 4.1 0.9
10 M	0543 1206 1801 ●	4.0 0.5 4.3		25 TU	0527 1130 1735	3.9 0.7 4.1
11 TU	0022 0613 1242 1832	0.7 4.0 0.6 4.2		26 W	0001 0555 1204 1806	0.8 4.0 0.6 4.2
12 W	0055 0642 1317 1902	0.8 4.0 0.8 4.1		27 TH	0032 0624 1242 1838	0.8 4.0 0.7 4.1
13 TH	0128 0710 1350 1932	0.9 3.9 1.0 3.9		28 F	0106 0659 1324 1915	0.8 4.0 0.8 3.9
14 F	0202 0739 1424 2003	1.1 3.8 1.4 3.6		29 SA	0145 0738 1410 1956	0.9 3.8 1.0 3.7
15 SA	0239 0811 1501 2036	1.3 3.6 1.6 3.3		30 SU	0230 0824 1504 2043	1.1 3.6 1.3 3.3
				31 M	0325 0922 1611 2145	1.4 3.4 1.5 3.0

NOVEMBER

Day	Time	m		Day	Time	m
1 TU	0437 1048 1732 ☽2353	1.6 3.2 1.7 2.8		16 W	0444 1023 1753 ☽	2.0 3.1 2.3
2 W	0601 1313 1905	1.7 3.2 1.7		17 TH	0025 0550 1225 1940	2.8 2.0 3.1 2.2
3 TH	0205 0731 1422 2031	2.9 1.6 3.5 1.5		18 F	0155 0659 1403 2044	2.9 1.9 3.2 2.0
4 F	0348 0843 1513 2127	3.3 1.4 3.7 1.3		19 SA	0241 0802 1444 2120	3.1 1.8 3.4 1.7
5 SA	0348 0937 1553 2209	3.3 1.1 3.9 1.1		20 SU	0317 0853 1520 2152	3.3 1.5 3.6 1.5
6 SU	0416 1022 1628 2245	3.6 0.9 4.0 1.0		21 M	0351 0937 1556 2224	3.5 1.3 3.8 1.2
7 M	0443 1103 1700 2319	3.7 0.8 4.1 0.9		22 TU	0423 1018 1631 2256	3.7 1.1 4.0 1.0
8 TU	0513 1142 1732 O2352	3.9 0.8 4.1 0.9		23 W	0454 1059 1706 ●2331	3.9 0.9 4.1 0.9
9 W	0543 1218 1803	4.0 0.9 4.1		24 TH	0528 1142 1743	4.0 0.8 4.1
10 TH	0024 0614 1253 1835	1.0 4.0 1.1 4.0		25 F	0008 0606 1227 1823	0.8 4.1 0.7 4.1
11 F	0058 0645 1327 1907	1.1 4.0 1.3 3.8		26 SA	0049 0647 1315 1905	0.8 4.0 0.8 3.9
12 SA	0134 0717 1401 1941	1.2 3.9 1.6 3.6		27 SU	0134 0732 1406 1951	0.9 3.9 1.0 3.6
13 SU	0213 0753 1440 2017	1.4 3.7 1.8 3.4		28 M	0223 0822 1502 2042	1.0 3.8 1.2 3.4
14 M	0256 0832 1528 2059	1.6 3.5 2.1 3.1		29 TU	0319 0921 1605 2144	1.2 3.6 1.4 3.1
15 TU	0346 0919 1630 2157	1.8 3.3 2.3 2.9		30 W	0422 1039 1716 ☾2312	1.4 3.4 1.6 2.9

DECEMBER

Day	Time	m		Day	Time	m
1 TH	0533 1228 1834	1.5 3.3 1.6		16 F	0450 1045 1802 ☽2343	1.9 3.2 2.1 2.9
2 F	0111 0651 1343 1950	2.9 1.5 3.4 1.6		17 SA	0546 1158 1909	1.9 3.2 2.1
3 SA	0222 0805 1440 2050	3.0 1.4 3.5 1.5		18 SU	0118 0647 1322 2009	3.0 1.8 3.3 1.9
4 SU	0308 0906 1524 2136	3.2 1.3 3.6 1.4		19 M	0220 0748 1427 2058	3.1 1.7 3.5 1.7
5 M	0340 0957 1602 2214	3.4 1.2 3.7 1.3		20 TU	0307 0848 1518 2143	3.3 1.5 3.6 1.4
6 TU	0412 1041 1636 2250	3.6 1.2 3.8 1.2		21 W	0350 0944 1604 2226	3.6 1.3 3.8 1.2
7 W	0446 1122 1710 2324	3.7 1.2 3.9 1.2		22 TH	0432 1037 1649 2309	3.8 1.0 3.9 1.0
8 TH	0520 1200 1743 O	3.9 1.3 3.9		23 F	0514 1129 1733 ●2354	4.0 0.9 4.0 0.8
9 F	0000 0555 1236 1818	1.2 3.9 1.4 3.8		24 SA	0559 1220 1818	4.1 0.8 4.0
10 SA	0037 0630 1312 1854	1.2 3.9 1.5 3.8		25 SU	0039 0644 1310 1903	0.7 4.1 0.8 3.9
11 SU	0116 0706 1349 1931	1.3 3.9 1.7 3.6		26 M	0126 0731 1402 1949	0.7 4.1 0.9 3.7
12 M	0155 0743 1428 2010	1.4 3.8 1.8 3.5		27 TU	0215 0820 1454 2036	0.8 4.0 1.0 3.5
13 TU	0234 0822 1511 2049	1.5 3.6 2.0 3.3		28 W	0306 0912 1548 2127	1.0 3.8 1.2 3.3
14 W	0315 0903 1559 2134	1.6 3.5 2.1 3.1		29 TH	0400 1010 1644 2224	1.1 3.6 1.4 3.1
15 TH	0400 0949 1656 2228	1.8 3.3 2.2 3.0		30 F	0458 1121 1745 ☾2337	1.3 3.4 1.6 2.9
				31 SA	0603 1244 1850	1.4 3.3 1.7

Chart Datum: 2·10 metres below Ordnance Datum (Newlyn)
HAT is 4·5 metres above Chart Datum

TIDES

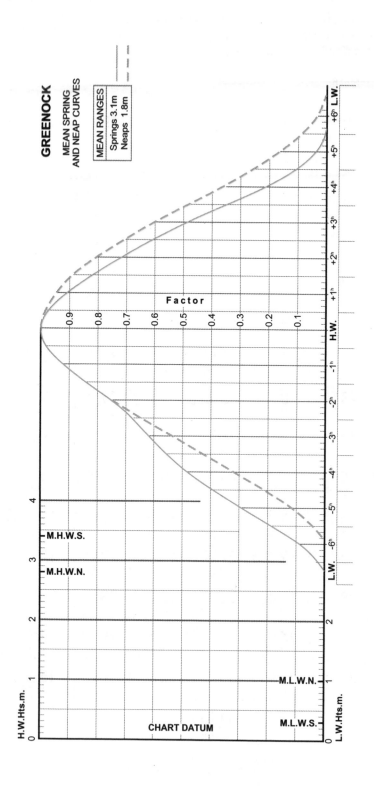

GREENOCK

MEAN SPRING
AND NEAP CURVES

MEAN RANGES
Springs 3.1m
Neaps 1.8m

Factor

0.9 0.8 0.7 0.6 0.5 0.4 0.3 0.2 0.1

H.W.

M.H.W.S.

M.H.W.N.

M.L.W.N.

M.L.W.S.

CHART DATUM

H.W.Hts.m.

L.W.Hts.m.

L.W.

SCOTLAND – GREENOCK

LAT 55°57′N   LONG 4°46′W

TIMES AND HEIGHTS OF HIGH AND LOW WATERS

Dates in amber are **SPRINGS**
Dates in grey are **NEAPS**

2022

JANUARY

Day	Time	m	Day	Time	m
1 SA	0352	0.5	**16** SU	0450	0.7
	1104	3.4		1130	3.4
	1630	0.5		1712	0.8
	2315	3.5			
2 SU ●	0445	0.4	**17** M ○	0005	3.1
	1153	3.5		0530	0.7
	1720	0.3		1208	3.5
				1747	0.7
3 M	0011	3.5	**18** TU	0044	3.2
	0536	0.4		0606	0.7
	1240	3.7		1243	3.6
	1809	0.2		1820	0.7
4 TU	0105	3.5	**19** W	0120	3.2
	0626	0.4		0640	0.7
	1326	3.7		1315	3.6
	1858	0.1		1851	0.6
5 W	0157	3.5	**20** TH	0155	3.2
	0715	0.5		0713	0.6
	1411	3.8		1349	3.6
	1946	0.1		1924	0.6
6 TH	0247	3.4	**21** F	0230	3.2
	0803	0.6		0748	0.6
	1456	3.8		1424	3.7
	2036	0.2		2000	0.5
7 F	0334	3.3	**22** SA	0306	3.2
	0852	0.7		0827	0.6
	1541	3.7		1502	3.7
	2127	0.4		2040	0.5
8 SA	0420	3.2	**23** SU	0344	3.2
	0941	0.8		0909	0.7
	1627	3.6		1542	3.6
	2221	0.5		2125	0.5
9 SU ☾	0506	3.1	**24** M	0423	3.1
	1033	0.9		0956	0.7
	1715	3.4		1623	3.6
	2321	0.6		2214	0.5
10 M	0552	3.0	**25** TU	0504	3.1
	1130	1.0		1047	0.8
	1807	3.2		1708	3.4
				2309	0.6
11 TU	0024	0.7	**26** W	0550	3.0
	0643	2.9		1146	0.9
	1235	1.1		1800	3.3
	1906	3.1			
12 W	0127	0.8	**27** TH	0010	0.7
	0740	2.9		0650	2.9
	1348	1.2		1253	1.0
	2015	3.0		1906	3.1
13 TH	0226	0.8	**28** F	0119	0.8
	0847	2.9		0820	2.9
	1453	1.1		1408	0.9
	2128	3.0		2034	3.1
14 F	0319	0.8	**29** SA	0232	0.8
	0952	3.1		0948	3.0
	1547	1.0		1520	0.7
	2231	3.0		2203	3.1
15 SA	0407	0.8	**30** SU	0340	0.7
	1046	3.2		1052	3.2
	1632	0.9		1621	0.5
	2322	3.1		2312	3.2
			31 M	0438	0.6
				1144	3.4
				1713	0.2

FEBRUARY

Day	Time	m	Day	Time	m
1 TU ●	0010	3.3	**16** W ○	0032	3.1
	0529	0.5		0548	0.6
	1231	3.6		1225	3.4
	1800	0.1		1801	0.5
2 W	0103	3.4	**17** TH	0108	3.1
	0616	0.4		0619	0.5
	1317	3.7		1257	3.5
	1845	0.0		1830	0.4
3 TH	0151	3.4	**18** F	0141	3.2
	0701	0.4		0650	0.5
	1400	3.7		1330	3.6
	1928	0.0		1900	0.3
4 F	0235	3.3	**19** SA	0213	3.2
	0744	0.4		0723	0.4
	1442	3.7		1406	3.6
	2011	0.1		1935	0.3
5 SA	0314	3.3	**20** SU	0245	3.2
	0825	0.5		0801	0.4
	1523	3.7		1443	3.7
	2054	0.2		2014	0.2
6 SU	0351	3.2	**21** M	0318	3.3
	0906	0.5		0842	0.4
	1602	3.6		1522	3.7
	2138	0.4		2057	0.2
7 M	0427	3.2	**22** TU	0353	3.2
	0948	0.7		0927	0.4
	1641	3.4		1602	3.6
	2226	0.6		2144	0.3
8 TU ☾	0504	3.1	**23** W	0429	3.2
	1034	0.8		1017	0.5
	1722	3.2		1644	3.5
	2320	0.8		2237	0.5
9 W	0545	3.0	**24** TH	0510	3.0
	1126	1.0		1115	0.7
	1807	3.0		1732	3.2
				2339	0.8
10 TH	0025	1.0	**25** F	0600	2.9
	0633	2.9		1227	0.9
	1236	1.2		1832	3.0
	1903	2.8			
11 F	0144	1.1	**26** SA	0054	1.0
	0733	2.8		0724	2.7
	1415	1.2		1355	0.9
	2024	2.7		2014	2.8
12 SA	0252	1.0	**27** SU	0224	1.0
	0859	2.8		0938	2.8
	1523	1.1		1515	0.6
	2214	2.7		2212	2.9
13 SU	0346	0.9	**28** M	0339	0.8
	1020	3.0		1043	3.1
	1613	0.9		1615	0.3
	2311	2.9		2316	3.1
14 M	0432	0.8			
	1111	3.2			
	1654	0.7			
	2354	3.0			
15 TU	0512	0.7			
	1151	3.3			
	1729	0.6			

MARCH

Day	Time	m	Day	Time	m
1 TU	0434	0.6	**16** W	0446	0.6
	1134	3.4		1124	3.2
	1704	0.1		1701	0.4
2 W ●	0007	3.2	**17** TH	0008	3.1
	0521	0.5		0520	0.5
	1219	3.5		1158	3.3
	1748	0.0		1732	0.3
3 TH	0053	3.3	**18** F ○	0044	3.1
	0603	0.3		0551	0.4
	1303	3.6		1231	3.4
	1828	-0.1		1801	0.2
4 F	0135	3.3	**19** SA	0117	3.2
	0642	0.3		0622	0.3
	1344	3.7		1307	3.5
	1905	0.0		1832	0.1
5 SA	0211	3.3	**20** SU	0148	3.2
	0719	0.3		0657	0.2
	1422	3.6		1345	3.6
	1942	0.1		1908	0.1
6 SU	0244	3.1	**21** M	0219	3.3
	0754	0.3		0735	0.2
	1459	3.6		1424	3.6
	2019	0.2		1949	0.1
7 M	0315	3.3	**22** TU	0252	3.3
	0830	0.4		0818	0.2
	1533	3.5		1504	3.6
	2057	0.4		2033	0.2
8 TU	0348	3.3	**23** W	0326	3.4
	0907	0.5		0904	0.2
	1608	3.3		1544	3.6
	2138	0.5		2121	0.3
9 W	0423	3.2	**24** TH	0403	3.3
	0947	0.6		0956	0.4
	1645	3.1		1627	3.4
	2225	0.8		2216	0.6
10 TH ☾	0501	3.1	**25** F	0444	3.1
	1033	0.8		1058	0.6
	1727	2.9		1715	3.1
	2322	1.0		2321	0.9
11 F	0544	2.9	**26** SA	0534	2.9
	1133	1.1		1219	0.8
	1818	2.6		1817	2.8
12 SA	0046	1.2	**27** SU	0047	1.1
	0639	2.7		0702	2.7
	1316	1.2		1354	0.7
	1930	2.5		2046	2.7
13 SU	0220	1.2	**28** M	0222	1.1
	0757	2.7		0927	2.8
	1453	1.1		1507	0.5
	2155	2.6		2214	2.9
14 M	0321	1.0	**29** TU	0332	0.8
	0945	2.8		1028	3.1
	1545	0.8		1602	0.2
	2250	2.8		2307	3.1
15 TU	0407	0.8	**30** W	0423	0.6
	1043	3.0		1116	3.4
	1626	0.6		1647	0.0
	2331	3.0		2352	3.2
			31 TH	0506	0.4
				1200	3.5
				1728	0.0

APRIL

Day	Time	m	Day	Time	m
1 F ●	0033	3.3	**16** SA ○	0011	3.2
	0545	0.3		0519	0.3
	1242	3.5		1159	3.4
	1805	0.0		1728	0.1
2 SA	0109	3.3	**17** SU	0046	3.2
	0620	0.3		0554	0.2
	1321	3.5		1240	3.5
	1838	0.1		1804	0.0
3 SU	0140	3.3	**18** M	0119	3.3
	0651	0.3		0632	0.1
	1357	3.5		1322	3.5
	1911	0.2		1845	0.0
4 M	0210	3.3	**19** TU	0153	3.4
	0722	0.3		0714	0.0
	1431	3.4		1405	3.6
	1945	0.3		1929	0.1
5 TU	0240	3.4	**20** W	0229	3.4
	0755	0.3		0759	0.1
	1504	3.4		1448	3.6
	2021	0.4		2016	0.2
6 W	0313	3.4	**21** TH	0306	3.4
	0830	0.4		0848	0.2
	1539	3.2		1531	3.4
	2100	0.6		2108	0.4
7 TH	0347	3.3	**22** F	0345	3.3
	0910	0.5		0945	0.3
	1615	3.1		1618	3.2
	2144	0.8		2207	0.7
8 F	0422	3.2	**23** SA	0429	3.2
	0954	0.7		1055	0.5
	1658	2.8		1712	3.0
	2236	1.0		2317	1.0
9 SA	0503	3.0	**24** SU	0526	2.9
	1051	1.0		1221	0.6
	1750	2.6		1831	2.7
	2349	1.2			
10 SU	0556	2.8	**25** M	0042	1.1
	1218	1.1		0716	2.8
	1859	2.5		1340	0.5
				2045	2.7
11 M	0128	1.3	**26** TU	0204	1.0
	0707	2.7		0902	2.8
	1404	1.0		1445	0.3
	2105	2.5		2153	2.9
12 TU	0241	1.1	**27** W	0309	0.8
	0846	2.7		1001	3.2
	1503	0.8		1537	0.2
	2212	2.8		2242	3.1
13 W	0331	0.9	**28** TH	0401	0.6
	0958	2.9		1050	3.3
	1546	0.5		1622	0.1
	2256	3.0		2325	3.2
14 TH	0411	0.7	**29** F	0444	0.4
	1042	3.1		1134	3.4
	1622	0.3		1702	0.1
	2335	3.1			
15 F	0446	0.5	**30** SA ●	0002	3.2
	1121	3.3		0522	0.4
	1655	0.2		1215	3.4
				1738	0.1

Chart Datum: 1·62 metres below Ordnance Datum (Newlyn)
HAT is 3·9 metres above Chart Datum

TIDES

TIDES

TIME ZONE (UT)
For Summer Time add ONE hour in **non-shaded areas**

SCOTLAND – GREENOCK
LAT 55°57'N   LONG 4°46'W
TIMES AND HEIGHTS OF HIGH AND LOW WATERS

Dates in amber are **SPRINGS**
Dates in grey are **NEAPS**

2022

MAY

Day	Time m	Time m	Time m	Time m
1 SU	0036 3.3	0555 0.3	1254 3.4	1811 0.2
16 M	0013 3.3	0529 0.1	1214 3.5	O 1740 0.0
2 M	0106 3.3	0625 0.3	1330 3.3	1843 0.3
17 TU	0052 3.4	0612 0.0	1302 3.5	1826 0.1
3 TU	0137 3.4	0654 0.3	1403 3.3	1916 0.4
18 W	0131 3.5	0658 0.0	1349 3.5	1914 0.2
4 W	0209 3.4	0727 0.4	1437 3.2	1953 0.5
19 TH	0211 3.5	0746 0.0	1437 3.4	2006 0.3
5 TH	0242 3.5	0803 0.4	1512 3.1	2033 0.6
20 F	0252 3.5	0840 0.1	1526 3.3	2102 0.5
6 F	0315 3.4	0843 0.5	1551 3.0	2117 0.8
21 SA	0336 3.4	0941 0.2	1620 3.1	2202 0.7
7 SA	0350 3.3	0929 0.7	1635 2.8	2208 1.0
22 SU	0425 3.2	1051 0.3	1723 2.9	◑ 2308 0.9
8 SU	0429 3.1	1025 0.8	1727 2.7	2310 1.1
23 M	0529 3.1	1205 0.4	1844 2.8	
9 M	0519 2.9	1137 0.9	1833 2.6 ◐	
24 TU	0019 1.0	0659 2.9	1312 0.4	2009 2.8
10 TU	0023 1.2	0624 2.8	1258 0.9	2000 2.6
25 W	0131 1.0	0824 3.0	1413 0.3	2113 2.9
11 W	0137 1.1	0742 2.8	1405 0.7	2118 2.8
26 TH	0235 0.8	0926 3.1	1506 0.2	2204 3.0
12 TH	0238 0.9	0856 2.9	1455 0.5	2210 2.9
27 F	0330 0.7	1018 3.2	1552 0.2	2248 3.1
13 F	0326 0.7	0953 3.1	1537 0.3	2254 3.1
28 SA	0417 0.5	1105 3.3	1634 0.2	2328 3.2
14 SA	0408 0.5	1040 3.3	1617 0.1	2334 3.2
29 SU	0457 0.5	1148 3.3	1711 0.3	
15 SU	0448 0.3	1127 3.4	1657 0.1	
30 M	0002 3.2	0533 0.4	1227 3.2	● 1747 0.4
31 TU	0036 3.3	0604 0.4	1304 3.2	1821 0.5

JUNE

Day	Time m	Time m	Time m	Time m
1 W	0108 3.4	0635 0.4	1338 3.1	1856 0.6
16 TH	0115 3.5	0646 0.0	1339 3.4	1904 0.3
2 TH	0141 3.5	0708 0.4	1413 3.1	1935 0.6
17 F	0159 3.6	0737 0.0	1433 3.3	1957 0.4
3 F	0215 3.5	0744 0.5	1450 3.0	2015 0.7
18 SA	0244 3.6	0831 0.0	1527 3.2	2052 0.5
4 SA	0249 3.5	0825 0.5	1530 3.0	2059 0.8
19 SU	0331 3.5	0928 0.1	1622 3.1	2147 0.6
5 SU	0324 3.4	0910 0.6	1615 2.9	2147 0.9
20 M	0421 3.4	1030 0.2	1719 3.0	2245 0.7
6 M	0403 3.2	1001 0.7	1705 2.8	2239 0.9
21 TU	0518 3.2	1134 0.3	1817 2.9	◑ 2345 0.8
7 TU	0449 3.1	1100 0.7	1801 2.7	◑ 2336 1.0
22 W	0624 3.1	1238 0.3	1916 2.9	
8 W	0544 3.0	1204 0.7	1904 2.7	
23 TH	0049 0.9	0735 3.0	1336 0.4	2015 2.8
9 TH	0037 1.0	0650 3.0	1306 0.6	2011 2.8
24 F	0155 0.9	0843 3.0	1431 0.4	2113 2.9
10 F	0140 0.9	0801 3.0	1403 0.5	2114 2.9
25 SA	0256 0.8	0943 3.0	1521 0.4	2205 3.0
11 SA	0239 0.8	0907 3.1	1455 0.3	2209 3.0
26 SU	0349 0.7	1036 3.1	1607 0.5	2252 3.1
12 SU	0332 0.5	1006 3.2	1544 0.2	2259 3.1
27 M	0435 0.6	1124 3.1	1649 0.5	2334 3.2
13 M	0422 0.3	1100 3.3	1632 0.2	2345 3.3
28 TU	0515 0.6	1207 3.1	1728 0.6	
14 TU	0509 0.2	1153 3.4	1721 0.2 O	
29 W	0011 3.3	0551 0.5	1245 3.0	1806 0.6
15 W	0030 3.4	0558 0.0	1246 3.4	1812 0.2
30 TH	0046 3.4	0624 0.5	1320 3.0	1843 0.6

JULY

Day	Time m	Time m	Time m	Time m
1 F	0119 3.5	0657 0.5	1356 3.0	1920 0.6
16 SA	0150 3.6	0725 -0.1	1428 3.2	1943 0.4
2 SA	0153 3.5	0731 0.5	1433 3.0	1958 0.7
17 SU	0235 3.7	0814 -0.1	1519 3.2	2032 0.4
3 SU	0227 3.5	0807 0.5	1512 3.0	2038 0.7
18 M	0321 3.6	0904 0.0	1606 3.1	2121 0.5
4 M	0303 3.5	0848 0.5	1553 3.0	2121 0.7
19 TU	0406 3.5	0957 0.2	1651 3.1	2211 0.6
5 TU	0341 3.4	0933 0.5	1636 2.9	2207 0.7
20 W	0452 3.4	1054 0.3	1733 3.0	◑ 2303 0.7
6 W	0423 3.3	1023 0.5	1722 2.9	2256 0.8
21 TH	0541 3.2	1154 0.5	1817 2.9	
7 TH	0510 3.2	1119 0.5	1812 2.8	◑ 2352 0.9
22 F	0000 0.9	0636 3.0	1256 0.6	1905 2.9
8 F	0605 3.1	1218 0.5	1909 2.8	
23 SA	0108 1.0	0741 2.8	1356 0.7	2002 2.8
9 SA	0052 0.9	0712 3.0	1319 0.5	2017 2.8
24 SU	0221 1.0	0901 2.8	1453 0.7	2113 2.9
10 SU	0158 0.8	0827 3.1	1420 0.5	2128 2.9
25 M	0325 0.9	1015 2.8	1545 0.7	2220 3.0
11 M	0303 0.7	0938 3.1	1519 0.4	2231 3.1
26 TU	0417 0.8	1110 2.9	1631 0.7	2312 3.2
12 TU	0403 0.4	1042 3.2	1615 0.4	2326 3.2
27 W	0500 0.6	1155 3.0	1714 0.6	2354 3.3
13 W	0456 0.2	1142 3.3	1709 0.3 O	
28 TH	0538 0.5	1235 3.0	1752 0.6 ●	
14 TH	0016 3.4	0547 0.0	1239 3.3	1801 0.3
29 F	0029 3.4	0612 0.5	1310 3.0	1828 0.6
15 F	0104 3.5	0636 -0.1	1335 3.3	1853 0.3
30 SA	0101 3.5	0643 0.5	1343 3.0	1901 0.6
31 SU	0132 3.5	0712 0.4	1416 3.0	1934 0.6

AUGUST

Day	Time m	Time m	Time m	Time m
1 M	0206 3.5	0744 0.4	1450 3.0	2010 0.6
16 TU	0302 3.7	0833 0.1	1534 3.2	2048 0.4
2 TU	0242 3.6	0819 0.4	1525 3.1	2050 0.6
17 W	0341 3.6	0917 0.2	1610 3.2	2130 0.5
3 W	0320 3.5	0900 0.4	1602 3.1	2133 0.6
18 TH	0420 3.4	1004 0.4	1645 3.1	2215 0.7
4 TH	0358 3.5	0946 0.4	1641 3.0	2220 0.7
19 F	0500 3.2	1059 0.7	1724 3.0	◐ 2305 0.9
5 F	0440 3.4	1038 0.5	1723 3.0	◑ 2313 0.8
20 SA	0543 3.0	1205 0.9	1808 2.9	
6 SA	0528 3.2	1137 0.6	1813 2.9	
21 SU	0010 1.1	0637 2.7	1322 1.0	1901 2.8
7 SU	0015 0.9	0628 3.0	1254 2.9	1921 2.8
22 M	0147 1.2	0754 2.6	1429 1.0	2013 2.8
8 M	0127 0.9	0749 2.9	1354 0.8	2056 2.8
23 TU	0304 1.0	1006 2.7	1526 0.9	2152 3.0
9 TU	0245 0.8	0923 2.8	1505 0.7	2216 3.0
24 W	0358 0.8	1100 2.8	1613 0.8	2253 3.2
10 W	0353 0.5	1040 3.1	1607 0.6	2315 3.3
25 TH	0441 0.7	1141 3.0	1655 0.7	2335 3.3
11 TH	0449 0.2	1142 3.2	1702 0.5	
26 F	0518 0.5	1219 3.0	1731 0.6	
12 F	0006 3.5	0538 0.0	1236 3.3	O 1751 0.4
27 SA	0009 3.4	0550 0.4	1252 3.1	● 1804 0.6
13 SA	0053 3.6	0623 -0.1	1327 3.3	1837 0.3
28 SU	0039 3.5	0619 0.4	1324 3.1	1834 0.6
14 SU	0138 3.7	0707 -0.1	1414 3.3	1922 0.3
29 M	0110 3.5	0645 0.4	1353 3.1	1905 0.5
15 M	0221 3.7	0750 -0.1	1456 3.2	2005 0.4
30 TU	0144 3.6	0714 0.3	1422 3.2	1939 0.5
31 W	0220 3.6	0749 0.3	1454 3.2	2018 0.5

Chart Datum: 1·62 metres below Ordnance Datum (Newlyn)
HAT is 3·9 metres above Chart Datum

TIME ZONE (UT)	SCOTLAND – GREENOCK	Dates in amber are SPRINGS
For Summer Time add ONE hour in **non-shaded areas**	LAT 55°57'N LONG 4°46'W	Dates in grey are NEAPS
	TIMES AND HEIGHTS OF HIGH AND LOW WATERS	**2022**

SEPTEMBER

Day	Time m	Day	Time m
1 TH	0258 3.6 / 0829 0.3 / 1529 3.2 / 2101 0.5	**16** F	0348 3.4 / 0917 0.6 / 1603 3.3 / 2129 0.7
2 F	0336 3.6 / 0913 0.4 / 1605 3.2 / 2148 0.6	**17** SA	0424 3.2 / 1004 0.9 / 1641 3.2 / ◑ 2215 0.9
3 SA	0415 3.5 / 1004 0.6 / 1645 3.1 / ◔ 2243 0.8	**18** SU	0505 3.0 / 1104 1.1 / 1724 3.0 / 2315 1.1
4 SU	0500 3.2 / 1105 0.8 / 1732 3.0 / 2349 0.9	**19** M	0556 2.7 / 1241 1.3 / 1817 2.9
5 M	0557 3.0 / 1218 1.0 / 1837 2.8	**20** TU	0109 1.3 / 0709 2.5 / 1404 1.3 / 1927 2.8
6 TU	0112 1.0 / 0723 2.8 / 1344 1.1 / 2042 2.8	**21** W	0237 1.1 / 0950 2.6 / 1502 1.1 / 2115 2.9
7 W	0242 0.8 / 0936 2.9 / 1505 0.9 / 2210 3.1	**22** TH	0331 0.9 / 1037 2.9 / 1549 0.9 / 2223 3.2
8 TH	0349 0.5 / 1047 3.1 / 1604 0.7 / 2305 3.4	**23** F	0413 0.7 / 1115 3.1 / 1629 0.7 / 2305 3.3
9 F	0440 0.2 / 1140 3.3 / 1653 0.5 / 2352 3.6	**24** SA	0448 0.5 / 1151 3.2 / 1704 0.6 / 2339 3.4
10 SA	0524 0.0 / 1226 3.3 / 1737 0.4 / ○	**25** SU	0520 0.4 / 1225 3.2 / 1734 0.6 / ●
11 SU	0036 3.7 / 0605 -0.1 / 1309 3.3 / 1818 0.4	**26** M	0010 3.5 / 0547 0.4 / 1255 3.2 / 1803 0.5
12 M	0119 3.7 / 0643 -0.1 / 1348 3.3 / 1856 0.4	**27** TU	0044 3.6 / 0614 0.3 / 1323 3.3 / 1834 0.5
13 TU	0159 3.7 / 0721 0.0 / 1423 3.3 / 1934 0.4	**28** W	0120 3.6 / 0645 0.3 / 1353 3.3 / 1910 0.4
14 W	0237 3.7 / 0758 0.2 / 1455 3.3 / 2010 0.4	**29** TH	0158 3.7 / 0722 0.3 / 1425 3.4 / 1951 0.4
15 TH	0313 3.6 / 0836 0.4 / 1528 3.3 / 2048 0.5	**30** F	0237 3.7 / 0803 0.3 / 1500 3.4 / 2035 0.5

OCTOBER

Day	Time m	Day	Time m
1 SA	0317 3.6 / 0849 0.5 / 1537 3.4 / 2125 0.6	**16** SU	0356 3.2 / 0924 1.0 / 1605 3.4 / 2138 0.9
2 SU	0358 3.5 / 0941 0.8 / 1618 3.3 / 2224 0.8	**17** M	0438 3.0 / 1017 1.3 / 1647 3.2 / ◑ 2236 1.2
3 M	0444 3.2 / 1045 1.0 / 1707 3.1 / ◔ 2339 1.0	**18** TU	0530 2.7 / 1141 1.5 / 1740 3.0
4 TU	0543 2.9 / 1209 1.3 / 1818 2.9	**19** W	0013 1.3 / 0643 2.6 / 1322 1.5 / 1847 2.9
5 W	0116 0.9 / 0743 2.7 / 1346 1.2 / 2039 2.9	**20** TH	0154 1.2 / 0900 2.7 / 1426 1.3 / 2018 3.0
6 TH	0237 0.7 / 0944 3.0 / 1500 1.0 / 2154 3.2	**21** F	0251 1.0 / 0958 2.9 / 1515 1.1 / 2135 3.1
7 F	0335 0.4 / 1039 3.2 / 1554 0.8 / 2246 3.5	**22** SA	0334 0.7 / 1038 3.1 / 1555 0.9 / 2222 3.3
8 SA	0423 0.2 / 1124 3.3 / 1638 0.6 / 2332 3.6	**23** SU	0411 0.6 / 1116 3.3 / 1629 0.7 / 2300 3.4
9 SU	0504 0.0 / 1209 3.4 / 1719 0.4 / ○	**24** M	0443 0.4 / 1150 3.3 / 1701 0.6 / 2337 3.5
10 M	0014 3.7 / 0542 0.0 / 1242 3.4 / 1756 0.4	**25** TU	0512 0.4 / 1223 3.4 / 1733 0.5 / ●
11 TU	0055 3.7 / 0618 0.1 / 1315 3.4 / 1830 0.4	**26** W	0015 3.6 / 0545 0.3 / 1253 3.4 / 1809 0.4
12 W	0134 3.7 / 0651 0.3 / 1346 3.4 / 1903 0.5	**27** TH	0057 3.7 / 0621 0.3 / 1326 3.5 / 1848 0.4
13 TH	0210 3.6 / 0725 0.4 / 1418 3.5 / 1937 0.5	**28** F	0139 3.7 / 0702 0.4 / 1402 3.6 / 1932 0.4
14 F	0244 3.5 / 0801 0.6 / 1452 3.5 / 2013 0.6	**29** SA	0221 3.7 / 0746 0.6 / 1440 3.6 / 2019 0.5
15 SA	0319 3.4 / 0840 0.8 / 1527 3.5 / 2053 0.7	**30** SU	0304 3.6 / 0836 0.7 / 1520 3.5 / 2114 0.6
		31 M	0349 3.4 / 0932 0.9 / 1604 3.4 / 2219 0.8

NOVEMBER

Day	Time m	Day	Time m
1 TU	0440 3.1 / 1040 1.2 / 1658 3.2 / ◐ 2341 0.9	**16** W	0509 2.8 / 1052 1.4 / 1705 3.2 / ◐ 2321 1.2
2 W	0551 2.9 / 1205 1.3 / 1821 3.0	**17** TH	0616 2.7 / 1211 1.5 / 1806 3.1
3 TH	0106 0.8 / 0802 2.9 / 1331 1.3 / 2016 3.1	**18** F	0045 1.2 / 0744 2.8 / 1325 1.4 / 1917 3.0
4 F	0215 0.6 / 0923 3.1 / 1439 1.1 / 2127 3.3	**19** SA	0153 1.0 / 0901 2.9 / 1424 1.2 / 2030 3.1
5 SA	0311 0.4 / 1014 3.2 / 1532 0.8 / 2219 3.5	**20** SU	0244 0.8 / 0953 3.1 / 1510 1.0 / 2129 3.3
6 SU	0358 0.3 / 1057 3.4 / 1617 0.7 / 2306 3.6	**21** M	0325 0.6 / 1036 3.2 / 1551 0.8 / 2218 3.4
7 M	0440 0.2 / 1136 3.4 / 1657 0.6 / 2349 3.7	**22** TU	0403 0.5 / 1115 3.3 / 1629 0.7 / 2304 3.5
8 TU	0518 0.3 / 1211 3.5 / 1733 0.5 / ○	**23** W	0440 0.4 / 1151 3.4 / 1708 0.5 / ● 2351 3.6
9 W	0030 3.6 / 0553 0.4 / 1243 3.5 / 1807 0.4	**24** TH	0520 0.4 / 1228 3.5 / 1749 0.4
10 TH	0108 3.6 / 0626 0.5 / 1315 3.6 / 1838 0.4	**25** F	0037 3.6 / 0602 0.4 / 1306 3.6 / 1833 0.4
11 F	0144 3.5 / 0700 0.6 / 1348 3.6 / 1911 0.6	**26** SA	0124 3.7 / 0648 0.5 / 1346 3.7 / 1920 0.4
12 SA	0219 3.4 / 0736 0.7 / 1423 3.7 / 1948 0.7	**27** SU	0211 3.6 / 0737 0.6 / 1428 3.7 / 2012 0.4
13 SU	0255 3.3 / 0815 0.9 / 1458 3.6 / 2028 0.8	**28** M	0259 3.5 / 0830 0.7 / 1512 3.7 / 2109 0.5
14 M	0334 3.2 / 0859 1.1 / 1535 3.5 / 2114 0.9	**29** TU	0350 3.3 / 0928 0.9 / 1600 3.5 / 2214 0.6
15 TU	0417 3.0 / 0949 1.2 / 1616 3.4 / 2209 1.1	**30** W	0448 3.2 / 1032 1.1 / 1658 3.4 / ◐ 2327 0.7

DECEMBER

Day	Time m	Day	Time m
1 TH	0601 3.0 / 1144 1.2 / 1813 3.3	**16** F	0539 2.9 / 1110 1.3 / 1726 3.2 / ◐ 2336 1.0
2 F	0039 0.7 / 0727 3.0 / 1258 1.2 / 1938 3.2	**17** SA	0639 2.8 / 1211 1.3 / 1824 3.2
3 SA	0144 0.6 / 0840 3.1 / 1406 1.1 / 2050 3.3	**18** SU	0039 1.0 / 0748 2.9 / 1315 1.3 / 1929 3.1
4 SU	0240 0.5 / 0936 3.2 / 1504 0.9 / 2148 3.4	**19** M	0140 0.9 / 0854 2.9 / 1416 1.1 / 2036 3.2
5 M	0330 0.5 / 1023 3.3 / 1553 0.8 / 2239 3.5	**20** TU	0235 0.8 / 0951 3.1 / 1511 0.9 / 2139 3.3
6 TU	0415 0.5 / 1105 3.4 / 1636 0.7 / 2325 3.5	**21** W	0326 0.6 / 1040 3.2 / 1601 0.7 / 2237 3.4
7 W	0455 0.5 / 1142 3.5 / 1715 0.6	**22** TH	0414 0.5 / 1126 3.4 / 1648 0.6 / 2331 3.5
8 TH	0008 3.5 / 0533 0.6 / 1217 3.6 / 1750 0.6 / ○	**23** F	0501 0.5 / 1209 3.5 / 1735 0.4 / ●
9 F	0048 3.4 / 0609 0.7 / 1251 3.6 / 1823 0.7	**24** SA	0024 3.5 / 0550 0.5 / 1252 3.7 / 1823 0.3
10 SA	0124 3.3 / 0644 0.7 / 1325 3.7 / 1857 0.7	**25** SU	0116 3.5 / 0639 0.5 / 1337 3.7 / 1912 0.2
11 SU	0200 3.3 / 0721 0.8 / 1400 3.7 / 1933 0.7	**26** M	0208 3.5 / 0730 0.5 / 1421 3.8 / 2004 0.2
12 M	0237 3.2 / 0800 0.9 / 1436 3.7 / 2012 0.8	**27** TU	0259 3.4 / 0822 0.6 / 1508 3.8 / 2058 0.3
13 TU	0317 3.1 / 0841 1.0 / 1512 3.6 / 2055 0.8	**28** W	0350 3.3 / 0915 0.7 / 1557 3.7 / 2155 0.4
14 W	0359 3.1 / 0926 1.1 / 1552 3.5 / 2142 0.9	**29** TH	0443 3.2 / 1010 0.8 / 1649 3.6 / 2257 0.5
15 TH	0446 3.0 / 1015 1.2 / 1636 3.4 / ◐ 2236 1.0	**30** F	0538 3.1 / 1110 1.0 / 1747 3.4 / ◐
		31 SA	0001 0.6 / 0636 3.0 / 1215 1.1 / 1852 3.3

Chart Datum: 1·62 metres below Ordnance Datum (Newlyn)
HAT is 3·9 metres above Chart Datum

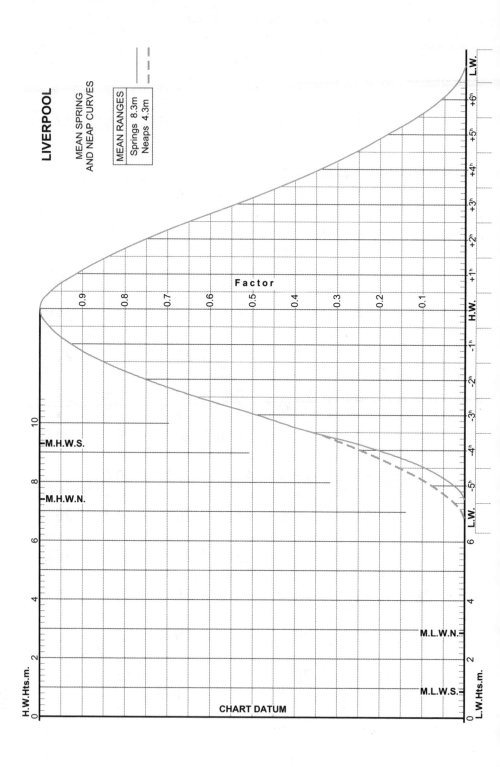

LIVERPOOL

MEAN SPRING
AND NEAP CURVES

MEAN RANGES	
Springs	8.3m
Neaps	4.3m

LIVERPOOL (GLADSTONE DOCK)
LAT 53°27'N   LONG 3°01'W
TIMES AND HEIGHTS OF HIGH AND LOW WATERS

Dates in amber are SPRINGS
Dates in grey are NEAPS

2022

JANUARY

Day	Time m	Time m	Time m	Time m
1 SA	0400 1.7	0931 9.0	1624 1.7	2157 9.1
2 SU	0454 1.4	1023 9.3	1721 1.3	● 2251 9.4
3 M	0545 1.2	1113 9.6	1814 1.0	2343 9.4
4 TU	0635 1.2	1203 9.7	1906 0.9	
5 W	0033 9.4	0723 1.3	1251 9.6	1956 1.0
6 TH	0121 9.2	0809 1.5	1338 9.4	2043 1.2
7 F	0208 8.8	0854 1.9	1426 9.1	2130 1.6
8 SA	0255 8.4	0939 2.3	1514 8.8	2216 2.0
9 SU	0344 8.0	1027 2.7	1605 8.3	○ 2305 2.5
10 M	0437 7.6	1120 3.1	1701 7.9	
11 TU	0000 2.9	0538 7.4	1222 3.3	1804 7.7
12 W	0100 3.1	0648 7.3	1329 3.4	1912 7.6
13 TH	0202 3.1	0756 7.4	1434 3.2	2016 7.7
14 F	0258 2.9	0852 7.7	1529 2.9	2111 7.9
15 SA	0346 2.7	0938 8.1	1617 2.6	2157 8.1
16 SU	0428 2.5	1018 8.4	1659 2.3	2237 8.4
17 M	0506 2.3	1054 8.6	1738 2.1	○ 2314 8.5
18 TU	0542 2.1	1128 8.8	1815 1.9	2348 8.7
19 W	0619 1.9	1202 8.9	1852 1.7	
20 TH	0022 8.7	0656 1.8	1235 9.0	1929 1.7
21 F	0056 8.7	0733 1.8	1309 9.0	2006 1.7
22 SA	0132 8.7	0810 1.9	1344 8.9	2043 1.8
23 SU	0210 8.6	0847 2.1	1422 8.8	2120 2.0
24 M	0250 8.4	0927 2.3	1505 8.6	2201 2.3
25 TU	0337 8.1	1012 2.6	1555 8.3	◑ 2251 2.5
26 W	0433 7.9	1109 2.8	1658 8.1	2356 2.7
27 TH	0543 7.7	1221 2.9	1815 7.9	
28 F	0117 2.7	0703 7.8	1346 2.8	1937 8.0
29 SA	0236 2.5	0816 8.2	1506 2.4	2050 8.3
30 SU	0344 2.1	0921 8.6	1615 1.9	2154 8.6
31 M	0444 1.7	1017 9.1	1716 1.3	2249 9.1

FEBRUARY

Day	Time m	Time m	Time m	Time m
1 TU	0538 1.4	1107 9.5	1810 0.9	● 2338 9.3
2 W	0626 1.1	1154 9.7	1858 0.7	
3 TH	0023 9.4	0712 1.1	1237 9.8	1942 0.7
4 F	0104 9.3	0753 1.2	1319 9.6	2022 0.9
5 SA	0144 9.0	0831 1.5	1358 9.4	2059 1.3
6 SU	0221 8.7	0906 1.9	1437 8.9	2134 1.9
7 M	0258 8.2	0942 2.4	1517 8.5	2208 2.4
8 TU	0340 7.8	1021 2.9	1604 7.9	◑ 2249 3.0
9 W	0431 7.4	1111 3.4	1703 7.4	2345 3.4
10 TH	0538 7.0	1224 3.7	1817 7.1	
11 F	0101 3.6	0703 7.0	1349 3.6	1940 7.1
12 SA	0218 3.5	0820 7.3	1500 3.2	2050 7.4
13 SU	0319 3.1	0916 7.7	1556 2.8	2141 7.8
14 M	0408 2.7	1000 8.2	1643 2.3	2222 8.2
15 TU	0450 2.3	1037 8.5	1724 1.9	2258 8.5
16 W	0529 2.0	1111 8.9	1801 1.6	○ 2331 8.8
17 TH	0606 1.7	1144 9.1	1838 1.3	
18 F	0003 9.0	0643 1.4	1216 9.2	1914 1.2
19 SA	0036 9.1	0719 1.3	1249 9.3	1949 1.2
20 SU	0110 9.1	0754 1.4	1323 9.3	2022 1.3
21 M	0146 9.0	0828 1.5	1359 9.1	2055 1.6
22 TU	0224 8.7	0903 1.8	1438 8.9	2131 1.9
23 W	0307 8.4	0944 2.2	1525 8.5	◐ 2216 2.4
24 TH	0400 8.0	1038 2.6	1627 8.0	2319 2.9
25 F	0513 7.6	1153 3.0	1755 7.6	
26 SA	0051 3.1	0644 7.5	1332 2.9	1931 7.6
27 SU	0223 2.8	0807 7.9	1501 2.5	2051 8.0
28 M	0337 2.3	0915 8.4	1612 1.8	2153 8.6

MARCH

Day	Time m	Time m	Time m	Time m
1 TU	0438 1.8	1010 9.0	1710 1.2	2242 9.0
2 W	0529 1.3	1056 9.4	1758 0.8	● 2325 9.3
3 TH	0613 1.0	1138 9.7	1840 0.6	
4 F	0004 9.4	0652 0.9	1216 9.7	1918 0.6
5 SA	0040 9.3	0728 1.0	1251 9.6	1952 0.9
6 SU	0113 9.1	0801 1.2	1327 9.3	2023 1.3
7 M	0145 8.8	0831 1.6	1400 9.0	2050 1.6
8 TU	0217 8.4	0901 2.1	1436 8.5	2116 2.3
9 W	0253 8.0	0932 2.7	1516 7.9	2147 2.9
10 TH	0336 7.5	1013 3.2	1608 7.3	◑ 2233 3.4
11 F	0436 7.0	1118 3.7	1722 6.8	2350 3.9
12 SA	0606 6.7	1259 3.8	1900 6.7	
13 SU	0132 3.8	0740 6.9	1426 3.4	2023 7.1
14 M	0248 3.3	0846 7.5	1529 2.8	2117 7.6
15 TU	0343 2.8	0932 8.0	1617 2.2	2157 8.1
16 W	0427 2.3	1009 8.5	1659 1.7	2232 8.6
17 TH	0507 1.8	1044 8.9	1738 1.3	2304 8.9
18 F	0545 1.4	1117 9.2	1815 1.0	○ 2337 9.2
19 SA	0623 1.1	1150 9.4	1851 0.8	
20 SU	0010 9.4	0659 1.0	1224 9.6	1926 0.8
21 M	0045 9.4	0734 1.0	1259 9.5	2000 1.0
22 TU	0122 9.2	0809 1.2	1337 9.3	2033 1.4
23 W	0201 9.0	0845 1.5	1419 8.9	2109 1.9
24 TH	0245 8.5	0927 2.0	1509 8.4	2154 2.5
25 F	0341 8.0	1023 2.6	1617 7.7	◑ 2301 3.0
26 SA	0501 7.5	1147 2.9	1753 7.3	
27 SU	0042 3.3	0635 7.5	1332 2.8	1931 7.5
28 M	0216 2.9	0759 7.9	1457 2.3	2047 8.0
29 TU	0328 2.3	0904 8.5	1602 1.6	2142 8.6
30 W	0425 1.7	0954 9.0	1654 1.1	2226 9.0
31 TH	0511 1.3	1036 9.3	1737 0.8	2304 9.2

APRIL

Day	Time m	Time m	Time m	Time m
1 F	0550 1.1	1115 9.5	1814 0.7	● 2339 9.3
2 SA	0626 1.0	1150 9.5	1847 0.8	
3 SU	0011 9.2	0659 1.0	1223 9.4	1918 1.0
4 M	0041 9.1	0730 1.2	1256 9.2	1945 1.4
5 TU	0111 8.8	0759 1.6	1328 8.8	2010 1.8
6 W	0142 8.5	0827 2.0	1402 8.4	2036 2.3
7 TH	0215 8.1	0857 2.5	1440 7.8	2107 2.8
8 F	0254 7.6	0935 3.0	1526 7.3	2149 3.4
9 SA	0347 7.1	1032 3.5	1633 6.8	◑ 2254 3.8
10 SU	0510 6.8	1204 3.7	1809 6.6	
11 M	0033 3.9	0648 6.9	1340 3.4	1938 6.9
12 TU	0202 3.5	0800 7.3	1447 2.8	2037 7.5
13 W	0303 2.9	0850 7.9	1539 2.2	2119 8.1
14 TH	0353 2.3	0931 8.4	1624 1.6	2156 8.6
15 F	0436 1.7	1008 8.9	1706 1.2	2231 9.0
16 SA	0517 1.3	1044 9.3	1746 0.9	○ 2306 9.3
17 SU	0557 1.0	1120 9.5	1824 0.7	2343 9.3
18 M	0636 0.8	1159 9.6	1901 0.7	
19 TU	0021 9.5	0715 0.8	1239 9.5	1938 0.9
20 W	0101 9.4	0753 1.1	1322 9.3	2015 1.4
21 TH	0145 9.0	0834 1.4	1409 8.8	2056 1.9
22 F	0234 8.6	0922 1.9	1506 8.2	2147 2.5
23 SA	0337 8.1	1026 2.4	1620 7.6	◐ 2259 3.0
24 SU	0457 7.7	1153 2.7	1750 7.4	
25 M	0034 3.1	0622 7.7	1323 2.5	1918 7.6
26 TU	0159 2.8	0739 8.0	1438 2.0	2027 8.0
27 W	0306 2.3	0848 8.5	1538 1.6	2119 8.5
28 TH	0359 1.9	0929 8.9	1627 1.3	2200 8.7
29 F	0444 1.5	1010 9.0	1707 1.2	2237 8.9
30 SA	0522 1.3	1047 9.2	1742 1.2	● 2310 9.0

TIDES

Chart Datum: 4·93 metres below Ordnance Datum (Newlyn)
HAT is 10·3m above Chart Datum

TIDES

LIVERPOOL (GLADSTONE DOCK)

LAT 53°27'N   LONG 3°01'W

TIMES AND HEIGHTS OF HIGH AND LOW WATERS

TIME ZONE (UT) — For Summer Time add ONE hour in **non-shaded** areas

Dates in amber are **SPRINGS** / Dates in grey are **NEAPS**

2022

MAY

Day	Time m	Day	Time m
1 SU	0556 1.3 / 1122 9.2 / 1813 1.2 / 2342 9.0	16 M	0531 1.1 / 1053 9.5 / 1757 0.8 / ○ 2318 9.5
2 M	0629 1.3 / 1156 9.1 / 1842 1.4	17 TU	0615 0.9 / 1138 9.5 / 1839 0.9
3 TU	0012 8.9 / 0700 1.5 / 1229 8.9 / 1910 1.6	18 W	0001 9.5 / 0659 0.9 / 1224 9.4 / 1921 1.1
4 W	0043 8.8 / 0730 1.7 / 1302 8.6 / 1938 1.9	19 TH	0046 9.4 / 0744 1.0 / 1313 9.2 / 2004 1.4
5 TH	0114 8.5 / 0800 2.0 / 1336 8.2 / 2007 2.3	20 F	0135 9.1 / 0832 1.3 / 1406 8.7 / 2051 1.9
6 F	0148 8.2 / 0833 2.4 / 1414 7.8 / 2041 2.7	21 SA	0230 8.7 / 0926 1.7 / 1507 8.2 / 2147 2.4
7 SA	0226 7.8 / 0913 2.8 / 1459 7.4 / 2123 3.2	22 SU	0334 8.3 / 1031 2.1 / 1616 7.8 / ○ 2256 2.8
8 SU	0315 7.4 / 1005 3.1 / 1557 7.0 / 2220 3.5	23 M	0444 8.1 / 1145 2.2 / 1731 7.6
9 M	0424 7.1 / 1118 3.3 / 1714 6.8 / ◑ 2339 3.7	24 TU	0012 2.9 / 0557 7.6 / 1257 2.2 / 1847 7.7
10 TU	0547 7.1 / 1242 3.2 / 1834 7.0	25 W	0125 2.7 / 0706 8.1 / 1403 2.1 / 1953 7.9
11 W	0102 3.4 / 0700 7.4 / 1353 2.7 / 1940 7.5	26 TH	0229 2.4 / 0806 8.3 / 1502 1.9 / 2046 8.2
12 TH	0202 2.9 / 0757 7.9 / 1451 2.2 / 2030 8.0	27 F	0324 2.2 / 0857 8.5 / 1551 1.8 / 2130 8.4
13 F	0307 2.4 / 0845 8.4 / 1542 1.7 / 2114 8.6	28 SA	0411 2.0 / 0941 8.6 / 1632 1.7 / 2208 8.6
14 SA	0358 1.9 / 0928 8.9 / 1630 1.3 / 2155 9.0	29 SU	0451 1.8 / 1020 8.7 / 1707 1.6 / 2242 8.7
15 SU	0445 1.4 / 1010 9.2 / 1714 1.0 / 2236 9.3	30 M	0527 1.7 / 1057 8.7 / 1740 1.7 / ● 2316 8.8
		31 TU	0602 1.7 / 1133 8.7 / 1811 1.8 / 2348 8.7

JUNE

Day	Time m	Day	Time m
1 W	0635 1.8 / 1208 8.6 / 1841 1.9	16 TH	0649 0.9 / 1217 9.3 / 1910 1.2
2 TH	0021 8.7 / 0708 1.9 / 1242 8.4 / 1913 2.0	17 F	0037 9.5 / 0740 0.9 / 1309 9.1 / 1958 1.4
3 F	0054 8.5 / 0742 2.0 / 1318 8.2 / 1946 2.3	18 SA	0129 9.3 / 0832 1.1 / 1403 8.8 / 2048 1.7
4 SA	0129 8.3 / 0818 2.3 / 1356 8.0 / 2023 2.6	19 SU	0223 9.0 / 0925 1.3 / 1458 8.5 / 2140 2.1
5 SU	0208 8.1 / 0858 2.5 / 1438 7.7 / 2106 2.8	20 M	0319 8.7 / 1020 1.7 / 1556 8.1 / 2237 2.4
6 M	0252 7.8 / 0945 2.7 / 1527 7.4 / 2156 3.1	21 TU	0418 8.4 / 1118 2.0 / 1657 7.8 / ○ 2337 2.6
7 TU	0347 7.6 / 1042 2.9 / 1627 7.3 / ○ 2257 3.2	22 W	0520 8.2 / 1218 2.2 / 1801 7.6
8 W	0452 7.5 / 1147 2.8 / 1733 7.3	23 TH	0040 2.8 / 0623 8.0 / 1319 2.4 / 1908 7.6
9 TH	0004 3.2 / 0559 7.6 / 1255 2.6 / 1839 7.6	24 F	0144 2.8 / 0726 8.0 / 1418 2.4 / 2007 7.8
10 F	0113 2.9 / 0702 7.9 / 1400 2.3 / 1939 8.0	25 SA	0244 2.6 / 0823 8.0 / 1510 2.4 / 2057 8.0
11 SA	0219 2.5 / 0759 8.3 / 1500 1.9 / 2033 8.4	26 SU	0337 2.5 / 0913 8.1 / 1556 2.3 / 2141 8.2
12 SU	0319 2.1 / 0852 8.7 / 1555 1.6 / 2123 8.8	27 M	0423 2.3 / 0958 8.3 / 1636 2.2 / 2220 8.4
13 M	0415 1.7 / 0943 9.0 / 1646 1.3 / 2211 9.2	28 TU	0504 2.1 / 1038 8.4 / 1712 2.1 / 2256 8.5
14 TU	0507 1.3 / 1034 9.3 / 1735 1.1 / ○ 2259 9.4	29 W	0542 2.0 / 1116 8.4 / 1746 2.1 / ● 2331 8.6
15 W	0559 1.0 / 1125 9.4 / 1823 1.1 / 2348 9.5	30 TH	0618 1.9 / 1152 8.4 / 1820 2.0

JULY

Day	Time m	Day	Time m
1 F	0005 8.6 / 0654 1.9 / 1227 8.4 / 1855 2.1	16 SA	0029 9.6 / 0735 0.7 / 1301 9.2 / 1950 1.2
2 SA	0039 8.6 / 0729 1.9 / 1302 8.4 / 1931 2.1	17 SU	0118 9.6 / 0823 0.7 / 1349 9.0 / 2036 1.4
3 SU	0114 8.5 / 0806 2.0 / 1338 8.2 / 2009 2.2	18 M	0205 9.4 / 0909 1.0 / 1435 8.7 / 2120 1.7
4 M	0150 8.4 / 0844 2.1 / 1417 8.1 / 2049 2.4	19 TU	0253 9.0 / 0954 1.4 / 1522 8.3 / 2205 2.1
5 TU	0229 8.3 / 0925 2.3 / 1458 7.9 / 2132 2.6	20 W	0341 8.6 / 1039 2.0 / 1611 7.9 / ◑ 2254 2.6
6 W	0313 8.1 / 1009 2.4 / 1546 7.8 / 2220 2.8	21 TH	0434 8.2 / 1129 2.4 / 1707 7.6 / 2350 2.9
7 TH	0403 8.0 / 1100 2.5 / 1641 7.7 / ◑ 2316 2.9	22 F	0533 7.8 / 1226 2.8 / 1812 7.4
8 F	0503 7.9 / 1201 2.6 / 1745 7.7	23 SA	0055 3.2 / 0640 7.5 / 1329 3.0 / 1923 7.4
9 SA	0021 2.9 / 0611 7.9 / 1311 2.5 / 1854 7.9	24 SU	0204 3.1 / 0749 7.5 / 1431 3.0 / 2027 7.6
10 SU	0134 2.7 / 0720 8.1 / 1422 2.3 / 1959 8.2	25 M	0307 2.9 / 0851 7.7 / 1526 2.8 / 2119 7.9
11 M	0246 2.3 / 0826 8.4 / 1526 2.0 / 2059 8.6	26 TU	0402 2.6 / 0942 7.9 / 1612 2.6 / 2203 8.2
12 TU	0352 1.9 / 0927 8.7 / 1624 1.6 / 2155 9.0	27 W	0448 2.3 / 1025 8.2 / 1653 2.4 / 2241 8.5
13 W	0453 1.5 / 1025 9.0 / 1719 1.4 / ○ 2248 9.3	28 TH	0528 2.1 / 1103 8.4 / 1730 2.2 / ● 2316 8.7
14 TH	0550 1.1 / 1119 9.2 / 1812 1.2 / 2339 9.5	29 F	0605 1.9 / 1137 8.5 / 1805 2.0 / 2350 8.8
15 F	0644 0.8 / 1211 9.3 / 1902 1.1	30 SA	0640 1.7 / 1211 8.6 / 1841 1.9
		31 SU	0022 8.9 / 0716 1.6 / 1243 8.6 / 1918 1.8

AUGUST

Day	Time m	Day	Time m
1 M	0055 8.9 / 0751 1.6 / 1317 8.6 / 1954 1.8	16 TU	0138 9.5 / 0841 1.0 / 1403 8.9 / 2051 1.5
2 TU	0128 8.8 / 0825 1.7 / 1351 8.5 / 2030 2.0	17 W	0218 9.2 / 0917 1.5 / 1441 8.5 / 2128 2.0
3 W	0202 8.7 / 0900 1.9 / 1428 8.4 / 2107 2.2	18 TH	0259 8.7 / 0953 2.1 / 1521 8.0 / 2207 2.3
4 TH	0239 8.5 / 0936 2.1 / 1509 8.2 / 2147 2.4	19 F	0344 8.1 / 1031 2.7 / 1610 7.5 / ◑ 2255 3.1
5 F	0323 8.3 / 1019 2.4 / 1559 7.9 / ◑ 2236 2.7	20 SA	0439 7.5 / 1122 3.3 / 1713 7.2
6 SA	0418 8.0 / 1114 2.7 / 1702 7.7 / 2340 2.9	21 SU	0002 3.5 / 0553 7.1 / 1234 3.6 / 1837 7.0
7 SU	0530 7.8 / 1230 2.8 / 1819 7.7	22 M	0127 3.6 / 0719 7.0 / 1355 3.6 / 1958 7.3
8 M	0103 2.9 / 0656 7.8 / 1355 2.7 / 1939 7.9	23 TU	0244 3.3 / 0834 7.3 / 1502 3.2 / 2059 7.7
9 TU	0228 2.6 / 0816 8.0 / 1509 2.4 / 2048 8.4	24 W	0343 2.8 / 0928 7.7 / 1554 2.9 / 2145 8.2
10 W	0342 2.0 / 0924 8.5 / 1613 1.9 / 2148 8.9	25 TH	0431 2.4 / 1009 8.1 / 1636 2.5 / 2222 8.5
11 TH	0446 1.5 / 1022 8.9 / 1710 1.5 / 2241 9.4	26 F	0511 2.0 / 1044 8.5 / 1714 2.1 / 2256 8.8
12 F	0544 0.9 / 1113 9.3 / 1802 1.2 / ○ 2329 9.7	27 SA	0547 1.7 / 1116 8.7 / 1749 1.8 / ● 2328 9.0
13 SA	0635 0.6 / 1200 9.4 / 1850 1.0	28 SU	0621 1.4 / 1148 9.0 / 1824 1.6 / 2359 9.2
14 SU	0014 9.8 / 0721 0.5 / 1243 9.4 / 1933 1.0	29 M	0655 1.3 / 1219 9.0 / 1859 1.5
15 M	0057 9.8 / 0802 0.6 / 1324 9.2 / 2013 1.2	30 TU	0029 9.2 / 0729 1.3 / 1250 9.0 / 1934 1.5
		31 W	0101 9.2 / 0802 1.4 / 1323 8.9 / 2008 1.7

Chart Datum: 4·93 metres below Ordnance Datum (Newlyn)
HAT is 10·3m above Chart Datum

LIVERPOOL (GLADSTONE DOCK)
LAT 53°27′N   LONG 3°01′W
TIMES AND HEIGHTS OF HIGH AND LOW WATERS

Dates in amber are **SPRINGS**
Dates in grey are **NEAPS**

2022

SEPTEMBER

Day	Time m	Time m	Day	Time m	Time m
1 TH	0134 9.0 / 0833 1.7	1359 8.7 / 2041 1.9	**16** F	0218 8.6 / 0905 2.3	1436 8.1 / 2123 2.7
2 F	0210 8.8 / 0906 2.0	1438 8.4 / 2119 2.3	**17** SA	0258 8.0 / 0935 2.9	1519 7.6 / ☽2204 3.2
3 SA	0253 8.5 / 0946 2.4	1526 8.1 / ☽2207 2.7	**18** SU	0350 7.3 / 1018 3.5	1619 7.1 / 2308 3.7
4 SU	0349 8.0 / 1041 2.9	1632 7.7 / 2316 3.0	**19** M	0504 6.8 / 1131 4.0	1749 6.8
5 M	0510 7.5 / 1205 3.2	1802 7.5	**20** TU	0049 3.8 / 0646 6.7	1316 4.0 / 1925 7.0
6 TU	0051 3.1 / 0651 7.5	1343 3.1 / 1931 7.8	**21** W	0216 3.4 / 0811 7.1	1435 3.6 / 2031 7.6
7 W	0224 2.6 / 0818 7.9	1502 2.6 / 2043 8.4	**22** TH	0316 2.9 / 0904 7.7	1528 3.0 / 2117 8.1
8 TH	0338 2.0 / 0924 8.5	1606 2.0 / 2141 9.0	**23** F	0403 2.3 / 0944 8.2	1611 2.5 / 2154 8.6
9 F	0440 1.3 / 1016 9.0	1700 1.5 / 2229 9.5	**24** SA	0442 1.9 / 1017 8.6	1649 2.0 / 2227 8.9
10 SA	0532 0.8 / 1100 9.4	1747 1.1 / ○2312 9.8	**25** SU	0519 1.5 / 1048 8.9	1725 1.7 / ●2258 9.2
11 SU	0616 0.5 / 1141 9.6	1829 0.9 / 2352 9.9	**26** M	0554 1.2 / 1118 9.1	1801 1.4 / 2329 9.4
12 M	0656 0.5 / 1218 9.5	1908 0.9	**27** TU	0629 1.1 / 1150 9.3	1836 1.3
13 TU	0030 9.8 / 0733 0.7	1253 9.3 / 1944 1.1	**28** W	0001 9.5 / 0703 1.1	1222 9.3 / 1912 1.3
14 W	0107 9.5 / 0806 1.1	1327 9.0 / 2017 1.6	**29** TH	0034 9.4 / 0736 1.3	1256 9.2 / 1946 1.5
15 TH	0142 9.1 / 0836 1.7	1400 8.6 / 2050 2.1	**30** F	0110 9.2 / 0808 1.6	1333 9.0 / 2021 1.8

OCTOBER

Day	Time m	Time m	Day	Time m	Time m
1 SA	0149 8.9 / 0842 2.0	1415 8.6 / 2101 2.2	**16** SU	0223 7.9 / 0852 3.0	1439 7.8 / 2125 3.2
2 SU	0236 8.4 / 0925 2.6	1508 8.1 / 2154 2.7	**17** M	0311 7.3 / 0932 3.6	1533 7.3 / ☽2222 3.7
3 M	0339 7.8 / 1025 3.1	1622 7.6 / 2311 3.1	**18** TU	0419 6.8 / 1036 4.0	1658 6.9 / 2358 3.9
4 TU	0511 7.3 / 1159 3.4	1757 7.5	**19** W	0556 6.6 / 1218 4.2	1834 7.0
5 W	0054 3.0 / 0653 7.4	1338 3.2 / 1924 7.9	**20** TH	0131 3.5 / 0726 7.0	1348 3.8 / 1946 7.5
6 TH	0221 2.4 / 0815 8.0	1453 2.6 / 2032 8.5	**21** F	0233 3.0 / 0824 7.7	1447 3.2 / 2036 8.0
7 F	0329 1.8 / 0914 8.6	1552 2.0 / 2125 9.1	**22** SA	0322 2.4 / 0905 8.1	1533 2.6 / 2115 8.5
8 SA	0424 1.2 / 0959 9.1	1642 1.5 / 2209 9.5	**23** SU	0404 1.9 / 0940 8.6	1615 2.1 / 2150 8.9
9 SU	0510 0.9 / 1039 9.3	1725 1.2 / ○2249 9.7	**24** M	0444 1.5 / 1013 9.0	1654 1.7 / 2224 9.2
10 M	0550 0.8 / 1116 9.4	1803 1.1 / 2327 9.8	**25** TU	0522 1.2 / 1046 9.3	1733 1.4 / ●2258 9.5
11 TU	0626 0.8 / 1150 9.4	1839 1.1	**26** W	0600 1.1 / 1120 9.5	1812 1.3 / 2334 9.6
12 W	0002 9.6 / 0659 1.1	1222 9.3 / 1913 1.3	**27** TH	0637 1.1 / 1157 9.5	1850 1.3
13 TH	0036 9.3 / 0729 1.5	1253 9.0 / 1945 1.7	**28** F	0012 9.5 / 0713 1.3	1235 9.4 / 1929 1.4
14 F	0110 8.9 / 0757 1.9	1325 8.7 / 2016 2.2	**29** SA	0053 9.4 / 0749 1.6	1317 9.1 / 2009 1.8
15 SA	0145 8.6 / 0823 2.5	1359 8.3 / 2047 2.7	**30** SU	0139 8.9 / 0829 2.1	1404 8.7 / 2056 2.2
			31 M	0233 8.3 / 0917 2.7	1503 8.2 / 2156 2.6

NOVEMBER

Day	Time m	Time m	Day	Time m	Time m
1 TU	0343 7.8 / 1024 3.2	1621 7.9 / ☽2318 2.8	**16** W	0340 7.1 / 1000 3.8	1607 7.2 / ☽2303 3.6
2 W	0512 7.5 / 1155 3.4	1746 7.8	**17** TH	0455 6.9 / 1116 4.0	1729 7.2
3 TH	0047 2.7 / 0641 7.6	1321 3.1 / 1905 8.1	**18** F	0026 3.5 / 0617 7.0	1240 3.8 / 1843 7.4
4 F	0203 2.2 / 0755 8.1	1430 2.6 / 2009 8.6	**19** SA	0135 3.1 / 0723 7.4	1349 3.3 / 1940 7.8
5 SA	0305 1.8 / 0851 8.5	1528 2.1 / 2101 9.0	**20** SU	0232 2.6 / 0814 7.9	1445 2.8 / 2028 8.3
6 SU	0358 1.5 / 0935 8.9	1616 1.7 / 2145 9.3	**21** M	0321 2.1 / 0857 8.4	1535 2.3 / 2110 8.7
7 M	0442 1.3 / 1014 9.1	1658 1.5 / 2224 9.4	**22** TU	0407 1.7 / 0936 8.9	1622 1.9 / 2150 9.1
8 TU	0520 1.3 / 1049 9.2	1736 1.4 / ○2301 9.4	**23** W	0450 1.4 / 1015 9.2	1707 1.6 / ○2231 9.4
9 W	0554 1.4 / 1123 9.2	1811 1.5 / 2337 9.3	**24** TH	0533 1.2 / 1055 9.5	1751 1.3 / 2314 9.5
10 TH	0625 1.5 / 1155 9.1	1845 1.6	**25** F	0614 1.2 / 1137 9.5	1835 1.3 / 2359 9.4
11 F	0011 9.0 / 0655 1.8	1226 8.9 / 1918 1.9	**26** SA	0656 1.4 / 1221 9.5	1919 1.3
12 SA	0045 8.7 / 0723 2.1	1258 8.7 / 1949 2.2	**27** SU	0046 9.2 / 0739 1.6	1308 9.3 / 2007 1.6
13 SU	0121 8.4 / 0752 2.5	1333 8.4 / 2022 2.4	**28** M	0138 8.9 / 0825 2.0	1401 9.0 / 2100 1.9
14 M	0159 8.0 / 0824 3.0	1412 8.0 / 2100 3.0	**29** TU	0236 8.5 / 0918 2.5	1502 8.6 / 2201 2.2
15 TU	0243 7.5 / 0905 3.4	1500 7.6 / 2151 3.4	**30** W	0341 8.1 / 1022 2.8	1610 8.3 / ☽2311 2.4

DECEMBER

Day	Time m	Time m	Day	Time m	Time m
1 TH	0454 7.8 / 1135 3.0	1721 8.2	**16** F	0401 7.3 / 1029 3.5	1623 7.6 / 2320 3.2
2 F	0022 2.4 / 0609 7.8	1248 2.9 / 1832 8.3	**17** SA	0503 7.3 / 1134 3.5	1729 7.5
3 SA	0129 2.3 / 0720 7.9	1355 2.7 / 1936 8.4	**18** SU	0027 3.1 / 0611 7.4	1244 3.4 / 1835 7.7
4 SU	0231 2.1 / 0819 8.2	1454 2.4 / 2031 8.6	**19** M	0135 2.8 / 0714 7.7	1352 3.0 / 1935 8.0
5 M	0325 2.0 / 0907 8.5	1546 2.2 / 2119 8.8	**20** TU	0236 2.5 / 0811 8.1	1455 2.6 / 2030 8.4
6 TU	0410 1.9 / 0949 8.7	1631 2.0 / 2202 8.9	**21** W	0331 2.1 / 0902 8.6	1551 2.2 / 2122 8.8
7 W	0449 1.9 / 1026 8.8	1711 1.9 / 2241 8.9	**22** TH	0422 1.7 / 0950 9.0	1644 1.8 / 2212 9.1
8 TH	0524 1.9 / 1101 8.9	1749 1.9 / ○2318 8.9	**23** F	0511 1.5 / 1037 9.3	1735 1.4 / ○2302 9.3
9 F	0557 1.9 / 1135 8.9	1824 1.9 / 2354 8.8	**24** SA	0559 1.3 / 1125 9.5	1826 1.2 / 2353 9.4
10 SA	0628 2.1 / 1208 8.9	1858 2.1	**25** SU	0646 1.3 / 1214 9.6	1917 1.1
11 SU	0029 8.6 / 0700 2.2	1241 8.7 / 1932 2.2	**26** M	0044 9.3 / 0734 1.4	1304 9.6 / 2008 1.1
12 M	0104 8.4 / 0732 2.4	1316 8.5 / 2006 2.4	**27** TU	0135 9.1 / 0823 1.7	1356 9.4 / 2059 1.3
13 TU	0141 8.1 / 0807 2.7	1353 8.3 / 2044 2.7	**28** W	0228 8.8 / 0912 2.0	1449 9.1 / 2151 1.6
14 W	0222 7.6 / 0846 3.0	1435 8.0 / 2128 2.9	**29** TH	0323 8.4 / 1005 2.3	1545 8.8 / 2246 1.9
15 TH	0307 7.6 / 0933 3.3	1524 7.7 / 2219 3.1	**30** F	0421 8.1 / 1102 2.6	1644 8.5 / ☽2344 2.3
			31 SA	0523 7.8 / 1204 2.9	1748 8.2

Chart Datum: 4·93 metres below Ordnance Datum (Newlyn)
HAT is 10·3m above Chart Datum

TIDES

325

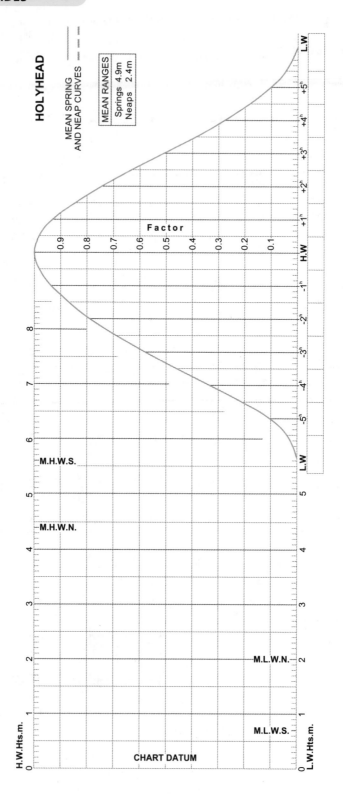

HOLYHEAD

MEAN SPRING
AND NEAP CURVES

MEAN RANGES	
Springs	4.9m
Neaps	2.4m

Factor

WALES – HOLYHEAD

LAT 53°19′N   LONG 4°37′W

TIMES AND HEIGHTS OF HIGH AND LOW WATERS

2022

JANUARY

Time	m	Time	m
1 0229	1.1	**16** 0317	1.7
SA 0847	5.5	SU 0935	5.1
1452	1.1	1545	1.5
2111	5.6	2153	5.0
2 0320	0.9	**17** 0352	1.5
SU 0936	5.7	M 1009	5.3
1545	0.8	1620	1.4
● 2204	5.7	○ 2227	5.1
3 0410	0.8	**18** 0425	1.4
M 1024	5.9	TU 1041	5.4
1637	0.6	1654	1.2
2255	5.7	2301	5.2
4 0458	0.8	**19** 0458	1.3
TU 1113	6.0	W 1114	5.5
1728	0.6	1728	1.1
2346	5.7	2335	5.2
5 0546	0.9	**20** 0532	1.2
W 1201	6.0	TH 1148	5.5
1818	0.6	1803	1.1
6 0035	5.5	**21** 0010	5.2
TH 0635	1.0	F 0608	1.2
1248	5.8	1223	5.5
1908	0.8	1839	1.1
7 0124	5.3	**22** 0047	5.2
F 0723	1.2	SA 0644	1.3
1337	5.6	1300	5.4
1959	1.0	1917	1.4
8 0215	5.0	**23** 0126	5.1
SA 0813	1.5	SU 0724	1.4
1427	5.4	1340	5.4
2051	1.3	1958	1.3
9 0308	4.7	**24** 0208	5.0
SU 0906	1.8	M 0808	1.5
1520	5.1	1423	5.2
◔ 2148	1.6	2045	1.4
10 0406	4.5	**25** 0257	4.8
M 1007	2.0	TU 0859	1.7
1619	4.8	1514	5.1
2249	1.9	◑ 2141	1.5
11 0512	4.4	**26** 0356	4.7
TU 1114	2.2	W 1001	1.8
1725	4.7	1618	4.9
2353	2.1	2249	1.7
12 0622	4.4	**27** 0509	4.6
W 1223	2.2	TH 1116	1.8
1835	4.6	1736	4.8
13 0055	2.0	**28** 0004	1.7
TH 0725	4.6	F 0627	4.7
1326	2.1	1233	1.8
1939	4.7	1858	4.9
14 0151	1.9	**29** 0116	1.6
F 0816	4.8	SA 0737	5.0
1421	1.9	1345	1.5
2031	4.8	2009	5.1
15 0237	1.8	**30** 0219	1.4
SA 0858	5.0	SU 0837	5.3
1506	1.7	1447	1.2
2115	4.9	2109	5.3
		31 0315	1.1
		M 0929	5.6
		1542	0.8
		2201	5.5

FEBRUARY

Time	m	Time	m
1 0404	0.9	**16** 0408	1.3
TU 1016	5.8	W 1023	5.4
1631	0.6	1635	1.0
● 2249	5.6	○ 2243	5.3
2 0449	0.7	**17** 0440	1.1
W 1102	6.0	TH 1055	5.6
1717	0.4	1707	0.8
2333	5.6	2315	5.4
3 0532	0.7	**18** 0512	0.9
TH 1145	6.0	F 1128	5.7
1801	0.5	1740	0.7
		2348	5.4
4 0015	5.5	**19** 0546	0.8
F 0614	0.8	SA 1202	5.7
1227	5.9	1814	0.7
1844	0.6		
5 0056	5.3	**20** 0022	5.4
SA 0655	0.9	SU 0621	0.9
1309	5.7	1237	5.7
1925	0.9	1850	0.8
6 0136	5.1	**21** 0059	5.3
SU 0736	1.2	M 0659	1.0
1350	5.4	1314	5.6
2007	1.2	1928	0.9
7 0217	4.9	**22** 0138	5.2
M 0820	1.5	TU 0740	1.1
1432	5.1	1355	5.4
2051	1.6	2012	1.2
8 0301	4.6	**23** 0223	5.0
TU 0909	1.9	W 0828	1.4
1520	4.8	1444	5.1
◐ 2142	1.9	◑ 2106	1.5
9 0355	4.4	**24** 0318	4.7
W 1009	2.2	TH 0930	1.7
1620	4.5	1548	4.8
2246	2.2	2216	1.8
10 0508	4.2	**25** 0433	4.5
TH 1127	2.4	F 1051	1.9
1739	4.3	1718	4.6
		2345	1.9
11 0003	2.3	**26** 0606	4.5
F 0635	4.3	SA 1224	1.8
1249	2.3	1857	4.6
1907	4.3		
12 0118	2.2	**27** 0108	1.8
SA 0747	4.5	SU 0728	4.8
1358	2.1	1343	1.5
2014	4.6	2013	4.9
13 0216	2.0	**28** 0216	1.5
SU 0838	4.7	M 0831	5.1
1449	1.8	1446	1.1
2102	4.7	2109	5.2
14 0300	1.8		
M 0918	5.0		
1528	1.5		
2139	4.9		
15 0336	1.5		
TU 0951	5.2		
1603	1.2		
2212	5.1		

MARCH

Time	m	Time	m
1 0309	1.2	**16** 0310	1.5
TU 0920	5.5	W 0924	5.2
1536	0.7	1535	1.1
2155	5.4	2146	5.1
2 0353	0.9	**17** 0342	1.2
W 1004	5.8	TH 0955	5.4
1619	0.5	1607	0.8
● 2235	5.5	2217	5.3
3 0433	0.7	**18** 0414	0.9
TH 1045	5.9	F 1027	5.6
1659	0.4	1639	0.6
2313	5.6	○ 2248	5.5
4 0511	0.6	**19** 0446	0.7
F 1124	5.9	SA 1101	5.8
1737	0.4	1711	0.5
2350	5.5	2321	5.6
5 0548	0.6	**20** 0520	0.6
SA 1202	5.8	SU 1136	5.8
1813	0.6	1745	0.5
		2357	5.6
6 0024	5.4	**21** 0556	0.6
SU 0625	0.8	M 1212	5.8
1238	5.7	1822	0.6
1849	0.8		
7 0058	5.2	**22** 0033	5.5
M 0702	1.0	TU 0636	0.7
1314	5.4	1251	5.6
1924	1.1	1902	0.8
8 0132	5.0	**23** 0113	5.3
TU 0740	1.3	W 0719	0.9
1351	5.1	1335	5.4
2002	1.5	1948	1.1
9 0209	4.7	**24** 0159	5.1
W 0822	1.7	TH 0810	1.2
1432	4.7	1427	5.0
2045	1.9	2044	1.6
10 0253	4.4	**25** 0257	4.8
TH 0915	2.1	F 0916	1.6
1525	4.4	1539	4.6
◑ 2140	2.3	◑ 2201	1.9
11 0356	4.2	**26** 0417	4.5
F 1029	2.4	SA 1047	1.8
1645	4.1	1723	4.4
2302	2.5	2337	2.1
12 0531	4.1	**27** 0556	4.5
SA 1206	2.4	SU 1222	1.7
1830	4.1	1901	4.6
13 0038	2.5	**28** 0102	1.9
SU 0707	4.3	M 0719	4.8
1326	2.1	1339	1.4
1950	4.3	2010	4.8
14 0148	2.2	**29** 0206	1.5
M 0808	4.6	TU 0818	5.1
1421	1.8	1436	1.0
2039	4.6	2059	5.1
15 0234	1.8	**30** 0255	1.2
TU 0905	5.4	W 0905	5.4
1501	1.4	1521	0.7
2115	4.9	2139	5.3
		31 0336	0.9
		TH 0945	5.6
		1559	0.5
		2214	5.4

APRIL

Time	m	Time	m
1 0412	0.7	**16** 0342	0.8
F 1022	5.8	SA 0955	5.6
1635	0.5	1606	0.7
● 2248	5.5	○ 2218	5.6
2 0448	0.6	**17** 0417	0.6
SA 1059	5.8	SU 1032	5.8
1708	0.5	1641	0.4
2321	5.5	2254	5.7
3 0522	0.7	**18** 0455	0.5
SU 1134	5.7	M 1110	5.8
1741	0.7	1719	0.4
2353	5.4	2332	5.7
4 0556	0.8	**19** 0535	0.5
M 1209	5.5	TU 1151	5.8
1814	0.9	1759	0.6
5 0025	5.3	**20** 0012	5.6
TU 0632	1.0	W 0619	0.6
1242	5.2	1235	5.6
1847	1.2	1844	0.8
6 0057	5.1	**21** 0057	5.4
W 0708	1.3	TH 0708	0.9
1317	5.0	1325	5.3
1922	1.5	1935	1.2
7 0131	4.8	**22** 0147	5.2
TH 0748	1.6	F 0805	1.2
1356	4.7	1425	4.9
2002	1.9	2036	1.7
8 0211	4.6	**23** 0250	4.9
F 0837	2.0	SA 0918	1.5
1446	4.3	1546	4.5
2053	2.2	◑ 2156	2.0
9 0306	4.3	**24** 0412	4.7
SA 0943	2.2	SU 1046	1.6
1559	4.1	1725	4.4
◑ 2205	2.5	2326	2.0
10 0431	4.1	**25** 0542	4.7
SU 1115	2.3	M 1211	1.5
1743	4.0	1849	4.6
2345	2.5		
11 0609	4.2	**26** 0043	1.8
M 1240	2.1	TU 0658	4.9
1908	4.2	1320	1.3
		1951	4.8
12 0102	2.3	**27** 0144	1.5
TU 0720	4.5	W 0756	5.1
1338	1.7	1414	1.0
2001	4.5	2037	5.0
13 0154	1.9	**28** 0232	1.3
W 0808	4.8	TH 0841	5.3
1421	1.4	1457	0.9
2039	4.9	2115	5.2
14 0233	1.5	**29** 0312	1.0
TH 0846	5.1	F 0921	5.4
1458	1.0	1534	0.8
2112	5.1	2148	5.3
15 0308	1.1	**30** 0349	0.9
F 0920	5.4	SA 0957	5.5
1532	0.7	1607	0.7
2144	5.4	● 2221	5.4

Chart Datum: 3·05 metres below Ordnance Datum (Newlyn)
HAT is 6·3m above Chart Datum

TIDES

TIME ZONE (UT)
For Summer Time add ONE hour in **non-shaded areas**

WALES – HOLYHEAD
LAT 53°19′N   LONG 4°37′W
TIMES AND HEIGHTS OF HIGH AND LOW WATERS

Dates in amber are **SPRINGS**
Dates in grey are **NEAPS**

2022

MAY

Day	Time	m	Day	Time	m
1 SU	0423 / 1033 / 1640 / 2253	0.8 / 5.5 / 0.8 / 5.4	16 M	0350 / 1005 / 1615 / 2229 ○	0.6 / 5.7 / 0.5 / 5.7
2 M	0458 / 1108 / 1712 / 2326	0.8 / 5.4 / 0.9 / 5.3	17 TU	0433 / 1050 / 1658 / 2313	0.5 / 5.8 / 0.6 / 5.7
3 TU	0532 / 1143 / 1744 / 2358	1.0 / 5.3 / 1.1 / 5.2	18 W	0519 / 1138 / 1744 / 2359	0.5 / 5.7 / 0.7 / 5.7
4 W	0607 / 1217 / 1817	1.1 / 5.1 / 1.3	19 TH	0609 / 1228 / 1834	0.6 / 5.5 / 0.9
5 TH	0030 / 0644 / 1253 / 1853	5.1 / 1.3 / 4.9 / 1.6	20 F	0048 / 0704 / 1324 / 1929	5.5 / 0.8 / 5.2 / 1.3
6 F	0105 / 0724 / 1332 / 1933	4.9 / 1.6 / 4.6 / 1.8	21 SA	0143 / 0806 / 1428 / 2032	5.3 / 1.0 / 4.9 / 1.6
7 SA	0145 / 0812 / 1420 / 2021	4.7 / 1.8 / 4.4 / 2.1	22 SU	0246 / 0915 / 1544 / 2144 ◗	5.1 / 1.3 / 4.6 / 1.8
8 SU	0235 / 0911 / 1524 / 2125	4.5 / 2.0 / 4.2 / 2.4	23 M	0359 / 1031 / 1705 / 2301	4.9 / 1.4 / 4.5 / 1.9
9 M	0344 / 1025 / 1649 / 2245 ◗	4.3 / 2.1 / 4.1 / 2.4	24 TU	0515 / 1144 / 1819	4.9 / 1.4 / 4.6
10 TU	0508 / 1142 / 1809	4.3 / 1.9 / 4.3	25 W	0011 / 0626 / 1249 / 1919	1.8 / 4.9 / 1.3 / 4.7
11 W	0002 / 0620 / 1244 / 1908	2.2 / 4.5 / 1.7 / 4.5	26 TH	0112 / 0724 / 1343 / 2007	1.6 / 5.0 / 1.2 / 4.9
12 TH	0101 / 0716 / 1333 / 1953	1.9 / 4.8 / 1.3 / 4.8	27 F	0203 / 0813 / 1428 / 2047	1.4 / 5.1 / 1.2 / 5.0
13 F	0148 / 0801 / 1415 / 2033	1.5 / 5.1 / 1.0 / 5.1	28 SA	0247 / 0855 / 1506 / 2123	1.3 / 5.2 / 1.1 / 5.1
14 SA	0229 / 0842 / 1455 / 2111	1.2 / 5.3 / 0.8 / 5.4	29 SU	0326 / 0934 / 1542 / 2157	1.2 / 5.2 / 1.1 / 5.2
15 SU	0309 / 0923 / 1534 / 2149	0.9 / 5.6 / 0.6 / 5.6	30 M	0403 / 1011 / 1615 / 2230 ●	1.1 / 5.2 / 1.1 / 5.3
			31 TU	0438 / 1047 / 1648 / 2303	1.1 / 5.2 / 1.2 / 5.3

JUNE

Day	Time	m	Day	Time	m
1 W	0514 / 1123 / 1721 / 2336	1.2 / 5.1 / 1.3 / 5.2	16 TH	0511 / 1131 / 1734 / 2349	0.5 / 5.6 / 0.8 / 5.7
2 TH	0549 / 1158 / 1755	1.2 / 5.0 / 1.4	17 F	0604 / 1224 / 1826	0.5 / 5.4 / 0.9
3 F	0010 / 0627 / 1234 / 1832	5.1 / 1.3 / 4.8 / 1.6	18 SA	0040 / 0700 / 1319 / 1920	5.7 / 0.6 / 5.2 / 1.1
4 SA	0046 / 0707 / 1314 / 1912	5.0 / 1.5 / 4.7 / 1.7	19 SU	0134 / 0757 / 1418 / 2017	5.5 / 0.8 / 5.0 / 1.4
5 SU	0127 / 0751 / 1400 / 1958	4.9 / 1.6 / 4.5 / 1.9	20 M	0231 / 0858 / 1520 / 2118	5.3 / 1.1 / 4.8 / 1.6
6 M	0213 / 0842 / 1453 / 2051	4.7 / 1.7 / 4.4 / 2.1	21 TU	0333 / 1001 / 1627 / 2224 ◗	5.1 / 1.3 / 4.6 / 1.8
7 TU	0308 / 0940 / 1557 / 2154	4.6 / 1.8 / 4.3 / 2.1	22 W	0437 / 1106 / 1734 / 2330	4.9 / 1.4 / 4.5 / 1.8
8 W	0412 / 1044 / 1706 / 2302	4.6 / 1.8 / 4.4 / 2.1	23 TH	0543 / 1209 / 1837	4.8 / 1.5 / 4.6
9 TH	0519 / 1146 / 1810	4.6 / 1.6 / 4.5	24 F	0034 / 0647 / 1306 / 1933	1.8 / 4.8 / 1.6 / 4.7
10 F	0005 / 0622 / 1243 / 1905	1.9 / 4.8 / 1.4 / 4.8	25 SA	0131 / 0743 / 1357 / 2020	1.7 / 4.8 / 1.5 / 4.8
11 SA	0102 / 0717 / 1334 / 1954	1.6 / 5.0 / 1.2 / 5.0	26 SU	0223 / 0832 / 1441 / 2100	1.6 / 4.9 / 1.5 / 4.9
12 SU	0153 / 0808 / 1422 / 2040	1.3 / 5.2 / 0.9 / 5.3	27 M	0307 / 0916 / 1521 / 2138	1.5 / 4.9 / 1.4 / 5.1
13 M	0242 / 0858 / 1509 / 2125	1.0 / 5.4 / 0.8 / 5.5	28 TU	0347 / 0955 / 1556 / 2213	1.4 / 5.0 / 1.4 / 5.2
14 TU	0330 / 0948 / 1556 / 2212 ○	0.8 / 5.6 / 0.7 / 5.6	29 W	0424 / 1032 / 1630 / 2246	1.3 / 5.0 / 1.4 / 5.2
15 W	0420 / 1038 / 1645 / 2300	0.6 / 5.6 / 0.7 / 5.7	30 TH	0500 / 1107 / 1704 / 2320	1.2 / 5.0 / 1.4 / 5.2

JULY

Day	Time	m	Day	Time	m
1 F	0535 / 1142 / 1738 / 2354	1.2 / 5.0 / 1.4 / 5.2	16 SA	0556 / 1214 / 1813	0.4 / 5.5 / 0.8
2 SA	0611 / 1218 / 1814	1.2 / 4.9 / 1.4	17 SU	0027 / 0646 / 1303 / 1901	5.9 / 0.5 / 5.3 / 0.9
3 SU	0030 / 0649 / 1256 / 1853	5.2 / 1.3 / 4.9 / 1.5	18 M	0115 / 0736 / 1352 / 1950	5.7 / 0.7 / 5.1 / 1.2
4 M	0108 / 0728 / 1336 / 1933	5.1 / 1.4 / 4.8 / 1.6	19 TU	0205 / 0826 / 1443 / 2042	5.5 / 1.0 / 4.9 / 1.4
5 TU	0149 / 0811 / 1420 / 2018	5.0 / 1.4 / 4.7 / 1.7	20 W	0256 / 0920 / 1537 / 2138 ◗	5.2 / 1.3 / 4.6 / 1.7
6 W	0233 / 0858 / 1510 / 2110	4.9 / 1.5 / 4.6 / 1.8	21 TH	0351 / 1017 / 1638 / 2242	4.9 / 1.6 / 4.5 / 1.9
7 TH	0325 / 0952 / 1608 / 2210 ◗	4.8 / 1.6 / 4.5 / 1.9	22 F	0454 / 1120 / 1746 / 2352	4.7 / 1.8 / 4.5 / 2.0
8 F	0424 / 1053 / 1714 / 2316	4.8 / 1.6 / 4.6 / 1.9	23 SA	0604 / 1225 / 1854	4.5 / 1.9 / 4.5
9 SA	0532 / 1158 / 1820	4.8 / 1.5 / 4.7	24 SU	0100 / 0715 / 1327 / 1954	2.0 / 4.5 / 1.9 / 4.6
10 SU	0022 / 0640 / 1300 / 1922	1.7 / 4.9 / 1.4 / 4.9	25 M	0202 / 0815 / 1420 / 2042	1.9 / 4.6 / 1.8 / 4.8
11 M	0125 / 0745 / 1359 / 2018	1.5 / 5.1 / 1.2 / 5.1	26 TU	0253 / 0903 / 1504 / 2123	1.7 / 4.7 / 1.7 / 5.0
12 TU	0224 / 0844 / 1454 / 2110	1.2 / 5.2 / 1.0 / 5.4	27 W	0335 / 0944 / 1542 / 2158	1.5 / 4.9 / 1.6 / 5.1
13 W	0320 / 0940 / 1546 / 2201 ○	0.9 / 5.4 / 0.9 / 5.6	28 TH	0411 / 1019 / 1615 / 2230	1.3 / 5.0 / 1.4 / 5.3
14 TH	0413 / 1033 / 1636 / 2250	0.6 / 5.5 / 0.8 / 5.8	29 F	0445 / 1052 / 1647 / 2302	1.2 / 5.0 / 1.3 / 5.4
15 F	0505 / 1124 / 1725 / 2339	0.5 / 5.6 / 0.7 / 5.9	30 SA	0517 / 1124 / 1720 / 2335	1.1 / 5.1 / 1.2 / 5.4
			31 SU	0551 / 1158 / 1754	1.0 / 5.1 / 1.2

AUGUST

Day	Time	m	Day	Time	m
1 M	0009 / 0625 / 1232 / 1829	5.4 / 1.0 / 5.1 / 1.2	16 TU	0048 / 0705 / 1317 / 1917	5.8 / 0.7 / 5.2 / 1.0
2 TU	0044 / 0700 / 1308 / 1905	5.4 / 1.0 / 5.0 / 1.3	17 W	0131 / 0747 / 1359 / 2002	5.6 / 1.0 / 5.0 / 1.3
3 W	0120 / 0737 / 1347 / 1945	5.3 / 1.2 / 4.9 / 1.4	18 TH	0215 / 0832 / 1444 / 2051	5.2 / 1.4 / 4.7 / 1.7
4 TH	0159 / 0818 / 1430 / 2031	5.2 / 1.4 / 4.8 / 1.6	19 F	0303 / 0922 / 1536 / 2150 ◗	4.9 / 1.8 / 4.5 / 2.0
5 F	0244 / 0907 / 1521 / 2126	5.0 / 1.5 / 4.7 / 1.8	20 SA	0401 / 1023 / 1645 / 2307	4.5 / 2.1 / 4.3 / 2.2
6 SA	0340 / 1008 / 1626 / 2236	4.8 / 1.6 / 4.6 / 1.9	21 SU	0519 / 1140 / 1810	4.3 / 2.3 / 4.3
7 SU	0453 / 1122 / 1745 / 2356	4.7 / 1.7 / 4.6 / 1.9	22 M	0030 / 0650 / 1257 / 1928	2.3 / 4.3 / 2.3 / 4.5
8 M	0618 / 1239 / 1902	4.7 / 1.7 / 4.8	23 TU	0143 / 0801 / 1401 / 2023	2.1 / 4.4 / 2.1 / 4.7
9 TU	0112 / 0738 / 1348 / 2007	1.6 / 4.9 / 1.5 / 5.1	24 W	0236 / 0850 / 1447 / 2104	1.8 / 4.7 / 1.9 / 5.0
10 W	0218 / 0842 / 1447 / 2102	1.3 / 5.1 / 1.2 / 5.4	25 TH	0317 / 0928 / 1523 / 2138	1.5 / 4.9 / 1.6 / 5.2
11 TH	0316 / 0937 / 1538 / 2151	0.9 / 5.4 / 1.0 / 5.7	26 F	0351 / 1000 / 1555 / 2208	1.3 / 5.0 / 1.4 / 5.4
12 F	0407 / 1025 / 1625 / 2237 ○	0.6 / 5.6 / 0.8 / 5.9	27 SA	0422 / 1030 / 1625 / 2239	1.1 / 5.2 / 1.2 / 5.5
13 SA	0453 / 1110 / 1709 / 2322	0.4 / 5.6 / 0.6 / 6.0	28 SU	0452 / 1059 / 1656 / 2310	0.9 / 5.3 / 1.0 / 5.6
14 SU	0538 / 1154 / 1752	0.3 / 5.6 / 0.7	29 M	0523 / 1131 / 1727 / 2342	0.8 / 5.3 / 1.0 / 5.6
15 M	0005 / 0622 / 1236 / 1834	6.0 / 0.4 / 5.4 / 0.8	30 TU	0554 / 1204 / 1800	0.8 / 5.3 / 1.0
			31 W	0015 / 0628 / 1238 / 1836	5.6 / 0.9 / 5.2 / 1.1

Chart Datum: 3·05 metres below Ordnance Datum (Newlyn)
HAT is 6·3m above Chart Datum

WALES – HOLYHEAD
LAT 53°19'N   LONG 4°37'W
TIMES AND HEIGHTS OF HIGH AND LOW WATERS

Dates in amber are SPRINGS
Dates in grey are NEAPS

2022

SEPTEMBER

Day	Time m	Day	Time m
1 TH	0050 5.5 / 0703 1.0 / 1314 5.2 / 1915 1.2	16 F	0135 5.2 / 0746 1.5 / 1356 4.8 / 2008 1.7
2 F	0129 5.3 / 0743 1.2 / 1356 5.0 / 2000 1.5	17 SA	0218 4.8 / 0829 1.9 / 1441 4.6 / 2103 2.1
3 SA	0213 5.1 / 0832 1.5 / 1446 4.8 / 2056 1.7	18 SU	0312 4.4 / 0925 2.3 / 1545 4.3 / 2219 2.4
4 SU	0311 4.8 / 0936 1.8 / 1554 4.6 / 2212 2.0	19 M	0433 4.1 / 1047 2.6 / 1717 4.2 / 2356 2.4
5 M	0435 4.6 / 1102 2.0 / 1726 4.6 / 2346 1.9	20 TU	0621 4.1 / 1223 2.6 / 1852 4.4
6 TU	0619 4.6 / 1232 2.0 / 1853 4.8	21 W	0115 2.2 / 0739 4.4 / 1333 2.3 / 1953 4.7
7 W	0110 1.7 / 0742 4.8 / 1344 1.7 / 2000 5.1	22 TH	0208 1.8 / 0826 4.7 / 1420 2.0 / 2034 5.0
8 TH	0216 1.2 / 0841 5.1 / 1440 1.3 / 2052 5.5	23 F	0248 1.5 / 0902 4.9 / 1455 1.7 / 2108 5.2
9 F	0309 0.8 / 0929 5.4 / 1526 1.0 / 2137 5.8	24 SA	0321 1.2 / 0932 5.1 / 1526 1.4 / 2138 5.5
10 SA	0353 0.5 / 1010 5.6 / 1608 0.7 / ○ 2218 6.0	25 SU	0351 1.0 / 1000 5.3 / 1556 1.1 / ● 2208 5.6
11 SU	0434 0.4 / 1049 5.6 / 1647 0.6 / 2259 6.1	26 M	0420 0.8 / 1029 5.5 / 1626 0.9 / 2240 5.8
12 M	0513 0.4 / 1127 5.6 / 1726 0.6 / 2339 6.0	27 TU	0451 0.7 / 1101 5.6 / 1658 0.8 / 2313 5.8
13 TU	0551 0.5 / 1205 5.5 / 1804 0.8	28 W	0523 0.7 / 1134 5.6 / 1733 0.8 / 2348 5.7
14 W	0018 5.8 / 0629 0.8 / 1241 5.3 / 1844 1.0	29 TH	0557 0.8 / 1209 5.5 / 1810 0.9
15 TH	0056 5.5 / 0707 1.1 / 1317 5.1 / 1924 1.4	30 F	0024 5.6 / 0635 1.0 / 1247 5.4 / 1852 1.1

OCTOBER

Day	Time m	Day	Time m
1 SA	0106 5.4 / 0718 1.3 / 1331 5.2 / 1940 1.4	16 SU	0142 4.7 / 0747 2.0 / 1359 4.7 / 2026 2.1
2 SU	0155 5.1 / 0810 1.7 / 1425 4.9 / 2043 1.8	17 M	0233 4.4 / 0839 2.4 / 1455 4.5 / ◑ 2135 2.4
3 M	0302 4.7 / 0921 2.0 / 1540 4.5 / ◑ 2209 2.0	18 TU	0349 4.1 / 0952 2.7 / 1620 4.3 / 2308 2.4
4 TU	0441 4.5 / 1056 2.2 / 1718 4.4 / 2346 1.9	19 W	0534 4.1 / 1131 2.7 / 1756 4.4
5 W	0625 4.6 / 1226 2.1 / 1843 4.9	20 TH	0029 2.2 / 0656 4.4 / 1248 2.5 / 1905 4.7
6 TH	0105 1.5 / 0739 4.8 / 1334 1.7 / 1947 5.3	21 F	0125 1.9 / 0747 4.7 / 1338 2.1 / 1952 5.0
7 F	0206 1.1 / 0831 5.2 / 1425 1.4 / 2035 5.6	22 SA	0207 1.5 / 0824 4.9 / 1417 1.8 / 2029 5.2
8 SA	0253 0.8 / 0912 5.4 / 1508 1.0 / 2117 5.8	23 SU	0242 1.2 / 0856 5.2 / 1450 1.4 / 2102 5.5
9 SU	0333 0.6 / 0949 5.6 / 1546 0.8 / ○ 2156 6.0	24 M	0314 1.0 / 0927 5.4 / 1520 1.1 / 2135 5.7
10 M	0410 0.5 / 1024 5.7 / 1623 0.7 / 2234 6.0	25 TU	0346 0.8 / 0958 5.6 / 1556 0.9 / ● 2209 5.8
11 TU	0446 0.6 / 1059 5.7 / 1700 0.6 / 2312 5.9	26 W	0419 0.7 / 1031 5.7 / 1631 0.8 / 2246 5.9
12 W	0521 0.8 / 1134 5.6 / 1737 0.9 / 2349 5.7	27 TH	0454 0.7 / 1108 5.8 / 1710 0.8 / 2325 5.8
13 TH	0555 1.0 / 1208 5.4 / 1814 1.1	28 F	0533 0.8 / 1147 5.7 / 1752 0.9
14 F	0025 5.4 / 0630 1.3 / 1242 5.2 / 1853 1.5	29 SA	0007 5.6 / 0616 1.1 / 1230 5.6 / 1839 1.1
15 SA	0102 5.1 / 0706 1.7 / 1318 5.0 / 1935 1.8	30 SU	0055 5.4 / 0704 1.4 / 1319 5.3 / 1934 1.4
		31 M	0152 5.0 / 0802 1.8 / 1418 5.1 / 2043 1.7

NOVEMBER

Day	Time m	Day	Time m
1 TU	0307 4.7 / 0917 2.1 / 1536 4.9 / ◑ 2209 1.8	16 W	0308 4.3 / 0906 2.5 / 1527 4.5 / 2210 2.3
2 W	0445 4.6 / 1047 2.2 / 1705 4.9 / 2335 1.7	17 TH	0431 4.2 / 1023 2.6 / 1648 4.5 / 2326 2.2
3 TH	0613 4.7 / 1208 2.0 / 1823 5.1	18 F	0550 4.3 / 1142 2.5 / 1800 4.6
4 F	0047 1.4 / 0720 5.0 / 1311 1.8 / 1924 5.3	19 SA	0027 1.9 / 0651 4.6 / 1242 2.2 / 1857 4.9
5 SA	0144 1.2 / 0809 5.2 / 1403 1.5 / 2013 5.5	20 SU	0116 1.7 / 0737 4.9 / 1329 1.9 / 1943 5.1
6 SU	0230 1.0 / 0850 5.4 / 1446 1.2 / 2055 5.7	21 M	0158 1.4 / 0816 5.1 / 1411 1.6 / 2024 5.4
7 M	0309 0.9 / 0925 5.6 / 1525 1.0 / 2134 5.7	22 TU	0236 1.1 / 0852 5.4 / 1450 1.3 / 2103 5.6
8 TU	0345 0.9 / 1000 5.6 / 1602 1.0 / ○ 2212 5.7	23 W	0314 0.9 / 0929 5.6 / 1529 1.0 / 2143 5.7
9 W	0420 0.9 / 1034 5.6 / 1638 1.0 / 2249 5.6	24 TH	0353 0.8 / 1007 5.8 / 1611 0.9 / 2226 5.8
10 TH	0454 1.1 / 1108 5.5 / 1715 1.1 / 2326 5.5	25 F	0434 0.8 / 1048 5.8 / 1655 0.8 / 2311 5.8
11 F	0527 1.2 / 1142 5.4 / 1752 1.3	26 SA	0518 0.9 / 1133 5.8 / 1743 0.8
12 SA	0001 5.2 / 0602 1.5 / 1215 5.3 / 1830 1.5	27 SU	0000 5.6 / 0606 1.1 / 1221 5.7 / 1836 1.0
13 SU	0038 5.0 / 0638 1.7 / 1250 5.1 / 1911 1.8	28 M	0054 5.4 / 0658 1.4 / 1313 5.5 / 1935 1.2
14 M	0117 4.8 / 0717 2.0 / 1331 4.9 / 1959 2.0	29 TU	0154 5.1 / 0758 1.7 / 1413 5.3 / 2041 1.4
15 TU	0205 4.5 / 0805 2.3 / 1420 4.7 / 2057 2.2	30 W	0305 4.8 / 0906 1.9 / 1522 5.2 / ◑ 2154 1.5

DECEMBER

Day	Time m	Day	Time m
1 TH	0424 4.7 / 1021 2.0 / 1637 5.1 / 2308 1.5	16 F	0328 4.4 / 0925 2.3 / 1543 4.7 / ◑ 2217 2.0
2 F	0541 4.7 / 1134 2.0 / 1749 5.1	17 SA	0436 4.4 / 1031 2.3 / 1650 4.7 / 2320 1.9
3 SA	0015 1.5 / 0647 4.9 / 1239 1.8 / 1853 5.2	18 SU	0543 4.5 / 1138 2.2 / 1755 4.8
4 SU	0114 1.4 / 0740 5.0 / 1335 1.7 / 1947 5.3	19 M	0019 1.8 / 0643 4.7 / 1238 2.0 / 1855 5.0
5 M	0203 1.3 / 0825 5.2 / 1423 1.5 / 2033 5.4	20 TU	0113 1.6 / 0735 5.0 / 1332 1.7 / 1948 5.1
6 TU	0246 1.3 / 0904 5.3 / 1506 1.3 / 2115 5.4	21 W	0202 1.3 / 0821 5.2 / 1422 1.4 / 2038 5.4
7 W	0324 1.2 / 0940 5.4 / 1546 1.3 / 2155 5.4	22 TH	0249 1.1 / 0906 5.5 / 1510 1.1 / 2126 5.5
8 TH	0400 1.3 / 1015 5.5 / 1624 1.3 / 2233 5.3	23 F	0335 1.0 / 0951 5.7 / 1558 0.9 / ○ 2216 5.7
9 F	0434 1.3 / 1050 5.5 / 1701 1.3 / 2309 5.3	24 SA	0422 0.9 / 1037 5.8 / 1648 0.7 / 2306 5.7
10 SA	0508 1.4 / 1124 5.4 / 1737 1.4 / 2345 5.2	25 SU	0510 0.9 / 1125 5.9 / 1739 0.7 / 2357 5.6
11 SU	0542 1.5 / 1157 5.4 / 1814 1.5	26 M	0559 1.0 / 1214 5.9 / 1832 0.7
12 M	0020 5.1 / 0618 1.7 / 1232 5.3 / 1853 1.6	27 TU	0049 5.5 / 0651 1.1 / 1305 5.8 / 1926 0.8
13 TU	0059 4.9 / 0656 1.8 / 1311 5.1 / 1935 1.7	28 W	0144 5.3 / 0744 1.3 / 1359 5.6 / 2023 1.0
14 W	0141 4.7 / 0739 2.0 / 1354 5.0 / 2022 1.9	29 TH	0242 5.0 / 0841 1.6 / 1456 5.4 / 2124 1.3
15 TH	0230 4.5 / 0827 2.2 / 1444 4.8 / 2116 2.0	30 F	0346 4.8 / 0944 1.8 / 1559 5.2 / ◑ 2228 1.5
		31 SA	0453 4.7 / 1051 1.9 / 1706 5.0 / 2334 1.6

Chart Datum: 3·05 metres below Ordnance Datum (Newlyn)
HAT is 6·3m above Chart Datum

TIDES

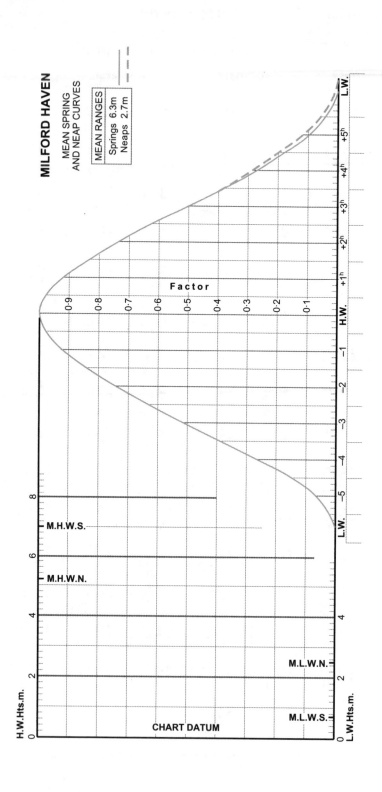

MILFORD HAVEN

MEAN SPRING
AND NEAP CURVES

MEAN RANGES
Springs 6.3m
Neaps 2.7m

WALES – MILFORD HAVEN
LAT 51°42′N   LONG 5°03′W
TIMES AND HEIGHTS OF HIGH AND LOW WATERS

Dates in amber are **SPRINGS**
Dates in grey are **NEAPS**

2022

JANUARY

	Time	m		Time	m
1 SA	0431	6.6	**16** SU	0518	6.1
	1055	1.3		1138	1.8
	1658	6.7		1738	6.1
	2324	1.1		2350	1.6
2 SU ●	0525	6.9	**17** M ○	0556	6.3
	1150	0.9		1215	1.6
	1753	7.0		1816	6.3
3 M	0015	0.9	**18** TU	0026	1.5
	0618	7.2		0632	6.5
	1242	0.7		1250	1.4
	1845	7.1		1851	6.4
4 TU	0104	0.8	**19** W	0100	1.4
	0708	7.3		0706	6.6
	1332	0.7		1324	1.3
	1935	7.0		1926	6.5
5 W	0152	0.9	**20** TH	0134	1.3
	0756	7.3		0740	6.7
	1420	0.7		1358	1.3
	2022	6.9		2000	6.5
6 TH	0238	1.0	**21** F	0209	1.3
	0843	7.1		0814	6.7
	1507	0.9		1433	1.3
	2107	6.6		2035	6.4
7 F	0323	1.3	**22** SA	0245	1.3
	0929	6.8		0850	6.6
	1553	1.3		1509	1.3
	2152	6.3		2111	6.3
8 SA	0407	1.6	**23** SU	0322	1.4
	1015	6.5		0928	6.5
	1638	1.6		1547	1.5
	2238	5.9		2151	6.2
9 SU ◑	0454	1.9	**24** M	0401	1.6
	1103	6.1		1010	6.3
	1726	2.0		1628	1.7
	2328	5.6		2235	5.9
10 M ◑	0546	2.2	**25** TU ◑	0446	1.8
	1157	5.8		1058	6.1
	1821	2.3		1717	1.9
				2329	5.7
11 TU	0026	5.3	**26** W	0541	2.1
	0648	2.5		1157	5.8
	1258	5.5		1820	2.1
	1925	2.4			
12 W	0134	5.2	**27** TH	0036	5.5
	0800	2.6		0654	2.2
	1406	5.4		1310	5.7
	2034	2.5		1942	2.2
13 TH	0243	5.3	**28** F	0154	5.6
	0909	2.5		0821	2.2
	1511	5.5		1431	5.7
	2136	2.3		2106	2.1
14 F	0344	5.5	**29** SA	0312	5.8
	1007	2.3		0941	1.9
	1608	5.7		1546	6.0
	2227	2.1		2217	1.7
15 SA	0435	5.8	**30** SU	0420	6.2
	1056	2.0		1047	1.4
	1657	5.9		1653	6.4
	2311	1.9		2316	1.3
			31 M	0520	6.7
				1145	0.9
				1749	6.7

FEBRUARY

	Time	m		Time	m
1 TU ●	0008	1.0	**16** W ○	0009	1.4
	0612	7.1		0614	6.5
	1236	0.7		1234	1.2
	1839	7.0		1834	6.5
2 W	0056	0.7	**17** TH	0043	1.1
	0700	7.3		0648	6.8
	1323	0.5		1307	1.0
	1924	7.1		1907	6.7
3 TH	0140	0.6	**18** F	0118	0.9
	0743	7.4		0722	6.9
	1406	0.5		1341	0.9
	2006	7.0		1941	6.8
4 F	0221	0.7	**19** SA	0152	0.8
	0825	7.3		0756	7.0
	1446	0.7		1414	0.8
	2045	6.8		2015	6.8
5 SA	0300	0.9	**20** SU	0226	0.8
	0904	7.0		0830	7.0
	1523	1.0		1448	0.9
	2122	6.5		2049	6.7
6 SU	0336	1.2	**21** M	0301	1.0
	0942	6.7		0906	6.8
	1559	1.5		1523	1.1
	2158	6.2		2126	6.5
7 M	0411	1.6	**22** TU	0338	1.2
	1019	6.2		0944	6.6
	1634	1.8		1600	1.4
	2236	5.8		2206	6.2
8 TU ◑	0448	2.0	**23** W	0418	1.5
	1100	5.8		1028	6.2
	1713	2.2		1644	1.8
	2319	5.4		2255	5.8
9 W	0533	2.4	**24** TH	0509	1.9
	1150	5.3		1124	5.7
	1806	2.6		1742	2.2
10 TH	0017	5.0	**25** F	0001	5.5
	0642	2.7		0622	2.3
	1300	5.0		1241	5.4
	1924	2.8		1912	2.5
11 F	0144	4.9	**26** SA	0131	5.3
	0817	2.8		0806	2.3
	1428	5.0		1418	5.3
	2054	2.7		2056	2.3
12 SA	0310	5.1	**27** SU	0303	5.6
	0940	2.6		0937	2.0
	1544	5.2		1546	5.7
	2202	2.4		2212	1.9
13 SU	0414	5.5	**28** M	0417	6.1
	1037	2.2		1045	1.5
	1639	5.6		1651	6.2
	2252	2.0		2311	1.4
14 M	0500	5.9			
	1121	1.8			
	1721	6.0			
	2333	1.7			
15 TU	0538	6.3			
	1159	1.5			
	1758	6.3			

MARCH

	Time	m		Time	m
1 TU	0514	6.6	**16** W	0511	6.2
	1139	1.0		1133	1.4
	1741	6.6		1732	6.3
				2344	1.3
2 W ●	0000	0.9	**17** TH	0547	6.6
	0601	7.1		1208	1.0
	1225	0.6		1806	6.6
	1825	7.0			
3 TH	0042	0.6	**18** F ○	0019	0.9
	0644	7.3		0622	6.9
	1306	0.4		1242	0.7
	1905	7.1		1841	6.9
4 F	0121	0.5	**19** SA	0054	0.7
	0723	7.4		0656	7.1
	1343	0.4		1316	0.6
	1942	7.1		1916	7.1
5 SA	0157	0.5	**20** SU	0129	0.5
	0759	7.3		0731	7.2
	1417	0.6		1351	0.5
	2016	6.9		1950	7.1
6 SU	0230	0.7	**21** M	0204	0.5
	0834	7.0		0807	7.2
	1449	0.8		1425	0.6
	2048	6.7		2026	7.0
7 M	0301	1.0	**22** TU	0240	0.7
	0906	6.7		0844	7.0
	1519	1.2		1501	0.9
	2118	6.3		2103	6.7
8 TU	0331	1.4	**23** W	0318	1.0
	0938	6.3		0923	6.6
	1548	1.6		1538	1.3
	2150	6.0		2144	6.3
9 W	0401	1.9	**24** TH	0400	1.4
	1012	5.8		1008	6.1
	1619	2.1		1622	1.8
	2225	5.5		2234	5.9
10 TH ◑	0437	2.3	**25** F	0453	1.9
	1053	5.3		1106	5.6
	1659	2.5		1723	2.3
	2312	5.1		2345	5.4
11 F	0532	2.7	**26** SA	0613	2.3
	1152	4.9		1232	5.2
	1809	2.9		1904	2.6
12 SA	0030	4.8	**27** SU	0122	5.3
	0717	3.0		0805	2.3
	1337	4.7		1417	5.2
	2005	3.0		2051	2.3
13 SU	0230	4.8	**28** M	0258	5.6
	0907	2.8		0932	1.9
	1515	4.9		1541	5.7
	2131	2.6		2204	1.8
14 M	0345	5.3	**29** TU	0407	6.1
	1010	2.3		1034	1.4
	1614	5.4		1638	6.2
	2225	2.1		2257	1.3
15 TU	0432	5.8	**30** W	0458	6.6
	1055	1.8		1123	0.9
	1655	5.9		1724	6.6
	2307	1.7		2342	0.9
			31 TH	0541	7.0
				1204	0.6
				1803	6.9

APRIL

	Time	m		Time	m
1 F ●	0020	0.7	**16** SA ○	0548	7.0
	0621	7.2		1211	0.7
	1240	0.5		1810	7.0
	1840	7.0			
2 SA	0055	0.6	**17** SU	0026	0.6
	0657	7.2		0627	7.2
	1314	0.5		1248	0.5
	1913	7.0		1848	7.2
3 SU	0128	0.6	**18** M	0104	0.5
	0730	7.1		0705	7.3
	1345	0.7		1326	0.5
	1944	6.9		1926	7.2
4 M	0159	0.8	**19** TU	0143	0.5
	0801	6.9		0745	7.2
	1415	0.9		1404	0.6
	2014	6.7		2005	7.1
5 TU	0229	1.1	**20** W	0223	0.7
	0832	6.6		0826	7.0
	1443	1.2		1443	0.9
	2043	6.4		2046	6.8
6 W	0257	1.4	**21** TH	0305	1.0
	0902	6.2		0910	6.6
	1510	1.6		1525	1.4
	2113	6.1		2132	6.4
7 TH	0326	1.8	**22** F	0352	1.4
	0934	5.8		1000	6.0
	1540	2.0		1614	1.9
	2146	5.7		2228	5.9
8 F	0401	2.2	**23** SA ◑	0452	1.9
	1012	5.3		1105	5.6
	1617	2.5		1722	2.3
	2229	5.2		2343	5.6
9 SA ◑	0450	2.7	**24** SU	0618	2.2
	1106	4.9		1230	5.2
	1715	2.9		1902	2.5
	2336	4.9			
10 SU	0621	2.9	**25** M	0113	5.5
	1237	4.6		0756	2.1
	1907	3.0		1404	5.3
				2034	2.2
11 M	0129	4.8	**26** TU	0238	5.8
	0815	2.8		0912	1.8
	1429	4.8		1519	5.7
	2043	2.7		2141	1.8
12 TU	0258	5.2	**27** W	0342	6.2
	0926	2.3		1010	1.4
	1532	5.3		1613	6.1
	2144	2.2		2232	1.4
13 W	0351	5.7	**28** TH	0432	6.5
	1015	1.8		1056	1.1
	1617	5.8		1657	6.5
	2229	1.7		2315	1.1
14 TH	0433	6.2	**29** F	0514	6.8
	1056	1.4		1135	0.9
	1656	6.3		1735	6.7
	2309	1.3		2352	0.9
15 F	0511	6.6	**30** SA ●	0552	6.9
	1134	1.0		1210	0.8
	1733	6.7		1810	6.8
	2348	0.9			

Chart Datum: 3·71 metres below Ordnance Datum (Newlyn)
HAT is 7·9m above Chart Datum

TIDES

WALES – MILFORD HAVEN
LAT 51°42′N   LONG 5°03′W
TIMES AND HEIGHTS OF HIGH AND LOW WATERS

TIME ZONE (UT)
For Summer Time add ONE hour in **non-shaded areas**

Dates in amber are **SPRINGS**
Dates in grey are **NEAPS**

2022

MAY

Day	Time m	Time m	Time m	Time m
1 SU	0026 0.9	0627 6.9	1242 1.0	1843 6.8
2 M	0059 0.9	0700 6.8	1314 1.0	1914 6.7
3 TU	0130 1.1	0732 6.6	1344 1.1	1944 6.6
4 W	0201 1.3	0803 6.4	1413 1.4	2015 6.4
5 TH	0231 1.5	0835 6.1	1442 1.7	2046 6.1
6 F	0303 1.8	0908 5.8	1515 2.0	2121 5.8
7 SA	0340 2.2	0947 5.4	1553 2.4	2204 5.4
8 SU	0428 2.5	1038 5.1	1647 2.7	2304 5.1
9 M ☽	0539 2.7	1151 4.8	1811 2.8	
10 TU	0026 5.0	0713 2.6	1322 4.9	1942 2.7
11 W	0153 5.2	0827 2.3	1435 5.3	2049 2.3
12 TH	0256 5.7	0923 1.9	1528 5.8	2142 1.8
13 F	0346 6.1	1011 1.4	1613 6.2	2229 1.4
14 SA	0431 6.6	1056 1.1	1656 6.7	2314 1.0
15 SU	0514 6.9	1139 0.8	1738 7.0	2358 0.7
16 M ○	0558 7.1	1222 0.6	1821 7.2	
17 TU	0041 0.6	0643 7.2	1304 0.6	1905 7.2
18 W	0126 0.6	0728 7.1	1348 0.7	1950 7.1
19 TH	0212 0.7	0815 6.9	1432 1.0	2037 6.9
20 F	0300 1.0	0904 6.5	1520 1.4	2129 6.5
21 SA	0353 1.4	0959 6.1	1614 1.8	2227 6.1
22 SU	0455 1.7	1102 5.7	1721 2.1	2335 5.9
23 M	0610 1.9	1215 5.4	1842 2.2	
24 TU	0050 5.8	0728 2.0	1332 5.5	2000 2.1
25 W	0203 5.9	0836 1.8	1441 5.7	2104 1.9
26 TH	0305 6.0	0933 1.6	1537 5.9	2157 1.6
27 F	0357 6.2	1021 1.4	1623 6.2	2242 1.5
28 SA	0442 6.4	1102 1.3	1704 6.3	2322 1.3
29 SU	0522 6.5	1139 1.3	1741 6.5	2359 1.3
30 M ●	0559 6.5	1213 1.2	1816 6.5	
31 TU	0033 1.3	0635 6.5	1247 1.3	1850 6.5

JUNE

Day	Time m	Time m	Time m	Time m
1 W	0107 1.3	0709 6.4	1319 1.4	1922 6.5
2 TH	0140 1.4	0742 6.2	1351 1.5	1955 6.3
3 F	0213 1.6	0816 6.1	1424 1.7	2029 6.2
4 SA	0248 1.8	0852 5.8	1459 1.9	2106 6.0
5 SU	0327 2.0	0931 5.6	1539 2.1	2148 5.7
6 M	0412 2.2	1018 5.4	1627 2.3	2240 5.5
7 TU ☽	0506 2.3	1115 5.2	1727 2.4	2341 5.4
8 W	0614 2.3	1222 5.2	1840 2.4	
9 TH	0050 5.5	0724 2.2	1332 5.4	1951 2.2
10 F	0157 5.7	0828 1.9	1435 5.7	2052 1.9
11 SA	0257 6.0	0926 1.6	1530 6.1	2149 1.6
12 SU	0352 6.4	1019 1.3	1622 6.5	2242 1.2
13 M	0445 6.7	1110 1.0	1712 6.8	2334 0.9
14 TU ○	0536 6.9	1200 0.8	1801 7.0	
15 W	0024 0.7	0627 6.9	1248 0.8	1851 7.1
16 TH	0115 0.7	0718 7.0	1337 0.8	1941 7.1
17 F	0205 0.7	0809 6.8	1426 1.0	2032 7.0
18 SA	0256 0.9	0900 6.6	1516 1.2	2124 6.8
19 SU	0349 1.1	0952 6.3	1608 1.5	2217 6.5
20 M	0444 1.4	1046 5.9	1704 1.8	2313 6.2
21 TU ◐	0542 1.7	1144 5.7	1806 2.0	
22 W	0014 5.9	0645 1.9	1247 5.5	1912 2.1
23 TH	0118 5.8	0748 2.0	1352 5.5	2018 2.1
24 F	0220 5.8	0848 2.0	1453 5.6	2117 2.0
25 SA	0318 5.8	0942 1.9	1548 5.8	2210 1.9
26 SU	0411 5.9	1029 1.8	1636 6.0	2255 1.8
27 M	0457 6.0	1112 1.7	1718 6.1	2337 1.6
28 TU	0538 6.1	1151 1.6	1756 6.3	
29 W ○	0015 1.6	0617 6.2	1227 1.5	1833 6.4
30 TH	0051 1.5	0653 6.2	1302 1.5	1908 6.4

JULY

Day	Time m	Time m	Time m	Time m
1 F	0126 1.5	0728 6.2	1336 1.5	1942 6.4
2 SA	0200 1.5	0803 6.1	1410 1.5	2016 6.3
3 SU	0235 1.6	0838 6.0	1446 1.6	2052 6.2
4 M	0312 1.7	0915 5.9	1523 1.8	2131 6.1
5 TU	0351 1.8	0955 5.8	1605 1.9	2213 5.9
6 W ◐	0435 1.9	1041 5.6	1651 2.1	2303 5.8
7 TH ◐	0525 2.0	1135 5.5	1747 2.2	
8 F	0000 5.7	0626 2.1	1238 5.5	1854 2.2
9 SA	0106 5.7	0735 2.1	1347 5.6	2007 2.1
10 SU	0216 5.8	0846 1.9	1454 5.9	2117 1.8
11 M	0323 6.1	0952 1.6	1556 6.2	2221 1.5
12 TU	0425 6.4	1052 1.3	1655 6.6	2320 1.1
13 W ○	0524 6.7	1147 1.1	1750 6.9	
14 TH	0015 0.8	0619 6.9	1239 0.9	1843 7.2
15 F	0108 0.6	0711 7.0	1329 0.8	1933 7.3
16 SA	0158 0.6	0800 6.9	1417 0.8	2022 7.2
17 SU	0246 0.6	0847 6.8	1503 0.9	2108 7.0
18 M	0332 0.9	0932 6.5	1548 1.2	2154 6.7
19 TU	0417 1.2	1017 6.2	1633 1.5	2240 6.4
20 W ◐	0502 1.6	1104 5.8	1720 1.9	2330 6.0
21 TH	0551 1.9	1156 5.5	1815 2.2	
22 F	0025 5.6	0649 2.2	1257 5.3	1921 2.4
23 SA	0130 5.4	0756 2.4	1407 5.3	2035 2.5
24 SU	0239 5.3	0904 2.4	1515 5.4	2142 2.3
25 M	0344 5.5	1003 2.2	1614 5.7	2236 2.1
26 TU	0439 5.7	1052 2.0	1701 5.9	2322 1.8
27 W	0524 5.9	1134 1.7	1742 6.2	
28 TH ●	0001 1.6	0603 6.1	1211 1.6	1819 6.4
29 F	0037 1.5	0639 6.3	1246 1.4	1853 6.5
30 SA	0111 1.3	0713 6.4	1320 1.3	1926 6.6
31 SU	0144 1.3	0746 6.4	1353 1.3	1959 6.6

AUGUST

Day	Time m	Time m	Time m	Time m
1 M	0217 1.2	0819 6.4	1427 1.3	2033 6.6
2 TU	0251 1.3	0853 6.3	1502 1.4	2107 6.5
3 W	0326 1.4	0928 6.2	1539 1.5	2145 6.3
4 TH	0403 1.6	1007 6.0	1618 1.8	2227 6.1
5 F ◐	0445 1.8	1054 5.8	1706 2.0	2318 5.8
6 SA	0537 2.1	1153 5.5	1808 2.2	
7 SU	0024 5.6	0650 2.3	1308 5.5	1932 2.3
8 M	0146 5.5	0819 2.2	1431 5.6	2100 2.1
9 TU	0307 5.7	0939 1.9	1545 6.0	2213 1.6
10 W	0419 6.1	1044 1.5	1649 6.5	2315 1.2
11 TH	0520 6.5	1140 1.1	1744 7.0	
12 F ○	0009 0.8	0613 6.9	1230 0.8	1834 7.3
13 SA	0058 0.5	0700 7.1	1316 0.6	1920 7.4
14 SU	0143 0.4	0743 7.1	1359 0.6	2003 7.4
15 M	0225 0.5	0824 7.0	1440 0.7	2044 7.2
16 TU	0304 0.7	0903 6.7	1518 1.0	2123 6.9
17 W	0341 1.1	0940 6.4	1554 1.4	2201 6.4
18 TH	0417 1.6	1018 6.0	1632 1.9	2241 5.9
19 F ◐	0455 2.1	1100 5.5	1715 2.3	2328 5.5
20 SA	0543 2.5	1154 5.2	1817 2.7	
21 SU	0033 5.1	0655 2.7	1315 5.0	1952 2.9
22 M	0202 4.9	0829 2.8	1448 5.1	2121 2.7
23 TU	0325 5.2	0942 2.5	1557 5.5	2221 2.3
24 W	0423 5.5	1034 2.1	1645 5.9	2306 1.9
25 TH	0507 5.9	1116 1.8	1724 6.2	2344 1.6
26 F	0544 6.2	1153 1.5	1758 6.5	
27 SA ●	0018 1.3	0618 6.4	1226 1.3	1832 6.7
28 SU	0050 1.1	0650 6.6	1259 1.1	1904 6.9
29 M	0121 1.0	0722 6.7	1331 1.0	1935 6.9
30 TU	0153 1.0	0754 6.7	1404 1.0	2008 6.9
31 W	0226 1.0	0826 6.7	1438 1.1	2041 6.8

Chart Datum: 3·71 metres below Ordnance Datum (Newlyn)
HAT is 7·9m above Chart Datum

TIME ZONE (UT)	WALES – MILFORD HAVEN	Dates in amber are SPRINGS
For Summer Time add ONE hour in **non-shaded areas**	LAT 51°42'N LONG 5°03'W	Dates in grey are NEAPS
	TIMES AND HEIGHTS OF HIGH AND LOW WATERS	**2022**

SEPTEMBER

Time	m	Time	m
1 0259	1.2	**16** 0333	1.7
0900	6.5	0934	6.1
TH 1512	1.3	F 1547	1.9
2116	6.6	2156	5.9
2 0333	1.5	**17** 0404	2.2
0937	6.2	1010	5.6
F 1550	1.6	SA 1623	2.4
2156	6.2	◗ 2236	5.4
3 0413	1.8	**18** 0443	2.6
1021	5.9	1057	5.2
SA 1636	2.0	SU 1718	2.9
◗ 2246	5.8	2335	4.9
4 0504	2.2	**19** 0551	3.0
1120	5.5	1215	4.9
SU 1740	2.4	M 1905	3.1
2357	5.4		
5 0622	2.5	**20** 0122	4.7
1246	5.3	0750	3.1
M 1920	2.5	TU 1417	4.9
		2057	2.9
6 0134	5.3	**21** 0302	5.0
0813	2.5	0917	2.7
TU 1424	5.5	W 1532	5.4
2100	2.2	2158	2.4
7 0309	5.6	**22** 0400	5.4
0937	2.1	1010	2.3
W 1544	6.0	TH 1618	5.9
2213	1.6	2241	1.9
8 0419	6.1	**23** 0441	5.9
1040	1.5	1050	1.8
TH 1644	6.6	F 1656	6.3
2309	1.1	2317	1.5
9 0513	6.6	**24** 0516	6.3
1131	1.0	1126	1.4
F 1733	7.1	SA 1730	6.6
2358	0.7	2350	1.2
10 0559	7.0	**25** 0549	6.6
1216	0.7	1159	1.1
SA 1817	7.4	SU 1802	6.9
○		●	
11 0040	0.4	**26** 0022	1.0
0641	7.2	0621	6.9
SU 1256	0.5	M 1232	0.9
1859	7.5	1835	7.1
12 0120	0.4	**27** 0054	0.8
0719	7.2	0654	7.0
M 1335	0.5	TU 1306	0.8
1937	7.5	1908	7.2
13 0156	0.5	**28** 0127	0.8
0755	7.1	0726	7.1
TU 1410	0.7	W 1340	0.8
2013	7.2	1942	7.1
14 0230	0.8	**29** 0200	0.9
0829	6.8	0800	7.0
W 1444	1.0	TH 1414	1.0
2048	6.9	2016	7.0
15 0302	1.2	**30** 0234	1.1
0902	6.5	0835	6.8
TH 1516	1.5	F 1450	1.3
2121	6.4	2054	6.7

OCTOBER

Time	m	Time	m
1 0310	1.5	**16** 0325	2.2
0914	6.4	0932	5.8
SA 1531	1.6	SU 1547	2.5
2136	6.2	2158	5.4
2 0352	1.9	**17** 0402	2.7
1001	6.0	1016	5.3
SU 1621	2.1	M 1637	2.9
2230	5.7	◗ 2253	4.9
3 0447	2.4	**18** 0500	3.1
1107	5.5	1125	5.0
M 1734	2.5	TU 1814	3.1
◗ 2351	5.3		
4 0620	2.7	**19** 0026	4.7
1243	5.3	0656	3.2
TU 1927	2.5	W 1323	4.9
		2009	3.0
5 0137	5.2	**20** 0219	4.9
0815	2.6	0832	2.9
W 1422	5.6	TH 1447	5.3
2059	2.1	2116	2.5
6 0308	5.6	**21** 0320	5.4
0932	2.1	0930	2.4
TH 1535	6.1	F 1538	5.8
2204	1.6	2202	2.0
7 0409	6.2	**22** 0403	5.9
1028	1.5	1013	1.9
F 1629	6.7	SA 1618	6.2
2255	1.1	2240	1.6
8 0457	6.7	**23** 0440	6.3
1114	1.0	1051	1.5
SA 1715	7.1	SU 1654	6.6
2338	0.7	2315	1.2
9 0538	7.0	**24** 0514	6.7
1155	0.8	1127	1.2
SU 1755	7.4	M 1729	7.0
○		2350	1.0
10 0016	0.6	**25** 0549	7.0
0616	7.2	1204	0.9
M 1232	0.7	TU 1804	7.2
1833	7.4	●	
11 0051	0.6	**26** 0025	0.8
0651	7.2	0625	7.2
TU 1307	0.7	W 1240	0.8
1909	7.3	1841	7.3
12 0125	0.7	**27** 0101	0.8
0724	7.1	0701	7.2
W 1340	0.9	TH 1318	0.8
1942	7.1	1919	7.2
13 0157	1.0	**28** 0138	0.9
0756	6.8	0739	7.1
TH 1412	1.2	F 1357	1.0
2014	6.7	1958	7.0
14 0227	1.4	**29** 0216	1.2
0827	6.5	0819	6.9
F 1442	1.6	SA 1438	1.3
2046	6.3	2041	6.7
15 0255	1.8	**30** 0257	1.5
0858	6.2	0904	6.5
SA 1512	2.0	SU 1524	1.6
2119	5.9	2130	6.2
		31 0345	2.0
		0958	6.1
		M 1622	2.1
		2231	5.7

NOVEMBER

Time	m	Time	m
1 0448	2.4	**16** 0431	2.8
1109	5.7	1050	5.3
TU 1743	2.4	W 1725	2.9
◗ 2353	5.4	◗ 2334	4.9
2 0624	2.6	**17** 0552	3.0
1238	5.6	1210	5.1
W 1921	2.3	TH 1858	2.9
3 0128	5.4	**18** 0104	4.9
0800	2.4	0725	2.9
TH 1404	5.9	F 1337	5.3
2041	2.0	2013	2.6
4 0247	5.8	**19** 0220	5.2
0910	2.0	0833	2.6
F 1512	6.3	SA 1441	5.6
2142	1.6	2109	2.2
5 0345	6.2	**20** 0312	5.7
1005	1.6	0925	2.1
SA 1605	6.7	SU 1529	6.1
2230	1.2	2155	1.8
6 0431	6.6	**21** 0356	6.2
1050	1.2	1011	1.7
SU 1649	6.9	M 1612	6.5
2312	1.0	2237	1.4
7 0512	6.8	**22** 0437	6.6
1130	1.1	1054	1.4
M 1730	7.1	TU 1654	6.8
2349	0.9	2318	1.1
8 0549	6.9	**23** 0518	6.9
1206	1.0	1136	1.1
TU 1807	7.1	W 1736	7.1
○		◐ 2359	1.0
9 0023	1.0	**24** 0559	7.1
0624	7.0	1219	0.9
W 1240	1.1	TH 1819	7.2
1842	7.0		
10 0056	1.1	**25** 0041	0.9
0657	6.9	0642	7.2
TH 1314	1.2	F 1302	0.9
1915	6.8	1903	7.2
11 0128	1.3	**26** 0123	1.0
0729	6.7	0726	7.2
F 1346	1.4	SA 1347	0.9
1948	6.6	1949	7.0
12 0159	1.5	**27** 0207	1.2
0801	6.5	0812	7.0
SA 1418	1.7	SU 1435	1.2
2021	6.2	2038	6.7
13 0229	1.9	**28** 0254	1.5
0834	6.2	0903	6.7
SU 1450	2.0	M 1526	1.4
2056	5.9	2132	6.3
14 0301	2.2	**29** 0347	1.8
0909	5.9	0959	6.4
M 1527	2.4	TU 1626	1.8
2135	5.5	2232	5.9
15 0339	2.5	**30** 0449	2.1
0952	5.6	1103	6.1
TU 1615	2.7	W 1736	2.0
2225	5.2	◗ 2340	5.6

DECEMBER

Time	m	Time	m
1 0606	2.3	**16** 0502	2.6
1215	5.9	1116	5.5
TH 1853	2.1	F 1746	2.6
		◗ 2353	5.2
2 0056	5.6	**17** 0609	2.7
0705	2.3	1221	5.4
F 1329	6.0	SA 1857	2.5
2005	2.0		
3 0208	5.7	**18** 0103	5.2
0834	2.1	0723	2.6
SA 1435	6.1	SU 1330	5.5
2106	1.8	2005	2.3
4 0309	6.0	**19** 0210	5.5
0932	1.8	0829	2.3
SU 1532	6.3	M 1434	5.8
2158	1.6	2105	2.1
5 0401	6.2	**20** 0309	5.9
1021	1.6	0928	2.0
M 1621	6.5	TU 1531	6.1
2243	1.5	2200	1.7
6 0445	6.4	**21** 0401	6.3
1105	1.5	1022	1.6
TU 1705	6.6	W 1624	6.5
2322	1.4	2251	1.4
7 0525	6.6	**22** 0451	6.7
1144	1.4	1114	1.3
W 1745	6.6	TH 1715	6.8
2359	1.4	2340	1.1
8 0602	6.6	**23** 0540	7.0
1221	1.4	1204	1.0
TH 1822	6.6	F 1805	7.0
○		●	
9 0034	1.4	**24** 0027	1.0
0638	6.7	0630	7.2
F 1256	1.5	SA 1253	0.8
1858	6.5	1856	7.1
10 0108	1.5	**25** 0115	0.9
0712	6.6	0719	7.3
SA 1330	1.6	SU 1343	0.8
1932	6.4	1946	7.0
11 0141	1.6	**26** 0203	1.0
0746	6.5	0809	7.2
SU 1404	1.7	M 1433	0.8
2006	6.2	2036	6.8
12 0213	1.8	**27** 0252	1.1
0820	6.3	0859	7.1
M 1438	1.9	TU 1523	1.0
2041	6.0	2126	6.6
13 0247	2.0	**28** 0341	1.3
0855	6.1	0950	6.8
TU 1514	2.1	W 1616	1.3
2119	5.8	2217	6.3
14 0324	2.2	**29** 0434	1.6
0935	5.9	1044	6.5
W 1556	2.3	TH 1710	1.6
2201	5.5	2312	5.9
15 0408	2.4	**30** 0531	1.9
1021	5.7	1141	6.2
TH 1645	2.5	F 1810	1.9
2252	5.3	◗	
		31 0012	5.7
		0636	2.1
		SA 1243	5.9
		1914	2.1

Chart Datum: 3·71 metres below Ordnance Datum (Newlyn)
HAT is 7·9m above Chart Datum

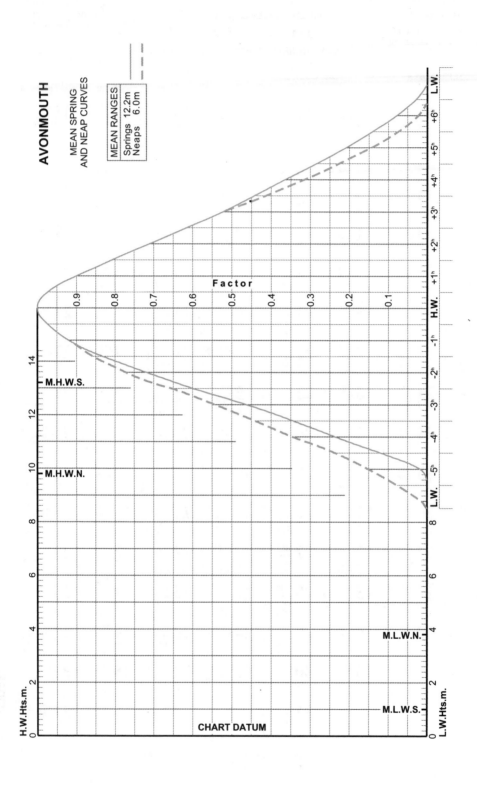

AVONMOUTH

MEAN SPRING
AND NEAP CURVES

MEAN RANGES
Springs 12.2m
Neaps 6.0m

AVONMOUTH
LAT 51°30'N LONG 2°44'W
TIMES AND HEIGHTS OF HIGH AND LOW WATERS

TIME ZONE (UT) — For Summer Time add ONE hour in **non-shaded areas**

Dates in amber are **SPRINGS**
Dates in grey are **NEAPS**

2022

JANUARY

Day	Time	m	Time	m	Time	m	Time	m
1 SA	0534	12.3	1217	2.0	1800	12.6		
2 SU	0048	1.8	0628	13.0	●1854	13.1		
3 M	0142	1.4	0719	13.4	1408	1.2	1946	13.4
4 TU	0234	1.2	0808	13.6	1459	1.1	2035	13.4
5 W	0321	1.2	0855	13.6	1546	1.1	2122	13.2
6 TH	0404	1.4	0941	13.3	1628	1.4	2207	12.8
7 F	0441	1.8	1025	12.8	1704	1.8	2249	12.2
8 SA	0513	2.1	1108	12.2	1737	2.3	2329	11.5
9 SU	0546	2.7	1152	11.5	☾1812	2.7		
10 M	0012	10.8	0624	3.2	1242	10.8	1855	3.2
11 TU	0104	10.3	0712	3.6	1344	10.3	1946	3.5
12 W	0210	10.0	0812	3.9	1451	10.2	2050	3.7
13 TH	0318	10.0	0925	3.9	1554	10.3	2203	3.5
14 F	0419	10.5	1043	3.4	1650	10.8	2311	3.0
15 SA	0513	11.0	1143	2.8	1740	11.3		
16 SU	0006	2.4	0600	11.6	1233	2.4	1826	11.7
17 M	0055	2.0	0643	12.1	1321	2.1	○1908	12.0
18 TU	0142	1.8	0724	12.3	1407	2.0	1949	12.1
19 W	0225	1.9	0803	12.4	1450	2.1	2028	12.1
20 TH	0304	2.0	0840	12.4	1526	2.2	2104	12.1
21 F	0337	2.1	0915	12.3	1556	2.2	2138	12.1
22 SA	0405	2.1	0949	12.3	1623	2.2	2211	12.0
23 SU	0435	2.1	1025	12.2	1654	2.2	2248	11.8
24 M	0509	2.2	1104	12.0	1730	2.3	2329	11.5
25 TU	0549	2.4	1150	11.6	☽1812	2.6		
26 W	0017	11.1	0637	2.9	1245	11.1	1903	3.1
27 TH	0118	10.6	0737	3.4	1355	10.6	2011	3.6
28 F	0239	10.3	0910	3.6	1523	10.6	2209	3.6
29 SA	0408	10.7	1053	3.2	1644	11.1	2332	2.9
30 SU	0519	11.6	1203	2.4	1750	11.9		
31 M	0035	2.2	0618	12.5	1303	1.7	1847	12.7

FEBRUARY

Day	Time	m	Time	m	Time	m	Time	m
1 TU	0133	1.5	0710	13.2	1400	1.1	●1938	13.2
2 W	0226	1.0	0759	13.7	1452	0.8	2025	13.5
3 TH	0314	0.8	0844	13.9	1537	0.6	2109	13.5
4 F	0355	0.9	0926	13.7	1616	0.8	2148	13.2
5 SA	0429	1.2	1004	13.3	1646	1.3	2222	12.7
6 SU	0453	1.7	1038	12.7	1709	1.8	2253	12.1
7 M	0513	2.2	1109	11.9	1732	2.3	2322	11.3
8 TU	0539	2.6	1143	11.1	1803	2.8	☽2357	10.6
9 W	0614	3.2	1226	10.2	1845	3.4		
10 TH	0045	9.9	0700	3.8	1328	9.5	1945	3.9
11 F	0201	9.4	0819	4.2	1459	9.4	2104	4.1
12 SA	0333	9.6	0947	4.0	1616	9.8	2227	3.6
13 SU	0443	10.3	1108	3.3	1716	10.6	2336	2.9
14 M	0537	11.1	1209	2.6	1805	11.4		
15 TU	0032	2.2	0624	11.9	1302	2.1	1850	11.9
16 W	0124	1.8	0707	12.4	1353	1.8	○1932	12.3
17 TH	0213	1.7	0747	12.7	1440	1.7	2011	12.5
18 F	0256	1.6	0824	12.8	1520	1.7	2047	12.6
19 SA	0332	1.6	0859	12.9	1552	1.8	2121	12.7
20 SU	0359	1.6	0933	12.9	1615	1.8	2153	12.6
21 M	0423	1.6	1007	12.8	1637	1.8	2227	12.4
22 TU	0451	1.7	1043	12.5	1706	1.9	2304	12.0
23 W	0524	2.0	1125	11.8	1742	2.4	2348	11.3
24 TH	0605	2.6	1215	11.0	1827	3.1		
25 F	0043	10.4	0700	3.4	1324	10.1	1929	3.9
26 SA	0210	9.8	0834	4.0	1508	9.9	2158	4.1
27 SU	0356	10.2	1045	3.5	1639	10.6	2324	3.1
28 M	0512	11.2	1155	2.4	1745	11.7		

MARCH

Day	Time	m	Time	m	Time	m	Time	m
1 TU	0025	2.1	0610	12.3	1253	1.5	1838	12.7
2 W	0120	1.3	0700	13.3	1347	0.8	●1925	13.4
3 TH	0211	0.7	0745	13.8	1436	0.4	2008	13.7
4 F	0257	0.4	0826	14.0	1519	0.3	2048	13.7
5 SA	0336	0.5	0904	13.8	1554	0.6	2122	13.4
6 SU	0407	1.0	0937	13.4	1620	1.2	2151	12.9
7 M	0426	1.5	1005	12.7	1636	1.7	2216	12.3
8 TU	0439	1.9	1030	12.0	1652	2.1	2240	11.6
9 W	0458	2.3	1057	11.2	1716	2.5	2308	10.9
10 TH	0526	2.8	1130	10.3	1749	3.2	☽2344	10.0
11 F	0605	3.6	1216	9.4	1839	4.0		
12 SA	0043	9.2	0715	4.4	1351	8.8	2012	4.5
13 SU	0244	9.0	0903	4.4	1542	9.2	2150	4.1
14 M	0412	9.8	1036	3.7	1649	10.2	2309	3.2
15 TU	0511	10.8	1146	2.7	1741	11.2		
16 W	0009	2.4	0559	11.7	1241	2.1	1826	12.0
17 TH	0103	1.8	0642	12.4	1332	1.6	1907	12.6
18 F	0152	1.5	0723	12.9	1419	1.4	○1946	12.9
19 SA	0236	1.3	0801	13.2	1500	1.3	2023	13.1
20 SU	0314	1.2	0837	13.3	1533	1.4	2058	13.2
21 M	0344	1.2	0912	13.3	1558	1.5	2131	13.1
22 TU	0407	1.3	0947	13.1	1618	1.6	2206	12.7
23 W	0433	1.5	1024	12.6	1644	1.8	2243	12.1
24 TH	0504	1.9	1105	11.8	1717	2.4	2326	11.2
25 F	0543	2.7	1155	10.7	☽1801	3.3		
26 SA	0023	10.2	0639	3.6	1310	9.7	1908	4.2
27 SU	0206	9.5	0851	4.2	1509	9.6	2158	4.1
28 M	0350	10.1	1036	3.3	1630	10.5	2310	3.0
29 TU	0459	11.3	1139	2.2	1730	11.7		
30 W	0006	1.9	0554	12.4	1232	1.2	1820	12.7
31 TH	0058	1.0	0640	13.3	1322	0.6	1904	13.4

APRIL

Day	Time	m	Time	m	Time	m	Time	m
1 F	0146	0.5	0722	13.7	1409	0.3	●1943	13.6
2 SA	0230	0.4	0801	13.8	1450	0.4	2020	13.6
3 SU	0308	0.6	0836	13.6	1524	0.8	2051	13.2
4 M	0338	1.1	0907	13.1	1549	1.3	2118	12.8
5 TU	0356	1.6	0933	12.5	1602	1.8	2141	12.2
6 W	0406	2.0	0956	11.9	1616	2.0	2204	11.7
7 TH	0424	2.2	1021	11.2	1638	2.4	2229	11.0
8 F	0451	2.6	1050	10.4	1708	3.0	2303	10.2
9 SA	0526	3.3	1133	9.5	☾1750	3.8	2355	9.4
10 SU	0622	4.2	1247	8.8	1911	4.5		
11 M	0136	8.9	0817	4.5	1457	9.0	2109	4.3
12 TU	0331	9.6	0955	3.8	1612	10.0	2233	3.5
13 W	0435	10.6	1111	2.9	1707	11.0	2337	2.6
14 TH	0525	11.6	1209	2.2	1753	12.0		
15 F	0031	1.9	0610	12.4	1300	1.6	1836	12.7
16 SA	0120	1.5	0652	13.0	1348	1.3	○1916	13.2
17 SU	0206	1.2	0732	13.4	1430	1.2	1955	13.4
18 M	0246	1.0	0812	13.6	1507	1.1	2033	13.5
19 TU	0321	1.0	0851	13.5	1537	1.3	2110	13.3
20 W	0352	1.1	0930	13.2	1603	1.5	2149	12.8
21 TH	0421	1.4	1011	12.5	1631	1.9	2229	12.1
22 F	0454	2.0	1055	11.6	1706	2.6	2316	11.1
23 SA	0537	2.8	1150	10.5	1754	3.5	◐	
24 SU	0022	10.2	0643	3.7	1315	9.7	1920	4.2
25 M	0209	9.9	0848	3.8	1455	9.9	2136	3.8
26 TU	0330	10.5	1010	3.0	1606	10.7	2242	2.8
27 W	0433	11.4	1109	2.1	1703	11.7	2336	1.9
28 TH	0525	12.3	1201	1.3	1751	12.5		
29 F	0026	1.2	0612	12.9	1249	0.9	1834	13.0
30 SA	0113	0.9	0653	13.2	1335	0.7	●1912	13.2

Chart Datum: 6·50 metres below Ordnance Datum (Newlyn)
HAT is 14·7m above Chart Datum

TIDES

AVONMOUTH
LAT 51°30'N   LONG 2°44'W
TIMES AND HEIGHTS OF HIGH AND LOW WATERS

TIME ZONE (UT)
For Summer Time add ONE hour in non-shaded areas

Dates in amber are **SPRINGS**
Dates in grey are **NEAPS**

2022

MAY

Day	Time m	Day	Time m
1 SU	0156 0.8 / 0731 13.2 / 1416 0.8 / 1947 13.1	16 M	0132 1.2 / 0705 13.3 / 1358 1.2 / ○ 1929 13.5
2 M	0235 1.0 / 0806 13.0 / 1451 1.2 / 2019 12.8	17 TU	0218 1.0 / 0749 13.5 / 1440 1.1 / 2011 13.6
3 TU	0307 1.4 / 0837 12.6 / 1516 1.6 / 2047 12.4	18 W	0300 0.9 / 0834 13.4 / 1519 1.2 / 2054 13.4
4 W	0327 1.9 / 0905 12.1 / 1533 1.9 / 2112 12.0	19 TH	0339 1.1 / 0919 13.1 / 1554 1.5 / 2138 12.9
5 TH	0341 2.1 / 0930 11.6 / 1550 2.1 / 2137 11.6	20 F	0418 1.4 / 1004 12.5 / 1630 2.0 / 2224 12.2
6 F	0401 2.3 / 0957 11.1 / 1614 2.4 / 2205 11.1	21 SA	0458 2.0 / 1053 11.7 / 1711 2.6 / 2316 11.4
7 SA	0429 2.6 / 1029 10.5 / 1646 2.8 / 2241 10.5	22 SU	0547 2.6 / 1151 10.8 / 1804 3.3
8 SU	0506 3.1 / 1112 9.9 / 1728 3.5 / 2332 9.8	23 M	0024 10.7 / 0652 3.1 / 1306 10.3 / 1923 3.7
9 M	0559 3.7 / 1216 9.4 / 1833 4.1 ◐	24 TU	0147 10.5 / 0813 3.2 / 1424 10.3 / 2053 3.5
10 TU	0048 9.5 / 0726 4.1 / 1348 9.3 / 2015 4.2	25 W	0257 10.8 / 0926 2.9 / 1528 10.8 / 2201 2.9
11 W	0229 9.7 / 0859 3.7 / 1518 10.0 / 2140 3.6	26 TH	0356 11.3 / 1027 2.4 / 1625 11.3 / 2257 2.3
12 TH	0344 10.5 / 1017 3.1 / 1621 10.9 / 2250 2.8	27 F	0449 11.8 / 1122 1.9 / 1714 11.9 / 2349 1.8
13 F	0441 11.4 / 1124 2.4 / 1714 11.8 / 2350 2.1	28 SA	0537 12.2 / 1211 1.6 / 1759 12.3
14 SA	0532 12.3 / 1221 1.9 / 1801 12.6	29 SU	0036 1.6 / 0620 12.4 / 1257 1.4 / 1839 12.5
15 SU	0043 1.6 / 0619 12.9 / 1311 1.5 / 1846 13.2	30 M	0120 1.5 / 0700 12.5 / 1339 1.4 / ● 1916 12.5
		31 TU	0201 1.6 / 0737 12.3 / 1417 1.6 / 1950 12.4

JUNE

Day	Time m	Day	Time m
1 W	0236 1.8 / 0811 12.1 / 1358 1.2 / 2023 12.1	16 TH	0245 1.0 / 0822 13.2 / 1508 1.2 / 2044 13.4
2 TH	0304 2.1 / 0844 11.8 / 1513 2.1 / 2054 11.8	17 F	0333 1.3 / 0912 13.0 / 1552 1.4 / 2132 13.1
3 F	0326 2.3 / 0915 11.4 / 1535 2.3 / 2123 11.5	18 SA	0418 1.3 / 1000 12.7 / 1634 1.7 / 2220 12.6
4 SA	0350 2.5 / 0946 11.1 / 1602 2.4 / 2154 11.2	19 SU	0502 1.6 / 1049 12.1 / 1716 2.2 / 2311 12.1
5 SU	0421 2.6 / 1020 10.8 / 1636 2.7 / 2231 10.8	20 M	0546 2.0 / 1140 11.5 / 1800 2.6
6 M	0459 2.9 / 1102 10.5 / 1718 3.0 / 2319 10.5	21 TU	0006 11.5 / 0634 2.4 / 1236 11.0 / ◐ 1852 3.0
7 TU	0548 3.1 / 1155 10.2 / 1812 3.4	22 W	0110 11.0 / 0727 2.8 / 1339 10.6 / 1951 3.3
8 W	0018 10.3 / 0649 3.4 / 1259 10.1 / 1923 3.6	23 TH	0214 10.9 / 0824 3.0 / 1441 10.6 / 2059 3.3
9 TH	0129 10.3 / 0801 3.4 / 1412 10.2 / 2041 3.5	24 F	0313 10.9 / 0928 3.0 / 1539 10.7 / 2207 3.1
10 F	0243 10.7 / 0917 3.1 / 1525 10.8 / 2158 3.0	25 SA	0408 11.0 / 1032 2.8 / 1633 11.0 / 2306 2.8
11 SA	0352 11.3 / 1034 2.7 / 1631 11.5 / 2308 2.5	26 SU	0500 11.3 / 1129 2.5 / 1723 11.4 / 2358 2.4
12 SU	0454 11.9 / 1141 2.2 / 1727 12.2	27 M	0547 11.6 / 1219 2.2 / 1807 11.8
13 M	0008 1.9 / 0550 12.5 / 1238 1.8 / 1819 12.9	28 TU	0045 2.1 / 0632 11.8 / 1305 1.9 / 1849 12.0
14 TU	0103 1.4 / 0642 13.0 / 1331 1.4 / ○ 1907 13.4	29 W	0130 2.0 / 0713 11.8 / 1348 1.9 / 1928 12.1
15 W	0155 1.1 / 0732 13.2 / 1421 1.2 / 1956 13.4	30 TH	0212 2.1 / 0752 11.8 / 1428 2.0 / 2006 12.0

JULY

Day	Time m	Day	Time m
1 F	0250 2.2 / 0830 11.7 / 1502 2.2 / 2042 11.9	16 SA	0329 0.8 / 0903 13.3 / 1550 1.1 / 2123 13.5
2 SA	0322 2.4 / 0905 11.5 / 1531 2.3 / 2115 11.7	17 SU	0415 0.8 / 0950 13.1 / 1631 1.3 / 2208 13.2
3 SU	0350 2.5 / 0939 11.4 / 1559 2.4 / 2148 11.5	18 M	0455 1.1 / 1033 12.7 / 1707 1.6 / 2252 12.7
4 M	0419 2.5 / 1012 11.3 / 1631 2.5 / 2223 11.4	19 TU	0530 1.5 / 1115 12.1 / 1739 2.1 / 2335 12.0
5 TU	0452 2.5 / 1049 11.1 / 1708 2.6 / 2303 11.2	20 W	0602 2.1 / 1156 11.4 / 1812 2.6
6 W	0532 2.6 / 1132 11.0 / 1751 2.8 / 2351 11.0	21 TH	0020 11.3 / 0638 2.6 / 1241 10.8 / 1852 3.2
7 TH	0618 2.8 / 1222 10.7 / 1843 3.0 ◐	22 F	0115 10.6 / 0722 3.1 / 1338 10.2 / 1944 3.6
8 F	0048 10.9 / 0713 3.0 / 1323 10.6 / 1947 3.3	23 SA	0220 10.2 / 0818 3.5 / 1446 10.0 / 2052 3.9
9 SA	0154 10.8 / 0819 3.2 / 1434 10.6 / 2107 3.3	24 SU	0325 10.1 / 0927 3.6 / 1552 10.2 / 2215 3.7
10 SU	0308 10.9 / 0946 3.2 / 1551 11.0 / 2233 2.9	25 M	0425 10.4 / 1042 3.3 / 1650 10.7 / 2323 3.1
11 M	0423 11.4 / 1110 2.8 / 1700 11.7 / 2343 2.3	26 TU	0520 10.8 / 1145 2.7 / 1742 11.3
12 TU	0528 12.0 / 1216 2.2 / 1759 12.4	27 W	0017 2.5 / 0609 11.3 / 1237 2.3 / 1828 11.8
13 W	0044 1.8 / 0627 12.5 / 1314 1.7 / ○ 1854 13.0	28 TH	0106 2.2 / 0654 11.7 / 1327 2.0 / ● 1911 12.1
14 TH	0142 1.3 / 0721 13.0 / 1411 1.4 / 1945 13.4	29 F	0155 2.1 / 0735 11.9 / 1413 1.9 / 1951 12.2
15 F	0238 1.0 / 0814 13.2 / 1503 1.1 / 2035 13.6	30 SA	0240 2.1 / 0815 11.9 / 1455 2.0 / 2028 12.2
		31 SU	0320 2.2 / 0852 11.9 / 1531 2.1 / 2103 12.1

AUGUST

Day	Time m	Day	Time m
1 M	0352 2.3 / 0925 11.9 / 1558 2.2 / 2135 12.1	16 TU	0436 0.9 / 1008 13.1 / 1647 1.4 / 2223 13.0
2 TU	0415 2.3 / 0956 11.8 / 1622 2.2 / 2206 12.0	17 W	0503 1.5 / 1041 12.4 / 1708 2.0 / 2256 12.2
3 W	0439 2.3 / 1029 11.7 / 1651 2.2 / 2242 11.9	18 TH	0524 2.1 / 1111 11.6 / 1729 2.5 / 2329 11.3
4 TH	0510 2.3 / 1105 11.5 / 1726 2.4 / 2323 11.6	19 F	0550 2.6 / 1143 10.8 / 1759 3.1 ◐
5 F	0547 2.5 / 1149 11.1 / 1808 2.8	20 SA	0007 10.4 / 0626 3.3 / 1226 10.0 / 1842 3.8
6 SA	0012 11.1 / 0632 2.9 / 1243 10.6 / 1901 3.3	21 SU	0106 9.5 / 0718 3.6 / 1338 9.4 / 1951 4.4
7 SU	0115 10.6 / 0730 3.5 / 1354 10.3 / 2018 3.7	22 M	0239 9.2 / 0835 4.3 / 1514 9.4 / 2124 4.4
8 M	0236 10.3 / 0903 3.8 / 1525 10.4 / 2213 3.5	23 TU	0357 9.6 / 1003 3.9 / 1625 10.1 / 2257 3.6
9 TU	0406 10.7 / 1055 3.3 / 1646 11.1 / 2333 2.7	24 W	0458 10.3 / 1119 3.1 / 1721 11.0 / 2357 2.8
10 W	0519 11.5 / 1206 2.5 / 1750 12.1	25 TH	0549 11.1 / 1217 2.4 / 1808 11.8
11 TH	0037 1.9 / 0620 12.3 / 1307 1.8 / 1845 13.0	26 F	0048 2.1 / 0634 11.8 / 1308 2.0 / 1851 12.3
12 F	0136 1.2 / 0713 13.0 / 1403 1.2 / ○ 1936 13.6	27 SA	0138 1.8 / 0715 12.2 / 1357 1.8 / ● 1931 12.6
13 SA	0230 0.7 / 0803 13.5 / 1454 0.8 / 2023 14.0	28 SU	0225 1.8 / 0754 12.4 / 1442 1.8 / 2008 12.7
14 SU	0319 0.6 / 0849 13.6 / 1539 0.7 / 2107 14.0	29 M	0307 1.8 / 0830 12.4 / 1519 1.9 / 2042 12.6
15 M	0402 0.5 / 0931 13.5 / 1617 0.9 / 2147 13.7	30 TU	0340 2.1 / 0903 12.4 / 1547 2.0 / 2113 12.6
		31 W	0403 2.1 / 0933 12.3 / 1607 2.1 / 2144 12.5

Chart Datum: 6·50 metres below Ordnance Datum (Newlyn)
HAT is 14·7m above Chart Datum

TIME ZONE (UT)
For Summer Time add ONE hour in **non-shaded areas**

AVONMOUTH
LAT 51°30'N LONG 2°44'W
TIMES AND HEIGHTS OF HIGH AND LOW WATERS

Dates in amber are **SPRINGS**
Dates in grey are **NEAPS**

2022

SEPTEMBER

Time m	Time m
1 0419 2.2 / 1004 12.2 / TH 1630 2.1 / 2218 12.3	**16** 0443 2.2 / 1028 11.7 / F 1647 2.6 / 2243 11.2
2 0444 2.2 / 1039 11.6 / F 1700 2.3 / 2257 11.8	**17** 0503 2.7 / 1054 10.9 / SA 1711 3.1 / ☽ 2313 10.3
3 0516 2.5 / 1120 11.3 / SA 1737 2.8 / ☽ 2343 11.0	**18** 0531 3.4 / 1128 10.0 / SU 1745 3.9 / 2356 9.3
4 0556 3.1 / 1211 10.6 / SU 1825 3.5	**19** 0615 4.2 / 1225 9.1 / M 1847 4.7
5 0045 10.1 / 0652 3.9 / M 1327 9.8 / 1943 4.3	**20** 0141 8.6 / 0745 4.8 / TU 1441 8.9 / 2045 4.9
6 0223 9.7 / 0849 4.4 / TU 1519 9.9 / 2215 3.9	**21** 0332 9.1 / 0932 4.4 / W 1559 9.8 / 2236 4.0
7 0405 10.3 / 1054 3.5 / W 1641 11.0 / 2329 2.7	**22** 0434 10.1 / 1057 3.4 / TH 1656 10.8 / 2337 2.9
8 0515 11.4 / 1159 2.4 / TH 1743 12.2	**23** 0524 11.1 / 1155 2.5 / F 1743 11.8
9 0028 1.6 / 0612 12.5 / F 1255 1.5 / 1834 13.3	**24** 0026 2.1 / 0608 11.9 / SA 1245 1.9 / 1825 12.5
10 0122 0.8 / 0700 13.3 / SA 1347 0.8 / ○ 1920 14.0	**25** 0114 1.7 / 0648 12.5 / SU 1333 1.7 / ● 1904 12.9
11 0213 0.3 / 0745 13.8 / SU 1435 0.5 / 2004 14.2	**26** 0200 1.5 / 0726 12.8 / M 1417 1.6 / 1941 13.0
12 0258 0.2 / 0826 13.9 / M 1518 0.5 / 2043 14.1	**27** 0241 1.6 / 0802 12.9 / TU 1455 1.6 / 2016 13.1
13 0338 0.4 / 0903 13.6 / TU 1553 0.9 / 2119 13.7	**28** 0316 1.7 / 0836 12.8 / W 1526 1.8 / 2049 13.0
14 0409 1.0 / 0936 13.1 / W 1618 1.6 / 2151 13.0	**29** 0340 1.9 / 0908 12.7 / TH 1548 1.9 / 2122 12.8
15 0429 1.7 / 1003 12.4 / TH 1632 2.1 / 2217 12.2	**30** 0358 2.1 / 0941 12.5 / F 1611 2.0 / 2158 12.4

OCTOBER

Time m	Time m
1 0421 2.2 / 1017 12.0 / SA 1639 2.3 / 2237 11.7	**16** 0425 2.8 / 1016 11.0 / SU 1636 3.1 / 2234 10.3
2 0452 2.6 / 1058 11.2 / SU 1715 2.9 / 2324 10.8	**17** 0452 3.3 / 1047 10.2 / M 1707 3.8 / ☽ 2312 9.5
3 0532 3.4 / 1152 10.3 / M 1805 3.8	**18** 0529 4.1 / 1135 9.3 / TU 1757 4.6
4 0031 9.8 / 0630 4.3 / TU 1322 9.6 / 1950 4.5	**19** 0025 8.7 / 0642 4.9 / W 1342 8.8 / 1957 5.0
5 0231 9.5 / 0925 4.5 / W 1519 10.0 / 2211 3.7	**20** 0252 8.9 / 0848 4.8 / TH 1522 9.6 / 2147 4.3
6 0400 10.4 / 1044 3.3 / TH 1630 11.2 / 2314 2.4	**21** 0358 9.9 / 1018 3.8 / F 1620 10.6 / 2300 3.2
7 0502 11.6 / 1141 2.1 / F 1726 12.4	**22** 0450 10.9 / 1120 2.9 / SA 1708 11.6 / 2352 2.4
8 0008 1.4 / 0553 12.7 / SA 1232 1.2 / 1814 13.4	**23** 0534 11.9 / 1211 2.2 / SU 1751 12.4
9 0058 0.7 / 0638 13.4 / SU 1321 0.7 / ○ 1858 14.0	**24** 0040 1.9 / 0616 12.5 / M 1258 1.8 / 1832 12.9
10 0145 0.3 / 0719 13.8 / M 1407 0.5 / 1938 14.1	**25** 0126 1.6 / 0655 13.0 / TU 1343 1.6 / ● 1911 13.2
11 0229 0.4 / 0757 13.8 / TU 1448 0.7 / 2016 13.9	**26** 0208 1.5 / 0732 13.2 / W 1423 1.5 / 1949 13.3
12 0306 0.7 / 0832 13.5 / W 1523 1.2 / 2049 13.4	**27** 0244 1.6 / 0809 13.2 / TH 1459 1.5 / 2026 13.3
13 0335 1.3 / 0902 13.0 / TH 1546 1.8 / 2118 12.7	**28** 0315 1.7 / 0846 13.1 / F 1530 1.7 / 2105 13.0
14 0353 1.9 / 0928 12.3 / F 1558 2.3 / 2143 12.0	**29** 0342 1.9 / 0924 12.7 / SA 1559 1.9 / 2145 12.5
15 0406 2.4 / 0951 11.7 / SA 1613 2.7 / 2207 11.2	**30** 0409 2.3 / 1004 12.1 / SU 1632 2.4 / 2228 11.7
	31 0443 2.8 / 1050 11.3 / M 1712 3.1 / 2320 10.7

NOVEMBER

Time m	Time m
1 0527 3.6 / 1150 10.4 / TU 1811 3.8 / ◑	**16** 0509 3.7 / 1113 9.9 / W 1738 4.1 / ☽ 2353 9.3
2 0034 9.9 / 0637 4.3 / W 1330 10.0 / 2011 4.1	**17** 0607 4.3 / 1226 9.4 / TH 1858 4.5
3 0222 9.9 / 0904 4.1 / TH 1500 10.5 / 2143 3.3	**18** 0126 9.1 / 0744 4.6 / F 1414 9.6 / 2036 4.3
4 0336 10.6 / 1015 3.2 / F 1604 11.4 / 2244 2.4	**19** 0259 9.7 / 0913 4.1 / SA 1526 10.3 / 2155 3.6
5 0435 11.6 / 1111 2.2 / SA 1659 12.4 / 2337 1.6	**20** 0401 10.6 / 1025 3.4 / SU 1622 11.2 / 2302 2.9
6 0525 12.5 / 1201 1.5 / SU 1746 13.1	**21** 0453 11.5 / 1125 2.7 / M 1712 12.0 / 2358 2.3
7 0025 1.1 / 0609 13.1 / M 1249 1.1 / 1830 13.5	**22** 0539 12.3 / 1218 2.1 / TU 1758 12.7
8 0112 0.8 / 0650 13.4 / TU 1334 1.0 / ○ 1910 13.5	**23** 0047 1.9 / 0623 12.9 / W 1306 1.7 / ● 1842 13.1
9 0154 0.9 / 0727 13.4 / W 1415 1.2 / 1947 13.3	**24** 0133 1.6 / 0705 13.3 / TH 1352 1.5 / 1926 13.3
10 0232 1.2 / 0801 13.1 / TH 1450 1.4 / 2021 12.9	**25** 0216 1.5 / 0747 13.4 / F 1436 1.4 / 2010 13.3
11 0303 1.6 / 0832 12.7 / F 1516 2.1 / 2051 12.3	**26** 0256 1.5 / 0830 13.3 / SA 1517 1.5 / 2054 13.1
12 0323 2.1 / 0900 12.2 / SA 1532 2.5 / 2119 11.7	**27** 0333 1.7 / 0914 13.0 / SU 1556 1.7 / 2140 12.6
13 0340 2.5 / 0926 11.7 / SU 1550 2.7 / 2145 11.1	**28** 0410 2.1 / 1000 12.5 / M 1638 2.1 / 2228 12.0
14 0402 2.7 / 0954 11.1 / M 1616 3.1 / 2215 10.5	**29** 0450 2.6 / 1051 11.8 / TU 1724 2.7 / 2321 11.2
15 0431 3.2 / 1027 10.5 / TU 1651 3.5 / 2255 9.9	**30** 0539 3.2 / 1151 11.1 / W 1822 3.2 / ◑

DECEMBER

Time m	Time m
1 0027 10.6 / 0646 3.7 / TH 1308 10.8 / 1938 3.4	**16** 0547 3.5 / 1152 10.3 / F 1819 3.6 / ◑
2 0148 10.4 / 0814 3.7 / F 1425 10.9 / 2055 3.2	**17** 0027 10.0 / 0647 3.8 / SA 1256 10.2 / 1925 3.8
3 0257 10.7 / 0929 3.3 / SA 1527 11.3 / 2200 2.8	**18** 0136 9.9 / 0801 3.9 / SU 1409 10.3 / 2041 3.7
4 0357 11.2 / 1030 2.8 / SU 1623 11.8 / 2257 2.3	**19** 0252 10.3 / 0921 3.7 / M 1522 10.8 / 2202 3.4
5 0450 11.8 / 1125 2.3 / M 1714 12.2 / 2349 1.9	**20** 0402 10.9 / 1036 3.1 / TU 1628 11.4 / 2313 2.8
6 0537 12.3 / 1214 1.9 / TU 1800 12.5	**21** 0502 11.7 / 1140 2.5 / W 1726 12.1
7 0036 1.6 / 0620 12.6 / W 1300 1.7 / 1843 12.6	**22** 0012 2.3 / 0555 12.4 / TH 1236 1.9 / 1819 12.7
8 0120 1.6 / 0659 12.7 / TH 1343 1.8 / ○ 1922 12.6	**23** 0105 1.8 / 0644 13.0 / F 1329 1.5 / ● 1909 13.1
9 0200 1.6 / 0736 12.6 / F 1421 2.0 / 1959 12.3	**24** 0156 1.5 / 0732 13.4 / SA 1421 1.3 / 1959 13.3
10 0236 1.9 / 0811 12.4 / SA 1454 2.3 / 2033 12.0	**25** 0245 1.4 / 0821 13.5 / SU 1510 1.2 / 2048 13.3
11 0304 2.2 / 0844 12.1 / SU 1519 2.6 / 2106 11.7	**26** 0331 1.4 / 0909 13.4 / M 1557 1.3 / 2137 13.0
12 0327 2.5 / 0915 11.7 / M 1542 2.8 / 2137 11.3	**27** 0415 1.6 / 0957 13.1 / TU 1642 1.5 / 2224 12.7
13 0352 2.7 / 0946 11.4 / TU 1609 2.9 / 2209 10.9	**28** 0456 1.9 / 1045 12.7 / W 1725 1.8 / 2311 12.1
14 0423 2.9 / 1019 11.0 / W 1644 3.1 / 2245 10.6	**29** 0538 2.3 / 1135 12.1 / TH 1808 2.3
15 0500 3.2 / 1100 10.6 / TH 1726 3.4 / 2330 10.2	**30** 0001 11.5 / 0623 2.8 / F 1231 11.5 / 1856 2.7
	31 0059 10.9 / 0714 3.2 / SA 1336 11.1 / 1949 3.1

Chart Datum: 6·50 metres below Ordnance Datum (Newlyn)
HAT is 14·7m above Chart Datum

TIDES

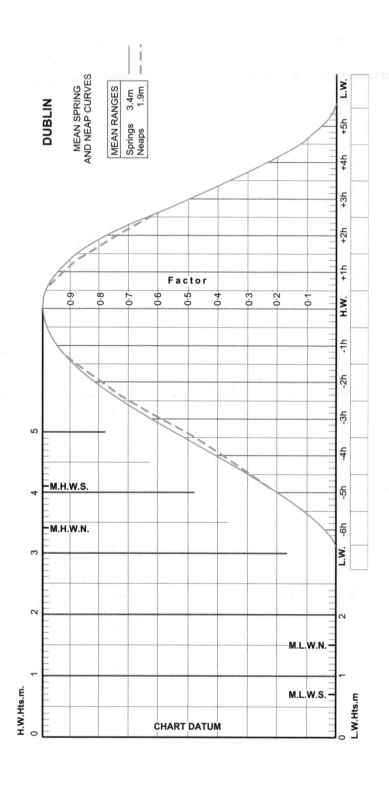

DUBLIN

MEAN SPRING
AND NEAP CURVES

MEAN RANGES	
Springs	3.4m
Neaps	1.9m

Factor

0·9
0·8
0·7
0·6
0·5
0·4
0·3
0·2
0·1

L.W.
+5h
+4h
+3h
+2h
+1h
H.W.
-1h
-2h
-3h
-4h
-5h
-6h
L.W.

H.W.Hts.m.
5
M.H.W.S.
4
M.H.W.N.
3
2
1
0
CHART DATUM

L.W.Hts.m
2
M.L.W.N.
1
M.L.W.S.
0

IRELAND – DUBLIN (NORTH WALL)
LAT 53°21'N   LONG 6°13'W
TIMES AND HEIGHTS OF HIGH AND LOW WATERS

Dates in amber are **SPRINGS**
Dates in grey are **NEAPS**

2022

JANUARY

Day	Time	m	Time	m	Time	m	Time	m
1 SA	0324	0.8	1000	4.0	1547	0.8	2228	4.1
16 SU	0420	1.3	1050	3.8	1643	1.1	2309	3.6
2 SU	0414	0.7	1050	4.2	1638	0.6	2321	4.1
17 M	0452	1.2	1125	3.9	1717	1.1	2343	3.7
3 M	0501	0.6	1137	4.3	1727	0.5		
18 TU	0521	1.1	1157	3.9	1748	1.0		
4 TU	0011	4.1	0547	0.7	1224	4.4	1817	0.4
19 W	0015	3.7	0549	1.1	1227	4.0	1819	0.9
5 W	0102	4.1	0632	0.7	1312	4.3	1907	0.5
20 TH	0048	3.7	0619	1.0	1302	4.0	1851	0.8
6 TH	0153	3.9	0720	0.9	1401	4.2	1958	0.6
21 F	0124	3.7	0654	1.0	1340	4.0	1928	0.8
7 F	0246	3.8	0810	1.0	1453	4.1	2051	0.7
22 SA	0204	3.7	0733	1.0	1422	4.0	2010	0.8
8 SA	0341	3.6	0903	1.2	1548	4.0	2145	0.9
23 SU	0248	3.7	0817	1.0	1506	3.9	2056	0.8
9 SU	0438	3.5	1000	1.4	1645	3.8	2242	1.1
24 M	0335	3.7	0905	1.1	1553	3.9	2146	0.9
10 M	0539	3.4	1101	1.5	1747	3.6	2342	1.3
25 TU	0427	3.6	0959	1.2	1645	3.8	2242	1.0
11 TU	0640	3.4	1206	1.6	1851	3.5		
26 W	0525	3.5	1101	1.3	1746	3.7	2347	1.1
12 W	0049	1.4	0741	3.4	1316	1.6	1954	3.5
27 TH	0631	3.5	1213	1.4	1857	3.6		
13 TH	0158	1.5	0837	3.5	1423	1.5	2053	3.5
28 F	0100	1.2	0743	3.5	1330	1.3	2014	3.6
14 F	0257	1.4	0927	3.6	1520	1.4	2146	3.5
29 SA	0212	1.1	0850	3.7	1442	1.1	2125	3.7
15 SA	0343	1.4	1011	3.7	1605	1.3	2230	3.6
30 SU	0316	1.0	0949	3.8	1543	0.9	2226	3.9
31 M	0409	0.8	1042	4.1	1636	0.6	2318	4.0

FEBRUARY

Day	Time	m	Time	m	Time	m	Time	m
1 TU	0455	0.7	1129	4.2	1723	0.4		
16 W	0500	1.0	1134	3.9	1722	0.8	2352	3.7
2 W	0005	4.0	0537	0.6	1212	4.3	1807	0.3
17 TH	0526	0.9	1204	4.0	1751	0.6		
3 TH	0049	4.0	0618	0.6	1255	4.3	1850	0.4
18 F	0022	3.8	0555	0.8	1236	4.0	1823	0.5
4 F	0131	3.9	0659	0.7	1338	4.2	1934	0.5
19 SA	0055	3.9	0628	0.7	1312	4.1	1859	0.5
5 SA	0214	3.8	0742	0.8	1422	4.1	2018	0.6
20 SU	0133	3.9	0706	0.7	1353	4.1	1940	0.5
6 SU	0257	3.6	0829	0.9	1508	3.9	2104	0.8
21 M	0215	3.9	0748	0.7	1436	4.0	2024	0.6
7 M	0344	3.5	0919	1.1	1557	3.7	2153	1.1
22 TU	0300	3.8	0835	0.8	1523	3.9	2113	0.8
8 TU	0437	3.3	1014	1.3	1652	3.5	2245	1.3
23 W	0350	3.7	0928	1.0	1616	3.7	2209	1.0
9 W	0539	3.2	1116	1.5	1759	3.3	2346	1.6
24 TH	0447	3.5	1031	1.2	1719	3.6	2316	1.2
10 TH	0646	3.2	1225	1.6	1911	3.2		
25 F	0558	3.4	1132	1.3	1841	3.4		
11 F	0100	1.7	0752	3.3	1347	1.6	2019	3.2
26 SA	0038	1.4	0722	3.4	1320	1.3	2011	3.4
12 SA	0228	1.6	0851	3.4	1459	1.4	2120	3.3
27 SU	0204	1.3	0839	3.6	1440	1.1	2125	3.6
13 SU	0324	1.5	0943	3.6	1547	1.3	2209	3.4
28 M	0312	1.1	0943	3.8	1542	0.8	2226	3.8
14 M	0402	1.3	1026	3.7	1623	1.1	2249	3.5
15 TU	0433	1.2	1103	3.8	1654	0.9	2323	3.6

MARCH

Day	Time	m	Time	m	Time	m	Time	m
1 TU	0403	0.9	1036	4.0	1630	0.5	2315	3.9
16 W	0406	1.1	1035	3.8	1623	0.7	2257	3.7
2 W	0446	0.7	1121	4.1	1712	0.4	2356	3.9
17 TH	0432	0.9	1106	3.9	1651	0.5	2324	3.8
3 TH	0524	0.6	1200	4.2	1751	0.3		
18 F	0459	0.7	1136	4.0	1721	0.4	2353	3.9
4 F	0031	3.9	0600	0.5	1235	4.2	1829	0.3
19 SA	0528	0.5	1208	4.1	1754	0.3		
5 SA	0104	3.8	0636	0.5	1311	4.1	1906	0.4
20 SU	0025	4.0	0602	0.4	1245	4.1	1831	0.3
6 SU	0137	3.7	0714	0.6	1350	4.0	1944	0.6
21 M	0102	4.0	0640	0.4	1326	4.1	1912	0.4
7 M	0213	3.6	0756	0.7	1431	3.8	2023	0.8
22 TU	0144	4.0	0724	0.5	1412	4.0	1957	0.5
8 TU	0253	3.5	0841	0.9	1514	3.6	2105	1.1
23 W	0231	3.9	0813	0.6	1502	3.9	2049	0.8
9 W	0336	3.4	0932	1.1	1603	3.4	2153	1.3
24 TH	0322	3.7	0910	0.9	1559	3.7	2148	1.1
10 TH	0430	3.2	1032	1.4	1706	3.2	2253	1.6
25 F	0422	3.5	1019	1.1	1710	3.4	2259	1.3
11 F	0547	3.1	1142	1.5	1830	3.0		
26 SA	0538	3.4	1145	1.2	1843	3.3		
12 SA	0006	1.8	0709	3.1	1302	1.6	1948	3.0
27 SU	0026	1.5	0710	3.4	1317	1.2	2011	3.4
13 SU	0143	1.8	0817	3.2	1427	1.4	2053	3.2
28 M	0154	1.4	0829	3.5	1434	1.0	2123	3.6
14 M	0257	1.6	0914	3.4	1518	1.2	2145	3.4
29 TU	0300	1.2	0933	3.8	1530	0.7	2219	3.7
15 TU	0336	1.3	0959	3.6	1554	0.9	2225	3.5
30 W	0348	0.9	1026	3.9	1615	0.5	2304	3.8
31 TH	0429	0.7	1109	4.0	1654	0.4	2341	3.8

APRIL

Day	Time	m	Time	m	Time	m	Time	m
1 F	0505	0.6	1145	4.1	1730	0.4		
16 SA	0427	0.6	1106	4.0	1651	0.2	2322	4.0
2 SA	0010	3.8	0540	0.5	1215	4.0	1805	0.4
17 SU	0501	0.4	1142	4.1	1726	0.2	2357	4.1
3 SU	0035	3.8	0614	0.5	1247	4.0	1838	0.5
18 M	0538	0.3	1222	4.2	1805	0.2		
4 M	0104	3.7	0650	0.6	1323	3.9	1911	0.7
19 TU	0037	4.1	0620	0.3	1307	4.1	1849	0.4
5 TU	0138	3.7	0729	0.7	1402	3.7	1946	0.9
20 W	0121	4.0	0707	0.4	1356	4.0	1938	0.6
6 W	0215	3.6	0811	0.9	1444	3.6	2025	1.1
21 TH	0211	3.9	0802	0.6	1452	3.8	2033	0.9
7 TH	0256	3.5	0900	1.1	1530	3.4	2109	1.3
22 F	0306	3.8	0906	0.8	1556	3.6	2137	1.2
8 F	0343	3.3	0958	1.3	1627	3.1	2208	1.6
23 SA	0410	3.6	1020	1.0	1714	3.4	2250	1.4
9 SA	0446	3.1	1106	1.4	1748	3.0	2325	1.8
24 SU	0531	3.5	1141	1.1	1840	3.4		
10 SU	0620	3.1	1221	1.5	1912	3.0		
25 M	0011	1.5	0657	3.5	1303	1.0	2000	3.4
11 M	0048	1.8	0738	3.1	1336	1.5	2019	3.1
26 TU	0131	1.4	0811	3.6	1413	0.9	2106	3.6
12 TU	0206	1.6	0837	3.3	1433	1.1	2111	3.3
27 W	0234	1.2	0914	3.8	1507	0.7	2159	3.7
13 W	0253	1.3	0923	3.5	1513	0.8	2151	3.5
28 TH	0323	1.0	1006	3.9	1552	0.6	2243	3.7
14 TH	0327	1.1	1000	3.7	1546	0.6	2223	3.7
29 F	0406	0.8	1050	3.9	1631	0.5	2319	3.8
15 F	0357	0.8	1033	3.9	1617	0.4	2251	3.9
30 SA	0444	0.7	1126	3.9	1707	0.6	2347	3.7

Chart Datum: 0·20 metres above Ordnance Datum (Dublin)
HAT is 4·5m above Chart Datum

TIDES

TIME ZONE (UT)	IRELAND – DUBLIN (NORTH WALL)	Dates in amber are SPRINGS
For Summer Time add ONE hour in **non-shaded areas**	LAT 53°21′N LONG 6°13′W	Dates in grey are NEAPS

TIMES AND HEIGHTS OF HIGH AND LOW WATERS

2022

MAY

Time	m	Time	m
1 SU	0519 0.7 / 1156 3.9 / 1740 0.6	**16** M	0436 0.4 / 1120 4.1 / 1703 0.3 / ○ 2335 4.1
2 M	0010 3.7 / 0555 0.7 / 1227 3.8 / 1812 0.7	**17** TU	0519 0.4 / 1206 4.1 / 1746 0.4
3 TU	0038 3.7 / 0631 0.7 / 1301 3.8 / 1844 0.9	**18** W	0018 4.1 / 0606 0.4 / 1256 4.1 / 1833 0.5
4 W	0112 3.7 / 0709 0.8 / 1339 3.7 / 1917 1.0	**19** TH	0106 4.1 / 0659 0.5 / 1350 4.0 / 1925 0.7
5 TH	0149 3.7 / 0751 0.9 / 1421 3.5 / 1955 1.2	**20** F	0159 4.0 / 0759 0.6 / 1450 3.8 / 2022 1.0
6 F	0230 3.6 / 0837 1.1 / 1507 3.4 / 2039 1.3	**21** SA	0258 3.9 / 0904 0.7 / 1556 3.6 / 2126 1.2
7 SA	0316 3.4 / 0932 1.2 / 1559 3.2 / 2134 1.5	**22** SU	0405 3.8 / 1014 0.9 / 1708 3.5 / ◔ 2233 1.4
8 SU	0412 3.3 / 1034 1.3 / 1706 3.1 / 2245 1.7	**23** M	0520 3.7 / 1126 0.9 / 1822 3.5 / 2345 1.4
9 M	0523 3.2 / 1140 1.3 / 1823 3.1 / ◔ 2359 1.7	**24** TU	0634 3.7 / 1237 0.9 / 1933 3.5
10 TU	0642 3.2 / 1244 1.2 / 1931 3.2	**25** W	0055 1.4 / 0743 3.7 / 1341 0.9 / 2036 3.6
11 W	0105 1.6 / 0745 3.3 / 1339 1.1 / 2024 3.3	**26** TH	0159 1.3 / 0845 3.8 / 1437 0.9 / 2129 3.6
12 TH	0158 1.3 / 0835 3.5 / 1426 0.8 / 2106 3.5	**27** F	0253 1.2 / 0938 3.8 / 1525 0.8 / 2214 3.7
13 F	0241 1.1 / 0917 3.7 / 1506 0.6 / 2143 3.7	**28** SA	0340 1.0 / 1025 3.8 / 1607 0.8 / 2251 3.7
14 SA	0319 0.8 / 0957 3.9 / 1544 0.4 / 2218 3.9	**29** SU	0422 0.9 / 1103 3.8 / 1644 0.9 / 2322 3.7
15 SU	0356 0.6 / 1038 4.0 / 1623 0.3 / 2255 4.0	**30** M	0501 0.9 / 1137 3.7 / ● 2349 3.7
		31 TU	0538 0.9 / 1209 3.7 / 1750 1.0

JUNE

Time	m	Time	m
1 W	0018 3.8 / 0615 0.9 / 1243 3.7 / 1822 1.0	**16** TH	0007 4.2 / 0559 0.4 / 1249 4.1 / 1821 0.6
2 TH	0052 3.8 / 0653 0.9 / 1320 3.6 / 1855 1.1	**17** F	0056 4.2 / 0653 0.5 / 1344 4.0 / 1913 0.8
3 F	0129 3.7 / 0733 1.0 / 1401 3.5 / 1932 1.2	**18** SA	0150 4.1 / 0751 0.5 / 1442 3.8 / 2007 1.0
4 SA	0209 3.7 / 0816 1.1 / 1445 3.4 / 2014 1.3	**19** SU	0247 4.1 / 0853 0.6 / 1543 3.7 / 2106 1.1
5 SU	0255 3.6 / 0904 1.1 / 1533 3.3 / 2103 1.4	**20** M	0349 4.0 / 0955 0.7 / 1646 3.6 / 2207 1.3
6 M	0344 3.5 / 0958 1.2 / 1626 3.3 / 2200 1.5	**21** TU	0455 3.9 / 1057 0.9 / 1750 3.5 / ◔ 2310 1.4
7 TU	0440 3.4 / 1054 1.2 / 1726 3.2 / ◔ 2303 1.5	**22** W	0602 3.8 / 1201 1.0 / 1854 3.5
8 W	0540 3.4 / 1152 1.1 / 1828 3.3	**23** TH	0014 1.4 / 0708 3.7 / 1303 1.1 / 1955 3.5
9 TH	0005 1.5 / 0643 3.5 / 1247 1.0 / 1926 3.4	**24** F	0120 1.4 / 0809 3.7 / 1403 1.1 / 2051 3.5
10 F	0102 1.4 / 0741 3.6 / 1340 0.9 / 2017 3.6	**25** SA	0221 1.3 / 0906 3.7 / 1456 1.1 / 2139 3.6
11 SA	0154 1.2 / 0835 3.7 / 1428 0.7 / 2104 3.7	**26** SU	0315 1.2 / 0957 3.7 / 1542 1.1 / 2221 3.7
12 SU	0243 0.9 / 0926 3.9 / 1515 0.6 / 2149 3.9	**27** M	0403 1.2 / 1040 3.6 / 1622 1.1 / 2256 3.7
13 M	0330 0.7 / 1016 4.0 / 1601 0.5 / 2234 4.0	**28** TU	0445 1.1 / 1117 3.6 / 1658 1.1 / 2328 3.8
14 TU	0418 0.6 / 1107 4.1 / 1646 0.5 / ○ 2320 4.1	**29** W	0523 1.0 / 1151 3.6 / 1731 1.1 / ●
15 W	0507 0.5 / 1157 4.1 / 1733 0.5	**30** TH	0000 3.8 / 0600 1.0 / 1225 3.6 / 1802 1.1

JULY

Time	m	Time	m
1 F	0032 3.8 / 0635 1.0 / 1300 3.6 / 1833 1.1	**16** SA	0044 4.3 / 0643 0.4 / 1330 4.0 / 1856 0.7
2 SA	0108 3.8 / 0710 1.0 / 1338 3.6 / 1907 1.1	**17** SU	0133 4.2 / 0735 0.4 / 1422 3.9 / 1945 0.8
3 SU	0146 3.8 / 0748 1.0 / 1418 3.6 / 1946 1.2	**18** M	0225 4.2 / 0829 0.5 / 1515 3.7 / 2037 1.0
4 M	0229 3.8 / 0829 1.0 / 1502 3.5 / 2030 1.2	**19** TU	0319 4.0 / 0924 0.7 / 1609 3.6 / 2132 1.1
5 TU	0314 3.7 / 0915 1.0 / 1549 3.5 / 2118 1.3	**20** W	0417 3.9 / 1019 0.9 / 1707 3.5 / ◔ 2229 1.3
6 W	0402 3.7 / 1005 1.0 / 1639 3.4 / 2210 1.3	**21** TH	0519 3.7 / 1117 1.1 / 1807 3.4 / 2331 1.4
7 TH	0455 3.6 / 1100 1.0 / 1734 3.4 / ◔ 2308 1.4	**22** F	0625 3.6 / 1218 1.3 / 1908 3.4
8 F	0553 3.6 / 1158 1.0 / 1834 3.4	**23** SA	0037 1.5 / 0731 3.5 / 1324 1.4 / 2008 3.4
9 SA	0010 1.3 / 0656 3.6 / 1258 1.0 / 1935 3.5	**24** SU	0150 1.5 / 0833 3.5 / 1428 1.4 / 2103 3.5
10 SU	0114 1.3 / 0802 3.7 / 1357 1.0 / 2034 3.7	**25** M	0256 1.4 / 0930 3.5 / 1521 1.4 / 2151 3.6
11 M	0216 1.1 / 0905 3.8 / 1453 0.9 / 2129 3.8	**26** TU	0348 1.3 / 1018 3.5 / 1604 1.3 / 2232 3.7
12 TU	0314 0.9 / 1004 3.9 / 1546 0.8 / 2221 4.0	**27** W	0430 1.1 / 1058 3.6 / 1640 1.2 / 2308 3.8
13 W	0409 0.7 / 1058 4.0 / 1635 0.7 / ○ 2309 4.2	**28** TH	0506 1.0 / 1133 3.6 / 1711 1.1 / ● 2340 3.9
14 TH	0501 0.5 / 1150 4.1 / 1722 0.6 / 2356 4.3	**29** F	0539 1.0 / 1205 3.6 / 1740 1.1
15 F	0552 0.4 / 1240 4.0 / 1808 0.7	**30** SA	0010 3.9 / 0610 0.9 / 1237 3.7 / 1808 1.0
		31 SU	0043 3.9 / 0640 0.8 / 1310 3.7 / 1839 1.0

AUGUST

Time	m	Time	m
1 M	0119 3.9 / 0713 0.8 / 1347 3.7 / 1915 1.0	**16** TU	0153 4.2 / 0757 0.5 / 1436 3.7 / 2003 0.9
2 TU	0158 3.9 / 0751 0.8 / 1428 3.7 / 1955 1.0	**17** W	0240 4.0 / 0845 0.7 / 1522 3.6 / 2053 1.0
3 W	0241 3.9 / 0835 0.8 / 1512 3.7 / 2040 1.0	**18** TH	0331 3.8 / 0934 1.0 / 1612 3.4 / 2148 1.2
4 TH	0326 3.8 / 0922 0.9 / 1559 3.6 / 2129 1.1	**19** F	0428 3.6 / 1027 1.3 / 1711 3.3 / ◔ 2248 1.3
5 F	0416 3.7 / 1015 1.0 / 1651 3.5 / 2225 1.3	**20** SA	0537 3.4 / 1126 1.5 / 1818 3.3 / 2357 1.6
6 SA	0514 3.6 / 1115 1.1 / 1753 3.4 / 2331 1.3	**21** SU	0652 3.3 / 1237 1.7 / 1926 3.3
7 SU	0623 3.5 / 1224 1.2 / 1903 3.5	**22** M	0119 1.6 / 0804 3.3 / 1400 1.7 / 2030 3.4
8 M	0047 1.4 / 0743 3.5 / 1336 1.2 / 2014 3.6	**23** TU	0240 1.5 / 0908 3.4 / 1503 1.5 / 2124 3.6
9 TU	0204 1.2 / 0857 3.7 / 1443 1.1 / 2117 3.8	**24** W	0333 1.3 / 0959 3.5 / 1546 1.4 / 2209 3.7
10 W	0311 1.0 / 0959 3.8 / 1540 0.9 / 2211 4.0	**25** TH	0412 1.1 / 1039 3.6 / 1619 1.2 / 2246 3.9
11 TH	0408 0.7 / 1053 4.0 / 1628 0.8 / 2259 4.2	**26** F	0444 0.9 / 1113 3.7 / 1648 1.1 / 2317 3.9
12 F	0457 0.4 / 1142 4.0 / 1711 0.6 / ○ 2343 4.3	**27** SA	0512 0.8 / 1142 3.7 / 1714 0.9 / ● 2345 4.0
13 SA	0542 0.3 / 1227 4.0 / 1753 0.6	**28** SU	0538 0.7 / 1210 3.8 / 1740 0.8
14 SU	0026 4.3 / 0627 0.3 / 1309 4.0 / 1834 0.6	**29** M	0014 4.0 / 0606 0.6 / 1240 3.8 / 1810 0.8
15 M	0109 4.3 / 0711 0.4 / 1352 3.8 / 1917 0.7	**30** TU	0048 4.1 / 0639 0.6 / 1315 3.8 / 1845 0.8
		31 W	0126 4.1 / 0716 0.6 / 1354 3.8 / 1924 0.8

Chart Datum: 0·20 metres above Ordnance Datum (Dublin)
HAT is 4·5m above Chart Datum

IRELAND – DUBLIN (NORTH WALL)
LAT 53°21′N LONG 6°13′W
TIMES AND HEIGHTS OF HIGH AND LOW WATERS

Dates in amber are **SPRINGS**
Dates in grey are **NEAPS**

2022

SEPTEMBER

Date	Time	m		Date	Time	m
1 TH	0208 / 0759 / 1437 / 2007	4.0 / 0.7 / 3.8 / 0.9		**16** F	0251 / 0849 / 1522 / 2111	3.8 / 1.1 / 3.5 / 1.2
2 F	0253 / 0846 / 1523 / 2057	3.9 / 0.9 / 3.7 / 1.0		**17** SA ☽	0343 / 0941 / 1615 / 2212	3.5 / 1.4 / 3.4 / 1.4
3 SA ☽	0345 / 0940 / 1617 / 2156	3.7 / 1.1 / 3.6 / 1.2		**18** SU	0450 / 1041 / 1727 / 2321	3.3 / 1.6 / 3.3 / 1.6
4 SU	0446 / 1045 / 1721 / 2309	3.6 / 1.3 / 3.4 / 1.4		**19** M	0616 / 1153 / 1847	3.1 / 1.8 / 3.3
5 M	0606 / 1204 / 1842	3.4 / 1.4 / 3.4		**20** TU	0045 / 0735 / 1325 / 1957	1.6 / 3.1 / 1.8 / 3.4
6 TU	0040 / 0740 / 1327 / 2003	1.4 / 3.4 / 1.4 / 3.6		**21** W	0215 / 0844 / 1437 / 2056	1.5 / 3.3 / 1.6 / 3.5
7 W	0206 / 0857 / 1438 / 2109	1.2 / 3.6 / 1.2 / 3.8		**22** TH	0307 / 0936 / 1520 / 2142	1.2 / 3.5 / 1.4 / 3.7
8 TH	0313 / 0959 / 1533 / 2203	0.9 / 3.8 / 1.0 / 4.0		**23** F	0343 / 1014 / 1552 / 2219	1.0 / 3.6 / 1.2 / 3.9
9 F	0404 / 1049 / 1618 / 2248	0.6 / 3.9 / 0.8 / 4.2		**24** SA	0413 / 1047 / 1620 / 2250	0.8 / 3.7 / 1.0 / 4.0
10 SA ○	0447 / 1132 / 1657 / 2329	0.4 / 4.0 / 0.6 / 4.3		**25** SU ●	0439 / 1114 / 1645 / 2317	0.6 / 3.8 / 0.8 / 4.1
11 SU	0527 / 1210 / 1734	0.3 / 4.0 / 0.6		**26** M	0505 / 1140 / 1711 / 2346	0.5 / 3.9 / 0.7 / 4.1
12 M	0005 / 0605 / 1244 / 1812	4.3 / 0.3 / 3.9 / 0.6		**27** TU	0534 / 1209 / 1741	0.5 / 4.0 / 0.6
13 TU	0043 / 0643 / 1319 / 1850	4.3 / 0.4 / 3.8 / 0.6		**28** W	0019 / 0607 / 1243 / 1817	4.2 / 0.5 / 4.0 / 0.6
14 W	0122 / 0722 / 1356 / 1932	4.1 / 0.6 / 3.8 / 0.8		**29** TH	0057 / 0645 / 1323 / 1857	4.1 / 0.5 / 4.0 / 0.7
15 TH	0205 / 0804 / 1437 / 2019	4.0 / 0.7 / 3.6 / 1.0		**30** F	0141 / 0728 / 1407 / 1943	4.1 / 0.7 / 3.9 / 0.8

OCTOBER

Date	Time	m		Date	Time	m
1 SA	0229 / 0818 / 1456 / 2037	3.9 / 0.9 / 3.8 / 1.0		**16** SU	0312 / 0900 / 1534 / 2142	3.5 / 1.5 / 3.5 / 1.4
2 SU	0326 / 0916 / 1553 / 2143	3.7 / 1.2 / 3.6 / 1.2		**17** M ☽	0414 / 1002 / 1639 / 2250	3.2 / 1.7 / 3.3 / 1.5
3 M ☽	0435 / 1028 / 1702 / 2306	3.5 / 1.5 / 3.5 / 1.4		**18** TU	0539 / 1116 / 1804	3.1 / 1.9 / 3.3
4 TU	0608 / 1154 / 1830	3.4 / 1.6 / 3.5		**19** W	0005 / 0701 / 1237 / 1919	1.6 / 3.1 / 1.9 / 3.3
5 W	0040 / 0740 / 1318 / 1952	1.3 / 3.4 / 1.5 / 3.6		**20** TH	0127 / 0809 / 1353 / 2019	1.5 / 3.3 / 1.7 / 3.5
6 TH	0202 / 0854 / 1426 / 2058	1.1 / 3.6 / 1.3 / 3.9		**21** F	0225 / 0901 / 1441 / 2107	1.2 / 3.5 / 1.5 / 3.7
7 F	0302 / 0951 / 1518 / 2151	0.8 / 3.8 / 1.1 / 4.1		**22** SA	0304 / 0941 / 1516 / 2145	1.0 / 3.6 / 1.2 / 3.8
8 SA	0349 / 1037 / 1601 / 2236	0.6 / 3.9 / 0.8 / 4.2		**23** SU	0335 / 1014 / 1545 / 2217	0.8 / 3.8 / 1.0 / 4.0
9 SU	0430 / 1124 / 1639 / 2314	0.4 / 4.0 / 0.7 / 4.2		**24** M ○	0404 / 1042 / 1613 / 2246	0.6 / 3.9 / 0.8 / 4.1
10 M	0507 / 1151 / 1716 / 2348	0.4 / 4.0 / 0.6 / 4.2		**25** TU ●	0433 / 1109 / 1643 / 2319	0.5 / 4.0 / 0.7 / 4.2
11 TU	0542 / 1220 / 1751	0.4 / 3.9 / 0.6		**26** W	0505 / 1140 / 1717 / 2355	0.4 / 4.1 / 0.6 / 4.2
12 W	0021 / 0617 / 1250 / 1829	4.2 / 0.6 / 3.9 / 0.7		**27** TH	0541 / 1217 / 1755	0.5 / 4.1 / 0.6
13 TH	0058 / 0651 / 1325 / 1909	4.0 / 0.7 / 3.8 / 0.8		**28** F	0037 / 0621 / 1259 / 1840	4.2 / 0.6 / 4.1 / 0.6
14 F	0138 / 0729 / 1403 / 1953	3.9 / 1.0 / 3.8 / 1.0		**29** SA	0124 / 0707 / 1346 / 1931	4.0 / 0.8 / 4.0 / 0.8
15 SA	0222 / 0811 / 1445 / 2044	3.7 / 1.2 / 3.6 / 1.2		**30** SU	0218 / 0811 / 1440 / 2031	3.9 / 1.1 / 3.9 / 1.0
				31 M	0321 / 0904 / 1541 / 2142	3.7 / 1.3 / 3.8 / 1.2

NOVEMBER

Date	Time	m		Date	Time	m
1 TU ☽	0438 / 1018 / 1654 / 2303	3.5 / 1.5 / 3.7 / 1.2		**16** W ☾	0455 / 1035 / 1709 / 2321	3.2 / 1.8 / 3.4 / 1.5
2 W	0605 / 1139 / 1816	3.5 / 1.6 / 3.7		**17** TH	0612 / 1147 / 1823	3.2 / 1.8 / 3.4
3 TH	0027 / 0727 / 1257 / 1932	1.2 / 3.5 / 1.5 / 3.8		**18** F	0027 / 0719 / 1252 / 1926	1.4 / 3.3 / 1.8 / 3.4
4 F	0141 / 0835 / 1402 / 2037	1.0 / 3.7 / 1.4 / 3.9		**19** SA	0125 / 0813 / 1346 / 2017	1.3 / 3.4 / 1.6 / 3.6
5 SA	0239 / 0930 / 1454 / 2132	0.8 / 3.8 / 1.2 / 4.0		**20** SU	0213 / 0856 / 1429 / 2100	1.1 / 3.6 / 1.4 / 3.7
6 SU	0327 / 1017 / 1540 / 2219	0.7 / 3.9 / 1.0 / 4.1		**21** M	0252 / 0933 / 1506 / 2139	0.9 / 3.8 / 1.1 / 3.9
7 M	0409 / 1057 / 1620 / 2259	0.6 / 4.0 / 0.9 / 4.1		**22** TU	0328 / 1006 / 1541 / 2217	0.7 / 3.9 / 0.9 / 4.0
8 TU ○	0446 / 1131 / 1658 / 2333	0.6 / 4.0 / 0.8 / 4.1		**23** W ●	0404 / 1040 / 1618 / 2257	0.6 / 4.1 / 0.7 / 4.1
9 W	0521 / 1159 / 1735	0.7 / 4.0 / 0.8		**24** TH	0441 / 1117 / 1659 / 2340	0.5 / 4.2 / 0.6 / 4.2
10 TH	0005 / 0555 / 1228 / 1813	4.0 / 0.8 / 3.9 / 0.8		**25** F	0522 / 1159 / 1743	0.6 / 4.2 / 0.6
11 F	0041 / 0628 / 1302 / 1853	3.9 / 0.9 / 3.9 / 0.9		**26** SA	0027 / 0606 / 1244 / 1832	4.1 / 0.7 / 4.2 / 0.6
12 SA	0120 / 0703 / 1339 / 1935	3.8 / 1.1 / 3.9 / 1.0		**27** SU	0118 / 0655 / 1335 / 1927	4.0 / 0.9 / 4.2 / 0.7
13 SU	0202 / 0742 / 1421 / 2023	3.6 / 1.3 / 3.8 / 1.2		**28** M	0216 / 0750 / 1431 / 2028	3.9 / 1.1 / 4.1 / 0.8
14 M	0250 / 0828 / 1507 / 2116	3.5 / 1.5 / 3.6 / 1.3		**29** TU	0321 / 0852 / 1533 / 2136	3.7 / 1.3 / 4.0 / 1.0
15 TU	0345 / 0926 / 1601 / 2216	3.3 / 1.7 / 3.5 / 1.4		**30** W ☾	0432 / 1001 / 1641 / 2247	3.6 / 1.4 / 3.9 / 1.0

DECEMBER

Date	Time	m		Date	Time	m
1 TH	0546 / 1112 / 1753	3.6 / 1.5 / 3.8		**16** F ☾	0505 / 1042 / 1714 / 2325	3.3 / 1.7 / 3.5 / 1.3
2 F	0000 / 0658 / 1224 / 1903	1.1 / 3.6 / 1.5 / 3.8		**17** SA	0607 / 1146 / 1814	3.3 / 1.7 / 3.5
3 SA	0108 / 0803 / 1329 / 2008	1.0 / 3.7 / 1.4 / 3.9		**18** SU	0022 / 0708 / 1244 / 1914	1.3 / 3.4 / 1.6 / 3.5
4 SU	0209 / 0900 / 1427 / 2106	1.0 / 3.8 / 1.3 / 3.9		**19** M	0117 / 0801 / 1337 / 2010	1.2 / 3.5 / 1.5 / 3.6
5 M	0302 / 0950 / 1517 / 2158	0.9 / 3.8 / 1.2 / 3.9		**20** TU	0208 / 0849 / 1427 / 2103	1.1 / 3.7 / 1.3 / 3.8
6 TU	0347 / 1033 / 1603 / 2242	0.9 / 3.9 / 1.1 / 3.9		**21** W	0255 / 0933 / 1514 / 2154	0.9 / 3.9 / 1.0 / 3.9
7 W	0427 / 1110 / 1644 / 2320	0.9 / 3.9 / 1.0 / 3.9		**22** TH	0340 / 1017 / 1600 / 2243	0.8 / 4.0 / 0.8 / 4.0
8 TH	0504 / 1141 / 1724 / 2354	1.0 / 3.9 / 1.0 / 3.8		**23** F ●	0425 / 1102 / 1647 / 2332	0.7 / 4.2 / 0.7 / 4.1
9 F	0537 / 1212 / 1802	1.0 / 4.0 / 1.0		**24** SA	0509 / 1147 / 1736	0.7 / 4.3 / 0.5
10 SA	0028 / 0610 / 1244 / 1841	3.8 / 1.1 / 4.0 / 1.0		**25** SU	0022 / 0556 / 1234 / 1827	4.1 / 0.7 / 4.3 / 0.5
11 SU	0104 / 0644 / 1320 / 1920	3.7 / 1.2 / 3.9 / 1.0		**26** M	0114 / 0644 / 1325 / 1920	4.1 / 0.8 / 4.3 / 0.5
12 M	0144 / 0720 / 1359 / 2001	3.6 / 1.3 / 3.9 / 1.1		**27** TU	0209 / 0736 / 1419 / 2017	4.0 / 0.9 / 4.2 / 0.6
13 TU	0227 / 0800 / 1442 / 2046	3.5 / 1.4 / 3.8 / 1.3		**28** W	0308 / 0833 / 1516 / 2116	3.8 / 1.0 / 4.1 / 0.7
14 W	0314 / 0846 / 1528 / 2134	3.4 / 1.5 / 3.7 / 1.3		**29** TH	0409 / 0933 / 1617 / 2217	3.7 / 1.2 / 4.0 / 0.9
15 TH	0406 / 0940 / 1618 / 2228	3.3 / 1.6 / 3.5 / 1.3		**30** F ☾	0513 / 1037 / 1721 / 2321	3.6 / 1.4 / 3.9 / 1.0
				31 SA	0618 / 1143 / 1827	3.5 / 1.5 / 3.8

Chart Datum: 0·20 metres above Ordnance Datum (Dublin)
HAT is 4·5m above Chart Datum

TIDES

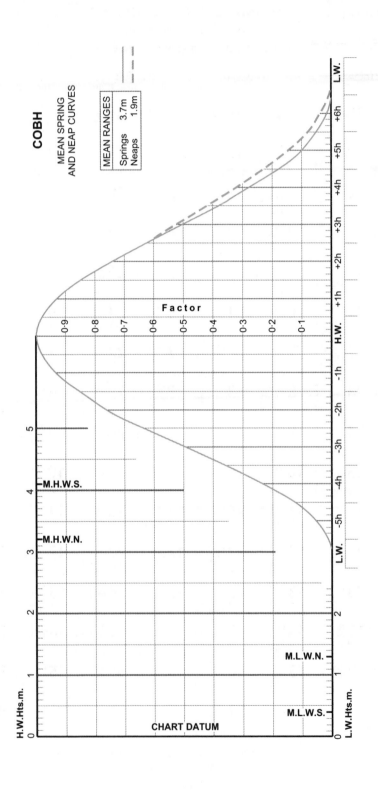

COBH

MEAN SPRING
AND NEAP CURVES

MEAN RANGES	
Springs	3.7m
Neaps	1.9m

IRELAND – COBH
LAT 51°51'N   LONG 8°18'W
TIMES AND HEIGHTS OF HIGH AND LOW WATERS

Dates in amber are **SPRINGS**
Dates in grey are **NEAPS**

2022

JANUARY

Day	Time	m	Day	Time	m
1 SA	0338 / 1017 / 1607 / 2245	4.0 / 0.7 / 4.0 / 0.6	16 SU	0426 / 1055 / 1645 / 2310	3.8 / 1.0 / 3.8 / 0.9
2 SU	0437 / 1113 / 1703 / ●2338	4.1 / 0.6 / 4.1 / 0.5	17 M	0508 / 1133 / 1725 / ○2345	3.9 / 0.9 / 3.9 / 0.8
3 M	0531 / 1205 / 1754	4.3 / 0.4 / 4.2	18 TU	0546 / 1207 / 1801	4.0 / 0.8 / 3.9
4 TU	0026 / 0621 / 1253 / 1842	0.4 / 4.3 / 0.4 / 4.1	19 W	0017 / 0621 / 1241 / 1834	0.8 / 4.0 / 0.8 / 3.9
5 W	0114 / 0709 / 1340 / 1929	0.4 / 4.3 / 0.5 / 4.1	20 TH	0050 / 0655 / 1315 / 1907	0.7 / 4.0 / 0.8 / 3.9
6 TH	0201 / 0756 / 1427 / 2014	0.4 / 4.2 / 0.6 / 3.9	21 F	0125 / 0729 / 1352 / 1942	0.8 / 4.0 / 0.8 / 3.9
7 F	0249 / 0843 / 1514 / 2100	0.6 / 4.0 / 0.7 / 3.8	22 SA	0204 / 0806 / 1430 / 2020	0.8 / 4.0 / 0.9 / 3.9
8 SA	0337 / 0931 / 1602 / 2146	0.7 / 3.8 / 0.9 / 3.6	23 SU	0245 / 0846 / 1511 / 2101	0.9 / 3.9 / 1.0 / 3.8
9 SU	0427 / 1019 / 1652 / ☽2235	0.9 / 3.7 / 1.1 / 3.5	24 M	0329 / 0929 / 1555 / 2147	0.9 / 3.8 / 1.1 / 3.7
10 M	0521 / 1112 / 1747 / 2330	1.1 / 3.5 / 1.2 / 3.3	25 TU	0417 / 1018 / 1645 / ☽2240	1.0 / 3.7 / 1.2 / 3.6
11 TU	0619 / 1210 / 1846	1.2 / 3.4 / 1.3	26 W	0514 / 1115 / 1747 / 2343	1.1 / 3.6 / 1.3 / 3.6
12 W	0033 / 0720 / 1312 / 1947	3.3 / 1.3 / 3.4 / 1.3	27 TH	0622 / 1221 / 1901	1.2 / 3.5 / 1.3
13 TH	0141 / 0821 / 1413 / 2046	3.3 / 1.3 / 3.4 / 1.3	28 F	0054 / 0738 / 1335 / 2020	3.5 / 1.2 / 3.5 / 1.2
14 F	0243 / 0918 / 1510 / 2141	3.4 / 1.2 / 3.5 / 1.2	29 SA	0210 / 0856 / 1450 / 2133	3.6 / 1.1 / 3.6 / 1.0
15 SA	0338 / 1010 / 1600 / 2229	3.6 / 1.1 / 3.7 / 1.0	30 SU	0325 / 1008 / 1559 / 2236	3.8 / 0.8 / 3.8 / 0.7
			31 M	0430 / 1107 / 1656 / 2329	4.0 / 0.6 / 3.9 / 0.5

FEBRUARY

Day	Time	m	Day	Time	m
1 TU	0523 / 1157 / 1746 ●	4.2 / 0.4 / 4.1	16 W	0528 / 1151 / 1745 ○	4.0 / 0.7 / 3.9
2 W	0016 / 0611 / 1242 / 1831	0.3 / 4.3 / 0.3 / 4.1	17 TH	0000 / 0603 / 1223 / 1818	0.6 / 4.0 / 0.6 / 4.0
3 TH	0100 / 0655 / 1325 / 1912	0.2 / 4.3 / 0.3 / 4.1	18 F	0031 / 0635 / 1256 / 1850	0.5 / 4.1 / 0.6 / 4.0
4 F	0143 / 0736 / 1406 / 1952	0.3 / 4.2 / 0.4 / 4.0	19 SA	0105 / 0708 / 1330 / 1922	0.5 / 4.1 / 0.6 / 4.0
5 SA	0224 / 0817 / 1445 / 2030	0.4 / 4.1 / 0.6 / 3.9	20 SU	0141 / 0742 / 1406 / 1957	0.5 / 4.0 / 0.6 / 4.0
6 SU	0305 / 0856 / 1525 / 2108	0.6 / 3.9 / 0.7 / 3.7	21 M	0220 / 0819 / 1443 / 2035	0.6 / 4.0 / 0.7 / 3.9
7 M	0345 / 0936 / 1604 / 2147	0.8 / 3.7 / 0.9 / 3.6	22 TU	0301 / 0900 / 1523 / 2117	0.7 / 3.9 / 0.9 / 3.8
8 TU	0428 / 1018 / 1647 / ☽2231	1.0 / 3.5 / 1.2 / 3.4	23 W	0347 / 0945 / 1610 / 2207	0.9 / 3.7 / 1.0 / 3.7
9 W	0517 / 1106 / 1740 / 2325	1.2 / 3.3 / 1.3 / 3.2	24 TH	0441 / 1040 / 1709 / 2309	1.0 / 3.5 / 1.2 / 3.5
10 TH	0617 / 1208 / 1845	1.4 / 3.2 / 1.4	25 F	0549 / 1150 / 1828	1.2 / 3.3 / 1.4
11 F	0037 / 0726 / 1325 / 1958	3.1 / 1.4 / 3.1 / 1.4	26 SA	0027 / 0713 / 1315 / 1959	3.3 / 1.3 / 3.2 / 1.3
12 SA	0203 / 0837 / 1439 / 2108	3.2 / 1.4 / 3.3 / 1.3	27 SU	0159 / 0845 / 1443 / 2123	3.4 / 1.1 / 3.3 / 1.0
13 SU	0312 / 0943 / 1539 / 2207	3.4 / 1.2 / 3.4 / 1.1	28 M	0321 / 1003 / 1554 / 2228	3.6 / 0.8 / 3.6 / 0.7
14 M	0406 / 1035 / 1628 / 2252	3.6 / 1.0 / 3.6 / 0.9			
15 TU	0450 / 1116 / 1709 / 2329	3.8 / 0.8 / 3.8 / 0.7			

MARCH

Day	Time	m	Day	Time	m
1 TU	0423 / 1059 / 1648 / 2319	3.9 / 0.5 / 3.9 / 0.4	16 W	0424 / 1049 / 1644 / 2302	3.7 / 0.7 / 3.7 / 0.6
2 W	0512 / 1145 / 1733 ●	4.1 / 0.3 / 4.1	17 TH	0501 / 1125 / 1720 / 2335	3.9 / 0.5 / 3.9 / 0.5
3 TH	0002 / 0555 / 1226 / 1814	0.2 / 4.2 / 0.2 / 4.1	18 F	0535 / 1158 / 1753 ○	4.0 / 0.4 / 4.0
4 F	0042 / 0634 / 1303 / 1851	0.2 / 4.3 / 0.2 / 4.1	19 SA	0006 / 0608 / 1231 / 1825	0.4 / 4.1 / 0.4 / 4.0
5 SA	0119 / 0710 / 1338 / 1925	0.2 / 4.2 / 0.3 / 4.0	20 SU	0041 / 0641 / 1305 / 1858	0.3 / 4.1 / 0.4 / 4.1
6 SU	0154 / 0745 / 1412 / 1958	0.3 / 4.1 / 0.5 / 3.9	21 M	0117 / 0717 / 1341 / 1933	0.3 / 4.1 / 0.4 / 4.0
7 M	0229 / 0820 / 1446 / 2030	0.5 / 3.9 / 0.6 / 3.8	22 TU	0157 / 0755 / 1420 / 2012	0.4 / 4.0 / 0.5 / 4.0
8 TU	0304 / 0854 / 1519 / 2105	0.7 / 3.8 / 0.9 / 3.6	23 W	0240 / 0836 / 1502 / 2055	0.5 / 3.8 / 0.7 / 3.8
9 W	0341 / 0930 / 1555 / 2145	0.9 / 3.5 / 1.1 / 3.4	24 TH	0327 / 0923 / 1550 / 2146	0.7 / 3.6 / 0.9 / 3.6
10 TH	0425 / 1012 / 1641 / ☽2233	1.2 / 3.3 / 1.3 / 3.2	25 F	0423 / 1019 / 1651 / ☽2250	1.0 / 3.4 / 1.1 / 3.4
11 F	0523 / 1106 / 1748 / 2339	1.4 / 3.1 / 1.5 / 3.0	26 SA	0533 / 1134 / 1813	1.2 / 3.1 / 1.3
12 SA	0637 / 1228 / 1911	1.5 / 2.9 / 1.5	27 SU	0016 / 0702 / 1309 / 1950	3.2 / 1.2 / 3.1 / 1.2
13 SU	0120 / 0756 / 1408 / 2031	3.0 / 1.4 / 3.0 / 1.4	28 M	0156 / 0841 / 1438 / 2115	3.3 / 1.0 / 3.3 / 0.9
14 M	0245 / 0909 / 1515 / 2137	3.2 / 1.2 / 3.3 / 1.1	29 TU	0312 / 0952 / 1543 / 2216	3.6 / 0.7 / 3.6 / 0.6
15 TU	0340 / 1006 / 1604 / 2225	3.5 / 0.9 / 3.5 / 0.8	30 W	0407 / 1044 / 1632 / 2303	3.9 / 0.4 / 3.8 / 0.3
			31 TH	0453 / 1126 / 1714 / 2344	4.1 / 0.3 / 4.0 / 0.2

APRIL

Day	Time	m	Day	Time	m
1 F	0533 / 1204 / 1752 ●	4.2 / 0.2 / 4.1	16 SA	0501 / 1127 / 1721 / ○2339	4.0 / 0.4 / 4.0 / 0.3
2 SA	0019 / 0609 / 1237 / 1826	0.2 / 4.2 / 0.2 / 4.1	17 SU	0538 / 1205 / 1757	4.1 / 0.3 / 4.1
3 SU	0053 / 0643 / 1309 / 1857	0.2 / 4.1 / 0.3 / 4.0	18 M	0017 / 0616 / 1242 / 1835	0.2 / 4.1 / 0.3 / 4.1
4 M	0124 / 0714 / 1340 / 1926	0.4 / 4.0 / 0.5 / 3.9	19 TU	0057 / 0655 / 1322 / 1915	0.2 / 4.1 / 0.3 / 4.1
5 TU	0156 / 0745 / 1410 / 1957	0.5 / 3.8 / 0.7 / 3.8	20 W	0140 / 0738 / 1405 / 1958	0.3 / 4.0 / 0.4 / 4.0
6 W	0228 / 0817 / 1440 / 2031	0.7 / 3.7 / 0.8 / 3.7	21 TH	0227 / 0823 / 1452 / 2045	0.5 / 3.8 / 0.6 / 3.8
7 TH	0303 / 0852 / 1515 / 2109	0.9 / 3.5 / 1.0 / 3.5	22 F	0318 / 0914 / 1545 / 2140	0.7 / 3.6 / 0.8 / 3.6
8 F	0345 / 0932 / 1559 / 2156	1.2 / 3.3 / 1.3 / 3.3	23 SA	0417 / 1014 / 1649 / ☽2248	0.9 / 3.3 / 1.0 / 3.4
9 SA	0441 / 1023 / 1703 / 2257	1.4 / 3.1 / 1.4 / 3.1	24 SU	0529 / 1130 / 1810	1.1 / 3.1 / 1.1
10 SU	0555 / 1135 / 1826	1.5 / 2.9 / 1.5	25 M	0015 / 0658 / 1300 / 1940	3.2 / 1.1 / 3.1 / 1.0
11 M	0025 / 0714 / 1319 / 1946	3.0 / 1.4 / 3.0 / 1.4	26 TU	0143 / 0824 / 1419 / 2055	3.4 / 0.9 / 3.3 / 0.8
12 TU	0201 / 0825 / 1435 / 2051	3.1 / 1.2 / 3.2 / 1.1	27 W	0250 / 0927 / 1518 / 2152	3.6 / 0.7 / 3.6 / 0.5
13 W	0300 / 0922 / 1526 / 2142	3.4 / 0.9 / 3.5 / 0.8	28 TH	0342 / 1018 / 1607 / 2239	3.8 / 0.5 / 3.8 / 0.4
14 TH	0345 / 1009 / 1607 / 2224	3.7 / 0.7 / 3.7 / 0.6	29 F	0427 / 1100 / 1649 / 2319	4.0 / 0.4 / 3.9 / 0.3
15 F	0424 / 1050 / 1645 / 2302	3.9 / 0.5 / 3.9 / 0.4	30 SA	0506 / 1137 / 1726 / ●2354	4.0 / 0.4 / 4.0 / 0.3

TIDES

Chart Datum: 0·13 metres above Ordnance Datum (Dublin)
HAT is 4·5m above Chart Datum

TIDES

IRELAND – COBH
LAT 51°51′N   LONG 8°18′W
TIMES AND HEIGHTS OF HIGH AND LOW WATERS

Dates in amber are **SPRINGS**
Dates in grey are **NEAPS**

2022

MAY

Day	Time m	Time m	Time m	Time m		Day	Time m	Time m	Time m	Time m
1 SU	0542 4.0	1210 0.4	1759 4.0			16 M	0510 4.1	1142 0.3	1733 4.1	2359 0.3
2 M	0026 0.4	0615 3.9	1241 0.5	1830 3.9		17 TU	0555 4.1	1227 0.3	1817 4.1	
3 TU	0056 0.5	0645 3.9	1310 0.6	1859 3.9		18 W	0044 0.3	0641 4.0	1311 0.3	1903 4.1
4 W	0126 0.7	0716 3.8	1339 0.7	1930 3.8		19 TH	0132 0.3	0728 3.9	1359 0.4	1951 4.0
5 TH	0158 0.8	0748 3.7	1411 0.9	2005 3.7		20 F	0222 0.4	0818 3.8	1450 0.5	2043 3.8
6 F	0234 1.0	0823 3.5	1447 1.0	2044 3.5		21 SA	0316 0.6	0912 3.6	1546 0.7	2140 3.6
7 SA	0317 1.2	0905 3.4	1532 1.2	2130 3.4		22 SU	0416 0.8	1012 3.4	1649 0.8	2246 3.5
8 SU	0411 1.2	0955 3.2	1631 1.3	2227 3.2		23 M	0524 0.9	1120 3.3	1801 0.9	
9 M	0518 1.4	1058 3.1	1744 1.4	2338 3.1		24 TU	0000 3.4	0641 0.9	1235 3.3	1917 0.9
10 TU	0630 1.3	1217 3.1	1857 1.3			25 W	0113 3.4	0752 0.9	1345 3.4	2023 0.8
11 W	0057 3.2	0737 1.2	1333 3.2	2001 1.1		26 TH	0215 3.6	0852 0.8	1443 3.5	2119 0.6
12 TH	0203 3.4	0834 1.0	1432 3.5	2055 0.9		27 F	0308 3.7	0943 0.7	1533 3.7	2207 0.6
13 F	0255 3.6	0925 0.7	1520 3.7	2143 0.6		28 SA	0354 3.8	1028 0.6	1617 3.8	2249 0.6
14 SA	0341 3.8	1012 0.6	1606 3.9	2229 0.5		29 SU	0436 3.8	1108 0.6	1657 3.8	2327 0.6
15 SU	0426 4.0	1058 0.4	1650 4.0	2314 0.3		30 M	0514 3.8	1143 0.6	1733 3.8	
						31 TU	0000 0.6	0549 3.8	1215 0.7	1806 3.8

JUNE

Day	Time m	Time m	Time m	Time m		Day	Time m	Time m	Time m	Time m
1 W	0030 0.7	0622 3.8	1245 0.7	1838 3.8		16 TH	0036 0.3	0631 4.0	1304 0.3	1856 4.1
2 TH	0101 0.8	0654 3.7	1316 0.8	1911 3.8		17 F	0126 0.3	0721 3.9	1354 0.3	1946 4.1
3 F	0135 0.9	0727 3.7	1350 0.9	1947 3.7		18 SA	0218 0.4	0812 3.8	1445 0.4	2038 3.9
4 SA	0213 1.0	0804 3.6	1429 1.0	2027 3.6		19 SU	0311 0.5	0904 3.7	1539 0.5	2132 3.8
5 SU	0256 1.1	0846 3.5	1513 1.1	2111 3.5		20 M	0406 0.7	0958 3.6	1635 0.7	2228 3.6
6 M	0345 1.2	0934 3.4	1605 1.2	2202 3.4		21 TU	0505 0.8	1055 3.4	1735 0.8	2328 3.5
7 TU	0442 1.2	1029 3.3	1704 1.2	2300 3.4		22 W	0607 0.9	1156 3.4	1839 0.9	
8 W	0544 1.2	1131 3.3	1808 1.2			23 TH	0031 3.4	0709 0.9	1259 3.3	1940 0.9
9 TH	0003 3.4	0649 1.2	1235 3.4	1912 1.1		24 F	0131 3.4	0808 0.9	1359 3.4	2037 0.9
10 F	0107 3.5	0748 1.0	1337 3.5	2010 0.9		25 SA	0227 3.5	0902 0.9	1453 3.5	2130 0.8
11 SA	0206 3.6	0845 0.9	1435 3.7	2106 0.7		26 SU	0318 3.6	0953 0.9	1544 3.6	2218 0.8
12 SU	0301 3.8	0940 0.7	1529 3.8	2201 0.6		27 M	0405 3.6	1038 0.8	1630 3.7	2300 0.8
13 M	0355 3.9	1033 0.5	1623 4.0	2255 0.4		28 TU	0449 3.7	1119 0.8	1711 3.8	2337 0.8
14 TU	0448 4.0	1125 0.4	1715 4.1	2346 0.3		29 W	0528 3.7	1154 0.8	1748 3.8	
15 W	0540 4.0	1215 0.3	1805 4.1			30 TH	0009 0.8	0605 3.7	1226 0.8	1823 3.8

JULY

Day	Time m	Time m	Time m	Time m		Day	Time m	Time m	Time m	Time m
1 F	0042 0.8	0639 3.7	1258 0.8	1857 3.8		16 SA	0117 0.3	0710 4.0	1342 0.2	1934 4.1
2 SA	0117 0.9	0713 3.7	1332 0.8	1932 3.8		17 SU	0205 0.3	0758 3.9	1430 0.3	2022 4.0
3 SU	0154 0.9	0749 3.7	1410 0.9	2010 3.7		18 M	0253 0.4	0845 3.8	1518 0.4	2109 3.9
4 M	0235 1.0	0828 3.6	1452 0.9	2050 3.7		19 TU	0341 0.6	0931 3.7	1606 0.6	2156 3.7
5 TU	0318 1.0	0911 3.6	1536 1.0	2135 3.6		20 W	0430 0.7	1018 3.5	1655 0.7	2245 3.6
6 W	0405 1.1	0958 3.5	1625 1.0	2224 3.6		21 TH	0521 0.9	1108 3.4	1749 0.9	2339 3.4
7 TH	0457 1.1	1051 3.5	1720 1.1	2319 3.6		22 F	0616 1.1	1205 3.3	1847 1.1	
8 F	0556 1.1	1149 3.5	1823 1.1			23 SA	0039 3.3	0716 1.2	1309 3.2	1949 1.1
9 SA	0020 3.5	0702 1.1	1252 3.5	1929 1.0		24 SU	0143 3.3	0818 1.2	1415 3.3	2050 1.1
10 SU	0125 3.6	0808 1.0	1357 3.6	2035 0.9		25 M	0244 3.3	0918 1.1	1515 3.4	2148 1.1
11 M	0230 3.6	0913 0.9	1502 3.7	2141 0.8		26 TU	0339 3.5	1013 1.0	1607 3.6	2237 0.9
12 TU	0333 3.7	1015 0.7	1605 3.9	2242 0.6		27 W	0428 3.6	1059 0.9	1653 3.7	2318 0.8
13 W	0434 3.9	1113 0.5	1703 4.0	2337 0.4		28 TH	0511 3.7	1136 0.8	1732 3.8	2352 0.8
14 TH	0530 4.0	1205 0.3	1756 4.1			29 F	0549 3.8	1208 0.7	1808 3.9	
15 F	0028 0.3	0621 4.0	1254 0.2	1846 4.2		30 SA	0024 0.7	0623 3.8	1239 0.7	1841 3.9
						31 SU	0057 0.7	0656 3.8	1311 0.7	1913 3.9

AUGUST

Day	Time m	Time m	Time m	Time m		Day	Time m	Time m	Time m	Time m
1 M	0132 0.8	0729 3.8	1346 0.7	1947 3.9		16 TU	0224 0.4	0815 3.9	1446 0.4	2036 3.9
2 TU	0209 0.8	0804 3.7	1424 0.8	2023 3.8		17 W	0305 0.5	0855 3.8	1527 0.6	2116 3.8
3 W	0247 0.9	0842 3.7	1505 0.8	2103 3.8		18 TH	0346 0.6	0934 3.6	1609 0.8	2157 3.6
4 TH	0328 0.9	0924 3.7	1548 0.9	2147 3.7		19 F	0430 1.0	1017 3.4	1655 1.0	2243 3.3
5 F	0413 1.0	1012 3.6	1638 1.0	2239 3.6		20 SA	0520 1.2	1108 3.2	1751 1.3	2341 3.2
6 SA	0508 1.1	1108 3.5	1739 1.1	2340 3.5		21 SU	0622 1.3	1217 3.1	1858 1.4	
7 SU	0617 1.2	1216 3.4	1853 1.2			22 M	0058 3.1	0735 1.4	1342 3.1	2012 1.4
8 M	0052 3.4	0738 1.2	1331 3.5	2012 1.1		23 TU	0216 3.2	0848 1.3	1453 3.3	2122 1.2
9 TU	0209 3.4	0855 1.0	1448 3.6	2128 0.9		24 W	0318 3.3	0951 1.1	1548 3.5	2217 1.0
10 W	0322 3.6	1003 0.8	1557 3.8	2233 0.6		25 TH	0409 3.6	1039 0.9	1633 3.7	2258 0.8
11 TH	0426 3.8	1102 0.5	1655 4.0	2328 0.4		26 F	0451 3.7	1116 0.7	1712 3.9	2331 0.7
12 F	0519 4.0	1153 0.3	1745 4.2			27 SA	0528 3.8	1146 0.6	1746 3.9	
13 SA	0015 0.2	0607 4.1	1238 0.2	1831 4.3		28 SU	0001 0.6	0602 3.9	1214 0.6	1817 4.0
14 SU	0100 0.2	0652 4.1	1322 0.1	1914 4.2		29 M	0032 0.6	0632 3.9	1244 0.6	1847 4.0
15 M	0143 0.2	0734 4.0	1405 0.2	1955 4.1		30 TU	0105 0.6	0703 3.9	1318 0.6	1918 4.0
						31 W	0140 0.7	0735 3.9	1355 0.6	1953 3.9

Chart Datum: 0·13 metres above Ordnance Datum (Dublin)
HAT is 4·5m above Chart Datum

TIME ZONE (UT)	IRELAND – COBH	Dates in amber are SPRINGS
For Summer Time add ONE hour in **non-shaded areas**	LAT 51°51′N LONG 8°18′W	Dates in grey are NEAPS
	TIMES AND HEIGHTS OF HIGH AND LOW WATERS	**2022**

SEPTEMBER

Time	m		Time	m
1 0216	0.7	**16** 0303	0.8
0811	3.8	0852	3.6
TH 1434	0.7	F 1525	0.9
2030	3.9	2111	3.6
2 0255	0.9	**17** 0341	1.1
0851	3.8	0931	3.4
F 1517	0.9	SA 1607	1.2
2113	3.8	◑ 2152	3.3
3 0340	1.0	**18** 0428	1.3
0938	3.5	1019	3.2
SA 1607	1.0	SU 1701	1.4
◔ 2205	3.6	2244	3.1
4 0435	1.2	**19** 0532	1.5
1037	3.5	1125	3.0
SU 1709	1.2	M 1813	1.6
2310	3.4		
5 0548	1.3	**20** 0004	3.0
1151	3.3	0655	1.5
M 1829	1.3	TU 1311	3.0
		1935	1.5
6 0032	3.2	**21** 0149	3.0
0719	1.3	0816	1.4
TU 1320	3.3	W 1431	3.2
2000	1.2	2051	1.3
7 0202	3.3	**22** 0255	3.3
0845	1.1	0923	1.1
W 1446	3.5	TH 1524	3.5
2123	0.9	2147	1.1
8 0318	3.6	**23** 0344	3.5
0955	0.7	1010	0.9
TH 1552	3.8	F 1607	3.7
2225	0.6	2228	0.8
9 0417	3.8	**24** 0424	3.7
1050	0.4	1046	0.7
F 1643	4.1	SA 1644	3.9
2315	0.4	2302	0.7
10 0505	4.0	**25** 0500	3.9
1137	0.2	1116	0.6
SA 1728	4.3	SU 1716	4.0
○ 2358	0.2	● 2333	0.6
11 0548	4.2	**26** 0532	4.0
1219	0.1	1145	0.5
SU 1809	4.3	M 1746	4.1
12 0037	0.2	**27** 0004	0.5
0628	4.2	0603	4.0
M 1257	0.1	TU 1216	0.5
1848	4.2	1817	4.1
13 0114	0.3	**28** 0037	0.5
0706	4.1	0634	4.0
TU 1335	0.3	W 1251	0.5
1924	4.0	1850	4.1
14 0151	0.4	**29** 0112	0.6
0741	4.0	0708	4.0
W 1411	0.4	TH 1329	0.6
1959	4.0	1926	4.0
15 0227	0.6	**30** 0150	0.7
0816	3.8	0745	3.9
TH 1447	0.7	F 1410	0.7
2035	3.8	2005	3.9

OCTOBER

Time	m		Time	m
1 0232	0.8	**16** 0259	1.1
0828	3.8	0855	3.5
SA 1456	0.9	SU 1527	1.3
2050	3.7	2112	3.4
2 0320	1.0	**17** 0344	1.4
0918	3.6	0942	3.3
SU 1550	1.1	M 1621	1.5
2145	3.5	◑ 2202	3.2
3 0420	1.2	**18** 0448	1.5
1021	3.4	1043	3.1
M 1656	1.3	TU 1733	1.6
◔ 2255	3.3	2312	3.0
4 0538	1.3	**19** 0612	1.6
1143	3.3	1219	3.0
TU 1820	1.4	W 1854	1.6
5 0025	3.2	**20** 0100	3.0
0713	1.3	0733	1.5
W 1322	3.3	TH 1352	3.2
1958	1.2	2007	1.4
6 0200	3.3	**21** 0217	3.3
0839	1.0	0838	1.2
TH 1441	3.6	F 1447	3.5
2115	0.9	2103	1.1
7 0310	3.6	**22** 0306	3.5
0943	0.7	0926	1.0
F 1539	3.9	SA 1529	3.7
2211	0.6	2148	0.9
8 0402	3.9	**23** 0347	3.8
1034	0.4	1006	0.8
SA 1626	4.2	SU 1606	3.9
2256	0.4	2226	0.7
9 0446	4.1	**24** 0424	3.9
1117	0.2	1041	0.6
SU 1707	4.3	M 1641	4.1
○ 2336	0.3	2302	0.6
10 0526	4.2	**25** 0459	4.1
1156	0.2	1117	0.5
M 1745	4.3	TU 1715	4.1
		● 2338	0.6
11 0011	0.3	**26** 0534	4.1
0604	4.2	1153	0.5
TU 1231	0.3	W 1750	4.2
1821	4.2		
12 0045	0.4	**27** 0014	0.5
0637	4.0	0611	4.1
W 1305	0.4	TH 1231	0.5
1853	4.1	1828	4.1
13 0118	0.6	**28** 0053	0.6
0709	4.0	0649	4.1
TH 1338	0.6	F 1313	0.6
1925	3.9	1908	4.1
14 0151	0.7	**29** 0135	0.7
0742	3.8	0731	4.0
F 1411	0.8	SA 1358	0.7
1958	3.8	1952	3.9
15 0224	0.9	**30** 0221	0.8
0816	3.7	0818	3.9
SA 1446	1.1	SU 1448	0.9
2032	3.6	2041	3.7
		31 0315	1.0
		0913	3.7
		M 1545	1.1
		2140	3.5

NOVEMBER

Time	m		Time	m
1 0419	1.2	**16** 0411	1.5
1020	3.5	1012	3.3
TU 1654	1.2	W 1654	1.6
◔ 2252	3.3	◑ 2233	3.2
2 0536	1.3	**17** 0524	1.5
1143	3.4	1121	3.2
W 1818	1.3	TH 1807	1.6
		2351	3.2
3 0019	3.2	**18** 0639	1.5
0705	1.2	1242	3.3
TH 1311	3.5	F 1916	1.4
1948	1.1		
4 0144	3.4	**19** 0110	3.3
0822	0.9	0743	1.3
F 1421	3.7	SA 1347	3.5
2055	0.9	2014	1.2
5 0248	3.7	**20** 0211	3.5
0922	0.7	0837	1.1
SA 1515	3.9	SU 1438	3.7
2147	0.7	2104	1.0
6 0339	3.9	**21** 0300	3.7
1011	0.5	0924	0.9
SU 1602	4.1	M 1522	3.9
2232	0.5	2150	0.8
7 0423	4.1	**22** 0344	3.9
1054	0.4	1009	0.7
M 1643	4.2	TU 1604	4.0
2311	0.5	2234	0.7
8 0503	4.1	**23** 0427	4.1
1133	0.4	1053	0.6
TU 1720	4.2	W 1647	4.1
○ 2347	0.5	● 2317	0.6
9 0539	4.1	**24** 0510	4.2
1207	0.5	1137	0.5
W 1755	4.1	TH 1730	4.2
10 0019	0.6	**25** 0000	0.5
0612	4.1	0554	4.2
TH 1240	0.7	F 1221	0.5
1827	4.0	1814	4.2
11 0050	0.7	**26** 0044	0.5
0644	4.0	0639	4.2
F 1311	0.8	SA 1307	0.6
1857	3.9	1859	4.1
12 0121	0.9	**27** 0130	0.6
0716	3.9	0727	4.1
SA 1343	1.0	SU 1355	0.7
1929	3.8	1948	3.9
13 0152	1.0	**28** 0220	0.7
0751	3.7	0818	4.0
SU 1418	1.2	M 1448	0.8
2004	3.7	2040	3.8
14 0228	1.2	**29** 0315	0.9
0830	3.6	0915	3.8
M 1459	1.3	TU 1545	1.0
2044	3.5	2138	3.6
15 0312	1.3	**30** 0416	1.0
0916	3.4	1017	3.7
TU 1550	1.5	W 1649	1.1
2133	3.4	◑ 2243	3.4

DECEMBER

Time	m		Time	m
1 0526	1.1	**16** 0437	1.4
1127	3.6	1037	3.5
TH 1803	1.2	F 1715	1.5
2356	3.4	◑ 2300	3.4
2 0641	1.1	**17** 0540	1.4
1240	3.6	1137	3.5
F 1918	1.1	SA 1820	1.4
3 0109	3.5	**18** 0004	3.4
0752	1.0	0646	1.3
SA 1346	3.7	SU 1240	3.5
2022	1.0	1923	1.3
4 0213	3.6	**19** 0109	3.5
0851	0.8	0747	1.2
SU 1442	3.8	M 1341	3.6
2116	0.9	2022	1.2
5 0307	3.8	**20** 0210	3.7
0943	0.8	0845	1.1
M 1532	3.9	TU 1438	3.8
2204	0.8	2117	1.0
6 0355	3.9	**21** 0306	3.8
1029	0.7	0941	0.9
TU 1616	4.0	W 1533	3.9
2246	0.8	2211	0.8
7 0438	4.0	**22** 0401	4.0
1110	0.7	1036	0.7
W 1656	4.0	TH 1626	4.0
2324	0.8	2302	0.7
8 0517	4.0	**23** 0454	4.1
1147	0.8	1127	0.6
TH 1733	4.0	F 1717	4.1
○ 2358	0.7	2351	0.5
9 0553	4.0	**24** 0544	4.2
1220	0.9	1216	0.5
F 1806	3.9	SA 1806	4.1
10 0029	0.8	**25** 0038	0.5
0627	4.0	0634	4.3
SA 1251	0.9	SU 1304	0.5
1839	3.9	1855	4.1
11 0100	0.9	**26** 0126	0.5
0700	3.9	0724	4.2
SU 1323	1.0	M 1353	0.5
1911	3.8	1944	4.0
12 0132	1.0	**27** 0215	0.5
0735	3.8	0814	4.1
M 1358	1.1	TU 1443	0.6
1946	3.7	2034	3.9
13 0208	1.1	**28** 0307	0.6
0813	3.7	0906	4.0
TU 1438	1.2	W 1535	0.8
2025	3.6	2125	3.8
14 0250	1.2	**29** 0401	0.8
0856	3.6	0959	3.8
W 1524	1.4	TH 1630	0.9
2110	3.5	2219	3.6
15 0340	1.3	**30** 0459	0.9
0944	3.5	1056	3.7
TH 1616	1.4	F 1729	1.0
2201	3.4	◑ 2317	3.5
		31 0601	1.0
		1156	3.6
		SA 1832	1.1

Chart Datum: 0·13 metres above Ordnance Datum (Dublin)
HAT is 4·5m above Chart Datum

TIDES

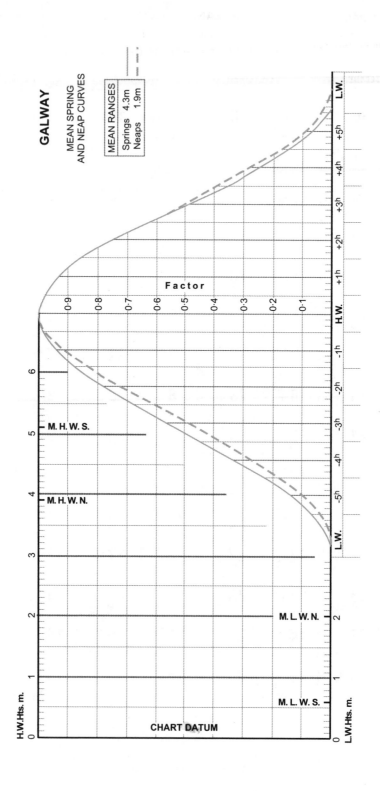

GALWAY

MEAN SPRING
AND NEAP CURVES

MEAN RANGES
Springs 4.3m
Neaps 1.9m

Factor

M. H. W. S.

M. H. W. N.

M. L. W. N.

M. L. W. S.

CHART DATUM

H.W.Hts. m.

L.W.Hts. m.

TIME ZONE (UT)
For Summer Time add ONE hour in **non-shaded areas**

IRELAND – GALWAY
LAT 53°16′N   LONG 9°03′W
TIMES AND HEIGHTS OF HIGH AND LOW WATERS

Dates in amber are **SPRINGS**
Dates in grey are **NEAPS**

2022

JANUARY

Day	Time m	Time m	Time m	Time m		Day	Time m	Time m	Time m	Time m
1 SA	0325 5.1	0932 1.0	1553 5.1	2155 1.0		16 SU	0412 4.6	1009 1.5	1637 4.5	2221 1.6
2 SU	0415 5.3	1021 0.8	1646 5.3	2242 0.9		17 M	0450 4.8	1047 1.3	1715 4.7	2258 1.4
3 M	0505 5.5	1109 0.7	1736 5.3	2329 0.9		18 TU	0527 4.9	1123 1.2	1752 4.8	2333 1.3
4 TU	0554 5.6	1157 0.6	1826 5.3			19 W	0603 5.0	1157 1.1	1829 4.8	
5 W	0015 1.0	0643 5.5	1244 0.7	1916 5.2		20 TH	0006 1.3	0637 5.0	1231 1.0	1904 4.8
6 TH	0102 1.1	0731 5.4	1331 0.9	2005 5.0		21 F	0041 1.3	0708 4.9	1306 1.0	1938 4.7
7 F	0149 1.3	0818 5.1	1419 1.1	2054 4.7		22 SA	0118 1.3	0741 4.9	1344 1.1	2014 4.6
8 SA	0240 1.6	0907 4.8	1511 1.4	2146 4.5		23 SU	0158 1.4	0821 4.8	1425 1.2	2056 4.5
9 SU	0337 1.8	0959 4.5	1608 1.6	2240 4.2		24 M	0242 1.5	0907 4.6	1511 1.4	2144 4.4
10 M	0442 2.0	1055 4.3	1711 1.9	2342 4.1		25 TU	0333 1.7	1002 4.5	1603 1.6	2241 4.3
11 TU	0549 2.1	1205 4.1	1815 2.0			26 W	0432 1.8	1104 4.3	1704 1.7	2346 4.2
12 W	0054 4.0	0655 2.1	1323 4.0	1917 2.0		27 TH	0541 1.9	1216 4.2	1819 1.8	
13 TH	0159 4.1	0754 2.0	1426 4.1	2011 2.0		28 F	0100 4.3	0708 1.8	1338 4.3	1952 1.7
14 F	0251 4.2	0845 1.9	1516 4.2	2059 1.9		29 SA	0214 4.5	0831 1.6	1450 4.6	2101 1.5
15 SA	0334 4.4	0930 1.7	1558 4.4	2141 1.7		30 SU	0315 4.9	0931 1.2	1548 4.9	2153 1.2
						31 M	0409 5.2	1021 0.9	1640 5.1	2240 1.0

FEBRUARY

Day	Time m	Time m	Time m	Time m		Day	Time m	Time m	Time m	Time m
1 TU	0458 5.4	1106 0.6	1728 5.3	2323 0.9		16 W	0512 4.9	1106 1.0	1734 4.8	2317 1.1
2 W	0544 5.6	1148 0.5	1814 5.4			17 TH	0545 5.0	1139 0.8	1808 4.9	2349 1.0
3 TH	0003 0.8	0629 5.6	1228 0.5	1858 5.3		18 F	0616 5.1	1210 0.7	1840 5.0	
4 F	0043 0.9	0712 5.5	1306 0.7	1940 5.1		19 SA	0021 0.9	0646 5.1	1243 0.7	1912 5.0
5 SA	0121 1.0	0753 5.3	1345 0.9	2021 4.9		20 SU	0057 0.8	0719 5.1	1320 0.7	1946 4.9
6 SU	0202 1.3	0835 4.9	1425 1.2	2102 4.6		21 M	0136 0.9	0757 5.0	1359 0.9	2026 4.7
7 M	0245 1.6	0918 4.6	1509 1.6	2146 4.3		22 TU	0218 1.1	0841 4.8	1442 1.1	2111 4.5
8 TU	0336 1.9	1004 4.3	1603 1.9	2233 4.1		23 W	0305 1.4	0933 4.5	1532 1.5	2206 4.3
9 W	0449 2.1	1056 4.0	1720 2.2	2327 3.9		24 TH	0401 1.6	1036 4.2	1632 1.8	2313 4.1
10 TH	0611 2.3	1201 3.8	1837 2.3			25 F	0512 1.9	1157 4.0	1753 2.0	
11 F	0043 3.8	0719 2.2	1356 3.8	1942 2.2		26 SA	0041 4.1	0701 1.9	1334 4.0	1959 1.9
12 SA	0228 4.0	0818 2.0	1502 4.0	2037 2.0		27 SU	0207 4.3	0840 1.5	1449 4.4	2106 1.6
13 SU	0320 4.2	0908 1.8	1546 4.2	2124 1.8		28 M	0310 4.7	0934 1.1	1545 4.7	2153 1.2
14 M	0400 4.5	0951 1.5	1624 4.5	2205 1.5						
15 TU	0437 4.7	1030 1.2	1700 4.7	2243 1.3						

MARCH

Day	Time m	Time m	Time m	Time m		Day	Time m	Time m	Time m	Time m
1 TU	0402 5.1	1018 0.8	1632 5.1	2233 0.9		16 W	0416 4.6	1006 1.0	1636 4.7	2220 1.1
2 W	0447 5.4	1057 0.5	1715 5.3	2310 0.7		17 TH	0447 4.8	1041 0.8	1708 4.9	2253 0.9
3 TH	0530 5.5	1131 0.4	1755 5.4	2344 0.6		18 F	0518 5.1	1113 0.5	1739 5.0	2324 0.7
4 F	0610 5.5	1204 0.4	1834 5.3			19 SA	0548 5.2	1144 0.4	1810 5.1	2357 0.5
5 SA	0017 0.7	0648 5.4	1235 0.6	1911 5.2		20 SU	0621 5.3	1217 0.4	1844 5.1	
6 SU	0050 0.8	0725 5.2	1308 0.8	1947 4.9		21 M	0033 0.5	0657 5.2	1254 0.5	1921 5.1
7 M	0125 1.0	0803 4.9	1343 1.1	2024 4.7		22 TU	0113 0.6	0738 5.1	1334 0.7	2001 4.9
8 TU	0201 1.4	0843 4.6	1419 1.5	2104 4.4		23 W	0156 0.9	0823 4.8	1418 1.1	2047 4.6
9 W	0241 1.7	0927 4.2	1458 1.9	2149 4.1		24 TH	0244 1.2	0916 4.4	1508 1.5	2142 4.3
10 TH	0327 2.0	1017 3.9	1543 2.2	2241 3.9		25 F	0342 1.6	1024 4.0	1613 1.9	2254 4.0
11 F	0532 2.3	1114 3.7	1804 2.4	2340 3.7		26 SA	0500 1.8	1153 3.8	1750 2.1	
12 SA	0649 2.3	1230 3.6	1914 2.3			27 SU	0033 4.0	0720 1.8	1335 3.9	2004 1.9
13 SU	0206 3.7	0751 2.1	1447 3.8	2012 2.1		28 M	0200 4.2	0837 1.4	1444 4.3	2059 1.5
14 M	0303 4.0	0843 1.7	1529 4.1	2101 1.8		29 TU	0300 4.6	0925 1.0	1533 4.7	2142 1.2
15 TU	0342 4.3	0927 1.4	1604 4.4	2143 1.4		30 W	0347 4.9	1004 0.7	1615 5.0	2218 0.9
						31 TH	0430 5.2	1038 0.5	1654 5.2	2251 0.7

APRIL

Day	Time m	Time m	Time m	Time m		Day	Time m	Time m	Time m	Time m
1 F	0509 5.3	1107 0.4	1731 5.2	2320 0.6		16 SA	0443 5.1	1042 0.5	1704 5.1	2256 0.5
2 SA	0546 5.3	1133 0.5	1806 5.2	2349 0.6		17 SU	0518 5.2	1114 0.3	1739 5.3	2331 0.4
3 SU	0622 5.2	1202 0.6	1840 5.1			18 M	0557 5.3	1150 0.3	1818 5.3	
4 M	0020 0.8	0658 5.0	1234 0.9	1914 4.9		19 TU	0010 0.4	0639 5.2	1229 0.5	1859 5.2
5 TU	0054 1.0	0735 4.8	1308 1.1	1951 4.7		20 W	0052 0.5	0724 5.0	1312 0.8	1944 5.0
6 W	0129 1.2	0814 4.5	1342 1.5	2031 4.4		21 TH	0139 0.8	0814 4.7	1400 1.2	2034 4.7
7 TH	0207 1.6	0858 4.2	1419 1.8	2116 4.1		22 F	0231 1.1	0912 4.3	1456 1.6	2133 4.3
8 F	0248 1.9	0947 3.9	1459 2.2	2206 3.9		23 SA	0335 1.5	1022 4.0	1609 2.0	2247 4.1
9 SA	0341 2.2	1042 3.7	1553 2.5	2302 3.7		24 SU	0459 1.7	1152 3.9	1757 2.1	
10 SU	0617 2.2	1146 3.5	1845 2.4			25 M	0022 4.0	0702 1.6	1323 4.0	1941 1.8
11 M	0009 3.6	0719 2.0	1412 3.7	1944 2.1		26 TU	0142 4.2	0813 1.3	1424 4.3	2036 1.5
12 TU	0227 3.8	0812 1.7	1457 4.0	2033 1.8		27 W	0239 4.5	0901 1.0	1511 4.6	2119 1.2
13 W	0308 4.2	0857 1.3	1531 4.3	2114 1.4		28 TH	0326 4.7	0940 0.8	1552 4.8	2155 1.0
14 TH	0341 4.5	0936 1.0	1601 4.6	2151 1.0		29 F	0407 4.9	1012 0.7	1629 5.0	2227 0.8
15 F	0411 4.8	1010 0.7	1631 4.9	2223 0.7		30 SA	0446 5.0	1038 0.7	1704 5.0	2254 0.8

Chart Datum: 0·20 metres above Ordnance Datum (Dublin)
HAT is 5·9m above Chart Datum

IRELAND – GALWAY
LAT 53°16'N LONG 9°03'W
TIMES AND HEIGHTS OF HIGH AND LOW WATERS

TIME ZONE (UT) — For Summer Time add ONE hour in non-shaded areas

Dates in amber are **SPRINGS** — Dates in grey are **NEAPS**

2022

MAY

Day	Time m	Day	Time m
1 SU	0522 5.0 / 1103 0.8 / 1738 5.0 / 2322 0.8	16 M	0451 5.2 / 1046 0.5 / 1712 5.3 / ○2308 0.4
2 M	0557 4.9 / 1133 1.0 / 1811 5.0 / 2355 0.9	17 TU	0536 5.3 / 1127 0.5 / 1756 5.4 / 2352 0.4
3 TU	0633 4.8 / 1206 1.1 / 1846 4.8	18 W	0624 5.2 / 1211 0.7 / 1843 5.3
4 W	0030 1.0 / 0711 4.6 / 1240 1.3 / 1924 4.7	19 TH	0038 0.5 / 0715 5.0 / 1258 0.9 / 1933 5.1
5 TH	0106 1.3 / 0751 4.4 / 1315 1.5 / 2003 4.5	20 F	0129 0.8 / 0809 4.7 / 1350 1.3 / 2027 4.8
6 F	0144 1.5 / 0834 4.2 / 1352 1.8 / 2046 4.2	21 SA	0225 1.1 / 0908 4.4 / 1451 1.6 / 2126 4.5
7 SA	0225 1.8 / 0921 3.9 / 1434 2.1 / 2134 4.0	22 SU	0331 1.3 / 1015 4.2 / 1605 1.9 / ○2235 4.3
8 SU	0315 2.0 / 1013 3.8 / 1527 2.3 / 2227 3.8	23 M	0448 1.5 / 1134 4.1 / 1732 1.9 / 2357 4.2
9 M	0530 2.1 / 1111 3.7 / 1806 2.4 / ○2327 3.7	24 TU	0615 1.5 / 1251 4.1 / 1855 1.8
10 TU	0639 1.9 / 1220 3.7 / 1906 2.1	25 W	0111 4.2 / 0730 1.4 / 1352 4.3 / 1958 1.6
11 W	0034 3.8 / 0734 1.7 / 1349 4.0 / 1956 1.8	26 TH	0210 4.3 / 0824 1.3 / 1441 4.4 / 2047 1.4
12 TH	0156 4.1 / 0820 1.4 / 1437 4.3 / 2039 1.5	27 F	0259 4.5 / 0907 1.2 / 1524 4.6 / 2127 1.2
13 F	0246 4.4 / 0900 1.1 / 1513 4.6 / 2115 1.1	28 SA	0342 4.6 / 0941 1.0 / 1602 4.7 / 2201 1.1
14 SA	0327 4.8 / 0935 0.8 / 1550 4.9 / 2150 0.8	29 SU	0421 4.6 / 1009 1.1 / 1637 4.8 / 2230 1.1
15 SU	0408 5.0 / 1009 0.6 / 1630 5.2 / 2228 0.5	30 M	0459 4.7 / 1038 1.2 / ●1712 4.8 / 2302 1.1
		31 TU	0536 4.7 / 1111 1.2 / 1748 4.8 / 2336 1.1

JUNE

Day	Time m	Day	Time m
1 W	0613 4.6 / 1146 1.3 / 1824 4.8	16 TH	0614 5.2 / 1201 0.8 / 1831 5.4
2 TH	0013 1.2 / 0652 4.5 / 1221 1.4 / 1902 4.7	17 F	0031 0.6 / 0706 5.1 / 1251 1.0 / 1923 5.2
3 F	0050 1.3 / 0731 4.4 / 1257 1.6 / 1940 4.6	18 SA	0123 0.7 / 0759 4.9 / 1343 1.2 / 2016 5.0
4 SA	0129 1.4 / 0812 4.3 / 1335 1.8 / 2019 4.3	19 SU	0217 0.9 / 0855 4.6 / 1441 1.5 / 2112 4.8
5 SU	0209 1.6 / 0855 4.1 / 1417 1.9 / 2102 4.2	20 M	0315 1.1 / 0954 4.4 / 1544 1.7 / 2212 4.5
6 M	0255 1.7 / 0943 4.0 / 1507 2.1 / 2152 4.0	21 TU	0419 1.3 / 1059 4.2 / 1654 1.8 / ○2319 4.3
7 TU	0350 1.8 / 1035 3.9 / 1611 2.2 / ○2246 4.0	22 W	0526 1.5 / 1207 4.2 / 1804 1.8
8 W	0500 1.8 / 1132 3.9 / 1738 2.1 / 2345 4.0	23 TH	0029 4.2 / 0633 1.6 / 1311 4.2 / 1910 1.8
9 TH	0624 1.7 / 1234 4.1 / 1856 1.9	24 F	0135 4.1 / 0735 1.6 / 1407 4.2 / 2008 1.7
10 F	0048 4.2 / 0726 1.5 / 1334 4.3 / 1950 1.6	25 SA	0230 4.2 / 0826 1.6 / 1455 4.3 / 2056 1.6
11 SA	0151 4.4 / 0815 1.3 / 1428 4.6 / 2037 1.3	26 SU	0318 4.4 / 0909 1.6 / 1537 4.5 / 2137 1.5
12 SU	0248 4.7 / 0859 1.0 / 1516 4.9 / 2121 0.9	27 M	0401 4.4 / 0945 1.5 / 1615 4.6 / 2213 1.4
13 M	0340 4.9 / 0942 0.8 / 1604 5.2 / 2206 0.7	28 TU	0440 4.5 / 1021 1.5 / 1652 4.7 / 2248 1.3
14 TU	0431 5.1 / 1027 0.7 / 1652 5.3 / ○2253 0.6	29 W	0519 4.5 / 1057 1.4 / ●1730 4.8 / 2324 1.2
15 W	0522 5.2 / 1113 0.8 / 1741 5.4 / 2341 0.5	30 TH	0557 4.6 / 1133 1.4 / 1807 4.8

JULY

Day	Time m	Day	Time m
1 F	0000 1.2 / 0636 4.6 / 1208 1.4 / 1844 4.7	16 SA	0023 0.5 / 0654 5.2 / 1241 0.9 / 1909 5.4
2 SA	0036 1.2 / 0713 4.5 / 1244 1.5 / 1919 4.6	17 SU	0110 0.5 / 0743 5.1 / 1328 1.0 / 1958 5.2
3 SU	0113 1.2 / 0750 4.4 / 1320 1.5 / 1953 4.5	18 M	0157 0.7 / 0832 4.9 / 1416 1.2 / 2047 5.0
4 M	0151 1.3 / 0827 4.3 / 1400 1.6 / 2030 4.4	19 TU	0246 1.0 / 0921 4.6 / 1509 1.5 / 2137 4.7
5 TU	0231 1.4 / 0909 4.2 / 1444 1.7 / 2115 4.3	20 W	0338 1.3 / 1013 4.3 / 1609 1.7 / ○2231 4.3
6 W	0317 1.5 / 0956 4.1 / 1536 1.8 / 2207 4.2	21 TH	0436 1.6 / 1110 4.1 / 1716 1.9 / 2333 4.1
7 TH	0409 1.6 / 1050 4.1 / 1635 1.9 / ○2305 4.2	22 F	0541 1.8 / 1218 4.0 / 1824 2.0
8 F	0508 1.6 / 1148 4.2 / 1741 1.8	23 SA	0052 3.9 / 0647 2.0 / 1330 4.0 / 1929 2.0
9 SA	0007 4.2 / 0615 1.6 / 1251 4.3 / 1855 1.7	24 SU	0204 3.9 / 0748 2.0 / 1431 4.1 / 2026 1.9
10 SU	0115 4.3 / 0728 1.5 / 1355 4.5 / 2005 1.5	25 M	0301 4.0 / 0840 1.9 / 1519 4.3 / 2114 1.7
11 M	0224 4.5 / 0834 1.3 / 1454 4.8 / 2104 1.2	26 TU	0347 4.2 / 0926 1.8 / 1600 4.5 / 2155 1.5
12 TU	0325 4.8 / 0929 1.1 / 1548 5.1 / 2157 0.9	27 W	0427 4.3 / 1006 1.6 / 1638 4.6 / 2233 1.3
13 W	0420 5.0 / 1019 1.0 / 1640 5.3 / ○2247 0.6	28 TH	0505 4.5 / 1044 1.4 / 1716 4.8 / ●2309 1.1
14 TH	0513 5.2 / 1108 0.9 / 1731 5.5 / 2336 0.5	29 F	0541 4.6 / 1119 1.3 / 1752 4.8 / 2344 1.0
15 F	0604 5.2 / 1155 0.8 / 1820 5.5	30 SA	0617 4.7 / 1153 1.2 / 1826 4.8
		31 SU	0017 1.0 / 0652 4.7 / 1226 1.2 / 1857 4.8

AUGUST

Day	Time m	Day	Time m
1 M	0051 0.9 / 0724 4.6 / 1300 1.2 / 1925 4.8	16 TU	0126 0.6 / 0800 5.0 / 1342 1.1 / 2015 5.0
2 TU	0126 1.0 / 0756 4.6 / 1337 1.3 / 1959 4.7	17 W	0206 1.0 / 0842 4.7 / 1425 1.4 / 2059 4.7
3 W	0204 1.1 / 0833 4.5 / 1419 1.4 / 2041 4.6	18 TH	0250 1.3 / 0925 4.4 / 1515 1.7 / 2145 4.3
4 TH	0246 1.2 / 0917 4.4 / 1505 1.5 / 2131 4.4	19 F	0341 1.7 / 1012 4.1 / 1626 2.0 / ○2236 4.0
5 F	0334 1.4 / 1009 4.2 / 1558 1.7 / 2229 4.2	20 SA	0452 2.1 / 1105 3.9 / 1748 2.2 / 2340 3.7
6 SA	0428 1.6 / 1110 4.2 / 1701 1.8 / 2336 4.1	21 SU	0610 2.2 / 1220 3.8 / 1857 2.1
7 SU	0534 1.8 / 1219 4.2 / 1820 1.8	22 M	0147 3.7 / 0718 2.2 / 1416 3.9 / 1958 2.0
8 M	0054 4.1 / 0702 1.8 / 1336 4.3 / 1956 1.6	23 TU	0251 3.8 / 0816 2.1 / 1508 4.1 / 2050 1.7
9 TU	0215 4.3 / 0830 1.6 / 1444 4.7 / 2104 1.3	24 W	0337 4.1 / 0905 1.7 / 1549 4.4 / 2134 1.5
10 W	0320 4.6 / 0928 1.3 / 1541 5.0 / 2157 0.9	25 TH	0414 4.3 / 0947 1.6 / 1625 4.6 / 2212 1.2
11 TH	0415 4.9 / 1017 1.0 / 1632 5.3 / 2243 0.6	26 F	0448 4.5 / 1025 1.3 / 1659 4.8 / 2248 1.0
12 F	0504 5.2 / 1101 0.8 / 1720 5.5 / ○2327 0.4	27 SA	0521 4.7 / 1100 1.1 / 1732 4.9 / ●2321 0.7
13 SA	0550 5.3 / 1143 0.7 / 1805 5.6	28 SU	0554 4.8 / 1131 1.0 / 1802 5.0 / 2353 0.7
14 SU	0007 0.3 / 0635 5.3 / 1222 0.7 / 1850 5.5	29 M	0624 4.8 / 1203 0.9 / 1829 5.0
15 M	0046 0.4 / 0718 5.2 / 1302 0.8 / 1933 5.3	30 TU	0024 0.6 / 0654 4.8 / 1236 0.9 / 1857 5.0
		31 W	0059 0.7 / 0724 4.9 / 1312 0.9 / 1931 4.9

Chart Datum: 0·20 metres above Ordnance Datum (Dublin)
HAT is 5·9m above Chart Datum

TIME ZONE (UT)
For Summer Time add ONE hour in **non-shaded areas**

IRELAND – GALWAY

LAT 53°16′N LONG 9°03′W

TIMES AND HEIGHTS OF HIGH AND LOW WATERS

Dates in amber are **SPRINGS**
Dates in grey are **NEAPS**

2022

SEPTEMBER

Date	Day	Time	m	Time	m	Time	m	Time	m
1	TH	0136	0.8	0759	4.7	1352	1.1	2013	4.7
2	F	0217	1.1	0842	4.5	1437	1.3	2102	4.4
3	SA	0303	1.4	0934	4.3	1529	1.6	◐ 2202	4.1
4	SU	0358	1.7	1039	4.1	1635	1.8	2317	3.9
5	M	0509	2.0	1158	4.0	1809	1.9		
6	TU	0049	3.9	0712	2.0	1329	4.2	2008	1.6
7	W	0218	4.2	0837	1.7	1441	4.6	2107	1.2
8	TH	0319	4.6	0927	1.3	1535	5.0	2152	0.7
9	F	0407	4.9	1009	0.9	1621	5.3	2232	0.4
10	SA	0450	5.2	1047	0.7	1704	5.5	○ 2309	0.3
11	SU	0531	5.3	1123	0.5	1746	5.6	2343	0.3
12	M	0611	5.3	1157	0.6	1825	5.5		
13	TU	0016	0.4	0649	5.2	1231	0.7	1904	5.3
14	W	0049	0.7	0725	5.0	1306	1.0	1943	5.0
15	TH	0125	1.0	0803	4.7	1344	1.3	2024	4.6
16	F	0203	1.4	0844	4.4	1426	1.7	2108	4.2
17	SA	0245	1.8	0929	4.1	1521	2.0	◑ 2158	3.9
18	SU	0341	2.2	1020	3.9	1716	2.2	2255	3.6
19	M	0542	2.4	1120	3.7	1828	2.2		
20	TU	0133	3.5	0652	2.3	1358	3.8	1930	2.0
21	W	0235	3.8	0750	2.1	1449	4.0	2023	1.7
22	TH	0317	4.1	0840	1.8	1528	4.3	2107	1.4
23	F	0352	4.3	0923	1.5	1602	4.6	2146	1.1
24	SA	0423	4.6	1001	1.2	1633	4.8	2221	0.8
25	SU	0453	4.8	1034	1.0	1703	5.0	● 2253	0.6
26	M	0522	4.9	1105	0.8	1731	5.1	2323	0.5
27	TU	0551	5.0	1136	0.7	1800	5.1	2355	0.5
28	W	0621	5.0	1210	0.6	1832	5.1		
29	TH	0030	0.6	0655	5.0	1248	0.7	1910	5.0
30	F	0109	0.8	0733	4.9	1329	0.9	1954	4.7

OCTOBER

Date	Day	Time	m	Time	m	Time	m	Time	m
1	SA	0151	1.1	0817	4.6	1415	1.2	2045	4.4
2	SU	0239	1.5	0911	4.3	1511	1.6	2150	4.0
3	M	0339	1.9	1020	4.1	1623	1.8	◐ 2312	3.8
4	TU	0503	2.2	1148	4.0	1837	1.9		
5	W	0056	3.9	0729	2.0	1324	4.2	2006	1.5
6	TH	0216	4.2	0831	1.6	1431	4.6	2057	1.0
7	F	0308	4.6	0915	1.2	1520	4.9	2138	0.7
8	SA	0351	4.9	0953	0.9	1604	5.2	2213	0.5
9	SU	0430	5.2	1028	0.7	1644	5.4	○ 2245	0.4
10	M	0508	5.3	1059	0.6	1723	5.4	2314	0.4
11	TU	0543	5.3	1130	0.6	1800	5.3	2344	0.6
12	W	0618	5.2	1202	0.8	1836	5.1		
13	TH	0016	0.8	0653	5.0	1236	1.0	1915	4.8
14	F	0051	1.2	0730	4.8	1313	1.3	1955	4.5
15	SA	0127	1.5	0811	4.5	1353	1.6	2039	4.2
16	SU	0205	1.9	0856	4.2	1439	2.0	2128	3.9
17	M	0246	2.3	0946	4.0	1639	2.2	◑ 2224	3.7
18	TU	0510	2.5	1043	3.8	1757	2.2	2330	3.5
19	W	0622	2.4	1153	3.7	1858	2.0		
20	TH	0201	3.7	0721	2.2	1414	3.9	1951	1.7
21	F	0244	4.0	0811	1.9	1454	4.2	2036	1.4
22	SA	0318	4.3	0854	1.5	1528	4.5	2116	1.1
23	SU	0348	4.6	0931	1.2	1558	4.8	2151	0.8
24	M	0416	4.8	1004	0.9	1627	5.0	2222	0.6
25	TU	0445	5.0	1035	0.7	1658	5.1	● 2253	0.5
26	W	0518	5.2	1109	0.6	1733	5.2	2327	0.5
27	TH	0553	5.2	1146	0.6	1813	5.2		
28	F	0005	0.6	0633	5.2	1227	0.7	1857	5.0
29	SA	0047	0.9	0716	5.0	1312	0.9	1946	4.7
30	SU	0133	1.2	0805	4.7	1402	1.2	2042	4.4
31	M	0226	1.6	0902	4.4	1503	1.5	2149	4.1

NOVEMBER

Date	Day	Time	m	Time	m	Time	m	Time	m
1	TU	0333	2.0	1012	4.2	1621	1.7	◐ 2310	3.9
2	W	0506	2.1	1137	4.1	1824	1.7		
3	TH	0045	4.0	0705	2.0	1306	4.2	1942	1.4
4	F	0156	4.3	0807	1.6	1409	4.5	2033	1.1
5	SA	0246	4.6	0853	1.3	1459	4.8	2114	0.9
6	SU	0328	4.9	0931	1.0	1542	5.0	2149	0.8
7	M	0406	5.0	1006	0.9	1622	5.1	2218	0.8
8	TU	0442	5.1	1036	0.8	1700	5.1	○ 2246	0.8
9	W	0516	5.1	1106	0.9	1737	5.0	2316	0.9
10	TH	0551	5.1	1139	1.0	1814	4.9	2350	1.1
11	F	0626	5.0	1214	1.1	1852	4.7		
12	SA	0025	1.4	0704	4.8	1252	1.3	1932	4.5
13	SU	0102	1.6	0744	4.6	1332	1.6	2016	4.3
14	M	0139	1.9	0828	4.4	1416	1.9	2103	4.0
15	TU	0221	2.2	0916	4.1	1516	2.1	2155	3.8
16	W	0317	2.4	1009	3.9	1711	2.2	◑ 2253	3.7
17	TH	0541	2.4	1108	3.8	1817	2.0		
18	F	0003	3.7	0644	2.3	1218	3.9	1913	1.8
19	SA	0142	4.0	0735	2.0	1350	4.1	2000	1.6
20	SU	0225	4.2	0819	1.7	1435	4.4	2041	1.3
21	M	0259	4.6	0858	1.4	1512	4.7	2116	1.0
22	TU	0333	4.9	0932	1.1	1549	5.0	2150	0.9
23	W	0410	5.1	1007	0.9	1630	5.1	● 2225	0.7
24	TH	0450	5.3	1046	0.7	1713	5.2	2305	0.7
25	F	0533	5.3	1128	0.6	1800	5.2	2347	0.8
26	SA	0618	5.3	1214	0.7	1849	5.1		
27	SU	0033	1.0	0707	5.2	1303	0.9	1941	4.8
28	M	0123	1.3	0758	5.0	1356	1.1	2038	4.6
29	TU	0220	1.6	0855	4.7	1457	1.3	2141	4.3
30	W	0326	1.9	0959	4.5	1609	1.5	◐ 2252	4.2

DECEMBER

Date	Day	Time	m	Time	m	Time	m	Time	m
1	TH	0447	2.0	1113	4.3	1735	1.6		
2	F	0010	4.2	0616	1.9	1231	4.3	1856	1.5
3	SA	0120	4.3	0727	1.8	1338	4.4	1956	1.4
4	SU	0215	4.5	0821	1.6	1432	4.6	2043	1.3
5	M	0301	4.6	0906	1.4	1519	4.7	2122	1.3
6	TU	0341	4.8	0945	1.3	1601	4.8	2155	1.3
7	W	0419	4.9	1019	1.2	1641	4.8	2225	1.3
8	TH	0455	4.9	1050	1.2	1719	4.8	○ 2258	1.3
9	F	0531	5.0	1125	1.2	1757	4.8	2334	1.4
10	SA	0608	4.9	1201	1.2	1836	4.7		
11	SU	0010	1.5	0646	4.9	1239	1.3	1915	4.6
12	M	0047	1.6	0724	4.7	1317	1.5	1956	4.4
13	TU	0125	1.8	0804	4.5	1357	1.6	2038	4.3
14	W	0204	2.0	0846	4.4	1441	1.8	2124	4.1
15	TH	0249	2.2	0932	4.2	1532	1.9	2214	4.0
16	F	0347	2.3	1024	4.1	1637	2.0	◑ 2309	4.0
17	SA	0505	2.3	1122	4.0	1800	2.0		
18	SU	0008	4.0	0634	2.2	1223	4.1	1906	1.8
19	M	0109	4.2	0732	1.9	1328	4.3	1957	1.6
20	TU	0206	4.5	0820	1.6	1428	4.6	2041	1.4
21	W	0256	4.8	0904	1.3	1520	4.8	2124	1.2
22	TH	0343	5.1	0948	1.1	1610	5.1	2208	1.0
23	F	0430	5.3	1033	0.8	1659	5.2	● 2253	0.9
24	SA	0518	5.4	1120	0.7	1750	5.3	2340	0.9
25	SU	0607	5.5	1208	0.7	1840	5.2		
26	M	0027	1.0	0658	5.4	1257	0.7	1932	5.1
27	TU	0117	1.2	0748	5.3	1348	0.9	2025	4.9
28	W	0209	1.4	0841	5.1	1442	1.1	2120	4.7
29	TH	0307	1.6	0937	4.8	1540	1.3	2219	4.4
30	F	0411	1.8	1038	4.5	1645	1.5	◐ 2325	4.3
31	SA	0522	1.9	1147	4.3	1756	1.7		

Chart Datum: 0·20 metres above Ordnance Datum (Dublin)
HAT is 5·9m above Chart Datum

TIDES

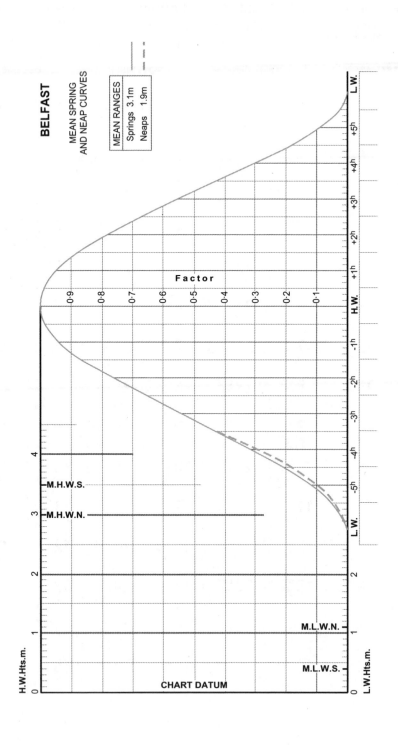

BELFAST

MEAN SPRING
AND NEAP CURVES

MEAN RANGES	
Springs	3.1m
Neaps	1.9m

TIME ZONE (UT)
For Summer Time add ONE hour in **non-shaded areas**

NORTHERN IRELAND – BELFAST
LAT 54°36′N LONG 5°55′W
TIMES AND HEIGHTS OF HIGH AND LOW WATERS

Dates in amber are **SPRINGS**
Dates in grey are **NEAPS**

2022

JANUARY

Day	Time m	Time m		Day	Time m	Time m
1 SA	0306 0.6 / 0930 3.4	1543 0.7 / 2156 3.6		16 SU	0357 0.9 / 1022 3.4	1620 0.8 / 2247 3.2
2 SU	0357 0.6 / 1022 3.6	1634 0.5 / ●2249 3.6		17 M	0434 0.9 / 1101 3.5	1656 0.8 / ○2324 3.2
3 M	0446 0.6 / 1113 3.7	1724 0.4 / 2343 3.6		18 TU	0510 0.8 / 1137 3.5	1732 0.7 / 2357 3.1
4 TU	0535 0.6 / 1203 3.7	1814 0.4		19 W	0547 0.8 / 1208 3.5	1808 0.6
5 W	0035 3.5 / 0625 0.7	1253 3.8 / 1906 0.4		20 TH	0022 3.1 / 0624 0.8	1236 3.5 / 1845 0.6
6 TH	0128 3.4 / 0715 0.8	1343 3.7 / 1957 0.4		21 F	0049 3.1 / 0702 0.8	1308 3.5 / 1922 0.5
7 F	0221 3.3 / 0805 0.8	1432 3.7 / 2050 0.4		22 SA	0125 3.1 / 0740 0.8	1347 3.5 / 2001 0.5
8 SA	0312 3.2 / 0858 0.9	1521 3.6 / 2144 0.6		23 SU	0208 3.1 / 0820 0.8	1429 3.5 / 2042 0.5
9 SU	0404 3.1 / 0948 1.0	1611 3.4 / ☾2243 0.7		24 M	0253 3.1 / 0903 0.8	1516 3.5 / 2129 0.6
10 M	0457 3.0 / 1045 1.1	1705 3.3 / 2344 0.9		25 TU	0344 3.0 / 0952 0.9	1608 3.4 / ☾2222 0.7
11 TU	0553 2.9 / 1151 1.2	1807 3.1		26 W	0440 3.0 / 1050 1.0	1709 3.3 / 2325 0.8
12 W	0043 1.0 / 0656 2.9	1258 1.2 / 1918 3.0		27 TH	0547 2.9 / 1203 1.1	1821 3.2
13 TH	0140 1.0 / 0758 3.0	1400 1.2 / 2026 3.0		28 F	0041 0.9 / 0702 3.0	1329 1.0 / 1937 3.2
14 F	0232 1.0 / 0852 3.1	1454 1.1 / 2120 3.1		29 SA	0156 0.8 / 0815 3.1	1439 0.8 / 2049 3.3
15 SA	0317 0.9 / 0940 3.3	1541 1.1 / 2206 3.1		30 SU	0258 0.8 / 0920 3.3	1538 0.6 / 2150 3.3
				31 M	0352 0.7 / 1016 3.5	1631 0.4 / 2245 3.4

FEBRUARY

Day	Time m	Time m		Day	Time m	Time m
1 TU	0441 0.6 / 1106 3.6	1720 0.3 / ●2335 3.4		16 W	0451 0.7 / 1116 3.4	1711 0.5 / ○2340 3.1
2 W	0528 0.6 / 1153 3.7	1807 0.2		17 TH	0527 0.6 / 1145 3.5	1746 0.4
3 TH	0022 3.4 / 0613 0.6	1238 3.7 / 1853 0.2		18 F	0000 3.1 / 0603 0.6	1208 3.5 / 1822 0.4
4 F	0109 3.3 / 0657 0.6	1323 3.7 / 1936 0.3		19 SA	0022 3.1 / 0638 0.6	1241 3.5 / 1857 0.3
5 SA	0154 3.2 / 0738 0.7	1407 3.6 / 2018 0.4		20 SU	0057 3.1 / 0714 0.5	1320 3.6 / 1934 0.3
6 SU	0238 3.1 / 0819 0.7	1450 3.5 / 2100 0.5		21 M	0138 3.2 / 0751 0.5	1403 3.6 / 2014 0.4
7 M	0321 3.1 / 0902 0.8	1534 3.4 / 2145 0.7		22 TU	0222 3.2 / 0833 0.6	1450 3.5 / 2058 0.5
8 TU	0406 3.0 / 0946 0.9	1621 3.2 / ☽2242 0.9		23 W	0310 3.1 / 0920 0.7	1542 3.3 / ☽2150 0.7
9 W	0454 2.9 / 1046 1.0	1713 3.0 / 2354 1.1		24 TH	0405 3.0 / 1018 0.9	1645 3.2 / 2253 0.9
10 TH	0549 2.9 / 1210 1.2	1815 2.8		25 F	0513 2.9 / 1140 1.0	1801 3.0
11 F	0100 1.1 / 0654 2.9	1324 1.2 / 1941 2.8		26 SA	0021 1.0 / 0637 2.8	1322 0.9 / 1929 3.0
12 SA	0159 1.1 / 0814 2.9	1425 1.1 / 2101 2.8		27 SU	0148 1.0 / 0806 2.9	1434 0.7 / 2048 3.1
13 SU	0251 1.0 / 0916 3.1	1517 0.9 / 2151 3.0		28 M	0253 0.8 / 0916 3.2	1534 0.5 / 2148 3.2
14 M	0335 0.9 / 1002 3.3	1559 0.7 / 2232 3.0				
15 TU	0414 0.8 / 1042 3.4	1636 0.6 / 2308 3.1				

MARCH

Day	Time m	Time m		Day	Time m	Time m
1 TU	0347 0.7 / 1009 3.4	1625 0.3 / 2237 3.3		16 W	0351 0.7 / 1012 3.2	1610 0.5 / 2241 3.1
2 W	0435 0.6 / 1055 3.5	1710 0.2 / ●2322 3.3		17 TH	0427 0.6 / 1044 3.3	1645 0.3 / 2308 3.1
3 TH	0517 0.5 / 1138 3.6	1752 0.2		18 F	0502 0.5 / 1110 3.4	1719 0.3 / ○2328 3.2
4 F	0004 3.3 / 0556 0.5	1219 3.6 / 1831 0.2		19 SA	0536 0.5 / 1138 3.5	1753 0.2 / 2355 3.2
5 SA	0045 3.2 / 0632 0.5	1259 3.6 / 1906 0.3		20 SU	0611 0.4 / 1214 3.6	1828 0.2
6 SU	0124 3.2 / 0707 0.5	1339 3.5 / 1940 0.4		21 M	0030 3.3 / 0647 0.4	1255 3.6 / 1906 0.2
7 M	0202 3.2 / 0743 0.6	1418 3.4 / 2015 0.6		22 TU	0111 3.3 / 0726 0.4	1341 3.5 / 1948 0.4
8 TU	0241 3.1 / 0822 0.6	1459 3.3 / 2053 0.7		23 W	0156 3.3 / 0809 0.5	1431 3.4 / 2034 0.5
9 W	0323 3.1 / 0904 0.8	1543 3.1 / 2137 0.9		24 TH	0245 3.2 / 0900 0.6	1528 3.2 / 2127 0.8
10 TH	0410 3.0 / 0953 1.0	1633 2.9 / ☽2237 1.2		25 F	0343 3.0 / 1003 0.8	1636 3.0 / ☽2235 1.0
11 F	0502 2.9 / 1107 1.1	1731 2.7		26 SA	0455 2.9 / 1141 0.9	1757 2.9
12 SA	0017 1.3 / 0604 2.8	1248 1.2 / 1844 2.6		27 SU	0014 1.1 / 0626 2.8	1317 0.8 / 1931 2.9
13 SU	0125 1.2 / 0717 2.8	1354 1.0 / 2039 2.7		28 M	0140 1.1 / 0759 3.0	1427 0.6 / 2042 3.0
14 M	0222 1.1 / 0843 2.9	1448 0.8 / 2130 2.8		29 TU	0246 0.9 / 0903 3.2	1525 0.4 / 2136 3.1
15 TU	0310 0.9 / 0934 3.1	1532 0.6 / 2208 3.0		30 W	0339 0.7 / 0953 3.4	1612 0.2 / 2221 3.2
				31 TH	0423 0.6 / 1036 3.5	1653 0.2 / 2303 3.2

APRIL

Day	Time m	Time m		Day	Time m	Time m
1 F	0500 0.5 / 1117 3.5	1729 0.2 / ●2341 3.2		16 SA	0433 0.5 / 1035 3.5	1646 0.2 / ○2256 3.3
2 SA	0534 0.5 / 1156 3.5	1802 0.3		17 SU	0507 0.4 / 1111 3.6	1722 0.2 / 2329 3.3
3 SU	0017 3.2 / 0607 0.5	1233 3.4 / 1833 0.4		18 M	0544 0.4 / 1152 3.6	1800 0.2
4 M	0052 3.2 / 0639 0.5	1309 3.4 / 1905 0.6		19 TU	0008 3.4 / 0624 0.3	1237 3.6 / 1843 0.3
5 TU	0127 3.3 / 0713 0.5	1346 3.3 / 1938 0.7		20 W	0052 3.4 / 0707 0.3	1327 3.5 / 1928 0.5
6 W	0205 3.3 / 0750 0.6	1426 3.2 / 2014 0.8		21 TH	0141 3.4 / 0756 0.4	1424 3.4 / 2019 0.7
7 TH	0246 3.2 / 0830 0.7	1509 3.0 / 2056 1.0		22 F	0235 3.3 / 0852 0.6	1527 3.2 / 2118 0.9
8 F	0331 3.1 / 0918 0.9	1559 2.8 / 2148 1.2		23 SA	0336 3.2 / 1005 0.7	1637 3.0 / ☽2232 1.1
9 SA	0422 3.0 / 1020 1.0	1657 2.7 / ☽2318 1.3		24 SU	0448 3.0 / 1140 0.8	1759 2.9
10 SU	0521 2.8 / 1206 1.1	1804 2.6		25 M	0001 1.2 / 0618 3.0	1303 0.6 / 1920 2.9
11 M	0046 1.3 / 0628 2.8	1317 1.0 / 1936 2.6		26 TU	0121 1.1 / 0739 3.1	1411 0.5 / 2023 3.0
12 TU	0147 1.2 / 0743 2.9	1413 0.8 / 2050 2.8		27 W	0227 0.9 / 0840 3.2	1505 0.3 / 2114 3.1
13 W	0238 1.0 / 0845 3.0	1458 0.6 / 2129 3.0		28 TH	0320 0.8 / 0929 3.4	1550 0.3 / 2158 3.2
14 TH	0321 0.8 / 0928 3.2	1537 0.4 / 2200 3.1		29 F	0403 0.7 / 1013 3.4	1628 0.3 / 2238 3.2
15 F	0358 0.6 / 1002 3.4	1612 0.3 / 2228 3.2		30 SA	0439 0.6 / 1054 3.4	1701 0.4 / ●2315 3.3

Chart Datum: 2·01 metres below Ordnance Datum (Belfast)
HAT is 3·9m above Chart Datum

TIDES

TIME ZONE (UT)
For Summer Time add ONE hour in **non-shaded areas**

NORTHERN IRELAND – BELFAST
LAT 54°36'N LONG 5°55'W
TIMES AND HEIGHTS OF HIGH AND LOW WATERS

Dates in amber are **SPRINGS**
Dates in grey are **NEAPS**

2022

MAY

Day	Time	m	Time	m		Day	Time	m	Time	m
1 SU	0511	0.6				16	0440	0.4		
	1131	3.4					1049	3.6		
	1732	0.5				M	1654	0.3		
	2349	3.3				○	2309	3.5		
2 M	0543	0.6				17	0522	0.4		
	1206	3.3					1135	3.6		
	1803	0.6				TU	1738	0.3		
							2354	3.5		
3 TU	0022	3.3	0616	0.6		18	0607	0.3		
	1239	3.3	1836	0.7		W	1227	3.6	1824	0.5
4 W	0057	3.4	0649	0.6		19	0043	3.5	0656	0.4
	1315	3.2	1909	0.8		TH	1322	3.4	1916	0.6
5 TH	0135	3.4	0725	0.6		20	0137	3.5	0750	0.4
	1355	3.1	1946	0.9		F	1422	3.3	2011	0.8
6 F	0216	3.3	0806	0.7		21	0233	3.4	0852	0.5
	1439	3.0	2029	1.0		SA	1525	3.2	2114	0.9
7 SA	0259	3.3	0852	0.8		22	0333	3.3	1004	0.6
	1529	2.9	2119	1.1		SU	1633	3.0	) 2222	1.0
8 SU	0346	3.1	0948	0.9		23	0439	3.2	1123	0.6
	1625	2.7	2224	1.3		M	1745	2.9	2335	1.1
9 M	0441	3.0	1104	1.0		24	0555	3.2	1236	0.6
	1729	2.7	) 2350	1.3		TU	1854	2.9		
10 TU	0543	2.9	1228	0.9		25	0046	1.1	0709	3.2
	1838	2.7				W	1340	0.5	1954	3.0
11 W	0100	1.2	0649	2.9		26	0152	1.0	0810	3.2
	1328	0.8	1944	2.8		TH	1435	0.5	2045	3.1
12 TH	0156	1.1	0751	3.1		27	0248	0.9	0902	3.3
	1416	0.6	2034	3.0		F	1520	0.5	2130	3.2
13 F	0242	0.9	0841	3.2		28	0335	0.8	0948	3.3
	1458	0.4	2115	3.1		SA	1558	0.5	2211	3.2
14 SA	0323	0.7	0925	3.4		29	0414	0.7	1030	3.3
	1536	0.3	2151	3.3		SU	1632	0.6	2249	3.3
15 SU	0401	0.6	1006	3.5		30	0450	0.7	1108	3.3
	1614	0.3	2229	3.4		M	1705	0.7	● 2323	3.3
						31	0524	0.7	1142	3.2
						TU	1739	0.8	2357	3.4

JUNE

Day	Time	m	Time	m		Day	Time	m	Time	m
1 W	0558	0.7	1215	3.2		16	0558	0.3	1219	3.5
	1813	0.8				TH	1812	0.6		
2 TH	0032	3.4	0632	0.7		17	0037	3.6	0651	0.3
	1250	3.1	1849	0.9		F	1315	3.4	1907	0.7
3 F	0110	3.5	0708	0.7		18	0131	3.6	0746	0.3
	1329	3.1	1927	0.9		SA	1414	3.3	2003	0.8
4 SA	0149	3.4	0747	0.7		19	0225	3.6	0845	0.4
	1412	3.0	2009	0.9		SU	1513	3.2	2101	0.9
5 SU	0229	3.4	0831	0.7		20	0320	3.5	0948	0.4
	1459	2.9	2057	1.0		M	1614	3.1	2201	0.9
6 M	0311	3.3	0920	0.8		21	0417	3.4	1054	0.5
	1551	2.8	2150	1.1		TU	1715	3.0	) 2302	1.0
7 TU	0359	3.2	1017	0.8		22	0520	3.3	1159	0.6
	1650	2.8	) 2248	1.2		W	1817	3.0		
8 W	0455	3.1	1120	0.8		23	0005	1.0	0629	3.2
	1751	2.8	2352	1.2		TH	1300	0.6	1916	3.0
9 TH	0557	3.1	1225	0.7		24	0110	1.0	0735	3.2
	1850	2.9				F	1356	0.7	2010	3.0
10 F	0056	1.1	0701	3.1		25	0210	1.0	0833	3.2
	1324	0.6	1945	3.0		SA	1445	0.7	2059	3.1
11 SA	0155	0.9	0800	3.3		26	0304	0.9	0924	3.2
	1416	0.5	2034	3.2		SU	1528	0.7	2144	3.2
12 SU	0246	0.8	0853	3.4		27	0351	0.8	1009	3.2
	1502	0.4	2120	3.3		M	1606	0.8	2224	3.3
13 M	0334	0.6	0943	3.5		28	0430	0.8	1049	3.2
	1548	0.4	2206	3.4		TU	1642	0.8	2302	3.4
14 TU	0421	0.5	1033	3.6		29	0507	0.8	1125	3.1
	1634	0.4	○ 2254	3.5		W	1718	0.8	● 2338	3.4
15 W	0509	0.4	1124	3.6		30	0541	0.7	1158	3.1
	1722	0.5	2345	3.6		TH	1754	0.9		

JULY

Day	Time	m	Time	m		Day	Time	m	Time	m
1 F	0013	3.5	0616	0.7		16	0026	3.7	0644	0.2
	1231	3.1	1831	0.9		SA	1302	3.4	1854	0.7
2 SA	0048	3.5	0652	0.7		17	0117	3.7	0735	0.2
	1305	3.0	1909	0.9		SU	1355	3.3	1945	0.7
3 SU	0122	3.5	0728	0.6		18	0207	3.7	0826	0.3
	1342	3.0	1949	0.9		M	1448	3.2	2036	0.8
4 M	0158	3.4	0808	0.6		19	0256	3.6	0919	0.4
	1423	3.0	2031	0.9		TU	1541	3.1	2127	0.8
5 TU	0238	3.4	0850	0.6		20	0346	3.5	1015	0.5
	1509	2.9	2116	0.9		W	1633	3.0	) 2222	0.9
6 W	0321	3.3	0937	0.6		21	0438	3.3	1116	0.7
	1600	2.9	2205	1.0		TH	1726	3.0	2323	1.0
7 TH	0411	3.2	1030	0.7		22	0535	3.1	1217	0.8
	1656	2.9	) 2259	1.0		F	1824	2.9		
8 F	0509	3.2	1130	0.7		23	0030	1.1	0645	3.0
	1757	2.9				SA	1316	0.9	1926	3.0
9 SA	0001	1.1	0615	3.2		24	0135	1.1	0801	2.9
	1235	0.7	1859	3.0		SU	1411	1.0	2026	3.1
10 SU	0112	1.0	0724	3.2		25	0236	1.0	0903	3.0
	1340	0.7	1958	3.1		M	1500	0.9	2118	3.2
11 M	0220	0.9	0828	3.3		26	0328	0.9	0952	3.0
	1439	0.6	2055	3.3		TU	1543	0.9	2204	3.3
12 TU	0319	0.8	0927	3.4		27	0411	0.8	1034	3.1
	1532	0.6	2150	3.4		W	1621	0.9	2244	3.4
13 W	0413	0.5	1022	3.5		28	0448	0.7	1112	3.1
	1622	0.6	○ 2243	3.5		TH	1657	0.8	● 2321	3.4
14 TH	0504	0.4	1116	3.5		29	0521	0.7	1146	3.0
	1712	0.6	2335	3.6		F	1732	0.8	2354	3.5
15 F	0554	0.3	1209	3.4		30	0555	0.6	1214	3.1
	1803	0.6				SA	1808	0.8		
						31	0022	3.5	0629	0.6
						SU	1237	3.0	1845	0.8

AUGUST

Day	Time	m	Time	m		Day	Time	m	Time	m
1 M	0051	3.5	0704	0.5		16	0142	3.7	0755	0.3
	1307	3.1	1922	0.8		TU	1416	3.2	2001	0.7
2 TU	0126	3.5	0739	0.5		17	0227	3.6	0837	0.5
	1346	3.1	2000	0.8		W	1501	3.2	2045	0.8
3 W	0205	3.5	0817	0.5		18	0312	3.4	0923	0.7
	1429	3.1	2040	0.8		TH	1546	3.1	2132	0.9
4 TH	0248	3.4	0900	0.5		19	0358	3.3	1017	0.9
	1516	3.1	2125	0.9		F	1634	3.0	◑ 2228	1.1
5 F	0336	3.4	0948	0.6		20	0449	3.0	1129	1.1
	1609	3.0	◔ 2216	1.0		SA	1726	3.0	2348	1.2
6 SA	0432	3.2	1045	0.8		21	0549	2.8	1238	1.2
	1711	3.0	2319	1.0		SU	1827	2.9		
7 SU	0541	3.1	1154	0.9		22	0103	1.2	0718	2.7
	1820	3.0				M	1338	1.2	1946	3.0
8 M	0045	1.1	0658	3.1		23	0208	1.1	0846	2.8
	1318	0.9	1932	3.0		TU	1433	1.1	2053	3.1
9 TU	0210	0.9	0813	3.1		24	0304	0.9	0937	2.9
	1429	0.8	2040	3.2		W	1519	1.0	2142	3.3
10 W	0313	0.7	0920	3.3		25	0348	0.8	1018	3.0
	1525	0.7	2141	3.4		TH	1558	0.9	2222	3.4
11 TH	0408	0.4	1016	3.4		26	0423	0.7	1053	3.1
	1614	0.6	2234	3.6		F	1634	0.8	2257	3.4
12 F	0458	0.3	1107	3.4		27	0456	0.6	1125	3.1
	1704	0.6	○ 2323	3.7		SA	1708	0.8	● 2326	3.5
13 SA	0544	0.2	1155	3.4		28	0529	0.5	1149	3.1
	1749	0.6				SU	1742	0.7	2348	3.5
14 SU	0010	3.7	0630	0.2		29	0601	0.5	1204	3.1
	1242	3.3	1834	0.6		M	1816	0.7		
15 M	0056	3.7	0713	0.2		30	0017	3.5	0634	0.4
	1329	3.3	1918	0.6		TU	1234	3.2	1851	0.7
						31	0054	3.5	0708	0.4
						W	1312	3.2	1927	0.7

Chart Datum: 2·01 metres below Ordnance Datum (Belfast)
HAT is 3·9m above Chart Datum

NORTHERN IRELAND – BELFAST
LAT 54°36′N   LONG 5°55′W
TIMES AND HEIGHTS OF HIGH AND LOW WATERS

Dates in amber are **SPRINGS**
Dates in grey are **NEAPS**

2022

SEPTEMBER

Date	Time	m	Time	m	Time	m	Time	m
1 TH	0135	3.6	0745	0.4	1354	3.2	2006	0.7
2 F	0219	3.5	0827	0.6	1440	3.2	2051	0.8
3 SA ◐	0309	3.4	0914	0.7	1532	3.1	2144	0.9
4 SU	0408	3.2	1012	0.9	1637	3.0	2253	1.1
5 M	0522	3.0	1127	1.1	1755	3.0		
6 TU	0043	1.1	0646	2.9	1312	1.2	1919	3.0
7 W	0205	0.9	0812	3.0	1424	1.0	2036	3.2
8 TH	0307	0.6	0918	3.2	1520	0.8	2134	3.4
9 F	0400	0.4	1009	3.3	1608	0.7	2223	3.6
10 SA ○	0446	0.2	1051	3.4	1651	0.6	2307	3.7
11 SU	0528	0.2	1137	3.4	1730	0.6	2350	3.7
12 M	0606	0.2	1219	3.4	1808	0.6		
13 TU	0032	3.7	0643	0.3	1300	3.3	1846	0.7
14 W	0114	3.6	0717	0.5	1341	3.3	1924	0.8
15 TH	0156	3.5	0753	0.6	1422	3.3	2004	0.8
16 F	0237	3.4	0832	0.8	1504	3.2	2047	0.9
17 SA ◐	0321	3.2	0915	1.1	1550	3.2	2138	1.1
18 SU	0411	3.0	1013	1.3	1642	3.1	2252	1.2
19 M	0508	2.8	1154	1.4	1741	3.0		
20 TU	0027	1.3	0621	2.6	1303	1.4	1852	3.0
21 W	0135	1.2	0824	2.7	1402	1.3	2019	3.1
22 TH	0232	1.0	0915	2.9	1451	1.1	2112	3.2
23 F	0317	0.8	0953	3.0	1532	0.9	2152	3.4
24 SA	0353	0.6	1025	3.1	1607	0.8	2225	3.5
25 SU ●	0426	0.5	1053	3.2	1641	0.7	2251	3.5
26 M	0458	0.5	1114	3.3	1714	0.7	2315	3.6
27 TU	0530	0.4	1133	3.3	1746	0.7	2347	3.6
28 W	0602	0.4	1204	3.4	1820	0.6		
29 TH	0026	3.6	0638	0.4	1243	3.4	1858	0.6
30 F	0110	3.6	0717	0.5	1326	3.4	1940	0.7

OCTOBER

Date	Time	m	Time	m	Time	m	Time	m
1 SA	0158	3.5	0801	0.7	1414	3.3	2028	0.8
2 SU	0252	3.3	0851	0.9	1509	3.2	2127	1.0
3 M ◐	0358	3.1	0953	1.2	1619	3.1	2249	1.1
4 TU	0517	3.0	1119	1.3	1743	3.0		
5 W	0041	1.0	0648	2.9	1304	1.3	1915	3.1
6 TH	0156	0.8	0809	3.1	1414	1.1	2027	3.3
7 F	0256	0.6	0907	3.2	1508	0.9	2121	3.5
8 SA	0345	0.4	0954	3.4	1554	0.8	2206	3.7
9 SU ○	0427	0.3	1036	3.4	1633	0.7	2249	3.7
10 M	0504	0.3	1115	3.5	1708	0.7	2329	3.7
11 TU	0538	0.4	1153	3.4	1742	0.7		
12 W	0008	3.6	0610	0.6	1230	3.4	1817	0.7
13 TH	0046	3.5	0643	0.7	1307	3.4	1853	0.8
14 F	0124	3.4	0717	0.8	1346	3.4	1932	0.8
15 SA	0205	3.3	0754	1.0	1428	3.4	2014	0.9
16 SU	0249	3.2	0836	1.2	1513	3.3	2102	1.1
17 M ◐	0338	3.0	0926	1.4	1604	3.2	2205	1.2
18 TU	0435	2.8	1049	1.5	1701	3.1	2343	1.3
19 W	0542	2.7	1222	1.5	1806	3.0		
20 TH	0055	1.2	0719	2.7	1325	1.4	1920	3.1
21 F	0153	1.0	0834	2.9	1417	1.2	2025	3.2
22 SA	0239	0.8	0913	3.1	1500	1.0	2109	3.4
23 SU	0317	0.7	0946	3.2	1537	0.9	2145	3.5
24 M	0352	0.5	1015	3.3	1611	0.8	2216	3.6
25 TU ●	0424	0.5	1040	3.4	1644	0.7	2248	3.7
26 W	0458	0.5	1107	3.5	1719	0.6	2325	3.7
27 TH	0534	0.5	1141	3.5	1757	0.6		
28 F	0007	3.7	0614	0.6	1222	3.6	1839	0.6
29 SA	0055	3.6	0657	0.7	1309	3.5	1925	0.7
30 SU	0149	3.5	0745	0.9	1402	3.5	2020	0.8
31 M	0250	3.3	0841	1.1	1502	3.4	2126	0.9

NOVEMBER

Date	Time	m	Time	m	Time	m	Time	m
1 TU ◐	0400	3.1	0949	1.3	1613	3.2	2255	1.0
2 W	0518	3.0	1115	1.4	1735	3.2	2358	1.2
3 TH	0026	0.9	0642	3.0	1242	1.3	1900	3.2
4 F	0137	0.7	0751	3.1	1352	1.2	2006	3.4
5 SA	0235	0.6	0845	3.3	1448	1.0	2059	3.5
6 SU	0322	0.5	0931	3.4	1533	0.9	2146	3.6
7 M	0403	0.5	1013	3.5	1611	0.8	2228	3.6
8 TU ○	0438	0.6	1052	3.5	1647	0.6	2308	3.6
9 W	0510	0.7	1129	3.5	1721	0.8	2346	3.5
10 TH	0543	0.8	1203	3.5	1756	0.8		
11 F	0021	3.4	0617	0.9	1238	3.6	1832	0.8
12 SA	0057	3.3	0651	1.0	1317	3.6	1909	0.9
13 SU	0137	3.3	0728	1.1	1358	3.5	1950	0.9
14 M	0221	3.1	0809	1.2	1442	3.5	2036	1.0
15 TU	0310	3.0	0859	1.3	1530	3.3	2131	1.1
16 W ◐	0405	2.9	0959	1.4	1623	3.2	2238	1.2
17 TH	0507	2.8	1117	1.5	1724	3.1	2358	1.2
18 F	0615	2.8	1233	1.4	1828	3.1		
19 SA	0102	1.0	0724	2.9	1331	1.3	1930	3.2
20 SU	0153	0.9	0818	3.1	1419	1.1	2023	3.3
21 M	0235	0.7	0900	3.3	1501	1.0	2107	3.5
22 TU	0314	0.6	0937	3.4	1539	0.8	2147	3.6
23 W ●	0352	0.5	1013	3.5	1618	0.7	2227	3.7
24 TH	0431	0.5	1048	3.6	1658	0.6	2311	3.7
25 F	0512	0.6	1129	3.6	1742	0.6	2359	3.7
26 SA	0557	0.7	1215	3.7	1829	0.6		
27 SU	0051	3.6	0646	0.8	1305	3.6	1921	0.6
28 M	0149	3.4	0739	0.9	1401	3.6	2019	0.7
29 TU	0251	3.3	0838	1.1	1500	3.5	2126	0.7
30 W	0357	3.2	0943	1.2	1605	3.4	2240	0.8

DECEMBER

Date	Time	m	Time	m	Time	m	Time	m
1 TH	0507	3.1	1054	1.2	1717	3.4	2356	0.8
2 F	0617	3.1	1206	1.2	1831	3.3		
3 SA	0104	0.7	0721	3.1	1315	1.2	1938	3.4
4 SU	0202	0.7	0816	3.2	1415	1.1	2034	3.4
5 M	0252	0.7	0905	3.3	1507	1.0	2124	3.5
6 TU	0335	0.7	0949	3.4	1550	0.9	2209	3.5
7 W	0412	0.8	1030	3.5	1629	0.9	2251	3.4
8 TH ○	0448	0.8	1108	3.5	1707	0.8	2329	3.4
9 F	0523	0.9	1144	3.6	1743	0.8		
10 SA	0003	3.3	0558	1.0	1218	3.6	1819	0.8
11 SU	0038	3.2	0633	1.0	1256	3.6	1855	0.8
12 M	0116	3.2	0711	1.1	1335	3.6	1933	0.8
13 TU	0157	3.1	0750	1.1	1415	3.5	2015	0.9
14 W	0241	3.0	0835	1.1	1457	3.4	2101	0.9
15 TH	0330	3.0	0925	1.2	1542	3.3	2152	1.0
16 F ◐	0425	2.9	1019	1.3	1633	3.2	2249	1.0
17 SA	0525	2.9	1120	1.3	1733	3.2	2352	1.0
18 SU	0626	2.9	1226	1.3	1836	3.2		
19 M	0054	0.9	0724	3.0	1329	1.2	1937	3.3
20 TU	0151	0.8	0816	3.2	1424	1.0	2032	3.4
21 W	0241	0.7	0903	3.3	1514	0.9	2122	3.5
22 TH	0327	0.7	0949	3.4	1601	0.7	2212	3.6
23 F ●	0413	0.6	1034	3.5	1647	0.6	2302	3.6
24 SA	0459	0.6	1122	3.6	1735	0.5	2354	3.6
25 SU	0547	0.7	1212	3.7	1825	0.4		
26 M	0048	3.5	0638	0.8	1303	3.7	1918	0.4
27 TU	0144	3.4	0731	0.8	1356	3.7	2013	0.4
28 W	0241	3.3	0826	0.9	1450	3.7	2111	0.5
29 TH	0340	3.2	0923	1.0	1546	3.6	2213	0.6
30 F ◐	0439	3.1	1022	1.0	1646	3.5	2318	0.7
31 SA	0541	3.1	1127	1.1	1752	3.3		

Chart Datum: 2·01 metres below Ordnance Datum (Belfast)
HAT is 3·9m above Chart Datum

TIDES

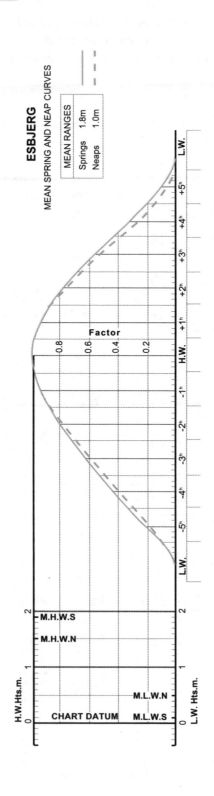

ESBJERG

MEAN SPRING AND NEAP CURVES

TIME ZONE -0100
(Danish Standard Time)
Subtract 1 hour for UT
For Danish Summer Time add
ONE hour in **non-shaded areas**

DENMARK – ESBJERG

LAT 55°28'N   LONG 8°27'E

TIMES AND HEIGHTS OF HIGH AND LOW WATERS

Dates in amber are **SPRINGS**
Dates in grey are **NEAPS**

2022

JANUARY

Day	Time	m		Day	Time	m
1 SA	0045 / 0650 / 1316 / 1924	1.9 / 0.3 / 2.0 / 0.2		**16** SU	0138 / 0747 / 1405 / 2003	1.9 / 0.4 / 1.8 / 0.4
2 SU	0152 / 0751 / 1430 / ● 2019	1.9 / 0.2 / 1.9 / 0.3		**17** M	0226 / 0832 / 1453 / 2042	1.9 / 0.3 / 1.8 / 0.4
3 M	0253 / 0847 / 1536 / 2108	1.9 / 0.1 / 1.9 / 0.3		**18** TU	0309 / 0912 / 1536 / ○ 2119	2.0 / 0.3 / 1.8 / 0.3
4 TU	0347 / 0939 / 1633 / 2154	2.0 / 0.1 / 1.9 / 0.3		**19** W	0348 / 0948 / 1613 / 2153	2.0 / 0.3 / 1.8 / 0.3
5 W	0434 / 1028 / 1722 / 2238	2.0 / 0.1 / 1.8 / 0.3		**20** TH	0421 / 1022 / 1645 / 2225	2.0 / 0.3 / 1.8 / 0.3
6 TH	0516 / 1115 / 1804 / 2322	2.1 / 0.1 / 1.7 / 0.3		**21** F	0449 / 1055 / 1712 / 2259	2.0 / 0.2 / 1.8 / 0.3
7 F	0557 / 1202 / 1844	2.1 / 0.2 / 1.7		**22** SA	0515 / 1130 / 1738 / 2334	2.0 / 0.2 / 1.8 / 0.3
8 SA	0006 / 0641 / 1250 / 1924	0.3 / 2.1 / 0.2 / 1.7		**23** SU	0544 / 1208 / 1809	2.1 / 0.2 / 1.8
9 SU	0054 / 0729 / 1341 / ● 2009	0.4 / 2.1 / 0.3 / 1.7		**24** M	0014 / 0620 / 1250 / 1849	0.3 / 2.1 / 0.2 / 1.8
10 M	0147 / 0822 / 1435 / 2059	0.4 / 2.0 / 0.3 / 1.7		**25** TU	0059 / 0705 / 1338 / ◑ 1939	0.3 / 2.1 / 0.2 / 1.8
11 TU	0245 / 0917 / 1533 / 2153	0.4 / 2.0 / 0.4 / 1.7		**26** W	0152 / 0801 / 1434 / 2039	0.3 / 2.0 / 0.3 / 1.8
12 W	0349 / 1015 / 1634 / 2250	0.5 / 1.9 / 0.4 / 1.7		**27** TH	0252 / 0907 / 1538 / 2148	0.3 / 2.0 / 0.3 / 1.8
13 TH	0456 / 1115 / 1733 / 2348	0.5 / 1.9 / 0.4 / 1.8		**28** F	0403 / 1022 / 1649 / 2305	0.4 / 1.9 / 0.4 / 1.8
14 F	0559 / 1214 / 1829	0.4 / 1.8 / 0.4		**29** SA	0520 / 1148 / 1801	0.4 / 1.9 / 0.4
15 SA	0045 / 0656 / 1312 / 1918	1.8 / 0.4 / 1.8 / 0.4		**30** SU	0027 / 0634 / 1316 / 1907	1.8 / 0.3 / 1.9 / 0.4
				31 M	0144 / 0740 / 1434 / 2005	1.8 / 0.2 / 1.9 / 0.3

FEBRUARY

Day	Time	m		Day	Time	m
1 TU	0249 / 0838 / 1536 / ● 2056	2.0 / 0.1 / 1.9 / 0.3		**16** W	0247 / 0849 / 1518 / ○ 2057	2.0 / 0.3 / 1.8 / 0.3
2 W	0343 / 0930 / 1627 / 2141	2.0 / 0.1 / 1.9 / 0.3		**17** TH	0329 / 0927 / 1558 / 2133	2.0 / 0.2 / 1.8 / 0.3
3 TH	0429 / 1016 / 1709 / 2223	2.1 / 0.1 / 1.8 / 0.3		**18** F	0406 / 1002 / 1631 / 2207	2.1 / 0.2 / 1.8 / 0.3
4 F	0507 / 1059 / 1743 / 2303	2.1 / 0.1 / 1.8 / 0.3		**19** SA	0436 / 1035 / 1658 / 2241	2.1 / 0.2 / 1.8 / 0.2
5 SA	0542 / 1140 / 1811 / 2344	2.1 / 0.2 / 1.7 / 0.3		**20** SU	0502 / 1109 / 1721 / 2316	2.1 / 0.2 / 1.8 / 0.2
6 SU	0616 / 1222 / 1840	2.1 / 0.2 / 1.7		**21** M	0527 / 1146 / 1745 / 2355	2.1 / 0.2 / 1.8 / 0.2
7 M	0027 / 0654 / 1304 / 1916	0.3 / 2.0 / 0.3 / 1.7		**22** TU	0559 / 1227 / 1819	2.1 / 0.2 / 1.8
8 TU	0112 / 0738 / 1350 / ◑ 2001	0.3 / 2.0 / 0.4 / 1.7		**23** W	0039 / 0642 / 1313 / ◑ 1905	0.2 / 2.1 / 0.2 / 1.8
9 W	0203 / 0828 / 1442 / 2054	0.4 / 1.9 / 0.4 / 1.7		**24** TH	0130 / 0737 / 1407 / 2004	0.3 / 2.0 / 0.3 / 1.8
10 TH	0301 / 0924 / 1540 / 2153	0.5 / 1.8 / 0.5 / 1.7		**25** F	0231 / 0847 / 1512 / 2119	0.4 / 1.9 / 0.4 / 1.7
11 F	0407 / 1027 / 1644 / 2257	0.5 / 1.8 / 0.5 / 1.7		**26** SA	0344 / 1015 / 1627 / 2248	0.4 / 1.8 / 0.5 / 1.7
12 SA	0517 / 1133 / 1747	0.5 / 1.7 / 0.5		**27** SU	0506 / 1154 / 1744	0.4 / 1.8 / 0.5
13 SU	0002 / 0623 / 1239 / 1845	1.8 / 0.5 / 1.7 / 0.5		**28** M	0020 / 0625 / 1322 / 1854	1.8 / 0.3 / 1.8 / 0.5
14 M	0104 / 0719 / 1339 / 1935	1.9 / 0.4 / 1.8 / 0.4				
15 TU	0159 / 0807 / 1433 / 2018	1.9 / 0.3 / 1.8 / 0.4				

MARCH

Day	Time	m		Day	Time	m
1 TU	0138 / 0732 / 1431 / 1952	1.9 / 0.2 / 1.9 / 0.4		**16** W	0124 / 0736 / 1403 / 1948	1.9 / 0.3 / 1.8 / 0.4
2 W	0241 / 0828 / 1526 / ● 2042	2.0 / 0.1 / 1.9 / 0.3		**17** TH	0216 / 0820 / 1450 / 2030	2.0 / 0.2 / 1.9 / 0.3
3 TH	0332 / 0916 / 1610 / 2125	2.1 / 0.1 / 1.9 / 0.3		**18** F	0301 / 0900 / 1531 / ○ 2108	2.1 / 0.2 / 1.9 / 0.3
4 F	0414 / 0959 / 1645 / 2205	2.1 / 0.1 / 1.8 / 0.2		**19** SA	0340 / 0936 / 1607 / 2145	2.1 / 0.1 / 1.9 / 0.2
5 SA	0448 / 1037 / 1711 / 2242	2.1 / 0.1 / 1.8 / 0.2		**20** SU	0414 / 1012 / 1636 / 2221	2.1 / 0.1 / 1.9 / 0.2
6 SU	0516 / 1113 / 1731 / 2319	2.1 / 0.2 / 1.8 / 0.2		**21** M	0443 / 1047 / 1659 / 2258	2.1 / 0.1 / 1.9 / 0.2
7 M	0543 / 1149 / 1754 / 2357	2.0 / 0.3 / 1.8 / 0.2		**22** TU	0510 / 1124 / 1722 / 2338	2.0 / 0.2 / 1.9 / 0.2
8 TU	0614 / 1225 / 1825	2.0 / 0.3 / 1.8		**23** W	0543 / 1205 / 1754	2.0 / 0.2 / 1.8
9 W	0038 / 0652 / 1305 / 1907	0.3 / 1.9 / 0.4 / 1.8		**24** TH	0022 / 0626 / 1252 / 1839	0.2 / 1.9 / 0.3 / 1.8
10 TH	0122 / 0738 / 1350 / ◑ 1958	0.4 / 1.8 / 0.5 / 1.8		**25** F	0114 / 0726 / 1346 / ◑ 1941	0.3 / 1.8 / 0.4 / 1.8
11 F	0214 / 0834 / 1442 / 2057	0.5 / 1.8 / 0.6 / 1.7		**26** SA	0217 / 0848 / 1451 / 2107	0.3 / 1.7 / 0.5 / 1.7
12 SA	0316 / 0939 / 1546 / 2205	0.5 / 1.7 / 0.6 / 1.7		**27** SU	0334 / 1027 / 1609 / 2245	0.4 / 1.7 / 0.6 / 1.8
13 SU	0429 / 1051 / 1657 / 2316	0.6 / 1.7 / 0.6 / 1.8		**28** M	0458 / 1200 / 1729	0.4 / 1.7 / 0.6
14 M	0542 / 1202 / 1804	0.5 / 1.7 / 0.6		**29** TU	0013 / 0616 / 1315 / 1838	1.9 / 0.3 / 1.8 / 0.5
15 TU	0024 / 0644 / 1307 / 1900	1.8 / 0.4 / 1.7 / 0.5		**30** W	0125 / 0720 / 1415 / 1935	2.0 / 0.2 / 1.9 / 0.4
				31 TH	0223 / 0812 / 1504 / 2024	2.1 / 0.1 / 1.9 / 0.3

APRIL

Day	Time	m		Day	Time	m
1 F	0311 / 0857 / 1543 / ● 2106	2.1 / 0.1 / 1.9 / 0.2		**16** SA	0225 / 0827 / 1458 / ○ 2040	2.1 / 0.2 / 1.9 / 0.2
2 SA	0351 / 0936 / 1614 / 2144	2.1 / 0.1 / 1.9 / 0.2		**17** SU	0309 / 0908 / 1537 / 2121	2.1 / 0.1 / 1.9 / 0.2
3 SU	0422 / 1011 / 1635 / 2220	2.1 / 0.2 / 1.9 / 0.2		**18** M	0349 / 0947 / 1610 / 2200	2.1 / 0.1 / 1.9 / 0.2
4 M	0447 / 1043 / 1652 / 2254	2.0 / 0.2 / 1.9 / 0.2		**19** TU	0425 / 1025 / 1638 / 2240	2.0 / 0.2 / 1.9 / 0.1
5 TU	0509 / 1115 / 1713 / 2329	2.0 / 0.3 / 1.9 / 0.2		**20** W	0459 / 1104 / 1704 / 2323	2.0 / 0.2 / 1.9 / 0.2
6 W	0535 / 1148 / 1743	1.9 / 0.4 / 1.9		**21** TH	0537 / 1147 / 1737	1.9 / 0.3 / 1.8
7 TH	0006 / 0610 / 1223 / 1821	0.3 / 1.8 / 0.4 / 1.8		**22** F	0011 / 0627 / 1234 / 1827	0.2 / 1.8 / 0.4 / 1.8
8 F	0046 / 0653 / 1303 / 1908	0.4 / 1.8 / 0.5 / 1.8		**23** SA	0105 / 0738 / 1329 / ◑ 1938	0.3 / 1.7 / 0.5 / 1.8
9 SA	0132 / 0747 / 1350 / ◑ 2006	0.4 / 1.7 / 0.6 / 1.8		**24** SU	0210 / 0905 / 1434 / 2109	0.3 / 1.6 / 0.6 / 1.8
10 SU	0229 / 0853 / 1448 / 2114	0.5 / 1.6 / 0.7 / 1.7		**25** M	0326 / 1031 / 1551 / 2257	0.4 / 1.6 / 0.6 / 1.8
11 M	0337 / 1006 / 1559 / 2226	0.6 / 1.6 / 0.7 / 1.8		**26** TU	0447 / 1147 / 1709 / 2355	0.4 / 1.7 / 0.6 / 1.9
12 TU	0451 / 1119 / 1712 / 2335	0.5 / 1.6 / 0.6 / 1.8		**27** W	0559 / 1252 / 1816	0.3 / 1.8 / 0.5
13 W	0559 / 1225 / 1816	0.4 / 1.7 / 0.5		**28** TH	0101 / 0659 / 1346 / 1913	2.0 / 0.2 / 1.8 / 0.3
14 TH	0039 / 0655 / 1323 / 1910	1.9 / 0.3 / 1.8 / 0.4		**29** F	0157 / 0749 / 1432 / 2001	2.1 / 0.2 / 1.9 / 0.3
15 F	0135 / 0744 / 1413 / 1957	2.0 / 0.2 / 1.9 / 0.3		**30** SA	0244 / 0832 / 1510 / ● 2044	2.1 / 0.2 / 1.9 / 0.2

Chart Datum: 0·69 metres below Dansk Normal Null
HAT is 2·2 metres above Chart Datum

TIDES

TIDES

TIME ZONE −0100
(Danish Standard Time)
Subtract 1 hour for UT
For Danish Summer Time add
ONE hour in **non-shaded areas**

DENMARK – ESBJERG
LAT 55°28′N   LONG 8°26′E
TIMES AND HEIGHTS OF HIGH AND LOW WATERS

Dates in amber are **SPRINGS**
Dates in grey are **NEAPS**

2022

MAY

Date	Time m	Time m	Time m	Time m
1 SU	0323 2.0	0909 0.2	1540 1.9	2122 2.0
2 M	0354 2.0	0943 0.3	1603 1.9	2157 0.2
3 TU	0418 1.9	1014 0.3	1621 1.9	2231 0.3
4 W	0439 1.8	1045 0.3	1643 1.9	2304 0.3
5 TH	0504 1.8	1116 0.4	1711 1.9	2339 0.3
6 F	0536 1.8	1149 0.4	1746 1.9	
7 SA	0016 0.4	0617 1.7	1226 0.5	1829 1.9
8 SU	0059 0.4	0707 1.7	1309 0.6	1922 1.8
9 M	0149 0.5	0809 1.6	1401 0.6	◐ 2024 1.8
10 TU	0249 0.5	0917 1.6	1504 0.6	2133 1.8
11 W	0357 0.5	1027 1.6	1615 0.6	2241 1.9
12 TH	0506 0.4	1133 1.7	1724 0.5	2347 1.9
13 F	0608 0.3	1234 1.8	1826 0.4	
14 SA	0048 2.0	0703 0.2	1330 1.9	1921 0.3
15 SU	0144 2.0	0753 0.2	1421 1.9	2010 0.2
16 M	0237 2.0	0839 0.2	1507 1.9	○ 2057 1.9
17 TU	0327 2.0	0923 0.2	1547 1.9	2141 0.2
18 W	0414 2.0	1005 0.2	1623 1.9	2226 0.1
19 TH	0500 1.9	1047 0.3	1657 1.9	2313 0.2
20 F	0550 1.8	1131 0.4	1738 1.9	
21 SA	0003 0.2	0647 1.7	1219 0.5	1834 1.9
22 SU	0058 0.3	0752 1.6	1313 0.5	◑ 1945 1.9
23 M	0201 0.3	0901 1.6	1415 0.6	2101 1.9
24 TU	0311 0.4	1009 1.6	1526 0.6	2215 1.9
25 W	0424 0.4	1114 1.7	1639 0.5	2324 2.0
26 TH	0532 0.3	1213 1.7	1746 0.4	
27 F	0027 2.0	0630 0.3	1307 1.8	1845 0.4
28 SA	0123 0.3	0719 0.3	1354 1.9	1935 0.3
29 SU	0212 0.3	0803 0.3	1435 1.9	2020 0.3
30 M	0254 1.9	0842 0.3	1509 1.9	● 2100 0.3
31 TU	0328 1.9	0916 0.3	1537 1.9	2137 0.3

JUNE

Date	Time m	Time m	Time m	Time m
1 W	0356 1.8	0949 0.4	1601 1.9	2211 0.3
2 TH	0420 1.8	1019 0.4	1625 1.9	2244 0.3
3 F	0446 1.7	1050 0.4	1652 1.9	2317 0.4
4 SA	0516 1.7	1122 0.4	1723 1.9	2352 0.4
5 SU	0551 1.7	1157 0.5	1801 1.9	
6 M	0032 0.4	0634 1.7	1237 0.5	1846 1.9
7 TU	0117 0.4	0726 1.7	1325 0.5	◐ 1940 1.9
8 W	0209 0.4	0825 1.7	1420 0.5	2041 1.9
9 TH	0308 0.4	0930 1.7	1524 0.5	2146 1.9
10 F	0414 0.4	1035 1.7	1633 0.5	2253 1.9
11 SA	0520 0.3	1140 1.8	1742 0.4	2359 1.9
12 SU	0623 0.3	1244 1.8	1845 0.4	
13 M	0106 2.0	0721 0.3	1344 1.8	1943 0.3
14 TU	0211 2.0	0813 0.3	1441 1.9	○ 2036 0.2
15 W	0314 1.9	0902 0.3	1532 1.9	2127 0.2
16 TH	0413 1.9	0948 0.3	1618 1.9	2215 0.1
17 F	0508 1.8	1032 0.4	1702 1.9	2304 0.2
18 SA	0559 1.7	1117 0.4	1747 1.9	2354 0.2
19 SU	0649 1.7	1204 0.4	1838 2.0	
20 M	0046 0.2	0739 1.6	1254 0.5	1935 2.0
21 TU	0143 0.3	0832 1.6	1350 0.5	◑ 2036 2.0
22 W	0244 0.3	0927 1.6	1453 0.5	2139 2.0
23 TH	0348 0.4	1024 1.7	1601 0.5	2242 1.9
24 F	0452 0.4	1121 1.7	1709 0.4	2343 1.9
25 SA	0552 0.4	1217 1.8	1812 0.4	
26 SU	0042 1.9	0645 0.4	1310 1.8	1907 0.4
27 M	0136 1.9	0732 0.4	1358 1.9	1956 0.3
28 TU	0224 1.8	0814 0.4	1440 1.9	2039 0.3
29 W	0305 1.8	0852 0.4	1516 1.9	● 2118 0.3
30 TH	0341 1.8	0927 0.4	1548 1.9	2154 0.3

JULY

Date	Time m	Time m	Time m	Time m
1 F	0411 1.7	0959 0.4	1616 1.9	2226 0.3
2 SA	0439 1.7	1029 0.4	1642 1.9	2258 0.3
3 SU	0505 1.7	1101 0.4	1709 1.9	2331 0.3
4 M	0532 1.7	1134 0.4	1740 2.0	
5 TU	0007 0.3	0605 1.7	1212 0.4	1817 2.0
6 W	0048 0.3	0646 1.7	1255 0.4	1902 2.0
7 TH	0134 0.3	0736 1.7	1345 0.4	◐ 1955 2.0
8 F	0227 0.3	0834 1.7	1443 0.4	2056 2.0
9 SA	0329 0.4	0938 1.7	1549 0.4	2204 1.9
10 SU	0437 0.4	1047 1.7	1702 0.4	2318 1.9
11 M	0547 0.4	1200 1.8	1815 0.4	
12 TU	0038 1.9	0653 0.4	1314 1.8	1921 0.3
13 W	0159 1.9	0752 0.4	1424 1.9	○ 2021 0.2
14 TH	0313 1.9	0845 0.4	1524 1.9	2115 0.2
15 F	0414 1.8	0933 0.4	1615 2.0	2205 0.1
16 SA	0505 1.8	1018 0.4	1700 2.0	2253 0.1
17 SU	0549 1.8	1101 0.3	1741 2.0	2339 0.2
18 M	0628 1.7	1145 0.3	1823 2.0	
19 TU	0026 0.2	0704 1.7	1231 0.3	1908 2.0
20 W	0114 0.3	0743 1.7	1320 0.4	◑ 1958 2.0
21 TH	0206 0.4	0829 1.7	1416 0.4	2052 1.9
22 F	0302 0.4	0921 1.7	1518 0.4	2151 1.9
23 SA	0403 0.5	1019 1.7	1625 0.5	2253 1.8
24 SU	0505 0.5	1120 1.7	1733 0.5	2356 1.8
25 M	0605 0.5	1221 1.8	1836 0.4	
26 TU	0058 1.8	0659 0.5	1319 1.8	1930 0.4
27 W	0154 1.7	0747 0.5	1410 1.9	2017 0.4
28 TH	0243 1.8	0829 0.5	1454 1.9	● 2058 0.3
29 F	0324 1.8	0906 0.4	1532 1.9	2134 0.3
30 SA	0359 1.8	0939 0.4	1605 2.0	2207 0.3
31 SU	0429 1.7	1010 0.4	1632 2.0	2238 0.3

AUGUST

Date	Time m	Time m	Time m	Time m
1 M	0453 1.7	1041 0.3	1655 2.0	2309 0.3
2 TU	0514 1.8	1114 0.3	1719 2.0	2343 0.3
3 W	0538 1.8	1149 0.3	1749 2.0	
4 TH	0020 0.2	0610 1.8	1230 0.3	1829 2.0
5 F	0103 0.3	0653 1.8	1317 0.3	◐ 1917 2.0
6 SA	0153 0.3	0746 1.8	1411 0.3	2017 1.9
7 SU	0252 0.4	0849 1.8	1517 0.4	2128 1.9
8 M	0401 0.5	1003 1.7	1633 0.4	2253 1.8
9 TU	0517 0.5	1128 1.7	1753 0.4	
10 W	0030 1.8	0631 0.5	1257 1.8	1906 0.3
11 TH	0159 1.8	0735 0.4	1414 1.9	2009 0.2
12 F	0309 1.8	0829 0.4	1514 2.0	○ 2103 0.1
13 SA	0404 1.8	0917 0.3	1604 2.0	2152 0.1
14 SU	0448 1.8	1001 0.3	1645 2.1	2235 0.1
15 M	0523 1.8	1042 0.3	1721 2.1	2317 0.1
16 TU	0551 1.8	1122 0.2	1755 2.1	2357 0.2
17 W	0615 1.8	1204 0.2	1830 2.0	
18 TH	0039 0.3	0646 1.8	1248 0.3	1912 2.0
19 F	0123 0.4	0726 1.8	1337 0.3	◑ 2000 1.9
20 SA	0211 0.5	0816 1.7	1432 0.5	2055 1.8
21 SU	0307 0.6	0915 1.7	1537 0.5	2159 1.7
22 M	0411 0.6	1021 1.7	1649 0.5	2308 1.7
23 TU	0519 0.6	1130 1.7	1759 0.5	
24 W	0017 1.7	0622 0.6	1237 1.8	1859 0.4
25 TH	0121 1.7	0716 0.5	1335 1.8	1950 0.4
26 F	0214 1.8	0802 0.5	1425 1.9	2032 0.3
27 SA	0259 1.8	0841 0.4	1507 2.0	● 2110 0.3
28 SU	0337 1.8	0916 0.3	1543 2.0	2143 0.2
29 M	0408 1.8	0949 0.3	1613 2.0	2215 0.2
30 TU	0432 1.8	1021 0.3	1637 2.0	2246 0.2
31 W	0452 1.8	1054 0.2	1659 2.0	2319 0.2

Chart Datum: 0·69 metres below Dansk Normal Null
HAT is 2·2 metres above Chart Datum

TIME ZONE –0100
(Danish Standard Time)
Subtract 1 hour for UT
For Danish Summer Time add
ONE hour in **non-shaded areas**

DENMARK – ESBJERG

LAT 55°28′N LONG 8°26′E

TIMES AND HEIGHTS OF HIGH AND LOW WATERS

Dates in amber are **SPRINGS**
Dates in grey are **NEAPS**

2022

SEPTEMBER

Time	m		Time	m
1 TH 0512 1.9 / 1129 0.2 / 1725 2.0 / 2356 0.2		**16**	0001 0.3 / 0555 1.9 / F 1216 0.2 / 1825 1.9	
2 F 0540 1.9 / 1209 0.2 / 1802 2.0		**17**	0040 0.4 / 0633 1.9 / SA 1300 0.3 / ◑ 1910 1.8	
3 SA 0037 0.3 / 0619 1.9 / 1255 0.2 / ◑ 1849 2.0		**18**	0122 0.5 / 0722 1.8 / SU 1350 0.4 / 2004 1.7	
4 SU 0126 0.3 / 0709 1.8 / 1350 0.2 / 1950 1.9		**19**	0212 0.6 / 0820 1.8 / M 1449 0.5 / 2108 1.7	
5 M 0224 0.4 / 0814 1.8 / 1456 0.4 / 2111 1.8		**20**	0313 0.6 / 0928 1.7 / TU 1600 0.5 / 2221 1.6	
6 TU 0335 0.5 / 0937 1.7 / 1617 0.4 / 2253 1.7		**21**	0425 0.7 / 1040 1.6 / W 1715 0.5 / 2334 1.6	
7 W 0456 0.6 / 1115 1.7 / 1741 0.4		**22**	0537 0.6 / 1150 1.8 / TH 1821 0.5	
8 TH 0036 1.7 / 0614 0.5 / 1248 1.8 / 1855 0.3		**23**	0041 1.7 / 0637 0.6 / F 1253 1.9 / 1914 0.4	
9 F 0155 1.8 / 0719 0.5 / 1401 2.0 / 1956 0.2		**24**	0137 1.8 / 0727 0.5 / SA 1347 2.0 / 1959 0.3	
10 SA 0255 1.9 / 0813 0.4 / 1458 2.1 / ○ 2048 0.1		**25**	0224 1.8 / 0810 0.4 / SU 1433 2.0 / ● 2038 0.2	
11 SU 0342 1.9 / 0859 0.3 / 1544 2.1 / 2132 0.1		**26**	0305 1.9 / 0848 0.3 / M 1513 2.0 / 2114 0.2	
12 M 0420 1.9 / 0941 0.2 / 1622 2.1 / 2212 0.1		**27**	0339 1.9 / 0924 0.2 / TU 1547 2.0 / 2148 0.2	
13 TU 0448 1.8 / 1020 0.2 / 1653 2.1 / 2249 0.2		**28**	0407 1.9 / 0959 0.2 / W 1615 2.0 / 2222 0.2	
14 W 0507 1.8 / 1058 0.2 / 1720 2.0 / 2325 0.2		**29**	0429 1.9 / 1034 0.2 / TH 1640 2.0 / 2257 0.2	
15 TH 0526 1.8 / 1136 0.2 / 1749 2.0		**30**	0449 1.9 / 1112 0.2 / F 1708 2.0 / 2334 0.2	

OCTOBER

Time	m		Time	m
1 SA 0517 1.9 / 1153 0.2 / 1745 1.9		**16**	0002 0.4 / 0554 1.9 / SU 1229 0.3 / 1828 1.8	
2 SU 0017 0.3 / 0556 1.9 / 1241 0.2 / 1835 1.8		**17**	0041 0.5 / 0641 1.9 / M 1314 0.4 / ◑ 1921 1.7	
3 M 0106 0.4 / 0648 1.9 / 1338 0.3 / ◑ 1945 1.7		**18**	0126 0.5 / 0737 1.8 / TU 1408 0.5 / 2025 1.6	
4 TU 0205 0.5 / 0759 1.8 / 1447 0.4 / 2122 1.7		**19**	0221 0.6 / 0841 1.8 / W 1512 0.5 / 2136 1.6	
5 W 0318 0.6 / 0933 1.8 / 1609 0.4 / 2304 1.7		**20**	0328 0.7 / 0951 1.8 / TH 1623 0.5 / 2247 1.6	
6 TH 0439 0.6 / 1112 1.8 / 1731 0.3		**21**	0441 0.7 / 1100 1.8 / F 1731 0.4 / 2353 1.7	
7 F 0029 1.7 / 0556 0.5 / 1234 1.9 / 1841 0.2		**22**	0548 0.6 / 1204 1.9 / SA 1829 0.3	
8 SA 0136 1.8 / 0659 0.4 / 1341 2.0 / 1939 0.1		**23**	0051 1.8 / 0644 0.5 / SU 1301 2.0 / 1919 0.3	
9 SU 0229 1.9 / 0752 0.3 / 1435 2.1 / ○ 2027 0.1		**24**	0142 1.9 / 0733 0.4 / M 1353 2.0 / 2003 0.2	
10 M 0313 1.9 / 0838 0.2 / 1519 2.1 / 2109 0.1		**25**	0228 1.9 / 0817 0.3 / TU 1438 2.0 / ● 2043 0.2	
11 TU 0346 1.9 / 0919 0.2 / 1555 2.1 / 2146 0.2		**26**	0307 1.9 / 0858 0.2 / W 1519 2.0 / 2122 0.2	
12 W 0411 1.9 / 0958 0.2 / 1623 2.0 / 2220 0.2		**27**	0342 1.9 / 0938 0.2 / TH 1556 1.9 / 2159 0.2	
13 TH 0428 1.9 / 1034 0.2 / 1646 2.0 / 2253 0.3		**28**	0410 1.9 / 1017 0.2 / F 1629 1.9 / 2238 0.2	
14 F 0448 1.9 / 1110 0.2 / 1712 1.9 / 2327 0.3		**29**	0435 1.9 / 1059 0.2 / SA 1703 1.9 / 2318 0.3	
15 SA 0517 1.9 / 1148 0.2 / 1746 1.8		**30**	0506 1.9 / 1144 0.2 / SU 1747 1.8	
		31	0002 0.4 / 0549 1.9 / M 1234 0.2 / 1847 1.7	

NOVEMBER

Time	m		Time	m
1 TU 0053 0.5 / 0648 1.9 / 1333 0.3 / ◑ 2008 1.7		**16**	0051 0.5 / 0703 1.9 / W 1333 0.4 / ◑ 1947 1.6	
2 W 0153 0.5 / 0808 1.9 / 1442 0.3 / 2136 1.6		**17**	0140 0.6 / 0801 1.9 / TH 1429 0.4 / 2052 1.6	
3 TH 0303 0.6 / 0937 1.9 / 1559 0.3 / 2256 1.7		**18**	0238 0.6 / 0905 1.9 / F 1531 0.4 / 2157 1.7	
4 F 0420 0.6 / 1059 1.9 / 1715 0.3		**19**	0344 0.6 / 1009 1.9 / SA 1636 0.4 / 2301 1.7	
5 SA 0006 1.7 / 0533 0.5 / 1212 2.0 / 1820 0.2		**20**	0453 0.5 / 1113 1.9 / SU 1739 0.3	
6 SU 0106 1.8 / 0636 0.4 / 1314 2.1 / 1915 0.2		**21**	0001 1.8 / 0557 0.5 / M 1213 2.0 / 1835 0.3	
7 M 0156 1.9 / 0729 0.3 / 1407 2.1 / 2002 0.2		**22**	0057 1.9 / 0654 0.4 / TU 1311 2.0 / 1926 0.2	
8 TU 0239 1.9 / 0816 0.2 / 1452 2.0 / ○ 2043 0.2		**23**	0149 1.9 / 0745 0.3 / W 1405 2.0 / ● 2013 0.2	
9 W 0313 1.9 / 0858 0.2 / 1529 2.0 / 2119 0.2		**24**	0237 1.9 / 0833 0.2 / TH 1456 2.0 / 2057 0.2	
10 TH 0339 1.9 / 0937 0.2 / 1556 1.9 / 2153 0.3		**25**	0320 1.9 / 0919 0.2 / F 1545 1.9 / 2140 0.2	
11 F 0400 1.9 / 1013 0.2 / 1620 1.8 / 2225 0.3		**26**	0359 1.9 / 1004 0.1 / SA 1632 1.8 / 2222 0.3	
12 SA 0423 2.0 / 1049 0.2 / 1646 1.8 / 2258 0.3		**27**	0436 1.9 / 1050 0.1 / SU 1721 1.8 / 2306 0.3	
13 SU 0452 2.0 / 1125 0.3 / 1719 1.8 / 2332 0.4		**28**	0514 1.9 / 1138 0.2 / M 1813 1.7 / 2352 0.4	
14 M 0529 2.0 / 1203 0.3 / 1759 1.7		**29**	0603 1.9 / 1230 0.2 / TU 1913 1.7	
15 TU 0009 0.4 / 0612 1.9 / 1245 0.4 / 1849 1.7		**30**	0042 0.4 / 0705 2.0 / W 1328 0.2 / ◑ 2018 1.7	

DECEMBER

Time	m		Time	m
1 TH 0139 0.5 / 0815 2.0 / 1432 0.3 / 2124 1.7		**16**	0107 0.5 / 0725 2.0 / F 1350 0.3 / ◑ 2006 1.7	
2 F 0244 0.5 / 0926 2.0 / 1541 0.3 / 2228 1.7		**17**	0158 0.5 / 0819 2.0 / SA 1444 0.4 / 2104 1.7	
3 SA 0354 0.5 / 1036 2.0 / 1649 0.3 / 2329 1.7		**18**	0256 0.5 / 0919 2.0 / SU 1544 0.4 / 2206 1.7	
4 SU 0504 0.4 / 1142 2.0 / 1751 0.3		**19**	0401 0.5 / 1022 1.9 / M 1649 0.3 / 2308 1.8	
5 M 0027 1.8 / 0608 0.3 / 1243 2.0 / 1846 0.2		**20**	0510 0.5 / 1126 1.9 / TU 1752 0.3	
6 TU 0119 1.9 / 0704 0.3 / 1338 2.0 / 1934 0.2		**21**	0011 1.8 / 0616 0.4 / W 1232 1.9 / 1852 0.3	
7 W 0205 1.9 / 0754 0.2 / 1426 1.9 / 2017 0.3		**22**	0113 1.9 / 0717 0.3 / TH 1339 1.9 / 1947 0.3	
8 TH 0244 1.9 / 0839 0.2 / 1506 1.9 / ○ 2055 0.3		**23**	0212 1.9 / 0813 0.2 / F 1444 1.9 / 2037 0.3	
9 F 0317 1.9 / 0919 0.2 / 1539 1.8 / 2130 0.3		**24**	0307 1.9 / 0905 0.2 / SA 1546 1.9 / 2125 0.3	
10 SA 0345 2.0 / 0957 0.3 / 1607 1.8 / 2204 0.3		**25**	0357 2.0 / 0954 0.1 / SU 1642 1.9 / 2210 0.3	
11 SU 0412 2.0 / 1032 0.3 / 1634 1.7 / 2236 0.4		**26**	0443 2.0 / 1043 0.1 / M 1734 1.8 / 2255 0.3	
12 M 0441 2.0 / 1107 0.3 / 1705 1.7 / 2309 0.4		**27**	0528 2.0 / 1131 0.1 / TU 1822 1.8 / 2340 0.3	
13 TU 0514 2.0 / 1143 0.3 / 1742 1.7 / 2344 0.4		**28**	0614 2.1 / 1221 0.1 / W 1910 1.7	
14 W 0552 2.0 / 1221 0.3 / 1824 1.7		**29**	0028 0.4 / 0706 2.1 / TH 1314 0.2 / 1959 1.7	
15 TH 0023 0.4 / 0636 2.0 / 1303 0.3 / 1912 1.7		**30**	0121 0.4 / 0802 2.1 / F 1411 0.2 / ◑ 2051 1.7	
		31	0219 0.5 / 0901 2.1 / SA 1512 0.3 / 2146 1.7	

TIDES

Chart Datum: 0·69 metres below Dansk Normal Null
HAT is 2·2 metres above Chart Datum

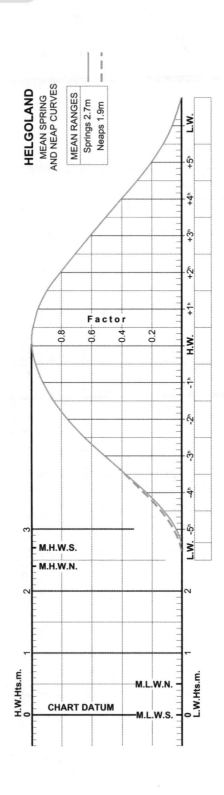

HELGOLAND
MEAN SPRING
AND NEAP CURVES

MEAN RANGES
Springs 2.7m
Neaps 1.9m

TIME ZONE -0100
(German Standard Time)
Subtract 1 hour for UT
For German Summer Time add
ONE hour in **non-shaded areas**

GERMANY – HELGOLAND
LAT 54°11'N LONG 7°53'E
TIMES AND HEIGHTS OF HIGH AND LOW WATERS

Dates in amber are **SPRINGS**
Dates in grey are **NEAPS**
2022

JANUARY

Day	Time	m	Time	m	Day	Time	m	Time	m
1 SA	0427 / 1007 / 1658 / 2235	0.6 / 3.1 / 0.6 / 3.0			16 SU	0525 / 1103 / 1741 / 2322	0.7 / 2.9 / 0.8 / 3.0		
2 SU	0529 / 1108 / 1755 / 2330	0.5 / 3.1 / 0.6 / 3.1			17 M	0609 / 1146 / 1822	0.7 / 2.9 / 0.6		
3 M	0625 / 1203 / 1848	0.4 / 3.1 / 0.6			18 TU	0001 / 0647 / 1224 / 1859	3.1 / 0.6 / 3.0 / 0.6		
4 TU	0022 / 0719 / 1256 / 1939	3.2 / 0.6 / 3.1 / 0.6			19 W	0037 / 0725 / 1301 / 1935	3.1 / 0.6 / 3.0 / 0.6		
5 W	0114 / 0812 / 1348 / 2028	3.3 / 0.6 / 3.1 / 0.6			20 TH	0112 / 0802 / 1337 / 2009	3.2 / 0.5 / 2.9 / 0.5		
6 TH	0203 / 0902 / 1437 / 2112	3.3 / 0.4 / 3.0 / 0.6			21 F	0147 / 0837 / 1412 / 2042	3.2 / 0.5 / 2.9 / 0.5		
7 F	0249 / 0946 / 1521 / 2152	3.3 / 0.4 / 2.9 / 0.6			22 SA	0220 / 0912 / 1447 / 2118	3.2 / 0.5 / 2.9 / 0.5		
8 SA	0332 / 1029 / 1604 / 2234	3.3 / 0.5 / 2.9 / 0.7			23 SU	0257 / 0950 / 1527 / 2159	3.2 / 0.5 / 2.9 / 0.6		
9 SU	0418 / 1112 / 1650 / 2319	3.2 / 0.7 / 2.8 / 0.8			24 M	0337 / 1031 / 1608 / 2239	3.1 / 0.5 / 2.8 / 0.6		
10 M	0506 / 1156 / 1738	3.1 / 0.8 / 2.8			25 TU	0417 / 1109 / 1648 / 2320	3.1 / 0.5 / 2.8 / 0.6		
11 TU	0008 / 0557 / 1245 / 1831	0.8 / 3.0 / 0.9 / 2.8			26 W	0501 / 1151 / 1734	3.0 / 0.6 / 2.7		
12 W	0105 / 0656 / 1344 / 1933	0.9 / 2.9 / 0.9 / 2.8			27 TH	0013 / 0558 / 1251 / 1837	0.7 / 2.9 / 0.6 / 2.7		
13 TH	0215 / 0804 / 1451 / 2041	0.9 / 2.9 / 0.9 / 2.8			28 F	0125 / 0713 / 1407 / 1954	0.7 / 2.9 / 0.7 / 2.8		
14 F	0327 / 0913 / 1557 / 2144	0.9 / 2.9 / 0.9 / 2.9			29 SA	0248 / 0835 / 1527 / 2111	0.7 / 2.9 / 0.7 / 2.9		
15 SA	0432 / 1013 / 1654 / 2238	0.8 / 2.9 / 0.9 / 3.0			30 SU	0409 / 0953 / 1642 / 2222	0.6 / 2.9 / 0.7 / 3.0		
					31 M	0521 / 1102 / 1748 / 2324	0.5 / 3.0 / 0.6 / 3.1		

FEBRUARY

Day	Time	m	Time	m	Day	Time	m	Time	m
1 TU	0623 / 1202 / 1844	0.4 / 3.0 / 0.6			16 W	0631 / 1209 / 1844	0.5 / 2.9 / 0.5		
2 W	0019 / 0716 / 1253 / 1932	3.2 / 0.4 / 3.1 / 0.6			17 TH	0020 / 0709 / 1245 / 1921	3.1 / 0.4 / 2.9 / 0.4		
3 TH	0107 / 0805 / 1338 / 2016	3.3 / 0.4 / 3.1 / 0.5			18 F	0055 / 0747 / 1321 / 1957	3.1 / 0.3 / 2.9 / 0.4		
4 F	0151 / 0848 / 1420 / 2056	3.4 / 0.4 / 3.0 / 0.5			19 SA	0129 / 0822 / 1355 / 2030	3.1 / 0.3 / 2.9 / 0.3		
5 SA	0231 / 0927 / 1458 / 2132	3.3 / 0.4 / 3.0 / 0.5			20 SU	0204 / 0857 / 1429 / 2105	3.1 / 0.3 / 2.9 / 0.3		
6 SU	0310 / 1003 / 1535 / 2208	3.3 / 0.5 / 2.9 / 0.5			21 M	0239 / 0932 / 1506 / 2142	3.1 / 0.3 / 2.9 / 0.3		
7 M	0348 / 1037 / 1611 / 2243	3.2 / 0.6 / 2.9 / 0.6			22 TU	0317 / 1009 / 1543 / 2220	3.1 / 0.3 / 2.9 / 0.4		
8 TU	0426 / 1108 / 1646 / 2317	3.1 / 0.7 / 2.9 / 0.7			23 W	0356 / 1043 / 1619 / 2256	3.0 / 0.4 / 2.8 / 0.4		
9 W	0504 / 1141 / 1725	3.0 / 0.8 / 2.8			24 TH	0436 / 1120 / 1702 / 2345	2.9 / 0.5 / 2.8 / 0.5		
10 TH	0000 / 0551 / 1230 / 1821	0.8 / 2.9 / 0.9 / 2.7			25 F	0531 / 1218 / 1805	2.8 / 0.7 / 2.7		
11 F	0105 / 0659 / 1343 / 1937	0.9 / 2.7 / 1.0 / 2.7			26 SA	0059 / 0651 / 1342 / 1930	0.6 / 2.7 / 0.8 / 2.7		
12 SA	0231 / 0823 / 1508 / 2059	0.9 / 2.6 / 0.9 / 2.7			27 SU	0233 / 0824 / 1514 / 2059	0.6 / 2.7 / 0.9 / 2.9		
13 SU	0355 / 0941 / 1623 / 2209	0.8 / 2.7 / 0.9 / 2.8			28 M	0404 / 0950 / 1636 / 2216	0.6 / 2.8 / 0.7 / 3.0		
14 M	0502 / 1043 / 1721 / 2301	0.7 / 2.8 / 0.7 / 2.9							
15 TU	0551 / 1130 / 1805 / 2343	0.6 / 2.9 / 0.6 / 3.0							

MARCH

Day	Time	m	Time	m	Day	Time	m	Time	m
1 TU	0519 / 1100 / 1742 / 2319	0.4 / 2.9 / 0.6 / 3.1			16 W	0527 / 1106 / 1741 / 2317	0.4 / 2.8 / 0.6 / 3.0		
2 W	0619 / 1156 / 1836	0.4 / 2.9 / 0.5			17 TH	0608 / 1145 / 1821 / 2355	0.3 / 2.9 / 0.4 / 3.0		
3 TH	0010 / 0708 / 1242 / 1920	3.2 / 0.3 / 3.0 / 0.5			18 F	0646 / 1221 / 1859	0.3 / 2.9 / 0.3		
4 F	0053 / 0748 / 1320 / 1958	3.3 / 0.3 / 3.0 / 0.4			19 SA	0030 / 0723 / 1257 / 1936	3.1 / 0.2 / 2.9 / 0.3		
5 SA	0131 / 0824 / 1354 / 2032	3.3 / 0.3 / 3.0 / 0.4			20 SU	0106 / 0800 / 1332 / 2011	3.1 / 0.2 / 3.0 / 0.2		
6 SU	0206 / 0858 / 1428 / 2105	3.3 / 0.4 / 3.0 / 0.4			21 M	0142 / 0835 / 1406 / 2046	3.1 / 0.2 / 3.0 / 0.2		
7 M	0241 / 0930 / 1501 / 2138	3.2 / 0.4 / 2.9 / 0.4			22 TU	0218 / 0909 / 1441 / 2122	3.1 / 0.2 / 3.0 / 0.2		
8 TU	0316 / 0959 / 1532 / 2208	3.1 / 0.5 / 2.9 / 0.4			23 W	0257 / 0945 / 1517 / 2201	3.1 / 0.3 / 2.9 / 0.3		
9 W	0348 / 1023 / 1600 / 2234	3.0 / 0.6 / 2.9 / 0.5			24 TH	0337 / 1021 / 1557 / 2242	3.0 / 0.4 / 2.9 / 0.3		
10 TH	0418 / 1047 / 1631 / 2307	2.8 / 0.7 / 2.8 / 0.7			25 F	0423 / 1103 / 1644 / 2335	2.8 / 0.5 / 2.8 / 0.4		
11 F	0458 / 1128 / 1720	2.7 / 0.9 / 2.7			26 SA	0523 / 1204 / 1751	2.7 / 0.7 / 2.8		
12 SA	0006 / 0603 / 1242 / 1838	0.8 / 2.5 / 1.0 / 2.6			27 SU	0052 / 0645 / 1331 / 1919	0.5 / 2.6 / 0.8 / 2.8		
13 SU	0136 / 0733 / 1418 / 2011	0.9 / 2.5 / 0.9 / 2.6			28 M	0229 / 0821 / 1507 / 2051	0.6 / 2.6 / 0.8 / 2.9		
14 M	0314 / 0905 / 1548 / 2134	0.7 / 2.5 / 0.8 / 2.7			29 TU	0401 / 0947 / 1628 / 2208	0.5 / 2.7 / 0.7 / 3.0		
15 TU	0433 / 1017 / 1654 / 2234	0.6 / 2.7 / 0.7 / 2.9			30 W	0512 / 1051 / 1729 / 2305	0.4 / 2.8 / 0.6 / 3.1		
					31 TH	0604 / 1139 / 1817 / 2351	0.3 / 2.9 / 0.5 / 3.2		

APRIL

Day	Time	m	Time	m	Day	Time	m	Time	m
1 F	0647 / 1219 / 1858	0.3 / 2.9 / 0.4			16 SA	0613 / 1149 / 1829	0.2 / 3.0 / 0.3		
2 SA	0031 / 0723 / 1254 / 1933	3.2 / 0.3 / 3.0 / 0.3			17 SU	0000 / 0652 / 1226 / 1908	3.1 / 0.2 / 3.0 / 0.3		
3 SU	0105 / 0755 / 1324 / 2004	3.2 / 0.3 / 3.0 / 0.3			18 M	0038 / 0731 / 1302 / 1946	3.1 / 0.2 / 3.0 / 0.2		
4 M	0138 / 0825 / 1355 / 2036	3.2 / 0.4 / 3.0 / 0.3			19 TU	0116 / 0808 / 1339 / 2025	3.1 / 0.2 / 3.0 / 0.2		
5 TU	0211 / 0854 / 1426 / 2108	3.1 / 0.4 / 3.0 / 0.3			20 W	0157 / 0846 / 1416 / 2105	3.1 / 0.2 / 3.0 / 0.2		
6 W	0244 / 0922 / 1456 / 2137	3.0 / 0.5 / 2.9 / 0.3			21 TH	0239 / 0924 / 1456 / 2148	3.0 / 0.3 / 3.0 / 0.2		
7 TH	0314 / 0946 / 1524 / 2203	2.9 / 0.5 / 2.9 / 0.4			22 F	0326 / 1006 / 1543 / 2237	2.9 / 0.4 / 2.9 / 0.2		
8 F	0345 / 1010 / 1554 / 2233	2.7 / 0.7 / 2.8 / 0.6			23 SA	0419 / 1056 / 1638 / 2337	2.7 / 0.5 / 2.9 / 0.4		
9 SA	0423 / 1047 / 1639 / 2326	2.6 / 0.9 / 2.7 / 0.8			24 SU	0524 / 1201 / 1748	2.6 / 0.7 / 2.8		
10 SU	0522 / 1155 / 1751	2.5 / 1.0 / 2.6			25 M	0054 / 0643 / 1324 / 1911	0.5 / 2.6 / 0.8 / 2.9		
11 M	0050 / 0648 / 1328 / 1922	0.8 / 2.5 / 0.9 / 2.6			26 TU	0223 / 0812 / 1454 / 2037	0.5 / 2.6 / 0.7 / 3.0		
12 TU	0228 / 0821 / 1502 / 2049	0.7 / 2.6 / 0.8 / 2.7			27 W	0347 / 0931 / 1610 / 2148	0.4 / 2.7 / 0.6 / 3.1		
13 W	0351 / 0937 / 1614 / 2153	0.5 / 2.6 / 0.7 / 2.9			28 TH	0450 / 1029 / 1705 / 2240	0.4 / 2.8 / 0.5 / 3.1		
14 TH	0449 / 1030 / 1705 / 2240	0.3 / 2.8 / 0.6 / 3.1			29 F	0536 / 1111 / 1748 / 2323	0.3 / 2.9 / 0.4 / 3.1		
15 F	0533 / 1111 / 1748 / 2321	0.3 / 2.9 / 0.4 / 3.1			30 SA	0615 / 1149 / 1829	0.3 / 2.9 / 0.4		

Chart Datum: 1·68 metres below Normal Null (German reference level)
HAT is 3·0 metres above Chart Datum

TIME ZONE −0100
(German Standard Time)
Subtract 1 hour for UT
For German Summer Time add ONE hour in **non-shaded areas**

GERMANY – HELGOLAND
LAT 54°11′N   LONG 7°53′E
TIMES AND HEIGHTS OF HIGH AND LOW WATERS

Dates in amber are **SPRINGS**
Dates in grey are **NEAPS**

2022

MAY

Day	Time	m	Day	Time	m
1 SU	0003 0652 1906	3.1 0.3 0.3	16 M	0618 1152 1838 ○	0.2 3.0 0.3
2 M	0039 0723 1255 1938	3.1 0.4 3.0 0.3	17 TU	0009 0700 1232 1922	3.1 0.2 3.1 0.2
3 TU	0111 0752 1325 2009	3.1 0.4 3.0 0.3	18 W	0052 0743 1314 2007	3.1 0.2 3.1 0.2
4 W	0143 0821 1356 2041	3.0 0.5 3.0 0.4	19 TH	0140 0828 1359 2055	3.1 0.3 3.1 0.1
5 TH	0216 0850 1428 2112	2.9 0.5 3.0 0.4	20 F	0229 0912 1445 2143	3.0 0.3 3.1 0.1
6 F	0249 0917 1459 2142	2.8 0.6 3.0 0.5	21 SA	0321 0959 1536 2237	2.8 0.4 3.0 0.2
7 SA	0323 0947 1532 2216	2.8 0.7 3.0 0.6	22 SU	0417 1052 1634 2338 ◑	2.7 0.5 3.0 0.3
8 SU	0403 1025 1615 2304	2.7 0.9 2.9 0.8	23 M	0520 1154 1741	2.6 0.6 3.0
9 M	0456 1123 1716 ◑	2.6 0.9 2.8	24 TU	0046 0631 1307 1854	0.4 2.6 0.7 3.0
10 TU	0013 0608 1242 1833	0.8 2.6 0.9 2.8	25 W	0202 0746 1425 2009	0.5 2.6 0.7 3.0
11 W	0137 0729 1408 1953	0.7 2.6 0.8 2.8	26 TH	0314 0857 1536 2115	0.5 2.7 0.6 3.1
12 TH	0257 0844 1521 2101	0.5 2.7 0.7 2.9	27 F	0414 0954 1631 2208	0.5 2.8 0.6 3.1
13 F	0358 0941 1618 2154	0.3 2.8 0.6 3.0	28 SA	0459 1037 1717 2252	0.5 2.9 0.5 3.1
14 SA	0448 1027 1707 2241	0.3 2.9 0.5 3.1	29 SU	0540 1117 1800 2334	0.5 3.0 0.5 3.1
15 SU	0534 1110 1754 2326	0.2 3.0 0.4 3.1	30 M	0619 1155 1840 ●	0.5 3.0 0.4
			31 TU	0013 0654 1229 1915	3.0 0.5 3.1 0.4

JUNE

Day	Time	m	Day	Time	m
1 W	0048 0725 1301 1948	3.0 0.5 3.1 0.4	16 TH	0038 0726 1258 1958	3.1 0.3 3.2 0.2
2 TH	0122 0756 1334 2022	3.0 0.5 3.1 0.5	17 F	0131 0817 1349 2051	3.0 0.4 3.2 0.2
3 F	0156 0827 1408 2054	2.9 0.6 3.1 0.5	18 SA	0224 0905 1439 2141	3.0 0.4 3.2 0.2
4 SA	0231 0859 1441 2128	2.9 0.6 3.1 0.6	19 SU	0316 0952 1529 2232	2.9 0.4 3.2 0.3
5 SU	0308 0933 1517 2206	2.8 0.7 3.1 0.7	20 M	0408 1042 1623 2326	2.8 0.5 3.2 0.4
6 M	0349 1013 1559 2250	2.8 0.8 3.1 0.7	21 TU	0504 1137 1721 ○	2.7 0.6 3.1
7 TU	0437 1102 1649 2343	2.7 0.9 3.0 0.7	22 W	0022 0603 1236 1822	0.5 2.7 0.7 3.1
8 W	0531 1202 1748	2.7 0.8 2.9	23 TH	0121 0704 1340 1926	0.6 2.7 0.7 3.0
9 TH	0047 0635 1312 1855	0.6 2.7 0.8 2.9	24 F	0223 0807 1448 2031	0.6 2.7 0.7 3.0
10 F	0155 0743 1422 2002	0.5 2.7 0.7 2.9	25 SA	0324 0908 1551 2131	0.6 2.8 0.6 3.0
11 SA	0259 0844 1526 2104	0.4 2.8 0.6 3.0	26 SU	0418 1001 1645 2222	0.7 2.9 0.7 3.0
12 SU	0357 0939 1625 2201	0.4 2.9 0.5 3.1	27 M	0507 1047 1734 2309	0.6 2.9 0.6 3.0
13 M	0453 1032 1721 2256	0.3 3.0 0.4 3.1	28 TU	0551 1130 1818 2352	0.6 3.1 0.5 3.1
14 TU	0547 1121 1814 2347	0.3 3.1 0.3 3.1	29 W	0630 1209 1857 ●	0.6 3.1 0.5
15 W	0637 1209 1905	0.3 3.1 0.2	30 TH	0031 0706 1244 1933	3.0 0.6 3.2 0.5

JULY

Day	Time	m	Day	Time	m
1 F	0107 0740 1319 2008	3.0 0.6 3.2 0.5	16 SA	0126 0809 1341 2044	3.1 0.4 3.4 0.3
2 SA	0142 0813 1352 2041	2.9 0.6 3.2 0.6	17 SU	0216 0856 1429 2132	3.0 0.4 3.4 0.3
3 SU	0216 0845 1425 2114	2.9 0.6 3.2 0.6	18 M	0303 0939 1514 2215	2.9 0.4 3.3 0.3
4 M	0252 0920 1501 2152	2.9 0.7 3.2 0.6	19 TU	0347 1021 1601 2300	2.9 0.5 3.3 0.4
5 TU	0332 1000 1542 2234	2.9 0.7 3.2 0.6	20 W	0433 1107 1650 2343 ◑	2.8 0.6 3.2 0.6
6 W	0416 1043 1624 2315	2.8 0.7 3.1 0.6	21 TH	0521 1153 1739	2.8 0.6 3.1
7 TH	0459 1128 1709	2.8 0.7 3.1	22 F	0027 0609 1244 1833	0.7 2.8 0.7 3.0
8 F	0000 0546 1220 1803	0.7 2.8 0.7 3.0	23 SA	0120 0707 1349 1937	0.7 2.8 0.8 2.9
9 SA	0056 0644 1325 1908	0.6 2.8 0.7 2.9	24 SU	0225 0814 1504 2049	0.8 2.8 0.8 2.9
10 SU	0202 0750 1437 2020	0.6 2.8 0.7 2.9	25 M	0335 0923 1615 2155	0.8 2.9 0.8 2.9
11 M	0312 0857 1549 2130	0.6 2.9 0.6 3.0	26 TU	0438 1022 1713 2250	0.8 3.0 0.7 3.0
12 TU	0421 1002 1658 2237	0.5 3.0 0.5 3.0	27 W	0529 1111 1801 2336	0.7 3.0 0.6 2.9
13 W	0526 1102 1800 ○ 2337	0.5 3.1 0.4 3.1	28 TH	0613 1152 1841 ●	0.6 3.1 0.6
14 TH	0625 1158 1858	0.5 3.2 0.3	29 F	0017 0651 1230 1918	2.9 0.6 3.2 0.6
15 F	0033 0718 1251 1952	3.1 0.5 3.3 0.3	30 SA	0053 0727 1304 1953	3.0 0.6 3.2 0.5
			31 SU	0127 0800 1336 2026	3.0 0.6 3.2 0.5

AUGUST

Day	Time	m	Day	Time	m
1 M	0200 0831 1408 2057	3.0 0.6 3.2 0.5	16 TU	0239 0916 1451 2148	3.0 0.4 3.3 0.4
2 TU	0233 0903 1442 2132	3.0 0.6 3.2 0.6	17 W	0317 0953 1531 2223	2.9 0.4 3.2 0.5
3 W	0310 0941 1520 2211	3.0 0.6 3.2 0.6	18 TH	0355 1030 1612 2257	2.9 0.5 3.1 0.5
4 TH	0350 1021 1559 2246	2.9 0.7 3.2 0.6	19 F	0432 1106 1652 2330 ◑	2.8 0.6 3.0 0.7
5 F	0427 1057 1637 2320	2.9 0.7 3.1 0.6	20 SA	0512 1147 1738	2.8 0.7 2.8
6 SA	0505 1139 1723	2.9 0.8 3.0	21 SU	0014 0604 1248 1842	0.9 2.7 0.9 2.7
7 SU	0008 0557 1241 1829	0.7 2.8 0.8 2.9	22 M	0123 0718 1412 2005	1.0 2.7 0.9 2.7
8 M	0119 0709 1403 1952	0.8 2.8 0.8 2.9	23 TU	0250 0842 1541 2128	1.0 2.8 0.9 2.7
9 TU	0243 0830 1530 2116	0.8 2.9 0.7 3.0	24 W	0410 0957 1653 2233	0.9 2.9 0.8 2.8
10 W	0404 0947 1648 2230	0.8 3.0 0.6 3.0	25 TH	0510 1052 1743 2321	0.8 3.0 0.7 2.9
11 TH	0517 1054 1756 2335	0.7 3.2 0.6 3.0	26 F	0554 1134 1822 2359	0.7 3.1 0.6 3.0
12 F	0618 1152 1853 ○	0.6 3.3 0.4	27 SA	0632 1210 1858 ●	0.6 3.1 0.6
13 SA	0029 0711 1243 1944	3.1 0.5 3.4 0.3	28 SU	0034 0707 1243 1932	3.0 0.6 3.2 0.5
14 SU	0116 0756 1328 2029	3.1 0.5 3.4 0.3	29 M	0107 0741 1316 2005	3.0 0.6 3.2 0.5
15 M	0159 0838 1411 2110	3.1 0.4 3.4 0.3	30 TU	0139 0812 1347 2035	3.0 0.6 3.3 0.5
			31 W	0210 0843 1419 2107	3.0 0.6 3.3 0.6

Chart Datum: 1·68 metres below Normal Null (German reference level)
HAT is 3·0 metres above Chart Datum

TIME ZONE -0100
(German Standard Time)
Subtract 1 hour for UT
For German Summer Time add
ONE hour in non-shaded areas

GERMANY – HELGOLAND

LAT 54°11′N   LONG 7°53′E

TIMES AND HEIGHTS OF HIGH AND LOW WATERS

Dates in amber are **SPRINGS**
Dates in grey are **NEAPS**

2022

SEPTEMBER

Time m	Time m
1 TH 0243 3.1 / 0917 0.6 / 1455 3.3 / 2141 0.6	**16** F 0315 2.9 / 0953 0.5 / 1533 3.0 / 2210 0.7
2 F 0319 3.0 / 0954 0.7 / 1533 3.2 / 2215 0.7	**17** SA 0346 2.9 / 1024 0.6 / 1608 2.9 / 2238 0.8
3 SA 0355 3.0 / 1030 0.7 / 1611 3.1 / ◖ 2249 0.8	**18** SU 0421 2.8 / 1059 0.8 / 1650 2.7 / 2318 1.0
4 SU 0433 2.9 / 1113 0.8 / 1659 3.0 / 2338 0.9	**19** M 0510 2.7 / 1155 1.0 / 1753 2.6
5 M 0528 2.9 / 1218 0.9 / 1810 2.9	**20** TU 0027 1.1 / 0625 2.7 / 1322 1.1 / 1920 2.6
6 TU 0055 1.0 / 0647 2.9 / 1349 0.9 / 1942 2.8	**21** W 0201 1.2 / 0758 2.7 / 1502 1.0 / 2054 2.6
7 W 0229 1.0 / 0818 2.9 / 1525 0.8 / 2114 2.9	**22** TH 0334 1.1 / 0924 2.8 / 1624 0.8 / 2208 2.8
8 TH 0358 0.9 / 0941 3.1 / 1647 0.7 / 2229 3.0	**23** F 0443 0.9 / 1025 3.0 / 1718 0.7 / 2257 2.9
9 F 0510 0.8 / 1048 3.2 / 1751 0.5 / 2329 3.1	**24** SA 0528 0.8 / 1107 3.1 / 1755 0.6 / 2332 3.0
10 SA 0608 0.6 / 1142 3.3 / 1843 0.4 / ○	**25** SU 0604 0.7 / 1142 3.2 / 1829 0.6 ●
11 SU 0017 3.1 / 0655 0.5 / 1228 3.4 / 1926 0.4	**26** M 0006 3.0 / 0640 0.6 / 1216 3.2 / 1904 0.5
12 M 0057 3.1 / 0736 0.5 / 1308 3.4 / 2004 0.4	**27** TU 0039 3.1 / 0715 0.6 / 1249 3.3 / 1937 0.5
13 TU 0133 3.1 / 0812 0.4 / 1345 3.4 / 2039 0.4	**28** W 0112 3.1 / 0747 0.6 / 1321 3.3 / 2009 0.5
14 W 0207 3.0 / 0847 0.4 / 1422 3.3 / 2112 0.5	**29** TH 0143 3.1 / 0819 0.6 / 1354 3.3 / 2039 0.6
15 TH 0242 3.0 / 0920 0.4 / 1458 3.2 / 2143 0.6	**30** F 0215 3.1 / 0852 0.6 / 1430 3.2 / 2112 0.6

OCTOBER

Time m	Time m
1 SA 0249 3.1 / 0930 0.6 / 1509 3.2 / 2147 0.7	**16** SU 0310 3.0 / 0951 0.7 / 1535 2.8 / 2159 0.9
2 SU 0328 3.0 / 1011 0.7 / 1554 3.0 / 2228 0.9	**17** M 0344 2.9 / 1026 0.9 / 1616 2.7 / ◖ 2237 1.1
3 M 0414 3.0 / 1102 0.8 / 1650 2.9 / ◖ 2325 1.0	**18** TU 0431 2.8 / 1117 1.1 / 1714 2.6 / 2341 1.2
4 TU 0516 2.9 / 1213 0.9 / 1807 2.8	**19** W 0539 2.8 / 1236 1.1 / 1835 2.6
5 W 0046 1.1 / 0639 2.9 / 1346 0.9 / 1940 2.8	**20** TH 0110 1.2 / 0708 2.8 / 1412 1.1 / 2007 2.6
6 TH 0223 1.1 / 0813 3.0 / 1523 0.8 / 2111 2.8	**21** F 0244 1.1 / 0835 2.9 / 1538 0.9 / 2125 2.7
7 F 0352 1.0 / 0935 3.2 / 1641 0.7 / 2222 2.9	**22** SA 0358 1.0 / 0942 3.1 / 1636 0.7 / 2217 2.9
8 SA 0458 0.8 / 1036 3.3 / 1737 0.6 / 2313 3.0	**23** SU 0448 0.8 / 1027 3.1 / 1716 0.6 / 2255 3.0
9 SU 0548 0.7 / 1124 3.3 / 1819 0.5 / ○ 2354 3.1	**24** M 0527 0.8 / 1105 3.2 / 1751 0.6 / 2329 3.1
10 M 0631 0.6 / 1205 3.3 / 1859 0.5 ●	**25** TU 0605 0.7 / 1142 3.2 / 1828 0.5 ●
11 TU 0031 3.1 / 0709 0.5 / 1243 3.3 / 1933 0.5	**26** W 0005 3.1 / 0643 0.6 / 1218 3.3 / 1904 0.5
12 W 0103 3.1 / 0744 0.5 / 1318 3.3 / 2004 0.5	**27** TH 0039 3.2 / 0719 0.6 / 1253 3.3 / 1939 0.5
13 TH 0135 3.1 / 0817 0.5 / 1353 3.2 / 2035 0.6	**28** F 0114 3.2 / 0756 0.6 / 1331 3.2 / 2014 0.6
14 F 0208 3.0 / 0850 0.5 / 1427 3.1 / 2105 0.7	**29** SA 0149 3.2 / 0833 0.5 / 1411 3.2 / 2050 0.6
15 SA 0239 3.0 / 0921 0.6 / 1500 3.0 / 2131 0.7	**30** SU 0227 3.1 / 0915 0.6 / 1455 3.1 / 2131 0.7
	31 M 0312 3.1 / 1003 0.6 / 1547 3.0 / 2219 0.9

NOVEMBER

Time m	Time m
1 TU 0406 3.1 / 1101 0.7 / 1649 2.8 / ◖ 2321 1.0	**16** W 0404 3.0 / 1052 1.0 / 1644 2.7 / ◖ 2307 1.1
2 W 0512 3.0 / 1213 0.8 / 1805 2.7	**17** TH 0501 2.9 / 1156 1.1 / 1750 2.6
3 TH 0039 1.1 / 0632 3.0 / 1340 0.9 / 1931 2.7	**18** F 0020 1.1 / 0614 2.9 / 1315 1.0 / 1908 2.6
4 F 0209 1.1 / 0759 3.1 / 1508 0.8 / 2055 2.8	**19** SA 0143 1.1 / 0732 2.9 / 1434 0.8 / 2022 2.7
5 SA 0333 1.0 / 0916 3.2 / 1619 0.8 / 2200 2.9	**20** SU 0257 1.0 / 0842 3.0 / 1537 0.7 / 2121 2.8
6 SU 0435 0.9 / 1014 3.3 / 1710 0.7 / 2247 3.0	**21** M 0355 0.9 / 0936 3.1 / 1625 0.6 / 2207 2.9
7 M 0522 0.8 / 1059 3.3 / 1750 0.7 / 2326 3.1	**22** TU 0443 0.8 / 1022 3.1 / 1709 0.6 / 2248 3.0
8 TU 0604 0.7 / 1140 3.3 / 1828 0.6 ○	**23** W 0528 0.7 / 1105 3.2 / 1751 0.6 / ● 2329 3.1
9 W 0002 3.1 / 0643 0.6 / 1218 3.2 / 1902 0.6	**24** TH 0612 0.6 / 1147 3.2 / 1833 0.6
10 TH 0036 3.1 / 0718 0.5 / 1253 3.2 / 1933 0.7	**25** F 0008 3.2 / 0654 0.5 / 1229 3.2 / 1914 0.6
11 F 0107 3.1 / 0752 0.5 / 1328 3.1 / 2004 0.7	**26** SA 0049 3.2 / 0738 0.5 / 1314 3.1 / 1957 0.6
12 SA 0140 3.1 / 0826 0.6 / 1402 3.0 / 2035 0.7	**27** SU 0132 3.2 / 0824 0.5 / 1402 3.1 / 2041 0.6
13 SU 0214 3.0 / 0859 0.6 / 1436 2.9 / 2104 0.8	**28** M 0217 3.2 / 0912 0.5 / 1452 3.0 / 2126 0.7
14 M 0246 3.1 / 0930 0.7 / 1512 2.8 / 2134 0.9	**29** TU 0306 3.2 / 1003 0.6 / 1545 2.9 / 2216 0.8
15 TU 0320 3.0 / 1006 0.9 / 1553 2.8 / 2213 1.0	**30** W 0401 3.2 / 1101 0.6 / 1645 2.8 / ◖ 2315 0.9

DECEMBER

Time m	Time m
1 TH 0504 3.1 / 1206 0.8 / 1753 2.8	**16** F 0428 3.0 / 1121 0.9 / 1708 2.7 / ◖ 2334 0.9
2 F 0024 1.0 / 0614 3.1 / 1318 0.8 / 1906 2.8	**17** SA 0522 2.9 / 1217 0.8 / 1806 2.7
3 SA 0140 1.0 / 0729 3.1 / 1432 0.8 / 2019 2.8	**18** SU 0038 0.9 / 0625 2.9 / 1322 0.8 / 1911 2.7
4 SU 0256 0.9 / 0842 3.2 / 1540 0.8 / 2124 2.9	**19** M 0147 0.9 / 0732 2.9 / 1427 0.7 / 2015 2.8
5 M 0401 0.9 / 0942 3.2 / 1634 0.8 / 2214 3.0	**20** TU 0254 0.9 / 0837 3.0 / 1529 0.7 / 2114 2.9
6 TU 0452 0.8 / 1031 3.2 / 1718 0.8 / 2256 3.1	**21** W 0356 0.8 / 0937 3.0 / 1626 0.6 / 2208 3.0
7 W 0538 0.7 / 1115 3.2 / 1759 0.7 / 2336 3.1	**22** TH 0454 0.7 / 1033 3.1 / 1720 0.6 / 2258 3.1
8 TH 0621 0.6 / 1156 3.1 / 1836 0.7	**23** F 0547 0.6 / 1125 3.1 / 1811 0.6 / ● 2346 3.2
9 F 0013 3.1 / 0659 0.6 / 1233 3.1 / 1910 0.7	**24** SA 0638 0.5 / 1215 3.1 / 1900 0.6
10 SA 0047 3.1 / 0734 0.6 / 1309 3.0 / 1943 0.7	**25** SU 0034 3.2 / 0729 0.4 / 1306 3.1 / 1950 0.6
11 SU 0122 3.2 / 0810 0.6 / 1345 2.9 / 2016 0.7	**26** M 0124 3.3 / 0822 0.4 / 1359 3.1 / 2039 0.6
12 M 0156 3.2 / 0844 0.6 / 1420 2.9 / 2047 0.7	**27** TU 0214 3.3 / 0913 0.4 / 1450 3.0 / 2125 0.6
13 TU 0229 3.1 / 0916 0.7 / 1455 2.8 / 2119 0.8	**28** W 0302 3.3 / 1002 0.5 / 1540 2.9 / 2211 0.7
14 W 0303 3.1 / 0952 0.8 / 1533 2.8 / 2156 0.9	**29** TH 0352 3.3 / 1052 0.5 / 1631 2.9 / 2302 0.7
15 TH 0342 3.1 / 1033 0.8 / 1618 2.7 / 2241 0.9	**30** F 0447 3.2 / 1145 0.7 / 1726 2.8 / ◖ 2356 0.8
	31 SA 0544 3.2 / 1240 0.8 / 1824 2.8

Chart Datum: 1·68 metres below Normal Null (German reference level)
HAT is 3·0 metres above Chart Datum

TIDES

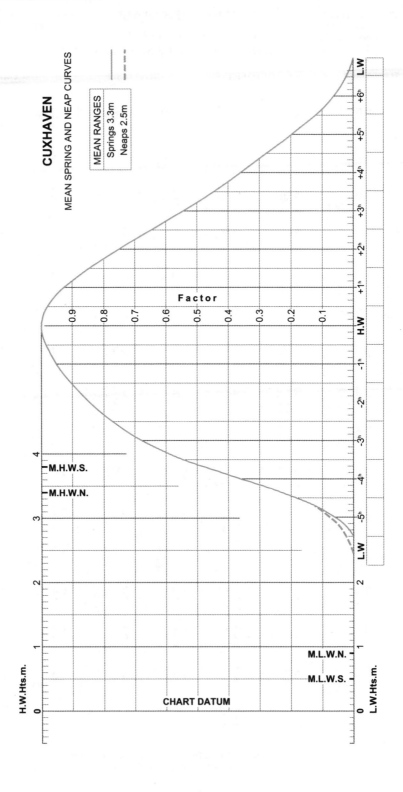

CUXHAVEN

MEAN SPRING AND NEAP CURVES

MEAN RANGES
Springs 3.3m
Neaps 2.5m

TIME ZONE -0100
(German Standard Time)
Subtract 1 hour for UT
For German Summer Time add
ONE hour in **non-shaded areas**

GERMANY – CUXHAVEN
LAT 53°52'N   LONG 8°43'E
TIMES AND HEIGHTS OF HIGH AND LOW WATERS

Dates in amber are **SPRINGS**
Dates in grey are **NEAPS**

2022

JANUARY

Time	m	Time	m
1 0545	0.6	**16** 0639	0.7
1121	3.6	1213	3.4
SA 1818	0.5	SU 1858	0.7
2351	3.6		
2 0650	0.5	**17** 0032	3.6
1223	3.6	0725	0.6
SU 1917	0.5	M 1258	3.4
●		1939	0.6
3 0046	3.6	**18** 0112	3.6
0747	0.6	0806	0.5
M 1319	3.6	TU 1338	3.5
2010	0.6	○ 2017	0.5
4 0138	3.8	**19** 0149	3.7
0841	0.4	0845	0.5
TU 1413	3.7	W 1416	3.5
2100	0.5	2053	0.5
5 0228	3.8	**20** 0224	3.7
0934	0.4	0922	0.5
W 1506	3.6	TH 1452	3.5
2150	0.5	2129	0.5
6 0318	3.9	**21** 0258	3.7
1024	0.4	0957	0.4
TH 1555	3.6	F 1527	3.4
2234	0.5	2201	0.5
7 0403	3.9	**22** 0332	3.7
1108	0.4	1031	0.4
F 1638	3.6	SA 1602	3.4
2312	0.5	2236	0.5
8 0446	3.8	**23** 0409	3.7
1148	0.5	1108	0.4
SA 1720	3.4	SU 1642	3.4
2351	0.6	2316	0.5
9 0530	3.8	**24** 0448	3.7
1229	0.6	1147	0.4
SU 1803	3.3	M 1722	3.4
☾		2355	0.5
10 0033	0.7	**25** 0528	3.6
0616	3.7	1223	0.4
M 1311	0.7	TU 1801	3.3
1849	3.3	☽	
11 0118	0.8	**26** 0034	0.5
0707	3.6	0610	3.5
TU 1356	0.8	W 1302	0.5
1940	3.3	1847	3.2
12 0213	0.8	**27** 0124	0.6
0806	3.5	0707	3.4
W 1453	0.9	TH 1359	0.6
2041	3.3	1948	3.2
13 0322	0.9	**28** 0234	0.6
0913	3.4	0822	3.3
TH 1601	0.9	F 1516	0.6
2148	3.3	2104	3.3
14 0436	0.8	**29** 0359	0.6
1022	3.4	0945	3.4
F 1709	0.9	SA 1640	0.6
2251	3.4	2223	3.4
15 0544	0.8	**30** 0524	0.6
1108	3.4	1105	3.4
SA 1808	0.8	SU 1759	0.6
2346	3.5	2335	3.5
		31 0639	0.4
		1216	3.5
		M 1908	0.5

FEBRUARY

Time	m	Time	m
1 0038	3.7	**16** 0052	3.5
0744	0.4	0749	0.4
TU 1317	3.5	W 1321	3.4
● 2005	0.5	○ 2002	0.4
2 0132	3.8	**17** 0130	3.6
0838	0.3	0829	0.3
W 1409	3.6	TH 1359	3.5
2055	0.5	2040	0.4
3 0220	3.9	**18** 0206	3.7
0927	0.3	0907	0.2
TH 1455	3.6	F 1435	3.5
2139	0.5	2117	0.3
4 0303	4.0	**19** 0241	3.7
1011	0.3	0942	0.2
F 1537	3.6	SA 1510	3.5
2218	0.4	2150	0.3
5 0344	3.9	**20** 0316	3.7
1049	0.4	1016	0.2
SA 1614	3.5	SU 1545	3.5
2253	0.4	2224	0.3
6 0423	3.8	**21** 0352	3.7
1123	0.4	1051	0.2
SU 1650	3.5	M 1621	3.4
2326	0.5	2301	0.3
7 0500	3.8	**22** 0430	3.7
1156	0.5	1127	0.4
M 1724	3.4	TU 1657	3.4
2359	0.6	2337	0.3
8 0537	3.6	**23** 0507	3.6
1225	0.6	1159	0.3
TU 1757	3.3	W 1733	3.3
☾		☾	
9 0029	0.6	**24** 0011	0.4
0613	3.5	0546	3.4
W 1253	0.7	TH 1232	0.4
1834	3.3	1814	3.3
10 0106	0.7	**25** 0054	0.5
0700	3.3	0641	3.3
TH 1336	0.9	F 1324	0.6
1928	3.2	1915	3.2
11 0207	0.8	**26** 0205	0.6
0806	3.2	0800	3.2
F 1446	0.9	SA 1446	0.7
2042	3.2	2039	3.3
12 0332	0.8	**27** 0339	0.6
0928	3.1	0933	3.2
SA 1612	0.9	SU 1622	0.7
2203	3.2	2209	3.4
13 0500	0.7	**28** 0515	0.5
1047	3.2	1101	3.3
SU 1732	0.8	M 1750	0.7
2314	3.3	2327	3.5
14 0612	0.6		
1151	3.3		
M 1834	0.7		
15 0009	3.5		
0706	0.5		
TU 1240	3.4		
1921	0.5		

MARCH

Time	m	Time	m
1 0636	0.4	**16** 0640	0.3
1213	3.4	1217	3.3
TU 1901	0.6	W 1857	0.5
2 0031	3.7	**17** 0027	3.5
0739	0.3	0725	0.2
W 1310	3.5	TH 1258	3.4
● 1957	0.5	1939	0.4
3 0122	3.8	**18** 0106	3.6
0829	0.3	0804	0.2
TH 1357	3.6	F 1335	3.5
2042	0.4	○ 2019	0.3
4 0205	3.9	**19** 0142	3.6
0911	0.3	0843	0.1
F 1436	3.6	SA 1412	3.5
2120	0.4	2057	0.2
5 0242	3.9	**20** 0218	3.7
0947	0.3	0919	0.1
SA 1510	3.6	SU 1447	3.5
2153	0.3	2132	0.2
6 0318	3.9	**21** 0254	3.7
1020	0.3	0954	0.1
SU 1543	3.6	M 1521	3.5
2225	0.3	2206	0.2
7 0353	3.8	**22** 0332	3.7
1050	0.4	1029	0.2
M 1614	3.5	TU 1556	3.5
2256	0.3	2242	0.2
8 0428	3.7	**23** 0411	3.6
1119	0.4	1103	0.2
TU 1644	3.4	W 1632	3.5
2324	0.3	2319	0.2
9 0459	3.5	**24** 0451	3.5
1141	0.5	1137	0.3
W 1711	3.4	TH 1710	3.4
2346	0.4	2356	0.3
10 0528	3.3	**25** 0534	3.3
1200	0.7	1213	0.5
TH 1740	3.3	F 1757	3.3
☾		☾	
11 0012	0.6	**26** 0043	0.4
0606	3.1	0633	3.2
F 1232	0.8	SA 1309	0.6
1827	3.2	1902	3.3
12 0105	0.7	**27** 0156	0.5
0709	3.0	0755	3.1
SA 1340	0.9	SU 1435	0.8
1942	3.1	2029	3.3
13 0233	0.8	**28** 0333	0.5
0838	2.9	0930	3.1
SU 1516	0.8	M 1614	0.8
2115	3.1	2201	3.5
14 0415	0.7	**29** 0511	0.5
1010	3.0	1057	3.2
M 1652	0.7	TU 1741	0.6
2238	3.2	2318	3.6
15 0540	0.5	**30** 0628	0.4
1124	3.2	1203	3.4
TU 1805	0.6	W 1847	0.5
2341	3.4		
		31 0016	3.7
		0723	0.3
		TH 1253	3.5
		1937	0.4

APRIL

Time	m	Time	m
1 0102	3.8	**16** 0033	3.6
0807	0.2	0732	0.1
F 1334	3.5	SA 1303	3.5
● 2019	0.3	○ 1949	0.3
2 0142	3.8	**17** 0112	3.7
0844	0.2	0812	0.1
SA 1410	3.6	SU 1341	3.6
2054	0.3	2029	0.2
3 0217	3.8	**18** 0150	3.7
0916	0.3	0850	0.1
SU 1440	3.6	M 1418	3.6
2125	0.3	2107	0.2
4 0250	3.8	**19** 0229	3.7
0945	0.3	0927	0.2
M 1509	3.6	TU 1454	3.6
2155	0.3	2145	0.2
5 0323	3.6	**20** 0311	3.6
1014	0.4	1004	0.2
TU 1539	3.5	W 1531	3.6
2225	0.3	2224	0.1
6 0356	3.5	**21** 0354	3.5
1041	0.4	1042	0.2
W 1608	3.5	TH 1611	3.5
2252	0.3	2305	0.1
7 0427	3.4	**22** 0441	3.4
1103	0.5	1121	0.3
TH 1635	3.4	F 1656	3.4
2315	0.4	2351	0.2
8 0456	3.3	**23** 0532	3.2
1122	0.6	1206	0.5
F 1704	3.3	SA 1751	3.4
2340	0.5	☾	
9 0532	3.1	**24** 0045	0.3
1152	0.8	0635	0.6
SA 1747	3.2	SU 1306	0.6
☾		1859	3.4
10 0026	0.7	**25** 0158	0.4
0630	3.0	0755	3.1
SU 1252	0.9	M 1428	0.7
1857	3.1	2022	3.4
11 0147	0.8	**26** 0329	0.5
0754	2.9	0924	3.1
M 1426	0.8	TU 1601	0.7
2028	3.1	2148	3.5
12 0328	0.6	**27** 0458	0.4
0928	3.0	1043	3.2
TU 1606	0.7	W 1722	0.6
2155	3.2	2259	3.7
13 0458	0.4	**28** 0606	0.4
1047	3.1	1142	3.3
W 1725	0.6	TH 1821	0.5
2301	3.4	2351	3.7
14 0602	0.2	**29** 0654	0.3
1142	3.3	1225	3.4
TH 1821	0.5	F 1906	0.4
2351	3.5		
15 0649	0.2	**30** 0034	3.8
1224	3.4	0734	0.3
F 1906	0.4	SA 1304	3.5
		● 1948	0.4

Chart Datum: 2·06 metres below Normal Null (German reference level)
HAT is 4·1 metres above Chart Datum

GERMANY – CUXHAVEN

LAT 53°52'N   LONG 8°43'E

TIMES AND HEIGHTS OF HIGH AND LOW WATERS

TIME ZONE –0100
(German Standard Time)
Subtract 1 hour for UT
For German Summer Time add
ONE hour in **non-shaded areas**

Dates in amber are **SPRINGS**
Dates in grey are **NEAPS**

2022

MAY

Day	Time m	Time m	Time m	Time m
1 SU	0114 3.8	0812 0.3	1340 3.6	2025 0.3
16 M	0039 3.7	0737 0.2	1307 3.6	1959 0.2 ○
2 M	0151 3.7	0844 0.3	1411 3.6	2057 0.3
17 TU	0122 3.7	0819 0.2	1348 3.7	2042 0.2
3 TU	0224 3.7	0912 0.4	1439 3.6	2127 0.3
18 W	0207 3.7	0901 0.2	1430 3.7	2127 0.2
4 W	0256 3.6	0940 0.4	1509 3.6	2158 0.4
19 TH	0255 3.6	0945 0.2	1514 3.7	2213 0.1
5 TH	0329 3.4	1007 0.5	1539 3.6	2227 0.4
20 F	0345 3.5	1028 0.3	1600 3.6	2301 0.1
6 F	0402 3.4	1033 0.6	1610 3.6	2256 0.5
21 SA	0437 3.3	1113 0.4	1650 3.6	2352 0.2
7 SA	0436 3.3	1059 0.7	1643 3.5	2327 0.6
22 SU	0532 3.2	1203 0.5	1747 3.6 ◐	
8 SU	0515 3.2	1132 0.8	1725 3.4	
23 M	0049 0.3	0634 3.1	1303 0.6	1853 3.6
9 M	0010 0.7	0607 3.1	1225 0.9	1825 3.3 ◑
24 TU	0155 0.4	0745 3.1	1414 0.7	2006 3.6
10 TU	0116 0.7	0717 3.0	1343 0.8	1942 3.3
25 W	0310 0.5	0901 3.1	1533 0.7	2121 3.6
11 W	0240 0.6	0839 3.1	1513 0.7	2102 3.3
26 TH	0426 0.5	1012 3.2	1647 0.6	2228 3.7
12 TH	0403 0.4	0955 3.4	1631 0.6	2211 3.4
27 F	0529 0.5	1108 3.3	1745 0.5	2320 3.7
13 F	0510 0.3	1055 3.3	1732 0.5	2305 3.6
28 SA	0616 0.4	1152 3.5	1832 0.5	
14 SA	0603 0.2	1142 3.5	1825 0.4	2353 3.7
29 SU	0004 3.7	0658 0.4	1232 3.6	1917 0.4
15 SU	0652 0.2	1226 3.5	1914 0.3	
30 M	0046 3.7	0738 0.4	1310 3.6	1958 0.4 ●
31 TU	0127 3.6	0814 0.4	1344 3.6	2034 0.4

JUNE

Day	Time m	Time m	Time m	Time m
1 W	0203 3.6	0845 0.5	1416 3.7	2106 0.4
16 TH	0153 3.6	0844 0.3	1414 3.8	2116 0.2
2 TH	0236 3.5	0914 0.5	1447 3.7	2139 0.5
17 F	0247 3.6	0934 0.3	1504 3.8	2209 0.2
3 F	0309 3.5	0944 0.5	1519 3.7	2211 0.5
18 SA	0341 3.5	1023 0.3	1554 3.8	2300 0.2
4 SA	0344 3.4	1013 0.6	1552 3.7	2244 0.6
19 SU	0433 3.4	1108 0.4	1644 3.8	2350 0.2
5 SU	0421 3.4	1046 0.7	1629 3.7	2320 0.6
20 M	0525 3.3	1156 0.5	1736 3.7	
6 M	0503 3.3	1124 0.8	1710 3.6	
21 TU	0042 0.3	0619 3.2	1248 0.6	1834 3.7 ◑
7 TU	0002 0.7	0550 3.3	1210 0.8	1800 3.5
22 W	0136 0.5	0718 3.2	1345 0.7	1935 3.7
8 W	0053 0.6	0645 3.2	1309 0.8	1900 3.5
23 TH	0233 0.5	0820 3.2	1449 0.7	2040 3.6
9 TH	0154 0.5	0749 3.2	1419 0.7	2007 3.4
24 F	0334 0.6	0923 3.3	1557 0.7	2145 3.6
10 F	0303 0.4	0857 3.2	1531 0.6	2114 3.5
25 SA	0437 0.6	1023 3.4	1702 0.7	2244 3.6
11 SA	0410 0.3	1000 3.3	1638 0.6	2216 3.6
26 SU	0533 0.6	1115 3.5	1758 0.7	2335 3.6
12 SU	0512 0.3	1056 3.4	1741 0.5	2314 3.6
27 M	0622 0.6	1201 3.6	1848 0.6	
13 M	0611 0.3	1148 3.5	1840 0.4	
28 TU	0022 3.6	0708 0.5	1244 3.6	1934 0.5 ○
14 TU	0009 3.6	0706 0.2	1238 3.6	1934 0.3 ○
29 W	0106 3.5	0749 0.5	1322 3.7	2014 0.5
15 W	0101 3.6	0756 0.3	1326 3.7	2025 0.2
30 TH	0145 3.5	0824 0.5	1358 3.7	2051 0.5

JULY

Day	Time m	Time m	Time m	Time m
1 F	0222 3.5	0858 0.5	1432 3.8	2127 0.5
16 SA	0242 3.6	0928 0.4	1457 3.9	2205 0.3
2 SA	0256 3.5	0930 0.6	1505 3.8	2159 0.5
17 SU	0333 3.6	1015 0.4	1544 4.0	2252 0.3
3 SU	0330 3.5	1001 0.6	1537 3.8	2232 0.6
18 M	0420 3.5	1057 0.4	1629 3.9	2335 0.3
4 M	0406 3.4	1035 0.7	1614 3.8	2309 0.6
19 TU	0504 3.4	1138 0.5	1715 3.8	
5 TU	0447 3.4	1115 0.7	1655 3.7	2350 0.6
20 W	0018 0.4	0550 3.3	1221 0.5	1803 3.8 ◑
6 W	0531 3.4	1157 0.7	1737 3.7	
21 TH	0100 0.5	0636 3.3	1304 0.6	1852 3.7
7 TH	0031 0.6	0615 3.3	1240 0.7	1822 3.6 ◐
22 F	0141 0.6	0724 3.3	1353 0.7	1947 3.5
8 F	0113 0.5	0703 3.3	1331 0.7	1916 3.5
23 SA	0230 0.7	0822 3.3	1455 0.7	2052 3.4
9 SA	0206 0.5	0801 3.3	1434 0.7	2022 3.5
24 SU	0334 0.8	0928 3.3	1610 0.8	2202 3.4
10 SU	0313 0.5	0907 3.3	1548 0.7	2133 3.5
25 M	0445 0.8	1035 3.4	1723 0.8	2307 3.4
11 M	0425 0.5	1000 3.4	1703 0.7	2244 3.5
26 TU	0550 0.8	1134 3.5	1825 0.7	
12 TU	0538 0.4	1119 3.5	1815 0.6	2351 3.6
27 W	0002 3.5	0644 0.7	1223 3.6	1915 0.6 ○
13 W	0645 0.4	1220 3.6	1920 0.5 ○	
28 TH	0049 3.5	0729 0.6	1305 3.7	1958 0.5 ●
14 TH	0052 3.6	0744 0.4	1315 3.7	2018 0.3
29 F	0131 3.5	0809 0.5	1343 3.7	2037 0.5
15 F	0148 3.6	0838 0.4	1407 3.9	2112 0.3
30 SA	0208 3.5	0845 0.5	1417 3.8	2114 0.5
31 SU	0243 3.5	0918 0.5	1450 3.8	2146 0.5

AUGUST

Day	Time m	Time m	Time m	Time m
1 M	0315 3.5	0949 0.6	1521 3.8	2217 0.5
16 TU	0356 3.5	1035 0.4	1606 3.9	2308 0.4
2 TU	0348 3.5	1021 0.6	1555 3.8	2251 0.5
17 W	0433 3.4	1110 0.5	1645 3.8	2343 0.4
3 W	0426 3.5	1059 0.6	1634 3.8	2330 0.5
18 TH	0511 3.4	1145 0.5	1725 3.7	
4 TH	0506 3.5	1138 0.6	1713 3.7	
19 F	0015 0.5	0547 3.3	1219 0.6	1805 3.5 ◑
5 F	0005 0.5	0544 3.4	1213 0.7	1750 3.6 ◐
20 SA	0045 0.7	0626 3.2	1255 0.7	1851 3.3
6 SA	0037 0.6	0622 3.4	1252 0.7	1837 3.5
21 SU	0124 0.8	0717 3.2	1351 0.8	1955 3.2
7 SU	0120 0.7	0715 3.3	1350 0.8	1943 3.4
22 M	0228 0.9	0830 3.2	1514 0.9	2117 3.1
8 M	0228 0.8	0826 3.3	1511 0.8	2106 3.4
23 TU	0354 1.0	0953 3.2	1646 0.9	2239 3.2
9 TU	0354 0.9	0947 3.4	1641 0.7	2230 3.5
24 W	0519 0.9	1108 3.4	1802 0.7	2345 3.3
10 W	0519 0.7	1104 3.5	1804 0.6	2346 3.5
25 TH	0624 0.7	1205 3.5	1857 0.6	
11 TH	0635 0.6	1212 3.7	1915 0.4	
26 F	0033 3.4	0711 0.6	1247 3.6	1940 0.5
12 F	0050 3.6	0739 0.5	1309 3.8	2014 0.4 ○
27 SA	0113 3.5	0751 0.6	1324 3.7	2018 0.5 ●
13 SA	0145 3.6	0832 0.5	1359 4.0	2106 0.3
28 SU	0149 3.5	0827 0.5	1358 3.8	2054 0.4
14 SU	0233 3.7	0918 0.4	1443 4.0	2152 0.3
29 M	0223 3.6	0902 0.5	1430 3.8	2127 0.4
15 M	0316 3.6	0959 0.4	1525 4.0	2232 0.3
30 TU	0255 3.6	0933 0.5	1501 3.8	2156 0.5
31 W	0326 3.6	1002 0.6	1534 3.8	2228 0.5

Chart Datum: 2·06 metres below Normal Null (German reference level)
HAT is 4·1 metres above Chart Datum

TIME ZONE -0100
(German Standard Time)
Subtract 1 hour for UT
For German Summer Time add
ONE hour in **non-shaded areas**

GERMANY – CUXHAVEN

LAT 53°52'N   LONG 8°43'E

TIMES AND HEIGHTS OF HIGH AND LOW WATERS

Dates in amber are **SPRINGS**
Dates in grey are **NEAPS**

2022

SEPTEMBER

Day	Time m	Day	Time m
1	0400 3.6 / 1037 0.6 / TH 1610 3.8 / 2302 0.6	16	0430 3.4 / 1109 0.4 / F 1648 3.6 / 2329 0.6
2	0436 3.6 / 1113 0.6 / F 1647 3.7 / 2335 0.6	17	0501 3.3 / 1136 0.6 / SA 1722 3.4 / ☽ 2353 0.7
3	0511 3.5 / 1147 0.7 / SA 1724 3.6 / ☽	18	0534 3.3 / 1206 0.7 / SU 1803 3.2
4	0006 0.7 / 0550 3.5 / SU 1225 0.7 / 1812 3.4	19	0026 0.9 / 0621 3.2 / M 1257 0.9 / 1904 3.0
5	0050 0.8 / 0644 3.3 / M 1326 0.8 / 1923 3.3	20	0129 1.1 / 0735 3.1 / TU 1421 1.0 / 2030 3.0
6	0204 1.0 / 0803 3.3 / TU 1455 0.8 / 2055 3.3	21	0302 1.1 / 0908 3.2 / W 1604 1.0 / 2204 3.1
7	0340 1.0 / 0934 3.4 / W 1635 0.8 / 2227 3.4	22	0441 1.0 / 1035 3.3 / TH 1730 0.8 / 2320 3.2
8	0514 0.8 / 1058 3.6 / TH 1803 0.6 / 2344 3.5	23	0556 0.9 / 1138 3.5 / F 1833 0.6
9	0630 0.7 / 1205 3.7 / F 1911 0.5	24	0010 3.4 / 0646 0.7 / SA 1221 3.6 / 1913 0.5
10	0045 3.5 / 0730 0.6 / SA 1258 3.9 / ○ 2005 0.4	25	0046 3.5 / 0724 0.6 / SU 1256 3.7 / ● 1949 0.5
11	0133 3.6 / 0818 0.5 / SU 1343 4.0 / 2049 0.4	26	0120 3.6 / 0801 0.6 / M 1330 3.8 / 2025 0.5
12	0214 3.6 / 0858 0.4 / M 1422 4.0 / 2127 0.4	27	0155 3.6 / 0837 0.5 / TU 1404 3.8 / 2059 0.4
13	0250 3.6 / 0934 0.4 / TU 1500 3.9 / 2202 0.4	28	0228 3.7 / 0910 0.5 / W 1436 3.8 / 2131 0.5
14	0324 3.6 / 1007 0.4 / W 1537 3.8 / 2233 0.4	29	0300 3.7 / 0941 0.6 / TH 1510 3.8 / 2201 0.5
15	0358 3.5 / 1039 0.4 / TH 1614 3.7 / 2303 0.5	30	0331 3.6 / 1013 0.6 / F 1545 3.8 / 2233 0.6

OCTOBER

Day	Time m	Day	Time m
1	0405 3.6 / 1049 0.6 / SA 1624 3.6 / 2307 0.7	16	0424 3.4 / 1105 0.6 / SU 1649 3.3 / 2313 0.8
2	0443 3.5 / 1127 0.6 / SU 1707 3.5 / 2344 0.8	17	0456 3.4 / 1134 0.8 / M 1728 3.2 / ☽ 2346 1.0
3	0529 3.4 / 1213 0.7 / M 1802 3.3 / ☽	18	0541 3.3 / 1221 1.0 / TU 1824 3.0
4	0036 0.9 / 0630 3.4 / TU 1320 0.8 / 1918 3.2	19	0043 1.1 / 0648 3.2 / W 1337 1.1 / 1944 3.0
5	0155 1.0 / 0753 3.4 / W 1453 0.8 / 2052 3.2	20	0212 1.2 / 0817 3.2 / TH 1515 1.0 / 2116 3.0
6	0334 1.0 / 0927 3.5 / TH 1634 0.8 / 2224 3.3	21	0351 1.1 / 0945 3.3 / F 1647 0.8 / 2236 3.2
7	0508 0.9 / 1050 3.7 / F 1758 0.7 / 2337 3.4	22	0511 0.9 / 1054 3.5 / SA 1751 0.6 / 2330 3.4
8	0619 0.7 / 1152 3.8 / SA 1857 0.5	23	0606 0.8 / 1141 3.6 / SU 1834 0.5
9	0029 3.5 / 0711 0.6 / SU 1239 3.9 / ○ 1943 0.5	24	0009 3.5 / 0647 0.7 / M 1219 3.7 / 1912 0.5
10	0112 3.6 / 0755 0.5 / M 1320 3.9 / 2022 0.4	25	0044 3.6 / 0727 0.6 / TU 1256 3.8 / ● 1950 0.5
11	0148 3.6 / 0832 0.4 / TU 1358 3.9 / 2057 0.5	26	0120 3.7 / 0806 0.6 / W 1332 3.8 / 2026 0.5
12	0221 3.6 / 0906 0.4 / W 1434 3.8 / 2128 0.5	27	0156 3.7 / 0843 0.5 / TH 1409 3.8 / 2101 0.5
13	0252 3.6 / 0937 0.4 / TH 1509 3.7 / 2157 0.5	28	0230 3.7 / 0918 0.5 / F 1447 3.8 / 2136 0.5
14	0323 3.5 / 1009 0.4 / F 1543 3.6 / 2224 0.6	29	0306 3.7 / 0954 0.5 / SA 1528 3.7 / 2211 0.6
15	0354 3.5 / 1038 0.5 / SA 1616 3.4 / 2249 0.7	30	0343 3.6 / 1034 0.5 / SU 1612 3.5 / 2250 0.7
		31	0426 3.6 / 1119 0.6 / M 1702 3.4 / 2335 0.8

NOVEMBER

Day	Time m	Day	Time m
1	0519 3.5 / 1213 0.7 / TU 1801 3.3 / ◑	16	0513 3.4 / 1200 1.0 / W 1754 3.1 / ◑
2	0032 0.9 / 0624 3.5 / W 1322 0.8 / 1916 3.2	17	0013 1.1 / 0609 3.4 / TH 1301 1.0 / 1859 3.1
3	0150 1.0 / 0744 3.5 / TH 1449 0.8 / 2043 3.2	18	0125 1.1 / 0722 3.2 / F 1420 0.9 / 2016 3.1
4	0321 1.0 / 0911 3.6 / F 1621 0.8 / 2208 3.2	19	0250 1.0 / 0841 3.3 / SA 1542 0.8 / 2132 3.2
5	0449 0.9 / 1029 3.7 / SA 1737 0.7 / 2314 3.4	20	0409 0.9 / 0952 3.4 / SU 1650 0.6 / 2234 3.3
6	0555 0.8 / 1128 3.8 / SU 1831 0.7	21	0511 0.8 / 1048 3.6 / M 1742 0.5 / 2321 3.5
7	0003 3.5 / 0644 0.7 / M 1213 3.9 / 1912 0.6	22	0602 0.7 / 1135 3.7 / TU 1828 0.5
8	0042 3.6 / 0726 0.6 / TU 1254 3.8 / ○ 1950 0.6	23	0002 3.6 / 0649 0.6 / W 1220 3.7 / ● 1913 0.5
9	0119 3.6 / 0805 0.5 / W 1333 3.8 / 2025 0.6	24	0044 3.6 / 0734 0.5 / TH 1302 3.7 / 1954 0.6
10	0152 3.6 / 0840 0.5 / TH 1409 3.7 / 2056 0.6	25	0124 3.7 / 0816 0.5 / F 1344 3.7 / 2036 0.6
11	0223 3.6 / 0913 0.5 / F 1444 3.6 / 2125 0.6	26	0205 3.7 / 0900 0.5 / SA 1431 3.7 / 2119 0.6
12	0255 3.6 / 0945 0.5 / SA 1518 3.5 / 2154 0.6	27	0248 3.7 / 0945 0.4 / SU 1520 3.6 / 2202 0.6
13	0326 3.6 / 1016 0.6 / SU 1552 3.4 / 2221 0.7	28	0333 3.7 / 1032 0.4 / M 1609 3.5 / 2246 0.6
14	0358 3.6 / 1045 0.7 / M 1626 3.3 / 2248 0.8	29	0421 3.7 / 1121 0.5 / TU 1701 3.4 / 2334 0.7
15	0432 3.5 / 1117 0.8 / TU 1703 3.2 / 2323 1.0	30	0514 3.7 / 1216 0.5 / W 1758 3.3

DECEMBER

Day	Time m	Day	Time m
1	0029 0.9 / 0615 3.7 / TH 1318 0.7 / 1903 3.2	16	0537 3.5 / 1231 0.8 / F 1818 3.2 / ◑
2	0136 0.9 / 0725 3.7 / F 1430 0.8 / 2016 3.2	17	0044 0.9 / 0631 3.4 / SA 1325 0.7 / 1915 3.1
3	0253 0.9 / 0840 3.7 / SA 1546 0.8 / 2131 3.3	18	0147 0.8 / 0734 3.4 / SU 1429 0.7 / 2020 3.2
4	0411 0.9 / 0953 3.7 / SU 1656 0.8 / 2236 3.4	19	0257 0.8 / 0841 3.4 / M 1537 0.6 / 2126 3.3
5	0518 0.8 / 1054 3.8 / M 1752 0.8 / 2327 3.5	20	0407 0.6 / 0947 3.5 / TU 1642 0.6 / 2226 3.4
6	0612 0.8 / 1144 3.8 / TU 1838 0.8	21	0512 0.7 / 1049 3.6 / W 1743 0.6 / 2321 3.5
7	0010 3.6 / 0658 0.7 / W 1228 3.7 / 1919 0.7	22	0613 0.6 / 1147 3.6 / TH 1840 0.6
8	0050 3.6 / 0741 0.6 / TH 1310 3.7 / 1958 0.6	23	0012 3.6 / 0708 0.5 / F 1240 3.6 / ● 1931 0.6
9	0127 3.6 / 0819 0.5 / F 1349 3.6 / 2031 0.6	24	0101 3.7 / 0759 0.5 / SA 1331 3.7 / 2021 0.6
10	0201 3.7 / 0854 0.5 / SA 1425 3.5 / 2103 0.6	25	0149 3.8 / 0850 0.4 / SU 1423 3.7 / 2111 0.6
11	0234 3.7 / 0929 0.5 / SU 1501 3.4 / 2135 0.6	26	0239 3.8 / 0944 0.4 / M 1517 3.6 / 2201 0.6
12	0308 3.7 / 1002 0.6 / M 1535 3.4 / 2204 0.7	27	0329 3.9 / 1035 0.4 / TU 1607 3.5 / 2247 0.6
13	0340 3.7 / 1033 0.6 / TU 1609 3.3 / 2234 0.7	28	0417 3.9 / 1123 0.4 / W 1656 3.4 / 2331 0.6
14	0414 3.6 / 1107 0.7 / W 1646 3.3 / 2310 0.8	29	0505 3.8 / 1211 0.5 / TH 1745 3.3
15	0452 3.6 / 1145 0.8 / TH 1729 3.2 / 2352 0.9	30	0019 0.7 / 0557 3.8 / F 1301 0.6 / ◑ 1837 3.3
		31	0110 0.8 / 0653 3.7 / SA 1354 0.7 / 1934 3.3

Chart Datum: 2·06 metres below Normal Null (German reference level)
HAT is 4·1 metres above Chart Datum

TIDES

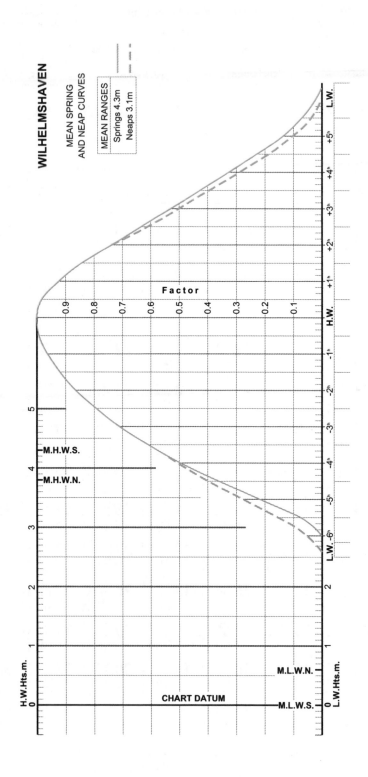

WILHELMSHAVEN

MEAN SPRING
AND NEAP CURVES

MEAN RANGES
Springs 4.3m
Neaps 3.1m

TIME ZONE -0100
(German Standard Time)
Subtract 1 hour for UT
For German Summer Time add
ONE hour in **non-shaded areas**

GERMANY – WILHELMSHAVEN

LAT 53°31′N   LONG 8°09′E

TIMES AND HEIGHTS OF HIGH AND LOW WATERS

Dates in amber are **SPRINGS**
Dates in grey are **NEAPS**

2022

JANUARY

Time	m		Time	m
1 0446	0.8	**16** 0541	0.9
1105	4.6	1156	4.4
SA 1719	0.7	SU 1802	0.9
2337	4.6		
2 0550	0.6	**17** 0014	4.6
1209	4.6	0629	0.8
SU 1821 ●	0.6	M 1241	4.6
		1845	0.8
3 0033	4.7	**18** 0054	4.6
0649	0.5	0710	0.7
M 1307	4.6	TU 1322	4.6
1916	0.6	○ 1924	0.7
4 0125	4.8	**19** 0131	4.7
0744	0.5	0748	0.6
TU 1401	4.7	W 1400	4.7
2009	0.7	2001	0.6
5 0215	4.9	**20** 0208	4.7
0837	0.4	0825	0.6
W 1454	4.6	TH 1437	4.6
2058	0.7	2037	0.6
6 0304	5.0	**21** 0243	4.8
0927	0.4	0901	0.5
TH 1542	4.6	F 1512	4.4
2141	0.6	2110	0.6
7 0349	4.9	**22** 0316	4.8
1011	0.5	0935	0.5
F 1624	4.5	SA 1548	4.4
2218	0.7	2143	0.6
8 0430	4.9	**23** 0353	4.8
1052	0.6	1011	0.5
SA 1704	4.4	SU 1627	4.4
2255	0.8	2221	0.6
9 0514	4.8	**24** 0434	4.7
1134	0.7	1050	0.5
SU 1745	4.3	M 1708	4.4
☽ 2336	0.9	2300	0.6
10 0559	4.7	**25** 0514	4.7
1217	0.9	1125	0.5
M 1828	4.2	TU 1746	4.3
		☽ 2338	0.7
11 0022	1.0	**26** 0556	4.5
0649	4.6	1203	0.6
TU 1302	1.0	W 1831	4.2
1919	4.2		
12 0116	1.1	**27** 0025	0.8
0747	4.4	0651	4.4
W 1358	1.1	TH 1258	0.8
2020	4.2	1933	4.2
13 0223	1.1	**28** 0133	0.9
0855	4.4	0805	4.3
TH 1505	1.2	F 1414	0.9
2129	4.2	2049	4.2
14 0337	1.1	**29** 0257	0.9
1004	4.4	0929	4.4
F 1614	1.1	SA 1539	0.9
2234	4.4	2208	4.4
15 0444	1.0	**30** 0421	0.8
1104	4.4	1050	4.4
SA 1713	1.0	SU 1700	0.8
2328	4.5	2320	4.5
		31 0537	0.7
		1203	4.5
		M 1811	0.7

FEBRUARY

Time	m		Time	m
1 0024	4.7	**16** 0037	4.6
0643	0.5	0650	0.6
TU 1306	4.6	W 1307	4.4
● 1912	0.7	○ 1907	0.6
2 0119	4.8	**17** 0115	4.6
0741	0.4	0730	0.5
W 1359	4.6	TH 1347	4.5
2003	0.6	1947	0.5
3 0207	5.0	**18** 0153	4.7
0831	0.4	0808	0.4
TH 1445	4.6	F 1424	4.5
2048	0.5	2024	0.4
4 0251	5.0	**19** 0229	4.7
0916	0.4	0845	0.3
F 1526	4.6	SA 1500	4.5
2126	0.5	2058	0.4
5 0332	5.0	**20** 0304	4.8
0954	0.4	0920	0.3
SA 1602	4.5	SU 1534	4.5
2159	0.5	2132	0.4
6 0410	4.9	**21** 0340	4.8
1030	0.5	0955	0.3
SU 1635	4.4	M 1610	4.5
2231	0.6	2207	0.4
7 0446	4.8	**22** 0418	4.7
1103	0.6	1030	0.4
M 1708	4.4	TU 1646	4.4
2303	0.6	2242	0.4
8 0521	4.7	**23** 0456	4.6
1133	0.7	1102	0.4
TU 1739	4.3	W 1720	4.4
☾ 2334	0.7	☾ 2314	0.5
9 0556	4.5	**24** 0534	4.5
1202	0.9	1134	0.6
W 1814	4.2	TH 1800	4.3
		2356	0.7
10 0011	0.9	**25** 0627	4.3
0642	4.2	1226	0.8
TH 1244	1.1	F 1901	4.2
1909	4.1		
11 0110	1.1	**26** 0103	0.8
0749	4.1	0745	4.2
F 1352	1.2	SA 1346	1.0
2025	4.1	2024	4.2
12 0232	1.1	**27** 0235	0.9
0913	4.1	0918	4.2
SA 1517	1.2	SU 1522	1.0
2148	4.2	2154	4.4
13 0400	1.0	**28** 0410	0.8
1032	4.2	1048	4.3
SU 1636	1.1	M 1651	0.9
2259	4.3	2313	4.6
14 0512	0.8		
1135	4.3		
M 1736	0.9		
2353	4.5		
15 0607	0.7		
1225	4.4		
TU 1824	0.7		

MARCH

Time	m		Time	m
1 0531	0.6	**16** 0539	0.6
1202	4.4	1203	4.3
TU 1804	0.8	W 1800	0.7
2 0018	4.7	**17** 0013	4.5
0637	0.5	0625	0.4
W 1302	4.5	TH 1246	4.4
● 1902	0.6	1844	0.5
3 0111	4.9	**18** 0053	4.6
0732	0.4	0706	0.3
TH 1349	4.6	F 1326	4.5
1950	0.6	○ 1926	0.4
4 0154	5.0	**19** 0131	4.7
0817	0.3	0745	0.2
F 1427	4.6	SA 1404	4.6
2028	0.5	2005	0.3
5 0232	5.0	**20** 0209	4.8
0853	0.3	0823	0.2
SA 1501	4.6	SU 1439	4.6
2101	0.4	2040	0.3
6 0308	4.9	**21** 0246	4.8
0926	0.4	0859	0.2
SU 1532	4.6	M 1514	4.6
2132	0.4	2114	0.3
7 0343	4.8	**22** 0322	4.8
0957	0.4	0933	0.3
M 1602	4.5	TU 1548	4.6
2202	0.4	2148	0.3
8 0417	4.7	**23** 0401	4.7
1026	0.5	1007	0.3
TU 1630	4.4	W 1623	4.5
2230	0.4	2222	0.3
9 0446	4.5	**24** 0440	4.5
1050	0.6	1039	0.4
W 1655	4.3	TH 1659	4.4
2253	0.5	2257	0.4
10 0513	4.3	**25** 0524	4.4
1110	0.8	1116	0.6
TH 1722	4.2	F 1744	4.3
2320	0.8	☾ 2343	0.6
11 0550	4.1	**26** 0621	4.2
1143	1.0	1211	0.9
F 1810	4.1	SA 1848	4.3
12 0010	1.0	**27** 0053	0.7
0653	3.9	0742	4.1
SA 1248	1.2	SU 1335	1.1
1927	4.0	2015	4.3
13 0134	1.1	**28** 0228	0.8
0824	3.8	0918	4.1
SU 1421	1.2	M 1514	1.1
2102	4.0	2148	4.5
14 0313	1.0	**29** 0406	0.7
0957	4.0	1046	4.2
M 1556	1.1	TU 1642	0.9
2226	4.2	2306	4.6
15 0439	0.8	**30** 0524	0.5
1111	4.2	1154	4.4
TU 1708	0.9	W 1748	0.7
2327	4.4		
		31 0005	4.8
		0622	0.4
		TH 1246	4.5
		1840	0.6

APRIL

Time	m		Time	m
1 0053	4.9	**16** 0022	4.7
0710	0.3	0633	0.3
F 1327	4.5	SA 1256	4.6
1925	0.5	○ 1856	0.4
2 0134	4.9	**17** 0103	4.8
0750	0.3	0715	0.2
SA 1402	4.6	SU 1335	4.6
2001	0.4	1937	0.3
3 0209	4.9	**18** 0143	4.8
0823	0.3	0754	0.2
SU 1431	4.6	M 1413	4.7
2032	0.3	2015	0.2
4 0242	4.8	**19** 0223	4.8
0852	0.4	0833	0.2
M 1500	4.6	TU 1449	4.7
2101	0.3	2052	0.2
5 0315	4.7	**20** 0304	4.7
0921	0.4	0909	0.3
TU 1529	4.5	W 1526	4.6
2131	0.4	2128	0.2
6 0347	4.5	**21** 0347	4.6
0949	0.5	0945	0.3
W 1556	4.5	TH 1604	4.6
2159	0.4	2206	0.2
7 0415	4.4	**22** 0432	4.4
1012	0.6	1022	0.5
TH 1621	4.4	F 1647	4.5
2223	0.5	2249	0.3
8 0442	4.2	**23** 0523	4.3
1033	0.8	1107	0.7
F 1648	4.3	SA 1739	4.4
2250	0.7	☾ 2343	0.5
9 0516	4.0	**24** 0625	4.1
1104	1.0	1208	0.9
SA 1731	4.2	SU 1847	4.4
☾ 2335	0.9		
10 0614	3.9	**25** 0055	0.6
1203	1.2	0743	4.1
SU 1843	4.1	M 1329	1.0
		2010	4.4
11 0050	1.1	**26** 0224	0.7
0740	3.8	0912	4.1
M 1333	1.2	TU 1501	1.0
2015	4.1	2137	4.6
12 0227	1.0	**27** 0354	0.6
0915	3.9	1033	4.2
TU 1510	1.1	W 1622	0.8
2143	4.2	2249	4.7
13 0356	0.7	**28** 0505	0.5
1034	4.1	1133	4.3
W 1629	0.9	TH 1722	0.7
2249	4.4	2343	4.8
14 0501	0.5	**29** 0555	0.4
1130	4.3	1218	4.5
TH 1724	0.6	F 1809	0.6
2338	4.6		
15 0549	0.3	**30** 0027	4.8
1215	4.5	0638	0.4
F 1811	0.5	SA 1257	4.5
		● 1853	0.6

Chart Datum: 2·7 metres below Normal Null (German reference level)
HAT is 5·1 metres above Chart Datum

TIDES

TIDES

TIME ZONE -0100
(German Standard Time)
Subtract 1 hour for UT
For German Summer Time add
ONE hour in **non-shaded areas**

GERMANY – WILHELMSHAVEN
LAT 53°31'N   LONG 8°09'E
TIMES AND HEIGHTS OF HIGH AND LOW WATERS

Dates in amber are **SPRINGS**
Dates in grey are **NEAPS**

2022

MAY

Day	Time	m	Time	m	Time	m	Time	m
1 SU	0108	4.8	0718	0.4	1332	4.6	1932	0.4
2 M	0144	4.8	0752	0.4	1401	4.6	2005	0.4
3 TU	0216	4.7	0820	0.4	1430	4.7	2035	0.4
4 W	0248	4.6	0849	0.5	1459	4.6	2105	0.4
5 TH	0320	4.5	0917	0.6	1528	4.6	2135	0.5
6 F	0351	4.4	0943	0.7	1556	4.6	2205	0.6
7 SA	0422	4.3	1011	0.8	1628	4.5	2237	0.7
8 SU	0458	4.1	1046	1.0	1710	4.4	2319	0.9
9 M ☽	0550	4.0	1138	1.1	1810	4.3		
10 TU	0021	1.0	0702	4.0	1253	1.1	1929	4.3
11 W	0141	0.9	0826	4.0	1419	1.0	2050	4.3
12 TH	0302	0.6	0944	4.2	1536	0.8	2158	4.5
13 F	0409	0.5	1044	4.3	1637	0.7	2253	4.6
14 SA	0504	0.3	1133	4.6	1729	0.6	2343	4.7
15 SU	0554	0.3	1219	4.6	1820	0.4		
16 M	0031	4.8	0641	0.2	1303	4.7	1906	0.3
17 TU	0116	4.8	0724	0.2	1344	4.8	1949	0.2
18 W	0202	4.8	0807	0.3	1427	4.8	2032	0.2
19 TH	0250	4.7	0850	0.3	1510	4.7	2116	0.1
20 F	0340	4.5	0932	0.4	1555	4.7	2201	0.2
21 SA	0430	4.4	1015	0.5	1642	4.7	2250	0.3
22 SU ☽	0524	4.2	1104	0.7	1737	4.6	2347	0.4
23 M	0624	4.1	1204	0.8	1842	4.6		
24 TU	0054	0.5	0733	4.1	1316	0.9	1955	4.6
25 W	0209	0.6	0848	4.1	1435	0.9	2111	4.6
26 TH	0326	0.6	0959	4.2	1549	0.8	2219	4.7
27 F	0431	0.5	1057	4.3	1648	0.7	2311	4.8
28 SA	0521	0.5	1142	4.5	1736	0.7	2355	4.8
29 SU	0603	0.5	1222	4.6	1822	0.6		
30 M ●	0038	4.7	0645	0.5	1301	4.6	1905	0.5
31 TU	0119	4.7	0722	0.5	1334	4.7	1942	0.4

JUNE

Day	Time	m	Time	m	Time	m	Time	m
1 W	0154	4.6	0754	0.5	1405	4.7	2015	0.5
2 TH	0227	4.5	0824	0.6	1437	4.7	2048	0.5
3 F	0301	4.5	0855	0.6	1509	4.7	2121	0.6
4 SA	0334	4.4	0925	0.7	1540	4.7	2154	0.6
5 SU	0408	4.3	0958	0.8	1615	4.7	2230	0.7
6 M	0447	4.3	1037	0.9	1656	4.6	2311	0.8
7 TU ☽	0534	4.2	1124	1.0	1746	4.6		
8 W ☾	0000	0.8	0630	4.1	1220	1.0	1846	4.5
9 TH	0058	0.7	0736	4.1	1327	0.9	1954	4.4
10 F	0205	0.6	0845	4.2	1438	0.8	2101	4.5
11 SA	0312	0.5	0949	4.3	1545	0.7	2204	4.6
12 SU	0414	0.4	1046	4.5	1646	0.6	2304	4.7
13 M	0514	0.4	1141	4.6	1745	0.5		
14 TU ○	0002	4.7	0611	0.3	1233	4.7	1840	0.3
15 W	0056	4.6	0702	0.3	1322	4.8	1931	0.3
16 TH	0149	4.7	0752	0.4	1411	4.9	2021	0.2
17 F	0243	4.7	0842	0.4	1501	4.9	2113	0.2
18 SA	0337	4.6	0929	0.4	1549	4.9	2202	0.2
19 SU	0427	4.4	1013	0.5	1637	4.9	2251	0.3
20 M	0517	4.3	1059	0.6	1728	4.8	2343	0.4
21 TU ☽	0609	4.2	1151	0.7	1824	4.8		
22 W ☾	0039	0.5	0704	4.2	1249	0.8	1924	4.7
23 TH	0137	0.6	0804	4.2	1353	0.9	2028	4.6
24 F	0239	0.7	0907	4.2	1501	0.9	2133	4.6
25 SA	0343	0.7	1008	4.3	1606	0.9	2233	4.6
26 SU	0441	0.8	1103	4.5	1703	0.8	2325	4.6
27 M	0531	0.7	1150	4.6	1755	0.7		
28 TU	0012	4.6	0616	0.7	1233	4.7	1842	0.6
29 W ●	0057	4.6	0657	0.6	1312	4.7	1924	0.5
30 TH	0136	4.5	0735	0.6	1347	4.8	2001	0.5

JULY

Day	Time	m	Time	m	Time	m	Time	m
1 F	0213	4.5	0810	0.6	1422	4.8	2036	0.6
2 SA	0247	4.5	0843	0.6	1455	4.8	2110	0.6
3 SU	0320	4.5	0915	0.7	1527	4.8	2143	0.6
4 M	0355	4.4	0948	0.7	1602	4.8	2219	0.7
5 TU	0434	4.4	1028	0.8	1642	4.8	2300	0.7
6 W	0517	4.3	1110	0.8	1724	4.7	2340	0.6
7 TH ☽	0600	4.3	1153	0.8	1808	4.6		
8 F ☾	0021	0.6	0647	4.3	1241	0.9	1901	4.5
9 SA	0113	0.6	0746	4.3	1344	0.9	2006	4.5
10 SU	0218	0.7	0853	4.3	1456	0.9	2118	4.5
11 M	0330	0.7	1002	4.4	1610	0.8	2232	4.6
12 TU	0443	0.6	1109	4.5	1720	0.7	2342	4.7
13 W ○	0551	0.5	1212	4.7	1825	0.4		
14 TH	0046	4.4	0653	0.5	1309	4.8	1924	0.3
15 F	0144	4.7	0748	0.5	1401	5.0	2020	0.3
16 SA	0239	4.7	0839	0.5	1452	5.1	2112	0.3
17 SU	0330	4.6	0926	0.5	1539	5.1	2159	0.2
18 M	0415	4.5	1005	0.5	1624	5.0	2242	0.3
19 TU	0457	4.4	1044	0.6	1708	4.9	2325	0.4
20 W ☽	0539	4.3	1127	0.7	1754	4.8		
21 TH	0008	0.6	0621	4.3	1211	0.8	1840	4.7
22 F ☾	0051	0.7	0706	4.2	1300	0.9	1933	4.5
23 SA	0140	0.9	0802	4.2	1401	1.0	2037	4.4
24 SU	0243	1.0	0911	4.3	1515	1.0	2149	4.4
25 M	0355	1.0	1021	4.4	1629	1.0	2256	4.4
26 TU	0500	0.9	1121	4.5	1732	0.8	2351	4.5
27 W	0553	0.8	1211	4.6	1823	0.7		
28 TH ●	0039	4.5	0638	0.7	1253	4.7	1908	0.6
29 F	0121	4.5	0720	0.7	1331	4.7	1947	0.6
30 SA	0159	4.6	0758	0.6	1407	4.8	2024	0.6
31 SU	0233	4.5	0833	0.6	1440	4.9	2058	0.5

AUGUST

Day	Time	m	Time	m	Time	m	Time	m
1 M	0306	4.5	0905	0.6	1511	4.9	2129	0.5
2 TU	0338	4.5	0937	0.7	1544	4.9	2203	0.6
3 W	0414	4.5	1013	0.7	1622	4.8	2241	0.6
4 TH	0453	4.5	1052	0.7	1700	4.8	2317	0.6
5 F ☽	0528	4.4	1127	0.8	1735	4.7	2348	0.7
6 SA	0604	4.4	1204	0.9	1820	4.5		
7 SU	0031	0.8	0656	4.3	1301	1.0	1925	4.4
8 M	0137	1.0	0808	4.3	1420	1.0	2048	4.4
9 TU	0301	1.0	0931	4.4	1547	0.9	2214	4.5
10 W	0426	0.9	1050	4.6	1708	0.7	2334	4.5
11 TH	0543	0.8	1200	4.7	1820	0.6		
12 F ○	0043	4.6	0650	0.7	1300	4.9	1922	0.4
13 SA	0140	4.7	0745	0.6	1351	5.1	2016	0.3
14 SU	0229	4.7	0831	0.5	1438	5.1	2102	0.3
15 M	0312	4.7	0911	0.5	1521	5.1	2142	0.3
16 TU	0350	4.6	0946	0.4	1601	5.0	2219	0.4
17 W	0425	4.5	1019	0.5	1639	4.9	2253	0.5
18 TH	0459	4.4	1053	0.6	1716	4.7	2326	0.6
19 F ☽	0532	4.3	1127	0.7	1752	4.5	2357	0.8
20 SA ☾	0606	4.2	1204	0.9	1835	4.3		
21 SU	0036	1.0	0656	4.1	1259	1.1	1938	4.1
22 M	0138	1.2	0810	4.1	1419	1.2	2101	4.1
23 TU	0304	1.2	0936	4.2	1551	1.1	2225	4.2
24 W	0428	1.1	1053	4.4	1709	1.0	2331	4.3
25 TH	0533	1.0	1150	4.5	1806	0.8		
26 F	0020	4.4	0621	0.8	1233	4.6	1849	0.7
27 SA ●	0101	4.5	0703	0.7	1310	4.7	1928	0.6
28 SU	0138	4.5	0742	0.7	1346	4.7	2005	0.6
29 M	0213	4.6	0818	0.6	1419	4.7	2040	0.5
30 TU	0245	4.6	0850	0.6	1451	4.9	2111	0.5
31 W	0316	4.6	0920	0.6	1522	4.9	2142	0.5

Chart Datum: 2·7 metres below Normal Null (German reference level)
HAT is 5·1 metres above Chart Datum

TIME ZONE -0100
(German Standard Time)
Subtract 1 hour for UT
For German Summer Time add
ONE hour in **non-shaded areas**

GERMANY – WILHELMSHAVEN

LAT 53°31′N   LONG 8°09′E

TIMES AND HEIGHTS OF HIGH AND LOW WATERS

Dates in amber are **SPRINGS**
Dates in grey are **NEAPS**

2022

SEPTEMBER

Time	m		Time	m
1 0348	4.6	**16** 0416	4.4
0953	0.7	1017	0.5
TH 1557	4.8	F 1637	4.6
2215	0.7	2241	0.7
2 0422	4.6	**17** 0444	4.3
1027	0.7	1045	0.7
F 1633	4.8	SA 1708	4.4
2247	0.7	◑ 2305	0.9
3 0455	4.5	**18** 0514	4.2
1100	0.8	1116	0.9
SA 1708	4.6	SU 1745	4.2
◔ 2318	0.8	2339	1.2
4 0531	4.4	**19** 0559	4.1
1136	0.9	1206	1.2
SU 1753	4.5	M 1845	4.0
5 0001	1.0	**20** 0040	1.4
0624	4.3	0713	4.1
M 1234	1.1	TU 1327	1.4
1903	4.3	2012	3.9
6 0112	1.2	**21** 0211	1.4
0742	4.3	0848	4.1
TU 1400	1.1	W 1508	1.3
2035	4.3	2147	4.0
7 0246	1.2	**22** 0349	1.3
0915	4.4	1016	4.3
W 1538	1.0	TH 1637	1.1
2210	4.4	2303	4.2
8 0420	1.1	**23** 0505	1.1
1041	4.6	1120	4.5
TH 1706	0.8	F 1739	0.9
2331	4.5	2354	4.4
9 0537	0.9	**24** 0555	0.9
1151	4.8	1203	4.6
F 1815	0.6	SA 1821	0.7
10 0035	4.6	**25** 0032	4.5
0639	0.7	0635	0.8
SA 1248	4.9	SU 1240	4.7
○ 1913	0.5	● 1859	0.6
11 0126	4.6	**26** 0108	4.6
0730	0.6	0715	0.7
SU 1335	5.0	M 1316	4.8
2001	0.4	1936	0.5
12 0208	4.7	**27** 0144	4.6
0811	0.5	0753	0.7
M 1416	5.1	TU 1351	4.9
2040	0.4	2012	0.5
13 0243	4.7	**28** 0217	4.7
0846	0.4	0826	0.6
TU 1454	5.0	W 1424	4.9
2114	0.4	2045	0.5
14 0316	4.6	**29** 0248	4.7
0918	0.4	0857	0.6
W 1531	4.9	TH 1457	4.9
2145	0.5	2115	0.6
15 0347	4.5	**30** 0319	4.7
0948	0.5	0928	0.7
TH 1606	4.8	F 1531	4.8
2215	0.6	2145	0.7

OCTOBER

Time	m		Time	m
1 0351	4.6	**16** 0405	4.4
1000	0.7	1013	0.8
SA 1609	4.6	SU 1632	4.3
2217	0.8	2225	1.0
2 0427	4.5	**17** 0435	4.4
1035	0.8	1044	1.0
SU 1651	4.5	M 1708	4.1
2253	1.0	◔ 2258	1.2
3 0510	4.4	**18** 0517	4.2
1119	0.9	1129	1.3
M 1743	4.3	TU 1803	3.9
◔ 2344	1.2	2354	1.5
4 0609	4.4	**19** 0625	4.2
1223	1.1	1242	1.4
TU 1857	4.2	W 1923	3.9
5 0100	1.3	**20** 0120	1.5
0731	4.4	0755	4.2
W 1353	1.1	TH 1416	1.4
2031	4.2	2056	4.0
6 0238	1.3	**21** 0257	1.4
0906	4.5	0925	4.3
TH 1534	1.0	F 1547	1.1
2205	4.3	2217	4.2
7 0411	1.2	**22** 0418	1.2
1031	4.7	1033	4.5
F 1659	0.8	SA 1653	0.9
2320	4.4	2312	4.4
8 0524	1.0	**23** 0513	1.0
1136	4.8	1121	4.6
SA 1802	0.7	SU 1739	0.7
		2352	4.5
9 0016	4.5	**24** 0556	0.9
0618	0.8	1201	4.7
SU 1226	4.9	M 1819	0.6
○ 1851	0.6		
10 0100	4.6	**25** 0030	4.6
0704	0.7	0638	0.7
M 1310	5.0	TU 1244	4.8
1933	0.5	● 1859	0.6
11 0138	4.6	**26** 0108	4.7
0743	0.5	0719	0.7
TU 1349	5.0	W 1318	4.8
2009	0.5	1937	0.5
12 0209	4.6	**27** 0144	4.7
0817	0.5	0756	0.6
W 1424	4.9	TH 1355	4.9
2040	0.5	2013	0.6
13 0239	4.6	**28** 0218	4.6
0847	0.5	0830	0.6
TH 1458	4.8	F 1433	4.8
2109	0.6	2047	0.6
14 0309	4.6	**29** 0253	4.7
0917	0.5	0905	0.6
F 1532	4.6	SA 1513	4.7
2136	0.7	2121	0.7
15 0338	4.5	**30** 0329	4.7
0946	0.6	0941	0.6
SA 1603	4.5	SU 1555	4.6
2201	0.8	2156	0.8
		31 0410	4.6
		1022	0.7
		M 1644	4.4
		2240	1.0

NOVEMBER

Time	m		Time	m
1 0500	4.5	**16** 0451	4.4
1114	0.9	1106	1.2
TU 1743	4.3	W 1732	4.0
◑ 2336	1.2	◑ 2322	1.3
2 0603	4.5	**17** 0547	4.3
1222	1.0	1204	1.3
W 1855	4.2	TH 1838	4.0
3 0052	1.3	**18** 0031	1.4
0723	4.5	0701	4.3
TH 1347	1.1	F 1319	1.2
2022	4.1	1957	4.0
4 0222	1.3	**19** 0153	1.3
0851	4.6	0821	4.3
F 1519	1.0	SA 1440	1.0
2147	4.2	2114	4.1
5 0350	1.2	**20** 0312	1.2
1010	4.7	0931	4.4
SA 1638	0.9	SU 1549	0.9
2255	4.4	2216	4.3
6 0458	1.0	**21** 0415	1.0
1111	4.9	1027	4.6
SU 1735	0.8	M 1643	0.7
2345	4.5	2303	4.5
7 0548	0.9	**22** 0507	0.9
1158	4.9	1116	4.7
M 1819	0.7	TU 1732	0.7
		2347	4.6
8 0027	4.6	**23** 0556	0.8
0632	0.8	1202	4.7
TU 1240	4.9	W 1818	0.6
○ 1900	0.7	●	
9 0104	4.6	**24** 0030	4.7
0713	0.7	0642	0.7
W 1320	4.8	TH 1247	4.8
1936	0.6	1902	0.6
10 0137	4.7	**25** 0111	4.7
0748	0.6	0725	0.6
TH 1356	4.7	F 1330	4.8
2007	0.7	1944	0.6
11 0207	4.7	**26** 0152	4.8
0820	0.6	0807	0.6
F 1430	4.6	SA 1417	4.7
2036	0.7	2027	0.6
12 0238	4.7	**27** 0235	4.8
0852	0.6	0851	0.5
SA 1505	4.5	SU 1505	4.6
2104	0.8	2110	0.7
13 0309	4.6	**28** 0318	4.8
0922	0.7	0935	0.5
SU 1537	4.4	M 1553	4.5
2131	0.9	2151	0.8
14 0338	4.6	**29** 0404	4.8
0952	0.8	1022	0.6
M 1608	4.4	TU 1644	4.4
2158	1.0	2236	0.9
15 0410	4.5	**30** 0455	4.7
1024	1.0	1115	0.8
TU 1644	4.2	W 1741	4.3
2233	1.2	◑ 2331	1.1

DECEMBER

Time	m		Time	m
1 0556	4.7	**16** 0518	4.5
1218	0.9	1133	1.0
TH 1845	4.2	F 1759	4.1
		◑ 2349	1.1
2 0037	1.2	**17** 0612	4.4
0705	4.6	1225	1.0
F 1329	1.0	SA 1857	4.1
1956	4.2		
3 0152	1.2	**18** 0049	1.1
0821	4.7	0714	4.4
SA 1445	1.0	SU 1327	0.9
2109	4.2	2002	4.1
4 0310	1.1	**19** 0158	1.1
0934	4.7	0822	4.4
SU 1557	1.0	M 1435	0.9
2215	4.4	2108	4.2
5 0418	1.0	**20** 0309	1.0
1036	4.8	0927	4.5
M 1657	0.9	TU 1542	0.8
2307	4.5	2209	4.4
6 0513	1.0	**21** 0414	1.0
1126	4.8	1030	4.5
TU 1744	0.9	W 1644	0.8
2352	4.6	2305	4.5
7 0600	0.9	**22** 0515	0.8
1212	4.8	1129	4.6
W 1826	0.8	TH 1743	0.7
		2358	4.6
8 0033	4.6	**23** 0612	0.7
0644	0.7	1225	4.7
TH 1255	4.7	F 1837	0.7
○ 1905	0.7	●	
9 0109	4.7	**24** 0048	4.7
0724	0.6	0704	0.6
F 1334	4.6	SA 1317	4.7
1940	0.7	1928	0.7
10 0143	4.7	**25** 0136	4.8
0759	0.6	0755	0.5
SA 1410	4.5	SU 1410	4.7
2011	0.7	2019	0.7
11 0217	4.7	**26** 0225	4.9
0833	0.7	0846	0.5
SU 1446	4.4	M 1504	4.6
2042	0.7	2108	0.7
12 0250	4.7	**27** 0314	4.9
0907	0.7	0937	0.5
M 1519	4.4	TU 1554	4.6
2112	0.8	2152	0.7
13 0321	4.7	**28** 0401	4.9
0938	0.8	1024	0.5
TU 1551	4.3	W 1641	4.4
2142	0.9	2234	0.8
14 0354	4.7	**29** 0449	4.9
1011	0.9	1112	0.6
W 1627	4.2	TH 1729	4.4
2217	1.0	2320	0.9
15 0432	4.6	**30** 0541	4.8
1049	1.0	1202	0.7
TH 1709	4.2	F 1820	4.3
2259	1.0	◑	
		31 0011	1.0
		0637	4.6
		SA 1255	0.9
		1914	4.3

Chart Datum: 2·7 metres below Normal Null (German reference level)
HAT is 5·1 metres above Chart Datum

TIDES

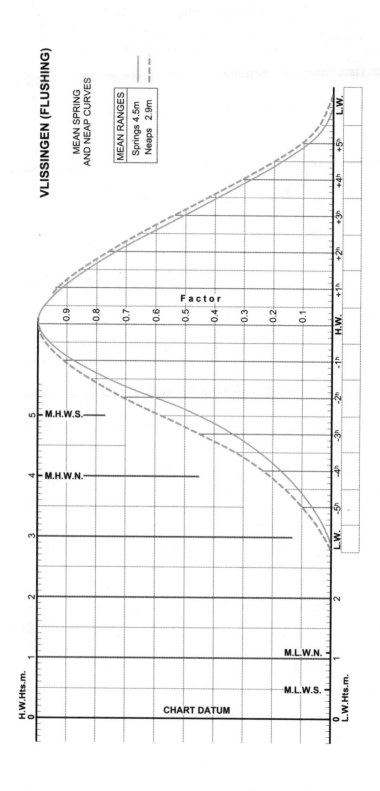

VLISSINGEN (FLUSHING)

MEAN SPRING
AND NEAP CURVES

MEAN RANGES
Springs 4.5m
Neaps 2.9m

TIME ZONE -0100
(Dutch Standard Time)
Subtract 1 hour for UT
For Dutch Summer Time add
ONE hour in **non-shaded areas**

NETHERLANDS – VLISSINGEN
LAT 51°27′N   LONG 3°36′E
TIMES AND HEIGHTS OF HIGH AND LOW WATERS

Dates in amber are **SPRINGS**
Dates in grey are **NEAPS**

2022

JANUARY

Day	Time	m	Day	Time	m
1 SA	0012 / 0635 / 1233 / 1905	4.8 / 0.8 / 4.8 / 0.6	**16** SU	0114 / 0724 / 1329 / 1936	4.3 / 1.0 / 4.4 / 1.0
2 SU	0104 / 0731 / 1324 / ●1955	4.8 / 0.7 / 5.0 / 0.6	**17** M	0151 / 0803 / 1405 / 2013	4.4 / 0.9 / 4.6 / 1.0
3 M	0154 / 0822 / 1414 / 2043	4.9 / 0.5 / 5.1 / 0.6	**18** TU	0224 / 0840 / 1439 / ○2048	4.6 / 0.8 / 4.7 / 0.9
4 TU	0242 / 0912 / 1503 / 2129	5.0 / 0.4 / 5.2 / 0.7	**19** W	0257 / 0917 / 1513 / 2124	4.7 / 0.7 / 4.8 / 0.9
5 W	0330 / 1001 / 1552 / 2214	4.9 / 0.4 / 5.1 / 0.8	**20** TH	0330 / 0955 / 1547 / 2200	4.7 / 0.6 / 4.8 / 0.9
6 TH	0417 / 1048 / 1641 / 2258	4.9 / 0.4 / 5.0 / 0.9	**21** F	0404 / 1033 / 1621 / 2236	4.7 / 0.5 / 4.8 / 0.9
7 F	0505 / 1135 / 1732 / 2343	4.8 / 0.4 / 4.9 / 1.0	**22** SA	0439 / 1110 / 1657 / 2312	4.7 / 0.5 / 4.8 / 0.9
8 SA	0554 / 1222 / 1824	4.7 / 0.5 / 4.7	**23** SU	0516 / 1148 / 1737 / 2351	4.7 / 0.6 / 4.7 / 0.9
9 SU	0030 / 0645 / 1310 / ◑1919	1.1 / 4.5 / 0.7 / 4.5	**24** M	0557 / 1228 / 1823	4.6 / 0.6 / 4.7
10 M	0122 / 0739 / 1403 / 2019	1.4 / 4.3 / 0.8 / 4.3	**25** TU	0034 / 0645 / 1314 / ◑1919	1.0 / 4.5 / 0.6 / 4.5
11 TU	0224 / 0841 / 1504 / 2129	1.4 / 4.1 / 1.0 / 4.1	**26** W	0126 / 0744 / 1409 / 2026	1.0 / 4.4 / 0.7 / 4.4
12 W	0334 / 0951 / 1618 / 2238	1.4 / 4.0 / 1.1 / 4.1	**27** TH	0230 / 0855 / 1515 / 2137	1.1 / 4.3 / 0.9 / 4.3
13 TH	0449 / 1059 / 1724 / 2338	1.4 / 4.1 / 1.1 / 4.1	**28** F	0346 / 1009 / 1633 / 2250	1.1 / 4.3 / 0.9 / 4.3
14 F	0551 / 1157 / 1815	1.3 / 4.2 / 1.1	**29** SA	0509 / 1119 / 1750 / 2357	1.1 / 4.4 / 0.9 / 4.4
15 SA	0030 / 0641 / 1247 / 1858	4.2 / 1.2 / 4.3 / 1.1	**30** SU	0623 / 1222 / 1852	0.9 / 4.7 / 0.8
			31 M	0055 / 0722 / 1318 / 1944	4.6 / 0.6 / 4.9 / 0.7

FEBRUARY

Day	Time	m	Day	Time	m
1 TU	0146 / 0815 / 1408 / ●2032	4.8 / 0.4 / 5.0 / 0.7	**16** W	0206 / 0823 / 1423 / ○2029	4.6 / 0.7 / 4.8 / 0.9
2 W	0232 / 0903 / 1454 / 2116	4.9 / 0.3 / 5.1 / 0.7	**17** TH	0238 / 0859 / 1455 / 2105	4.7 / 0.5 / 4.9 / 0.8
3 TH	0317 / 0948 / 1539 / 2158	5.0 / 0.2 / 5.2 / 0.7	**18** F	0310 / 0935 / 1527 / 2141	4.8 / 0.4 / 5.0 / 0.7
4 F	0359 / 1031 / 1622 / 2238	5.0 / 0.2 / 5.1 / 0.8	**19** SA	0343 / 1013 / 1600 / 2218	4.9 / 0.4 / 5.0 / 0.7
5 SA	0441 / 1112 / 1706 / 2316	4.9 / 0.3 / 5.0 / 0.9	**20** SU	0417 / 1050 / 1636 / 2254	4.9 / 0.3 / 5.0 / 0.7
6 SU	0523 / 1150 / 1749 / 2355	4.9 / 0.4 / 4.8 / 1.0	**21** M	0453 / 1127 / 1714 / 2331	4.9 / 0.4 / 4.9 / 0.7
7 M	0606 / 1229 / 1834	4.7 / 0.6 / 4.5	**22** TU	0532 / 1206 / 1757	4.9 / 0.4 / 4.8
8 TU	0036 / 0650 / 1311 / ◑1920	1.1 / 4.5 / 0.8 / 4.3	**23** W	0012 / 0617 / 1249 / ◐1849	0.7 / 4.8 / 0.5 / 4.6
9 W	0125 / 0740 / 1403 / 2013	1.2 / 4.2 / 1.0 / 4.0	**24** TH	0101 / 0713 / 1341 / 1954	0.8 / 4.6 / 0.7 / 4.3
10 TH	0234 / 0841 / 1513 / 2126	1.3 / 4.0 / 1.2 / 3.8	**25** F	0205 / 0826 / 1449 / 2110	1.0 / 4.3 / 0.9 / 4.1
11 F	0353 / 1006 / 1631 / 2259	1.4 / 3.8 / 1.3 / 3.8	**26** SA	0326 / 0949 / 1615 / 2234	1.1 / 4.2 / 1.1 / 4.0
12 SA	0508 / 1126 / 1739	1.4 / 3.9 / 1.3	**27** SU	0458 / 1111 / 1741 / 2349	1.1 / 4.3 / 1.0 / 4.2
13 SU	0003 / 0613 / 1226 / 1833	3.9 / 1.2 / 4.1 / 1.2	**28** M	0617 / 1220 / 1845	0.8 / 4.5 / 0.9
14 M	0053 / 0704 / 1312 / 1916	4.1 / 1.0 / 4.3 / 1.1			
15 TU	0132 / 0746 / 1350 / 1954	4.4 / 0.9 / 4.6 / 1.0			

MARCH

Day	Time	m	Day	Time	m
1 TU	0048 / 0716 / 1314 / 1935	4.5 / 0.6 / 4.8 / 0.8	**16** W	0105 / 0721 / 1324 / 1930	4.3 / 0.8 / 4.6 / 0.9
2 W	0136 / 0805 / 1359 / ●2019	4.7 / 0.3 / 5.0 / 0.7	**17** TH	0139 / 0758 / 1357 / 2005	4.6 / 0.6 / 4.8 / 0.8
3 TH	0218 / 0849 / 1440 / 2059	4.9 / 0.2 / 5.1 / 0.7	**18** F	0210 / 0833 / 1428 / ○2041	4.8 / 0.4 / 5.0 / 0.7
4 F	0257 / 0929 / 1519 / 2137	5.0 / 0.2 / 5.1 / 0.7	**19** SA	0242 / 0909 / 1500 / 2118	4.9 / 0.3 / 5.1 / 0.6
5 SA	0336 / 1008 / 1558 / 2214	5.0 / 0.2 / 5.1 / 0.7	**20** SU	0316 / 0947 / 1535 / 2156	5.0 / 0.2 / 5.1 / 0.5
6 SU	0414 / 1044 / 1637 / 2249	5.0 / 0.3 / 5.0 / 0.7	**21** M	0351 / 1026 / 1612 / 2234	5.1 / 0.2 / 5.1 / 0.5
7 M	0451 / 1118 / 1714 / 2322	4.9 / 0.4 / 4.8 / 0.8	**22** TU	0429 / 1104 / 1651 / 2313	5.1 / 0.3 / 5.0 / 0.5
8 TU	0529 / 1150 / 1752 / 2355	4.8 / 0.6 / 4.6 / 0.9	**23** W	0509 / 1144 / 1735 / 2356	5.0 / 0.4 / 4.8 / 0.6
9 W	0607 / 1223 / 1830	4.6 / 0.8 / 4.3	**24** TH	0555 / 1228 / 1826	4.9 / 0.5 / 4.5
10 TH	0030 / 0650 / 1303 / ◑1915	1.0 / 4.3 / 1.0 / 4.0	**25** F	0047 / 0652 / 1322 / ◐1933	0.7 / 4.6 / 0.8 / 4.2
11 F	0118 / 0745 / 1413 / 2013	1.2 / 4.0 / 1.3 / 3.7	**26** SA	0153 / 0811 / 1435 / 2056	0.9 / 4.2 / 1.1 / 3.9
12 SA	0310 / 0902 / 1550 / 2149	1.4 / 3.7 / 1.4 / 3.5	**27** SU	0319 / 0941 / 1610 / 2226	1.0 / 4.1 / 1.2 / 3.9
13 SU	0429 / 1051 / 1704 / 2331	1.4 / 3.7 / 1.4 / 3.7	**28** M	0455 / 1108 / 1737 / 2342	1.0 / 4.3 / 1.1 / 4.1
14 M	0540 / 1159 / 1805	1.2 / 4.0 / 1.2	**29** TU	0610 / 1216 / 1837	0.7 / 4.6 / 0.9
15 TU	0024 / 0638 / 1246 / 1852	4.0 / 1.0 / 4.3 / 1.0	**30** W	0037 / 0704 / 1305 / 1922	4.4 / 0.5 / 4.8 / 0.8
			31 TH	0120 / 0749 / 1344 / 2002	4.6 / 0.3 / 5.0 / 0.7

APRIL

Day	Time	m	Day	Time	m
1 F	0158 / 0828 / 1421 / ●2039	4.8 / 0.2 / 5.0 / 0.7	**16** SA	0137 / 0802 / 1357 / ○2013	4.8 / 0.4 / 5.1 / 0.6
2 SA	0235 / 0906 / 1457 / 2114	4.9 / 0.2 / 5.0 / 0.6	**17** SU	0212 / 0840 / 1432 / 2052	4.8 / 0.3 / 5.2 / 0.5
3 SU	0311 / 0941 / 1533 / 2150	5.0 / 0.3 / 5.0 / 0.6	**18** M	0248 / 0920 / 1510 / 2133	5.1 / 0.2 / 5.2 / 0.4
4 M	0346 / 1015 / 1608 / 2223	5.0 / 0.4 / 4.9 / 0.7	**19** TU	0326 / 1001 / 1549 / 2215	5.2 / 0.3 / 5.1 / 0.4
5 TU	0421 / 1047 / 1642 / 2255	4.9 / 0.5 / 4.7 / 0.7	**20** W	0407 / 1042 / 1632 / 2258	5.2 / 0.3 / 5.0 / 0.4
6 W	0455 / 1116 / 1715 / 2324	4.8 / 0.7 / 4.5 / 0.8	**21** TH	0450 / 1124 / 1718 / 2345	5.0 / 0.5 / 4.7 / 0.5
7 TH	0530 / 1144 / 1749 / 2354	4.6 / 0.9 / 4.3 / 0.9	**22** F	0540 / 1212 / 1813	4.8 / 0.7 / 4.4
8 F	0609 / 1219 / 1829	4.3 / 1.0 / 4.1	**23** SA	0040 / 0644 / 1310 / ◐1925	0.6 / 4.5 / 0.9 / 4.1
9 SA	0034 / 0659 / 1309 / ◑1926	1.1 / 4.0 / 1.3 / 3.8	**24** SU	0150 / 0808 / 1428 / 2047	0.8 / 4.3 / 1.1 / 3.9
10 SU	0214 / 0818 / 1514 / 2046	1.3 / 3.7 / 1.5 / 3.5	**25** M	0315 / 0934 / 1606 / 2213	0.9 / 4.2 / 1.2 / 3.9
11 M	0351 / 1001 / 1627 / 2244	1.3 / 3.7 / 1.4 / 3.6	**26** TU	0445 / 1057 / 1725 / 2324	0.8 / 4.3 / 1.1 / 4.1
12 TU	0459 / 1121 / 1729 / 2345	1.1 / 4.0 / 1.2 / 3.9	**27** W	0554 / 1159 / 1820	0.6 / 4.6 / 0.9
13 W	0600 / 1211 / 1819	0.9 / 4.3 / 1.0	**28** TH	0016 / 0644 / 1245 / 1903	4.4 / 0.4 / 4.8 / 0.8
14 TH	0028 / 0646 / 1250 / 1858	4.3 / 0.7 / 4.7 / 0.9	**29** F	0058 / 0726 / 1324 / 1940	4.6 / 0.4 / 4.9 / 0.7
15 F	0103 / 0725 / 1323 / 1935	4.6 / 0.5 / 4.9 / 0.7	**30** SA	0136 / 0804 / 1400 / ●2016	4.7 / 0.3 / 4.9 / 0.7

Chart Datum: 2·56 metres below NAP Datum
HAT is 5·4 metres above Chart Datum

TIME ZONE –0100
(Dutch Standard Time)
Subtract 1 hour for UT
For Dutch Summer Time add
ONE hour in **non-shaded areas**

NETHERLANDS – VLISSINGEN

LAT 51°27′N   LONG 3°36′E

TIMES AND HEIGHTS OF HIGH AND LOW WATERS

Dates in amber are **SPRINGS**
Dates in grey are **NEAPS**

2022

MAY

Day	Time m	Time m	Time m	Time m		Day	Time m	Time m	Time m	Time m
1 SU	0211 4.8	0839 0.4	1435 4.9	2051 0.6		16 M	0142 5.0	0812 0.3	1406 5.1	○ 2029 0.5
2 M	0246 4.9	0914 0.4	1509 4.8	2127 0.6		17 TU	0223 5.1	0855 0.3	1447 5.1	2114 0.4
3 TU	0321 4.9	0947 0.5	1542 4.7	2202 0.6		18 W	0305 5.2	0939 0.4	1531 5.0	2200 0.4
4 W	0355 4.8	1019 0.7	1614 4.6	2235 0.7		19 TH	0350 5.1	1023 0.5	1617 4.9	2247 0.4
5 TH	0429 4.7	1049 0.8	1646 4.5	2304 0.8		20 F	0438 5.0	1109 0.6	1708 4.6	2338 0.4
6 F	0503 4.5	1118 1.0	1720 4.3	2335 0.9		21 SA	0533 4.8	1159 0.8	1807 4.4	
7 SA	0540 4.3	1152 1.1	1759 4.1			22 SU	0036 0.5	0643 4.6	1259 1.0	☽ 1916 4.2
8 SU	0016 1.0	0627 4.1	1239 1.3	1853 3.9		23 M	0145 0.6	0758 4.4	1416 1.1	2028 4.1
9 M	0119 1.1	0743 3.9	1417 1.4	☽ 2010 3.7		24 TU	0300 0.7	0914 4.3	1542 1.2	2144 4.0
10 TU	0308 1.1	0905 3.8	1544 1.4	2135 3.7		25 W	0420 0.7	1029 4.4	1658 1.1	2252 4.2
11 W	0412 1.0	1027 4.0	1643 1.2	2251 3.9		26 TH	0526 0.6	1129 4.6	1753 1.0	2346 4.4
12 TH	0511 0.9	1125 4.3	1734 1.0	2342 4.3		27 F	0617 0.5	1218 4.7	1837 0.9	
13 F	0602 0.7	1209 4.7	1819 0.9			28 SA	0032 4.5	0659 0.5	1300 4.7	1915 0.7
14 SA	0024 4.6	0647 0.5	1247 4.7	1902 0.7		29 SU	0113 4.6	0736 0.5	1339 4.7	1952 0.7
15 SU	0103 4.8	0729 0.4	1326 5.1	1945 0.6		30 M	0150 4.7	0812 0.6	1415 4.7	● 2029 0.7
						31 TU	0226 4.7	0847 0.6	1449 4.7	2106 0.6

JUNE

Day	Time m	Time m	Time m	Time m		Day	Time m	Time m	Time m	Time m
1 W	0301 4.7	0921 0.7	1522 4.6	2143 0.6		16 TH	0251 5.1	0922 0.5	1518 4.9	2150 0.3
2 TH	0335 4.7	0955 0.8	1554 4.5	2220 0.7		17 F	0339 5.1	1009 0.6	1607 4.8	2240 0.3
3 F	0410 4.6	1028 0.9	1627 4.4	2254 0.7		18 SA	0430 5.0	1056 0.7	1700 4.7	2332 0.3
4 SA	0446 4.5	1100 1.0	1703 4.3	2328 0.8		19 SU	0527 4.9	1146 0.9	1756 4.6	
5 SU	0523 4.4	1136 1.1	1742 4.2			20 M	0027 0.4	0629 4.7	1242 1.0	1855 4.4
6 M	0007 0.8	0607 4.2	1219 1.2	1830 4.1		21 TU	0125 0.5	0733 4.6	1345 1.1	☽ 1957 4.3
7 TU	0059 0.9	0707 4.1	1316 1.3	☽ 1933 4.0		22 W	0226 0.6	0839 4.4	1454 1.2	2103 4.2
8 W	0208 0.9	0818 4.1	1434 1.3	2044 3.9		23 TH	0336 0.7	0949 4.4	1610 1.2	2210 4.2
9 TH	0315 0.9	0926 4.2	1544 1.2	2152 4.1		24 F	0447 0.7	1052 4.4	1715 1.1	2311 4.3
10 F	0415 0.8	1030 4.4	1642 1.1	2253 4.3		25 SA	0543 0.7	1147 4.5	1806 1.0	
11 SA	0514 0.7	1125 4.6	1737 0.9	2345 4.6		26 SU	0004 4.4	0629 0.7	1236 4.5	1850 0.9
12 SU	0609 0.6	1214 4.8	1830 0.7			27 M	0052 4.5	0709 0.8	1320 4.5	1931 0.8
13 M	0032 4.8	0700 0.5	1300 5.0	1921 0.6		28 TU	0135 4.5	0747 0.8	1359 4.5	2010 0.8
14 TU	0118 5.0	0748 0.4	1345 5.0	○ 2011 0.5		29 W	0213 4.6	0823 0.8	1434 4.6	● 2049 0.7
15 W	0204 5.1	0835 0.4	1431 5.0	2100 0.4		30 TH	0248 4.6	0859 0.9	1507 4.6	2127 0.7

JULY

Day	Time m	Time m	Time m	Time m		Day	Time m	Time m	Time m	Time m
1 F	0322 4.7	0935 0.9	1539 4.6	2205 0.6		16 SA	0330 5.1	0955 0.7	1556 4.9	2230 0.3
2 SA	0357 4.6	1010 1.0	1613 4.5	2242 0.7		17 SU	0419 5.1	1041 0.8	1643 4.9	2318 0.3
3 SU	0432 4.6	1044 1.0	1648 4.5	2318 0.7		18 M	0510 5.0	1127 0.9	1732 4.8	
4 M	0507 4.5	1119 1.1	1724 4.4	2354 0.7		19 TU	0004 0.3	0602 4.9	1213 1.0	1823 4.7
5 TU	0546 4.5	1157 1.1	1805 4.3			20 W	0052 0.4	0656 4.7	1303 1.1	☽ 1916 4.5
6 W	0035 0.7	0632 4.4	1242 1.1	1854 4.3		21 TH	0142 0.6	0754 4.5	1401 1.2	2014 4.3
7 TH	0123 0.7	0730 4.4	1335 1.2	☽ 1955 4.2		22 F	0239 0.8	0859 4.3	1508 1.2	2122 4.2
8 F	0219 0.8	0836 4.4	1439 1.1	2103 4.3		23 SA	0349 0.9	1010 4.2	1623 1.3	2233 4.1
9 SA	0322 0.8	0941 4.4	1549 1.1	2209 4.4		24 SU	0501 1.0	1116 4.2	1732 1.2	2338 4.2
10 SU	0429 0.8	1046 4.5	1659 1.0	2312 4.5		25 M	0558 1.0	1213 4.3	1827 1.1	
11 M	0537 0.7	1146 4.7	1806 0.8			26 TU	0035 4.3	0645 1.0	1303 4.4	1914 1.0
12 TU	0009 4.7	0638 0.6	1240 4.8	1905 0.6		27 W	0123 4.4	0726 1.0	1345 4.4	1955 0.9
13 W	0102 4.9	0731 0.6	1331 4.9	○ 2000 0.5		28 TH	0202 4.5	0803 0.9	1419 4.5	● 2033 0.8
14 TH	0152 5.0	0821 0.6	1420 4.9	2051 0.4		29 F	0235 4.6	0839 1.0	1451 4.6	2109 0.7
15 F	0241 5.1	0909 0.6	1508 4.9	2141 0.3		30 SA	0308 4.7	0915 0.9	1522 4.7	2146 0.6
						31 SU	0340 4.8	0950 0.9	1555 4.7	2223 0.6

AUGUST

Day	Time m	Time m	Time m	Time m		Day	Time m	Time m	Time m	Time m
1 M	0412 4.8	1025 1.0	1627 4.7	2258 0.6		16 TU	0444 5.1	1100 0.9	1702 5.0	2334 0.4
2 TU	0445 4.8	1058 1.0	1700 4.7	2333 0.6		17 W	0529 4.9	1140 1.0	1746 4.8	
3 W	0520 4.7	1133 1.0	1737 4.6			18 TH	0013 0.5	0615 4.7	1222 1.0	1832 4.7
4 TH	0008 0.6	0600 4.7	1212 1.0	1819 4.6		19 F	0055 0.7	0704 4.4	1310 1.2	☽ 1923 4.4
5 F	0049 0.6	0648 4.6	1258 1.0	☽ 1911 4.5		20 SA	0146 0.9	0758 4.2	1416 1.3	2024 4.1
6 SA	0139 0.7	0751 4.5	1357 1.1	2019 4.4		21 SU	0254 1.2	0912 3.9	1535 1.4	2150 3.9
7 SU	0241 0.8	0901 4.4	1510 1.1	2134 4.3		22 M	0414 1.3	1043 3.8	1655 1.4	2314 4.0
8 M	0356 0.9	1015 4.3	1633 1.1	2248 4.4		23 TU	0526 1.3	1151 4.0	1802 1.2	
9 TU	0516 0.9	1127 4.4	1752 0.9	2356 4.6		24 W	0017 4.2	0622 1.2	1243 4.2	1856 1.0
10 W	0624 0.8	1229 4.6	1857 0.7			25 TH	0105 4.4	0707 1.1	1325 4.4	1938 0.9
11 TH	0054 4.8	0720 0.8	1322 4.8	1951 0.5		26 F	0143 4.6	0744 1.1	1358 4.6	2013 0.8
12 F	0145 5.0	0809 0.7	1409 4.9	○ 2041 0.3		27 SA	0215 4.8	0818 1.0	1428 4.7	● 2047 0.7
13 SA	0231 5.2	0855 0.7	1453 5.0	2127 0.2		28 SU	0245 4.9	0852 0.9	1458 4.8	2121 0.6
14 SU	0316 5.2	0938 0.8	1537 5.0	2212 0.2		29 M	0315 5.0	0926 0.9	1528 4.9	2156 0.5
15 M	0400 5.2	1020 0.8	1619 5.0	2254 0.3		30 TU	0346 5.0	1000 0.9	1600 4.9	2232 0.5
						31 W	0418 5.0	1035 0.9	1633 4.9	2306 0.5

Chart Datum: 2·56 metres below NAP Datum
HAT is 5·4 metres above Chart Datum

TIME ZONE −0100
(Dutch Standard Time)
Subtract 1 hour for UT
For Dutch Summer Time add
ONE hour in **non-shaded areas**

NETHERLANDS – VLISSINGEN

LAT 51°27′N   LONG 3°36′E

TIMES AND HEIGHTS OF HIGH AND LOW WATERS

Dates in amber are **SPRINGS**
Dates in grey are **NEAPS**

2022

SEPTEMBER

Time m	Time m
1 TH 0453 4.9 / 1109 0.9 / 1709 4.9 / 2342 0.6	**16** F 0536 4.7 / 1144 1.0 / 1751 4.7
2 F 0532 4.9 / 1147 0.9 / 1749 4.8	**17** SA 0011 0.9 / 0616 4.4 / 1223 1.2 / ◑ 1835 4.4
3 SA 0021 0.6 / 0617 4.7 / 1232 0.9 / ◑ 1838 4.7	**18** SU 0053 1.2 / 0701 4.1 / 1317 1.4 / 1930 4.1
4 SU 0110 0.8 / 0715 4.4 / 1330 1.1 / 1945 4.4	**19** M 0202 1.4 / 0758 3.8 / 1457 1.5 / 2050 3.8
5 M 0213 1.0 / 0831 4.2 / 1449 1.2 / 2111 4.2	**20** TU 0335 1.6 / 0957 3.8 / 1616 1.5 / 2244 3.8
6 TU 0336 1.2 / 0956 4.1 / 1621 1.2 / 2237 4.3	**21** W 0451 1.5 / 1121 3.8 / 1729 1.3 / 2350 4.1
7 W 0507 1.2 / 1118 4.2 / 1746 1.0 / 2351 4.5	**22** TH 0554 1.4 / 1215 4.1 / 1828 1.1
8 TH 0617 1.0 / 1221 4.5 / 1850 0.7	**23** F 0037 4.4 / 0642 1.2 / 1255 4.4 / 1911 0.9
9 F 0049 4.8 / 0711 0.9 / 1311 4.7 / 1941 0.5	**24** SA 0114 4.7 / 0719 1.1 / 1328 4.6 / 1945 0.8
10 SA 0135 5.1 / 0756 0.8 / 1353 4.9 / ○ 2026 0.3	**25** SU 0146 4.9 / 0751 1.0 / 1357 4.8 / ● 2017 0.6
11 SU 0216 5.2 / 0838 0.8 / 1433 5.0 / 2108 0.3	**26** M 0215 5.0 / 0824 0.9 / 1427 5.0 / 2051 0.5
12 M 0256 5.2 / 0917 0.8 / 1513 5.1 / 2148 0.3	**27** TU 0245 5.1 / 0858 0.8 / 1458 5.1 / 2126 0.5
13 TU 0336 5.2 / 0956 0.8 / 1552 5.1 / 2226 0.4	**28** W 0317 5.2 / 0934 0.8 / 1531 5.1 / 2203 0.5
14 W 0416 5.1 / 1033 0.9 / 1632 5.1 / 2302 0.5	**29** TH 0351 5.1 / 1011 0.8 / 1607 5.1 / 2240 0.5
15 TH 0456 4.9 / 1108 0.9 / 1711 4.9 / 2336 0.7	**30** F 0428 5.1 / 1048 0.8 / 1644 5.1 / 2318 0.6

OCTOBER

Time m	Time m
1 SA 0508 4.9 / 1129 0.8 / 1726 5.0 / 2359 0.7	**16** SU 0536 4.4 / 1147 1.1 / 1756 4.4
2 SU 0554 4.7 / 1216 0.9 / 1816 4.7	**17** M 0007 1.3 / 0616 4.1 / 1227 1.3 / ◑ 1845 4.1
3 M 0049 1.0 / 0653 4.3 / 1317 1.1 / ◑ 1927 4.4	**18** TU 0056 1.6 / 0709 3.8 / 1415 1.4 / 2000 3.8
4 TU 0156 1.2 / 0814 4.0 / 1441 1.2 / 2101 4.2	**19** W 0256 1.7 / 0825 3.6 / 1535 1.5 / 2150 3.7
5 W 0328 1.4 / 0945 3.9 / 1617 1.2 / 2232 4.2	**20** TH 0410 1.6 / 1034 3.6 / 1644 1.4 / 2310 4.0
6 TH 0504 1.3 / 1109 4.1 / 1740 0.9 / 2347 4.6	**21** F 0514 1.5 / 1133 4.0 / 1747 1.1 / 2359 4.3
7 F 0610 1.1 / 1209 4.4 / 1839 0.7	**22** SA 0605 1.3 / 1215 4.3 / 1833 0.9
8 SA 0039 4.8 / 0658 1.0 / 1254 4.7 / 1925 0.5	**23** SU 0037 4.6 / 0644 1.1 / 1249 4.6 / 1909 0.8
9 SU 0120 5.0 / 0739 0.9 / 1333 4.9 / ○ 2006 0.4	**24** M 0110 4.9 / 0718 1.0 / 1321 4.8 / 1943 0.6
10 M 0158 5.1 / 0818 0.8 / 1411 5.0 / 2044 0.4	**25** TU 0141 5.1 / 0753 0.9 / 1354 5.0 / ● 2019 0.5
11 TU 0235 5.1 / 0855 0.8 / 1449 5.1 / 2122 0.4	**26** W 0214 5.2 / 0830 0.8 / 1428 5.2 / 2057 0.5
12 W 0313 5.1 / 0932 0.8 / 1526 5.1 / 2157 0.5	**27** TH 0249 5.2 / 0909 0.7 / 1505 5.2 / 2136 0.5
13 TH 0350 5.0 / 1007 0.8 / 1603 5.0 / 2231 0.7	**28** F 0327 5.2 / 0950 0.7 / 1544 5.2 / 2216 0.6
14 F 0426 4.8 / 1042 0.9 / 1639 4.9 / 2302 0.9	**29** SA 0407 5.1 / 1032 0.7 / 1625 5.1 / 2257 0.7
15 SA 0501 4.6 / 1114 1.0 / 1716 4.7 / 2333 1.1	**30** SU 0451 4.9 / 1117 0.7 / 1711 5.0 / 2342 0.9
	31 M 0540 4.6 / 1209 0.8 / 1806 4.7

NOVEMBER

Time m	Time m
1 TU 0035 1.1 / 0643 4.2 / 1313 1.0 / ◑ 1924 4.3	**16** W 0020 1.5 / 0635 4.0 / 1302 1.3 / ◑ 1919 3.9
2 W 0145 1.4 / 0805 4.0 / 1436 1.1 / 2052 4.2	**17** TH 0132 1.7 / 0743 3.8 / 1446 1.4 / 2037 3.8
3 TH 0320 1.5 / 0930 3.9 / 1606 1.0 / 2219 4.3	**18** F 0320 1.7 / 0904 3.7 / 1550 1.3 / 2202 3.9
4 F 0451 1.4 / 1049 4.1 / 1724 0.9 / 2329 4.6	**19** SA 0421 1.5 / 1028 3.9 / 1650 1.1 / 2306 4.2
5 SA 0553 1.2 / 1147 4.4 / 1819 0.7	**20** SU 0514 1.4 / 1123 4.2 / 1743 1.0 / 2351 4.6
6 SU 0019 4.6 / 0639 1.1 / 1232 4.6 / 1903 0.6	**21** M 0600 1.2 / 1205 4.5 / 1827 0.8
7 M 0100 4.9 / 0718 0.9 / 1312 4.9 / 1942 0.5	**22** TU 0030 4.8 / 0641 1.0 / 1244 4.8 / 1907 0.7
8 TU 0138 5.0 / 0756 0.9 / 1350 4.9 / ○ 2019 0.5	**23** W 0107 5.0 / 0722 0.8 / 1323 5.0 / ● 1949 0.6
9 W 0215 5.0 / 0833 0.8 / 1427 5.0 / 2055 0.6	**24** TH 0146 5.1 / 0805 0.7 / 1402 5.2 / 2031 0.5
10 TH 0252 4.9 / 0910 0.8 / 1503 5.0 / 2130 0.7	**25** F 0226 5.2 / 0849 0.6 / 1443 5.2 / 2114 0.6
11 F 0327 4.8 / 0947 0.8 / 1539 4.9 / 2204 0.9	**26** SA 0308 5.1 / 0935 0.6 / 1526 5.2 / 2157 0.6
12 SA 0401 4.7 / 1022 0.9 / 1615 4.8 / 2235 1.0	**27** SU 0352 5.0 / 1021 0.6 / 1612 5.1 / 2242 0.8
13 SU 0434 4.5 / 1055 1.0 / 1651 4.6 / 2306 1.2	**28** M 0440 4.8 / 1111 0.6 / 1702 4.9 / 2330 0.9
14 M 0509 4.4 / 1127 1.1 / 1729 4.4 / 2338 1.3	**29** TU 0533 4.6 / 1205 0.7 / 1802 4.7
15 TU 0547 4.2 / 1204 1.2 / 1814 4.2	**30** W 0024 1.1 / 0637 4.3 / 1308 0.8 / ◑ 1916 4.5

DECEMBER

Time m	Time m
1 TH 0130 1.3 / 0747 4.2 / 1419 0.9 / 2031 4.4	**16** F 0043 1.4 / 0703 4.1 / 1329 1.1 / ◑ 1943 4.1
2 F 0251 1.4 / 0900 4.1 / 1536 0.9 / 2148 4.4	**17** SA 0144 1.5 / 0808 4.0 / 1438 1.1 / 2051 4.1
3 SA 0416 1.4 / 1013 4.2 / 1654 0.8 / 2256 4.5	**18** SU 0304 1.5 / 0918 4.0 / 1542 1.1 / 2158 4.2
4 SU 0523 1.3 / 1114 4.3 / 1751 0.7 / 2350 4.6	**19** M 0410 1.4 / 1024 4.2 / 1644 1.0 / 2259 4.5
5 M 0613 1.1 / 1205 4.5 / 1837 0.7	**20** TU 0509 1.2 / 1120 4.5 / 1742 0.8 / 2351 4.7
6 TU 0037 4.7 / 0655 1.0 / 1250 4.7 / 1917 0.7	**21** W 0604 1.0 / 1210 4.7 / 1835 0.7
7 W 0119 4.8 / 0735 0.9 / 1332 4.8 / 1955 0.7	**22** TH 0038 4.9 / 0656 0.8 / 1257 4.9 / 1924 0.6
8 TH 0159 4.8 / 0813 0.8 / 1411 4.8 / ○ 2031 0.8	**23** F 0124 5.0 / 0747 0.7 / 1343 5.1 / ● 2011 0.6
9 F 0236 4.7 / 0851 0.8 / 1448 4.8 / 2106 0.9	**24** SA 0209 5.0 / 0836 0.5 / 1428 5.2 / 2057 0.6
10 SA 0311 4.7 / 0929 0.8 / 1524 4.8 / 2141 0.9	**25** SU 0255 5.0 / 0925 0.5 / 1515 5.2 / 2144 0.7
11 SU 0344 4.6 / 1007 0.8 / 1559 4.7 / 2214 1.1	**26** M 0342 4.9 / 1014 0.4 / 1604 5.1 / 2230 0.8
12 M 0417 4.5 / 1042 0.9 / 1635 4.6 / 2247 1.2	**27** TU 0431 4.8 / 1104 0.4 / 1656 5.0 / 2318 0.9
13 TU 0451 4.4 / 1116 0.9 / 1712 4.5 / 2319 1.3	**28** W 0523 4.7 / 1156 0.5 / 1752 4.9
14 W 0528 4.3 / 1151 1.0 / 1752 4.3 / 2356 1.4	**29** TH 0008 1.0 / 0619 4.6 / 1250 0.5 / 1853 4.7
15 TH 0610 4.2 / 1233 1.1 / 1841 4.2	**30** F 0103 1.2 / 0718 4.4 / 1346 0.7 / ◑ 1957 4.5
	31 SA 0206 1.3 / 0821 4.4 / 1449 0.8 / 2105 4.4

Chart Datum: 2·56 metres below NAP Datum
HAT is 5·4 metres above Chart Datum

TIDES

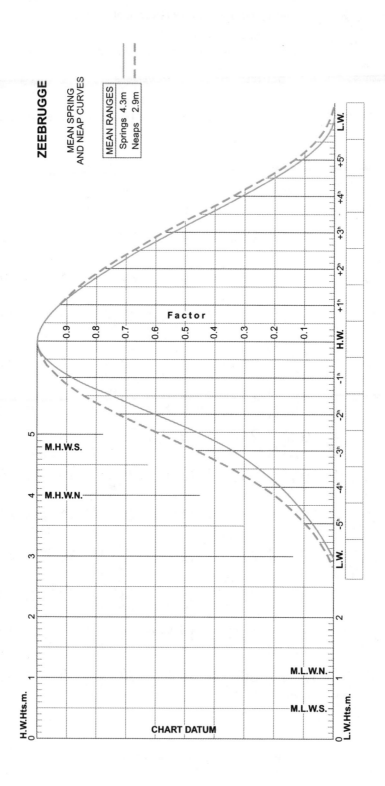

ZEEBRUGGE

MEAN SPRING
AND NEAP CURVES

MEAN RANGES
Springs 4.3m
Neaps 2.9m

Factor

0.9
0.8
0.7
0.6
0.5
0.4
0.3
0.2
0.1

H.W.

L.W.

M.H.W.S.

M.H.W.N.

M.L.W.N.

M.L.W.S.

CHART DATUM

H.W.Hts.m.

L.W.Hts.m.

TIME ZONE -0100
(Belgian Standard Time)
Subtract 1 hour for UT
For Belgian Summer Time add
ONE hour in non-shaded areas

Dates in amber are **SPRINGS**
Dates in grey are **NEAPS**

2022

TIMES AND HEIGHTS OF HIGH AND LOW WATERS

JANUARY

Time	m		Time	m
1 SA 0613	0.9	**16** SU 0054	4.2
1211	4.6	0713	1.0
1837	0.7	1310	4.3
		1921	1.1
2 SU 0043	4.6	**17** M 0131	4.3
0704	0.8	0744	0.9
1303	4.7	1345	4.3
●1926	0.7	1947	1.1
3 M 0131	4.6	**18** TU 0202	4.3
0752	0.6	0810	0.9
1350	4.8	1415	4.4
2012	0.7	○2012	1.1
4 TU 0215	4.6	**19** W 0230	4.3
0838	0.5	0838	0.8
1437	4.9	1443	4.5
2057	0.8	2043	1.0
5 W 0259	4.6	**20** TH 0257	4.4
0923	0.5	0911	0.7
1523	4.9	1514	4.6
2142	0.8	2118	0.9
6 TH 0344	4.6	**21** F 0328	4.5
1010	0.4	0947	0.6
1610	4.8	1549	4.7
2227	0.9	2156	0.9
7 F 0430	4.6	**22** SA 0404	4.6
1058	0.4	1027	0.5
1700	4.7	1629	4.7
2315	1.0	2238	0.9
8 SA 0520	4.5	**23** SU 0444	4.6
1149	0.5	1110	0.5
1753	4.6	1713	4.7
		2322	0.9
9 SU 0006	1.1	**24** M 0529	4.5
0613	4.4	1156	0.6
1244	0.6	1802	4.6
☽1851	4.4		
10 M 0102	1.2	**25** TU 0011	1.0
0712	4.2	0621	4.4
1343	0.8	1249	0.7
1953	4.0	☽1859	4.4
11 TU 0206	1.4	**26** W 0108	1.2
0816	4.1	0721	4.3
1447	1.0	1352	0.8
2058	4.0	2004	4.3
12 W 0317	1.4	**27** TH 0219	1.3
0925	4.0	0830	4.2
1553	1.1	1506	1.0
2207	4.0	2116	4.1
13 TH 0430	1.4	**28** F 0341	1.3
1035	4.0	0945	4.1
1659	1.1	1620	1.0
2314	4.0	2231	4.1
14 F 0537	1.3	**29** SA 0457	1.2
1138	4.1	1059	4.2
1758	1.1	1728	1.0
		2340	4.1
15 SA 0009	4.1	**30** SU 0602	1.0
0631	1.1	1204	4.4
1229	4.2	1827	0.9
1846	1.1		
		31 M 0036	4.3
		0656	0.8
		1257	4.6
		1916	0.9

FEBRUARY

Time	m		Time	m
1 TU 0121	4.4	**16** W 0137	4.3
0742	0.6	0750	0.8
1342	4.7	1351	4.5
●2000	0.8	○1952	1.0
2 W 0202	4.6	**17** TH 0205	4.4
0826	0.4	0818	0.6
1424	4.9	1421	4.7
2042	0.8	2024	0.8
3 TH 0243	4.7	**18** F 0234	4.6
0908	0.3	0852	0.4
1507	4.8	1453	4.8
2123	0.7	2101	0.7
4 F 0325	4.8	**19** SA 0307	4.7
0952	0.2	0930	0.3
1550	4.9	1530	4.9
2205	0.7	2141	0.6
5 SA 0408	4.8	**20** SU 0344	4.8
1036	0.2	1010	0.3
1635	4.9	1608	4.9
2248	0.8	2221	0.7
6 SU 0452	4.7	**21** M 0423	4.8
1121	0.3	1051	0.3
1722	4.7	1650	4.8
2330	0.9	2302	0.7
7 M 0537	4.6	**22** TU 0505	4.7
1206	0.5	1133	0.5
1809	4.4	1734	4.7
		2345	0.9
8 TU 0014	1.1	**23** W 0552	4.6
0625	4.3	1219	0.6
1256	0.8	1824	4.4
☽1900	4.1		
9 W 0104	1.3	**24** TH 0034	1.0
0719	4.0	0646	4.4
1358	1.1	1316	0.9
2000	3.8	1925	4.1
10 TH 0224	1.5	**25** F 0140	1.3
0827	3.8	0755	4.1
1511	1.3	1437	1.1
2116	3.6	2046	3.8
11 F 0350	1.5	**26** SA 0318	1.4
0952	3.6	0925	3.9
1622	1.4	1602	1.2
2238	3.6	2217	3.7
12 SA 0504	1.4	**27** SU 0443	1.2
1109	3.7	1053	4.0
1728	1.4	1717	1.2
2343	3.8	2333	3.9
13 SU 0606	1.3	**28** M 0552	1.0
1206	3.9	1159	4.3
1823	1.3	1818	1.0
14 M 0031	4.0		
0652	1.1		
1248	4.1		
1900	1.2		
15 TU 0108	4.1		
0724	0.9		
1322	4.3		
1925	1.1		

MARCH

Time	m		Time	m
1 TU 0026	4.2	**16** W 0033	4.1
0645	0.7	0649	0.9
1248	4.5	1250	4.4
1904	0.9	1854	1.0
2 W 0107	4.4	**17** TH 0104	4.3
0728	0.5	0719	0.6
1328	4.7	1321	4.6
●1944	0.8	1926	0.8
3 TH 0144	4.6	**18** F 0134	4.6
0808	0.3	0752	0.4
1407	4.9	1353	4.9
2023	0.7	○2002	0.6
4 F 0223	4.8	**19** SA 0207	4.8
0848	0.2	0829	0.2
1446	5.0	1428	5.0
2101	0.6	2041	0.5
5 SA 0302	4.9	**20** SU 0242	4.9
0929	0.1	0908	0.2
1527	5.0	1506	5.0
2140	0.6	2122	0.5
6 SU 0342	4.9	**21** M 0321	5.0
1009	0.1	0949	0.2
1608	4.9	1545	5.0
2219	0.6	2202	0.5
7 M 0423	4.8	**22** TU 0400	4.9
1049	0.3	1029	0.3
1649	4.7	1626	4.8
2255	0.7	2242	0.6
8 TU 0502	4.6	**23** W 0442	4.8
1126	0.6	1110	0.5
1727	4.4	1709	4.6
2330	0.9	2323	0.8
9 W 0540	4.4	**24** TH 0528	4.6
1201	0.9	1155	0.7
1805	4.1	1757	4.3
10 TH 0004	1.2	**25** F 0011	1.0
0620	4.0	0621	4.3
1240	1.3	1251	1.1
☽1847	3.7	☽1857	3.9
11 F 0047	1.5	**26** SA 0119	1.2
0711	3.7	0735	4.0
1417	1.6	1419	1.3
2002	3.4	2028	3.6
12 SA 0308	1.6	**27** SU 0304	1.3
0856	3.4	0916	3.8
1542	1.7	1547	1.4
2150	3.3	2204	3.6
13 SU 0422	1.5	**28** M 0425	1.1
1029	3.5	1044	4.0
1647	1.6	1701	1.2
2305	3.5	2316	3.9
14 M 0524	1.3	**29** TU 0533	0.9
1131	3.8	1146	4.3
1744	1.4	1802	1.1
2356	3.8		
15 TU 0614	1.1	**30** W 0007	4.2
1215	4.1	0625	0.6
1824	1.2	1232	4.6
		1846	0.9
		31 TH 0047	4.4
		0708	0.4
		1310	4.8
		1924	0.8

APRIL

Time	m		Time	m
1 F 0123	4.7	**16** SA 0101	4.7
0747	0.2	0722	0.3
1347	4.9	1324	5.0
●2001	0.6	1937	0.5
2 SA 0200	4.8	**17** SU 0138	4.9
0825	0.2	0803	0.2
1424	4.9	1402	5.1
2038	0.5	2019	0.4
3 SU 0238	4.9	**18** M 0217	5.0
0903	0.2	0844	0.2
1503	4.9	1442	5.0
2114	0.5	2101	0.4
4 M 0317	4.9	**19** TU 0258	5.0
0941	0.3	0926	0.2
1541	4.8	1523	4.9
2150	0.6	2142	0.5
5 TU 0354	4.8	**20** W 0340	4.9
1016	0.5	1008	0.4
1617	4.6	1605	4.7
2223	0.7	2224	0.6
6 W 0429	4.5	**21** TH 0423	4.7
1047	0.7	1050	0.6
1649	4.3	1649	4.4
2253	0.9	2307	0.8
7 TH 0501	4.3	**22** F 0511	4.5
1114	1.0	1137	0.9
1719	4.0	1739	4.1
2322	1.1	2359	0.9
8 F 0534	4.0	**23** SA 0608	4.2
1144	1.3	1238	1.2
1751	3.8	1844	3.8
2358	1.3	☽	
9 SA 0616	3.7	**24** SU 0116	1.1
1225	1.6	0729	4.0
1836	3.5	1405	1.4
☽		2015	3.6
10 SU 0059	1.6	**25** M 0245	1.1
0734	3.4	0904	3.9
1455	1.7	1524	1.4
2049	3.3	2141	3.7
11 M 0335	1.5	**26** TU 0358	0.9
0937	3.5	1023	4.1
1600	1.6	1635	1.2
2212	3.4	2249	4.0
12 TU 0434	1.3	**27** W 0504	0.7
1044	3.8	1123	4.4
1655	1.4	1737	1.1
2308	3.7	2341	4.3
13 W 0524	1.0	**28** TH 0600	0.5
1132	4.1	1209	4.6
1740	1.2	1823	0.9
2350	4.1		
14 TH 0606	0.8	**29** F 0023	4.5
1212	4.5	0645	0.4
1819	0.9	1249	4.7
		1902	0.8
15 F 0026	4.4	**30** SA 0102	4.8
0644	0.5	0724	0.3
1248	4.8	1326	4.8
1858	0.7	●1939	0.7

Chart Datum: 0·23 metres below TAW Datum
HAT is 5·6 metres above Chart Datum

TIDES

TIDES

TIME ZONE -0100
(Belgian Standard Time)
Subtract 1 hour for UT
For Belgian Summer Time add
ONE hour in **non-shaded areas**

BELGIUM – ZEEBRUGGE
LAT 51°21'N   LONG 3°12'E
TIMES AND HEIGHTS OF HIGH AND LOW WATERS

Dates in amber are **SPRINGS**
Dates in grey are **NEAPS**

2022

MAY

#	Time	m	#	Time	m
1 SU	0139	4.7	16 M	0112	4.9
	0802	0.3		0737	0.3
	1403	4.8		1338	4.9
	2015	0.6		○1957	0.5
2 M	0217	4.8	17 TU	0155	4.9
	0838	0.4		0821	0.3
	1440	4.7		1421	4.8
	2050	0.6		2041	0.5
3 TU	0254	4.7	18 W	0238	4.9
	0913	0.5		0905	0.4
	1516	4.5		1504	4.7
	2124	0.6		2125	0.5
4 W	0329	4.6	19 TH	0323	4.8
	0944	0.7		0949	0.6
	1549	4.4		1548	4.5
	2155	0.7		2210	0.6
5 TH	0401	4.4	20 F	0410	4.7
	1011	0.9		1035	0.8
	1617	4.2		1636	4.3
	2224	0.9		2258	0.7
6 F	0431	4.2	21 SA	0502	4.5
	1038	1.1		1125	1.0
	1645	4.0		1729	4.1
	2255	1.0		2356	0.8
7 SA	0504	4.1	22 SU	0603	4.3
	1110	1.3		1228	1.2
	1718	3.9		1834	3.9 ☽
	2332	1.1			
8 SU	0547	3.9	23 M	0107	0.8
	1152	1.4		0719	4.1
	1804	3.7		1342	1.3
				1952	3.8
9 M	0028	1.3	24 TU	0219	0.8
	0654	3.7		0838	4.1
	1311	1.6		1452	1.3
	☾1935	3.5		2107	3.9
10 TU	0244	1.3	25 W	0325	0.8
	0840	3.7		0949	4.2
	1509	1.5		1559	1.2
	2113	3.6		2213	4.1
11 W	0343	1.1	26 TH	0430	0.7
	0950	3.9		1051	4.4
	1606	1.3		1704	1.1
	2215	3.8		2310	4.3
12 TH	0435	0.9	27 F	0530	0.6
	1045	4.2		1142	4.5
	1657	1.1		1758	0.9
	2304	4.1		2358	4.4
13 F	0523	0.7	28 SA	0620	0.5
	1132	4.5		1227	4.6
	1744	0.9		1841	0.8
	2348	4.4			
14 SA	0609	0.5	29 SU	0042	4.5
	1215	4.8		0702	0.5
	1829	0.7		1308	4.6
				1920	0.8
15 SU	0030	4.7	30 M	0122	4.6
	0653	0.3		0740	0.6
	1256	4.9		●1346	4.5
	1913	0.5		1956	0.7
			31 TU	0200	4.5
				0815	0.7
				1423	4.5
				2030	0.7

JUNE

#	Time	m	#	Time	m
1 W	0236	4.5	16 TH	0224	4.8
	0846	0.8		0847	0.6
	1457	4.3		1449	4.6
	2102	0.7		2112	0.5
2 TH	0310	4.4	17 F	0311	4.8
	0915	1.0		0933	0.7
	1527	4.2		1535	4.5
	2133	0.8		2200	0.5
3 F	0340	4.3	18 SA	0400	4.7
	0943	1.1		1021	0.9
	1554	4.1		1624	4.4
	2204	0.8		2250	0.5
4 SA	0411	4.2	19 SU	0453	4.6
	1013	1.1		1112	1.0
	1624	4.1		1716	4.3
	2237	0.9		2345	0.5
5 SU	0447	4.2	20 M	0550	4.5
	1049	1.2		1208	1.1
	1700	4.0		1814	4.2
	2318	1.0			
6 M	0531	4.1	21 TU	0045	0.6
	1133	1.3		0655	4.4
	1748	3.9		1309	1.2
				☽1919	4.1
7 TU	0013	1.0	22 W	0147	0.6
	0630	4.1		0802	4.3
	1236	1.4		1413	1.2
	☾1855	3.9		2026	4.1
8 W	0140	1.0	23 TH	0249	0.7
	0746	4.0		0908	4.2
	1406	1.4		1519	1.2
	2015	3.9		2132	4.1
9 TH	0251	0.9	24 F	0354	0.7
	0858	4.1		1013	4.2
	1516	1.2		1628	1.2
	2122	4.0		2236	4.2
10 F	0349	0.8	25 SA	0458	0.8
	0958	4.3		1114	4.3
	1614	1.1		1731	1.1
	2220	4.2		2334	4.3
11 SA	0444	0.7	26 SU	0555	0.8
	1053	4.5		1206	4.3
	1710	0.9		1824	1.0
	2313	4.4			
12 SU	0536	0.6	27 M	0025	4.3
	1144	4.6		0643	0.8
	1802	0.8		1252	4.4
	2359	4.6		1907	0.9
13 M	0627	0.5	28 TU	0108	4.4
	1232	4.7		0723	0.9
	1852	0.7		1332	4.3
				1944	0.9
14 TU	0051	4.8	29 W	0147	4.4
	0715	0.5		0755	1.0
	1319	4.7		1408	4.3
	○1939	0.6		●2016	0.8
15 W	0138	4.8	30 TH	0222	4.3
	0802	0.5		0823	1.1
	1404	4.6		1439	4.3
	2026	0.5		2045	0.8

JULY

#	Time	m	#	Time	m
1 F	0253	4.3	16 SA	0259	4.9
	0850	1.1		0918	0.8
	1508	4.2		1520	4.6
	2115	0.8		2146	0.3
2 SA	0323	4.3	17 SU	0346	4.9
	0921	1.0		1004	0.8
	1536	4.3		1606	4.7
	2148	0.7		2234	0.3
3 SU	0355	4.4	18 M	0435	4.8
	0955	1.0		1051	0.8
	1608	4.3		1654	4.6
	2225	0.7		2324	0.3
4 M	0431	4.4	19 TU	0526	4.7
	1034	1.0		1140	0.9
	1645	4.3		1745	4.6
	2306	0.7			
5 TU	0514	4.5	20 W	0015	0.4
	1117	1.0		0621	4.6
	1729	4.3		1231	1.0
	2354	0.7		☽1841	4.4
6 W	0603	4.4	21 TH	0110	0.6
	1209	1.1		0720	4.4
	1822	4.3		1328	1.2
				1941	4.2
7 TH	0051	0.8	22 F	0211	0.8
	0702	4.4		0822	4.2
	1310	1.2		1436	1.3
	☾1925	4.2		2047	4.1
8 F	0156	0.8	23 SA	0317	1.0
	0808	4.3		0931	4.0
	1421	1.2		1552	1.3
	2032	4.2		2200	4.0
9 SA	0303	0.8	24 SU	0426	1.1
	0914	4.3		1043	4.0
	1533	1.2		1704	1.3
	2138	4.2		2311	4.0
10 SU	0408	0.8	25 M	0531	1.1
	1018	4.3		1145	4.1
	1640	1.1		1805	1.1
	2242	4.3			
11 M	0509	0.8	26 TU	0008	4.1
	1119	4.4		0625	1.1
	1741	0.9		1234	4.2
	2342	4.4		1854	1.0
12 TU	0607	0.7	27 W	0053	4.3
	1215	4.4		0706	1.1
	1836	0.8		1315	4.2
				1931	0.9
13 W	0037	4.6	28 TH	0130	4.3
	0658	0.7		0736	1.1
	1305	4.5		1348	4.3
	○1926	0.7		●2000	0.9
14 TH	0126	4.7	29 F	0203	4.4
	0746	0.7		0801	1.1
	1351	4.5		1418	4.3
	2013	0.5		2027	0.8
15 F	0213	4.8	30 SA	0232	4.5
	0832	0.8		0829	1.0
	1435	4.6		1445	4.4
	2059	0.4		2057	0.7
			31 SU	0302	4.6
				0902	0.9
				1515	4.5
				2131	0.6

AUGUST

#	Time	m	#	Time	m
1 M	0335	4.7	16 TU	0411	5.0
	0938	0.8		1025	0.7
	1548	4.6		1628	4.9
	2209	0.5		2256	0.2
2 TU	0411	4.8	17 W	0457	4.9
	1018	0.8		1108	0.8
	1625	4.7		1713	4.8
	2248	0.5		2342	0.4
3 W	0451	4.8	18 TH	0544	4.7
	1059	0.8		1151	0.9
	1705	4.7		1800	4.6
	2330	0.5			
4 TH	0535	4.7	19 F	0029	0.7
	1142	0.9		0634	4.6
	1751	4.6		1238	1.1
				☽1852	4.3
5 F	0016	0.6	20 SA	0125	1.0
	0625	4.6		0730	4.0
	1232	1.0		1340	1.4
	☽1845	4.5		1956	4.0
6 SA	0111	0.8	21 SU	0240	1.3
	0723	4.4		0843	3.8
	1332	1.2		1518	1.5
	1948	4.3		2120	3.8
7 SU	0221	0.9	22 M	0354	1.4
	0832	4.2		1008	3.7
	1455	1.3		1633	1.4
	2102	4.2		2244	3.8
8 M	0339	1.0	23 TU	0502	1.4
	0949	4.1		1119	3.8
	1617	1.2		1739	1.3
	2221	4.2		2346	4.0
9 TU	0450	1.0	24 W	0600	1.4
	1103	4.1		1210	4.0
	1726	1.1		1830	1.1
	2331	4.3			
10 W	0553	1.0	25 TH	0031	4.2
	1205	4.2		0643	1.3
	1825	0.9		1250	4.2
				1907	0.9
11 TH	0028	4.6	26 F	0106	4.4
	0646	0.9		0711	1.2
	1253	4.4		1322	4.4
	1914	0.6		1935	0.8
12 F	0115	4.8	27 SA	0137	4.6
	0732	0.8		0736	1.0
	1336	4.6		1350	4.5
	○1959	0.4		●2002	0.6
13 SA	0159	4.9	28 SU	0206	4.7
	0816	0.8		0806	0.9
	1418	4.8		1418	4.7
	2043	0.3		2034	0.5
14 SU	0242	5.0	29 M	0237	4.9
	0858	0.7		0841	0.7
	1500	4.9		1449	4.8
	2127	0.2		2109	0.4
15 M	0326	5.1	30 TU	0311	5.0
	0941	0.7		0919	0.6
	1543	5.0		1524	4.9
	2211	0.1		2147	0.3
			31 W	0347	5.0
				0958	0.6
				1601	4.9
				2226	0.4

Chart Datum: 0·23 metres below TAW Datum
HAT is 5·6 metres above Chart Datum

TIME ZONE -0100
(Belgian Standard Time)
Subtract 1 hour for UT
For Belgian Summer Time add ONE hour in **non-shaded areas**

BELGIUM – ZEEBRUGGE
LAT 51°21'N   LONG 3°12'E
TIMES AND HEIGHTS OF HIGH AND LOW WATERS

Dates in amber are **SPRINGS**
Dates in grey are **NEAPS**
2022

SEPTEMBER

Day	Time m	Day	Time m
1 TH	0425 5.0 / 1037 0.7 / 1640 4.9 / 2305 0.5	16 F	0508 4.6 / 1113 0.9 / 1722 4.6 / 2344 0.9
2 F	0506 4.8 / 1117 0.8 / 1723 4.8 / 2347 0.6	17 SA ◑	0548 4.3 / 1150 1.1 / 1805 4.3
3 SA ◑	0552 4.6 / 1201 1.0 / 1812 4.6	18 SU	0025 1.3 / 0632 3.9 / 1234 1.4 / 1857 3.9
4 SU	0037 0.9 / 0646 4.3 / 1257 1.2 / 1913 4.3	19 M	0149 1.6 / 0741 3.6 / 1443 1.6 / 2033 3.6
5 M	0148 1.2 / 0757 4.0 / 1428 1.4 / 2037 4.1	20 TU	0320 1.7 / 0925 3.5 / 1557 1.6 / 2207 3.6
6 TU	0321 1.3 / 0930 3.8 / 1602 1.3 / 2211 4.1	21 W	0425 1.7 / 1042 3.6 / 1700 1.4 / 2312 3.9
7 W	0436 1.3 / 1053 4.0 / 1713 1.1 / 2324 4.3	22 TH	0523 1.5 / 1136 3.9 / 1753 1.1 / 2358 4.2
8 TH	0541 1.1 / 1152 4.2 / 1811 0.8	23 F	0607 1.3 / 1216 4.2 / 1831 0.9
9 F	0017 4.6 / 0633 1.0 / 1238 4.5 / 1859 0.5	24 SA	0034 4.5 / 0639 1.1 / 1248 4.5 / 1902 0.7
10 SA ○	0101 4.9 / 0736 0.8 / 1318 4.7 / 1941 0.3	25 SU ●	0105 4.8 / 0708 0.9 / 1318 4.7 / 1933 0.5
11 SU	0141 5.1 / 0756 0.7 / 1357 4.9 / 2022 0.2	26 M	0136 5.0 / 0742 0.7 / 1349 4.9 / 2007 0.3
12 M	0221 5.2 / 0837 0.6 / 1437 5.1 / 2104 0.1	27 TU	0209 5.1 / 0819 0.6 / 1422 5.0 / 2045 0.3
13 TU	0302 5.2 / 0917 0.5 / 1518 5.1 / 2146 0.1	28 W	0245 5.2 / 0858 0.5 / 1459 5.1 / 2124 0.3
14 W	0344 5.1 / 0957 0.6 / 1600 5.1 / 2227 0.3	29 TH	0322 5.1 / 0937 0.6 / 1537 5.1 / 2203 0.4
15 TH	0426 4.9 / 1036 0.7 / 1642 4.9 / 2306 0.6	30 F	0401 5.0 / 1016 0.7 / 1616 5.0 / 2242 0.6

OCTOBER

Day	Time m	Day	Time m
1 SA	0441 4.8 / 1055 0.8 / 1659 4.6 / 2323 0.8	16 SU	0508 4.2 / 1112 1.1 / 1725 4.2 / 2333 1.4
2 SU	0526 4.5 / 1139 1.0 / 1749 4.5	17 M ◑	0542 3.9 / 1149 1.4 / 1808 3.9
3 M ◑	0013 1.1 / 0619 4.1 / 1237 1.2 / 1853 4.2	18 TU	0014 1.7 / 0628 3.6 / 1356 1.6 / 1932 3.6
4 TU	0130 1.4 / 0737 3.8 / 1418 1.4 / 2029 4.0	19 W	0237 1.9 / 0830 3.4 / 1516 1.6 / 2118 3.6
5 W	0306 1.5 / 0918 3.7 / 1545 1.2 / 2202 4.1	20 TH	0342 1.8 / 0952 3.6 / 1614 1.4 / 2225 3.9
6 TH	0420 1.4 / 1036 4.0 / 1654 1.0 / 2310 4.5	21 F	0437 1.5 / 1050 3.9 / 1706 1.1 / 2315 4.2
7 F	0524 1.2 / 1133 4.3 / 1752 0.7 / 2359 4.7	22 SA	0524 1.3 / 1133 4.2 / 1748 0.9 / 2356 4.6
8 SA	0615 1.0 / 1218 4.6 / 1839 0.5	23 SU	0602 1.0 / 1210 4.5 / 1826 0.6
9 SU ○	0043 5.0 / 0657 0.8 / 1257 4.8 / 1921 0.3	24 M	0031 4.9 / 0639 0.8 / 1244 4.8 / 1902 0.4
10 M	0122 5.1 / 0736 0.7 / 1336 5.0 / 2001 0.2	25 TU ●	0106 5.1 / 0717 0.6 / 1319 5.0 / 1940 0.3
11 TU	0200 5.1 / 0815 0.6 / 1415 5.1 / 2040 0.3	26 W	0142 5.2 / 0756 0.5 / 1356 5.1 / 2020 0.3
12 W	0240 5.1 / 0853 0.5 / 1455 5.1 / 2120 0.3	27 TH	0220 5.2 / 0837 0.5 / 1435 5.1 / 2101 0.4
13 TH	0320 5.0 / 0931 0.6 / 1535 5.0 / 2157 0.5	28 F	0259 5.0 / 0918 0.6 / 1516 5.1 / 2141 0.5
14 F	0358 4.8 / 1007 0.7 / 1613 4.8 / 2231 0.8	29 SA	0340 4.9 / 0958 0.7 / 1558 4.9 / 2222 0.7
15 SA	0435 4.5 / 1040 0.9 / 1649 4.5 / 2302 1.1	30 SU	0422 4.6 / 1040 0.8 / 1643 4.7 / 2306 1.0
		31 M	0508 4.3 / 1128 1.0 / 1736 4.5 / 2359 1.3

NOVEMBER

Day	Time m	Day	Time m
1 TU ◑	0606 4.0 / 1235 1.1 / 1847 4.2	16 W	0554 3.8 / 1218 1.4 / 1843 3.8
2 W	0121 1.5 / 0729 3.8 / 1406 1.2 / 2020 4.1	17 TH	0046 1.8 / 0717 3.6 / 1425 1.4 / 2018 3.8
3 TH	0245 1.5 / 0858 3.8 / 1521 1.0 / 2142 4.3	18 F	0249 1.7 / 0851 3.7 / 1524 1.3 / 2129 4.0
4 F	0356 1.4 / 1011 4.1 / 1628 0.8 / 2248 4.5	19 SA	0347 1.5 / 0954 3.9 / 1616 1.1 / 2226 4.3
5 SA	0501 1.2 / 1108 4.4 / 1728 0.6 / 2340 4.7	20 SU	0439 1.3 / 1045 4.2 / 1705 0.9 / 2313 4.5
6 SU	0554 1.0 / 1156 4.6 / 1818 0.5	21 M	0526 1.1 / 1130 4.5 / 1750 0.7 / 2356 4.8
7 M	0024 4.9 / 0638 0.8 / 1238 4.8 / 1901 0.4	22 TU	0610 0.8 / 1212 4.7 / 1833 0.5
8 TU ○	0104 5.0 / 0718 0.7 / 1318 4.9 / 1941 0.4	23 W ○	0038 4.9 / 0653 0.7 / 1253 4.9 / 1916 0.4
9 W	0143 5.0 / 0756 0.7 / 1357 5.0 / 2019 0.5	24 TH	0119 5.0 / 0736 0.6 / 1334 5.0 / 1958 0.5
10 TH	0222 4.9 / 0833 0.6 / 1437 4.9 / 2056 0.6	25 F	0200 4.9 / 0819 0.6 / 1417 5.0 / 2041 0.6
11 F	0300 4.7 / 0910 0.7 / 1515 4.8 / 2130 0.8	26 SA	0242 4.8 / 0902 0.6 / 1500 4.9 / 2124 0.7
12 SA	0336 4.5 / 0943 0.8 / 1550 4.6 / 2200 1.0	27 SU	0324 4.7 / 0946 0.7 / 1546 4.8 / 2208 0.9
13 SU	0408 4.3 / 1015 0.9 / 1624 4.4 / 2228 1.2	28 M	0410 4.5 / 1032 0.7 / 1635 4.7 / 2256 1.1
14 M	0439 4.2 / 1046 1.1 / 1658 4.2 / 2259 1.4	29 TU	0500 4.3 / 1126 0.8 / 1732 4.5 / 2353 1.3
15 TU	0511 4.0 / 1123 1.2 / 1739 4.0 / 2338 1.6	30 W ◑	0559 4.1 / 1231 0.9 / 1841 4.3

DECEMBER

Day	Time m	Day	Time m
1 TH	0103 1.4 / 0711 4.0 / 1343 0.9 / 1959 4.3	16 F ◑	0010 1.5 / 0629 4.0 / 1308 1.2 / 1917 4.1
2 F	0214 1.4 / 0827 4.0 / 1450 0.8 / 2112 4.3	17 SA	0127 1.5 / 0742 3.9 / 1424 1.1 / 2028 4.1
3 SA	0323 1.3 / 0937 4.2 / 1556 0.8 / 2218 4.4	18 SU	0248 1.5 / 0853 4.0 / 1525 1.0 / 2132 4.2
4 SU	0431 1.2 / 1039 4.3 / 1701 0.7 / 2316 4.6	19 M	0352 1.3 / 0954 4.1 / 1622 0.9 / 2230 4.4
5 M	0533 1.1 / 1134 4.5 / 1757 0.6	20 TU	0450 1.2 / 1050 4.3 / 1716 0.8 / 2324 4.5
6 TU	0006 4.7 / 0622 0.9 / 1222 4.6 / 1844 0.6	21 W	0544 1.0 / 1143 4.5 / 1807 0.7
7 W	0051 4.7 / 0705 0.8 / 1306 4.7 / 1925 0.7	22 TH	0014 4.6 / 0634 0.8 / 1232 4.7 / 1855 0.7
8 TH ○	0131 4.7 / 0744 0.8 / 1346 4.7 / 2002 0.8	23 F ○	0100 4.7 / 0720 0.7 / 1319 4.8 / 1941 0.7
9 F	0210 4.6 / 0820 0.8 / 1425 4.6 / 2036 0.9	24 SA	0145 4.7 / 0806 0.6 / 1404 4.8 / 2026 0.7
10 SA	0246 4.5 / 0854 0.8 / 1501 4.5 / 2107 1.0	25 SU	0229 4.6 / 0851 0.6 / 1450 4.9 / 2111 0.8
11 SU	0319 4.4 / 0926 0.8 / 1534 4.4 / 2135 1.1	26 M	0313 4.6 / 0937 0.5 / 1537 4.9 / 2157 0.9
12 M	0349 4.3 / 0957 0.9 / 1606 4.3 / 2204 1.2	27 TU	0359 4.6 / 1026 0.5 / 1627 4.8 / 2245 1.0
13 TU	0419 4.2 / 1030 0.9 / 1640 4.3 / 2237 1.3	28 W	0448 4.5 / 1118 0.5 / 1721 4.7 / 2338 1.1
14 W	0452 4.1 / 1108 1.0 / 1720 4.2 / 2317 1.4	29 TH	0542 4.4 / 1214 0.6 / 1821 4.6
15 TH	0534 4.1 / 1156 1.1 / 1810 4.1	30 F ◑	0035 1.2 / 0643 4.3 / 1313 0.6 / 1926 4.4
		31 SA	0136 1.3 / 0749 4.2 / 1416 0.7 / 2033 4.3

Chart Datum: 0·23 metres below TAW Datum
HAT is 5·6 metres above Chart Datum

TIDES

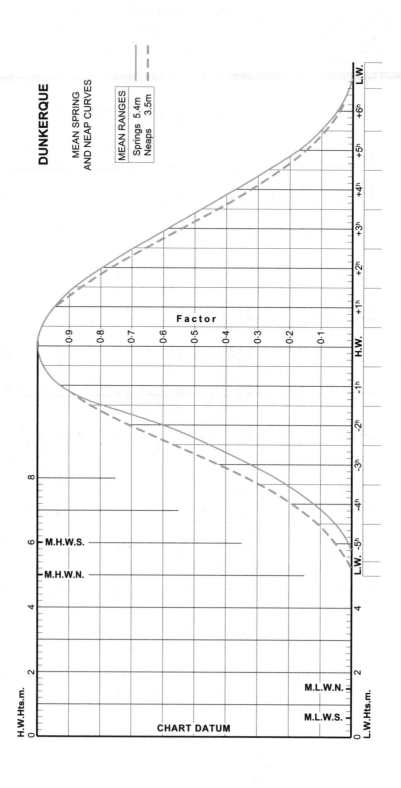

DUNKERQUE

MEAN SPRING
AND NEAP CURVES

MEAN RANGES
Springs 5.4m
Neaps   3.5m

TIME ZONE -0100
(French Standard Time)
Subtract 1 hour for UT
For French Summer Time add
ONE hour in **non-shaded areas**

FRANCE – DUNKERQUE

LAT 51°03′N   LONG 2°22′E

Dates in amber are **SPRINGS**
Dates in grey are **NEAPS**

2022

TIMES AND HEIGHTS OF HIGH AND LOW WATERS

JANUARY

Day	Time m	Time m	Day	Time m	Time m
1 SA	0547 1.1 / 1109 5.8	1816 0.8 / 2342 5.8	**16** SU	0636 1.3	1205 5.4 / 1855 1.2
2 SU	0642 0.9 / 1203 6.0	1910 0.7 ●	**17** M	0027 5.4 / 0713 1.1	1242 5.8 / 1930 1.1
3 M	0033 5.9 / 0734 0.7	1255 6.2 / 2000 0.6	**18** TU	0101 5.6 / 0749 1.0	1316 5.6 / 2005 1.1 ○
4 TU	0123 6.0 / 0824 0.5	1347 6.2 / 2049 0.7	**19** W	0132 5.7 / 0825 0.8	1348 5.7 / 2041 1.0
5 W	0212 6.0 / 0913 0.5	1438 6.2 / 2136 0.8	**20** TH	0205 5.7 / 0901 0.8	1423 5.8 / 2117 1.0
6 TH	0259 5.9 / 1001 0.5	1528 6.1 / 2223 0.9	**21** F	0240 5.7 / 0937 0.7	1459 5.8 / 2152 1.0
7 F	0346 5.8 / 1048 0.6	1616 5.8 / 2308 1.1	**22** SA	0314 5.7 / 1013 0.8	1535 5.7 / 2227 1.1
8 SA	0430 5.6 / 1135 0.8	1705 5.5 / 2354 1.1	**23** SU	0347 5.6 / 1050 0.8	1611 5.6 / 2304 1.1
9 SU	0518 5.4 / 1224 1.0	1758 5.3	**24** M	0424 5.5 / 1129 0.9	1653 5.5 / 2345 1.2
10 M	0043 1.5 / 0611 5.2	1317 1.3 / 1900 5.0	**25** TU	0510 5.4 / 1214 1.0	1748 5.3 ◐
11 TU	0140 1.7 / 0716 5.0	1416 1.4 / 2007 4.9	**26** W	0034 1.4 / 0610 5.3	1311 1.2 / 1852 5.2
12 W	0242 1.7 / 0827 4.9	1519 1.5 / 2110 4.8	**27** TH	0139 1.5 / 0719 5.2	1425 1.3 / 2003 5.1
13 TH	0347 1.7 / 0931 4.9	1625 1.5 / 2208 4.9	**28** F	0301 1.6 / 0835 5.1	1544 1.3 / 2125 5.1
14 F	0453 1.6 / 1028 5.1	1727 1.5 / 2302 5.1	**29** SA	0420 1.4 / 0958 5.3	1700 1.1 / 2241 5.3
15 SA	0551 1.4 / 1120 5.2	1816 1.3 / 2348 5.3	**30** SU	0534 1.2 / 1108 5.6	1808 0.9 / 2342 5.6
			31 M	0637 0.9 / 1205 5.9	1905 0.8

FEBRUARY

Day	Time m	Time m	Day	Time m	Time m
1 TU	0033 5.8 / 0729 0.6	1255 6.1 / 1953 0.6 ●	**16** W	0045 5.5 / 0731 0.8	1301 5.7 / 1948 0.9 ○
2 W	0118 5.9 / 0816 0.4	1341 6.2 / 2038 0.6	**17** TH	0116 5.7 / 0807 0.7	1332 5.8 / 2023 0.8
3 TH	0201 6.0 / 0901 0.3	1427 6.1 / 2120 0.7	**18** F	0147 5.8 / 0843 0.5	1404 5.9 / 2058 0.7
4 F	0242 6.0 / 0944 0.3	1509 6.0 / 2201 0.8	**19** SA	0218 5.9 / 0919 0.5	1437 5.9 / 2133 0.7
5 SA	0321 5.9 / 1024 0.5	1550 5.8 / 2238 0.9	**20** SU	0249 5.9 / 0954 0.5	1509 5.9 / 2206 0.7
6 SU	0359 5.8 / 1103 0.6	1628 5.6 / 2315 1.1	**21** M	0320 5.8 / 1029 0.5	1543 5.8 / 2241 0.9
7 M	0437 5.6 / 1148 0.9	1708 5.4 / 2354 1.3	**22** TU	0356 5.8 / 1105 0.7	1623 5.6 / 2318 1.0
8 TU	0519 5.4 / 1221 1.2	1754 5.1 ◐	**23** W	0440 5.6 / 1146 0.9	1715 5.4 ◐
9 W	0038 1.5 / 0609 5.0	1312 1.5 / 1852 4.8	**24** TH	0004 1.2 / 0538 5.4	1239 1.1 / 1821 5.1
10 TH	0137 1.8 / 0717 4.7	1416 1.7 / 2009 4.5	**25** F	0106 1.5 / 0652 5.1	1355 1.4 / 1941 4.9
11 F	0247 1.9 / 0841 4.6	1530 1.8 / 2128 4.5	**26** SA	0235 1.6 / 0823 5.0	1526 1.5 / 2119 4.8
12 SA	0407 1.9 / 0957 4.7	1652 1.7 / 2235 4.7	**27** SU	0407 1.5 / 0959 5.1	1654 1.3 / 2240 5.1
13 SU	0524 1.6 / 1100 4.9	1755 1.5 / 2328 5.0	**28** M	0529 1.2 / 1108 5.5	1804 1.0 / 2338 5.4
14 M	0617 1.3 / 1148 5.2	1838 1.3			
15 TU	0010 5.3 / 0657 1.1	1228 5.5 / 1914 1.1			

MARCH

Day	Time m	Time m	Day	Time m	Time m
1 TU	0629 0.8 / 1201 5.8	1855 0.8	**16** W	0630 1.0 / 1204 5.5	1849 1.0
2 W	0025 5.7 / 0718 0.5	1247 6.0 / 1939 0.6	**17** TH	0021 5.5 / 0706 0.7	1238 5.7 / 1923 0.8
3 TH	0105 5.9 / 0801 0.3	1327 6.1 / 2019 0.6	**18** F	0052 5.7 / 0741 0.5	1308 5.9 / 1958 0.7 ○
4 F	0140 6.0 / 0842 0.3	1406 6.1 / 2057 0.6	**19** SA	0121 5.9 / 0817 0.4	1338 6.0 / 2033 0.6
5 SA	0216 6.0 / 0920 0.3	1443 6.0 / 2133 0.7	**20** SU	0150 6.0 / 0854 0.3	1409 6.0 / 2109 0.6
6 SU	0251 6.0 / 0955 0.4	1518 5.9 / 2206 0.9	**21** M	0221 6.0 / 0930 0.3	1443 6.0 / 2144 0.6
7 M	0325 5.9 / 1028 0.6	1551 5.7 / 2239 0.9	**22** TU	0256 6.0 / 1006 0.4	1520 5.9 / 2219 0.7
8 TU	0359 5.7 / 1059 0.8	1624 5.5 / 2312 1.1	**23** W	0335 5.9 / 1044 0.6	1603 5.7 / 2258 0.9
9 W	0436 5.5 / 1133 1.1	1702 5.1 / 2348 1.4	**24** TH	0422 5.7 / 1126 0.9	1657 5.4 / 2346 1.1
10 TH	0519 5.1 / 1214 1.5	1751 4.8	**25** F	0525 5.4 / 1222 1.2	1808 5.0 ◐
11 F	0037 1.7 / 0618 4.7	1314 1.8 / 1903 4.4	**26** SA	0053 1.4 / 0644 5.0	1346 1.5 / 1934 4.7
12 SA	0148 2.0 / 0744 4.4	1436 2.0 / 2038 4.3	**27** SU	0227 1.6 / 0825 4.9	1522 1.6 / 2116 4.7
13 SU	0317 2.0 / 0919 4.4	1612 1.9 / 2202 4.5	**28** M	0402 1.4 / 0956 5.1	1648 1.3 / 2230 5.1
14 M	0448 1.8 / 1033 4.8	1725 1.6 / 2301 4.9	**29** TU	0519 1.0 / 1059 5.5	1750 1.0 / 2324 5.4
15 TU	0548 1.4 / 1124 5.1	1812 1.3 / 2344 5.2	**30** W	0614 0.7 / 1149 5.8	1837 0.8
			31 TH	0006 5.7 / 0659 0.5	1230 5.9 / 1918 0.7

APRIL

Day	Time m	Time m	Day	Time m	Time m
1 F	0041 5.8 / 0739 0.4	1305 6.0 / 1954 0.7 ●	**16** SA	0017 5.7 / 0710 0.5	1235 5.9 / 1928 0.7 ○
2 SA	0114 5.9 / 0816 0.4	1339 6.0 / 2029 0.6	**17** SU	0047 5.9 / 0748 0.4	1307 6.0 / 2006 0.6
3 SU	0148 6.0 / 0851 0.4	1413 6.0 / 2103 0.6	**18** M	0120 6.0 / 0827 0.3	1342 6.1 / 2044 0.5
4 M	0221 6.0 / 0923 0.5	1445 5.9 / 2135 0.7	**19** TU	0156 6.1 / 0907 0.3	1420 6.1 / 2123 0.5
5 TU	0254 5.9 / 0954 0.7	1516 5.7 / 2207 0.8	**20** W	0237 6.1 / 0947 0.4	1504 5.9 / 2204 0.6
6 W	0326 5.7 / 1024 0.9	1547 5.5 / 2238 1.0	**21** TH	0323 6.0 / 1029 0.7	1554 5.7 / 2249 0.8
7 TH	0401 5.5 / 1055 1.2	1623 5.2 / 2313 1.3	**22** F	0419 5.6 / 1118 1.0	1655 5.3 / 2343 1.1
8 F	0442 5.1 / 1133 1.5	1710 4.8 / 2356 1.6	**23** SA	0526 5.4 / 1222 1.3	1804 5.0 ◐
9 SA	0539 4.7 / 1226 1.8	1819 4.4 ◐	**24** SU	0056 1.3 / 0643 5.1	1347 1.5 / 1928 4.7
10 SU	0058 1.9 / 0659 4.4	1343 2.1 / 1945 4.3	**25** M	0225 1.4 / 0821 5.0	1513 1.5 / 2102 4.8
11 M	0223 2.0 / 0829 4.4	1523 2.0 / 2115 4.4	**26** TU	0349 1.2 / 0941 5.2	1629 1.3 / 2208 5.1
12 TU	0359 1.7 / 0952 4.7	1642 1.6 / 2221 4.8	**27** W	0459 0.9 / 1039 5.5	1727 1.0 / 2259 5.4
13 W	0505 1.3 / 1047 5.1	1734 1.3 / 2308 5.2	**28** TH	0551 0.7 / 1126 5.7	1812 0.9 / 2338 5.6
14 TH	0553 1.0 / 1129 5.5	1814 1.0 / 2346 5.5	**29** F	0635 0.6 / 1204 5.8	1851 0.8
15 F	0632 0.7 / 1204 5.7	1851 0.8	**30** SA	0013 5.7 / 0713 0.6	1238 5.8 / 1926 0.8 ●

Chart Datum: 2·69 metres below IGN Datum
HAT is 6·4 metres above Chart Datum

TIDES

TIME ZONE -0100
(French Standard Time)
Subtract 1 hour for UT
For French Summer Time add
ONE hour in **non-shaded areas**

FRANCE – DUNKERQUE
LAT 51°03'N   LONG 2°22'E
TIMES AND HEIGHTS OF HIGH AND LOW WATERS

Dates in amber are **SPRINGS**
Dates in grey are **NEAPS**

2022

MAY

Time	m		Time	m
1 SU 0046 / 0747 / 1311 / 2000	5.8 / 0.6 / 5.8 / 0.7		**16** M 0014 / 0720 / 1356 / 1940 ○	5.9 / 0.5 / 5.6 / 0.6
2 M 0121 / 0820 / 1345 / 2034	5.9 / 0.6 / 5.8 / 0.7		**17** TU 0054 / 0803 / 1320 / 2023	6.0 / 0.4 / 6.0 / 0.5
3 TU 0154 / 0853 / 1416 / 2108	5.8 / 0.7 / 5.7 / 0.7		**18** W 0138 / 0847 / 1406 / 2108	6.1 / 0.4 / 6.0 / 0.5
4 W 0227 / 0925 / 1447 / 2141	5.8 / 0.9 / 5.6 / 0.9		**19** TH 0228 / 0934 / 1457 / 2156	6.1 / 0.6 / 5.8 / 0.6
5 TH 0301 / 0957 / 1521 / 2214	5.6 / 1.0 / 5.4 / 1.0		**20** F 0323 / 1023 / 1554 / 2247	6.0 / 0.8 / 5.6 / 0.7
6 F 0338 / 1029 / 1559 / 2249	5.4 / 1.3 / 5.2 / 1.2		**21** SA 0422 / 1118 / 1652 / 2346	5.7 / 1.0 / 5.4 / 0.9
7 SA 0421 / 1107 / 1647 / 2331	5.1 / 1.5 / 4.9 / 1.5		**22** SU 0524 / 1223 / 1755	5.5 / 1.3 / 5.1
8 SU 0517 / 1157 / 1751	4.8 / 1.7 / 4.6		**23** M 0055 / 0635 / 1335 / 1911	1.1 / 5.2 / 1.4 / 5.0
9 M 0026 / 0625 / 1301 / 1901 ◑	1.6 / 4.6 / 1.9 / 4.5		**24** TU 0209 / 0801 / 1448 / 2031	1.1 / 5.1 / 1.4 / 5.0
10 TU 0135 / 0738 / 1424 / 2016	1.7 / 4.6 / 1.9 / 4.5		**25** W 0321 / 0911 / 1555 / 2133	1.0 / 5.2 / 1.3 / 5.1
11 W 0300 / 0854 / 1547 / 2126	1.6 / 4.8 / 1.6 / 4.8		**26** TH 0426 / 1007 / 1653 / 2223	0.9 / 5.4 / 1.2 / 5.3
12 TH 0413 / 0957 / 1646 / 2220	1.3 / 5.1 / 1.3 / 5.1		**27** F 0521 / 1054 / 1741 / 2306	0.8 / 5.5 / 1.1 / 5.4
13 F 0508 / 1044 / 1734 / 2301	1.0 / 5.4 / 1.1 / 5.4		**28** SA 0606 / 1135 / 1822 / 2345	0.8 / 5.6 / 1.0 / 5.6
14 SA 0554 / 1124 / 1816 / 2337	0.7 / 5.7 / 0.9 / 5.7		**29** SU 0644 / 1212 / 1900	0.8 / 5.6 / 0.9
15 SU 0637 / 1200 / 1858	0.6 / 5.8 / 0.7		**30** M 0023 / 0720 / 1248 / 1935 ●	5.6 / 0.9 / 5.6 / 0.9
			31 TU 0059 / 0754 / 1323 / 2011	5.7 / 0.9 / 5.6 / 0.8

JUNE

Time	m		Time	m
1 W 0135 / 0828 / 1356 / 2047	5.7 / 0.9 / 5.6 / 0.8		**16** TH 0130 / 0835 / 1400 / 2100	6.1 / 0.6 / 5.9 / 0.5
2 TH 0209 / 0903 / 1429 / 2123	5.6 / 1.0 / 5.5 / 0.9		**17** F 0225 / 0926 / 1454 / 2151	6.1 / 0.6 / 5.8 / 0.5
3 F 0245 / 0938 / 1505 / 2158	5.6 / 1.1 / 5.4 / 1.0		**18** SA 0321 / 1018 / 1547 / 2243	6.0 / 0.8 / 5.7 / 0.5
4 SA 0325 / 1012 / 1546 / 2234	5.4 / 1.3 / 5.3 / 1.1		**19** SU 0416 / 1111 / 1640 / 2338	5.8 / 0.9 / 5.5 / 0.7
5 SU 0408 / 1050 / 1632 / 2314	5.2 / 1.4 / 5.1 / 1.2		**20** M 0512 / 1207 / 1734	5.6 / 1.1 / 5.4
6 M 0458 / 1135 / 1724	5.1 / 1.5 / 4.9		**21** TU 0036 / 0614 / 1306 / 1837 ◑	0.8 / 5.4 / 1.3 / 5.2
7 TU 0001 / 0553 / 1228 / 1820 ◑	1.3 / 4.9 / 1.6 / 4.8		**22** W 0138 / 0724 / 1407 / 1945	1.0 / 5.2 / 1.4 / 5.1
8 W 0058 / 0652 / 1331 / 1921	1.4 / 4.9 / 1.7 / 4.8		**23** TH 0240 / 0829 / 1509 / 2048	1.0 / 5.1 / 1.4 / 5.1
9 TH 0204 / 0754 / 1445 / 2022	1.4 / 4.9 / 1.6 / 4.9		**24** F 0342 / 0926 / 1609 / 2144	1.1 / 5.1 / 1.4 / 5.2
10 F 0317 / 0856 / 1553 / 2122	1.2 / 5.1 / 1.4 / 5.1		**25** SA 0442 / 1019 / 1706 / 2235	1.1 / 5.2 / 1.3 / 5.2
11 SA 0421 / 0953 / 1651 / 2214	1.0 / 5.3 / 1.2 / 5.4		**26** SU 0535 / 1113 / 1756 / 2322	1.1 / 5.3 / 1.2 / 5.3
12 SU 0516 / 1043 / 1743 / 2302	0.8 / 5.6 / 1.0 / 5.6		**27** M 0620 / 1152 / 1839	1.1 / 5.4 / 1.1
13 M 0607 / 1130 / 1832 / 2350	0.7 / 5.8 / 0.8 / 5.8		**28** TU 0006 / 0659 / 1232 / 1918	5.4 / 1.1 / 5.4 / 1.0
14 TU 0656 / 1218 / 1920 ○	0.6 / 5.9 / 0.7		**29** W 0047 / 0735 / 1309 / 1955 ●	5.5 / 1.0 / 5.5 / 0.9
15 W 0039 / 0745 / 1308 / 2009	6.0 / 0.6 / 5.9 / 0.6		**30** TH 0123 / 0811 / 1343 / 2032	5.6 / 1.0 / 5.5 / 0.9

JULY

Time	m		Time	m
1 F 0157 / 0847 / 1415 / 2108	5.6 / 1.1 / 5.5 / 0.9		**16** SA 0219 / 0916 / 1443 / 2141	6.2 / 0.6 / 5.9 / 0.3
2 SA 0233 / 0923 / 1451 / 2144	5.6 / 1.1 / 5.5 / 0.9		**17** SU 0311 / 1004 / 1530 / 2229	6.1 / 0.7 / 5.9 / 0.4
3 SU 0310 / 0958 / 1530 / 2219	5.5 / 1.2 / 5.4 / 0.9		**18** M 0400 / 1051 / 1616 / 2317	5.9 / 0.9 / 5.7 / 0.5
4 M 0350 / 1034 / 1609 / 2256	5.4 / 1.2 / 5.3 / 1.0		**19** TU 0449 / 1137 / 1702	5.7 / 1.0 / 5.6
5 TU 0431 / 1112 / 1649 / 2337	5.3 / 1.3 / 5.2 / 1.1		**20** W 0004 / 0538 / 1224 / 1751 ◑	0.7 / 5.5 / 1.2 / 5.4
6 W 0515 / 1155 / 1734	5.2 / 1.4 / 5.1		**21** TH 0055 / 0633 / 1316 / 1849	1.0 / 5.2 / 1.4 / 5.2
7 TH 0023 / 0605 / 1246 / 1828	1.1 / 5.2 / 1.5 / 5.1		**22** F 0150 / 0735 / 1415 / 1956	1.2 / 5.2 / 1.6 / 5.1
8 F 0118 / 0702 / 1347 / 1927	1.2 / 5.1 / 1.5 / 5.1		**23** SA 0250 / 0840 / 1519 / 2104	1.4 / 4.9 / 1.6 / 4.9
9 SA 0225 / 0804 / 1501 / 2031	1.2 / 5.1 / 1.5 / 5.1		**24** SU 0357 / 0944 / 1629 / 2207	1.5 / 4.9 / 1.6 / 5.0
10 SU 0337 / 0909 / 1611 / 2137	1.2 / 5.2 / 1.4 / 5.3		**25** M 0506 / 1044 / 1735 / 2305	1.5 / 5.0 / 1.4 / 5.1
11 M 0443 / 1015 / 1715 / 2241	1.0 / 5.4 / 1.2 / 5.5		**26** TU 0603 / 1136 / 1825 / 2355	1.4 / 5.2 / 1.2 / 5.3
12 TU 0545 / 1116 / 1815 / 2340	0.9 / 5.6 / 0.9 / 5.8		**27** W 0646 / 1220 / 1905	1.3 / 5.3 / 1.1
13 W 0643 / 1211 / 1910 ○	0.8 / 5.7 / 0.7		**28** TH 0036 / 0722 / 1257 / 1941 ●	5.4 / 1.2 / 5.5 / 0.9
14 TH 0034 / 0737 / 1303 / 2002	6.0 / 0.7 / 5.9 / 0.5		**29** F 0112 / 0756 / 1329 / 2016	5.6 / 1.1 / 5.6 / 0.8
15 F 0127 / 0827 / 1354 / 2052	6.1 / 0.6 / 5.9 / 0.4		**30** SA 0144 / 0831 / 1359 / 2051	5.7 / 1.0 / 5.6 / 0.8
			31 SU 0216 / 0905 / 1431 / 2126	5.7 / 1.0 / 5.7 / 0.7

AUGUST

Time	m		Time	m
1 M 0249 / 0939 / 1505 / 2200	5.7 / 1.0 / 5.6 / 0.7		**16** TU 0333 / 1021 / 1542 / 2246	6.0 / 0.8 / 5.9 / 0.5
2 TU 0324 / 1012 / 1536 / 2234	5.7 / 1.0 / 5.6 / 0.8		**17** W 0413 / 1100 / 1622 / 2325	5.8 / 1.0 / 5.7 / 0.8
3 W 0356 / 1046 / 1607 / 2309	5.6 / 1.1 / 5.5 / 0.8		**18** TH 0454 / 1139 / 1705	5.5 / 1.2 / 5.5
4 TH 0431 / 1123 / 1645 / 2349	5.5 / 1.2 / 5.4 / 1.0		**19** F 0006 / 0538 / 1223 / 1754 ◑	1.1 / 5.2 / 1.4 / 5.2
5 F 0516 / 1206 / 1736 ●	5.4 / 1.3 / 5.3		**20** SA 0054 / 0633 / 1319 / 1859	1.4 / 4.9 / 1.7 / 4.9
6 SA 0037 / 0616 / 1301 / 1842	1.1 / 5.2 / 1.5 / 5.2		**21** SU 0155 / 0747 / 1428 / 2022	1.7 / 4.6 / 1.9 / 4.7
7 SU 0141 / 0724 / 1418 / 1956	1.3 / 5.1 / 1.6 / 5.1		**22** M 0310 / 0908 / 1552 / 2142	1.9 / 4.6 / 1.9 / 4.7
8 M 0302 / 0841 / 1542 / 2120	1.4 / 5.0 / 1.5 / 5.2		**23** TU 0439 / 1022 / 1714 / 2249	1.8 / 4.7 / 1.6 / 4.9
9 TU 0422 / 1006 / 1701 / 2239	1.3 / 5.2 / 1.3 / 5.4		**24** W 0544 / 1119 / 1808 / 2340	1.6 / 5.0 / 1.3 / 5.2
10 W 0536 / 1115 / 1809 / 2340	1.1 / 5.4 / 1.0 / 5.8		**25** TH 0629 / 1202 / 1848	1.3 / 5.3 / 1.1
11 TH 0638 / 1209 / 1905	0.9 / 5.7 / 0.6		**26** F 0020 / 0704 / 1237 / 1921	5.5 / 1.2 / 5.5 / 0.9
12 F 0032 / 0729 / 1256 / 1954 ○	6.0 / 0.7 / 5.9 / 0.4		**27** SA 0053 / 0735 / 1308 / 1954 ●	5.7 / 1.0 / 5.7 / 0.7
13 SA 0120 / 0816 / 1340 / 2040	6.2 / 0.6 / 6.0 / 0.3		**28** SU 0123 / 0808 / 1336 / 2027	5.8 / 0.9 / 5.8 / 0.6
14 SU 0206 / 0859 / 1422 / 2124	6.2 / 0.6 / 6.0 / 0.3		**29** M 0152 / 0841 / 1404 / 2101	5.9 / 0.9 / 5.8 / 0.6
15 M 0250 / 0941 / 1503 / 2206	6.1 / 0.7 / 6.0 / 0.3		**30** TU 0221 / 0914 / 1433 / 2135	5.9 / 0.9 / 5.8 / 0.6
			31 W 0250 / 0946 / 1500 / 2208	5.9 / 1.0 / 5.8 / 0.7

Chart Datum: 2·69 metres below IGN Datum
HAT is 6·4 metres above Chart Datum

TIME ZONE -0100
(French Standard Time)
Subtract 1 hour for UT
For French Summer Time add
ONE hour in **non-shaded areas**

FRANCE – DUNKERQUE
LAT 51°03′N   LONG 2°22′E
TIMES AND HEIGHTS OF HIGH AND LOW WATERS

Dates in amber are **SPRINGS**
Dates in grey are **NEAPS**

2022

SEPTEMBER

Day	Time m	Day	Time m
1 TH	0320 5.8 / 1018 1.0 / 1531 5.8 / 2241 0.8	**16** F	0409 5.6 / 1058 1.2 / 1622 5.6 / 2320 1.2
2 F	0355 5.7 / 1053 1.1 / 1609 5.7 / 2319 0.9	**17** SA ◐	0448 5.3 / 1136 1.5 / 1706 5.2
3 SA ◑	0438 5.5 / 1134 1.3 / 1700 5.5	**18** SU	0001 1.6 / 0537 4.9 / 1225 1.8 / 1806 4.8
4 SU	0005 1.2 / 0540 5.2 / 1229 1.5 / 1813 5.2	**19** M	0059 2.0 / 0649 4.5 / 1335 2.1 / 1934 4.5
5 M	0111 1.5 / 0700 4.9 / 1351 1.7 / 1941 5.0	**20** TU	0222 2.2 / 0825 4.3 / 1509 2.1 / 2111 4.5
6 TU	0244 1.6 / 0834 4.8 / 1529 1.7 / 2123 5.1	**21** W	0404 2.1 / 0952 4.6 / 1642 1.8 / 2225 4.8
7 W	0416 1.5 / 1007 5.0 / 1656 1.3 / 2240 5.5	**22** TH	0516 1.7 / 1051 4.9 / 1739 1.4 / 2315 5.2
8 TH	0533 1.2 / 1111 5.4 / 1802 0.9 / 2336 5.8	**23** F	0601 1.4 / 1134 5.3 / 1820 1.1 / 2354 5.5
9 F	0629 0.9 / 1200 5.7 / 1853 0.5	**24** SA	0636 1.2 / 1209 5.6 / 1853 0.8
10 SA ○	0023 6.1 / 0715 0.6 / 1241 6.0 / 1938 0.4	**25** SU ●	0026 5.8 / 0707 1.0 / 1239 5.8 / 1925 0.7
11 SU	0104 6.2 / 0757 0.4 / 1317 6.1 / 2020 0.3	**26** M	0055 5.9 / 0739 0.9 / 1305 5.9 / 1958 0.6
12 M	0143 6.2 / 0836 0.3 / 1354 6.1 / 2059 0.3	**27** TU	0121 6.0 / 0812 0.8 / 1331 6.0 / 2033 0.5
13 TU	0221 6.1 / 0913 0.4 / 1431 6.1 / 2136 0.5	**28** W	0148 6.0 / 0846 0.8 / 1359 6.0 / 2107 0.6
14 W	0258 6.0 / 0949 0.6 / 1507 6.0 / 2211 0.7	**29** TH	0219 6.0 / 0920 0.8 / 1430 6.0 / 2141 0.8
15 TH	0334 5.8 / 1023 1.0 / 1543 5.8 / 2245 0.9	**30** F	0251 6.0 / 0953 0.9 / 1505 6.0 / 2216 0.8

OCTOBER

Day	Time m	Day	Time m
1 SA	0330 5.8 / 1030 1.1 / 1548 5.8 / 2256 1.1	**16** SU	0407 5.3 / 1100 1.5 / 1628 5.2 / 2321 1.7
2 SU	0417 5.5 / 1114 1.3 / 1644 5.5 / 2345 1.4	**17** M ◐	0453 4.9 / 1145 1.8 / 1725 4.8
3 M ◑	0525 5.1 / 1213 1.6 / 1807 5.1	**18** TU	0012 2.1 / 0601 4.5 / 1246 2.1 / 1845 4.5
4 TU	0100 1.7 / 0652 4.8 / 1345 1.8 / 1942 4.9	**19** W	0128 2.3 / 0727 4.3 / 1413 2.2 / 2020 4.5
5 W	0241 1.8 / 0834 4.8 / 1525 1.6 / 2123 5.1	**20** TH	0313 2.2 / 0902 4.5 / 1551 1.9 / 2143 4.8
6 TH	0412 1.6 / 0959 5.1 / 1648 1.2 / 2231 5.6	**21** F	0430 1.9 / 1008 4.9 / 1655 1.5 / 2236 5.2
7 F	0521 1.2 / 1057 5.5 / 1748 0.8 / 2323 5.9	**22** SA	0521 1.5 / 1055 5.3 / 1740 1.1 / 2317 5.5
8 SA	0612 0.9 / 1142 5.8 / 1835 0.5	**23** SU	0559 1.2 / 1132 5.6 / 1817 0.9 / 2351 5.8
9 SU ○	0006 6.1 / 0654 0.6 / 1218 6.0 / 1916 0.4	**24** M	0633 1.0 / 1202 5.8 / 1852 0.7
10 M	0042 6.2 / 0732 0.8 / 1250 6.1 / 1955 0.4	**25** TU ●	0019 5.9 / 0707 0.9 / 1229 5.9 / 1927 0.6
11 TU	0116 6.1 / 0808 0.8 / 1325 6.1 / 2031 0.5	**26** W	0047 6.0 / 0743 0.8 / 1258 6.1 / 2004 0.6
12 W	0150 6.1 / 0843 0.8 / 1400 6.1 / 2105 0.7	**27** TH	0118 6.1 / 0819 0.8 / 1331 6.1 / 2041 0.6
13 TH	0225 6.0 / 0917 0.9 / 1435 6.0 / 2138 0.9	**28** F	0154 6.1 / 0857 0.8 / 1409 6.1 / 2120 0.7
14 F	0258 5.8 / 0951 1.0 / 1510 5.8 / 2210 1.1	**29** SA	0233 6.0 / 0936 0.9 / 1452 6.0 / 2200 0.9
15 SA	0331 5.6 / 1025 1.2 / 1546 5.6 / 2243 1.4	**30** SU	0319 5.8 / 1019 1.0 / 1544 5.8 / 2246 1.2
		31 M	0415 5.4 / 1109 1.3 / 1650 5.5 / 2343 1.5

NOVEMBER

Day	Time m	Day	Time m
1 TU ◑	0526 5.1 / 1216 1.5 / 1807 5.2	**16** W ◑	0526 4.7 / 1209 1.8 / 1804 4.7
2 W	0104 1.8 / 0645 4.9 / 1346 1.6 / 1939 5.1	**17** TH	0040 2.1 / 0635 4.5 / 1315 1.9 / 1916 4.6
3 TH	0234 1.8 / 0822 4.9 / 1513 1.4 / 2108 5.3	**18** F	0159 2.2 / 0750 4.6 / 1440 1.8 / 2034 4.8
4 F	0354 1.5 / 0937 5.2 / 1628 1.1 / 2211 5.6	**19** SA	0326 1.9 / 0905 4.8 / 1555 1.6 / 2140 5.1
5 SA	0458 1.3 / 1032 5.5 / 1726 0.8 / 2301 5.8	**20** SU	0427 1.6 / 1001 5.1 / 1650 1.2 / 2228 5.4
6 SU	0548 1.1 / 1115 5.7 / 1812 0.7 / 2342 5.9	**21** M	0514 1.4 / 1045 5.4 / 1735 1.0 / 2307 5.6
7 M	0629 1.0 / 1151 5.9 / 1852 0.6	**22** TU	0556 1.2 / 1120 5.7 / 1817 0.8 / 2342 5.8
8 TU ○	0017 6.0 / 0706 0.9 / 1224 6.0 / 1929 0.7	**23** W ●	0636 1.0 / 1155 5.9 / 1858 0.7
9 W	0050 6.0 / 0742 0.9 / 1300 6.0 / 2003 0.8	**24** TH	0017 6.0 / 0716 0.9 / 1232 6.1 / 1939 0.7
10 TH	0124 5.9 / 0816 0.9 / 1335 6.0 / 2037 0.9	**25** F	0056 6.1 / 0758 0.8 / 1314 6.2 / 2022 0.7
11 F	0158 5.9 / 0851 0.9 / 1410 5.9 / 2110 1.0	**26** SA	0139 6.1 / 0842 0.7 / 1400 6.2 / 2107 0.8
12 SA	0231 5.7 / 0926 1.0 / 1445 5.7 / 2143 1.2	**27** SU	0226 6.0 / 0928 0.8 / 1451 6.1 / 2155 0.9
13 SU	0304 5.5 / 1001 1.2 / 1523 5.5 / 2216 1.5	**28** M	0319 5.8 / 1018 0.9 / 1548 5.9 / 2247 1.2
14 M	0342 5.3 / 1037 1.4 / 1605 5.2 / 2254 1.7	**29** TU	0416 5.5 / 1113 1.1 / 1650 5.6 / 2346 1.4
15 TU	0427 5.0 / 1118 1.6 / 1658 4.9 / 2340 2.0	**30** W ◑	0516 5.3 / 1218 1.2 / 1757 5.4

DECEMBER

Day	Time m	Day	Time m
1 TH	0055 1.6 / 0625 5.1 / 1332 1.3 / 1919 5.2	**16** F ◑	0002 1.8 / 0548 4.9 / 1230 1.6 / 1823 4.9
2 F	0209 1.6 / 0749 5.0 / 1446 1.2 / 2038 5.3	**17** SA	0057 1.9 / 0648 4.8 / 1331 1.6 / 1924 4.9
3 SA	0319 1.6 / 0900 5.2 / 1555 1.1 / 2139 5.4	**18** SU	0205 1.9 / 0751 4.8 / 1444 1.5 / 2028 5.0
4 SU	0423 1.4 / 0956 5.3 / 1655 1.0 / 2230 5.5	**19** M	0320 1.7 / 0853 5.0 / 1553 1.4 / 2128 5.2
5 M	0517 1.3 / 1043 5.5 / 1745 0.9 / 2315 5.6	**20** TU	0423 1.5 / 0951 5.2 / 1652 1.2 / 2222 5.4
6 TU	0603 1.2 / 1125 5.6 / 1828 0.9 / 2354 5.7	**21** W	0518 1.3 / 1042 5.5 / 1744 1.0 / 2311 5.6
7 W	0643 1.1 / 1205 5.7 / 1906 1.0	**22** TH	0608 1.1 / 1130 5.8 / 1833 0.8 / 2357 5.8
8 TH ○	0031 5.7 / 0721 1.0 / 1243 5.8 / 1942 1.0	**23** F	0657 0.9 / 1217 6.0 / 1922 0.8
9 F	0107 5.7 / 0757 1.0 / 1321 5.8 / 2016 1.1	**24** SA	0044 5.9 / 0746 0.8 / 1307 6.1 / 2011 0.7
10 SA	0142 5.7 / 0834 1.0 / 1356 5.8 / 2051 1.1	**25** SU	0133 6.0 / 0835 0.6 / 1358 6.2 / 2101 0.7
11 SU	0215 5.6 / 0910 1.0 / 1431 5.7 / 2125 1.3	**26** M	0223 6.0 / 0925 0.6 / 1450 6.1 / 2151 0.8
12 M	0249 5.5 / 0945 1.2 / 1509 5.5 / 2200 1.4	**27** TU	0314 5.9 / 1016 0.6 / 1543 6.0 / 2241 1.0
13 TU	0326 5.4 / 1020 1.2 / 1549 5.4 / 2235 1.5	**28** W	0404 5.7 / 1108 0.7 / 1637 5.8 / 2333 1.2
14 W	0408 5.2 / 1057 1.4 / 1634 5.2 / 2315 1.7	**29** TH	0456 5.5 / 1203 0.9 / 1735 5.5
15 TH	0454 5.0 / 1140 1.5 / 1726 5.0	**30** F ◑	0029 1.3 / 0552 5.3 / 1302 1.0 / 1841 5.3
		31 SA	0128 1.5 / 0659 5.2 / 1405 1.2 / 1951 5.2

Chart Datum: 2·69 metres below IGN Datum
HAT is 6·4 metres above Chart Datum

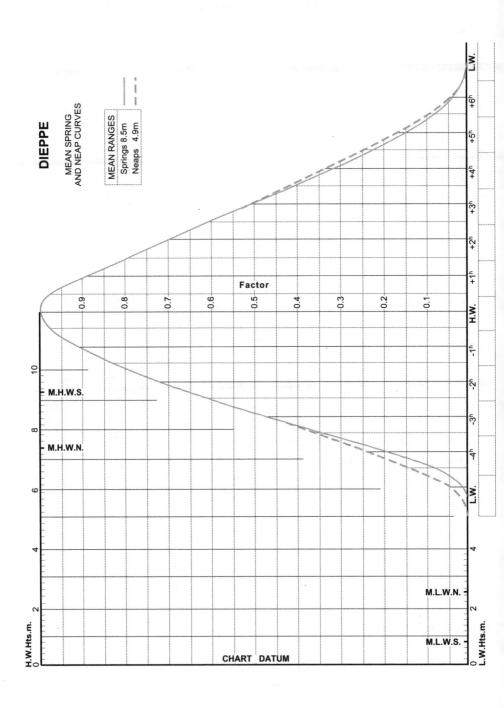

DIEPPE

MEAN SPRING
AND NEAP CURVES

MEAN RANGES
Springs 8.5m
Neaps 4.9m

TIME ZONE -0100
(French Standard Time)
Subtract 1 hour for UT
For French Summer Time add
ONE hour in **non-shaded areas**

FRANCE – DIEPPE
LAT 49°56'N   LONG 1°05'E
TIMES AND HEIGHTS OF HIGH AND LOW WATERS

Dates in amber are **SPRINGS**
Dates in grey are **NEAPS**

2022

	JANUARY				FEBRUARY				MARCH				APRIL		
	Time m		Time m		Time m		Time m		Time m		Time m		Time m		Time m
1	0435 1.5 / 1008 8.8 / SA 1707 1.2 / 2236 8.9	**16**	0516 2.1 / 1048 8.1 / SU 1742 1.8 / 2312 8.2	**1**	0621 1.1 / 1148 9.3 / TU 1852 0.7 ●	**16**	0622 1.5 / 1148 8.7 / W 1847 1.2 ○	**1**	0519 1.5 / 1051 8.8 / TU 1751 1.0 / 2319 9.0	**16**	0516 1.8 / 1046 8.3 / W 1741 1.4 / 2308 8.6	**1**	0643 0.8 / 1200 9.4 / F 1902 0.6 ●	**16**	0607 1.0 / 1131 9.1 / SA 1832 0.7 / ○ 2351 9.3
2	0533 1.2 / 1102 9.2 / SU 1804 0.9 / ● 2331 9.2	**17**	0558 1.9 / 1127 8.4 / M 1822 1.6 / 2349 8.4	**2**	0016 9.3 / 0715 0.9 / W 1236 9.5 / 1943 0.5	**17**	0009 8.8 / 0700 1.3 / TH 1224 8.9 / 1924 1.0	**2**	0616 1.0 / 1139 9.2 / W 1843 0.6 ●	**17**	0558 1.4 / 1124 8.8 / TH 1823 1.0 / 2345 8.9	**2**	0018 9.3 / 0719 0.8 / SA 1235 9.4 / 1935 0.7	**17**	0650 0.8 / 1209 9.4 / SU 1911 0.6
3	0629 1.0 / 1154 9.4 / M 1858 0.7	**18**	0637 1.7 / 1203 8.6 / TU 1900 1.4 / ○	**3**	0102 9.4 / 0803 0.8 / TH 1320 9.5 / 2027 0.5	**18**	0045 9.0 / 0737 1.1 / F 1259 9.1 / 2000 0.8	**3**	0003 9.3 / 0704 0.8 / TH 1222 9.5 / 1928 0.5	**18**	0639 1.1 / 1200 9.1 / F 1902 0.7 / ○	**3**	0051 9.3 / 0750 0.8 / SU 1308 9.3 / 2004 0.8	**18**	0028 9.5 / 0730 0.6 / M 1248 9.5 / 1949 0.5
4	0022 9.3 / 0721 0.9 / TU 1244 9.5 / 1950 0.6	**19**	0026 8.6 / 0713 1.6 / W 1239 8.7 / 1937 1.3	**4**	0144 9.4 / 0845 0.8 / F 1401 9.4 / 2105 0.7	**19**	0119 9.1 / 0813 1.0 / SA 1334 9.2 / 2034 0.8	**4**	0043 9.4 / 0745 0.7 / F 1301 9.6 / 2005 0.5	**19**	0020 9.2 / 0717 0.8 / SA 1236 9.3 / 1939 0.6	**4**	0122 9.2 / 0818 1.0 / M 1340 9.1 / 2029 1.0	**19**	0106 9.5 / 0808 0.6 / TU 1327 9.5 / 2025 0.7
5	0112 9.3 / 0812 1.0 / W 1333 9.4 / 2039 0.7	**20**	0101 8.7 / 0749 1.5 / TH 1314 8.8 / 2013 1.3	**5**	0223 9.2 / 0921 1.1 / SA 1440 9.2 / 2139 1.0	**20**	0154 9.1 / 0847 1.0 / SU 1409 9.1 / 2107 0.9	**5**	0120 9.4 / 0821 0.7 / SA 1337 9.5 / 2037 0.6	**20**	0055 9.4 / 0753 0.7 / SU 1311 9.4 / 2013 0.5	**5**	0152 9.0 / 0844 1.2 / TU 1410 8.8 / 2053 1.4	**20**	0144 9.4 / 0845 0.7 / W 1407 9.2 / 2101 1.0
6	0200 9.2 / 0859 1.1 / TH 1420 9.2 / 2124 0.9	**21**	0137 8.7 / 0825 1.5 / F 1350 8.8 / 2047 1.3	**6**	0300 8.9 / 0953 1.4 / SU 1517 8.7 / 2207 1.4	**21**	0228 9.0 / 0921 1.1 / M 1444 9.0 / 2138 1.1	**6**	0154 9.3 / 0851 0.9 / SU 1411 9.2 / 2104 0.9	**21**	0130 9.4 / 0828 0.7 / M 1347 9.4 / 2046 0.6	**6**	0220 8.6 / 0908 1.6 / W 1439 8.3 / 2117 1.8	**21**	0224 9.1 / 0924 1.0 / TH 1450 8.8 / 2141 1.4
7	0246 9.0 / 0943 1.4 / F 1505 8.9 / 2206 1.2	**22**	0213 8.7 / 0900 1.5 / SA 1427 8.7 / 2122 1.4	**7**	0335 8.5 / 1022 1.8 / M 1554 8.4 / 2236 1.9	**22**	0304 8.8 / 0955 1.4 / TU 1522 8.7 / 2212 1.4	**7**	0226 9.0 / 0917 1.2 / M 1443 8.9 / 2128 1.3	**22**	0205 9.3 / 0903 0.8 / TU 1424 9.2 / 2118 0.9	**7**	0247 8.2 / 0934 2.0 / TH 1509 7.8 / 2146 2.3	**22**	0308 8.5 / 1008 1.5 / F 1539 8.2 / 2229 2.0
8	0331 8.6 / 1025 1.7 / SA 1551 8.4 / 2246 1.7	**23**	0249 8.5 / 0937 1.6 / SU 1504 8.5 / 2158 1.5	**8**	0411 8.0 / 1057 2.3 / TU 1633 7.6 / ◖ 2312 2.4	**23**	0342 8.5 / 1034 1.7 / W 1604 8.2 / ◖ 2253 1.9	**8**	0256 8.6 / 0941 1.6 / TU 1513 8.3 / 2152 1.8	**23**	0242 9.0 / 0937 1.1 / W 1503 8.8 / 2153 1.4	**8**	0317 7.6 / 1008 2.5 / F 1545 7.1 / 2226 2.9	**23**	0402 7.9 / 1103 2.0 / SA 1645 7.5 / ◖ 2333 2.5
9	0416 8.2 / 1107 2.1 / SU 1638 8.0 / ◖ 2327 2.1	**24**	0328 8.4 / 1015 1.8 / M 1545 8.3 / 2236 1.8	**9**	0453 7.4 / 1141 2.7 / W 1724 7.0	**24**	0428 8.0 / 1124 2.1 / TH 1659 7.7 / 2349 2.3	**9**	0325 8.1 / 1009 2.1 / W 1545 7.7 / 2222 2.3	**24**	0321 8.6 / 1017 1.5 / TH 1547 8.2 / 2236 1.9	**9**	0359 7.0 / 1057 3.0 / SA 1642 6.5 / ◖ 2324 3.4	**24**	0521 7.3 / 1203 2.5 / SU 1816 7.2
10	0504 7.7 / 1154 2.4 / M 1730 7.5	**25**	0410 8.1 / 1059 2.0 / TU 1631 8.0 / ◖ 2322 2.0	**10**	0001 2.9 / 0551 6.9 / TH 1244 3.1 / 1839 6.6	**25**	0533 7.5 / 1230 2.4 / F 1820 7.2	**10**	0356 7.5 / 1047 2.6 / TH 1624 7.0 / ◖ 2304 2.9	**25**	0408 8.0 / 1108 2.0 / F 1644 7.5 / ◖ 2334 2.5	**10**	0509 6.4 / 1211 3.4 / SU 1828 6.3	**25**	0104 2.7 / 0657 7.2 / M 1352 2.3 / 1947 7.4
11	0014 2.5 / 0559 7.4 / TU 1250 2.7 / 1832 7.2	**26**	0501 7.9 / 1153 2.2 / W 1729 7.7	**11**	0112 3.2 / 0717 6.7 / F 1412 3.2 / 2010 6.6	**26**	0108 2.7 / 0709 7.3 / SA 1403 2.5 / 2000 7.3	**11**	0442 6.9 / 1140 3.1 / F 1730 6.4	**26**	0518 7.2 / 1218 2.5 / SA 1816 7.1	**11**	0058 3.6 / 0710 6.3 / M 1359 3.4 / 2006 6.7	**26**	0235 2.4 / 0821 7.6 / TU 1513 1.9 / 2058 8.0
12	0113 2.7 / 0706 7.2 / W 1356 2.8 / 1943 7.1	**27**	0020 2.3 / 0608 7.6 / TH 1300 2.4 / 1847 7.5	**12**	0246 3.2 / 0843 6.9 / SA 1534 2.8 / 2121 7.0	**27**	0248 2.5 / 0841 7.6 / SU 1534 2.1 / 2124 7.8	**12**	0008 3.4 / 0606 6.3 / SA 1306 3.4 / 1924 6.3	**27**	0101 2.8 / 0705 7.1 / SU 1358 2.5 / 2001 7.2	**12**	0241 3.1 / 0833 6.9 / TU 1519 2.6 / 2107 7.4	**27**	0348 1.8 / 0924 8.2 / W 1618 1.4 / 2151 8.5
13	0221 2.8 / 0817 7.2 / TH 1506 2.7 / 2051 7.2	**28**	0135 2.4 / 0731 7.6 / F 1424 2.3 / 2011 7.6	**13**	0401 2.8 / 0944 7.3 / SU 1634 2.3 / 2213 7.6	**28**	0410 2.0 / 0955 8.2 / M 1648 1.5 / 2228 8.4	**13**	0154 3.6 / 0805 6.4 / SU 1454 3.1 / 2052 6.8	**28**	0246 2.6 / 0840 7.5 / M 1531 2.0 / 2120 7.9	**13**	0345 2.4 / 0927 7.6 / W 1615 1.9 / 2153 8.0	**28**	0446 1.4 / 1013 8.6 / TH 1710 1.1 / 2235 8.8
14	0330 2.6 / 0917 7.5 / F 1607 2.4 / 2146 7.5	**29**	0302 2.2 / 0856 7.8 / SA 1544 1.9 / 2125 8.0	**14**	0456 2.3 / 1030 7.9 / M 1724 1.9 / 2255 8.1			**14**	0330 3.0 / 0947 7.0 / M 1605 2.5 / 2146 7.4	**29**	0408 2.0 / 0947 8.2 / TU 1642 1.4 / 2216 8.5	**14**	0436 1.8 / 1011 8.2 / TH 1704 1.4 / 2234 8.6	**29**	0533 1.2 / 1055 8.9 / F 1753 1.0 / 2314 9.0
15	0428 2.4 / 1006 7.8 / SA 1658 2.0 / 2232 7.9	**30**	0416 1.8 / 0956 8.4 / SU 1652 1.4 / 2229 8.5	**15**	0541 1.9 / 1110 8.3 / TU 1807 1.5 / 2333 8.5			**15**	0429 2.4 / 1005 7.7 / TU 1657 1.9 / 2229 8.1	**30**	0511 1.4 / 1037 8.6 / W 1738 1.0 / 2302 9.0	**15**	0523 1.3 / 1052 8.7 / F 1749 1.0 / 2313 9.0	**30**	0612 1.1 / 1133 9.0 / SA 1829 1.0 / ● 2349 9.0
		31	0521 1.4 / 1055 8.9 / M 1755 1.0 / 2326 9.0							**31**	0601 1.0 / 1121 9.2 / TH 1824 0.7 / 2342 9.2				

Chart Datum: 4·43 metres below IGN Datum
HAT is 10·1 metres above Chart Datum

383

TIDES

TIME ZONE -0100
(French Standard Time)
Subtract 1 hour for UT
For French Summer Time add
ONE hour in **non-shaded areas**

FRANCE – DIEPPE
LAT 49°56'N   LONG 1°05'E
TIMES AND HEIGHTS OF HIGH AND LOW WATERS

Dates in amber are **SPRINGS**
Dates in grey are **NEAPS**

2022

MAY

Day	Times / m	Day	Times / m
1 SU	0646 1.0 / 1207 9.0 / 1900 1.0	16 M ○	0620 0.8 / 1142 9.2 / 1843 0.7
2 M	0021 9.0 / 0717 1.0 / 1239 9.0 / 1930 1.1	17 TU	0002 9.4 / 0705 0.7 / 1226 9.4 / 1926 0.7
3 TU	0051 9.0 / 0748 1.1 / 1311 8.8 / 1958 1.3	18 W	0044 9.4 / 0749 0.6 / 1310 9.4 / 2008 0.8
4 W	0122 8.8 / 0816 1.3 / 1343 8.6 / 2025 1.6	19 TH	0128 9.3 / 0833 0.7 / 1356 9.2 / 2051 1.1
5 TH	0152 8.5 / 0843 1.6 / 1414 8.2 / 2052 1.9	20 F	0214 9.0 / 0917 1.0 / 1445 8.8 / 2137 1.5
6 F	0221 8.1 / 0910 2.0 / 1446 7.8 / 2123 2.3	21 SA	0305 8.6 / 1007 1.3 / 1540 8.3 / 2230 1.9
7 SA	0254 7.7 / 0945 2.4 / 1524 7.3 / 2203 2.8	22 SU ◑	0404 8.0 / 1104 1.7 / 1645 7.8 / 2335 2.2
8 SU	0336 7.1 / 1031 2.8 / 1617 6.9 / 2258 3.1	23 M	0515 7.6 / 1213 2.0 / 1758 7.6
9 M ◐	0438 6.7 / 1136 3.0 / 1737 6.6	24 TU	0050 2.3 / 0630 7.5 / 1327 2.0 / 1912 7.6
10 TU	0014 3.2 / 0609 6.6 / 1301 3.0 / 1906 6.8	25 W	0203 2.2 / 0744 7.7 / 1436 1.9 / 2020 7.9
11 W	0140 3.0 / 0734 6.9 / 1421 2.6 / 2013 7.4	26 TH	0309 1.9 / 0848 8.0 / 1537 1.7 / 2116 8.2
12 TH	0251 2.4 / 0836 7.5 / 1524 2.0 / 2107 8.0	27 F	0407 1.7 / 0941 8.2 / 1630 1.6 / 2203 8.4
13 F	0349 1.9 / 0928 8.1 / 1619 1.5 / 2154 8.5	28 SA	0455 1.5 / 1025 8.4 / 1714 1.5 / 2243 8.6
14 SA	0442 1.4 / 1014 8.6 / 1710 1.1 / 2238 8.9	29 SU	0536 1.4 / 1104 8.5 / 1752 1.4 / 2319 8.6
15 SU	0532 1.1 / 1059 9.0 / 1758 0.9 / 2320 9.2	30 M ●	0613 1.4 / 1140 8.6 / 1826 1.4 / 2353 8.7
		31 TU	0648 1.3 / 1214 8.6 / 1901 1.4

JUNE

Day	Times / m	Day	Times / m
1 W	0025 8.7 / 0722 1.3 / 1248 8.6 / 1934 1.5	16 TH ○	0030 9.3 / 0736 0.7 / 1300 9.3 / 1957 0.9
2 TH	0058 8.6 / 0755 1.4 / 1323 8.4 / 2006 1.7	17 F	0119 9.3 / 0826 0.7 / 1350 9.2 / 2047 1.0
3 F	0132 8.4 / 0825 1.6 / 1357 8.2 / 2036 1.9	18 SA	0210 9.1 / 0916 0.8 / 1442 8.9 / 2136 1.3
4 SA	0205 8.1 / 0857 1.9 / 1432 7.9 / 2109 2.2	19 SU	0301 8.8 / 1006 1.1 / 1534 8.6 / 2228 1.6
5 SU	0241 7.8 / 0932 2.1 / 1512 7.6 / 2149 2.4	20 M	0355 8.4 / 1057 1.4 / 1627 8.2 / 2321 1.9
6 M	0323 7.5 / 1016 2.4 / 1558 7.3 / 2238 2.7	21 TU ○	0451 8.1 / 1150 1.7 / 1724 7.9
7 TU	0415 7.2 / 1110 2.5 / 1656 7.2 / 2338 2.8	22 W	0018 2.1 / 0551 7.7 / 1246 2.0 / 1825 7.7
8 W	0518 7.1 / 1213 2.6 / 1804 7.2	23 TH	0118 2.2 / 0656 7.6 / 1346 2.1 / 1930 7.6
9 TH	0045 2.7 / 0630 7.2 / 1322 2.4 / 1913 7.4	24 F	0220 2.2 / 0803 7.6 / 1446 2.1 / 2033 7.7
10 F	0154 2.4 / 0739 7.5 / 1429 2.1 / 2015 7.9	25 SA	0320 2.1 / 0903 7.7 / 1544 2.1 / 2128 7.9
11 SA	0259 2.0 / 0841 7.9 / 1532 1.7 / 2111 8.3	26 SU	0415 2.0 / 0955 7.9 / 1636 2.0 / 2214 8.1
12 SU	0400 1.6 / 0936 8.4 / 1631 1.4 / 2203 8.7	27 M	0503 1.8 / 1040 8.1 / 1720 1.8 / 2255 8.2
13 M	0457 1.2 / 1029 8.7 / 1725 1.1 / 2252 9.0	28 TU	0546 1.7 / 1119 8.2 / 1801 1.7 / 2331 8.3
14 TU	0552 1.0 / 1119 9.0 / 1817 1.0 / 2341 9.2	29 W	0626 1.6 / 1156 8.3 / 1840 1.7
15 W ○	0645 0.8 / 1209 9.2 / 1908 0.9	30 TH	0007 8.4 / 0704 1.5 / 1232 8.4 / 1917 1.7

JULY

Day	Times / m	Day	Times / m
1 F	0042 8.5 / 0740 1.5 / 1308 8.4 / 1952 1.7	16 SA	0112 9.4 / 0821 0.5 / 1342 9.3 / 2042 0.9
2 SA	0118 8.4 / 0814 1.5 / 1344 8.4 / 2025 1.8	17 SU	0201 9.3 / 0909 0.6 / 1429 9.2 / 2128 1.0
3 SU	0153 8.3 / 0848 1.6 / 1420 8.3 / 2100 1.9	18 M	0247 9.1 / 0953 0.8 / 1514 8.9 / 2211 1.3
4 M	0229 8.2 / 0923 1.7 / 1457 8.1 / 2137 2.0	19 TU	0332 8.8 / 1034 1.2 / 1558 8.6 / 2251 1.6
5 TU	0308 8.0 / 1001 1.9 / 1536 7.9 / 2218 2.1	20 W	0417 8.3 / 1113 1.6 / 1643 8.1 / 2334 2.0
6 W	0350 7.8 / 1043 2.0 / 1620 7.7 / 2304 2.3	21 TH	0506 7.8 / 1156 2.1 / 1733 7.7
7 TH ○	0438 7.6 / 1132 2.2 / 1712 7.6 / 2359 2.4	22 F	0024 2.4 / 0602 7.4 / 1248 2.4 / 1833 7.3
8 F	0534 7.5 / 1229 2.3 / 1814 7.6	23 SA	0125 2.6 / 0711 7.1 / 1352 2.7 / 1945 7.2
9 SA	0101 2.3 / 0643 7.5 / 1336 2.2 / 1925 7.7	24 SU	0235 2.6 / 0826 7.1 / 1503 2.7 / 2054 7.3
10 SU	0213 2.2 / 0757 7.7 / 1450 2.1 / 2033 8.0	25 M	0341 2.4 / 0931 7.4 / 1607 2.4 / 2151 7.6
11 M	0325 1.8 / 0906 8.1 / 1559 1.7 / 2135 8.4	26 TU	0438 2.1 / 1022 7.7 / 1700 2.2 / 2237 7.9
12 TU	0431 1.5 / 1008 8.5 / 1701 1.4 / 2233 8.8	27 W	0527 1.9 / 1104 8.0 / 1745 1.9 / 2316 8.2
13 W ○	0532 1.1 / 1106 8.8 / 1800 1.2 / 2328 9.1	28 TH	0610 1.6 / 1142 8.3 / 1826 1.7 / 2353 8.4
14 TH	0632 0.8 / 1201 9.1 / 1858 1.0	29 F	0650 1.5 / 1218 8.5 / 1904 1.6
15 F	0021 9.3 / 0728 0.6 / 1253 9.3 / 1952 0.9	30 SA	0028 8.6 / 0727 1.4 / 1253 8.6 / 1939 1.5
		31 SU	0103 8.7 / 0802 1.3 / 1327 8.7 / 2013 1.5

AUGUST

Day	Times / m	Day	Times / m
1 M	0137 8.7 / 0836 1.3 / 1401 8.7 / 2047 1.5	16 TU	0223 9.3 / 0927 0.7 / 1445 9.1 / 2141 1.2
2 TU	0212 8.6 / 0908 1.3 / 1435 8.6 / 2120 1.6	17 W	0301 9.0 / 0958 1.2 / 1522 8.7 / 2212 1.6
3 W	0246 8.5 / 0940 1.5 / 1510 8.4 / 2155 1.7	18 TH	0339 8.5 / 1028 1.7 / 1559 8.2 / 2245 2.1
4 TH	0323 8.3 / 1015 1.7 / 1547 8.2 / 2233 1.9	19 F ◑	0418 7.8 / 1102 2.2 / 1639 7.6 / 2327 2.6
5 F ○	0403 8.0 / 1055 2.0 / 1630 7.9 / 2320 2.2	20 SA	0506 7.2 / 1148 2.8 / 1733 7.1
6 SA	0453 7.7 / 1146 2.3 / 1726 7.7	21 SU	0026 3.0 / 0616 6.7 / 1257 3.2 / 1854 6.7
7 SU	0019 2.4 / 0559 7.4 / 1253 2.5 / 1843 7.5	22 M	0150 3.2 / 0751 6.6 / 1429 3.2 / 2026 6.8
8 M	0136 2.4 / 0726 7.4 / 1420 2.5 / 2008 7.7	23 TU	0314 2.9 / 0911 7.0 / 1546 2.8 / 2132 7.3
9 TU	0302 2.1 / 0849 7.7 / 1540 2.1 / 2122 8.1	24 W	0419 2.4 / 1004 7.5 / 1643 2.3 / 2219 7.8
10 W	0416 1.7 / 1000 8.3 / 1649 1.6 / 2226 8.6	25 TH	0509 1.9 / 1046 8.1 / 1729 1.9 / 2258 8.2
11 TH	0522 1.2 / 1101 8.8 / 1753 1.2 / 2323 9.1	26 F	0553 1.6 / 1122 8.5 / 1809 1.6 / 2334 8.6
12 F ○	0625 0.8 / 1154 9.2 / 1851 0.9	27 SA ●	0632 1.3 / 1157 8.7 / 1846 1.4
13 SA	0013 9.4 / 0721 0.5 / 1242 9.5 / 1943 0.7	28 SU	0009 8.8 / 0709 1.1 / 1231 8.9 / 1921 1.2
14 SU	0059 9.6 / 0809 0.4 / 1326 9.5 / 2028 0.7	29 M	0042 9.0 / 0743 1.0 / 1304 9.0 / 1954 1.2
15 M	0142 9.5 / 0851 0.5 / 1407 9.4 / 2107 0.8	30 TU	0115 9.1 / 0815 1.0 / 1336 9.0 / 2027 1.2
		31 W	0148 9.0 / 0846 1.1 / 1409 9.0 / 2059 1.3

Chart Datum: 4·43 metres below IGN Datum
HAT is 10·1 metres above Chart Datum

TIME ZONE -0100
(French Standard Time)
Subtract 1 hour for UT
For French Summer Time add
ONE hour in **non-shaded areas**

FRANCE – DIEPPE
LAT 49°56'N   LONG 1°05'E
TIMES AND HEIGHTS OF HIGH AND LOW WATERS

Dates in amber are **SPRINGS**
Dates in grey are **NEAPS**

2022

SEPTEMBER

Day	Time	m	Time	m	Time	m	Time	m
1 TH	0222	8.9	0916	1.3	1442	8.8	2131	1.5
2 F	0257	8.6	0947	1.3	1517	8.5	2206	1.8
3 SA	0335	8.2	1024	2.0	1558	8.1	◐2251	2.1
4 SU	0424	7.7	1115	2.4	1654	7.6	2351	2.5
5 M	0533	7.2	1227	2.8	1820	7.2		
6 TU	0116	2.7	0716	7.1	1408	2.8	2001	7.4
7 W	0255	2.3	0849	7.6	1536	2.2	2121	8.0
8 TH	0412	1.7	0959	8.3	1646	1.6	2222	8.7
9 F	0519	1.1	1053	9.0	1747	1.1	2313	9.2
10 SA	0616	0.7	1140	9.4	1839	0.8	○2358	9.5
11 SU	0705	0.5	1223	9.6	1924	0.7		
12 M	0039	9.7	0746	0.5	1302	9.6	2003	0.7
13 TU	0117	9.6	0822	0.6	1338	9.5	2037	0.9
14 W	0153	9.4	0852	0.9	1412	9.2	2105	1.2
15 TH	0227	9.0	0918	1.3	1444	8.8	2131	1.6
16 F	0300	8.4	0942	1.8	1515	8.2	2159	2.1
17 SA	0333	7.8	1006	2.1	1548	7.6	◐2235	2.7
18 SU	0413	7.1	1054	3.0	1634	6.9	2328	3.2
19 M	0519	6.5	1201	3.6	1757	6.4		
20 TU	0058	3.5	0714	6.3	1353	3.7	1953	6.5
21 W	0244	3.2	0844	6.8	1521	3.1	2105	7.0
22 TH	0352	2.6	0936	7.5	1617	2.4	2152	7.7
23 F	0442	2.0	1017	8.1	1701	1.9	2231	8.3
24 SA	0525	1.5	1054	8.6	1741	1.5	2307	8.7
25 SU	0604	1.2	1129	8.9	1819	1.2	2342	9.0
26 M	0641	1.0	1201	9.1	●1855	1.1		
27 TU	0016	9.2	0716	0.9	1236	9.3	1930	1.0
28 W	0049	9.3	0749	0.9	1308	9.3	2004	1.0
29 TH	0123	9.3	0821	1.0	1342	9.2	2037	1.1
30 F	0158	9.1	0853	1.2	1417	9.0	2110	1.3

OCTOBER

Day	Time	m	Time	m	Time	m	Time	m
1 SA	0235	8.8	0925	1.6	1454	8.6	2147	1.7
2 SU	0316	8.3	1006	2.1	1538	8.0	2234	2.2
3 M	0408	7.6	1101	2.6	1639	7.4	◐2338	2.6
4 TU	0528	7.1	1221	3.0	1820	7.1		
5 W	0114	2.8	0721	7.1	1410	2.8	2001	7.4
6 TH	0254	2.3	0846	7.8	1533	2.1	2114	8.1
7 F	0407	1.6	0947	8.5	1638	1.5	2208	8.8
8 SA	0506	1.1	1036	9.1	1732	1.0	2254	9.3
9 SU	0556	0.8	1118	9.4	1817	0.8	○2336	9.5
10 M	0639	0.7	1157	9.5	1857	0.9		
11 TU	0013	9.5	0715	0.7	1233	9.5	1932	0.9
12 W	0049	9.4	0747	0.9	1306	9.3	2002	1.0
13 TH	0122	9.2	0815	1.2	1337	9.1	2030	1.3
14 F	0154	8.9	0841	1.5	1408	8.7	2056	1.7
15 SA	0226	8.4	0906	2.0	1438	8.2	2123	2.2
16 SU	0257	7.8	0935	2.5	1509	7.6	2156	2.7
17 M	0334	7.2	1014	3.1	1550	7.0	2243	3.2
18 TU	0432	6.6	1101	3.6	1703	6.4	2359	3.6
19 W	0618	6.3	1257	3.8	1859	6.4		
20 TH	0151	3.4	0755	6.7	1435	3.3	2019	6.9
21 F	0307	2.8	0853	7.4	1534	2.6	2111	7.6
22 SA	0359	2.2	0938	8.1	1621	2.0	2154	8.2
23 SU	0445	1.6	1017	8.6	1704	1.5	2233	8.7
24 M	0527	1.3	1054	9.0	1745	1.2	2310	9.0
25 TU	0607	1.0	1130	9.2	1825	1.0	●2346	9.2
26 W	0645	0.9	1206	9.4	1903	0.9		
27 TH	0022	9.4	0722	0.9	1241	9.4	1941	0.9
28 F	0100	9.4	0758	1.0	1319	9.3	2018	1.0
29 SA	0139	9.2	0834	1.3	1358	9.1	2056	1.3
30 SU	0221	8.8	0913	1.7	1440	8.6	2138	1.6
31 M	0308	8.3	0959	2.2	1531	8.0	2230	2.1

NOVEMBER

Day	Time	m	Time	m	Time	m	Time	m
1 TU	0408	7.7	1100	2.7	1642	7.5	◐2339	2.5
2 W	0535	7.3	1226	2.9	1817	7.3		
3 TH	0113	2.5	0708	7.4	1401	2.6	1942	7.6
4 F	0238	2.1	0824	7.9	1515	2.0	2051	8.2
5 SA	0345	1.6	0922	8.5	1615	1.5	2144	8.7
6 SU	0441	1.3	1010	8.9	1706	1.2	2229	9.0
7 M	0527	1.1	1051	9.2	1749	1.1	2310	9.1
8 TU	0607	1.1	1129	9.2	1826	1.1	○2347	9.2
9 W	0641	1.1	1203	9.2	1900	1.1		
10 TH	0021	9.1	0712	1.2	1236	9.1	1932	1.4
11 F	0054	8.9	0743	1.4	1308	8.9	2002	1.4
12 SA	0128	8.7	0813	1.7	1340	8.6	2031	1.7
13 SU	0201	8.3	0841	2.1	1411	8.2	2059	2.1
14 M	0234	7.9	0911	2.5	1445	7.7	2131	2.5
15 TU	0311	7.4	0949	3.0	1525	7.2	2215	2.9
16 W	0402	6.9	1042	3.3	1625	6.8	◐2315	3.2
17 TH	0517	6.7	1156	3.5	1750	6.6		
18 F	0038	3.3	0644	6.8	1323	3.3	1912	6.9
19 SA	0159	2.9	0754	7.3	1434	2.8	2016	7.4
20 SU	0303	2.4	0848	7.8	1530	2.2	2107	7.9
21 M	0356	1.9	0934	8.4	1621	1.7	2153	8.4
22 TU	0445	1.5	1016	8.8	1708	1.4	2236	8.8
23 W	0531	1.2	1057	9.1	1754	1.1	●2318	9.1
24 TH	0615	1.1	1138	9.3	1838	1.0		
25 F	0000	9.3	0658	1.1	1220	9.4	1922	0.9
26 SA	0043	9.3	0740	1.1	1303	9.4	2005	0.9
27 SU	0128	9.2	0824	1.3	1348	9.1	2050	1.1
28 M	0216	8.9	0909	1.6	1438	8.7	2138	1.4
29 TU	0309	8.4	1001	2.0	1534	8.3	2232	1.8
30 W	0411	8.0	1103	2.3	1640	7.9	◐2337	2.1

DECEMBER

Day	Time	m	Time	m	Time	m	Time	m
1 TH	0521	7.7	1216	2.5	1753	7.7		
2 F	0051	2.2	0634	7.7	1330	2.4	1906	7.7
3 SA	0202	2.1	0745	7.9	1439	2.1	2014	7.9
4 SU	0307	1.9	0847	8.2	1540	1.8	2112	8.2
5 M	0404	1.7	0939	8.5	1633	1.6	2201	8.5
6 TU	0453	1.6	1023	8.7	1718	1.5	2245	8.6
7 W	0534	1.6	1103	8.8	1757	1.4	2323	8.7
8 TH	0610	1.5	1139	8.8	1833	1.4	○2359	8.7
9 F	0646	1.5	1213	8.8	1908	1.4		
10 SA	0034	8.7	0721	1.6	1247	8.7	1943	1.5
11 SU	0109	8.5	0755	1.8	1321	8.6	2015	1.7
12 M	0144	8.4	0826	2.0	1355	8.3	2046	1.9
13 TU	0219	8.1	0858	2.3	1430	8.0	2118	2.2
14 W	0256	7.8	0934	2.5	1509	7.7	2156	2.4
15 TH	0338	7.5	1018	2.8	1554	7.4	2243	2.7
16 F	0428	7.2	1111	2.9	1650	7.1	◐2340	2.8
17 SA	0530	7.1	1214	2.9	1757	7.1		
18 SU	0045	2.8	0640	7.2	1322	2.8	1908	7.2
19 M	0154	2.6	0747	7.6	1431	2.5	2014	7.6
20 TU	0302	2.2	0846	8.0	1535	2.0	2112	8.1
21 W	0403	1.9	0939	8.4	1633	1.6	2204	8.5
22 TH	0458	1.5	1029	8.8	1727	1.3	2254	8.9
23 F	0551	1.3	1117	9.1	1819	1.0	●2344	9.1
24 SA	0641	1.1	1206	9.3	1910	0.8		
25 SU	0033	9.3	0731	1.0	1255	9.4	2000	0.9
26 M	0124	9.3	0822	1.1	1345	9.3	2050	0.8
27 TU	0214	9.1	0912	1.2	1436	9.1	2139	1.0
28 W	0305	8.8	1002	1.5	1527	8.8	2228	1.3
29 TH	0357	8.5	1052	1.8	1620	8.4	2318	1.6
30 F	0451	8.1	1146	2.1	1717	8.0	◐	
31 SA	0011	2.0	0549	7.8	1245	2.3	1819	7.7

Chart Datum: 4·43 metres below IGN Datum
HAT is 10·1 metres above Chart Datum

TIDES

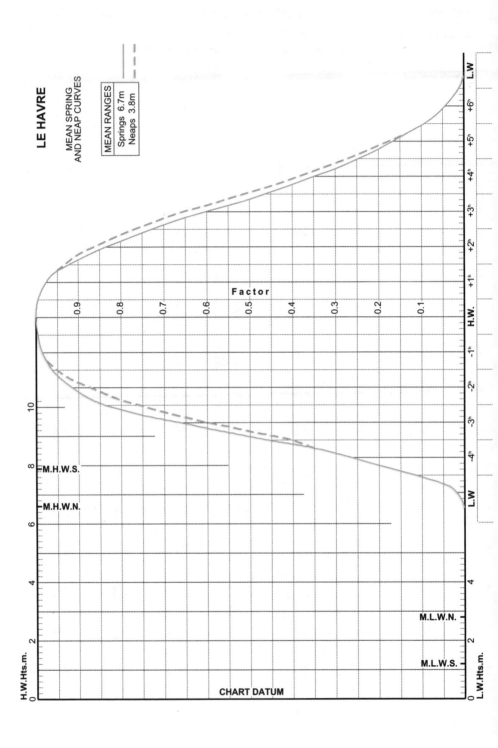

LE HAVRE

MEAN SPRING
AND NEAP CURVES

MEAN RANGES	
Springs	6.7m
Neaps	3.8m

<table>
<tr><td>

TIME ZONE -0100
(French Standard Time)
Subtract 1 hour for UT
For French Summer Time add
ONE hour in **non-shaded areas**

</td><td>

FRANCE – LE HAVRE

LAT 49°29'N   LONG 0°07'E

TIMES AND HEIGHTS OF HIGH AND LOW WATERS

</td><td>

Dates in amber are **SPRINGS**
Dates in grey are **NEAPS**

2022

</td></tr>
</table>

JANUARY

Time	m	Time	m
1 SA	0347 1.8 / 0915 7.8 / 1619 1.6 / 2144 7.8	**16** SU	0426 2.4 / 0954 7.3 / 1654 2.1 / 2221 7.3
2 SU ●	0445 1.6 / 1006 8.0 / 1716 1.3 / 2237 8.0	**17** M	0509 2.2 / 1029 7.4 / 1734 1.9 / 2257 7.4
3 M	0540 1.4 / 1056 8.1 / 1811 1.1 / 2327 8.1	**18** TU ○	0548 2.1 / 1104 7.6 / 1812 1.8 / 2331 7.5
4 TU	0634 1.3 / 1138 8.2 / 1903 1.0	**19** W	0624 2.0 / 1138 7.7 / 1848 1.7
5 W	0016 8.1 / 0725 1.3 / 1232 8.1 / 1952 1.0	**20** TH	0006 7.6 / 0700 1.9 / 1212 7.7 / 1924 1.6
6 TH	0104 8.0 / 0812 1.5 / 1319 8.0 / 2037 1.2	**21** F	0041 7.6 / 0736 1.9 / 1249 7.7 / 1959 1.6
7 F	0151 7.8 / 0855 1.8 / 1405 7.7 / 2119 1.6	**22** SA	0118 7.5 / 0812 1.9 / 1327 7.6 / 2035 1.7
8 SA	0238 7.5 / 0937 2.1 / 1452 7.4 / 2158 2.0	**23** SU	0157 7.4 / 0849 2.1 / 1407 7.4 / 2110 1.9
9 SU ◐	0326 7.2 / 1018 2.5 / 1541 7.1 / 2238 2.4	**24** M	0238 7.3 / 0927 2.2 / 1449 7.2 / 2148 2.1
10 M	0417 6.9 / 1103 2.8 / 1637 6.8 / 2324 2.8	**25** TU ◑	0321 7.1 / 1009 2.5 / 1535 7.0 / 2233 2.4
11 TU	0514 6.7 / 1156 3.1 / 1740 6.6	**26** W	0413 6.9 / 1100 2.7 / 1635 6.9 / 2329 2.7
12 W	0020 3.0 / 0617 6.7 / 1302 3.2 / 1851 6.5	**27** TH	0520 6.8 / 1207 2.8 / 1755 6.7
13 TH	0129 3.1 / 0725 6.7 / 1417 3.0 / 2003 6.6	**28** F	0048 2.8 / 0644 6.9 / 1338 2.7 / 1925 6.9
14 F	0241 3.0 / 0826 6.9 / 1518 2.7 / 2100 6.9	**29** SA	0218 2.6 / 0801 7.2 / 1458 2.3 / 2038 7.2
15 SA	0338 2.7 / 0914 7.1 / 1609 2.4 / 2144 7.1	**30** SU	0329 2.2 / 0903 7.5 / 1604 1.8 / 2138 7.6
		31 M	0434 1.8 / 0958 7.8 / 1709 1.4 / 2230 7.8

FEBRUARY

Time	m	Time	m
1 TU	0537 1.5 / 1047 8.0 / 1808 1.2 / ● 2318 8.0	**16** W ○	0536 2.0 / 1048 7.6 / 1800 1.6 / 2314 7.6
2 W	0632 1.3 / 1133 8.1 / 1858 0.9	**17** TH	0614 1.7 / 1123 7.7 / 1836 1.4 / 2348 7.7
3 TH	0004 8.1 / 0718 1.1 / 1217 8.2 / 1941 0.8	**18** F	0650 1.5 / 1157 7.8 / 1911 1.2
4 F	0047 8.0 / 0758 1.2 / 1259 8.1 / 2018 1.0	**19** SA	0023 7.8 / 0725 1.4 / 1233 7.9 / 1945 1.2
5 SA	0127 7.9 / 0833 1.4 / 1339 7.9 / 2052 1.3	**20** SU	0059 7.8 / 0759 1.4 / 1310 7.8 / 2019 1.3
6 SU	0205 7.6 / 0906 1.8 / 1417 7.6 / 2121 1.8	**21** M	0136 7.7 / 0833 1.6 / 1347 7.7 / 2051 1.5
7 M	0242 7.3 / 0936 2.2 / 1455 7.2 / 2150 2.3	**22** TU	0213 7.5 / 0907 1.8 / 1426 7.5 / 2125 1.9
8 TU	0319 7.0 / 1008 2.7 / 1538 6.8 / ◑ 2223 2.8	**23** W	0251 7.3 / 0944 2.2 / 1508 7.2 / 2204 2.3
9 W	0405 6.7 / 1050 3.1 / 1636 6.4 / 2310 3.2	**24** TH	0337 7.0 / 1030 2.5 / 1606 6.8 / 2257 2.8
10 TH	0508 6.4 / 1149 3.4 / 1754 6.1	**25** F	0445 6.7 / 1135 2.9 / 1736 6.5
11 F	0019 3.5 / 0629 6.2 / 1318 3.5 / 1928 6.2	**26** SA	0021 3.1 / 0626 6.6 / 1317 2.9 / 1920 6.7
12 SA	0157 3.5 / 0754 6.4 / 1446 3.2 / 2040 6.5	**27** SU	0203 2.9 / 0752 6.9 / 1445 2.5 / 2035 7.0
13 SU	0313 3.1 / 0855 6.7 / 1547 2.7 / 2127 6.9	**28** M	0322 2.4 / 0857 7.3 / 1601 1.9 / 2133 7.5
14 M	0408 2.7 / 0937 7.0 / 1637 2.3 / 2205 7.2		
15 TU	0455 2.3 / 1014 7.3 / 1720 1.9 / 2239 7.4		

MARCH

Time	m	Time	m
1 TU	0436 1.9 / 0949 7.6 / 1709 1.4 / 2221 7.8	**16** W	0431 2.2 / 0949 7.3 / 1656 1.8 / 2213 7.5
2 W ●	0536 1.4 / 1035 7.9 / 1802 1.0 / 2304 7.9	**17** TH	0514 1.8 / 1024 7.6 / 1737 1.5 / 2248 7.7
3 TH	0622 1.1 / 1117 8.0 / 1844 0.8 / 2344 8.0	**18** F ○	0552 1.5 / 1059 7.8 / 1814 1.2 / 2323 7.9
4 F	0701 1.0 / 1156 8.1 / 1920 0.8	**19** SA	0629 1.3 / 1135 8.0 / 1849 1.0 / 2359 8.0
5 SA	0021 8.0 / 0734 1.1 / 1234 8.1 / 1950 1.0	**20** SU	0704 1.1 / 1212 8.0 / 1924 1.0
6 SU	0056 7.9 / 0804 1.3 / 1309 7.9 / 2018 1.3	**21** M	0035 8.0 / 0739 1.1 / 1249 8.0 / 1957 1.1
7 M	0129 7.7 / 0831 1.6 / 1342 7.6 / 2043 1.7	**22** TU	0112 7.9 / 0813 1.3 / 1328 7.8 / 2030 1.4
8 TU	0159 7.4 / 0855 2.1 / 1413 7.2 / 2105 2.2	**23** W	0149 7.7 / 0847 1.6 / 1408 7.5 / 2103 1.8
9 W	0228 7.1 / 0919 2.5 / 1446 6.8 / 2131 2.8	**24** TH	0228 7.4 / 0924 2.0 / 1453 7.1 / 2143 2.4
10 TH	0300 6.7 / 0952 3.0 / 1530 6.3 / ◑ 2211 3.3	**25** F ◑	0316 7.0 / 1010 2.5 / 1555 6.7 / 2239 2.9
11 F	0350 6.3 / 1045 3.5 / 1652 6.0 / 2318 3.8	**26** SA	0430 6.6 / 1120 2.9 / 1738 6.5
12 SA	0527 6.0 / 1211 3.7 / 1844 5.9	**27** SU	0014 3.2 / 0619 6.5 / 1310 2.9 / 1917 6.6
13 SU	0103 3.8 / 0713 6.0 / 1406 3.5 / 2010 6.3	**28** M	0158 2.9 / 0743 6.8 / 1441 2.4 / 2027 7.0
14 M	0244 3.4 / 0826 6.4 / 1518 2.9 / 2100 6.7	**29** TU	0322 2.4 / 0845 7.2 / 1558 1.9 / 2120 7.4
15 TU	0343 2.8 / 0911 6.9 / 1610 2.3 / 2138 7.2	**30** W	0430 1.8 / 0934 7.5 / 1657 1.4 / 2203 7.7
		31 TH	0520 1.4 / 1016 7.8 / 1742 1.1 / 2241 7.8

APRIL

Time	m	Time	m
1 F ●	0600 1.2 / 1054 7.9 / 1818 1.0 / 2317 7.9	**16** SA	0520 1.5 / 1030 7.8 / 1742 1.2 / ○ 2254 7.9
2 SA	0634 1.1 / 1130 7.9 / 1849 1.1 / 2351 7.9	**17** SU	0600 1.2 / 1109 8.0 / 1821 1.0 / 2331 8.0
3 SU	0703 1.2 / 1205 7.9 / 1917 1.2	**18** M	0639 1.0 / 1148 8.0 / 1859 1.0
4 M	0023 7.8 / 0731 1.4 / 1238 7.7 / 1943 1.5	**19** TU	0010 8.1 / 0718 1.0 / 1229 8.0 / 1936 1.1
5 TU	0053 7.6 / 0757 1.8 / 1310 7.5 / 2006 1.8	**20** W	0050 8.0 / 0755 1.1 / 1312 7.8 / 2011 1.4
6 W	0121 7.4 / 0820 2.0 / 1340 7.2 / 2028 2.3	**21** TH	0130 7.7 / 0831 1.5 / 1356 7.5 / 2048 1.9
7 TH	0147 7.2 / 0842 2.4 / 1410 6.8 / 2052 2.8	**22** F	0214 7.4 / 0911 1.9 / 1447 7.1 / 2132 2.5
8 F	0218 6.8 / 0910 2.9 / 1449 6.4 / 2128 3.3	**23** SA ◑	0308 7.0 / 1001 2.4 / 1556 6.7 / 2236 3.0
9 SA	0301 6.3 / 0957 3.4 / 1553 6.0 / ◑ 2230 3.8	**24** SU	0428 6.6 / 1122 2.8 / 1736 6.6
10 SU	0417 5.9 / 1119 3.7 / 1753 5.9	**25** M	0017 3.1 / 0605 6.6 / 1302 2.7 / 1900 6.7
11 M	0011 3.9 / 0619 5.9 / 1308 3.5 / 1921 6.2	**26** TU	0146 2.8 / 0722 6.8 / 1422 2.4 / 2006 7.1
12 TU	0155 3.5 / 0739 6.3 / 1430 3.0 / 2019 6.7	**27** W	0300 2.3 / 0822 7.1 / 1532 1.9 / 2056 7.4
13 W	0300 2.9 / 0832 6.8 / 1526 2.4 / 2102 7.1	**28** TH	0402 1.9 / 0910 7.4 / 1627 1.6 / 2137 7.6
14 TH	0351 2.3 / 0914 7.2 / 1616 1.8 / 2140 7.5	**29** F	0450 1.6 / 0950 7.6 / 1709 1.5 / 2214 7.7
15 F	0437 1.8 / 0952 7.6 / 1701 1.5 / 2216 7.8	**30** SA ●	0528 1.5 / 1028 7.7 / 1743 1.4 / 2248 7.7

Chart Datum: 4·38 metres below IGN Datum
HAT is 8·4 metres above Chart Datum

TIDES

TIME ZONE -0100
(French Standard Time)
Subtract 1 hour for UT
For French Summer Time add ONE hour in **non-shaded areas**

FRANCE – LE HAVRE
LAT 49°29'N   LONG 0°07'E
TIMES AND HEIGHTS OF HIGH AND LOW WATERS

Dates in amber are **SPRINGS**
Dates in grey are **NEAPS**

2022

MAY

Date	Time	m	Date	Time	m
1 SU	0600 / 1103 / 1813 / 2320	1.4 / 7.7 / 1.5 / 7.7	**16** M	0530 / 1043 / 1752 / ○ 2305	1.3 / 7.9 / 1.2 / 8.0
2 M	0630 / 1137 / 1842 / 2350	1.5 / 7.6 / 1.6 / 7.7	**17** TU	0615 / 1127 / 1835 / 2348	1.1 / 8.0 / 1.1 / 8.0
3 TU	0659 / 1210 / 1910	1.6 / 7.5 / 1.8	**18** W	0658 / 1213 / 1918	1.0 / 7.9 / 1.3
4 W	0021 / 0726 / 1243 / 1936	7.6 / 1.7 / 7.4 / 2.0	**19** TH	0032 / 0741 / 1301 / 2000	8.0 / 1.1 / 7.8 / 1.6
5 TH	0050 / 0752 / 1315 / 2001	7.4 / 2.0 / 7.1 / 2.4	**20** F	0118 / 0824 / 1350 / 2044	7.8 / 1.4 / 7.5 / 2.0
6 F	0119 / 0817 / 1348 / 2028	7.2 / 2.4 / 6.9 / 2.8	**21** SA	0207 / 0911 / 1446 / 2136	7.5 / 1.8 / 7.2 / 2.4
7 SA	0153 / 0847 / 1428 / 2104	6.9 / 2.7 / 6.5 / 3.2	**22** SU	0305 / 1009 / 1555 / ◑ 2246	7.1 / 2.2 / 6.9 / 2.7
8 SU	0238 / 0930 / 1523 / 2159	6.5 / 3.1 / 6.3 / 3.5	**23** M	0418 / 1123 / 1714	6.8 / 2.5 / 6.8
9 M	0340 / 1038 / 1650 / ☽ 2324	6.2 / 3.4 / 6.1 / 3.6	**24** TU	0002 / 0536 / 1235 / 1825	2.8 / 6.7 / 2.5 / 6.8
10 TU	0511 / 1209 / 1821	6.1 / 3.3 / 6.3	**25** W	0112 / 0646 / 1342 / 1929	2.7 / 6.8 / 2.4 / 7.0
11 W	0053 / 0803 / 1328 / 1925	3.4 / 6.3 / 3.0 / 6.7	**26** TH	0216 / 0747 / 1444 / 2022	2.4 / 7.0 / 2.2 / 7.2
12 TH	0202 / 0739 / 1431 / 2015	2.9 / 6.7 / 2.5 / 7.1	**27** F	0316 / 0839 / 1539 / 2106	2.2 / 7.2 / 2.1 / 7.4
13 F	0259 / 0830 / 1526 / 2059	2.4 / 7.1 / 2.0 / 7.4	**28** SA	0407 / 0923 / 1624 / 2144	2.0 / 7.3 / 2.0 / 7.5
14 SA	0352 / 0915 / 1618 / 2141	1.9 / 7.4 / 1.6 / 7.7	**29** SU	0448 / 1003 / 1703 / 2219	1.9 / 7.4 / 1.9 / 7.5
15 SU	0442 / 0959 / 1706 / 2223	1.6 / 7.7 / 1.4 / 7.9	**30** M	0525 / 1040 / 1738 / ○ 2252	1.8 / 7.4 / 1.9 / 7.5
			31 TU	0600 / 1115 / 1812 / 2324	1.8 / 7.4 / 1.9 / 7.5

JUNE

Date	Time	m	Date	Time	m
1 W	0632 / 1149 / 1843 / 2356	1.8 / 7.4 / 2.0 / 7.5	**16** TH	0645 / 1203 / 1907	1.1 / 7.9 / 1.4
2 TH	0702 / 1223 / 1913	1.9 / 7.3 / 2.2	**17** F	0020 / 0735 / 1253 / 1958	8.0 / 1.2 / 7.8 / 1.5
3 F	0028 / 0732 / 1257 / 1943	7.4 / 2.0 / 7.1 / 2.4	**18** SA	0110 / 0826 / 1345 / 2049	7.9 / 1.3 / 7.7 / 1.8
4 SA	0101 / 0803 / 1333 / 2015	7.2 / 2.2 / 7.0 / 2.6	**19** SU	0200 / 0916 / 1438 / 2140	7.6 / 1.5 / 7.4 / 2.1
5 SU	0138 / 0836 / 1413 / 2053	7.0 / 2.5 / 6.8 / 2.9	**20** M	0254 / 1007 / 1535 / 2234	7.3 / 1.9 / 7.2 / 2.3
6 M	0222 / 0917 / 1502 / 2140	6.8 / 2.7 / 6.6 / 3.1	**21** TU	0352 / 1100 / 1635 / ☽ 2329	7.1 / 2.2 / 7.0 / 2.6
7 TU	0314 / 1010 / 1602 / 2243	6.6 / 2.9 / 6.5 / 3.2	**22** W	0454 / 1154 / 1737	6.9 / 2.4 / 6.9
8 W	0417 / 1116 / 1713 / 2352	6.5 / 2.9 / 6.5 / 3.1	**23** TH	0025 / 0558 / 1250 / 1839	2.7 / 6.8 / 2.6 / 6.9
9 TH	0529 / 1225 / 1822	6.5 / 2.8 / 6.7	**24** F	0125 / 0703 / 1350 / 1939	2.7 / 6.8 / 2.4 / 6.9
10 F	0101 / 0638 / 1333 / 1922	2.9 / 6.7 / 2.5 / 7.0	**25** SA	0226 / 0805 / 1449 / 2032	2.6 / 6.8 / 2.6 / 7.1
11 SA	0208 / 0740 / 1438 / 2016	2.5 / 7.0 / 2.2 / 7.3	**26** SU	0322 / 0858 / 1541 / 2117	2.4 / 7.0 / 2.4 / 7.2
12 SU	0310 / 0837 / 1538 / 2107	2.1 / 7.3 / 1.9 / 7.6	**27** M	0411 / 0943 / 1628 / 2156	2.3 / 7.1 / 2.3 / 7.3
13 M	0408 / 0931 / 1634 / 2155	1.7 / 7.5 / 1.6 / 7.8	**28** TU	0455 / 1023 / 1710 / 2232	2.1 / 7.2 / 2.2 / 7.4
14 TU	0502 / 1022 / 1717 / ○ 2244	1.4 / 7.7 / 1.4 / 7.9	**29** W	0535 / 1059 / 1749 / ● 2306	2.0 / 7.3 / 2.2 / 7.4
15 W	0554 / 1112 / 1817 / 2332	1.2 / 7.9 / 1.4 / 8.0	**30** TH	0612 / 1134 / 1825 / 2339	1.9 / 7.3 / 2.2 / 7.4

JULY

Date	Time	m	Date	Time	m
1 F	0647 / 1209 / 1859	1.9 / 7.3 / 2.2	**16** SA	0010 / 0733 / 1243 / 1955	8.1 / 1.0 / 7.9 / 1.3
2 SA	0013 / 0721 / 1243 / 1933	7.5 / 1.9 / 7.3 / 2.2	**17** SU	0058 / 0821 / 1330 / 2041	8.0 / 1.0 / 7.8 / 1.5
3 SU	0048 / 0755 / 1319 / 2008	7.4 / 2.0 / 7.2 / 2.3	**18** M	0144 / 0904 / 1417 / 2123	7.8 / 1.2 / 7.6 / 1.7
4 M	0125 / 0829 / 1358 / 2044	7.3 / 2.1 / 7.1 / 2.5	**19** TU	0230 / 0944 / 1502 / 2203	7.6 / 1.6 / 7.4 / 2.1
5 TU	0205 / 0906 / 1439 / 2124	7.2 / 2.3 / 7.0 / 2.6	**20** W	0316 / 1021 / 1548 / ◑ 2244	7.3 / 2.1 / 7.1 / 2.5
6 W	0249 / 0946 / 1525 / 2210	7.0 / 2.4 / 6.9 / 2.7	**21** TH	0406 / 1102 / 1640 / 2332	6.9 / 2.5 / 6.8 / 2.8
7 TH	0337 / 1033 / 1618 / ☽ 2303	6.9 / 2.6 / 6.8 / 2.8	**22** F	0504 / 1152 / 1740	6.6 / 2.9 / 6.7
8 F	0434 / 1130 / 1719	6.8 / 2.7 / 6.8	**23** SA	0031 / 0613 / 1256 / 1849	3.0 / 6.5 / 3.1 / 6.6
9 SA	0005 / 0541 / 1237 / 1828	2.8 / 6.8 / 2.7 / 6.9	**24** SU	0141 / 0731 / 1407 / 2001	3.0 / 6.5 / 3.1 / 6.7
10 SU	0119 / 0656 / 1357 / 1938	2.6 / 6.8 / 2.5 / 7.1	**25** M	0247 / 0840 / 1511 / 2057	2.9 / 6.7 / 2.9 / 6.9
11 M	0236 / 0809 / 1509 / 2041	2.3 / 7.1 / 2.2 / 7.4	**26** TU	0343 / 0930 / 1604 / 2141	2.6 / 6.9 / 2.7 / 7.1
12 TU	0342 / 0913 / 1610 / 2138	1.9 / 7.4 / 1.9 / 7.7	**27** W	0433 / 1010 / 1651 / 2218	2.3 / 7.1 / 2.4 / 7.3
13 W	0442 / 1010 / 1710 / ○ 2230	1.6 / 7.6 / 1.6 / 7.9	**28** TH	0518 / 1045 / 1734 / ● 2251	2.1 / 7.3 / 2.2 / 7.4
14 TH	0541 / 1103 / 1809 / 2321	1.3 / 7.8 / 1.5 / 8.0	**29** F	0558 / 1119 / 1813 / 2325	1.9 / 7.4 / 2.1 / 7.5
15 F	0639 / 1154 / 1905	1.1 / 7.9 / 1.4	**30** SA	0635 / 1152 / 1848 / 2358	1.8 / 7.4 / 2.0 / 7.6
			31 SU	0710 / 1226 / 1922	1.7 / 7.5 / 1.9

AUGUST

Date	Time	m	Date	Time	m
1 M	0032 / 0743 / 1301 / 1956	7.6 / 1.7 / 7.6 / 1.9	**16** TU	0119 / 0837 / 1346 / 2052	8.0 / 1.2 / 7.8 / 1.6
2 TU	0108 / 0816 / 1337 / 2030	7.6 / 1.7 / 7.4 / 2.0	**17** W	0158 / 0908 / 1423 / 2123	7.7 / 1.6 / 7.5 / 2.0
3 W	0145 / 0848 / 1414 / 2104	7.5 / 1.9 / 7.3 / 2.2	**18** TH	0236 / 0936 / 1500 / 2154	7.4 / 2.1 / 7.2 / 2.5
4 TH	0223 / 0922 / 1452 / 2142	7.3 / 2.1 / 7.2 / 2.4	**19** F	0317 / 1005 / 1541 / ◑ 2231	7.0 / 2.6 / 6.8 / 3.0
5 F	0304 / 1000 / 1535 / 2225	7.1 / 2.4 / 7.0 / 2.6	**20** SA	0409 / 1047 / 1638 / 2328	6.5 / 3.2 / 6.5 / 3.4
6 SA	0353 / 1048 / 1631 / 2322	6.9 / 2.6 / 6.8 / 2.8	**21** SU	0524 / 1155 / 1759	6.2 / 3.6 / 6.3
7 SU	0501 / 1153 / 1749	6.7 / 2.9 / 6.8	**22** M	0054 / 0700 / 1331 / 1931	3.5 / 6.1 / 3.6 / 6.3
8 M	0041 / 0631 / 1328 / 1916	2.9 / 6.6 / 2.9 / 6.9	**23** TU	0220 / 0823 / 1450 / 2040	3.2 / 6.4 / 3.3 / 6.6
9 TU	0215 / 0758 / 1451 / 2029	2.6 / 6.9 / 2.5 / 7.3	**24** W	0323 / 0914 / 1548 / 2124	2.8 / 6.8 / 2.8 / 7.0
10 W	0326 / 0907 / 1558 / 2129	2.1 / 7.3 / 2.1 / 7.6	**25** TH	0416 / 0951 / 1637 / 2159	2.4 / 7.1 / 2.4 / 7.3
11 TH	0431 / 1003 / 1703 / 2221	1.6 / 7.7 / 1.7 / 7.9	**26** F	0501 / 1024 / 1720 / 2232	2.0 / 7.4 / 2.1 / 7.5
12 F	0537 / 1053 / 1806 / ○ 2309	1.2 / 7.9 / 1.4 / 8.1	**27** SA	0542 / 1057 / 1757 / ● 2305	1.8 / 7.6 / 1.9 / 7.7
13 SA	0634 / 1140 / 1851 / 2354	1.0 / 8.0 / 1.2 / 8.2	**28** SU	0618 / 1130 / 1831 / 2338	1.6 / 7.7 / 1.7 / 7.8
14 SU	0722 / 1224 / 1940	0.8 / 8.1 / 1.1	**29** M	0651 / 1203 / 1904	1.6 / 7.7 / 1.6
15 M	0038 / 0802 / 1306 / 2018	8.1 / 0.9 / 8.0 / 1.3	**30** TU	0011 / 0722 / 1236 / 1936	7.6 / 1.4 / 7.8 / 1.6
			31 W	0046 / 0754 / 1311 / 2009	7.8 / 1.5 / 7.9 / 1.7

Chart Datum: 4·38 metres below IGN Datum
HAT is 8·4 metres above Chart Datum

TIME ZONE -0100
(French Standard Time)
Subtract 1 hour for UT
For French Summer Time add
ONE hour in **non-shaded areas**

FRANCE – LE HAVRE

LAT 49°29'N   LONG 0°07'E

TIMES AND HEIGHTS OF HIGH AND LOW WATERS

Dates in amber are **SPRINGS**
Dates in grey are **NEAPS**

2022

SEPTEMBER

Time	m		Time	m
1 0122	7.7	**16** 0158	7.4
0826	1.6	0850	2.2
TH 1346	7.6	F 1414	7.3
2042	1.9	2106	2.5
2 0158	7.5	**17** 0233	7.0
0857	2.0	0914	2.8
F 1422	7.3	SA 1448	6.9
2117	2.2	☽ 2137	3.0
3 0237	7.2	**18** 0317	6.5
0932	2.3	0951	3.4
SA 1503	7.1	SU 1536	6.4
☾ 2157	2.5	2228	3.5
4 0328	6.9	**19** 0434	6.1
1018	2.8	1057	3.9
SU 1600	6.8	M 1708	6.0
2253	2.9	2359	3.8
5 0443	6.6	**20** 0624	6.0
1126	3.2	1250	4.0
M 1731	6.6	TU 1855	6.1
6 0020	3.1	**21** 0149	3.5
0630	6.5	0753	6.3
TU 1319	3.2	W 1427	3.5
1911	6.8	2010	6.6
7 0206	2.7	**22** 0258	3.0
0759	6.9	0845	6.8
W 1445	2.7	TH 1525	2.9
2024	7.2	2056	6.9
8 0320	2.1	**23** 0349	2.4
0902	7.4	0922	7.2
TH 1555	2.1	F 1612	2.4
2120	7.6	2132	7.3
9 0428	1.6	**24** 0434	2.0
0953	7.8	0955	7.5
F 1701	1.6	SA 1653	2.0
2208	8.0	2205	7.6
10 0530	1.2	**25** 0514	1.7
1037	8.0	1028	7.7
SA 1755	1.3	SU 1730	1.7
○ 2251	8.2	● 2238	7.9
11 0619	0.9	**26** 0549	1.4
1119	8.1	1101	7.9
SU 1838	1.1	M 1805	1.4
2332	8.2	2312	8.0
12 0658	0.9	**27** 0623	1.3
1159	8.1	1135	7.9
M 1915	1.1	TU 1839	1.4
		2346	8.0
13 0012	8.2	**28** 0656	1.3
0732	1.0	1209	8.0
TU 1236	8.0	W 1913	1.4
1947	1.3		
14 0049	8.0	**29** 0022	8.0
0802	1.3	0730	1.3
W 1311	7.8	TH 1244	7.9
2016	1.6	1947	1.5
15 0124	7.8	**30** 0059	7.8
0828	1.7	0803	1.6
TH 1343	7.6	F 1320	7.7
2042	2.0	2021	1.7

OCTOBER

Time	m		Time	m
1 0139	7.6	**16** 0200	6.9
0835	2.0	0838	2.9
SA 1358	7.5	SU 1407	6.9
2056	2.1	2059	3.0
2 0223	7.2	**17** 0240	6.5
0912	2.5	0913	3.4
SU 1444	7.1	M 1450	6.5
2138	2.5	☽ 2144	3.5
3 0319	6.9	**18** 0344	6.1
1001	3.0	1013	3.9
M 1549	6.8	TU 1607	6.1
☾ 2237	3.0	2307	3.8
4 0445	6.5	**19** 0539	6.0
1118	3.4	1158	4.0
TU 1731	6.6	W 1806	6.0
5 0022	3.1	**20** 0055	3.6
0634	6.6	0701	6.3
W 1321	3.2	TH 1341	3.6
1905	6.8	1922	6.4
6 0202	2.6	**21** 0213	3.1
0751	7.0	0759	6.7
TH 1441	2.6	F 1443	3.0
2013	7.3	2014	6.8
7 0314	2.0	**22** 0307	2.5
0849	7.5	0842	7.2
F 1548	2.0	SA 1531	2.5
2105	7.7	2055	7.3
8 0417	1.5	**23** 0353	2.1
0934	7.8	0919	7.6
SA 1645	1.5	SU 1614	2.0
2149	8.0	2132	7.6
9 0509	1.2	**24** 0435	1.7
1015	8.0	0954	7.8
SU 1732	1.3	M 1655	1.7
○ 2229	8.1	2208	7.9
10 0552	1.1	**25** 0515	1.5
1053	8.1	1030	8.0
M 1810	1.2	TU 1734	1.5
2307	8.1	● 2244	8.0
11 0626	1.1	**26** 0552	1.3
1129	8.0	1105	8.1
TU 1843	1.3	W 1812	1.3
2344	8.1	2322	8.1
12 0657	1.3	**27** 0630	1.3
1203	8.0	1142	8.1
W 1913	1.4	TH 1850	1.3
13 0019	7.9	**28** 0001	8.0
0725	1.6	0707	1.4
TH 1235	7.8	F 1221	8.0
1941	1.7	1927	1.4
14 0053	7.7	**29** 0043	7.9
0750	1.9	0743	1.6
F 1305	7.6	SA 1301	7.8
2006	2.1	2005	1.6
15 0126	7.3	**30** 0127	7.6
0813	2.4	0820	2.0
SA 1335	7.3	SU 1345	7.6
2030	2.5	2043	2.0
		31 0217	7.3
		0901	2.5
		M 1437	7.2
		2129	2.5

NOVEMBER

Time	m		Time	m
1 0320	6.9	**16** 0309	6.4
0956	3.0	0944	3.6
TU 1548	6.9	W 1523	6.3
☽ 2236	2.9	☾ 2224	3.5
2 0450	6.7	**17** 0436	6.3
1130	3.3	1103	3.8
W 1724	6.7	TH 1656	6.2
		2348	3.5
3 0024	2.9	**18** 0600	6.4
0620	6.8	1228	3.6
TH 1310	3.0	F 1820	6.4
1845	6.9		
4 0146	2.5	**19** 0104	3.2
0730	7.2	0702	6.7
F 1422	2.5	SA 1339	3.2
1949	7.3	1920	6.7
5 0252	2.0	**20** 0208	2.7
0825	7.5	0753	7.1
SA 1524	2.0	SU 1438	2.7
2041	7.6	2009	7.1
6 0349	1.7	**21** 0303	2.3
0909	7.7	0837	7.4
SU 1617	1.7	M 1529	2.2
2125	7.8	2054	7.5
7 0437	1.5	**22** 0352	1.9
0949	7.9	0918	7.7
M 1701	1.5	TU 1617	1.8
2205	7.9	2136	7.7
8 0517	1.5	**23** 0439	1.6
1026	7.9	0958	7.9
TU 1738	1.5	W 1703	1.5
○ 2243	7.9	● 2219	7.9
9 0551	1.5	**24** 0523	1.5
1100	7.9	1039	8.0
W 1811	1.5	TH 1747	1.3
2319	7.9	2302	8.0
10 0622	1.6	**25** 0607	1.4
1133	7.9	1121	8.1
TH 1842	1.6	F 1831	1.2
2354	7.7	2347	8.0
11 0652	1.8	**26** 0649	1.5
1205	7.7	1205	8.1
F 1912	1.8	SA 1914	1.3
12 0028	7.6	**27** 0034	7.9
0721	2.1	0731	1.7
SA 1236	7.6	SU 1251	7.9
1940	2.1	1957	1.5
13 0102	7.3	**28** 0123	7.7
0748	2.5	0815	2.0
SU 1308	7.3	M 1340	7.7
2007	2.4	2042	1.8
14 0137	7.0	**29** 0216	7.4
0817	2.9	0904	2.4
M 1342	7.0	TU 1435	7.4
2038	2.8	2136	2.2
15 0217	6.7	**30** 0319	7.1
0852	3.3	1007	2.7
TU 1424	6.7	W 1542	7.1
2119	3.2	☽ 2245	2.5

DECEMBER

Time	m		Time	m
1 0434	7.0	**16** 0337	6.6
1125	2.9	1018	3.3
TH 1658	6.9	F 1550	6.6
		☾ 2249	3.1
2 0000	2.5	**17** 0444	6.6
0548	7.0	1120	3.3
F 1238	2.8	SA 1701	6.5
1810	7.0	2352	3.0
3 0109	2.5	**18** 0554	6.7
0654	7.1	1234	3.2
SA 1344	2.6	SU 1813	6.7
1915	7.1		
4 0212	2.3	**19** 0057	2.9
0752	7.3	0655	6.9
SU 1446	2.3	M 1334	2.9
2012	7.3	1916	6.9
5 0310	2.1	**20** 0207	2.6
0840	7.5	0751	7.2
M 1541	2.1	TU 1442	2.5
2101	7.5	2015	7.2
6 0359	2.0	**21** 0311	2.2
0923	7.6	0843	7.5
TU 1627	1.9	W 1543	2.1
2144	7.6	2108	7.5
7 0442	1.9	**22** 0408	1.9
1002	7.7	0932	7.7
W 1707	1.8	TH 1637	1.7
2224	7.6	2200	7.7
8 0519	1.9	**23** 0500	1.6
1037	7.7	1020	7.9
TH 1743	1.8	F 1729	1.4
○ 2302	7.6	● 2249	7.9
9 0555	1.9	**24** 0551	1.5
1111	7.7	1108	8.0
F 1818	1.8	SA 1819	1.2
2337	7.6	2339	8.0
10 0629	2.0	**25** 0641	1.4
1144	7.7	1156	8.1
SA 1851	1.8	SU 1910	1.1
11 0012	7.5	**26** 0028	8.0
0702	2.2	0732	1.5
SU 1217	7.6	M 1245	8.1
1924	2.0	2000	1.2
12 0047	7.3	**27** 0119	7.9
0734	2.4	0822	1.6
M 1251	7.4	TU 1335	7.9
1956	2.2	2050	1.4
13 0122	7.2	**28** 0210	7.7
0806	2.6	0912	1.9
TU 1326	7.2	W 1426	7.7
2029	2.5	2140	1.7
14 0159	7.0	**29** 0303	7.5
0842	2.9	1003	2.2
W 1405	7.0	TH 1521	7.4
2106	2.7	2229	2.0
15 0243	6.8	**30** 0400	7.2
0924	3.1	1055	2.5
TH 1452	6.8	F 1620	7.1
2152	2.9	☽ 2321	2.3
		31 0501	7.0
		1152	2.7
		SA 1724	6.9

Chart Datum: 4·38 metres below IGN Datum
HAT is 8·4 metres above Chart Datum

TIDES

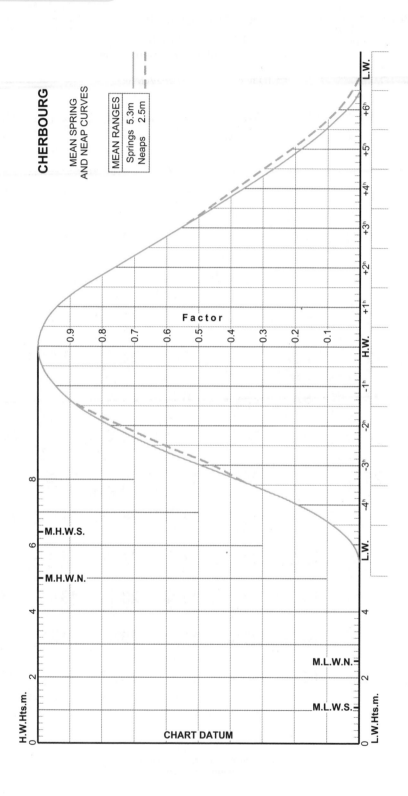

CHERBOURG

MEAN SPRING
AND NEAP CURVES

MEAN RANGES	
Springs	5.3m
Neaps	2.5m

Factor

TIME ZONE -0100
(French Standard Time)
Subtract 1 hour for UT
For French Summer Time add ONE hour in **non-shaded areas**

FRANCE – CHERBOURG

LAT 49°39'N   LONG 1°38'W

TIMES AND HEIGHTS OF HIGH AND LOW WATERS

Dates in amber are SPRINGS
Dates in grey are NEAPS

2022

JANUARY

Day	Time	m	Time	m	Time	m	Time	m
1 SA	0135	1.6	0716	6.2	1406	1.6	1945	6.2
16 SU	0217	2.2	0755	5.7	1446	1.9	2023	5.7
2 SU ●	0231	1.4	0808	6.4	1502	1.2	2040	6.4
17 M	0257	2.0	0833	5.9	1524	1.7	2100	5.8
3 M	0325	1.3	0859	6.6	1555	1.0	2133	6.5
18 TU ○	0334	1.9	0908	6.0	1600	1.6	2135	5.9
4 TU	0417	1.2	0949	6.7	1645	0.9	2224	6.4
19 W	0410	1.8	0942	6.1	1636	1.5	2209	6.0
5 W	0506	1.3	1038	6.6	1734	0.9	2312	6.3
20 TH	0446	1.7	1016	6.2	1711	1.4	2243	6.0
6 TH	0553	1.5	1125	6.5	1820	1.1	2358	6.1
21 F	0521	1.7	1051	6.2	1747	1.5	2320	5.9
7 F	0638	1.7	1210	6.3	1904	1.4		
22 SA	0557	1.7	1128	6.1	1822	1.5	2357	5.8
8 SA	0042	5.8	0723	1.9	1254	5.8	1947	1.8
23 SU	0634	1.8	1206	6.0	1900	1.7		
9 SU ☽	0126	5.5	0809	2.3	1341	5.6	2033	2.1
24 M	0036	5.7	0715	2.0	1246	5.8	1942	1.9
10 M	0213	5.3	0900	2.5	1432	5.3	2124	2.4
25 TU ☽	0118	5.5	0803	2.2	1331	5.5	2032	2.1
11 TU	0309	5.1	1001	2.7	1534	5.0	2227	2.6
26 W	0209	5.3	0901	2.4	1429	5.3	2134	2.3
12 W	0416	5.0	1112	2.6	1647	5.0	2336	2.6
27 TH	0318	5.2	1013	2.5	1549	5.2	2253	2.4
13 TH	0526	5.1	1219	2.6	1758	5.0		
28 F	0446	5.3	1135	2.4	1723	5.3		
14 F	0039	2.5	0625	5.3	1316	2.4	1855	5.2
29 SA	0013	2.2	0602	5.5	1251	2.0	1838	5.5
15 SA	0132	2.4	0713	5.5	1404	2.2	1942	5.5
30 SU	0124	2.0	0705	5.9	1357	1.6	1941	5.9
31 M	0226	1.6	0802	6.2	1457	1.2	2038	6.2

FEBRUARY

Day	Time	m	Time	m	Time	m	Time	m
1 TU ●	0322	1.4	0854	6.5	1550	0.9	2129	6.4
16 W ○	0321	1.8	0854	6.0	1545	1.4	2120	6.0
2 W	0411	1.2	0943	6.7	1637	0.8	2215	6.5
17 TH	0357	1.5	0928	6.2	1620	1.1	2154	6.1
3 TH	0456	1.1	1027	6.7	1720	0.8	2257	6.4
18 F	0431	1.4	1002	6.4	1654	1.1	2227	6.2
4 F	0537	1.1	1108	6.6	1800	0.9	2335	6.3
19 SA	0506	1.3	1036	6.4	1728	1.1	2301	6.1
5 SA	0615	1.3	1146	6.4	1836	1.2		
20 SU	0540	1.3	1111	6.4	1802	1.1	2336	6.1
6 SU	0010	6.0	0651	1.6	1222	6.1	1910	1.6
21 M	0615	1.4	1146	6.2	1837	1.3		
7 M	0043	5.7	0724	2.0	1256	5.7	1944	2.0
22 TU	0010	6.0	0652	1.6	1223	6.0	1915	1.6
8 TU ☽	0117	5.4	0804	2.4	1335	5.3	2023	2.4
23 W	0047	5.7	0735	1.9	1304	5.6	2001	2.0
9 W	0158	5.1	0851	2.7	1423	4.9	2114	2.8
24 TH	0133	5.4	0829	2.3	1359	5.2	2101	2.4
10 TH	0257	4.8	1000	2.9	1543	4.6	2232	3.0
25 F	0239	5.1	0943	2.5	1527	4.9	2228	2.7
11 F	0427	4.7	1133	2.9	1727	4.6		
26 SA	0426	5.0	1119	2.5	1721	5.0		
12 SA	0002	2.9	0555	4.9	1248	2.7	1837	4.9
27 SU	0005	2.5	0554	5.3	1246	2.1	1840	5.3
13 SU	0110	2.7	0653	5.2	1344	2.3	1926	5.2
28 M	0123	2.1	0701	5.7	1355	1.7	1943	5.8
14 M	0201	2.4	0738	5.5	1430	2.0	2008	5.5
15 TU	0244	2.0	0817	5.8	1509	1.7	2045	5.8

MARCH

Day	Time	m	Time	m	Time	m	Time	m
1 TU	0224	1.7	0758	6.1	1452	1.2	2034	6.1
16 W	0220	2.0	0753	5.7	1443	1.6	2020	5.9
2 W	0315	1.3	0846	6.4	1539	0.9	2118	6.4
17 TH	0257	1.7	0830	6.1	1519	1.3	2056	6.1
3 TH	0359	1.1	0929	6.6	1621	0.7	2157	6.5
18 F ○	0333	1.4	0906	6.3	1555	1.0	2130	6.3
4 F	0438	1.0	1007	6.7	1658	0.7	2231	6.5
19 SA	0409	1.1	0941	6.5	1629	0.9	2204	6.4
5 SA	0513	1.0	1043	6.6	1731	0.9	2304	6.3
20 SU	0444	1.0	1015	6.6	1704	0.9	2238	6.5
6 SU	0546	1.2	1116	6.4	1802	1.1	2333	6.1
21 M	0519	1.0	1051	6.5	1739	1.0	2312	6.4
7 M	0616	1.5	1146	6.1	1831	1.5		
22 TU	0555	1.1	1127	6.3	1814	1.2	2347	6.1
8 TU	0001	5.8	0646	1.8	1215	5.7	1859	1.9
23 W	0633	1.4	1204	6.0	1853	1.6		
9 W	0028	5.5	0717	2.2	1245	5.3	1931	2.4
24 TH	0025	5.8	0716	1.8	1248	5.6	1940	2.1
10 TH ☽	0059	5.2	0756	2.6	1324	4.8	2013	2.8
25 F	0112	5.4	0812	2.2	1347	5.1	2044	2.6
11 F	0144	4.8	0852	2.9	1433	4.5	2123	3.2
26 SA	0223	5.0	0931	2.5	1531	4.8	2223	2.8
12 SA	0309	4.5	1035	3.1	1652	4.4	2321	3.2
27 SU	0417	4.9	1116	2.5	1724	4.9		
13 SU	0518	4.6	1215	2.9	1816	4.7		
28 M	0005	2.6	0547	5.2	1243	2.1	1839	5.3
14 M	0044	2.9	0627	4.9	1317	2.4	1904	5.1
29 TU	0118	2.1	0652	5.6	1346	1.6	1932	5.8
15 TU	0138	2.5	0713	5.3	1403	2.0	1943	5.5
30 W	0213	1.7	0743	6.0	1436	1.2	2016	6.1
31 TH	0258	1.3	0821	6.3	1518	1.0	2054	6.3

APRIL

Day	Time	m	Time	m	Time	m	Time	m
1 F ●	0337	1.1	0906	6.5	1555	0.9	2129	6.4
16 SA ○	0301	1.3	0835	6.3	1522	1.0	2100	6.4
2 SA	0412	1.1	0940	6.5	1628	0.9	2200	6.4
17 SU	0340	1.1	0913	6.5	1600	0.9	2136	6.5
3 SU	0444	1.1	1013	6.5	1658	1.1	2229	6.3
18 M	0419	0.9	0952	6.6	1638	0.9	2213	6.6
4 M	0514	1.2	1044	6.3	1727	1.3	2257	6.1
19 TU	0457	0.9	1030	6.5	1716	1.0	2250	6.5
5 TU	0542	1.5	1113	6.0	1754	1.6	2323	5.9
20 W	0537	1.0	1111	6.3	1755	1.3	2329	6.2
6 W	0610	1.8	1141	5.6	1821	2.0	2348	5.6
21 TH	0620	1.3	1153	6.0	1839	1.8		
7 TH	0642	2.1	1209	5.3	1852	2.4		
22 F	0012	5.9	0708	1.7	1243	5.5	1931	2.2
8 F	0017	5.3	0716	2.5	1246	4.9	1930	2.8
23 SA ☽	0105	5.5	0808	2.1	1350	5.1	2043	2.6
9 SA ☽	0057	4.9	0805	2.8	1346	4.5	2033	3.2
24 SU	0222	5.1	0930	2.4	1534	4.9	2222	2.8
10 SU	0208	4.5	0930	3.0	1551	4.4	2226	3.3
25 M	0404	5.0	1106	2.3	1710	5.0	2351	2.5
11 M	0414	4.5	1124	2.9	1735	4.7		
26 TU	0525	5.3	1222	2.0	1815	5.4		
12 TU	0001	3.0	0542	4.8	1233	2.5	1825	5.1
27 W	0055	2.1	0626	5.6	1320	1.7	1905	5.7
13 W	0058	2.5	0633	5.2	1322	2.1	1906	5.5
28 TH	0147	1.8	0716	5.9	1408	1.4	1946	6.0
14 TH	0142	2.1	0716	5.7	1404	1.6	1945	5.8
29 F	0230	1.5	0758	6.1	1448	1.3	2023	6.2
15 F	0222	1.6	0756	6.0	1444	1.3	2023	6.2
30 SA ●	0308	1.4	0836	6.2	1523	1.2	2056	6.2

Chart Datum: 3·33 metres below IGN Datum
HAT is 7·0 metres above Chart Datum

TIDES

391

TIDES

TIME ZONE -0100
(French Standard Time)
Subtract 1 hour for UT
For French Summer Time add
ONE hour in **non-shaded areas**

FRANCE – CHERBOURG
LAT 49°39'N   LONG 1°38'W
TIMES AND HEIGHTS OF HIGH AND LOW WATERS

Dates in amber are **SPRINGS**
Dates in grey are **NEAPS**

2022

MAY

Day	Time	m	Day	Time	m
1 SU	0342	1.3	16 M	0310	1.1
	0911	6.2		0845	6.4
	1555	1.3		1532	1.0
	2126	6.2		○ 2108	6.5
2 M	0414	1.3	17 TU	0355	1.0
	0943	6.2		0930	6.5
	1625	1.4		1615	1.0
	2156	6.2		2150	6.6
3 TU	0444	1.4	18 W	0440	0.9
	1015	6.0		1015	6.4
	1654	1.6		1659	1.2
	2224	6.1		2233	6.5
4 W	0513	1.6	19 TH	0525	1.0
	1045	5.8		1101	6.2
	1723	1.8		1745	1.4
	2252	5.9		2318	6.3
5 TH	0544	1.8	20 F	0614	1.3
	1115	5.6		1150	5.9
	1753	2.1		1835	1.8
	2321	5.6			
6 F	0616	2.1	21 SA	0007	6.0
	1148	5.3		0707	1.6
	1825	2.4		1245	5.6
	2354	5.4		1931	2.2
7 SA	0652	2.4	22 SU	0104	5.6
	1227	5.0		0807	1.9
	1906	2.8		1352	5.2
				☽ 2042	2.5
8 SU	0036	5.0	23 M	0215	5.3
	0739	2.6		0919	2.1
	1323	4.7		1513	5.1
	2005	3.0		2201	2.5
9 M	0137	4.8	24 TU	0334	5.2
	0848	2.8		1037	2.2
	☽ 1450	4.6		1630	5.1
	☾ 2130	3.1		2316	2.4
10 TU	0308	4.7	25 W	0446	5.3
	1019	2.8		1145	2.1
	1626	4.7		1734	5.3
	2259	2.9			
11 W	0436	4.8	26 TH	0018	2.2
	1133	2.5		0547	5.5
	1730	5.1		1241	1.9
				1825	5.6
12 TH	0003	2.6	27 F	0110	2.0
	0539	5.2		0639	5.6
	1230	2.1		1330	1.8
	1819	5.4		1909	5.8
13 F	0055	2.1	28 SA	0156	1.8
	0629	5.6		0726	5.8
	1318	1.7		1412	1.7
	1902	5.8		1948	5.9
14 SA	0141	1.7	29 SU	0236	1.7
	0716	5.9		0807	5.9
	1404	1.4		1449	1.6
	1945	6.1		2024	6.0
15 SU	0226	1.4	30 M	0312	1.6
	0800	6.2		0844	5.9
	1448	1.1		1524	1.7
	2026	6.4		● 2057	6.0
			31 TU	0347	1.6
				0919	5.9
				1557	1.7
				2129	6.0

JUNE

Day	Time	m	Day	Time	m
1 W	0420	1.6	16 TH	0428	1.0
	0953	5.8		1006	6.3
	1629	1.8		1650	1.3
	2200	6.0		2224	6.5
2 TH	0452	1.7	17 F	0519	1.0
	1025	5.7		1058	6.2
	1702	2.0		1741	1.4
	2231	5.9		2313	6.4
3 F	0526	1.8	18 SA	0610	1.1
	1059	5.6		1149	6.0
	1735	2.1		1833	1.7
	2304	5.7			
4 SA	0559	2.0	19 SU	0004	6.2
	1135	5.4		0702	1.3
	1810	2.3		1242	5.8
	2341	5.5		1926	1.9
5 SU	0638	2.2	20 M	0057	5.9
	1216	5.2		0755	1.6
	1851	2.5		1336	5.5
				2023	2.2
6 M	0024	5.3	21 TU	0153	5.6
	0722	2.3		0851	1.9
	1304	5.0		1434	5.3
	1943	2.7		☽ 2123	2.4
7 TU	0115	5.1	22 W	0252	5.4
	0816	2.5		0951	2.1
	1404	4.9		1536	5.2
	☽ 2046	2.8		2228	2.4
8 W	0219	5.0	23 TH	0356	5.2
	0920	2.5		1054	2.2
	1514	4.9		1639	5.2
	2156	2.7		2331	2.4
9 TH	0328	5.0	24 F	0500	5.2
	1030	2.4		1154	2.3
	1623	5.1		1739	5.3
	2304	2.5			
10 F	0436	5.2	25 SA	0029	2.3
	1135	2.2		0601	5.3
	1724	5.4		1248	2.2
				1832	5.4
11 SA	0005	2.2	26 SU	0121	2.2
	0539	5.5		0655	5.4
	1233	1.9		1337	2.1
	1818	5.7		1918	5.6
12 SU	0101	1.9	27 M	0207	2.0
	0636	5.8		0742	5.5
	1327	1.6		1420	2.0
	1908	6.0		1958	5.7
13 M	0154	1.5	28 TU	0248	1.9
	0730	6.1		0824	5.6
	1418	1.4		1500	2.0
	1957	6.3		2036	5.8
14 TU	0246	1.3	29 W	0326	1.8
	0823	6.2		0903	5.7
	1509	1.3		1537	1.9
	○ 2046	6.4		2111	5.9
15 W	0337	1.1	30 TH	0402	1.7
	0915	6.3		0938	5.7
	1600	1.2		1613	1.9
	2135	6.5		2144	5.9

JULY

Day	Time	m	Day	Time	m
1 F	0438	1.7	16 SA	0513	0.8
	1012	5.7		1052	6.3
	1648	2.0		1734	1.3
	2217	5.9		2306	6.6
2 SA	0512	1.7	17 SU	0600	0.9
	1046	5.7		1140	6.2
	1722	2.0		1821	1.4
	2252	5.9		2352	6.4
3 SU	0548	1.8	18 M	0646	1.1
	1122	5.6		1224	6.0
	1758	2.1		1905	1.6
	2329	5.8			
4 M	0623	1.9	19 TU	0036	6.1
	1200	5.5		0729	1.4
	1836	2.2		1306	5.7
				1950	1.9
5 TU	0008	5.6	20 W	0119	5.8
	0701	2.0		0812	1.8
	1241	5.4		1348	5.5
	1918	2.3		☽ 2037	2.3
6 W	0051	5.5	21 TH	0205	5.4
	0745	2.1		0858	2.2
	1326	5.3		1436	5.2
	2007	2.4		2131	2.5
7 TH	0138	5.3	22 F	0300	5.1
	0835	2.2		0953	2.5
	1417	5.2		1536	5.0
	☽ 2105	2.5		2238	2.7
8 F	0233	5.2	23 SA	0408	4.9
	0935	2.3		1101	2.7
	1518	5.2		1649	5.0
	2211	2.5		2348	2.6
9 SA	0339	5.2	24 SU	0526	4.9
	1044	2.3		1210	2.6
	1629	5.3		1759	5.1
	2322	2.3			
10 SU	0454	5.3	25 M	0051	2.5
	1154	2.2		0633	5.1
	1740	5.5		1310	2.5
				1854	5.3
11 M	0029	2.1	26 TU	0145	2.3
	0607	5.5		0726	5.3
	1259	1.9		1401	2.3
	1842	5.8		1940	5.5
12 TU	0131	1.7	27 W	0231	2.0
	0712	5.8		0810	5.5
	1359	1.7		1444	2.2
	1939	6.1		2020	5.7
13 W	0230	1.4	28 TH	0311	1.8
	0811	6.0		0849	5.7
	1457	1.5		1523	2.0
	○ 2033	6.4		● 2057	5.9
14 TH	0327	1.1	29 F	0348	1.7
	0908	6.2		0924	5.8
	1553	1.3		1559	1.9
	2126	6.5		2131	6.0
15 F	0422	0.9	30 SA	0423	1.6
	1002	6.3		0958	5.9
	1645	1.2		1634	1.8
	2217	6.6		2203	6.1
			31 SU	0457	1.5
				1030	5.9
				1707	1.7
				2237	6.1

AUGUST

Day	Time	m	Day	Time	m
1 M	0530	1.5	16 TU	0618	1.0
	1104	5.9		1153	6.2
	1741	1.8		1834	1.5
	2312	6.1			
2 TU	0603	1.5	17 W	0005	6.3
	1138	5.8		0653	1.4
	1815	1.8		1227	5.9
	2347	6.0		1910	1.8
3 W	0637	1.6	18 TH	0040	5.9
	1214	5.7		0727	1.8
	1851	2.0		1300	5.6
				1947	2.0
4 TH	0023	5.8	19 F	0117	5.4
	0714	1.8		0804	2.3
	1250	5.6		1338	5.2
	1933	2.1		☽ 2033	2.6
5 F	0103	5.6	20 SA	0203	5.0
	0757	2.1		0851	2.7
	1333	5.4		1430	4.9
	☽ 2023	2.4		2136	2.9
6 SA	0151	5.4	21 SU	0313	4.7
	0850	2.3		1003	3.0
	1428	5.2		1553	4.7
	2128	2.5		2308	3.0
7 SU	0256	5.2	22 M	0457	4.6
	1001	2.5		1137	3.0
	1546	5.2		1732	4.8
	2249	2.5			
8 M	0428	5.1	23 TU	0027	2.8
	1128	2.5		0619	4.9
	1719	5.3		1251	2.8
				1836	5.1
9 TU	0010	2.3	24 W	0126	2.3
	0559	5.3		0712	5.2
	1246	2.2		1345	2.5
	1831	5.6		1923	5.5
10 W	0121	1.9	25 TH	0213	2.1
	0708	5.7		0753	5.5
	1353	1.9		1429	2.2
	1931	6.0		2002	5.8
11 TH	0224	1.4	26 F	0253	1.8
	0808	6.0		0830	5.8
	1453	1.5		1506	1.9
	2026	6.4		2038	6.0
12 F	0321	1.1	27 SA	0328	1.6
	0903	6.3		0904	6.0
	1546	1.3		1540	1.7
	○ 2118	6.6		● 2112	6.2
13 SA	0413	0.8	28 SU	0402	1.4
	0952	6.5		0936	6.1
	1634	1.1		1613	1.6
	2205	6.8		2144	6.3
14 SU	0458	0.7	29 M	0434	1.3
	1036	6.5		1008	6.2
	1717	1.1		1646	1.5
	2248	6.8		2216	6.4
15 M	0540	0.8	30 TU	0506	1.2
	1116	6.4		1039	6.2
	1757	1.2		1718	1.5
	2328	6.6		2249	6.4
			31 W	0538	1.3
				1112	6.2
				1750	1.5
				2322	6.3

Chart Datum: 3·33 metres below IGN Datum
HAT is 7·0 metres above Chart Datum

TIME ZONE -0100
(French Standard Time)
Subtract 1 hour for UT
For French Summer Time add
ONE hour in **non-shaded areas**

FRANCE – CHERBOURG

LAT 49°39′N   LONG 1°38′W

TIMES AND HEIGHTS OF HIGH AND LOW WATERS

Dates in amber are **SPRINGS**
Dates in grey are **NEAPS**

2022

SEPTEMBER

	Time m		Time m
1	0610 1.5 / 1145 6.0 / TH 1825 1.7 / 2356 6.0	**16**	0001 5.9 / 0643 2.0 / F 1214 5.7 / 1901 2.2
2	0644 1.7 / 1219 5.8 / F 1904 2.0	**17**	0033 5.4 / 0715 2.5 / SA 1246 5.3 / ◑ 1942 2.7
3	0034 5.7 / 0711 2.1 / SA 1259 5.5 / ◐ 1952 2.3	**18**	0113 5.0 / 0756 2.9 / SU 1330 4.9 / 2036 3.0
4	0122 5.4 / 0817 2.5 / SU 1355 5.2 / 2058 2.6	**19**	0220 4.6 / 0904 3.3 / M 1453 4.6 / 2222 3.2
5	0234 5.0 / 0936 2.8 / M 1526 5.0 / 2233 2.7	**20**	0430 4.5 / 1105 3.3 / TU 1701 4.7
6	0431 4.9 / 1120 2.8 / TU 1715 5.2	**21**	0000 2.9 / 0600 4.8 / W 1229 3.0 / 1812 5.0
7	0006 2.4 / 0603 5.3 / W 1245 2.4 / 1827 5.6	**22**	0100 2.5 / 0647 5.2 / TH 1322 2.6 / 1857 5.4
8	0119 1.9 / 0708 5.7 / TH 1350 1.9 / 1926 6.1	**23**	0145 2.1 / 0725 5.6 / F 1403 2.2 / 1935 5.8
9	0218 1.4 / 0802 6.1 / F 1445 1.5 / 2017 6.5	**24**	0223 1.8 / 0801 5.9 / SA 1439 1.9 / 2011 6.1
10	0309 1.0 / 0850 6.4 / SA 1532 1.2 / ○ 2102 6.8	**25**	0258 1.5 / 0835 6.2 / SU 1512 1.6 / ● 2045 6.4
11	0354 0.8 / 0932 6.6 / SU 1614 1.0 / 2144 6.9	**26**	0332 1.3 / 0908 6.3 / M 1546 1.4 / 2118 6.5
12	0435 0.7 / 1010 -6.6 / M 1652 1.0 / 2222 6.8	**27**	0405 1.1 / 0940 6.4 / TU 1619 1.3 / 2151 6.6
13	0511 0.9 / 1044 6.5 / TU 1727 1.2 / 2257 6.6	**28**	0438 1.1 / 1011 6.5 / W 1653 1.3 / 2224 6.6
14	0543 1.1 / 1116 6.3 / W 1759 1.5 / 2330 6.3	**29**	0511 1.2 / 1044 6.4 / TH 1727 1.4 / 2258 6.4
15	0614 1.5 / 1145 6.0 / TH 1829 1.8	**30**	0545 1.4 / 1118 6.2 / F 1803 1.6 / 2335 6.1

OCTOBER

	Time m		Time m
1	0621 1.8 / 1155 6.0 / SA 1844 1.9	**16**	0637 2.6 / 1205 5.4 / SU 1904 2.6
2	0017 5.7 / 0704 2.2 / SU 1239 5.6 / 1935 2.3	**17**	0036 5.0 / 0716 3.0 / M 1245 5.0 / ◑ 1953 3.0
3	0111 5.3 / 0801 2.7 / M 1342 5.2 / ◐ 2048 2.6	**18**	0139 4.6 / 0818 3.3 / TU 1359 4.7 / 2121 3.2
4	0237 4.9 / 0933 3.0 / TU 1528 5.0 / 2231 2.7	**19**	0338 4.5 / 1012 3.4 / W 1602 4.6 / 2312 3.0
5	0440 5.0 / 1123 2.8 / W 1710 5.3	**20**	0517 4.8 / 1147 3.1 / TH 1728 4.9
6	0004 2.3 / 0601 5.4 / TH 1241 2.3 / 1818 5.7	**21**	0018 2.7 / 0607 5.2 / F 1242 2.7 / 1817 5.3
7	0110 1.8 / 0657 5.8 / F 1339 1.9 / 1911 6.2	**22**	0105 2.2 / 0647 5.6 / SA 1324 2.3 / 1858 5.7
8	0203 1.4 / 0744 6.2 / SA 1427 1.5 / 1958 6.6	**23**	0144 1.9 / 0723 6.0 / SU 1402 1.9 / 1936 6.1
9	0248 1.1 / 0826 6.5 / SU 1510 1.2 / ○ 2039 6.7	**24**	0221 1.5 / 0759 6.2 / M 1438 1.6 / 2012 6.4
10	0328 0.9 / 0903 6.6 / M 1548 1.1 / 2117 6.8	**25**	0258 1.3 / 0834 6.5 / TU 1515 1.3 / ● 2048 6.6
11	0404 1.0 / 0937 6.6 / TU 1623 1.2 / 2152 6.7	**26**	0334 1.2 / 0909 6.6 / W 1552 1.2 / 2125 6.6
12	0437 1.1 / 1008 6.5 / W 1655 1.3 / 2225 6.5	**27**	0410 1.1 / 0944 6.6 / TH 1630 1.2 / 2202 6.6
13	0508 1.4 / 1038 6.3 / TH 1725 1.5 / 2256 6.2	**28**	0448 1.2 / 1020 6.5 / F 1708 1.3 / 2241 6.4
14	0537 1.7 / 1107 6.1 / F 1756 1.9 / 2327 5.8	**29**	0525 1.5 / 1059 6.4 / SA 1749 1.5 / 2323 6.1
15	0605 2.1 / 1134 5.8 / SA 1827 2.2 / 2358 5.4	**30**	0608 1.9 / 1142 6.1 / SU 1836 1.8
		31	0012 5.7 / 0657 2.3 / M 1233 5.6 / 1933 2.2

NOVEMBER

	Time m		Time m
1	0113 5.3 / 0801 2.7 / TU 1342 5.3 / ◐ 2049 2.5	**16**	0111 4.9 / 0748 3.1 / W 1322 4.9 / ◑ 2031 3.0
2	0247 5.1 / 0936 2.9 / W 1522 5.2 / 2225 2.5	**17**	0233 4.7 / 0907 3.3 / TH 1450 4.8 / 2157 3.0
3	0428 5.2 / 1111 2.7 / TH 1649 5.4 / 2346 2.2	**18**	0403 4.8 / 1036 3.1 / F 1615 4.9 / 2314 2.7
4	0538 5.5 / 1221 2.3 / F 1753 5.7	**19**	0509 5.1 / 1144 2.8 / SA 1720 5.2
5	0047 1.8 / 0631 5.8 / SA 1315 1.9 / 1846 6.1	**20**	0010 2.4 / 0558 5.5 / SU 1235 2.4 / 1810 5.6
6	0137 1.5 / 0716 6.1 / SU 1402 1.6 / 1931 6.3	**21**	0057 2.0 / 0640 5.8 / M 1320 2.0 / 1855 5.9
7	0220 1.3 / 0756 6.3 / M 1443 1.4 / 2012 6.4	**22**	0141 1.7 / 0721 6.2 / TU 1403 1.7 / 1938 6.2
8	0258 1.3 / 0832 6.4 / TU 1520 1.4 / ○ 2050 6.5	**23**	0223 1.4 / 0801 6.4 / W 1446 1.4 / ● 2020 6.4
9	0333 1.3 / 0905 6.4 / W 1554 1.4 / 2124 6.4	**24**	0305 1.3 / 0841 6.6 / TH 1529 1.2 / 2103 6.5
10	0406 1.5 / 0936 6.4 / TH 1627 1.5 / 2158 6.2	**25**	0348 1.3 / 0922 6.6 / F 1613 1.1 / 2147 6.5
11	0437 1.6 / 1007 6.3 / F 1659 1.6 / 2230 6.0	**26**	0431 1.3 / 1004 6.6 / SA 1658 1.2 / 2233 6.4
12	0508 1.9 / 1037 6.1 / SA 1731 1.9 / 2303 5.8	**27**	0517 1.5 / 1049 6.5 / SU 1745 1.4 / 2321 6.1
13	0539 2.2 / 1108 5.8 / SU 1803 2.2 / 2337 5.5	**28**	0605 1.8 / 1138 6.2 / M 1837 1.6
14	0613 2.6 / 1141 5.5 / M 1841 2.5	**29**	0014 5.8 / 0700 2.2 / TU 1233 5.9 / 1935 1.8
15	0016 5.1 / 0653 2.9 / TU 1222 5.2 / 1927 2.8	**30**	0117 5.5 / 0803 2.5 / W 1339 5.6 / ◐ 2042 2.1

DECEMBER

	Time m		Time m
1	0234 5.3 / 0919 2.6 / TH 1457 5.4 / 2157 2.2	**16**	0140 5.0 / 0817 2.9 / F 1352 5.1 / 2051 2.6
2	0351 5.3 / 1038 2.6 / F 1611 5.4 / 2310 2.2	**17**	0244 5.0 / 0922 2.9 / SA 1458 5.0 / 2158 2.6
3	0459 5.4 / 1145 2.4 / SA 1716 5.6	**18**	0352 5.1 / 1032 2.8 / SU 1607 5.1 / 2306 2.5
4	0011 2.0 / 0555 5.6 / SU 1243 2.1 / 1813 5.8	**19**	0457 5.3 / 1138 2.5 / M 1714 5.3
5	0104 1.9 / 0643 5.9 / M 1332 1.9 / 1903 5.9	**20**	0007 2.2 / 0554 5.6 / TU 1237 2.2 / 1813 5.6
6	0149 1.8 / 0726 6.0 / TU 1416 1.8 / 1947 6.0	**21**	0103 1.9 / 0645 5.9 / W 1331 1.9 / 1908 5.9
7	0230 1.7 / 0805 6.1 / W 1455 1.7 / 2028 6.1	**22**	0154 1.7 / 0734 6.2 / TH 1422 1.5 / 2000 6.2
8	0307 1.7 / 0840 6.2 / TH 1532 1.6 / ○ 2105 6.1	**23**	0245 1.5 / 0822 6.4 / F 1513 1.3 / ● 2051 6.4
9	0342 1.8 / 0914 6.2 / F 1607 1.6 / 2140 6.0	**24**	0335 1.4 / 0909 6.6 / SA 1604 1.1 / 2141 6.4
10	0416 1.8 / 0947 6.2 / SA 1641 1.7 / 2214 5.9	**25**	0425 1.3 / 0958 6.7 / SU 1654 1.0 / 2232 6.4
11	0450 2.0 / 1020 6.1 / SU 1714 1.8 / 2249 5.8	**26**	0515 1.4 / 1047 6.6 / M 1744 1.0 / 2322 6.3
12	0524 2.2 / 1053 5.9 / M 1750 2.0 / 2324 5.6	**27**	0605 1.5 / 1138 6.5 / TU 1835 1.2
13	0559 2.4 / 1128 5.7 / TU 1826 2.2	**28**	0014 6.1 / 0656 1.8 / W 1229 6.2 / 1926 1.5
14	0002 5.4 / 0637 2.6 / W 1208 5.5 / 1907 2.4	**29**	0106 5.8 / 0749 2.0 / TH 1322 5.9 / 2019 1.8
15	0046 5.2 / 0723 2.7 / TH 1254 5.3 / 1954 2.5	**30**	0201 5.5 / 0846 2.3 / F 1419 5.6 / 2116 2.1
		31	0301 5.3 / 0949 2.4 / SA 1522 5.4 / 2219 2.3

Chart Datum: 3·33 metres below IGN Datum
HAT is 7·0 metres above Chart Datum

TIDES

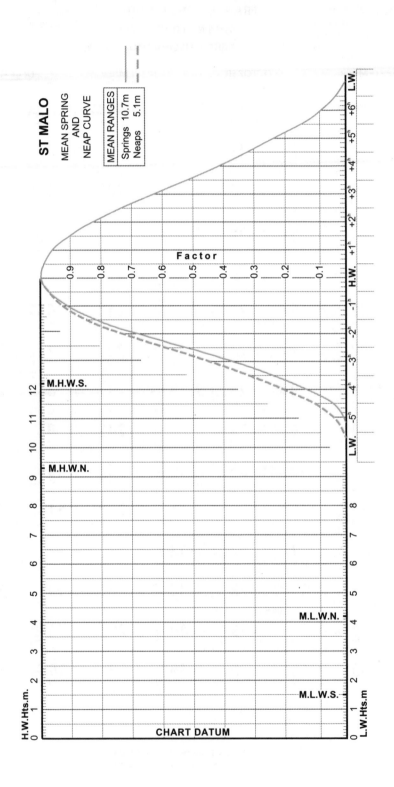

ST MALO

MEAN SPRING
AND
NEAP CURVE

MEAN RANGES	
Springs	10.7m
Neaps	5.1m

TIME ZONE -0100
(French Standard Time)
Subtract 1 hour for UT
For French Summer Time add
ONE hour in **non-shaded** areas

FRANCE – ST MALO
LAT 48°38'N   LONG 2°02'W
TIMES AND HEIGHTS OF HIGH AND LOW WATERS

Dates in amber are **SPRINGS**
Dates in grey are **NEAPS**

2022

JANUARY

Time	m	Time	m
1 0529 11.3 / 1223 2.2 / SA 1757 11.5		**16** 0028 3.4 / 0606 10.5 / SU 1256 3.2 / 1833 10.5	
2 0052 2.0 / 0624 11.9 / SU 1322 1.6 / ● 1852 11.9		**17** 0112 3.0 / 0645 10.9 / M 1337 2.8 / 1911 10.8	
3 0148 1.7 / 0716 12.3 / M 1417 1.3 / 1945 12.2		**18** 0151 2.7 / 0722 11.2 / TU 1416 2.5 / ○ 1948 11.0	
4 0241 1.5 / 0806 12.5 / TU 1509 1.2 / 2034 12.2		**19** 0229 2.5 / 0757 11.4 / W 1454 2.4 / 2022 11.2	
5 0329 1.5 / 0853 12.5 / W 1557 1.2 / 2120 12.0		**20** 0306 2.4 / 0832 11.6 / TH 1530 2.3 / 2057 11.3	
6 0414 1.8 / 0938 12.2 / TH 1641 1.6 / 2204 11.6		**21** 0342 2.3 / 0907 11.6 / F 1606 2.3 / 2132 11.2	
7 0457 2.2 / 1021 11.7 / F 1722 2.1 / 2246 11.0		**22** 0417 2.4 / 0942 11.5 / SA 1641 2.4 / 2207 11.0	
8 0537 2.8 / 1103 11.0 / SA 1802 2.8 / 2327 10.4		**23** 0453 2.6 / 1019 11.2 / SU 1717 2.7 / 2244 10.6	
9 0616 3.4 / 1146 10.3 / SU 1842 3.5 / ◑		**24** 0530 3.0 / 1057 10.7 / M 1754 3.1 / 2323 10.2	
10 0010 9.8 / 0659 4.0 / M 1236 9.6 / 1927 4.0		**25** 0611 3.4 / 1141 10.2 / TU 1838 3.5 / ◐	
11 0104 9.3 / 0751 4.5 / TU 1339 9.1 / 2023 4.4		**26** 0012 9.8 / 0703 3.8 / W 1238 9.8 / 1935 3.9	
12 0213 9.0 / 0859 4.7 / W 1455 9.0 / 2133 4.5		**27** 0119 9.5 / 0812 4.1 / TH 1355 9.5 / 2053 4.0	
13 0328 9.1 / 1013 4.5 / TH 1606 9.2 / 2241 4.2		**28** 0244 9.5 / 0938 3.9 / F 1524 9.6 / 2219 3.8	
14 0431 9.5 / 1117 4.1 / F 1703 9.6 / 2339 3.8		**29** 0408 9.9 / 1059 3.4 / SA 1645 10.1 / 2335 3.2	
15 0522 10.0 / 1210 3.6 / SA 1751 10.1		**30** 0520 10.7 / 1210 2.6 / SU 1752 10.9	
		31 0042 2.5 / 0619 11.4 / M 1314 1.9 / 1850 11.5	

FEBRUARY

Time	m	Time	m
1 0142 1.9 / 0712 12.1 / TU 1412 1.3 / ● 1940 12.0		**16** 0138 2.6 / 0708 11.3 / W 1404 2.3 / ○ 1933 11.3	
2 0235 1.4 / 0759 12.5 / W 1502 1.0 / 2025 12.3		**17** 0218 2.2 / 0744 11.7 / TH 1443 1.9 / 2008 11.6	
3 0321 1.2 / 0842 12.7 / TH 1546 0.9 / 2107 12.3		**18** 0256 1.8 / 0818 12.0 / F 1520 1.6 / 2042 11.8	
4 0402 1.3 / 0922 12.6 / F 1625 1.1 / 2144 12.0		**19** 0332 1.6 / 0853 12.2 / SA 1555 1.5 / 2116 11.9	
5 0438 1.7 / 0959 12.1 / SA 1659 1.7 / 2218 11.5		**20** 0406 1.6 / 0927 12.1 / SU 1628 1.7 / 2149 11.7	
6 0510 2.2 / 1033 11.4 / SU 1729 2.4 / 2250 10.9		**21** 0439 1.9 / 1001 11.8 / M 1659 2.0 / 2221 11.3	
7 0538 3.0 / 1105 10.6 / M 1756 3.2 / 2322 10.1		**22** 0511 2.4 / 1035 11.3 / TU 1732 2.6 / 2256 10.7	
8 0606 3.7 / 1140 9.8 / TU 1827 3.9 / ◑ 2358 9.4		**23** 0547 3.0 / 1114 10.5 / W 1809 3.3 / ◑ 2338 10.0	
9 0642 4.4 / 1224 9.0 / W 1910 4.6		**24** 0633 3.7 / 1204 9.8 / TH 1900 4.0	
10 0051 8.7 / 0739 5.0 / TH 1340 8.4 / 2021 5.1		**25** 0039 9.4 / 0740 4.2 / F 1324 9.1 / 2020 4.5	
11 0222 8.4 / 0915 5.2 / F 1527 8.3 / 2158 5.0		**26** 0219 9.0 / 0917 4.3 / SA 1515 9.0 / 2204 4.3	
12 0359 8.7 / 1047 4.8 / SA 1643 8.9 / 2314 4.5		**27** 0404 9.4 / 1051 3.7 / SU 1646 9.7 / 2331 3.6	
13 0502 9.3 / 1150 4.1 / SU 1735 9.5		**28** 0518 10.4 / 1207 2.8 / M 1751 10.6	
14 0010 3.8 / 0549 10.0 / M 1239 3.4 / 1818 10.2			
15 0056 3.2 / 0630 10.7 / TU 1323 2.8 / 1857 10.8			

MARCH

Time	m	Time	m
1 0041 2.6 / 0614 11.3 / TU 1309 1.9 / 1842 11.5		**16** 0032 3.2 / 0605 10.6 / W 1259 2.7 / 1832 10.9	
2 0136 1.8 / 0701 12.1 / W 1402 1.2 / ● 1927 12.1		**17** 0115 2.5 / 0644 11.4 / TH 1341 2.0 / 1909 11.5	
3 0225 1.3 / 0744 12.6 / TH 1447 0.9 / 2007 12.4		**18** 0156 1.9 / 0721 11.9 / F 1421 1.5 / ○ 1945 12.0	
4 0305 1.1 / 0823 12.8 / F 1526 0.8 / 2043 12.4		**19** 0236 1.4 / 0757 12.4 / SA 1459 1.2 / 2019 12.3	
5 0341 1.1 / 0858 12.6 / SA 1559 1.1 / 2116 12.2		**20** 0313 1.2 / 0832 12.6 / SU 1535 1.1 / 2053 12.4	
6 0411 1.5 / 0930 12.2 / SU 1627 1.6 / 2146 11.8		**21** 0348 1.2 / 0907 12.5 / M 1608 1.3 / 2126 12.2	
7 0437 2.0 / 0959 11.6 / M 1651 2.3 / 2212 11.1		**22** 0421 1.5 / 0941 12.1 / TU 1639 1.8 / 2159 11.7	
8 0500 2.7 / 1026 10.8 / TU 1712 3.1 / 2238 10.4		**23** 0454 2.0 / 1016 11.4 / W 1711 2.5 / 2234 11.0	
9 0520 3.5 / 1052 9.9 / W 1735 3.9 / 2305 9.6		**24** 0530 2.8 / 1055 10.6 / TH 1748 3.4 / 2317 10.1	
10 0546 4.3 / 1123 9.0 / TH 1808 4.7 / ◑ 2342 8.8		**25** 0615 3.6 / 1148 9.6 / F 1840 4.2 / ◑	
11 0629 5.0 / 1218 8.1 / F 1906 5.4		**26** 0021 9.2 / 0726 4.3 / SA 1317 8.8 / 2009 4.8	
12 0100 8.1 / 0756 5.5 / SA 1443 7.8 / 2107 5.6		**27** 0215 8.8 / 0911 4.4 / SU 1518 8.9 / 2203 4.5	
13 0319 8.1 / 1015 5.2 / SU 1619 8.4 / 2248 5.0		**28** 0359 9.4 / 1048 3.7 / M 1642 9.7 / 2328 3.6	
14 0435 8.9 / 1126 4.4 / M 1712 9.3 / 2346 4.1		**29** 0506 10.4 / 1158 2.7 / TU 1738 10.7	
15 0524 9.8 / 1215 3.5 / TU 1754 10.1		**30** 0028 2.6 / 0557 11.3 / W 1254 1.9 / 1823 11.5	
		31 0118 1.9 / 0640 12.0 / TH 1341 1.4 / 1903 12.0	

APRIL

Time	m	Time	m
1 0202 1.5 / 0720 12.4 / F 1422 1.2 / 1940 12.3		**16** 0125 1.8 / 0651 12.0 / SA 1350 1.5 / ○ 1915 12.2	
2 0239 1.3 / 0756 12.5 / SA 1456 1.2 / 2013 12.3		**17** 0208 1.3 / 0730 12.4 / SU 1431 1.1 / 1951 12.5	
3 0311 1.4 / 0829 12.3 / SU 1525 1.4 / 2044 12.1		**18** 0249 1.1 / 0808 12.6 / M 1510 1.0 / 2028 12.6	
4 0339 1.7 / 0859 12.0 / M 1551 1.8 / 2111 11.8		**19** 0327 1.1 / 0845 12.5 / TU 1546 1.3 / 2104 12.3	
5 0403 2.1 / 0926 11.4 / TU 1613 2.4 / 2136 11.2		**20** 0404 1.4 / 0923 12.1 / W 1621 1.8 / 2141 11.8	
6 0424 2.7 / 0951 10.7 / W 1634 3.1 / 2200 10.6		**21** 0440 2.0 / 1003 11.4 / TH 1657 2.6 / 2222 11.0	
7 0445 3.4 / 1016 9.9 / TH 1656 3.9 / 2226 9.8		**22** 0521 2.7 / 1049 10.4 / F 1739 3.5 / 2311 10.1	
8 0509 4.2 / 1044 9.1 / F 1726 4.7 / 2258 9.0		**23** 0612 3.6 / 1149 9.5 / SA 1838 4.3 / ◐	
9 0547 4.9 / 1129 8.3 / SA 1816 5.4 / ◐ 2359 8.2		**24** 0024 9.3 / 0726 4.2 / SU 1320 8.9 / 2009 4.7	
10 0656 5.4 / 1340 7.8 / SU 1959 5.7		**25** 0207 9.1 / 0903 4.2 / M 1503 9.1 / 2149 4.3	
11 0221 8.0 / 0915 5.4 / M 1533 8.2 / 2201 5.2		**26** 0337 9.6 / 1028 3.6 / TU 1618 9.8 / 2304 3.5	
12 0349 8.7 / 1041 4.6 / TU 1632 9.1 / 2304 4.3		**27** 0439 10.4 / 1132 2.8 / W 1710 10.6	
13 0444 9.6 / 1134 3.6 / W 1717 10.0 / 2353 3.3		**28** 0000 2.8 / 0528 11.1 / TH 1224 2.3 / 1754 11.2	
14 0529 10.5 / 1221 2.7 / TH 1757 10.9		**29** 0048 2.2 / 0611 11.6 / F 1309 1.9 / 1833 11.6	
15 0040 2.5 / 0611 11.3 / F 1306 2.0 / 1837 11.6		**30** 0130 2.0 / 0650 11.8 / SA 1347 1.8 / ● 1908 11.8	

TIDES

Chart Datum: 6·29 metres below IGN Datum
HAT is 13·6 metres above Chart Datum

TIDES

TIME ZONE -0100
(French Standard Time)
Subtract 1 hour for UT
For French Summer Time add
ONE hour in **non-shaded areas**

FRANCE – ST MALO
LAT 48°38'N   LONG 2°02'W
TIMES AND HEIGHTS OF HIGH AND LOW WATERS

Dates in amber are **SPRINGS**
Dates in grey are **NEAPS**

2022

MAY

Time	m		Time	m
1 0205	1.9		**16** 0137	1.5
0726	11.9		0700	12.2
SU 1420	1.8		M 1401	1.4
1941	11.9		○ 1923	12.4
2 0236	1.9		**17** 0223	1.2
0758	11.7		0744	12.4
M 1449	2.0		TU 1445	1.3
2011	11.8		2005	12.5
3 0305	2.1		**18** 0307	1.2
0828	11.5		0827	12.3
TU 1516	2.2		W 1527	1.5
2038	11.5		2047	12.3
4 0331	2.4		**19** 0350	1.4
0856	11.1		0912	11.9
W 1541	2.6		TH 1608	2.0
2105	11.1		2131	11.8
5 0356	2.8		**20** 0433	1.9
0924	10.6		0959	11.3
TH 1606	3.2		F 1651	2.6
2133	10.6		2219	11.2
6 0421	3.4		**21** 0520	2.6
0953	9.9		1050	10.5
F 1632	3.8		SA 1739	3.3
2202	10.0		2313	10.4
7 0449	4.0		**22** 0614	3.2
1026	9.3		1150	9.8
SA 1704	4.5		SU 1840	4.0
2239	9.3		◑	
8 0528	4.5		**23** 0020	9.8
1114	8.6		0720	3.7
SU 1753	5.0		M 1303	9.4
2336	8.7		1955	4.3
9 0628	5.0		**24** 0139	9.6
1241	8.2		0836	3.8
M 1911	5.3		TU 1425	9.3
◑			2114	4.1
10 0115	8.4		**25** 0257	9.7
0801	5.1		0948	3.6
TU 1424	8.4		W 1535	9.7
2051	5.1		2223	3.7
11 0245	8.8		**26** 0400	10.1
0934	4.5		1050	3.2
W 1534	9.1		TH 1631	10.2
2206	4.3		2320	3.2
12 0349	9.5		**27** 0452	10.5
1039	3.7		1145	2.6
TH 1628	9.9		F 1717	10.7
2304	3.5			
13 0442	10.3		**28** 0009	2.9
1134	2.9		0538	10.9
F 1714	10.7		SA 1229	2.7
2357	2.7		1759	11.0
14 0530	11.1		**29** 0052	2.7
1225	2.2		0619	11.0
SA 1758	11.5		SU 1309	2.6
			1836	11.2
15 0048	2.0		**30** 0129	2.6
0616	11.8		0657	11.1
SU 1315	1.7		M 1344	2.5
1841	12.0		● 1911	11.3
			31 0203	2.5
			0732	11.1
			TU 1416	2.5
			1943	11.3

JUNE

Time	m		Time	m
1 0235	2.5		**16** 0253	1.4
0804	11.0		0818	12.0
W 1447	2.6		TH 1515	1.7
2013	11.2		2038	12.3
2 0307	2.7		**17** 0343	1.4
0835	10.8		0907	11.9
TH 1518	2.9		F 1603	1.9
2044	11.0		2127	12.0
3 0337	2.9		**18** 0431	1.7
0907	10.5		0957	11.5
F 1548	3.2		SA 1650	2.3
2116	10.7		2216	11.6
4 0408	3.3		**19** 0519	2.1
0941	10.1		1046	11.0
SA 1619	3.6		SU 1738	2.8
2151	10.3		2306	11.0
5 0441	3.6		**20** 0608	2.7
1019	9.7		1136	10.4
SU 1655	4.0		M 1828	3.4
2231	9.8		2359	10.4
6 0521	4.0		**21** 0659	3.2
1104	9.3		1230	9.9
M 1741	4.4		TU 1923	3.8
2320	9.4		◑	
7 0611	4.3		**22** 0058	9.9
1202	8.9		0754	3.6
TU 1839	4.6		W 1331	9.5
◑			2023	4.0
8 0024	9.1		**23** 0204	9.7
0714	4.4		0854	3.8
W 1314	8.9		TH 1439	9.5
1950	4.6		2128	4.1
9 0138	9.2		**24** 0311	9.6
0827	4.3		0956	3.8
TH 1426	9.2		F 1543	9.7
2104	4.2		2231	3.9
10 0248	9.6		**25** 0412	9.8
0939	3.8		1055	3.7
F 1530	9.8		SA 1639	10.0
2212	3.7		2327	3.6
11 0350	10.1		**26** 0505	10.0
1045	3.2		1148	3.5
SA 1627	10.4		SU 1727	10.3
2314	3.0			
12 0448	10.8		**27** 0016	3.3
1145	2.6		0552	10.3
SU 1721	11.1		M 1234	3.2
			1810	10.6
13 0012	2.4		**28** 0059	3.1
0543	11.3		0635	10.5
M 1241	2.2		TU 1315	3.1
1811	11.7		1848	10.8
14 0108	1.9		**29** 0139	2.9
0636	11.7		0713	10.6
TU 1335	1.8		W 1353	2.9
○ 1901	12.1		1924	11.0
15 0202	1.5		**30** 0216	2.8
0727	12.0		0749	10.7
W 1426	1.7		TH 1429	2.9
1950	12.3		1958	11.1

JULY

Time	m		Time	m
1 0251	2.8		**16** 0337	1.2
0823	10.7		0901	12.1
F 1504	2.9		SA 1558	1.6
2031	11.1		2120	12.4
2 0326	2.8		**17** 0425	1.3
0857	10.7		0947	11.9
SA 1538	3.0		SU 1642	1.8
2106	11.0		2204	12.1
3 0400	2.9		**18** 0508	1.6
0932	10.6		1029	11.5
SU 1612	3.1		M 1723	2.3
2141	10.8		2246	11.6
4 0435	3.1		**19** 0547	2.2
1008	10.3		1109	10.9
M 1647	3.3		TU 1802	2.9
2219	10.5		2327	10.9
5 0511	3.3		**20** 0625	2.9
1046	10.0		1150	10.3
TU 1726	3.6		W 1841	3.5
2259	10.2		◑	
6 0551	3.6		**21** 0011	10.1
1128	9.7		0704	3.6
W 1810	3.9		TH 1235	9.7
2345	9.9		1926	4.1
7 0638	3.8		**22** 0105	9.5
1219	9.5		0753	4.2
TH 1903	4.1		F 1333	9.2
◑			2026	4.5
8 0042	9.6		**23** 0214	9.1
0734	4.0		0856	4.5
F 1322	9.4		SA 1449	9.0
2009	4.1		2140	4.6
9 0151	9.6		**24** 0332	9.0
0844	3.9		1009	4.5
SA 1434	9.6		SU 1603	9.2
2125	3.9		2252	4.3
10 0304	9.8		**25** 0440	9.3
1000	3.7		1116	4.2
SU 1546	10.0		M 1703	9.7
2238	3.4		2351	3.9
11 0415	10.2		**26** 0534	9.7
1112	3.2		1210	3.7
M 1652	10.6		TU 1752	10.2
2345	2.8			
12 0521	10.8		**27** 0040	3.4
1217	2.7		0619	10.2
TU 1754	11.2		W 1257	3.4
			1833	10.6
13 0048	2.2		**28** 0123	3.1
0623	11.3		0659	10.5
W 1318	2.2		TH 1338	3.0
○ 1850	11.8		● 1911	11.0
14 0149	1.7		**29** 0203	2.8
0720	11.8		0736	10.8
TH 1416	1.8		F 1417	2.8
1943	12.2		1945	11.2
15 0246	1.3		**30** 0240	2.6
0813	12.0		0810	11.0
F 1509	1.6		SA 1453	2.6
2033	12.5		2019	11.4
			31 0316	2.4
			0844	11.1
			SU 1528	2.5
			2053	11.5

AUGUST

Time	m		Time	m
1 0350	2.4		**16** 0444	1.4
0917	11.2		1002	11.9
M 1601	2.5		TU 1657	1.9
2126	11.5		2217	11.9
2 0422	2.4		**17** 0516	2.1
0949	11.1		1035	11.3
TU 1633	2.6		W 1727	2.7
2159	11.3		2250	11.1
3 0454	2.6		**18** 0543	2.9
1022	10.8		1107	10.5
W 1707	2.9		TH 1755	3.5
2234	10.9		2324	10.2
4 0528	3.0		**19** 0612	3.7
1056	10.4		1141	9.8
TH 1743	3.3		F 1827	4.2
2311	10.4		◑	
5 0605	3.4		**20** 0005	9.3
1137	10.0		0649	4.5
F 1826	3.8		SA 1228	9.0
◑ 2358	9.9		1918	4.9
6 0652	3.9		**21** 0111	8.5
1231	9.6		0752	5.1
SA 1925	4.2		SU 1349	8.5
			2048	5.3
7 0104	9.5		**22** 0258	8.3
0757	4.2		0930	5.2
SU 1348	9.3		M 1535	8.6
2047	4.3		2228	4.9
8 0231	9.4		**23** 0424	8.8
0927	4.2		1055	4.7
M 1520	9.5		TU 1646	9.2
2216	3.8		2336	4.2
9 0401	9.7		**24** 0519	9.4
1053	3.7		1154	4.0
TU 1643	10.2		W 1735	10.0
2332	3.1			
10 0517	10.4		**25** 0024	3.5
1206	3.0		0603	10.1
W 1749	11.1		TH 1241	3.4
			1815	10.6
11 0040	2.3		**26** 0107	3.0
0620	11.2		0641	10.7
TH 1312	2.3		F 1322	2.9
1845	11.9		1852	11.2
12 0143	1.6		**27** 0146	2.5
0714	11.9		0717	11.2
F 1410	1.7		SA 1400	2.5
○ 1935	12.5		● 1927	11.6
13 0238	1.1		**28** 0223	2.2
0803	12.3		0750	11.5
SA 1500	1.3		SU 1437	2.2
2021	12.8		2001	11.9
14 0326	0.8		**29** 0259	1.9
0846	12.5		0823	11.7
SU 1545	1.2		M 1511	2.0
2103	12.8		2033	12.1
15 0408	0.9		**30** 0332	1.8
0926	12.3		0854	11.8
M 1624	1.4		TU 1543	1.9
2141	12.5		2105	12.1
			31 0403	1.9
			0925	11.7
			W 1614	2.1
			2136	11.8

Chart Datum: 6·29 metres below IGN Datum
HAT is 13·6 metres above Chart Datum

TIME ZONE -0100
(French Standard Time)
Subtract 1 hour for UT
For French Summer Time add
ONE hour in **non-shaded areas**

FRANCE – ST MALO
LAT 48°38'N   LONG 2°02'W
TIMES AND HEIGHTS OF HIGH AND LOW WATERS

Dates in amber are **SPRINGS**
Dates in grey are **NEAPS**

2022

SEPTEMBER

Date	Time m	Time m		Date	Time m	Time m
1 TH	0433 2.2 / 0956 11.4	1645 2.5 / 2208 11.4		**16** F	0459 3.0 / 1024 10.7	1710 3.5 / 2239 10.1
2 F	0502 2.7 / 1027 10.9	1718 3.0 / 2243 10.7		**17** SA	0521 3.9 / 1052 9.9	1735 4.3 / 2311 9.2 ◐
3 SA	0536 3.3 / 1104 10.3	1757 3.7 / 2327 10.0 ◐		**18** SU	0552 4.7 / 1128 9.0	1816 5.1
4 SU	0619 4.0 / 1154 9.6	1854 4.3		**19** M	0005 8.3 / 0648 5.5	1243 8.2 / 1944 5.7
5 M	0034 9.2 / 0726 4.6	1322 9.0 / 2026 4.6		**20** TU	0224 7.9 / 0847 5.7	1504 8.2 / 2203 5.3
6 TU	0223 8.9 / 0913 4.7	1519 9.2 / 2210 4.1		**21** W	0403 8.5 / 1033 5.1	1621 9.0 / 2315 4.5
7 W	0406 9.5 / 1051 4.0	1643 10.1 / 2330 3.1		**22** TH	0456 9.3 / 1130 4.2	1709 9.8 / 2359 3.6
8 TH	0518 10.4 / 1204 3.0	1744 11.2		**23** F	0536 10.2 / 1214 3.4	1748 10.7
9 F	0036 2.2 / 0613 11.4	1306 2.1 / 1834 12.1		**24** SA	0039 2.9 / 0613 10.9	1255 2.7 / 1825 11.4
10 SA	0132 1.4 / 0700 12.1	1358 1.4 / 1919 12.7 ○		**25** SU	0119 2.3 / 0648 11.5	1334 2.2 / 1901 11.9 ●
11 SU	0222 0.9 / 0742 12.5	1443 1.1 / 2000 13.0		**26** M	0157 1.9 / 0723 11.9	1412 1.8 / 1935 12.3
12 M	0304 0.8 / 0822 12.7	1522 1.0 / 2038 12.9		**27** TU	0233 1.6 / 0756 12.2	1447 1.6 / 2008 12.4
13 TU	0341 1.0 / 0857 12.5	1556 1.4 / 2112 12.6		**28** W	0307 1.5 / 0828 12.2	1522 1.6 / 2041 12.4
14 W	0411 1.5 / 0928 12.1	1624 2.0 / 2143 11.9		**29** TH	0339 1.6 / 0859 12.1	1554 1.8 / 2113 12.1
15 TH	0437 2.2 / 0957 11.4	1648 2.7 / 2212 11.1		**30** F	0410 2.0 / 0930 11.7	1625 2.3 / 2147 11.5

OCTOBER

Date	Time m	Time m		Date	Time m	Time m
1 SA	0440 2.6 / 1004 11.1	1659 2.9 / 2224 10.8		**16** SU	0443 4.0 / 1013 10.0	1659 4.3 / 2234 9.2
2 SU	0514 3.4 / 1043 10.3	1741 3.7 / 2311 9.8		**17** M	0512 4.7 / 1046 9.1	1736 5.0 / 2320 8.4 ◐
3 M	0601 4.2 / 1139 9.5	1843 4.4		**18** TU	0602 5.5 / 1148 8.3	1847 5.6
4 TU	0029 9.0 / 0717 4.9	1326 8.9 / 2025 4.6		**19** W	0128 7.9 / 0743 5.9	1408 8.1 / 2106 5.5
5 W	0232 8.9 / 0917 4.8	1520 9.4 / 2209 4.0		**20** TH	0318 8.3 / 0947 5.4	1535 8.8 / 2228 4.7
6 TH	0404 9.6 / 1048 3.9	1633 10.4 / 2322 3.0		**21** F	0415 9.2 / 1048 4.4	1627 9.7 / 2317 3.8
7 F	0506 10.7 / 1155 2.8	1727 11.4		**22** SA	0457 10.1 / 1134 3.5	1710 10.5
8 SA	0021 2.1 / 0554 11.6	1248 2.0 / 1813 12.2		**23** SU	0000 3.0 / 0536 10.9	1217 2.8 / 1750 11.3
9 SU	0111 1.4 / 0637 12.2	1335 1.5 / 1855 12.6 ○		**24** M	0042 2.3 / 0614 11.6	1259 2.2 / 1828 11.9
10 M	0156 1.1 / 0716 12.5	1416 1.3 / 1933 12.8		**25** TU	0123 1.8 / 0650 12.1	1341 1.7 / 1905 12.3 ●
11 TU	0234 1.2 / 0751 12.5	1451 1.4 / 2009 12.6		**26** W	0203 1.5 / 0726 12.4	1421 1.5 / 1942 12.5
12 W	0306 1.4 / 0824 12.3	1522 1.7 / 2041 12.3		**27** TH	0241 1.5 / 0800 12.5	1459 1.5 / 2018 12.5
13 TH	0334 1.8 / 0853 12.0	1548 2.2 / 2110 11.7		**28** F	0316 1.6 / 0836 12.3	1535 1.7 / 2055 12.1
14 F	0358 2.4 / 0920 11.4	1612 2.8 / 2137 10.9		**29** SA	0351 2.0 / 0912 11.9	1612 2.2 / 2134 11.5
15 SA	0420 3.2 / 0946 10.8	1634 3.5 / 2203 10.1		**30** SU	0426 2.7 / 0952 11.3	1651 2.8 / 2218 10.7
				31 M	0507 3.5 / 1039 10.4	1740 3.6 / 2314 9.8

NOVEMBER

Date	Time m	Time m		Date	Time m	Time m
1 TU	0601 4.3 / 1146 9.6	1848 4.2 ◐		**16** W	0538 5.1 / 1120 8.8	1814 5.1
2 W	0038 9.1 / 0724 4.7	1325 9.3 / 2022 4.3		**17** TH	0020 8.3 / 0649 5.4	1252 8.5 / 1939 5.2
3 TH	0220 9.2 / 0907 4.5	1500 9.7 / 2151 3.8		**18** F	0201 8.4 / 0824 5.3	1424 8.8 / 2112 4.8
4 F	0342 9.8 / 1028 3.7	1608 10.4 / 2258 3.0		**19** SA	0313 9.0 / 0943 4.6	1530 9.4 / 2218 4.1
5 SA	0439 10.6 / 1129 2.9	1700 11.2 / 2353 2.3		**20** SU	0407 9.8 / 1041 3.8	1622 10.2 / 2310 3.3
6 SU	0526 11.3 / 1219 2.3	1746 11.8		**21** M	0452 10.6 / 1132 3.1	1708 10.9 / 2359 2.6
7 M	0041 1.9 / 0607 11.8	1304 2.0 / 1827 12.1		**22** TU	0535 11.3 / 1221 2.4	1753 11.6
8 TU	0123 1.7 / 0645 12.1	1344 1.9 / 1905 12.1 ○		**23** W	0047 2.1 / 0616 11.9	1309 1.9 / 1836 12.0
9 W	0159 1.8 / 0721 12.1	1418 1.9 / 1940 12.0		**24** TH	0132 1.7 / 0657 12.2	1355 1.6 / 1918 12.3
10 TH	0230 2.0 / 0753 12.0	1449 2.1 / 2012 11.7		**25** F	0216 1.6 / 0738 12.4	1439 1.5 / 2001 12.3 ●
11 F	0259 2.2 / 0822 11.7	1517 2.4 / 2042 11.3		**26** SA	0259 1.7 / 0820 12.3	1523 1.6 / 2045 12.1
12 SA	0327 2.7 / 0851 11.3	1545 2.9 / 2111 10.8		**27** SU	0340 2.0 / 0904 12.0	1607 2.0 / 2132 11.6
13 SU	0353 3.2 / 0920 10.8	1612 3.4 / 2142 10.1		**28** M	0424 2.5 / 0951 11.5	1654 2.5 / 2222 10.9
14 M	0421 3.9 / 0950 10.2	1641 4.1 / 2216 9.4		**29** TU	0512 3.2 / 1044 10.8	1747 3.1 / 2319 10.2
15 TU	0453 4.5 / 1027 9.5	1718 4.6 / 2301 8.8		**30** W	0608 3.8 / 1147 10.2	1848 3.5 ◐

DECEMBER

Date	Time m	Time m		Date	Time m	Time m
1 TH	0026 9.7 / 0717 4.1	1301 9.8 / 1959 3.8		**16** F	0613 4.6 / 1154 9.2	1846 4.5
2 F	0144 9.5 / 0834 4.2	1419 9.8 / 2112 3.7		**17** SA	0040 8.9 / 0715 4.7	1304 9.1 / 1952 4.5
3 SA	0259 9.7 / 0947 3.8	1529 10.2 / 2218 3.3		**18** SU	0155 9.0 / 0827 4.6	1418 9.3 / 2105 4.2
4 SU	0401 10.2 / 1050 3.4	1626 10.6 / 2316 3.0		**19** M	0303 9.4 / 0940 4.1	1525 9.7 / 2215 3.7
5 M	0452 10.7 / 1144 3.0	1715 11.0		**20** TU	0403 10.0 / 1045 3.5	1625 10.4 / 2317 3.1
6 TU	0006 2.7 / 0537 11.1	1231 2.7 / 1800 11.2		**21** W	0457 10.7 / 1145 2.8	1720 11.0
7 W	0049 2.5 / 0618 11.4	1312 2.5 / 1841 11.3		**22** TH	0013 2.5 / 0548 11.4	1241 2.2 / 1812 11.5
8 TH	0127 2.5 / 0655 11.5	1349 2.5 / 1918 11.3 ○		**23** F	0107 2.1 / 0637 11.9	1335 1.8 / 1904 11.9
9 F	0201 2.6 / 0730 11.5	1423 2.5 / 1953 11.2		**24** SA	0159 1.8 / 0726 12.2	1427 1.5 / 1954 12.1
10 SA	0234 2.6 / 0802 11.4	1456 2.6 / 2026 11.0		**25** SU	0250 1.7 / 0815 12.4	1519 1.4 / 2044 12.1
11 SU	0306 2.8 / 0833 11.2	1529 2.8 / 2058 10.7		**26** M	0339 1.7 / 0903 12.3	1608 1.4 / 2132 11.9
12 M	0338 3.1 / 0906 10.9	1601 3.2 / 2131 10.4		**27** TU	0427 2.0 / 0952 12.0	1656 1.7 / 2221 11.5
13 TU	0410 3.5 / 0940 10.5	1633 3.6 / 2207 9.9		**28** W	0514 2.4 / 1040 11.5	1744 2.2 / 2309 10.9
14 W	0444 3.9 / 1017 10.1	1709 3.9 / 2247 9.5		**29** TH	0602 2.9 / 1130 10.9	1832 2.8 / 2359 10.3
15 TH	0523 4.3 / 1100 9.6	1752 4.3 / 2336 9.1 ◐		**30** F	0652 3.4 / 1225 10.3	1923 3.3
				31 SA	0055 9.8 / 0748 3.9	1327 9.8 / 2020 3.8

Chart Datum: 6·29 metres below IGN Datum
HAT is 13·6 metres above Chart Datum

TIDES

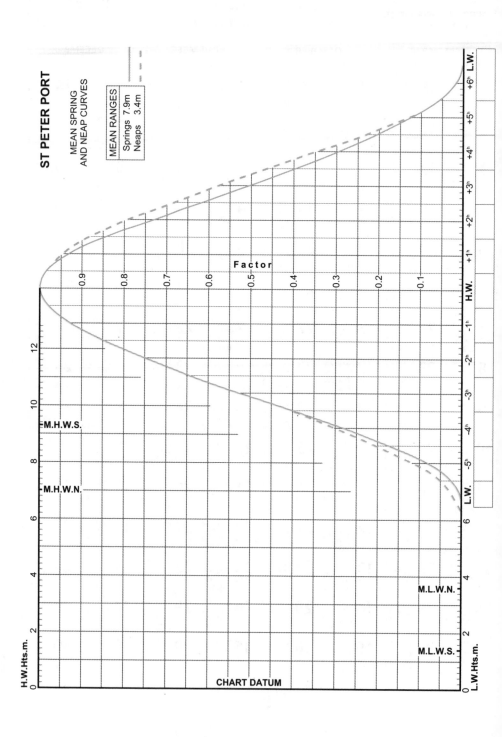

ST PETER PORT

MEAN SPRING
AND NEAP CURVES

MEAN RANGES	
Springs	7.9m
Neaps	3.4m

TIME ZONE (UT)
For Summer Time add ONE hour in **non-shaded areas**

CHANNEL ISLES – ST PETER PORT
LAT 49°27′N   LONG 2°32′W
TIMES AND HEIGHTS OF HIGH AND LOW WATERS

Dates in amber are **SPRINGS**
Dates in grey are **NEAPS**

2022

JANUARY

Time m	Time m
1 SA 0455 8.7 / 1123 1.9 / 1722 8.7 / 2349 1.8	**16** SU 0526 8.0 / 1153 2.7 / 1751 8.0
2 SU 0549 9.1 / 1219 1.5 / 1817 9.0 ●	**17** M 0006 2.6 / 0607 8.4 / 1232 2.4 / ○1832 8.2
3 M 0042 1.5 / 0640 9.4 / 1310 1.2 / 1909 9.2	**18** TU 0045 2.3 / 0645 8.6 / 1310 2.1 / 1911 8.4
4 TU 0132 1.3 / 0729 9.6 / 1400 1.0 / 1958 9.3	**19** W 0122 2.1 / 0722 8.7 / 1347 2.0 / 1948 8.5
5 W 0219 1.3 / 0816 9.6 / 1447 1.1 / 2044 9.1	**20** TH 0158 2.1 / 0757 8.8 / 1423 1.9 / 2022 8.5
6 TH 0304 1.5 / 0901 9.4 / 1532 1.3 / 2128 8.8	**21** F 0233 2.1 / 0832 8.7 / 1457 2.0 / 2056 8.4
7 F 0347 1.9 / 0945 9.0 / 1616 1.7 / 2211 8.4	**22** SA 0307 2.2 / 0906 8.6 / 1531 2.1 / 2130 8.3
8 SA 0430 2.4 / 1029 8.5 / 1659 2.3 / 2254 7.9	**23** SU 0342 2.4 / 0943 8.4 / 1606 2.3 / 2207 8.1
9 SU 0514 2.9 / 1114 7.9 / 1744 2.8 / ☾2340 7.4	**24** M 0420 2.6 / 1024 8.2 / 1646 2.6 / 2250 7.8
10 M 0603 3.4 / 1206 7.4 / 1834 3.3	**25** TU 0505 2.9 / 1112 7.9 / 1734 2.9 / ☾2342 7.5
11 TU 0035 7.0 / 0701 3.7 / 1307 7.0 / 1933 3.6	**26** W 0601 3.2 / 1211 7.5 / 1835 3.2
12 W 0142 6.9 / 0811 3.8 / 1418 6.9 / 2040 3.7	**27** TH 0049 7.3 / 0716 3.3 / 1326 7.3 / 1956 3.3
13 TH 0254 7.0 / 0922 3.7 / 1526 7.0 / 2145 3.5	**28** F 0214 7.3 / 0845 3.2 / 1453 7.4 / 2125 3.1
14 F 0354 7.3 / 1021 3.4 / 1621 7.3 / 2239 3.2	**29** SA 0337 7.7 / 1008 2.8 / 1612 7.7 / 2241 2.7
15 SA 0443 7.7 / 1110 3.0 / 1709 7.6 / 2325 2.9	**30** SU 0445 8.2 / 1115 2.2 / 1717 8.2 / 2343 2.1
	31 M 0542 8.8 / 1213 1.6 / 1813 8.7

FEBRUARY

Time m	Time m
1 TU 0036 1.6 / 0634 9.3 / 1304 1.1 / ●1903 9.1	**16** W 0030 2.2 / 0631 8.6 / 1256 1.9 / ○1857 8.6
2 W 0125 1.2 / 0721 9.6 / 1351 0.8 / 1948 9.4	**17** TH 0109 1.8 / 0708 8.9 / 1334 1.6 / 1933 8.8
3 TH 0209 1.0 / 0805 9.8 / 1434 0.7 / 2030 9.4	**18** F 0145 1.6 / 0744 9.1 / 1408 1.4 / 2007 8.9
4 F 0250 1.1 / 0845 9.6 / 1514 0.9 / 2108 9.2	**19** SA 0220 1.5 / 0819 9.2 / 1441 1.4 / 2039 8.9
5 SA 0327 1.3 / 0923 9.3 / 1550 1.3 / 2142 8.8	**20** SU 0253 1.5 / 0851 9.1 / 1513 1.5 / 2111 8.8
6 SU 0401 1.8 / 0958 8.8 / 1623 1.9 / 2215 8.3	**21** M 0325 1.7 / 0925 8.9 / 1545 1.8 / 2145 8.5
7 M 0433 2.4 / 1031 8.1 / 1655 2.6 / 2247 7.7	**22** TU 0359 2.0 / 1002 8.5 / 1620 2.2 / 2222 8.1
8 TU 0506 3.0 / 1108 7.5 / 1730 3.2 / ☾2325 7.2	**23** W 0438 2.5 / 1044 8.0 / 1702 2.7 / ☾2308 7.7
9 W 0547 3.6 / 1153 6.9 / 1816 3.7	**24** TH 0528 3.0 / 1139 7.4 / 1758 3.3
10 TH 0016 6.7 / 0650 4.0 / 1301 6.5 / 1925 4.1	**25** F 0011 7.2 / 0642 3.4 / 1257 7.0 / 1924 3.6
11 F 0139 6.5 / 0814 4.1 / 1436 6.4 / 2049 4.1	**26** SA 0148 6.9 / 0829 3.5 / 1445 6.9 / 2117 3.5
12 SA 0314 6.7 / 0943 3.9 / 1556 6.8 / 2207 3.7	**27** SU 0330 7.3 / 1006 3.0 / 1612 7.4 / 2239 2.9
13 SU 0419 7.2 / 1047 3.4 / 1651 7.2 / 2304 3.2	**28** M 0440 8.0 / 1112 2.3 / 1714 8.1 / 2337 2.2
14 M 0508 7.7 / 1135 2.8 / 1736 7.7 / 2350 2.7	
15 TU 0550 8.2 / 1218 2.3 / 1817 8.2	

MARCH

Time m	Time m
1 TU 0534 8.7 / 1205 1.6 / 1804 8.7	**16** W 0527 8.1 / 1153 2.2 / 1754 8.2
2 W 0026 1.5 / 0622 9.3 / 1251 1.0 / ●1849 9.2	**17** TH 0007 2.1 / 0607 8.6 / 1232 1.6 / 1833 8.7
3 TH 0110 1.1 / 0705 9.7 / 1334 0.7 / 1930 9.5	**18** F 0047 1.6 / 0645 9.1 / 1310 1.2 / ○1909 9.1
4 F 0151 0.8 / 0745 9.8 / 1412 0.6 / 2007 9.5	**19** SA 0124 1.2 / 0721 9.4 / 1345 1.0 / 1943 9.3
5 SA 0227 0.8 / 0822 9.7 / 1447 0.8 / 2040 9.4	**20** SU 0159 1.0 / 0756 9.5 / 1419 0.9 / 2016 9.3
6 SU 0300 1.1 / 0855 9.4 / 1518 1.2 / 2109 9.0	**21** M 0233 1.0 / 0831 9.5 / 1451 1.1 / 2049 9.2
7 M 0329 1.5 / 0924 8.9 / 1545 1.8 / 2136 8.5	**22** TU 0306 1.2 / 0905 9.2 / 1524 1.5 / 2123 8.9
8 TU 0354 2.1 / 0952 8.2 / 1610 2.4 / 2203 7.9	**23** W 0340 1.7 / 0942 8.7 / 1559 2.0 / 2200 8.3
9 W 0419 2.8 / 1021 7.6 / 1635 3.1 / 2232 7.4	**24** TH 0419 2.3 / 1025 8.0 / 1640 2.7 / 2246 7.7
10 TH 0448 3.4 / 1057 6.9 / 1709 3.7 / ☾2310 6.8	**25** F 0510 2.9 / 1120 7.3 / 1738 3.4 / ☾2352 7.1
11 F 0536 4.0 / 1151 6.4 / 1812 4.2	**26** SA 0630 3.5 / 1250 6.7 / 1916 3.9
12 SA 0017 6.3 / 0716 4.3 / 1340 6.1 / 1957 4.4	**27** SU 0141 6.8 / 0831 3.5 / 1449 6.8 / 2118 3.6
13 SU 0208 6.5 / 0901 4.1 / 1530 6.5 / 2133 4.0	**28** M 0324 7.3 / 1000 2.9 / 1606 7.5 / 2229 2.9
14 M 0354 6.8 / 1020 3.5 / 1629 7.1 / 2238 3.4	**29** TU 0428 8.0 / 1058 2.2 / 1700 8.1 / 2321 2.1
15 TU 0444 7.5 / 1111 2.8 / 1713 7.7 / 2326 2.7	**30** W 0517 8.7 / 1146 1.5 / 1745 8.7
	31 TH 0006 1.5 / 0601 9.2 / 1228 1.0 / 1826 9.2

APRIL

Time m	Time m
1 F 0047 1.1 / 0642 9.5 / 1307 0.8 / ●1903 9.4	**16** SA 0016 1.5 / 0614 9.1 / 1239 1.1 / ○1838 9.2
2 SA 0125 0.9 / 0719 9.6 / 1343 0.8 / 1938 9.5	**17** SU 0056 1.1 / 0654 9.5 / 1317 0.9 / 1915 9.5
3 SU 0159 0.9 / 0754 9.5 / 1416 1.0 / 2008 9.3	**18** M 0134 0.8 / 0732 9.6 / 1354 0.8 / 1952 9.5
4 M 0229 1.2 / 0824 9.2 / 1444 1.3 / 2036 9.0	**19** TU 0211 0.8 / 0810 9.5 / 1430 1.0 / 2028 9.4
5 TU 0256 1.6 / 0852 8.7 / 1509 1.9 / 2102 8.6	**20** W 0248 1.1 / 0848 9.2 / 1506 1.4 / 2106 9.0
6 W 0320 2.1 / 0919 8.2 / 1532 2.5 / 2127 8.1	**21** TH 0327 1.6 / 0929 8.6 / 1545 2.1 / 2148 8.4
7 TH 0343 2.7 / 0947 7.6 / 1555 3.1 / 2155 7.5	**22** F 0411 2.2 / 1017 7.9 / 1632 2.8 / 2238 7.8
8 F 0410 3.3 / 1020 7.0 / 1626 3.6 / 2230 7.0	**23** SA 0509 2.9 / 1119 7.2 / 1737 3.5 / ☾2350 7.2
9 SA 0451 3.8 / 1109 6.5 / 1720 4.2 / 2329 6.5	**24** SU 0635 3.3 / 1252 6.8 / 1918 3.8
10 SU 0623 4.2 / 1244 6.1 / 1909 4.4	**25** M 0132 7.0 / 0821 3.3 / 1433 7.0 / 2100 3.4
11 M 0119 6.3 / 0815 4.1 / 1445 6.4 / 2048 4.1	**26** TU 0300 7.4 / 0936 2.8 / 1541 7.5 / 2204 2.8
12 TU 0305 6.7 / 0936 3.5 / 1551 7.0 / 2158 3.4	**27** W 0401 8.0 / 1031 2.2 / 1632 8.1 / 2254 2.2
13 W 0404 7.4 / 1032 2.8 / 1638 7.6 / 2250 2.7	**28** TH 0449 8.5 / 1117 1.7 / 1715 8.6 / 2338 1.8
14 TH 0451 8.0 / 1117 2.2 / 1720 8.3 / 2334 2.1	**29** F 0533 8.9 / 1158 1.4 / 1755 8.9
15 F 0533 8.6 / 1159 1.6 / 1800 8.8	**30** SA 0017 1.4 / 0613 9.1 / 1236 1.2 / ●1832 9.1

Chart Datum: 5·06 metres below Ordnance Datum (Local)
HAT is 10·3 metres above Chart Datum

TIDES

TIME ZONE (UT)
For Summer Time add ONE hour in **non-shaded areas**

CHANNEL ISLES – ST PETER PORT
LAT 49°27'N   LONG 2°31'W
TIMES AND HEIGHTS OF HIGH AND LOW WATERS

Dates in amber are **SPRINGS**
Dates in grey are **NEAPS**

2022

MAY

Day	Time	m	Time	m
1 SU	0054 / 0650 / 1311 / 1906	1.3 / 9.2 / 1.2 / 9.0	16 M	0026 / 0625 / 1249 / 1848	1.2 / 9.3 / 1.1 / 9.4
2 M	0128 / 0724 / 1343 / 1937	1.3 / 9.1 / 1.4 / 9.1	17 TU	0110 / 0709 / 1331 / 1930	0.9 / 9.4 / 1.0 / 9.5
3 TU	0158 / 0755 / 1411 / 2006	1.5 / 8.8 / 1.7 / 8.8	18 W	0154 / 0753 / 1413 / 2012	0.9 / 9.4 / 1.2 / 9.4
4 W	0226 / 0824 / 1437 / 2033	1.8 / 8.5 / 2.1 / 8.5	19 TH	0237 / 0838 / 1456 / 2056	1.1 / 9.1 / 1.5 / 9.1
5 TH	0252 / 0853 / 1503 / 2101	2.2 / 8.1 / 2.6 / 8.1	20 F	0322 / 0925 / 1541 / 2143	1.5 / 8.6 / 2.1 / 8.6
6 F	0319 / 0923 / 1530 / 2131	2.7 / 7.6 / 3.1 / 7.6	21 SA	0413 / 1017 / 1633 / 2238	2.0 / 8.0 / 2.7 / 8.0
7 SA	0349 / 0959 / 1605 / 2209	3.2 / 7.1 / 3.5 / 7.2	22 SU	0514 / 1120 / 1739 / 2346	2.6 / 7.5 / 3.2 / 7.6
8 SU	0432 / 1048 / 1657 / 2304	3.6 / 6.7 / 4.0 / 6.8	23 M	0628 / 1236 / 1901	2.9 / 7.2 / 3.4
9 M	0545 / 1203 / 1821	3.9 / 6.4 / 4.2	24 TU	0105 / 0748 / 1355 / 2023	7.4 / 3.0 / 7.2 / 3.3
10 TU	0025 / 0723 / 1339 / 1955	6.6 / 3.9 / 6.5 / 4.0	25 W	0221 / 0858 / 1502 / 2127	7.5 / 2.8 / 7.5 / 3.0
11 W	0158 / 0841 / 1454 / 2107	6.8 / 3.4 / 7.0 / 3.4	26 TH	0324 / 0954 / 1555 / 2219	7.8 / 2.5 / 7.8 / 2.6
12 TH	0309 / 0942 / 1549 / 2204	7.3 / 2.9 / 7.6 / 2.8	27 F	0415 / 1041 / 1640 / 2305	8.1 / 2.2 / 8.2 / 2.3
13 F	0404 / 1033 / 1637 / 2255	7.9 / 2.3 / 8.2 / 2.2	28 SA	0500 / 1124 / 1721 / 2346	8.3 / 2.0 / 8.5 / 2.0
14 SA	0453 / 1121 / 1722 / 2342	8.5 / 1.8 / 8.7 / 1.6	29 SU	0542 / 1204 / 1759	8.5 / 1.9 / 8.6
15 SU	0540 / 1206 / 1805	9.0 / 1.3 / 9.1	30 M	0023 / 0621 / 1239 / 1835	1.9 / 8.6 / 1.9 / 8.7
			31 TU	0059 / 0657 / 1313 / 1909	1.9 / 8.6 / 1.9 / 8.7

JUNE

Day	Time	m	Time	m
1 W	0131 / 0731 / 1344 / 1941	1.9 / 8.4 / 2.1 / 8.6	16 TH	0143 / 0743 / 1404 / 2003	1.0 / 9.2 / 1.3 / 9.4
2 TH	0202 / 0804 / 1414 / 2012	2.1 / 8.2 / 2.4 / 8.4	17 F	0232 / 0833 / 1452 / 2051	1.0 / 9.1 / 1.5 / 9.2
3 F	0233 / 0836 / 1445 / 2043	2.4 / 8.0 / 2.6 / 8.1	18 SA	0321 / 0922 / 1540 / 2140	1.3 / 8.8 / 1.8 / 8.9
4 SA	0305 / 0910 / 1517 / 2117	2.7 / 7.7 / 3.0 / 7.8	19 SU	0412 / 1012 / 1631 / 2231	1.7 / 8.4 / 2.3 / 8.5
5 SU	0339 / 0947 / 1555 / 2157	3.0 / 7.3 / 3.3 / 7.5	20 M	0505 / 1106 / 1725 / 2326	2.1 / 7.9 / 2.7 / 8.0
6 M	0422 / 1033 / 1641 / 2246	3.2 / 7.1 / 3.6 / 7.2	21 TU	0602 / 1203 / 1825	2.5 / 7.6 / 3.1
7 TU	0517 / 1130 / 1743 / 2347	3.4 / 6.9 / 3.7 / 7.1	22 W	0026 / 0703 / 1305 / 1931	7.6 / 2.8 / 7.3 / 3.3
8 W	0627 / 1238 / 1856	3.5 / 6.9 / 3.7	23 TH	0132 / 0806 / 1410 / 2038	7.4 / 3.0 / 7.3 / 3.3
9 TH	0057 / 0741 / 1348 / 2010	7.2 / 3.3 / 7.1 / 3.4	24 F	0238 / 0907 / 1510 / 2138	7.4 / 3.0 / 7.4 / 3.1
10 F	0209 / 0847 / 1454 / 2116	7.4 / 3.0 / 7.5 / 2.9	25 SA	0337 / 1001 / 1603 / 2230	7.5 / 2.9 / 7.6 / 2.9
11 SA	0315 / 0948 / 1552 / 2215	7.8 / 2.5 / 8.0 / 2.4	26 SU	0428 / 1050 / 1649 / 2315	7.7 / 2.8 / 7.9 / 2.7
12 SU	0414 / 1044 / 1646 / 2310	8.2 / 2.1 / 8.5 / 1.9	27 M	0514 / 1133 / 1731 / 2357	7.9 / 2.6 / 8.1 / 2.5
13 M	0509 / 1136 / 1737	8.6 / 1.7 / 8.9	28 TU	0556 / 1213 / 1810	8.0 / 2.4 / 8.3
14 TU	0002 / 0602 / 1227 / 1827	1.5 / 9.0 / 1.4 / 9.2	29 W	0035 / 0636 / 1249 / 1848	2.3 / 8.2 / 2.3 / 8.5
15 W	0053 / 0653 / 1316 / 1915	1.2 / 9.2 / 1.3 / 9.4	30 TH	0111 / 0714 / 1325 / 1924	2.2 / 8.2 / 2.3 / 8.5

JULY

Day	Time	m	Time	m
1 F	0147 / 0750 / 1400 / 1959	2.2 / 8.2 / 2.3 / 8.4	16 SA	0226 / 0826 / 1446 / 2042	0.8 / 9.3 / 1.2 / 9.6
2 SA	0221 / 0825 / 1434 / 2033	2.3 / 8.1 / 2.5 / 8.3	17 SU	0313 / 0911 / 1531 / 2127	0.9 / 9.1 / 1.4 / 9.3
3 SU	0255 / 0900 / 1508 / 2107	2.4 / 7.9 / 2.6 / 8.1	18 M	0357 / 0955 / 1614 / 2210	1.2 / 8.8 / 1.8 / 8.9
4 M	0330 / 0935 / 1543 / 2143	2.6 / 7.8 / 2.8 / 7.9	19 TU	0441 / 1038 / 1657 / 2254	1.7 / 8.4 / 2.3 / 8.3
5 TU	0407 / 1013 / 1623 / 2225	2.8 / 7.6 / 3.0 / 7.7	20 W	0524 / 1121 / 1741 / 2340	2.3 / 7.8 / 2.8 / 7.7
6 W	0450 / 1058 / 1709 / 2314	2.9 / 7.4 / 3.2 / 7.6	21 TH	0611 / 1209 / 1831	2.9 / 7.4 / 3.3
7 TH	0540 / 1150 / 1805	3.1 / 7.3 / 3.3	22 F	0033 / 0705 / 1307 / 1933	7.2 / 3.4 / 7.0 / 3.7
8 F	0011 / 0642 / 1252 / 1914	7.5 / 3.2 / 7.3 / 3.3	23 SA	0141 / 0808 / 1417 / 2046	6.9 / 3.6 / 6.9 / 3.7
9 SA	0119 / 0754 / 1403 / 2030	7.4 / 3.1 / 7.4 / 3.1	24 SU	0256 / 0917 / 1526 / 2156	6.8 / 3.6 / 7.1 / 3.5
10 SU	0232 / 0907 / 1515 / 2142	7.6 / 2.9 / 7.7 / 2.7	25 M	0401 / 1018 / 1622 / 2251	7.1 / 3.4 / 7.4 / 3.2
11 M	0344 / 1015 / 1620 / 2247	7.9 / 2.6 / 8.2 / 2.2	26 TU	0454 / 1109 / 1710 / 2338	7.4 / 3.1 / 7.8 / 2.8
12 TU	0450 / 1117 / 1719 / 2348	8.2 / 2.2 / 8.6 / 1.8	27 W	0539 / 1153 / 1753	7.7 / 2.8 / 8.1
13 W	0549 / 1215 / 1814	8.6 / 1.8 / 9.1	28 TH	0019 / 0621 / 1233 / 1833	2.5 / 8.0 / 2.5 / 8.4
14 TH	0044 / 0646 / 1309 / 1907	1.3 / 9.0 / 1.4 / 9.4	29 F	0058 / 0700 / 1311 / 1911	2.2 / 8.3 / 2.2 / 8.6
15 F	0137 / 0737 / 1359 / 1956	1.0 / 9.2 / 1.2 / 9.6	30 SA	0135 / 0737 / 1347 / 1946	2.0 / 8.4 / 2.1 / 8.7
			31 SU	0210 / 0812 / 1422 / 2020	2.0 / 8.4 / 2.1 / 8.7

AUGUST

Day	Time	m	Time	m
1 M	0242 / 0844 / 1454 / 2052	2.0 / 8.4 / 2.2 / 8.6	16 TU	0332 / 0927 / 1547 / 2141	1.0 / 9.1 / 1.5 / 9.1
2 TU	0314 / 0916 / 1526 / 2125	2.1 / 8.3 / 2.3 / 8.4	17 W	0408 / 1002 / 1621 / 2216	1.6 / 8.6 / 2.1 / 8.5
3 W	0346 / 0949 / 1600 / 2200	2.3 / 8.1 / 2.5 / 8.2	18 TH	0441 / 1035 / 1654 / 2251	2.3 / 8.0 / 2.7 / 7.8
4 TH	0421 / 1026 / 1638 / 2242	2.5 / 7.9 / 2.8 / 7.9	19 F	0516 / 1115 / 1732 / 2332	3.0 / 7.4 / 3.4 / 7.1
5 F	0502 / 1111 / 1725 / 2333	2.8 / 7.6 / 3.1 / 7.6	20 SA	0559 / 1158 / 1827	3.7 / 6.8 / 4.0
6 SA	0555 / 1208 / 1828	3.1 / 7.3 / 3.3	21 SU	0032 / 0705 / 1313 / 1949	6.5 / 4.1 / 6.5 / 4.2
7 SU	0039 / 0708 / 1324 / 1954	7.3 / 3.4 / 7.2 / 3.4	22 M	0215 / 0830 / 1453 / 2127	6.4 / 4.2 / 6.6 / 4.0
8 M	0204 / 0839 / 1452 / 2125	7.2 / 3.4 / 7.4 / 3.1	23 TU	0344 / 0955 / 1604 / 2235	6.7 / 3.9 / 7.1 / 3.5
9 TU	0332 / 1003 / 1609 / 2240	7.5 / 3.0 / 7.9 / 2.5	24 W	0439 / 1052 / 1653 / 2323	7.2 / 3.6 / 7.6 / 3.0
10 W	0445 / 1112 / 1712 / 2343	8.0 / 2.4 / 8.5 / 1.9	25 TH	0523 / 1137 / 1735	7.7 / 2.9 / 8.1
11 TH	0545 / 1210 / 1807	8.6 / 1.8 / 9.1	26 F	0003 / 0603 / 1216 / 1815	2.5 / 8.1 / 2.4 / 8.5
12 F	0038 / 0639 / 1301 / 1857	1.3 / 9.1 / 1.3 / 9.6	27 SA	0040 / 0641 / 1254 / 1852	2.1 / 8.5 / 2.0 / 8.8
13 SA	0127 / 0726 / 1348 / 1943	0.8 / 9.4 / 1.0 / 9.9	28 SU	0116 / 0717 / 1329 / 1927	1.8 / 8.7 / 1.8 / 9.0
14 SU	0212 / 0810 / 1431 / 2025	0.6 / 9.6 / 0.9 / 9.9	29 M	0150 / 0750 / 1403 / 2000	1.6 / 8.9 / 1.7 / 9.1
15 M	0254 / 0850 / 1510 / 2105	0.6 / 9.5 / 1.0 / 9.6	30 TU	0221 / 0821 / 1434 / 2031	1.5 / 8.9 / 1.7 / 9.1
			31 W	0251 / 0851 / 1505 / 2102	1.7 / 8.7 / 1.8 / 8.9

Chart Datum: 5·06 metres below Ordnance Datum (Local)
HAT is 10·3 metres above Chart Datum

CHANNEL ISLES – ST PETER PORT

LAT 49°27'N LONG 2°31'W

TIMES AND HEIGHTS OF HIGH AND LOW WATERS

2022

SEPTEMBER

	Time	m		Time	m
1 TH	0321 0922 1536 2135	1.9 8.5 2.1 8.6	**16** F	0357 0950 1609 2206	2.4 8.1 2.8 7.7
2 F	0353 0956 1611 2214	2.3 8.2 2.5 8.1	**17** SA	0422 1019 1637 2239	3.2 7.5 3.3 7.0 ◑
3 SA	0431 1038 1655 2302	2.8 7.8 3.0 7.6 ◔	**18** SU	0454 1057 1722 2330	3.8 6.9 4.1 6.4
4 SU	0521 1134 1758	3.3 7.3 3.5	**19** M	0558 1205 1858	4.4 6.4 4.5
5 M	0011 0640 1301 1939	7.0 3.8 7.0 3.7	**20** TU	0128 0747 1419 2056	6.1 4.6 6.4 4.3
6 TU	0158 0834 1449 2127	6.9 3.8 7.2 3.3	**21** W	0325 0930 1541 2213	6.5 4.2 6.9 3.7
7 W	0338 1005 1706 2240	7.3 3.2 7.9 2.5	**22** TH	0417 1029 1629 2258	7.1 3.5 7.5 3.0
8 TH	0445 1108 1706 2336	8.0 2.4 8.6 1.8	**23** F	0458 1112 1710 2337	7.7 2.9 8.1 2.4
9 F	0537 1200 1755	8.7 1.7 9.3	**24** SA	0536 1151 1748	8.3 2.3 8.6
10 SA	0024 0624 1245 1841	1.1 9.3 1.2 9.8 ○	**25** SU	0013 0613 1228 1825	1.9 8.7 1.9 9.0 ●
11 SU	0108 0706 1328 1922	0.7 9.6 0.8 10.0	**26** M	0049 0649 1304 1901	1.5 9.0 1.5 9.3
12 M	0149 0746 1407 2001	0.5 9.7 0.8 10.0	**27** TU	0123 0722 1338 1934	1.3 9.2 1.4 9.4
13 TU	0227 0821 1443 2036	0.7 9.6 1.0 9.7	**28** W	0155 0754 1410 2007	1.3 9.2 1.4 9.4
14 W	0300 0854 1514 2108	1.1 9.2 1.4 9.1	**29** TH	0226 0825 1442 2039	1.4 9.1 1.6 9.2
15 TH	0330 0923 1543 2137	1.7 8.7 2.1 8.5	**30** F	0257 0857 1515 2114	1.7 8.8 1.9 8.7

OCTOBER

	Time	m		Time	m
1 SA	0330 0933 1551 2154	2.2 8.4 2.4 8.1	**16** SU	0341 0941 1559 2203	3.3 7.6 3.5 7.1
2 SU	0409 1016 1638 2244	2.9 7.8 3.1 7.4	**17** M	0409 1016 1637 2249	3.9 7.0 4.1 6.5 ◑
3 M	0503 1117 1748	3.5 7.2 3.6	**18** TU	0502 1116 1808	4.4 6.5 4.5 ◐
4 TU	0003 0634 1258 1946	6.8 4.0 6.9 3.8	**19** W	0030 0700 1320 2004	6.1 4.7 6.4 4.4
5 W	0209 0842 1449 2126	6.8 3.8 7.3 3.2	**20** TH	0241 0843 1457 2127	6.4 4.3 6.8 3.8
6 TH	0337 0959 1557 2229	7.5 3.1 8.0 2.4	**21** F	0340 0949 1551 2218	7.1 3.7 7.4 3.1
7 F	0432 1053 1649 2318	8.2 2.3 8.7 1.7	**22** SA	0422 1035 1634 2300	7.7 3.0 8.0 2.5
8 SA	0518 1140 1734	8.9 1.7 9.3	**23** SU	0501 1116 1713 2338	8.3 2.4 8.6 2.0
9 SU	0002 0600 1222 1817	1.2 9.3 1.2 9.7 ○	**24** M	0539 1155 1752	8.8 1.9 9.0
10 M	0043 0640 1302 1856	0.9 9.6 1.0 9.8	**25** TU	0016 0616 1233 1830	1.6 9.1 1.5 9.4 ●
11 TU	0121 0716 1339 1933	0.8 9.7 1.0 9.7	**26** W	0052 0651 1311 1907	1.3 9.4 1.3 9.4
12 W	0155 0749 1412 2006	1.0 9.5 1.2 9.4	**27** TH	0128 0727 1347 1944	1.3 9.5 1.3 9.5
13 TH	0226 0819 1442 2035	1.4 9.2 1.7 8.9	**28** F	0203 0802 1424 2021	1.4 9.3 1.4 9.2
14 F	0253 0847 1508 2103	2.0 8.7 2.2 8.4	**29** SA	0239 0839 1501 2101	1.7 9.0 1.8 8.7
15 SA	0317 0913 1532 2131	2.6 8.2 2.9 7.7	**30** SU	0317 0920 1544 2146	2.3 8.6 2.4 8.1
			31 M	0401 1010 1637 2244	2.9 7.9 3.0 7.4

NOVEMBER

	Time	m		Time	m
1 TU	0502 1117 1755	3.6 7.4 3.5 ◐	**16** W	0438 1049 1726 2341	4.2 6.8 4.1 6.5
2 W	0009 0640 1254 1940	7.0 3.9 7.2 3.5	**17** TH	0602 1211 1901	4.4 6.6 4.2
3 TH	0157 0826 1427 2104	7.1 3.7 7.5 3.0	**18** F	0122 0738 1345 2021	6.5 4.3 6.8 3.8
4 F	0313 0936 1532 2203	7.6 3.1 8.1 2.4	**19** SA	0239 0851 1453 2123	6.9 3.8 7.3 3.3
5 SA	0406 1028 1623 2251	8.2 2.4 8.6 1.9	**20** SU	0333 0947 1546 2213	7.5 3.2 7.8 2.8
6 SU	0451 1113 1708 2334	8.7 1.8 9.0 1.4	**21** M	0418 1035 1633 2259	8.1 2.6 8.3 2.2
7 M	0531 1155 1749	9.1 1.6 9.3	**22** TU	0501 1120 1717 2342	8.6 2.1 8.8 1.8
8 TU	0013 0610 1234 1829	1.4 9.3 1.4 9.3 ○	**23** W	0542 1204 1801	9.0 1.7 9.1 ●
9 W	0051 0646 1310 1905	1.4 9.3 1.5 9.2	**24** TH	0024 0624 1247 1844	1.5 9.3 1.4 9.3
10 TH	0124 0719 1343 1938	1.6 9.2 1.7 9.0	**25** F	0106 0705 1330 1928	1.4 9.5 1.3 9.3
11 F	0155 0749 1413 2009	1.9 9.0 2.0 8.6	**26** SA	0148 0747 1413 2012	1.5 9.4 1.4 9.1
12 SA	0223 0818 1441 2038	2.3 8.6 2.4 8.2	**27** SU	0230 0831 1458 2057	1.7 9.2 1.7 8.8
13 SU	0249 0847 1509 2109	2.7 8.2 2.9 7.7	**28** M	0315 0918 1547 2148	2.2 8.8 2.1 8.3
14 M	0316 0918 1540 2143	3.2 7.7 3.4 7.2	**29** TU	0405 1011 1644 2246	2.7 8.3 2.6 7.8
15 TU	0349 0955 1620 2229	3.7 7.3 3.8 6.8	**30** W	0506 1114 1751 2357	3.2 7.9 2.9 7.4 ◔

DECEMBER

	Time	m		Time	m
1 TH	0623 1230 1909	3.5 7.6 3.1	**16** F	0515 1123 1755	3.9 7.1 3.7 ◐
2 F	0117 0747 1347 2023	7.3 3.5 7.6 3.0	**17** SA	0005 0625 1229 1906	6.9 4.0 7.0 3.7
3 SA	0231 0858 1454 2125	7.5 3.2 7.8 2.7	**18** SU	0118 0741 1342 2017	6.9 3.8 7.2 3.5
4 SU	0330 0955 1550 2218	7.9 2.8 8.1 2.5	**19** M	0229 0851 1450 2121	7.3 3.3 7.5 3.1
5 M	0419 1044 1639 2304	8.2 2.5 8.4 2.3	**20** TU	0330 0952 1550 2219	7.7 2.9 7.9 2.6
6 TU	0502 1128 1723 2345	8.5 2.1 8.5 2.1	**21** W	0424 1047 1646 2312	8.2 2.4 8.4 2.2
7 W	0542 1209 1804	8.7 2.1 8.6	**22** TH	0514 1140 1738	8.7 1.9 8.7
8 TH	0023 0620 1246 1842	2.1 8.9 2.0 8.7 ○	**23** F	0003 0603 1231 1830	1.8 9.1 1.5 9.0 ●
9 F	0059 0655 1321 1918	2.1 8.9 1.9 8.6	**24** SA	0052 0652 1321 1919	1.6 9.3 1.3 9.2
10 SA	0131 0728 1354 1951	2.2 8.8 2.0 8.4	**25** SU	0141 0740 1410 2008	1.5 9.5 1.2 9.2
11 SU	0202 0801 1425 2024	2.4 8.6 2.4 8.1	**26** M	0228 0827 1458 2056	1.5 9.5 1.2 9.0
12 M	0233 0832 1457 2058	2.7 8.3 2.7 7.8	**27** TU	0315 0915 1547 2145	1.7 9.2 1.5 8.7
13 TU	0305 0906 1531 2133	3.0 8.0 3.0 7.5	**28** W	0403 1005 1636 2234	2.0 8.9 1.9 8.3
14 W	0340 0943 1609 2213	3.3 7.6 3.3 7.2	**29** TH	0454 1056 1728 2327	2.5 8.4 2.3 7.9
15 TH	0422 1027 1655 2302	3.7 7.3 3.6 7.0	**30** F	0550 1153 1825	2.9 7.9 2.8 ◐
			31 SA	0027 0654 1256 1928	7.5 3.3 7.6 3.1

Chart Datum: 5·06 metres below Ordnance Datum (Local)
HAT is 10·3 metres above Chart Datum

TIDES

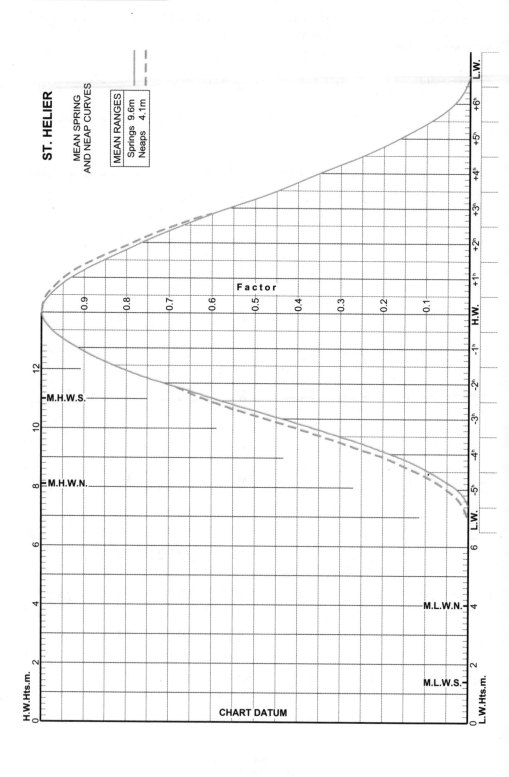

ST. HELIER

MEAN SPRING
AND NEAP CURVES

MEAN RANGES
Springs 9.6m
Neaps 4.1m

Factor

0.9 0.8 0.7 0.6 0.5 0.4 0.3 0.2 0.1

H.W.Hts.m.

M.H.W.S.

M.H.W.N.

CHART DATUM

H.W.

L.W.

M.L.W.N.

M.L.W.S.

L.W.Hts.m.

L.W.

CHANNEL ISLES – ST HELIER
LAT 49°11'N LONG 2°07'W
TIMES AND HEIGHTS OF HIGH AND LOW WATERS

TIME ZONE (UT)
For Summer Time add ONE hour in **non-shaded areas**

Dates in amber are **SPRINGS**
Dates in grey are **NEAPS**

2022

JANUARY

Day	Time m	Time m	Time m	Time m
1 SA	0444 10.1	1124 2.1	1711 10.3	2353 1.9
2 SU	0539 10.7	1223 1.6	1807 10.7 ●	
3 M	0048 1.6	0632 11.1	1317 1.2	1900 10.9
4 TU	0141 1.4	0721 11.2	1409 1.1	1949 10.9
5 W	0230 1.5	0808 11.2	1458 1.2	2036 10.7
6 TH	0316 1.9	0853 10.9	1544 1.5	2119 10.3
7 F	0359 2.1	0936 10.4	1626 2.0	2201 9.8
8 SA	0440 2.6	1017 9.8	1707 2.6	2242 9.2
9 SU	0521 3.1	1101 9.2	1748 3.1	☾ 2327 8.7
10 M	0606 3.7	1151 8.6	1836 3.7	
11 TU	0021 8.3	0702 4.1	1254 8.2	1936 4.0
12 W	0130 8.1	0812 4.2	1409 8.1	2045 4.0
13 TH	0243 8.2	0924 4.1	1519 8.2	2151 3.8
14 F	0346 8.5	1025 3.7	1617 8.6	2246 3.5
15 SA	0437 9.0	1116 3.2	1705 9.0	2333 3.1
16 SU	0520 9.4	1200 2.8	1747 9.4	
17 M	0015 2.7	0559 9.8	1240 2.5	○ 1825 9.7
18 TU	0054 2.4	0636 10.1	1318 2.2	1901 9.9
19 W	0131 2.3	0711 10.3	1354 2.1	1936 10.0
20 TH	0206 2.2	0746 10.4	1429 2.0	2011 10.1
21 F	0240 2.1	0821 10.4	1502 2.0	2046 10.1
22 SA	0314 2.2	0857 10.3	1536 2.1	2121 9.9
23 SU	0350 2.4	0933 10.1	1612 2.4	2158 9.6
24 M	0428 2.7	1012 9.7	1651 2.9	2239 9.2
25 TU	0510 3.1	1057 9.2	1736 3.1	☾ 2329 8.8
26 W	0603 3.5	1154 8.8	1835 3.5	
27 TH	0034 8.5	0715 3.7	1308 8.5	1955 3.7
28 F	0157 8.5	0841 3.6	1435 8.6	2122 3.5
29 SA	0320 8.9	1003 3.1	1557 9.0	2239 2.9
30 SU	0432 9.6	1114 2.4	1705 9.7	2346 2.3
31 M	0532 10.3	1218 1.7	1803 10.3	

FEBRUARY

Day	Time m	Time m	Time m	Time m
1 TU	0043 1.7	0625 10.9	1313 1.2	● 1854 10.8
2 W	0135 1.3	0713 11.3	1403 0.9	1940 11.0
3 TH	0221 1.1	0757 11.4	1447 0.8	2021 11.0
4 F	0302 1.2	0837 11.3	1526 1.0	2058 10.8
5 SA	0339 1.5	0913 10.9	1600 1.5	2132 10.3
6 SU	0410 2.0	0837 10.3	1630 2.1	2204 9.7
7 M	0439 2.7	1019 9.5	1658 2.8	2236 9.0
8 TU	0509 3.3	1054 8.8	1730 3.5	☾ 2314 8.4
9 W	0547 4.0	1140 8.0	1814 4.2	
10 TH	0008 7.8	0647 4.5	1255 7.5	1927 4.6
11 F	0138 7.5	0821 4.6	1436 7.5	2104 4.5
12 SA	0309 7.8	0951 4.3	1553 7.9	2219 4.0
13 SU	0413 8.4	1053 3.6	1647 8.6	2313 3.4
14 M	0502 9.0	1142 3.0	1731 9.2	2359 2.8
15 TU	0543 9.6	1225 2.4	1810 9.7	
16 W	0040 2.3	0621 10.1	1305 2.0	○ 1846 10.1
17 TH	0119 2.0	0657 10.5	1342 1.7	1921 10.4
18 F	0155 1.7	0732 10.8	1417 1.5	1955 10.6
19 SA	0229 1.5	0807 11.0	1450 1.4	2029 10.7
20 SU	0302 1.5	0841 10.9	1522 1.5	2103 10.6
21 M	0335 1.7	0916 10.7	1555 1.8	2137 10.2
22 TU	0410 2.1	0951 10.2	1628 2.3	2212 9.6
23 W	0447 2.6	1030 9.5	1706 2.9	☾ 2254 9.0
24 TH	0533 3.3	1121 8.8	1759 3.6	2355 8.4
25 F	0641 3.8	1237 8.1	1923 4.1	
26 SA	0129 8.1	0821 3.9	1423 8.0	2111 3.9
27 SU	0313 8.4	0957 3.3	1558 8.7	2237 3.2
28 M	0429 9.3	1112 2.5	1704 9.5	2342 2.3

MARCH

Day	Time m	Time m	Time m	Time m
1 TU	0526 10.2	1212 1.6	1756 10.3	
2 W	0036 1.6	0615 10.9	1303 1.0	● 1842 10.9
3 TH	0123 1.1	0658 11.3	1347 0.7	1922 11.2
4 F	0204 0.9	0737 11.5	1426 0.7	1958 11.2
5 SA	0239 1.0	0813 11.4	1458 0.9	2030 11.0
6 SU	0310 1.3	0845 11.0	1526 1.4	2059 10.6
7 M	0336 1.8	0914 10.4	1551 2.0	2126 10.0
8 TU	0400 2.4	0940 9.7	1614 2.7	2151 9.3
9 W	0424 3.1	1007 8.9	1638 3.4	2219 8.6
10 TH	0453 3.8	1039 8.1	1713 4.2	☾ 2258 7.9
11 F	0539 4.5	1136 7.3	1815 4.8	
12 SA	0017 7.3	0710 4.9	1351 7.0	2007 5.0
13 SU	0231 7.3	0911 4.6	1528 7.6	2148 4.4
14 M	0346 8.0	1025 3.8	1624 8.3	2248 3.6
15 TU	0436 8.8	1116 3.0	1707 9.1	2335 2.8
16 W	0518 9.5	1201 2.3	1745 9.8	
17 TH	0017 2.2	0557 10.2	1242 1.8	1822 10.3
18 F	0058 1.7	0634 10.7	1321 1.4	○ 1858 10.8
19 SA	0135 1.3	0711 11.1	1357 1.1	1933 11.1
20 SU	0211 1.1	0746 11.3	1431 1.0	2008 11.2
21 M	0245 1.0	0822 11.3	1503 1.1	2042 11.0
22 TU	0318 1.2	0857 10.9	1536 1.5	2115 10.5
23 W	0352 1.7	0932 10.3	1609 2.2	2151 9.8
24 TH	0430 2.4	1012 9.4	1647 3.0	2233 9.0
25 F	0516 3.2	1104 8.5	1741 3.8	☾ 2337 8.3
26 SA	0629 3.8	1230 7.8	1915 4.3	
27 SU	0124 7.9	0818 3.9	1429 7.9	2109 4.0
28 M	0310 8.4	0954 3.2	1555 8.7	2230 3.1
29 TU	0419 9.3	1102 2.3	1652 9.6	2329 2.2
30 W	0511 10.2	1156 1.6	1738 10.4	
31 TH	0018 1.6	0556 10.8	1241 1.1	1819 10.8

APRIL

Day	Time m	Time m	Time m	Time m
1 F	0101 1.2	0636 11.2	1322 0.9	● 1856 11.1
2 SA	0138 1.1	0712 11.3	1356 1.0	1929 11.1
3 SU	0210 1.1	0745 11.3	1425 1.2	1958 10.9
4 M	0237 1.4	0814 10.8	1450 1.5	2025 10.6
5 TU	0302 1.8	0841 10.3	1514 2.0	2050 10.1
6 W	0326 2.3	0906 9.6	1538 2.7	2114 9.5
7 TH	0350 3.0	0931 8.9	1603 3.4	2139 8.8
8 F	0419 3.7	1000 8.1	1635 4.1	2213 8.1
9 SA	0501 4.3	1048 7.4	1730 4.7	☾ 2317 7.4
10 SU	0618 4.8	1251 7.0	1908 5.0	
11 M	0134 7.2	0813 4.7	1445 7.4	2059 4.6
12 TU	0303 7.9	0940 4.0	1544 8.2	2207 3.8
13 W	0357 8.7	1036 3.1	1629 9.1	2258 2.9
14 TH	0442 9.5	1124 2.4	1710 9.8	2344 2.2
15 F	0524 10.2	1209 1.7	1750 10.5	
16 SA	0027 1.6	0604 10.8	1250 1.3	○ 1829 11.0
17 SU	0108 1.2	0644 11.2	1330 1.0	1906 11.3
18 M	0147 0.9	0723 11.4	1407 0.9	1944 11.3
19 TU	0224 0.9	0801 11.3	1443 1.1	2021 11.1
20 W	0302 1.1	0840 10.9	1519 1.6	2058 10.6
21 TH	0340 1.7	0921 10.2	1557 2.3	2139 9.9
22 F	0422 2.4	1006 9.3	1641 3.1	2228 9.1
23 SA	0516 3.2	1106 8.4	1742 3.8	2339 8.3
24 SU	0633 3.7	1236 8.0	1917 4.1	
25 M	0121 8.2	0811 3.6	1418 8.2	2054 3.7
26 TU	0250 8.7	0933 3.0	1531 8.9	2206 3.0
27 W	0354 9.4	1035 2.3	1625 9.6	2302 2.3
28 TH	0444 10.0	1126 1.8	1710 10.2	2349 1.8
29 F	0528 10.5	1211 1.5	1749 10.5	
30 SA	0030 1.6	0607 10.7	1248 1.5	● 1825 10.7

Chart Datum: 5·88 metres below Ordnance Datum (Local)
HAT is 12·2 metres above Chart Datum

TIDES

TIME ZONE (UT)
For Summer Time add ONE hour in **non-shaded areas**

CHANNEL ISLES – ST HELIER
LAT 49°11'N   LONG 2°07'W
TIMES AND HEIGHTS OF HIGH AND LOW WATERS

Dates in amber are **SPRINGS**
Dates in grey are **NEAPS**

2022

MAY

Day	Time m	Time m	Time m	Time m
1 SU	0106 1.6	0642 10.7	1321 1.5	1857 10.7
16 M	0037 1.3	0616 11.1	1300 1.2	1840 11.2 ○
2 M	0136 1.6	0715 10.6	1349 1.7	1927 10.6
17 TU	0122 1.0	0700 11.2	1344 1.1	1922 11.3
3 TU	0204 1.7	0745 10.4	1417 1.9	1954 10.4
18 W	0206 1.0	0745 11.1	1426 1.3	2005 11.1
4 W	0232 2.0	0813 10.0	1444 2.3	2021 10.0
19 TH	0250 1.2	0830 10.7	1509 1.7	2049 10.6
5 TH	0259 2.4	0841 9.5	1511 2.8	2048 9.5
20 F	0335 1.6	0917 10.1	1553 2.3	2136 10.0
6 F	0328 2.9	0909 8.9	1540 3.4	2116 8.9
21 SA	0424 2.2	1008 9.4	1644 2.9	2230 9.3
7 SA	0400 3.5	0942 8.3	1615 3.9	2153 8.3
22 SU	0520 2.8	1109 8.7	1746 3.5	2337 8.8 ◑
8 SU	0442 4.0	1031 7.7	1706 4.4	2251 7.8
23 M	0629 3.2	1223 8.4	1902 3.7	
9 M	0546 4.4	1157 7.4	1823 4.7 ◐	
24 TU	0056 8.6	0745 3.3	1342 8.5	2020 3.5
10 TU	0028 7.6	0713 4.6	1340 7.6	1955 4.5
25 W	0212 8.8	0855 3.0	1450 8.8	2127 3.1
11 W	0201 7.9	0838 3.9	1449 8.2	2111 3.8
26 TH	0316 9.2	0955 2.7	1547 9.3	2224 2.7
12 TH	0305 8.6	0944 3.2	1541 9.0	2210 3.1
27 F	0409 9.5	1047 2.4	1634 9.7	2313 2.4
13 F	0357 9.4	1038 2.5	1628 9.7	2302 2.3
28 SA	0455 9.8	1133 2.2	1715 10.0	2355 2.3
14 SA	0444 10.1	1128 1.9	1713 10.4	2351 1.7
29 SU	0536 10.0	1212 2.2	1752 10.1	
15 SU	0530 10.7	1216 1.5	1756 10.9	
30 M	0032 2.2	0613 10.1	1246 2.1	1827 10.2 ●
31 TU	0105 2.1	0648 10.1	1318 2.2	1859 10.3

JUNE

Day	Time m	Time m	Time m	Time m
1 W	0137 2.1	0721 10.0	1350 2.3	1930 10.2
16 TH	0154 1.1	0735 10.9	1416 1.4	1956 11.1
2 TH	0209 2.3	0753 9.8	1421 2.5	2001 9.9
17 F	0244 1.2	0825 10.7	1505 1.6	2044 10.8
3 F	0241 2.5	0825 9.4	1453 2.8	2032 9.6
18 SA	0334 1.4	0914 10.3	1553 2.0	2133 10.4
4 SA	0313 2.8	0858 9.1	1526 3.1	2106 9.2
19 SU	0423 1.8	1004 9.8	1642 2.5	2223 9.9
5 SU	0348 3.2	0935 8.6	1603 3.5	2145 8.8
20 M	0514 2.3	1054 9.3	1734 2.9	2316 9.3
6 M	0429 3.5	1020 8.3	1649 3.9	2235 8.4
21 TU	0607 2.8	1149 8.9	1830 3.3 ◐	
7 TU	0520 3.8	1119 8.0	1744 4.1	2340 8.2 ◑
22 W	0015 8.9	0704 3.1	1251 8.6	1932 3.5
8 W	0623 3.9	1231 8.0	1857 4.1	
23 TH	0121 8.7	0805 3.3	1356 8.6	2037 3.5
9 TH	0054 8.3	0736 3.7	1343 8.3	2011 3.8
24 F	0227 8.7	0906 3.2	1459 8.7	2138 3.4
10 F	0205 8.6	0846 3.3	1447 8.8	2119 3.2
25 SA	0328 8.8	1003 3.2	1554 9.0	2233 3.2
11 SA	0308 9.2	0950 2.8	1543 9.5	2219 2.6
26 SU	0421 9.1	1054 3.0	1642 9.3	2322 2.9
12 SU	0405 9.8	1048 2.3	1636 10.1	2315 2.1
27 M	0508 9.3	1139 2.8	1724 9.6	
13 M	0459 10.3	1143 1.9	1727 10.6	
28 TU	0004 2.7	0550 9.5	1219 2.6	1803 9.8
14 TU	0009 1.6	0552 10.7	1235 1.6	1818 10.9 ○
29 W	0042 2.5	0628 9.6	1256 2.5	1839 9.9
15 W	0102 1.3	0644 10.9	1326 1.4	1907 11.1
30 TH	0119 2.4	0705 9.7	1332 2.5	1914 10.0

JULY

Day	Time m	Time m	Time m	Time m
1 F	0154 2.3	0740 9.7	1407 2.5	1948 10.0
16 SA	0239 0.9	0817 10.9	1459 1.3	2036 11.2
2 SA	0229 2.4	0814 9.6	1441 2.6	2022 9.9
17 SU	0327 1.0	0903 10.7	1544 1.5	2120 10.9
3 SU	0303 2.5	0848 9.5	1515 2.7	2057 9.7
18 M	0411 1.3	0945 10.3	1626 1.9	2202 10.4
4 M	0334 2.7	0924 9.2	1551 2.9	2134 9.4
19 TU	0451 1.9	1026 9.8	1706 2.5	2243 9.7
5 TU	0414 2.9	1002 9.0	1630 3.2	2214 9.1
20 W	0531 2.5	1107 9.2	1747 3.1	2328 9.1 ◑
6 W	0455 3.1	1045 8.7	1715 3.5	2302 8.8
21 TH	0612 3.2	1154 8.6	1834 3.6	
7 TH	0543 3.4	1138 8.5	1810 3.7 ◐	
22 F	0022 8.5	0703 3.7	1253 8.2	1935 4.0
8 F	0000 8.6	0641 3.5	1241 8.5	1916 3.7
23 SA	0131 8.1	0807 4.0	1405 8.1	2048 4.1
9 SA	0109 8.6	0751 3.5	1353 8.6	2031 3.5
24 SU	0247 8.1	0919 4.0	1516 8.3	2158 3.8
10 SU	0222 8.8	0906 3.2	1503 9.1	2143 3.0
25 M	0354 8.3	1022 3.7	1615 8.7	2256 3.4
11 M	0332 9.3	1016 2.8	1608 9.6	2249 2.4
26 TU	0448 8.8	1115 3.3	1704 9.2	2344 3.0
12 TU	0438 9.8	1120 2.3	1709 10.2	2352 1.9
27 W	0533 9.2	1200 2.9	1746 9.6	
13 W	0539 10.3	1221 1.9	1805 10.7 ○	
28 TH	0026 2.6	0614 9.5	1241 2.6	1824 9.9 ●
14 TH	0052 1.4	0636 10.7	1317 1.5	1859 11.1
29 F	0106 2.4	0651 9.7	1319 2.4	1900 10.1
15 F	0148 1.1	0729 10.9	1410 1.3	1949 11.3
30 SA	0143 2.2	0726 9.9	1355 2.3	1935 10.3
31 SU	0218 2.1	0759 10.0	1428 2.2	2008 10.3

AUGUST

Day	Time m	Time m	Time m	Time m
1 M	0250 2.0	0832 10.0	1502 2.2	2042 10.3
16 TU	0345 1.1	0917 10.7	1558 1.7	2132 10.7
2 TU	0323 2.1	0905 9.9	1535 2.3	2115 10.1
17 W	0418 1.8	0949 10.1	1630 2.3	2205 9.9
3 W	0356 2.3	0939 9.7	1610 2.6	2150 9.8
18 TH	0447 2.5	1021 9.4	1659 3.1	2239 9.1
4 TH	0430 2.6	1014 9.3	1647 3.0	2229 9.3
19 F	0517 3.3	1056 8.7	1734 3.8	2320 8.2 ◑
5 F	0508 3.1	1056 8.9	1732 3.4	2317 8.9 ◐
20 SA	0556 4.1	1144 8.0	1826 4.4	
6 SA	0557 3.5	1152 8.5	1832 3.7	
21 SU	0026 7.6	0700 4.6	1307 7.6	1955 4.7
7 SU	0023 8.5	0707 3.8	1309 8.4	1954 3.8
22 M	0212 7.4	0837 4.7	1448 7.8	2131 4.4
8 M	0149 8.4	0836 3.7	1438 8.6	2122 3.4
23 TU	0337 7.8	1000 4.2	1615 8.3	2238 3.8
9 TU	0318 8.7	1001 3.3	1557 9.2	2239 2.7
24 W	0434 8.5	1057 3.6	1648 9.0	2327 3.1
10 W	0434 9.4	1113 2.6	1703 10.0	2346 2.0
25 TH	0518 9.1	1143 3.0	1729 9.6	
11 TH	0536 10.1	1215 1.9	1759 10.7	
26 F	0009 2.6	0557 9.6	1224 2.5	1807 10.0
12 F	0046 1.3	0630 10.7	1310 1.4	1850 11.3 ○
27 SA	0049 2.2	0632 10.0	1302 2.2	1842 10.4 ●
13 SA	0139 0.9	0718 11.1	1400 1.1	1936 11.6
28 SU	0126 1.9	0705 10.3	1338 1.9	1915 10.7
14 SU	0227 0.6	0801 11.2	1444 1.0	2018 11.6
29 M	0200 1.7	0738 10.5	1411 1.7	1948 10.9
15 M	0309 0.7	0841 11.1	1523 1.2	2057 11.2
30 TU	0232 1.6	0810 10.6	1443 1.7	2021 10.9
31 W	0303 1.6	0841 10.5	1515 1.8	2053 10.6

Chart Datum: 5·88 metres below Ordnance Datum (Local)
HAT is 12·2 metres above Chart Datum

CHANNEL ISLES – ST HELIER
LAT 49°11'N   LONG 2°07'W
TIMES AND HEIGHTS OF HIGH AND LOW WATERS

Dates in amber are **SPRINGS**
Dates in grey are **NEAPS**

2022

SEPTEMBER

Day	Time m	Day	Time m
1 TH	0333 1.9 / 0913 10.2 / 1548 2.2 / 2126 10.2	**16** F	0402 2.7 / 0937 9.5 / 1613 3.1 / 2153 9.0
2 F	0405 2.4 / 0945 9.7 / 1622 2.7 / 2201 9.6	**17** SA	0426 3.5 / 1004 8.8 / 1641 3.9 / ◐ 2225 8.1
3 SA	0439 3.0 / 1022 9.1 / 1703 3.3 / ◐ 2245 8.8	**18** SU	0458 4.3 / 1041 8.0 / 1726 4.6 / 2318 7.4
4 SU	0525 3.7 / 1115 8.5 / 1803 3.9 / 2353 8.2	**19** M	0557 4.9 / 1158 7.3 / 1856 5.0
5 M	0639 4.2 / 1242 8.0 / 1937 4.1	**20** TU	0142 7.0 / 0753 5.1 / 1422 7.4 / 2103 4.8
6 TU	0139 7.9 / 0827 4.2 / 1435 8.3 / 2119 3.6	**21** W	0320 7.6 / 0936 4.6 / 1537 8.1 / 2215 4.0
7 W	0324 8.5 / 1001 3.5 / 1558 9.0 / 2238 2.7	**22** TH	0413 8.4 / 1034 3.8 / 1624 8.9 / 2302 3.2
8 TH	0435 9.4 / 1110 2.6 / 1658 10.1 / 2341 1.8	**23** F	0453 9.1 / 1118 3.0 / 1704 9.6 / 2343 2.5
9 F	0529 10.3 / 1206 1.8 / 1748 10.9	**24** SA	0529 9.8 / 1158 2.4 / 1740 10.2
10 SA	0034 1.1 / 0617 10.9 / 1256 1.2 / ○ 1834 11.5	**25** SU	0022 2.0 / 0605 10.3 / 1237 1.9 / ● 1815 10.7
11 SU	0122 0.7 / 0659 11.3 / 1340 0.9 / 1915 11.7	**26** M	0059 1.7 / 0638 10.7 / 1313 1.6 / 1850 11.0
12 M	0204 0.6 / 0737 11.4 / 1420 0.9 / 1953 11.6	**27** TU	0135 1.2 / 0711 10.9 / 1348 1.4 / 1923 11.2
13 TU	0240 0.8 / 0812 11.2 / 1454 1.2 / 2027 11.3	**28** W	0208 1.3 / 0744 11.0 / 1421 1.4 / 1957 11.2
14 W	0311 1.3 / 0843 10.8 / 1523 1.7 / 2058 10.9	**29** TH	0239 1.5 / 0816 10.9 / 1454 1.6 / 2031 10.9
15 TH	0338 1.9 / 0911 10.2 / 1549 2.4 / 2126 9.9	**30** F	0311 1.8 / 0848 10.5 / 1527 2.0 / 2104 10.3

OCTOBER

Day	Time m	Day	Time m
1 SA	0343 2.4 / 0922 9.9 / 1603 2.6 / 2141 9.5	**16** SU	0348 3.6 / 0925 8.9 / 1605 3.9 / 2147 8.2
2 SU	0419 3.1 / 1001 9.2 / 1647 3.4 / 2229 8.7	**17** M	0420 4.3 / 0958 8.1 / 1646 4.6 / ◐ 2234 7.4
3 M	0509 3.9 / 1058 8.4 / 1754 4.0 / ◐ 2348 7.9	**18** TU	0514 5.0 / 1101 7.4 / 1806 5.0
4 TU	0634 4.4 / 1241 7.9 / 1939 4.1	**19** W	0047 7.0 / 0656 5.2 / 1331 7.3 / 2009 4.9
5 W	0152 7.9 / 0831 4.2 / 1438 8.4 / 2119 3.5	**20** TH	0240 7.5 / 0850 4.8 / 1457 7.9 / 2131 4.2
6 TH	0324 8.6 / 0956 3.4 / 1550 9.3 / 2229 2.6	**21** F	0335 8.3 / 0954 4.0 / 1546 8.7 / 2222 3.4
7 F	0424 9.6 / 1057 2.4 / 1643 10.2 / 2325 1.7	**22** SA	0416 9.0 / 1041 3.2 / 1627 9.5 / 2305 2.7
8 SA	0512 10.4 / 1148 1.7 / 1729 11.0	**23** SU	0454 9.8 / 1123 2.5 / 1705 10.1 / 2347 2.1
9 SU	0013 1.2 / 0555 11.0 / 1233 1.3 / ○ 1811 11.4	**24** M	0530 10.3 / 1204 2.0 / 1743 10.7
10 M	0056 1.0 / 0633 11.3 / 1313 1.1 / 1849 11.5	**25** TU	0026 1.7 / 0606 10.8 / 1243 1.6 / ● 1820 11.1
11 TU	0133 1.0 / 0708 11.3 / 1349 1.2 / 1924 11.4	**26** W	0104 1.4 / 0642 11.1 / 1321 1.4 / 1857 11.3
12 W	0206 1.2 / 0739 11.1 / 1419 1.5 / 1956 11.0	**27** TH	0141 1.3 / 0718 11.2 / 1358 1.3 / 1935 11.2
13 TH	0234 1.6 / 0808 10.8 / 1447 1.9 / 2025 10.5	**28** F	0216 1.5 / 0754 11.1 / 1435 1.5 / 2013 10.9
14 F	0259 2.2 / 0835 10.3 / 1512 2.5 / 2052 9.8	**29** SA	0252 1.9 / 0830 10.7 / 1512 1.9 / 2052 10.3
15 SA	0323 2.8 / 0859 9.6 / 1536 3.2 / 2118 9.0	**30** SU	0329 2.4 / 0910 10.0 / 1554 2.6 / 2136 9.5
		31 M	0412 3.2 / 0957 9.3 / 1646 3.3 / 2233 8.7

NOVEMBER

Day	Time m	Day	Time m
1 TU	0510 3.9 / 1103 8.5 / 1800 3.8 / ◐ 2357 8.1	**16** W	0447 4.6 / 1034 7.8 / 1728 4.6 / ◐ 2337 7.4
2 W	0639 4.3 / 1241 8.2 / 1935 3.8	**17** TH	0602 4.9 / 1206 7.5 / 1855 4.7
3 TH	0142 8.2 / 0818 4.0 / 1417 8.6 / 2100 3.3	**18** F	0123 7.5 / 0736 4.8 / 1345 7.8 / 2022 4.3
4 F	0301 8.8 / 0933 3.3 / 1525 9.4 / 2204 2.6	**19** SA	0235 8.0 / 0854 4.2 / 1450 8.4 / 2127 3.7
5 SA	0358 9.6 / 1031 2.5 / 1618 10.1 / 2257 2.0	**20** SU	0326 8.7 / 0951 3.5 / 1539 9.1 / 2218 3.0
6 SU	0445 10.2 / 1121 2.0 / 1703 10.6 / 2343 1.7	**21** M	0409 9.5 / 1041 2.8 / 1624 9.8 / 2306 2.4
7 M	0526 10.6 / 1205 1.7 / 1744 10.8	**22** TU	0451 10.1 / 1127 2.2 / 1707 10.4 / 2351 1.9
8 TU	0024 1.6 / 0603 10.8 / 1243 1.6 / ○ 1822 10.9	**23** W	0532 10.6 / 1212 1.7 / ● 1750 10.8
9 W	0100 1.6 / 0638 10.9 / 1317 1.7 / 1856 10.8	**24** TH	0034 1.6 / 0614 11.0 / 1255 1.5 / 1834 11.1
10 TH	0131 1.8 / 0709 10.8 / 1347 1.9 / 1928 10.5	**25** F	0117 1.5 / 0656 11.2 / 1339 1.4 / 1918 11.0
11 F	0200 2.0 / 0739 10.6 / 1416 2.2 / 1959 10.2	**26** SA	0159 1.6 / 0738 11.1 / 1422 1.5 / 2003 10.8
12 SA	0227 2.4 / 0807 10.2 / 1444 2.6 / 2028 9.6	**27** SU	0241 1.9 / 0823 10.8 / 1508 1.8 / 2050 10.3
13 SU	0255 2.9 / 0835 9.7 / 1513 3.1 / 2057 9.0	**28** M	0326 2.3 / 0909 10.3 / 1556 2.2 / 2140 9.7
14 M	0325 3.5 / 0904 9.1 / 1545 3.7 / 2130 8.4	**29** TU	0416 2.9 / 1001 9.7 / 1651 2.6 / 2238 9.1
15 TU	0359 4.1 / 0940 8.4 / 1626 4.2 / 2216 7.8	**30** W	0515 3.4 / 1103 9.1 / 1756 3.2 / ◐ 2345 8.6

DECEMBER

Day	Time m	Day	Time m
1 TH	0626 3.7 / 1217 8.8 / 1909 3.3	**16** F	0519 4.2 / 1108 8.2 / 1754 4.1 / ◐ 2356 7.9
2 F	0103 8.5 / 0744 3.7 / 1335 8.8 / 2022 3.2	**17** SA	0624 4.4 / 1218 8.1 / 1903 4.1
3 SA	0217 8.8 / 0854 3.4 / 1445 9.1 / 2125 2.9	**18** SU	0110 8.0 / 0740 4.2 / 1333 8.3 / 2017 3.9
4 SU	0319 9.2 / 0955 3.0 / 1543 9.5 / 2221 2.6	**19** M	0219 8.4 / 0852 3.8 / 1440 8.7 / 2124 3.4
5 M	0410 9.6 / 1048 2.6 / 1633 9.8 / 2310 2.4	**20** TU	0319 9.0 / 0954 3.2 / 1539 9.3 / 2224 2.9
6 TU	0455 9.9 / 1134 2.4 / 1717 10.0 / 2353 2.3	**21** W	0412 9.6 / 1051 2.6 / 1634 9.9 / 2318 2.4
7 W	0535 10.2 / 1215 2.3 / 1757 10.1	**22** TH	0503 10.2 / 1145 2.0 / 1727 10.4
8 TH	0030 2.3 / 0612 10.3 / 1251 2.2 / 1834 10.1	**23** F	0010 1.9 / 0553 10.7 / 1237 1.6 / ● 1820 10.7
9 F	0104 2.3 / 0646 10.4 / 1324 2.3 / 1909 10.1	**24** SA	0101 1.7 / 0643 11.0 / 1328 1.3 / 1910 10.9
10 SA	0136 2.4 / 0718 10.3 / 1356 2.4 / 1942 9.9	**25** SU	0150 1.5 / 0732 11.2 / 1419 1.2 / 2000 10.9
11 SU	0208 2.6 / 0750 10.1 / 1428 2.6 / 2015 9.6	**26** M	0239 1.6 / 0820 11.1 / 1508 1.3 / 2049 10.6
12 M	0239 2.8 / 0822 9.8 / 1500 2.9 / 2048 9.2	**27** TU	0327 1.8 / 0908 10.8 / 1557 1.6 / 2137 10.2
13 TU	0311 3.2 / 0855 9.4 / 1534 3.2 / 2122 8.8	**28** W	0415 2.2 / 0956 10.4 / 1646 2.0 / 2225 9.7
14 W	0346 3.6 / 0931 9.0 / 1611 3.6 / 2202 8.4	**29** TH	0504 2.6 / 1045 9.8 / 1736 2.5 / 2316 9.2
15 TH	0427 3.9 / 1014 8.5 / 1657 3.9 / 2251 8.1	**30** F	0556 3.1 / 1139 9.3 / 1829 3.0 / ◐
		31 SA	0012 8.8 / 0655 3.5 / 1241 8.8 / 1929 3.3

Chart Datum: 5·88 metres below Ordnance Datum (Local)
HAT is 12·2 metres above Chart Datum

TIDES

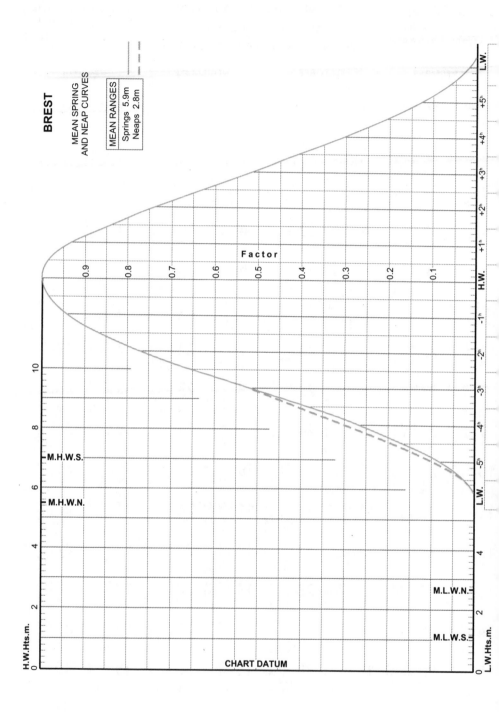

BREST

MEAN SPRING
AND NEAP CURVES

MEAN RANGES
Springs 5.9m
Neaps 2.8m

TIME ZONE -0100
(French Standard Time)
Subtract 1 hour for UT
For French Summer Time add
ONE hour in **non-shaded areas**

FRANCE – BREST

LAT 48°23'N   LONG 4°30'W

TIMES AND HEIGHTS OF HIGH AND LOW WATERS

Dates in amber are **SPRINGS**
Dates in grey are **NEAPS**

2022

JANUARY

#	Time	m	Time	m	#	Time	m	Time	m
1 SA	0320	6.7	1548	6.8	16 SU	0402	6.2	1623	6.2
	0941	1.5	2209	1.4		1026	2.1	2237	2.1
2 SU	0414	7.1	1641	7.0	17 M	0439	6.4	1700	6.3
	1036	1.1	● 2301	1.2		1104	1.9	2314	1.9
3 M	0506	7.3	1732	7.1	18 TU	0515	6.5	1735	6.4
	1128	0.9	2351	1.1		1140	1.7	O 2349	1.8
4 TU	0555	7.4	1821	7.1	19 W	0550	6.7	1810	6.5
	1218	0.7				1215	1.6		
5 W	0040	1.1	1306	1.0	20 TH	0025	1.7	1249	1.6
	0643	7.4	1908	6.9		0625	6.7	1845	6.5
6 TH	0128	1.3	1354	1.2	21 F	0100	1.7	1324	1.6
	0730	7.2	1955	6.6		0659	6.7	1920	6.5
7 F	0215	1.6	1441	1.5	22 SA	0137	1.7	1401	1.7
	0816	6.9	2041	6.4		0735	6.6	1957	6.3
8 SA	0302	1.9	1529	1.9	23 SU	0215	1.8	1441	1.9
	0902	6.5	2128	6.0		0813	6.5	2038	6.2
9 SU	0351	2.2	1619	2.3	24 M	0257	2.0	1525	2.1
	0951	6.1	◐ 2220	5.6		0855	6.3	2125	6.0
10 M	0444	2.6	1715	2.6	25 TU	0345	2.2	1617	2.3
	1045	5.7	2319	5.4		0945	6.0	◑ 2222	5.8
11 TU	0544	2.8	1817	2.8	26 W	0442	2.4	1719	2.5
	1149	5.5				1046	5.8	2329	5.7
12 W	0025	5.4	1258	5.4	27 TH	0551	2.5	1833	2.5
	0651	2.9	1922	2.8		1200	5.7		
13 TH	0132	5.5	1403	5.5	28 F	0046	5.7	1323	5.8
	0758	2.8	2023	2.7		0708	2.5	1950	2.4
14 F	0231	5.7	1458	5.7	29 SA	0203	6.0	1439	6.1
	0857	2.6	2114	2.5		0825	2.1	2100	2.0
15 SA	0320	5.9	1544	6.0	30 SU	0310	6.4	1542	6.5
	0945	2.3	2158	2.3		0932	1.7	2200	1.6
					31 M	0407	6.9	1636	6.8
						1029	1.3	2253	1.3

FEBRUARY

#	Time	m	Time	m	#	Time	m	Time	m
1 TU	0458	7.2	1725	7.0	16 W	0459	6.6	1718	6.6
	1120	0.9	● 2342	1.1		1122	1.6	O 2332	1.6
2 W	0545	7.4	1810	7.1	17 TH	0533	6.8	1752	6.8
	1207	0.8				1156	1.3		
3 TH	0027	1.0	1251	0.8	18 F	0007	1.4	1230	1.2
	0629	7.5	1851	7.0		0607	7.0	1825	6.9
4 F	0110	1.0	1333	1.0	19 SA	0041	1.3	1304	1.2
	0710	7.3	1930	6.8		0641	7.1	1859	6.8
5 SA	0151	1.3	1412	1.3	20 SU	0117	1.3	1339	1.3
	0748	7.0	2006	6.5		0715	7.0	1934	6.7
6 SU	0230	1.6	1450	1.7	21 M	0154	1.4	1416	1.5
	0825	6.7	2043	6.2		0751	6.8	2012	6.5
7 M	0310	2.0	1530	2.2	22 TU	0234	1.6	1458	1.8
	0903	6.2	2122	5.8		0830	6.6	2055	6.2
8 TU	0352	2.4	1615	2.6	23 W	0320	2.0	1546	2.2
	0945	5.7	◑ 2210	5.4		0915	6.2	2147	5.9
9 W	0442	2.8	1711	3.0	24 TH	0414	2.3	1647	2.6
	1040	5.3	2315	5.2		1014	5.7	2257	5.6
10 TH	0548	3.1	1824	3.2	25 F	0523	2.6	1807	2.8
	1157	5.1				1134	5.4		
11 F	0038	5.1	1326	5.1	26 SA	0025	5.5	1315	5.5
	0711	3.2	1945	3.1		0650	2.6	1940	2.6
12 SA	0200	5.3	1438	5.4	27 SU	0156	5.8	1440	5.8
	0830	2.9	2050	2.8		0820	2.3	2056	2.2
13 SU	0300	5.6	1527	5.7	28 M	0305	6.3	1539	6.3
	0926	2.6	2138	2.5		0928	1.8	2154	1.7
14 M	0344	5.9	1607	6.0					
	1009	2.2	2219	2.1					
15 TU	0423	6.3	1644	6.3					
	1046	1.9	2256	1.8					

MARCH

#	Time	m	Time	m	#	Time	m	Time	m
1 TU	0400	6.8	1628	6.7	16 W	0357	6.3	1618	6.4
	1022	1.3	2243	1.3		1019	1.8	2230	1.7
2 W	0447	7.2	1711	7.0	17 TH	0433	6.6	1653	6.7
	1109	0.9	● 2328	1.0		1055	1.4	2307	1.4
3 TH	0529	7.4	1750	7.1	18 F	0508	7.0	1727	7.0
	1151	0.8				1130	1.1	O 2342	1.1
4 F	0009	0.9	1229	0.8	19 SA	0543	7.2	1800	7.1
	0608	7.4	1826	7.1		1205	1.0		
5 SA	0047	1.0	1305	1.0	20 SU	0018	1.0	1240	0.9
	0644	7.3	1859	6.9		0617	7.3	1835	7.1
6 SU	0122	1.2	1339	1.3	21 M	0054	1.0	1316	1.0
	0716	7.1	1929	6.7		0652	7.2	1910	7.0
7 M	0156	1.5	1411	1.7	22 TU	0133	1.1	1354	1.3
	0748	6.7	2000	6.3		0729	7.0	1949	6.7
8 TU	0230	1.9	1444	2.2	23 W	0215	1.4	1436	1.7
	0820	6.2	2032	5.9		0810	6.6	2032	6.3
9 W	0306	2.4	1521	2.6	24 TH	0301	1.9	1526	2.2
	0855	5.7	2110	5.5		0857	6.1	2127	5.9
10 TH	0349	2.8	1609	3.1	25 F	0358	2.3	1630	2.7
	0939	5.3	◑ 2205	5.1		0958	5.6	◑ 2242	5.5
11 F	0447	3.2	1720	3.4	26 SA	0511	2.6	1758	2.9
	1052	4.9	2335	4.9		1128	5.3		
12 SA	0615	3.3	1859	3.3	27 SU	0020	5.5	1319	5.4
	1240	4.8				0647	2.7	1937	2.7
13 SU	0119	5.0	1412	5.1	28 M	0151	5.8	1435	5.8
	0756	3.1	2020	3.0		0815	2.3	2048	2.2
14 M	0231	5.4	1503	5.5	29 TU	0254	6.3	1527	6.3
	0858	2.7	2112	2.6		0917	1.8	2141	1.7
15 TU	0318	5.8	1543	6.0	30 W	0344	6.7	1611	6.7
	0942	2.2	2153	2.1		1006	1.3	2226	1.3
					31 TH	0427	7.0	1650	6.9
						1049	1.1	2307	1.1

APRIL

#	Time	m	Time	m	#	Time	m	Time	m
1 F	0506	7.2	1725	7.0	16 SA	0437	7.0	1657	7.1
	1127	1.0	● 2344	1.0		1059	1.1	O 2314	1.0
2 SA	0541	7.2	1757	7.0	17 SU	0514	7.2	1734	7.3
	1202	1.0				1137	0.9	2353	0.9
3 SU	0019	1.1	1234	1.2	18 M	0552	7.3	1811	7.3
	0614	7.1	1826	6.9		1215	0.9		
4 M	0051	1.3	1305	1.4	19 TU	0033	0.9	1254	1.0
	0644	6.9	1855	6.7		0631	7.2	1850	7.1
5 TU	0123	1.6	1335	1.8	20 W	0115	1.0	1336	1.3
	0714	6.6	1924	6.4		0712	7.0	1933	6.8
6 W	0156	1.9	1406	2.2	21 TH	0201	1.4	1422	1.8
	0745	6.2	1954	6.0		0758	6.5	2022	6.4
7 TH	0230	2.3	1440	2.6	22 F	0252	1.8	1516	2.3
	0818	5.7	2029	5.6		0851	6.0	2122	6.0
8 F	0310	2.7	1524	3.0	23 SA	0353	2.2	1625	2.7
	0859	5.3	2117	5.2		0959	5.5	◑ 2241	5.6
9 SA	0403	3.1	1627	3.3	24 SU	0509	2.5	1754	2.8
	1003	4.9	◑ 2239	4.9		1130	5.3		
10 SU	0522	3.3	1802	3.4	25 M	0012	5.6	1304	5.5
	1145	4.8				0638	2.5	1921	2.6
11 M	0023	5.0	1323	5.0	26 TU	0130	5.9	1412	5.8
	0700	3.2	1932	3.1		0755	2.2	2026	2.2
12 TU	0143	5.3	1422	5.5	27 W	0230	6.2	1502	6.2
	0813	2.7	2031	2.6		0853	1.8	2117	1.8
13 W	0236	5.7	1505	5.9	28 TH	0318	6.6	1545	6.5
	0901	2.3	2116	2.1		0941	1.5	2201	1.5
14 TH	0319	6.2	1544	6.4	29 F	0400	6.8	1622	6.7
	0942	1.8	2156	1.7		1022	1.4	2241	1.4
15 F	0359	6.6	1621	6.8	30 SA	0438	6.9	1656	6.8
	1021	1.4	2235	1.3		1059	1.3	● 2317	1.3

Chart Datum: 3·64 metres below IGN Datum
HAT is 7·9 metres above Chart Datum

TIDES

TIDES

TIME ZONE -0100
(French Standard Time)
Subtract 1 hour for UT
For French Summer Time add ONE hour in **non-shaded areas**

FRANCE – BREST
LAT 48°23'N   LONG 4°30'W
TIMES AND HEIGHTS OF HIGH AND LOW WATERS

Dates in amber are **SPRINGS**
Dates in grey are **NEAPS**

2022

MAY

Day	Time	m	Day	Time	m
1 SU	0512 / 1132 / 1727 / 2350	6.9 / 1.3 / 6.8 / 1.4	**16** M	0447 / 1110 / 1709 / 2330	7.1 / 1.0 / 7.2 / 0.9
2 M	0544 / 1204 / 1756	6.8 / 1.5 / 6.7	**17** TU	0530 / 1153 / 1752	7.2 / 1.0 / 7.3
3 TU	0023 / 0615 / 1235 / 1826	1.5 / 6.6 / 1.6 / 6.6	**18** W	0015 / 0615 / 1238 / 1837	0.9 / 7.1 / 1.1 / 7.1
4 W	0055 / 0647 / 1306 / 1856	1.7 / 6.4 / 1.9 / 6.4	**19** TH	0102 / 0703 / 1325 / 1925	1.0 / 6.8 / 1.4 / 6.9
5 TH	0129 / 0719 / 1338 / 1928	2.0 / 6.1 / 2.2 / 6.1	**20** F	0152 / 0754 / 1415 / 2019	1.3 / 6.5 / 1.8 / 6.5
6 F	0204 / 0754 / 1413 / 2004	2.3 / 5.7 / 2.5 / 5.7	**21** SA	0247 / 0851 / 1512 / 2120	1.7 / 6.1 / 2.2 / 6.2
7 SA	0244 / 0837 / 1456 / 2052	2.6 / 5.4 / 2.9 / 5.4	**22** SU	0349 / 0957 / 1619 / 2231	2.0 / 5.7 / 2.5 / 5.9
8 SU	0334 / 0935 / 1553 / 2200	2.9 / 5.1 / 3.1 / 5.2	**23** M	0459 / 1113 / 1734 / 2345	2.3 / 5.5 / 2.6 / 5.8
9 M	0439 / 1055 / 1709 / 2326	3.0 / 5.0 / 3.2 / 5.1	**24** TU	0612 / 1229 / 1848	2.3 / 5.6 / 2.5
10 TU	0600 / 1218 / 1832	3.0 / 5.1 / 3.0	**25** W	0055 / 0720 / 1334 / 1951	5.9 / 2.2 / 5.8 / 2.3
11 W	0043 / 0713 / 1325 / 1938	5.3 / 2.7 / 5.4 / 2.6	**26** TH	0155 / 0818 / 1427 / 2045	6.1 / 2.0 / 6.0 / 2.0
12 TH	0144 / 0810 / 1418 / 2031	5.7 / 2.3 / 5.9 / 2.2	**27** F	0246 / 0908 / 1512 / 2132	6.2 / 1.9 / 6.2 / 1.8
13 F	0234 / 0859 / 1503 / 2118	6.1 / 1.9 / 6.3 / 1.7	**28** SA	0330 / 0951 / 1552 / 2213	6.3 / 1.8 / 6.4 / 1.7
14 SA	0320 / 0943 / 1546 / 2202	6.6 / 1.5 / 6.7 / 1.4	**29** SU	0409 / 1029 / 1627 / 2251	6.4 / 1.7 / 6.5 / 1.7
15 SU	0404 / 1027 / 1627 / 2246	6.9 / 1.2 / 7.0 / 1.1	**30** M	0445 / 1104 / 1701 / 2326	6.4 / 1.7 / 6.6 / 1.7
			31 TU	0520 / 1138 / 1733	6.4 / 1.8 / 6.5

JUNE

Day	Time	m	Day	Time	m
1 W	0000 / 0554 / 1211 / 1805	1.8 / 6.3 / 1.9 / 6.4	**16** TH	0003 / 0606 / 1226 / 1829	0.9 / 7.0 / 1.2 / 7.2
2 TH	0034 / 0628 / 1244 / 1838	1.9 / 6.2 / 2.0 / 6.3	**17** F	0054 / 0657 / 1317 / 1920	0.9 / 6.8 / 1.3 / 7.0
3 F	0110 / 0702 / 1319 / 1913	2.0 / 6.0 / 2.2 / 6.1	**18** SA	0145 / 0749 / 1408 / 2012	1.2 / 6.6 / 1.6 / 6.8
4 SA	0146 / 0739 / 1355 / 1950	2.2 / 5.8 / 2.4 / 5.9	**19** SU	0239 / 0843 / 1502 / 2107	1.4 / 6.3 / 1.9 / 6.5
5 SU	0225 / 0821 / 1437 / 2035	2.4 / 5.6 / 2.6 / 5.7	**20** M	0334 / 0939 / 1600 / 2205	1.7 / 5.9 / 2.1 / 6.1
6 M	0310 / 0911 / 1526 / 2130	2.6 / 5.4 / 2.8 / 5.5	**21** TU	0432 / 1039 / 1701 / 2306	2.0 / 5.7 / 2.3 / 5.9
7 TU	0404 / 1011 / 1626 / 2235	2.7 / 5.3 / 2.8 / 5.4	**22** W	0533 / 1142 / 1804	2.3 / 5.6 / 2.5
8 W	0506 / 1119 / 1734 / 2344	2.7 / 5.3 / 2.8 / 5.5	**23** TH	0009 / 0635 / 1245 / 1908	5.8 / 2.4 / 5.6 / 2.5
9 TH	0613 / 1225 / 1842	2.6 / 5.5 / 2.6	**24** F	0111 / 0736 / 1345 / 2007	5.7 / 2.4 / 5.7 / 2.4
10 F	0048 / 0716 / 1326 / 1943	5.7 / 2.3 / 5.8 / 2.3	**25** SA	0209 / 0831 / 1438 / 2101	5.8 / 2.3 / 5.8 / 2.3
11 SA	0147 / 0814 / 1421 / 2039	6.0 / 2.0 / 6.2 / 1.9	**26** SU	0300 / 0920 / 1524 / 2148	5.9 / 2.2 / 6.0 / 2.1
12 SU	0242 / 0907 / 1512 / 2131	6.3 / 1.7 / 6.5 / 1.5	**27** M	0345 / 1003 / 1605 / 2230	6.0 / 2.1 / 6.2 / 2.0
13 M	0334 / 0958 / 1601 / 2222	6.6 / 1.4 / 6.9 / 1.2	**28** TU	0425 / 1042 / 1642 / 2307	6.1 / 2.0 / 6.3 / 1.9
14 TU	0425 / 1048 / 1650 / 2313	6.9 / 1.2 / 7.1 / 1.0	**29** W	0503 / 1118 / 1717 / 2344	6.2 / 2.0 / 6.3 / 1.9
15 W	0516 / 1137 / 1739	7.0 / 1.1 / 7.2	**30** TH	0538 / 1153 / 1751	6.2 / 2.0 / 6.4

JULY

Day	Time	m	Day	Time	m
1 F	0019 / 0614 / 1228 / 1826	1.8 / 6.2 / 2.0 / 6.4	**16** SA	0044 / 0648 / 1306 / 1909	0.8 / 6.9 / 1.1 / 7.2
2 SA	0054 / 0649 / 1303 / 1900	1.9 / 6.1 / 2.0 / 6.3	**17** SU	0133 / 0735 / 1354 / 1956	0.9 / 6.8 / 1.3 / 7.0
3 SU	0129 / 0724 / 1339 / 1937	1.9 / 6.0 / 2.1 / 6.2	**18** M	0220 / 0821 / 1441 / 2042	1.2 / 6.5 / 1.5 / 6.7
4 M	0206 / 0802 / 1417 / 2016	2.0 / 5.9 / 2.2 / 6.1	**19** TU	0307 / 0906 / 1529 / 2129	1.5 / 6.2 / 1.9 / 6.3
5 TU	0245 / 0844 / 1500 / 2100	2.2 / 5.8 / 2.3 / 5.9	**20** W	0355 / 0954 / 1619 / 2219	1.9 / 5.8 / 2.2 / 5.9
6 W	0330 / 0932 / 1548 / 2151	2.3 / 5.6 / 2.5 / 5.8	**21** TH	0447 / 1048 / 1715 / 2317	2.3 / 5.6 / 2.5 / 5.6
7 TH	0421 / 1028 / 1645 / 2251	2.4 / 5.6 / 2.5 / 5.7	**22** F	0544 / 1150 / 1819	2.6 / 5.4 / 2.7
8 F	0521 / 1131 / 1750 / 2357	2.5 / 5.6 / 2.5 / 5.7	**23** SA	0023 / 0648 / 1259 / 1928	5.4 / 2.8 / 5.4 / 2.8
9 SA	0627 / 1237 / 1858	2.4 / 5.7 / 2.4	**24** SU	0134 / 0755 / 1406 / 2034	5.4 / 2.7 / 5.5 / 2.6
10 SU	0105 / 0734 / 1344 / 2005	5.8 / 2.2 / 6.0 / 2.1	**25** M	0237 / 0854 / 1502 / 2129	5.5 / 2.6 / 5.7 / 2.4
11 M	0212 / 0838 / 1446 / 2108	6.1 / 2.0 / 6.3 / 1.8	**26** TU	0328 / 0943 / 1548 / 2213	5.7 / 2.4 / 6.0 / 2.2
12 TU	0316 / 0938 / 1545 / 2207	6.4 / 1.7 / 6.7 / 1.4	**27** W	0411 / 1024 / 1627 / 2252	5.9 / 2.2 / 6.2 / 2.0
13 W	0414 / 1034 / 1639 / 2302	6.6 / 1.4 / 7.0 / 1.1	**28** TH	0449 / 1102 / 1703 / 2328	6.1 / 2.0 / 6.3 / 1.8
14 TH	0508 / 1126 / 1731 / 2354	6.9 / 1.2 / 7.2 / 0.9	**29** F	0524 / 1137 / 1737	6.2 / 1.9 / 6.5
15 F	0559 / 1217 / 1821	7.0 / 1.1 / 7.3	**30** SA	0002 / 0557 / 1211 / 1810	1.7 / 6.3 / 1.8 / 6.6
			31 SU	0036 / 0630 / 1245 / 1843	1.6 / 6.4 / 1.7 / 6.6

AUGUST

Day	Time	m	Day	Time	m
1 M	0109 / 0704 / 1319 / 1917	1.6 / 6.4 / 1.7 / 6.6	**16** TU	0153 / 0749 / 1411 / 2008	1.1 / 6.7 / 1.4 / 6.8
2 TU	0142 / 0737 / 1354 / 1951	1.7 / 6.3 / 1.8 / 6.5	**17** W	0232 / 0826 / 1452 / 2046	1.5 / 6.3 / 1.8 / 6.4
3 W	0218 / 0814 / 1433 / 2029	1.8 / 6.2 / 2.0 / 6.3	**18** TH	0312 / 0904 / 1535 / 2128	2.0 / 6.0 / 2.2 / 5.9
4 TH	0257 / 0854 / 1516 / 2113	2.0 / 6.0 / 2.2 / 6.0	**19** F	0356 / 0949 / 1624 / 2220	2.5 / 5.6 / 2.7 / 5.4
5 F	0343 / 0945 / 1607 / 2207	2.2 / 5.8 / 2.4 / 5.8	**20** SA	0449 / 1050 / 1728 / 2332	2.9 / 5.2 / 3.0 / 5.1
6 SA	0438 / 1046 / 1709 / 2315	2.4 / 5.6 / 2.5 / 5.6	**21** SU	0558 / 1213 / 1849	3.1 / 5.1 / 3.1
7 SU	0546 / 1200 / 1824	2.6 / 5.6 / 2.6	**22** M	0102 / 0721 / 1340 / 2012	5.0 / 3.1 / 5.2 / 2.9
8 M	0036 / 0705 / 1320 / 1945	5.6 / 2.5 / 5.8 / 2.3	**23** TU	0220 / 0833 / 1444 / 2111	5.3 / 2.9 / 5.5 / 2.6
9 TU	0159 / 0822 / 1435 / 2058	5.8 / 2.3 / 6.1 / 1.9	**24** W	0313 / 0924 / 1530 / 2155	5.6 / 2.5 / 5.9 / 2.2
10 W	0310 / 0928 / 1537 / 2159	6.2 / 1.9 / 6.6 / 1.4	**25** TH	0354 / 1005 / 1608 / 2232	5.9 / 2.2 / 6.2 / 1.9
11 TH	0408 / 1025 / 1631 / 2253	6.6 / 1.5 / 7.0 / 1.0	**26** F	0429 / 1041 / 1643 / 2307	6.2 / 1.9 / 6.5 / 1.7
12 F	0459 / 1116 / 1720 / 2343	6.9 / 1.1 / 7.3 / 0.8	**27** SA	0503 / 1115 / 1716 / 2340	6.4 / 1.7 / 6.7 / 1.5
13 SA	0546 / 1204 / 1806	7.1 / 1.0 / 7.5	**28** SU	0535 / 1149 / 1748	6.6 / 1.5 / 6.9
14 SU	0029 / 0630 / 1248 / 1849	0.7 / 7.1 / 0.9 / 7.4	**29** M	0012 / 0606 / 1222 / 1820	1.3 / 6.7 / 1.4 / 6.9
15 M	0112 / 0711 / 1331 / 1929	0.8 / 7.0 / 1.1 / 7.2	**30** TU	0044 / 0638 / 1255 / 1852	1.3 / 6.7 / 1.4 / 6.9
			31 W	0116 / 0710 / 1329 / 1925	1.4 / 6.7 / 1.5 / 6.8

Chart Datum: 3·64 metres below IGN Datum
HAT is 7·9 metres above Chart Datum

TIME ZONE -0100
(French Standard Time)
Subtract 1 hour for UT
For French Summer Time add
ONE hour in **non-shaded areas**

FRANCE – BREST

LAT 48°23'N   LONG 4°30'W

TIMES AND HEIGHTS OF HIGH AND LOW WATERS

Dates in amber are **SPRINGS**
Dates in grey are **NEAPS**

2022

SEPTEMBER

Time	m		Time	m
1 0151	1.5	**16** 0229	2.1	
TH 0744	6.5		0817	6.1
1407	1.7	F 1452	2.3	
2001	6.5		2040	5.8
2 0228	1.8	**17** 0307	2.6	
F 0823	6.2		0855	5.6
1449	2.0	SA 1537	2.8	
2043	6.2	◑ 2126	5.3	
3 0312	2.2	**18** 0354	3.0	
SA 0911	5.9		0950	5.2
1539	2.3	SU 1637	3.2	
◑ 2136	5.8	2240	4.9	
4 0407	2.6	**19** 0505	3.4	
SU 1015	5.6		1124	5.0
1644	2.6	M 1807	3.4	
2250	5.4			
5 0521	2.8	**20** 0028	4.8	
M 1140	5.5		0643	3.4
1807	2.7	TU 1309	5.1	
		1945	3.1	
6 0026	5.4	**21** 0157	5.1	
TU 0654	2.8		0806	3.1
1315	5.7	W 1419	5.4	
1940	2.5	2045	2.7	
7 0201	5.7	**22** 0248	5.6	
W 0819	2.4		0857	2.6
1431	6.2	TH 1503	5.9	
2054	1.9	2127	2.3	
8 0308	6.2	**23** 0327	6.0	
TH 0923	1.9		0937	2.2
1529	6.7	F 1540	6.3	
2152	1.4	2203	1.9	
9 0400	6.7	**24** 0401	6.3	
F 1015	1.4		1013	1.8
1619	7.2	SA 1615	6.6	
2241	1.0	2237	1.6	
10 0445	7.0	**25** 0434	6.7	
SA 1101	1.0		1047	1.5
1703	7.5	SU 1648	6.9	
○ 2325	0.7	● 2310	1.3	
11 0527	7.2	**26** 0507	6.9	
SU 1144	0.9		1121	1.2
1744	7.6	M 1721	7.1	
		2343	1.2	
12 0007	0.7	**27** 0539	7.0	
M 0605	7.2		1155	1.2
1224	0.9	TU 1753	7.2	
1822	7.5			
13 0045	0.9	**28** 0016	1.1	
TU 0640	7.1		0611	7.1
1302	1.1	W 1230	1.2	
1857	7.2	1826	7.1	
14 0120	1.2	**29** 0050	1.2	
W 0712	6.8		0644	7.0
1338	1.4	TH 1306	1.3	
1931	6.8	1901	7.0	
15 0155	1.6	**30** 0126	1.5	
TH 0744	6.5		0720	6.8
1414	1.8	F 1345	1.6	
2004	6.3	1939	6.6	

OCTOBER

Time	m		Time	m
1 0206	1.8	**16** 0228	2.7	
SA 0801	6.4		0816	5.7
1430	2.0	SU 1459	2.8	
2023	6.2	2048	5.3	
2 0252	2.3	**17** 0312	3.1	
SU 0851	6.0		0906	5.3
1524	2.4	M 1555	3.2	
2121	5.7	◑ 2155	5.0	
3 0351	2.7	**18** 0416	3.4	
M 1002	5.6		1030	5.0
1633	2.7	TU 1717	3.4	
◑ 2245	5.3	2338	4.8	
4 0513	3.0	**19** 0550	3.5	
TU 1138	5.5		1216	5.1
1806	2.8	W 1854	3.2	
5 0034	5.4	**20** 0110	5.1	
W 0654	2.9		0719	3.2
1313	5.8	TH 1332	5.4	
1938	2.4	2000	2.8	
6 0159	5.8	**21** 0207	5.5	
TH 0813	2.4		0816	2.8
1421	6.3	F 1422	5.8	
2044	1.9	2045	2.4	
7 0256	6.3	**22** 0248	6.0	
F 0910	1.8		0859	2.3
1514	6.8	SA 1502	6.3	
2136	1.4	2124	1.9	
8 0342	6.7	**23** 0325	6.4	
SA 0957	1.4		0938	1.9
1559	7.2	SU 1539	6.6	
2221	1.1	2201	1.6	
9 0424	7.1	**24** 0401	6.7	
SU 1040	1.1		1015	1.5
1640	7.4	M 1615	7.0	
○ 2302	0.9	2238	1.3	
10 0501	7.2	**25** 0436	7.0	
M 1120	1.0		1052	1.3
1718	7.4	TU 1651	7.2	
2340	0.9	● 2313	1.1	
11 0536	7.2	**26** 0510	7.2	
TU 1157	1.1		1129	1.1
1753	7.3	W 1727	7.3	
		2350	1.1	
12 0014	1.1	**27** 0546	7.2	
W 0608	7.1		1207	1.1
1232	1.3	TH 1804	7.2	
1826	7.0			
13 0047	1.4	**28** 0028	1.2	
TH 0638	6.8		0623	7.1
1306	1.6	F 1247	1.2	
1857	6.7	1843	7.0	
14 0120	1.8	**29** 0108	1.5	
F 0709	6.5		0704	6.9
1341	2.0	SA 1331	1.5	
1930	6.3	1927	6.6	
15 0153	2.2	**30** 0153	1.9	
SA 0740	6.1		0751	6.5
1417	2.4	SU 1421	1.9	
2005	5.8	2018	6.1	
		31 0244	2.3	
			0848	6.1
		M 1519	2.3	
		2124	5.7	

NOVEMBER

Time	m		Time	m
1 0348	2.7	**16** 0339	3.2	
TU 1002	5.8		0944	5.3
◑ 2250	5.4	W 1626	3.2	
		◑ 2239	5.0	
2 0511	2.9	**17** 0450	3.3	
W 1132	5.7		1108	5.2
1800	2.6	TH 1745	3.1	
3 0024	5.5	**18** 0000	5.1	
TH 0641	2.7		0611	3.0
1255	6.0	F 1225	5.4	
1920	2.3	1856	2.9	
4 0137	5.9	**19** 0107	5.4	
F 0752	2.3		0718	2.9
1359	6.3	SA 1326	5.7	
2021	1.9	1952	2.5	
5 0232	6.3	**20** 0158	5.8	
SA 0847	1.9		0811	2.4
1450	6.7	SU 1416	6.1	
2112	1.6	2039	2.1	
6 0317	6.6	**21** 0243	6.2	
SU 0934	1.6		0858	2.0
1535	6.9	M 1500	6.5	
2156	1.4	2123	1.7	
7 0358	6.9	**22** 0325	6.6	
M 1016	1.4		0941	1.7
1615	7.1	TU 1542	6.8	
2236	1.3	2204	1.5	
8 0435	7.0	**23** 0405	6.9	
TU 1055	1.3		1023	1.4
1652	7.1	W 1624	7.0	
○ 2312	1.3	● 2246	1.3	
9 0508	7.0	**24** 0446	7.2	
W 1132	1.4		1106	1.2
1726	7.0	TH 1706	7.2	
2346	1.5	2328	1.2	
10 0540	6.9	**25** 0527	7.3	
TH 1206	1.5		1150	1.1
1759	6.8	F 1749	7.1	
11 0019	1.7	**26** 0012	1.3	
F 0612	6.8		0611	7.2
1241	1.7	SA 1236	1.2	
1832	6.5	1835	7.0	
12 0052	1.9	**27** 0058	1.5	
SA 0647	6.5		0658	7.0
1316	2.0	SU 1325	1.4	
1906	6.2	1925	6.6	
13 0126	2.3	**28** 0147	1.7	
SU 0717	6.2		0750	6.7
1352	2.4	M 1418	1.7	
1942	5.8	2020	6.3	
14 0203	2.6	**29** 0242	2.1	
M 0754	5.9		0848	6.4
1433	2.7	TU 1516	2.0	
2025	5.5	2124	5.9	
15 0245	2.9	**30** 0344	2.4	
TU 0839	5.5		0955	6.1
1522	3.0	W 1623	2.2	
2121	5.2	◑ 2236	5.7	

DECEMBER

Time	m		Time	m
1 0455	2.6	**16** 0400	2.9	
TH 1108	6.0		1006	5.5
1736	2.4	F 1640	2.9	
2351	5.7	◑ 2251	5.3	
2 0609	2.5	**17** 0503	3.0	
F 1220	6.0		1113	5.5
1846	2.3	SA 1746	2.8	
		2358	5.4	
3 0100	5.8	**18** 0611	2.9	
SA 0717	2.4		1221	5.6
1325	6.1	SU 1851	2.6	
1948	2.1			
4 0158	6.1	**19** 0100	5.7	
SU 0816	2.1		0716	2.6
1420	6.3	M 1323	5.9	
2042	2.0	1950	2.4	
5 0248	6.3	**20** 0157	6.0	
M 0907	1.9		0815	2.3
1508	6.5	TU 1420	6.2	
2128	1.8	2044	2.0	
6 0331	6.5	**21** 0250	6.4	
TU 0953	1.8		0909	1.9
1551	6.6	W 1513	6.5	
2210	1.8	2135	1.7	
7 0411	6.6	**22** 0340	6.7	
W 1034	1.7		1000	1.5
1630	6.6	TH 1603	6.8	
2248	1.7	2225	1.5	
8 0447	6.7	**23** 0428	7.0	
TH 1112	1.7		1050	1.2
1706	6.6	F 1653	7.0	
2324	1.8	● 2313	1.3	
9 0521	6.7	**24** 0517	7.2	
F 1148	1.7		1139	1.0
1742	6.5	SA 1742	7.1	
2359	1.9			
10 0555	6.6	**25** 0002	1.2	
SA 1223	1.8		0606	7.3
1816	6.4	SU 1229	1.0	
		1832	7.0	
11 0033	2.0	**26** 0052	1.3	
SU 0629	6.5		0655	7.3
1259	2.0	M 1319	1.0	
1851	6.2	1922	6.8	
12 0109	2.2	**27** 0142	1.4	
M 0704	6.3		0745	7.1
1335	2.2	TU 1410	1.3	
1928	6.0	2014	6.6	
13 0145	2.4	**28** 0233	1.6	
TU 0740	6.1		0837	6.8
1413	2.4	W 1504	1.6	
2007	5.7	2107	6.3	
14 0224	2.6	**29** 0328	1.9	
W 0820	5.9		0932	6.5
1454	2.6	TH 1559	1.9	
2052	5.5	2204	6.0	
15 0308	2.8	**30** 0425	2.2	
TH 0908	5.7		1031	6.2
1542	2.8	F 1659	2.2	
2146	5.4	◑ 2305	5.7	
		31 0527	2.4	
			1134	5.9
		SA 1802	2.4	

Chart Datum: 3·64 metres below IGN Datum
HAT is 7·9 metres above Chart Datum

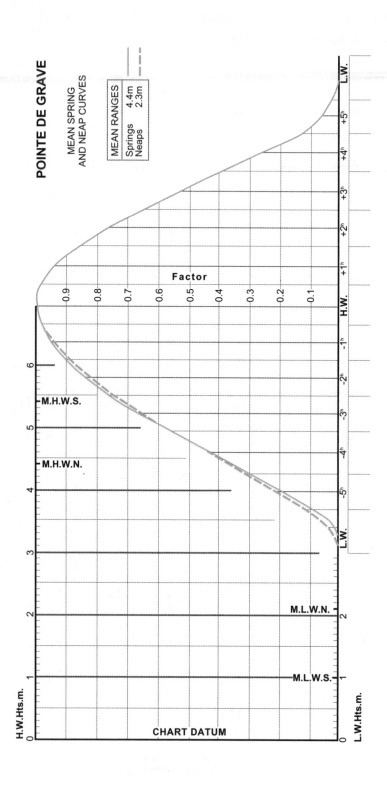

POINTE DE GRAVE

MEAN SPRING
AND NEAP CURVES

MEAN RANGES
Springs 4.4m
Neaps 2.3m

TIME ZONE -0100
(French Standard Time)
Subtract 1 hour for UT
For French Summer Time add
ONE hour in **non-shaded areas**

FRANCE – POINTE DE GRAVE

LAT 45°34'N   LONG 1°04'W

TIMES AND HEIGHTS OF HIGH AND LOW WATERS

Dates in amber are **SPRINGS**
Dates in grey are **NEAPS**

2022

JANUARY

Day	Time	m		Day	Time	m
1 SA	0335	5.2		**16** SU	0413	4.8
	0928	1.4			1015	1.7
	1607	5.2			1635	4.7
	2157	1.3			2225	1.7
2 SU ●	0428	5.4		**17** M	0448	4.9
	1024	1.2			1053	1.6
	1701	5.4			1711	4.8
	2249	1.2			2302	1.6
3 M	0519	5.6		**18** TU ○	0523	5.0
	1118	1.0			1130	1.5
	1752	5.4			1745	4.9
	2339	1.1			2338	1.5
4 TU	0610	5.6		**19** W	0556	5.1
	1208	1.0			1206	1.4
	1841	5.3			1819	4.9
5 W	0028	1.2		**20** TH	0014	1.5
	0659	5.6			0630	5.1
	1257	1.0			1242	1.4
	1929	5.2			1852	4.9
6 TH	0114	1.2		**21** F	0050	1.4
	0747	5.4			0705	5.1
	1343	1.2			1317	1.4
	2016	5.0			1928	4.8
7 F	0200	1.4		**22** SA	0126	1.5
	0834	5.2			0741	5.0
	1428	1.4			1353	1.5
	2103	4.7			2006	4.8
8 SA	0247	1.6		**23** SU	0204	1.5
	0922	4.9			0822	4.9
	1515	1.6			1431	1.6
	2153	4.5			2050	4.6
9 SU ◑	0337	1.8		**24** M	0244	1.6
	1012	4.7			0909	4.8
	1606	1.8			1513	1.7
	2249	4.3			2142	4.5
10 M	0432	2.0		**25** TU ◑	0331	1.8
	1110	4.5			1004	4.7
	1703	2.0			1603	1.8
	2357	4.2			2245	4.4
11 TU	0534	2.1		**26** W	0429	1.9
	1218	4.3			1112	4.5
	1806	2.2			1707	2.0
					2357	4.4
12 W	0107	4.2		**27** TH	0538	2.0
	0640	2.2			1222	4.5
	1328	4.3			1822	2.0
	1913	2.2				
13 TH	0205	4.3		**28** F	0114	4.5
	0747	2.2			0656	1.9
	1426	4.4			1352	4.6
	2014	2.1			1939	1.9
14 F	0253	4.5		**29** SA	0225	4.8
	0846	2.0			0812	1.7
	1515	4.5			1504	4.8
	2105	2.0			2049	1.7
15 SA	0335	4.6		**30** SU	0327	5.0
	0934	1.9			0920	1.5
	1557	4.6			1604	5.0
	2147	1.8			2149	1.5
				31 M	0421	5.3
					1019	1.2
					1656	5.2
					2243	1.2

FEBRUARY

Day	Time	m		Day	Time	m
1 TU ●	0511	5.5		**16** W ○	0506	5.0
	1112	1.0			1113	1.4
	1743	5.3			1727	5.0
	2332	1.1			2322	1.4
2 W	0558	5.6		**17** TH	0539	5.2
	1159	0.9			1148	1.2
	1827	5.3			1800	5.0
					2358	1.2
3 TH	0017	1.0		**18** F	0612	5.2
	0641	5.6			1223	1.2
	1243	0.9			1833	5.1
	1908	5.2				
4 F	0059	1.1		**19** SA	0033	1.2
	0723	5.5			0645	5.3
	1323	1.0			1257	1.1
	1946	5.0			1906	5.1
5 SA	0139	1.2		**20** SU	0107	1.2
	0801	5.3			0721	5.2
	1402	1.2			1331	1.2
	2021	4.8			1942	5.0
6 SU	0218	1.4		**21** M	0143	1.2
	0838	5.0			0759	5.1
	1440	1.5			1406	1.3
	2055	4.6			2021	4.9
7 M	0259	1.6		**22** TU	0220	1.4
	0916	4.7			0842	4.9
	1521	1.7			1445	1.5
	2134	4.4			2108	4.7
8 TU ◑	0344	1.9		**23** W	0304	1.6
	1001	4.4			0934	4.7
	1608	2.0			1532	1.8
	2228	4.1			2208	4.5
9 W	0439	2.2		**24** TH	0359	1.8
	1104	4.1			1042	4.4
	1706	2.3			1633	2.0
	2350	4.0			2326	4.3
10 TH	0548	2.4		**25** F	0512	2.0
	1232	4.0			1214	4.3
	1819	2.4			1758	2.2
11 F	0121	4.0		**26** SA	0100	4.4
	0706	2.4			0644	2.0
	1354	4.1			1351	4.4
	1937	2.4			1931	2.1
12 SA	0226	4.2		**27** SU	0219	4.6
	0820	2.2			0811	1.8
	1454	4.2			1503	4.6
	2041	2.2			2046	1.8
13 SU	0315	4.4		**28** M	0321	5.0
	0914	2.0			0918	1.5
	1540	4.4			1559	4.9
	2128	2.0			2144	1.5
14 M	0355	4.7				
	0958	1.8				
	1619	4.6				
	2209	1.7				
15 TU	0431	4.9				
	1036	1.5				
	1654	4.8				
	2246	1.5				

MARCH

Day	Time	m		Day	Time	m
1 TU	0413	5.2		**16** W	0405	4.8
	1012	1.2			1010	1.5
	1646	5.1			1627	4.9
	2233	1.2			2221	1.5
2 W ●	0458	5.4		**17** TH	0439	5.1
	1059	1.0			1047	1.3
	1727	5.3			1701	5.1
	2317	1.0			2258	1.2
3 TH	0539	5.5		**18** F ○	0513	5.2
	1141	0.9			1122	1.1
	1804	5.3			1734	5.2
	2359	0.9			2334	1.1
4 F	0617	5.5		**19** SA	0547	5.4
	1221	0.9			1157	1.0
	1839	5.3			1807	5.3
5 SA	0037	1.0		**20** SU	0010	1.0
	0652	5.4			0622	5.4
	1256	1.0			1232	1.0
	1910	5.1			1842	5.3
6 SU	0112	1.1		**21** M	0045	1.0
	0725	5.2			0659	5.3
	1330	1.2			1307	1.1
	1938	4.9			1919	5.2
7 M	0146	1.3		**22** TU	0122	1.1
	0756	5.0			0738	5.2
	1402	1.4			1343	1.2
	2007	4.7			1959	5.0
8 TU	0220	1.6		**23** W	0201	1.2
	0828	4.7			0823	4.9
	1436	1.7			1423	1.5
	2039	4.5			2047	4.8
9 W	0258	1.9		**24** TH	0246	1.5
	0907	4.4			0917	4.6
	1514	2.0			1511	1.8
	2121	4.2			2148	4.5
10 TH	0344	2.2		**25** F ◑	0342	1.8
	1000	4.1			1031	4.3
	1605	2.4			1615	2.1
	2228	4.0			2314	4.3
11 F	0452	2.4		**26** SA	0502	2.1
	1130	3.9			1221	4.2
	1723	2.6			1750	2.3
12 SA	0022	3.9		**27** SU	0054	4.4
	0622	2.5			0644	2.0
	1316	3.9			1350	4.3
	1854	2.6			1926	2.1
13 SU	0148	4.0		**28** M	0210	4.6
	0746	2.3			0806	1.8
	1425	4.1			1456	4.6
	2009	2.3			2035	1.8
14 M	0245	4.3		**29** TU	0309	4.9
	0846	2.1			0906	1.5
	1513	4.4			1546	4.9
	2101	2.0			2128	1.5
15 TU	0328	4.6		**30** W	0357	5.2
	0931	1.8			0954	1.2
	1552	4.6			1627	5.1
	2143	1.7			2214	1.2
				31 TH	0438	5.3
					1037	1.0
					1703	5.2
					2251	1.1

APRIL

Day	Time	m		Day	Time	m
1 F	0514	5.4		**16** SA ○	0443	5.3
	1116	1.0			1050	1.1
	1736	5.2			1704	5.3
	2334	1.0			2306	1.1
2 SA	0548	5.4		**17** SU	0521	5.4
	1152	1.0			1128	1.0
	1806	5.2			1741	5.4
					2344	0.9
3 SU	0009	1.1		**18** M	0600	5.5
	0620	5.3			1206	1.0
	1225	1.1			1820	5.4
	1834	5.1				
4 M	0042	1.2		**19** TU	0024	0.9
	0650	5.2			0641	5.4
	1255	1.3			1244	1.1
	1901	5.0			1901	5.3
5 TU	0114	1.4		**20** W	0104	1.0
	0720	5.0			0726	5.2
	1325	1.5			1324	1.3
	1930	4.8			1946	5.1
6 W	0145	1.6		**21** TH	0147	1.2
	0752	4.7			0815	4.9
	1355	1.8			1408	1.5
	2002	4.6			2039	4.9
7 TH	0219	1.9		**22** F	0236	1.5
	0829	4.4			0915	4.5
	1430	2.1			1500	1.8
	2040	4.4			2145	4.6
8 F	0259	2.1		**23** SA ◑	0336	1.8
	0916	4.1			1039	4.3
	1514	2.3			1609	2.1
	2134	4.1			2312	4.5
9 SA ◑	0359	2.4		**24** SU	0459	2.0
	1036	3.9			1219	4.2
	1626	2.6			1742	2.2
	2312	3.9				
10 SU	0530	2.5		**25** M	0040	4.5
	1227	3.9			0631	1.9
	1801	2.6			1336	4.4
					1906	2.1
11 M	0054	4.0		**26** TU	0151	4.7
	0657	2.4			0744	1.7
	1340	4.1			1435	4.6
	1920	2.4			2010	1.8
12 TU	0159	4.3		**27** W	0247	4.9
	0803	2.1			0840	1.5
	1432	4.3			1522	4.8
	2019	2.1			2102	1.5
13 W	0247	4.5		**28** TH	0333	5.0
	0852	1.8			0927	1.3
	1514	4.6			1600	4.9
	2106	1.8			2147	1.3
14 TH	0328	4.8		**29** F	0412	5.1
	0934	1.5			1008	1.2
	1551	4.9			1634	5.0
	2147	1.5			2228	1.2
15 F	0406	5.1		**30** SA ●	0447	5.2
	1013	1.3			1046	1.2
	1628	5.1			1705	5.1
	2227	1.2			2306	1.2

Chart Datum: 2·83 metres below IGN Datum
HAT is 6·1 metres above Chart Datum

TIDES

TIME ZONE -0100
(French Standard Time)
Subtract 1 hour for UT
For French Summer Time add
ONE hour in **non-shaded areas**

FRANCE – POINTE DE GRAVE
LAT 45°34'N   LONG 1°04'W
TIMES AND HEIGHTS OF HIGH AND LOW WATERS

Dates in amber are **SPRINGS**
Dates in grey are **NEAPS**

2022

MAY

Day	Time m	Time m	Time m	Time m		Day	Time m	Time m	Time m	Time m
1 SU	0520 5.2	1120 1.3	1735 5.1	2341 1.3		16 M	0457 5.4	1100 1.1	1718 5.4	○ 2320 1.0
2 M	0551 5.1	1152 1.3	1804 5.1			17 TU	0543 5.4	1143 1.0	1803 5.4	
3 TU	0013 1.3	0622 5.0	1833 5.0			18 W	0005 0.9	0631 5.3	1226 1.1	1851 5.4
4 W	0044 1.5	0653 4.8	1252 1.6	1903 4.9		19 TH	0051 1.0	0721 5.1	1311 1.3	1942 5.2
5 TH	0117 1.6	0726 4.6	1324 1.8	1937 4.7		20 F	0138 1.2	0816 4.8	1359 1.5	2039 5.0
6 F	0151 1.8	0804 4.4	1400 2.0	2016 4.5		21 SA	0231 1.4	0919 4.6	1454 1.8	2144 4.8
7 SA	0231 2.0	0850 4.2	1444 2.2	2106 4.3		22 SU	0331 1.7	1035 4.4	1601 2.0	☽ 2259 4.6
8 SU	0324 2.2	0957 4.0	1545 2.4	2219 4.1		23 M	0443 1.8	1155 4.3	1718 2.0	
9 M	0437 2.3	1130 4.0	1705 2.5	☽ 2351 4.1		24 TU	0013 4.6	0559 1.9	1305 4.4	1831 2.0
10 TU	0556 2.3	1244 4.1	1819 2.3			25 W	0119 4.6	0707 1.8	1403 4.5	1934 1.8
11 W	0101 4.3	0704 2.1	1341 4.4	1922 2.1		26 TH	0216 4.7	0805 1.7	1450 4.7	2029 1.7
12 TH	0156 4.5	0801 1.8	1428 4.6	2016 1.8		27 F	0303 4.8	0854 1.6	1529 4.8	2117 1.6
13 F	0244 4.8	0849 1.6	1511 4.9	2105 1.6		28 SA	0343 4.9	0937 1.5	1603 4.9	2200 1.5
14 SA	0329 5.1	0934 1.3	1553 5.1	2151 1.3		29 SU	0420 4.9	1016 1.5	1637 4.9	2239 1.5
15 SU	0413 5.3	1017 1.2	1635 5.3	2236 1.1		30 M	0455 4.9	1051 1.5	1709 5.0	● 2315 1.5
						31 TU	0529 4.9	1123 1.5	1741 5.0	2349 1.5

JUNE

Day	Time m	Time m	Time m	Time m		Day	Time m	Time m	Time m	Time m
1 W	0602 4.8	1156 1.6	1813 4.9			16 TH	0625 5.3	1214 1.2	1845 5.4	
2 TH	0022 1.6	0636 4.7	1229 1.7	1846 4.8		17 F	0042 1.0	0718 5.1	1302 1.3	1938 5.3
3 F	0057 1.7	0710 4.6	1304 1.8	1921 4.7		18 SA	0132 1.1	0812 4.9	1352 1.4	2033 5.2
4 SA	0134 1.8	0747 4.5	1342 1.9	2000 4.6		19 SU	0223 1.3	0908 4.7	1444 1.6	2129 5.0
5 SU	0214 1.9	0830 4.3	1425 2.0	2047 4.5		20 M	0317 1.5	1009 4.5	1541 1.7	2229 4.8
6 M	0300 2.0	0925 4.2	1516 2.2	2144 4.4		21 TU	0415 1.7	1113 4.4	1643 1.8	☽ 2331 4.6
7 TU	0355 2.1	1034 4.1	1617 2.2	☽ 2252 4.3		22 W	0517 1.8	1220 4.3	1748 1.9	
8 W	0458 2.1	1144 4.2	1722 2.2			23 TH	0036 4.5	0621 1.9	1322 4.3	1852 1.9
9 TH	0001 4.4	0602 2.0	1246 4.4	1825 2.0		24 F	0137 4.5	0723 1.9	1414 4.4	1953 1.9
10 F	0103 4.5	0704 1.9	1341 4.6	1925 1.8		25 SA	0230 4.5	0819 1.8	1459 4.5	2047 1.8
11 SA	0200 4.7	0802 1.7	1433 4.8	2023 1.6		26 SU	0316 4.6	0908 1.8	1538 4.7	2135 1.7
12 SU	0255 4.9	0856 1.5	1522 5.1	2118 1.4		27 M	0358 4.7	0950 1.7	1615 4.8	2218 1.7
13 M	0349 5.1	0947 1.3	1612 5.2	2211 1.2		28 TU	0437 4.7	1028 1.7	1651 4.9	2256 1.6
14 TU	0441 5.2	1037 1.2	1702 5.4	○ 2302 1.0		29 W	0513 4.7	1104 1.6	1726 4.9	● 2332 1.6
15 W	0533 5.3	1125 1.1	1753 5.5	2353 1.0		30 TH	0548 4.7	1139 1.6	1759 4.9	

JULY

Day	Time m	Time m	Time m	Time m		Day	Time m	Time m	Time m	Time m
1 F	0008 1.6	0622 4.7	1214 1.6	1833 4.9		16 SA	0035 0.9	0707 5.2	1253 1.1	1925 5.5
2 SA	0044 1.6	0656 4.7	1250 1.7	1907 4.9		17 SU	0122 1.0	0755 5.0	1339 1.2	2013 5.3
3 SU	0120 1.6	0731 4.6	1327 1.7	1944 4.8		18 M	0207 1.1	0841 4.8	1425 1.3	2100 5.1
4 M	0157 1.7	0809 4.5	1405 1.8	2025 4.7		19 TU	0252 1.3	0927 4.6	1513 1.5	2148 4.8
5 TU	0235 1.7	0853 4.4	1448 1.9	2111 4.6		20 W	0339 1.6	1017 4.4	1604 1.8	☽ 2240 4.6
6 W	0319 1.8	0946 4.3	1536 1.9	2206 4.5		21 TH	0431 1.8	1117 4.2	1703 2.0	2341 4.3
7 TH	0409 1.9	1048 4.3	1632 2.0	☽ 2309 4.5		22 F	0531 2.0	1229 4.2	1808 2.1	
8 F	0508 1.9	1154 4.4	1736 2.0			23 SA	0052 4.2	0637 2.1	1337 4.2	1918 2.1
9 SA	0016 4.5	0614 1.9	1259 4.5	1843 1.9		24 SU	0159 4.2	0745 2.1	1433 4.3	2023 2.0
10 SU	0124 4.6	0722 1.8	1402 4.7	1950 1.7		25 M	0255 4.3	0844 2.0	1519 4.5	2118 1.9
11 M	0232 4.8	0826 1.7	1502 4.9	2054 1.5		26 TU	0342 4.4	0932 1.9	1559 4.7	2202 1.8
12 TU	0335 4.9	0927 1.5	1559 5.2	2156 1.3		27 W	0422 4.6	1013 1.8	1636 4.8	2242 1.6
13 W	0433 5.1	1023 1.3	1653 5.4	○ 2252 1.1		28 TH	0459 4.7	1050 1.7	1710 4.9	● 2318 1.5
14 TH	0527 5.2	1115 1.2	1745 5.5	2345 0.9		29 F	0533 4.8	1126 1.6	1744 5.0	2354 1.4
15 F	0618 5.3	1205 1.1	1836 5.5			30 SA	0606 4.8	1201 1.5	1816 5.0	
						31 SU	0029 1.4	0637 4.8	1235 1.5	1848 5.0

AUGUST

Day	Time m	Time m	Time m	Time m		Day	Time m	Time m	Time m	Time m
1 M	0102 1.4	0710 4.8	1309 1.5	1922 5.0		16 TU	0142 1.1	0804 4.9	1359 1.2	2022 5.1
2 TU	0135 1.4	0744 4.7	1343 1.5	1958 4.9		17 W	0221 1.3	0840 4.7	1439 1.5	2101 4.8
3 W	0209 1.5	0822 4.7	1420 1.6	2039 4.8		18 TH	0300 1.6	0918 4.4	1523 1.8	2144 4.5
4 TH	0246 1.6	0906 4.5	1501 1.7	2128 4.6		19 F	0345 1.9	1006 4.2	1616 2.1	☽ 2241 4.2
5 F	0329 1.8	1002 4.4	1552 1.9	☽ 2228 4.5		20 SA	0440 2.2	1121 4.0	1724 2.3	
6 SA	0424 1.9	1110 4.4	1656 2.0	2341 4.4		21 SU	0004 4.0	0551 2.4	1300 4.0	1846 2.4
7 SU	0534 2.0	1228 4.4	1813 2.0			22 M	0133 4.0	0713 2.4	1409 4.2	2003 2.2
8 M	0105 4.4	0654 2.0	1346 4.6	1932 1.9		23 TU	0236 4.2	0824 2.2	1500 4.5	2100 2.0
9 TU	0225 4.6	0812 1.9	1453 4.9	2047 1.6		24 W	0324 4.4	0914 2.0	1541 4.6	2144 1.8
10 W	0331 4.8	0919 1.6	1551 5.2	2150 1.3		25 TH	0403 4.6	0955 1.8	1616 4.8	2222 1.6
11 TH	0427 5.1	1016 1.3	1644 5.4	2245 1.0		26 F	0438 4.7	1032 1.6	1649 5.0	2258 1.4
12 F	0517 5.2	1107 1.1	1732 5.6	○ 2335 0.9		27 SA	0510 4.9	1107 1.4	1721 5.1	● 2332 1.3
13 SA	0603 5.3	1154 1.0	1818 5.6			28 SU	0541 5.0	1141 1.3	1752 5.2	
14 SU	0021 0.8	0646 5.3	1238 1.0	1902 5.6		29 M	0006 1.2	0612 5.0	1214 1.3	1824 5.2
15 M	0103 0.9	0726 5.1	1319 1.1	1943 5.4		30 TU	0038 1.2	0643 5.0	1247 1.3	1856 5.2
						31 W	0110 1.3	0716 5.0	1319 1.3	1931 5.1

Chart Datum: 2·83 metres below IGN Datum
HAT is 6·1 metres above Chart Datum

TIME ZONE -0100
(French Standard Time)
Subtract 1 hour for UT
For French Summer Time add
ONE hour in **non-shaded areas**

FRANCE – POINTE DE GRAVE

LAT 45°34'N LONG 1°04'W

Dates in amber are **SPRINGS**
Dates in grey are **NEAPS**

2022

TIMES AND HEIGHTS OF HIGH AND LOW WATERS

SEPTEMBER

Day	Time m	Day	Time m
1 TH	0142 1.4 / 0752 4.9 / 1354 1.4 / 2010 4.9	**16** F	0220 1.7 / 0826 4.6 / 1442 1.9 / 2055 4.4
2 F	0217 1.5 / 0834 4.7 / 1434 1.6 / 2058 4.7	**17** SA ◑	0258 2.0 / 0908 4.3 / 1529 2.2 / 2148 4.1
3 SA ◑	0259 1.8 / 0928 4.5 / 1524 1.8 / 2201 4.4	**18** SU	0348 2.4 / 1014 4.0 / 1638 2.5 / 2319 3.9
4 SU	0353 2.0 / 1041 4.3 / 1630 2.1 / 2325 4.3	**19** M	0504 2.6 / 1212 4.0 / 1811 2.6
5 M	0509 2.2 / 1215 4.3 / 1759 2.1	**20** TU	0103 3.9 / 0636 2.6 / 1337 4.1 / 1936 2.4
6 TU	0107 4.3 / 0645 2.2 / 1341 4.6 / 1933 1.9	**21** W	0210 4.1 / 0753 2.4 / 1432 4.4 / 2033 2.1
7 W	0225 4.5 / 0810 2.0 / 1448 4.9 / 2046 1.6	**22** TH	0257 4.4 / 0846 2.1 / 1514 4.6 / 2116 1.8
8 TH	0326 4.8 / 0913 1.6 / 1542 5.2 / 2143 1.3	**23** F	0335 4.6 / 0927 1.8 / 1549 4.9 / 2154 1.6
9 F	0416 5.1 / 1005 1.3 / 1630 5.5 / 2232 1.0	**24** SA	0408 4.8 / 1004 1.6 / 1621 5.1 / 2229 1.4
10 SA ○	0500 5.3 / 1051 1.0 / 1713 5.6 / 2316 0.9	**25** SU ●	0440 5.0 / 1039 1.4 / 1653 5.2 / 2303 1.2
11 SU	0540 5.3 / 1134 0.9 / 1754 5.7 / 2358 0.8	**26** M	0512 5.1 / 1114 1.2 / 1725 5.3 / 2337 1.2
12 M	0618 5.3 / 1215 0.9 / 1832 5.6	**27** TU	0543 5.2 / 1148 1.2 / 1757 5.4
13 TU	0036 1.0 / 0652 5.2 / 1252 1.1 / 1908 5.4	**28** W	0010 1.2 / 0616 5.2 / 1222 1.2 / 1831 5.3
14 W	0111 1.2 / 0724 5.0 / 1328 1.3 / 1942 5.1	**29** TH	0043 1.2 / 0651 5.2 / 1257 1.2 / 1908 5.2
15 TH	0145 1.4 / 0754 4.8 / 1404 1.5 / 2016 4.8	**30** F	0118 1.4 / 0729 5.0 / 1334 1.4 / 1950 4.9

OCTOBER

Day	Time m	Day	Time m
1 SA	0155 1.6 / 0814 4.8 / 1417 1.6 / 2042 4.6	**16** SU	0219 2.1 / 0830 4.4 / 1450 2.2 / 2108 4.1
2 SU	0240 1.9 / 0911 4.6 / 1508 1.9 / 2152 4.3	**17** M ◑	0305 2.4 / 0927 4.2 / 1551 2.5 / 2234 3.9
3 M ◑	0337 2.2 / 1032 4.4 / 1620 2.1 / 2335 4.2	**18** TU	0415 2.7 / 1111 4.0 / 1722 2.6
4 TU	0501 2.4 / 1215 4.4 / 1802 2.2	**19** W	0018 3.9 / 0546 2.7 / 1247 4.1 / 1847 2.5
5 W	0111 4.3 / 0645 2.3 / 1335 4.7 / 1932 1.9	**20** TH	0127 4.1 / 0703 2.5 / 1348 4.3 / 1950 2.2
6 TH	0219 4.6 / 0801 1.9 / 1436 5.0 / 2035 1.6	**21** F	0217 4.4 / 0802 2.2 / 1434 4.6 / 2037 1.9
7 F	0313 4.9 / 0857 1.6 / 1527 5.3 / 2125 1.3	**22** SA	0256 4.6 / 0848 1.9 / 1512 4.9 / 2116 1.6
8 SA	0358 5.1 / 0945 1.3 / 1611 5.5 / 2210 1.1	**23** SU	0332 4.9 / 0928 1.6 / 1547 5.1 / 2153 1.3
9 SU ○	0437 5.3 / 1029 1.1 / 1650 5.6 / 2251 1.0	**24** M	0406 5.1 / 1006 1.4 / 1622 5.3 / 2229 1.3
10 M	0512 5.3 / 1110 1.0 / 1727 5.6 / 2329 1.0	**25** TU ●	0440 5.3 / 1043 1.2 / 1657 5.4 / 2305 1.2
11 TU	0546 5.3 / 1148 1.1 / 1802 5.5	**26** W	0515 5.4 / 1121 1.1 / 1734 5.4 / 2342 1.2
12 W	0005 1.1 / 0618 5.2 / 1223 1.2 / 1835 5.3	**27** TH	0552 5.4 / 1159 1.1 / 1813 5.4
13 TH	0038 1.3 / 0647 5.1 / 1257 1.4 / 1906 5.0	**28** F	0020 1.2 / 0632 5.3 / 1239 1.2 / 1855 5.2
14 F	0109 1.6 / 0717 4.9 / 1331 1.6 / 1939 4.8	**29** SA	0059 1.4 / 0716 5.2 / 1321 1.3 / 1944 4.9
15 SA	0142 1.8 / 0750 4.7 / 1407 1.9 / 2017 4.4	**30** SU	0142 1.6 / 0808 5.0 / 1408 1.6 / 2042 4.6
		31 M	0231 1.9 / 0911 4.7 / 1504 1.9 / 2201 4.4

NOVEMBER

Day	Time m	Day	Time m
1 TU ◐	0333 2.2 / 1035 4.6 / 1619 2.1 / 2339 4.3	**16** W ◐	0334 2.5 / 1009 4.2 / 1626 2.5 / 2317 4.0
2 W	0458 2.3 / 1204 4.6 / 1753 2.1	**17** TH	0449 2.6 / 1139 4.2 / 1741 2.4
3 TH	0058 4.5 / 0627 2.2 / 1317 4.8 / 1911 1.9	**18** F	0029 4.1 / 0600 2.5 / 1247 4.3 / 1848 2.3
4 F	0200 4.7 / 0737 1.9 / 1416 5.0 / 2010 1.6	**19** SA	0124 4.4 / 0702 2.3 / 1342 4.5 / 1943 2.0
5 SA	0251 4.9 / 0832 1.6 / 1506 5.2 / 2100 1.4	**20** SU	0211 4.6 / 0756 2.0 / 1428 4.8 / 2030 1.8
6 SU	0333 5.1 / 0920 1.4 / 1548 5.3 / 2143 1.3	**21** M	0252 4.9 / 0844 1.8 / 1510 5.0 / 2113 1.6
7 M	0410 5.2 / 1004 1.3 / 1626 5.4 / 2223 1.2	**22** TU	0332 5.1 / 0928 1.5 / 1552 5.2 / 2154 1.4
8 TU	0444 5.2 / 1044 1.2 / 1701 5.3 / 2300 1.3	**23** W ●	0412 5.3 / 1012 1.3 / 1634 5.3 / 2236 1.3
9 W	0517 5.2 / 1122 1.3 / 1735 5.3 / 2334 1.4	**24** TH	0453 5.4 / 1057 1.2 / 1718 5.4 / 2319 1.2
10 TH	0549 5.2 / 1157 1.4 / 1809 5.1	**25** F	0537 5.5 / 1141 1.1 / 1803 5.3
11 F	0007 1.5 / 0621 5.1 / 1230 1.5 / 1841 4.9	**26** SA	0002 1.2 / 0623 5.4 / 1227 1.1 / 1853 5.2
12 SA	0039 1.7 / 0652 5.0 / 1305 1.7 / 1915 4.7	**27** SU	0047 1.4 / 0714 5.3 / 1314 1.3 / 1946 5.0
13 SU	0113 1.9 / 0727 4.8 / 1341 1.9 / 1954 4.5	**28** M	0134 1.5 / 0809 5.1 / 1405 1.4 / 2047 4.7
14 M	0151 2.1 / 0806 4.6 / 1423 2.1 / 2041 4.2	**29** TU	0227 1.8 / 0912 5.0 / 1501 1.7 / 2159 4.5
15 TU	0235 2.3 / 0857 4.3 / 1515 2.3 / 2148 4.1	**30** W ◐	0328 1.9 / 1024 4.8 / 1608 1.8 / 2316 4.4

DECEMBER

Day	Time m	Day	Time m
1 TH	0439 2.0 / 1137 4.7 / 1723 1.9	**16** F ◐	0354 2.3 / 1026 4.4 / 1635 2.2 / 2319 4.2
2 F	0028 4.5 / 0554 2.0 / 1246 4.8 / 1834 1.9	**17** SA	0456 2.3 / 1136 4.4 / 1739 2.2
3 SA	0131 4.6 / 0701 1.9 / 1348 4.8 / 1936 1.8	**18** SU	0023 4.3 / 0559 2.2 / 1241 4.5 / 1841 2.1
4 SU	0223 4.7 / 0800 1.8 / 1440 4.9 / 2029 1.7	**19** M	0120 4.5 / 0700 2.1 / 1340 4.6 / 1939 1.9
5 M	0307 4.9 / 0853 1.6 / 1525 5.0 / 2115 1.6	**20** TU	0212 4.7 / 0758 1.9 / 1436 4.8 / 2033 1.7
6 TU	0346 5.0 / 0939 1.6 / 1605 5.0 / 2157 1.5	**21** W	0302 5.0 / 0854 1.6 / 1528 5.0 / 2124 1.5
7 W	0422 5.1 / 1022 1.5 / 1642 5.1 / 2235 1.5	**22** TH	0350 5.2 / 0948 1.4 / 1619 5.2 / 2214 1.4
8 TH	0457 5.1 / 1101 1.5 / 1718 5.0 / 2310 1.6	**23** F ●	0429 5.4 / 1039 1.2 / 1710 5.3 / 2303 1.2
9 F	0531 5.1 / 1137 1.5 / 1752 5.0 / 2345 1.6	**24** SA	0529 5.5 / 1130 1.1 / 1800 5.3 / 2351 1.2
10 SA	0604 5.1 / 1212 1.6 / 1826 4.9	**25** SU	0620 5.5 / 1220 1.0 / 1852 5.3
11 SU	0019 1.7 / 0637 5.0 / 1248 1.7 / 1901 4.7	**26** M	0040 1.2 / 0711 5.5 / 1309 1.1 / 1944 5.1
12 M	0055 1.8 / 0712 4.9 / 1325 1.8 / 1937 4.6	**27** TU	0129 1.3 / 0804 5.4 / 1359 1.2 / 2038 4.9
13 TU	0132 1.9 / 0749 4.7 / 1404 1.9 / 2017 4.4	**28** W	0218 1.5 / 0859 5.2 / 1449 1.4 / 2134 4.7
14 W	0213 2.1 / 0832 4.6 / 1447 2.1 / 2107 4.3	**29** TH	0311 1.6 / 0956 5.0 / 1544 1.6 / 2236 4.5
15 TH	0300 2.2 / 0923 4.4 / 1536 2.2 / 2209 4.2	**30** F ◐	0409 1.8 / 1057 4.8 / 1643 1.8 / 2342 4.4
		31 SA	0513 1.9 / 1204 4.6 / 1748 1.9

Chart Datum: 2·83 metres below IGN Datum
HAT is 6·1 metres above Chart Datum

TIDES

Practical Boat Owner

SUBSCRIBE NOW! FOR JUST £1

GREAT SUBSCRIBER BENEFITS

Each issue is packed with the best boat-owning advice, DIY tips and sailing adventures

Enjoy the luxury of home delivery

Never miss an issue of Britain's best practical marine magazine

3 ISSUES FOR JUST £1

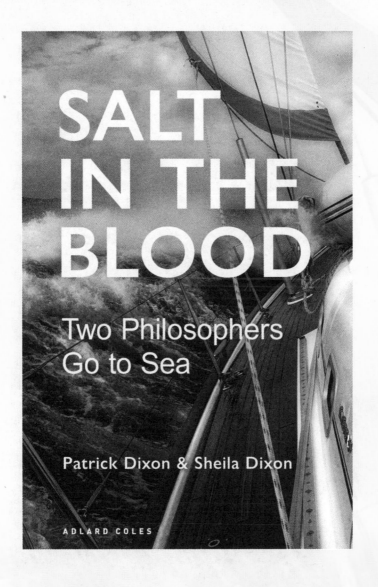

SALT IN THE BLOOD

Two Philosophers Go to Sea

Patrick Dixon & Sheila Dixon

ADLARD COLES

An inspirational personal story
filled with practical advice
for all those who have salt in the blood